# CHILTON'S GUIDE TO AUTOMATIC TRANSMISSION REPAIR – 1980-84 IMPORT CARS & TRUCKS

| | |
|---|---|
| **Senior Vice President** | Ronald A. Hoxter |
| **Publisher and Editor-In-Chief** | Kerry A. Freeman, S.A.E. |
| **Executive Editors** | Dean F. Morgantini, S.A.E., W. Calvin Settle, Jr., S.A.E. |
| **Managing Editor** | Nick D'Andrea |
| **Special Products Manager** | Ken Grabowski, A.S.E., S.A.E. |
| **Senior Editors** | Jacques Gordon, Michael L. Grady, Debra McCall, Kevin M. G. Maher, Richard J. Rivele, S.A.E., Richard T. Smith, Jim Taylor, Ron Webb |
| **Project Managers** | Martin J. Gunther, Will Kessler, A.S.E., Richard Schwartz |
| **Production Manager** | Andrea Steiger |
| **Product Systems Manager** | Robert Maxey |
| **Director of Manufacturing** | Mike D'Imperio |

ONE OF THE *ABC PUBLISHING COMPANIES,*
A PART OF *CAPITAL CITIES/ABC, INC.*

Manufactured in USA
© 1988 Chilton Book Company
Chilton Way, Radnor, PA 19089
ISBN 0–8019–7891–2
Library of Congress Card Catalog No. 88–48013
3456789012   5432109876

# ACKNOWLEDGEMENTS

**Chilton Book Company expresses appreciation to the following firms for their cooperation and technical assistance:**

ATRA—Automatic Transmission Rebuilders Association, Ventura, California
    Special Thanks to: Mr. Gene Lewis—Executive Director
                    Mr. John Maloney—National President
                    Mr. Robert D. Cherrnay—Technical Director
                    Mr. Michael Abell—Service Engineering
                    Mr. C. W. Smith—Technical Staff
ASC—Automotive Service Councils, Inc.® Elmhurst, Illinois
    Special Thanks to: Mr. Del Wright—Chairman of the Board
                    Mr. John F. Mullins, Jr.—Vice Chairman of the Board
                    Mr. George W. Merwin, III—President
American Motors Corporation and Regie Nationale des Usines Renault, Detroit, Michigan
American Honda Motor Company, Gardena, California
American Isuzu Motors, Inc., Whittier, California
Audi, Division of Volkswagen of America Incorporated, Englewood Cliffs, New Jersey
Brandywine Transmission Service, Inc., Wilmington, Delaware
Borg Warner Transmission Service Center, Ramsey, New Jersey
    Special Thanks to: Mr. Michael LePore
Chrysler Corporation, Detroit, Michigan
Detroit Diesel Allison, Division of General Motors Corporation, Indianapolis, Indiana
Ford Motor Company, Dearborn, Michigan
Fuji Heavy Industries, Ltd., Tokyo, Japan
General Motors Corporation, Flint, Michigan
Hydra-Matic, Division of General Motors Corporation, Ypsilanti, Michigan
Jaguar, Rover, Triumph Motor Company, Inc., Leonia, New Jersey
Japanese Automatic Transmission Company, Tokyo, Japan
Lee's Auto Service, Trainer, Chester, Pennsylvania
Mazda Motors of America, Incorporated, Montvale, New Jersey
Mercedes Benz of North America, Incorporated, Montvale, New Jersey
Nissan Motor Corporation of USA, Carson, California
Ralph's Garage, Chester, Pennsylvania
Seuro Transmissions, Incorporated, Pittsburgh, Pennsylvania
Subaru of America, Incorporated, Pennsauken, New Jersey
Toyota Motor Sales USA, Incorporated, Torrence, California
Transmissions By Lucille, Pittsburgh, Pennsylvania
Volkswagen of America, Incorporated, Englewood Cliffs, New Jersey
Volvo of America Corporation, Rockleigh, New Jersey
ZF of North America, Inc., Chicago, Illinois

# CONTENTS

## IMPORT CARS, LIGHT TRUCKS & VANS
## TRANSMISSIONS AND TRANSAXLES

## PART NUMBERS

Part numbers listed in this reference are not recomendations by Chilton for any product by brand name. They are references that can be used with interchange manuals and aftermarket supplier catalogs to locate each brand supplier's discrete part number.

Although information in this manual is based on industry sources and is complete as possible at the time of publication, the possibilty exists that some car manufacturers made later changes which could not be included here. While striving for total accuracy, Chilton Book Company cannot assume responsibity for any errors, changes or omissions that may occur in the compilation of this data.

No part of this publication may be reproduced, transmitted or stored in any form or by any means, electronic or mechanical, including photocopy, recording, or by information storage or retrieval system withiout prior written permission from the publisher.

There are 14 major sections in this manual. And each is appropriately numbered for easy location:

1. **General Information**
2. **Audi/VW — Type 089,90 Transaxle**
3. **Borg Warner — Model 66**
4. **Honda — 3 & 4 Speed Transaxle**
5. **Jatco — Transmissions/Transaxles**
6. **Mercedes-Benz — W4A040, W4A020**
7. **Mitsubishi — Km171, 172 Transaxle**
8. **Renault — MBI, MJ Transaxle**
9. **Subaru — 4WD (with Lock-Up Converter) Transaxle**
10. **Toyota — Transmissions/Transaxle**
11. **Volvo — AW70, AW71 with OD**
12. **ZF-4HP22**
13. **Metric Information & Mechanic's Data**
14. **Oil Flow Circuits (Color)**

Further, each Transmission/Transaxle section is indexed and organized by the following functions:

**Applications**
**General Description**
**Modifications**
**Trouble Diagnosis**
**On Car Services**
**Removal and Installation Procedures**
**Bench Overhaul**
**Specifications**
**Special Tools**

Graphic symbols throughout the manual aid in the location of sections and speed the pinpointing of information.

## METRIC NOTICE

Certain parts are dimensioned in the metric system. Many fasteners are metric and should not be replaced with a customary inch fastener.

It is important to note that during any maintenance procedure or repair, the metric fastener should be salvaged for reassembly. If the fastener is not reusable, then the equivalent fastener should be used.

A mismatched or incorrect fastener can result in component damage or possibly, personal injury.

## SAFETY NOTICE

Proper service and repair procedures are vital to the safe, reliable operation of all motor vehicles, as well as the personal safety of those performing repairs. This manual outlines procedures for servicing and repairing vehicles using safe, effective methods. The procedures contain many NOTES, CAUTIONS and WARNINGS which should be followed along with standard safety procedures to eliminate the possiblity of personal injury or improper service which could damage the vehicle of compromise its safety.

It is important to note that repair procedures and techniques, tools and parts for servicing motor vehicles, as well as the skill and experience of the individual performing the work, vary widely. It is not possible to anticipate all of the conceivable ways or conditions under which vehicles may be serviced, or to provide cautions to all of the possible hazards that may result. Standard and accepted safety precautions and equipment should be used when handling toxic or flammable fluids, and safety goggles or other protection should be used when handling toxic or flammable fluids, and safety goggles or other protection should be used during cutting, grinding, chiseling, prying or any process than can cause material removal or projectiles.

Some procedures require the use of tools especialy designed for a specific purpose. Before substituting another tool or procedure, you must be completely satisfied that neither your personal safety, nor the performance of the vehicle will be endangered.

# INDEX

# GENERAL INFORMATION

## Introduction

This concise, but comprehensive service manual places emphasis on diagnosing, troubleshooting, adjustments, testing, disassembly and assembly of the automatic transmission.

This manual will consist of the following major sections:
1. General Information section
2. Import Car Automatic Transmission/Transaxle section
3. Import Truck Automatic Transmission section
4. Modification section
5. Correction section.

Within the Automatic Transmission sections, the following information is included:
1. Transmission Application Chart.
2. General description—to include:
   a. Model and type.
   b. Capacities.
   c. Fluid specifications.
   d. Checking fluid level.
3. Transmission modifications
4. Trouble diagnosis—to include:
   a. Hydraulic system operation
   b. Oil pressure test.
   c. Air pressure test.
   d. Stall test.
   e. Control pressure specifications.
   f. Shift speed specifications (when available).
5. On Car services—to include:
   a. Adjustments.
   b. Removal and installation.
6. Transmission/Transaxle removal and installation.
7. Bench overhaul—to include:
   a. Transmission/transaxle disassembly.
   b. Internal component disassembly and assembly.
   c. Transmission/transaxle assembly.
8. Specifications.
9. Factory recommended tools.

## Metric Fasteners And Inch System

Metric bolt sizes and bolt pitch are more commonly used for all fasteners on the automatic transmissions/transaxles now being manufactured. The metric bolt sizes and thread pitches are very close to the dimensions of the similar inch system fasteners and for this reason, replacement fasteners must have the same measurement and strength as those removed.

Do not attempt to interchange metric fasteners for inch system fasteners. Mismatched and incorrect fasteners can result in dam-

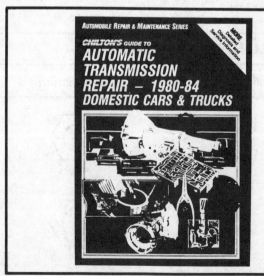

Companion manual—"Chilton's Guide to Automatic Transmission Repair, 1980-84 Domestic Cars & Trucks"

## (ENGLISH) INCH SYSTEM Bolt, 1/2-13x1

G- Grade Marking
(bolt strength)
L- Length, (inches)**
T- Thread Pitch
(thread/inch)
D- Nominal Diameter
(inches)

## METRIC SYSTEM Bolt M12-1.75x25

P- Property Class*
(bolt strength)
L- Length (millimeters)**
T- Thread Pitch (thread width
crest to crest mm)
D- Nominal Diameter
(millimeters)

*The property class is an Arabic numeral distinguishable from the slash SAE English grade system.
**The length of all bolts is measured from the underside of the head to the end.

**Comparison of the English Inch and Metric system bolt and thread nomenclature**(© Ford Motor Co.)

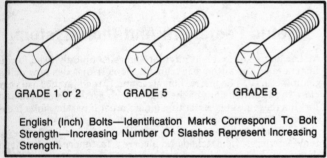

GRADE 1 or 2        GRADE 5        GRADE 8

English (Inch) Bolts—Identification Marks Correspond To Bolt
Strength—Increasing Number Of Slashes Represent Increasing
Strength.

**Typical English Inch bolt head identification marks**
(© Ford Motor Co.)

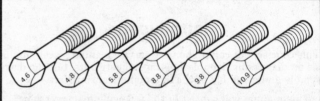

Metric Bolts—Identification Class Numbers Correspond To Bolt
Strength—Increasing Numbers Represent Increasing Strength.
Common Metric Fastener Bolt Strength Property Are 9.8 And 10.9
With The Class Identification Embossed On The Bolt Head.

**Typical Metric bolt head identification marks**
(© Ford Motor Co.)

## (ENGLISH) INCH SYSTEM

| Grade | Identification |
|---|---|
| Hex Nut Grade 5 | 3 Dots |
| Hex Nut Grade 8 | 6 Dots |

Increasing dots represent increasing strength.

## METRIC SYSTEM

| Class | Identification |
|---|---|
| Hex Nut Property Class 9 | Arabic 9 |
| Hex Nut Property Class 10 | Arabic 10 |

May also have blue finish or paint daub on hex flat.
Increasing numbers represent increasing strength.

**Comparison of English Inch and Metric hex nut strength identification marks**(© Ford Motor Co.)

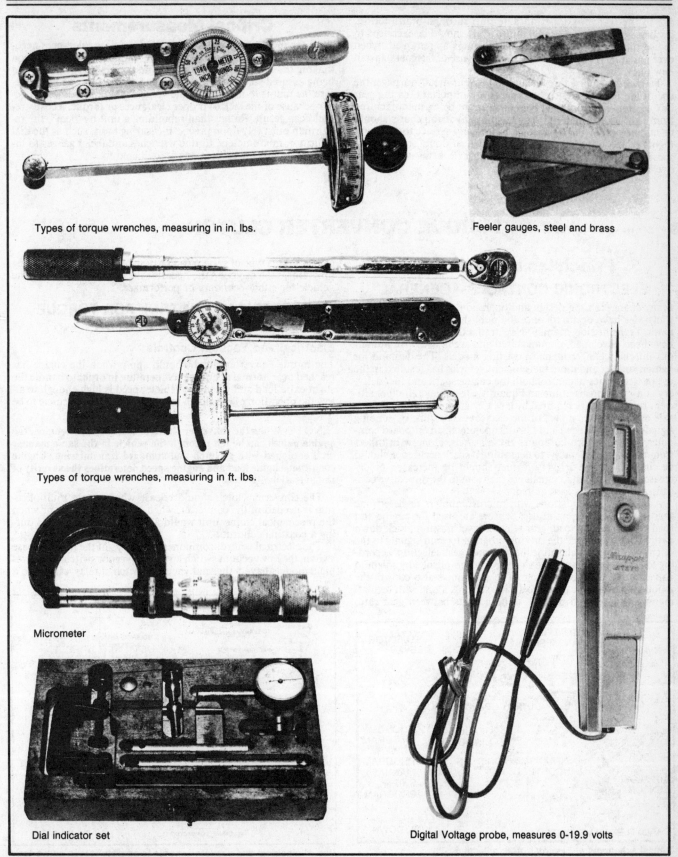

Types of torque wrenches, measuring in in. lbs.

Feeler gauges, steel and brass

Types of torque wrenches, measuring in ft. lbs.

Micrometer

Dial indicator set

Digital Voltage probe, measures 0-19.9 volts

**Typical precision measuring tools**

age to the transmission/transaxle unit through malfunction, breakage or possible personal injury. Care should be exercised to re-use the fasteners in their same locations as removed, when ever possible. If any doubt exists in the re-use of fasteners, install new ones.

To avoid stripped threads and to prevent metal warpage, the use of the torque wrench becomes more important, as the gear box assembly and internal components are being manufactured from light weight material. The torque conversion charts should be understood by the repairman, to properly service the requirements of the torquing procedures. When in doubt, refer to the specifications for the transmission/transaxle being serviced or overhauled.

## Critical Measurements

With the increase use of transaxles and the close tolerances needed throughout the drive train, more emphasis is placed upon making the critical bearing and gear measurements correctly and being assured that correct preload and turning torque exists before the unit is re-installed in the vehicle. Should a comeback occur because of the lack of proper clearances or torque, a costly rebuild can result. Rather than rebuilding a unit by "feel", the repairman must rely upon precise measuring tools, such as the dial indicator, micrometers, torque wrenches and feeler gauges to insure that correct specifications are adhered to.

# TORQUE CONVERTER CLUTCH

## Principles of Operation

### ELECTRONIC CONTROLS—GENERAL

Many changes in the design and operation of the transmission/transaxles have occurred since the publishing of our first Automatic Transmission Manual. New transaxles and transmissions have been developed, manufactured and are in use, with numerous internal changes made in existing models. The demand for lighter, smaller and more fuel efficient vehicles has resulted in the use of electronics to control both the engine spark and fuel delivery at a more precise time and quantity, to achieve the fuel efficient results that are required by law. Certain transmission/transaxle assemblies are a part of the electronic controls, by sending signals of vehicle speed and throttle opening to an on-board computer, which in turn computes these signals, along with others from the engine assembly, to determine if spark occurence should be changed or the delivery fo fuel should be increased or decreased. The computed signals are then sent to the respective controls and/or sensors as required.

Automatic transmissions with microcomputers to determine gear selections are now in use. Sensors are used for engine and road speeds, engine load, gear selector lever position, kick down switch and a status of the driving program to send signals to the microcomputer to determine the optimum gear selection, according to a preset program. The shifting is accomplished by solenoid valves in the hydraulic system. The electronics also control the modulated hydraulic pressure during shifting, along with regulating engine torque to provide smooth shifts between gear ratio changes. This type of system can be designed for different driving programs, such as giving the operator the choice of operating the vehicle for either economy or performace.

### ELECTRICAL CONTROL FOR TORQUE CONVERTER CLUTCH

#### Electrical and Vacuum Controls

The torque converter clutch should apply when the engine has reached near normal operating temperature in order to handle the slight extra load and when the vehicle speed is high enough to allow the operation of the clutch to be smooth and the vehicle to be free of engine pulses.

**NOTE: When the converter clutch is coupled to the engine, the engine pulses can be felt through the vehicle in the same manner as if equipped with a clutch and standard transmission. Engine condition, engine load and engine speed determines the severity of the pulsations.**

The converter clutch should release when torque multiplication is needed in the converter, when coming to a stop, or when the mechanical connection would affect exhaust emissions during a coasting condition.

The electrical control components consists of the brake release switch, the low vacuum switch and the governor switch. Some vehicle models have a thermal vacuum switch, a relay valve and a

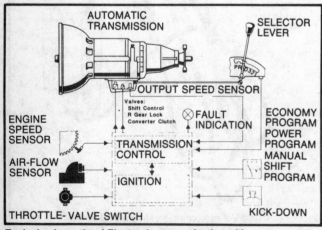

Typical schematic of Electronic gear selection with microcomputer control (© ZF of North America, Inc.)

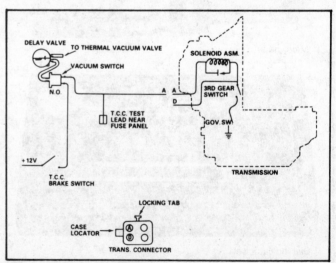

Use of electrical and vacuum controls to operate torque converter clutch (© General Motors Corp.)

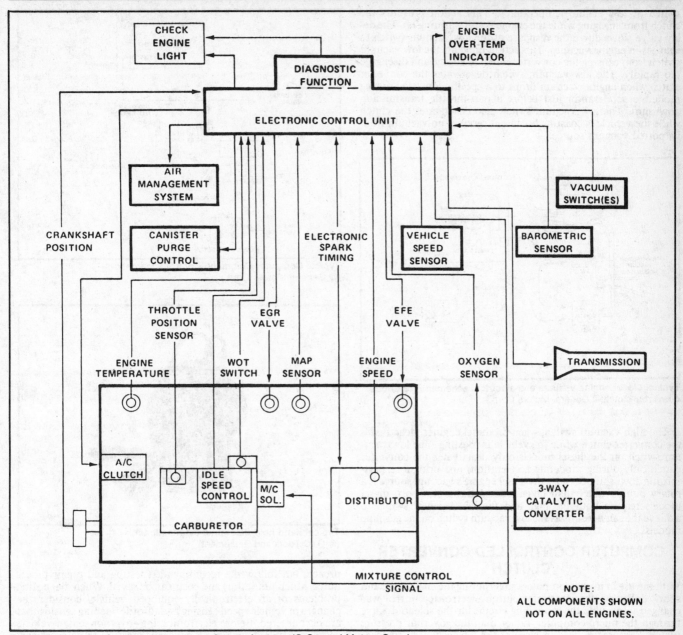

**Typical schematic of a computer command control system**(© General Motors Corp.)

delay valve. Diesel engines use a high vacuum switch in addition to certain above listed components. These various components control the flow of current to the apply valve solenoid. By controlling the current flow, these components activate or deactivate the solenoid, which in turn engages or disengages the transmission converter clutch, depending upon the driving conditions as mentioned previously. The components have the two basic circuits, electrical and vacuum.

## ELECTRICAL CURRENT FLOW

All of the components in the electrical circuit must be closed or grounded before the solenoid can open the hydraulic circuit to engage the converter clutch. The circuit begins at the fuse panel and flows to the brake switch and as long as the brake pedal is not depressed, the current will flow to the low vacuum switch on the gasoline engines and to the high vacuum switch on the diesel engines. These two switches open or close the circuit path to the so-

lenoid, dependent upon the engine or pump vacuum. If the low vacuum switch is closed (high vacuum switch on diesel engines), the current continues to flow to the transmission case connector, into the solenoid and to the governor pressure switch. When the vehicle speed is approximately 35-50 mph, the governor switch grounds to activate the solenoid. The solenoid, in turn, opens a hydraulic circuit to the converter clutch assembly, engaging the unit.

It should be noted that external vacuum controls include the thermal vacuum valve, the relay valve, the delay valve, the low vacuum switch and a high vacuum switch (used on diesel engines). Keep in mind that all of the electrical or vacuum components may not be used on all engines, at the same time.

## VACUUM FLOW

The vacuum relay valve works with the thermal vacuum valve to keep the engine vacuum from reaching the low vacuum valve switch at low engine temperatures. This action prevents the clutch from engaging while the engine is still warming up. The delay valve slows down the response of the low vacuum switch to changes in engine vacuum. This action prevents the low vacuum switch from causing the converter clutch to engage and disengage too rapidly. The low vacuum switch deactivates the converter clutch when engine vacuum drops to a specific low level during moderate acceleration just before a part-throttle transmission downshift. The low vacuum switch also deactivates the clutch while the vehicle is coasting because it receives no vacuum from its ported vacuum source.

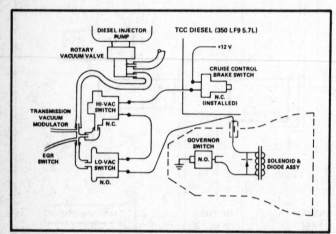

**Typical diesel engine vacuum and electrical schematic for torque converter clutch**(© General Motors Corp.)

The high vacuum switch, when on diesel engines, deactivates the converter clutch while the vehicle is coasting. The low vacuum switch on the diesel models only deactivates the converter clutch only during moderate acceleration, just prior to a part-throttle downshift. Because the diesel engine's vacuum source is a rotary pump, rather than taken from a carburetor port, diesel models require both the high and the low vacuum switch to achieve the same results as the low vacuum switch on the gasoline models.

## COMPUTER CONTROLLED CONVERTER CLUTCH

With the use of micro-computers governoring the engine fuel and spark delivery, the converter clutch electronic control was changed to provide the grounding circuit for the solenoid valve through the micro-computer, rather than the governor pressure switch. Sensors are used in place of the formerly used switches and send signals back to the micro-computer to indicate if the engine is in its proper mode to accept the mechanical lock-up of the converter clutch.

Normally a coolant sensor, a throttle position sensor, an engine vacuum sensor and a vehicle speed sensor are used to signal the micro-computer when the converter clutch can be applied. Should a sensor indicate the need for the converter clutch to be deactivated, the grounding circuit to the transmission solenoid valve would be interrupted and the converter clutch would be released.

### Diagnostic Precautions

We have entered into the age of electronics and with it, the need for the diagnostician to increase the skills needed for this particular field. By learning the basic components, their operation, the testing procedures and by applying a "common sense" approach to the diagnosis procedures, repairs can be made accurately and quickly. Avoid the "short-cut" and "parts replacement" ap-

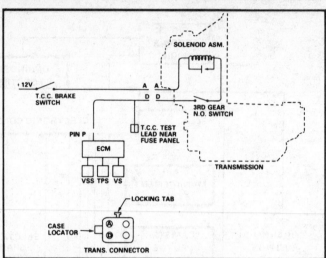

**Typical Computer Command Control schematic**
(© General Motors Corp.)

**Typical hand held Electronic diagnostic tool**
(© OTC Tools and Equipment)

proach, but follow the recommended testing and repair procedures. Much time effort and costs can be saved. When diagnosing problems of an electronically equipped vehicle, consider the changes in vehicle speed sensing and throttle opening sensing that are encountered. Before electronics, the governor sensed vehicle speed and by allowing more governor pressure to be produced, overcame throttle and main line pressures to move the shifting valves. Now, the vehicle speed is sensed from a small electric producing generator, mounted on or near the speedometer or cable and is activated by the rotation of the speedometer cable. This signal is then directed to the micro-computer for computation on when the converter clutch should be engaged or disengaged.

The governor operation still remains the same as to the shifting and producing of governor pressure, but its importance of being the vehicle speed sensor has now diminished. A throttle positioner switch has been added to the carburetor to more precisely identify the position of the throttle plates in regards to vehicle speed and load. The throttle cable or modulator are still used to control the throttle pressure within the transmission/transaxle assemblies. Added pressure switches are mounted to the various passages of the valve bodies to sense gear changes, by allowing electrical current to either pass through or be blocked by the switches. The repairman must be attentive when overhauling or replacing the valve body, to be sure the correct pressure switch is installed in the correct hydraulic passage, because the switches have either normally closed (N.C.) contacts or normally open (N.O.) contacts and would be identified on the electrical schematic as such. To interchange switches would cause malfunctions and possible costly repairs to both the transmission and to the electronic system components.

The many types of automatic transmissions that employ the electronic controlled converter clutch, do not follow the same electronic or hydraulic routings nor have the same sensors, oil pressure switches and vacuum sensing applications. Therefore, before diagnosing a fault in the converter clutch assembly, the electric, the electronic or hydraulic circuits, identify the automatic transmission as to its model designation and code.

**NOTE: Refer to the proper diagnostic outline in the individual automatic transmission outline or to the General Motors Turbo Hydra-Matic Converter Clutch Diagnostic outline, at the beginning of the General Motors Automatic Transmission Sections.**

## HYDRAULIC CONVERTER CLUTCH OPERATION

Numerous automatic transmissions rely upon hydraulic pressures to sense, determine when and to apply the converter clutch assembly. This type of automatic transmission unit is considered to be a self-contained unit with only the shift linkage, throttle cable or modulator valve being external. Specific valves, located within the valve body or oil pump housing, are caused to be moved when a sequence of events occur within the unit. For example, to engage the converter clutch, most all automatic transmissions require the gear ratio to be in the top gear before the converter clutch control valves can be placed in operation. The governor and throttle pressures must maintain specific fluid pressures at various points within the hydraulic circuits to aid in the engagement or disengagement of the converter clutch. In addition, check valves must properly seal and move to exhaust pressured fluid at the correct time to avoid "shudders" or "chuckles" during the initial application and engagement of the converter clutch.

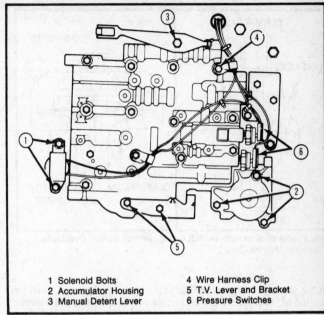

| | |
|---|---|
| 1 Solenoid Bolts | 4 Wire Harness Clip |
| 2 Accumulator Housing | 5 T.V. Lever and Bracket |
| 3 Manual Detent Lever | 6 Pressure Switches |

**Valve body components and pressure switches**
(© General Motors Corp.)

## CENTRIFUGAL TORQUE CONVERTER CLUTCH OPERATION

A torque converter has been in use that mechanically locks up centrifugally without the use of electronics or hydraulic pressure. At specific input shaft speeds, brake-like shoes move outward from the rim of the turbine assembly, to engage the converter housing, locking the converter unit mechanically together for a 1:1 ratio. Slight slippage can occur at the low end of the rpm scale,

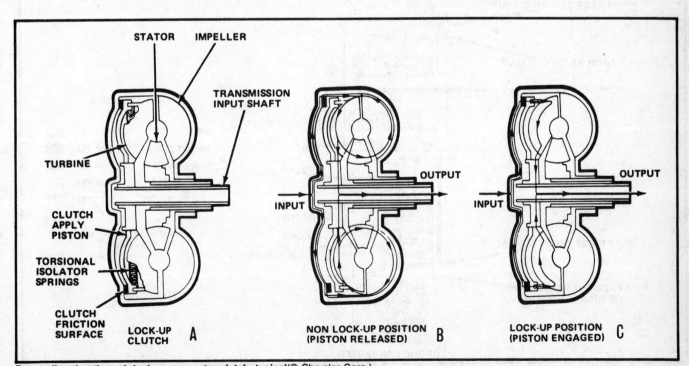

**Power direction through lock-up converter clutch, typical** (© Chrysler Corp.)

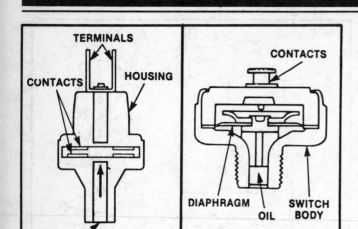

Comparison of pressure switch and governor switch terminals (© General Motors Corp.)

## MECHANICAL CONVERTER LOCK-UP OPERATION

An other type of converter lock-up is the Ford Motor Company's AOD Automatic Overdrive transmission, which uses a direct drive input shaft splined to the damper assembly of the torque converter cover to the direct clutch, bypassing the torque converter reduction components. A second shaft encloses the direct drive input shaft and is coupled between the converter turbine and the reverse clutch or forward clutch, depending upon their applied phase. With this type of unit, when in third gear, the input shaft torque is split, 30% hydraulic and 70% mechanical. When in the overdrive or fourth gear, the input torque is completely mechanical and the transmission is locked mechanically to the engine.

## CONFIRMING LOCK-UP OF TORQUE CONVERTER

To confirm the lock-up of the torque converter has occurred, check the engine rpm with a tachometer while the vehicle is being driven. If the torque converter is locked-up, the engine rpm will decrease approximately 200-400 rpm, at the time of lock-up.

# Overdrive Units

With need for greater fuel economy, the automatic transmission/transaxles were among the many vehicle components that have been modified to aid in this quest. Internal changes have been made and in some cases, additions of a fourth gear to provide the

but the greater the rpm, the tighter the lock-up. Again, it must be mentioned, that when the converter has locked-up, the vehicle may respond in the same manner as driving with a clutch and standard transmission. This is considered normal and does not indicate converter clutch or transmission problems. Keep in mind if engines are in need of tune-ups or repairs, the lock-up "shudder" or "chuckle" feeling may be greater.

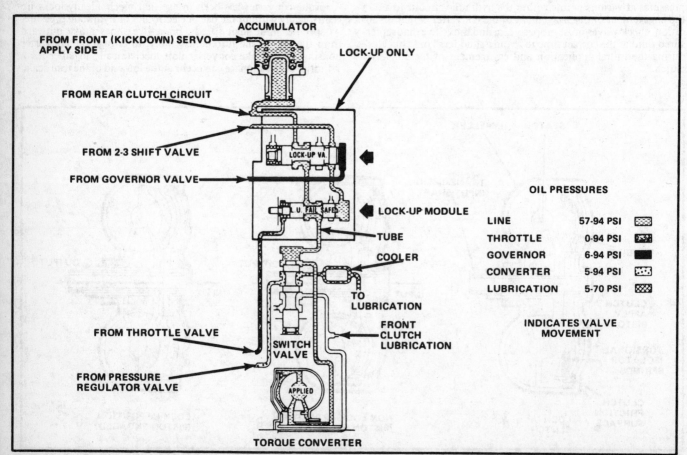

Typical hydraulic schematic for the lock-up converter controls. Note governor pressure reaction area on the lock-up valve(© Chrysler Corp.)

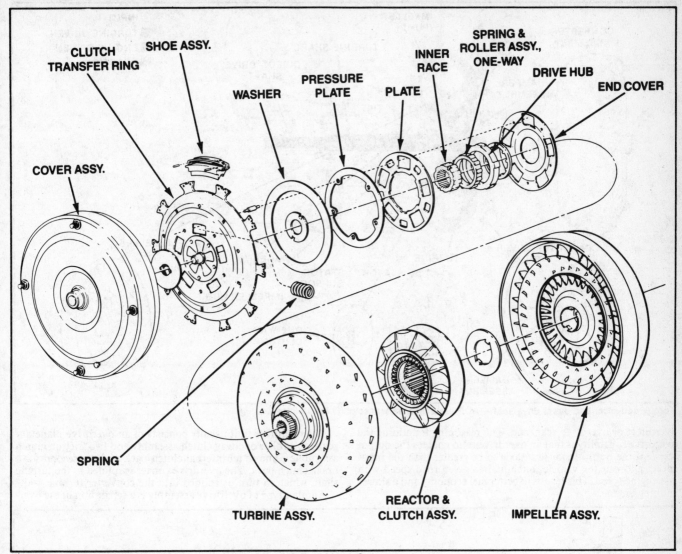

Exploded view of centrifugal type torque converter clutch(© Ford Motor Co.)

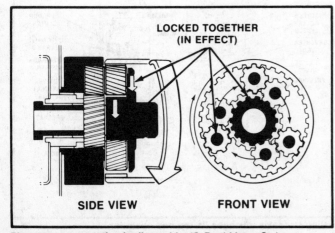

Planetary gear rotation in direct drive(© Ford Motor Co.)

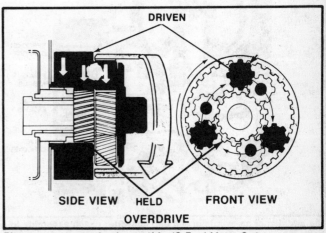

Planetary gear rotation in overdrive(© Ford Motor Co.)

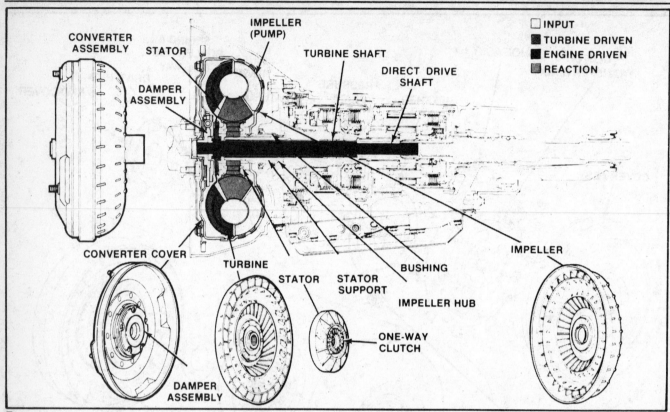

INPUT
TURBINE DRIVEN
ENGINE DRIVEN
REACTION

Torque converter and direct drive shaft—AOD automatic transmission(© Ford Motor Co.)

overdirect or overdrive gear ratio. The reasoning for adding the overdrive capability is that an overdrive ratio enables the output speed of the transmission/transaxle to be greater than the input speed, allowing the vehicle to maintain a given road speed with less engine speed. This results in better fuel economy and a slower running engine.

The overdrive unit usually consists of an overdrive planetary gear set, a roller one-way clutch assembly and two friction clutch assemblies, one as an internal clutch pack and the second for a brake clutch pack. The overdrive carrier is splined to the turbine shaft, which in turn, is splined into the converter turbine.

Another type of overdrive assembly is a separation of the over-

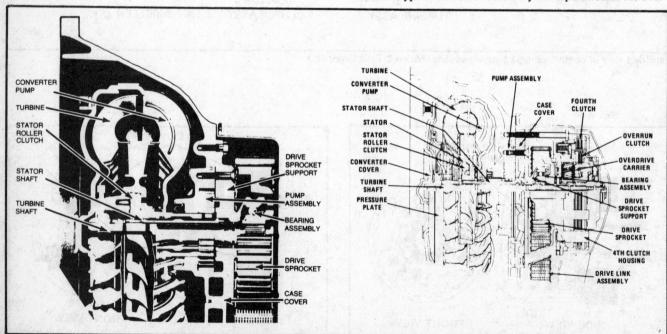

The addition of an overdrive unit and converter clutch assembly to an existing transaxle, changes its top end operation (© General Motors Corp.)

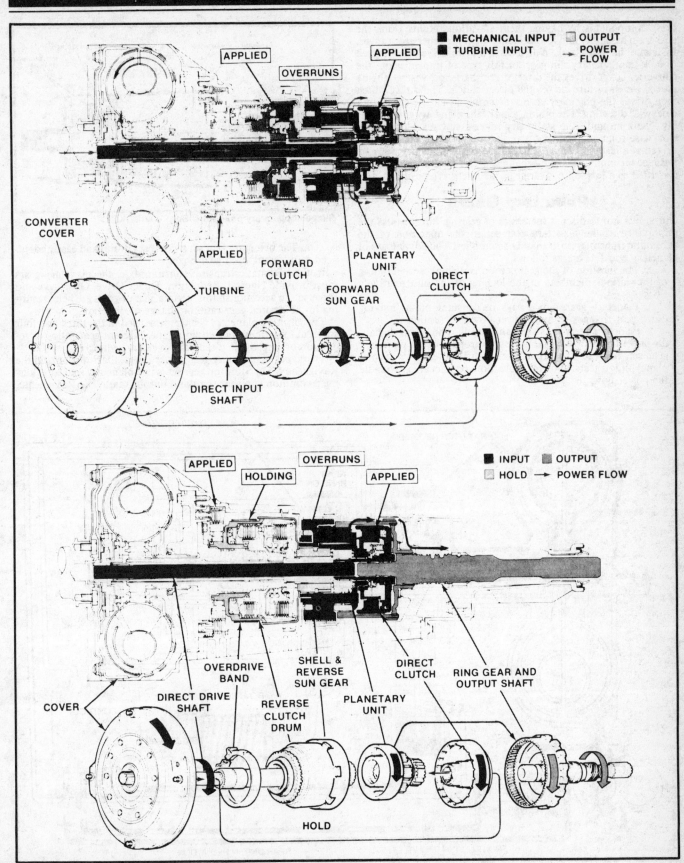

Comparison of direct drive and overdrive power flows(© Ford Motor Co.)

drive components by having them at various points along the gear train assembly and also utilizing them for other gear ranges. Instead of having a brake clutch pack, an overdrive band is used to lock the planetary sun gear. In this type of transmission, the converter cover drives the direct drive shaft clockwise at engine speed, which in turn drives the direct clutch. The direct clutch then drives the planetary carrier assembly at engine speed in a clockwise direction. The pinion gears of the planetary gear assembly "walk around" the stationary reverse sun gear, again in a clockwise rotation. The ring gear and output shaft are therefore driven at a faster speed by the rotation of the planetary pinions. Because the input is 100% mechanical drive, the converter can be classified as a lock-up converter in the overdrive position.

## Planetary Gears

Our aim is not to discuss the basics of gearing, but to stress the importance of the planetary gear set in the operation of the automatic transmission/transaxle assemblies. The advantages of planetary gear sets are as follows;

a. The location of the gear components makes the holding of the various members or the locking of the unit relatively easy.

b. Planetary gears are always in constant mesh, making quick gear changes without power flow interruption.

c. Planetary gears are strong and sturdy. The gears can handle larger torque loads as it is passed through the the planetary gear set, because the torque load is distributed over several planet pinion gears, allowing more tooth contact area to handle the power flow.

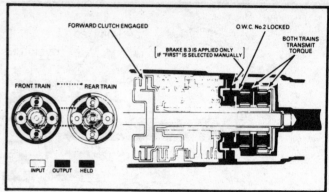

Simpson planetary gear set (© Borg Warner, Ltd.)

d. The planetary gear set is compact in size and easily adapted to different sized gear boxes.

In the automatic transmission/transaxle, the planetary gears must provide Neutral, Reduction, Direct Drive, Overdrive and Reverse. To accomplish this, certain gear or gears are held, resulting in the desired gear ratio or change of direction.

Two or more planetary gear sets are used in the three and four speed automatic units, providing the different gear ratios in reduction or to provide a separate overdrive ratio.

Two types of planetary gear sets are used, the Simpson and the Ravigneaux. The Simpson gear set is two planetary gear sets sharing a common sun gear shaft and output shaft. The Ravigneaux

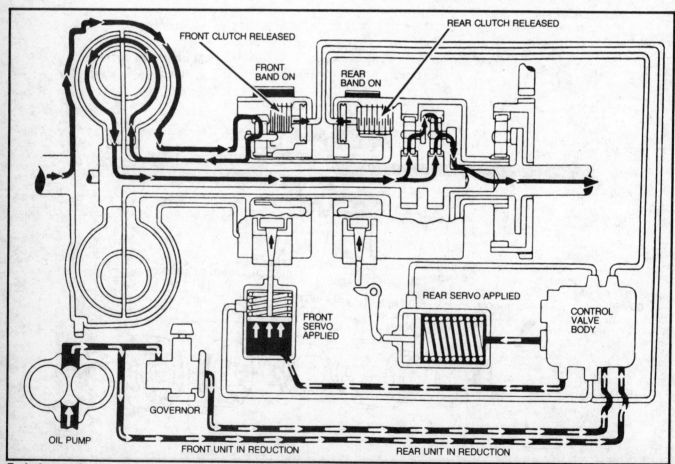

Typical power flow through an automatic transmission, using clutches, bands and planetary gear sets, with servo application illustrated

gear set utilizes a dual pinion planetary carrier, two sun gears and a ring gear. The pinion gears consists of short pinions (primary) and long pinions (secondary). Most automatic gear boxes use the Simpson type planetary gear assemblies.

## HOLDING OR LOCKING-UP COMPONENTS OF THE PLANETARY GEARS

The holding or locking-up of the planetary gears is accomplished by hydraulic pressure, directed to a specific component, by the opening or closing of fluid passages in the transmission/transaxle assembly by spool type valves, either operated manually or automatically. The holding components are either clutch packs, internal or external, bands or overrunning "one-way" clutch units. Depending upon the design of the transmission/transaxle assembly, would dictate the holding of a specific part of the planetary gear unit by the holding components. It is important for the repairman to refer to the clutch and band application chart to determine the holding components in a particular gear ratio.

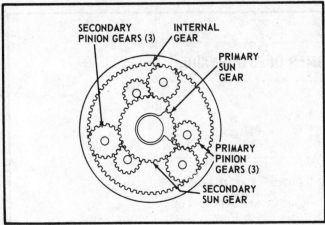

Ravigneaux planetary gear set(© General Motors Corp.)

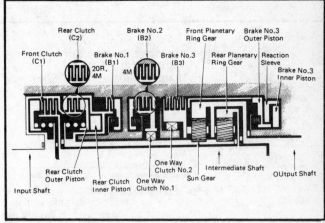

Typical component arrangement using clutch brakes instead of bands(© Toyota Motor Co.)

# DIAGNOSING AUTOMATIC TRANSMISSION/TRANSAXLE MALFUNCTIONS

Diagnosing automatic transmission problems is simplified following a definite procedure and understanding the basic operation of the individual transmission that is being inspected or serviced. Do not attempt to "short-cut" the procedure or take for granted that another technician has performed the adjustments or the critical checks. It may be an easy task to locate a defective or burned-out unit, but the technician must be skilled in locating the primary reason for the unit failure and must repair the malfunction to avoid having the same failure occur again.

Each automatic transmission manufacturer has developed a diagnostic procedure for their individual transmissions. Although the operation of the units are basically the same, many differences will appear in the construction, method of unit application and the hydraulic control systems.

The same model transmissions can be installed in different makes of vehicles and are designed to operate under different load stresses, engine applications and road conditions. Each make of vehicle will have specific adjustments or use certain outside manual controls to operate the individual unit, but may not interchange with another transmission/vehicle application from the same manufacturer.

The identification of the transmission is most important so that the proper preliminary inspections and adjustments may be done and if in need of a major overhaul, the correct parts may be obtained and installed to avoid costly delays.

## CUSTOMER EXPLANATION OF MALFUNCTION

The customer should be approached and questioned in a professional, but friendly and courteous manner as to the malfunction that could exist in the gearbox. By evaluating the answers, a pattern could emerge as to why this problem exists, what to do to correct it and what should be done to prevent a recurrence. Should the vehicle be towed because of apparent transmission failure, the cause should be determined before the unit is re-

Obtaining customer explanation of malfunction(© Ford Motor Co.)

moved to be certain a stalled engine, a broken or worn drive line component, broken drive plate or lack of fluid could be the cause. Again, question the owner/driver as to what happened, when and where the malfunction took place, such as engine flare-up, starting from a stop and/or on a hill. From the answers given, usually the correct diagnosis can be determined. Physical inspection of the vehicle components is the next step, to verify that either the outer components are at fault or the unit must be removed for overhaul.

## SYSTEMATIC DIAGNOSIS

Transmission/transaxle manufacturers have compiled diagnostic aids for the use of technicians when diagnosing malfunctions through oil pressure tests or road test procedures. Diagnostic symptom charts, operational shift speed charts, oil pressure specifications, clutch and band application charts and oil flow schematics are some of the aids available.

Numerous manufacturers and re-manufacturers require a diag-

---

| AUTOMATIC TRANSMISSION | CUSTOMER QUESTIONNAIRE |
|---|---|

1. How long have you had the condition?          R. O. _____

   □ Since car was new
   □ Recently (when?) _____
   □ Came on gradually          □ Suddenly

2. Describe the condition?

|  | P-R-N-D-2-1 SELECTOR POSITION(S) | CHECK AS APPROPRIATE WHICH GEAR? | | |
|---|---|---|---|---|
| | | HIGH | INTERMEDIATE | LOW |
| □ Slow Engagement | | | | |
| □ Rough Engagement | | | | |
| □ Slip | | | | |
| □ No Drive | | | | |
| □ No Upshift | | | | |
| □ No Downshift | | | | |
| □ Slip During Shift | | | | |
| □ Wrong Shift Speed(s) | | | | |
| □ Rough Shift | | | | |
| □ Mushy Shift | | | | |
| □ Erratic Shift | | | | |
| □ Engine "runaway or "buzzy" | | | | |
| □ No Kickdown | | | | |
| □ Starts in high gear in D | | | | |
| □ Starts in intermediate gear in D | | | | |
| □ Oil leak (where?) | | | | |

3. Which of the following cause or affect the condition?

   □ Transmission cold          □ Engine at fast (cold) idle
   □ After warm-up              □ Normal idle
   □ High speed                 □ Wet road
   □ Cruising speed             □ Dry road
   □ Low Speed                  □ Braking
   □ Accelerating               □ Coasting down

4. Does the engine need a tune-up?

   □ Yes          □ No          □ When was last tune-up? _____

5. Describe any strange noises

   □ Rumble                     □ Squeak
   □ Knock                      □ Grind
   □ Chatter                    □ Hiss
   □ Snap or pop                □ Scrape
   □ Buzz                       □ Other (describe)_____
   □ Whine

Ford Parts and Service Division
Training and Publications Department

**SERVICE ADVISOR HELPER**

---

**Customer questionnaire, published by Ford Motor Co., for use by their Dealer body diagnostic personnel. Typical of other manufacturers** (© Ford Motor Co.)

nosis check sheet be filled out by the diagnostician, pertaining to the operation, fluid level, oil pressures (idling and at various speeds), verification of adjustments and possible causes and the needed correction of the malfunctions. In certain cases, authorization must be obtained before repairs can be done, with the diagnostic check sheet accompanying the request for payment or warranty claim, along with the return of defective parts.

It is a good policy to use the diagnostic check sheet for the evaluation of all transmission/transaxles diagnosis and include the completed check sheet in the owners service file, should future reference be needed.

Many times, a rebuilt unit is exchanged for the defective unit, saving down time for the owner and vehicle. However, if the diagnostic check sheet would accompany the removed unit to the rebuilder, more attention could be directed to verifying and repairing the malfunctioning components to avoid costly comebacks of the rebuilt unit, at a later date. Most large volume rebuilders employ the use of dynamometers, as do the new unit manufacturers, to verify proper build-up of the unit and its correct operation before it is put in service.

### GENERAL DIAGNOSIS

Should the diagnostician not use a pre-printed check sheet for the diagnosing of the malfunctioning unit, a sequence for diagnosis of the gear box is needed to proceed in an orderly manner. A suggested sequence is as follows:
1. Inspect and correct the fluid level.
2. Inspect and adjust the throttle or kick-down linkage.
3. Inspect and adjust the manual linkage.
4. Install one or more oil pressure gauges to the transmission as instructed in the individual transmission sections.

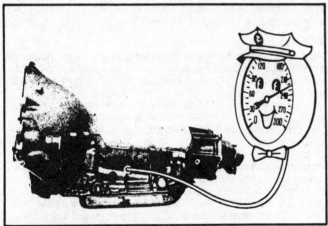

Use the oil pressure gauge(© General Motors Corp.)

5. Road test the vehicle (with owner if possible).

**NOTE: During the road test, use all the selector ranges while noting any differences in operation or changes in oil pressures, so that the unit or hydraulic circuit can be isolated that is involved in the malfunction.**

## Engine Performance

When engine performance has declined due to the need of an engine tune-up or a system malfunction, the operation of the transmission is greatly affected. Rough or slipping shift and overheating of the transmission and fluid can occur, which can develop into serious internal transmission problems. Complete the adjustments or repairs to the engine before the road test is attempted or transmission adjustments made.

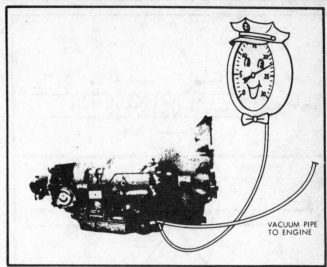

Use the vacuum gauge as required(© General Motors Corp.)

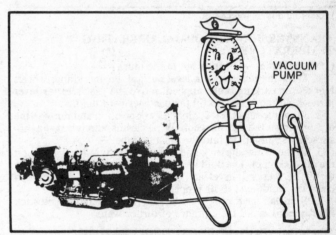

Using the hand operated vacuum pump as required
(© General Motors Corp.)

## Inspection of the Fluid Level

Most automatic transmissions are designed to operate with the fluid level between the ADD or ONE PINT and FULL marks on the dipstick indicator, with the fluid at normal operating temperature. The normal operating temperature is attained by operating the engine-transmission assembly for at least 8 to 15 miles of driving or its equivalent. The fluid temperature should be in the range of 150° to 200°F when normal operating temperature is attained.

**NOTE: If the vehicle has been operated for long periods at high speed or in extended city traffic during hot weather, an accurate fluid level check cannot be made until the fluid cools, normally 30 minutes after the vehicle has been parked, due to fluid heat in excess of 200° F.**

The transmission fluid can be checked during two ranges of temperature.
1. Transmission at normal operating temperature.
2. Transmission at room temperature.

During the checking procedure and adding of fluid to the transmission, it is most important not to overfill the reservoir to avoid foaming and loss of fluid through the breather, which can cause slippage and transmission failure.

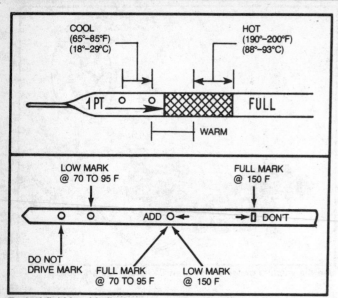

**Typical fluid level indicators**

### TRANSMISSION AT NORMAL OPERATING TEMPERATURE

**(150° to 200° F.—Dipstick hot to the touch)**

1. With the vehicle on a level surface, engine idling, wheels blocked or parking brake applied, move the gear selector lever through all the ranges to fill the passages with fluid.
2. Place the selector lever in the Park position and remove the dipstick from the transmission. Wipe clean and reinsert the dipstick to its full length into the dipstick tube.
3. Remove the dipstick and observe the fluid level mark on the dipstick stem. The fluid level should be between the ADD and the FULL marks. If necessary, add fluid through the filler tube to bring the fluid level to its proper height.
4. Reinstall the dipstick and be sure it is sealed to the dipstick filler tube to avoid the entrance of dirt or water.

### TRANSMISSION AT ROOM TEMPERATURE

**(65° to 95° F.—Dipstick cool to touch)**

—————————— CAUTION ——————————

*The automatic transmissions are sometimes overfilled because the fluid level is checked when the transmission has not been operated and the fluid is cold and contracted. As the transmission is warmed to normal operating temperature, the fluid level can change as much as ¼ inch.*

1. With the vehicle on a level surface, engine idling, wheels blocked or parking brake applied, move the selector lever through all the ranges to fill the passages with fluid.
2. Place the selector lever in the Park position and remove the dipstick from the transmission. Wipe clean and re-insert it back into the dipstick tube.
3. Remove the dipstick and observe the fluid level mark on the dipstick stem. The fluid should be directly below the FULL indicator.

**NOTE:** Most dipsticks will have either one mark or two marks, such as dimples or holes in the stem of the dipstick, to indicate the cold level, while others may be marked HOT or COLD levels.

4. Add enough fluid, as necessary, to the transmission, but do not overfill.

—————————— CAUTION ——————————

*This operation is most critical, due to the expansion of the fluid under heat.*

## FLUID TYPE SPECIFICATIONS

The automatic transmission fluid is used for numerous functions such as a power-transmitting fluid in the torque converter, a hydraulic fluid in the hydraulic control system, a lubricating agent for the gears, bearings and bushings, a friction-controlling fluid for the bands and clutches and a heat transfer medium to carry the heat to an air or cooling fan arrangement.

Because of the varied automatic transmission designs, different frictional characteristics of the fluids are required so that one fluid cannot assure freedom from chatter or squawking from the bands and clutches. Operating temperatures have increased sharply in many new transmissions and the transmission drain intervals have been extended or eliminated completely. It is therefore most important to install the proper automatic transmission fluid into the automatic transmission designed for its use.

### Types of Automatic Transmission Fluid

#### DEXRON® II

This fluid supersedes the Dexron® type fluid and meets a more severe set of performance requirements, such as improved high temperature oxidation resistance and low temperature fluidity. The Dexron® II is recommended for use in all General Motors, Chrysler, American Motors and certain imported vehicles automatic transmissions. This fluid can replace all Dexron® fluid with a B- number designation.

Container Identification number—D-XXXXX

#### DEXRON® II—SERIES D

This fluid was developed and is used in place of the regular Dexron® II fluids.

The container identification is with a "D" prefix to the qualification number on the top of the container.

#### TYPE F

Ford Motor Company began developing its own specifications for automatic transmission fluid in 1959 and again updated its specifications in 1967, requiring fluid with different frictional characteristics and identified as Type F fluid.

Beginning with the 1977 model year, a new Type CJ fluid was specified for use with the C-6 and newly introduced Jatco model PLA-A transmissions. This new fluid is not interchangeable with the Type F fluid.

Prior to 1967, all Ford automatic transmissions use fluids in containers marked with qualification number IP-XXXXXX, meeting Ford specification number ESW-M2C33-D.

Fluids in containers marked with qualification number 2P-XXXXXX meets Ford specification ESW-M2C33-F and is used in the Ford automatic transmissions manufactured since 1967, except the 1977 and later C-6, the Automatic Overdrive, and Jatco models PLA-A, PLA-A1, PLA-A2 transmissions.

The container identification number for the new fluid is Ford part number D7AZ-19582-A and carries a qualification number ESP-M2C138-CJ.

#### TYPE CJ

—————————— CAUTION ——————————

*The CJ fluid is NOT compatible with clutch friction material of other Ford transmissions and must only be used in the 1977 and later C-6, the Automatic Overdrive and Jatco models PLA-A, PLA-A1 and PLA-A2 automatic transmissions.*

*Do not mix or interchange the fluids through refills or topping off as the Type F and the Type CJ fluids are not compatible.*

A technical bulletin has been issued by Ford Motor Company, dated 1978, advising the compatibility of Dexron® II, series D fluid with the CJ fluid. It can be substituted or mixed, if necessary, in the 1977 and later C-6, the Automatic Overdrive and the Jatco PLA-A, PLA-A1 and PLA-A2 automatic transmissions.

With approved internal modifications, CJ or Dexron® II, series D automatic transmission fluid can be used in the past models of the C-4 transmissions. To insure the proper fluid is installed or added, a mylar label is affixed or is available to be affixed to the dipstick handle with the proper fluid designation on the label.

## TYPE H

With the introduction of the C-5 automatic Transmission, Ford Motor Company developed a new type fluid, designated "H", meeting Ford's specification ESP-M2C166-H. This fluid contains a special detergent which retains in suspension, particles generated during normal transmission operation. This suspension of particles results in a dark discoloration of the fluid and does not indicate need for service. It should be noted that the use of other fluids in the C-5 automatic transmission could result in a shuddering condition.

## TYPE G

The type G fluid is an improvement over the type F fluid and meets Ford Motor Company specification of M2C-33G.

Type G fluid has the capability of reducing oxidization at higher transmission operating temperatures. Should an automatic transmission be filled with type G fluid, type F fluid can be used to top off the level. However, the more type F fluid that is mixed with the type G fluid, will proportionally reduce the maximum working temperature of the type G fluid.

## FLUID CONDITION

During the checking of the fluid level, the fluid condition should be inspected for color and odor. The normal color of the fluid is deep red or orange-red and should not be a burned brown or black color. If the fluid color should turn to a green/brown shade at an early stage of transmission operation and have an offensive odor, but not a burned odor, the fluid condition is considered normal and not a positive sign of required maintenance or transmission failure.

With the use of absorbent white paper, wipe the dipstick and examine the stain for black, brown or metallic specks, indicating clutch, band or bushing failure, and for gum or varnish on the dipstick or bubbles in the fluid, indicating either water or antifreeze in the fluid.

Should there be evidence of water, anti-freeze or specks of residue in the fluid, the oil pan should be removed and the sediment inspected. If the fluid is contaminated or excessive solids are found in the removed oil pan, the transmission should be disassembled, completely cleaned and overhauled. In addition to the cleaning of the transmission, the converter and transmission cooling system should be cleaned and tested.

### Fluid Overfill Problems

When the automatic transmission is overfilled with fluid, the rotation of the internal units can cause the fluid to become aerated. This aeration of the fluid causes air to be picked up by the oil pump and causes loss of control and lubrication pressures. The fluid can also be forced from the transmission assembly through the air vent, due to the aerated condition.

### Fluid Underfill Problems

When the fluid is low in the transmission, slippage and loss of unit engagement can result, due to the fluid not being picked up by the pump. This condition is evident when first starting after the vehicle has been sitting and cooled to room temperature, in cold weather, making a turn or driving up a hill. This condition should be corrected promptly to avoid costly transmission repairs.

# Throttle Valve and Kickdown Control Inspection

Inspect the throttle valve and kickdown controls for proper operation, prior to the road test. Refer to the individual transmission section for procedures.

## THROTTLE VALVE CONTROLS

The throttle valve can be controlled by linkage, cable or engine vacuum.

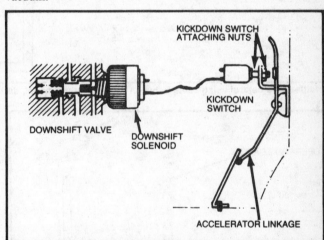

**Typical kickdown switch and controls**(© Ford Motor Co.)

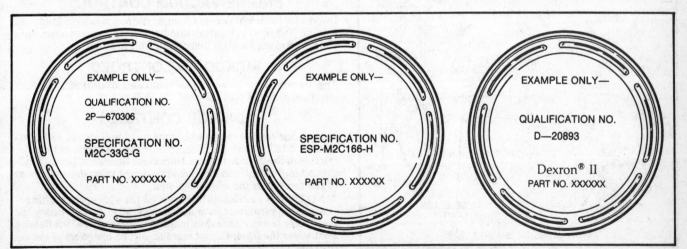

**Comparison of types H, G and Dexron® II identifying codes found on container tops—typical**

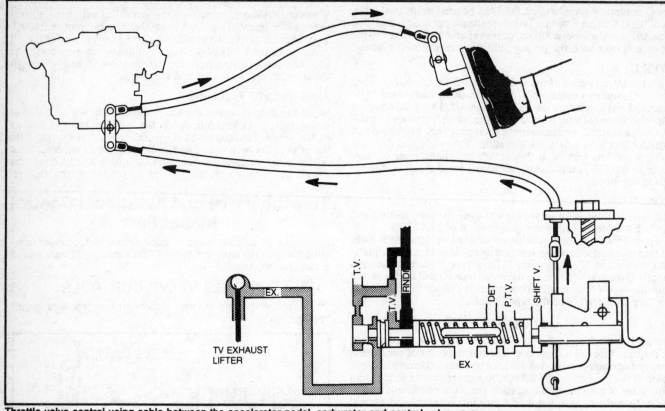

**Throttle valve control using cable between the accelerator pedal, carburetor and control valve** (© Borg Warner, Ltd.)

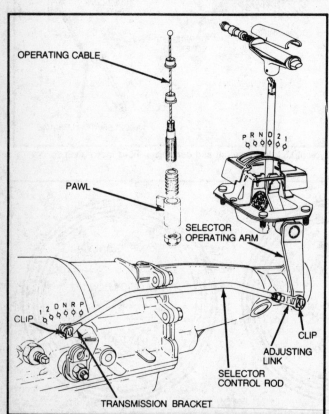

**Manual Control linkage phasing—typical**(© Ford Motor Co.)

## LINKAGE CONTROL

Inspect the linkage for abnormal bends, looseness at the bellcrank connections and linkage travel at the wide open throttle stop. Be sure the linkage operates without binding and returns to the closed position upon release of the accelerator.

## CABLE CONTROL

Inspect the cable for sharp bends or crimps, secured retainers, freedom of cable movement throughout the full throttle position and the return to the closed throttle position without binding or sticking, and connection of the throttle return spring.

## ENGINE VACUUM CONTROLS

Inspect for sufficient engine vacuum, vacuum hose condition and routing, and signs of transmission fluid in the vacuum hoses indicating a leaking vacuum diaphragm (modulator).

## KICKDOWN CONTROLS

The transmission kickdown is controlled by linkage, cable or electrical switches and solenoid.

## LINKAGE CONTROLS

The linkage control can be a separate rod connected to and operating in relation with the carburetor throttle valves, or incorporated with the throttle linkage. Inspect for looseness, bends, binding and movement into the kickdown detent upon the movement of the throttle to the wide open stop.

NOTE: It is a advisable to inspect for the wide open throttle position at the carburetor from inside the vehicle, by depressing the accelerator pedal, rather than inspecting movement of the linkage from under the hood. Carpet matting, dirt or looseness of the accelerator can prevent the opening of the throttle to operate the kickdown linkage.

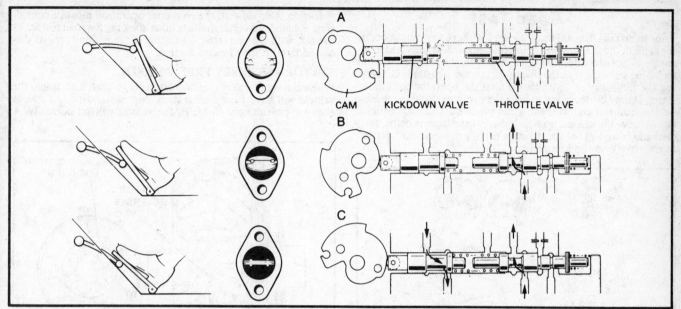

Typical throttle and kickdown valve operation through three possible operating positions of the throttle plates and accelerator pedal (© Borg Warner, Ltd.)

## CABLE CONTROLS

The kickdown cable control can be a separate cable or used with the throttle valve control cable. It operates the kickdown valve at the wide open throttle position. Inspect for kinks and bends on bracket retention of the cable. Inspect for freedom of movement of the cable and see that the cable drops into the kickdown detent when the accelerator pedal is fully depressed and the throttle valves are fully open.

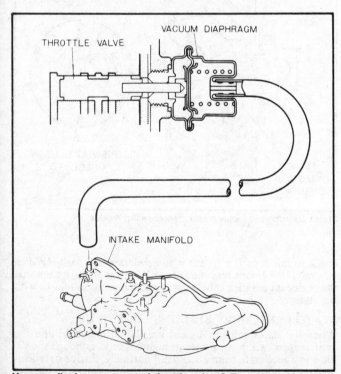

Vacuum diaphragm operated throttle valve(© Toyo Kogyo Co. Ltd.)

## ELECTRICAL CONTROLS

The electrical kickdown controls consist of a switch, located on the accelerator linkage and a solenoid control, either mounted externally on the transmission case or mounted internally on the control valve body, in such a position as to operate the kickdown valve upon demand of the vehicle operator. Inspect the switch for proper operation which should allow electrical current to pass through, upon closing of the switch contacts by depressing the accelerator linkage. Inspect the wire connector at the transmission case or the terminals of the externally mounted solenoid for current with the switch contacts closed. With current present at the solenoid, either externally or internally mounted, a clicking noise should be heard, indicating that the solenoid is operating.

### Manual Linkage Control Inspection

The manual linkage adjustment is one of the most critical, yet the most overlooked, adjustment on the automatic transmission. The controlling quadrant, either steering column or console mounted, must be properly phased with the manual control valve detent. Should the manual valve be out of adjustment or position, hydraulic leakage can occur within the control valve assembly and can result in delay of unit engagement and/or slippage of the clutches and bands upon application. The partial opening of apply passages can also occur for clutches and bands not in applying sequence, and result in dragging of the individual units or bands during transmission operation.

Inspect the selector lever and quadrant, the linkage or cable control for looseness, excessive wear or binding. Inspect the engine/transmission assembly for excessive lift during engine torque application, due to loose or broken engine mounts, which can pull the manual valve out of position in the control valve detent.

─────── CAUTION ───────

*The neutral start switch should be inspected for operation in Park and Neutral positions, after any adjustments are made to the manual linkage or cable.*

## Road Test

Prior to driving the vehicle on a road test, have the vehicle operator explain the malfunction of the transmission as fully and as accurate as possible. Because the operator may not have the same technical knowledge as the diagnostician, ask questions concerning the malfunction in a manner that the operator can understand. It may be necessary to have the operator drive the vehicle on the road test and to identify the problem. The diagnostician can observe the manner in which the transmission is being operated and can point out constructive driving habits to the operator to improve operation reliability.

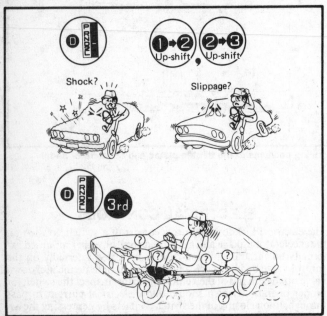

Road Test vehicle to determine malfunctions(© Toyota Motor Co.)

Many times, an actual transmission malfunction can occur without the operator's knowledge, due to slight slippages occurring and increasing in duration while the vehicle is being driven. Had the operator realized that a malfunction existed, minor adjustments possibly could have been done to avoid costly repairs.

As noted previously in this section, be aware of the engine's performance. For example, if a vacuum modulator valve is used to control the throttle pressure, an engine performing poorly cannot send the proper vacuum signals to the transmission for proper application of the throttle pressure and control pressure, in the operation of the bands and clutches. Slippages and changes in shift points can occur.

Perform the road test with the customer, whenever possible, to determine the cause of the malfunction

During the road test, the converter operation must be considered. Related converter malfunctions affecting the road test are as follows, with the converter operation, diagnosis and repairs discussed later in the General Section.

### STATOR ASSEMBLY FREE WHEELS

When the stator roller clutch freewheels in both directions, the vehicle will have poor acceleration from a standstill. At speeds above approximately 45 MPH, the vehicle will act normally. A

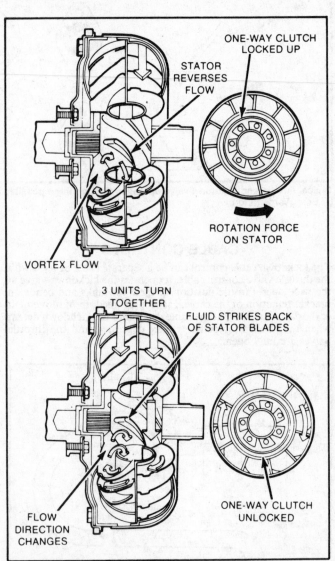

Stator operation in lock-up and freewheeling modes

check to make on the engine is to accelerate to a high RPM in neutral. If the engine responds properly, this is an indication that the engine is operating satisfactorily and the problem may be with the stator.

### STATOR ASSEMBLY REMAINS LOCKED UP

When the stator remains locked up, the engine RPM and the vehicle speed will be restricted at higher speeds, although the vehicle will accelerate from a standstill normally. Engine overheating may be noticed and visual inspection of the converter may reveal a blue color, resulting from converter overheating.

## Clutch and Band Application

During the road test, operate the transmission/transaxle in each gear position and observe the shifts for signs of any slippage, variation, sponginess or harshness. Note the speeds at which the upshifts and downshifts occur. If slippage and engine flare-up occurs in any gears, clutch, band or overrunning clutch problems are indicated and depending upon the degree of wear, a major overhaul may be indicated.

The clutch and band application chart in each transmission/transaxle section provides a basis for road test analysis to determine the internal units applied or released in a specific gear ratio.

**NOTE: Certain transmission/transaxles use brake clutches in place of bands and are usually indicated as B-1 and B-2 on the unit application chart. These components are diagnosed in the same manner as one would diagnose a band equipped gearbox.**

### EXAMPLES

Using the Borg Warner Model 66 Clutch and Band application chart as a guide, the following conditions can be determined.

1. A customer complaint is a slippage in third speed and reverse. By referring to the clutch and band application chart, the commonly applied component is the rear clutch unit, applied in both third speed and reverse. By having a starting point, place the gear selector in the reverse position and if the slippage is present and slippage is verified on the road in third speed, all indications would point to rear clutch failure.

Broken input shaft can operate intermittently at low torque applications, until worn smooth as illustrated

2. A customer complaint is a flare-up of engine speed during the 1-2 shift, D position, with a delayed application or sponginess in the second gear. By referring to the clutch and band application chart, the application of the components can be located during each shift and gear ratio level. With the front clutch unit applied in each of the gear ranges and the front band applied only in the second speed, the complaint can then be pinpointed to either the front band being out of adjustment, worn out or a servo apply problem. Because the front clutch is applied in the three forward speeds and no apparent slippage or flare-up occurs in the first or third speeds, the front clutch unit is not at fault.

Many times, malfunctions occur within a unit that are not listed on a diagnosis chart. Such malfunctions could be breakage of servo or clutch return springs, stripped serrated teeth from mated components or broken power transfer shaft, just to name a few. When a malfunction of this type occurs, it can be difficult to diagnose, but by applying the information supplied in a clutch and band application chart, the use of an oil pressure gauge, when necessary, and using a "common sense" approach, the malfunction can be determined.

### SUMMARY OF ROAD TEST

This process of elimination is used to locate the unit that is malfunctioning and to confirm the proper operation of the transmission. Although the slipping unit can be defined, the actual cause of the malfunction cannot be determined by the band and clutch application charts. It is necessary to perform hydraulic and air pressure tests to determine if a hydraulic or mechanical component failure is the cause of the malfunction.

## Pressure Tests

### OIL PRESSURE GAUGE

The oil pressure gauge is the primary tool used by the diagnostician to determine the source of malfunctions of the automatic transmissions.

Oil pressure gauges are available with different rates, ranging from 0-100, 0-300 and 0-500 PSI that are used to measure the pressures in the various hydraulic circuits of the automatic transmissions. The high-rated pressure gauges (0-300, 0-500 PSI) are used to measure the control line pressures while the low-rated gauge (0-100 PSI) is used to measure the governor, lubrication and throttle pressures on certain automatic transmissions.

The gauges may be an individual unit with a 4- to 10-foot hose attached, or may be part of a console unit with other gauges, normally engine tachometer and vacuum. The diagnostician's preference dictates the type used.

## CLUTCH AND BAND APPLICATION CHART
### Borg Warner Model 66

| Gear | Front Clutch | Rear Clutch | Front Band | Rear Band | One-Way Clutch |
|------|------|------|------|------|------|
| Drive 1st | Applied | — | — | — | Holding |
| Drive 2nd | Applied | — | Applied | — | — |
| Drive 3rd | Applied | Applied | — | — | — |
| 1—Low | Applied | — | — | Applied | — |
| 2—1st | Applied | — | — | — | Holding |
| 2—2nd | Applied | — | Applied | — | — |
| Reverse | — | Applied | — | Applied | — |

**NOTE: Rear band is released in "N", but applied in "P" for constructional reasons only.**

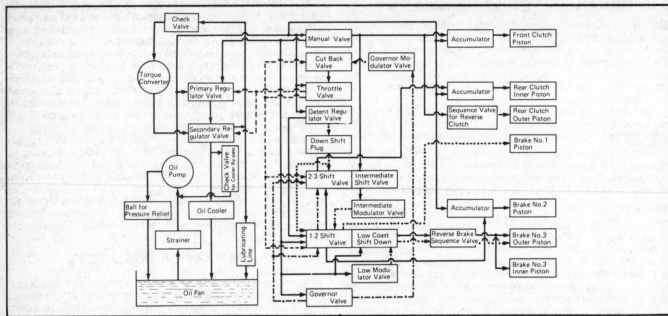

**Typical hydraulic control system**(© Toyota Motor Co.)

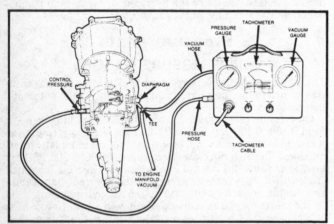

**Typical installation of oil pressure and vacuum gauges on transmission**(© Ford Motor Co.)

## CONTROL PRESSURE TESTING

The methods of obtaining control pressure readings when conducting a pressure test, vary from manufacturer to manufacturer when vacuum modulators are used to modulate the throttle pressures. Since engine vacuum is the controlling factor as the vehicle is being driven, the amount of vacuum must be controlled when testing. The use of a motorized vacuum pump, a hand held mechanically operated vacuum pump or an air bleed valve may be recommended by the manufacturer.

Before any vacuum tests are performed on the modulator, the engine, being the primary vacuum source, must be checked to ascertain that vacuum is available to the modulator. The hose at the modulator should be disconnected and a vacuum gauge attached to the hose. With the brakes set and the engine idling at normal operating temperature, the engine vacuum reading should be in

To measure the hydraulic pressures, select a gauge rated over the control pressure specifications and install the hose fitting into the control pressure line tap, located either along the side or the rear of the transmission case. Refer to the individual automatic transmission sections for the correct locations, since many transmission cases have more than one pressure tap to check pressures other than the control pressure.

The pressure gauges can be used during a road test, but care must be exercised in routing the hose from under the vehicle to avoid dragging or being entangled with objects on the roadway.

The gauge should be positioned so the dial is visible to the diagnostician near the speedometer area. If a console of gauges is used, the console is normally mounted on a door window or on the vehicle dash.

### CAUTION

*During the road test, traffic safety must be exercised. It is advisable to have a helper to assist in the reading or recording of the results during the road test.*

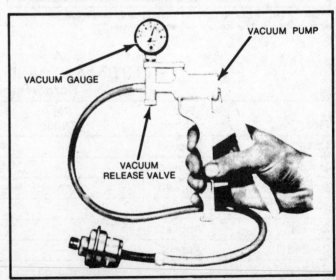

**Typical vacuum pump used to test vacuum diaphragms on and off the transmission**(© Ford Motor Co.)

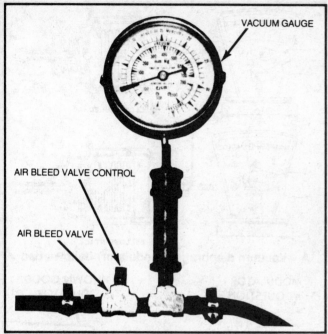

AIR BLEED VALVE CONTROL

AIR BLEED VALVE

VACUUM GAUGE

**Air bleed with vacuum gauge attached**

the 17 to 20 in. Hg range. Should the vacuum be low, check the vacuum reading at the engine and compare the two readings. If the vacuum reading is lower at the modulator end of the hose than at the engine, look for leaking or defective hoses or lines. If both readings are low, the engine is not producing sufficient vacuum to properly operate the modulator at road speeds or under specific road conditions, which could result in transmission malfunctions and premature internal wear. To correct this condition, the reason for the low engine vacuum would have to be determined and repaired.

—————— **CAUTION** ——————

*To install a rebuilt unit under this type of vacuum condition would invite operational problems.*

An air bleed valve was placed in the vacuum line from the engine to the modulator to control the amount of vacuum reacting on the diaphragm, simply by allowing more or less atmospheric air to enter the vacuum line, controlled by a screw valve. This type of testing has been replaced by the use of the hand held mechanical vacuum pump, in most cases.

### Testing Control Pressure—Typical

To illustrate a typical control pressure test, the following explanation is given concerning the accompanying chart.

**NOTE: Refer to the individual transmission sections for correct specifications.**

## TRANSMISSION MALFUNCTION RELATED TO OIL PRESSURE

| ③ Drive Brakes Applied 1000 RPM | ③ Reverse Brakes Applied 1000 RPM | ③ Super or Lo Brakes Applied 1000 RPM | Neutral Brakes Applied 1000 RPM | ③ Drive 1000 RPM Brakes on Detent* Activated | Drive Idle | ① Drive 30 MPH Closed Throttle | Drive—from 1000 to 3000 RPM Wheels free to move | Pressure Test Conditions |
|---|---|---|---|---|---|---|---|---|
| | | | | | | | **0″ vacuum to modulator** | |
| 60-90 | 85-150 | 85-110 | 55-70 | 90-110 | 60-85 | 55-70 | Pressure drop of 10 PSI or more | Normal Results Note2 |
| | | | | | | | DROP | Malfunction in Control Valve Assembly |
| | | | | | | | NO DROP | Malfunction in Governor or Governor Feed System |
| ALL PRESSURES HIGH WITH LESS THAN 35 PSI BETWEEN PRESSURE READINGS | | | | | | | — | Malfunction in Detent System |
| ALL PRESSURES HIGH WITH MORE THAN 35 PSI BETWEEN PRESSURE READINGS | | | | | | | — | Malfunction in Modulator |
| Low | | | | | | Low to Normal | — | Oil Leak in Feed System to the Direct Clutch |
| Low | Low to Normal | | | Low to Normal | | Low to Normal | — | Oil Leak in Feed System to the Forward Clutch |
| | | | | Low | | | — | Detent System |

*Columns 1–7 above fall under: 15-20″ vacuum applied to modulator*

A blank space = Normal pressure
A dash (—) in space = Pressure reading has no meaning
① Coast for 30 mph—read before reaching 20 mph

② If high line pressures are experienced see "High Line Pressures" note.

③ Cable pulled or blocked thru detent position or downshift switch closed by hand

NOTE: It is assumed the oil pressure gauge, the vacuum gauge, the vacuum pump, and the tachometer are attached to the engine/transmission assembly, while having the brakes locked and the wheels chocked. The fluid temperature should be at normal operating temperature.

1. Start the engine and allow to idle.

2. Apply 15-20 inches of vacuum to the vacuum modulator with the vacuum hand pump.

3. Place the selector lever in the Drive position and increase the engine speed to 1000 RPM. The pressure reading should be 60-90 PSI, as indicated on the chart.

4. Taking another example from the chart, place the selector lever in the Super or Low position and increase the engine speed to 1000 RPM. As indicated on the chart, the pressure should read 85-110 PSI.

5. Referring to the chart column to test pressures with the detent activated, the following must be performed. Place the selector lever in the Drive position and increase the engine speed to 1000 RPM. With the aid of a helper, if necessary, pull the detent cable through the detent, or if the transmission is equipped with an electrical downshift switch, close the switch by hand. The pressure reading should be 90-110 PSI, as indicated on the chart.

6. A pressure test conditions column is included in the chart to assist the diagnostician in determining possible causes of transmission malfunctions from the hydraulic system.

--- CAUTION ---

*Do not use the above pressure readings when actually testing the control pressures. The above readings are only used as a guide for the chart explanation. Refer to the individual transmission section for the correct specifications and pressure readings.*

## HIGH CONTROL PRESSURE

If a condition of high control pressure exists, the general causes can be categorized as follows.

1. Vacuum leakage or low vacuum
2. Vacuum modulator damaged
3. Pump pressure excessive
4. Control valve assembly
5. Throttle linkage or cable misadjusted

## LOW CONTROL PRESSURE

If a condition of low control pressure exists, the general causes can be categorized as follows.

1. Transmission fluid low
2. Vacuum modulator defective
3. Filter assembly blocked or air leakage
4. Oil pump defective
5. Hydraulic circuit leakage
6. Control valve body

## NO CONTROL PRESSURE RISE

If a control pressure rise does not occur as the vacuum drops or the throttle valve linkage/cable is moved, the mechanical connection between the vacuum modulator or throttle valve linkage/cable and the throttle valve should be inspected. Possible broken or disconnected parts are at fault.

## Vacuum Modulator

### TESTING

A defective vacuum modulator can cause one or more of the following conditions.

a. Engine burning transmission fluid
b. Transmission overheating
c. Harsh upshifts
d. Delayed shifts
e. Soft up and down shifts

Whenever a vacuum modulator is suspected of malfunctioning, a vacuum check should be made of the vacuum supply.

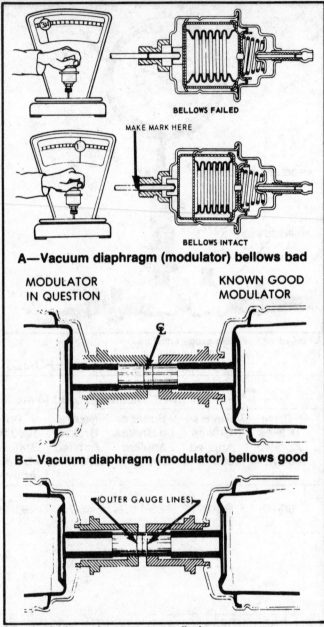

**A—Vacuum diaphragm (modulator) bellows bad**

MODULATOR IN QUESTION          KNOWN GOOD MODULATOR

**B—Vacuum diaphragm (modulator) bellows good**

**Other methods used to test vacuum diaphragms**

1. Disconnect the vacuum line at the transmission vacuum modulator connector pipe.

2. With the engine running, the vacuum gauge should show an acceptable level of vacuum for the altitude at which the test is being performed.

3. If the vacuum reading is low, check for broken, split or crimped hoses and for proper engine operation.

4. If the vacuum reading is acceptable, accelerate the engine quickly. The vacuum should drop off and return immediately upon release of the accelerator. If the gauge does not register a change in the vacuum reading, indications are that the vacuum lines are plugged, restricted or connected to a reservoir supply.

5. Correct the vacuum supply as required.

When the vacuum supply is found to be sufficient, the vacuum modulator must be inspected and this can be accomplished on or off the vehicle.

## On Vehicle Tests

1. Remove the vacuum line and attach a vacuum pump to the modulator connector pipe.

2. Apply 18 inches of vacuum to the modulator. The vacuum should remain at 18 inches without leaking down.

3. If the vacuum reading drops sharply or will not remain at 18 inches, the diaphragm is leaking and the unit must be replaced.

4. If transmission fluid is present on the vacuum side of the diaphragm or in the vacuum hose, the diaphragm is leaking and the unit must be replaced.

**NOTE: Gasoline or water vapors may settle on the vacuum side of the diaphragm. Do not diagnose as transmission fluid.**

## Off Vehicle Tests

1. Remove the vacuum modulator from the transmission.

2. Attach a vacuum pump to the vacuum modulator connector pipe and apply 18 inches of vacuum.

3. The vacuum should hold at 18 inches, if the diaphragm is good and will drop to zero if the diaphragm is leaking.

4. With the control rod in the transmission side of the vacuum modulator, apply vacuum to the connector pipe. The rod should move inward with light finger pressure applied to the end of the rod. When the vacuum is released, the rod will move outward by pressure from the internal spring.

## Stall Speed Tests

The stall speed test is performed to evaluate the condition of the transmission as well as the condition of the engine.

The stall speed is the maximum speed at which the engine can drive the torque converter impeller while the turbine is held stationary. Since the stall speed is dependent upon the engine and torque converter characteristics, it can vary with the condition of the engine as well as the condition of the automatic transmission, so it is most important to have a properly performing engine before a stall speed test is attempted, thereby eliminating the engine from any malfunction that may be present.

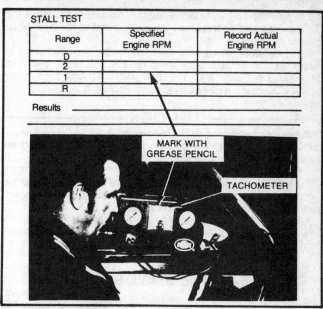

| STALL TEST | | | |
|---|---|---|---|
| Range | Specified Engine RPM | Record Actual Engine RPM | |
| D | | | |
| 2 | | | |
| 1 | | | |
| R | | | |

Results _____

MARK WITH GREASE PENCIL

TACHOMETER

**Preparation for stall test**(© Ford Motor Co.)

Because engines perform differently between high and low altitudes, the stall speeds given in specification charts are for vehicles tested at sea level and cannot be considered representative of stall speed tests performed at higher altitudes. Unless specific stall speed tests specification charts are available for use at higher altitudes, representative stall speeds can be determined by testing several vehicles known to be operating properly, averaging the results and recording the necessary specifications for future reference.

## PERFORMING THE STALL SPEED TESTS

1. Attach a tachometer to the engine and an oil pressure gauge to the transmission control pressure tap. Position the tachometer and oil pressure gauge so the operator can read the dials.

2. Mark the specified maximum engine RPM on the tachometer clear cover with a grease pencil so that the operator can immediately check the stall speed to see if it is over or under specifications.

3. Start the engine and bring to normal operating temperature.

4. Check the transmission fluid level and correct as necessary.

5. Apply the parking brake and chock the wheels.

— CAUTION —

*Do not allow anyone in front of the vehicle during the preparation or during the stall speed test.*

## EFFECT OF ALTITUDE ON ENGINE VACUUM

| Elevation in Feet | Number of Engine Cylinders | | |
|---|---|---|---|
| | FOUR | SIX | EIGHT |
| Zero to 1000 | 18 to 20 | 19 to 21 | 21 to 22 |
| 1000 to 2000 | 17 to 19 | 18 to 20 | 19 to 21 |
| 2000 to 3000 | 16 to 18 | 17 to 19 | 18 to 20 |
| 3000 to 4000 | 15 to 17 | 16 to 18 | 17 to 19 |
| 4000 to 5000 | 14 to 16 | 15 to 17 | 16 to 18 |
| 5000 to 6000 | 13 to 15 | 14 to 16 | 15 to 17 |

## SAMPLE STALL TEST DIAGNOSIS CHART

| Selector Lever Range | Specified Engine RPM | Actual Engine RPM | Control Pressure PSI | Holding Members Applied |
|---|---|---|---|---|
| D (Drive) | | | | |
| 1 | | | | |
| 2 | | | | |
| R (Reverse) | | | | |

**NOTE:** The range identifications are to be taken from the selector quadrant of the vehicle being tested. Before stall test, fill in the specified engine RPM and the holding members applied columns from the clutch and band application and specification charts of the automatic transmission being tested.

6. Apply the service brakes and place the selector lever in the "D" position and depress the accelerator pedal to the wide open throttle position.

7. Do not hold the throttle open any longer than necessary to obtain the maximum engine speed reading and never over five (5) seconds for each test. The stall will occur when no more increase in engine RPM at wide open throttle is noted.

— CAUTION —

*If the engine speed exceeds the maximum limits of the stall speed specifications, release the accelerator immediately as internal transmission slippage is indicated.*

8. Shift the selector lever into the Neutral position and operate the engine from 1000 to 1500 RPM for at least 30 seconds to two minutes to cool the transmission fluid.

9. If necessary, the stall speed test can be performed in other forward and reverse gear positions. Observe the transmission fluid cooling procedure between each test as outlined in step 8.

## RESULTS OF THE STALL SPEED TESTS

The stall speed RPM will indicate possible problems. If the engine RPM is high, internal transmission slippage is indicated. If the engine RPM is low, engine or converter problems can exist.

The transmission will not upshift during the stall test and by knowing what internal transmission members are applied in each test range, an indication of a unit failure can be pinpointed.

It is recommended a chart be prepared to assist the diagnostician in the determination of the stall speed results in comparison to the specified engine RPM, and should include the range and holding member applied.

### LOW ENGINE RPM ON STALL SPEED TEST

The low engine RPM stall speed indicates either the engine is not performing properly or the converter stator one-way clutch is not holding. By road testing the vehicle, the determination as to the defect can be made.

If the stator is not locked by the one-way clutch, the performance of the vehicle will be poor up to approximately 30-35 MPH. If the engine is in need of repairs or adjustments, the performance of the vehicle will be poor at all speeds.

### HIGH ENGINE RPM ON STALL SPEED TEST

When the engine RPM is higher than specifications, internal transmission unit slippage is indicated. By following the holding member application chart, the defective unit can be pinpointed.

It must be noted that a transmission using a one-way overrunning clutch while in the "D" position, first gear, and having a band applied in the "2" position, first gear (for vehicle braking purposes while going downhill), may have the band slipping unnoticed during the stall test, because the overruning clutch will hold. To determine this, a road test must be performed to place the transmission in a range where the band is in use without the overrunning clutch.

### NORMAL ENGINE RPM ON STALL SPEED TEST

When the engine RPM is within the specified ranges, the holding members of the transmission are considered to be operating properly.

A point of interest is if the converter oneway clutch (overrunning) is seized and locks the stator from turning either way, the engine RPM will be normal during the test, but the converter will be in reduction at all times and the vehicle will probably not exceed a speed of 50-60 miles per hour. If this condition is suspected, examine the fluid and the converter exterior for signs of overheating, since an extreme amount of heat is generated when the converter remains in constant reduction.

## Transmission Noises

During the stall speed test and the road test, the diagnostician must be alert to any abnormal noises from the transmission area or any excessive movement of the engine/transmission assembly during torque application or transmission shifting.

— CAUTION —

*Before attempting to diagnose automatic transmission noises, be sure the noises do not orginate from the engine components, such as the water pump, alternator, air conditioner compressor, power steering or the air injection pump. Isolate these components by removing the proper drive belt and operate the engine. Do not operate the engine longer than two minutes at a time to avoid overheating.*

1. Whining or siren type noises—Can be considered normal if occurring during a stall speed test, due to the fluid flow through the converter.

2. Whining noise (continual with vehicle stationary)—If the noise increases and decreases with the engine speed, the following defects could be present.
   a. Oil level low
   b. Air leakage into pump (defective gasket, "O"-ring or porosity of a part)
   c. Pump gears damaged or worn
   d. Pump gears assembled backward
   e. Pump crescent interference

3. Buzzing noise—This type of noise is normally the result of a pressure regulator valve vibrating or a sealing ring broken or worn out and will usually come and go, depending upon engine/transmission speed.

4. Rattling noise (constant)—Usually occurring at low engine speed and resulting from the vanes stripped from the impeller or turbine face or internal interference of the converter parts.

5. Rattling noise (intermittent)—Reflects a broken flywheel or flex plate and usually occurs at low engine speed with the transmission in gear. Placing the transmission in "N" or "P" will change the rattling noise or stop it for a short time.

6. Gear noise (one gear range)—This type of noise will normally indicate a defective planetary gear unit. Upon shifting into another gear range, the noise will cease. If the noise carries over to the next gear range, but at a different pitch, defective thrust bearings or bushings are indicated.

7. Engine vibration or excessive movement—Can be caused by transmission filler or cooler lines vibrating due to broken or disconnected brackets. If excessive engine/transmission movement is noted, look for broken engine/transmission mounts.

— CAUTION —

*When necessary to support an engine equipped with metal safety tabs on the mounts, be sure the metal tabs are not in contact with the mount bracket after the engine/transmission assembly is again supported by the mounts. A severe vibration can result.*

8. Squeal at low vehicle speeds—Can result from a speedometer driven gear seal, a front pump seal or rear extension seal being dry.

The above list of noises can be used as a guide. Noises other than the ones listed can occur around or within the transmission assembly. A logical and common sense approach will normally result in the source of the noise being detected.

## Air Pressure Tests

The automatic transmission have many hidden passages and hydraulic units that are controlled by internal fluid pressures, supplied through tubes, shafts and valve movements.

The air pressure test are used to confirm the findings of the fluid pressure tests and to further pinpoint the malfunctioning area. The air pressure test can also confirm the hydraulic unit operation after repairs have been made.

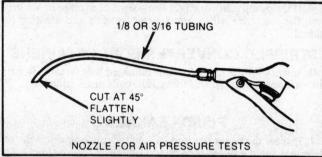

Type of air nozzle to be used in the air pressure tests
(© Ford Motor Co.)

To perform the air pressure test, the control valve body must be removed from the transmission case, exposing the case passages. By referring to the individual transmission section, identify each passage before any attempt is made to proceed with the air pressure test.

—————————— CAUTION ——————————

*It is a good practice to protect the diagnostician's face and body with glasses and protective clothing and the surrounding area from the oil spray that will occur when air pressure is applied to the various passages.*

NOTE: The air pressure should be controlled to approximately 25 psi and the air should be clean and dry.

When the passages have been identified and the air pressure applied to a designated passage, reaction can be seen, heard and felt in the various units. Should air pressure be applied to a clutch apply passage, the piston movement can be felt and a soft dull thud should be heard. Some movement of the unit assembly can be seen.

When air pressure is applied to a servo apply passage, the servo rod or arm will move and tighten the band around the drum. Upon release of the air pressure, spring tension should release the servo piston.

When air pressure is applied to the governor supply passage, a whistle, click or buzzing noise may be heard.

When failures have occurred within the transmission assembly and the air pressure tests are made, the following problems may exist.
1. No clutch piston movement
2. Hissing noise and excessive fluid spray
3. Excessive unit movement
4. No servo band apply or release

## Torque Converter

The torque converter is a simple, but yet complex torque multiplication unit, designed and applied to specific engine/transmis-

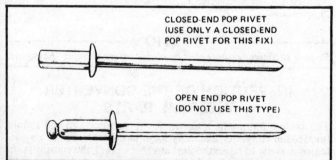

Comparison of closed end "POP" rivet and open end "POP" rivet

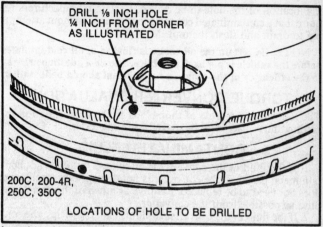

Location of hole to be drilled in the converters of models THM 325, 200C, 200-4R, 250C and 350C transmissions
(© General Motors Corp.)

sion/transaxle applications. Manufacturers apply different ratings for their application to a specific engine. An example is the use of the "K" factor method by several of the vehicle manufacturers to indicate the performance curve of a given engine size. The larger the "K" factor, the smaller the engine size, which gives more engine break-away torque at lower speeds.
**Example:**

$$K = \frac{RPM}{\sqrt{Torque\ (Nm)}}$$

$$K = \frac{2200}{\sqrt{100}}$$

$$K = \frac{2200}{10}$$

$$K = 220$$

NOTE: Torque of 100 N•m is usually constant for the finding of the "K" factor.

NOTE: Performance cars are rated differently.

Regardless of the type of rating used, the correct torque converter must be coupled to the specific engine/transmission/transaxle assembly to achieve the desired operational efficiency. Converter rebuilders are supplying quality rebuilt units to the trade, that in most cases, equal the performance of the new converter units. In cases where problems occur, it is generally the use of a converter assembly that does not match the desired performance curve of the engine/transmission/transaxle assembly.

## DRAINING AND FLUSHING THE CONVERTER

When the converter has become filled with contaminated fluid that can be flushed out and the converter reused, the different manufacturers recommend procedures that should be followed for their respective converters. All recommend the use of a commercial flushing machine, if available. Certain converters will have drain plugs that can be removed to allow the fluid to drain. Other manufacturers recommend the drilling of drain holes and the use of a rivet plug to close the hole after the fluid has been drained and the converter flushed. With the use of lock-up converters, the drilling of a drain hole in the converter shell must be done correctly or the lock-up mechanism can be damaged. Various after-market suppliers have drill and tap guide kits available to drill a hole in the converter, tap threads in the shell and install a threaded plug or a kit with a drill, pop rivets and instructions on the location of the hole to be drilled. Certain manufacturers require that a contaminated converter be replaced without attempting to drain and flush the unit.

NOTE: Be certain the oil cooler is flushed of all contaminates before the vehicle is put back in service. Should a question arise as to the efficiency of the cooler, a replacement should be installed.

### TORQUE CONVERTER EVALUATION

The following is a "rule of thumb" as to the determination regarding the replacement or usage of the converter.

### CONTAMINATED FLUID

1. If the fluid in the converter is discolored but does not contain metal particles, the converter is not damaged internally and does not need to be replaced. Remove as much of the discolored fluid as possible from the converter.

2. If the fluid in the converter contains metal particles, the converter is damaged internally and must be replaced.

3. If the fluid contamination was due to burned clutch plates, overheated fluid or engine coolant leakage, the unit should be flushed. The degree of contamination would have to be decided by the repairman in regards to either the replacement or flushing of the unit.

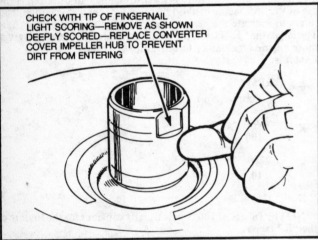

CHECK WITH TIP OF FINGERNAIL
LIGHT SCORING—REMOVE AS SHOWN
DEEPLY SCORED—REPLACE CONVERTER
COVER IMPELLER HUB TO PREVENT
DIRT FROM ENTERING

Checking converter hub for light or heavy scoring
(© Ford Motor Co.)

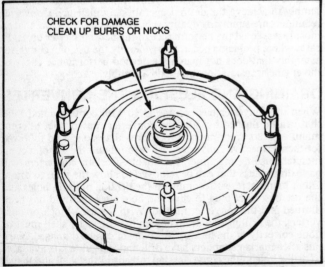

CHECK FOR DAMAGE
CLEAN UP BURRS OR NICKS

Checking converter cover for nicks or burrs(© Ford Motor Co.)

4. If the pump gears or cover show signs of damage or are broken, the converter will contain metal particles and must be replaced.

### STRIPPED CONVERTER BOLT RETAINERS

1. Inspect for the cause, such as damaged bolt threads. Repair the stripped bolt retainers, using Heli-coils or its equivalent.

### FLUID LEAKAGE

1. Inspect the converter hub surface for roughness, scoring or wear that could damage the seal or bushing. If the roughness can be felt with a fingernail, the front seal could be damaged. Repair the hub surface with fine crocus cloth, if possible, and replace the front seal.

2. Inspect the inside of the bell housing. If fluid is present, leakage is indicated and the converter should be leak tested. If leaks are found in the converter, the unit should be replaced.

—————— CAUTION ——————
*Do not attempt to re-weld the converter.*

### CONVERTER NOISE OR SLIPPAGE

1. Check for loose or missing flywheel to converter bolts, a cracked flywheel, a broken converter pilot, or other engine parts that may be vibrating. Correct as required.

NOTE: Most converter noises occur under light throttle in the "D" position and with the brakes applied.

2. Inspect the converter for excessive end play by the use of the proper checking tools. Replace the converter if the turbine end play exceeds the specifications (usually 0.050 in.).

3. Inspect the converter for damages to the internal roller bearings, thrust races and roller clutch. The thrust roller bearing and thrust races can be checked by viewing them when looking into the converter neck or feeling through the opening to make sure they are not cracked, broken or mispositioned.

4. Inspect the stator clutch by either inserting a protected finger into the splined inner race of the roller clutch or using special tools designed for the purpose, and trying to turn the race in either direction. The inner race should turn freely in a clockwise direction, but not turn or be very difficult to turn in a counterclockwise direction. The converter must be replaced if the roller bearings, thrust races or roller clutch are damaged.

### CONVERTER VIBRATION

1. Isolate the cause of the vibration by disconnecting other engine driven parts one at a time. If the converter is determined to be the cause of the vibration, check for loss of balance weights and should they be missing, replace the converter. If the weights are in place, relocate the converter 120 degrees at a time to cancel out engine and converter unbalanced conditions. Washers may be used on the converter to flywheel bolts to isolate an area of unbalance.

—————— CAUTION ——————
*Be sure sufficient clearance is available before starting the engine.*

### INSPECTION OF THE CONVERTER INTERNAL PARTS

The average automatic transmission repair shop can and should inspect the converter assembly for internal wear before any attempt is made to reuse the unit after rebuilding the transmission unit. Special converter checking tools are needed and can be obtained through various tool supply channels.

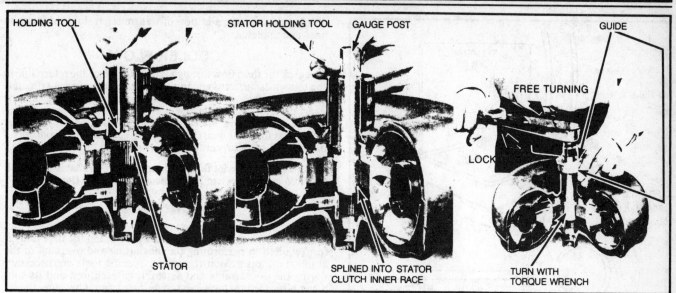

**Preparing tool to inspect converter stator overrunning clutch operation(© Ford Motor Co.)**

## CHECKING CONVERTER END PLAY (STATOR AND TURBINE)

1. Place the converter on a flat surface with the flywheel side down and the converter hub opening up.
2. Insert the special end play checking tool into the drive hub opening until the tool bottoms.

NOTE: Certain end play checking tools have a dual purpose, to check the stator and turbine end play and to check the stator one-way clutch operation. The dual purpose tool will have an expandable sleeve (collet) on the end, along with splines to engage the internal splines of the stator one-way clutch inner race.

3. Install the cover or guide plate over the converter hub and tighten the screw nut firmly to expand the split sleeve (collet) in the turbine hub.
4. Attach a dial indicator tool on the tool screw and position the indicator tip or button on the converter hub or the cover. Zero the dial indicator.
5. Lift the screw upward as far as it will go, carrying the dial indicator with it. Read the measurement from the indicator dial. The reading represents the converter end play.
6. Refer to the individual automatic transmission sections for the permissible converter end play.
7. Remove the tools from the converter assembly. Do not leave the split sleeve (collet) in the turbine hub.

## STATOR TO IMPELLER INTERFERENCE CHECK

1. Place the transmission oil pump assembly on a flat surface with the stator splines up.
2. Carefully install the converter on oil pump and engage the stator splines.
3. Hold the pump assembly and turn the converter counterclockwise.
4. The converter should turn freely with no interference. If a slight rubbing noise is heard, this is considered normal, but if a binding or loud scraping noise is heard, the converter should be replaced.

## STATOR-TO-TURBINE INTERFERENCE CHECK

1. Place the converter assembly on a flat surface with the flywheel side down and the converter hub opening up.

2. Install the oil pump on the converter hub. Install the input shaft into the converter and engage the turbine hub splines.
3. While holding the oil pump and converter, rotate the input shaft back and forth.
4. The input shaft should turn freely with only a slight rubbing noise. If a binding or loud scraping noise is heard, the converter should be replaced.

## STATOR ONE-WAY CLUTCH CHECK

Because the stator one-way clutch must hold the stator for torque multiplication at low speed and free-wheel at high speeds during the coupling phase, the stator assembly must be checked while the converter is out of the vehicle.

1. Have the converter on a flat surface with the flywheel side down and the hub opening up.
2. Install the stator race holding tool into the converter hub opening and insert the end into the groove in the stator to prevent the stator from turning.
3. Place the special tool post, without the screw and split sleeve (collet), into the converter hub opening. Engage the splines of the tool post with the splines of the stator race. Install the cover or guide plate to hold the tool post in place.
4. With a torque wrench, turn the tool post in a clockwise manner. The stator should turn freely.
5. Turn the tool post with the torque wrench in a counterclockwise rotation and the lock-up clutch should lock up with a 10 ft.-lb. pull.
6. If the lock-up clutch does not lock up, the one-way clutch is defective and the converter should be replaced.

Certain vehicle manufacturers do not recommend the use of special tools or the use of the pump cover stator shaft as a testing device for the stator one-way clutch unit. Their recommendations are to insert a finger into the converter hub opening and contact the splined inner race of the one-way clutch. An attempt should be made to rotate the stator inner race in a clockwise direction and the race should turn freely. By turning the inner race in a counter-clockwise rotation, it should either lock-up or turn with great difficulty.

── **CAUTION** ──

*Care should be exercised to remove any metal burrs from the converter hub before placing a finger into the opening. Personal injury could result.*

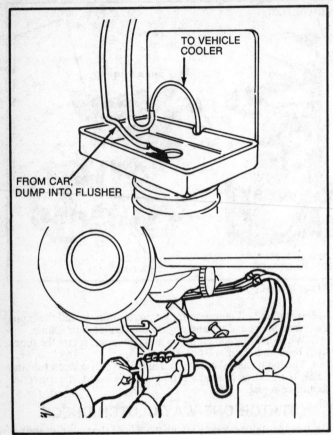

TO VEHICLE COOLER

FROM CAR, DUMP INTO FLUSHER

**Two methods of flushing transmission cooler and lines**

## CONVERTER LOCK-UP CLUTCH AND PISTON

Unless a direct malfunction occurs and/or fluid contamination exists from the converter clutch unit, it is extremely difficult to diagnose an internal wear problem. The diagnostician should exercise professional expertise when the determination is made to replace or reuse the converter unit, relating to mileage, type of operation and wear of related parts within the gearbox.

## Flushing the Fluid Cooler and Lines

Much reference has been made to the importance of flushing the transmission/transaxle fluid coolers and lines during an overhaul procedure. With the increased use of converter clutch units and the necessary changes to the internal fluid routings, the passage of contaminated fluid, sludge or metal particles to the fluid cooler is more predominate. In most cases, the fluid returning from the fluid cooler is directed to the lubrication system and should the system be deprived of lubricating fluid due to blockage, premature unit failure will occur.

### GENERAL FLUSHING PROCEDURES

Two methods of flushing the fluid cooling system can be used.
  a. Disconnect both fluid lines from the cooler and the transmission/transaxle and flush each line and cooler separately.
  b. Disconnect both fluid lines from the transmission /transaxle assemblies, leaving the lines attached to the cooler. Add a length of hose to the return line and place in a container. Flush both lines and the cooler at the same time.
When flushing the cooling components, use a commercial flushing fluid or its equivalent. Reverse flush the lines and cooler with the flushing fluid and pulsating air pressure. Continue the flushing process until clean flushing fluid appears. Remove the

flushing fluid by the addition of transmission fluid through the lines and cooler.

## COOLER FLOW

To check the fluid flow through the cooler, place the return line to the transmission/transaxle in a clean container of approximately one quart capacity. Overfill the transmission/transaxle by one quart of fluid, start the engine with the shift in the neutral position. Run the engine for exactly twenty (20) seconds. If the cooler flow is less than one quart in the twenty (20) seconds, have the radiator fluid cooler reconditioned or replaced.

NOTE: Commercial flushing machines are available that flush the fluid cooling system and measure the rate of flow.

## Special Tools

There are an unlimited amount of special tools and accessories available to the transmission rebuilder to lessen the time and effort required in performing the diagnosing and overhaul of the automatic transmission/transaxles. Specific tools are necessary during the disassembly and assembly of each unit and its subassemblies. Certain tools can be fabricated, but it becomes the responsibility of the repair shop operator to obtain commercially manufactured tools to insure quality rebuilding and to avoid costly "come backs."

The commercial labor saving tools range from puller sets, bushing and seal installer sets, compression tools and presses (both mechanically and hydraulically operated), holding fixtures, oil pump aligning tools (a necessity on most automatic transmissions) to work bench arrangements, degreaser tanks, steam cleaners, converter flushing machines, transmission jacks and lifts, to name a few. For specific information concerning the various tools, a parts and tool supplier should be consulted.

In addition to the special tools, a complete tool chest with the necessary hand tools should be available to the repairman.

## BASIC MEASURING TOOLS

The use of the basic measuring tools has become more critical in the rebuilding process. The increased use of front drive transaxles, in which both the automatic transmission and the final drive gears are located, has required the rebuilder to adhere to specifications and tolerances more closely than ever before.

Bearings must be torqued or adjusted to specific preloads in order to meet the rotating torque drag specifications. The end play and backlash of the varied shafts and gears must be measured to avoid excessive tightness or looseness. Critical tensioning bolts must be torqued to their specifications to avoid warpage of components and proper mating of others.

Dial indicators must be protected and used as a delicate measuring instrument. A mutilated or un-calibrated dial indicator invites premature unit failure and destruction. Torque wrenches are available in many forms, some cheaply made and others, accurate and durable under constant use. To obtain accurate readings and properly applied torque, recalibration should be applied to the torque wrenches periodically, regardless of the type used. Micrometers are used as precise measuring tools and should be properly stored when not in use. Instructions on the recalibration of the micrometers and a test bar usually accompany the tool when it is purchased.

Other measuring tools are available to the rebuilder and each in their own way, must be protected when not in use to avoid causing mis-measuring in the fitting of a component to the unit. A good example of poorly cared-for tools is the lowly feeler gauge blades. Many times a bent and wrinkled blade is used to measure clearances that, if incorrect, can cause the failure of a rebuilt unit. Why risk the failure of a $1000.00 unit because of a $2.98 feeler gauge? Good tools and the knowledge of how to use them reflects upon the longevity of the rebuilt unit.

## STANDARD TORQUE SPECIFICATIONS AND CAPSCREW MARKINGS

Newton/Metre has been designated as the world standard for measuring torque and will gradually replace the foot-pound and kilogram-meter torque measuring standard. Torquing tools are still being manufactured with foot-pounds and kilogram-meter scales, along with the new Newton-Metre standard. To assist the repairman, foot-pounds, kilogram-meter and Newton-Metre are listed in the following charts, and should be followed as applicable.

### U. S. BOLTS

| SAE Grade Number | 1 or 2 | | | 5 | | | 6 or 7 | | | 8 | | |
|---|---|---|---|---|---|---|---|---|---|---|---|---|
| Capscrew Head Markings — Manufacturer's marks may vary. Three-line markings on heads shown below, for example. Indicate SAE Grade 5.  |  | | |  | | |  | | |  | | |
| Usage | Used Frequently | | | Used Frequently | | | Used at Times | | | Used at Times | | |
| Quality of Material | Indeterminate | | | Minimum Commercial | | | Medium Commercial | | | Best Commercial | | |
| Capacity Body Size (inches)—(Thread) | Ft-Lb | kgm | Nm | Ft-Lb | kgm | Nm | Ft-Lb | kgm | Nm | Ft-Lb | kgm | Nm |
| ¼-20 | 5 | 0.6915 | 6.7791 | 8 | 1.1064 | 10.8465 | 10 | 1.3630 | 13.5582 | 12 | 1.6596 | 16.2698 |
| -28 | 6 | 0.8298 | 8.1349 | 10 | 1.3830 | 13.5582 | | | | 14 | 1.9362 | 18.9815 |
| ⁵/₁₆-18 | 11 | 1.5213 | 14.9140 | 17 | 2.3511 | 23.0489 | 19 | 2.6277 | 25.7605 | 24 | 3.3192 | 32.5396 |
| -24 | 13 | 1.7979 | 17.6256 | 19 | 2.6277 | 25.7605 | | | | 27 | 3.7341 | 36.6071 |
| ³/₈-16 | 18 | 2.4894 | 24.4047 | 31 | 4.2873 | 42.0304 | 34 | 4.7022 | 46.0978 | 44 | 6.0852 | 59.6560 |
| -24 | 20 | 2.7660 | 27.1164 | 35 | 4.8405 | 47.4536 | | | | 49 | 6.7767 | 66.4351 |
| ⁷/₁₆-14 | 28 | 3.8132 | 37.9629 | 49 | 6.7767 | 66.4351 | 55 | 7.6065 | 74.5700 | 70 | 9.6810 | 94.9073 |
| -20 | 30 | 4.1490 | 40.6745 | 55 | 7.6065 | 74.5700 | | | | 18 | 10.7874 | 105.7538 |
| ½-13 | 39 | 5.3937 | 52.8769 | 75 | 10.3725 | 101.6863 | 85 | 11.7555 | 115.2445 | 105 | 14.5215 | 142.3609 |
| -20 | 41 | 5.6703 | 55.5885 | 85 | 11.7555 | 115.2445 | | | | 120 | 16.5860 | 162.6960 |
| ⁹/₁₆-12 | 51 | 7.0533 | 69.1467 | 110 | 15.2130 | 149.1380 | 120 | 16.5960 | 162.6960 | 155 | 21.4365 | 210.1490 |
| -18 | 55 | 7.6065 | 74.5700 | 120 | 16.5960 | 162.6960 | | | | 170 | 23.5110 | 230.4860 |
| ⁵/₈-11 | 83 | 11.4789 | 112.5329 | 150 | 20.7450 | 203.3700 | 167 | 23.0961 | 226.4186 | 210 | 29.0430 | 284.7180 |
| -18 | 95 | 13.1385 | 128.8027 | 170 | 23.5110 | 230.4860 | | | | 240 | 33.1920 | 325.3920 |
| ¾-10 | 105 | 14.5215 | 142.3609 | 270 | 37.3410 | 366.0660 | 280 | 38.7240 | 379.6240 | 375 | 51.8625 | 508.4250 |
| -16 | 115 | 15.9045 | 155.9170 | 295 | 40.7985 | 399.9610 | | | | 420 | 58.0860 | 568.4360 |
| ⁷/₈- 9 | 160 | 22.1280 | 216.9280 | 395 | 54.6285 | 535.5410 | 440 | 60.8520 | 596.5520 | 605 | 83.6715 | 820.2590 |
| -14 | 175 | 24.2025 | 237.2650 | 435 | 60.1605 | 589.7730 | | | | 675 | 93.3525 | 915.1650 |
| 1- 8 | 236 | 32.5005 | 318.6130 | 590 | 81.5970 | 799.9220 | 660 | 91.2780 | 894.8280 | 910 | 125.8530 | 1233.7780 |
| -14 | 250 | 34.5750 | 338.9500 | 660 | 91.2780 | 849.8280 | | | | 990 | 136.9170 | 1342.2420 |

## SUGGESTED TORQUE FOR COATED BOLTS AND NUTS

| Metric Sizes | | 6&6.3 | 8 | 10 | 12 | 14 | 16 | 20 |
|---|---|---|---|---|---|---|---|---|
| Nuts and All Metal Bolts | N·m | 0.4 | 0.8 | 1.4 | 2.2 | 3.0 | 4.2 | 7.0 |
| | In. Lbs. | 4.0 | 7.0 | 12 | 18 | 25 | 35 | 57 |
| Adhesive or Nylon Coated Bolts | N·m | 0.4 | 0.6 | 1.2 | 1.6 | 2.4 | 3.4 | 5.6 |
| | In. Lbs. | 4.0 | 5.0 | 10 | 14 | 20 | 28 | 46 |

| Inch Sizes | | ¼ | ⁵/₁₆ | ³/₈ | ⁷/₁₆ | ½ | ⁹/₁₆ | ⁵/₈ | ¾ |
|---|---|---|---|---|---|---|---|---|---|
| Nuts and All Metal Bolts | N·m | 0.4 | 0.6 | 1.4 | 1.8 | 2.4 | 3.2 | 4.2 | 6.2 |
| | In. Lbs. | 4.0 | 5.0 | 12 | 15 | 20 | 27 | 35 | 51 |
| Adhesive or Nylon Coated Bolts | N·m | 0.4 | 0.6 | 1.0 | 1.4 | 1.8 | 2.6 | 3.4 | 5.2 |
| | In. Lbs. | 4.0 | 5.0 | 9.0 | 12 | 15 | 22 | 28 | 43 |

## METRIC BOLTS

| Description | Torque ft-lbs. (Nm) | | | |
|---|---|---|---|---|
| Thread for general purposes (size x pitch) (mm) | Head mark 4 | | Head mark 7 | |
| 6 x 1.0 | 2.2 to 2.9 | (3.0 to 3.9) | 3.6 to 5.8 | (4.9 to 7.8) |
| 8 x 1.25 | 5.8 to 8.7 | (7.9 to 12) | 9.4 to 14 | (13 to 19) |
| 10 x 1.25 | 12 to 17 | (16 to 23) | 20 to 29 | (27 to 39) |
| 12 x 1.25 | 21 to 32 | (29 to 43) | 35 to 53 | (47 to 72) |
| 14 x 1.5 | 35 to 52 | (48 to 70) | 57 to 85 | (77 to 110) |
| 16 x 1.5 | 51 to 77 | (67 to 100) | 90 to 120 | (130 to 160) |
| 18 x 1.5 | 74 to 110 | (100 to 150) | 130 to 170 | (180 to 230) |
| 20 x 1.5 | 110 to 140 | (150 to 190) | 190 to 240 | (160 to 320) |
| 22 x 1.5 | 150 to 190 | (200 to 260) | 250 to 320 | (340 to 430) |
| 24 x 1.5 | 190 to 240 | (260 to 320) | 310 to 410 | (420 to 550) |

CAUTION: Bolts threaded into aluminum require much less torque.

## DECIMAL AND METRIC EQUIVALENTS

| Fractions | Decimal In. | Metric mm. | Fractions | Decimal In. | Metric mm. |
|---|---|---|---|---|---|
| 1/64 | .015625 | .397 | 33/64 | .515625 | 13.097 |
| 1/32 | .03125 | .794 | 17/32 | .53125 | 13.494 |
| 3/64 | .046875 | 1.191 | 35/64 | .546875 | 13.891 |
| 1/16 | .0625 | 1.588 | 9/16 | .5625 | 14.288 |
| 5/64 | .078125 | 1.984 | 37/64 | .578125 | 14.684 |
| 3/32 | .09375 | 2.381 | 19/32 | .59375 | 15.081 |
| 7/64 | .109375 | 2.778 | 39/64 | .609375 | 15.478 |
| 1/8 | .125 | 3.175 | 5/8 | .625 | 15.875 |
| 9/64 | .140625 | 3.572 | 41/64 | .640625 | 16.272 |
| 5/32 | .15625 | 3.969 | 21/32 | .65625 | 16.669 |
| 11/64 | .171875 | 4.366 | 43/64 | .671875 | 17.066 |
| 3/16 | .1875 | 4.763 | 11/16 | .6875 | 17.463 |
| 13/64 | .203125 | 5.159 | 45/64 | .703125 | 17.859 |
| 7/32 | .21875 | 5.556 | 23/32 | .71875 | 18.256 |
| 15/64 | .234375 | 5.953 | 47/64 | .734375 | 18.653 |
| 1/4 | .250 | 6.35 | 3/4 | .750 | 19.05 |
| 17/64 | .265625 | 6.747 | 49/64 | .765625 | 19.447 |
| 9/32 | .28125 | 7.144 | 25/32 | .78125 | 19.844 |
| 19/64 | .296875 | 7.54 | 51/64 | .796875 | 20.241 |
| 5/16 | .3125 | 7.938 | 13/16 | .8125 | 20.638 |
| 21/64 | .328125 | 8.334 | 53/64 | .828125 | 21.034 |
| 11/32 | .34375 | 8.731 | 27/32 | .84375 | 21.431 |
| 23/64 | .359375 | 9.128 | 55/64 | .859375 | 21.828 |
| 3/8 | .375 | 9.525 | 7/8 | .875 | 22.225 |
| 25/64 | .390625 | 9.922 | 57/64 | .890625 | 22.622 |
| 13/32 | .40625 | 10.319 | 29/32 | .90625 | 23.019 |
| 27/64 | .421875 | 10.716 | 59/64 | .921875 | 23.416 |
| 7/16 | .4375 | 11.113 | 15/16 | .9375 | 23.813 |
| 29/64 | .453125 | 11.509 | 61/64 | .953125 | 24.209 |
| 15/32 | .46875 | 11.906 | 31/32 | .96875 | 24.606 |
| 31/64 | .484375 | 12.303 | 63/64 | .984375 | 25.003 |
| 1/2 | .500 | 12.7 | 1 | 1.00 | 25.4 |

## Work Area

The size of the work area depends upon the space available within the service shop to perform the rebuilding operation by having the necessary benches, tools, cleaners and lifts arranged to provide the most logical and efficient approach to the removal, disassembly, assembly and installation of the automatic transmission. Regardless of the manner in which the work area is arranged, it should be well lighted, ventilated and clean.

## Precautions to Observe When Handling Solvents

All solvents are toxic or irritating to the skin to some degree. The amount of toxicity or irritation normally depends upon the skin exposure to the solvent. It is a good practice to avoid skin contact with solvent by using rubber gloves and parts drainers when cleaning the transmission parts.

### CAUTION

*Do not, under any circumstances, wash grease from hands or arms by dipping into the solvent tank and air drying with compressed air. Blood poison can result.*

## Drive Line Service

Drive line vibrations can affect the operation and longevity of the automatic transmission/transaxles and should be diagnosed during the road test and inspected during the unit removal phase. The drive shafts are designed for specific applications and the disregard for the correct application can result in drive shaft failure with extremely violent and hazardous consequences. A replace-

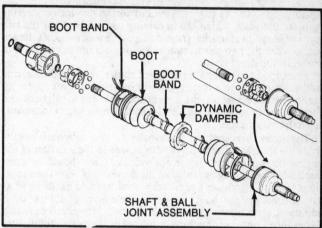

**Typical front drive axle assembly using CV joint components on both ends of shaft**(© Toyo Kogyo Co. Ltd.)

ment shaft assembly must always be of the same design and material specifications as the original to assure proper operation.

Natural drive line vibrations are created by the fluctuations in the speed of the drive shaft as the drive line angle is changed during a single revolution of the shaft. With the increased use of the front drive transaxles, the drive shafts and universal joints must transfer the driving power to the front wheels and at the same time, compensate for steering action on turns. Special universal joints were developed, one a constant velocity (CV) or double offset type, and a second type known as the tripod joint. The constant velocity joint uses rolling balls in curved grooves to obtain

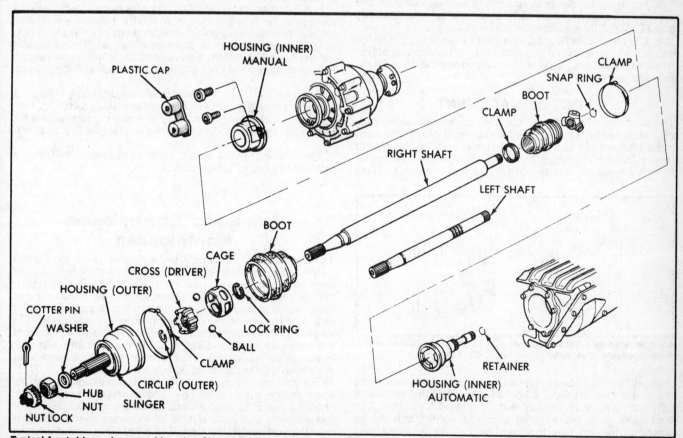

**Typical front drive axle assembly using CV and Tri-pot joint components**(© Chrysler Corp.)

uniform motion. As the joint rotates in the driving or steering motion, the balls, which are in driving contact between the two halfs of the joint coupling, remain in a plane which bisects the angle between the two shafts, thus cancelling out the fluctuations of speed in the drive shaft.

The tripod type uses a three legged spider, with needle bearing and balls incased in a three grooved housing. With the spider attached to the driveshaft, the joint assembly is free to roll back and forth in the housing grooves as the shaft length varies in normal drive line operation.

The front driveshafts are normally of two different lengths from the transaxle to the drive wheels, due to the location of the engine/transaxle mounting in the vehicle. Care should be exercised when removing or replacing the driveshafts, as to their locations (mark if necessary), removal procedures and handling so as not to damage the boots covering the universal joints, or if equipped, with boots covering the transaxle driveshaft opening. Should the boots become torn or otherwise damaged, premature failure of the universal joint would result due to the loss of lubricant and entrance of contaminates.

## ATTACHMENT OF THE DRIVESHAFT TO THE TRANSAXLE

The attachment of the driveshafts to the transaxle is accomplished in a number of ways and if not familiar with the particular shaft attachment, do not pry or hammer until the correct procedure is known.

The shafts can be attached by one of the following methods:

1. Driveshaft flange to transaxle stub shaft flange, bolted together. Mark flanges and remove bolts.
2. Circlips inside differential housing. Remove differential cover, compress circlips and push axle shafts outward.
3. Spring loaded circlip mounted in groove on axle shaft and mating with a groove in the differential gear splines. Is usually pryed or taped from differential gear with care.
4. Universal joint housing, axle shaft flange or axle shaft stub end pinned to either the differential stub shaft or differential gear flange with a roll pin. Mark the two components and drive the pin from the units.

## BOOT REPLACEMENT

The most common repairs to the front driveshafts are boot replacement and boot retaining ring replacement. Many automatic transmission repair shops are requested to perform this type of repairs for their customers. EOM and after-market replacement boots are available, with special tools used to crimp and tighten

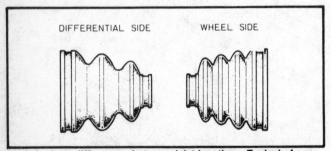

**Look for boot differences between joint locations. Typical of one manufacturer's drive axle**(© Toyo Kogyo Co. Ltd.)

the retaining rings. Most boot replacement procedures require the removal of the driveshafts. A boot kit is available that provides a split boot that can be installed without driveshaft removal. The boot is then sealed with a special adhesive along its length and the procedure finished with the installation of the boot retaining rings.

## DRIVE LINE DIAGNOSIS—FRONT WHEEL DRIVE

### Clicking Noise In Turns

1. Worn or damaged outboard joint. (Check for cut or damaged seals).

### "Clunk" When Accelerating From "Coast" To "Drive"

1. Worn or damaged inboard joint

### Shudder Or Vibration During Acceleration

1. Excessive joint angle
   a. Excessive toe-in.
   b. Incorrect spring heights.
2. Worn or damaged inboard or outboard joints.
3. Sticking inboard joint assembly (Double Offset Design).
4. Sticking spider assembly (Tri-Pot Design).

### Vibration At Highway Speeds

1. Out of balance front wheels or tires.
2. Out of round front tires.

# Towing

Proper towing is important for the safe and reliable transfer of an inoperative vehicle from one point to another.

The basic towing instructions and procedures are general in nature and the towing procedures may not apply to the same make, model or vehicle throughout the model years without procedure changes, modification to equipment or the use of auxiliary equipment designed for a specific purpose.

It is important to minimize the risk of personal injury, to avoid damage to the towed vehicle or to render it unsafe while being towed. There are many conceivable methods of towing with possible hazardous consequences for each method. Therefore, it is the responsibility of the tow truck operator to determine the correct connection of the towing apparatus in a safe and secure manner.

Towing manuals are available from varied sources, explaining the vehicle manufacturer's recommended lifting procedures, towing speeds and towing distances. The operating instructions for the towing truck should be understood and followed by the operator.

The disabled vehicle should never be pushed or pulled on a highway because of safety reasons.

# Automatic Transmission Identification

The need to identify automatic transmissions occurs when transmission units are obtained; for example, through bulk buying for overhaul and storage as replacement units. To assist the repairman in coupling the proper transmission to the vehicle/engine combination, a listing is given of automatic transmission codes and their corresponding vehicle model and engine usage. The torque converter identification is difficult, as most replacement converters are rebuilt and distributed to suppliers for resale. The transmission model and serial number should be considered when converter replacement is required.

The following listings contain the transmission models or codes for the most commonly used automatic transmissions. Should a model or code be needed for a non-listed vehicle or transmission, refer to the individual transmission section and, if available, the model or code will be noted along with the model and code location.

# AMERICAN CAR MANUFACTURER'S BODY CODES

## AMERICAN MOTORS CORPORATION

| Year | Series | Model |
|---|---|---|
| 1980-82 | 01 | Concord |
| 1980-83 | 30 | Eagle |
| 1980-83 | 40 | Spirit |
| 1980 | 40 | AMX |
| 1981-83 | 50 | SX-4, Kammback |
| 1980 | 60 | Pacer |

## Chrysler Corporation

| Year | Series | Model |
|---|---|---|
| 1980-82 | L | M-Horizon/TC3, Z-Omni/024 |
| 1984 | L | M-Horizon/turismo, Z-Omni/Charger |
| 1980 | F | H-Volare, N-Aspen |
| 1980-81 | M | B-Caravelle, F-LeBaron, G-Diplomat |
| 1982 | M | V-Dodge 400, C-LeBaron, G-Diplomat |
| 1984 | M | G-Diplomat/Gran Fury, F-New Yorker/Fifth Avenue |
| 1980-84 | J | X-Mirida, S-Cordoba |
| 1980-81 | R | J-Gran Fury, E-Saint Regis, T-Newport/New Yorker |
| 1982 | R | B-Gran Fury, F-New Yorker |
| 1981-84 | Y | Y-Imperial |
| 1981-84 | K | D-Aries, P-Reliant |
| 1984 | CV | V-Dodge 400, C-LeBaron |
| 1984 | E | E-Chrysler E class, New Yorker, Dodge 600, 600ES |

## Ford Motor Company

| Year | Series | Model |
|---|---|---|
| 1980-82 | | LTD, Marquis, Continental |
| 1984 | L | LTD, Marquis, Continental |
| 1980-82 | | Thunderbird, Cougar |
| 1984 | S | Thunderbird, Cougar |
| 1980-82 | | Town Car, Mark VI |
| 1984 | Panther | LTD Crown Victoria, Grand Marquis, Town Car, Mark VI |
| 1980-82 | | Fairmont, Zephyr, Mustang, Capri |

## Ford Motor Company

| Year | Series | Model |
|---|---|---|
| 1984 | Fox | Fairmont, Zephyr, Mustang, Capri |
| 1980 | | Pinto, Bobcat |
| 1980-82 | | Granada, Monarch① |
| 1981-82 | | Escort, Lynx, EXP, LN7 |
| 1984 | Erika | Escort, Lynx, EXP, LN7 |
| 1984 | Topaz | Tempo, Topaz |

① 1980 only

## General Motors Corporation

| Year | Series | Model |
|---|---|---|
| 1980-81 | A | Century, Regal, Malibu, El Camino, Monte Carlo, Cutlass, LeMans, Grand AM, Safari |
| 1982-84 | A | Century, Celebrity, Ciera, 6000 |
| 1980-81 | B | LeSabre, Estate Wagon, Impala, Caprice, Delta 88, Catalina, Bonneville |
| 1982-84 | B | LeSabre, Impala, Caprice, Delta 88 |
| 1980-84 | C | Electra, Limited, Fleetwood Cp.① Deville, Ninety-Eight |
| 1980-84 | E | Riviera, Eldorado, Toronado |
| 1980 | H | Skyhawk, Monza, Starfire, Sunbird |
| 1980-84 | X | Skylark, Citation, Omega, Phoenix |
| 1982-84 | J | Skyhawk, Cimarron, Firenza, Cavalier, 2000 |
| 1980-82 | D | Fleetwood Sedan, Limousine |
| 1984 | D | Fleetwood, Limousine |
| 1980-84 | K | Seville |
| 1980-84 | Z | Commercial Chassis |
| 1980-84 | F | Camaro, Firebird |
| 1980-84 | T | Chevette |
| 1982-84 | T | 1000 |
| 1980-84 | Y | Corvette |
| 1982-84 | G | Regal, Malibu, El Camino, Monte Carlo, Cutlass, Bonneville, Grand Prix |

① 1984 Fleetwood Brougham

## GENERAL MOTORS CORPORATION
### Automatic Transmission/Transaxle Listing

| Year | Model | Engine | Trans. code |
|------|-------|--------|-------------|
| | **THM 125 (M34,MD9)** | | |
| 1980-81 | Skylark, Citation, Omega | 151 eng. | PZ |
| | Phoenix | 173 eng. | CT,CV |
| 1982-84 | Century, Celebrity, Citation, Ciera, Omega, Phoenix, 6000 | 151 eng. | PL,PW,PI,PD,PZ |
| | | 173 eng. | CE,CL,CT,CW,CC |
| | Century, Ciera | 3.0L eng. | BL,BF |
| | Century, Celebrity, Ciera 6000 | 260 eng. (diesel) | OP |
| | Cavalier, Cimarron, Firenza, Skyhawk, J2000 | 112 eng. (1.8L) | PG,P3,C1,CU,CF,C3,HV,CA,CJ,PE, PJ |
| | Cavalier, Cimarron, Firenza, Skyhawk | 122 eng. (2.0L) | CB,CA,CF |
| | Fiero | 151 eng. | PF |
| | **THM 180 (MD2,MD3)** | | |
| 1980-81 | Chevette | 1.6L eng. | Trans. Code unavailable |
| | **THM 180 C** | | |
| 1982 | Chevette, T1000 | 1.6L eng. | VQ |
| 1983 | Chevette, T1000 | 1.6L eng. | JY,TN |
| 1984 | Chevette, T1000 | 1.6L eng. | TP |
| | **THM 200 (MV9, M29)** | | |
| 1980 | Chevette | 1.6L eng. | CN |
| | Monza, Starfire, Sunbird | 151 eng. | PB,PY |
| | El Camino, Grand Am, LeMans, Malibu, Monte Carlo | 229 eng. | CA,CK |
| | Century, Grand Am, Grand Prix, LeMans, Cutlass, Regal | 231 eng. | BZ |
| | Bonneville, Catalina, Century, Grand Am, Grand Prix, LeMans Regal | 260 eng. | PG |
| | Delta 88 | 260 eng. | OW |
| | Caprice, Impala | 267 eng. | CE |
| | Century, Grand AM, Grand Prix, LeMans, LeSabre, Regal | 301 eng. | PW |
| | Firebird | 301 eng. | PD |
| | Cutlass, El Camino, Malibu, Monte Carlo | 305 eng. | CC |
| | Bonneville, Catalina, LeSabre, | 350 eng. (Gas) | BA |
| | Delta 88 | 350 eng. (Gas) | OS |
| | Bonneville, Catalina, Cutlass, Delta 88, Electra, LeSabre, Olds. 98 | 350 eng. (Diesel) | OT |
| | DeVille, Fleetwood | 350 eng. (Diesel) | AS |
| 1981 | Chevette | 1.6L eng. | CN |
| | Chevette | 1.8L eng. (Diesel) | CY |
| | Starfire | 151 eng. | PB,PY |
| | El Camino, Grand Prix, LeMans, Malibu, Monte Carlo | 229 eng. | CA |

## GENERAL MOTORS CORPORATION
### Automatic Transmission/Transaxle Listing

| Year | Model | Engine | Trans. code |
|---|---|---|---|
| 1981 | Century, Cutlass, El Camino. Grand Prix, LeMans, Malibu, Monte Carlo, Regal | 231 eng. | BZ |
| | Delta 88 | 260 eng. | OW |
| | Bonneville, Catalina, Century, Grand Prix, LeMans, Regal | 260 eng. | DW,PG |
| | Firebird | 260 eng. | PF |
| | Camaro, El Camino, Malibu, Monte Carlo | 267 eng. | CE |
| | Cutlass | 267 eng. | WA |
| | Grand Prix, LeMans | 301 eng. | PD,PE |
| | Cutlass, El Camino, Malibu, Monte Carlo | 305 eng. | CC |
| | LeSabre | 307 eng. | OG |
| | Bonneville, Catalina, Caprice, Century, Cutlass, Delta 88, Electra, Grand Prix, Impala, LeMans, LeSabre, Olds. 98, Regal | 350 eng. (Diesel) | OT |
| | DeVille, Fleetwood | 350 eng. (Diesel) | AS |
| 1982-83 | Chevette, T1000 | 1.8L eng. (Diesel) | JY,CY |
| | Cutlass, El Camino, Malibu, Monte Carlo, Regal | 260 eng. (Diesel) | OR |
| 1984 | Chevette, T1000 | 1.8L eng. (Diesel) | JY |
| | Bonneville, Caprice, Cutlass, Delta 88, El Camino, Grand Prix, Impala, LeSabre, Monte Carlo, Parisienne, Regal | 231 eng. | BH |
| | Cutlass | 260 eng. (Diesel) | OR |
| | Cutlass, Delta 88, LeSabre | 307 eng. | OI |
| | Bonneville, Caprice, Cutlass, Delta 88, El Camino, Grand Prix, Impala, LeSabre, Monte Carlo, Parisienne | 350 eng. (Diesel) | OU |
| | **THM 200-4R (MW9)** | | |
| 1981 | DeVille, Fleetwood, LeSabre | 252 eng. | BM,BY |
| | Caprice, Impala | 305 eng. | CU |
| | Bonneville, Catalina, Delta 88, Electra, Olds. 98 | 307 eng. | OG |
| 1982-83 | Regal | 231 eng. | BR |
| | DeVille, Electra, Fleetwood LeSabre, Olds. 98 | 252 eng. (V-6) | BY |
| | Regal | 252 eng. (V-6) | BT |
| | DeVille, Fleetwood | 252 eng. (V-8) | AA,AP |
| | Caprice, Impala | 267 eng. | CQ |
| | Caprice, Impala | 305 eng. | CR |

### GENERAL MOTORS CORPORATION
### Automatic Transmission/Transaxle Listing

| Year | Model | Engine | Trans. code |
|------|-------|--------|-------------|
| 1982-83 | Cutlass | 307 eng. | OZ |
| | Electra, LeSabre | 307 eng. | OG |
| | Caprice, Delta 88, Deville, Electra, Fleetwood, Impala, LeSabre, Olds. 98, | 350 eng. (Diesel) | OM |
| | **THM 250 (M31)** | | |
| 1980 | Caprice, Impala | 229 eng. | WK |
| | Firebird | 260 eng. | MC |
| | Caprice, Impala, El Camino, Malibu, Monte Carlo | 267 eng. | WH,XL |
| | Bonneville, Catalina, Century, Grand AM, Grand Prix, LeMans, LeSabre, Regal | 301 eng. | MD,TB |
| | Cutlass, El Camino, Malibu, Monte Carlo | 305 eng. | WL |
| | Delta 88 | 307 eng. | TT |
| 1981 | Camaro, Caprice, Impala | 229 eng. | TA |
| | Cutlass, El Camino, Grand Prix LeMans, Malibu, Monte Carlo | 231 eng. | XX |
| | El Camino, Malibu, Monte Carlo | 267 eng. | XS |
| | El Camino, Malibu, Monte Carlo | 305 eng. | XK |
| | Cutlass, Delta 88, LeSabre | 307 eng. | XL,XA |
| 1982-84 | Caprice, El Camino, Impala, Malibu, Monte Carlo | 229 eng. | XP,XE |
| | Bonneville, Cutlass, El Camino, Grand Prix, Malibu, Monte Carlo Regal | 231 eng. | WK |
| | Bonneville, El Camino, Grand Prix, Malibu, Monte Carlo, Caprice | 305 eng. | XK |
| | Cutlass | 307 eng. | XN |
| | Delta 88, LeSabre | 307 eng. | XL |
| | El Camino, Monte Carlo | 229 eng. | CH |
| | Regal | 231 eng. | BQ |
| | LeSabre, Electra, Regal | 252 eng. (V6) | BY,BT |
| | Fleetwood | 252 eng. (V8) | AA,AP |
| | Cutlass, Regal | 260 eng. (Diesel) | OF,OY |
| | Cutlass, Regal | 305 eng. | HG |
| | Bonneville, El Camino, Grand Prix, Monte Carlo | 305 eng. | CQ,CR |
| | Delta 88, Electra, LeSabre, Olds. 98 | 307 eng. | OG,OJ,OZ |
| | Bonneville, Cutlass, Delta 88, El Camino, Electra, Grand Prix, LeSabre, Monte Carlo, Olds. 98, Parisienne, Regal | 350 eng. (Diesel) | OM |

## GENERAL MOTORS CORPORATION
### Automatic Transmission/Transaxle Listing

| Year | Model | Engine | Trans. code |
|------|-------|--------|-------------|
| | | **THM 325 (M32)** | |
| 1980-81 | Riviera | 231 eng. | BJ |
| | Riviera, Toronado | 252 eng. | BE |
| | Eldorado, Seville | 252 eng. | AG |
| | Riviera, Toronado | 307 eng. | OH |
| | Riviera, Toronado | 350 eng. (Gas) | OJ |
| | Eldorado, Seville | 350 eng. (Gas) | AJ |
| | Riviera, Toronado | 350 eng. (Diesel) | OK |
| | Eldorado, Seville | 350 eng. (Diesel) | AK |
| | Eldorado, Seville | 368 eng. | AF |
| | | **THM 325 4SP. (M57)** | |
| 1982-84 | Riviera | 231 eng. | BJ |
| | Eldorado, Seville | 252 eng. (V-6) | AM |
| | Eldorado, Seville | 252 eng. (V-8) | AB,AJ,AE |
| | Riviera, Toronado | 252 eng. | BE |
| | Riviera, Toronado | 307 eng. | OJ |
| | Eldorado, Seville | 350 eng. (Diesel) | AL |
| | Riviera, Toronado | 350 eng. (Diesel) | OK |
| | | **THM 350** | |
| 1980 | Caprice, Impala | 229 eng. | JA,XY |
| | Bonneville, Catalina, Caprice, Century, Cutlass, Delta 88, El Camino, Grand Am, Grand Prix, Impala, LeMans, Malibu, Monte Carlo | 231 eng. | KJ,KT,KC,KS,KH |
| | Camaro, Firebird | 231 eng. | KF |
| | Skyhawk, Starfire, Sunbird | 231 eng. | KA |
| | DeVille, Electra, Fleetwood LeSabre | 252 eng. | KD |
| | Cutlass | 260 eng. | LC,LD |
| | Camaro, El Camino, Malibu, Monte Carlo | 267 eng. | JJ,JN |
| | Bonneville, Catalina, Grand Am, Grand Prix, LeMans | 301 eng. | MS |
| | Camaro, Firebird | 301 eng. | MJ,MT |
| | Bonneville, Caprice, Catalina, Century, Cutlass, El Camino, Grand Am, Grand Prix, Impala, LeMans, Malibu, Monte Carlo, Regal | 305 eng. | JE,JK,LJ |
| | Camaro, Firebird | 305 eng. | JK,JD |
| | Corvette | 305 eng. | JC |
| | Bonneville, Catalina, Delta 88, LeSabre | 350 eng. (Gas) | KN,LA,TV |
| | Camaro | 350 eng. (Gas) | JL |

## GENERAL MOTORS CORPORATION
### Automatic Transmission/Transaxle Listing

| Year | Model | Engine | Trans. code |
|---|---|---|---|
| | **THM 350** | | |
| 1980 | Caprice, El Camino, Impala, Malibu, Monte Carlo | 350 eng. (Diesel) | JS |
| 1981 | Bonneville, Catalina, Caprice, Century, Cutlass, Delta 88, El Camino, Grand Prix, LeMans, LeSabre, Impala, Malibu, Monte Carlo, Regal | 231 eng. | KD,KT |
| | Camaro, Firebird | 231 eng. | KY |
| | Electra, LeSabre | 252 eng. | KK |
| | Cutlass, Grand Prix, LeMans | 260 eng. | LC |
| | Firebird | 301 eng. | MC |
| | Grand Prix, LeMans | 301 eng. | MA |
| | Camaro | 350 eng. (Gas) | JC |
| | Corvette | 350 eng. (Gas) | JD |
| | Bonneville, Catalina, Caprice, Delta 88, Impala, LeSabre | 350 eng. (Diesel) | LA,LD |
| 1982 | Caprice, El Camino, Impala, Malibu, Monte Carlo | 229 eng. | WP |
| | Caprice, El Camino, Impala, Malibu, Monte Carlo | 267 eng. | WC |
| | Bonneville, Cutlass, El Camino, Grand Prix, Malibu, Monte Carlo, Regal | 350 eng. (Diesel) | WX |
| | Caprice, Delta 88, Electra, Impala, LeSabre, Olds. 98 | 350 eng. (Diesel) | WT |
| | **THM 350C—(Lock-up Converter)** | | |
| 1980 | Caprice, Impala | 267 eng. | TZ |
| | El Camino, Malibu, Monte Carlo | 267 eng. | XN |
| | Bonneville, Catalina, LeSabre | 301 eng. | WB |
| | Corvette | 305 eng. | TW |
| | Caprice, Cutlass, El Camino, Impala, Malibu, Monte Carlo | 305 eng. | WD |
| | Delta 88 | 307 eng. | WA |
| | All Models | 350R eng. (Gas) | TY |
| | Bonneville, Catalina | 350X eng. (Gas) | TV |
| | Bonneville, Catalina, Caprice, Delta 88, Impala, LeSabre | 350 eng. (Diesel) | WC |
| 1981 | El Camino, Malibu, Monte Carlo | 229 eng. | WP |
| | Caprice, Cutlass, El Camino, Impala, Malibu, Monte Carlo | 267 eng. | WC |
| | Camaro, Caprice, El Camino, Impala, Malibu, Monte Carlo | 305 eng. | WD |
| | Caprice, El Camino, Impala, Malibu, Monte Carlo | 350 eng. (Gas) | WE |
| | Caprice, Impala | 350 eng. (Diesel) | WS,WW |

## GENERAL MOTORS CORPORATION
### Automatic Transmission/Transaxle Listing

| Year | Model | Engine | Trans. code |
|------|-------|--------|-------------|
| | **THM 350C—(Lock-up Converter)** | | |
| 1982 | Bonneville, Caprice, El Camino Cutlass, Delta 88, Impala, Electra, Grand Prix, Malibu, Monte Carlo, Regal | 231 eng. | KA |
| | Bonneville, Electra, Grand Prix, Regal | 252 eng. | KE,KK |
| | Cutlass, Delta 88 | 260 eng. | LA |
| | Bonneville, El Camino, Grand Prix, Malibu, Monte Carlo | 350 eng. (Diesel) | LB |
| | Caprice, Delta 88, Electra, Impala, Regal | 350 eng. (Diesel) | LD |
| 1983 | Bonneville, Caprice, Cutlass, Delta 88, Electra, Impala Grand Prix, Regal | 231 eng. | KA |
| | Electra | 252 eng. | KE,KK |
| | Bonneville, El Camino, Grand Prix, Malibu, Monte Carlo | 305 eng. | WD,WE |
| | Caprice, Delta 88, Impala | 350 eng. (Diesel) | LD,LJ |
| | Bonneville, Cutlass, El Camino, Grand Prix, Malibu, Monte Carlo | 350 eng. (Diesel) | LB |
| | Electra, Regal | 350 eng. (Diesel) | LB,LJ |
| 1984 | El Camino, Monte Carlo | 305 eng. | WS |
| | Impala, Caprice | 305 eng. | WW |
| | **THM 400 (M40)** | | |
| 1980 | Electra, LeSabre | 350 eng. | BB,OB |
| | Fleetwood, DeVille | 368 eng. | AB,AD,AE |
| | Limo, Comm. Ch. | 368 eng. | AD,AN |
| 1981-84 | Fleetwood, DeVille | 368 eng. | AE |
| | Limo | 368 eng. | AN |
| | Comm. Ch. | 368 eng. | AD |
| | **THM 700 (MD8)** | | |
| 1982 | Caprice, Impala | 267 eng. | Y4,YL |
| | Caprice, Impala | 305 eng. | Y3,YK |
| | Corvette | 350 eng. (Gas) | YA |
| 1983 | Caprice, Impala | 305 eng. | YK |
| 1984 | Camaro, Firebird | 151 eng. | PQ |
| | Camaro, Firebird | 173 eng. | YF |
| | Camaro, Firebird | 305 eng. | YG,YP |
| | Caprice, Impala, Parisienne | 305 eng. | YK |
| | Corvette | 350 eng. | Y9,YW |
| | **THM 440-T4 (ME9)** | | |
| 1984 | Celebrity, Century, Ciera, 6000 | 260 eng. (Diesel) | OB,OV |

## CHRYSLER CORPORATION
### Transmission Listing

| Year | Assy. No. | Engine Cu. In. | Type Trans. | Other Information |
|------|-----------|----------------|-------------|-------------------|
| | | | | **AMERICAN MOTORS CORPORATION CARS** |
| 1980 | 3235770 | 2.5 Litre | A-904 | Standard—Non-Lockup (4 Cyl) |
| | 3237269 | 258 | A-904 | Standard—Lockup |
| | 3236581 | 258 | A-998 | 4-Wheel Drive—Non-Lockup |
| | 3238455 | 258 | A-998 | Export Non-Lockup |
| | 3238767 | 282 | A-998 | Mexico—Lockup |
| | 3235220 | 258/304 | A-999 | Jeep CJ 4-Wheel Drive—Non-Lockup |
| | 5359402 | 258/360 | A-727 | Jeep SR 4-Wheel Drive—Non-Lockup |
| 1981 | 3238777 | 2.5 Litre | A-904 | Wide Ratio—Non Lockup |
| | 3238772 | 2.5 Litre | A-904 | 4x4 Wide Ratio—Non Lockup |
| | 3238778 | 2.5 Litre | A-904 | CJ-7 4x4 Wide Ratio—Non Lockup |
| | 3240107 | 258 | A-904 | Standard—Lockup |
| | 3238771 | 258 | A-998 | 4x4 Eagle—Lockup |
| | 3240296 | 258/282 | A-998 | VAM—Lockup |
| | 3238773 | 258/304 | A-999 | CJ-7 4x4 Lockup (2.73 Axle) |
| | 3239816 | 258/304 | A-999 | CJ-7 4x4 Lockup (3.31 Axle) |
| | 3240219 | 258 | A-999 | CJ-7 4x4 Export—Non Lockup |
| | 3238774 | 360 | A-727 | Sr Jeep 4x4 Lockup (2.73 Axle) |
| | 3239817 | 258/360 | A-727 | Sr Jeep 4x4 Lockup (3.31-3.73 Axle) |
| | 3240255 | 258/360 | A-727 | Sr Jeep 4x4 Export—Non Lockup |
| 1982 | 3238772 | 2.5 Litre | A-904 | 4x4—Non-Lockup |
| | 3238777 | 2.5 Litre | A-904 | Non-Lockup |
| | — | 2.5 Litre | A-904 | CJ7 4x4—Non-Lockup |
| | 5567640 | 2.5 Litre | A-904 | AM General-Post Office Trucks |
| | 3240229 | 258 | A-904 | Lock-up |
| | 3241099 | 258 | A-998 | 4x4 Eagle-Lockup |
| | 3241100 | 6 & V8 | A-998 | VAM—Non-Lockup |
| | 3240231 | 258 | A-999 | CJ7 4x4—Lockup |
| | 3240231 | 258 | A-999 | SR Jeep 4x4—Lockup (2.73 Axle) |
| | — | 258/304 | A-999 | CJ7 4x4—Lockup (3.31 Axle) |
| | 3241098 | 258 | A-999 | CJ7 4x4 Export—Non-Lockup |
| | 3238774 | 360 | A-727 | SR Jeep 4x4—Lockup (2.73 Axle) |
| | 3239817 | 258/360 | A-727 | SR Jeep 4x4—Lockup (3.31/3.73 Axle) |
| | 3240255 | 258/360 | A-727 | SR Jeep 4x4 Export—Non-Lockup |
| 1983-84 | 8933000864 | 2.5 Litre | A-904 | 4x4—Non Lockup |
| | 8933000863 | 2.5 Litre | A-904 | Non Lockup |
| | 8923000028 | 2.5 Litre | A-904 | AM General—Post Office Truck |
| | 8953000847 | 2.46 Litre | A-904 | XJ 4x4—Lockup |
| | 3240229 | 258 | A-904 | Lockup |
| | 8933000916 | 258 | A-998 | 4x4 Eagle—Lockup |
| | 3241100 | 6 & 8 | A-998 | VAM—Non Lockup |
| | 8933000913 | 258 | A-999 | CJ7-8 4x4—Lockup |
| | | | | SJ 4x4—Lockup (2.73 Axle) |
| | 8933000917 | 258 | A-999 | CJ 4x4 Export—Non Lockup |
| | 8933000915 | 360 | A-727 | SJ 4x4—Lockup (2.73 Axle) |
| | 8933000914 | 258/360 | A-727 | SJ 4x4—Lock (3.31/3.73 Axle) |
| | 8933000918 | 258/360 | A-727 | SJ 4x4 Export—Non Lockup |

## CHRYSLER CORPORATION
### Transmission Listing

| Year | Assy. No. | Engine Cu. In. | Type Trans. | Other Information |
|------|-----------|----------------|-------------|-------------------|
| | | | **CHRYSLER CORPORATION CARS** | |
| 1980 | 4130951 | 225 | A-904 | Standard—Lockup |
| | 4130953 | 225 | A-904 | Wide Ratio Gear Set—Lockup |
| | 4202095 | 225 | A-904 | Wide Ratio Gear Set—Non-Lockup |
| | 4130952 | 225 | A-904 | Heavy Duty—Lockup |
| | 4202094 | 225 | A-904 | Heavy Duty—Non-Lockup |
| | 4130955 | 318 | A-998 | Standard—Lockup |
| | 4130956 | 318 | A-998 | Wide Ratio Gear Set—Lockup |
| | 4130957 | 360 | A-999 | Standard—Lockup |
| | 4202084 | 1.6 Litre | A-904 | MMC (Colt-Arrow)—Non-Lockup |
| | 4202085 | 2.0 Litre | A-904 | MMC (Colt-Arrow) Non-Lockup |
| | 4202086 | 2.6 Litre | A-904 | MMC (Colt-Arrow) Non-Lockup |
| | 4202064 | 318 | A-727 | Standard—Lockup |
| | 4130976 | 360 | A-727 | Hi-Performance—Lockup |
| | 4058376 | 360 | A-727 | Hi-Performance—Non-Lockup |
| | 5224442 | 1.7 Litre | A-404 | Federal & California—3.48 Axle |
| 1981 | 4202662 | 225 | A-904 | Wide Ratio—Non Lockup |
| | 4202663 | 225 | A-904 | Wide Ratio—Lockup |
| | 4202664 | 225 | A-904 | Heavy Duty—Wide Ratio—Non Lockup |
| | 4058383 | 225 | A-904T | Heavy Duty—Wide Ratio—Lockup |
| | 4058398 | 318 | A-999 | Wide Ratio—Lockup |
| | 4202675 | 318 | A-999 | Wide Ratio—Lockup |
| | 4202729 | 318 | A-999 | "Imperial"-Wide Ratio—Lockup |
| | 4202572 | 1.6 Litre | A-904 | MMC (Arrow-Colt)—Non Lockup |
| | 4202573 | 2.0 Litre | A-904 | MMC (Arrow-Colt)—Non Lockup |
| | 4202574 | 2.6 Litre | A-904 | MMC (Arrow-Colt)—Non Lockup |
| | 4202571 | 318 | A-727 | Hi-Performance—Lockup |
| | 4058393 | 360 | A-727 | Export—Non-Lockup |
| 1982 | 4202662 | 225 | A-904 | Non-Lockup |
| | 4202663 | 225 | A-904 | Lockup |
| | 4202664 | 225 | A-904 | Heavy Duty—Non Lockup |
| | 4058383 | 225 | A-904T | Heavy Duty—Lockup Also used in truck |
| | 4058398 | 318 | A-999 | Lockup—Also used in truck |
| | 4202675 | 318 | A-999 | Lockup |
| | 4202729 | 318 | A-999 | "Imperial" lockup |
| | 4269051 | 1.6 Litre | A-904 | MMC Non-Lockup |
| | 4269052 | 2.0 Litre | A-904 | MMC Non-Lockup |
| | 4269053 | 2.6 Litre | A-904 | MMC Non-Lockup |
| | 4202571 | 318 HP | A-727 | Hi-Performance Lockup |
| | 4058393 | 360 | A-727 | Export—Non-Lockup |
| 1983 | 4202662 | 225 | A-904 | Non-Lockup |
| | 4202663 | 225 | A-904 | Lockup |
| | 4202664 | 225 | A-904 | Heavy Duty—Non Lockup |
| | 4058398 | 318 | A-999 | Lockup-Also used in Truck |
| | 4202675 | 318 | A-999 | Lockup |
| | 4202729 | 318 | A-999 | "Imperial" lockup |
| | 4269932 | 1.6 Litre | A-904 | MMC Non Lockup |
| | 4269933 | 2.0 Litre | A-904 | MMC Non Lockup |
| | 4269934 | 2.6 Litre | A-904 | MMC Non-Lockup |

## CHRYSLER CORPORATION
### Transmission Listing

| Year | Assy. No. | Engine Cu. In. | Type Trans. | Other Information |
|------|-----------|----------------|-------------|-------------------|
| 1983 | 4202898 | 2.6 Litre | A-904 | MMC 4x4 Non Lockup |
|      | 4202571 | 318 HP | A-727 | Hi-Performance Lockup |
|      | — | 360 | A-727 | Export—Non Lockup |
| 1984 | 4295512 | 2.2 Litre | Transaxle | 2.78 Overall Ratio |
|      | 4295763 | 2.2 Litre | Transaxle | 3.22 Overall Ratio |
|      | 4295513 | 2.2 Litre (E.F.I) | Transaxle | 3.02 Overall Ratio |
|      | 4329827 | 2.2 Litre (Turbo) | Transaxle | 3.02 Overall Ratio |
|      | 4295515 | 2.6 Litre | Transaxle | 3.02 Overall Ratio |
|      | 4295517 | 2.6 Litre | Transaxle | 3.22 Overall Ratio |
|      | 4295887 | 318 | A904 | Lock-up 2.24 Axle |
|      | 4329436 | 318 | A904 | Lock-up 2.26 Axle |
|      | 4058398 | 318 | A904 | Lock-up 2.94 Axle |
|      | 4329631 | 318 | A904 | Non Lock-up 2.94 Axle |

### DODGE TRUCK TRANSMISSIONS

| Year | Assy. No. | Engine Cu. In. | Type Trans. | Other Information |
|------|-----------|----------------|-------------|-------------------|
| 1980 | 4058376 | 360 | A-727 | Hi-Perf. Long Extension—Non-Lockup |
|      | 4058371 | 225 | A-727 | Long Extension—Lockup |
|      | 4058355 | 225 | A-727 | 4-Wheel Drive—Lockup |
|      | 4058351 | 318/360 | A-727 | Short Extension—Lockup |
|      | 4058375 | 318/360 | A-727 | Short Extension—Non-Lockup |
|      | 4058373 | 318/360 | A-727 | Long Extension—Lockup |
|      | 4058374 | 318/360 | A-727 | Long Heavy Duty Ext.—Lockup |
|      | 4058372 | 318/360 | A-727 | Long Heavy Duty Ext.—Non-Lockup |
|      | 4058356 | 318/360 | A-727 | 4-Wheel Drive-Lockup |
|      | 4058358 | 318/360 | A-727 | 4-Wheel Drive—Non-Lockup |
|      | 4058336 | 446 | A-727 | Medium Extension—Non-Lockup |
| 1981 | 4058383 | 225 | A-904T | Wide Ratio—Lockup |
|      | 4058398 | 318 | A-999 | Wide Ratio—Lockup |
|      | 4058384 | 225 | A-727 | Long Ext.—Lockup |
|      | 4058385 | 225 | A-727 | 4x4—Lockup |
|      | 4058388 | 318/360 | A-727 | Short Ext.—Lockup |
|      | 4058389 | 318/360 | A-727 | Short Ext.—Non-Lockup |
|      | 4058392 | 318/360 | A-727 | Long Ext.—Lockup |
|      | 4058394 | 318/360 | A-727 | HD Long Ext.—Lockup |
|      | 4058395 | 318/360 | A-727 | HD Long Ext.—Non Lockup |
|      | 4058396 | 318/360 | A-727 | 4x4—Lockup |
|      | 4058397 | 318/360 | A-727 | 4x4—Non-Lockup |
| 1982 | 4058383 | 225 | A-904T | Lockup |
|      | 4058398 | 318 | A-999 | Lockup |
|      | 4058384 | 225 | A-727 | Long Ext.—Lockup |
|      | 4058385 | 225 | A-727 | 4x4—Lockup |
|      | 4058388 | 318/360 | A-727 | Short Ext.—Lockup |
|      | 4058389 | 318/360 | A-727 | Short Ext.—Non-Lockup |
|      | 4058394 | 318/360 | A-727 | HD Long Ext.—Lockup |
|      | 4058395 | 318/360 | A-727 | HD Long Ext.—Non-Lockup |
|      | 4058396 | 318/360 | A-727 | 4x4—Lockup |
|      | 4058397 | 318/360 | A-727 | 4x4—Non-Lockup |

## CHRYSLER CORPORATION
### Transmission Listing

| Year | Assy. No. | Engine Cu. In. | Type Trans. | Other Information |
|------|-----------|----------------|-------------|-------------------|
| | | | | |
| **DODGE TRUCK TRANSMISSIONS** | | | | |
| 1983 | 4058383 | 225 | A-904T | Lockup |
| | 4058398 | 318 | A-999 | Lockup |
| | 4058384 | 225 | A-727 | Long Ext.—Lockup |
| | — | 225 | A-727 | 4x4—Lockup |
| | — | 318/360 | A-727 | Short Ext.—Lockup |
| | 4058389 | 318/360 | A-727 | Short Ext.—Non-Lockup |
| | — | 318/360 | A-727 | HD Long Ext.—Lockup |
| | 4058395 | 318/360 | A-727 | HD Long Ext.—Non Lockup |
| | — | 318/360 | A-727 | 4x4—Lockup |
| | 4058397 | 318/360 | A-727 | 4x4—Non Lockup |
| 1984 | 4058384 | 225 | A-727 | Long Ext.—Lockup |
| | 4295941 | 225 | A-727 | Long Ext.—Non Lockup |
| | 4329438 | 318 | A-727 | Long Ext. |
| | 4329468 | 360 | A-727 | Long Ext. |
| | 4329482 | 318/360 | A-727 | Short Ext. |
| | 4329458 | 318 | A-727 | 4x4 |
| | 4329488 | 360 | A-727 | 4x4 |
| | 4058383 | 225 | A-904 | Long Ext. |
| | 4058398 | 318 | A-999 | Long Ext.—Lockup |

### Other Transmission Usage

| Year | Assy. No. | Engine Cu. In. | Type Trans. | Other Information |
|------|-----------|----------------|-------------|-------------------|
| **EXPORT** | | | | |
| 1980 | 4193341 | — | A-727 | Aston-Martin—Non-Lockup |
| | 4193390 | — | A-727 | Aston-Martin—Lockup |
| | 4058377 | 225/Diesel | A-727 | United Kingdon Export Short Ext. |
| **AM GENERAL TRANSMISSION** | | | | |
| | 5565798 | 2.0L | A-904 | Standard—Non-Lockup (4 Cyl) |
| **INTERNATIONAL HARVESTER CORP. TRANSMISSION** | | | | |
| | 492448-C91 | 304/345 | A-727 | Scout 4-Wheel Drive—Non-Lockup |
| **MARINE AND INDUSTRIAL TRANSMISSIONS** | | | | |
| | 4142312 | 225 | A-727 | Short Extension—Non-Lockup |
| | 4142313 | 225 | A-727 | Medium Extension—Non-Lockup |
| | 4142321 | 318/360 | A-727 | Medium Extension—Non-Lockup |
| | 4142362 | Diesel | A-727 | Short Extension—Non-Lockup |
| | 4142363 | Diesel | A-727 | Medium Extension—Non-Lockup |
| | 4142364 | Diesel | A-727 | Long Extension—Non-Lockup |
| **EXPORT** | | | | |
| 1981 | 4025739 | — | A-727 | Aston-Martin Lockup |
| | 4058387 | 225/Diesel | A-727 | UK Export—Short Ext.—Non Lockup |
| **MARINE & INDUSTRIAL TRANSMISSIONS** | | | | |
| | 4142312 | 225 | A-727 | Short Ext.—Non Lockup |
| | 4142313 | 225 | A-727 | Medium Ext.—Non Lockup |
| | 4142321 | 318/360 | A-727 | Medium Ext.—Non Lockup |
| **MARINE AND INDUSTRIAL TRANSMISSIONS** | | | | |
| | 4142362 | Diesel | A-727 | Short Ext.—Non Lockup |
| | 4142363 | Diesel | A-727 | Medium Ext.—Non Lockup |
| | 4142364 | Diesel | A-727 | Long Ext.—Non Lockup |

## CHRYSLER CORPORATION
### Transmission Listing

#### Other Transmission Usage

| | | | | |
|---|---|---|---|---|
| **EXPORT** | | | | |
| 1982 | 4058387 | 225/Diesel | A-727 | UK Export—Short Non-Lockup |
| | 4025739 | — | A-727 | Aston Martin—Lockup |
| | 4202717 | — | A-727 | Roadmaster Rail—Medium Non-Lockup |
| | 3836023 | — | A-727 | Land Rover 4x4—Non-Lockup |
| | 3836024 | Diesel | A-727 | IVECO—Medium Ext—Non-Lockup |
| **MARINE AND INDUSTRIAL TRANSMISSIONS** | | | | |
| | 4142312 | 225 | A-727 | Short Ext—Non-Lockup |
| | 4142313 | 225 | A-727 | Medium Ext—Non-Lockup |
| | 4142321 | 318/360 | A-727 | .Medium Ext—Non-Lockup |
| | 4142362 | Diesel | A-727 | Short Ext—Non-Lockup |
| | 4142363 | Diesel | A-727 | Medium Ext—Non-Lockup |
| | 4142364 | Diesel | A-727 | Long Ext—Non-Lockup |
| **EXPORT** | | | | |
| 1983 | 4058387 | 225/Diesel | A-727 | UK Export-Short Non-Lockup |
| | 4025739 | — | A-727 | Aston Martin-Lockup |
| | 4202717 | — | A-727 | Roadmaster Rail—Med. Non-Lockup |
| | 3836023 | — | A-727 | Land Rover 4x4—Non Lockup |
| | 3836024 | Diesel | A-727 | IVECO—Med. Ext. Non-Lockup |
| | 3836040 | — | A-727 | Maserati—Lockup |
| **MARINE AND INDUSTRIAL TRANSMISSIONS** | | | | |
| | 4142312 | 225 | A-727 | Short Ext—Non Lockup |
| | 4142313 | 225 | A-727 | Med. Ext—Non Lockup |
| | 4142321 | 318/360 | A-727 | Med. Ext—Non Lockup |
| | 4142362 | Diesel | A-727 | Short Ext—Non Lockup |
| | 4142363 | Diesel | A-727 | Med. Ext—Non Lockup |
| | 4142364 | Diesel | A-727 | Long Ext—Non Lockup |

## FORD MOTOR CO.
### Automatic Transmission/Transaxle Listing

| Year | Model | Engine | Trans-code |
|---|---|---|---|
| **C-3 TRANS.** | | | |
| 1980 | Pinto—Bobcat | 2.3L eng. | 80DT-AA,-AB |
| | Mustang—Capri | 2.3L eng. wo/turbo | 800T-CA,-CB |
| | | 2.3L eng. w/turbo | 800T-CDA,-CDB |
| | | 200 eng. | 80DT-EA,-EB |
| | Fairmont—Zephyr | 2.3L eng. wo/turbo | 80DT-CA,-CB,-HA,-HB |
| | | 2.3L eng. w/turbo | 80DT-CDA,-CDB |
| | | 200 eng. | 80DT-EA,-EB,-LA,-LB,-CEB |
| | Thunderbird—Cougar | 200 eng. | 80DT-LB |
| 1981 | Mustang—Capri | 2.3L eng. | 81DT-CFA,-CHA |
| | | 200 eng. | 81DT-DAA,-DAB,-DEA,-DEB |
| | Cougar-XR7—Granada Fairmont—Zephyr | 2.3L eng. | 81DT-CFA,-CHA,-CKA,-CMA |
| | | 200 eng. | 81DT-DAA,-DAB,-DDA,-DDB,-DEA-DEB,-DGA,-DGB |
| | Thunderbird | 200 eng. | 81DT-DDA,-DDB,-DGA,-DGB |

## FORD MOTOR CO.
### Automatic Transmission/Transaxle Listing

| Year | Model | Engine | Trans-code |
|---|---|---|---|
| 1982 | Mustang—Capri | 2.3L eng.<br>200 eng. | 82DT-AAA,-ACA<br>82DT-BBA |
| | Cougar-XR7—Granada | 2.3L eng. | 82DT-AAA,-ABA,-ACA,-ADA,-ARA |
| | Fairmont—Zephyr | 2.3L eng.<br>200 eng. | 82DT-AAA,-ABA,-ACA,-ADA<br>82DT-BAA,-BBA |
| 1983 | Mustang—Capri | 2.3L eng. | 83DT-AAB |
| | LTD—Marquis | 2.3L eng. | 83DT-AAB,-ABB,-AGB,-AHB |
| | Fairmont—Zephyr | 2.3L eng.<br>200 eng. | 83DT-AAB,-ABB<br>83DT-BAA,-BBA |
| | Cougar-XR7—Thunderbird | 232 eng.<br>255 eng. | PKA-BH1,2,3<br>PKA-AH5,6,7,8 |
| | Lincoln Continental | 232 eng.<br>302 eng. | PKA-BF1,2,3,4<br>PKA-BD1,2,3,4 |
| | Lincoln Towncar—Mark VI | 302 eng. | PKA-M8-M13,14,15,16-BC1,2,3 |
| 1983 | Ford—Mercury | 302 eng.<br>351 eng. | PKA-AG17-AU17-AY12-BB12<br>PKA-C25-AS17 |
| | Cougar-XR7—Thunderbird | 232 eng.<br>302 eng. | PKA-BR-BT<br>PKA-K |
| | Lincoln Continental | 302 eng. | PKA-BD12 |
| | Lincoln Towncar—Mark VI | 302 eng. | PKA-M25-BC5 |
| | Marquis—LTD | 232 eng. | PKA-BR-BT |
| 1984 | Ford—Mercury | 302 eng.<br><br>351 eng. | PKA-AG23,24-AU23,24<br>  -AY18,19-BB18,19<br>PKA-C31,32-AS,23 |
| | Mustang—Capri | 232 eng.<br>302 eng. | PKA-BZ,1-CD,1<br>PKA-BW,1 |
| | Cougar-XR7—LTD<br>Marquis—Thunderbird | 232 eng. | PKA-BT6,7-CB6,7 |
| | Cougar-XR7—Thunderbird | 302 eng. | PKA-K6,7 |
| | Lincoln Continental | 302 eng. | PKA-BD18 |
| | Lincoln Towncar | 302 eng. | PKA-M31-BC12 |
| | Lincoln Mark VII | 302 eng. | PKA-BV |
| | **ATX TRANS.** | | |
| 1981 | Escort—Lynx | 1.6L eng. | PMA-A1,2 |
| | LN7—EXP | 1.6L eng. | PMA-K,1 |
| 1982 | Escort—Lynx—LN7—EXP | 1.6L eng.<br>1.6L eng.(H.O.) | PMA-A3-K2<br>PMA-R |
| 1983 | Escort—Lynx—LN7—EXP | 1.6L eng.<br>1.6L eng.w/E.F.I.<br>1.6L eng.(H.O.) | PMA-K3,PMB-A1<br>PMA-P<br>PMA-R1 |
| 1984 | Tempo—Topaz<br>Tempo, Topaz | 2.3L eng.<br>2.3L eng.(Canada) | PMA-N<br>PMA-AA |
| | Escort—Lynx—EXP | 1.6L eng.w/E.F.I.<br>1.6L eng.(w/H.O.) | PMA-U1,2-PMB,D<br>PMA-V3-PMB-C2 |
| | Tempo—Topaz | 2.3L eng. | PMA-N-N1-N2 |

# GENERAL INFORMATION

## FORD MOTOR CO.
## Automatic Transmission/Transaxle Listing

| Year | Model | Engine | Trans-code |
|------|-------|--------|------------|
| | | **C-3 TRANS.** | |
| 1984 | Mustang—Capri | 140 eng. | 84DT-AAA,-ACA,-AJA |
| | LTD—Marquis | 140 eng. | 83DT-AGB,-AHB<br>84DT-ABA,-ACA,-ADA,-AKA |
| | Thunderbird—Cougar XR7 | 140 eng. | 84DT-AEA,-AFA |
| | | **C-4 TRANS.** | |
| 1980 | Ford—Mercury | 302 eng. | PEE-DZ3,4,5,6,7,-EA3,4,5,6,7-EM3,4-FC1,2-FE1,2,3,4,5 |
| | Mustang—Capri | 2.3L eng.<br>200 eng.<br>255 eng. | PEJ-AC1,2,3<br>PEB-P4,5,6,7<br>PEM-B1,2,3,4-E1,2,3,4-N1,2,3,4 |
| | Granada—Monarch | 250 eng.<br>255 eng.<br>302 eng. | PEL-A1,2,3-B1,2,3,-C1-D1<br>PEM-J1,2,3,4-K1,2,3,4-P1-R1<br>PEE-CW5,6,7,8,9-FP1,2,3,4-FR1,2,3,4 |
| | Pinto—Bobcat | 2.3L eng. | PEJ-Z1,2,3 |
| | Fairmont—Zephyr | 2.3L eng.<br>200 eng.<br><br>255 eng. | PEJ-AC1,2,3-AD1,2,3<br>PEB-N6,7,8,9,-P4,5,6,7-S3,4-T1,2,3,4-U1,2,3<br>PEM-C1,2,3,4-D1,2,3,4-E1,2,3,4-G1-H1,2,3,4-M1,2,3,4-L1,2,3,4-N1,2,3,4 |
| | Cougar—Thunderbird | 200 eng.<br>255 eng.<br>302 eng. | PEB-T3,4<br>PEM-D1,2,3,4-L1,2,3,4<br>PEE-F1,2,3,4-FN1,2,3,4 |
| | Versailles | 302 eng. | PEE-EY2,3,4,5,6-FV1,2,3,4 |
| 1981 | Mustang—Capri | 2.3L eng.<br>200 eng.<br>255 eng. | PEJ-AC3-AC4<br>PEB-P8,P9,P10-A1-B1<br>PEM-E5-E6-W-W1-AD-AD1-AK-AK1 |
| | Fairmont—Zephyr | 2.3L eng.<br>200 eng.<br><br>255 eng. | PEJ-AC3-AC4-AD3-AD4<br>PEB-N10-N11—P8,P9,P10,U4-U5-Z-Z1<br>PEM-C5-C6-D5-D6-E5-E6-AC-AC1-AD-AD1-AL-AL1-AM-AM1-AN-AN1-AN2 |
| | Cougar-XR7 | 2.3L eng.<br>200 eng.<br><br>255 eng. | PEJ-AC3-AC4-AD3-AD4<br>PEB-N10-N11-P8,P9,P10-Z-Z1<br>PEN-A-A1-B-B1<br>PEM-C5-C6-D6-D5-E5-E6-AC-AC1-AD-AD1-AE-AE1-AL-AL1-AM-AM1-AN-AN1-AN2 |
| | Granada | 2.3L eng.<br>200 eng.<br><br>255 eng. | PEJ-AC3-AC4-AD3-AD4<br>PEB-N10-N11-P8-P9-P10<br>PEN-A-A1-B-B1<br>PEM-C5-C6-E5-E6-AC-AC1-AD-AD1-AL-AL1-AM-AM1-AN-AN1-AN2 |
| | Thunderbird | 200 eng. | PEB-A-Z1-D5-D6-AC-AC1-AE-AE1-AN2 |

## FORD MOTOR CO.
## Automatic Transmission/Transaxle Listing

| Year | Model | Engine | Trans-code |
|------|-------|--------|------------|
| | | **C-5 TRANS.** | |
| 1982 | Mustang—Capri | 200 eng. | PEN-G-W |
| | | 255 eng. | PEM-AM3-AP |
| | Cougar-XR7—Granada | 200 eng. | PEB-Z2-C-G-J-K-P-S |
| | | 232 eng. | PEP-B-D-E-F-G-H-N-P |
| | Fairmont—Zephyr | 200 eng. | PEN-C-G-P-V-W |
| | | 255 eng. | PEM-AL3 |
| 1983 | Mustang—Capri | 232 eng. | PEP-B1-R |
| | Cougar-XR7—Thunderbird | 232 eng. | PEP-V-W |
| | Fairmont—Zephyr | 200 eng. | PEN-G1-P1-AA-AB-BA-CA |
| | Marquis—LTD | 200 eng. | PEN-S1-U-Y-Z |
| | | 232 eng. | PEP-R-W |
| 1984 | Mustang—Capri | 232 eng. | PEP-AF |
| | Cougar-XR7—Thunderbird | 232 eng. | PEP-AD-AE |
| | LTD—Marquis | 232 eng. | PEP-AC-AE-Z |
| | | **C-6 TRANS.** | |
| 1980 | Ford—Mercury | 302 eng. | PDG-BH5-CU5 |
| | | 351 eng. | PGD-DD-DE-DG |
| | | **FMX TRANS.** | |
| 1980 | Ford—Mercury | 302 eng. | PHB-BH2-BH3 |
| | | 351 eng. | PHB-BK-BK1-BP-BP1-BT-BT1-BU-BU1 |
| 1981 | Ford—Mercury | 302 eng. | PHB-BH2,3-BN |
| | | **JATCO TRANS.** | |
| 1980 | Granada—Monarch | 250 eng. | PLA-A2-A3 |
| | | **A.O.T. TRANS.** | |
| 1980 | Ford—Mercury | 302 eng. | PKA-E1,2,3,4,5,6-W1,2,3 |
| | | 351 eng. | PKA-C1,2,3,4,5,6-R1,2,3,4,5,6 T1,2,3,4,5,6-Z1,2,3,4,5,6 |
| | Cougar-XR7—Thunderbird | 302 eng. | PKA-Y1,2,3,4,5,6 |
| | Lincoln—Mark VI | 302 eng. | PKA-M1m2m3m4m5m6 |
| | | 351 eng. | PKA-D1,2,3,4,5,6-U1,2,3,4,5,6 |
| 1981 | Ford—Mercury | 255 eng. | PKA-AF-AF5-AT-AT5 |
| | | 302 eng. | PKA-E6-AG-AG5-AG50-AL-AV-AU5 |
| | | 351 eng. | PKA-C6-C8-C13-R8-T8-Z8-AR-AS-AS5-AV |
| | Cougar-XR7—Thunderbird | 255 eng. | PKA-AH-AH5 |
| | | 302 eng. | PKA-Y8 |
| | Lincoln—Mark VI | 302 eng. | PKA-=M8-M13 |
| 1982 | Ford | 255 eng. | PKA-AF5,6-AT5 |
| | | 302 eng. | PKA-AG-AG5-AU5-AU6-AY,1-BB,1 |
| | | 351 eng. | PKA-C13,14-AS5,6 |
| | Mercury | 255 eng. | PKA-AF,5,6,7,8,-AT,5,6,7,8 |
| | | 302 eng. | PKA-AG-AG5,6,7,8-AU-AU5,6,7,8-AY1,2,3-BB1,2,3 |
| | | 351 eng. | PKA-C13,14,15,16-AS-AS5,6,7,8 |

# INDEX

# AUDI/VOLKSWAGEN TRANSAXLE TYPE 089 • 090

## APPLICATIONS

### Application

**Audi 4000, 5000**
**Volkswagen Rabbit, Scirocco, Jetta, Dasher, Quantom, Vanagon**
**Fiat Strada**

## GENERAL DESCRIPTION

The series 010, types 089, 090 automatic transaxle is a fully automatic three speed unit, containing a three piece torque converter, forward and reverse planetary gear sets, three multiple disc clutches, and one band. The final drive unit is part of the transaxle assembly, containing the differential assembly. Shift control is by manually operated linkage.

### Transmission and Converter Identification

#### TRANSMISSION

Code letters and numbers are stamped on the top of the transmission case, as well as on a pad on the front of the converter housing by the dipstick handle. These code letters and numbers denote the series of the transmission, the model code, and the date of manufacture. These numbers are important when ordering service replacement parts.

Transmission code letters and date of manufacture

Example:     KJ        03        03        1

            Code letters    day    month    year (81)

**Typical transaxle identification marking locations**
(©Volkswagen of America, Inc.)

#### CONVERTER

The torque converter will have a letter stamped on the outside of one of the lugs. It is important to make note of the letter for parts ordering.

## Transmission Metric Fasteners

These transmissions are of metric design, and metric bolt sizes and thread pitches are used for all fasteners on these transmissions.

The metric fastener dimensions are very close to the dimensions of the familiar inch system fasteners, and for this reason, replacement fasteners must have the same measurement and strength as those removed.

Do not attempt to interchange metric fasteners for inch system fasteners. Mismatched or incorrect fasteners can result in damage to the transmission unit through malfunctions, breakage or possible personal injury.

Care should be taken to reuse the fasteners in the same locations as removed, whenever possible.

**NOTE: All threaded case holes must be checked for quality of their threads, especially the bolt holes for the mount brackets. It is virtually impossible to rethread these bolt holes after the transaxle has been installed in the vehicle.**

## Capacities

The fluid quantities are approximate and the correct fluid level should be determined by the dipstick indicator for the correct level.
Dry fill—6.4 U.S. quarts (6 Liters).
Refill—3.2 U.S. quarts (3 Liters).

## Fluid Specifications

Use only Dexron® or Dexron® II automatic transmission fluid or its equivalent to fill, refill or correct the fluid level.

### CHECKING THE FLUID LEVEL

When checking the fluid level, the vehicle engine/transaxle assembly must be at normal operating temperature and positioned on a level surface. The following procedure is suggested.

1. Start the engine and allow to idle, set the parking brake and move the selector lever through the detents, returning it to the Neutral position.
2. Remove the dipstick, clean and re-insert it. Remove the dipstick and note the level of the fluid on the dipstick indicator. The level must be between the upper and lower marks on the indicator. Add fluid as required to correct the level. Do not overfill.

 **MODIFICATIONS**

### DELETION OF CASE STRAINER

**SERIES 010**

As of automatic transaxle serial number 21040, the fluid strainer, located in the pressure channel has been deleted. During repairs on the transaxles prior to serial number 21040, do not re-install the fluid strainer in the pressure channel.

### DELETION OF GOVERNOR STRAINER

**TYPE 089**

As of automatic transaxle serial number 09040, the fluid strainer, located in the governor assembly, has been deleted. During repairs on the transaxles prior to transmission serial number 08040, do not re-install the fluid strainer in the governor assembly.

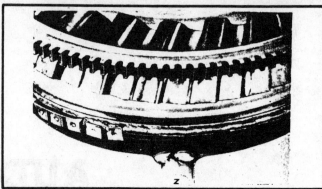
Location of Converter code letter (©Volkswagen of America, Inc.)

### OIL PUMP SHAFT SPLINE CHANGE

**TYPES 090, 089**

To aid in the assembly, the oil pump shaft splines have been lengthened and tapered for easier insertion into the converter. New pump shafts can be installed in earlier transaxles. Part numbers remain unchanged.
**Type 090—Old Shaft**
Measured between the inner shoulder edges
Part number 090323561—20.047 inches (509.2 mm).
**Type 090—New Shaft**
Overall length measurement
Part number 090323561—21.523 inches (546.7 mm).
**Type 089—Old Shaft**
Measured between the inner shoulder edges
Part number 089323561—17.838 inches (453.1 mm).
**Type 089—New Shaft**
Overall length measurement
Part number 089323561—19.315 inches (490.6 mm).

### LEFT AND RIGHT DRIVE FLANGE REPLACEMENT

**TYPE 089**

The drive flange oil seal contact surface has been widened and the shaft shortened. The new shaft can be installed in older transaxles without determining the end play and inserting adjusting shims. Measurement is made from the forward edge of the seal surface to the inner end of the shaft.
**New Shaft Dimensions**
Right—Part number 089409356—1.931 inches (49.05 mm).
Left—Part number 089409355—2.894 inches (73.5 mm).
**Old Shaft Dimensions**
Right—Part number 082409356—1.970 inches (50.05 mm).
Left—Part number 082409355—2.933 inches (74.5 mm).

### SPRING IDENTIFICATION TABLE— VALVE BODY ASSEMBLIES

**TYPE 089—AUDI, VANAGON**

These tables allows identification of the springs by their dimensions. Coil diameter and free length can vary between new and used springs, due to settling, so check the spring wire thickness and number of coils first, as a means of spring identification. Use the inner coil diameter and free length, if necessary.

——————— **CAUTION** ———————

*Several springs of the valve body may have the same dimensions. However, do not interchange them because the tolerances of each spring is different.*

**NOTE: The part numbers are listed for identification only and the springs are available by special order only.**

## VALVE BODY SPRING IDENTIFICATION TABLE
### Audi—Transaxle Type 089

| Description | Coils | Wire thickness mm (in.) | Free length[1] mm (in.) | Inner diameter[2] of coil mm (in.) | As of transm. No. |
|---|---|---|---|---|---|
| 1 Spring/throttle pressure limiting valve | 14.5 | 1.1 (0.042) | 35.3 (1.388) | 7.7 (0.302) | |
| 2 Spring/main pressure limiting valve | 11.0 | 1.2 (0.472) | 32.4 (1.274) | 7.7 (0.302) | |
| 3 Spring/main pressure valve | 16.5 16.5 | 1.5 (0.059) 1.5 (0.059) | 71.6 (2.818) 77.0 (3.031) | 11.9 (0.468) 11.9 (0.468) | 23 079 |
| 4 Spring/control valve 3—2 | 12.5 | 1.0 (0.039) | 32.4 (1.274) | 7.7 (0.302) | |
| 5 Spring/throttle pressure valve | 16.0 | 1.25 (0.048) | 43.3 (1.703) | 7.75 (0.304) | |
| 6 Spring/shift valve 1—2 | 6.5 9.5 | 0.9 (0.035) 0.8 (0.031) | 19.9 (0.783) 26.0 (1.024) | 8.1 (0.317) 8.2 (0.323) | alternative |
| 7 Spring/converter pressure valve | 12.5 8.5 | 1.0 (0.039) 1.25 (0.049) | 32.4 (1.274) 22.2 (0.874) | 7.7 (0.302) 7.7 (0.302) | gradual |
| 8 Spring/modulator pressure valve | 12.0 11.5 | 0.7 (0.027) 0.8 (0.031) | 18.7 (0.736) 28.6 (1.125) | 5.3 (0.208) 7.75 (0.305) | 11 098[3] |
| 9 Spring/shift valve 2—3 | 6.5 9.5 | 0.9 (0.035) 0.8 (0.031) | 19.9 (0.783) 26.0 (1.024) | 8.1 (0.317) 8.2 (0.323) | alternative |
| 10 Spring/kickdown control valve 3—2 | 11.5 | 0.9 (0.035) | 28.4 (1.118) | 8.1 (0.317) | |
| 11 Spring/apply valve 1st/reverse gear brake | 11.5 | 0.9 (0.035) | 28.4 (1.118) | 8.1 (0.317) | |

[1] Free length can vary due to tolerances and settling
[2] Inner coil diameter is within tolerance of ±0.3 mm (0.012 in.)
[3] Valve changed from 8 mm (0.315 in.) to 11 mm (0.433 in.)

## VALVE BODY SPRING IDENTIFICATION TABLE
### Vanagon—Transaxle Type 089, 090

| Description | Coils | Wire thickness mm (in.) | Free length[1] mm (in.) | Inner diameter[2] of coil mm (in.) |
|---|---|---|---|---|
| 1. Spring/throttle pressure limiting valve | 14.5 | 1.1 (0.042) | 37.9 (1.492) | 7.7 (0.302) |
| 2. Spring/main pressure limiting valve | 12.5 | 1.2 (0.047) | 27.5 (1.083) | 7.6 (0.299) |
| 3. Spring/main pressure valve | 16.5 | 1.4 (0.055) | 69.2 (2.724) | 11.9 (0.468) |
| 4. Spring/control valve 3-2 | 16.5 | 1.1 (0.042) | 44 (1.732) | 7.75 (0.304) |
| 5. Spring/throttle pressure valve | 11.5 | 0.8 (0.032) | 28.6 (1.126) | 7.75 (0.304) |
| 6. Spring/shift valve 1-2 | 6.5 | 0.9 (0.035) | 19.9 (0.783) | 8.1 (0.317) |
| 7. Spring/shift valve 2-3 | 8.5 | 0.8 (0.032) | 17.4 (0.685) | 6.95 (0.274) |
| 8. Spring/modulator pressure valve | 12.5 | 1.0 (0.039) | 32.4 (1.274) | 7.7 (0.302) |
| 9. Spring/converter pressure valve | 8.5 | 1.25 (0.049) | 22.2 (0.874) | 7.7 (0.302) |
| 10. Spring/kickdown control valve 3-2 | 11.5 | 0.9 (0.035) | 28.4 (1.118) | 8.1 (0.317) |
| 11. Spring/apply valve 1st/reverse gear brake | 10.5 | 0.63 (0.025) | 36.3 (1.429) | 9.0 (0.354) |

[1] Free length can vary due to tolerances and settling
[2] Inner coil diameter is within tolerance of ± 0.3 mm

## OPERATING LEVER, PARK LOCK, MANUAL VALVE AND OPERATING LEVER MODIFICATION

### SERIES 10 TRANSAXLE

Three versions of the modifications have been made. The manual valves have been modified with necessary changes made to the operating levers. The operating lever parking lock assembly has been modified with necessary changes made to the operating rod assembly. The modified parts must be installed in their proper combination of either of the three versions.

## THRUST WASHER MODIFICATION

### SERIES 10 TRANSAXLE

Earlier thrust washer for the direct reverse clutch to oil pump was steel/bronze and plastic and the thrust washer for the forward clutch was steel/bronze. A new plastic thrust washer with three outer lugs has been released for use between the direct reverse clutch and the oil pump, and between the forward clutch and the direct reverse clutch. The new plastic thrust washer can be installed in earlier transaxle assemblies.

## OIL PUMP AND FORWARD CLUTCH MODIFICATIONS

### SERIES 10 TRANSAXLES

The in-service oil pump used a locating lug type thrust washer between the oil pump and the forward clutch. The forward clutch housing used a drilled area, 180° apart, to seat the thrust washer and the contact area of the oil pump was machined. The new oil pump thrust washer contact area is not machined and a three piece thrust bearing assemlby is now used in place of the single thrust washer. The forward clutch housing is not drilled, since it

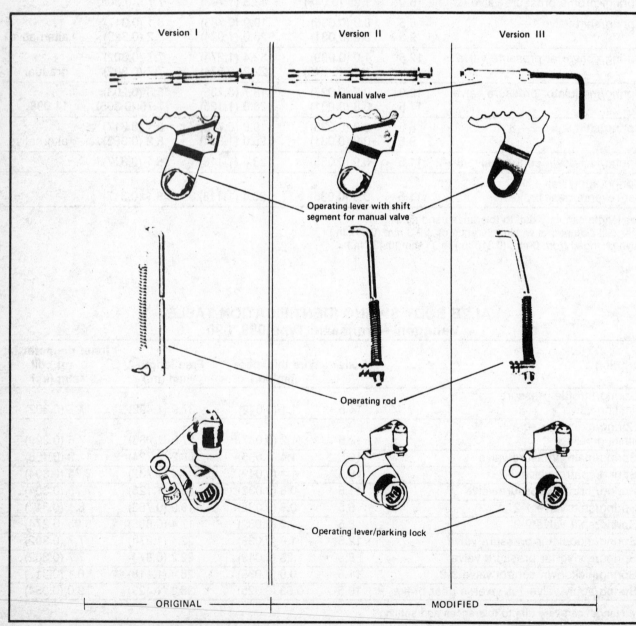

Operating lever modifications (©Volkswagen of America, Inc.)

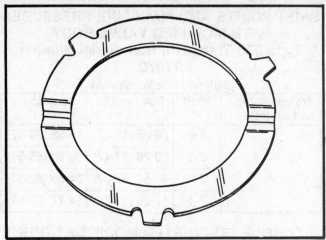

**New style thrust washers** (©Volkswagen of America, Inc.)

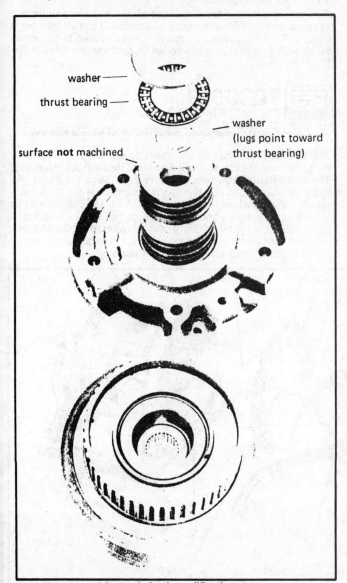

washer —
thrust bearing —
washer
(lugs point toward
thrust bearing)
surface **not** machined

**New oil pump and forward clutch modifications**
(©Volkswagen of America, Inc.)

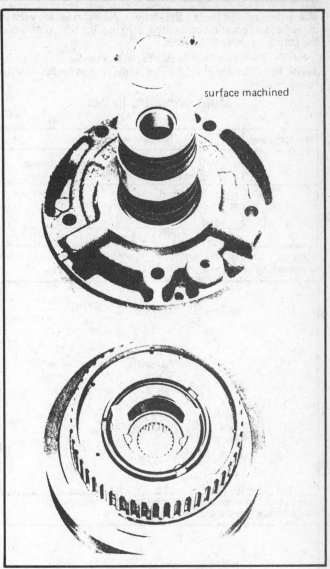

surface machined

**Old style oil pump and forward clutch modifications**
(©Volkswagen of America, Inc.)

is not necessary to locate the lugs of the bearing in the clutch housing. Care must be exercised during the assembly of the units, not to interchange any of the components, new to old or old to new, as transaxle failure will result.

## TURBINE SHAFT MODIFICATION

### Series 10 Transaxle

The turbine shaft splines have been modified from the forward clutch/oil pump assembly that uses a thrust washer, to a turbine shaft grooved for a circlip on the end of the splines, used with the forward clutch/oil pump using the new thrust bearing modification. The new shaft must always be installed with a circlip, never without. The new shaft and circlip can be installed in the transaxle using the forward clutch/oil pump and thrust washer.

## VALVE BODY MODIFICATION

**TYPE 090 FROM SERIAL NUMBER 17070**
**TRANSAXLE CODE-NG, VALVE BODY CODE-BH**

The new valve body can be installed in transaxles from serial number 01068. Modifications have been made to the separation plate markings and check ball locations. New springs are used in the shift and operation calibration, affecting the shift points and the main line pressure settings.

NOTE: For Valve Body Spring Identification chart, refer to the Spring Identification chart for Audi and Vanagon in this Modification Section.

## Main pressure in bar
### (psi)

| Transmission code letters | Selector lever position | | |
|---|---|---|---|
| | Drive idle speed ① | Drive full throttle | Reverse idle speed |
| NG | speed higher than 50 km/h (32 mph) | — | car stationary |
| | 2.9-3.0 (41-42) | 5.85-5.95 (83-84) | 9.1-9.7 (129-138) |

*Carry out this test on dynamometer:
—accelerate up to 50 km (32 mph)
—release accelerator pedal (idle speed)
—check pressure on gauge

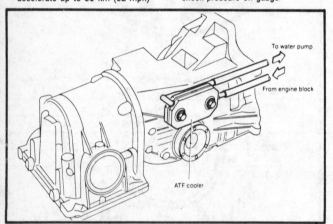

**Location of transaxle fluid cooler on varied transaxles** (©Volkswagen of America, Inc.)

## SHIFT POINTS AND MAIN LINE PRESSURES WITH MODIFIED VALVE BODY
## Type 090 Transaxle from Serial Number 17070
### Shift points in km/h (mph)

| Transmission code letters | Shift | Full throttle | Kickdown |
|---|---|---|---|
| NG | 1-2 | 25-36 (16-22) | 49-52 (30-32) |
| | 2-3 | 60-76 (37-47) | 89-90 (55-56) |
| | 3-2 | 43-60 (27-37) | 84-86 (52-53) |
| | 2-1 | 17-20 (11-12) | 44-47 (27-29) |

## TORQUE CONVERTER MODIFICATIONS
**TYPE 090 TRANSAXLE**

Torque converters coded Z, using modified impeller and turbine vanes, are used in later transaxle assemblies. The part number is 090323571. This new torque converter can be used in earlier vehicles with torque converters coded D, part number 033325571-D.

# TROUBLE DIAGNOSIS

The VW/Audi and Fiat Strada transaxle assemblies are basically the same, except in their configuration of the final drive housing. The transmission units are the same, both using the Series 010 transmissions. However, the major difference is the nomenclature of the internal components by VW/Audi and Fiat Strada. To aid the repairman, separate transmission band and clutch application charts, diagnosis charts and double keyed exploded views are used, along with component nomenclature changes noted in the disassembly and assembly text as required.

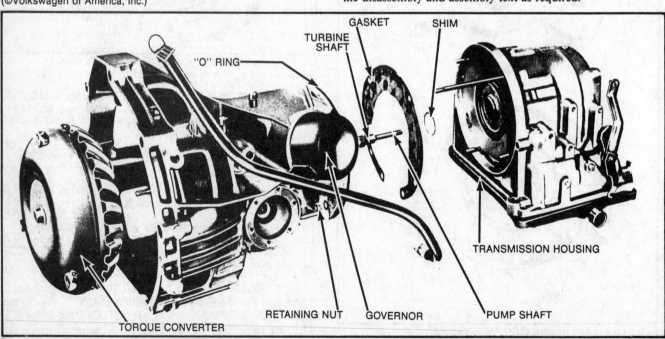

**Transaxle type used with Audi models, Jetta and Vanagon. Note final drive configuration** (©Volkswagen of America, Inc.)

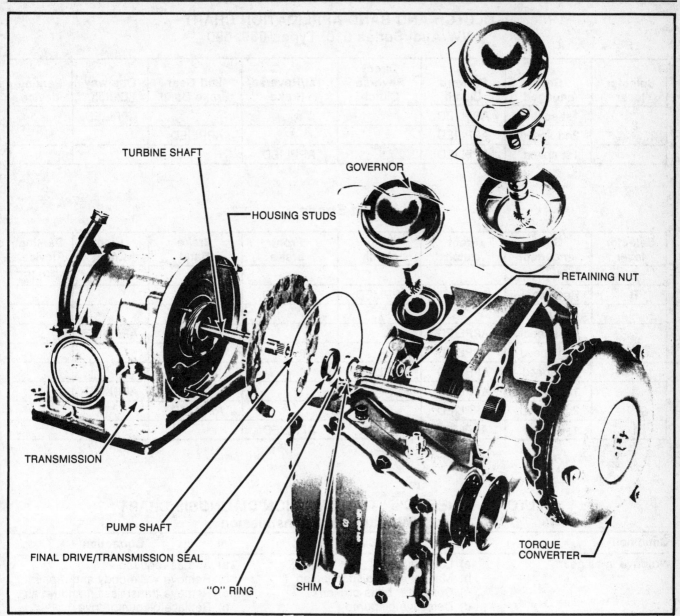

TURBINE SHAFT

GOVERNOR

HOUSING STUDS

RETAINING NUT

TRANSMISSION

PUMP SHAFT

FINAL DRIVE/TRANSMISSION SEAL

"O" RING

SHIM

TORQUE CONVERTER

Transaxle type used with Rabbit, Scirocco, Fiat Strada. Note final drive configuration (©Volkswagen of America, Inc.)

## CLUTCH AND BAND APPLICATION CHART
### VW/Audi Series 010, Types 089, 090

| Selector lever | Gear engaged | Forward Clutch | Direct Reverse Clutch | 1st/Reverse Brake | 2nd Gear Brake Band | One-way Clutch | Parking device |
|---|---|---|---|---|---|---|---|
| P | Park | | | | | | APPLIED |
| R | Reverse | | APPLIED | APPLIED | | | |
| N | Neutral | | | | | | |
| D | 1st speed | APPLIED | | | | APPLIED | |
| | 2nd speed | APPLIED | | | APPLIED | | |
| | 3rd speed | APPLIED | APPLIED | | | | |

## CLUTCH AND BAND APPLICATION CHART
### VW/Audi Series 010, Types 089, 090

| Selector lever | Gear engaged | Forward Clutch | Direct Reverse Clutch | 1st/Reverse Brake | 2nd Gear Brake Band | One-way Clutch | Parking device |
|---|---|---|---|---|---|---|---|
| 2 | 1st speed | APPLIED | | | | APPLIED | |
| | 2nd speed | APPLIED | | | APPLIED | | |
| 1 | 1st speed | APPLIED | | APPLIED | | | |

### Fiat Strada

| Selector lever | Gear engaged | Front clutch | Rear clutch | Front brake | Brake Band | Free wheel | Parking device |
|---|---|---|---|---|---|---|---|
| P | Park | | | | | | APPLIED |
| R | Reverse | | APPLIED | APPLIED | | | |
| N | Neutral | | | | | | |
| D | 1st speed | APPLIED | | | | APPLIED | |
| | 2nd speed | APPLIED | | | APPLIED | | |
| | 3rd speed | APPLIED | APPLIED | | | | |
| 2 | 1st speed | APPLIED | | | | APPLIED | |
| | 2nd speed | APPLIED | | | APPLIED | | |
| 1 | 1st speed | APPLIED | | APPLIED | | | |

## CHILTON'S THREE "C's" TRANSMISSION DIAGNOSIS CHART
### Audi/VW Automatic Transmission

| Condition | Cause | Correction |
|---|---|---|
| No drive in all gears | a) Low fluid level<br>b) Manual valve disconnected<br>c) Converter bolts broken<br>d) Defective oil pump | a) Add as required<br>b) Remove valve body and repair<br>c) Remove transmission and repair<br>d) Replace oil pump/drive |
| No drive in forward gears | a) Defective oil pump<br>b) Forward planetary failed | a) Overhaul clutch<br>b) Replace planetary |
| No drive in 1st gear | a) One-way clutch failed<br>b) Defective forward clutch | a) Replace clutch<br>b) Overhaul clutch |
| No drive in 2nd gear | a) 2nd gear brake band failed | a) Overhaul transmission replace band |
| No drive in 3rd gear | a) Direct and reverse clutch failed | a) Overhaul clutch |
| No drive in Reverse | a) 1st and reverse clutch failure<br>b) Direct and reverse clutch failed<br>c) Defective forward clutch | a) Overhaul transmission replace clutch components<br>b) Overhaul clutch<br>c) Overhaul clutch |
| Drive in Neutral | a) Forward clutch seized | a) Overhaul clutch |

## CHILTON'S THREE "C's" TRANSMISSION DIAGNOSIS CHART
### Audi/VW Automatic Transmission

| Condition | Cause | Correction |
|---|---|---|
| No 2nd gear upshift | a) Defective governor<br>b) Accumulator cover loose<br><br>c) Valve body dirty<br><br>d) 2nd gear brake band failed | a) Overhaul or replace<br>b) Check accumulator, cover and seals<br>c) Clean, change filter and fluid<br>d) Overhaul transmission and replace band |
| No 3rd gear upshift | a) Governor dirty<br><br>b) Valve body dirty<br><br>c) 2-3 Shift valve sticking<br>d) Check balls out of place | a) Remove, disassemble and clean<br>b) Clean, change filter and fluid<br>c) Clean valve body<br>d) Remove valve body, replace check balls as required |
| Noisy in Drive during start | a) 1st gear one-way clutch failed | a) Replace clutch and affected parts |
| Shift speed above or below normal speed | a) Governor dirty<br><br>b) Valve body dirty | a) Remove, disassemble and clean<br>b) Clean, change filter and fluid |
| No kickdown | a) Accelerator cable out of adjustment | a) Adjust cable to specifications |

## CHILTON'S THREE "C's" TRANSMISSION DIAGNOSIS CHART
### Fiat Strada

| Condition | Cause | Correction |
|---|---|---|
| Low oil level | a) Oil leaking from inlet<br>b) Oil leaking from seals | a) Correct inlet leakage<br>b) Replace seals |
| Oil escaping from inlet piping | a) High oil level<br>b) Clogged transmission vent valve<br>c) Leak in oil pump suction line | a) Correct oil level<br>b) Clean vent valve<br>c) Correct oil pump suction leakage |
| Oil leakage at transmission bell housing | a) Oil leaking from converter<br>b) Transmission bell housing seal<br>c) Capscrew securing housing to transmission case | a) Replace or repair converter<br>b) Replace bell housing seal<br>c) Reseal capscrew and torque properly |
| Oil leakage near transmission case | a) Selector valve sealing ring<br><br>b) Oil sump gasket<br>c) Sealing ring on oil inlet piping<br>d) Oil pressure point connector | a) Replace selector valve sealing ring<br>b) Replace oil pan gasket<br>c) Replace sealing ring<br>d) Tighten port plug |
| Low oil pressure | a) Low oil level<br>b) Clogged oil filter<br>c) Leak in oil pump suction line<br>d) Leak in hydraulic circuit<br><br>e) Oil pressure regulator valve spring out of adjustment | a) Correct fluid level<br>b) Replace oil filter<br>c) Repair suction line leakage<br>d) Locate hydraulic circuit leakage and repair<br>e) Adjust or replace regulator valve spring |
| High oil pressure | a) Main pressure regulator valve spring out of adjustment | a) Adjust or replace regulator valve spring |

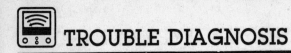 

## CHILTON'S THREE "C's" TRANSMISSION DIAGNOSIS CHART
### Fiat Strada

| Condition | Cause | Correction |
| --- | --- | --- |
| "P" difficult to disengage | a) Selector lever linkage jammed | a) Correct binding or jammed condition |
| No take off with selector lever at "D", "2", "1" or "R" | a) Low oil level<br>b) Oil filter clogged<br>c) Selector lever linkage disconnected<br>d) Input shaft failed<br>e) Oil pressure regulator valve stuck open<br>f) Defective oil pump | a) Correct oil level<br>b) Replace oil filter<br>c) Reconnect selector lever linkage<br>d) Install new input shaft<br>e) Correct pressure regulator valve operation<br>f) Replace oil pump |
| Take off only after repeated movement of selector lever | Selector valve not aligned with valve body ports:<br>a) Distorted or badly adjusted connecting cable<br>b) Nut securing sector to shaft loose | <br><br>a) Adjust or replace the connecting cable<br>b) Tighten the retaining nut |
| No take off after shift from "P" to "D", "2" or "1" | a) Parking device stuck in engagement position | a) Correct binding or jammed condition |
| Sudden take off at high engine rpm | a) Front clutch piston seized<br>b) Low oil level<br>c) Defective oil pump<br>d) Oil filter missing | a) Overhaul unit as required<br>b) Correct fluid level<br>c) Replace oil pump<br>d) Install oil filter |
| Bumpy take off  Smooth only in "R" | a) Low oil pressure<br>b) Pressure regulator valve stuck | a) Correct oil pressure<br>b) Correct pressure regulator valve operation |
| No take off in "D" or "2", only in "1" and "R" | a) Defective free wheel | a) Overhaul unit as required |
| No take off in "D", "2" and "1" ("R" only) | a) Defective front clutch | a) Overhaul unit as required |
| No take off in "R" | a) Defective front brake<br>b) Defective rear clutch | a) Overhaul unit as required<br>b) Overhaul unit as required |
| Take off in "N" | a) Selector lever linkage incorrectly adjusted | a) Adjust linkage correctly |
| No) 1-2 upshift with selector lever at "D" or "2" (transmission locked in 1st) | a) Centrifugal speed governor valve sticking<br>b) 1-2 shift valve stuck in 1st<br>c) Leaking seals on oil pump hub<br>d) Leaking governor hydraulic circuit<br>e) Clogged governor filter<br>f) Worn brake hand | a) Free up governor valve<br>b) Free up 1-2 shift valve<br>c) Replace seals on oil pump hub<br>d) Locate and repair leaking governor hydraulic circuit<br>e) Remove or replace governor filter<br>f) Replace brake band |
| No 2-3 upshift with selector lever at "D" (transmission locked in 2nd) | a) 2-3 shift valve stuck in 2nd<br>b) Leaking governor hydraulic circuit | a) Free up 2-3 shift valve<br>b) Locate and repair leaking governor hydraulic circuit |
| Upshifts in "D" and "2" only with throttle valve completely open | a) Modulator and relief valves stuck<br>b) Kick-down valve or control cable stuck | a) Free up modulator and relief valves<br>b) Free up or replace valve or cable |
| Upshifts in "D" and "2" only with throttle valve partially open | a) Kick-down valve cable incorrectly adjusted<br>b) Kick-down valve cable failed | a) Correct kick-down cable adjustment<br>b) Replace kick-down cable or adjust |

## CHILTON'S THREE "C's" TRANSMISSION DIAGNOSIS CHART
### Fiat Strada

| Condition | Cause | Correction |
|---|---|---|
| No downshift with kick-down actuated | a) Kick-down valve cable failed<br>b) Kick-down valve cable incorrectly adjusted | a) Replace kick-down cable and adjust<br>b) Correct kick-down cable adjustment |
| Downshift at high speeds | a) Loss of pressure in governor | a) Correct governor oil pressure loss |
| Rough 3-2 downshift with kick-down actuated and at high speed | a) Rear brake incorrectly adjusted<br>b) 3-2 shift valve seized or defective spring | a) Correct rear brake adjustment<br>b) Free up 3-2 shift valve or replace spring |
| During downshift with kick-down actuated, engine idles and revs up | a) Low oil pressure<br>b) Excessive band brake play or loose adjusting screw | a) Correct low oil pressure malfunction<br>b) Adjust band |
| Engine braking minimal with lever at "1" | a) Selector lever linkage incorrectly adjusted<br>b) Front clutch piston and front brake stuck | a) Adjust selector lever linkage<br>b) Overhaul unit as required |
| Engine braking minimal with lever at "2" | a) Selector lever linkage incorrectly adjusted<br>b) Front clutch piston and front brake stuck | a) Adjust selector lever linkage<br>b) Overhaul unit as required |
| Car not restrained with lever at "P" | a) Selector lever linkage incorrectly adjusted<br>b) Parking release spring failed<br>c) Parking pawl stop failed | a) Adjust selector lever linkage<br>b) Replace parking release spring<br>c) Replace parking pawl stop |
| Excessive noise in all gears | a) Excessive play between sun and planet gears<br>b) Defective thrust bearings<br>c) Worn bushings<br>d) Excessive end float<br>e) Parking release spring unhooked or incorrectly installed<br>f) Nuts securing bell housing to transmission case | a) Replace necessary gears<br>b) Replace thrust bearings<br>c) Replace bushings<br>d) Correct end play<br>e) Connect parking release spring or install correctly<br>f) Tighten nuts securely |
| Screech on starting | a) Converter defective | a) Replace converter assembly |
| Excessive quantity of ferrous deposits in oil | a) Oil pump<br>b) Clutch hub worn | a) Replace oil pump, clean and examine unit for wear<br>b) Replace clutch hub, clean and examine unit for wear |
| Excessive quantity of aluminum deposits in oil | a) End float adjustment thrust washer | a) Replace thrust washer, clean and examine unit for wear) |

### "E" Mode Transaxles

| Condition | Cause | Correction |
|---|---|---|
| Transmission does not disengage from engine with closed throttle and selector lever in position E | a) Accelerator cable incorrectly adjusted<br>b) Selector lever cable incorrectly adjusted<br>c) Main pressure too high<br>d) Declutching valve in valve body sticking | a) Adjust accelerator cable<br>b) Adjust selector lever cable<br>c) Adjust accelerator cable<br>d) Disassemble valve body and check declutch valve |

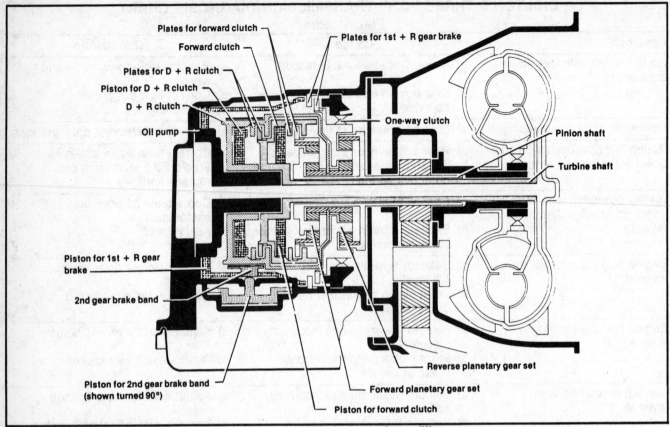

Plates for forward clutch

Forward clutch

Plates for D + R clutch

Piston for D + R clutch

D + R clutch

Oil pump

Plates for 1st + R gear brake

One-way clutch

Pinion shaft

Turbine shaft

Piston for 1st + R gear brake

2nd gear brake band

Piston for 2nd gear brake band (shown turned 90°)

Reverse planetary gear set

Forward planetary gear set

Piston for forward clutch

**Cross section of the transaxle shifting components. Refer to key list for nomenclature differences** (©Volkswagen of America, Inc.)

# HYDRAULIC CONTROL SYSTEM

The power flow from the torque converter flows to the planetary gears by means of the the turbine shaft, through the hollow drive pinion. All three forward gears and reverse are obtained by driving or holding either the sun gear, planetary gear carrier or annulus (internal ring) gear.

The hydraulic control system directs the path and pressure of the fluid so that the proper element can be applied as needed. The valve body directs the pressure to the proper clutch or band servo. There are three ways in which these control valves are operated.

1. The manual valve is connected to the selector lever by a cable. Shifting the lever moves the manual valve to change the range of the transaxle.

2. The kick down valve and the modulated pressure valves are operated and controlled by a mechanical cable, connected to the accelerator linkage.

3. The governor controls the pressure relative to speed and so makes the transaxle sensitive to changes in vehicle speed.

With the engine running, the oil pump supplies the torque converter with fluid. The fluid is passed through the impeller, and at low speeds, the oil is redirected by the stator to the converter turbine in such a manner that it actually assists in delivering power or mulitplying engine torque. As the impeller speed increases, the direction of the oil leaving the turbine changes and flows against the stator vanes in such a manner that the stator is now impeding the flow of oil. At this point, the roller clutch in the converter re-

leases and the stator revolves freely on its shaft. Once the stator becomes inactive, there is no further multiplication of torque within the converter. At this point, the converter is merely acting as a fluid coupling at approximately a one-to-one ratio.

The converter is attached to planetary gears by the turbine shaft, so that a smooth gear change can be made without interrupting the flow of power from the engine. Various ratios (3 forward and 1 reverse) can be obtained by holding, releasing or driving different parts of the planetary gear set.

To accomplish this, three multiple disc clutches, one band and a one-way clutch are used. The clutches and the band are applied and released by oil pressure, while the one-way clutch mechanically prevents the rotation of the front brake/front planetary hub assembly when the transaxle is in the DRIVE position, first speed ratio and under an application of torque from the engine.

The valve body controls the shifting of the transmission, dependent upon the engine load and the road speed.

## Major Components

### CLUTCHES

Multiple disc clutches are used with-in the rear clutch drum and the front clutch drum. A third multiple disc clutch is used as a brake clutch, between the front brake/front planet hub and the case. This brake clutch replaces the low/reverse band, as used in the Series 003 transaxle models.

### BAND

The second gear brake band is used to stop the rotation of the direct/reverse clutch drum by hydraulic application, providing a second speed ratio. The band is applied in the second gear when

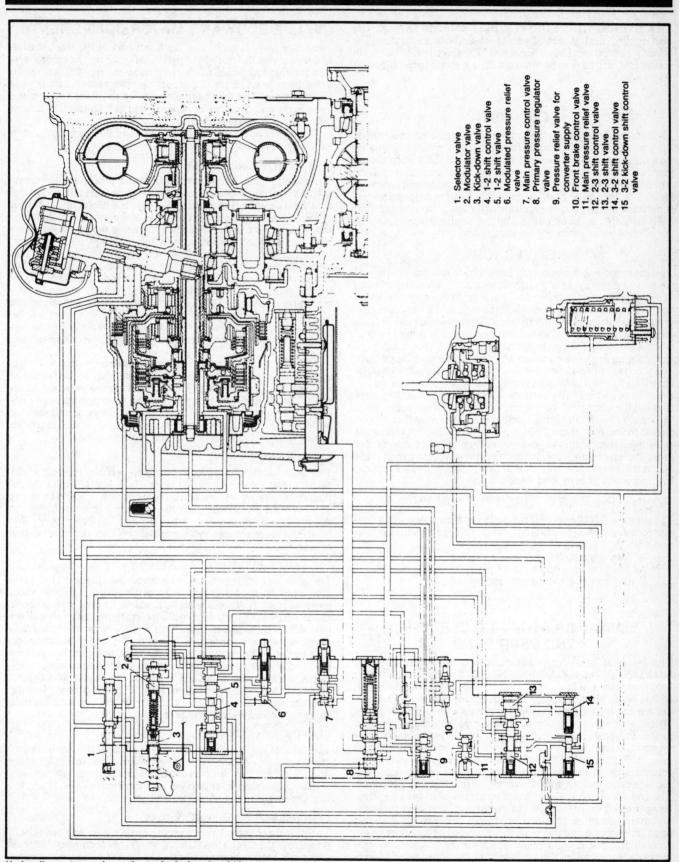

1. Selector valve
2. Modulator valve
3. Kick-down valve
4. 1-2 shift control valve
5. 1-2 shift valve
6. Modulated pressure relief valve
7. Main pressure control valve
8. Primary pressure regulator valve
9. Pressure relief valve for converter supply
10. Front brake control valve
11. Main pressure relief valve
12. 2-3 shift control valve
13. 2-3 shift valve
14. 3-2 shift control valve
15. 3-2 kick-down shift control valve

**Hydraulic system schematic, typical of series 010 transaxles** (©Volkswagen of America, Inc.)

the gear selector is in the DRIVE or INTERMEDIATE range. It is also applied during second gear downshifts or kickdown. The band has an external adjusting screw. The throttle relay lever, in most cases, will have to be removed to gain access to the adjusting screw.

## OIL PUMP

The transaxle uses a gear type oil pump, mounted on the front of the gear box assembly and is driven by the converter through a long input shaft. The oil pump draws filtered fluid from the oil pan and sends it, under pressure, to the main pressure regulator valve, located in the valve body. A main pressure relief valve is located in the valve body to prevent excessive high pressures, should the main pressure regulator valve fail. A second pressure relief is located in the oil pump, utilizing a ball and spring, should the control valve assembly fail completely.

## GOVERNOR

The governor is a conventional design in that it has centrifugal weights and springs, and is driven by a shaft which is, in turn, driven by a gear in the differential housing. In this way, the governor only rotates when the vehicle is moving, and it produces governor oil pressure in relation to the road speed of the vehicle. This pressure is then directed to the valve body and it is used to control the gearshift timing and gearshift operation. The main pressure coming from the oil pump acts against the centrifugal force and presses the two-stage governor valve and at the same time the centrifugal weight, until the proper governor pressure is set between the different valve surfaces. The governor valve then stays at about the same position even though the speed increases, while the weight presses the spring together until the spring disc is positioned correctly at about 20-22 mph. At this point, the increasing centrifugal force from the governor valve alone accounts for any more increase in pressure. In this way, the governor can provide an exacting amount of pressure at low road speeds and prevent high pressures at high road speeds.

## PRIMARY THROTTLE VALVE

The primary throttle valve is controlled by a cable assembly connected to the carburetor throttle linkage, and operates in conjunction with the opening of the throttle plates.
1. At idle, approx. 5-6 psi
2. At full throttle, approx. 45-48 psi
3. With vaccum disconnected, approx. 48 psi

## ACCUMULATOR AND SERVO—
## 2ND GEAR BAND

The 2nd gear band accumulator controls the pressure for the band apply. When the shift from 1st to 2nd is made, the drum is held gradually to allow a smooth shift and to keep the shift from feeling harsh to the operator. A free-moving piston which is under tension by a spring receives oil pressure to both sides of the piston. When the gearshift selector is moved from the 1st position to the 2nd position, oil from the shift valve in the valve body which is main line pressure, regulated by a jet or orifice is supplied to the underside of the 2nd gear band servo as well as the accumulator. At the beginning of the shift, the accumulator piston is pressed down against its spring by this main line pressure. The 2nd gear band is also released by means of its return spring, being pressed downward. At the moment of gear change, throttled main line pressure is delivered from below to the 2nd gear band servo piston and this same throttle pressure is applied to the accumulator piston from below which moves it upward against the main line pressure. By thus balancing the pressures and forces involved, a smooth shift is obtained.

## VALVE BODY AND MAJOR COMPONENTS

The valve body is located in the lower part of the transmission and it contains the rest of the parts that make up the control system for the hydraulics of the transmission. In addition to the valve body itself, there is a separator plate as well as a thicker transfer plate. The separator plate serves as a seal between the valve body and the transfer plate, as well as a connection for the different oil passages and openings.

There are a number of different valves in the valve body, each with a specific function. These are listed below.

### MAIN PRESSURE VALVE

The main pressure valve controls the main pressure of the transaxle. This oil controls the operation of the clutches and bands and the transaxle operation in general. There is a preset spring as well as throttle pressure acting on one side of the spring. On the other side and working in the opposite direction is the oil pressure that is to be regulated, and it acts on two different sized surfaces. When the gearshift selector is in Neutral, Drive, 2nd or 1st, this oil is directed by the manual valve to a second area on the valve and thus works against the spring and throttle pressures. When the oil pressure exceeds the spring and throttle pressures, the main pressure valve is pushed against the spring and allows the oil to flow to the converter valve so that the converter will be filled with oil. As the pressure builds up, the valve is pushed further and allows the excess pressure to return to the pump suction circuit.

The oil pressure with a closed throttle is determined by the setting of the spring tension which is originally set at the factory at the time the governor is calibrated. *This setting must not be altered.* The oil pressures acting against the main pressure valve depend on engine speed, throttle position, road speed and selector lever position. In this way, the main pressure valve delivers an appropriate pressure according to the requirements.

### MODULATOR VALVE

The modulator valve limits the main oil pressure to about 86-88 psi at a road speed of approximately 16-18 MPH. Under the influence of the governor pressure, the valve moves against a spring and connects the primary throttle pressure line with the line to the pressure limiting valve. When the pressure drops below this limit, the valve returns to its original position and cuts off this connection.

### PRESSURE LIMITING VALVE

The pressure limiting valve continues to limit the main line pressure from the modulator valve by restricting the throttle valve pressure going to the main pressure valve. At road speeds above about 15-18 MPH, the face of the pressure limiting valve slides past the modulator valve against the factory preset spring tension, and restricts the flow from a second primary throttle pressure line. Another passage feeds the main line pressure valve a throttled primary pressure which is limited to approximately 27-29 psi, while the main pressure is limited to a maximum of about 86-88 psi. At speeds lower than 16-18 MPH, the primary throttle pressure flows unrestricted by means of the pressure limiting valve to the main pressure valve.

### MANUAL VALVE

The manual valve is connected to the gear shift selector lever and cable assembly. According to the position of the lever, the main line oil pressure is directed to the various points and circuits. When the gearshift lever is in the Park position, a valve blocks the main pressure inlet and the flow of pressure.

### CONVERTER PRESSURE VALVE

The purpose of the converter pressure valve is to limit the flow of pressure to the torque converter. The valve is open when the pressure reads below about 60-62 psi. The flow of oil to the converter will then be unrestricted. However, when the pressure rises above this limit, the valve is pushed against a spring and the flow of oil is then restricted so that the converter will not be subjected to a pressure above 62-65 psi.

## KICK-DOWN VALVE

The kick-down valve is used to provide added fluid pressure to the shift valves, causing either a downshift from third to second, second to first or a delay in the upshift when added acceleration is needed. The kick-down valve is operated by a mechanical cable, connected between the carburetor throttle linkage and the transaxle valve body. The kick-down and throttle valves work in conjunction with each other, since both are controlled by the mechanical cable.

## 1-2 SHIFT VALVE

The 1-2 shift valve engages 1st and 2nd gear according to the amount of governor pressure by either relieving oil pressure or applying oil pressure to the feed end of the 2nd gear servo.

When starting out in Drive or 2nd, the valve spring and the throttle pressure oil push the valve into the 1st position. The line pressure to the valve is then closed and the feed to the 2nd band servo receives no oil pressure. As the speed increases, the governor pressure overcomes the spring force and the throttle pressure, and the valve is pushed against the spring into the 2nd gear position.

At this point the main line pressure opens up and the feed side of the 2nd gear servo, as well as the underside of the accumulator, receive oil pressure. The band is applied and 2nd gear is engaged. The governor pressure is reinforced by the main line pressure which acts on the area between the valve diameters. In this way, the valve is held in the 2nd gear position even at speeds which are below the upshift speed. This prevents the continuous up and down shifting which might occur in this range when the speed remains almost constant. When starting off in 1st gear position, both surfaces of this valve are under main line pressure.

## 2-3 SHIFT VALVE

The 2-3 shift valve shifts the transaxle from 2nd gear to 3rd according to the governor pressure, the secondary throttle pressure and the position of the kickdown valve. It can also shift back from 3rd to 2nd by exhausting the oil from the release side of the 2nd gear servo and the direct and reverse clutch piston. At low speeds, the valve spring and the throttle pressure hold the valve in the 2nd gear position. The main oil line from the manual valve is then closed. As the speed increases, and the governor pressure becomes greater than the spring force and the throttle pressure, the valve snaps to the 3rd gear position. The main line pressure opens and oil is supplied to the release side of the 2nd gear band as well as to the direct and reverse clutch. As soon as main line pressure enters, it acts against the valve and prevents the valve from moving to an off position. The main pressure holds the valve in the 3rd gear position unitl the road speed drops below the upshift speed. This gives a speed difference between upshifting and downshifting which should fit in with normal driving practice and prevent continuous up and downshifting.

## 2-3 CONTROL VALVE

The purpose of this valve is to vary the restriction of the main line pressure as it is fed from the 1-2 shift valve to the feed side of the 2nd gear band, according to the road speed and engine load. This smooths out the 3-2 downshift under all driving conditions. When kickdowns are made at high speed, as well as shifts made at low speeds without throttle, the governor pressure takes over to hold the valve against the stop against primary throttle pressure. The pressure from the 1-2 shift valve to the 2nd gear band is then restricted by a small jet that is near the 2-3 valve. This causes a delay in the band apply after the direct clutch is released and gives the engine time to accelerate to its new speed. When downshifts are made with throttle at medium speeds, the primary throttle pressure predominates and the result is that the valve is pressed to its stop against regulator pressure. The pressure line from the 1-2 shift valve is then connected to the feed side of the band by an additional large jet, and since the engine needs less time to change speed, the band is applied quicker.

# E-MODE
# AUTOMATIC TRANSAXLE

A modified version of the Series 010 (Types 089, 090) transaxles has been released and is used in 1982 and later selected vehicles. When the transaxle is placed in the "E" position, the drive between the transaxle and the differential is disengaged when ever the accelerator pedal is released. The vehicle will "freewheel" on deceleration and at idle because the transaxle is then in the Neutral mode. If the selector lever is placed in any other position, the transaxle will operate in its normal manner.

In order to obtain the freewheeling mode, the forward clutch and the valve body were modified. To control the operation of the forward clutch, two new valves were added to the valve body and several other valves were modified.

The new valves are the forward clutch release valve and the forward clutch engagement valve with a separate plate clutch.

The modification of existing valves affects the manual valve and the transfer plate. In addition, a de-clutching valve has been added to the kickdown valve.

## Manual Valve Modification

The manual valve has an additional position "E" along with the valve body channels being redesigned.

### DECLUTCHING VALVE

The declutching valve was added to the kickdown valve and opens as soon as the accelerator pedal is released.

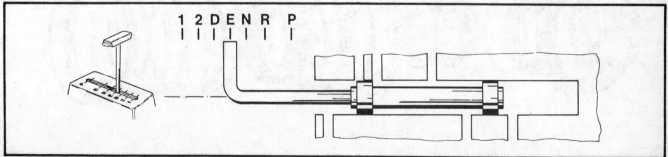

**Manual valve in "E" position** (©Volkswagen of America, Inc.)

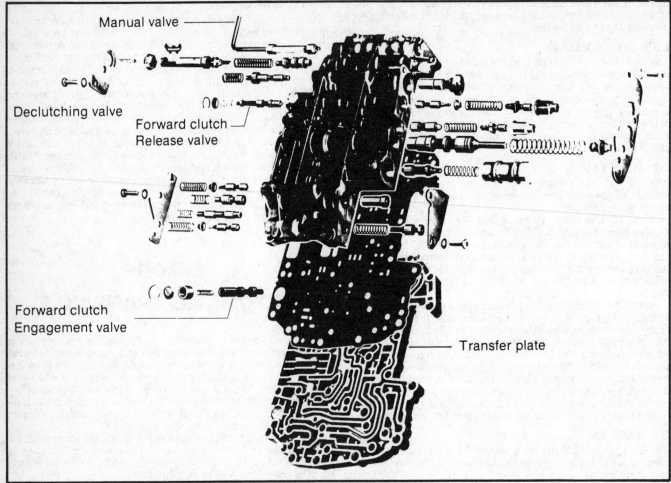

Manual valve

Declutching valve

Forward clutch
Release valve

Forward clutch
Engagement valve

Transfer plate

**Exploded view of E-Mode transaxle valve body assembly** (©Volkswagen of America, Inc.)

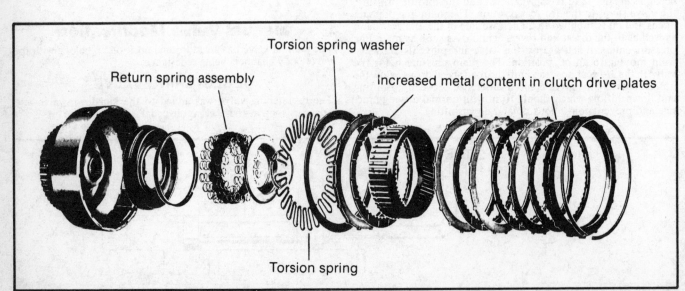

Torsion spring washer

Return spring assembly

Increased metal content in clutch drive plates

Torsion spring

**Exploded view of "E" mode forward clutch components** (©Volkswagen of America, Inc.)

## FORWARD CLUTCH VALVE

The release valve controls the main pressure for the forward clutch in conjunction with the throttle pressure.

## FORWARD CLUTCH ENGAGEMENT VALVE

In conjunction with the plate valve, the engagement valve ensures that the forward clutch engages quickly and smoothly.

## Operation

### SELECTOR LEVER IN "E" POSITION
### FORWARD CLUTCH RELEASED

1. As the accelerator pedal is released, throttle pressure on the forward clutch release valve is reduced by the mechanical opening of the declutching valve.

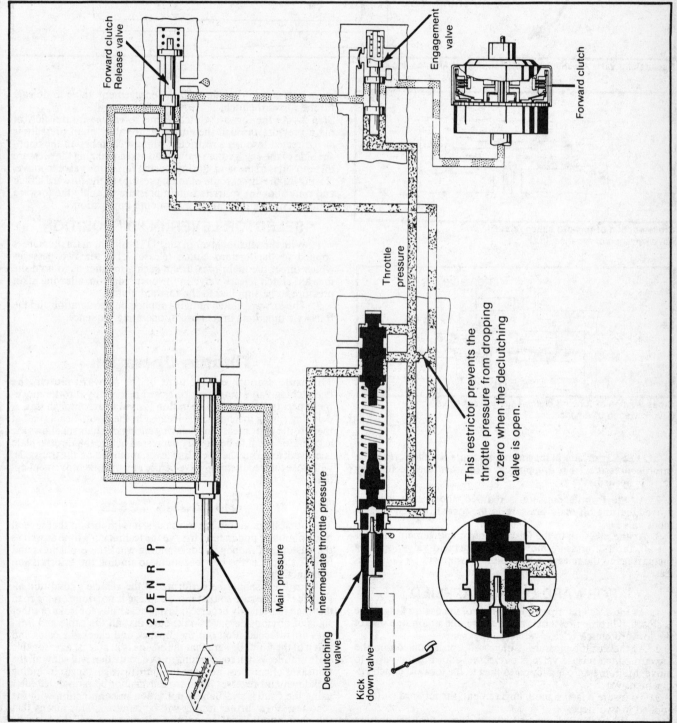

**Selector lever in "E" position and forward clutch released** (©Volkswagen of America, Inc.)

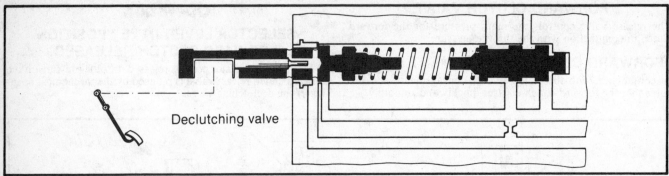

**Declutching valve mechanism** (©Volkswagen of America, Inc.)

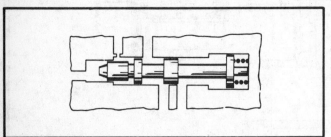

**Cross section of forward clutch release valve**
(©Volkswagen of America, Inc.)

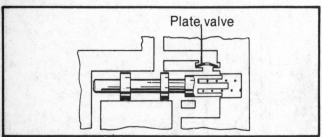

**Cross section of forward clutch engagement valve**
(©Volkswagen of America, Inc.)

**NOTE: A restrictor in the throttle pressure circuit prevents the throttle pressure from dropping to zero when the declutching valve is opened.**

2. As the throttle pressure is reduced, the release valve is moved, cutting off main pressure to the forward clutch engagement valve.

3. As the pressure to the forward clutch engagement valve is cut off, throttle pressure moves the engagement valve, opening the passage to the release valve, so the forward clutch can be released.

### FORWARD CLUTCH APPLIED

1. As the accelerator pedal is depressed, the declutching valve is closed. Throttle pressure is allowed to build up on one side of the forward clutch release valve.

2. As the throttle pressure is increased, spring tension on the forward clutch release valve is overcome, allowing the valve to move. Main pressure is allowed to flow to the forward clutch engagement valve.

3. To insure a fast, smooth engagement, the forward clutch is applied in two steps.

**Step 1**—When the declutching valve is closed, throttle pressure builds up and moves the forward clutch release valve, allowing main pressure to flow through the engagement valve to quickly fill the forward clutch.

**Step 2**—As the forward clutch begins to engage from a flow of main pressure through the engagement valve, main pressure is also directed through a restrictor, filling a chamber on the opposite side of the engagement valve land and equalizing the pressure on both sides of the land. Spring tension forces the valve to move, closing off the direct route of main pressure to the forward clutch and only allowing restricted main pressure to apply the forward clutch, resulting in a quick, but smooth application.

### SELECTOR LEVER IN "D" POSITION

1. With the selector lever in the "D" position, main pressure is applied to the forward clutch release valve via two passages which direct the main pressure in such a manner as to hold the forward clutch release valve in the open position, allowing main pressure to be supplied to the forward clutch.

2. The forward clutch remains applied on deceleration and the transaxle functions in its normal operating sequence.

## Throttle Operation

To insure smooth engagement of the forward clutch, the declutching valve must first be closed before any throttle movement occurs. A two stage operation is used to accomplish this. A delaying spring mechanism is located in the throttle cable end at the throttle plate area. This delaying spring mechanism allows the accelerator pedal to be slightly depressed before the throttle plate is moved, assuring the operating lever, mounted on the transaxle, will close the declutching valve before any throttle movement occurs.

## Diagnosis Tests

To troubleshoot automatic transaxles, it is important that several basic points be understood to save the technician's time as well as the customer's money. Understanding what the problem is and how it started is the best beginning to finding the transmission malfunction.

A road test should be performed if the vehicle's condition allows for it. Use care so that more damage is not done on the road test than has already occurred. Inspect carefully for leaks or other signs of obvious damage. Make sure that all the cable and linkages are attached. Pull out the dipstick and check the color and smell of the fluid. Be sure that the engine is in at least a reasonable state of tune. When road testing, pick a route that will show all the transaxle operations, and try the unit in each range, including kickdown and reverse. If the trouble cannot be pinpointed after using the Clutch and Band Application in conjunction with the road test, then further testing will be required. This means that the shift points, stall speed and oil pressure will have to be checked.

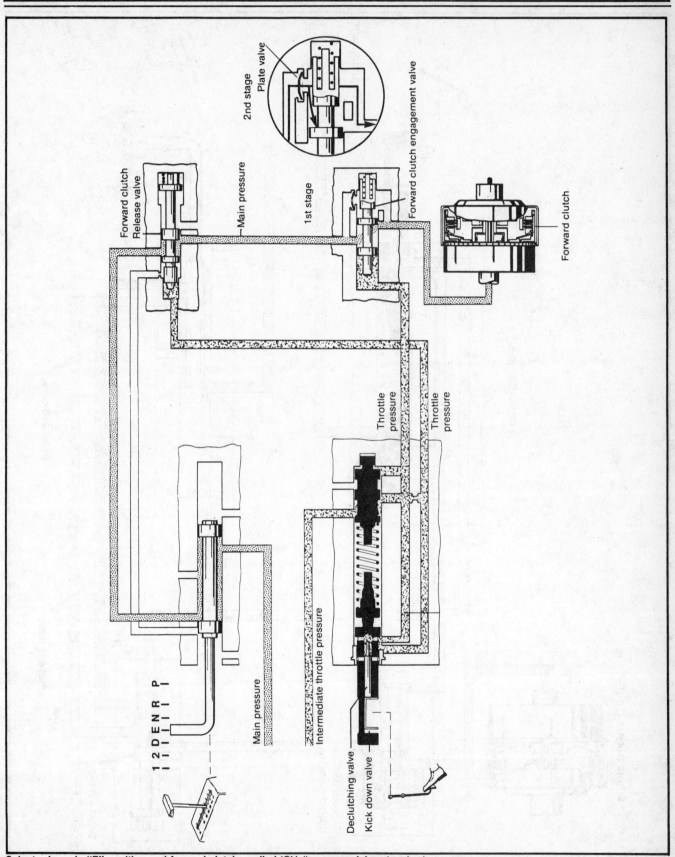

2nd stage

Plate valve

Forward clutch engagement valve

Forward clutch

Forward clutch
Release valve

Main pressure

1st stage

Throttle pressure

Throttle pressure

Main pressure

Intermediate throttle pressure

1 2 D E N R P

Declutching valve

Kick down valve

**Selector lever in "E" position and forward clutch applied** (©Volkswagen of America, Inc.)

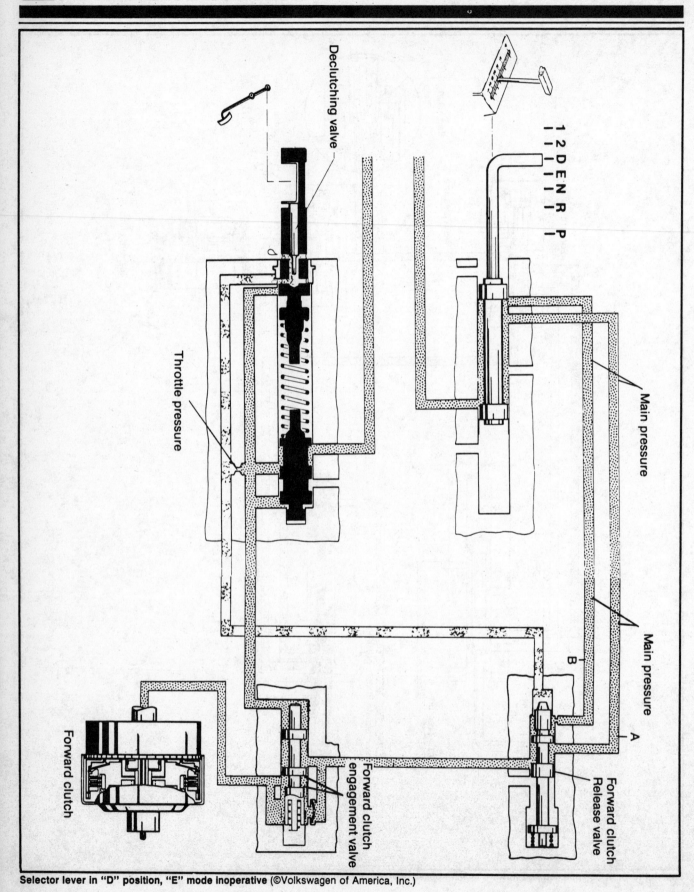

Declutching valve

Throttle pressure

1 2 D E N R P

Main pressure

Main pressure

B

A

Forward clutch
Release valve

Forward clutch
engagement valve

Forward clutch

Selector lever in "D" position, "E" mode inoperative (©Volkswagen of America, Inc.)

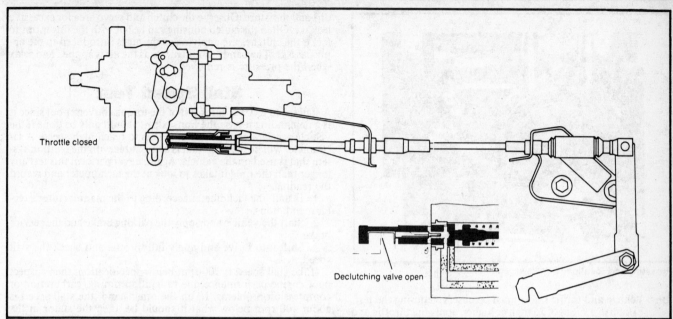

**Throttle closed and declutching valve open** (©Volkswagen of America, Inc.)

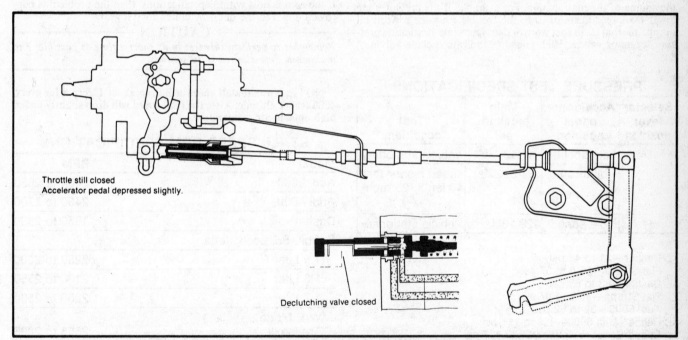

**Throttle closed, accelerator pedal slightly depressed, declutching valve closed** (©Volkswagen of America, Inc.)

## Pressure Test

The pressure test port is located near the mid-section of the transaxle housing, next to the band servo. The pressure gauge to be used should have at least a 150 psi capacity.

1. Connect the pressure gauge hose to the pressure port and route the hose so that the gauge can be read from the drivers position.

2. Start the engine and apply the brakes. The engine/transaxle assembly must be at normal operating temperature.

3. Place the selector lever in the "D" position and allow the engine to idle. Observe the pressure reading and refer to the pressure specifications for the specific pressure required for the vehicle.

4. Place the selector lever in reverse and allow the engine to idle. Observe the pressure reading and refer to the pressure specifications for the specified pressure required for the vehicle.

5. For the full throttle pressure test, the manufacturer recommends the test be done on a dynamometer. However, if the test is done on the road, the pressure hose must be protected from drag-

**Pressure port location** (©Volkswagen of America, Inc.)

ging. Vehicle and traffic safety must be observed during the test.

6. Establish a speed of 25 mph or higher, apply full throttle and observe the pressure gauge reading. Refer to the pressure specifications for the specified pressure required for the vehicle.

The pressure tests should be carefully reviewed to help locate the source of the malfunction. For example, if the pressures are lower than specifications, then the trouble could be a worn oil pump, internal leaks past worn or damaged seals, or sticking pressure regulator valves. High pressures indicate sticking valves.

## PRESSURE TEST SPECIFICATIONS

| Selector lever position | Accelerator pedal position | Main pressure psi | Test conditions |
|---|---|---|---|
| D | idle speed* | 41-42①⑤ | vehicle stationary |
|  | full throttle | 83-84②⑥ | speed higher than 40 km/h (25 mph). ④ |
| R | idle speed | 129-138③⑦ | vehicle stationary |

① Dasher—41 to 43 psi
Fiat Strada—55.5 to 57 psi
② Dasher—83 to 85 psi
Fiat Strada—89.6 to 91 psi
Audi 5000—80 to 82 psi
③ Dasher/Audi 5000—108 to 117 psi
Rabbit/Scirocco/Jetta—109 to 117 psi
(Model EQ to S/N 16079—100 to 109 psi)
Fiat Strada—104 to 105.3 psi
④ For safety reasons, the manufacturer recommends the test be made on a dynamometer.
⑤ "E" mode transaxle—42-44 psi
⑥ "E" mode transaxle—85-86 psi
⑦ "E" mode transaxle—131-145 psi

## Air Pressure Test

Air can be applied to appropriate passages so that the operation of the bands and clutches can be checked. Use a reduced amount of air pressure and make certain that the air is relatively free from dirt and moisture. Observe the clutch and servo area for excessive leakage. Often the clutch housing can be felt with the finger tips to feel if the clutches are applying as the air is introduced to the apply passage. The bands should move as the air is applied and relax when the pressure is removed.

## Stall Speed Test

A stall speed test is a quick test of the torque converter but since it is a demanding test on the transaxle, it should only be done if the vehicle accelerates poorly or if it fails to reach high speed. A tachometer will be required that is compatible with the ignition system that is used on the vehicle. Again, never perform this test any longer than the time it takes to look at the tachometer and record the reading.

1. Install the tachometer according to the manufacturer's recommendations.
2. Start the vehicle and apply the parking brake and the service brake.
3. Shift into Drive and apply full throttle and check the stall speed.

If the stall speed is 200 rpm below specification, then suspect poor engine performance due to ignition timing, carburetion or compression problems. If, on the other hand, the stall speed is about 400 rpm below what it should be, then the stator in the torque converter is bad. If the stall speed is too high, then the fault is in the forward clutch or the one-way clutch for 1st gear. As a further double check, run the test again in 1st gear on the selector. If the rpm is now within specifications, then the problem is narrowed down to the one-way clutch for 1st gear.

--- **CAUTION** ---

*Remember to perform this test in as short a time as possible. The maximum time allowed is 20 seconds.*

NOTE: Normal stall speed will drop about 125 rpm for every 4000 feet of altitude. Also, the stall speed will drop slightly under high outside air temperature.

## STALL SPEED RPM SPECIFICATIONS

| Model | RPM |
|---|---|
| Audi 5000 | 2400 to 2650 |
| Audi 4000 | 2450 to 2700 |
| Dasher | 1950 to 2550 |
| Rabbit, Scirocco, Jetta |  |
|    1.5 Liter | 2250 to 2500 |
|    1.6 Liter | 2100 to 2350 |
|    1.7 Liter | 2200 to 2500 |
|    W/E Mode Transaxle | 2555 to 2805 |
| Fiat Strada | 2260 |

## Road Test

If the transaxle is operative, the vehicle should be road tested in each gear range and under all possible road conditions. The shift points should be noted and recorded, checked against specifications and malfunction probabilities listed. The shifts should be smooth and take place quickly, without a lag in the acceleration. Listen for any signs of engine flare-up during the shifts, which would indicate a slipping brake band or clutches. Check the transaxle for abnormal fluid leakages.

If the shift point are incorrect or the transaxle does not have a kick-down, check and verify the accelerator cable for proper adjustment.

## SHIFT POINTS AT VARIED VEHICLE SPEEDS

(Shift points in mph)

### AUDI 4000

| Shift | Full throttle | Kickdown |
|-------|---------------|----------|
| 1-2 | 20-28 | 34-37 |
| 2-3 | 48-61 | 66-67 |
| 3-2 | 35-48 | 62-64 |
| 2-1 | 14-16 | 29-31 |

### AUDI 5000

| | | |
|-------|---------------|----------|
| 1-2 | 24-30 | 42-46 |
| 2-3 | 58-62 | 75-77 |
| 3-2 | 36-43 | 72-74 |
| 2-1 | 16-18 | 39-43 |

### DASHER, QUANTUM

| | | |
|-------|---------------|----------|
| 1-2 | 19-24 | 35-39 |
| 2-3 | 49-53 | 64-66 |
| 3-2 | 30-36 | 61-63 |
| 2-1 | 14-17 | 31-35 |

### RABBIT/SCIROCCO/JETTA

| | | |
|-------|---------------|----------|
| 1-2 | 20-23 | 36-39 |
| 2-3 | 51-54 | 68-69 |
| 3-2 | 31-36 | 64-65 |
| 2-1 | 15-17 | 32-35 |

### Trans. TB

| | | |
|-------|---------------|----------|
| 1-2 | 32-46 | 55-59 |
| 2-3 | 78-98 | 105-107 |
| 3-2 | 56-77 | 99-101 |
| 2-1 | 23-26 | 47-51 |

### Trans. EQ up to 17 07 0

| | | |
|-------|---------------|----------|
| 1-2 | 32-43 | 53-57 |
| 2-3 | 78-94 | 103-104 |
| 3-2 | 57-73 | 96-99 |
| 2-1 | 22-25 | 46-50 |

### Trans. EQ up to 16 07 0

| | | |
|-------|---------------|----------|
| 1-2 | 32-37 | 58-63 |
| 2-3 | 82-87 | 109-111 |
| 3-2 | 50-58 | 103-105 |
| 2-1 | 24-27 | 52-56 |

### FIAT STRADA

| | | |
|-----------|------|------------------|
| D to 2 | —— | Below 70 |
| D or 2 to 1 | —— | Below 40 |
| 1 to 2 | 40 | |
| 2 to 3 | 70 | |
| 3 to 2 | —— | Below 64 (Manual) |
| 2 to 1 | —— | Below 32 (Manual) |

 ON CAR SERVICES

# ADJUSTMENTS

## Throttle Linkages

The 010 Series (Type 089, 090) transaxles, use a mechanical throttle valve system, controlled by cables from the accelerator pedal, to the transaxle and back to the carburetor or fuel injection throttle plate(s). It is most important the cable assemblies be free of kinks, bends or high operating resistance and the choke plate off, with the fast idle cam in the off position on carbureted models. The accelerator pedal height is an important factor in the adjustment of the cables and where dimensions are available, will be noted for the specific applications.

### Adjustments

**QUANTUM, AUDI 4000**

1. Verify the throttle valve is closed and operating lever has freedom of movement.

2. Loosen the lock nuts on the throttle cable bracket, located on the cylinder head.

3. Pull the sleeve of the throttle cable in the direction of the throttle plates. Turn the rear adjusting nut against the bracket and lock into position with the front adjusting nut.

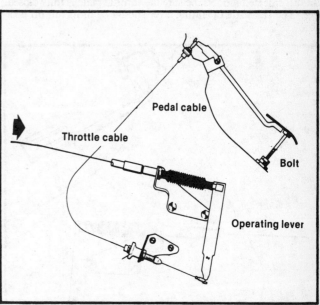

**Pedal and throttle cable arrangement, Quantum and Audi 4000 models** (©Volkswagen of America, Inc.)

4. From inside the vehicle, remove the accelerator pedal stop. On vehicles equipped with air conditioning, remove the switch.

5. Using a metric bolt, M8 x 135 mm, thread two nuts on the bolts, with the bottom of the last nut to the top of the bolt head, giving a dimension of 4⅞ inch (124 mm). Lock the inner nut against the lower outer bolt to maintain this dimension.

6. Install this bolt in place of the accelerator pedal stop, being sure the bolt head touches the pedal plate only, not the pedal rod.

7. Adjust the pedal cable so the accelerator pedal touches the substituted pedal stop, while the operating lever on the transaxle housing is in the closed throttle position.

8. Remove the substituted bolt from under the accelerator pedal, install the original pedal stop and if equipped with air conditioning, install the switch.

## Verifying Adjustment

1. Depress the accelerator pedal until resistance is felt at the full throttle position, without going to the kick-down position.
2. The throttle lever must contact its stop.
3. Depress the accelerator pedal to its full stop and note the cable attaching trunnion at the throttle plate lever. The spring coils at the trunnion must be pressed together.
4. The operating lever on the transaxle housing must be in contact with its kick-down stop.

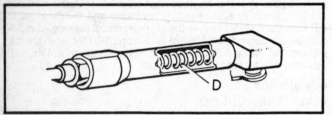

**Spring coils (D) within cable trunnion** (©Volkswagen of America, Inc.)

## Adjustments
### RABBIT, SCIROCCO, JETTA

1. Verify the throttle plates are fully closed, the choke is off and the fast idle cam is in the off position on carbureted engines. On fuel injected models, be sure the throttle plate is fully closed.
2. The transaxle operating lever should be in its full off position.

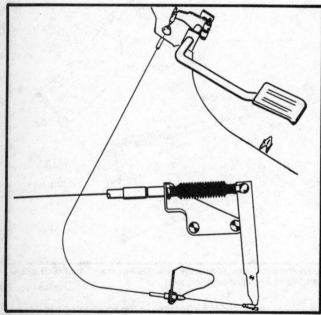

**Pedal and accelerator cable arrangement, Rabbit, Scirocco, Jetta, Dasher similar** (©Volkswagen of America, Inc.)

3. Check to ascertain if the ball socket on the end of the cable can be install without tension, on the ball stud of the operating lever. If so, the cable is properly adjusted.
4. If necessary to adjust, turn the adjusting nut until the correct tension is obtained. Tighten any lock nuts that were loosened.

## Verifying Adjustment

1. Press the accelerator to the floor, against its stop, which would be the kick-down position. Hold pedal down.
2. Be sure all play has been removed from the operating lever. If necessary, loosen the adjusting nut on the transaxle bracket and adjust to eliminate all free play. Recheck this adjustment several times to make sure it is correct. Tighten lock nut and recheck again. Readjust, if necessary.

## Adjustment
### FIAT STRADA

1. Check to verify accelerator pedal travel is four inches. If applicable, include the floor mat thickness measurement in the adjustment. Bend the accelerator pedal rod as required.
2. With the accelerator pedal fully depressed, including the kick down position, be sure the linkage is at its full travel. Adjust as required.
3. Be sure the carburetor pedal and throttle plates close properly after adjustment.

## Adjustment
### AUDI 5000

1. On this application there is to be found two sections of linkage as well as a cable. One linkage is the connection between the throttle body and the rocker lever, or bellcrank. The other linkage is the one that connects the transmission operating lever to the bellcrank. It has, on its lower end, an adjustable sliding plate. The cable runs from the accelerator pedal to the transaxle. Begin adjustment by setting the throttle valve to the idle position. Press the rocker lever (bellcrank) back to the stop.
2. Remove the adjustable ball joint from its stud on the rocker lever and adjust as necessary. Again, the object is to obtain a free fit without forcing anything, and without any free-play.
3. Down at the transaxle, loosen the bolt holding the sliding adjusting plate to the linkage, and adjust for a free fit without play or tension.
4. To adjust the accelerator cable, make sure that the pedal is in the idle position. Carefully measure the distance from the stop on the floor to the pedal plate. It should be 80mm (3¼ inch). Adjust the cable end on the transmission to correct this figure if necessary. Double-check that the throttle is fully open when the accelerator pedal is pressed before the kickdown position. On the linkage that runs to the transmission, on the upper end at the ball joint, there is a kickdown take-up spring incorporated into the linkage. This spring must not be compressed after making this adjustment.

### DASHER

1. Check that the throttle valve on the injection system is closed, that is, at the idle position. Remove the ball socket from the transaxle operating lever.
2. Push the transaxle lever to the zero-throttle position. If the ball end on the cable can be installed without placing the cable in tension, then the adjustment is correct. If the ball end will not fit properly, loosen the locknut on the bracket in the engine compartment that holds the cable. Turn the adjusting nut until the ball end can be attached without forcing.
3. Double-check that the transaxle lever is still in the zero-throttle position and then tighten the locknut.
4. The accelerator cable from the pedal to the transaxle operating lever must also be checked. Remove the cover under the dashboard to provide access to the top of the accelerator linkage.
5. Locate the arm on the end of the accelerator pedal and the clamping bolt. Loosen this bolt, but do not remove.
6. From a piece of stiff wire such as welding rod or brazing rod, make a support for the accelerator pedal that is 105mm (4¼ inch) from the pedal stop on the floor to the deepest part of the curve under the pedal. Double-check that the transaxle operating lever has not moved from its zero throttle position.

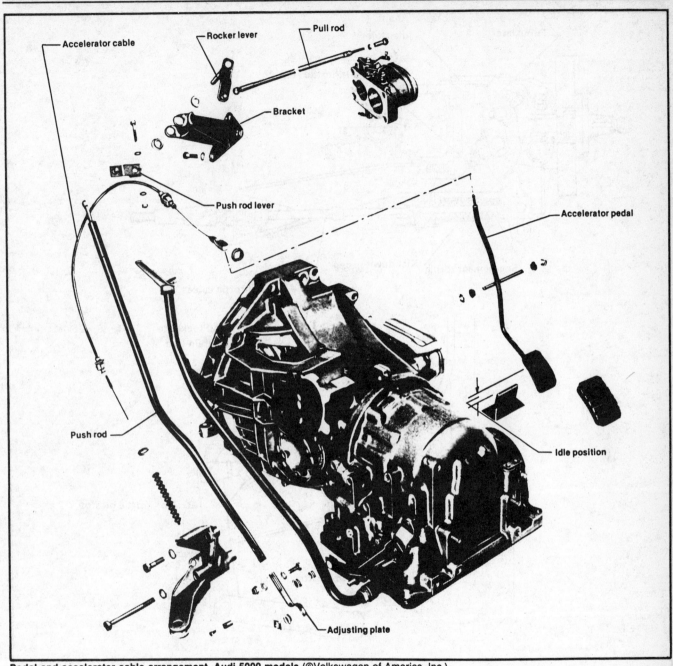

Pedal and accelerator cable arrangement, Audi 5000 models (©Volkswagen of America, Inc.)

7. Pull the relay bracket or lever slowly to take up the slack in the cable. Tighten the clamp bolt. Remove the wire support and push the accelerator pedal down to the stop. The operating lever on the transaxle must be on the kickdown stop without any play.

─────────── CAUTION ───────────

*On all of the above adjustments, it is of the utmost importance that when assembling the different pieces of linkage to their pivots and brackets, that none of the pieces are under tension or pressure or being forced to fit in any way. Many problems that appear to be transaxle malfunctions are caused by improper throttle linkage adjustments.*

### Adjustment
### RABBIT, JETTA
### WITH DIESEL ENGINE AND "E" MODE TRANSAXLE

─────────── CAUTION ───────────

*When adjusting the accelerator linkage and the pedal cable, always place the selector lever in the "P" position and set the parking brake when the engine is running.*

NOTE: The throttle controls must be readjusted whenever the idle or full throttle stop screws have been turned.

1. Set the parking brake and place the selector lever in the "P" position.

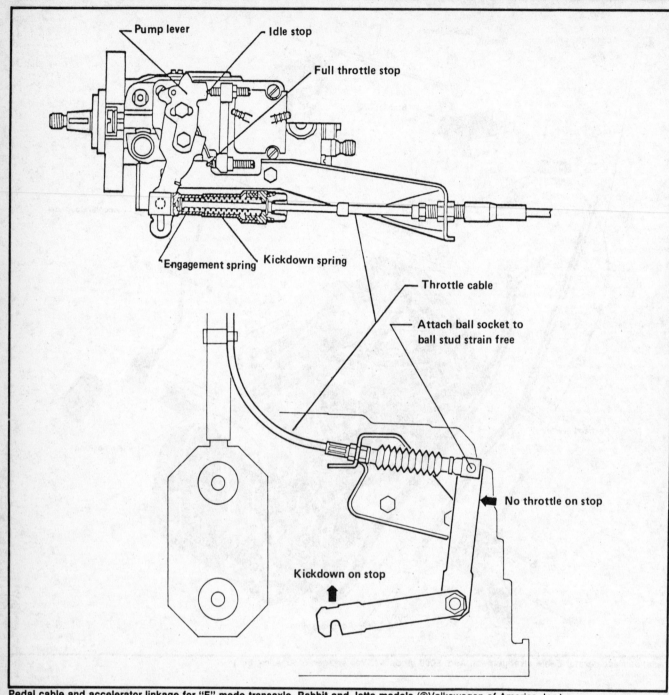

Pump lever          Idle stop

Full throttle stop

Engagement spring   Kickdown spring

Throttle cable

Attach ball socket to
ball stud strain free

No throttle on stop

Kickdown on stop

**Pedal cable and accelerator linkage for "E" mode transaxle, Rabbit and Jetta models** (©Volkswagen of America, Inc.)

2. Remove the plastic injection pump cover and check the idle and maximum engine speeds. Adjust as required.

3. Loosen the accelerator pedal cable adjuster at the bracket before the operating lever. Disconnect the cable at the operating lever.

4. Remove the circlip and ball socket on the pump lever.

5. Adjust the ball stud travel from the idle stop to the full throttle stop by moving the ball stud in the pump lever slot. The travel should be 1.259 ± 0.040 inch (32 ± 1 mm).

6. Remove the rubber boot from the delay spring mechanism and loosen the adjusting nuts on the throttle cable.

7. Push the transaxle lever to the closed throttle position and pull the cable housing away from the delay spring mechanism.

**NOTE: Be sure the delay spring is not compressed.**

8. With the cable housing in this position, tighten the adjusting nuts, attach the ball socket to the ball stud and install the circlip.

9. Connect the accelerator cable to the lever.

10. Press the accelerator cable into the kick-down position. With the aid of a helper, adjust the accelerator cable adjuster so that the transaxle lever contacts the stop.

NOTE: Be sure the accelerator kick-down spring (delay spring mechanism) is compressed.

11. Lock the accelerator cable adjusting nut.

12. Operate the cable and be sure the accelerator pedal cable is at stop and the cable is free of any tension.

### Checking Accelerator Cable

1. Push the pump lever against the idle stop. The delay spring mechanism must not be compressed.

2. Move the transaxle operating lever to the closed throttle position, and press the accelerator pedal into the full throttle position. Push the pump lever against the full throttle stop.

NOTE: The kick-down spring must not be compressed.

3. Press the accelerator pedal past the full throttle point to the stop. The transaxle lever must be against the stop and the kick-down spring (delay spring mechanism) compressed.

## Band Adjustment

The adjuster for the band is on the side of the case. The adjustment procedure is;

1. Center the band by first torquing the adjusting screw to 87 in. lbs. (10 N•m). Loosen the screw and then retighten to a torque of 43 in. lbs (5 N•m).

2. Carefully loosen the adjuster screw exactly 2½ turns. Hold the screw so that it does not turn, and tighten the locknut.

### ——————— CAUTION ———————

*Loc-Tite® or similar substance is used on the band adjusting bolt to case threads. If the bolt cannot be easily turned, it should be heated to break the seal prior to turning the bolt in the case to prevent damage to the case threads.*

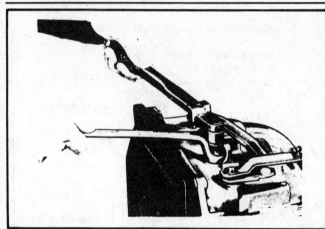

Adjustment of Band, typical. Shift or operating lever may have to be repositioned (©Volkswagen of America, Inc.)

## Manual Linkage

Depending on the vehicle, the adjustment is done either at the transaxle or at the selector lever. If the adjustment calls for the removal of the console, the following points may prove helpful.

1. The shifter handle is usually retained by a set screw. Remove the set screw and the handle should pull up and off.

2. The shifter pattern indicator can be removed by prying off in most cases. It is held on by plastic clips. "Brush type" covers may be held on by screws. Check carefully.

3. The console itself is held on by a few Phillips-head screws. It is extremely important that the selector lever cable be carefully adjusted to avoid burned clutches. Adjust the selector cable as follows.

1. Place the selector lever in Neutral and start the engine. Allow to idle.

2. Apply the parking brake and the service brakes, and then place the selector lever in Reverse. Take note of any reduction in engine speed. There should be a noticeable reduction in speed as the clutch applies. Speed up the engine slightly with the accelerator pedal to increase the idle speed.

3. Keep the accelerator pedal in this position and place the selector lever in Park. The engine speed must increase, indicating that the direct and reverse clutch is disengaged. The engine speed should increase, not drop. If the engine speed does not increase, when placing the lever in Park, or if it drops when pulling the lever against the stop (NOT actually shifting into Reverse ) thus indicating a partial apply of the clutch, then the setting is incorrect and must be adjusted. Operating the transaxle with the controls not in complete travel will result in the unit burning up in only a few miles of operation. This is an important point to watch with the 010 series transmissions. The detent gate that is normally found in the transmission shifter assembly, in the driver's compartment, has been eliminated on late model units so that the detents that are felt are in the transmission only.

### Adjustment

#### QUANTAM, AUDI 5000, 4000, FIAT STRADA

1. Remove the console.

2. Shift the selector lever ino Park.

3. Loosen the clamp nut under the shifter selector lever.

4. Press the selector lever to the rear stop to remove cable slack.

5. Tighten the clamp nut.

6. Check operation. Install console.

#### RABBIT, SCIROCCO

1. Place the selector lever in Park. Make sure that it is fully engaged.

2. Loosen the clamp screw nut on the transaxle lever.

3. Move the transaxle operating lever all the way counterclockwise, and tighten the clamp nut.

4. Check operation.

#### DASHER

1. Remove the console. Shift the selector lever into park.

2. Loosen the cable clamp nut. This nut is located directly under the shifter lever, and retains the swivel and washers to the forward end of the cable.

3. Move the lever on the transaxle into Park, and push fully

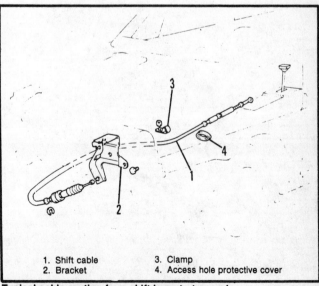

1. Shift cable       3. Clamp
2. Bracket           4. Access hole protective cover

**Typical cable routing from shift lever to transaxle** (©Volkswagen of America, Inc.)

# ON CAR SERVICES

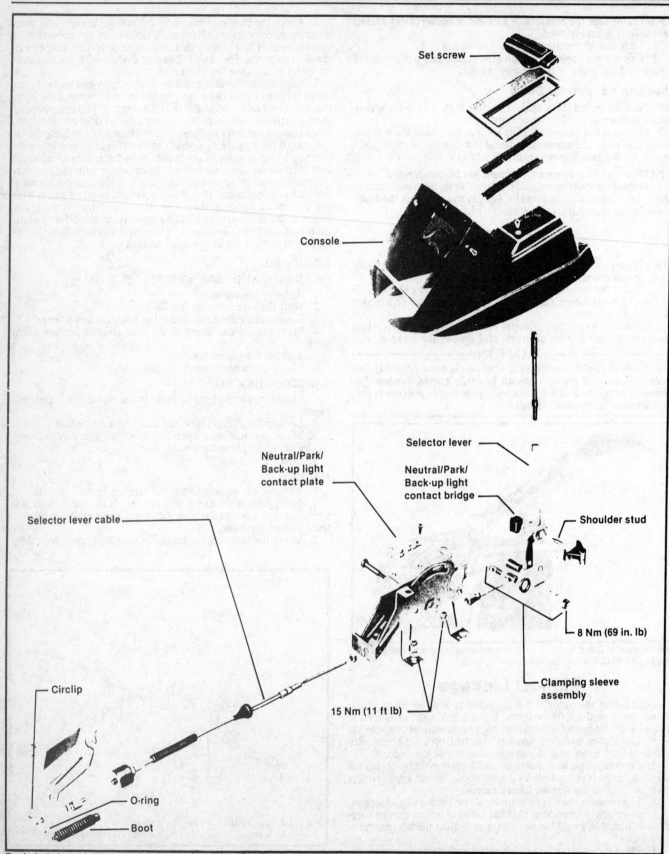

Set screw

Console

Selector lever

Neutral/Park/
Back-up light
contact plate

Neutral/Park/
Back-up light
contact bridge

Shoulder stud

Selector lever cable

8 Nm (69 in. lb)

Clamping sleeve
assembly

Circlip

15 Nm (11 ft lb)

O-ring

Boot

**Exploded view of shift selector mechanism, typical of all models except Vanagon (©Volkswagen of America, Inc.)**

against the stop. This removes all slack from the cable and the linkage.

4. Tighten the clamp nut and replace the console.
5. Check operation.

**VANAGON**

1. Loosen the shift rod bolt.
2. Shift the selector lever into the "P" position.
3. Push the transaxle operating lever to the rear and into the "P" position.
4. Push the shift rod to the rear and tighten the shift rod bolt.
5. Check shifting detents for proper operation. The engine must not start unless the shift lever is in the "P" or "N" positions.

## Neutral Safety Switch

The neutral safety switch used on these applications is mounted on the transaxle selector lever in the driver's compartment. In each case, the switch can be found working off a portion of the selector lever. Removal of the lever cover or console will be required to adjust the switch. Note that there are elongated holes in the switch for the mounting screws. The mouting screws are loosened and the switch moved as necessary so that the starter will operate in Park and Neutral only. This adjustment is important since a dangerous situation can occur if the transaxle were allowed to start in gear.

# SERVICES
## Fluid Change

1. Raise and safely support vehicle.
2. Place a large drain pan under the transaxle. If the unit has a drain plug, remove it and allow to drain. If the unit does not have a drain plug, the filler tube connection can be loosened to allow most of the fluid to drain. It is often advantageous to drain the fluid when hot, when many of the contaminates are in suspension. However, be carefull since transaxle fluid temperatures often reach 300°F.

3. After the fluid has drained, install the drain plug, or filler tube connection if removed. Lower the vehicle and add 2 quarts of Dexron® type automatic transmission fluid.

## Oil Pan

### Removal and Installation

The oil pan can be removed while the transaxle is in the vehicle. Along with the pan, the valve body and other internal components can be inspected, and serviced. The following procedure can be used.

1. Raise and safely support vehicle.
2. Place a large drain pan under the transaxle. If the unit has a drain plug, remove it and allow to drain. If the unit does not have a drain plug, the filler tube connection can be loosened to allow most of the fluid to drain. In any case, the filler tube will have to be removed to allow pan removal.
3. Remove the oil pan retaining screws. Remove the oil pan. If the pan is stuck, tap gently with a rubber mallet. Prying the pan off is not recommended since the gasket surfaces can be damaged. Inspect the oil pan carefully for debris to help get an indication of the condition of the transaxle internal components. Remove the fluid strainer and clean or replace as required.
4. Install the strainer and make sure that the oil pan is thoroughly clean. See that there are no traces of gasket material on either the pan flange or the transaxle gasket rail. Install the pan, taking care to see that the new gasket on the pan is smooth and straight. The pan bolts are only snugged down. Working diagonally, torque the screws to only 7 foot-pounds. Allow the gasket to "set" for about five minutes and retorque to 14 foot-pounds.
5. Lower the vehicle and, following the information in the section "Fluid Change," refill the transaxle and check the fluid level carefully.

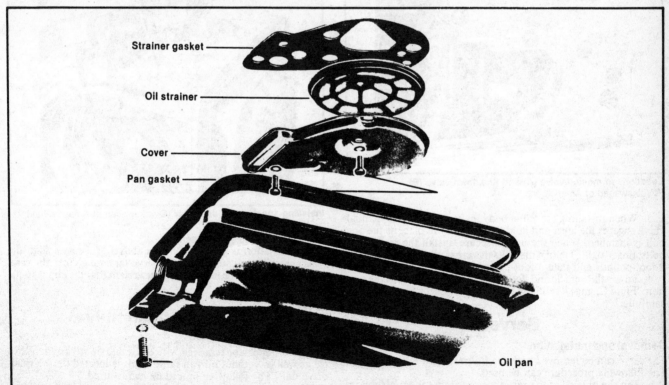

Strainer gasket

Oil strainer

Cover

Pan gasket

Oil pan

**Oil pan and filter assembly—later models** (©Volkswagen of America, Inc.)

## Valve Body

### Removal and Installation

The valve body can be removed on these units with the transaxle still in the vehicle. The following procedure can be used.

1. Following the information given above, drain the oil and remove the oil pan.

2. Remove all but one of the retaining bolts. This is important because otherwise the valve body, separator plate and transfer plate will come apart and the check balls will fall out of place. After all but the last bolt is removed, carefully remove this last bolt while holding these valve body components together. Carefully lower the assembly, holding it firmly to keep the parts intact. The factory does not recommend that the valve body be disassembled or even the three major parts separated (since the check valves may become lost) unless the fluid was extremely dirty. The valve body components are very fragile and easily damaged.

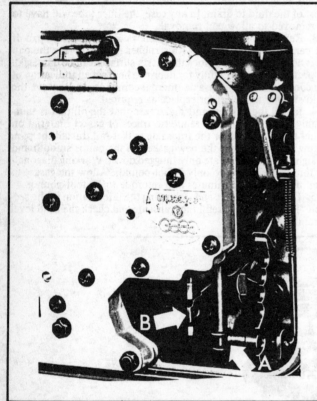

Locations of manual valve (A) and Kickdown valve (B) (©Volkswagen of America, Inc.)

3. When installing the valve body make sure that the manual valve engages the lever and hold the assembly in place as the one bolt is installed. When the unit is secure, install the rest of the bolts, finger-tight. Tighten the bolts in a cross pattern, first to only 2 foot-pounds and then 4 foot-pounds.

4. Lower the vehicle and, following the information in the section "Fluid Change," refill the transaxle and check the fluid level carefully.

## Servos

### Removal and Installation

The servo can be removed with the transaxle still in the vehicle. The following procedure can be used.

1. Tap the outside of the servo piston so that the pressure on the circlip will be released. Remove the circlip.

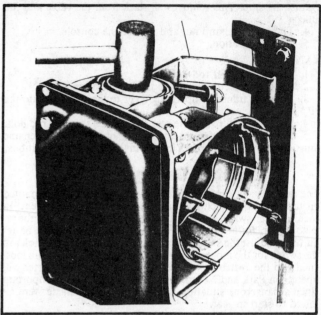

Removing servo piston retaining clip (©Volkswagen of America, Inc.)

Installing servo piston assembly (©Volkswagen of America, Inc.)

2. Remove the servo assembly.

3. Installation is a reversal of the above. Make sure that the seals are well lubricated. Press the servo far enough into the case that the circlip can be installed. Make certain that the clip is in its proper place.

## Governor Assembly

### Removal and Installation

The governor can be removed with the transaxle still in the vehicle as well as without oil pan removal. It is located on the final drive unit. The following procedure can be used.

1. Locate the round, pressed steel cover on the side of the final drive unit. Note that the governor usually will need only cleaning.

**Governor assembly location on transaxle**
(©Volkswagen of America, Inc.)

If, however, the valve body is replaced, then the governor will have to be replaced regardless of the condition of the original governor. This is because the valve body and the governor have been calibrated to work together. With the cover removed from the final drive, pull the governor from the case.

2. Check the drive gear and the thrust plate for wear. Again, because the governor affects the pressure and thereby the operation of the valve body, and replacement of the governor will affect pressure. For this reason, replacement governor shafts are available, so that the valve portion can remain with the unit for which it was calibrated.

3. Installation is a reversal of the above procedure. Be sure to check the seal at the innermost end of the governor shaft bore in the final drive housing. This is especially important if the hypoid oil in the final drive has been contaminated by the automatic transmission fluid. Pry out any defective seals and replace them. Install the new seal with the lip outward, toward the governor body. Note too that the design of the governor changed with the 010 series, serial number ET 27 016. Operation and removal is the same. For overhaul information, see the section "Unit Disassembly and Assembly."

# REMOVAL & INSTALLATION

## AUDI 5000

### Removal

1. Disconnect the battery ground strap and remove the windshield washer reservoir.

2. Note that this model uses a cooler for the transmission. Remove the hoses at the cooler and clamp them shut.

3. Unsnap the ball connection at the upper end of the accelerator linkage rod, remove the speedometer cable and remove the upper engine to transaxle mounting bolts.

4. The engine will have to be supported since mounts will be removed. The factory tool is a bar-like arrangement that is placed

across the engine compartment, supported by the inner flanges on the top of the fenders. A hook is attached and is fitted to the lifting ring on the engine. Once this lifting fixture is in place, take the weight off the engine by lifting with the hook slightly.

5. Locate the guard plate that is under the subframe. Remove this plate as well as the exhaust pipe bracket from the transaxle. Remove the front exhaust pipe.

6. Remove the guard plate that should be found on the right driveshaft (axle). Unbolt the driveshafts at the transaxle end of the shaft. Remove the starter motor.

7. Remove the shifter cable holder from the transaxle, and disconnect the cable from the operating lever on the the transaxle. Remove the accelerator linkage rod from the transaxle by removing the retaining clip. Also, disconnect the accelerator cable from the lever.

8. Remove the right side guard plate from the subframe. Remove the transaxle mounts from the subframe.

9. Working through the starter opening, remove the torque converter bolts.

10. Support the transaxle with a suitable jack and raise slightly to take the weight off the remaining mounting bolts. Remove the lower engine to transaxle bolts. Remove the rear subframe mounting bolts.

11. Move the driveshafts to the rear and carefully separate the engine and transaxle. Lower the transaxle carefully and remove from the vehicle. Be careful that the torque converter does not fall from the case. Run a length of wire across the opening to hold the converter in place.

### Installation

1. The installation is basically a reversal of the above sequence, with the following points to watch. Use care to see that the transaxle and final drive assembly is balanced on the jack. Lift the transaxle assembly and install to the engine.

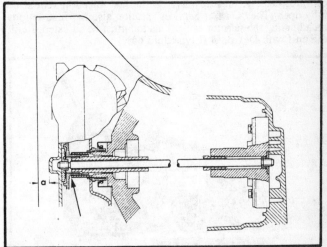

**Correct installation of oil pump drive shaft during transaxle installation** (©Volkswagen of America, Inc.)

─────────── CAUTION ───────────

*It is very important that the torque converter be fully seated. The distance from the face of the transmission case to the pilot or hub of the converter must be 10mm or 0.393 inch. The torque converter must move freely by hand. If the torque converter should slip off the one-way clutch support, the converter will probably pull the oil pump shaft out of the oil pump. This will result in severe damage to the transmission when the transaxle is bolted into place. It is important to check the distance mentioned above very carefully.*

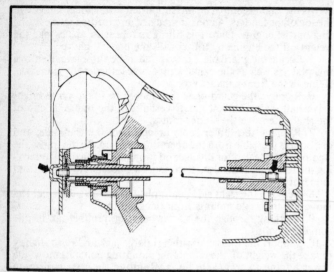

**Incorrect installation of oil pump drive shaft, should converter slip off the one-way clutch support. Internal damage will result** (©Volkswagen of America, Inc.)

2. Install the lower engine to transaxle bolts, install the subframe and install the transaxle mounts on the subframe. Converter bolts are torqued to 22 foot-pounds.

3. It is absolutely necessary that, once the transaxle is installed, the accelerator cable and the accelerator linkage rod be adjusted. Refer to the section "On Car Services" for specific instructions. Also, check the accelerator pedal adjustment. Press the pedal to the full throttle position, but not into the kick-down position. Make sure that the kick-down take-up spring on the linkage is not compressed. The throttle valve on the fuel injection should be fully open. The "On Car Services" section also has instructions on adjusting the selector cable. This too must be adjusted. Refill the unit with Dexron® II type fluid only.

**Typical removal and installation of transaxle on a lifting device tool** (©Volkswagen of America, Inc.)

## RABBIT, SCIROCCO, JETTA

### Removal

1. Remove both the battery ground strap and the positive cable at the battery.

2. Remove the speedometer cable at the transaxle.

3. Remove the two upper engine to transaxle bolts. Loosen the left transaxle mount, which is the one near the battery. The weight will have to be taken off the engine. The factory tool for this consists of a bar that spans the engine compartment and rests on the fender ledge, or inner flange. A threaded rod from the bar with a hook arrangement is designed to fit into the lifting ring on the engine. By taking the weight of the mounts with the threaded hook, the mounts can be disconnected as needed and the engine will still be secure.

4. Remove the rear transaxle mount.

5. Disconnect the driveshafts (axles) at the transaxle.

6. Remove the starter motor. Do not overlook the third bolt that is between the engine and starter.

7. Remove the converter plate and transaxle shield.

8. Remove the torque converter from the drive plate. Install transmission jack.

9. Place the selector lever in Park and remove the cable connection. Remove the cable bracket, disconnect the accelerator cable and the pedal cable.

10. Remove the left transaxle carrier, or mount. Remove the lower bolt and nut holding the transaxle. Check for any missed bolts and then move the transmission and jack away from the engine. Carefully lower the transaxle away from the car. Make sure that the torque converter does not fall. A length of wire across the opening of the case will hold converter in place until the transaxle can be secured in the disassembly fixture and the torque converter removed.

### Installation

1. Installation is basically a reversal of the above sequence, with the following points to watch. Use care to see that the transaxle and final drive assembly is balanced on the jack.

2. Check the torque converter by turning as a check that it is not out of position. It is possible to install the unit with the converter out of alignment so that it will jam when the transaxle is tightened.

3. Be sure to torque the engine to transaxle bolts 40 foot-pounds.

4. Check the engine to transaxle alignment. The left mount must be in the center of the space provided for it in the mount on the body.

5. Torque the driveshaft bolts to 30 ft. lbs. and the converter bolts to 22 foot-pounds.

6. See the section "On Car Services" for information on the selector cable and accelerator/pedal cable adjustments. Refill the unit with Dexron® type fluid.

## DASHER

### Removal

1. Remove the battery ground strap and disconnect the speedometer cable from the final drive. Remove the two upper transaxle to engine bolts. Support the engine with support tool.

2. Remove the nuts from the exhaust manifold and disconnect the head pipe.

3. Remove the converter cover plate.

4. Remove the starter motor.

5. Working through the starter opening, remove the torque converter bolts. Remove exhaust pipe bracket and cable bracket. Disconnect cable from transaxle lever.

6. Remove the bolts holding the driveshafts (axles) at the final drive and position them out of the way. Mechanic's wire can be used to tie the shafts out of the way.

7. The left ball joint is held on by two bolts. Mark the position of the left ball joint so that it can be reinstalled in the same place to avoid the need for a front end alignment. Remove the bolts and then reassemble with the ball joint moved out for clearance.

8. Remove the through bolt from the mount and remove the mount from the body.

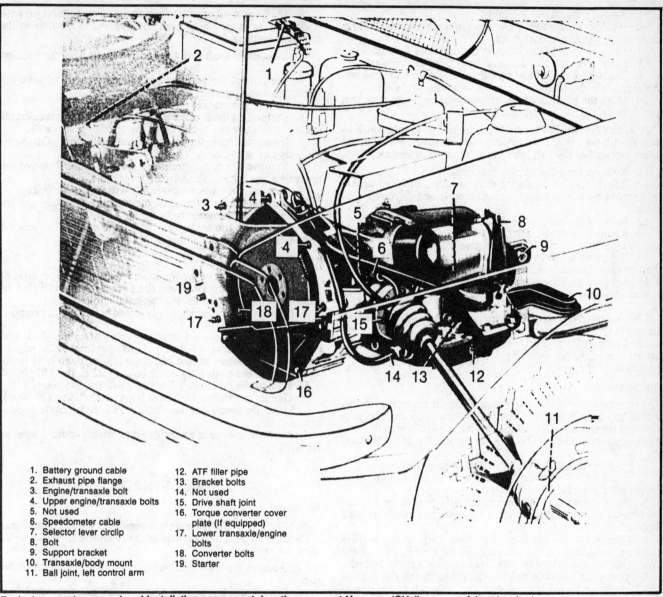

1. Battery ground cable
2. Exhaust pipe flange
3. Engine/transaxle bolt
4. Upper engine/transaxle bolts
5. Not used
6. Speedometer cable
7. Selector lever circlip
8. Bolt
9. Support bracket
10. Transaxle/body mount
11. Ball joint, left control arm
12. ATF filler pipe
13. Bracket bolts
14. Not used
15. Drive shaft joint
16. Torque converter cover plate (If equipped)
17. Lower transaxle/engine bolts
18. Converter bolts
19. Starter

**Typical transaxle removal and installation component, locations, except Vanagon (©Volkswagen of America, Inc.)**

9. Remove the third upper engine to transaxle bolt.
10. Loosen the two lower engine to transmission bolts. Support the transaxle with a jack and lift slightly. Remove the bolts and move the transaxle to the rear and carefuly lower. Be careful that the torque converter does not fall from the case. Run a length of wire across the opening to hold the converter in place.

### Installation

1. The installation is basically the reversal of the above sequence, with the following points to watch. Use care to see that the transmisison and final drive assembly is balanced on the jack. Lift the transaxle assembly and install to the engine.

#### — CAUTION —

*It is very important that the torque converter be fully seated. The distance from the face of the transaxle case to the pilot or hub of the converter must be 30mm or 1³/₁₆ inch. The torque converter must move freely by hand. If the torque converter should slip off the one-way clutch support, the converter will pull the oil pump shaft out of the oil pump. This will result in severe damage to the transaxle*

*when the transaxle is bolted to the engine. The transaxle to engine bolts should be torqued to 40 foot-pounds.*

2. Install the mounts and crossmember making sure that everything lines up.
3. Return the ball joint to its original position, and torque the nuts to 47 ft. lbs. The driveshaft bolts get torqued to 30 foot-pounds, the converter bolts to 22 foot-pounds.
4. Attach the selector lever cable to the transaxle. Install the exhaust system components as required.

### AUDI 4000, QUANTUM

#### Removal

1. Disconnect the battery ground strap.
2. Remove the coolant hose and the upper engine/transaxle bolts.
3. Install the engine support tool and raise the vehicle.
4. Remove both front stop bolts.

5. Remove the starter assembly.

6. Working through the starter hole in the converter housing, remove the three converter bolts.

7. Remove the coolant hoses at the transaxle fluid cooler.

8. Disconnect the speedometer cable from the transaxle.

9. Disconnect the left and right drive shafts from the transaxle flanges. Tie the shafts to the body with wire.

10. Mark the position of the left ball joint on the control arm and remove the ball joint/control arm bolts.

**NOTE: The ball joint assembly can be held away from the lower arm with the use of a six to eight inch metal bar, bolted to the lower arm and to the ball joint and used as an extension.**

11. Remove the exhaust pipe brackets.

12. Remove the holder for the selector cable from the transaxle. Remove the circlip from the selector cable and disconnect the cable.

13. Remove the selector cable bracket on the transaxle.

14. Remove the center bolt from the engine mount and lift the engine assembly slightly with the engine support tool.

15. Remove the bracket for the throttle and the pedal cable on the transaxle housing.

16. Support the transaxle assembly with a lifting device, such as a transmission jack or its equivalent. Raise the assembly slightly.

17. Remove the lower engine/transaxle bolts and separate the transaxle from the engine.

18. Carefully lower the transaxle from underneath the vehicle. Secure the converter assembly to prevent its falling from the transaxle.

### Installation

The installation of the transaxle is basically the reversal of the removal sequence. Be sure the transaxle is secured on the lifting device and the converter is retained in place. The following installation points should be noted during the installation of the transaxle.

1. Push the pump shaft fully into the pump splines.

2. Install the converter into the transaxle before attempting to install the transaxle.

3. When installing the converter, carefully push it on the one-way clutch support. Check to see if the converter can be rotated by hand.

4. When the converter is properly seated, the distance from the front flat surface of the converter to the leading edge of the converter housing should be 0.393 inch (approximately 10 mm).

5. Attach the transaxle to the engine and install the engine/transaxle bolts. Install the remaining components in reverse of their removal. Align the engine/transaxle mounts before tightening bolts.

6. Adjust the throttle cable and selector lever cable as necessary.

7. Install transmission fluid and correct the level as required.

8. Check the camber setting of the left wheel to verify the correct replacement of the ball joint and bolts.

9. The tightening torques are as follows;

| | |
|---|---|
| Drive shaft/flange bolts | 33 ft. lbs. (45 N•m) |
| Torque converter bolts | 22 ft. lbs. (30 N•m) |
| Transaxle/engine bolts | 40 ft. lbs. (55 N•m) |
| Ball joint/control arm | 48 ft. lbs. (65 N•m) |
| Mount to body | 30 ft. lbs. (40 N•m) |
| Mount to transaxle | 40 ft. lbs. (55 N•m) |

## VANAGON

### Removal

1. Remove the battery ground strap and the fan housing grille.

2. Remove the three torque converter bolts through the hole on top of the transaxle housing.

**NOTE: To gain access to the torque converter bolts, the crankshaft must be rotated until each bolt appears in the hole in the transaxle housing.**

3. Disconnect the left and right drive shafts from the transaxle.

4. Disconnect the wiring from the starter and remove the starter assembly.

5. Loosen the bracket for the dipstick tube.

6. Disconnect the accelerator linkage. Pry off the accelerator cable and remove the circlip from the selector lever cable.

7. Install an engine support tool from the bottom of the vehicle body to the engine.

8. Remove the engine/transaxle ground strap. Remove the mounting bracket and the selector lever cable.

9. Support the transaxle assembly with a lifting device.

10. Remove the rear transaxle mount from the body and remove the engine/transaxle bolts.

11. Lower the transaxle from under the vehicle. Secure the converter to prevent its falling from the transaxle.

### Installation

1. The installation of the transaxle is basically the reversal of the removal sequence. However, there are certain points that attention should be given during the installation.

2. Be sure the pump shaft is fully seated before the converter is installed.

3. The converter should rotate by hand when installed. The proper distance from the flat of the converter front to the edge of the converter housing should be ⅜ inch (approximately 10 mm).

4. Tighten the engine/transaxle bolts to 22 ft. lbs. (30 N•m).

5. Tighten the drive shaft bolts to 33 ft. lbs. (45 N•m).

6. Tighten the torque converter bolts to 22 ft. lbs. (30 N•m).

7. Make the necessary accelerator and pedal cable adjustments.

8. Refill the transaxle assembly and correct the fluid level as required.

## FIAT STRADA

### Removal

**NOTE: The engine/transaxle assembly must be removed and replaced as a unit. The transaxle can be separated from the engine after the removal.**

1. Remove the hood, (scribe location), the jack and the spare tire.

2. Disconnect the battery negative and positive battery cables.

3. Drain the cooling system completely.

4. If equipped with A/C, slowly bleed the freon from the system.

--- **CAUTION** ---

*Wear protective gloves and clothing. Do not discharge the freon near an open flame, as a toxic gas may result.*

5. Remove the air cleaner assembly and its connecting hoses. Plug the openings on the engine to prevent dirt from entering.

6. Mark the electrical wiring to identify during assembly, and remove from the electrical components.

7. Remove the fuel system hoses from the carburetor and vapor cannister. Mark hoses for identification during assembly.

8. Remove the accelerator cable. Disconnect the A/C compressor delivery hose and the compressor return hose, if equipped with A/C.

9. Disconnect the heater hoses and the top on bottom radiator hoses.

10. Raise the vehicle and support safely.

11. Remove the front wheel assemblies. Remove the left and

right splash shields from the fender wells and from the front center.

12. Separate the strut assemblies from the hub carriers by the removal of the retaining bolts.

13. Remove the tie rod end retaining nuts and separate the end from the hub carrier.

14. Remove the Allen headed cap screws from the drive axle flanges, along with the retaining plates. Discard the Allen headed cap screws. New ones must be used during the installation.

15. Remove the catalytic converter (all models), and the front exhaust pipe from the vehicle on air pump equipped models.

--- CAUTION ---

*Allow the catalytic converter to cool before attempting to remove.*

16. Disconnect the speedometer cable from the transaxle.

17. Place the selector lever in the "1" position and remove the "E" clip and washer. Slide the shift cable eyelet off the pin on the transaxle lever. Remove the nut to free the clamp and lay the shift cable to one side.

18. Attach a lifting sling to the engine/transaxle assembly and place a jack under the center engine mount.

19. Remove the bolts to separate the engine mount from the body.

NOTE: Do not remove the bolt unless the mount is damaged.

20. Remove two bolts attaching the right engine mount to the mounting bracket. Do not remove the right engine mount from the engine.

21. Remove the two upper bolts while only loosening the lower bolts and remove the right mount mounting bracket.

22. Remove the bolt and washer from the left engine mount.

23. Separate the sway bar from the mounting bracket. Remove the mounting bracket from the body.

24. Slowly remove the jack supporting the center engine mount. Lower the engine/transaxle assembly from the engine compartment.

25. Support the engine transaxle/assembly and remove the bolts to separate the flywheel from the converter. Remove accelerator cable from transaxle.

26. Remove the bolts from the converter housing to engine and separate the transaxle from the engine. Prevent the torque converter from falling from the assembly during the separation sequence.

### Installation

1. The installation of the engine transaxle assembly is basically the reversal of the removal sequence. The engine/transaxle must be joined before the unit is raised into position in the engine compartment.

Note: The torque converter coupled to the engine of the Fiat Strada, utilizes a four lug flywheel-to-converter attachment instead of the usual three lug attachment, although three lug unit maybe encountered. The final drive unit configuration is different from the Audi/VW model usage.

2. Using new Allen headed cap screws, torque to 31 ft. lbs. when installing the drive shafts to the transaxle flanges.

3. Torque the engine/transaxle bolts to 21.7 ft. lbs.

## BENCH OVERHAUL

### Before Disassembly

When servicing the series 10 transaxles it is recommended that the technician be aware of the importance of cleanliness. Cleanliness is an important factor in the overhaul of the transaxle. Be-

fore opening up the transaxle the outside of the unit should be thoroughly cleaned, preferably with high-pressure cleaning equipment such as a car wash spray unit. Dirt entering the transaxle internal parts will negate all the effort and time spent on the overhaul.

During the inspection and reassembly, all parts should be cleaned with solvent then dried with compressed air. Wiping cloths and rags should not be used to dry parts since lint will find its way into the valve body passages. Lube seals with Dexron® II and use ordinary unmedicated petroleum jelly to hold the thrust washers and ease the assembly of seals, since it will not leave a harmful residue as grease often will. Do not use solvent on neoprene seals, friction plates or composition thrust washers if they are to be re-used.

Before installing bolts into aluminum parts, always dip the threads into clean transmission fluid. Anti-seize compound can also be used to prevent bolts from galling the aluminum and seizing. Always use a torque wrench to keep from stripping the threads. Take care with the seals when installing them, especially the smaller O-rings. The slightest damage can cause leaks. Aluminum parts are very susceptible to damage and so great care should be used when handling them. The internal snap rings should be expanded and the external snap rings compressed if they are to be re-used. This will help insure proper seating when installed.

## Converter Inspection

The torque converter that is used on these units is of conventional design. It is a sealed, welded unit and so it cannot be disassembled for service or repair. There are, however, a few checks that should be made on the torque converter.

The torque converter contains approximately 2 quarts of transmission fluid. The fluid can be drained through the hub, since there is no drain plug on these units. The factory recommends a plastic tube and container arrangement to siphon the fluid from the converter. However, the converter can be inverted and the

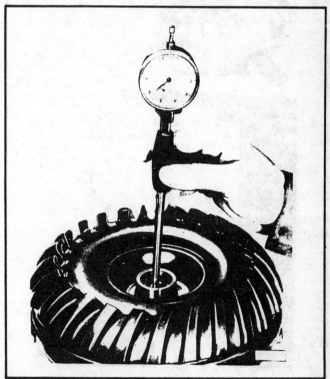

**Measuring converter bushing for wear**
(©Volkswagen of America, Inc.)

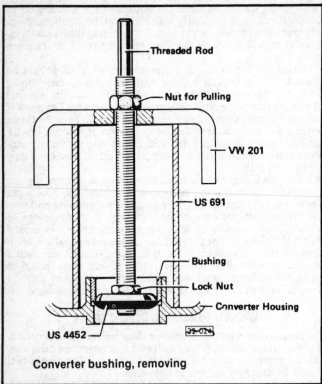

Threaded Rod

Nut for Pulling

VW 201

US 691

Bushing

Lock Nut

Converter Housing

US 4452

Converter bushing, removing

Suggested tool and method for converter bushing removal (©Volkswagen of America, Inc.)

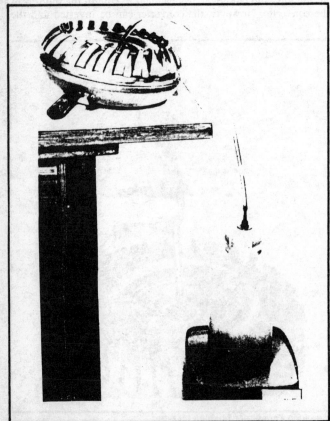

Method used to drain converter (©Volkswagen of America, Inc.)

fluid drained into a pan. The fluid that is drained from the torque converter can help in diagnosing the condition of the converter.

1. If the oil in the converter is discolored but does not contain metal bits or particles, the converter is not damaged and need not be replaced. Remember that fluid color is no longer a good indicator of transmission fluid condition. In the past, dark color was associated with overheated transmission fluid. It is not a positive sign of transaxle failure with the newer fluids.

2. If the oil in the converter contains metal particles, the converter is damaged internally and must be replaced. The oil may have an "aluminum paint" appearance.

3. If the cause of the oil contamination was due to burned clutch plates or overheated oil, the converter is contaminated and should be cleaned or replaced.

The converter should be checked carefully for damage, especially around the seal area. The bushing can be collapsed to remove it since the design of the hub prevents it from being driven all the way through. Remove any sharp edges or burrs from the seal surface. A silicone type seal is used on these transaxles and it is driven into place in the front housing. Since this type of seal is soft, a great amount of care is needed to see that the seal surface on the converter is smooth and clean. Also, the seal itself should not be exposed to any type of solvent. If the case is to be washed with solvent, the seal must be replaced, usually as the last item before installation of the converter at the completion of the overhaul.

The converter bushing can also be checked for wear with an internal dial indicator. The wear limit is 34.25mm or 1.348 inch. The maximum out of round is 0.03mm or 0.001 inch. The bushing can be replaced. The inside diameter must be 1.340 to 1.341 inch (34.03 to 34.05mm).

The most important point to remember when working with the converter actually involves the oil pump. Since the drive shaft for the oil pump extends into the converter area, the technician must make absolutely certain that the pump shaft is installed all the way into the pump drive splines. Also, when the converter is installed on the one-way clutch support, make certain that the converter is not tilted or misaligned. If the converter slips off of the clutch housing, remove it and check the oil pump shaft again. The converter can pull the shaft forward and disengage the shaft from the pump. The shaft then drops down on the pump end, unseen, and when the transmission is installed and tightened down, the shaft will cause a great amount of internal damage as it is pushed through the pump castings. The importance of checking this oil pump shaft and the proper handling of the converter cannot be over-emphasized.

## Transaxle Separation and Transmission Disassembly

NOTE: To aid the repairman in identifying the internal transmission components, the VW/Audi nomenclature will be used with the Fiat Strada nomenclature in parenthesis, with the abbreviation F/S preceding it.

1. Remove the converter assembly. Drain all fluid and oil from both the transmission and final drive units.

NOTE: When the transmission and final drive units are assembled as a unit assembly, it is known as a "Transaxle assembly". Otherwise, each is known by its unit name, transmission or final drive.

2. Mount the transaxle assembly on a holding fixture, if available.

3. Remove the oil pump shaft, the governor and the oil filler pipe with dipstick.

4. Remove the retaining nuts and separate the transmission unit from the final drive. Remove the turbine (input) shaft.

5. Remove the capscrews retaining the flange and remove the flange and gasket. Remove the oil pan.

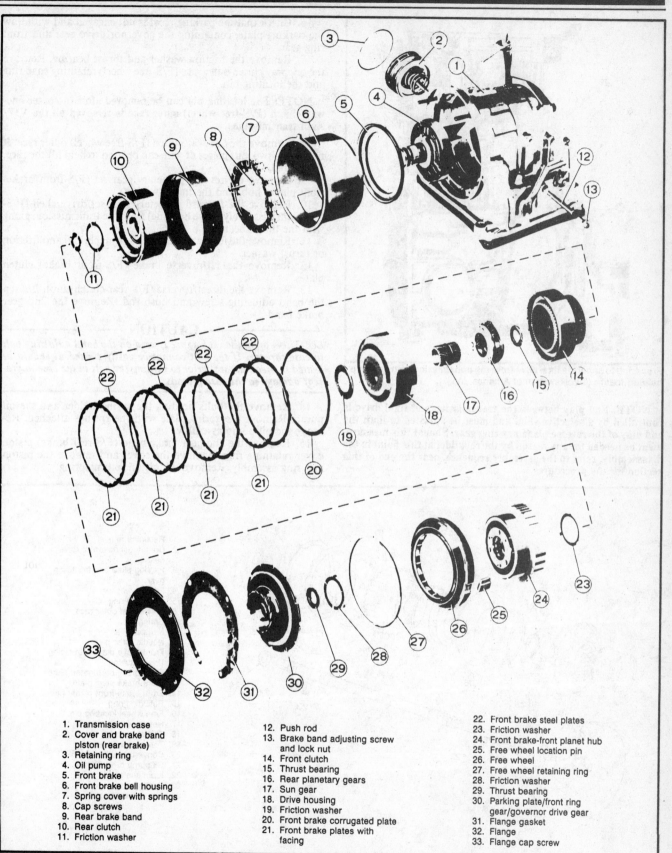

**Exploded view of internal transaxle components** (©Volkswagen of America, Inc.)

1. Transmission case
2. Cover and brake band piston (rear brake)
3. Retaining ring
4. Oil pump
5. Front brake
6. Front brake bell housing
7. Spring cover with springs
8. Cap screws
9. Rear brake band
10. Rear clutch
11. Friction washer

12. Push rod
13. Brake band adjusting screw and lock nut
14. Front clutch
15. Thrust bearing
16. Rear planetary gears
17. Sun gear
18. Drive housing
19. Friction washer
20. Front brake corrugated plate
21. Front brake plates with facing

22. Front brake steel plates
23. Friction washer
24. Front brake-front planet hub
25. Free wheel location pin
26. Free wheel
27. Free wheel retaining ring
28. Friction washer
29. Thrust bearing
30. Parking plate/front ring gear/governor drive gear
31. Flange gasket
32. Flange
33. Flange cap screw

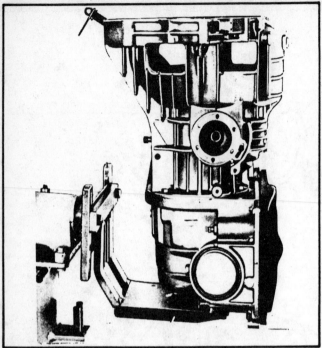

Preparing to separate final drive from the transmission with unit on a holding fixture (©Volkswagen of America, Inc.)

NOTE: End play between the transmission and final drive is controlled by a selective shim and must be adjusted to limit the end play of the reverse planetary ring gear. Should this measurement be needed for any reason by the rebuilder at this point in the disassembly, refer to the assembly sequence, near the end of this section for the procedures.

6. Check that the parking pawl is not engaged and withdraw the parking plate, containing the governor drive gear and front ring gear.

7. Remove the friction washer and thrust bearing. Remove the one way clutch outer race (F/S-free wheel) retaining snap ring and the locating pin.

NOTE: The locating pin can be removed after the outer one-way clutch (F/S-free wheel) outer race is removed on the VW/Audi transmissions.

8. Remove the one-way clutch (F/S-free wheel) outer race. If necessary, two stiff pieces of wire can be used to help lift the race, if required.

9. Remove the reverse planetary gear set (F/S-front brake-front planet hub) and the thrust washer.

10. Remove the forward planetary gear set/drive shell (F/S-rear planet assembly/drive housing) from the transmission, along with the thrust bearing.

11. Remove the forward clutch (F/S-front clutch) and friction or thrust washer.

12. Remove the 1st/reverse brake (F/S-front brake) clutch plates.

13. Remove the direct/reverse (F/S-rear clutch) unit. Loosen the band adjusting screw and push rod. Remove the 2nd gear brake band.

---
### CAUTION
---

*Loc-Tite® or similar substance is used on the band adjusting bolt to case threads. If the bolt cannot be easily turned, it should be heated to break the seal prior to turning the bolt in the case to prevent damage to the case threads.*

---

14. Remove the bolts holding the spring holder and the oil pump. Remove the spring plate with the springs attached. Remove the oil pump assembly.

15. Remove the 2nd gear brake band (F/S-rear brake) piston cover retaining ring. Remove the cover and remove the piston and ring assembly. Remove the piston return spring.

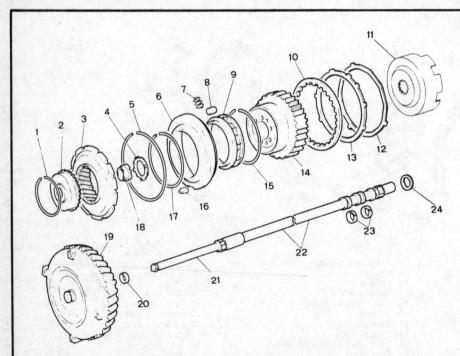

1. Retaining ring
2. Centrifugal governor drive gear
3. Parking plate and front ring gear
4. Friction washer
5. Retaining ring
6. Free wheel outer race
7. Spring
8. Needle roller
9. Needle roller cage
10. Front brake plate with facing
11. Drive housing
12. Front brake corrugated plate
13. Front brake steel plate
14. Front brake-front planet hub
15. Retaining ring
16. Free wheel locating pin
17. Retaining ring
18. Thrust bearing
19. Torque converter
20. Converter hub housing
21. Oil pump drive shaft
22. Input shaft
23. Sealing rings
24. Thrust washer

Exploded view of front section of transmission with Fiat nomenclature (©Volkswagen of America, Inc.)

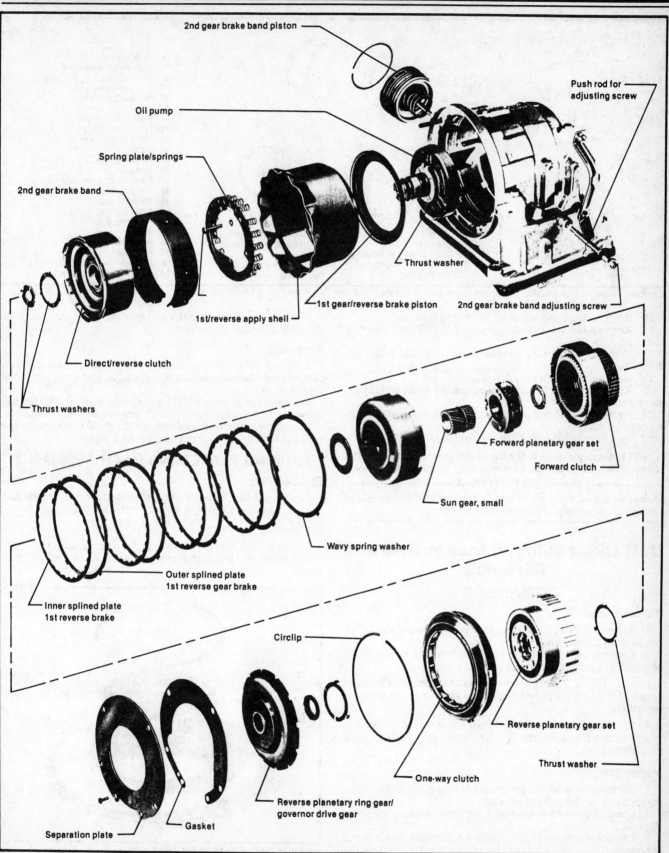

2nd gear brake band piston

Oil pump

Push rod for adjusting screw

Spring plate/springs

2nd gear brake band

Thrust washer

Direct/reverse clutch

1st/reverse apply shell

1st gear/reverse brake piston

2nd gear brake band adjusting screw

Thrust washers

Forward planetary gear set

Forward clutch

Sun gear, small

Wavy spring washer

Outer splined plate
1st reverse gear brake

Inner splined plate
1st reverse brake

Circlip

Reverse planetary gear set

Thrust washer

One-way clutch

Reverse planetary ring gear/
governor drive gear

Separation plate

Gasket

**Exploded view of transmission components with Audi/VW nomenclature** (©Volkswagen of America, Inc.)

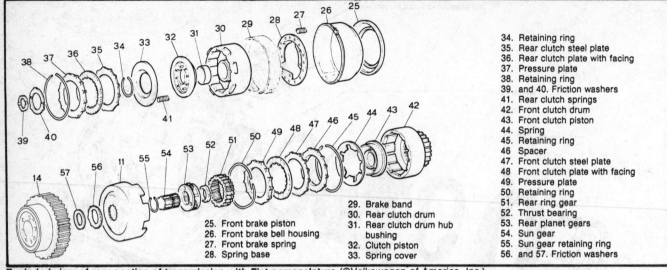

34. Retaining ring
35. Rear clutch steel plate
36. Rear clutch plate with facing
37. Pressure plate
38. Retaining ring
39. and 40. Friction washers
41. Rear clutch springs
42. Front clutch drum
43. Front clutch piston
44. Spring
45. Retaining ring
46. Spacer
47. Front clutch steel plate
48. Front clutch plate with facing
49. Pressure plate
50. Retaining ring
51. Rear ring gear
52. Thrust bearing
53. Rear planet gears
54. Sun gear
55. Sun gear retaining ring
56. and 57. Friction washers

29. Brake band
30. Rear clutch drum
31. Rear clutch drum hub bushing
32. Clutch piston
33. Spring cover

25. Front brake piston
26. Front brake bell housing
27. Front brake spring
28. Spring base

**Exploded view of rear section of transmission with Fiat nomenclature** (©Volkswagen of America, Inc.)

16. Remove the band adjusting screw and push rod.

17. Remove the 1st/reverse apply shell (F/S-front brake bell housing).

18. Remove the 1st reverse brake piston (F/S-front brake piston).

19. Remove the oil filter and retaining screws

20. Remove the valve body retaining bolts and carefully remove the valve body from the case.

21. Remove the accumulator piston spring and piston from the bore in the case.

22. Remove the oil pump filter, if equipped.

NOTE: During repairs to the transaxles prior to serial number 21040, do not re-install the oil pump filter in the pressure bore.

─────────── CAUTION ───────────

*Pistons with moulded seals should be replaced and not be reused during the reassembly of the transaxle components.*

# Unit Disassembly, Inspection and Assembly
## GOVERNOR

### Disassembly

1. Remove the two screws and lock plate retaining the governor shaft to the governor body.

2. Remove and discard the oil filter from the circuit plate. Note the position of the circuit plate and remove.

NOTE: During repairs to the transaxles prior to the serial number 08040, do not re-install the fluid strainer in the governor assembly.

3. Remove the counter weight from the governor housing.

4. Remove the circlip, the flyweight, valve and spring, cap and centralizer shaft.

### Inspection

1. Thoroughly flush the governor housing oil passages. Blow compressed air through the passages.

2. Check the governor housing for scoring, burrs or deposits. Replace if required.

3. Check the governor valve spring for damaged or weakened condition.

4. Check the valve for scores or burrs.

5. Check the governor shaft and gear for being bent, worn or damaged. Replace as rquired.

### Assembly

1. Install the centralizer shaft and cup, spring and valve into the governor housing. Install the flyweight and retain with the circlip.

2. Install the counter weight and circuit plate. Install the circuit plate in the same position as it was when it was removed.

3. Assemble the shaft assembly to the governor housing and retain it with the two screws and the lock plate.

## PARKING PLATE/RING GEAR ASSEMBLY

### Disassembly

1. Remove the retaining ring and separate the drive gear hub from the parking plate/ring gear.

### Inspection

1. Inspect the parking plate teeth for damage and side wear.

2. Inspect the drive and ring gear teeth for scores or being worn.

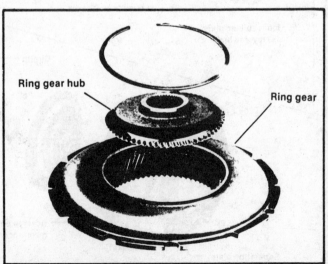

Ring gear hub

Ring gear

**Exploded view of parking plate/ring gear**
(©Volkswagen of America, Inc.)

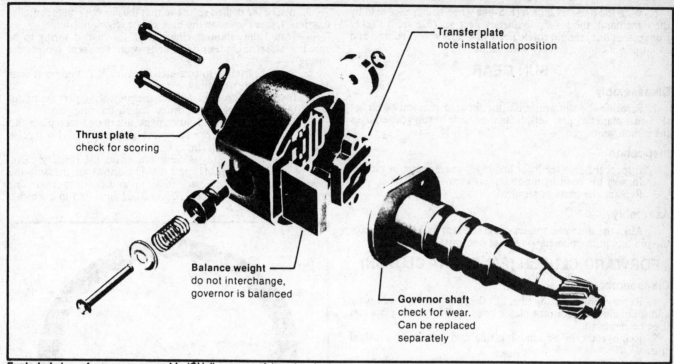

**Transfer plate**
note installation position

**Thrust plate**
check for scoring

**Balance weight**
do not interchange,
governor is balanced

**Governor shaft**
check for wear.
Can be replaced
separately

**Exploded view of governor assembly** (©Volkswagen of America, Inc.)

3. Replace the components as required.

## Assembly

1. Mate the splines of the drive gear hub and parking plate/ring gear. Install the retaining ring.

## ONE-WAY CLUTCH (F/S-FREE WHEEL)

### Disassembly

1. Mark the position of the cage to the outer race.
2. Remove the retaining rings, top and bottom.
3. Tap the cage lightly and remove the cage from the outer ring.
4. Disassemble the rollers and the springs, noting their direction for assembly.

### Inspection

1. Inspect the springs for distortion or breakage.
2. Inspect the rollers and outer race for wear, galling or brinnelling.
3. Replace the worn or damaged parts.

### Assembly

1. Position the lower retaining ring in the outer ring.
2. Heat the outer ring to 300°F. (150°C.) on a hot plate.
3. Using gloves and two sets of pliers, place the cage on top of the outer ring, aligning the previously made marks, and install the cage into the outer ring quickly. Be sure the cage "dogs" are securely positioned in the appropriate outer ring grooves. Rotate the cage slightly immediately after installation, if necessary.

NOTE: **The cage quickly absorbs the heat from the outer ring and will lock-up. If the cage is not correctly positioned, do not force it, but remove it and repeat the operation.**

4. When the unit has cooled down, install the springs and rollers in the cage. Install the top retaining ring.
5. Install the one-way clutch (F/S-free wheel) on the reverse planetary gear set (F/S-front brake/front planet hub).

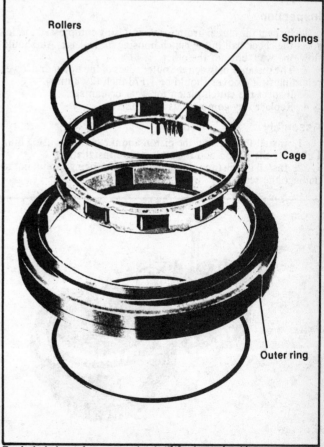

**Rollers**

**Springs**

**Cage**

**Outer ring**

**Exploded view of one-way clutch (F/S - front clutch)**
(©Volkswagen of America, Inc.)

6. With the one-way clutch (F/S-free wheel) outer race held by the right hand, the reverse planetary gear set (F/S-front brake/front planet hub) should rotate freely in a clockwise direction and lock-up in a counterclockwise direction.

## SUN GEAR

### Disassembly

1. Separate the sun gear from the forward planetary gear set (F/S-rear planetary gear set). Note short side of sun gear engages the pinion gears.

### Inspection

1. Inspect the gear teeth for breakage, wear, scores or chips.
2. Inspect the bushing for abnormal wear.
3. Replace the parts as required.

### Assembly

1. Align the short end splines of the sun gear with the splines of the pinions in the planetary gear set and install in place.

## FORWARD CLUTCH (F/S-FRONT CLUTCH)

### Disassembly

1. Remove the retaining ring. Lift the ring gear, pressure plate and set of clutches from the clutch housing. The thrust plate can then be removed.
2. Remove the lower retaining ring and remove the dished spring.
3. Remove the piston assembly from the clutch housing.
4. Remove the seals from the clutch housing hub and the piston.

### Inspection

1. Inspect the clutch drum for wear. Using compressed air, inspect the check ball in the clutch housing for leakage. Air should flow one way, but not the other.
2. The distance between the outer edges of the upper and lower retaining ring grooves should be 1.173 inch (29.8 mm).
3. Inspect the clutch piston for wear or damage.
4. Replace any components as required.

### Assembly

1. Install the seals on the piston and the clutch housing hub. Lubricate the piston and the seals before installation.
2. Install the piston in the clutch housing, being careful not to damage the seals.

**Measuring end play of forward clutch pack**
(©Volkswagen of America, Inc.)

3. Install the dished spring so that the convex end (or smaller diameter), faces towards the base of the clutch housing.
4. Install the retaining ring. Check the dished spring to be sure it is under slight tension. If no tension is present, replace the spring.
5. Soak the friction lined clutch plates in A/T fluid for at least 15 minutes before assembly.
6. Install the thrust plate with the projecting part facing towards the base of the clutch drum. Install the ring gear.
7. Starting with a lined clutch plate, alternate a steel plate and a lined plate. Install the pressure plate next to a lined clutch plate and install the retaining ring.
8. After the assembly is complete, check the running clearance of the clutch pack. Using a dial indicator tool, measure the movement of the clutch pack in an up and down motion. The proper clearance should be 0.020 to 0.035 inch (0.5 to 0.9 mm).

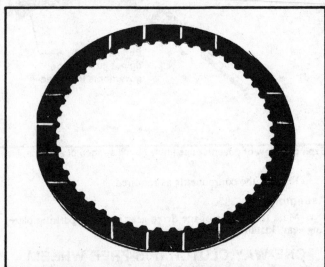

**Grooved plates used in forward clutch assembly**
(©Volkswagen of America, Inc.)

9. Should the measurement be out of specifications, pressure plates of different thicknesses are available to allow clearance adjustment.
10. To test the assembly, install the forward clutch (F/S-front clutch) and the direct/reverse (F/S-rear clutch) with the thrust washers, on the oil pump.
11. Apply compressed air to the "A" port as illustrated.
12. The piston must compress the clutch plates under air pressure and release them when the air pressure is removed.

## DIRECT/REVERSE CLUTCH (F/S-REAR CLUTCH)

### Disassembly

1. Remove the clutch pack retaining snap ring and remove the clutch pack assembly.
2. Install a special spring compressor tool and compress the spring cover in the clutch housing. Remove the retaining ring, release the compressor tool and remove. Remove the spring cover, the springs and the piston.

### Inspection

1. Inspect the clutch drum bushing. The bushing can be replaced, if required. The old bushing can be used to press the new bushing into a measurement of 0.067 inch (1.7 mm) below the top edge.
2. Inspect the clutch drum for wear or damage.

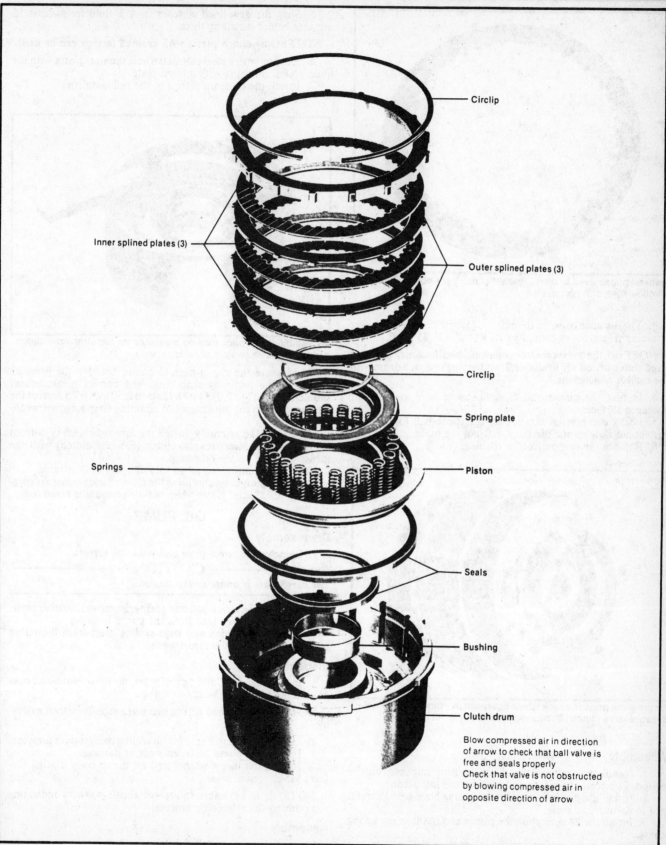

Circlip

Inner splined plates (3)

Outer splined plates (3)

Circlip

Spring plate

Springs

Piston

Seals

Bushing

Clutch drum

Blow compressed air in direction
of arrow to check that ball valve is
free and seals properly
Check that valve is not obstructed
by blowing compressed air in
opposite direction of arrow

**Exploded view of forward clutch (F/S - rear clutch) (©Volkswagen of America, Inc.)**

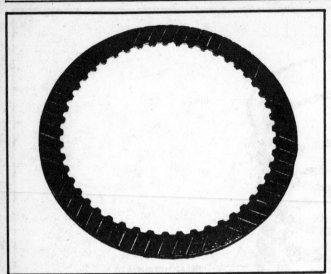

**Grooved plates used in direct/reverse clutch assembly**
(©Volkswagen of America, Inc.)

3. The distance between the outer edges of the upper and lower retaining ring grooves should be 1.230 inch (31.25 mm).

**NOTE: If the measurement is out of specifications, different sized clutch drums are available. Install only the clutch drum with the correct dimensions.**

4. Inspect the piston and clutch housing bore for wear or damaged surfaces.

5. Using compressed air, inspect the check ball for leakage. Air should flow in one direction, but not the other.

6. Replace the components as required.

**Air pressure ports to check clutch operation. A - forward clutch, B - direct/reverse clutch** (©Volkswagen of America, Inc.)

## Assembly

1. Install the seals on the clutch housing hub and on the piston. Lubricate the piston and seals before installation.

2. Install the piston in the clutch housing bore, being careful not to damage the seals.

3. Install the 24 springs on the piston and position the spring cover.

4. Install the compresing tool. Compress the springs and install the spring cover retaining ring. Remove the tool.

5. Soak the new lined clutches in A/T fluid for at least 15 minutes before installing them.

**NOTE: Only clutch plates with grooved facings can be used.**

6. Starting with a steel plate, alternate the steel plates with the lined plates, finishing with a lined plate.

7. Install the pressure plate and the retaining ring.

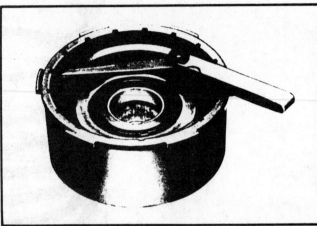

**Measuring clutch pack running clearance on direct/reverse clutch assembly** (©Volkswagen of America, Inc.)

8. Measure the clutch pack clearance between the pressure plate and the retaining snap ring. The correct measurement should be 0.0807 to 0.0984 inch (2.05 to 2.50 mm). To correct the clearance, different thicknesses of retaining snap rings are available.

9. To test the assembly, install the forward clutch (F/S-front clutch) and the direct/reverse clutch (F/S-rear clutch) with the thrust washers, on the oil pump.

10. Apply compressed air to the "B" port as illustrated.

11. The piston must compress the clutch plates under air pressure and release the plates when the air pressure is removed.

## OIL PUMP

### Disassembly

1. Remove the cover plate and retaining screws.

─────────── CAUTION ───────────
*The cover plate is under spring tension.*

2. Remove the check ball and spring. Remove the drive plate, drive gear and driven gear from the pump housing.

3. Remove the small and large sealing rings from the pump body hub. Remove the thrust washer.

### Inspection

1. Inspect the drive and driven gears, the drive plate, and cover plate for abnormal wear or damage.

**NOTE: The drive and driven gears are supplied as an assembly.**

2. Inspect the pump housing hub sealing ring grooves for wear.

3. Inspect the pump body for wear or damage.

4. Inspect the thrust washer and oil pump body mating surfaces for abnormal wear.

**NOTE: It is advisable to replace thrust washers indicating wear during the rebuilding process.**

### Assembly

1. Lubricate and install the drive gear, driven gears and the drive plate.

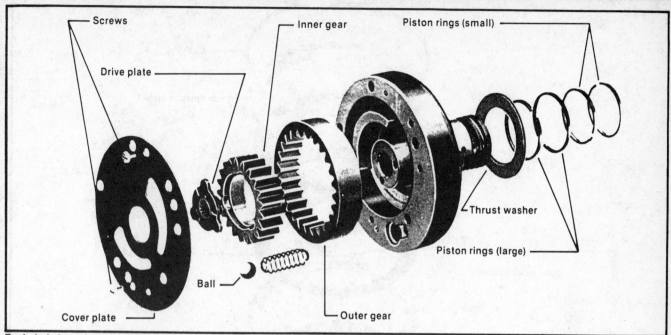

**Exploded view of oil pump assembly** (©Volkswagen of America, Inc.)

NOTE: **Install the driven gear with the code letter facing towards the cover plate.**

2. Install the spring and check ball in the pump housing.

3. Install the cover plate and retain with the retaining capscrews.

4. Install the thrust washer, the large seal rings and the small seal rings. Be sure the seal rings are hooked together at their ends.

5. After the assembly, insert the oil pump drive shaft and check that the gear rotate freely.

## 2ND GEAR BRAKE BAND PISTON (F/S-REAR BRAKE)

### Disassembly

1. The piston assembly can be disassembled by removing the circlip from the piston shaft.

─────────────── CAUTION ───────────────

*The piston shaft is under spring tension. Upon disassembly, do not lose the shim from between the piston and the accumulator spring.*

2. Remove the seals from the piston and cover.

NOTE: **"O" ring seals are used on the cover, while lip seals are used on the piston. Note the positioning of the lip seals.**

### Inspection

1. Inspect the springs for distortion or being broken.

2. Inspect the piston and cover assemblies for wear or damage. Inspect the piston diameter.

### Assembly

1. Install the piston shaft, shim and spring into the piston and retain with the circlip.

NOTE: **If the piston is replaced, the unit is pre-assembled and adjusted.**

2. Lubricate and install the "O" ring seals in the cover assembly.

3. Lubricate and install the lip seals on the piston with the small seal lip facing the bottom of the cover and the large seal lip facing the open end of the cover.

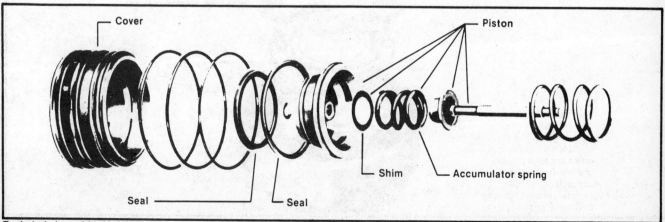

**Exploded view of brake band piston** (©Volkswagen of America, Inc.)

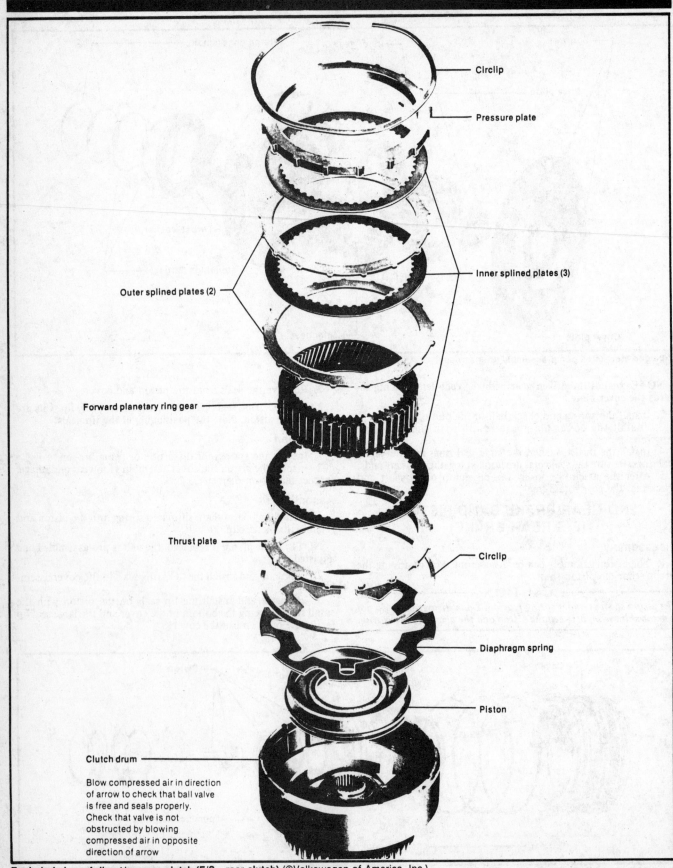

Circlip

Pressure plate

Inner splined plates (3)

Outer splined plates (2)

Forward planetary ring gear

Thrust plate

Circlip

Diaphragm spring

Piston

Clutch drum

Blow compressed air in direction
of arrow to check that ball valve
is free and seals properly.
Check that valve is not
obstructed by blowing
compressed air in opposite
direction of arrow

Exploded view of direct/reverse clutch (F/S - rear clutch) (©Volkswagen of America, Inc.)

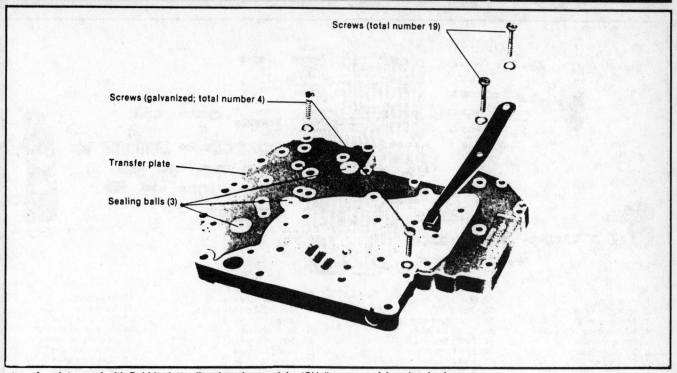

Screws (total number 19)

Screws (galvanized; total number 4)

Transfer plate

Sealing balls (3)

**transfer plate used with Rabbit, Jetta diesel engine models** (©Volkswagen of America, Inc.)

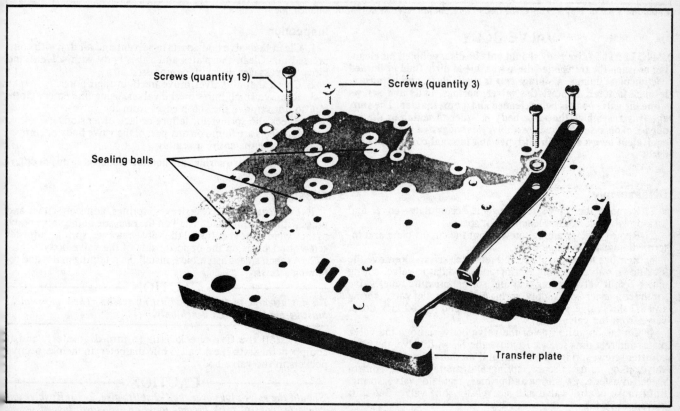

Screws (quantity 19)

Screws (quantity 3)

Sealing balls

Transfer plate

**separation plate and transfer plate. Note location of three sealing balls in transfer plate**
(©Volkswagen of America, Inc.)

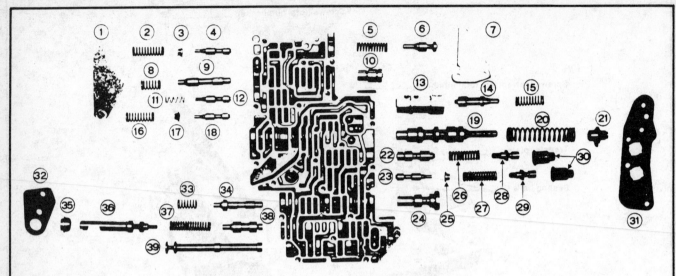

**Exploded view of Fiat Strada valve body components** (©Volkswagen of America, Inc.)

1. Valve plate
2. Spring for valve
3. Seat for spring
4. 3-2 kick-down shift valve
5. Spring for valve
6. 3-2 shift valve
7. Valve plate
8. Spring for valve
9. 2-3 shift control valve
10. 2-3 shift valve
11. Spring for valve

12. Main relief valve
13. Sleeve
14. Front brake control valve
15. Spring for valve
16. Spring for valve
17. Seat for spring
18. Pressure relief valve for converter supply
19. Primary regulator valve
20. Spring for valve
21. Adjuster screw for valve

22. Main control valve
23. Modulated pressure relief valve
24. 1-2 shift valve
25. Seat for spring
26. Spring for valve
27. Spring for valve
28. Adjuster screw for valve
29. Adjuster screw for valve
30. Plugs for adjuster screws

31. Valve plate
32. Valve plate
33. Spring for valve
34. 1-2 shift control valve
35. Bushing for valve
36. Kick-down valve
37. Spring for valve
38. Modulator valve
39. Selector valve

## VALVE BODY

NOTE: The valve body should only be disassembled for cleaning or when the transaxle failure was due to dirty fluid or burned friction plate linings. A storage tray is available from the transaxle manufacturer, to store the valves, springs, balls and screws while the valve body is being cleaned and/or overhauled. The storage tray resembles the valve body in order to mantian the sequence of disassembly and assembly. It is suggested the tray or its equivalent be used. Different types and internal components are used.

### Disassembly

1. Remove the screws retaining the accumulator cover and kick-down valve control lever detent spring.
2. Remove the retaining screws from the circuit plate and intermediate plate to valve body.
3. Remove the valve plates and retaining screws. Remove the kick-down valve, bushing, spring and modulator valve, spring and 1-2 shift valve, spring seat and spring, pressure relief valve for the converter fluid supply, spring and main relief valve, spring and 2-3 shift valve, spring and spring seat and the 3-2 kick-down valve from the valve body.
4. On the opposite side of the valve body, remove the valve plates and retaining screws. Remove the 1-2 shift valve, the plug, adjuster screw, spring, spring seat and modulated pressure relief valve, plug, adjuster screw, spring and main pressure control valve, adjuster screw, spring and primary regulator valve, spring, front brake control valve and sleeve, 2-3 shift valve, 3-2 shift valve and spring.
5. Remove the five (6 mm diameter) check balls, and if equipped, the sixth ball, (3 mm diameter). Mark the locations of each ball for reference during the assembly

### Inspection

1. Clean the valve body parts in solvent and air dry with compressed air. Clean the plates and valve body with solvent and blow the passages dry with compressed air.
2. Check that all valves move freely in their bores.
3. Remove small burrs on the valves, using fine emery cloth, but do not remove the sharp edges from the valves.
4. Check the springs for failure or lack of tension.
5. If defects are found on any part of the valve body or components, replace the entire assembly.

NOTE: The valve springs are not interchangeable due to different tension values.

### Assembly

1. Lubricate the valves, sleeves, springs, adjuster screws and plugs with A/T fluid and install on the one side of the valve body, as they were removed. Install the valves, sleeves, springs, adjuster screws and plugs on the opposite side of the valve body.
2. As each side is assembled, install the retaining plates and retaining screws.

— CAUTION —

*Do not attempt to turn the adjusting screws. Their adjustment must be made on a test bench only.*

3. Install the five check balls (6 mm diameter), and if equipped, the sixth check ball (3 mm diameter) in their respective pockets in the valve body.

— CAUTION —

*Should the valve plugs over the 1-2 shift valve, 2-3 shift valve and converter control valve become loose or dislodged, loss of second gear or third gear and the lack of proper converter charging can occur.*

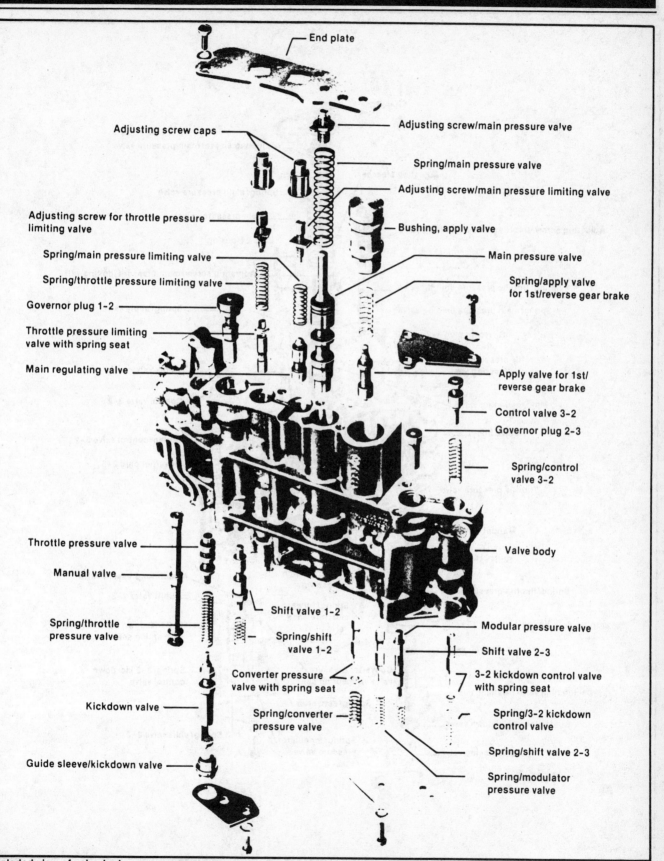

- End plate
- Adjusting screw caps
- Adjusting screw/main pressure valve
- Spring/main pressure valve
- Adjusting screw/main pressure limiting valve
- Adjusting screw for throttle pressure limiting valve
- Bushing, apply valve
- Spring/main pressure limiting valve
- Main pressure valve
- Spring/throttle pressure limiting valve
- Spring/apply valve for 1st/reverse gear brake
- Governor plug 1-2
- Throttle pressure limiting valve with spring seat
- Main regulating valve
- Apply valve for 1st/reverse gear brake
- Control valve 3-2
- Governor plug 2-3
- Spring/control valve 3-2
- Valve body
- Throttle pressure valve
- Manual valve
- Spring/throttle pressure valve
- Shift valve 1-2
- Modular pressure valve
- Spring/shift valve 1-2
- Shift valve 2-3
- Converter pressure valve with spring seat
- 3-2 kickdown control valve with spring seat
- Kickdown valve
- Spring/converter pressure valve
- Spring/3-2 kickdown control valve
- Spring/shift valve 2-3
- Guide sleeve/kickdown valve
- Spring/modulator pressure valve

**Exploded view of valve body components of one type of Audi/VW transaxle models (©Volkswagen of America, Inc.)**

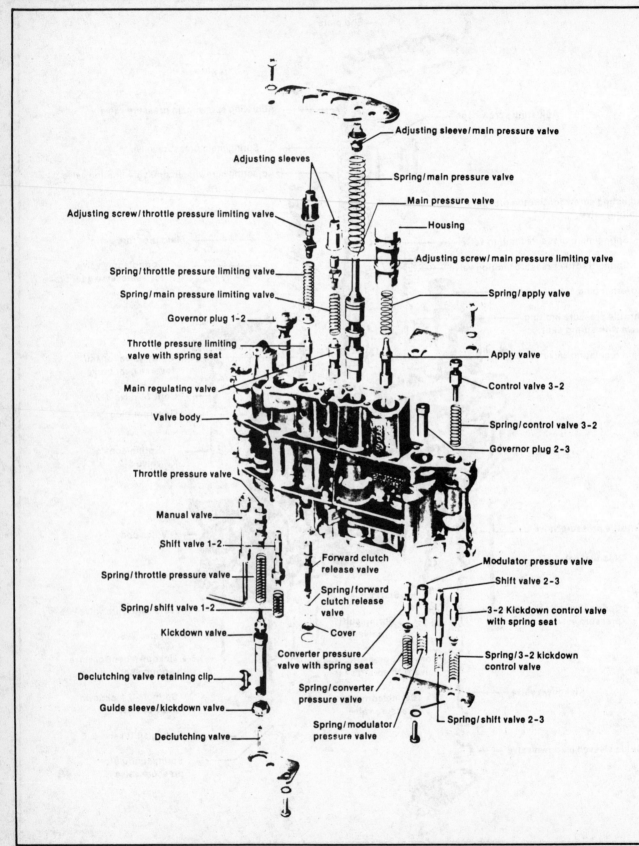

Exploded view of "E" mode valve body used with Rabbit, Jetta diesel engine models (©Volkswagen of America, Inc.)

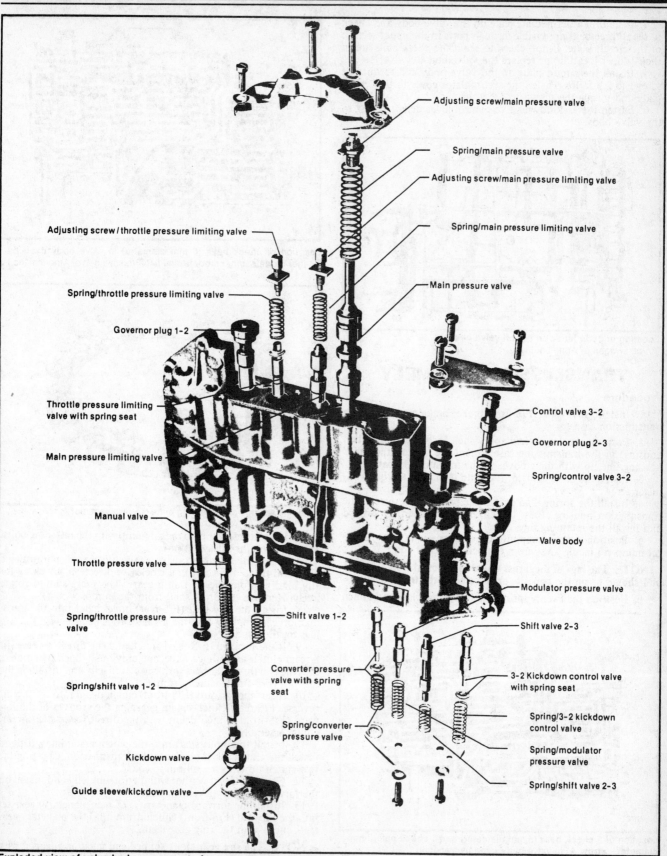

Adjusting screw/main pressure valve

Spring/main pressure valve

Adjusting screw/main pressure limiting valve

Spring/main pressure limiting valve

Adjusting screw / throttle pressure limiting valve

Spring/throttle pressure limiting valve

Main pressure valve

Governor plug 1-2

Throttle pressure limiting valve with spring seat

Control valve 3-2

Governor plug 2-3

Main pressure limiting valve

Spring/control valve 3-2

Manual valve

Valve body

Throttle pressure valve

Modulator pressure valve

Spring/throttle pressure valve

Shift valve 1-2

Shift valve 2-3

Spring/shift valve 1-2

Converter pressure valve with spring seat

3-2 Kickdown control valve with spring seat

Spring/converter pressure valve

Spring/3-2 kickdown control valve

Spring/modulator pressure valve

Kickdown valve

Guide sleeve/kickdown valve

Spring/shift valve 2-3

**Exploded view of valve body components for second type of Audi/VW transaxle models** (©Volkswagen of America, Inc.)

4. Install the intermediate plate on the valve body and check to see if three balls are visible through ports in the upper section of the circuit plate. If not, check to see if the check balls are in their proper location, or replace the valve body.

5. Install the circuit plate on the valve body and torque the screws to 2.9 ft. lbs. Fasten the accumulator cover to the circuit plate and torque the screws to 2.2 ft. lbs.

6. Fasten the kick-down valve control lever detent spring to the valve body.

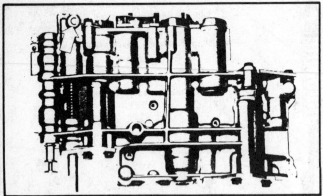

Location of code letter on typical valve body (©Volkswagen of America, Inc.)

## TRANSMISSION ASSEMBLY

### Procedure

1. Install 1st/reverse (F/S-front brake) brake piston into the transmission case.

2. Position the 1st/reverse apply shell (F/S-front brake bell housing) in the transmission case so that the lugs on the shell/housing line up with the grooves in the transmission case.

3. Install the band actuator rod until it touches the band adjuster screw.

4. Install the spring, 2nd gear brake piston and cover in the transmission housing. Press the cover/piston assembly inward and install the retaining ring.

5. Position the oil pump into the transmission case with the oil pump rib facing away from the band actuator rod.

**NOTE: The lugs of the thrust washer straddle the oil pump rib and should be on the opposite or top side of the transmission.**

6. Position the twenty springs on the spring plate and attach

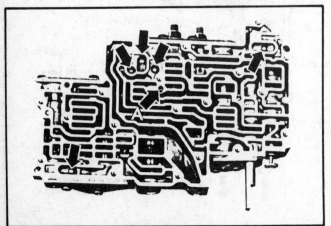

Location of 5 check balls (6 mm diameter) and 1 check ball (3 mm diameter - arrow A) in valve body used by Vanagon (©Volkswagen of America, Inc.)

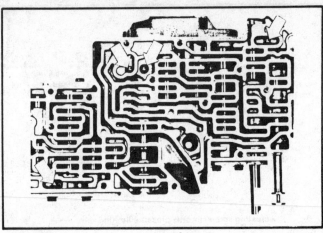

Location of check balls (6 mm diameter) in valve body used by Dasher models, other models similar (©Volkswagen of America, Inc.)

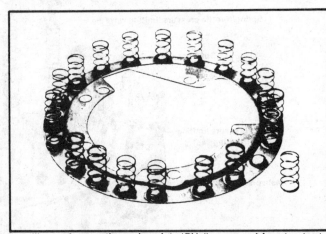

Installing springs on the spring plate (©Volkswagen of America, Inc.)

the spring plate assembly to the oil pump with the retaining bolts. Torque to 61 *inch* lbs. (7 N•m).

7. Insert the oil pump drive shaft into the oil pump drive plate and rotate the shaft in a clockwise direction, checking for any binding from the oil pump gears. The gears should rotate freely. Remove the drive shaft from the pump.

8. Install the 2nd gear (F/S-rear) brake band into the transmission case making sure the actuator rods engage with the two lugs on the band.

9. If the forward (F/S-rear) clutch and the direct/reverse (F/S-rear) clutch assemblies have not previously been assembled, coat the two thrust washers with petroleum jelly and install on the forward (F/S-front) clutch drum.

10. Install the forward (F/S-front) clutch drum into the direct/reverse (F/S-rear) clutch drum, engaging the grooves of the forward (F/S-front) clutch drum with the direct/reverse (F/S-rear) clutch assembly.

11. Install the input shaft into the clutch assemblies, lift and install the clutch assemblies into the transmission, engaging the two clutch units to the oil pump collar.

12. Coat the thrust washer with petroleum jelly and install on the forward (F/S-front) clutch hub.

13. Install the forward planetary (F/S-rear planetary) gear set into the forward (F/S-front) clutch drum until the planetary gear teeth mesh with the ring gear teeth.

**NOTE: The sun gear short splined end must be engaged with the planetary gear teeth when the planetary gear set is installed.**

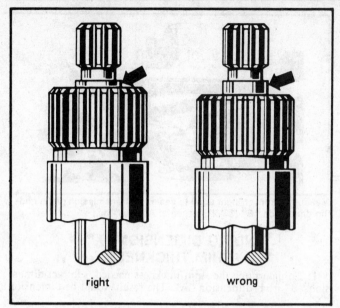

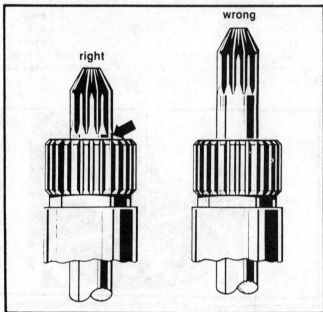

**Checking pump shaft for full engagement, both old style (A), and new style (B)** (©Volkswagen of America, Inc.)

14. Install the drive shell/housing, along with the thrust washer, on the sun gear.

15. Install the reverse-planetary gear set (F/S-front brake-front planet hub) into the transmission case until the sun gear meshes with the planet gear teeth. Install the thrust washer, coated with petroleum jelly, on the planet carrier hub.

16. Install the 1st/reverse (F/S-front) brake plates, starting with the wavy spring washer (F/S-front brake corrugated plate), a steel plate, followed by a lined plate. Alternate the clutch plates, steel to lined, until all are installed.

17. Coat the thrust washer with petroleum jelly and install. Install the one-way clutch (F/S-free wheel) into the transmission case. Rotate the reverse planetary gear set (F/S-front brake-front planet hub) in a clockwise direction while pressing the one-way clutch (F/S-free wheel) into operating position.

NOTE: To verify the correct operation of the one-way clutch (F/S-free wheel), position the transmission in the upright position and while holding the one-way clutch (F/S-free wheel) outer race stationary, the reverse planetary gear set (F/S-front brake-front planet hub) should rotate freely in a clockwise direction and lock-up in a counterclockwise direction.

18. Install the one-way clutch (F/S-free wheel) outer race locating pin in the housing of the transmission case.

19. An indicator of correct assembly of the transmission components, is the installation of the outer race retaining snap ring without interference from the assembly.

NOTE: The snap ring opening must be opposite the locating pin.

20. Position the transmission horizontally. Loosen the band adjusting lock nut and tighten the adjusting screw to 87 *inch* lbs. (10 N•m). Loosen and retighten the adjusting screw to 43 *inch* lbs. (5 N•m). Loosen the adjusting screw exactly 2½ turns and tighten the lock nut.

21. Install the reverse planetary ring gear/governor drive gear (F/S-parking plate/front ring gear/governor drive gear) on the reverse planetary gear set (F/S-front brake-front planet hub).

22. Install the flange with the two gaskets. Install the retaining cap screws.

23. Install the valve body and accumulator piston and spring into its bore in the transmisssion case. Install the valve body to the transmission housing, connecting the manual valve and the kick-down valve. Tighten all bolts diagonally and to a torque of 35 *inch* lbs. (4 N•m).

24. Install the gasket, oil strainer, cover and attach with the retaining screws. Torque to 26 *inch* lbs. (3 N•m).

25. Using a new gasket, install the oil pan and install the retaining bolts. Torque to 14 ft. lbs. (20 N•m).

## Assembly of Transmission and Final Drive

End play between the transmission and final drive must be measured and adjusted as required to limit the end play movement of the reverse planetary ring gear (F/S-front brake-front planet hub), before the two units are assembled.

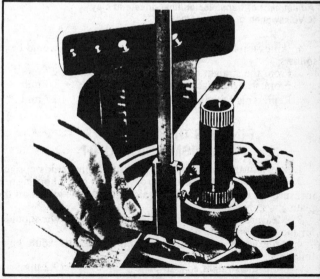

**Measuring from straight edge to final drive housing, finding dimension "A"** (©Volkswagen of America, Inc.)

## FINDING DIMENSION "A"— FINAL DRIVE UNIT

1. Have the final drive unit in an upright position with the seal, sealing ring and thrust washer removed.
2. Using a straight edge laid across the face of the final drive unit, measure the distance from the top face of the straight edge to the top of the oil sleeve bushing, with a depth measuring tool. Record the reading.
3. Measure the distance from the straight edge to the face of the final drive housing and record the measurement.

NOTE: This measurement is the thickness of the straight edge tool.

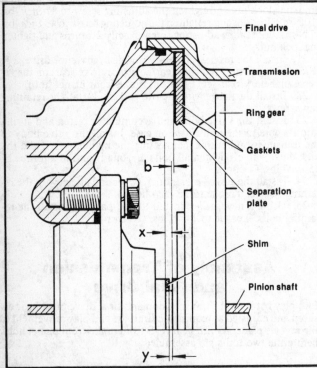

Adjustment of transmission/final drive end play
(©Volkswagen of America, Inc.)

4. An example of the measurements and results would be as follows;

| | |
|---|---|
| From the straight edge to oil sleeve bushing | 18.7 mm |
| From straight edge to final drive surface | −8.0 mm |
| Represents Dimension "A" | 10.7 mm |

## FINDING DIMENSION "B"— TRANSMISSION UNIT

1. Position the transmission with its attaching studs upright.
2. Lay the straight edge tool across the face of the housing and measure the distance from the straight edge to the gasket on the plate.
3. Measure the distance from the straight edge to the shoulder for the shim on the plate.
4. An example of the measurements and results would be as follows;

| | |
|---|---|
| From the straight edge to plate | 19.2 mm |
| From the straight edge to shoulder | −10.0 mm |
| Represents dimension "B" | 9.2 mm |

Measuring from straight edge to gasket on transmission plate, finding dimension "B" (©Volkswagen of America, Inc.)

## FINDING DIMENSION "X"— SHIM THICKNESS

1. To determine the shim thickness needed, subtract dimension "B" from dimension "A". The result would be dimension "X".
2. An example of finding dimension "X" would be as follows;

| | | |
|---|---|---|
| Dimension "A" | | 10.7 mm |
| Dimension "B" | (Subtract) | −9.2 mm |
| Dimension "X" | | 1.5 mm |

3. Shims are available in two thicknesses, 0.4 and 1.2 mm.
4. From the following chart, determine the shim or shim combination and to be used to correct dimension "X."

Measuring from straight edge to shoulder for shims, finding dimension "B" (©Volkswagen of America, Inc.)

Measuring from straight edge to pinion bearing spacer on pinion shaft, finding dimension "A" (©Volkswagen of America, Inc.)

## ALLOWABLE END PLAY—DIMENSION "Y"

An allowable end play clearance, described as dimension "Y", is constant and should be between 0.23 to 0.84 mm or 0.009 to 0.033 inch. This measurement must be included in the stacking of the proposed thrust washer(s), as determined in the preceding steps. An example of the inclusion of the end play clearance is as follows;

1. As the previous examples explained how to find dimensions "A" and "B", resulting in dimension "X", the theoretical use of thrust washers to this dimension would be the use of two 0.4 mm washers, for a total of 0.8 mm. Using the dimension "X" of 1.5 mm and subtracting 0.8 mm from it, the result is 0.7 mm which falls within the 0.23 to 0.84 mm allowable end play.

| Dimension "X" | 1.5 mm |
|---|---|
| 2 x 0.4 mm shim | − 0.8 mm |
| Dimension "Y" | 0.7 mm |

### JOINING OF UNITS

1. Install the oil seal, thrust washer and turbine shaft with "O" ring seals.
2. Install final drive outer "O" ring seal and lubricate.
3. Have the transmission in an upright position and carefully set the final drive unit onto the transmission mating surface and studs. Install the retaining nuts and torque to 22 ft. lbs. (30 N•m).
4. Place the assembled transaxle horizontal and install the oil pump shaft. Be sure the shaft engages the oil pump drive plate correctly.
5. Install the converter assembly and retain it with a holding bar.

# **S**PECIFICATIONS

## CAPACITIES

| Dry fill | 6.4 US Quarts (6 Liters) |
|---|---|
| Refill | 3.2 US Quarts (3 Liters) |

## BAND ADJUSTMENT

1st torque—87 in. lbs. and release

2nd torque—43 in. lbs.

Loosen adjuster screw exactly 2½ turn

Tighten adjusting screw nut 14 ft. lbs. (18 N•m)

## PRESSURE TEST SPECIFICATIONS

| Selector lever position | Accelerator pedal position | Main pressure psi | Test conditions |
|---|---|---|---|
| D | idle speed* | 41-42①⑤ | vehicle stationary |
| | full throttle | 83-84②⑥ | speed higher than 40 km/h (25 mph). ④ |
| R | idle speed | 129-138③⑦ | vehicle stationary |

①Dasher—41 to 43 psi
　Fiat Strada—55.5 to 57 psi
②Dasher—83 to 85 psi
　Fiat Strada—89.6 to 91 psi
　Audi 5000—80 to 82 psi
③Dasher/Audi 5000—108 to 117 psi
　Rabbit/Scirocco/Jetta—109 to 117 psi
　(Model EQ to S/N 16079—100 to 109 psi)
　Fiat Strada—104 to 105.3 psi
④For safety reasons, the manufacturer recommends the test be made on a dynamometer.
⑤"E" mode transaxle—42-44 psi
⑥"E" mode transaxle—85-86 psi
⑦"E" mode transaxle—131-145 psi

## STALL SPEED RPM SPECIFICATIONS

| Model | RPM |
|---|---|
| Audi 5000 | 2400 to 2650 |
| Audi 4000 | 2450 to 2700 |
| Dasher | 1950 to 2550 |
| Rabbit, Scirocco, Jetta | |
| 1.5 Liter | 2250 to 2500 |
| 1.6 Liter | 2100 to 2350 |
| 1.7 Liter | 2200 to 2500 |
| W/E Mode Transaxle | 2555 to 2805 |
| Fiat Strada | 2260 |

## END PLAY SHIM CHART

| Measured End Play mm (in.) | Number and Size of Shims |
|---|---|
| 0.23-0.84 (.009-.033) | No shim |
| 0.85-1.24 (.034-.049) | One 0.4mm shim |
| 1.25-1.64 (.050-.065) | Two 0.4mm shims |
| 1.65-2.04 (.066-.081) | One 1.2mm shim |
| 2.05-2.44 (.082-.097) | One 0.4mm and one 1.2mm shim |
| 2.45-2.84 (.098-.113) | Two 0.4mm and one 1.2mm shim |
| 2.85-3.24 (.114-.129) | Two 1.2mm shims |
| 3.25-3.64 (.130-.145) | One 0.4mm and two 1.2mm shims |
| 3.65-3.88 (.146-.155) | Two 0.4mm and two 1.2mm shims |

NOTE: Shims are available in two sizes: 0.4mm, part no. 010 323 345 A and 1.2mm, part no. 010 323 346 A

SPECIAL TOOLS

ASSORTED DRIVERS

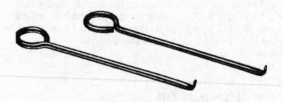

HOOKS FOR REMOVING ONE-WAY CLUTCH

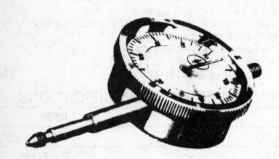

DIAL INDICATOR

GEAR PULLER

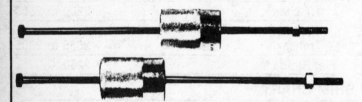

SLIDE HAMMERS

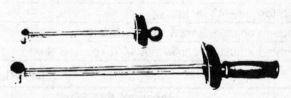

TORQUE WRENCHES

CROSS POINT BLADE SOCKET

CROSS POINT BLADE

PULLER FOR REAR CLUTCH DRUM HUB BUSHING

TORQUE SCREWDRIVER

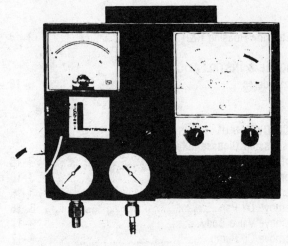

ROAD PERFORMANCE TESTER

SNAP RING PLIERS

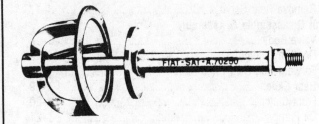

CLUTCH SPRING COMPRESSOR

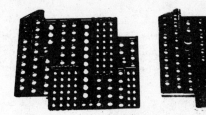

VALVE AND SPRING WASHING CONTAINER

## TORQUE SPECIFICATIONS

| | |
|---|---|
| Drive shaft/flange bolts | 33 ft. lbs. (45 N•m) |
| Torque converter bolts | 22 ft. lbs. (30 N•m) |
| Transaxle/engine bolts | 40 ft. lbs. (55 N•m) |
| Ball joint/control arm | 48 ft. lbs. (65 N•m) |
| Mount to body | 30 ft. lbs. (40 N•m) |
| Mount to transaxle | 40 ft. lbs. (55 N•m) |
| Oil Pan | 14 ft. lbs. (18 N•m) |
| Valve Body | 35 In. lbs. (4 N•m) |

# INDEX

# BORG WARNER MODEL66

## TRANSMISSION AND CONVERTER IDENTIFICATION

### Transmission

The Borg Warner Model 66 automatic transmission is identified by a yellow name plate which will have Model 66 and the number "6606" stamped on the name plate, this automatic transmission is used in all XJ6 4.2 models. All automatic transmissions used in the XJ6 3.4 model will have a golden brown name plate which will have Model 66 and the number "6067" stamped on the name plate.

### Converter

The torque converter is a welded unit and cannot be disassembled for service by the average repair shop. New and rebuilt units are available.

### Transmission Metric Fasteners

The metric fastener dimensions are very close to the dimensions of the familiar inch system fasteners, and for this reason, replacement fasteners must have the same measurement and strength as those removed.

Do not attempt to interchange metric fasteners for inch system fasteners. Mismatched or incorrect fasteners can result in damage to the transmission unit through malfunctions, breakage or possible personal injury.

Care should be taken to reuse the fasteners in the same locations as removed.

### Fluid Capacities

The Jaguar XJ6 4.2 has an automatic transmission fluid capacity of 8.7 quarts. The Jaguar XJ6 3.4 has a fluid capacity of 7.6 quarts. These figures include the torque converter, if the converter has not been drained use between 2.5 and 3.0 quarts of automatic transmission fluid. Always bring the transmission up to operating temperature and recheck the fluid level. Never overfill the transmission.

## APPLICATIONS

### BORG WARNER MODEL 66 APPLICATION CHART

| Type | Model | Transmission Identification |
|------|-------|------------------------------|
| Jaguar | XJ6 4.2 | 6066 |
| | XJ6 3.4 | 6067 |
| Rover | 3500 Series | —— |

## GENERAL DESCRIPTION

The Borg Warner Model 66 automatic transmission is a three speed unit consisting of a planetary gear set, hydraulic control system, oil pump, clutches and bands and a torque converter.

The planetary gear set provides three forward speeds and reverse. It consists of two sun gears, two sets of pinions, a pinion (planet) carrier and a ring gear. There are six selector lever positions (P,R,N,D,2, and 1) with provision for manually holding the low and 2nd gears and for kickdown shifts.

The hydraulic control system includes the governor, throttle cable, manual linkage and the valve body all affecting the application or release of the clutches and bands. Governor pressure varies in direct relation to vehicle speed. The throttle cable controls throttle pressure in relation to engine speed. The valve body controls the application of the bands and clutches to hold the planetary gear set.

The oil pump is located directly behind the torque converter and is mechanically connected to engine output. This means that pressure is always supplied while the engine is running.

Mechanical torque multiplication is increased hydraulically by the torque converter. The converter provides a continuous range of torque multiplication from 1:1 to 2.3:1

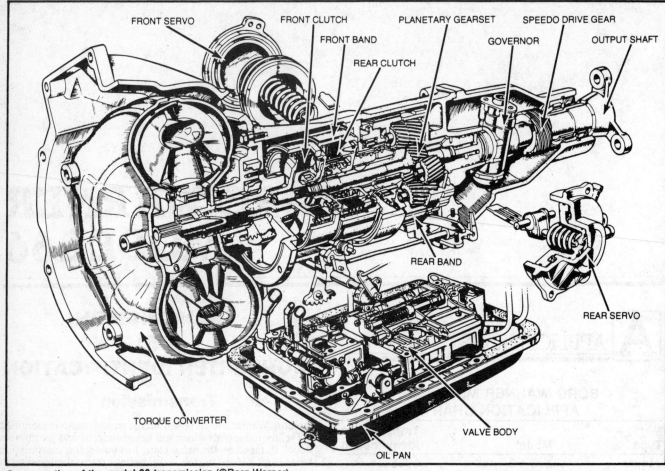

**Cross section of the model 66 transmission (©Borg Warner)**

## Checking Fluid Level

The automatic transmission, when at normal operating temeprature, is designed to operate with its fluid level between the MIN and MAX mark on the transmission dipstick.

1. With the vehicle on a level surface, foot brakes applied and the engine running at idle, move the selector lever through each range. Allow time in each range for the transmission to engage. Return the lever to Park.

2. With the engine still running remove the dipstick, wipe it clean and replace it.

3. Once again remove the dipstick and note the reading on the HOT side of the stick. Add the proper amount of transmission fluid to bring the fluid level to the MAX mark on the dipstick.

4. The difference between the MAX and MIN marks on the dipstick represent approximately 1 quart of automatic transmission fluid.

# Ⓜ MODIFICATIONS

## Transmission Oil Pump Assembly

A groove has been added to the oil pump/converter bush to improve lubrication of the bush. This groove stops short of the front edge of the bush to prevent the oil seal from being swamped. A tin/aluminum pump drive gear bush is also being used. The new stator support will have an increased diameter bush to accommodate the increased diameter input shaft. A large pump suction tube is being used to ensure that the end of the tube is immersed in transmission fluid at all times.

## Input Shaft and Front Clutch Assembly

An input shaft of larger diameter is being used on all later Borg Warner model 66 automatic transmissions.

## Rear Clutch and Front Drum Assembly

To improve the lubrication path to the rear clutch and the front band the following changes were made to the rear clutch and front drum assembly:

1. The rear clutch piston face (clutch plate side) now has four slots at right angles to one another to improve the oil flow from the inside diameter of the clutch pack.

2. The four wide grooves on the inside diameter of the front drum (steel clutch late splines area) have been deepened to enable more oil flow around the plates.

3. Between the outside and inside diameter of the front drum, so that they line up with the four deepened grooves, four holes have been drilled to enable an oil feed to the front band to be maintained.

4. The rearmost lubrication groove between the three sealing ring grooves of the front drum has also been deepened and the

holes size increased in order to improve the oil flow.

5. The lubrication feed hole in the reverse sun gear has been increased in diameter

## One-Way Clutch Assembly

An upgraded first gear one-way clutch assembly has been introduced which has 30 sprags instead of the 24 sprags on earlier assemblies. The center support of the transmission now has increased diameter rear clutch and lubrication drillings.

## Carrier Assembly

An improved lubrication oil flow has been achieved by introducing a wider bush into the carrier cover which has opposing helical oil grooves. Non-crowned shaved short pinions have also been introduced. These pinions have no identification groove in order to improve their durability.

## Output Shaft Lubrication Hole

The lubrication hole in the output shaft has been increased in diameter to allow a better flow of automatic transmission fluid.

## Maincase and Servos

The front clutch and governor feed hole in the rear of the maincase has been increased 5.0 mm. The rear servo piston and cover have been strengthened for increased service life.

## Transmission Oil Pan

A new deeper oil pan is now being used in order to ensure that the oil pump suction pipe is at all times below the fluid level. An oil filter spacer is now being used on the transmission because of the deep oil pan.

## Transmission Cooler and Line Cleaning

It is important that the cooler lines and the cooler are thoroughly flushed to remove any contaminated automatic transmission fluid before being completely re-connected to the transmission. If this precaution is not taken the transmission overhaul could be completely wasted. A small amount of thrust washer debris or burnt friction material will very rapidly spread throughout a transmission and torque converter.

## Manual Level Cross Shaft Greasing

It is advisable to grease the manual valve lever cross shaft when installing the front servo cover. This is done to eliminate the possibility of the cross shaft corroding in the bore of the servo cover due to the ingress of salt and other foreign matter. It is essential that lithium based grease BB NO. 3 be used, as this type of grease is compatible with the rubber O-ring. Also it is important that the following procedure be used to apply the grease, in order to reduce the possibility of grease being forced past the O-ring and into the transmission.

1. Remove the front servo cover. After cleaning the cross shaft bore in the servo cover apply a small amount of grease into the cross shaft bore hole of the front servo cover.

2. Wipe off any excess grease from the front servo cover gasket face, it is important that this face be clean.

3. Install the gasket and replace the cover. Torque the front servo cover bolts 13 to 18 ft. lbs.

4. Remove any excess grease on the protruding end of the cross shaft.

## Dimpled Thrust Washers in Torque Converter Assembly

In order to improve durability and stop the spinning of the bearing thrust race, all in service 11 inch torque converters are now using a dimpled bearing thrust race. The following is a list of improved torque converters incorporating this design change together with the old style torque converter that it replaces.

## Torque Converter Modification

The torque converter has an increased spline size to accommodate the larger input shaft. The stator one-way clutch inner race has a revised profile adding to its increase in hardness. A Torrington race has been introduced into the impeller side of the stator, the impeller blades also have a rib formed in them giving them added strength. Six impeller blades are welded in two equally spaced places at the impeller shell to strengthen the assembly. The blower ring has been deleted and the converter mounting bosses are welded to the front cover.

Should this unit require repair, new and rebuilt units are available from parts supplier outlets.

## Pressure Take Off Plug Improvement

In order to aid in the removal and installation of the pressure take off plug a new hexagon headed plug has been introduced which will replace the hexagon allen key head plug that is currently being used. The new plug can be installed in service if required in place of the old plug. When installing the new plug be sure that the torque is 6 to 8 ft. lbs. when the transmission is cold.

## Kickdown 3-2 Flare Up Model 66 4.2 Series

Some model 66 automatic transmissions installed in the 4.2 series have a kickdown 3-2 flare up condition occurring at about 50 miles per hour. To correct this problem the front band adjustment must be checked and set to the correct setting. This adjustment is very important as misadjustment can cause this kickdown 3-2 problem. The procedure is as follows.

1. Loosen the locknut.

2. Adjust the square ended adjusting screw to 5 foot pounds.

3. Back off the adjusting screw ⅝ ths. of a turn.

4. Retighten the locknut to 35 ft. lbs. This will ensure that the adjusting screw will not turn.

If correct adjustment of the front band does not cure the problem, a modification in the form of a change to the servo orifice control valve spring should be done. The valve body assembly should be installed with a new spring Part Number 35-296 in place of the old spring Part Number 04-66-156-018F. The difference being that the new spring is 27.5 mm long and the old spring is 32.0 mm long.

## REVISED TORQUE CONVERTER ASSEMBLIES

| Old Style Torque Converter | Improved Torque Converter | Automatic Transmission |
| --- | --- | --- |
| 0466-511-049X (Ident. 6049) | 0466-511-061C (Ident. 6061) | Model 66 4.2 Series |
| 0466-511-055M (Ident. 6055) | 0466-511-067H (Ident. 6067) | Model 66 3.4 Series |

## Automatic Transmission Fluid

Model 66 automatic transmissions are filled at the factory with type "G" automatic transmission fluid. The type "G" automatic transmission fluid is an improvement to the type "F" automatic tranmsmission fluid in that it has the capability of reducing oxidation at elevated temperatures. When transmissions are filled with type "G" automatic transmission fluid type "F" automatic transmission fluid can be used for topping off. The more type "F" automatic transmission fluid is used in the system, the more temperature will be reduced.

 TROUBLE DIAGNOSIS

### CLUTCH AND BAND APPLICATION CHART
#### Borg Warner Model 66

| | Front Clutch | Rear Clutch | Front Band | Rear Band | One-Way Clutch |
|---|---|---|---|---|---|
| Drive 1st gear | Applied | — | — | — | Holding |
| Drive 2nd gear | Applied | — | Applied | — | — |
| Drive 3rd gear | Applied | Applied | — | — | — |
| 1—Low gear | Applied | — | — | Applied | — |
| 2—1st gear | Applied | — | — | — | Holding |
| 2—2nd gear | Applied | — | Applied | — | — |
| Reverse gear | — | Applied | — | Applied | — |

NOTE: Rear band is released in "N", but applied in "P" for constructional reasons only.

### CHILTON'S THREE "C's" TRANSMISSION DIAGNOSIS CHART
#### Borg Warner Model 66

| Condition | Cause | Correction |
|---|---|---|
| No starter action in "P" or "N"; Starter motor action in all other selector lever positions; Back-up lights inoperative. | a) Neutral safety switch out of adjustment or defective | a) Replace or adjust switch as needed |
| Excessive thump into "D", "1" or "R" | a) Engine idle too high<br>b) Throttle cable out of adjustment<br>c) Valves sticking in control valve body | a) Adjust idle speed<br>b) Adjust or replace throttle cable<br>c) Clean control valve body or replace it necessary |
| Vehicle moves with selector lever in "N" | a) Manual linkage out of adjustment<br>b) Fault in front clutch support housing<br>c) Fault in stator support shaft bearing<br>d) Fault in forward sun gear shaft seals | a) Adjust manual linkage<br>b) Replace front clutch support housing<br>c) Replace stator support shaft bearing<br>d) Replace forward sun gear shaft seals |
| Stall speed above specification and transmission grabs in selector lever position "1" and "R" | a) Throttle cable out of adjustment<br>b) Filter clogged<br>c) Valve body sticking<br>d) Oil pump defect | a) Adjust or replace throttle cable<br>b) Replace fluid and filter<br>c) Clean valve body and replace fluid and filter<br>d) Repair or replace oil pump |

## CHILTON'S THREE "C's" TRANSMISSION DIAGNOSIS CHART
### Borg Warner Model 66

| Condition | Cause | Correction |
|---|---|---|
| Grabs in position "1" only | a) Front clutch<br>b) Stator support shaft bearing | a) Repair or replace front clutch<br>b) Replace stator support shaft bearing |
| Grabs in position "R" only | a) Rear band out of adjustment<br>b) Rear servo gasket<br>c) Rear clutch<br>d) Defect in rear brake band | a) Adjust rear band<br>b) Replace rear servo gasket<br>c) Repair or replace rear clutch<br>d) Replace rear brake band |
| Stall speed below 1150 rpm | a) Torque converter bad | a) Replace torque converter |
| Heavy engagement of all selector lever positions except park | a) Manual linkage out of adjustment | a) Adjust manual linkage |
| Parking pawl does not hold vehicle | a) Manual linkage out of adjustment<br>b) Parking lock linkage, pawl or gear faulty | a) Adjust manual linkage<br>b) Replace as needed |
| No drive in "D", "2", "1" or "R" | a) Fluid level low<br>b) Manual linkage out of adjustment<br>c) Throttle cable out of adjustment | a) Adjust fluid to proper level<br>b) Adjust manual linkage<br>c) Adjust throttle cable |
| No drive in selector position "D", "2" or "1" | a) Output shaft oil seals<br>b) Governor pressure tube loose<br>c) Front clutch faulty<br>d) Stator support shaft bearing faulty<br>e) Sun gear shaft seals | a) Replace oil seals<br>b) Repair or replace tube<br>c) Replace front clutch<br>d) Replace stator support shaft bearing<br>e) Replace sun gear shaft seals |
| No drive in "D" 1st gear | a) One-way clutch faulty | a) Replace one-way clutch |
| No drive in "D" 1st gear but moves in "1" | a) One-way clutch installed backwards | a) Install one-way clutch properly |
| No 2nd gear in position "D" or "2" | a) Front band out of adjustment<br>b) Front servo gasket<br>c) Front servo tubes loose<br>d) Valve body sticking | a) Adjust front band<br>b) Replace front servo gasket<br>c) Tighten or replace tubes<br>d) Clean or replace valve body |
| No 3rd gear in position "D", "R" normal | a) Valve body sticking<br>b) Governor sticking | a) Clean or replace valve body<br>b) Clean or replace governor |
| Slips in "D" 2nd gear | a) Front band out of adjustment | a) Adjust front band |

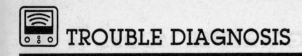 

### CHILTON'S THREE "C's" TRANSMISSION DIAGNOSIS CHART
#### Borg Warner Model 66

| Condition | Cause | Correction |
|---|---|---|
| Slips in "D" of "1" 1st gear and "R" | a) Rear band out of adjustment | a) Adjust rear band |
| No engine braking in "1" and no movement in "R" | a) Rear band worn out or not adjusted | a) Adjust or replace rear band |
|  | b) Rear servo gasket faulty | b) Replace rear servo gasket |
|  | c) Rear servo pressure tubes loose | c) Repair or replace tubes |
| Faulty or sticky kickdown; faulty part-throttle shifts points | a) Throttle cable out of adjustment | a) Adjust throttle cable |
|  | b) Filter clogged | b) Replace fluid and filter |
|  | c) Oil pump and/or O-ring faulty | c) Repair and/or replace pump or O-ring |
|  | d) Valves sticking | d) Clean or replace valve body |
|  | e) Governor sticking | e) Clean or replace governor |
|  | f) Output shaft oil seals faulty | f) Replace oil seals |
|  | g) Governor pressure tube leaks | g) Repair or replace tube |
| Improper or hesitant kickdown and improper part throttle shift points | a) Throttle cable out of adjustment | a) Adjust throttle cable |
|  | b) Valves sticking | b) Clean or replace valve body |
|  | c) Oil pump faulty | c) Repair or replace oil pump |
|  | d) Vacuum leak at intake manifold | d) Replace intake manifold gasket |
|  | e) Governor sticking | e) Clean or replace governor |
|  | g) Governor pressure tube loose | g) Repair or replace tube |
| Improper 1-2 shift | a) Valves sticking | a) Clean or replace valve body |
| Improper 2-3 shift | a) Valves sticking | a) Clean or replace valve body |
| No upshift | a) Governor sticking | a) Clean or replace governor |
|  | b) Output shaft seals faulty | b) Replace seals |
|  | c) Governor pressure tube loose | c) Repair or replace tube |
| No "D" 3rd gear and "R" inoperative | a) Valves sticking | a) Clean or replace valve body |
|  | b) Rear clutch pressure tube loose | b) Repair or replace tube |
|  | c) Faulty piston rings in intermediate shaft hub | c) Replace piston rings |
| Reduced maximum speed in all gears and transmission is overheating | a) Torque converter one-way clutch locked, will not free wheel | a) Replace converter |

## CHILTON'S THREE "C's" TRANSMISSION DIAGNOSIS CHART
### Borg Warner Model 66

| Condition | Cause | Correction |
|---|---|---|
| Rough and delayed shifts | a) Throttle cable out of adjustment | a) Adjust or replace throttle cable |
| | b) Sticking regulator valve | b) Clean or replace valve body |
| | c) Fluid intake filter clogged | c) Replace filter |
| | d) Oil pump faulty | d) Repair or replace oil pump |
| | e) O-ring on pump pick-up pipe faulty | e) Replace O-ring |
| Engine races into and out of 2nd gear | a) Front brake band out of adjustment | a) Adjust front brake band |
| | b) Front servo seals faulty or front servo tube loose | b) Replace front servo seal and/or repair tube |
| | c) Front brake band worn | c) Replace band |
| | d) Valves sticking | d) Clean valve body |
| Engine races as 2-3 and 3-2 shifts are occuring | a) Rear clutch feed tube leaks | a) Tighten or replace tube |
| | b) Rear clutch worn | b) Replace rear clutch |
| | c) Rear clutch seal rings | c) Replace seal rings |
| | d) Valves sticking | d) Clean valve body |
| Whining when engine is running | a) Oil pump gears and/or converter bushing | a) Replace pump gears and/or converter bushing |
| Irregular noises from the gearbox but not in "D" 3rd gear | a) Planetary gearset broken | a) Replace broken parts |
| Whine for short time after starting vehicle, only when vehicle has sat 12 hours or more | a) Converter valve faulty—will not affect performance | a) Replace converter valve |

## DIAGNOSTIC TEST RESULTS CHART

| Condition | Cause | Correction |
|---|---|---|
| Low control pressure | a) Low fluid level | a) Correct fluid level |
| | b) Manual valve out of adjustment | b) Adjust manual linkage |
| | c) Downshift cable out of adjustment | c) Adjust cable |
| | d) Filter clogged | d) Replace filter |
| | e) Oil suction tube or O-ring faulty | e) Replace pipe or O-ring |
| | f) Oil pump faulty | f) Overhaul pump |
| High control pressure | a) Downshift cable out of adjustment | a) Adjust cable |
| | b) Throttle or regulator valve sticking | b) Clean valve body |

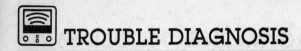

## DIAGNOSTIC TEST RESULTS CHART

| Condition | Cause | Correction |
|---|---|---|
| Stall rpm high in "1" and "R" | a) Downshift cable out of adjustment | a) Adjust cable |
| | b) Valve sticking | b) Clean the valve body |
| | c) Filter clogged | c) Replace the filter |
| | d) Suction or O-ring leaks | d) Replace O-ring or suction tube |
| | e) Oil pump faulty | e) Overhaul oil pump |
| Stall rpm high in "1" only | a) Front clutch support housing seals | a) Replace seals |
| | b) Forward sun gear shaft seals | b) Replace seals |
| Stall rpm high in "R" only | a) Rear band worn or out of adjustment | a) Adjust band and/or replace if needed |
| | b) Rear servo piston seal or rear servo tube fit | b) Replce seal or tube as needed |
| | c) Rear clutch feed tube leaks | c) Repair fit or replace tube |
| | d) Rear clutches worn or faulty sealing rings | d) Replace rear clutches or seal rings as needed |
| Stall rpms under 1,300 <br><br> Road test vehicle | | |
| Poor acceleration all speeds | a) Engine condition | a) Repair engine |
| Poor acceleration under 30 mph and normal over 30 mph | a) Converter one-way clutch slips | a) Replace converter |
| Shift speed off specification at kickdown | a) Downshift cable out of adjustment | a) Adjust cable |
| | b) Governor valve sticking | b) Clean or replace valve |
| | c) Output shaft rings or governor tube seals faulty | c) Replace as needed |
| Shift speed off 1-2 shift only | a) Valves sticking | a) Clean valve body |
| Shift speed off 2-3 shift only | a) Valves sticking | a) Clean valve body |
| No upshifts | a) Valves sticking | a) Clean valve body |
| | b) Output shaft seal rings or governor shaft seal faulty | b) Replace as needed |
| No upshift and no reverse | a) Valves sticking | a) Clean valve body |
| Reduces maximum shift in all ratios and converter overheats reduced top speed to approximately 50 MPH | a) Converter one-way clutch seized | a) Replace converter |

## Hydraulic Control System

In diagnosing automatic transmission problems it is helpful to have a better understanding of the hydraulic control system. The hydraulic control system consists of a valve body, oil pump, clutch and band apply passages and pistons, and the governor. The gear ratio of the automatic transmission is determined by the planetary gear units which are controlled by the clutches and bands.

## Major components

### PUMP

The impeller of the torque converter drives the oil pump, which is an internal/external gear type unit, whenever the engine is running. The pump takes transmission fluid from the oil pan, through a strainer, and delivers it under pressure to the hydraulic system.

## GOVERNOR

The governor is mounted on the output (driven) shaft and revolves with the output shaft whenever the vehicle is in motion. Governor movement speed varies directly with the speed of the vehicle. The centrifugal force of the governor rotation controls the two governor valve ports. These ports are connected to the system by passages drilled into the shaft. Automatic transmission fluid enters one port, at line pressure, from the manual valve and returns to the shift valves at governor pressure through the second port. The governor pressure increases as the speed of the vehicle increases.

## VALVE BODY

The valve body incorporates the pressure regulator system, the flow control system and check valves. This unit controls the automatic up and down shifting, kickdown shifts and manual shifts.

Contained in the valve body are the secondary regulator valve, downshift valve, primary regulator valve, manual valve, both the 1-2 and 2-3 shift valves, servo orifice control valve, throttle valve and the modulator plug and valve.

## CONTROL PRESSURE

### Test

Before pressure testing check the fluid and adjust to the proper level. Also, check and adjust the throttle linkage.
1. Attach a tachometer to the engine.
2. Raise the vehicle and support it safely.
3. Connect a pressure gauge to the main control pressure port.
4. Check the pressure in "D" and at idle speed.
5. Leave the gauges connected and lower the vehicle.
6. While operating the vehicle on level ground, check the main control pressure at kickdown.
7. Road test and record shift speed points and compare to specifications.

# DIAGNOSIS TESTS

## Stall Test

With all four wheels blocked, both foot and hand brake applied, and test gauges attached, place the selector lever in "D" and depress the accelerator to the floor. Record the highest rpm and compare the results to the figures below.

| RPM | Condition |
|---|---|
| Under 1300 | Stator free wheel spin |
| 1950 to 2100 | Normal |
| Over 2500 | Clutch slip |

Repeat the stall test in "1" and "R" and record the results for comparison with the above information. Be sure not to exceed ten seconds per stall test and always run the engine at approximately 1000 rpm in "N" between tests to cool the transmission.

## Air Pressure Test

If internal fluid pressure leakage or clutch and band problems are indicated, the problems can be pinpointed by air pressure testing.
1. Raise the vehicle and support it safely.
2. Drain the transmission fluid and remove the pan.
3. Remove the fluid pressure tubes and using reduced com-

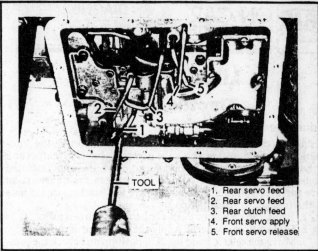

| | |
|---|---|
| 1. | Rear servo feed |
| 2. | Rear servo feed |
| 3. | Rear clutch feed |
| 4. | Front servo apply |
| 5. | Front servo release |

Oil delivery tube removal with pulling tool (©Borg Warner)

pressed air (approximately 25 psi) apply the air at the pressure holes and listen for leakage and the movement of the elements.
4. Remove the extension housing and air test at the 3 holes in the rear transmission cover.

## Road Test

Road testing should follow the complete procedure detailed below. The automatic transmission should be at normal working operative temperature. Refer to the Gear Change Speeds chart for any appropriate testing information.
1. With the brakes applied and the engine idling, move the automatic transmission selector lever from "N" to "R", then from "N" to "D", then from "N" to "2" and finally, from "N" to "1". Be sure that engagement is felt with each gear selection.
2. Check the stall speed.
3. Place the selector lever in "D" and accelerate with minimum throttle opening to check the speed of the first gear to second gear shift.
4. Continue with minimum throttle and check the speed of the second gear to third gear shift.
5. Once again, place the selector lever in "D" and accelerate with maximum throttle opening (kickdown) to check the speed of the first gear to second gear shift.
6. Continue with maximum throttle and check the speed of the second gear to the third gear shift.
7. Check for kickdown shift from third gear to second gear.
8. Check for kickdown shift from second gear to first gear.
9. Check for kickdown shift from third gear to first gear.
10. Check for (roll-out) downshift with minimum throttle from second gear to first gear.
11. Check for part throttle downshift from third gear to second gear.

Should a problem be apparent during the road test, refer to Chiltons three C's Diagnosis Chart.

 **ON CAR SERVICES**

# ADJUSTMENTS
## Throttle Linkage

### Adjustment

Install a pressure gauge to the control pressure port on the automatic transmission case. It may be necessary to lift the carpet and remove the access plate in order to remove the plug from the transmission case. There is a bracket between the transmission case and the rear mount. Do not remove this bracket, use the hole in the bracket to reach the port.

1. Bring the engine to normal operating temperature.
2. Block all four wheels. Apply the hand and foot brakes.
3. Move the selector into the "D" position and check the pressure to 60-75 psi at idle.
4. Increase the engine speed to 1200 rpm and check the pressure to 75-115 psi.

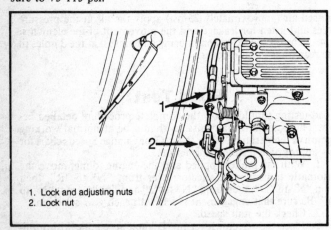

1. Lock and adjusting nuts
2. Lock nut

**Downshift cable adjustment (©Borg Warner)**

5. If the pressures do not agree with the specifications above, adjust the downshift cable as follows.
6. Shut the engine off and put the selector lever in "N".
7. Loosen the locknut on the downshift cable.
8. Using the adjuster nut on the outer cable, adjust the length of the cable to alter the pressure. Increase the cable length to increase the pressure and decrease the cable length to decrease the pressure.
9. The ferrule on the inner cable should be .010 inch from the threaded end of the outer cable. Lock the locknut.
10. Remove the pressure gauge and replace the plug.
11. Replace the access plate and carpeting as required.
12. Check the fluid level and road test the vehicle.

## Front and Rear Band

### Adjustment

Both the front and rear band adjustment should be checked and adjusted after 1,000 miles on a new vehicle and every 15,000 miles thereafter. It may be necessary to remove the access plate in the left footwell in order to reach the front band.

1. Loosen the locknut on the adjuster screw.
2. Back off the adjuster screw 2 or 3 turns.
3. Torque the adjuster screw to 5 ft. lbs. and back off ¾ of a turn.
4. Hold the adjuster screw and torque the locknut to 35 ft. lbs.

## Manual Linkage

### Adjustment

1. Remove the console cover.
2. Take off the split pin and washer securing the cable to the lever and detach the cable.
3. Place the selector lever in "1" and the lever on the transmission in the "1" position.
4. Adjust the lock nuts on the holding bracket at the console until the cable can be connected to the selector lever without moving the lever.
5. Tighten the lock nuts and secure the cable with a new split pin.
6. Replace the console cover.

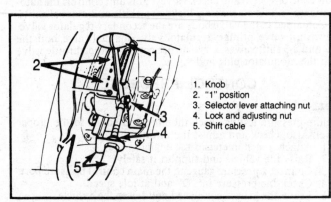

1. Knob
2. "1" position
3. Selector lever attaching nut
4. Lock and adjusting nut
5. Shift cable

**Manual linkage adjustment (©Borg Warner)**

## Neutral Safety Switch

### Adjustment

1. Disconnect the battery.
2. Remove the gearshift knob.
3. Pry the electric window switch from the center console. Do not disconnect the window switches.
4. Remove the 2 screws and lift the lettered selector panel to gain access to the cigar lighter and door switch terminals.
5. Disconnect the door lock and cigar lighter terminals and remove the selector panel.
6. Remove the positive connector from the safety switch.

**NOTE: The safety switch is grounded.**

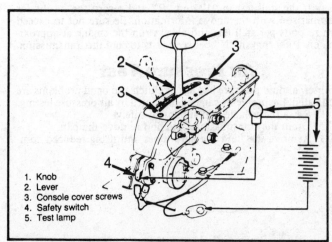

1. Knob
2. Lever
3. Console cover screws
4. Safety switch
5. Test lamp

**Neutral safety switch adjustment (©Borg Warner)**

7. Connect a test lamp in series with a battery and the safety switch.

8. Place the selector lever in "N" and loosen the lock nut on the safety switch.

9. Move the switch until the test lamp lights.

10. Tighten the lock nut and check to see if the light is on in "P" and off in the other positions.

11. Disconnect the test lamp, and connect the position wire to the switch.

12. Connect the cigar lighter and door lock switches.

13. Refit the selector cover panel.

14. Install the window switch and gearshift knob.

15. Connect the battery cable.

16. Check the operation of the windows, cigar lighter and door locks.

# SERVICES

## Throttle Linkage

### Removal and Installation

1. Remove the automatic transmission pan from the transmission assembly. Disconnect the cable from the downshift cam.

2. Position cable removal tool CWB-62 or equivalent on the plastic ferrule, push upwards until ferrule, together with cable, is pressed out of the transmission case.

3. Remove the split pin, washer and clevis pin securing clevis to throttle linkage; discard the split pin.

4. Loosen the lock nut and withdraw the downshift cable.

5. Place new O-ring on plastic ferrule.

6. Lubricate the ferrule with fresh transmission fluid.

— CAUTION —

*Do not lubricate inner cable.*

7. Press the ferrule into the case and connect the cable to the cam.

8. Connect the clevis to the throttle linkage; use a new split pin.

9. With accelerator pedal released and throttle levers resting on idle screws adjust cable until heel of downshift cam just makes contact with downshift valve.

10. With accelerator pedal depressed check that the lobe of the cam fully depresses the downshift valve.

11. Install pan and gasket on case.

12. Refill transmission with fluid.

13. Check and adjust throttle pressure if necessary.

## Fluid Change Interval

For normal service vehicles every 24,000 miles is sufficient for changing the automatic transmission fluid and filter. For severe service vehicles a shorter service interval should be used.

1. Raise and support the vehicle safely.

2. Drain the automatic transmission fluid.

3. Remove the automatic transmission pan.

4. Remove the oil filter attaching bolts and remove the filter from the transmission assembly.

5. After cleaning the pan to transmission mating surfaces install a new oil filter.

6. Using a new transmission pan gasket install the transmission pan.

7. Fill the automatic transmission with three quarts of the proper type of automatic transmission fluid. Be sure to check the fluid level on the dipstick.

8. Start the engine and bring the transmission to normal operating temperature, then check the fluid level and correct as required.

## Valve Body

### Removal and Installation

1. Move the selector lever to the "P" position. Raise and support the vehicle on a hoist.

2. Drain the automatic transmission and remove the pan.

3. Disconnect the downshift cable from the cam.

4. Using a suitable and safe tool, pry the tubes from the transmission. Be careful not to damage these tubes.

5. Take note of the placement of the magnet and remove it.

6. Remove the valve body to casing bolts.

7. Remove the valve body using care not to drop the manual valve.

**NOTE: Extreme care must be taken to be sure that the removal of the valve body does not damage the torque converter feed, pump feed or pump outlet pipes.**

8. When installing the valve body in the transmission case be sure that the tubes are correctly located in the valve body. The valve body may be tapped gently with a soft mallet to be sure that correct location is obtained.

9. Align the pin on the detent lever so that it engages with the groove machined in the manual valve.

10. Install the valve body retaining bolts. Be sure that the shortest bolt is installed in front.

11. Reconnect the kickdown cable to the cam.

12. Install the transmission oil pan using a new pan gasket.

13. Fill the transmission with the proper type transmission fluid to the "MAX" mark on the transmission dipstick. Run the engine until it reaches normal operating temperature and adjust the fluid level as required.

14. Lower the vehicle and road test.

## Front Servo

### Removal and Installation

1. Drain the automatic transmission and remove the pan.

2. Remove the valve body.

3. Remove the servo assembly along with the push rod and spring. Discard the servo cover gasket.

4. The brake band strut may fall out, if so, recover it.

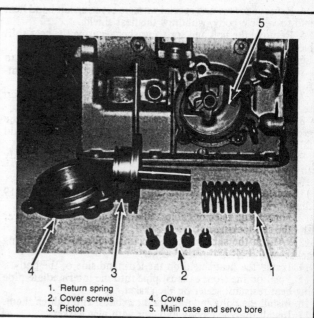

1. Return spring
2. Cover screws
3. Piston
4. Cover
5. Main case and servo bore

**Front servo exploded view (©Borg Warner)**

5. Using petroleum jelly, install a new gasket on the servo body. Set the strut in position on the brake band.

6. Insert the push rod and spring into the case and make sure that the strut is in the slot in the end of the push rod.

7. Install the servo cover bolts and torque them to 19 ft. lbs.

8. Install the valve body and adjust the brake band.

9. Install the transmission pan. Fill the transmission with the proper type of automatic transmission fluid. Road test and adjust as required.

## Rear Servo

### Removal and Installation

1. Drain the automatic transmission and remove the transmission oil pan. Remove the valve body assembly.

2. Remove the nuts and bolts securing the intermediate exhaust pipe to the front pipe.

3. Separate intermediate pipe from front pipe and remove and discard the gasket.

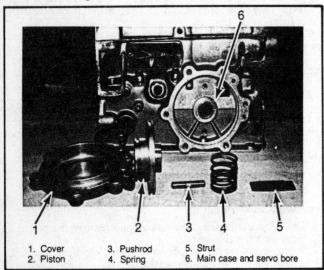

| | | |
|---|---|---|
| 1. Cover | 3. Pushrod | 5. Strut |
| 2. Piston | 4. Spring | 6. Main case and servo bore |

**Rear servo exploded view (©Borg Warner)**

4. Remove screws and special washers securing left hand heat shield to vehicle body; withdraw the heat shield.

5. Remove the bolt and spring washer securing the gear shift cable connecting block to the mounting bracket.

6. Remove the self-locking nut holding the selector lever to the selector shaft. Withdraw the lever and selector cable assembly.

7. Mark the position of the rear servo to the transmission case.

8. Remove the rear servo attaching bolts and withdraw the servo, push rod and spring. Recover the brake band strut, should it fall out.

9. To install, position a new gasket on the rear servo body with petroleum jelly.

10. Position the brake band strut in the case.

11. Install the rear servo attaching bolts and torque them to 19 ft. lbs.

12. Install the selector cable and attach the cable to the lever with the self locking nut.

13. Attach the shift cable connecting block to the mounting bracket with bolt and spring washer.

14. Install the heat shield on the left-hand side of the body.

15. Position the front exhaust pipe into the intermediate pipe using heat resistant sealer on the gasket.

16. Install the bolts and nuts on the exhaust and tighten them.

17. Install the valve body and pan with new gasket.

18. Adjust the rear band and fill the transmission with fluid.

## Governor

### Removal and Installation

1. Remove rear extension housing.

2. Slide speedometer drive gear off output shaft.

3. Move selector lever to "N".

4. Rotate the output shaft to a position from which the governor securing plug can be removed.

5. Note the fitted position of the governor and remove the plug.

6. Slide the governor off the output shaft.

7. Depress the governor weight and remove the snap ring.

8. Take the stem, spring and valve from the governor body.

9. Replace parts as needed.

10. Install the valve, spring and stem into the governor body.

11. Depress the governor weight and install the snap ring.

12. Slide the governor on the output shaft, aligning the blind hole on the shaft.

13. Install the securing plug and spring washer. Make sure that the end of the plug enters the blind hole in the output shaft.

14. Torque the plug to 16.5 ft. lbs.

15. Slide the speedometer drive gear on the output shaft.

16. Install the extension housing and check the fluid level.

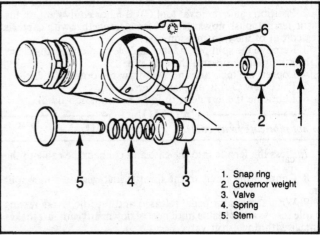

| | |
|---|---|
| 1. Snap ring | |
| 2. Governor weight | |
| 3. Valve | |
| 4. Spring | |
| 5. Stem | |

**Governor exploded view (©Borg Warner)**

## Rear Extension Housing

### Removal and Installation

1. Disconnect the battery cables.

2. Set the engine lifting hook tool through the engine support bracket and the rear engine lifting eyelet.

3. Remove the center mounting nut from the rear support. Take off the nuts and washers from the front end of the strengthening plate.

4. Unfasten the heat shield.

5. Position a jack to support the engine mounting and remove the bolts.

6. Lower the jack and remove the mounting.

7. Remove the bolts securing the support plate to the floor pan.

8. Remove the bolts and nuts fastening the drive shaft to output flange.

9. Lower the engine slightly. Be careful not to damage the heater control valve.

10. Place the transmission selector lever in "P".

11. Remove the output flange center bolt and take off the output flange.

12. Disconnect the speedometer right angle drive. Remove the driven gear plate and the driven gear.

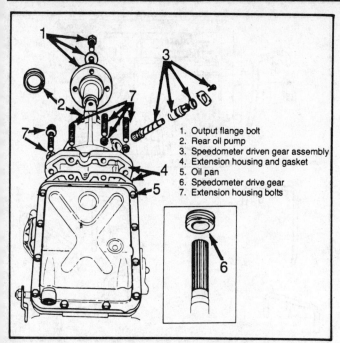

1. Output flange bolt
2. Rear oil pump
3. Speedometer driven gear assembly
4. Extension housing and gasket
5. Oil pan
6. Speedometer drive gear
7. Extension housing bolts

**Rear extension housing exploded view** (©Borg Warner)

13. Remove the selector cable mounting bracket.

14. Note the location of the stud type bolts and then remove all of the extension housing to case bolts.

15. Withdraw the extension housing and remove the gasket.

16. Pry the rear oil seal out of the extension housing and install a new one.

17. Using a new gasket install the extension housing and the selector cable mounting bracket on the transmission case.

18. Torque the extension to case bolts to 42.5 ft. lbs.

19. Secure the selector cable connect block to the mounting bracket.

20. Replace the speedometer driven gear O-ring and install the driven gear and plate.

21. Connect the speedometer cable and right angle drive.

22. Install the output flange and torque the center bolt to 40-50 ft. lbs.

23. Raise the engine slightly on the support tool.

24. Refasten the drive shaft to the output flange.

25. Fasten rear engine mounting support to transmission tunnel.

26. Use the bolts and special washers to secure the rear engine mounting support plate to the floor pan.

27. Position a jack to support the rear engine mount in place and install the attaching bolts.

28. Install the center mounting nut on the rear engine mount.

29. Remove the engine lifting tool from the engine compartment.

30. Connect the battery.

31. Check the fluid level.

## REMOVAL & INSTALLATION

### Transmission Assembly

#### Removal

1. Position the vehicle on a hoist and support it safely. Disconnect the battery.

2. Remove the dipstick from the dipstick tube and remove the bolt holding the dipstick tube to the manifold.

3. Remove the bolts holding the upper fan cowl to the lower fan cowl. Slacken the bolts securing the cowl bracket to the radiator in order to facilitate the removal of the top cowl.

4. Remove and discard the split pin securing the kickdown cable to the throttle bellcrank, withdraw the clevis pin and washer; slacken the locknut and disconnect the cable.

5. Remove the union nut holding the dipstick tube to the transmission oil pan. Remove the dipstick tube. Drain the transmission fluid.

6. Disconnect the exhaust system. Remove the exhaust heat shields from the floor pan.

7. Position the transmission jack to the automatic transmission.

8. Remove the bolts securing the crash plate to the automatic transmission case studs. Remove the nut securing the crash plate to the rear mounting bolt.

9. Remove the bolts, spacers and washers securing the rear engine mounting to the floor pan.

10. Remove the bolts holding the driveshaft tunnel spreader plate to the floor pan.

11. Position the engine support bracket and locate the hook at the engine rear lifting eye. Turn the adjusting nut to take the weight of the engine. Be sure not to damage the heater control valve.

12. Remove the rubber pad from the top of the transmission.

13. Remove the nut holding the selector lever bellcrank to the cross shaft and remove the bellcrank.

14. Remove the bolt securing the selector cable trunnion to the mounting bracket.

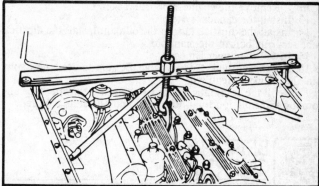

**Engine support tool** (©Borg Warner)

15. Remove the bolts securing the tie plate to the engine oil pan and transmission converter housing front cover plate. Remove the cover plate.

16. Rotate the engine until a torque converter securing bolt is accessible; knock back the lock tab and remove the bolt; repeat this procedure for the three remaining torque converter securing bolts.

17. Remove and discard the tab washers.

18. Remove the bolt and washer securing the breather pipe clip.

19. Remove the screw securing the oil cooler pipe clamp plate to the sump bracket.

20. Disconnect the transmission oil lines and breather pipes from the transmission case.

21. Disconnect the speedometer cable from the drive pinion. Disconnect the electrical wires from the starter and solenoid.

22. Be sure that the transmission is secured to the transmission jack.

23. Remove the nut, bolts and washers securing the torque converter housing to the engine block. Remove the starter and spacer.

24. Lower the transmission jack and carefully remove the auto-

matic transmission from the vehicle.

25. Remove the torque converter from the input shaft.

### Installation

1. Install the torque converter to the input shaft. Be sure that the torque converter is correctly engaged on the input shaft spline.

2. Position and secure the automatic transmission on the transmission jack.

3. Install the rubber pad on top of the transmission unit. Raise the transmission unit and install it in its proper place. Install the bolts securing the torque converter housing to the engine. Do not tighten these bolts until the starter and spacer have been installed.

4. Align the torque converter to drive plate holes with new tab washers. Do not tighten until all four bolts are installed. Be sure to bend over the tab washers.

5. Reconnect the electrical connections to the starter and solenoid. Install the oil cooler lines to the transmission. Install the breather pipe.

6. Install the torque converter front cover, and the tie plate between the engine oil pan and the torque converter housing.

7. Install the driveshaft.

8. Install the gear selector bellcrank to the cross shaft. Secure and align the gear selector lever trunnion to the mounting plate.

9. Reconnect the speedometer cable to the drive pinion.

10. Install the driveshaft tunnel spreader plate, exhaust heat shield and the rear engine mounting.

11. Install the crash plate and secure the bolts to the transmission case studs.

12. Remove the transmission jack from the transmission assembly. Remove the engine support bracket.

13. Install the exhaust system.

14. Install the dipstick tube to the oil pan. Install the dipstick tube securing bolt to the manifold.

15. Install the upper fan cowl.

16. Reconnect the kickdown cable. Be sure to use a new split pin and adjust as required.

17. Refill the automatic transmission with the proper type automatic transmission fluid. Road test and adjust as required.

**BENCH OVERHAUL**

### Before Disassembly

Thoroughly clean the transmission before teardown and maintain a high standard of cleanliness during all transmission repair work. Use lint free rags. Install new gaskets and O-rings. Clean all metal parts with industrial solvent and lubricate them with transmission fluid before installation.

Soak new clutches in clean transmission fluid before installing them.

### Converter Inspection

Check the converter by doing the stall test and road test on the vehicle.

The converter is a sealed unit and must be replaced as a unit.

### Transmission

#### Disassembly

1. Remove the torque converter housing bolts. Lift the converter housing from the transmission.

2. Remove the dipstick tube and drain the transmission fluid,

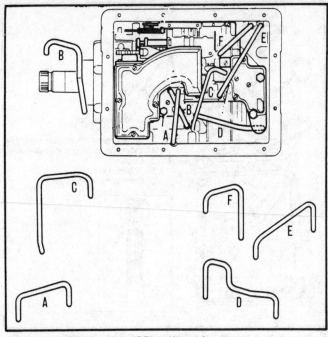

**Oil pressure tube location** (©Borg Warner)

if not previously done.

3. Invert the automatic transmission and position the selector in the "P" mode.

4. Remove the speedometer driven gear housing and the driven gear.

5. Take off the bolt securing the output flange and remove the flange.

6. Remove the extension housing bolts.

**NOTE: Record the position of the regular bolts, stud type bolts and spacers for installation.**

7. Withdraw the extension housing and remove the gasket.

8. Replace the rear oil seal.

9. Slide the speedometer drive off the output shaft.

10. Remove the oil pan bolts and pan from the case. Discard the gasket.

11. Take the magnet from the valve body.

12. Note the position of the oil tubes and without damaging them pry the tubes out. Do not pry out the tube under the valve body until after the valve body is removed.

13. Disconnect the throttle cable from the cam.

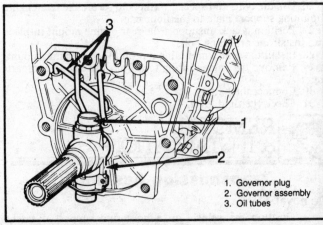

1. Governor plug
2. Governor assembly
3. Oil tubes

**Governor assembly location** (©Borg Warner)

14. Remove the valve body and then remove the final fluid tube.

15. Carefully pry or pull the oil cooler tube out of the case, without damaging it.

16. Remove the oil tube retaining plate.

17. Using suitable long-nosed pliers, withdraw the pump inlet tube.

18. Take out the pump outlet pipe.

19. Withdraw the converter feed tube.

20. Scribe alignment marks on the oil pump and transmission case.

21. Remove the oil pump to transmission case bolts and washers.

22. Support the stator tube and withdraw the oil pump.

23. Discard the gasket and the bronze thrust washer.

24. Remove the plug and spring washer securing the governor on the output shaft.

25. Slide the governor off the shaft. Note the position of the governor for installation.

26. Carefully pry the governor feed, governor return and lubrication tubes from the case.

27. Loosen the locknut and unscrew the front brake band adjuster. If the strut falls, recover it.

28. Loosen the locknut and unscrew the rear brake band adjuster. If the strut falls recover it.

29. Remove the front clutch assembly together with the input shaft.

30. Remove one steel and one bronze washer. Discard the bronze washer.

31. Take out the rear clutch assembly. Remove and discard the sealing rings.

32. Note the fitted position of the front brake band; compress and withdraw the brake band.

33. Withdraw the forward sun gear shaft.

34. Remove the small needle roller bearing from the input end of the forward sun gear shaft.

35. Take the flange backing washer and large needle bearing from the output end of the forward sun gear shaft.

36. Remove the metal sealing rings from the input end of the shaft and discard them.

37. Remove the fiber sealing ring from the output end of the shaft and discard it.

38. Remove the bolts and lockwashers securing the center support.

39. Push the output shaft forward to displace the center support and sun gear assembly.

40. Withdraw the center support and sun gear assembly from the case and remove the needle bearing from the input end of the sun gear assembly.

41. Separate the center support from the sun gear assembly.

42. Pull the output shaft towards the rear of the transmission.

43. Note the installed position of the rear brake band. Compress and remove the rear brake band.

44. Withdraw the output shaft and ring gear assembly.

45. Remove the bronze thrust washer and discard it.

46. Remove the front servo to case attaching bolts.

47. Take out the front servo, operating rod and spring; remove and discard the gasket.

48. Scribe alignment marks on the rear servo and transmission case.

49. Remove the rear servo to case attaching bolts.

50. Withdraw the rear servo, operating rod and spring; remove and discard the O-rings and gasket.

51. Remove the plate securing the parking pawl and the rear servo lever pivot pin.

52. Take out the rear servo pivot pin and operating lever.

53. Remove the parking pawl pivot pin, pawl and torsion spring.

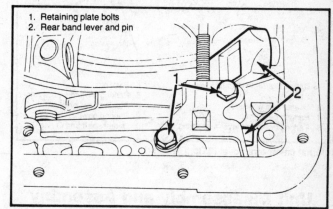

1. Retaining plate bolts
2. Rear band lever and pin

**Parking brake pawl retaining plate (©Borg Warner)**

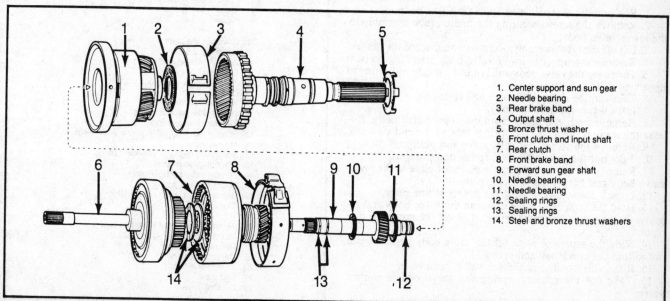

1. Center support and sun gear
2. Needle bearing
3. Rear brake band
4. Output shaft
5. Bronze thrust washer
6. Front clutch and input shaft
7. Rear clutch
8. Front brake band
9. Forward sun gear shaft
10. Needle bearing
11. Needle bearing
12. Sealing rings
13. Sealing rings
14. Steel and bronze thrust washers

**Exploded view of the model 66 gear train (©Borg Warner)**

54. Release the clip and remove the pin locating the manual valve lever.

55. Take out the detent shaft, manual lever, spacer and washers. Remove and discard the O-ring and oil seal.

56. Remove the parking brake rod from the parking pawl.

57. Remove the torsion spring from the parking brake rod operating lever.

58. Using a punch, drive out the operating lever pivot pin; withdraw the lever and spring.

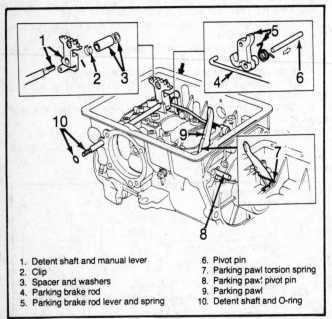

1. Detent shaft and manual lever
2. Clip
3. Spacer and washers
4. Parking brake rod
5. Parking brake rod lever and spring
6. Pivot pin
7. Parking pawl torsion spring
8. Parking pawl pivot pin
9. Parking pawl
10. Detent shaft and O-ring

**Internal linkage removal (©Borg Warner)**

## Unit Disassembly and Assembly

### VALVE BODY

1. Remove the manual valve from the valve body.

2. Remove the screws securing the suction tube assembly to the lower valve body.

3. Lift off the tube assembly. Remove and discard the gasket.

4. Remove the upper to lower valve body attaching bolts.

5. Turn over the valve body and remove the cam mounting to upper valve body bolts.

6. Take out the downshift valve and spring.

7. Lift off the upper valve body.

8. Remove both end plates from the upper valve body. Release the tension slowly on the springs behind the end plates.

9. Remove the spring, 1-2 shift valve and plunger.

10. Take out the 2-3 shift valve, spring and plunger.

11. Remove the screws holding the collector plate to the lower valve body and lift off the collector plate.

12. Loosen the screws holding the governor line plate.

13. Hold the separating plate down on the valve body and remove the governor line plate screws. Lift off the governor line plate.

14. Slide the separator plate off the valve body being careful not to lose the check ball and spring.

15. If the valve body has a check valve, remove it.

16. Take out the retainer, spring and servo orifice control valve.

17. Withdraw the retaining pin, plug, modulator valve and spring.

18. Remove the throttle valve spring retainer and the throttle valve retainer.

19. Take out the throttle valve and spring.

20. Remove the screw, spacer and detent spring.

21. If the roller arm is peened to the valve body, swing the arm clear to remove the regulator valve retaining plate.

22. Release the spring tension slowly when removing the regulator valve retaining plate.

23. Remove the spring, sleeve and primary regulator valve.

24. Take out the spring and secondary regulator valve.

25. Check all springs to specification.

26. Check all valves for free movement and the bores for dam-

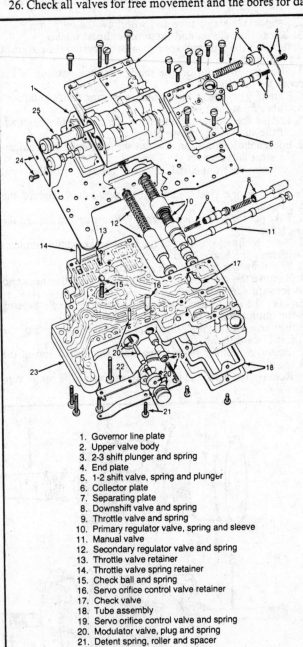

1. Governor line plate
2. Upper valve body
3. 2-3 shift plunger and spring
4. End plate
5. 1-2 shift valve, spring and plunger
6. Collector plate
7. Separating plate
8. Downshift valve and spring
9. Throttle valve and spring
10. Primary regulator valve, spring and sleeve
11. Manual valve
12. Secondary regulator valve and spring
13. Throttle valve retainer
14. Throttle valve spring retainer
15. Check ball and spring
16. Servo orifice control valve retainer
17. Check valve
18. Tube assembly
19. Servo orifice control valve and spring
20. Modulator valve, plug and spring
21. Detent spring, roller and spacer
22. Cam mounting arm
23. Lower valve body
24. End plate
25. 2-3 shift valve

**Exploded view of the valve body assembly (©Borg Warner)**

age. If the valves or the valve body is damaged, replace the component.

27. Install the secondary regulator valve and spring.

28. Insert the primary regulator valve, sleeve and spring.

29. Install the regulator valve retaining plate.

30. Attach the detent roller spring and assembly with a screw and spacer.

31. Insert the throttle valve, spring, spring retainer and valve retainer.

32. Install the spring, modulator valve, plug and retaining pin.

33. Insert the servo orifice control valve, spring and retainer.

34. Set in the check valve, if equipped.

35. Install the spring and the check ball.

36. Set the separator plate and while holding the plate down attach the governor line plate with the attaching bolts.

37. Insert the plunger, spring and 2-3 shift valve.

38. install the plunger, 1-2 shift valve and spring.

39. Install the two end plates on the upper valve body.

40. Set the upper valve body on the lower valve body.

41. Insert the spring and downshift valve.

42. Install the cam mounting arm on the valve body with the attaching screws.

43. Turn the valve body over and install the upper to lower valve body attaching screws.

44. Using a new gasket install the suction tube assembly on the lower valve body.

45. Set in the manual valve.

## ONE-WAY CLUTCH

**NOTE: No overhaul of this assembly is possible. In the event of defects, the unit must be replaced.**

1. Remove the assembly from the transmission after taking note of its installed position.

2. Check the sprag faces for flat spots.

3. Install the one-way clutch assembly in the planet carrier. Be sure that the lip faces out and that the clutch is fully seated in the recess.

## FORWARD SUN GEAR SHAFT

1. Check the shaft for any obstructions in its passages. If any obstructions are encountered, clear them with compressed air.

2. Check the splines, sealing rings and the sealing ring grooves for burrs or damage.

3. Check the large and small needle roller bearings for wear and damage.

## REAR CLUTCH ASSEMBLY

1. Compress the piston return spring and remove the snap ring.

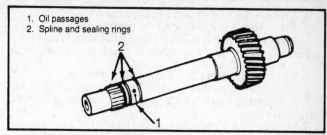

1. Oil passages
2. Spline and sealing rings

**Forward sun gear shaft** (©Borg Warner)

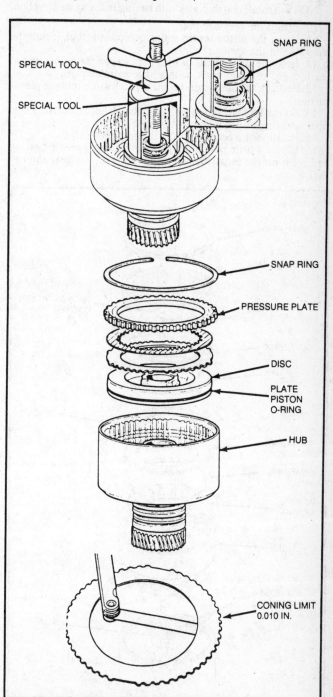

SPECIAL TOOL

SPECIAL TOOL

SNAP RING

SNAP RING

PRESSURE PLATE

DISC

PLATE
PISTON
O-RING

HUB

CONING LIMIT
0.010 IN.

**Exploded view of the rear clutch assembly** (©Borg Warner)

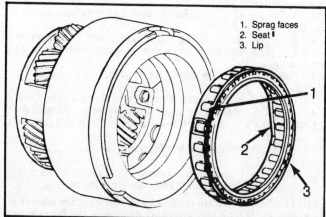

1. Sprag faces
2. Seat
3. Lip

**One-way clutch assembly** (©Borg Warner)

2. Remove the tool, retainer and spring.

3. Take the large snap ring off the pressure plate.

4. Remove the pressure plate, clutch discs and clutch plates.

5. Apply air pressure to the hole in the clutch housing to remove the clutch piston.

6. Remove the piston seal and install a new one.

7. Check the outer clutch coning for not less than 0.010 in.

8. Lubricate the piston with clean fluid and install it in the clutch drum.

9. Starting with a steel plate, install alternately the discs and plates.

NOTE: Install clutch plates with coning in the same direction.

10. Install the pressure plate.

11. Using the piston return spring compressor tool, install the snap ring in the spring retainer.

12. Hold the large needle bearing in place, on the output end of the forward sun gear shaft, with a little petroleum jelly.

13. Position the flanged end of the thrust washer into the planet carrier.

14. Set the forward sun gear shaft in the planet carrier; fit a new fiber seal ring on the output end of the shaft.

15. Position the center support in the planet carrier.

16. Smear a little petroleum jelly on the small needle bearing and set it on the thrust washer on the forward sun gear shaft.

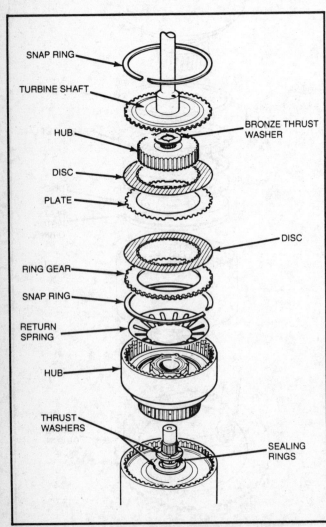

Exploded view of the front clutch assembly (©Borg Warner)

17. Install the rear clutch on the forward sun gear shaft and put new seal rings on the input end of the shaft.

18. Stagger the gaps in the seal rings when installing them.

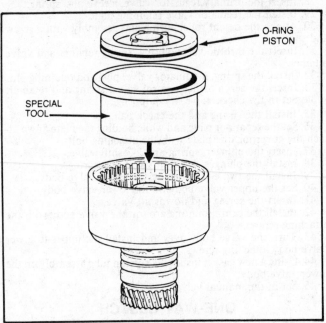

Front clutch piston installation (©Borg Warner)

## FRONT CLUTCH ASSEMBLY

1. Remove the snap ring and take out the turbine shaft.

2. Remove and discard the bronze thrust washer.

3. Remove the clutch hub, four plates and five discs.

4. Take off the snap ring and return spring.

5. Apply compressed air in the clutch housing to remove the piston.

6. Remove the plain or Belleville washers from under the piston.

7. Take the O-ring off the piston.

8. Coat a new O-ring with clean transmission fluid and install it on the piston.

9. Place the plain and Belleville washers in the housing.

NOTE: Some later transmissions have all Belleville and no plain washers. Install the Belleville washers in three opposing pairs.

10. Soak a new oil seal in transmission fluid and insert it, open end outward, into the housing.

11. Lubricate with transmission fluid and install the piston in the housing.

12. Set in the return spring and secure it with the snap ring.

13. Put the steel washer and a new bronze washer on the forward sun gear shaft.

14. Stagger the gaps on the input end of the sun gear shaft sealing rings.

15. Install the front clutch hub on the rear clutch hub and shaft.

16. Install the clutch plates and discs alternately starting with the heavier plate with no notches in it. Five plates and five discs are installed.

17. Align the teeth inside the discs and insert the clutch hub into the discs.

18. Set a new bronze thrust washer in the recess of the hub.

19. Install the turbine shaft and secure it with the snap ring.

NOTE: Never separate the front and rear clutches after they are assembled. Doing this will cause damage to the forward sun gear sealing rings.

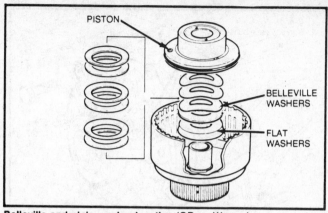

Belleville and plain washer location (©Borg Warner)

## OIL PUMP ASSEMBLY

1. Remove the pump body to pump adaptor bolts.
2. If it is necessary to tap the adaptor to separate it from the body, use a hide or hard rubber mallet.
3. Mark the gears with die marker before removing them.
4. Remove the gears and inspect the pump body and gears for wear or damage.
5. Replace the O-ring and oil seal with new parts.
6. Soak new parts and seals in transmission fluid.
7. Set the gears into the pump body using the alignment marks to position them.
8. Install the pump body to adaptor bolts and torque them alternately a little at a time to 2.5 ft. lbs.

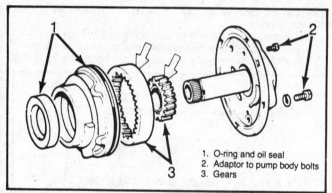

1. O-ring and oil seal
2. Adaptor to pump body bolts
3. Gears

Exploded view of the oil pump (©Borg Warner)

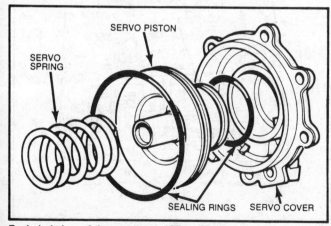

Exploded view of the rear servo (©Borg Warner)

## FRONT SERVO ASSEMBLY

1. Remove the piston and the return spring from the front servo assembly.
2. Check the spring and the fluid passages. Replace parts as required.
3. When installing the spring and piston coat the new O-rings with automatic transmission fluid.

## REAR SERVO ASSEMBLY

1. Remove the piston and the return spring from the rear servo assembly.
2. Replace parts as required.
3. When installing the piston and spring coat the new O-rings with automatic transmission fluid.

## GOVERNOR ASSEMBLY

1. Depress the governor stem and remove the snap ring.
2. Take the govenor weight, spring, stem and valve from the governor body.
3. Replace parts or entire assembly as needed.
4. Install the valve, spring, stem and weight. Secure the stem with a new snap ring.

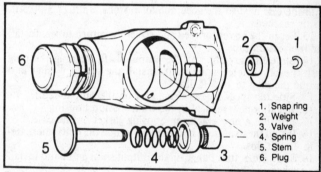

1. Snap ring
2. Weight
3. Valve
4. Spring
5. Stem
6. Plug

Exploded view of the governor assembly (©Borg Warner)

## Transmission

### Assembly

1. Smear the large bronze thrust washer with petroleum jelly and position it lug side into the case.
2. Set the output shaft into the case.
3. Postion the front and rear brake bands in the case.
4. Align the oil holes in the center support with the oil holes in the case and insert the clutch assemblies as a unit into the case.
5. Make sure that the planet gears are fully engaged with the ring gear.
6. Install the center support bolts and finger tighten only at this time.
7. Put a new bronze washer on the oil pump, with the lugs facing the pump.

**NOTE: The oil pump thrust washer is selective to obtain proper end play. Two washer thicknesses are available. It is recommended that the thinner thrust washer be used, since it almost always gives proper end play.**

8. Install the oil pump, with a new gasket, on the case.
9. Coat a new O-ring with transmission fluid and set it in the oil pump inlet tube.
10. Install the oil pump inlet and outlet tubes and secure them with the retaining plate. Torque the retaining plate bolts to 1.75 ft. lbs.
11. Torque the oil pump bolts in a diagonal pattern to 19 ft. lbs.
12. Tighten the center support bolts in small amounts, starting

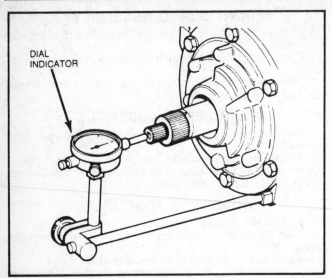

DIAL INDICATOR

**Checking total end play** (©Borg Warner)

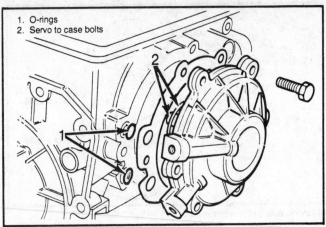

1. O-rings
2. Servo to case bolts

**Rear servo O-ring installation** (©Borg Warner)

with the one next to the accumulator pistons, until 17.3-20.3 ft. lbs. is reached.

13. Set in the governor feed and governor return tubes. Install the lubrication tube.

14. Slide the governor on the output shaft, aligning the plug with the blind hole in the shaft. Install the spring washer and torque the plug to 16.5 ft. lbs.

15. Side the speedometer drive gear on the output shaft.

16. Install a new oil seal in the transmission housing.

17. Position a new extension housing gasket on the case.

18. Install the extension housing and torque the bolts alternately to 42.5 ft. lbs.

19. Slide the output flange on the output shaft and hand install the washer and bolt.

20. Move the selector lever until the parking pawl engages with the gear.

21. Torque the output flange bolt to 40-50 ft. lbs.

22. Install a dial runout gauge on the end of the turbine shaft.

23. Insert a suitable lever between the front clutch and the front of the case. Ease the gear train to the rear of the case and zero the dial indicator.

24. Insert a lever between the ring gear and rear clutch, and ease the gear train forward. End play should read between .008 and 0.29 in. If end play exceeds .029 in. install the proper selective thrust washers to correct it.

25. Remove the dial indicator gauge.

26. Lubricate and install a new O-ring on the speedometer driven gear shaft.

27. Insert the driven gear shaft and secure it with it's cover and two bolts.

28. Using a new gasket, install the front servo. Torque the bolts alternately to 19 ft. lbs.

29. Set the front brake band strut in the case. Insert the proper end of the strut in the slot on the servo rod.

30. Tighten the front band adjusting screw until contact is made with the brake band.

31. Install a new O-ring in the rear servo body oil holes.

32. Using a new gasket, install the servo assembly. Make sure that the operating rod is in the detent of the operating lever.

33. Install the rear band strut in the case.

34. Tighten the rear band adjusting screw until contact is made with the band.

35. Torque the rear servo to case bolts to 19 ft. lbs.

36. Insert the oil tube that extends under the valve body.

37. Install the valve body and torque the bolts to 6.75 ft. lbs.

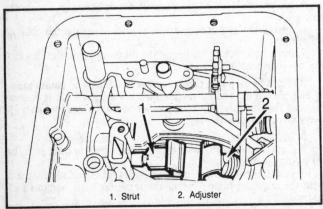

1. Strut
2. Adjuster

**Front band strut location** (©Borg Warner)

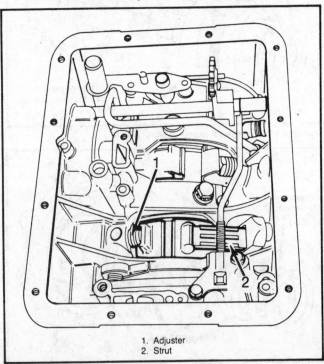

1. Adjuster
2. Strut

**Rear brake band strut location** (©Borg Warner)

38. Connect the throttle cable to the cam.
39. Fit in the remaining oil tubes.
40. Install the magnet on the valve body.
41. Install the transmission oil pan, using a new gasket. Torque the bolts to 5.75 ft. lbs.
42. Fasten the dipstick and the breather to the transmission case.

43. Install the converter housing. Torque the bolts at the top of the housing 20 to 30 ft. lbs. Torque the bolts at the bottom of the housing 30 to 50 ft. lbs.
44. Tighten the front and rear band adjusting screws to 5 ft. lbs., and then back them off ¾ of a turn.
45. Tighten both band adjusting lock nuts to 35 ft. lbs. Hold the adjusting screws from turning while tightening the lock nuts.

# SPECIFICATIONS

## VALVE SPRING IDENTIFICATION

| Description | Length | Diameter | Number of Coils | Color |
|---|---|---|---|---|
| Secondary regulator valve | 2.593 in. | .480-.490 in. | 23 | Blue |
| Primary regulator valve | 2.94 in. | .604-.610 in. | 14 | Blue |
| Servo orifice control valve | 1.08 in. | .198-.208 in. | 17 | Yellow |
| 2-3 shift valve | 1.59 in. | .275-.285 in. | 22.5 | Yellow |
| 1-2 shift valve | 1.094 in. | .230-.240 in. | 13 | Plain |
| Throttle return valve | .807 in. | .136-.146 in. | 28 | Yellow |
| Modulator valve | 1.069 in. | .150-.160 in. | 19 | Plain |
| Throttle valve | 1.175-1.185 in. | .230-.240 in. | 18 | Green |
| Dump ball valve | .70 in. | .210-.230 in. | 16 | Plain or white |

# SPECIAL TOOLS

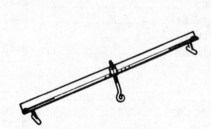

ENGINE SUPPORT

FRONT SERVO ADJUSTER ADAPTOR

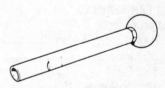

THROTTLE CABLE MOUNTING SEAL REMOVER

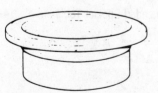

REAR CLUTCH PISTON REPLACER

FRONT CLUTCH PISTON REPLACER

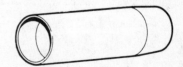

ACCUMULATOR PISTON ASSEMBLY SLEEVE

# INDEX

# HONDA
# 3 SPEED • 4 SPEED
# Automatic Transaxle

## A APPLICATIONS

### HONDA AUTOMATIC TRANSAXLE APPLICATION CHART

| Year | Model | Transaxle Type |
|------|-------|----------------|
| 1981 and Later | Civic | 3 speed unit |
| 1981-82 | Accord | 3 speed unit |
| 1983 and Later | Accord | 4 speed unit |
| 1981-82 | Prelude | 3 speed unit |
| 1983 and Later | Prelude | 4 speed unit |

## G GENERAL DESCRIPTION

### Three Speed Transaxle

The three speed Honda automatic transaxle is a combination of a three element torque converter and a dual shaft automatic transaxle which provides three forward speeds and one reverse speed. The entire unit is placed in line with the engine assembly.

Later Civic's are equipped with a lock up torque converter. The lock up mechanism engages above thirty miles per hour in drive. Lock up of the torque converter is prevented by a servo valve, which unless the throttle is opened sufficiently, the converter will not engage.

### Four Speed Transaxle

The four speed Honda automatic transaxle is a combination of a three element torque converter and a dual shaft automatic transaxle which provides four forward speeds and one reverse speed.

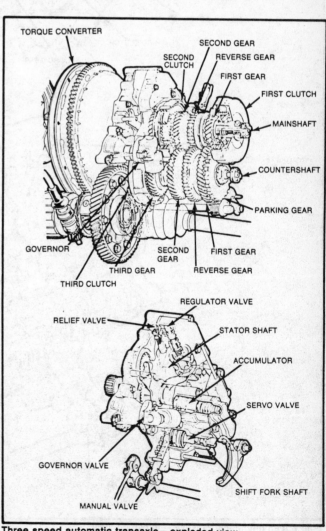

Three speed automatic transaxle—exploded view

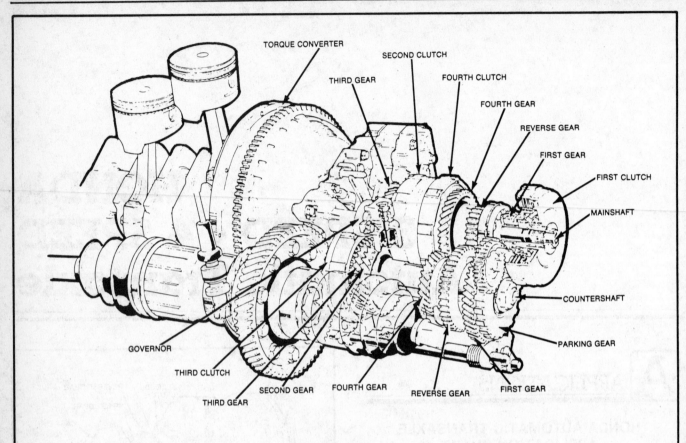

TORQUE CONVERTER

SECOND CLUTCH

THIRD GEAR

FOURTH CLUTCH

FOURTH GEAR

REVERSE GEAR

FIRST GEAR

FIRST CLUTCH

MAINSHAFT

COUNTERSHAFT

PARKING GEAR

GOVERNOR

THIRD CLUTCH

SECOND GEAR

THIRD GEAR

FOURTH GEAR

REVERSE GEAR

FIRST GEAR

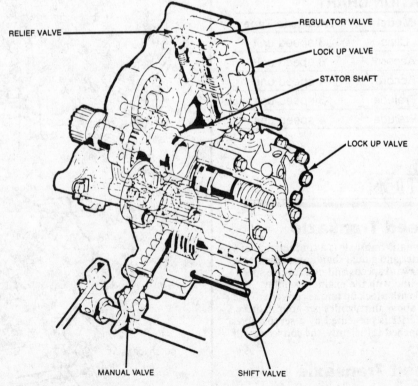

RELIEF VALVE

REGULATOR VALVE

LOCK UP VALVE

STATOR SHAFT

LOCK UP VALVE

MANUAL VALVE

SHIFT VALVE

Four speed automatic transaxle—exploded view

The entire unit is placed in line with the engine assembly.

The Honda four speed automatic transaxle is equipped with a lock up torque converter. When the transaxle is in D4 and at speeds above forty three miles per hour, the torque converter will utilize the lock up function. Lock up of the torque converter is prevented by a servo valve, which unless the throttle is opened sufficiently, the torque converter will not engage.

## Transaxle and Torque Converter Identification

### TRANSAXLE

Both the three speed automatic transaxle and the four speed automatic transaxle identification numbers are stamped on a plate, which is located on top of the automatic transaxle assembly. This plate can be viewed from the top the engine compartment.

### TORQUE CONVERTER

Torque converter usage differs with the type of engine and the type of vehicle that the automatic transaxle is being used in. Some early model three speed Honda torque converters can be disassembled. However, should problems exist within the torque converter replacement of the unit is recommended.

## Metric Fasteners

Metric bolt sizes and thread pitches are used for all fasteners in both the Honda three speed and the Honda four speed automatic transaxles.

The metric fasteners have dimensions that are very close to the dimensions of the familiar inch system fasteners, and for this reason, replacement fasteners must have the same measurement and strength as those removed.

The fasteners should be reused in the same locations as removed. Do not interchange metric fasteners for the inch system fasteners, as mismatched or incorrect fasteners can result in damages to the transmission unit through malfunctions, breakage or possible personal injury.

## Checking Transaxle Fluid Level

The transaxle fluid should be at normal operating temperature, the engine stopped and the vehicle on a level surface.

**NOTE: The dipstick is screwed into the transaxle case.**

1. Unscrew the dipstick and remove if from the transaxle.
2. Wipe the dipstick clean and reinsert into the transaxle.

**IMPORTANT Do not screw the dipstick in.**

3. Remove the dipstick and read the fluid level as indicated on the dipstick.
4. Correct the fluid level, as required. Use the proper grade and type automatic transmission fluid.

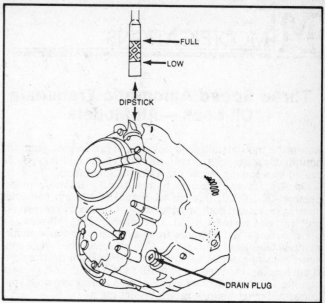

**Three speed transaxle dipstick location**

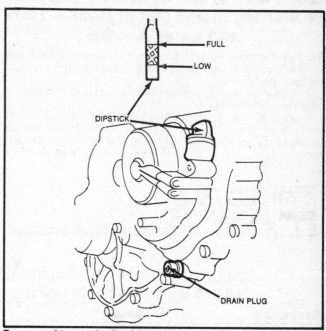

**Four speed transaxle dipstick location**

## FLUID CAPACITIES
### Honda Three Speed and Four Speed Automatic Transmissions

| Year | Transmission | Model | Oil Drain (refil) | Dry Refil |
|---|---|---|---|---|
| 1981-83 | Three speed | Civic | 2.6 quarts | 5.2 quarts |
| 1984 and Later | Three speed | Civic | 2.9 quarts | 5.6 quarts |
| 1981-82 | Three speed | Accord | 2.6 quarts | 5.2 quarts |
| 1983 and Later | Four speed | Accord | 3.0 quarts | 6.0 quarts |
| 1981-82 | Three speed | Prelude | 2.6 quarts | 5.2 quarts |
| 1983 and Later | Four speed | Prelude | 3.0 quarts | 6.0 quarts |

MODIFICATIONS

## Three Speed Automatic Transaxle Oil Leak—All Models

Automatic transmission fluid leaking, not just seeping, from the bottom of the automatic transaxle between the housings can be caused by a leaking torque converter housing gasket.

On Accords and Preludes from automatic transaxle model number AK-3000001 through AK-3056816 the torque converter housing gasket and both housings must be replaced to correct the problem. Use parts kit H/C-123152 when making this repair.

On Accords and Preludes from automatic transaxle model number AK-3056817 on, and all Civics, replace the torque converter housing gasket. Use parts kit H/C-106589 for the two dowel pin housing and parts kit H/C-106883 for the three dowel pin housing. If either kit comes equipped with a black two dowel pin torque converter housing gasket, do not use it.

## Lock Up Torque Converter Slipping or Shifting In and Out of Gear—1983 and Later Accord

The lock up torque converter may cause a surge or shifting feeling by continually locking and unlocking. To correct this problem, perform the following;
1. Check the throttle control cable and bracket. If necessary, adjust to specification.
2. Road test the vehicle at 55 mph on a level road and observe the tachometer for signs of torque converter surging. Do not use the cruise control when road testing the vehicle. If the torque converter still surges, shorten the throttle cable one turn clockwise and try the road test again. If the problem still exists shorten the cable again. The cable can be shortened approximately three millimeters shorter than specification.

**NOTE: Adjusting the cable more than three millimeters cause harsh shifting on part throttle upshifts and closed throttle downshifts.**

3. Retest the vehicle at 55 mph with the cruise control engaged. If the torque converter surges with the cruise control engaged, but is okay with it disengaged, adjust the cruise control cable at the actuator to its minimum specification.

## Mainshaft Bushing Seizure—1983 and Later Accord and Prelude

On some Accords and Preludes, insufficient clearance between the automatic transaxle bushing and the fourth clutch feed pipe can result in inadequate lubrication of the bushing. In extreme cases the bushing will overheat and seize itself onto the clutch feed pipe. When this happens, some of the transmission fluid will be diverted, resulting in clutch slippage in D3 and D4, or transaxle lock up when the unit is shifted into reverse.

In order to correct the problem the automatic transaxle must be removed from the vehicle. Disassemble the transaxle and inspect all parts for wear, damage and contamination. Clean and replace all damaged parts as required. In all cases, replace the mainshaft and end cover, including the first and fourth clutch feed pipes.

When replacing the fourth clutch feed pipe, follow the procedure below;
1. Install the O-ring in the fourth clutch feed pipe guide. Slip the guide onto the pipe.
2. Install the feed pipe in the end cover so that the tabs on the end of the feed pipe fit into the slots in the end cover.
3. Use a long metal tube, which is longer and smaller in diameter than the feed pipe, to tap the feed pipe down until it bottoms in the end cover.
4. Use a center punch to stake the feed pipe in place.
5. Install the end cover on the transaxle.

## TROUBLE DIAGNOSIS

### CHILTON'S THREE "C's" AUTOMATIC TRANSAXLE DIAGNOSIS CHART
#### 1981-83 Honda Civic, 1981-82 Honda Accord and Prelude—Three speed

| Condition | Cause | Correction |
|---|---|---|
| Vehicle will not move | a) Low fluid level<br>b) Stuck regulator valve or damaged spring<br>c) Stuck servo shaft<br>d) Damaged mainshaft<br>e) Manual shift out of adjustment<br>f) Damaged final gear<br>g) Broken flex plate<br>h) Filter clogged | a) Correct fluid level as required<br>b) Free stuck regulator valve or replace damaged spring<br>c) Correct as required<br>d) Replace mainshaft as required<br>e) Adjust manual shift<br>f) Replace final gear as required<br>g) Replace flex plate<br>h) Replace filter |
| Vehicle does not move in D1 but will move in 2, D2 and D3 | a) Manual shift out of adjustment<br>b) Worn or damaged one way clutch<br>c) Damaged low gear<br>d) First clutch piston stuck or O-ring | a) Adjust manual shift as required<br>b) Repair or replace one way clutch<br>c) Replace low gear as required<br>d) Repair or replace piston or O-ring seal as required |

## CHILTON'S THREE "C's" AUTOMATIC TRANSAXLE DIAGNOSIS CHART
### 1981-83 Honda Civic, 1981-82 Honda Accord and Prelude—Three speed

| Condition | Cause | Correction |
|---|---|---|
| Vehicle does not move in D1 but will move in 2, D2 and D3 | e) First clutch feed pipe or O-ring damaged<br>f) Worn or burnt first clutch disc<br>g) First clutch check ball stuck | e) Repair or replace component as required<br>f) Replace first clutch disc as required<br>g) Free stuck check ball as required |
| Vehicle does not move in 2, but okay in drive | a) Manual shift out of adjustment | a) Adjust manual shift as required |
| Vehicle does not move in reverse, but okay in drive and 2 | a) Stuck servo shaft<br><br>b) Damaged reverse gear | a) Correct servo shaft blockage as required<br>b) Replace reverse gear as required |
| Engine vibrates at idle | a) Lack of engine power | a) Correct engine as required |
| Up shift speed too high | a) Faulty governor valve<br>b) Throttle control cable out of adjustment<br>c) Defective throttle valve "A"<br>d) Defective modulator valve | a) Repair or replace governor valve<br>b) Adjust throttle control cable as required<br>c) Replace defective part as required<br>d) Replace modulator valve as required |
| Jumps from D1 to D3 while selector is in drive | a) Defective 2-3 shift valve | a) Replace defective shift valve as required |
| All up shift points too early | a) Throttle cable out of adjustment<br>b) Defective throttle valve "A"<br>c) Defective modulator valve | a) Adjust throttle cable<br>b) Replace defective valve as required<br>c) Replace modulator valve as required |
| D1 and D2 upshift point too early | a) Faulty 1-2 shift valve | a) Repair or replace shift valve as required |
| D2 and D3 upshift point too early | a) Defective 2-3 shift valve | a) Repair or replace shift valve as required |
| Harsh shift from D1 to D2 | a) Faulty second clutch piston<br>b) Damaged second clutch piston O-ring<br>c) Worn or damaged second clutch sealing rings<br>d) Worn or burnt second clutch disc<br>e) Second clutch check ball stuck<br>f) Defective second accumulator<br>g) No second ball check valve | a) Repair or replace piston<br>b) Replace O-ring<br><br>c) Replace sealing srings as required<br><br>d) Replace disc as required<br>e) Correct as required<br>f) Repair or replace accumulator as required<br>g) Install second ball check valve |
| Engine races in shifting from D2 into D3 | a) Defective throttle valve "B"<br>b) Defective third accumulator<br>c) Defective orifice control valve<br>d) Foreign matter stuck in main orifice<br>e) Defective third clutch piston<br>f) Damaged third clutch piston O-ring<br>g) Damaged third clutch feed pipe or O-ring<br>h) Worn or burnt third clutch disc | a) Repair or replace defective part<br>b) Repair or replace as required<br>c) Replace orifice control valve<br>d) Correct as required<br><br>e) Repair or replace as required<br>f) Replace O-ring<br><br>g) Repair or replace defective part as required<br>h) Correct defective part as required |
| Engine vibrates when shifting from D2 into D3 | a) Faulty second clutch piston or damaged O-ring seal<br>b) Second clutch check ball stuck | a) Repair or replace defective component as required<br>b) Correct as required |

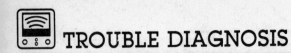 

### CHILTON'S THREE "C's" AUTOMATIC TRANSAXLE DIAGNOSIS CHART
#### 1981-83 Honda Civic, 1981-82 Honda Accord and Prelude—Three speed

| Condition | Cause | Correction |
|---|---|---|
| Engine vibrates when shifting from D2 into D3 | c) Worn or damaged second clutch sealing rings | c) Correct as required |
| | d) Worn or burned second clutch disc | d) Replace second clutch disc as required |
| | e) Foreign matter stuck in second orifice | e) Correct as required |
| | f) Foreign matter stuck in separator port orifice | f) Correct as required |
| Vehicle creeps forward in neutral | a) Shift cable out of adjustment | a) Adjust shift cable as required |
| | b) Faulty first clutch piston or damaged O-ring | b) Repair or replace defective part as required |
| | c) Damaged first clutch feed pipe or O-ring | c) Repair or replace defective part as necessary |
| | d) Faulty matter stuck in first clutch check valve | d) Correct as required |
| | e) Worn or burnt first clutch disc | e) Replace first clutch disc |
| | f) Fluid level too high | f) Check fluid level |
| | g) Burnt needle bearings | g) Correct as required |
| | h) Burnt thrust washer | h) Correct as required |
| | i) Improper clutch clearance | i) Correct as required |
| | j) Faulty second clutch piston or damaged O-ring seal | j) Repair or replace defective component as required |
| | k) Foreign matter stuck in second clutch check valve | k) Correct as required |
| | l) Worn or damaged second clutch sealing ring | l) Replace sealing ring |
| | m) Worn or burnt second clutch disc | m) Replace clutch disc |
| | n) Defective third clutch piston or stuck O-ring | n) Replace piston or O-ring as required |
| | o) Foreign matter stuck in third clutch check valve | o) Correct as required |
| | p) Damaged third clutch feed pipe or O-ring | p) Repair or replace components as required |
| | q) Worn or burnt third clutch disc | q) Replace third clutch disc |
| Excessive time lag from neutral to drive | a) Faulty first clutch piston or O-ring seal | a) Repair or replace first clutch piston or O-ring seal |
| | b) Foreign matter stuck in first clutch piston check valve | b) Correct as required |
| | c) Damaged first clutch feed pipe or O-ring seal | c) Replace feed pipe or O-ring seal |
| | d) Worn or damaged first clutch sealing rings | d) Replace components as required |
| | e) Worn or burnt first clutch disc | e) Repair or replace as required |
| | f) Foreign matter stuck in low orifice | f) Correct as required |
| Excessive time lag from neutral to reverse | a) Stuck servo shaft | a) Correct as required |
| | b) Faulty second clutch piston or O-ring seal | b) Repair or replace second clutch piston or O-ring |
| | c) Foreign matter stuck in second clutch check ball valve | c) Correct as required |
| | d) Damaged second clutch feed pipe or O-ring | d) Replace feed pipe or O-ring as required |
| | e) Worn or burnt second clutch disc | e) Replace second clutch disc as required |

## CHILTON'S THREE "C's" AUTOMATIC TRANSAXLE DIAGNOSIS CHART
### 1984 and Later Honda Civic—Three speed

| Condition | Cause | Correction |
|---|---|---|
| Vehicle runs but does not move | a) Fluid level low<br>b) Stuck regulator valve or damaged spring<br>c) Stuck servo shaft<br>d) Damaged mainshaft<br>e) Damaged final gear<br>f) Broken flex plate | a) Correct fluid level<br>b) Replace regulator valve or spring as required<br>c) Repair as required<br>d) Replace mainshaft<br>e) Repair or replace as required<br>f) Replace flex plate |
| Vehicle does not move in D1 but does move in D3 and D3 | a) Manual shift out of adjustment<br>b) Worn or damaged one way clutch<br>c) Damaged low gear<br>d) First clutch piston stuck or O-ring damaged<br>e) Foreign matter stuck in first clutch check valve<br>f) Damaged first clutch feed pipe or O-ring<br>g) Worn or damaged first clutch sealing rings<br>h) Worn or damaged first clutch disc | a) Adjust manual shift<br>b) Repair or replace one way clutch<br>c) Repair or replace low gear as needed<br>d) Repair or replace first clutch piston or O-ring<br>e) Correct as required<br><br>f) Repair or replace feed pipe and O-ring as required<br>g) Replace sealing rings as required<br><br>h) Replace clutch disc as required |
| Vehicle does not move in 2, but is movable in D | a) Manual shift out of adjustment<br>b) Damaged second gear<br>c) Second clutch piston stuck or O-ring<br>d) Foreign matter stuck in second clutch check valve<br>e) Worn or damaged second clutch sealing rings<br>f) Worn or damaged second clutch disc | a) Adjust manual shift as required<br>b) Repair or replace second gear as required<br>c) Repair or replace components as required<br>d) Correct as required<br><br>e) Replace sealing rings as required<br><br>f) Replace clutch disc as required |
| Engine vibrates at idle | a) Lack of engine power<br>b) Broken flex plate | a) Correct as required<br>b) Correct as required |
| Selector lever jumps from D1 into D3 from drive | a) Defective 2-3 shift valve | a) Correct defective shift valve as required |
| Up shift points too early | a) Faulty governor valve<br>b) Throttle cable out of adjustment<br>c) Defective throttle valve "A"<br>d) Cable housing damaged | a) Repair or replace as required<br>b) Adjust cable at transmission<br>c) Replace as required<br>d) Repair or replace as required |
| D1 and D2 up shift point too early | a) Faulty governor valve<br>b) Defective 1-2 shift valve | a) Repair or replace as required<br>b) Repair or replace shift valve as required |
| D2 and D3 up shift point too early | a) Faulty governor valve<br>b) Defective 2-3 shift valve | a) Repair or replace as required<br>b) Repair or replace shift valve as required |
| Harsh shift from D1 to D2 or from D2 to D3 | a) Second clutch piston stuck or O-ring damaged<br>b) Foreign matter stuck in second clutch check valve<br>c) Worn or damaged second clutch sealing rings | a) Repair or replace piston or O-ring as required<br>b) Correct as required<br><br>c) Repair or replace as required |

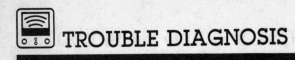

## CHILTON'S THREE "C's" AUTOMATIC TRANSAXLE DIAGNOSIS CHART
### 1984 and Later Honda Civic—Three speed

| Condition | Cause | Correction |
|---|---|---|
| Harsh shift from D1 to D2 or from D2 to D3 | d) Worn or burnt second clutch disc<br>e) Defective throttle valve "R"<br>f) Defective second accumulator | d) Replace second clutch disc as needed<br>e) Correct as required<br>f) Repair or replace as required |
| Harsh shift from D2 to D1 | a) Defective throttle valve "B"<br>b) Defective third accumulator<br>c) Defective clutch pressure control valve<br>d) Defective third orifice control valve<br>e) Foreign matter stuck in third ball check valve | a) Correct as required<br>b) Repair or replace as required<br>c) Repair or replace pressure control valve as required<br>d) Replace defective third clutch orifice valve<br>e) Correct as required |
| Harsh shift from D3 to D2 | a) Defective throttle valve "B"<br>b) Defective second accumulator<br>c) Foreign matter stuck in third ball check valve | a) Correct as required<br>b) Replace or repair as required<br>c) Correct as required |
| Engine races in shifting from D2 into D3 | a) Defective throttle valve "B"<br>b) Defective third accumulator<br>c) Defective second orifice control valve<br>d) Foreign matter stuck in third orifice<br>e) Defective third clutch piston<br>f) Damaged third clutch piston O-ring<br>g) Damaged third clutch feed pipe or O-ring<br>h) Worn or burnt third clutch disc<br>i) Defective clutch pressure control valve | a) Repair or replace defective part<br>b) Repair or replace as required<br>c) Replace orifice control valve<br>d) Correct as required<br>e) Repair or replace as required<br>f) Replace O-ring<br>g) Repair or replace defective part as required<br>h) Correct defective part as required<br>i) Replace clutch pressure control valve as required |
| Engine vibrates when shifting from D2 to D3 | a) Faulty second clutch piston or damaged O-ring seal<br>b) Second clutch check ball stuck<br>c) Worn or damaged second clutch sealing rings<br>d) Worn or burned second clutch disc<br>e) Foreign matter stuck in second orifice<br>f) Foreign matter stuck in separator port orifice<br>g) Defective throttle valve "B"<br>h) Defective third accumulator<br>i) Foreign matter stuck in third ball check valve | a) Repair or replace defective components as required<br>b) Correct as required<br>c) Correct as required<br>d) Replace second clutch disc as required<br>e) Correct as required<br>f) Correct as required<br>g) Correct as required<br>h) Repair or replace accumulator<br>i) Correct as required |
| Vehicle creeps forward in neutral | a) Shift cable out of adjustment<br>b) Faulty first clutch piston or damaged O-ring<br>c) Damaged first clutch feed pipe or O-ring<br>d) Faulty matter stuck in first clutch check valve<br>e) Worn or burnt first clutch disc<br>f) Fluid level too high | a) Adjust shift cable as required<br>b) Repair or replace defective part as required<br>c) Repair or replace defective part as necessary<br>d) Correct as required<br>e) Replace first clutch disc<br>f) Check fluid level |

## CHILTON'S THREE "C's" AUTOMATIC TRANSAXLE DIAGNOSIS CHART
### 1984 and Later Honda Civic—Three speed

| Condition | Cause | Correction |
|---|---|---|
| Vehicle creeps forward in neutral | g) Burnt needle bearings | g) Correct as required |
| | h) Burnt thrust washer | h) Correct as required |
| | i) Improper clutch clearance | i) Correct as required |
| | j) Faulty second clutch piston or damaged O-ring seal | j) Repair or replace defective component as required |
| | k) Foreign matter stuck in second clutch check valve | k) Correct as required |
| | l) Worn or damaged second clutch sealing ring | l) Replace sealing ring |
| | m) Worn or burnt second clutch disc | m) Replace clutch disc |
| | n) Defective third clutch piston or stuck O-ring | n) Replace piston or O-ring as required |
| | o) Foreign matter stuck in third clutch check valve | o) Correct as required |
| | p) Damaged third clutch feed pipe or O-ring | p) Repair or replace components as required |
| | q) Worn or burnt third clutch disc | q) Replace third clutch disc |
| Excessive time lag from neutral | a) Faulty first clutch piston or O-ring seal | a) Repair or replace first clutch piston or O-ring seal |
| | b) Foreign matter stuck in first clutch piston check valve | b) Correct as required |
| | c) Damaged first clutch feed pipe or O-ring seal | c) Replace feed pipe or O-ring seal |
| | d) Worn or damaged first clutch sealing rings | d) Replace components as required |
| | e) Worn or burnt first clutch disc | e) Repair or replace as required |
| | f) Foreign matter stuck in first orifice | f) Correct as required |
| Excessive time lag from neutral to reverse | a) Shift cable out of adjustment | a) Adjust as required |
| | b) Servo shaft stuck | b) Correct as required |
| | c) Defective 2-3 shift valve | c) Repair or replace shift valve |

## CHILTON'S THREE "C's" AUTOMATIC TRANSAXLE DIAGNOSIS CHART
### 1983 and Later Honda Accord and Prelude—Four Speed

| Condition | Cause | Correction |
|---|---|---|
| Engine runs but vehicle does not move | a) Low fluid level | a) Correct fluid level |
| | b) Stuck regulator valve or damaged spring | b) Correct regulator valve or spring as required |
| | c) Damaged mainshaft | c) Replace mainshaft as required |
| | d) Damaged final gear | d) Repair or replace as required |
| | e) Damaged flex plate | e) Replace flex plate |
| Vehicle does not move in D3 or D4, but does move in D2 | a) Manual shift out of adjustment | a) Adjust manual shift as required |
| | b) Worn or damaged one way clutch | b) Repair or replace as required |
| | c) Stuck first clutch piston or damaged O-ring seal | c) Repair or replace defective components as required |
| | d) Damaged first clutch feed pipe or O-ring | d) Repair or replace parts as required |
| | e) Foreign matter stuck in first clutch check valve | e) Correct as required |
| | f) Worn or burnt first clutch disc | f) Replace clutch disc as required |
| | g) Defective CPC valve | g) Repair or replace valve as required |

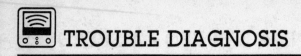

## CHILTON'S THREE "C's" AUTOMATIC TRANSAXLE DIAGNOSIS CHART
### 1983 and Later Honda Accord and Prelude—Four Speed

| Condition | Cause | Correction |
|---|---|---|
| Vehicle does not move in D2, but does move in D3 and D4 | a) Manual shift out of adjustment | a) Adjust manual shift as required |
| | b) Damaged second gear | b) Repair or replace second gear as needed |
| | c) Stuck second clutch piston or damaged O-ring | c) Repair or replace defective components as required |
| | d) Foreign matter stuck in second clutch check valve | d) Correct as required |
| | e) Worn or damaged second clutch sealing rings | e) Replace second clutch sealing rings as required |
| | f) Worn or burnt second clutch disc | f) Replace clutch disc as required |
| Vehicle does not move in reverse, but okay in D3, D4 and D2 | a) Stuck servo shaft | a) Correct as required |
| | b) Manual shift out of adjustment | b) Adjust shift linkage as required |
| | c) Damaged reverse gear | c) Repair or replace gear as required |
| | d) Defective 2-3 shift valve | d) Repair or replace defective shift valve |
| | e) Stuck fourth clutch piston or damaged O-ring | e) Repair or replace defective components as required |
| | f) Foreign matter stuck in fourth clutch check valve | f) Correct as required |
| | g) Worn or damaged fourth clutch sealing rings | g) Correct as required |
| | h) Worn or burnt fourth clutch disc | h) Replace clutch disc as required |
| Engine vibrates at idle | a) Lack of engine power | a) Correct as required |
| | b) Improper clutch clearance | b) Correct clutch clearance as required |
| Up shift speed too high | a) Faulty governor valve | a) Repair or replace governor valve as required |
| | b) Throttle control cable out of adjustment | b) Adjust cable as required at transmission case |
| | c) Defective throttle valve "A" | c) Repair or replace throttle valve |
| | d) Defective modulator valve | d) Repair or replace valve as required |
| Jumps from first to third in D3 | a) Defective 2-3 shift valve | a) Repair or replace defective 2-3 shift valve as required |
| Jumps from first to fourth in D4 | a) Defective 2-3 shift valve | a) Repair or replace defective shift valve as required |
| | b) Defective 3-4 shift valve | b) Repair or replace defective valve as required |
| Up shift points are too early or late | a) Faulty governor valve | a) Repair or replace governor valve |
| | b) Throttle cable out of adjustment | b) Adjust throttle cable |
| | c) Defective throttle valve "A" | c) Repair or replace valve as required |
| | d) Defective modulator valve | d) Repair or replace valve as required |
| Early or late up shift point— first to second | a) Faulty governor valve | a) Repair or replace valve as required |
| | b) Defective 1-2 shift valve | b) Repair or replace shift valve as required |
| Early or late shift point— second to third | a) Faulty governor valve | a) Repair or replace valve |
| | b) Defective 2-3 shift valve | b) Repair or replace valve |
| Early or late up shift point— third to fourth | a) Faulty governor valve | a) Repair or replace valve |
| | b) Defective 3-4 shift valve | b) Repair or replace valve |

## CHILTON'S THREE "C's" AUTOMATIC TRANSAXLE DIAGNOSIS CHART
### 1983 and Later Honda Accord and Prelude—Four Speed

| Condition | Cause | Correction |
|---|---|---|
| Harsh shift from first to second | a) Stuck second clutch piston or damaged O-ring | a) Repair or replace defective component as required |
| | b) Foreign matter stuck in second clutch check valve | b) Correct as required |
| | c) Worn or damaged second clutch sealing rings | c) Replace second clutch sealing rings as required |
| | d) Worn or burnt second clutch disc | d) Replace clutch disc as required |
| | e) Defective throttle valve "B" | e) Repair or replace valve |
| | f) Defective second accumulator | f) Repair or replace accumulator |
| Harsh shift from second to third | a) Defective throttle valve "B" | a) Repair or replace defective valve |
| | b) Defective third accumulator | b) Repair or replace accumulator |
| | c) Defective second orifice control valve | c) Replace defective orifice control valve |
| | d) Stuck third clutch piston or damaged O-ring | d) Repair or replace defective components as required |
| | e) Foreign matter stuck in third clutch check valve | e) Correct as required |
| | f) Damaged third clutch feed pipe or O-ring | f) Repair or replace defective component as required |
| | g) Worn or burnt third clutch disc | g) Replace clutch disc as required |
| Harsh shift from third to fourth | a) Defective throttle valve "B" | a) Repair or replace valve |
| | b) Defective fourth accumulator | b) Repair or replace accumulator |
| | c) Stuck fourth clutch piston or damaged O-ring | c) Repair or replace defective components as required |
| | d) Foreign matter stuck in fourth clutch check valve | d) Correct as required |
| | e) Worn or damaged fourth clutch sealing rings | e) Correct as required |
| | f) Worn or burnt fourth clutch disc | f) Replace clutch as required |
| | g) Lack of engine power | g) Correct as required |
| Vehicle creeps forward in neutral | a) Shift cable out of adjustment | a) Adjust shift cable |
| | b) Fluid level too high | b) Adjust fluid level |
| | c) Burnt needle bearings | c) Correct as required |
| | d) Burnt thrust washer | d) Replace thrust washer |
| | e) Improper clutch clearance | e) Correct clutch clearance |
| | f) Stuck first clutch piston or damaged O-ring seal | f) Repair or replace defective components as required |
| | g) Damaged first clutch feed pipe or O-ring | g) Repair or replace parts as required |
| | h) Foreign matter stuck in first clutch check valve | h) Correct as required |
| | i) Worn or burnt first clutch disc | i) Replace clutch disc as required |
| | j) Stuck second clutch piston or damaged O-ring | j) Repair or replace defective component as required |
| | k) Foreign matter stuck in second clutch check valve | k) Correct as required |
| | l) Worn or damaged second clutch sealing rings | l) Replace second clutch sealing rings as required |
| | m) Worn or burnt second clutch disc | m) Replace clutch disc as required |
| | n) Stuck third clutch piston or damaged O-ring | n) Repair or replace defective components as required |
| | o) Foreign matter stuck in third clutch check valve | o) Correct as required |

## CHILTON'S THREE "C's" AUTOMATIC TRANSAXLE DIAGNOSIS CHART
### 1983 and Later Honda Accord and Prelude—Four Speed

| Condition | Cause | Correction |
|---|---|---|
| Vehicle creeps forward in neutral | p) Damaged third clutch feed pipe or O-ring | p) Repair or replace defective component as required |
| | q) Worn or burnt third clutch disc | q) Replace clutch disc as required |
| | r) Stuck fourth clutch piston or damaged O-ring | r) Repair or replace defective components as required |
| | s) Foreign matter stuck in fourth clutch check valve | s) Correct as required |
| | t) Worn or damaged fourth clutch sealing rings | t) Correct as required |
| | u) Worn or burnt fourth clutch disc | u) Replace clutch disc as required |
| Excessive time lag from neutral to D3 and D4 | a) Foreign matter stuck in first orifice | a) Correct as required |
| | b) Stuck first clutch piston or damaged O-ring seal | b) Repair or replace defective components as required |
| | c) Damaged first clutch feed pipe or O-ring | c) Repair or replace parts as required |
| | d) Foreign matter stuck in first clutch check valve | d) Correct as required |
| | e) Worn or burnt first clutch disc | a) Replace clutch disc as required |
| Excessive time lag from neutral to reverse | a) Stuck servo shaft | a) Repair or replace as required |
| | b) Defective 2-3 shift valve | b) Repair or replace valve as required |
| | c) Stuck fourth clutch piston or damaged O-ring | c) Repair or replace defective components as required |
| | d) Foreign matter stuck in fourth clutch check valve | d) Correct as required |
| | e) Worn or damaged fourth clutch sealing rings | e) Correct as required |
| | f) Worn or burnt fourth clutch disc | a) Replace clutch disc as required |

# Hydraulic Control System

## THREE SPEED TRANSAXLE

The Honda three speed automatic transaxle hydraulic control system incorporates the valve body assembly, which includes a main valve body and regulator valve. This assembly is bolted to the torque converter case through a separator plate.

The main valve body contains a manual valve, 1-2 shift valve, 2-3 shift valve, pressure relief valve, orifice control valve, torque converter check valve and the oil pump gear.

The servo valve body includes the shift fork shaft, throttle control valves, throttle modulator valve, and the accumulator pistons.

The regulator valve regulates the fluid pressure within the hydraulic control system. Fluid from the regulator passes through the manual valve to the various control valves.

The first and third clutches receive fluid from the valves through their respective feed pipes.

## FOUR SPEED TRANSAXLE

The Honda four speed automatic transaxle hydraulic control system incorporates the valve body assembly, which includes a main valve body and regulator valve. This assembly is bolted to the torque converter case through a separator plate.

The main valve body contains a manual valve, 1-2 shift valve, 2-3 shift valve, 3-4 shift valve, pressure relief valve, orifice control valve, torque converter check valve and the oil pump gear.

The servo valve body includes the shift fork shaft, throttle control valves, throttle modulator valve, and the accumulator pistons.

The regulator valve regulates the fluid pressure within the hydraulic control system. Fluid from the regulator passes through the manual valve to the various control valves.

The first, third and fourth clutches receive fluid from the valves through their respective feed pipes.

# Diagnosis Tests

## CONTROL PRESSURE TEST

Control pressure tests should be performed whenever slippage, delay or harshness is felt in the shifting of the automatic transaxle. These tests can pinpoint the differences between mechanical and hydraulic failures within the transaxle. Before making any tests be sure that the transaxle is full of fluid, the engine is in tune, the transaxle is up to operating temperature and that all external linkage is adjusted properly.

### Line Pressure Test

1. Raise the vehicle and support it safely.
2. Install the gauge set to the proper transaxle pressure test ports.
3. Start the engine and run at 2000 rpm.
4. With the selector lever in neutral or park the specification should be 107-114 psi.

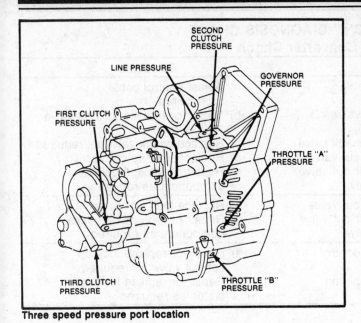

**Three speed pressure port location**

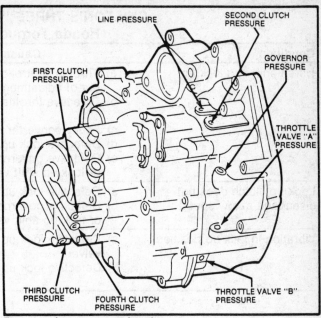

**Four speed pressure port location**

5. If the vehicle is equipped with a three speed transaxle the specification should be 100-114 psi for the rest of the gear selections.

6. If the vehicle is equipped with a four speed transaxle the specification should be 100-114 psi in D3 or D4 and 71-114 psi for the rest of the gear selections.

7. When reinstalling the pressure port plugs, do not reuse the aluminum washers.

### Throttle Pressure Test

1. Raise the vehicle and support it safely.
2. Install the gauge set to the proper transaxle pressure test ports.
3. Start the engine and run at 1000 rpm. Disconnect the throttle control cable at the throttle lever.
4. Read the pressure with the lever released it should be zero.
5. Manually push the lever up to simulate full throttle. Read and record the specification on the gauge. For the three speed transaxles before 1984 the specification should be 90-93 psi. For three speed transaxles beginning with 1984 the specification should be 78-82 psi. For all four speed transaxles the specification should be 86-88 psi.
6. When reinstalling the pressure port plugs, do not reuse the aluminum washers.

### Governor Pressure Test

1. Raise the vehicle and support it safely.
2. Install the gauge set to the proper transaxle pressure test ports.
3. Start the engine and run the vehicle at a speed of 38 mph.
4. With the selector lever in drive (D3 if vehicle is equipped with a four speed transaxle) record the pressure reading.
5. For 1981-83 three speed transaxles, the specification should be 46-49 psi. For 1984 and later three speed transaxles and all four speed transaxles, the specification should be 31-33 psi.
6. When reinstalling the pressure port plugs, do not reuse the aluminum washers.

### Stall Speed Test

1. Raise the vehicle and support it safely.
2. Connect an engine tachometer and start the engine.
3. Once the engine has reached normal operating temperature, position the selector lever in drive (D3 if the vehicle is equipped with a four speed transaxle).

4. Fully depress the gas pedal for six to eight seconds, and note the engine speed.

**NOTE: To prevent damage to the automatic transaxle, do not test stall speed for more than ten seconds at a time.**

5. Allow two minutes for the transaxle to cool and then repeat the test in 2 (D4 and 2 if the vehicle is equipped with a four speed transaxle) and reverse.
6. All stall speed readings must be the same in all selector positions.
7. For 1981-83 three speed transaxles the specification should be 2400-2500 rpm. For all 1984 and later three speed transaxles the specification should be 2700 rpm. For all four speed transaxles the specification should be 2400 rpm.

## AIR PRESSURE TEST

Air pressure testing should be done in moderation to avoid excessive fluid spray and damage to the internal parts during disassembly and assembly, through partial retention of units.

## ROAD TEST

1. Road test using all selective ranges, noting when discrepancies in operation or oil pressure occur.
2. Attempt to isolate the unit or circuit involved in the malfunction.
3. If engine performance indicates an engine tune-up is required, this should be performed before road testing is completed or transaxle correction attempted. Poor engine performance can result in rough shifting or other malfunctions.

## Converter Clutch Operation and Diagnosis

### TORQUE CONVERTER CLUTCH

**Three Speed Transaxle**

When the Honda three speed automatic transaxle is in drive and at speeds above thirty miles per hour, pressurized fluid is bled off from the back of the torque converter through an oil passage causing the lock up function of the torque converter to take place. As

## CHILTON'S THREE "C's" DIAGNOSIS CHART
### Honda Torque Converter Clutch

| Condition | Cause | Correction |
|---|---|---|
| Harsh shift into lock up | a) Throttle control cable out of adjustment | a) Adjust control cable as required |
| | b) Defective throttle valve "B" | b) Repair or replace throttle valve "B" as required |
| | c) Faulty converter check valve | c) Replace check valve as required |
| | d) Defective lock up cut valve | d) Replace lock up cut valve |
| | e) Defective governor cut valve or lock up shift valve | e) Repair or replace defective component as required |
| Lock up clutch does not disengage at low speed | a) Defective lock up cut valve | a) Replace lock up cut valve |
| | b) Defective governor cut valve or lock up shift valve | b) Repair or replace defective component as required |
| Vibration in lock up position | a) Defective lock up control valve | a) Repair or replace lock up control valve as required |
| | b) Defective lock up piston | b) Repair or replace lock up piston as required |

this function occurs the mainshaft rotates at the same speed as the engine crankshaft.

The lock up valve body is bolted to the top of the regulator body, and includes the lock up shift valve. The lock up shift valve controls the engagement of the lock up function according to vehicle speed and throttle pressure.

The lock up control is integrated with the regulator valve body and regulates the torque converter oil pressure in relation to vehicle speed and throttle opening. The lock up cut out valve is the servo valve. It prevents the lock up function from taking place when the throttle is not opened sufficiently.

### Four Speed Transaxle

When the Honda four speed automatic transaxle is in drive and at speeds above forty three miles per hour, pressurized fluid is drained from the back of the torque converter through an oil passage causing the lock up function of the torque converter to occur. As this takes place the mainshaft rotates at the same speed as the engine crankshaft.

The pressure control valve body is bolted to the top of the regulator body and includes the pressure control shift valve and pressure control timing valve. The pressure control shift valve controls the range of lock-up according to vehicle speed and throttle pressure. The timing valve senses when the transaxle is in fourth gear.

The clutch pressure control valve is bolted to the top of the servo valve and prevents the lock up function from taking place when the throttle is not opened sufficiently.

## ON CAR SERVICES

# Adjustments
## NEUTRAL SAFETY SWITCH

**Adjustment**

1. Move the selector lever through park, reverse and neutral to check the continuity of the switch.
2. Replace the switch if there is not continuity between the terminals.

3. To replace the switch, remove the console. Remove the switch retaining bolts and electrical connections. Remove the switch from its mounting.
4. When installing, position the slider on the switch in the neutral position.
5. Shift the selector lever in the neutral position. Align the switch lug with the actuator rod.
6. Continue the installation in the reverse order of the removal position.

## SHIFT INDICATOR

**Adjustment**

1. Check that the index mark of the indicator aligns with the N mark of the shift indicator panel when the transaxle is in neutral.
2. If not aligned, remove panel mounting screws and adjust by moving panel.

## SHIFT CABLE ADJUSTMENT

**Adjustment**

1. Remove the console assembly.
2. Shift the selector lever into drive. Remove the lock pin from the cable adjuster.
3. Check that the hole in the adjuster is in line with the hole in the shift cable.

**NOTE: There are two holes in end of the shift cable. They are positioned 90° apart to allow cable adjustments in ¼ turn increments.**

4. If not perfectly aligned, loosen locknut on shift cable and adjust as required.
5. Tighten the locknuts. Install lock pin on adjuster.

**NOTE: If the lock pin binding as you reinstall it, the cable is still out of adjustment and must be readjusted.**

6. Start engine and check shift lever in all gears.

## THROTTLE CONTROL CABLE BRACKET

**Adjustment**

1. Disconnect the throttle control cable from the throttle control lever.
2. Bend down the lock tabs of the lock plate and remove the two bolts to free the bracket.

3. Loosely install a new lock plate.

4. Position the special tool between the throttle control lever and the bracket.

**NOTE: The special tool is designed so that the distance between the lever and the bracket is 3.287 in. when it is installed.**

5. Position the bracket so that there is no binding between the bracket and the special tool. Then tighten the two bolts, bend up the lock plate tabs against the bolts heads.

**NOTE: Make sure the control lever doesn't get pulled toward the bracket side as you tighten the bolts.**

## THROTTLE CONTROL CABLE

### Adjustment

1. Check that the carburetor throttle cable play is correct.

2. Be sure that the engine has reached operating temperature. The electric fan should come on twice.

3. Be sure that the idle speed is within specification. Check that the choke is functioning properly.

4. Be sure that the distance between the throttle control lever and the throttle control bracket is correct.

5. With the engine off, disconnect the throttle control cable from the throttle control lever.

6. Disconnect the vacuum tube from the dash pot and connect the vacuum pump and keep vacuum applied.

7. Attach a weight of about 2.6 lbs to the accelerator pedal. Raise the pedal, then release it, this will allow the weight to remove the normal free play from the throttle cable. Secure the cable.

8. Lay the end of the throttle control cable on the battery.

9. Adjust the distance between the throttle control cable end and the locknut to 3.3 inch.

10. Insert the end of throttle control cable in the groove of the throttle control lever.

11. Insert the throttle control cable in the bracket and secure it with the locknut. Be sure that the cable is not kinked or twisted.

12. Check that the cable moves freely by depressing the accelerator.

13. Remove the weight on the accelerator pedal and push the pedal to make sure that there is the specified play at the throttle control lever.

14. Start the engine and check the synchronization between the carburetor and the throttle control cable.

**NOTE: The throttle control lever should start to move as engine speed increases.**

15. If the throttle control lever moves before engine speed increases, turn the cable lock nut counter clockwise and re-tighten the other lock nut.

16. If the throttle control lever moves after engine speed increases, turn the lock nut clockwise and re-tighten the other lock nut.

## Services

### FLUID CHANGE

1. Raise the vehicle and support safely.

2. Remove the transmission drain plug and allow the fluid to drain into a waste container. Remove the dipstick to aid in the draining.

3. When the fluid draining is complete, install the drain plug and tighten securely.

4. Fill with new fluid through the dipstick opening.

**NOTE: The fluid refill may be less because of the fluid remaining in the units and the recesses of the case.**

## REMOVAL & INSTALLATION

### Removal
#### 1981-83 CIVIC

1. Disconnect the negative battery cable.

2. Position the selector lever in neutral.

3. Disconnect the battery cable from the starter. Disconnect the water temperature sending unit wiring and the ignition timing thermosensor wiring.

4. Disconnect and plug the transaxle oil cooler lines at the transaxle.

5. Remove the starter mounting bolt on the transaxle side and the top transaxle mounting bolt.

6. Loosen the front wheel nuts. Raise the vehicle and support it safely.

7. Drain the transaxle and reinstall the drain plug.

8. Remove the throttle control cable.

9. Remove the cable clip and then pull the speedometer cable out of the holder.

10. Do not remove the holder or the speedometer gear may fall into the transaxle housing.

11. Remove the nut and washer from each end of the stabilizer bar. Remove both mounting brackets and then remove the bar.

12. Disconnect right and left lower arm ball joints and tie-rod end ball joints using ball joint remover tool, or you can remove pivot bolts from lower control arms instead.

13. Turn the right steering knuckle outward as far as it will go. Position a suitable tool against inboard CV joint, pry right axle out of transaxle housing approximately ½ inch (to force its spring clip out of groove inside differential gear splines), then pull it out the rest of the way. Repeat on opposite side.

14. Place a jack under engine oil pan and raise engine just enough to take weight off mounts.

15. Remove engine damper from center beam.

16. Remove front and rear torque rods, and rear torque rod brackets.

17. Remove rear engine mount and its bracket.

18. Cut a block of wood, 1" x 2" x 4", and place between the center beam and the oil pan, then lower the jack and let engine rest on center beam.

19. Remove engine damper bracket and torque converter cover plate from the transaxle.

20. Remove engine-side starter mounting bolt, then remove starter.

21. Raise transmission jack securely against the transaxle.

22. Remove center console and shift indicator.

23. Remove lock pin from adjuster and shift cable.

24. Remove both bolts and pull shift cable out of housing.

25. Unbolt torque converter from drive plate by rotating crank and removing eight bolts.

26. Remove two remaining the transaxle mounting bolts.

27. Roll the transaxle away from engine to clear the two dowel pins, then lower the jack.

28. Reinstall center beam, then remove hoist.

#### 1984 AND LATER CIVIC

1. Disconnect the negative battery cable.

2. Position the selector lever in the neutral position.

3. Disconnect the battery cable from the starter. Disconnect the transaxle ground cable.

4. Disconnect and plug the transaxle oil cooler lines at the transaxle.

5. Remove the two starter mounting bolts. Remove the top three transaxle mounting bolts.

6. Loosen the front wheel nuts. Raise the vehicle and support it safely.

7. Drain the transaxle and reinstall the drain plug.
8. Remove the throttle control cable.
9. Remove the cable clip and then pull the speedometer cable out of the holder.
10. Do not remove the holder or the speedometer gear will fall into the transaxle housing.
11. Remove the engine and wheelwell splash shields from the front end of the frame.
12. Remove the exhaust header pipe.
13. Disconnect the right and left lower arm ball joints and tie rod end ball joints using the ball joint remover.

**NOTE: Make sure the floor jack is positioned securely under the lower control arm, at the ball joint. Otherwise torsion bar tension on the lower control arm may cause the arm to jump suddenly away from the steering knuckle as the ball joint is being removed.**

14. Turn the right steering knuckle outward as far as it will go. Position a suitable tool against the inboard CV joint, pry right axle out of the transaxle housing approximately ½ inch (to force its spring clip out of groove inside deferential gear splines), then pull it out the rest of the way. Repeat on opposite side.
15. Attach a chain hoist to the bolt near the distributor, then lift the engine slightly to unload the mounts.
16. Raise the transmission jack and secure it against the transaxle assembly.
17. Remove the bolts from the front transaxle mount.
18. Remove the transaxle housing bolts from the engine torque bracket.
19. Remove the torque converter housing bolts from the rear transaxle mount.
20. Remove the torque converter cover plate.
21. Remove the drive plate bolts.
22. Remove the cotter pin from the shift cable control pin, then pull out the control pin.
23. Remove the cable holder and carefully remove the shift cable.

**NOTE: Be careful not to lose the shift cable bushing.**

24. Remove the one remaining transaxle mounting bolt from the engine side.
25. Pull the transaxle away from engine to clear the two dowel pins, then lower the jack.
26. Remove torque converter from the transaxle.

### 1981 AND LATER ACCORD AND PRELUDE

1. Disconnect the negative battery cable.
2. Position the selector lever in neutral.
3. Disconnect the battery cable from the starter. Disconnect the wire from the solenoid.
4. Disconnect and plug the transaxle oil cooler lines at the transaxle.
5. Remove the starter mounting bolt on the transaxle side and the top transaxle mounting bolt.
6. Loosen the front wheel nut. Raise the vehicle and support it safely.
7. Drain the transaxle. Reinstall the transaxle drain plug.
8. Remove the throttle control cable.
9. On some vehicles it may be necessary to remove the right front wheel well fender shield.
10. If the vehicle is not equipped with power steering, remove the cable clip and pull the speedometer cable out of the housing. Do not remove the holder because the speedometer gear may fall into the transaxle housing.
11. If the vehicle is equipped with power steering, remove the speed sensor along with the speedometer cable and hoses.
12. Remove the transaxle-side starter motor mounting bolt and two upper transaxle mounting bolts.
13. Place transmission jack securely beneath transaxle, and hook hanger plate with hoist; make sure hoist chain is tight.
14. Remove subframe center beam.

15. Remove the ball joint pinch bolt from the right side lower control arm, then use a lead or brass hammer to tap the control arm free of the kunckle.
16. Remove the right side radius rod.
17. Disconnect the stabilizer bar at the right side lower control arm.
18. Detach stabilizer spring from radius rods.
19. Remove front self-locking nuts from radius rods on each side.
20. Remove lower arm bolt from both sides of sub frame.
21. Turn right side steering knuckle to its most outboard position. Pry CV joint out approximately ½ in., then pull CV joint out of transaxle housing.

**NOTE: Do not pull on the driveshaft or knuckle since this may cause the inboard CV joint to separate; pull on the inboard CV joint.**

22. Remove engine-side starter motor bolt. Detach starter motor and lower through chassis.
23. Remove the transaxle damper bracket located in front of torque converter cover plate.
24. Remove torque converter cover plate.
25. Disconnect the shift cable from transaxle.
26. Wire the shift cable away from the transaxle assembly.
27. Remove both bolts and pull shift cable out of housing.
28. Unbolt torque converter assembly from drive plate by removing eight bolts.
29. Remove the three rear engine mounting bolts from the transaxle housing. Remove the rear engine mount.
30. Remove the lower transaxle mounting bolt.
31. Pull the transaxle assembly away from the engine in order to clear the two dowel pins.
32. Pry the left side CV joint out about ½ in. Pull the transaxle out and lower the assembly on the transmission jack.
33. Remove the torque converter assembly from the transaxle.

### Installation
#### 1981-83 CIVIC

1. Slide torque converter onto mainshaft.
2. Position the transaxle on the transmission jack, and raise to engine level.
3. Check that the two dowel pins are installed in torque converter housing.
4. Align dowel pins with holes in block; align torque converter bolt heads with holes in drive plate.
5. If you left the front end connected on driver's side, insert left axle (with new spring clip on the end) into differential as you roll the transaxle up to the engine.
6. Secure the transaxle to engine with two lower mounting bolts.
7. Attach the torque converter to the drive plate with the eight bolts, and torque to 9 ft. lbs. Rotate crank as necessary to tighten bolts to ½ torque, then final torque, in a criss-cross pattern. Check for free rotation after tightening last bolt.
8. Secure cable retainer to guide (below shift console).
9. Remove transmission jack.
10. Install the torque converter cover plate and damper bracket.
11. Place a jack under engine oil pan and raise engine only enough to align bolt holes for rear motor mount bracket.

**NOTE: Place a flat piece of wood on the jack lifting pad, to prevent damage to oil pan.**

12. Install rear engine mount and bracket.
13. Install starter with engine-side mounting bolt and torque to 33 ft. lbs.
14. Install front and rear torque rods and brackets.
15. Install new 26mm spring clip on end of each axle.

16. Turn right steering knuckle fully outward, and slide axle into differential until you feel its spring clip engage side gear. Repeat on left side or, if left axle is already in, check to be sure spring clip has engaged side gear.

17. Reconnect lower arm and tie rod end ball joints. Torque lower arm nuts to 25 ft. lbs. and the tie rod nuts to 32 ft. lbs.

18. Install stabilizer bar. Torque end nuts and bracket bolts to 31 ft. lbs.

19. Install the front wheels. Lower the vehicle from the lift.

20. Insert the speedometer cable into the gear holder and secure the cable with the clip. Install the boot.

21. Install the transaxle side starter mounting bolt. Install the top transaxle mounting bolt. Torque all bolts to 33 ft. lbs.

22. Connect the transaxle oil cooler lines.

23. Install the forward bolt for the rear torque rod bracket. Attach the shift control cable to the shift lever with the pin and clip. Install the center console as required.

24. Connect all necessary electrical wiring.

25. Connect the negative battery cable. Fill the transaxle with the proper grade and type automatic transmission fluid. Adjust the shift cable.

26. Install and adjust throttle control cable as required. Road test the vehicle.

## 1984 AND LATER CIVIC

1. Slide the torque converter onto mainshaft.

2. Position the transaxle on the transmission jack, and raise to engine level.

3. Check that the two dowel pins are installed in torque converter housing.

4. Align dowel pins with holes in block; align torque converter bolt heads with holes in drive plate.

5. If you left the front end connected on driver's side, insert left axle (with new spring clip on the end) into differential as you roll the transaxle up to the engine.

**NOTE: New 26mm spring clips must be used on both axles.**

6. Secure the transaxle to engine with engine side mounting bolt and torque to 50 ft. lbs.

7. Attach torque converter to drive plate with eight bolts, and torque to 9 ft. lbs. Rotate crank as necessary to tighten bolts to ½ torque, then final torque, in a criss-cross pattern. Check for free rotation after tightening last bolt.

8. Install the shift cable.

9. Remove the transmission jack.

10. Install the torque converter cover plate.

11. Install the rear transmission mount and torque its bolts to 47 ft. lbs.

12. Install the engine torque bracket and torque the retaining bolts to 33 ft. lbs.

13. Loosely install the front transaxle mounting bolts.

14. Install the starter mounting bolts and torque to 33 ft. lbs.

15. Install a new 26mm spring clip on end of each axle.

16. Turn right steering knuckle fully outward, and slide axle into differential until you feel its spring clip engage side gear. Repeat on left side or, if left axle is already in, check to be sure spring clip has engaged side gear.

17. Reconnect the lower arm ball joints and torque to 33 ft. lbs.

18. Reconnect the tie-rod end ball joints and torque to 33 ft. lbs.

19. Install the splash shields and exhaust header pipe.

20. Install the front wheels. Lower the vehicle.

21. Remove the chain hoist.

22. Insert the speedometer cable into the gear holder and secure it with the clip. Install the boot.

23. Install the three top transaxle mounting bolts. Torque them to 42 ft. lbs.

24. Connect the transaxle oil cooler lines.

25. Attach the shift control cable to the shift lever with the retaining pin and clip. Install the center console as required.

26. Connect all electrical wiring.

27. Connect the negative battery cable. Fill the transaxle with the proper grade and type automatic transmission fluid.

28. Start the engine and check for proper shift cable adjustment. Adjust the cable as required.

29. Install and set the throttle control cable as required.

30. Road test the vehicle and check for leaks.

## 1981 and Later Accord and Prelude

1. Attach the shift cable to the shift arm with the retaining pin. Secure the cable to the edge of the transaxle housing with the cable holder and bolt. Torque the bolt to 9 ft. lbs.

2. Install torque converter on the transaxle.

3. Place the transaxle on transmission jack, and raise to engine level.

4. Hook hanger plate with hoist and make hoist chain tight.

5. Check that the two dowel pins are installed in the transaxle housing.

6. Install new 26mm spring clips on the end of each axle.

7. Align dowel pins with holes in block; align torque converter bolt head with holes in drive plate.

8. Fit the left axle into the differential as you raise the transaxle up to the engine.

9. Secure the transaxle to engine with the two lower mounting bolts.

10. Install rear and front engine mounts on the transaxle housing, torque to 28 ft. lbs.

11. Install the front transaxle mount bolts and torque them to 28 ft. lbs.

12. Attach torque converter to drive plate with eight bolts, and torque to 9 ft. lbs. Rotate crank as necessary to tighten bolts to ½ torque, then the final torque, in a crisscross pattern. Check for free rotation after tightening the last bolts.

13. Remove the transmission jack.

14. Install torque converter cover plate, torque two bolts (in oil pan flange). Torque bolts to 9 ft. lbs.

15. Install damper bracket, torque two nuts to 40 ft. lbs. and three bolts to 22 ft. lbs.

16. Remove the hoist from the transaxle assembly.

17. Install the starter mount bolts, and troque them to 33 ft. lbs.

18. Install the rear torque rod and brackets.

19. Turn right steering knuckle fully outward, and slide axle into differential until you feel its spring clip engage side the gear. Check that the left axle spring clip is engaged in its side gear.

20. Reconnect ball joint to knuckle, then torque its bolt to 40 ft. lbs. Reinstall the damper fork and torque its bolt to 32 ft. lbs.

21. Install the speedometer cable. Align the tab on the cable end with the slot in the holder. Install the clip so the bent leg is on the groove. After installation pull the cable to be sure that its secure.

22. Install the front tires and wheels. Lower the vehicle to the ground.

23. Install the transaxle side starter mounting bolts. Torque to 33 ft. lbs. Install the top transaxle mounting bolt and torque to 33 ft. lbs.

24. Connect the transaxle oil cooler lines to the transaxle assembly.

25. Connect all necessary wiring and electrical connectors.

26. Connect the negative battery cable. Fill the transaxle with the proper grade and type automatic transmission fluid.

27. Install and connect the shift cable. Install the console assembly as required.

28. Start the engine and shift the transaxle through all the gears. If the shift cable is out of adjustment correct it.

29. Install the throttle cable and adjust it as required. Road test the vehicle.

## BENCH OVERHAUL

### Before Disassembly

1. Clean the exterior of the automatic transaxle before any attempt is made to disassemble the unit. This procedure is done to prevent dirt or other foreign material from entering the transaxle and damaging the internal parts.

#### — CAUTION —

*If steam cleaning is done to the exterior of the automatic transaxle immediate disassembly should be done to avoid rust from condensation, which will form on the internal parts of the transaxle.*

2. Handle all automatic transaxle parts carefully to avoid nicking or burring the bearing or mating surface.
3. Lubricate all internal parts with automatic transmission fluid before assembling.
4. Do not use other lubricants except on gaskets and thrust washers, as may be indicated. Gaskets and thrust washers may be coated with petroleum jelly in place of other lubricants.
5. Always use new gaskets and seals during the assembly.
6. Tighten all nuts and bolts to the specified torque.

### Torque Converter Inspection

Some three speed automatic transaxles are equipped with a torque converter that can be disassembled. Only qualified repair shops that have special equipment should attempt disassembly and reassembly of the torque converter.

### THREE SPEED TRANSAXLE

#### Disassembly

1. Locate alignment marks on the converter cover and converter pump. If not visible, scribe marks so that the converter cover and pump may be reassembled in the same position.
2. Remove the retaining bolts holding the converter cover to the starter ring gear.
3. Separate the converter cover from the pump body with the use of a plastic or rawhide hammer.
4. Remove the turbine thrust washer and remove the turbine from the converter pump.
5. Remove the serrated thrust washer from between the turbine and the stator.
6. Remove the stator from the pump body, along with the thrust washer.
7. Remove the snap rings from the stator and remove the front and rear side plates. Push the one-way clutch assembly from the stator body.

#### — CAUTION —

*As the one-way clutch assembly is removed from the stator, the rollers and springs may become disengaged and fall from the assembly. Do not lose the rollers or springs.*

#### Inspection

1. Inspect the cover for cracks, nicks and burrs on the sealing surfaces.
2. Inspect the thrust washers for overheating indications, extreme wear and a galling condition.
3. Inspect the turbine and converter pump cover for broken or damaged vanes, nicks and burrs, and thrust washer wear surfaces for scores.

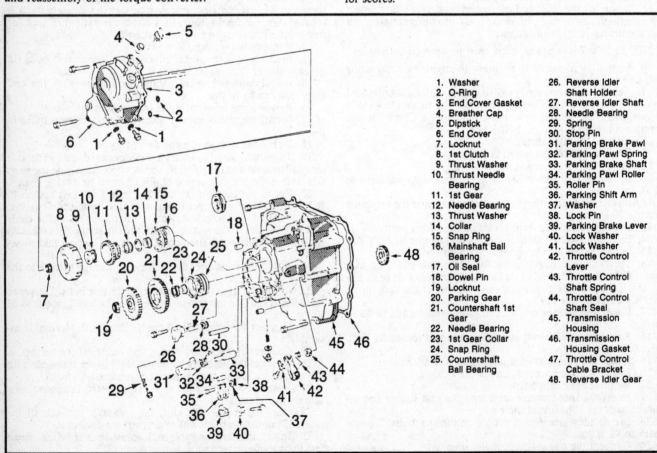

| | |
|---|---|
| 1. Washer | 26. Reverse Idler Shaft Holder |
| 2. O-Ring | 27. Reverse Idler Shaft |
| 3. End Cover Gasket | 28. Needle Bearing |
| 4. Breather Cap | 29. Spring |
| 5. Dipstick | 30. Stop Pin |
| 6. End Cover | 31. Parking Brake Pawl |
| 7. Locknut | 32. Parking Pawl Spring |
| 8. 1st Clutch | 33. Parking Brake Shaft |
| 9. Thrust Washer | 34. Parking Pawl Roller |
| 10. Thrust Needle Bearing | 35. Roller Pin |
| 11. 1st Gear | 36. Parking Shift Arm |
| 12. Needle Bearing | 37. Washer |
| 13. Thrust Washer | 38. Lock Pin |
| 14. Collar | 39. Parking Brake Lever |
| 15. Snap Ring | 40. Lock Washer |
| 16. Mainshaft Ball Bearing | 41. Lock Washer |
| 17. Oil Seal | 42. Throttle Control Lever |
| 18. Dowel Pin | 43. Throttle Control Shaft Spring |
| 19. Locknut | 44. Throttle Control Shaft Seal |
| 20. Parking Gear | 45. Transmission Housing |
| 21. Countershaft 1st Gear | 46. Transmission Housing Gasket |
| 22. Needle Bearing | 47. Throttle Control Cable Bracket |
| 23. 1st Gear Collar | 48. Reverse Idler Gear |
| 24. Snap Ring | |
| 25. Countershaft Ball Bearing | |

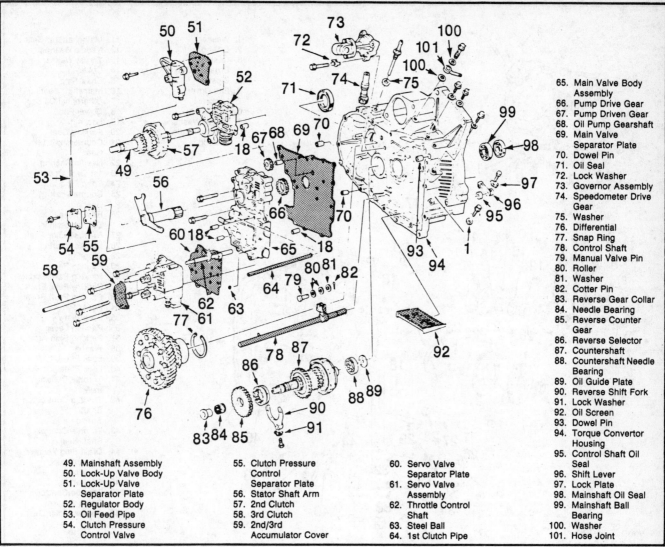

| | |
|---|---|
| 65. | Main Valve Body Assembly |
| 66. | Pump Drive Gear |
| 67. | Pump Driven Gear |
| 68. | Oil Pump Gearshaft |
| 69. | Main Valve Separator Plate |
| 70. | Dowel Pin |
| 71. | Oil Seal |
| 72. | Lock Washer |
| 73. | Governor Assembly |
| 74. | Speedometer Drive Gear |
| 75. | Washer |
| 76. | Differential |
| 77. | Snap Ring |
| 78. | Control Shaft |
| 79. | Manual Valve Pin |
| 80. | Roller |
| 81. | Washer |
| 82. | Cotter Pin |
| 83. | Reverse Gear Collar |
| 84. | Needle Bearing |
| 85. | Reverse Counter Gear |
| 86. | Reverse Selector |
| 87. | Countershaft |
| 88. | Countershaft Needle Bearing |
| 89. | Oil Guide Plate |
| 90. | Reverse Shift Fork |
| 91. | Lock Washer |
| 92. | Oil Screen |
| 93. | Dowel Pin |
| 94. | Torque Convertor Housing |
| 95. | Control Shaft Oil Seal |
| 96. | Shift Lever |
| 97. | Lock Plate |
| 98. | Mainshaft Oil Seal |
| 99. | Mainshaft Ball Bearing |
| 100. | Washer |
| 101. | Hose Joint |

| | | | |
|---|---|---|---|
| 49. | Mainshaft Assembly | 55. | Clutch Pressure Control Separator Plate |
| 50. | Lock-Up Valve Body | 56. | Stator Shaft Arm |
| 51. | Lock-Up Valve Separator Plate | 57. | 2nd Clutch |
| 52. | Regulator Body | 58. | 3rd Clutch |
| 53. | Oil Feed Pipe | 59. | 2nd/3rd Accumulator Cover |
| 54. | Clutch Pressure Control Valve | | |

| | | | |
|---|---|---|---|
| 60. | Servo Valve Separator Plate | 63. | Steel Ball |
| 61. | Servo Valve Assembly | 64. | 1st Clutch Pipe |
| 62. | Throttle Control Shaft | | |

**Three speed transaxle—exploded view**

4. Inspect the stator for broken vanes and the operation of the one-way clutch. Using the stator torque converter shaft, installed in the one-way clutch from the pump side (thinner vanes up), the one-way clutch should turn in a counterclockwise direction and lock-up in a clockwise direction.

5. Inspect the one-way clutch springs and rollers for breakage, distortion, galling and indentations on the stator cam.

6. Inspect the converter hub surface and serrations for damage. Inspect the O-ring groove for burrs.

### Assembly

1. Hold the stator with the thinner vanes up and place the stator cam with the wide shoulder upward, into the stator body. Place a roller into the opening between the stator cam and the stator ring. Insert a spring on the deep side of the roller pocket and continue the roller/spring installation, with the center of the spring against the roller.

2. Install the stator side plates and the snap rings and lock into place. Install side plates with grooved side out.

3. Inspect the one-way clutch operation. With the thinner vane side up (converter pump side), the one-way clutch should free-wheel in a counterclockwise rotation and lock up in a clockwise rotation.

4. Place the converter pump body on a flat surface with the vanes up. Install the thrust washer in the converter pump.

5. Place the stator assembly in the pump body, with the thicker vanes up and the stator resting on the thrust washer.

6. Place the serrated thrust washer in the stator, being sure the washer is flush with the stator surface.

7. Install the large O-ring on the pump body and set the turbine in place over the stator assembly.

8. Install the thrust washer in the turbine center and install the converter cover, aligning the match marks.

9. Slide the starter ring gear up over the pump cover and install the bolts through the converter cover and into the starter ring gear. The flat side of the ring gear should be towards the torque converter cover.

## Transaxle Disassembly

### TRANSAXLE HOUSING

#### Disassembly

**THREE AND FOUR SPEED TRANSAXLES**

1. Remove the transaxle dipstick. Remove the end cover retaining bolts. Remove the end cover.

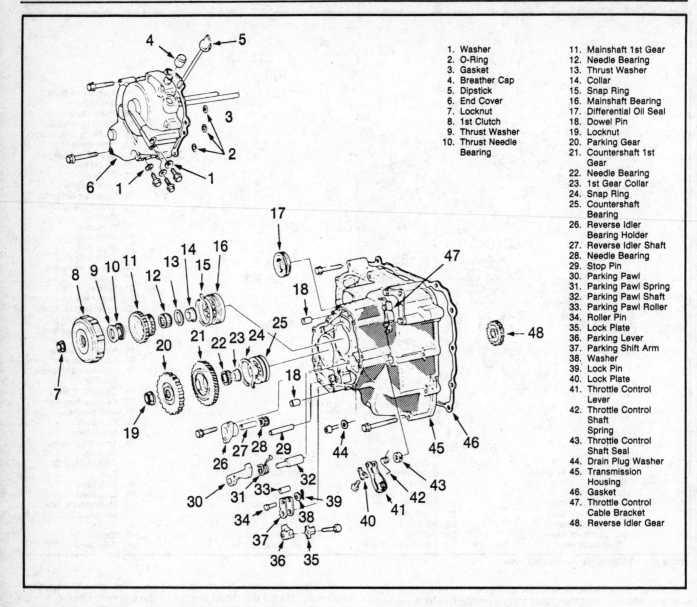

1. Washer
2. O-Ring
3. Gasket
4. Breather Cap
5. Dipstick
6. End Cover
7. Locknut
8. 1st Clutch
9. Thrust Washer
10. Thrust Needle
    Bearing
11. Mainshaft 1st Gear
12. Needle Bearing
13. Thrust Washer
14. Collar
15. Snap Ring
16. Mainshaft Bearing
17. Differential Oil Seal
18. Dowel Pin
19. Locknut
20. Parking Gear
21. Countershaft 1st
    Gear
22. Needle Bearing
23. 1st Gear Collar
24. Snap Ring
25. Countershaft
    Bearing
26. Reverse Idler
    Bearing Holder
27. Reverse Idler Shaft
28. Needle Bearing
29. Stop Pin
30. Parking Pawl
31. Parking Pawl Spring
32. Parking Pawl Shaft
33. Parking Pawl Roller
34. Roller Pin
35. Lock Plate
36. Parking Lever
37. Parking Shift Arm
38. Washer
39. Lock Pin
40. Lock Plate
41. Throttle Control
    Lever
42. Throttle Control
    Shaft
    Spring
43. Throttle Control
    Shaft Seal
44. Drain Plug Washer
45. Transmission
    Housing
46. Gasket
47. Throttle Control
    Cable Bracket
48. Reverse Idler Gear

2. Shift the transaxle into the park position. Lock the mainshaft in place by using the mainshaft holder.

3. Remove the end cover gasket, dowel pins and O-rings.

4. Pry the staked edge of the locknut flange out of the notch in the first clutch.

5. Remove the mainshaft locknut. Be careful as the mainshaft locknut is left hand threaded.

6. Remove the first clutch assembly. Remove the thrust washer, needle bearing and the first gear from the transaxle.

7. Remove the needle bearing and the thrust washer from the mainshaft.

8. Pry the staked edge of the locknut out of the notch in the parking gear. Remove the countershaft locknut and the parking pawl stop pin.

9. Remove the parking pawl, shaft and spring from the transaxle case.

10. Remove the parking gear and first gear countershaft as a complete unit.

11. From the countershaft, remove the needle bearing and the first gear collar. From the mainshaft, remove the O-ring and the first gear collar.

12. Remove the reverse idler bearing holder.

13. Bend down the tab on the lock plate which is under the parking shift arm bolt. Remove the bolt. Remove the parking shift arm spring.

14. Bend down the tab on the throttle control lever bolt lock plate, then remove the bolt. Remove the throttle control lever and spring from throttle valve shaft.

15. Remove the retaining bolts as indicated in the retaining bolt illustration.

**NOTE: Retaining bolt number one will not come all the way out of the transaxle housing because the throttle control cable bracket is in the way. Just unscrew the bracket so that it is free of the threads in the converter housing and leave it in place. If you remove the bracket you will have to readjust it upon installation.**

16. Align the control shaft spring pin with the cutout in the transaxle housing.

17. Install the transaxle housing puller. Screw in the puller and separate the transaxle housing from the rest of the transaxle assembly.

18. Remove the puller from the transaxle housing.

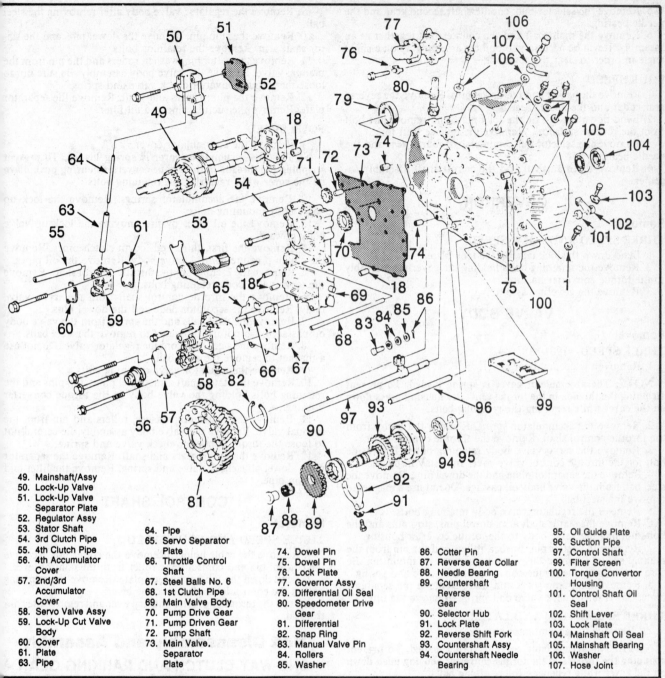

49. Mainshaft/Assy
50. Lock-Up Valve
51. Lock-Up Valve Separator Plate
52. Regulator Assy
53. Stator Shaft
54. 3rd Clutch Pipe
55. 4th Clutch Pipe
56. 4th Accumulator Cover
57. 2nd/3rd Accumulator Cover
58. Servo Valve Assy
59. Lock-Up Cut Valve Body
60. Cover
61. Plate
63. Pipe

64. Pipe
65. Servo Separator Plate
66. Throttle Control Shaft
67. Steel Balls No. 6
68. 1st Clutch Pipe
69. Main Valve Body
70. Pump Drive Gear
71. Pump Driven Gear
72. Pump Shaft
73. Main Valve. Separator Plate

74. Dowel Pin
75. Dowel Pin
76. Lock Plate
77. Governor Assy
79. Differential Oil Seal
80. Speedometer Drive Gear
81. Differential
82. Snap Ring
83. Manual Valve Pin
84. Rollers
85. Washer

86. Cotter Pin
87. Reverse Gear Collar
88. Needle Bearing
89. Countershaft Reverse Gear
90. Selector Hub
91. Lock Plate
92. Reverse Shift Fork
93. Countershaft Assy
94. Countershaft Needle Bearing

95. Oil Guide Plate
96. Suction Pipe
97. Control Shaft
99. Filter Screen
100. Torque Convertor Housing
101. Control Shaft Oil Seal
102. Shift Lever
103. Lock Plate
104. Mainshaft Oil Seal
105. Mainshaft Bearing
106. Washer
107. Hose Joint

Four speed transaxle—exploded view

## MAINSHAFT AND COUNTERSHAFT

### Removal

#### THREE SPEED—1981-83

1. Remove the gasket, dowel pins and the first and third oil feed pipes.
2. Remove the reverse idler gear collar, needle bearing and the countershaft reverse gear.
3. Bend down the tab on the lock plate and remove the bolt on the reverse shift fork.
4. Remove the reverse shift fork and the selector sleeve as a complete unit.

5. Remove the countershaft second gear. Remove the mainshaft and the countershaft together. It will be necessary to pull the assembly up on a slight angle in order to clear the governor.

#### THREE SPEED—1984 AND LATER

1. Remove the gasket and the dowel pins. Remove and clean the magnet.
2. Remove the reverse gear collar, needle bearing and the countershaft reverse gear.
3. Bend down the tab on the lock plate and remove the reverse shift retaining bolt.
4. Remove the reverse shift fork and the selector sleeve as a unit.

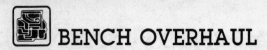
5. Remove the selector hub, countershaft second gear and the needle bearing.

6. Remove the mainshaft and the countershaft together as an assembly. It will be necessary to pull the assembly up on a slight angle in order to clear the governor.

**FOUR SPEED**

1. Remove the gasket and the dowel pins. Remove the reverse gear collar and the needle bearing.

2. Bend down the tab on the lock plate and remove the bolt from the reverse shift fork. Remove the reverse shift fork.

3. Remove the selector hub, countershaft fourth gear and the needle bearing.

4. Remove the mainshaft and the countershaft assembly together.

## GOVERNOR

### Removal

**THREE SPEED AND FOUR SPEED**

1. Bend down the lock tabs on the lock plate.

2. Remove the retaining bolts holding the governor assembly to the torque converter housing.

3. Remove the governor assembly.

## VALVE BODY

### Removal

**THREE SPEED—1981-83**

1. Remove the accumulator cover.

NOTE: The accumulator cover is spring loaded. To prevent stripping the threads in the torque converter housing press down on the cover while removing the retaining bolts.

2. Remove the accumulator spring. Remove the E-clip from the throttle control shaft. Remove the throttle control shaft.

3. Remove the servo valve body retaining bolts. The inside bolt for the throttle control valve cover may stay in place.

4. Remove the separator plate and the dowel pins. Remove the steel ball from the valve body oil passage. Do not use a magnet to remove the steel ball.

5. Remove the regulator valve body retaining bolts.

6. Remove the stator shaft arm, dowel pins, stop pins and the bolts holding the valve body to the torque coverter housing.

7. Remove the cotter pin, washer, rollers and the pin from the manual valve. Remove the valve body from its mounting. Be sure not to loose the torque converter check valve and spring.

8. Remove the pump gears and shaft. Remove the separator plate, dowel pins, check valve and spring. Remove the filter.

**THREE SPEED—1984 AND LATER**

1. Remove the accumulator cover.

NOTE: The accumulator cover is spring loaded. To prevent stripping the threads in the torque converter housing push down on the cover while removing the retaining bolts.

2. Remove the accumulator springs. Remove the lock up valve body mounting bolts.

3. Slide up on the lock up valve body. Remove the oil feed pipe and the lock up valve body.

4. Remove the first and third clutch pipes. Remove the clutch pressure control valve and the clutch pressure control valve separator plate.

5. Remove the servo valve body retaining bolts and remove the servo valve body.

6. Remove the E-clip from the throttle control shaft. Remove the throttle control shaft.

7. Remove the servo valve separator plate and dowel pins.

8. Remove the steel balls from the valve body oil passage. Do not use a magnet to remove the balls.

9. Remove the regulator valve body after removing the steel ball.

10. Remove the stop pin. Remove the dowel pins and the stator shaft arm. Remove the retaining bolts.

11. Remove the cotter pin, washer, rollers and the pin from the manual valve. Remove the valve body assembly. Be sure not to loose the torque converter check valve and spring.

12. Remove the pump gears and shaft. Remove the separator plate. Remove the suction pipe and oil filter.

**FOUR SPEED**

1. Remove the accumulator cover.

NOTE: The accumulator cover is spring loaded. To prevent stripping the threads in the torque converter housing push down on the cover while removing the retaining bolts.

2. Remove the accumulator springs. Remove the lock up valve body mounting bolts.

3. Remove the oil pipes by first moving the lock up valve body upward.

4. Remove the first, third and fourth clutch pipes. Remove the clutch pressure control valve body. Remove the oil pipes.

5. Remove the E-clip from the throttle control shaft. Remove the servo valve body retaining bolts.

6. Remove the throttle control shaft from the servo valve body. Remove the separator plate and the dowel pins.

7. Remove the steel balls and the spring from the valve body oil passages. Do not use a magnet to remove the steel balls.

8. Remove the steel ball from the regulator valve. Do not use a magnet to remove the steel ball.

9. Remove the regulator valve retaining bolts.

10. Remove the stator shaft arm, dowel pins, stop pins and the retaining bolts holding the valve body to the torque converter housing.

11. Remove the cotter pin, washer, rollers and pin from the manual valve. Remove the valve body assembly. Be careful not to loose the torque converter check valve and spring.

12. Remove the pump gears and shaft. Remove the separator plate, dowel pins check valve and spring. Remove the filter and suction pipe.

## CONTROL SHAFT

### Removal

**THREE SPEED AND FOUR SPEED**

1. Remove the cable holder. Remove the cotter pin. Remove the control pin and control lever roller from the control lever.

2. Bend down the tab on the lock plate. Remove the retaining bolt in the control lever. Remove the lever.

3. Turn the torque converter housing over and remove the control rod.

# Unit Disassembly and Assembly

## ONE WAY CLUTCH AND PARKING GEAR

### Disassembly

1. Separate the countershaft first gear from the parking gear by turning the parking gear assembly counterclockwise.

2. Remove the one way clutch assembly by prying it upward using a suitable tool.

3. Inspect all parts for wear, scoring or damage. Replace defective components as required.

### Assembly

1. Assemble the components in the reverse order of the disassembly procedure.

2. Once the components are assembled, hold the countershaft first gear and turn the parking gear in a counterclockwise direction, it must turn freely.

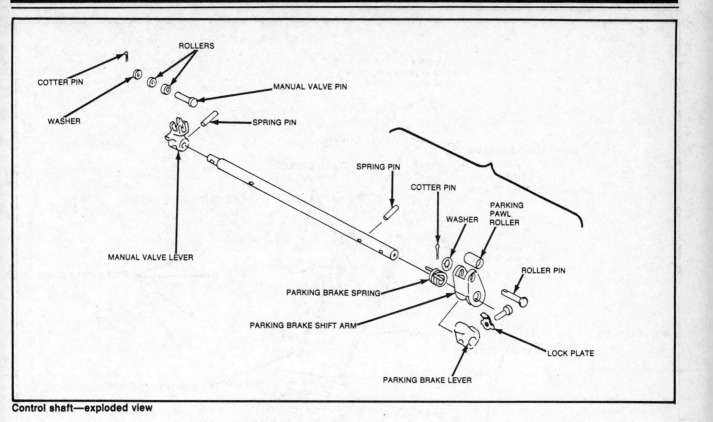

**Control shaft—exploded view**

## VALVE BODY

### Disassembly

1. Position the valve body assembly in a suitable holding fixture.
2. Remove the retaining bolts securing the shift valve covers.
3. Remove the internal components from inside the valve body after removing each of the shift valve covers.
4. Remove the torque converter check spring and valve from the top of the valve body.
5. Remove the pump driven gear and the drive gear from the valve body.
6. Remove the valve spring cap, relief valve spring and the valve.
7. Remove the orifice control spring seat, spring and the second gear orifice control valve.
8. Remove the detent spring, rollers and manual valve from the valve body assembly.
9. Inspect all parts for wear, damage and scoring. Repair or replace defective components as required.

### Assembly

1. Before reassembly coat all parts with clean automatic transmission fluid.
2. Slide the spring into the hole in the big end of the shift valve. While holding the steel balls in place, position the sleeve over the valve.
3. Position the shift spring in the valve. Install the assembly into the valve body and retain it in place with the valve cover.
4. Position the relief spring into the relief valve. Install the assembly into the valve body. Be sure to install the relief valve first.
5. Compress the relief valve spring and then slip the check valve cap into place with the recessed side facing the spring.

6. Install the manual valve, detent rollers and spring into the valve body.
7. Install the pump gears and shaft into the valve body. Measure the thrust clearance of the driven gear to the valve body. It should be 0.001-0.002 in. The service limit specification is 0.003 in.
8. Measure the side clearance of the drive and driven gears. It should be 0.004-0.006 in. for 1981-83 three speed transaxles and 0.008-0.010 in. for all other transaxles. The service limit specification is 0.002-0.004 in.
9. Lay the valve body assembly aside until the transaxle is ready to be reassembled.

## REGULATOR VALVE BODY

### Disassembly

1. Hold the retainer in place while removing the lock bolt. Once the lock bolt is removed, slowly release the retainer.
2. On 1984 and later three speed transaxles, hold the lock up valve cover in place and remove the screws. Remove the spring and the control valve.
3. On four speed transaxles it may also be necessary to hold the lock up valve in place and remove the screws, while removing the spring and the control valve.
4. Clean all parts and check for wear, damage or scoring. Repair or replace defective components as required. Coat all parts with transmission fluid.

### Assembly

1. Install the pressure regulator valve along with the inner and outer springs.
2. Install the reaction spring, spring seat and the retainer.
3. Align the hole in the retainer with the hole in the valve body. Press the retainer into the valve body and tighten the lock bolt.

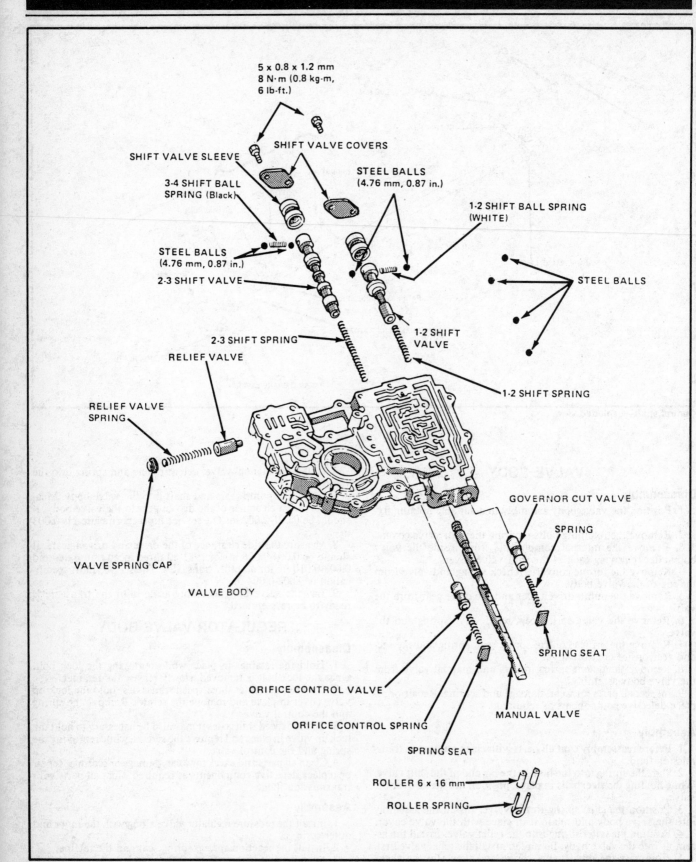

5 x 0.8 x 1.2 mm
8 N·m (0.8 kg·m, 6 lb-ft.)

SHIFT VALVE COVERS

SHIFT VALVE SLEEVE

STEEL BALLS (4.76 mm, 0.87 in.)

3-4 SHIFT BALL SPRING (Black)

1-2 SHIFT BALL SPRING (WHITE)

STEEL BALLS (4.76 mm, 0.87 in.)

2-3 SHIFT VALVE

STEEL BALLS

2-3 SHIFT SPRING

1-2 SHIFT VALVE

RELIEF VALVE

1-2 SHIFT SPRING

RELIEF VALVE SPRING

GOVERNOR CUT VALVE

SPRING

SPRING SEAT

VALVE SPRING CAP

VALVE BODY

ORIFICE CONTROL VALVE

ORIFICE CONTROL SPRING

MANUAL VALVE

SPRING SEAT

ROLLER 6 x 16 mm

ROLLER SPRING

Three speed valve body—exploded view

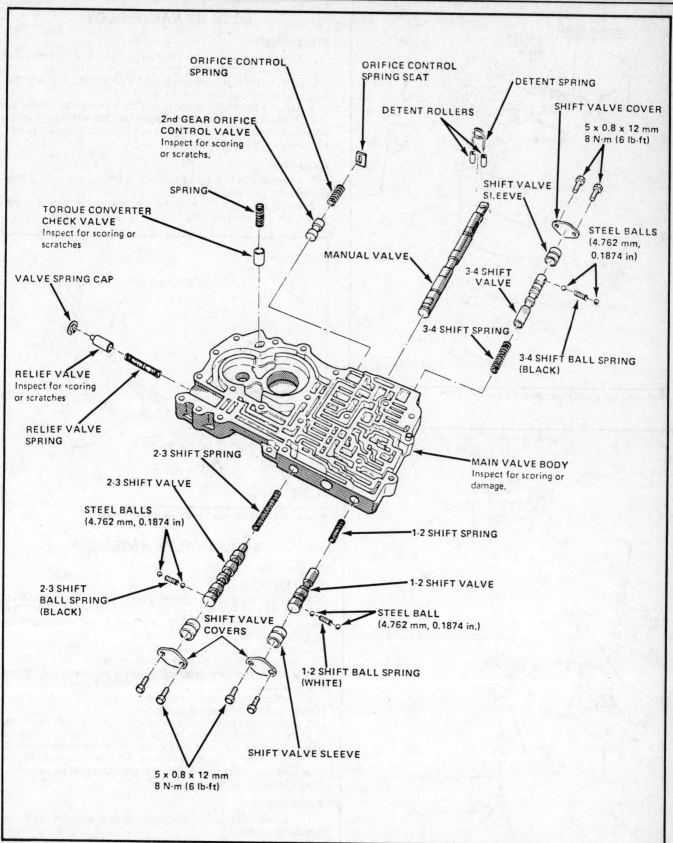

**Four speed valve body—exploded view**

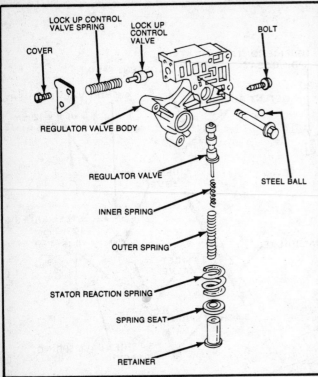

Regulator valve body—exploded view

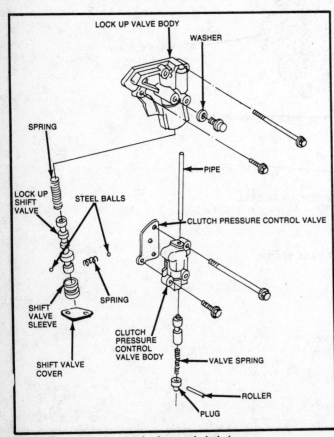

Three speed lock up valve body—exploded view

## LOCK UP VALVE BODY

### Disassembly

1. Remove the shift valve cover retaining bolts. Remove the shift valve sleeve, valve and spring.
2. Remove the clutch pressure control valve plug. Remove the roller, spring and control valve.
3. Remove the clutch pressure control valve separator plate.
4. Clean and inspect all parts. Repair or replace defective components as required. Coat all parts in clean automatic transmission fluid before installation.

### Assembly

1. Assemble the lock up valve body in the reverse order of the disassembly procedure.
2. Install the assembly onto the regulator valve body. Set the unit aside unti the transaxle is ready to be reassembled.

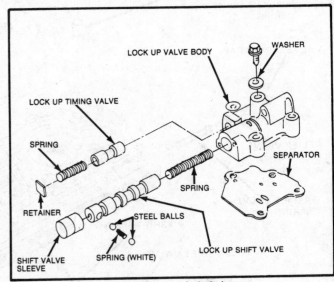

Four speed lock up valve body—exploded view

## SERVO VALVE ASSEMBLY

### Disassembly

#### THREE SPEED

1. Remove the throttle valve retainer. Remove the outer throttle valve "B", spring "B" and the inner throttle valve "B". Remove the outer throttle valve "A", spring "A" and the inner throttle valve "A".
2. Remove the lock up valve seat, spring and valve, if the vehicle is equipped with a lock up torque converter.
3. Remove the modulator valve spring retainer plate, spring and modulator valve.
4. Remove the accumulator cover. Remove the accumulator pistons and their related components.
5. Remove the servo valve along with the servo return spring.
6. Do not adjust or remove the throttle pressure adjustment bolt, it has been pre set at the factory for the proper shift points.
7. Clean all parts and check for wear, scoring or damage. Repair or replace parts as required. Before installation coat all parts with clean automatic transmission fluid.

### Assembly

1. Assemble the servo valve in the reverse order of the disassembly procedure.
2. Once the component has been assembled, set it aside until the automatic transaxle is ready to be reassembled.

## ACCUMULATOR SPRING SELECTION CHART

| Component | Three Speed (81-83) | Three Speed (84- Later) | Four Speed |
|---|---|---|---|
| Servo valve return spring | 1.20 inch | 1.44 inch | 1.59 inch |
| Second accumulator spring | 3.70 inch | 3.91 inch | 3.28 inch |
| Third accumulator spring | 3.70 inch | 3.70 inch | 4.21 inch |
| Fourth accumulator spring | — | — | 3.72 inch |

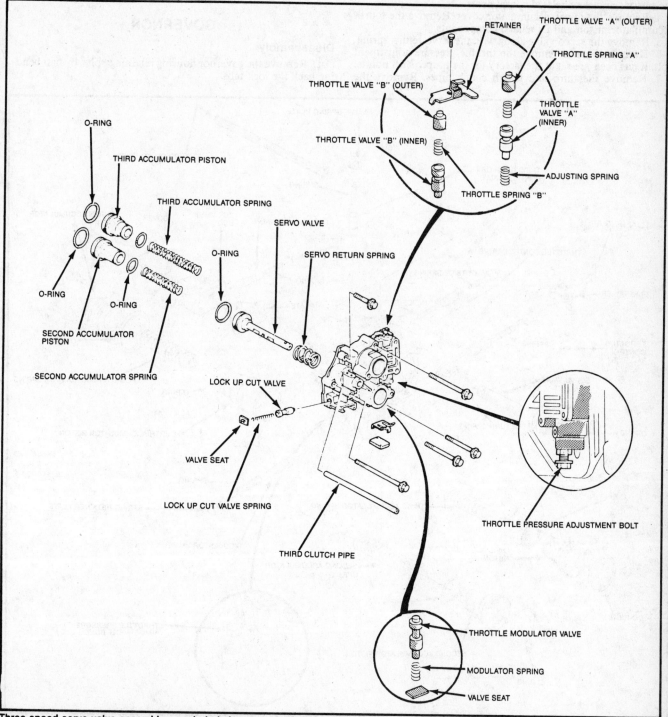

**Three speed servo valve assembly—exploded view**

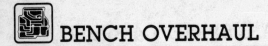
## Disassembly
### FOUR SPEED

1. Remove the throttle valve retainer. Remove the outer throttle valve "B", spring "B" and the inner throttle valve "B". Remove the outer throttle valve "A", spring "A" and the inner throttle valve "A".

2. Remove the modulator valve spring, retainer plate and spring and the modulator valve.

3. Remove the second and third accumulator cover. Remove the pistons and their related components.

4. Remove the fourth accumulator cover. Remove the fourth accumulator piston and its related components.

5. Remove the servo valve along with the servo return spring.

6. Do not adjust or remove the throttle pressure adjustment bolt, it has been pre set at the factory for the proper shift points.

7. Remove the third and fourth clutch pipes. Remove the clutch pressure control valve body and its related components.

8. Clean all parts and check for wear, scoring or damage. Repair or replace parts as required. Before installation coat all parts with clean automatic transmission fluid.

## Assembly

1. Assemble the servo valve in the reverse order of the disassembly procedure.

2. Once the component has been assembled, set it aside until the automatic transaxle is ready to be reassembled.

## GOVERNOR

### Disassembly

1. Remove the governor housing retaining bolts, by first bending back the lock tabs.

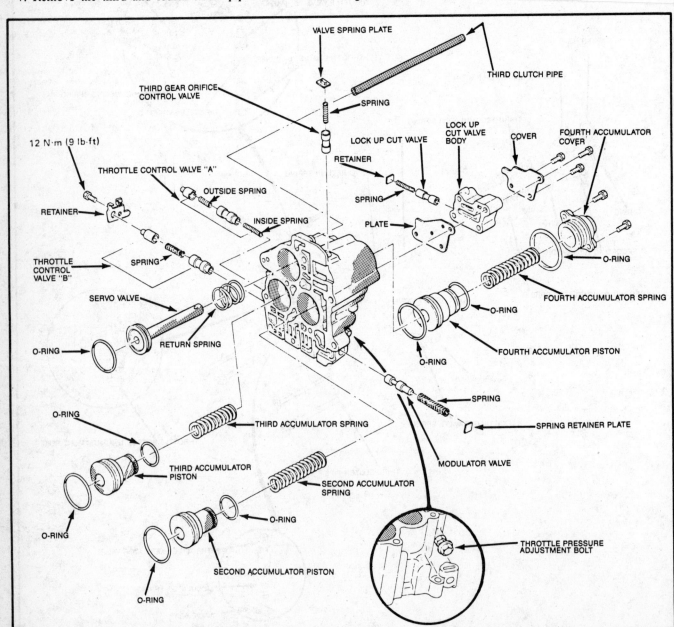

**Four speed servo valve assembly—exploded view**

2. Remove the governor housing E-clip and remove the governor housing internal components.

3. Remove the snap ring and gear from the governor holder. Remove the key and the dowel pins along with the pipe from the governor assembly shaft.

4. Clean and inspect all parts for wear, scoring or damage. Repair or replace components as required.

## Assembly

1. Inspect the inside of the governor housing where the secondary weight sits for smoothness, correct as required.

2. Assemble the governor in the reverse order of the disassembly procedure. Be sure to use new lock tabs.

3. Set the governor aside until the transaxle is ready for reassembly.

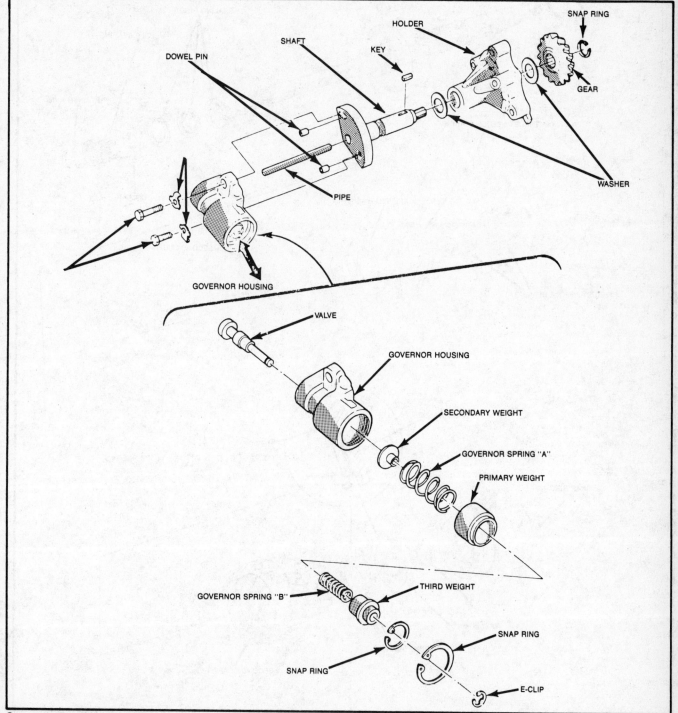

Governor assembly—exploded view

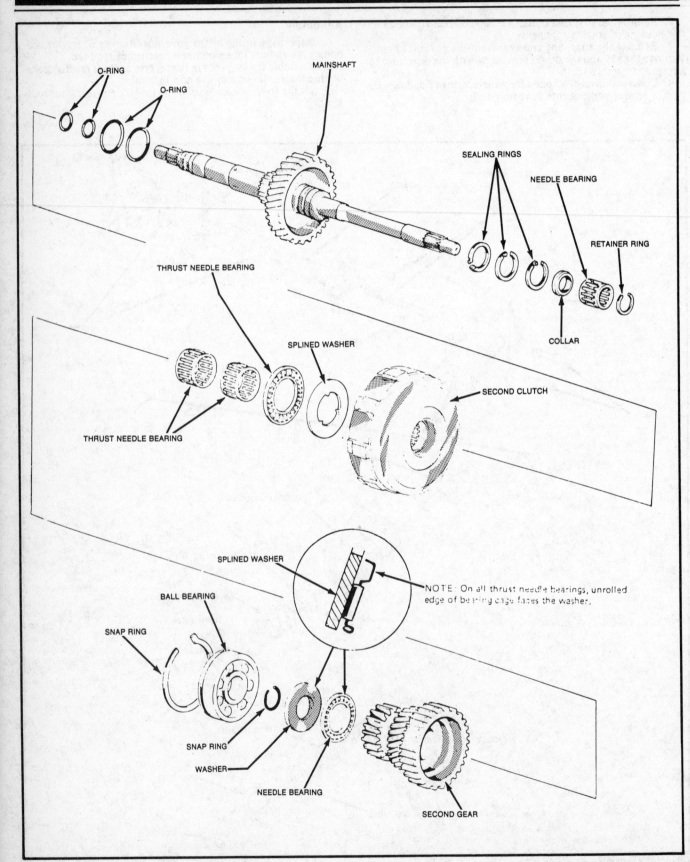

Three speed mainshaft assembly—exploded view

## MAINSHAFT

### Disassembly

#### THREE SPEED—1981-83

1. Remove the snap ring from the rear of the mainshaft assembly. Remove the needle bearing, spacer collar and the metal sealing rings. Discard the metal sealing rings.
2. Remove the snap ring from the front of the mainshaft assembly.
3. Remove and discard the O-ring seals. Remove the thrust washer, thrust needle bearing, and needle bearing.
4. Lift the second gear assembly from the mainshaft.
5. Separate the second gear assembly from the second clutch unit. Be sure not to lose the thrust needle bearing and the splined washer.
6. Clean and inspect all parts for wear, damage or scoring. Repair or replace defective components as required.
7. Coat all parts with clean automatic transmission fluid before reassembly.

### Assembly

1. Assemble the mainshaft assembly in the reverse order of the disassembly procedure.
2. Check the mainshaft clearance measurement and replace the thrust washers as required.
3. Set the mainshaft assembly aside until the automatic transaxle is ready for reassembly.

#### THREE SPEED—1984 AND LATER

1. Remove the snap ring from the rear of the mainshaft assembly. Remove the needle bearing, spacer collar and the metal sealing rings. Discard the metal sealing rings.
2. Remove the snap ring from the front of the mainshaft assembly.
3. Remove the ball bearing, snap ring, washer, needle bearing and the second gear assembly.
4. Remove the second clutch assembly and separate it from the thrust needle bearing and splined washer.
5. Remove and discard the O-rings from the mainshaft assembly.
6. Clean and inspect all parts for wear, damage or scoring. Repair or replace defective components as required.
7. Coat all parts with clean automatic transmission fluid before reassembly.

### Assembly

1. Assemble the mainshaft assembly in the reverse order of the disassembly procedure.
2. Check the mainshaft clearance measurement and replace the thrust washers as required.
3. Set the mainshaft assembly aside until the automatic transaxle is ready for reassembly.

### FOUR SPEED

1. Remove the snap ring from the rear of the mainshaft assembly. Remove the needle bearing, spacer collar and the metal sealing rings. Discard the metal sealing rings.
2. Remove the snap ring from the front of the mainshaft assembly.
3. Remove the ball bearings, thrust needle bearing, snap ring, washer and the fourth gear assembly.
4. Remove the needle bearings, thrust needle bearing, fourth gear collar, thrust washer and the second and fourth clutch assembly.
5. Remove the remaining washers, gears, bearings and O-rings from the mainshaft assembly. Discard the O-rings.
6. Clean and inspect all parts for wear, damage or scoring. Repair or replace defective components as required.
7. Coat all parts with clean automatic transmission fluid before reassembly.

### Assembly

1. Assemble the mainshaft assembly in the reverse order of the disassembly procedure.
2. Check the mainshaft clearance measurement and replace the thrust washers as required.
3. Set the mainshaft assembly aside until the automatic transaxle is ready for reassembly.

## COUNTERSHAFT

### Disassembly

#### THREE SPEED—1981-83

1. Remove the locknut. Remove the needle bearing, second gear, spacer collar, thrust washer and the needle bearing.
2. Remove the third gear assembly, thrust needle bearing, splined thrust washer and the third clutch assembly from the countershaft. Remove and discard the O-rings.
3. Clean and inspect all parts for wear, damage and scoring. Repair or replace defective components as required.
4. Coat all parts with clean automatic transmission fluid before reassembly.

### Assembly

1. Assemble the countershaft in the reverse order of the disassembly procedure.
2. Check the countershaft clearance measurement and replace thrust washers as required.
3. Set the countershaft assembly aside until the automatic transaxle is ready to be reassembled.

### Disassembly

#### THREE SPEED—1984 AND LATER

1. Remove the lock ring. Remove the reverse collar and needle bearing. Remove the reverse gear along with the reverse gear selector and the selector hub.
2. Remove the second gear assembly, needle bearing, and the splined thrust washer from the countershaft.
3. Remove the third gear assembly, needle bearing and the splined thrust washer from the countershaft assembly.
4. Remove the third clutch assembly and discard the O-ring seals.
5. Clean and inspect all parts for wear, damage and scoring. Repair or replace defective components as required.
6. Coat all parts with clean automatic transmission fluid before reassembly.

### Assembly

1. Assemble the countershaft in the reverse order of the disassembly procedure.
2. Check the countershaft clearance measurement and replace thrust washers as required.
3. Set the countershaft assembly aside until the automatic transaxle is ready to be reassembled.

### Disassembly

#### FOUR SPEED

1. Remove the snap ring. Remove the roller bearing, reverse gear collar and the needle bearing.
2. Remove the reverse gear, reverse gear selector and the selector hub from the countershaft.
3. Remove the fourth gear, needle bearing, spacer collar and second gear.
4. Remove the cotter washers, thrust needle bearing and the third gear assembly.
5. Remove the third clutch assembly, by first removing the thrust needle bearing, needle bearing and the splined thrust washer.
6. Remove and discard the O-rings from the countershaft assembly.

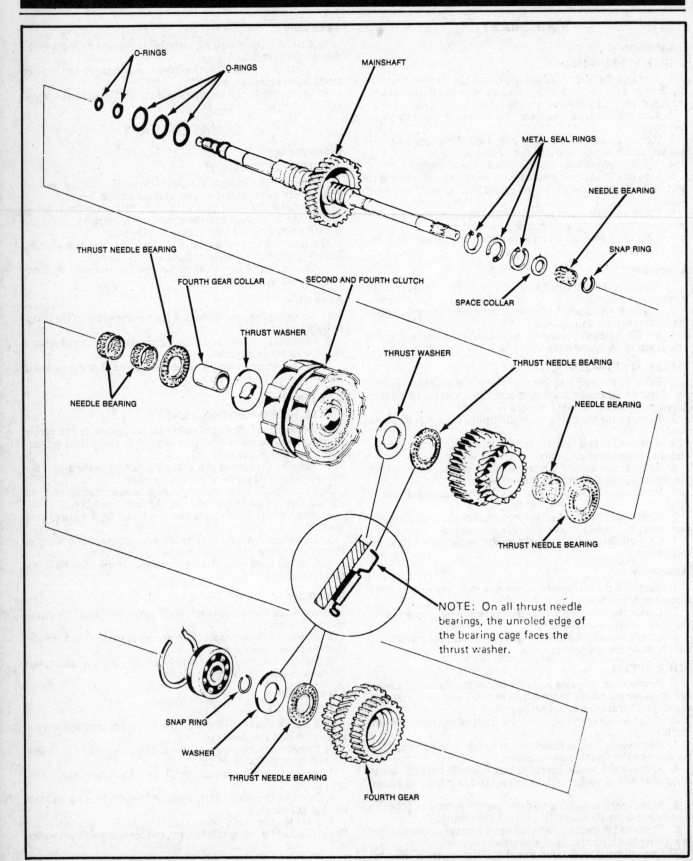

O-RINGS

O-RINGS

MAINSHAFT

METAL SEAL RINGS

NEEDLE BEARING

THRUST NEEDLE BEARING

FOURTH GEAR COLLAR

SECOND AND FOURTH CLUTCH

SNAP RING

SPACE COLLAR

THRUST WASHER

NEEDLE BEARING

THRUST WASHER

THRUST NEEDLE BEARING

NEEDLE BEARING

THRUST NEEDLE BEARING

NOTE: On all thrust needle bearings, the unroled edge of the bearing cage faces the thrust washer.

SNAP RING

WASHER

THRUST NEEDLE BEARING

FOURTH GEAR

Four speed mainshaft assembly—exploded view

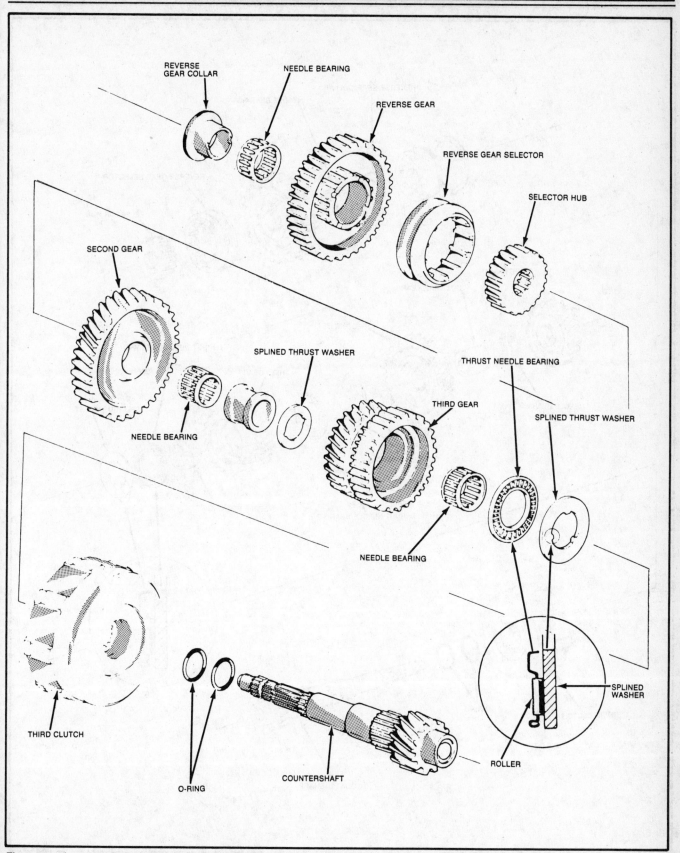

**Three speed countershaft assembly—exploded view**

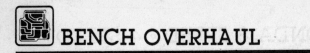 

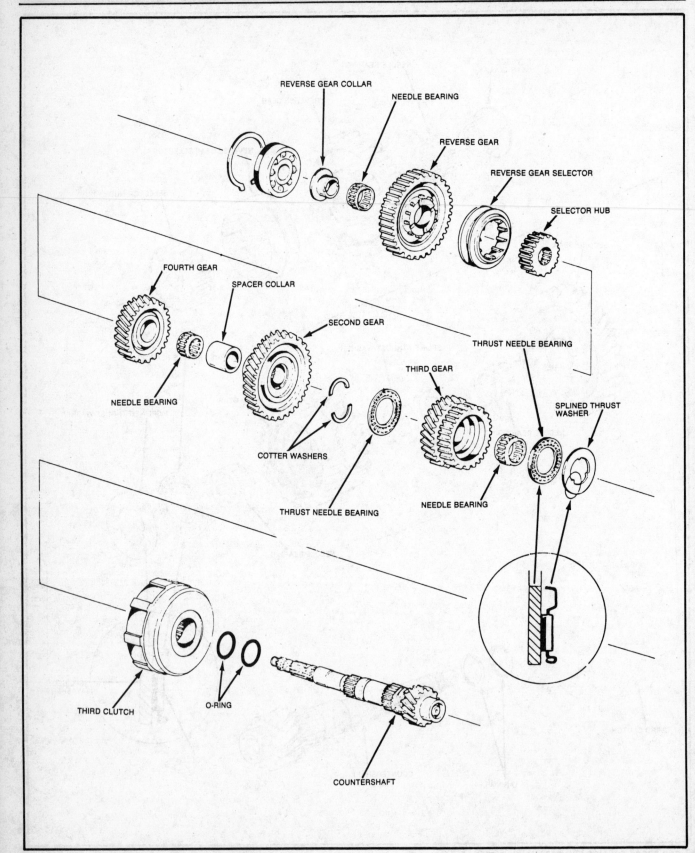

Four speed countershaft assembly—exploded view

7. Clean and inspect all parts for wear, damage and scoring. Repair or replace defective components as required.

8. Coat all parts with clean automatic transmission fluid before reassembly.

## Assembly

1. Assemble the countershaft in the reverse order of the disassembly procedure.

2. Check the countershaft clearance measurement and replace thrust washers as required.

3. Set the countershaft assembly aside until the automatic transaxle is ready to be reassembled.

## THRUST WASHER SELECTION CHART— ALL TRANSAXLES

| Type | Part Number | Thickness (inches) |
|---|---|---|
| A | 90411-PA9-010 | 0.117-0.118 |
| B | 90412-PA9-010 | 0.119-0.120 |
| C | 90413-PA9-010 | 0.121-0.122 |
| D | 90414-PA9-010 | 0.123-0.124 |
| E | 90415-PA9-010 | 0.125-0.126 |
| F | 90418-PA9-010 | 0.127-0.128 |
| G | 90419-PA9-010 | 0.129-0.130 |
| H | 90420-PA9-010 | 0.131-0.132 |
| I | 90421-PA9-010 | 0.133-0.134 |

## MAINSHAFT/COUNTERSHAFT CLEARANCE MEASUREMENTS

### THREE SPEED

1. Remove the mainshaft and the countershaft bearings from the transaxle housing.

2. Assemble the mainshaft and the countershaft together. On all thrust needle bearings the unrolled edge of the bearing cage faces the thrust washer.

3. Install the mainshaft assembly into the torque converter housing. Install the mainshaft holder to prevent the shafts from turning. Torque the locknut to 25 ft. lbs.

4. Hold the parking gear on the countershaft and torque the retaining nut to 25 ft. lbs.

5. Measure the thrust washer clearances using the proper feeler gauge. Make all measurements before changing the thrust washers.

6. On the mainshaft, measure the clearance between the shoulder on the washer and the thrust needle bearing.

7. If the clearance is not within specification, measure the thickness of the second clutch splined thrust washer (third gear thrust needle bearing on three speed transaxles 1984 and later) and select the correct washer to give correct clearance.

8. The correct specification is 0.003-0.006 in.

9. On the countershaft, measure the clearance between the shoulder on the selector hub and the shoulder on the second gear.

10. The correct clearance should be 0.003-0.006 in. If the correct clearance is not obtained, select a new washer to give the correct clearance.

11. Leave the feeler gauge in place while measuring the clearance for third gear. Measure the clearance between the thrust washer and third gear.

12. The clearance should be 0.003-0.006 in. If the correct clearance is not obtained, select a replacement thrust washer to obtain correct clearance.

## THRUST WASHER SELECTION CHART— THREE SPEED TRANSAXLES

| Type | Part Number | Thickness (inches) |
|---|---|---|
| A | 90401-PA9-010 | 0.089-0.091 |
| B | 90402-PA9-010 | 0.091-0.093 |
| C | 90403-PA9-010 | 0.093-0.094 |
| D | 90404-PA9-010 | 0.095-0.096 |
| E | 90407-PA9-000 | 0.097-0.098 |
| F | 90408-PA9-000 | 0.099-0.100 |
| G | 90409-PA9-000 | 0.101-0.102 |

### FOUR SPEED

1. Remove the mainshaft and the countershaft bearings from the transaxle housing.

2. Assemble the mainshaft and the countershaft together. On all thrust needle bearings the unrolled edge of the bearing cage faces the thrust washer.

3. Install the mainshaft assembly into the torque converter housing. Install the mainshaft holder to prevent the shafts from turning. Torque the locknut to 25 ft. lbs.

4. Hold the parking gear on the countershaft and torque the retaining nut to 35 ft. lbs.

5. Measure the thrust washer clearances using the proper feeler gauge. Make all measurements before changing the thrust washers.

6. On the countershaft, measure the clearance between the shoulder on the selector hub and the shoulder on fourth gear.

7. The clearance should be 0.003-0.006 in. If the clearance is not within the specification given, select the proper thrust washer to bring the clearance to within specification.

8. Leave the feeler gauge in the fourth gear measurement position while measuring second gear.

9. Second gear clearance should be 0.003-0.006 in. If clearance is not within specification select the proper thrust washer to bring the clearance within specification.

## SPACER COLLAR SELECTION CHART— FOUR SPEED TRANSAXLES

| Type | Part Number | Thickness (inches) |
|---|---|---|
| A | 90503-PC9-000 | 1.534-1.535 |
| B | 90508-PC9-000 | 1.536-1.537 |
| C | 90504-PC9-000 | 1.538-1.539 |
| D | 90509-PC9-000 | 1.540-1.541 |
| E | 90505-PC9-000 | 1.542-1.543 |
| F | 90510-PC9-000 | 1.544-1.545 |
| G | 90507-PC9-000 | 1.546-1.547 |

10. Slide out the third gear. Measure and record the clearance between second and third gears. Slide third gear in and again measure the clearance between second and third gears. Be sure to leave the feeler gauge in the fourth gear measuring slot while measuring second gear clearance. Calculate the difference between the two readings to determine the actual clearance between the two gears.

11. On the mainshaft, measure the clearance between the shoulder of the second gear and third gear.

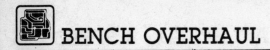

12. The correct clearance should be 0.003-0.006 in. If the clearance is not within the specification given, select the proper thrust washer to bring the clearance within specification.

## CLUTCH ASSEMBLY

### Disassembly
#### THREE SPEED

NOTE: The first, second and third clutch assemblies are all the same.

1. Remove the snap ring. Remove the end plate, clutch discs and clutch plates from the clutch assembly.
2. Install the clutch spring compressor tool and compress the assembly in order to remove the snap ring.
3. Remove the tool. Remove the snap ring, spring retainer and the spring.
4. Apply compressed air to the clutch drum and remove the clutch piston assembly. Remove and discard the O-ring seals.
5. Clean and inspect all parts for wear, damage and scoring. Replace defective parts, clutch discs and plates as required.
6. Before reassembly soak the clutch discs in clean automatic transmission fluid for about thirty minutes. Coat all parts with transmission fluid.

### Assembly

1. Install a new O-ring on the clutch piston. Make sure that the spring washer is properly positioned.
2. Install the piston in the clutch drum. Apply pressure and rotate the assembly to ensure proper seating.
3. Install the return spring and the retainer. Position the snap ring on the spring retainer.
4. Assemble the spring compressor tool on the clutch assembly. Compress the unit until the snap ring is seated in its retaining groove. Remove the tool.
5. Starting with a clutch plate, alternately install the clutch discs and plates. Install the clutch end plate with the flat side toward the disc. Install the snap ring.
6. Measure the clearance between the clutch end plate and the top clutch disc. It should be 0.016-0.028 in. for the first clutch, 0.026-0.031 in. for the second clutch and 0.016-0.024 in. for the third clutch.

### END PLATE SELECTION CHART

| Part Number | Plate Number | Thickness (inches) |
|---|---|---|
| 22551-PA9-010 | one | 0.091-0.094 |
| 22552-PA9-010 | two | 0.094-0.098 |
| 22553-PA9-010 | three | 0.098-0.102 |
| 22554-PA9-010 | four | 0.102-0.106 |
| 22555-PA9-010 | five | 0.106-0.110 |
| 22556-PA9-010 | six | 0.110-0.114 |
| 22557-PA9-010 | seven | 0.114-0.118 |
| 22558-PA9-010 | eight | 0.118-0.122 |
| 22559-PA9-010 | nine | 0.122-0.126 |
| 22560-PA9-010 | ten | 0.126-0.130 |

7. If the reading is not within specification select a new clutch end plate as required.
8. Check for clutch engagement by blowing compressed air into the oil passage of the clutch drum hub. Remove air pressure and check that the clutch releases.
9. Set the clutch assembly aside until you are ready to reassemble the automatic transaxle.

### Disassembly
#### FOUR SPEED

NOTE: The first and third clutches are identical but are not interchangeable. The second and fourth clutches are also identical but not interchangeable.

1. Remove the snap ring. Remove the end plate, clutch discs and clutch plates from the clutch assembly.
2. Install the clutch spring compressor tool and compress the assembly in order to remove the snap ring.
3. Remove the tool. Remove the snap ring, spring retainer and the spring.
4. Apply compressed air to the clutch drum and remove the clutch piston assembly. Remove and discard the O-ring seals.
5. Clean and inspect all parts for wear, damage and scoring. Replace defective parts, clutch discs and plates as required.
6. Before reassembly soak the clutch discs in clean automatic transmission fluid for about thirty minutes. Coat all parts with transmission fluid.

### Assembly

1. Install a new O-ring on the clutch piston. Make sure that the spring washer is properly positioned.
2. Install the piston in the clutch drum. Apply pressure and rotate the assembly to ensure proper seating.
3. Install the return spring and the retainer. Position the snap ring on the spring retainer.
4. Assemble the spring compressor tool on the clutch assembly. Compress the unit until the snap ring is seated in its retaining groove. Remove the tool.
5. Starting with a clutch plate, alternately install the clutch discs and plates. Install the clutch end plate with the flat side toward the disc. Install the snap ring.
6. Measure the clearance between the clutch end plate and the top clutch disc. It should be 0.016-0.028 in. for the first clutch, 0.026-0.031 in. for the second clutch and 0.016-0.023 in. for the third and fourth clutch.

### END PLATE SELECTION CHART

| Part Number | Plate Number | Thickness (inches) |
|---|---|---|
| 22551-PC9-000 | one | 0.094 |
| 22552-PC9-000 | two | 0.098 |
| 22553-PC9-000 | three | 0.102 |
| 22554-PC9-000 | four | 0.106 |
| 22555-PC9-000 | five | 0.110 |
| 22556-PC9-000 | six | 0.114 |
| 22557-PC9-000 | seven | 0.118 |
| 22558-PC9-000 | eight | 0.122 |
| 22559-PC9-000 | nine | 0.126 |
| 22560-PC9-000 | ten | 0.130 |

7. If the reading is not within specification select a new clutch end plate as required.
8. Check for clutch engagement by blowing compressed air into the oil passage of the clutch drum hub. Remove air pressure and check that the clutch releases.
9. Set the clutch assembly aside until you are ready to reassemble the automatic transaxle.

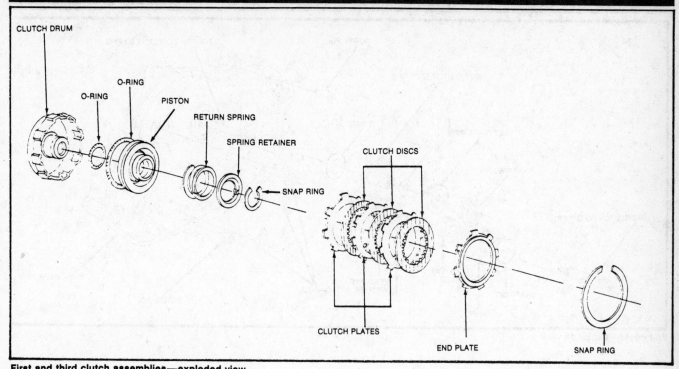

**First and third clutch assemblies—exploded view**

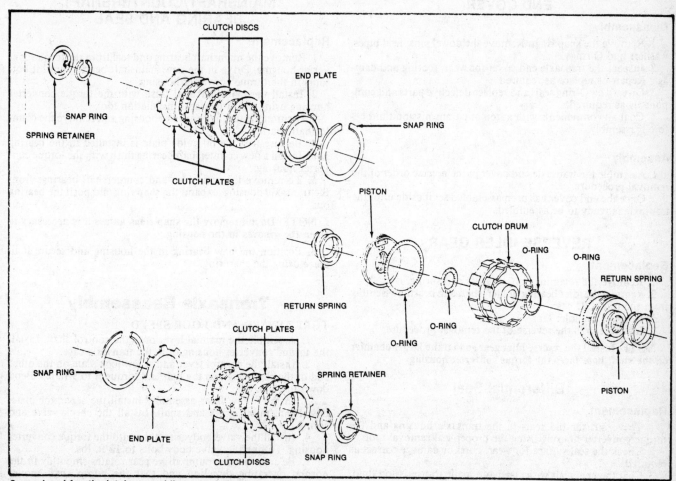

**Second and fourth clutch assemblies—exploded view**

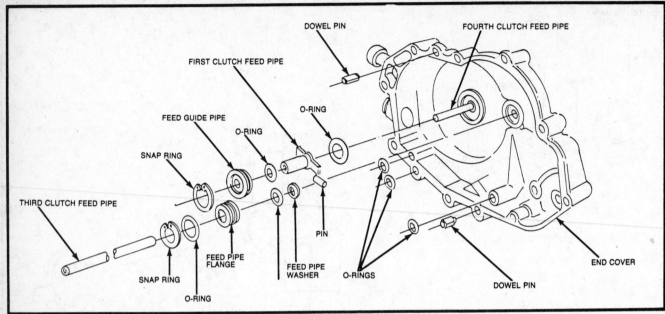

**End cover—exploded view**

Labels in figure: DOWEL PIN, FOURTH CLUTCH FEED PIPE, FIRST CLUTCH FEED PIPE, O-RING, FEED GUIDE PIPE, O-RING, SNAP RING, THIRD CLUTCH FEED PIPE, SNAP RING, O-RING, FEED PIPE FLANGE, FEED PIPE WASHER, PIN, O-RINGS, DOWEL PIN, END COVER

## END COVER

### Disassembly

1. Remove the snap rings. Remove the dowel pins, feed pipes, washers and O-rings.
2. Inspect the transaxle end cover for wear, scoring and damage. Repair or replace as required.
3. Discard all O-ring seals and replace defective parts and components as required.
4. Coat all components with automatic transmission fluid before reassembly.

### Assembly

1. Assemble the transaxle end cover in the reverse order of the removal procedure.
2. Once the end cover has been assembled set it aside until the transaxle is ready to be assembled.

## REVERSE IDLER GEAR

### Replacement

1. Remove the retaining bolt, washers and spring, if used.
2. Remove the idler bearing holder, shaft and bearing assembly from the transaxle case.
3. Remove the idler gear.
4. Installation is the reverse of the removal procedure.

NOTE: Install the reverse idler gear so that the larger chamfer on the shaft bore faces the torque converter housing.

## Differential Seal

### Replacement

1. Drive out the old seals in the transaxle housing and the torque converter housing using the proper seal removal tools.
2. Check the seal surface for wear, burrs or damage correct as required.
3. Coat the new seals with clean automatic transmission fluid. Install the seals using the proper seal installation tools.

## MAINSHAFT/COUNTERSHAFT BEARING AND SEAL

### Replacement

1. Remove the mainshaft bearing and seal from the torque converter housing. Drive in the new mainshaft bearing until it bottoms in the torque converter housing.
2. Install the mainshaft seal flush with the torque converter housing using the proper seal installation tool.
3. Position the torque converter housing and remove the countershaft bearing.
4. Be sure that the oil guide plate is installed in the bearing hole. Install a new countershaft bearing flush with the torque converter housing.
5. To remove the mainshaft and countershaft bearings from the transaxle housing, expand the snap ring and push the bearing out.

NOTE: Do not remove the snap rings unless it is necessary to clean the grooves in the housing.

6. Position the new bearing in the housing and secure it in place using the snap ring.

## Transaxle Reassembly

### THREE SPEED AND FOUR SPEED

1. Assemble the manual lever onto the control shaft. Install the torque converter housing onto the transaxle case.
2. Install the control lever and a new lock plate on the other end of the shaft. Tighten the bolt and torque it to 9 ft. lbs. Bend down the lock tab.
3. Install a new filter assembly. Install the separator plate, dowel pin, pump gears and shaft. Install the check valve and spring.
4. Install the valve body assembly onto the torque converter housing. Torque the valve body bolts to 12 ft. lbs.
5. Be sure that the pump drive gear rotates smoothly in the normal operating direction and that the pump shaft moves smoothly in both axial and normal operating directions.

6. Install the stator shaft arm, stop pin and the dowel pins. Install the regulator valve and torque the retaining bolts to 9 ft. lbs.

7. Install the steel ball or balls into the valve body oil passage or passages.

8. Install the separator plate. Install the throttle control shaft and the dowel pins.

9. Install the servo assembly. Be sure to use the proper retaining bolts in the proper retaining holes. Torque the retaining bolts to 9 ft. lbs.

10. Put the roller on each side of the manual valve stem. Attach the valve to the lever with the pin. Secure the assembly in place using the lock pin.

11. On 1984 and later three speed transaxles, install the first and third clutch feed pipes. Install the clutch pressure control separator plate onto the servo body and then install the clutch pressure control body. Install the lock up separator plate onto the regulator body. Install the oil feed pipe into the clutch pressure control body.

12. On all four speed transaxles, install the clutch pressure control valve body, cover, and separator plate onto the servo body. Install and torque the clutch pressure control valve body bolts to 9 ft. lbs. Install the first, third and fourth clutch feed pipes. Install the separator plate. Position the oil pass pipes between the pressure control valve and the clutch pressure control valve body and slide the assembly into place. Install the pressure control valve body bolts and torque them to 9 ft. lbs.

13. Install the accumulator springs. Install the accumulator cover and torque the retaining bolts to 9 ft. lbs., in a criss cross method. On the four speed transaxle, install the fourth accumulator cover and torque the retaining bolts to 9 ft. lbs.

14. Install the governor valve using new lock plates. Torque the retaining bolts to 9 ft. lbs. and bend the lock tabs.

15. Position the countershaft in place. Position the mainshaft in place. Do not tap on the shafts with a hammer to drive them in place.

16. Install the countershaft second gear. On all four speed transaxles, install the countershaft fourth gear and the needle bearing.

17. Assemble the reverse shift fork and the selector sleeve. Install these two components as an assembly on the countershaft.

**NOTE: Install the sleeve with the grooved side down and the unmarked side up. Check for wear on the surface of the sleeve and the shift fork.**

18. Install the reverse shift fork over the servo valve stem. Align the hole in the stem with the hole in the fork. Install the bolt and the lock plate. Torque the bolt to 10 ft. lbs. and bend down the lock tab.

19. Install the countershaft reverse gear, needle bearing and reverse gear collar.

20. On 1984 and later three speed transaxles install the magnet.

21. Install a new gasket, the dowel pins and the oil feed pipes into the torque converter housing.

22. Position the automatic transaxle housing on the torque converter housing.

**NOTE: Be sure main valve control shaft lines up with hole in housing and that reverse idler gear meshes with mainshaft and countershaft, or housing will not go on.**

23. Install the retaining bolts and torque them in two steps. First to 20 ft. lbs. and then to 28 ft. lbs.

**NOTE: When tightening the transaxle housing bolts, take care that you do not distort or damage the throttle control bracket; distortion or damage to bracket will change the transaxle shift points.**

24. Install the throttle control lever and spring on the throttle control shaft. Install the bolt and a new lock plate. Torque the retaining bolt to 6 ft. lbs. and bend down the lock plate.

25. Install the parking shift arm and spring on the shift shaft with the retaining bolt and a new lock plate. Torque the bolt to 10 ft. lbs. and bend down the lock tab.

**NOTE: The spring should put clockwise tension on the shift arm and force it against the stop pin.**

26. Install the first gear collar and needle bearing on the countershaft. Install the collar on the mainshaft.

27. Install the reverse idler bearing holder. Install the O-rings on the mainshaft assembly.

28. Install the countershaft first gear and the parking gear on the countershaft.

29. Install the stop pin, parking pawl shaft and the pawl release spring.

**NOTE: The end of the parking pawl release spring fits into the hole in the parking pawl. The release spring should put clockwise tension on the pawl which will force it away from the parking gear.**

30. Shift the transaxle into the park position. Install the countershaft lock nut. Stake the lock nut flange into the gear groove.

31. Install the needle bearing and the thrust washer onto the mainshaft. Install the first gear, needle bearing and thrust washer onto the mainshaft.

32. Install the first clutch assembly on the mainshaft. Install the mainshaft lock nut. This nut has left hand threads. Stake the lock nut flange into the groove of the first clutch.

33. Install the gasket, dowel pins and O-rings on the transaxle housing. Install the end cover and torque the retaining bolts to 9 ft. lbs.

34. Install the transaxle cooler line fittings on the transaxle assembly.

35. Install the torque converter on the mainshaft assembly.

## TORQUE SPECIFICATIONS

| Item | Torque (ft. lbs.) |
|---|---|
| Drive plate to crankshaft bolts | 34-38 |
| Converter to drive plate bolts | 7 -10 |
| Control cable mounting bolts | 7 -10 |
| Center crossmember mounting bolts | 14-18 |
| Center mount bracket bolts | 14-18 |
| Starter retaining bolts | 29-36 |

## SPECIAL TOOLS

Special tools needed for the disassembly and assembly of the Honda three and four speed transaxles are listed below.

1. Oil pressure gauge or gauge set with the installation attachments
2. Mainshaft holder
3. Clutch drum return spring compressor
4. Mainshaft locknut wrench
5. Transaxle case puller, slide hammer type
6. Ball joint remover
7. Lifting cable for engine and/or transaxle
8. Mechanics tool kit
9. Torque wrench, ft. lbs.
10. Bearing remover, slide hammer type
11. Hand operated air nozzle
12. Feeler gauge and straight edge
13. Bearing driver
14. Seal driver

# INDEX

# JATCO
# L3N71B•4N71B•L4N71B•E4N71B•JM600

## APPLICATIONS

| | | |
|---|---|---|
| Datsun | 1982 810 Maxima, 200SX, 210 | L3N71B |
| Nissan | 1983-84 810 Maxima | L4N71B |
| | 1983-84 720 Pick-up W/2WD | L3N71B |
| | 1984 300ZX | E4N71B |
| Chrysler | (Mitsubishi) 1984 Conquest | L4N71B |
| | | (JM600) |

## GENERAL DESCRIPTION

The L3N71B transmission is a three speed, fully automatic unit, consisting of two multiple disc clutches, a multiple disc brake, a brake band, a one way clutch, two planetary gear sets and a three element torque converter, housing hydraulically operated lock-up converter components.

The L4N71B Chrysler/Mitsubishi JM600 transmissions are four speed, fully automatic unit, consisting of three multiple disc clutches, a multiple disc brake, two brake bands, a one way clutch, three planetary gear sets and a three element torque converter, housing hydraulically operated lock-up converter compo-nents. The fourth speed has an overdrive ratio of 0.686.

A hydraulic control system operates the friction elements and the automatic up and down shifts.

The E4N71B automatic transmission is based on the L4N71B model and can provide lock-up in all forward speeds (1 through 4) by electronic control, through a microcomputer. Either a standard or power shifting pattern is automatically selected by programs set in the lock-up control unit, depending upon the position of the accelerator and the vehicle speed.

## Transmission and Converter Identification

### TRANSMISSION

The transmission can be identified by a plate attached to the right side of the case. The plate contains the model and serial numbers. An identification of the number arrangements can be determined from the serial number in the following manner;
Example: 2601234

1. The first digit, in this case, 2, denotes the year, 1982.
2. The second digit or letter, in this case, 6, denotes the month of production. 6 = June
1 = January, 2 = February, 3 = March, 4 = April, 5 = May, 6 = June, 7 = July, 8 = August, 9 = September, X = October, Y = November, Z = December.
3. The next five digits represents the serial number for the month of transmission production.

## AUTOMATIC TRANSMISSION MODEL CODE DESIGNATION

| Year | Engine Model | Transmission Model Code | Transmission Model |
|---|---|---|---|
| 1982 | L24E | X6701 | L3N71B |
| | LD28 | X6700 | L3N71B |
| 1983-84 | L24E | X8708 | L4N71B |
| | LD28 | X8707 | L4N71B |
| 1984 | VG30E | X8075 | E4N71B |
| | VG30E w/Turbo | X8006 | 4N71B (Non-Lockup) |
| 1984 | — | JM600 | L4N71B |

## CONVERTER

The torque converters are identified by a letter or letters, stamped on the unit.

1982    Gasoline engine model L24E—converter code GC
      Diesel engine model LD28—converter code GB

1983-84   Gasoline engine model L24E—converter code GL
      Diesel engine model LD28—converter code GD

1984    Engine model VG30E-less turbo—converter code GK
      Engine model VG30E-with turbo—converter code GC

1984    Conquest (Chrysler/Mitsubishi) converter Code GKA

## Transmission Metric Fasteners

Metric bolt sizes and thread pitches are used for all fasteners on the Jatco transmissions. The metric fastener dimensions are close to the dimensions of the familiar inch system fasteners, and for this reason, replacement fasteners must have the same measurement and strength as those removed.

─────────── CAUTION ───────────

*Do not attempt to interchange metric fasteners for inch system fasteners. Mismatched or incorrect fasteners can result in damage to the transmission unit through malfunctions, breakage or possible personal injury.*

──────────────────────────────

Care should be taken to re-use the fasteners in the same locations as removed, whenever possible.

## Transmission Fluid Capacity

L4N71B, E4N71B, JM600—7⅜ US quarts (7.0 Liters)
L3N71B—6½ US quarts (6.1 Liters)

## TRANSMISSION FLUID LEVEL CHECK

The automatic transmissions are designed to operate with the oil level between the "L" and the "F" or "H" markings on the dipstick. The "L" mark on the dipstick indicates the transmission is approximately ⅞ US pint (0.4 liter) low. Only Dexron® transmission fluid or its equivalent can be used.

### Checking Fluid Level

1. Operate the vehicle to bring the transmission to its normal operating temperature of between 122°-176° F. (50°-80° C.).

2. Park the vehicle on a level surface, apply the brakes and leave the engine running with the selector lever in the PARK position.

3. Slowly move the selector lever through the entire shift detent pattern and return it to the PARK position.

4. Remove the dipstick from the transmission tube, clean it and replace it back into the tube. Seat it fully to the tube.

5. Remove the dipstick and read the level as indicated.

6. Correct the level as required and recheck.

**NOTE: Overfilling of the transmission can cause fluid loss during vehicle operation. Underfilling can cause lack of fluid pressure to the internal components, resulting in transmission failure.**

# M MODIFICATIONS

No known modifications were made to the L3N71B, L4N71B, JM600 or E4N71B automatic transmissions at time of printing.

# TROUBLE DIAGNOSIS

**NOTE:** The nomenclature of the various applying members differ in varied applications, although each perform the same function. Where required, both names will be given to a specific unit for easier identification. Examples are as follows;

1. The rear clutch is the same as the forward clutch.
2. The front clutch is the same as the reverse and high clutch.
3. The rear band is the same as the intermediate band.

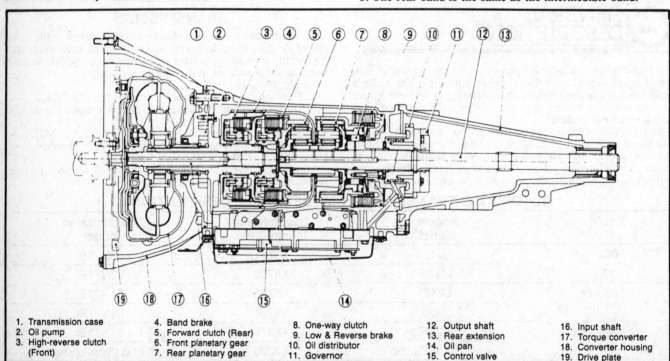

| | | |
|---|---|---|
| 1. Transmission case | 4. Band brake | 8. One-way clutch | 12. Output shaft | 16. Input shaft |
| 2. Oil pump | 5. Forward clutch (Rear) | 9. Low & Reverse brake | 13. Rear extension | 17. Torque converter |
| 3. High-reverse clutch (Front) | 6. Front planetary gear | 10. Oil distributor | 14. Oil pan | 18. Converter housing |
| | 7. Rear planetary gear | 11. Governor | 15. Control valve | 19. Drive plate |

**Cross section of L3N71B automatic transmission** (© Nissan Motor Co. of USA)

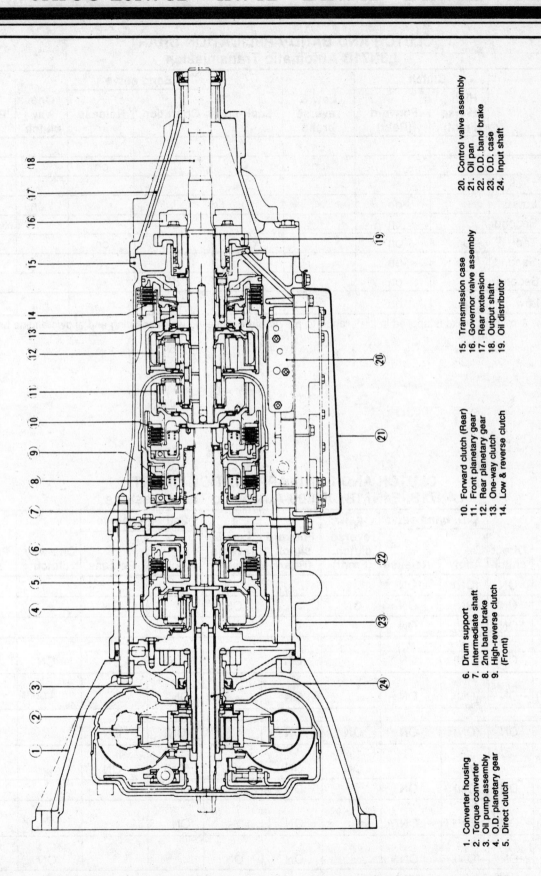

1. Converter housing
2. Torque converter
3. Oil pump assembly
4. O.D. planetary gear
5. Direct clutch
6. Drum support
7. Intermediate shaft
8. 2nd band brake
9. High-reverse clutch (Front)
10. Forward clutch (Rear)
11. Front planetary gear
12. Rear planetary gear
13. One-way clutch
14. Low & reverse clutch
15. Transmission case
16. Governor valve assembly
17. Rear extension
18. Output shaft
19. Oil distributor
20. Control valve assembly
21. Oil pan
22. O.D. band brake
23. O.D. case
24. Input shaft

**Cross section of L4N71B, E4N71B, JM600 automatic transmission (© Nissan Motor Co. of USA)**

## CLUTCH AND BAND APPLICATION CHART
### L3N71B Automatic Transmission

| Range | | Clutch | | Low & reverse brake | Lock-up | Band servo | | One way clutch | Parking pawl |
|---|---|---|---|---|---|---|---|---|---|
| | | High-reverse (Front) | Forward (Rear) | | | Operation | Release | | |
| Park | | | | on | | | | | on |
| Reverse | | on | | on | | | on | | |
| Neutral | | | | | | | | | |
| Drive | D1 Low | | on | | | | | on | |
| | D2 Second | | on | | | on | | | |
| | D3 Top | on | on | | on | (on) | on | | |
| 2 | Second | | on | | | on | | | |
| 1 | 1₂ Second | | on | | | on | | | |
| | 1₁ Low | | on | on | | | | | |

**NOTE:** The low & reverse brake is applied in "1₁" range to prevent free wheeling when coasting and allows engine braking.

## CLUTCH AND BAND APPLICATION CHART
### L4N71B, E4N71B, JM600 Automatic Transmissions

| Range | | Direct clutch | O.D. band servo | | High-reverse clutch (Front) | Forward clutch (Rear) | Low & reverse brake | 2nd band servo | | One-way clutch | Parking pawl |
|---|---|---|---|---|---|---|---|---|---|---|---|
| | | | Apply | Release | | | | Apply | Release | | |
| Park | | ON | (ON) | ON | | | ON | | | | ON |
| Reverse | | ON | (ON) | ON | ON | | ON | | ON | | |
| Neutral | | ON | (ON) | ON | | | | | | | |
| D | D₁ (Low) | ON | (ON) | ON | | ON | | | | ON | |
| | D₂ (Second) | ON | (ON) | ON | | ON | | ON | | | |
| | D₃ (Top) | ON | (ON) | ON | ON | ON | | (ON) | ON | | |
| | D₄ (O.D.) | | ON | | ON | ON | | (ON) | ON | | |
| 2 | Second | ON | (ON) | ON | | ON | | ON | | | |
| 1 | 1₂ (Second) | ON | (ON) | ON | | ON | | ON | | | |
| | 1₁ (Low) | ON | (ON) | ON | | ON | ON | | | ON | |

**NOTE:** The low & reverse brake is applied in "1₁" range to prevent free wheeling when coasting and allows engine braking.

## CHILTON'S THREE "C's" AUTOMATIC TRANSMISSION DIAGNOSIS CHART
### L3N71B, L4N71B, JM600 and E4N71B Automatic Transmission Models

| Condition | Cause | Correction |
|---|---|---|
| Engine does not start in "N", "P" ranges | a) Range select linkage<br>b) Neutral safety switch<br>c) Ignition switch and starter motor<br>d) Lock-up solenoid<br>e) Lock-up control unit and/or sensors | a) Adjust linkage<br>b) Adjust or replace<br>c) Repair or replace<br>d) Test, repair or replace solenoid<br>e) Test repair or replace lock-up control unit and or sensors |
| Engine starts in range other than "N" and "P" | a) Range select linkage<br>b) Neutral safety switch | a) Adjust linkage<br>b) Adjust or replace |
| Vehicle moves in "N" range | a) Range select linkage<br>b) Manual control valve<br>c) Rear clutch<br>d) Fluid quality not to specifications | a) Adjust linkage<br>b) Adjust range select linkage/renew valve<br>c) Renew rear clutch<br>d) Drain and replace fluid |
| Vehicle will not move in "D" range (but moves in "2", "1" and "R" ranges) | a) Range select linkage<br>b) Throttle valve pressure<br>c) Manual control valve<br>d) One way clutch of transmission | a) Adjust linkage<br>b) Correct throttle valve or passage per air test<br>c) Adjust range select linkage/renew valve<br>d) Renew clutch |
| Vehicle will not move in "D", "1" or "2" ranges but moves in "R" range Clutch slips, very poor acceleration | a) Oil level<br>b) Range select linkage<br>c) Throttle valve pressure<br>d) Manual control valve<br>e) Leakage of fluid passage<br>f) Engine adjustment and brake defects<br>g) Rear clutch<br>h) Front Clutch | a) Add if needed<br>b) Adjust linkage<br>c) Correct throttle valve or passage per air test<br>d) Adjust range select linkage/renew valve<br>e) Correct as per air test<br>f) Repair as needed<br>g) Renew rear clutch<br>h) Renew front clutch |
| Sharp shock shifting from "N" to "D" range | a) Vacuum diaphragm and hoses<br>b) Engine idle rpm<br>c) Throttle valve pressure<br>d) Rear clutch<br>e) Control Valve | a) Renew diaphragm and hoses<br>b) Set engine idle rpm<br>c) Correct throttle valve or passage per air test<br>d) Renew rear clutch<br>e) Clean, repair or replace control valve assembly |

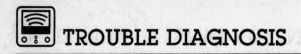 

### CHILTON'S THREE "C's" AUTOMATIC TRANSMISSION DIAGNOSIS CHART
### L3N71B, L4N71B, JM600 and E4N71B Automatic Transmission Models

| Condition | Cause | Correction |
|---|---|---|
| Vehicle will not move in "R" range (but moves in "D", "2" and "1" ranges). Clutch slips, very poor acceleration. | a) Oil level<br>b) Range select linkage<br>c) Throttle valve pressure<br>d) Manual control valve assembly<br>e) Leakage of passage<br>f) Rear clutch<br>g) Front clutch<br>h) Low and reverse brake<br>i) Front clutch check ball | a) Add if needed<br>b) Adjust linkage<br>c) Correct throttle valve or passage per air test<br>d) Adjust range select linkage/renew valve assembly<br>e) Correct as per air test<br>f) Renew rear clutch<br>g) Renew front clutch<br>h) Renew low and reverse brake<br>i) Repair or renew |
| Vehicle will not move in any range | a) Oil level<br>b) Range select linkage<br>c) Throttle valve pressure<br>d) Manual control valve<br>e) Leakage of fluid passage<br>f) Oil pump<br>g) Parking linkage<br>h) Lock-up control<br>i) Lock-up system sensors<br>j) Lock-up solenoid | a) Add if needed<br>b) Adjust linkage<br>c) Correct throttle valve or passage per air test<br>d) Adjust range select linkage/renew valve<br>e) Correct as per air test<br>f) Repair or renew<br>g) Repair or renew<br>h) Test, repair or replace lock-up control<br>i) Test, repair or replace system sensors<br>j) Test, repair or replace lock-up solenoid |
| Clutches or brakes slip When starting to mcve | a) Oil level<br>b) Range select linkage<br>c) Throttle valve pressure<br>d) Manual control valve<br>e) Leakage of fluid passage<br>f) Oil pump<br>g) Vacuum modulator and/or hoses | a) Add if needed<br>b) Adjust linkage<br>c) Correct throttle valve or passage per air test<br>d) Adjust range select linkage/renew valve<br>e) Correct as per air test<br>f) Repair or renew<br>g) Repair or renew |
| Excessive creep | a) High engine idle rpm | a) Adjust idle rpm |
| Vehicle braked in "R" range | a) Band servo<br>b) Leakage of fluid passage<br>c) Rear clutch<br>d) Band brake<br>e) Parking linkage | a) Renew band servo<br>b) Correct as per air test<br>c) Renew rear clutch<br>d) Renew band brake<br>e) Repair/renew linkage |

## CHILTON'S THREE "C's" AUTOMATIC TRANSMISSION DIAGNOSIS CHART
### L3N71B, L4N71B, JM600 and E4N71B Automatic Transmission Models

| Condition | Cause | Correction |
|---|---|---|
| No creep at all | a) Oil level | a) Add if needed |
| | b) range select linkage | b) Adjust linkage |
| | c) Low engine idle rpm | c) Adjust idle rpm |
| | d) Manual control valve | d) Adjust range select linkage/renew valve |
| | e) Rear clutch | e) Renew rear clutch |
| | f) Front clutch | f) Renew front clutch |
| | g) Oil pump | g) Repair or renew oil pump |
| | h) Leakage of fluid passage | h) Correct as per air test |
| | i) Direct Clutch | i) Renew direct clutch |
| Failure to change gear from "1st" to "2nd" | a) Range linkage | a) Adjust linkage |
| | b) Vacuum diaphragm and hoses | b) Renew diaphragm/hoses |
| | c) Downshift solenoid kickdown switch and wiring | c) Repair wiring and adjust or renew the solenoid downshift kickdown switch |
| | d) Manual control valve | d) Adjust range select linkage/renew valve |
| | e) Band servo | e) Renew band servo |
| | f) Leakage of fluid passage | f) Correct as per air test |
| | g) Front clutch | g) Renew front clutch |
| | h) Front clutch check ball | h) Renew front clutch check ball |
| | i) Governor valve | i) Repair or replace governor assembly |
| Failure to change gear from "2nd" to "3rd" | a) Range select linkage | a) Adjust linkage |
| | b) Vacuum diaphragm and hoses | b) Renew diaphragm/hoses |
| | c) Downshift solenoid kickdown switch and wiring | c) Repair wiring and adjust or renew the downshift solenoid kickdown switch |
| | d) Manual control valve | d) Adjust range select linkage/renew valve |
| | e) Governor valve | e) Overhaul governor/renew governor |
| | f) Band servo | f) Renew band servo |
| | g) Leakage of fluid passage | g) Correct as per air test |
| | h) Band brake | h) Renew band brake |
| | i) Front clutch | i) Renew front clutch |

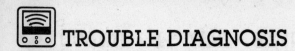

## CHILTON'S THREE "C's" AUTOMATIC TRANSMISSION DIAGNOSIS CHART
### L3N71B, L4N71B, JM600 and E4N71B Automatic Transmission Models

| Condition | Cause | Correction |
|---|---|---|
| Failure to Change gear from "3rd" to "4th" | a) Range selector linkage | a) Adjust range selector linkage |
| | b) Vacuum diaphragm or hoses | b) Renew diaphragm/hoses |
| | c) Kickdown solenoid, switch or wiring | c) Repair or renew solenoid, switch or wiring |
| | d) Oil quality | d) Correct oil quality |
| | e) Control valve assembly | e) Clean or renew control valve Assembly |
| | f) Governor | f) Clean or renew governor assembly |
| | g) Band servo | g) Repair or renew band servo components |
| | h) Component or oil passage leakage | h) Air test passages for case and components |
| | i) O.D. band | i) Adjust or renew O.D. band |
| Too high gear change point from "1st" to "2nd" and from "2nd" to "3rd" | a) Vacuum diaphragm and hoses | a) Renew diaphragm/hoses |
| | b) Downshift solenoid kickdown switch and wiring | b) Repair wiring and adjust or renew the downshift solenoid kickdown switch |
| | c) Manual control valve | c) Adjust range select linkage/renew valve |
| | d) Governor valve | d) Overhaul governor/ renew governor |
| | e) Leakage of fluid passage | e) Correct as per air test |
| Too high a gear change point from "1st" to "2nd", from "2nd" to "3rd", from "3rd" to "4th" | a) Vacuum diaphragm or hoses | a) Renew diaphragm/hoses |
| | b) Kickdown solenoid, switch or wiring | b) Repair or renew solenoid, switch or wiring |
| | c) Line pressure | c) Test line pressure with gauge and correct as required |
| | d) Oil quality | d) Correct oil quality |
| | e) Control valve assembly | e) Clean or renew control valve assembly |
| | f) Governor | f) Clean or renew governor assembly |
| | g) Oil passage leakage | g) Air test passages for case and components |
| Gear change directly from "1st" to "3rd" occurs | a) Manual control valve | a) Adjust range select linkage/renew valve |
| | b) Governor valve | b) Overhaul governor/ renew governor |
| | c) Leakage of fluid passage | c) Correct as per air test |
| | d) Band brake | d) Renew band brake |
| Gear change directly from "2nd" to "4th" occurs | a) Oil quality | a) Correct oil quality |
| | b) Control valve assembly | b) Clean or renew control valve assembly |
| | c) Oil passage leakage | c) Air test passages for case and component leakage |
| | d) Governor | d) Clean or renew governor assembly |
| | e) Forward clutch (rear) | e) Renew forward clutch (rear) |
| | f) Front clutch | f) Renew front clutch |

## CHILTON'S THREE "C's" AUTOMATIC TRANSMISSION DIAGNOSIS CHART
### L3N71B, L4N71B, JM600 and E4N71B Automatic Transmission Models

| Condition | Cause | Correction |
|---|---|---|
| Too sharp shock in change from "1st" to "2nd" | a) Vacuum diaphragm and hoses | a) Renew diaphragm/hoses |
| | b) Manual control valve | b) Adjust range select linkage/renew valve |
| | c) Band servo | c) Renew band servo |
| | d) Band brake | d) Renew band brake |
| | e) Torque converter | e) Renew torque converter |
| | f) Lock-up control unit and sensors | f) Test, repair or replace lock-up control unit and/or sensors |
| | g) Lock-up control solenoid | g) Test/repair or replace lock-up control solenoid |
| Too sharp shock in change from "2nd" to "3rd" | a) Vacuum diaphragm and hoses | a) Renew diaphragm/hoses |
| | b) Downshift solenoid kickdown switch and wiring | b) Repair wiring and adjust or renew the downshift solenoid kickdown switch |
| | c) Throttle valve pressure | c) Correct throttle valve or passage per air test |
| | d) Manual control valve | d) Adjust range select linkage/renew valve |
| | e) Band servo | e) Renew band servo |
| | f) Front clutch | f) Renew front clutch |
| | g) Torque converter | g) Renew torque converter |
| | h) Lock-up control unit and sensors | h) Test, repair or replace lock-up control unit and/or sensors |
| | i) Lock-up control solenoid | i) Test, repair or replace lock-up control solenoid |
| Too sharp shock in change from "3rd" to "4th" | a) Vacuum diaphragm and hoses | a) Renew diaphragm/hoses |
| | b) Line pressure | b) Test line pressure with gauge and correct as required |
| | c) Control valve assembly | c) Clean or renew control valve assembly |
| | d) Oil passage leakage | d) Air test passages for case and component leakage |
| | e) Band servo | e) Renew band servo components |
| | f) O.D. band or servo | f) Renew O.D. band or servo |
| | g) Lock-up solenoid | g) Test, repair or renew lock-up solenoid |
| | h) Lock-up control unit and/or sensors | h) Test, repair or renew lock-up control unit and/or sensors |
| | i) Torque converter | i) Renew torque converter |
| | j) Lock-up control valve | j) Repair or renew lock-up control valve |

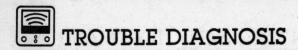

## CHILTON'S THREE "C's" AUTOMATIC TRANSMISSION DIAGNOSIS CHART
### L3N71B, L4N71B, JM600 and E4N71B Automatic Transmission Models

| Condition | Cause | Correction |
|---|---|---|
| Almost no shock or slipping in change from "1st" to "2nd" | a) Oil level <br> b) Range select linkage <br> c) Vacuum diaphragm and hoses <br> d) Throttle valve pressure <br><br> e) Manual control valve <br><br> f) Band servo <br> g) Leakage of fluid passage <br> h) Band brake | a) Add if needed <br> b) Adjust linkage <br> c) Renew diaphragm/hoses <br> d) Correct throttle valve or passage per air test <br> e) Adjust range select linkage/renew valve <br> f) Renew band servo <br> g) Correct as per air test <br> h) Renew band brake |
| Almost no shock or engine runaway on "2nd" to "3rd" shift | a) Oil level <br> b) Range select linkage <br> c) Vacuum diaphragm and hoses <br> d) Throttle valve pressure <br><br> e) Manual control valve <br><br> f) Band servo <br> g) Leakage of fluid passage <br> h) Front clutch <br> i) Front clutch check ball | a) Add if needed <br> b) Adjust linkage <br> c) Renew diaphragm/hoses <br> d) Correct throttle valve or passage per air test <br> e) Adjust range select linkage/renew valve <br> f) Renew band servo <br> g) Correct as per air test <br> h) Renew front clutch <br> i) Renew front clutch check ball |
| Almost no shock or slipping in change from "3rd" to "4th" | a) Oil level <br> b) range select linkage <br> c) Vacuum diaphragm and hoses <br> d) Line pressure <br><br> e) Oil quality <br> f) Control valve <br><br> g) Oil passage leakage <br><br> h) Band servo <br> i) O.D. band | a) Correct oil level <br> b) Adjust range select linkage <br> c) Renew diaphragm/hoses <br> d) Test line pressure with gauge and correct as required <br> e) Correct oil quality <br> f) Clean or renew control valve assembly <br> g) Air test passages for case and component leakage <br> h) Renew band servo components <br> i) Renew O.D. band |
| Vehicle braked by gear change from "1st" to "2nd" | a) Manual control valve <br><br> b) Front clutch <br> c) Low and reverse brake <br><br> d) One-way clutch of transmission | a) Adjust range select linkage/renew valve <br> b) Renew front clutch <br> c) Renew low and reverse brake <br> d) Renew one-way clutch of transmission |
| Vehicle braked by gear change from "2nd" to "3rd" | a) Manual control valve <br><br> b) Band servo <br> c) Brake band | a) Adjust range select linkage <br> b) Renew band servo <br> c) Renew brake band |

## CHILTON'S THREE "C's" AUTOMATIC TRANSMISSION DIAGNOSIS CHART
### L3N71B, L4N71B, JM600 and E4N71B Automatic Transmission Models

| Condition | Cause | Correction |
|---|---|---|
| Vehicle braked by gear change from "3rd" to "4th" | a) Oil quality | a) Correct oil quality |
| | b) Direct clutch | b) Renew direct clutch components |
| | c) Control valve assembly | c) Clean or renew control valve assembly |
| | d) High-reverse clutch (front) | d) Renew high-reverse (front) clutch components |
| Maximum speed not attained, acceleration poor | a) Oil level | a) Add if needed |
| | b) Range select linkage | b) Adjust linkage |
| | c) Throttle valve pressure | c) Correct throttle valve or passage per air test |
| | d) High stall rpm | d) Renew torque converter |
| | e) Manual control valve | e) Adjust range select linkage/renew valve |
| | f) Band servo | f) Repair/renew band servo |
| | g) Rear clutch | g) Renew rear clutch |
| | h) Front clutch | h) Renew front clutch |
| | i) Band brake | i) Renew band brake |
| | j) Low and reverse brake | j) Renew low and reverse brake |
| | k) Oil pump | k) Repair or renew oil pump |
| Failure to change from "4th" to "3rd" | a) Vacuum diaphragm and hoses | a) Renew diaphragm/hoses |
| | b) Control valve assembly | b) Clean or renew control valve assembly |
| | c) Governor | c) Clean or renew governor assembly |
| | d) Oil passage leakage | d) Air test passages for case and component leakage |
| | e) Oil quality | e) Correct oil quality |
| | f) Direct clutch | f) Renew direct clutch components |
| | g) High-reverse clutch (front) | g) Renew high-reverse (front) clutch components |
| | h) O.D. band | h) Renew O.D. band |
| | i) O.D. cancel switch | i) Test, repair or replace O.D. cancel switch |
| | j) O.D. cancel solenoid | j) Test, repair or replace O.D. cancel solenoid |
| | k) Lock-up solenoid | k) Test, repair or replace lock-up solenoid |
| | l) O.D. cancel valve | l) Repair or replace O.D. cancel valve |
| Failure to change gear from "2nd" to "1st" or from "3rd" to "1st" | a) Vacuum diaphragm and hoses | a) Renew diaphragm/hoses |
| | b) Manual control valve | b) Adjust range select linkage/renew valve |
| | c) Governor valve | c) Overhaul governor/renew governor |
| | d) Band servo | d) Renew band servo |
| | e) Band brake | e) Renew band brake |
| | f) Leakage of fluid pressure passage | f) Correct as per air test |
| | g) One-way clutch of transmission | g) Renew one-way clutch of transmission |

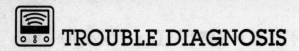

## CHILTON'S THREE "C's" AUTOMATIC TRANSMISSION DIAGNOSIS CHART
### L3N71B, L4N71B, JM600 and E4N71B Automatic Transmission Models

| Condition | Cause | Correction |
|---|---|---|
| Failure to change from "3rd" to "2nd" and from "4th" to "2nd" | a) Vacuum diaphragm and hoses<br>b) Control valve assembly<br><br>c) Governor<br>d) band servo (2nd and O.D.)<br>e) Oil passage leakage<br><br>f) Oil quality<br>g) High-reverse (front) clutch<br>h) O.D. band<br>i) 2nd band brake | a) Renew vacuum diaphragm/hoses<br>b) Clean or renew vacuum diaphragm/hoses<br>c) Clean or renew governor assembly<br>d) Renew band servo components<br>e) Air test passages for case and component leakage<br>f) Correct oil quality<br>g) Renew high-reverse (front) clutch components<br>h) Renew O.D. band components<br>i) Renew 2nd band brake |
| Gear change shock felt during deceleration by releasing accelerator pedal | a) Range select linkage<br>b) Vacuum diaphragm and hoses<br>c) Downshift solenoid kickdown switch and wiring<br><br><br>d) Throttle valve pressure<br><br>e) Manual control valve<br><br>f) Governor valve<br><br>g) Leakage of fluid pressure passage<br>h) Accumulor | a) Adjust linkage<br>b) Renew diaphragm/hoses<br><br>c) Repair wiring and adjust or renew the downshift solenoid kickdown switch<br>d) Correct throttle valve or passage per air test<br>e) Adjust range select linkage/renew valve<br>f) Overhaul governor/renew governor<br>g) Correct as per air test<br>h) Repair accumulor |
| Too high change point from "3rd" to "2nd" and from "2nd" to "1st" | a) Range select linkage<br>b) Vacuum diaphragm and hoses<br>c) Downshift solenoid kickdown switch and wiring<br><br><br>d) Throttle valve pressure<br><br>e) Manual control valve<br><br>f) Governor valve<br><br>g) Leakage at fluid passage | a) Adjust linkage<br>b) Renew diaphragm/hoses<br><br>c) Repair wiring and adjust or renew the downshift solenoid kickdown switch<br>d) Correct throttle valve or passage per air test<br>e) Adjust range select linkage/renew valve<br>f) Overhaul governor/renew governor<br>g) Correct per air test |

## CHILTON'S THREE "C's" AUTOMATIC TRANSMISSION DIAGNOSIS CHART
### L3N71B, L4N71B, JM600 and E4N71B Automatic Transmission Models

| Condition | Cause | Correction |
|---|---|---|
| Too high a change point from "4th" to "3rd", from "3rd" to "2nd", from "2nd" to "1st" | a) Range selector linkage<br>b) Vacuum diaphragm and hoses<br>c) Kickdown solenoid, switches wiring<br>d) Line pressure<br>e) Control valve assembly<br>f) Governor<br>g) Oil passage leakage<br>h) Lock-up control unit and sensors | a) Adjust range selector linkage<br>b) Renew diaphragm/hoses<br>c) Repair or renew solenoid, switches, wiring<br>d) Test line pressure with gauge and correct as required<br>e) Clean or renew control valve assembly<br>f) Clean or renew governor assembly<br>g) Air test passages for case and component leakage<br>h) Test, repair or replace lock-up control and/or sensors |
| Failure to change from "3rd" to "2nd" | a) Vacuum diaphragm and hoses<br>b) Manual control valve<br>c) Governor valve<br>d) Band servo<br>e) Leakage of fluid pressure passage<br>f) Front clutch<br>g) Band brake | a) Renew diaphragm/hoses<br>b) Adjust range select linkage/renew valve<br>c) Overhaul governor/renew governor<br>d) Renew band servo<br>e) Correct as per air test<br>f) Renew front clutch<br>g) Renew band brake |
| Kickdown operates or engine overruns when depressing pedal in "3rd" beyond kickdown speed limit | a) Range select linkage<br>b) Vacuum diaphragm and hoses<br>c) Main line pressure<br>d) Manual control valve<br>e) Governor valve<br>f) Leakage of fluid pressure passage<br>g) Front clutch | a) Adjust linkage<br>b) Renew diaphragm/hoses<br>c) Correct main line or passage per air test<br>d) Adjust range select linkage/renew valve assembly<br>e) Overhaul governor/renew governor<br>f) Correct as per air test<br>g) Renew front clutch |
| No kickdown by depressing pedal in "3rd" within kickdown speed | a) Vacuum diaphragm and hoses<br>b) Downshift solenoid kickdown switch and wiring<br>c) Manual control valve<br>d) Governor valve<br>e) Band brake<br>f) Leakage at fluid passage | a) Renew diaphragm/hoses<br>b) Repair wiring and adjust or renew the solenoid downshift kickdown switch<br>c) Adjust range select linkage/renew valve assembly<br>d) Overhaul governor/renew governor<br>e) Renew band brake<br>f) Correct per air test |

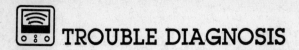 

### CHILTON'S THREE "C's" AUTOMATIC TRANSMISSION DIAGNOSIS CHART
### L3N71B, L4N71B, JM600 and E4N71B Automatic Transmission Models

| Condition | Cause | Correction |
|---|---|---|
| Engine Races extremely fast or slips in changing from "4th" to "3rd" when depressing pedal | a) Vacuum diaphragm and hoses | a) Renew vacuum diaphragm/hoses |
| | b) Main line pressure | b) Test line pressure with gauge and correct as required |
| | c) Control valve assembly | c) Clean or renew control valve assembly |
| | d) Band servo | d) Renew band servo components |
| | e) Oil passage leakage | e) Air test passages for case or component leakage |
| | f) Oil quality | f) Correct oil quality |
| | g) Direct clutch | g) Renew direct clutch components |
| | h) High-reverse (front) clutch and/or check ball | h) Renew high-reverse (front) clutch components and check ball for sealing |
| | i) O.D. band | i) Renew O.D. band |
| Kickdown does not operate with pedal depressed in "4th" within kickdown speed | a) Kickdown solenoid, switch and wire | a) Test, repair or renew as required |
| | b) Vacuum diaphragm and hoses | b) Renew diaphragm/hoses |
| | c) Fluid Quality | c) Drain and refill with new fluid |
| | d) Control valve assembly | d) Clean or replace control valve assembly |
| | e) Governor | e) Clean or replace governor |
| | f) High-reverse clutch (front) | f) Renew clutch assembly |
| | g) Direct clutch | g) Renew clutch assembly |
| | h) Leakage of fluid in pressure | h) Correct as per air test |
| Kickdown operates or engine overruns when depressing pedal in "4th" beyond kick-down vehicle speed limit | a) Range selector linkage | a) Adjust linkage |
| | b) Vacuum diaphragm and hoses | b) Renew diaphragm/hoses |
| | c) Line pressure | c) Correct line-pressure |
| | d) Fluid quality | d) Drain and refill with new fluid |
| | e) Control valve assembly | e) Clean or replace control valve assembly |
| | f) Governor | f) Clean or replace governor |
| | g) Leakage of fluid in pressure passage | g) Correct as per air test |
| | h) O.D. band brake | h) Correct O.D. band as required |
| Shift pattern does not change | a) Vacuum diaphragm or hoses | a) Renew diaphragm/hoses |
| | b) O.D. cancel switch | b) Test, repair or renew O.D. cancel switch |
| | c) Kickdown switch, solenoid, or wires | c) Test, repair or renew kickdown switch, solenoid or wires |
| | d) O.D. cancel solenoid | d) Test, repair or renew O.D. cancel solenoid |
| | e) Engine lack of power or braking problem | e) Adjust engine components as required. Check brake drag |
| | f) Lock-up control unit or sensors | f) Test, repair or renew lock-up unit or sensors |

## CHILTON'S THREE "C's" AUTOMATIC TRANSMISSION DIAGNOSIS CHART
### L3N71B, L4N71B, JM600 and E4N71B Automatic Transmission Models

| Condition | Cause | Correction |
|---|---|---|
| Engine races extremely or slips in changing from "3rd" to "2nd" when depressing pedal | a) Vacuum diaphragm and hoses<br>b) Main line pressure<br>c) Manual control valve<br>d) Band servo<br>e) Leakage of fluid pressure passage<br>f) Front clutch | a) Renew diaphragm/hoses<br>b) Correct main line or passage as per air test<br>c) Adjust range select linkage/renew valve assembly<br>d) Renew band servo<br>e) Correct as per air test<br>f) Renew front clutch |
| Failure to change from "3rd" to "2nd" when changing lever into "2" range | a) Range select linkage<br>b) Main line pressure<br>c) Manual control valve<br>d) Band servo<br>e) Band brake<br>f) Leakage of fluid pressure passage | a) Adjust linkage<br>b) Correct main line or passage per air test<br>c) Adjust range select linkage/renew valve assembly<br>d) Renew band servo<br>e) Renew band brake<br>f) Correct as per air test |
| Gear change from "2nd" to "1st" or from "2nd" to "3rd" in "2" range | a) Range select linkage<br>b) Main line pressure<br>c) Manual control valve | a) Adjust linkage<br>b) Correct main line or passage per air test<br>c) Adjust range select linkage/renew valve assembly |
| No shock on change from "1" range to "2" range or engine races extremely | a) Oil level<br>b) Range select linkage<br>c) Vacuum diaphragm and hoses<br>d) Engine idle rpm<br>e) High stall speed<br>f) Manual control valve<br>g) Transmission air check to determine if band servo is working<br>h) Oil pump | a) Add if needed<br>b) Adjust linkage<br>c) Renew diaphragm/hoses<br>d) Set idle rpm<br>e) Renew band brake<br>f) Adjust range select linkage/renew valve assembly<br>g) Repair or renew servo<br>h) Repair or renew |
| Failure to shift from "3rd" to "2nd" when shifting lever into "1" range | a) Range select linkage<br>b) Main line pressure<br>c) Manual control valve<br>d) Governor valve<br>e) Band servo<br>f) Leakage of fluid pressure passage<br>g) Low and reverse brake bands | a) Adjust linkage<br>b) Correct main line or passage per air test<br>c) Adjust range select linkage/renew valve assembly<br>d) Overhaul governor/renew governor<br>e) Renew band servo<br>f) Correct as per air test<br>g) Renew low and reverse brake bands |

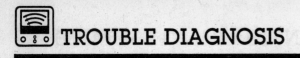 

## CHILTON'S THREE "C's" AUTOMATIC TRANSMISSION DIAGNOSIS CHART
### L3N71B, L4N71B, JM600 and E4N71B Automatic Transmission Models

| Condition | Cause | Correction |
|---|---|---|
| No engine braking in range "1" | a) Range select linkage<br>b) Main line pressure<br><br><br>c) Manual control valve<br><br>d) Leakage of fluid pressure passage<br>e) Low and reverse brake bands | a) Adjust linkage<br>b) Correct main line or passage per air test<br>c) Adjust range select linkage/renew valve assembly<br>d) Correct as per air test<br>e) Renew low and reverse brake bands |
| Gear change from "1st" to "2nd" or from "2nd" to "3rd" in "1" range | a) Range select linkage<br>b) Manual control valve<br><br>c) Leakage of fluid pressure passage | a) Adjust linkage<br>b) Adjust range select linkage/renew valve assembly<br>c) Correct as per air test |
| Does not change from "2nd" to "1st" in "1" range | a) Oil level<br>b) Range select linkage<br>c) Manual control valve<br><br>d) Governor valve<br><br>e) Band servo<br>f) Leakage of fluid pressure passage<br>g) Low and reverse brake | a) Add if needed<br>b) Adjust linkage<br>c) Adjust range select linkage/renew valve assembly<br>d) Overhaul governor/renew governor<br>e) Renew band servo<br>f) Correct as per air test<br>g) Renew low and reverse brake |
| Large shock in changing from "2nd" to "1st" in "1" range | a) Vacuum diaphragm and hoses<br>b) High engine stall rpm<br><br>c) Manual control valve | a) Renew diaphragm/hoses<br>b) Renew low and reverse brake<br>c) Adjust range select linkage/renew valve assembly |
| Transmission overheats | a) Oil level<br>b) Band servo<br>c) Cooler fluid pressure<br><br><br>d) Restricted or no rear lubrication<br>e) Manual control valve<br><br>f) Leakage of fluid pressure passage<br>g) Front clutch<br>h) Band brake<br>i) Low and reverse brake<br>j) Line pressure<br><br>k) "O" ring in input shaft<br>l) Torque converter<br>m) Lock-up orifice in oil pump cover<br>n) Oil pump | a) Add if needed<br>b) Renew band servo<br>c) Correct cooler fluid or passage per air test<br>d) Check passages<br><br>e) Adjust range select linkage/renew valve assembly<br>f) Correct as per air test<br>g) Renew front clutch<br>h) Renew band brake<br>i) Renew low and reverse brake<br>j) Test line pressure with gauge and correct as required<br>k) Renew "O" ring in input shaft<br>l) Renew torque converter<br>m) Inspect orifice, clean or renew plate or oil pump assembly<br>n) Renew oil pump assembly |

## CHILTON'S THREE "C's" AUTOMATIC TRANSMISSION DIAGNOSIS CHART
### L3N71B, L4N71B, JM600 and E4N71B Automatic Transmission Models

| Condition | Cause | Correction |
|---|---|---|
| Vehicle moves changing into "P" range or parking gear does not disengage when shifted out of "P" range | a) Range select linkage | a) Adjust linkage |
| Oil shoots out during operation. White smoke from exhaust during operation | a) Oil level<br>b) Vacuum diaphragm and hoses<br>c) Main line pressure<br><br>d) Restricted or no rear lubrication<br>e) Manual control valve<br><br>f) Leakage of fluid pressure passage<br>g) Rear clutch<br>h) Band brake<br>i) Low and reverse brake<br><br>j) Oil pump<br>k) One-way clutch torque converter<br>l) Planetary gear | a) Add if needed<br>b) Renew vacuum diaphragm/hoses<br>c) Correct main line or passage per air test<br>d) Check passages<br><br>e) Adjust range select linkage/renew valve assembly<br>f) Correct as per air test<br>g) Renew rear clutch<br>h) Renew band brake<br>i) Renew low and reverse brake<br>j) Renew oil pump<br>k) Renew one-way clutch torque converter<br>l) Renew planetary gear |
| Offensive smell at fluid fill pipe | a) Oil level<br>b) Rear clutch<br>c) Front clutch<br>d) Band brake<br>e) Low and reverse brake<br><br>f) Oil pump<br>g) Leakage of fluid pressure passage<br>h) One-way clutch torque converter | a) Add if needed<br>b) Renew rear clutch<br>c) Renew front clutch<br>d) Renew band brake<br>e) Renew low and reverse brake<br>f) Renew oil pump<br>g) Correct as per air test<br>h) Renew one-way clutch torque converter |
| Transmission noise in "P" and "N" ranges | a) Oil level<br>b) Main line pressure<br><br>c) Oil pump | a) Add if needed<br>b) Correct main line or passage per air test<br>c) Renew oil pump |
| Transmission noise in "D", "2", "1" and "R" ranges | a) Oil level<br>b) Main line pressure<br><br>c) Rear clutch<br>d) Oil pump<br>e) One-way clutch of transmission<br>f) Planetary gear<br>g) Torque converter | a) Add if needed<br>b) Correct main line or passage per air test<br>c) Renew rear clutch<br>d) Renew oil pump<br>e) Renew one-way clutch of transmission<br>f) Renew planetary gear<br>g) Renew torque converter |

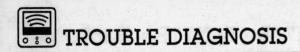 

## CHILTON'S THREE "C's" AUTOMATIC TRANSMISSION DIAGNOSIS CHART
### L3N71B, L4N71B, JM600 and E4N71B Automatic Transmission Models

| Condition | Cause | Correction |
|---|---|---|
| Transmission shifts to O.D. even if O.D. cancel switch is turned to "ON" | a) O.D. cancel switch and/or wiring | a) Inspect, renew cancel switch if necessary and/or repair wiring |
| | b) O.D. cancel solenoid | b) Renew O.D. cancel solenoid |
| | c) O.D. cancel valve | c) Clean or renew O.D. cancel valve |
| | d) Lock-up control unit and sensors | d) Test, repair or renew lock-up control unit and sensors |
| Lamp inside O.D. cancel switch does not glow, even if ignition switch is turned to "ON" (engine not started) | a) O.D. cancel switch and/or wiring | a) Inspect, renew cancel switch or components, as required. Repair wiring as required |
| | b) Lock-up control unit and sensors | b) Test repair or renew lock-up control unit and sensors |
| Lamp inside O.D. cancel switch does not glow, even if transmission is shifted to O.D. | a) O.D. cancel switch and/or wiring | a) Inspect, renew cancel switch or components, as required. Repair wiring as required |
| | b) O.D. indicator switch | b) Repair or renew O.D. indicator switch |
| Lamp inside power shift switch does not glow even if shift pattern is turned to "power" pattern | a) O.D. cancel switch | a) Test, repair or renew O.D. cancel switch |
| | b) Lock-up control unit and sensors | b) Test, repair or renew lock-up control unit or sensors |
| Lock-up does not occur in any range (E4N71B) | a) Lock-up solenoid | a) Test, repair or renew lock-up solenoid |
| | b) Lock-up control unit and sensors | b) Test, repair or renew lock-up control unit or sensors |
| | c) Torque converter | c) Renew torque converter |
| | d) Lock-up control valve | d) Renew lock-up control valve |
| Lock-up does not occur in "4th" gear (L4N71B) | a) Governor | a) Clean or renew governor |
| | b) O.D. band servo | b) Repair O.D. band servo |
| | c) Lock-up control valve | c) Clean or renew lock-up control valve |
| | d) O.D. brake band | d) Renew O.D. brake band |
| Large jolt changing from lock-up "OFF" to "ON" | a) Fluid quality | a) Drain and replace fluid |
| | b) Line pressure | b) Correct line pressure to specs. |
| | c) Governor | c) Clean or renew governor |
| | d) Lock-up control unit and sensors | d) Test, repair or renew lock-up control unit or sensors |
| | e) Lock-up control valve | e) Clean or renew lock-up control valve |
| | f) O.D. brake band | f) Renew O.D. brake band |
| Torque converter not locked-up | a) Governor tube | a) Repair or renew governor tube |
| | b) Governor | b) Clean or renew governor |
| | c) Line pressure | c) Test line pressure with gauge and correct as required |
| | d) "O" ring in input shaft | d) Renew "O" ring in input shaft |
| | e) Torque converter | e) Renew torque converter |
| | f) Lock-up control valve | f) Clean or renew lock-up control valve |
| | g) Lock-up orifice in oil pump cover | g) Inspect orifice, clean or renew plate or oil pump assembly |
| | h) Oil pump | h) Renew oil pump assembly |

## CHILTON'S THREE "C's" AUTOMATIC TRANSMISSION DIAGNOSIS CHART
### L3N71B, L4N71B, JM600 and E4N71B Automatic Transmission Models

| Condition | Cause | Correction |
|---|---|---|
| Lock-up piston slips | a) Line pressure | a) Test line pressure with gauge and correct as required |
| | b) "O" ring in input shaft | b) Renew "O" ring in input shaft |
| | c) Torque converter | c) Renew torque converter |
| | d) Lock-up orifice in oil pump cover | d) Inspect orifice, clean or renew plate or oil pump assembly |
| | e) Oil pump | e) Renew oil pump assembly |
| Lock-up points extremely high or low | a) Governor tube | a) Repair or renew governor tube |
| | b) Governor | b) Clean or renew governor |
| | c) Lock-up control valve | c) Clean or renew lock-up control valve |
| Engine stalls in R, D, 2, and 1 ranges | a) Torque converter | a) Renew torque converter |
| | b) Lock-up valve | b) Clean or renew lock-up valve |

## Preparation for Trouble Diagnosis

A logical and orderly diagnosis outline, with charts, is provided with clutch and band application charts, shift speed and governor pressures, main control pressures and a basic oil flow schematic to assist the repairman in diagnosing the problems, causes and extent of repairs needed to bring the automatic transmission back to its acceptable level of operation.

Preliminary checks and adjustments should be made to the manual linkage, accelerator and downshift switch control. Transmission oil level must be checked, both visually and by smell, to determine if the fluid level is correct and to observe the condition of the fluid, should any foreign material be present in the fluid. Smelling the fluid will indicate if internal damage has been done to the bands and/or clutches, through excessive slippage or overheating of the transmission.

It is most important to locate the defects and their causes and to properly repair them, avoiding a reoccurrence of the same problem which results in costly and time consuming repairs for a second time.

## Hydraulic Control System

Hydraulic pressure, clutch and band applications control the changing of the gear ratios in the automatic transmissions. The clutches and bands are applied or released by the force of the fluid pressure, controlled by a system of valves and control mechanisms.

1. Screen or filter cleans foreign material from the fluid supply before entering the oil pump.
2. The oil pump supplies the oil pressure to the transmission and its components.
3. Converter pressure relief valve prevents excessive pressure build-up in the converter.
4. The torque converter is a fluid coupler, torque multiplier and a lock-up unit.
5. The rear (forward) clutch is applied in all forward gears.
6. The high-reverse (front) clutch is applied in reverse and high gears.
7. The low and reverse clutch brake is applied in Park, Reverse and range "1" low gear.
8. The rear lubrication passages lubricate the rear transmission components.
9. The front lubrication passages lubricate the front transmission components.
10. The oil cooler system removes heat from the transmission fluid as it flows through a cooler in the engine's cooling system.
11. Drain back valve prevents loss of fluid in the hydraulic circuits when the engine is stopped.
12. Throttle control valve regulates the throttle pressure in relation to the engine manifold vacuum through vacuum diaphragm assembly.

NOTE: A vacuum pump is used on the diesel engine to control the vacuum supply to the vacuum diaphragm.

13. The brake band servo is applied in the "2" speed and pressure released when the transmission is in "3" gear.
14. Pressure modifier valve uses throttle pressure, controlled by governor pressure, to modify the main line pressure from the regulator valve. It also modifies harsh shifting caused by excessive pump pressure.
15. Vacuum diaphragm moves the throttle valve in relation to the engine vacuum changes or controlled vacuum from the diesel engine installed vacuum pump.
16. Throttle back-up valve increases throttle pressure output to increase line pressure when the manual valve is shifted to either "2" or "1" range.
17. Governor provides road speed signals to the transmission control valve assembly and causes either up or down shifting.
18. Oil pressure regulator valve is used to control main line pressure.
19. Throttle solenoid downshift valve overrides normal upshifts to provide forced downshifts on full acceleration.
20. Manual selector valve moves with the shift selector and direct main line pressure to the various oil passages, applying units to provide the necessary gear ratios.
21. 1-2 shift valve controls the upshifts from "1st" to "2nd" and downshifts from "2nd" to "1st"
22. The 2-3 shift valve controls the upshift from "2nd" to "3rd" and downshifts from "3rd" to "2nd".
23. The 3-4 shift valve controls the upshift from "3rd" to "4th" and downshifts from "4th" to "3rd".
24. Second lock-up valve applies the brake band servo in "D," 1, and 2 ranges. The second lock-up valve locks out the 1-2 shift valve in the "2" range.
25. The speed cut valve controls the opening and closing of the line pressure passage to the high-reverse (front) clutch, dependent upon the governor pressure which is generated in proportion to car road speed.
26. When in operation, the lock-up control valve drains fluid from the front of the lock-up piston, located in the torque converter. As the fluid is drained, the turbine runner is coupled to the pump impeller, giving mechanical lock-up, rather than a fluid coupling effect.

27. The overdrive cancel solenoid and switch allow or prevent engagement of the overdrive unit, on demand of the operator.

28. Overdrive cancel valve works in conjunction with the overdrive cancel solenoid to allow or prevent the engagement of the overdrive unit.

29. The shift valve train system applies and exhausts the fluid pressures to the servos and clutch assemblies for upshifts and downshifts automatically on demand.

30. The Kickdown system forces downshifts by overriding the governor/throttle valve control of the shift valves.

## Diagnosis Tests

### OIL PRESSURE CIRCUITS

To utilize the oil flow charts for diagnosing transmission problems, the repairman must have an understanding of the oil pressure circuits and how each circuit affects the operation of the transmission, by the use of controlled oil pressure.

Control (line) pressure is a regulated main line pressure, developed by the operation of the front pump. It is directed to the main regulator valve, where predetermined spring pressure automatically moves the regulator valve to control the pressure of the oil at a predetermined rate, by opening the valve and exhausting excessive pressured oil back into the sump and holding the valve closed to build up pressure when needed.

Therefore, it is most important during the diagnosis phase to test main line control pressure to determine if high or low pressure exists. Do not attempt to adjust a pressure regulator valve spring to obtain more or less control pressure. Internal transmission damage may result.

The manual valve is the controlling agent of the automatic transmission. It is manually operated to a specific range, which in turn directs fluid pressure to the varied applying units, providing the necessary gear ratios to operate the vehicle under different road conditions and engine loads.

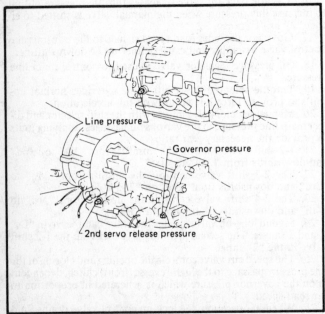

**Pressure test port locations on the four speed automatic transmissions. The L4N71B, JM600 models utilize a pipe to the converter from the governor pressure port** (© Nissan Motor Co. of USA)

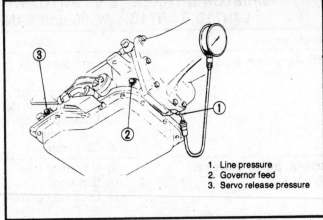

1. Line pressure
2. Governor feed
3. Servo release pressure

**Installation of pressure gauge to line pressure port—L3N71B models illustrated** (© Nissan Motor Co. of USA)

## PRELIMINARY CHECKS

### Verifying Malfunctions

1. Obtain as much information from the vehicle operator as to the nature of the malfunction.

2. Determine when the condition exists, only when first started, during the engine/transmission warm up period, after the assemblies have reached normal operating temperature of 122-176° F. (50-80° C.) or during all driving phases.

3. Verify fluid level and fluid condition, noting its color, texture and odor. Some common forms of contaminations are as follows;

  a. Dark or black fluid with a burned odor can indicate worn or burned friction material.

  b. Dark or black fluid without a burned odor can indicate a slight engine coolant leakage or addition of various types of additives.

  c. Milky white color of the fluid would indicate water contamination from the cooling system or from an outside source, such as road water or from a flood.

  d. Varnished fluid, light to dark brown and tacky, can indicate over or under filling, which in turn can cause overheating of the fluid and cause the fluid to oxidize.

4. Verify the engine idle of the vehicle is set to specifications.

5. Verify the shift linkage detents align with the detents in the transmission. In many cases, failure of the transmission can be traced to improperly adjusted manual control valve linkage.

### ROAD TEST

A road test can be made to determine the condition of the transmission internal components through their applications and releases during the gear ratio changes, which occur automatically. Spin-up, dragging or harshness is normally produced during the shifting, either up or down. By referring to the clutch and band application chart for the components engaged during a particular gear range, the malfunctioning component can normally be pinpointed.

It is suggested by the manufacturer that an oil pressure gauge (0-400 psi) be installed on the transmission at the main line pressure port before any road-test is performed. A tachometer and vacuum gauge should also be install in such a manner that all hoses from the gauges be routed to avoid ground contact while the vehicle is in motion.

— CAUTION —

*Road safety must be paramount with the gauges read and the results recorded by one person, while a second person operates the vehicle.*

A road test sequence should be followed. It may be necessary to repeat a sequence under different throttle conditions, such as light, medium, full or wide open throttle. Each sequence should have its results recorded.

## Before The Road Test

1. Check that engine can only be started in the "P" and "N" ranges and that the vehicle is locked in position with the selector lever in the "P" range. Record the results.
2. Shift the selector lever into the "R" (Reverse) range. Note the initial engagement. Drive the vehicle in the reverse range to detect slippage or other malfunctions. Record the results.
3. Move the selector lever to the "N" range. There should be no forward or rearward movement. Record the results.
4. Shift the selector lever to the "D" range and note the engagement of the internal components, note the results.
5. Shift the gear selector lever to the "2" range and note the gear engagement. Record the results.
6. Shift the selector lever to the "1" range and note the gear engagement. Record the results.
7. Record the line pressure and vacuum readings at each range position.

## During Road Test

1. Using a pre-selected road test course, drive the vehicle through all automatic shifts and in all gear ranges.
2. Note the shift timing and check that the torque converter locks up at its speed of approximately 42 mph.

**NOTE: Because the shock of the torque converter lock-up is very slight, it is advisable to have a tachometer connected to the engine, to determine the loss of rpm (200-400 rpm) as the converter locks up. Certa in vehicle/transmission applications have a lock-up light indicator mounted either on the console or the dash, to alert the operator of the converter clutch lock-up.**

3. During the road test, note the shift quality and timing, check for slippage or hesitation during the shifts, harshness, overlapping of unit application during the shift, noise or other malfunctions.

## ROAD TEST GUIDE FOR L3N71B MODELS

### "D" RANGE

1. Check the vehicle speeds and the engine rpm as the automatic transmission upshifts from "1st" to "2nd", from "2nd" to "3rd" and when the torque converter has locked up, on a light acceleration with engine vacuum approximately at 4 inches.
2. On quick acceleration, check the shifts as was done in step one. The engine vacuum would be at zero inches.
3. Running at speeds of 19, 25, 31, 37 and 43 mph in "D" range, check the kick down operation from "3rd" to "2nd" and from "2nd" to "1st".
4. With the accelerator pedal released and engine vacuum approximately 18 inches or more, check the downshifting from "3rd" to "2nd" and from "2nd" to "1st".
5. With the accelerator pedal released and engine vacuum at 18 inches or more while driving at 30 mph, manually move the gear selector lever from the "D" position to the "1" position. The transmission should automatically shift to the "2nd" gear of the "1" position and engine braking should occur. As the vehicle slows, the transmission will downshift from the "2nd" gear to the "1st" gear while in the "1" position. Again, engine braking should occur.
6. With the accelerator pedal released, quick shift the selector lever into the "2" position while driving at 30 mph. A downshift from "3rd" to "2nd" should take place and engine braking should occur. Verify that the transmission remains in the "2nd" gear, regardless of vehicle speed.

### "1" RANGE

1. Check for proper upshifting of the transmission from "1st" to "2nd" while in the "1" range. "3rd" gear is not attainable.

### "2" RANGE

1. Check the transmisison for being locked into the "2nd" gear and not upshifting or downshifting, regardless of vehicle speed.

## ROAD TEST GUIDE FOR L4N71B AND TM600 MODELS

### "D" RANGE

1. On a light acceleration and with engine vacuum at approximately 4 inches, check the vehicle speeds and the engine rpm as the automatic transmission upshifts from "1st" to "2nd", from "2nd" to "3rd" and from "3rd" to "4th", with the O.D. cancel switch in the off position. Verify the torque converter lock-up with either the indicator light or with a tachometer attached to the engine.
2. On quick acceleration, check the upshifts as was done in step one. The engine vacuum would be at zero inches.
3. Running at speeds of 19, 25, 31, 37, 43 and 62 mph in the "D" range, check the kickdown operation from "4th" to "3rd" and from "3rd" to "2nd", both in and out of the O.D. mode.
4. With the accelerator pedal released and the engine vacuum approximately 18 inches or more, check the down shifting from the "4th" to "3rd", "3rd" to "2nd" and "2nd" to "1st" with the transmission in the O.D. mode. Check the down shifting with the transmission out of the O.D. mode from "3rd" to "2nd" and from "2nd" to "1st".
5. With the accelerator pedal released and the engine vacuum at 18 inches or more, traveling at a speed of 30 mph, manually move the gear selector lever from the "D" position to the "1" position. The transmission should automatically shift to the "2nd" gear of the "1" position and engine braking should occur. As the vehicle slows, the transmission will downshift from the "2nd" gear to the "1st" gear while in the "1" position. Again, engine braking should occur.
6. Quick shift the selector lever into the "2" position while releasing the accelerator pedal. Have the vehicle traveling at a road speed of 30 mph. A downshift from the "3rd" to "2nd" should take place and engine braking should occur. Verify that the transmission remains in the "2nd" gear, regardless of vehicle speed.

### "1" RANGE

1. Check for proper transmission upshifting from "1st" to "2nd" while in the "1" range. The transmission should not shift into "3rd" gear.

### "2" RANGE

1. Check the transmission for being locked into the "2nd" gear and not upshifting or downshifting, regardless of vehicle speed.

### O.D. CANCEL SWITCH OPERATION

1. Verify that the transmission will not shift into the overdrive mode while the O.D. cancel switch is in the "ON" position.

### O.D. INDICATOR LAMP

1. With the ignition switch in the "ON" position, without the engine operating, the O.D. indicator lamp should glow and go out as soon as the engine is started.
2. Verify the indicator lamp glows when the transmission is shifted into O.D. with the O.D. cancel switch in the "OFF" position.

## ROAD TEST GUIDE FOR E4N71B MODELS

### "P" RANGE

1. Place the control lever in "P" range and start the engine. Stop the engine and repeat the procedure in all other ranges and neutral.

2. Stop vehicle on a slight upgrade and place control lever in "P" range. Release parking brake to make sure vehicle remains locked.

### "R" RANGE

1. Manually shift the control lever from "P" to "R", and note shift quality.

2. Drive the vehicle in reverse long enough to detect slippage or other abnormalities.

### "N" RANGE

1. Manually shift the control lever from "R" and "D" to "N" and note quality.

2. Release parking brake with control lever in "N" range. Lightly depress accelerator pedal to make sure vehicle does not move. (When vehicle is new or soon after clutches have been replaced, vehicle may move slightly. This is not a problem.)

### "D" RANGE

1. Manually shift the gear selector from "N" to "D" range, and note shift quality.

2. Drive the vehicle in "D" range. Record, on the symptom chart, respective vehicle speeds at which upshifting and downshifting occur. These speeds are to be read at several different intake manifold vacuum levels. Also, determine the timing at which shocks are encountered during shifting and which clutches are engaged.

3. Check to determine if shifting speed changes when accelerator pedal is depressed slowly and when it is depressed quickly.

4. Check to determine if shifting to overdrive gear cannot be made while power shift switch is "ON."

5. When vehicle is being driven in the 40-53 mph (65-85 km/h) speed range in "D₃" at half to light throttle position, fully depress accelerator pedal to make sure it downshifts from 3rd to 2nd gear.

6. When vehicle is being driven in the 16-22 mph (25-35 km/h) speed range in "D " range at half to light throttle position, fully depress accelerator pedal to make sure it downshifts from 2nd to 1st gear.

### "2" RANGE

1. While vehicle is being driven in "2" range, make sure that it does not shift into 1st or 3rd gear, despite speed changes.

2. Shift control lever to "D" range and allow vehicle to operate at 25-31 mph (40-50 km/h). Then, shift to "2" range to make sure it downshifts to 2nd gear.

### "1" RANGE

1. Shift control lever to "1" range and allow vehicle to run. Ensure that it does not upshift from 1st to 2nd gear although vehicle speed increases.

2. While vehicle is being driven in "1" range, release accelerator pedal to make sure that engine compression acts as a brake.

3. Shift control lever to "D" or "2" range and allow vehicle to run at 12-19 mph (20-30 km/h). Then, shift control lever to "1" range to make sure the downshift to 1st gear is made.

## CONTROL PRESSURE SYSTEM TESTS

Control pressure tests should be performed whenever slippage, delay or harshness is felt in the shifting of the transmission. Throttle and modulator pressure changes can cause these problems also, but are generated from the control pressures and therefore reflect any problems arising from the control pressure system.

The control pressure is first checked in all ranges without any throttle pressure input, and then checked as the throttle pressure is increased by lowering the vacuum supply to the vacuum diaphragm with the use of the stall test.

The control pressure tests should define differences between mechanical or hydraulic failures of the transmission.

The transmissions are provided with three pressure test ports, line pressure, governor pressure and servo release pressure. Only the main line pressure test ports on the transmissions and the governor pressure test ports are of any value to the diagnostician in determining transmission malfunctions.

### Testing

1. Install pressure gauges to the main line pressure test port and if equipped, to the governor pressure test port.

2. Install a tachometer and vacuum gauge to the engine.

3. Block the wheels and apply the parking brake.

4. Operate the engine/transmission in the ranges as listed on the accompanying charts and at the engine vacuum as specified.

5. Record the actual pressure readings in each test and compare them with specifications.

**NOTE: Look for a steady rise in pressure as the vehicle speed increases under a light load and pressure should not drop between shifts more than 14 psi. Excessive pressure drop could indicate internal leakages.**

### Precautions Before Idle Tests

1. Be sure manifold vacuum is above 15 in. Hg. If lower, check for engine conditions and/or vacuum leaks and repair.

2. Make sure the manifold vacuum changes with throttle plate opening. Check by accelerating quickly and observing the vacuum reading.

### Possible Malfunctions Due to Low Line Pressure

If line pressure does not rise, first check to make sure that vacuum hose is connected properly.

1. When line pressure is low at all positions, the problem may be due to:

a. Wear on interior of oil pump

b. Oil leakage at or around oil pump, control valve body, transmission case or governor

c. Sticking pressure regulator valve

d. Sticking pressure modifier valve

2. When line pressure is low at a particular position, the problem may be due to the following:

a. If oil leaks at or around forward clutch (rear) or governor, line pressure is low in "D", "2" or "1" range but is normal in "R" range.

b. If oil leaks at or around low and reverse brake circuit, line pressure becomes low in "R" or "P" range but is normal in "D", "2" or "1" range.

3. When line pressure is high, pressure regulator valve may have stuck.

## LINE PRESSURE
### At Stall Point

| Range | Line Pressure (psi) |
|---|---|
| **L24E ENGINE MODEL WITH L4N71B TRANSMISSION** | |
| R | 203-230 |
| D | 141-158 |
| 2 | 145-166 |
| 1 | 141-158 |
| **LD28 ENGINE MODEL WITH L4N71B TRANSMISSION** | |
| R | 242-270 |
| D | 134-156 |
| 2 | 142-171 |
| 1 | 134-156 |

**NOTE:** For the LD28 Engine models, set the engine vacuum at 5.91 in. Hg to measure line pressure.

## LINE PRESSURE
### At Idle

| Range | Line Pressure (psi) |
|---|---|
| **L24E ENGINE MODEL WITH L4N71B TRANSMISSION** | |
| R | 60-80 |
| D | 46-54 |
| 2 | 85-166 |
| 1 | 46-54 |
| **LD28 ENGINE MODEL WITH L4N71B TRANSMISSION** | |
| R | 43-100 |
| D | 43-57 |
| 2 | 85-171 |
| 1 | 43-57 |

**NOTE:** For the LD28 Engine models, set the engine vacuum at 23.62 in. Hg to measure line pressure.

### Possible Malfunctions Due to Cut-down Pressure

1. When cut-down point disappears, the problem may be due to:
    a. Sticking pressure modifier valve
    b. Sticking governor valve
    c. Oil leaks at oil passage
2. When cut-down point is too low or too high, the problem may be due to:
    a. Incorrect springs (at pressure modifier valve or governor valve)
    b. Oil leaks at oil passage

## LINE PRESSURE
### E4N71B Automatic Transmission

| Engine | Range | Line Pressure (psi) |
|---|---|---|
| | **AT IDLE** | |
| VG30E | R | 65-85 |
| W/O Turbo | D | 40-54 |
| | 2 | 114-156 |
| | 1 | 40-54 |
| VG30E | R | 44-64 |
| W/Turbo | D | 40-54 |
| | 2 | 114-164 |
| | 1 | 40-54 |
| | **AT STALL TEST** | |
| VG30E | R | 284-347 |
| W/O Turbo | D | 156-178 |
| | 2 | 156-185 |
| | 1 | 156-178 |
| VG30E | R | 284-341 |
| W/Turbo | D | 242-273 |
| | 2 | 242-273 |
| | 1 | 242-273 |

## LINE PRESSURE
### At Stall Point

| Range | Line Pressure (psi) |
|---|---|
| **L24E ENGINE MODEL WITH L3N71B TRANSMISSION** | |
| R | 203-230 |
| D | 141-158 |
| 2 | 145-166 |
| 1 | 141-158 |
| **LD28 ENGINE MODEL WITH L3N71B TRANSMISSION** | |
| R | 279-301 |
| D | 148-173 |
| 2 | 142-171 |
| 1 | 148-173 |

**NOTE:** For the LD 28 Engine models, set the engine vacuum at 5.91 in. Hg to measure line pressure.

## MAIN LINE PRESSURE CUT BACK POINT
### L4N71B Transmission

| Intake Manifold Vacuum (in.-Hg) | Vehicle Speed (mph) | Propeller Shaft Rotation (rpm) |
|---|---|---|
| **L24E ENGINE MODELS** | | |
| 0 | 22-27 | 1190-1440 |
| 3.94 | 11-16 | 600-850 |
| **LD28 ENGINE MODEL** | | |
| 5.91 | 14-19 | 730-1030 |
| 13.78 | 9-12 | 470-670 |

**NOTE:** This indication of line pressure change from high to low values occurs as the output shaft rotation is gradually increased from a "stall point." The cut down point should occur at the above speeds.

## LINE PRESSURE
### At Idle

| Range | Line Pressure (psi) |
|---|---|
| **L24E ENGINE MODEL WITH L3N71B TRANSMISSION** | |
| R | 60-80 |
| D | 46-54 |
| 2 | 85-166 |
| 1 | 46-54 |
| **LD28 ENGINE MODEL WITH L3N71B TRANSMISSION** | |
| R | 105-119 |
| D | 55-70 |
| 2 | 85-171 |
| 1 | 55-70 |

**NOTE:** For the LD28 engine models, set the engine vacuum to 23.62 in. Hg to measure line pressure.

## LINE PRESSURE AND VEHICLE SPEED AT SHIFT POINTS
### L4N71B Transmission

| Intake Manifold Vacuum① (in. Hg) | Shift | Vehicle Speed (mph) | Propeller Shaft Revolutions (rpm) | Line Pressure (psi) |
|---|---|---|---|---|
| | | **L24 ENGINE (GASOLINE)** | | |
| 0 (Kickdown) | D-1 to 2 | 34-39 | 1790-2040 | 77-100 |
| | D-2 to 3 | 60-65 | 3170-3420 | 77-100 |
| | D-3 to 4 | — | — | — |
| | D-4 to 3 | — | — | — |
| | D-3 to 2 | 60-55 | 3130-2880 | 77-100 |
| | D-2 to 1 | 30-25 | 1580-1330 | 77-100 |
| 3.94 | D-1 to 2 | 13-17 | 680-930 | 64-87 |
| | D-2 to 3 | 35-40 | 1860-2110 | 64-87 |
| | D-3 to 4 | 58-63 | 3050-3300 | 64-87 |
| | D-4 to 3 | 37-33 | 1970-1720 | 64-87 |
| | D-3 to 2 | 22-18 | 1190-940 | 64-87 |
| | D-2 to 1 | 11-7 | 600-350 | 64-87 |
| 0 (Full throttle) | 1-2 to 1 | 30-25 | 1600-1350 | 80-102 |
| 11.81 | 1-2 to 1 | 30-25 | 1600-1350 | 80-102 |
| | | **LD28 ENGINE (DIESEL)** | | |
| 5.91 (Kickdown) | D-1 to 2 | 25-30 | 1320-1570 | 82-100 |
| | D-2 to 3 | 50-55 | 2640-2890 | 82-100 |
| | D-3 to 4 | — | — | — |
| | D-4 to 3 | — | — | — |
| | D-3 to 2 | 50-45 | 2630-2380 | 82-100 |
| | D-2 to 1 | 25-21 | 1320-1070 | 82-100 |
| 13.78 | D-1 to 2 | 9-14 | 470-720 | 68-82 |
| | D-2 to 3 | 32-36 | 1650-1900 | 68-82 |
| | D-3 to 4 | 44-49 | 2330-2580 | 68-82 |
| | D-4 to 3 | 35-30 | 1860-1610 | 68-82 |
| | D-3 to 2 | 24-19 | 1280-1030 | 68-82 |
| | D-2 to 1 | 11-7 | 600-350 | 68-82 |
| 5.91 (Full Throttle) | 1-2 to 1 | 25-21 | 1320-1070 | 80-102 |
| 23.62 | 1-2 to 1 | 25-21 | 1320-1070 | 80-102 |

① LD28 Diesel engine uses a vacuum pump and regulator instead of engine manifold vacuum.

## LINE PRESSURE AND VEHICLE SPEED AT SHIFT POINTS
### L3N71B Transmission

| Intake Manifold Vacuum① (in. Hg) | Shift | Vehicle Speed (mph) | Propeller Shaft Revolutions (rpm) | Line Pressure (psi) |
|---|---|---|---|---|
| | | **L24 ENGINE (GASOLINE)** | | |
| 0 (Kickdown) | D-1 to 2 | 36-41 | 1790-2040 | 77-100 |
| | D-2 to 3 | 63-68 | 3170-3420 | 77-100 |
| | D-3 to 2 | 62-57 | 3130-2880 | 77-100 |
| | D-2 to 1 | 31-26 | 1580-1330 | 77-100 |
| 3.94 | D-1 to 2 | 14-18 | 680-930 | 64-87 |
| | D-2 to 3 | 37-42 | 1860-2110 | 64-87 |
| | D-3 to 2 | 24-19 | 1190-940 | 64-87 |
| | D-2 to 1 | 12-7 | 600-350 | 64-87 |
| 0 (Full Throttle) | 1-2 to 1 | 32-27 | 1600-1350 | 80-102 |
| 11.81 | 1-2 to 1 | 32-27 | 1600-1350 | 80-102 |
| | | **LD28 ENGINE (DIESEL)** | | |
| 5.91 (Kickdown) | D-1 to 2 | 28-34 | 1320-1570 | 82-100 |
| | D-2 to 3 | 56-62 | 2640-2890 | 82-100 |
| | D-3 to 2 | 56-51 | 2630-2380 | 82-100 |
| | D-2 to 1 | 28-23 | 1320-1070 | 82-100 |
| 13.78 | D-1 to 2 | 10-15 | 470- 720 | 68-82 |
| | D-2 to 3 | 35-41 | 1650-1900 | 68-82 |
| | D-3 to 2 | 27-22 | 1280-1030 | 68-82 |
| | D-2 to 1 | 13-7 | 600-350 | 68-82 |
| 5.91 (Full Throttle) | 1-2 to 1 | 28-23 | 1320-1070 | 80-102 |
| 23.62 | 1-2 to 1 | 28-23 | 1320-1070 | 80-102 |

① LD28 Diesel engine uses a vacuum pump and regulator instead of engine manifold vacuum.

## LINE PRESSURE
### JM600 Automatic Transmission

| Range | Line pressure (psi) |
|---|---|
| **LINE PRESSURE AT IDLE** | |
| R | 44- 64 |
| D | 40- 54 |
| 2 | 114-164 |
| 1 | 40- 54 |
| **LINE PRESSURE AT STALL POINT** | |
| R | 284-341 |
| D | 242-273 |
| 2 | 242-259 |
| 1 | 249-273 |

## MAIN LINE PRESSURE CUT BACK POINT
### L3N71B Transmission

| Intake Manifold Vacuum (in.-Hg) | Vehicle Speed (mph) | Propeller Shaft Rotation (rpm) |
|---|---|---|
| **L24E ENGINE MODELS** | | |
| 0 | 24-29 | 1190-1440 |
| 3.94 | 12-17 | 600-850 |
| **LD28 ENGINE MODEL** | | |
| 5.91 | 16-22 | 730-1030 |
| 13.78 | 13-17 | 590-790 |

**NOTE:** This indication of line pressure change from high to low values occurs as the output shaft rotation is gradually increased from a "stall point." The cut down point should occur at the above speeds.

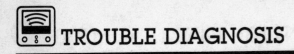

## LINE PRESSURE AND VEHICLE SPEEDS AT SHIFT POINTS
### E4N71B Automatic Transmission

| Engine | Intake Manifold Vacuum (in. Hg) | Gearshift | Vehicle Speed (mph) | Propeller Shaft Revolution (rpm) | Line Pressure (psi) |
|---|---|---|---|---|---|
| VG30E W/O Turbo | 1. Disconnect harness from lock-up control unit. Road test the vehicle to determine if all items listed in the → chart are within their specified values. | | 2. Reconnect harness to lock-up control unit. Road test the vehicle to see if shifting corresponds to the specified shift schedule pattern. | | |
| | 0 (Kickdown) | D₁ → D₂ | 37-42 | 1900-2150 | 114-137 |
| | | D₂ → D₃ | 63-68 | 3250-3500 | 114-137 |
| | | D₃ → D₄ | — | — | — |
| | | D₄ → D₃ | — | — | — |
| | | D₃ → D₂ | 55-60 | 2850-3100 | 108-131 |
| | | D₂ → D₁ | 26-31 | 1350-1600 | 108-131 |
| | 3.94 | D₁ → D₂ | 7-14 | 400- 700 | 80-102 |
| | | D₂ → D₃ | 29-37 | 1500-1900 | 80-102 |
| | | D₃ → D₄ | 42-52 | 2150-2650 | 80-102 |
| | | D₄ → D₃ | 16-25 | 800-1300 | 71- 94 |
| | | D₃ → D₂ | 9-19 | 450- 950 | 71- 94 |
| | | D₂ → D₁ | 7-12 | 350- 600 | 71-131 |
| | 0 (Full throttle) | 1₂ → 1₁ | 26-31 | 1350-1600 | 105-128 |
| | 11.81 | 1₂ → 1₁ | 24-29 | 1250-1500 | 92-114 |
| VG30E W/Turbo | 13.78 (Kickdown) | D₁ → D₂ | 37-43 | 1850-2150 | 92-125 |
| | | D₂ → D₃ | 64-70 | 3150-3450 | 92-125 |
| | | D₃ → D₄ | — | — | — |
| | | D₄ → D₃ | — | — | — |
| | | D₃ → D₂ | 53-58 | 2600-2900 | 92-125 |
| | | D₂ → D₁ | 29-34 | 1400-1700 | 92-125 |
| | 7.87 | D₁ → D₂ | 10-16 | 500- 800 | 46- 68 |
| | | D₂ → D₃ | 13-21 | 650-1050 | 46- 68 |
| | | D₃ → D₄ | 25-35 | 1250-1750 | 46- 68 |
| | | D₄ → D₃ | 13-23 | 650-1150 | 46- 68 |
| | | D₃ → D₂ | 7-17 | 350- 850 | 46- 68 |
| | | D₃ → D₁ | 7-12 | 350- 600 | 46- 77 |
| | 13.78 (Full throttle) | 1₂ → 1₁ | 29-34 | 1400-1700 | 85-108 |
| | 17.72 | 1₂ → 1₁ | 27-34 | 1350-1650 | 85-108 |

## VEHICLE SPEED AT SHIFT POINTS
### JM600 Automatic Transmission

| Intake Manifold Vacuum (in. Hg) | Gearshift | Car speed (mph) | Output shaft speed (rpm) |
|---|---|---|---|
| 13.8 | $D_1 \rightarrow D_2$ | 37-42 | 1,800-2,100 |
| | $D_2 \rightarrow D_3$ | 63-69 | 3,100-3,400 |
| | $D_3 \rightarrow D_4$ | — | — |
| | $D_4 \rightarrow D_3$ | — | — |
| | $D_3 \rightarrow D_2$ | 52-58 | 2,550-2,850 |
| | $D_2 \rightarrow D_1$ | 27-34 | 1,350-1,650 |
| 0 | $D_1 \rightarrow D_2$ | 14-21 | 700-1,000 |
| | $D_2 \rightarrow D_3$ | 42-50 | 2,050-2,450 |
| | $D_3 \rightarrow D_4$ | 61-71 | 3,020-3,520 |
| | $D_4 \rightarrow D_3$ | 34-44 | 1,670-2,170 |
| | $D_3 \rightarrow D_2$ | 21-31 | 1,050-1,550 |
| | $D_2 \rightarrow D_1$ | 7-12 | 350- 600 |
| 7.9 | $D_1 \rightarrow D_2$ | 10-16 | 500- 800 |
| | $D_2 \rightarrow D_3$ | 12-21 | 600-1,000 |
| | $D_3 \rightarrow D_4$ | 25-35 | 1,260-1,760 |
| | $D_4 \rightarrow D_3$ | 11-21 | 560-1,060 |
| | $D_3 \rightarrow D_2$ or $D_3 \rightarrow D_1$ | 7-17 | 350- 850 |
| | $D_2 \rightarrow D_1$ | 7-12 | 350- 600 |
| 13.8 | $1_2 \rightarrow 1_1$ | 27-34 | 1,350-1,650 |
| 17.8 | $1_2 \rightarrow 1_1$ | 26-32 | 1,300-1,600 |

## LINE PRESSURE CUT-DOWN POINT
### E4N71B Automatic Transmission

| Engine | Intake Manifold Vacuum (in. Hg) | Vehicle Speed (mph) | Propeller Shaft Revolutions (rpm) |
|---|---|---|---|
| VG30E | 0 | 17-23 | 900-1200 |
| W/O Turbo | 3.94 | 7-14 | 400-700 |
| VG30E | 13.78 | 18-24 | 1200-1600 |
| W/Turbo | 7.87 | 8-14 | 400-800 |

NOTE: The cut-down point indicates a point where line pressure changes from a high to a low value.

### STALL TEST

The stall test is an application of engine torque, through the transmission and drive train to locked-up wheels, held by the vehicle's brakes. The engine's speed is increased until the rpms are stabilized. Given ideal engine operating conditions and no slippage from transmission clutches, bands or torque converter, the engine will stabilize at a specified test rpm.

### Performing the Stall Test

1. Check the engine oil level and start the engine bringing it up to operating temperature.
2. Check the transmission fluid level and correct as necessary. Attach a calibrated tachometer to the engine and a 0-400 psi oil pressure gauge to the transmission control pressure tap on the right side of the case.
3. Mark the specified maximum engine rpm on the tachometer cover plate with a grease pencil to easily check if the stall speed is over or under specifications.
4. Apply the parking brake and block both front and rear wheels.

—— CAUTION ——
*Do not allow anyone in front of the vehicle while performing the stall test.*

5. While holding the brake pedal with the left foot, place the selector lever in "D" position and slowly depress the accelerator.
6. Read and record the engine rpm when the accelertor pedal is fully depressed and the engine rpm is stabilized. Read and record the oil pressure reading at the high engine rpm point.

NOTE: The stall test must be made within five seconds.

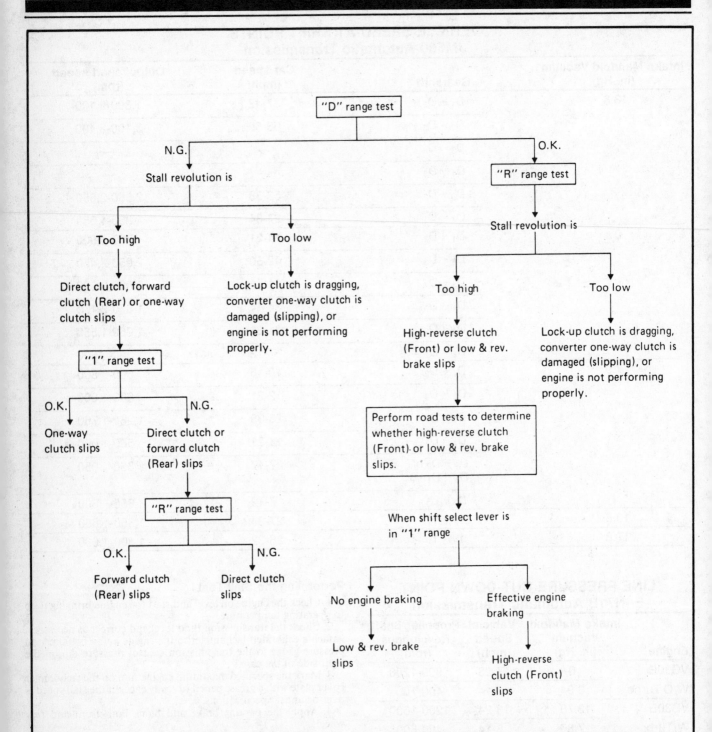

If converter one-way clutch is frozen, vehicle will have poor high speed performance. If converter one-way clutch is slipping, vehicle will be sluggish up to 50 or 60 km/h (30 or 40 MPH).

**Stall test analysis** (© Nissan Motor Co. of USA)

7. Shift the selector lever into the "N" position and increase the engine rpm to approximately 1000-1200 rpms. Hold this engine speed for one to two minutes to cool the transmission and fluid.

8. Make similar tests in the "2", "1" and "R" positions.

**NOTE: If at any time the engine rpm races above the maximum as per specifications, indications are that a clutch unit or band is slipping and the stall test should be stopped before more damage is done to the internal parts.**

## Results of Stall Test
### HIGH ENGINE RPM

If a slipping condition occurs during the stall test, indicated by high engine rpm, the selector lever position at the time of slippage provides an indication as to what holding member of the transmission is defective.

By determining the holding member involved, several possible causes of slippage can be diagnosed.
1. Slips in all ranges, control pressure low
2. Slips in "D", "1" or "2", rear clutch
3. Slips in 1st gear only, one-way clutch
4. Slips in "R" only, front clutch or low and reverse brake
Perform a road test to confirm these conditions.

### LOW ENGINE RPM

When low stall speed is indicated, the converter one-way clutch is not holding, lock-up clutch is dragging or the engine is in need of a major tune-up. To determine which is at fault, perform a road test and observe the operation of the transmission and the engine. If the converter one-way clutch does not lock the stator, acceleration will be poor up to approximately 30 MPH. Above 30 MPH acceleration will be normal. With poor engine performance acceleration will be poor at all speeds. When the one-way clutch is seized and locks the stator from turning either way, the stall test rpm will be normal. However, on a road test the vehicle will not go any faster than 50-55 MPH because of the 2:1 reduction ratio in the converter.

If slippage was indicated by high engine rpm, the road test will help identify the problem area observing the transmission operation during upshifts, both automatic and manual.

## STALL SPEEDS

| | |
|---|---|
| 1982 and later L3N71B Transmission Model | 1800 to 2100 rpm |
| 1983 and later L4N71B Transmission Model | |
| With L24E Engine | 1800 to 2100 rpm |
| With LD28 Engine | 1650 to 1950 rpm |
| 1984 E4N71B Transmission Model | |
| With VG30E w/o Turbo | 2150 to 2450 rpm |
| With VG30E Turbo | 2500 to 2800 rpm |
| 1984 Conquest (L4N71B/JM600) | 2350 to 2650 rpm |

## Precautions If Stall Test is Used On Pressure Rise Test

(Refer to stall test procedures.)
1. Do not operate engine/transmission at stall for longer than 5 seconds per test.
2. Operate the engine between 1000 and 1200 rpm at the end of a test for approximately one to two minutes for cooling (in neutral).
3. Release the accelerator immediately in case of slippage or spin-up of the transmission to avoid more damage to the unit.

## AIR PRESSURE TESTS

The control pressure test results and causes of abnormal pressures are to be used as a guide. Further testing or inspection could be necessary before repairs are made. If the pressures are found to be low in a clutch, servo or passageway, a verfication can be accomplished by removing the valve body and performing an air pressure test. This test can serve two purposes:

1. To determine if a malfunction of a clutch or band is caused by fluid leakage in the system or is the result of a mechanical failure.
2. To test the transmission for internal fluid leakage during the rebuilding and before completing the assembly.

### Procedure

1. Obtain an air nozzle and adjust for 25 psi.
2. Apply air pressure (25 psi) to the passages as illustrated.

### Vacuum Diaphragm

The modulated throttle system, which adjusts throttle pressure for the control of the shift valves, is operated by engine manifold vacuum through a vacuum diaphragm and must be inspected whenever a transmission defect is apparent.

### Preparation of Vacuum Test

Before the vacuum diaphragm test is performed, check the engine vacuum supply and the condition and routing of the supply lines.

With the engine idling, remove the vacuum line at the vacuum diaphragm and install a vacuum gauge. There must be a steady, acceptable vacuum reading for the altitude at which the test is being performed.

If the vacuum is low, check for a vacuum leak or poor engine performance. If the vacuum is steady and acceptable, acclerate the engine sharply and observe the vacuum gauge reading. The vacuum should drop off rapidly at acceleration and return to the original reading immediately upon release of the accelerator.

If the vacuum reading does not change or changes slowly, check the vacuum supply lines for being plugged, restricted or connected to a vacuum reservoir supply. Repair the system as required.

## MANIFOLD VACUUM TESTS
### GASOLINE ENGINE

1. With the engine idling, remove the vacuum supply hose from the modulator nipple and check the hose end for the presence of engine vacuum with an appropriate gauge.
2. If vacuum is present, accelerate the engine and allow it to return to idle. A drop in vacuum should be noted during acceleration and a return to normal vacuum at idle.
3. If manifold vacuum is not present, check for breaks or restrictions in the vacuum lines and repair.

### DIESEL ENGINE (LD28 ENGINE MODEL)

An engine operated vacuum pump is used to supply the vacuum needed to operate the transmission diaphragm and other vehicle vacuum operated components.

### Vacuum Pump Inspection

1. Install a vacuum gauge between the vacuum pump and the vacuum diaphragm.
2. Start the engine and run it at idle speed of 600-750 rpm.
3. With the vacuum diaphragm not operating, the vacuum reading on the gauge should be 22.44-24.80 in. Hg.

## VACUUM DIAPHRAGM TESTS

1. Apply at least 18 in. Hg. to the modulator vacuum nipple and observe the vacuum reading. The vacuum should hold.
2. If the vacuum does not hold, the diaphragm is leaking and the modulator assembly must be replaced.

**NOTE: A leaking diaphragm causes harsh gear engagements and delayed or no up-shifts due to maximum throttle pressure developed.**

### Additional Vacuum Diaphragm Testing
#### ON THE CAR TEST

The vacuum diaphragm is tested on the vehicle with the aid of an outside vacuum source, which can be adjusted to maintain a certain amount of vacuum. Apply 18 inches Hg. to the vaccum diaphragm vacuum nipple, through a hose connected to the outside vacuum source. The vacuum should hold at the applied level without any leakdown. If the vacuum level drops off, the vacuum diaphragm is leaking and must be replaced.

## OFF CAR TEST

With the vacuum diaphragm removed from the automatic transmission, apply 18 inches Hg. to the diaphragm vacuum nipple.

The vacuum level should remain and not drop off. If the vacuum level drops, the diaphragm is leaking and the unit should be replaced.

A second test can be made with the diaphragm removed from the transmission. Insert the control rod into the valve end of the diaphragm and apply vacuum to the nipple. Hold a finger over the control rod and release the vacuum supply hose. The control rod should be moved outward by the pressure of the internal return spring. If the control rod does not move outward, a broken return spring is indicated.

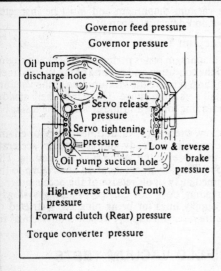

Governor feed pressure
Governor pressure
Oil pump discharge hole
Servo release pressure
Servo tightening pressure
Low & reverse brake pressure
Oil pump suction hole
High-reverse clutch (Front) pressure
Forward clutch (Rear) pressure
Torque converter pressure

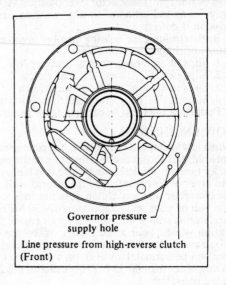

Governor pressure supply hole
Line pressure from high-reverse clutch (Front)

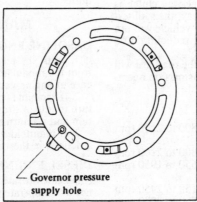

Governor pressure supply hole

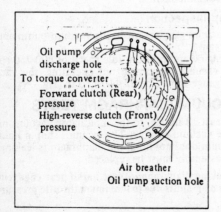

Oil pump discharge hole
To torque converter
Forward clutch (Rear) pressure
High-reverse clutch (Front) pressure
Air breather
Oil pump suction hole

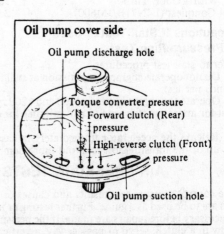

Oil pump cover side
Oil pump discharge hole
Torque converter pressure
Forward clutch (Rear) pressure
High-reverse clutch (Front) pressure
Oil pump suction hole

**Fluid passage identification—L3N71B models** (© Nissan Motor Co. of USA)

## ON CAR SERVICES

## Adjustments

Varied adjustments can be made and certain internal components can be removed and/or replaced with the transmission assembly remaining in the vehicle. A list of the serviceable components are as follows:

Manual linkage
Inhibitor (safety start) switch
Vacuum diaphragm and/or rod
Downshift solenoid
Kick down switch
Vacuum diaphragm (modulator) adjustment—LD28 Diesel Engine models
O.D. cancel switch and O.D. indicator light
Band Adjustment—
    Internal
    O.D. band
Control valve assembly
Extension oil seal
Parking linkage components
Governor valve assembly

### MANUAL LINKAGE

#### Adjustment

1. Move the shift linkage through all detents with the selector lever. If the detents cannot be felt or the pointer indicating the gear range is improperly aligned, the linkage needs to be adjustment.
2. Place the gear selector lever in the Range "1" or "D" position.
3. Loosen the locknuts at the bottom of the gear selector lever to rod trunnion. Move the rod through the trunnion until the "D" or Range "1" is properly aligned and the transmission is in the "D" or Range "1" position.
4. Tighten the lock nuts to hold the trunnion in place.
5. Recheck the "P" and range "1" positions. Be sure the full detent can be felt when in the "P" position.
6. If the adjustment cannot be properly made, inspect the levers and rod for damage or worn grommets. Repair as necessary.

### INHIBITOR (SAFETY START) SWITCH

#### Adjustment

1. The two major functions of the inhibitor switch are to illuminate the back-up lights when the selector lever is in the "R" position and to allow the engine to start when the transmission is in the "P" or "N" detents.
2. With the manual linkage properly adjusted, place the transmission manual lever in the "N" position, vertical position and third detent from the rear of the transmission.
3. Remove the screw from the alignment pin hole at the bottom of the switch. Loosen the two switch retaining screws.
4. Insert a 0.079 inch diameter alignment pin in the alignment pin hole, and inward through the hole in the inner switch rotor.
5. Tighten the switch attaching bolts 3.6-5.1 ft. lbs. and remove the alignment pin.
6. The switch can be tested, using a continuity tester or by checking the starting of the engine in the "P" and "N" positions only.

### VACUUM DIAPHRAGM

#### Adjustment

The vacuum diaphragms used in production are non-adjustable.

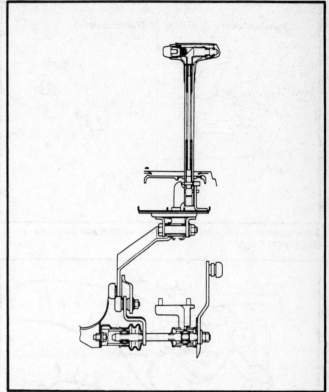

Shift linkage arrangement—JM600 models (© Chrysler Corp.)

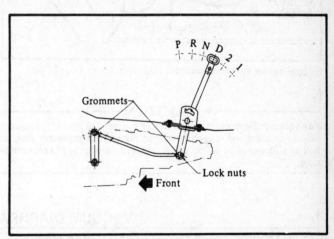

Shift linkage—typical of the L3N71B, 4N71B, L4N71B transmissions (© Nissan Motor Co. of USA)

However, adjustable diaphragms are sometimes available through the aftermarket supply. Should the transmission be equipped with the adjustable type, the following method of adjustment can be accomplished.

1. Remove the vacuum supply hose from the diaphragm's vacuum nipple.
2. Using a small screwdriver, turn the adjusting screw, located in the vacuum nipple, clockwise to increase the throttle pressure and counterclockwise to decrease the throttle pressure. One complete turn of the adjusting screw will change the throttle pressure approximately 2-3 psi.
3. After the adjustments are made, reinstall the vacuum supply hose and make the necessary pressure tests as required.

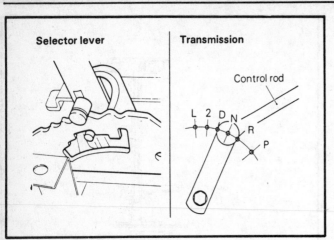

Selector lever detent and transmission control arm positions
(© Chrysler Corp.)

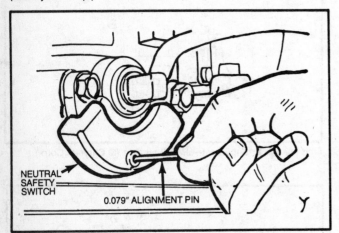

Neutral safety switch adjustment (© Nissan Motor Co. of USA)

— CAUTION —

*The vacuum diaphragm should not be adjusted to provide pressures below the specified ranges to change the shift engagement feel, as soft or slipping shift points could result in damage to the transmission.*

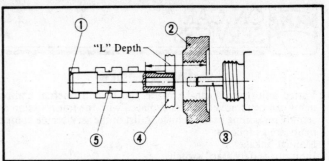

Measurement for correct vacuum modulator rod
(© Nissan Motor Co. of USA)

## VACUUM DIAPHRAGM ROD

### Adjustment

The manufacturer's recommended adjustment of the vacuum diaphragm is the select the correct rod length between the diaphragm and the throttle valve in the valve body assembly. When the correct rod length is selected, the shift pattern of the transmission should be within specifications.

1. Disconnect the vacuum supply hose from the diaphragm and remove the diaphragm from the transmission case.
2. Using a depth gauge, measure the distance between the rod seat in the throttle valve when fully seated in the valve body, and the surface of the indented diaphragm seat on the transmission case. This distance is considered "L" depth.
3. From the accompanying chart, select the proper length diaphragm rod and install.
4. Install the diaphragm and seat properly with its sealing ring. Install the vacuum hose to the diaphragm nipple.
5. Road test for proper operation or perform the pressure test as previously outlined.

## VACUUM MODULATOR

### Adjustment

#### LD28 DIESEL ENGINE MODELS

1. Install a vacuum gauge between the vacuum pump and the vacuum modulator.
2. Start the engine and operate at 600-750 rpm.
3. Be sure the vacuum pump is operating properly. With the vacuum modulator not operating, the vacuum should read 22.44-24.80 in. Hg.
4. With the engine at 600-750 rpm, adjust the vacuum modula-

## VACUUM DIAPHRAGM ROD SELECTION

| Measured depth "L" mm (in) | Rod length mm (in) | Part number Nissan | Chrysler |
|---|---|---|---|
| Under 25.55 (1.0059) | 29.0 (1.142) | 31932-X0103 | MD610614 |
| 25.65-26.05 (1.0098-1.0256) | 29.5 (1.161) | 31932-X0104 | MD610615 |
| 26.15-26.55 (1.0295-1.0453) | 30.0 (1.181) | 31932-X0100 | MD610616 |
| 26.65-27.05 (1.0492-1.0650) | 30.5 (1.201) | 31932-X0102 | MD610617 |
| Over 27.15 (1.0689) | 31.0 (1.220) | 31932-X0101 | MD610618 |

tor to attain a vacuum of 23.62 ± 1.18 in. Hg. Vacuum at full throttle state should be 7.09 ± 1.18 in. Hg at 5000 rpm.

5. Adjustments would be made at the throttle lever adjusting rod to modulator assembly.

---
**CAUTION**

*Do not attempt to adjust the modulator assembly with the engine at no load and operating at 5000 rpm. This adjustment should only be done on the road, through a trial and error method or on a chassis dynamometer.*

---

## KICKDOWN SWITCH

### Adjustment

1. Fully depress the accelerator pedal. A click should be heard just before the pedal bottoms out.
2. If the switch requires adjustment, loosen the locknut and extend the switch until the pedal lever makes contact with the switch and the switch clicks.

---
**CAUTION**

*Do not allow the switch to make contact too soon. This would cause the transmission to downshift on part throttle.*

---

NOTE: If the switch is internally shorted, continuity is present through the switch in any position. Check with a continuity tester.

# Band Adjustment
## SECOND BAND SERVO

### Adjustment

1. Remove the fluid and the oil pan from the transmission.
2. Loosen the locknut.
3. Torque the band servo piston stem 9-11 ft. lbs.
4. Back off the band adjusting servo piston stem two complete turns.

---
**CAUTION**

*Do not back off the adjusting stem excessively as the anchor block could fall out of place.*

---

5. While holding the adjusting stem, tighten the locknut to 11-29 ft. lbs. torque.
6. Using a new gasket, install the oil pan and fill the transmission with Dexron® fluid.

## OVERDRIVE BAND

### Adjustment

1. Remove the O.D. servo cover and gasket.

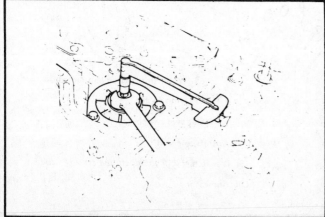

**Adjustment of 2nd band** (© Chrysler Corp.)

2. Loosen the servo piston stem locknut.
3. Tighten the servo piston stem 5.1-7.2 ft. lbs. Back off the stem two complete turns.
4. While holding the servo piston stem, tighten the locknut 11-29 ft. lbs.
5. Install the servo cover and gasket. Check the fluid level of the transmission and correct.

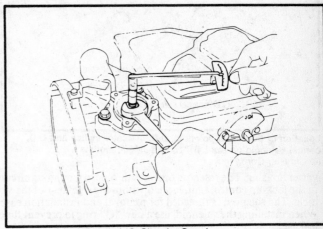

**Adjustment of O.D. band** (© Chrysler Corp.)

# Service
## DOWNSHIFT SOLENOID

### Removal and Installation

1. Disconnect the solenoid wiring harness.
2. Place a pan underneath the downshift solenoid and remove it and its "O" ring seal. Fluid will drain into the pan.
3. Install a new solenoid with a lubricated "O" ring into its bore in the case. Tighten securely.
4. Connect the downshift solenoid wiring harness and refill the transmission with Dexron® II fluid.

## O.D. CANCEL SWITCH AND
## O.D. INDICATOR LIGHT

### Removal and Installation

**E4N71B, JM600 and L4N71B TRANSMISSIONS**

The cancel switch and the indicator light are located on the center console box and can be replaced, if necessary, by the removal of the switch.

## O.D. CANCEL SOLENOID

### Removal and Installation

**E4N71B, JM600 and L4N71B TRANSMISSIONS**

The O.D. Cancel switch is located on the left side of the overdrive unit of the transmission assembly. Confirm that a clicking noise is heard when power is applied. The switch is replaced by unscrewing the switch from the case and installing a new switch and "O" ring in its place. Correct the transmission level.

NOTE: Have a drain pan placed under the cancel switch area, before removal, to catch the fluid that will drain from the switch bore.

## LOCK-UP CONTROL SOLENOID

### Removal and Installation

**E4N71B TRANSMISSION**

The lock-up control solenoid is located on the left side of the con-

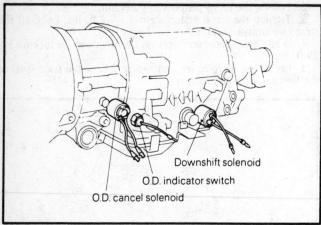

Location of downshift solenoid, O.D. indicator switch and O.D. cancel solenoid on the L4N71B and JM600 models
(© Chrysler Corp.)

verter housing. The solenoid operates through a grounding circuit in the lock-up control unit, located within the right rear of the vehicle. The solenoid is threaded for removal and installation ease. When installing the solenoid, use a new "O" ring to prevent fluid leakage.

## LOW TEMPERATURE SENSOR

### Removal and Installation
### E4N71B TRANSMISSION

A sensor is mounted within the transmission and its function is to prevent converter lock-up if the transmission fluid temperature is below 68°F. (20°C.) by being inter-connected to the Lock-up Con-

trol Unit. A supplied voltage from the Lock-up Control Unit of 5 volts is required to activate this portion of the Low Temperature Sensor/Lock-up Control Unit operation when the fluid temperature is above the minimum requirements for converter clutch lock-up.

## Troubleshooting and Diagnosis
### E4N71B TRANSMISSIONS

### CONTROL VALVE ASSEMBLY

**Removal**

1. Drain the fluid and remove the oil pan from the transmission.
2. Remove the kickdown solenoid, the vacuum diaphragm and rod.
3. Remove the retaining bolts from the control valve assembly. Three different lengths are used.
4. Carefully lower the valve body from the transmission. Remove the manual valve from the control valve assembly to avoid having it drop from the assembly.

**Installation**

1. Install the manual valve into the control valve assembly and position to the bottom of the transmission case.
2. With the manual control valve in the neutral position and the selector lever in the neutral position, align the groove in the valve with the control lug on the linkage.
3. Install the retaining bolts, placing the three different length bolts in their proper locations.
4. Torque the bolts 4.0-5.4 ft. lbs.
5. Operate the controls to be certain the manual valve can be moved in each detent.

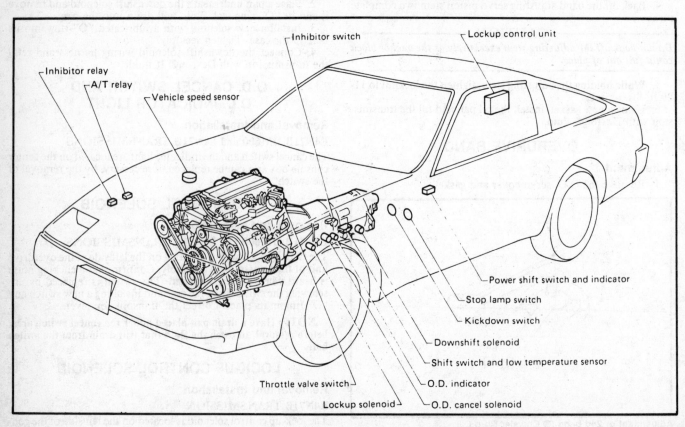

## LOCK-UP CONTROL UNIT
### E4N71B Transmissions
Check Voltage between No. 22 terminal (Ground) and each terminal

| Terminal No. | Input/Output Signal Source | Test Procedure | Desired Results | |
|---|---|---|---|---|
| 1 | Downshift solenoid | Measure when depressing and releasing accelerator pedal. | 0V if turned on 12V if turned off | |
| 2 | Lock-up solenoid | Measure while driving vehicle in "D" range. | 0V if turned on 12V if turned off | |
| 3 | Throttle sensor (power source) | Connect tester to terminals 3 and 5. | 5V at all times | |
| 4 | Throttle sensor | Measure while operating accelerator pedal. | Full-close throttle: Full-open throttle: | 0.4V 4V |
| 5 | Throttle sensor (ground) | — | — | |
| 6 | O.D. cancel solenoid | Measure while operating O.D. cancel switch. | 0V if turned on 12V if turned off | |
| 7 | Power shift indicator lamp | Measure while depressing accelerator pedal in "D" range with driving. | 0V if turned on 12V if turned off | |
| 8 | Idle contact switch | Measure while operating accelerator pedal. | Full-close throttle: Part-open throttle: | 12V 0V |
| 9 | Full throttle contact switch | | Throttle opening Over ½: Below ¼: | 12V 0V |
| 10 | Inhibitor "2" range switch | Measure with control lever set to "2" range or other ranges. | 12V if set to "2" range 0V if set to other ranges | |
| 11 | Vehicle speed sensor | Check voltage variation while running vehicle over 1 m (3 ft) at very low speed | Voltage must vary from 0V to more than 5V | |
| 12 | 1-2 shift switch | Jack up rear wheels, set lever to D range, and measure while accelerating with a slightly open throttle. | D1 range: D2, D3, and D4 ranges: | 0V 5V |
| 13 | A.S.C.D. cruise signal | Measure by repeatedly releasing vehicle speed setting during A.S.C.D. driving. | 12V if A.S.C.D. is set 0V if A.S.C.D. is released | |
| 14 | Brake switch | Measure while operating brake pedal | Braking condition: Non-braking condition: | 12V 0V |
| 15 | A.S.C.D. O.D. cut signal | Measure by turning on and off accelerator switch during A.S.C.D. driving at D4 speed. | 0V if accelerator switch is on 5V if accelerator switch is off | |
| | 3-4 shift switch | Jack up rear wheels, set lever to D range, and measure while accelerating with a slightly open throttle. | D1, D2, and D3 ranges: D4 range: | 0V 5V |
| 16 | 2-3 shift switch | | D1 and D2 ranges: D3 and D4 ranges: | 0V 5V |
| 17 | Power source | Make ground connection. | 12V at all times | |
| 18 | Power shift switch | Measure while operation power shift switch. | 0V if turned on 12V if turned off | |

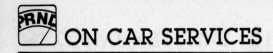

## LOCK-UP CONTROL UNIT
### E4N71B Transmissions
Check Voltage between No. 22 terminal (Ground) and each terminal

| Terminal No. | Input/Output Signal Source | Test Procedure | Desired Results |
|---|---|---|---|
| 19 | Low-temperature sensor | When checking in installed state, refer to the items on the right. Remove sensor from transmission and make continuity test. | Continuity test<br>Zero continuity at 20°C (68°F) or higher<br>Continuity at 10°C (50°F) or lower<br>(Reference)<br>5V if oil temp. is over 20°C (68°F)<br>0V if oil temp. is below 10°C (50°F) |
| 20 | — | — | — |
| 21 | Kickdown switch | Measure while operating accelerator pedal. | Full-open accelerator: 0V<br>Less than full open: 5V |
| 22 | Ground | — | — |

A.S.C.D.: Automatic Speed Control Device
O.D.: Overdrive

## LOCK-UP CONTROL RUNNING TEST
### E4N71B Transmissions

| Order of Inspection | Test Items | Test Procedure |
|---|---|---|
| 1 | Lock-up signals | • Connect tester to control unit connector terminals, Nos. 2 and 22 and check lock-up signals while running vehicle.<br>  Proper indication:<br>    0V if lock-up solenoid is on.<br>    12V if lock-up solenoid is off. |
| 2 | Wires for output signals | Check if connector between control unit and lock-up solenoid is properly connected. Also, check connector for continuity. |
| 3 | Lock-up solenoid | • Check if O-ring is installed to tip of solenoid.<br>• Check operation of solenoid by applying 12V voltage. |
| 4 | Wires for input signals | Check if connections are properly made between control unit and following sensors. Also, check connectors for conduction.<br>• Throttle sensor (Idle, high-throttle side)<br>• Inhibitor switch (2 range)<br>• Shift switches (1-2, 2-3 and 3-4)<br>• Low-temperature sensor<br>• Kickdown switch<br>• Vehicle speed sensor<br>• O.D. switch |
| 5 | Input signals | Check item given on inspection-4 |

## OVERDRIVE CONTROL RUNNING TEST
### E4N71B Transmissions

| Order of Inspection | Test Item | Test Procedure |
|---|---|---|
| 1 | O.D. solenoid | Turn on key and set O.D. switch to "O.D. release" position to see if O.D. solenoid clicks. |
| 2 | Input signals | Inspect following items<br>• Shift switches (1-2, 2-3 and 3-4)<br>• Vehicle speed sensor<br>• Low-temperature sensor<br>• Full throttle contact switch<br>• Kickdown switch |

## POWER SHIFT INDICATOR DIAGNOSIS
### E4N71B Transmissions

| Order of Inspection | Test Item | Test Procedure |
|---|---|---|
| 1 | Vehicle speed sensor | 1. Connect tester to connector terminals, Nos. 11 and 22, of lock-up control unit.<br>2. Check voltage variation by running vehicle over 1 m (3 ft) at very slow speed.<br>  Proper indication:<br>  Voltage must vary from 0V to over 5V. |
| 2 | Throttle sensor | 1. Connect tester to connector terminals, Nos. 4 and 22, of lock-up control unit.<br>2. Measure voltage while operating accelerator pedal.<br>  Proper indication:<br>  Accelerator pedal in full-close throttle position: 0V<br>  Accelerator pedal in full-open throttle position: 4V |

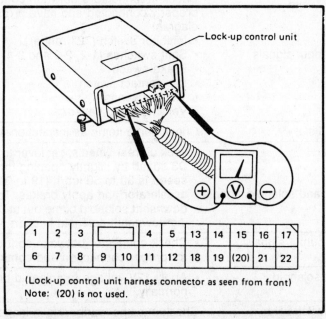

**Testing of lock-up control unit and harness connection terminal location** (© Nissan Motor Co. of USA)

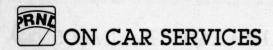

## AUTOMATIC SPEED CONTROL DEVICE RUNNING TEST
### E4N71B Transmissions

| Order of Inspection | Test Item | Test Procedure |
|---|---|---|
| 1 | O.D. cancel solenoid signals | Jack up rear wheels, set lever to D range, and accelerate up to D4 speed by slightly opening throttle. Then, when vehicle speed is 30 to 80 km/h (19 to 50 mph), completely close accelerator and apply brakes over 0.7 second. To check if signals to turn on O.D. cancel solenoid come out at this time, check item "O.D. cancel solenoid" in chart. |
| 2 | A.S.C.D. cruise signals | 1. Connect tester to connector terminals, Nos. 13 and 22, of lock-up control unit. 2. Measure by repeatedly releasing vehicle speed setting during A.S.C.D. driving. Proper indication: A.S.C.D. is set: 12V A.S.C.D. is released: OV |

## DOWNSHIFT CONTROL RUNNING TEST
### E4N71B Transmissions

| Order of Inspection | Test Items | Test Procedure |
|---|---|---|
| 1 | O.D. cancel solenoid signals | • Jack up rear wheels, set lever to D range, and accelerate up to D4 speed by slightly opening throttle. Then, when vehicle speed is 30 to 80 km/h (19 to 50 MPH), completely close accelerator and apply brakes over 0.7 second. To check if signals to turn on O.D. cancel solenoid come out at this time, check item "O.D. cancel solenoid" in chart |
| 2 | Wires for output signals | • Check connector between control unit and O.D. cancel solenoid for proper connection and continuity. |
| 3 | O.D. cancel solenoid | • Apply 12V voltage to solenoid proper to see if it operates normally. |
| 4 | Wires for input signals | Check if connectors between control unit and sensors are properly connected and have proper continuity. Refer to circuit diagram<br>• Inhibitor switch ("2" range)<br>• Shift switches (1-2, 2-3 and 3-4)<br>• Brake switch<br>• Idle contact switch<br>• Throttle sensor<br>• Vehicle speed sensor |
| 5 | Input signals | Check same items as inspection-4 in chart |
| 6 | Downshift and solenoid signals | • Jack up rear wheels, set lever to D range, and accelerate up to D3 speed by slightly opening throttle. Then, when vehicle speed is 30 to 50 km/h (19 to 31 MPH), completely close accelerator and apply brakes. To check if signals to turn on downshift solenoid come out at this time, check items concerning downshift solenoid in chart |
| 7 | Wires for output signals | • Check connector between control unit and downshift solenoid for proper connection and continuity. |
| 8 | Downshift solenoid | • Apply 12V voltage to solenoid proper to see if it operates normally. |
| 9 | 3-4 shift switch wires | Check in same manner as in inspection-4, above. |
| 10 | 3-4 shift switch signals | Check in same manner as in inspection-5, above. |

## KICKDOWN CONTROL RUNNING TEST
### E4N71B Transmissions

| Order of Inspection | Test Item | Test Procedure |
|---|---|---|
| 1 | Downshift solenoid signals | Listen for a "click" to be emitted by downshift solenoid when accelerator pedal is fully depressed and ignition switch is "ON". |
| 2 | Kickdown switch signals | Connect tester to connector terminals, Nos. 21 and 22, of lock-up control unit. Measure while operating accelerator pedal.<br>Full-open accelerator: 0V<br>Less than full open: 5V |
| 3 | Wires for kickdown switch | Check connector between kickdown switch and control unit for proper connection and continuity. |
| 4 | Input signal wiring | Check connector between downshift solenoid and control unit for proper connection and continuity. |
| 5 | Downshift solenoid | Apply 12V voltage to solenoid proper to see if it functions normally. |

## SHIFT PATTERN CHANGE CONTROL RUNNING TEST
### E4N71B Transmissions

| Order of Inspection | Test Item | Test Procedure |
|---|---|---|
| 1 | Power shift indicator lamp signals | • Jack up rear wheels and accelerate in D range. When vehicle speed goes over 13 km/h (8 MPH), turn on power shift switch.<br>• Jack up rear wheels and quickly depress accelerator pedal while in D range. To confirm if signals come out to turn on power shift indicator lamp in the above condition, check power shift indicator lamp |
| 2 | Power shift indicator lamp wirings | • Check connector between control unit and power shift indicator lamp for proper connection and continuity. |
| 3 | Input wiring | Check connectors between control unit and following sensors for proper connections and continuity.<br>• Power shift switch<br>• Throttle sensor<br>• Vehicle speed sensor |
| 4 | Input signals | Check same items as inspection-3. |
| 5 | Input wiring | Check connectors between control unit and following sensors for proper connections and continuity.<br>• Inhibitor switch ("2" range)<br>• Shift switches (1-2, 2-3, and 3-4) |
| 6 | Input signals | Check same items as inspection-5. |
| 7 | Output wiring | Check connector between control unit and downshift solenoid for proper connections and continuity. |
| 8 | Downshift solenoid | • Apply 12V voltage to solenoid proper to see if it functions normally. |
| 9 | Input wiring | • Check connector between control unit and 3-4 shift switch for proper connections and continuity. |
| 10 | Input signals | Check item "3-4 shift switch" in chart. |
| 11 | Output wiring | Check connector between control unit and O.D. cancel solenoid for connections and continuity. |
| 12 | O.D. cancel solenoid | Apply 12V voltage to solenoid proper to see if it functions normally. |

## AUTOMATIC SPEED CONTROL DEVICE RUNNING TEST
### E4N71B Transmissions

| Order of Inspection | Test Item | Test Procedure |
|---|---|---|
| 3 | A.S.C.D. wiring harness | Refer to A.S.C.D. Electrical diagram. |
| 4 | A.S.C.D. controller | Refer to A.S.C.D. Electrical diagram. |
| 5 | A.S.C.D. O.D. cut signals | 1. Connect tester to connector terminals, Nos. 15 and 22, of lock-up control unit.<br>2. Measure by repeatedly releasing vehicle speed setting during A.S.C.D. driving in D4 speed.<br>Proper indication:<br>Accelerator pedal is depressed: 0V<br>Accelerator pedal is released: 5V |
| 6 | A.S.C.D wiring harness | Refer to A.S.C.D. Electrical diagram. |
| 7 | Output signal wiring | Check connector between control unit and O.D. cancel solenoid for connections and continuity. |
| 8 | O.D. cancel solenoid | Apply 12V voltage to solenoid proper to see if it operates normally. |

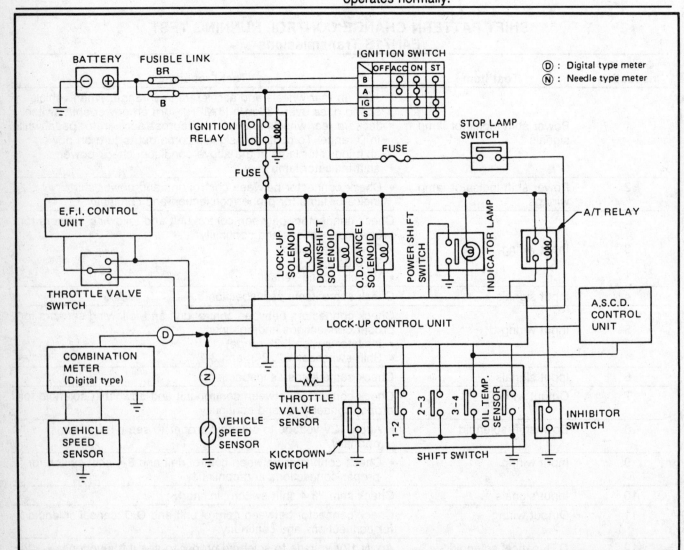

Lock-up control system electrical schematic—E4N71B models (© Nissan Motor Co. of USA)

6. With new "O" rings, install the kickdown solenoid and the vacuum diaphragm with its rod.

7. Using a new gasket, install the oil pan and torque the retaining bolts 3.6-5.1 ft. lbs.

8. Complete any other assembly and refill the transmission with the correct fluid. Correct the level as required.

## EXTENSION OIL SEAL

### Replacement

1. Remove the propeller shaft assembly.

2. With a seal removing tool, remove the seal from the extension housing.

3. Apply a coat of transmission fluid to the oil seal surface and drive the seal into the bore of the extension housing with a seal driver tool.

4. Coat the yoke of the drive shaft with vaseline and install in place.

5. Correct the fluid level of the transmission.

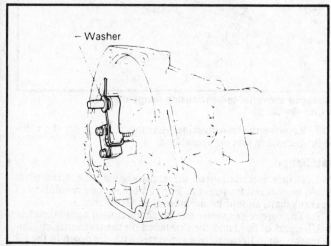

**Parking mechanism in the extension housing (© Chrysler Corp.)**

## PARKING MECHANISM COMPONENTS

### Removal

1. Drain the fluid by removing the oil pan assembly.

2. Remove the propeller shaft from the transmission.

3. Remove the speedometer cable and speedometer pinion.

4. Support the transmission with a wood block and a jack-type support. Remove the rear support mounting bolts.

5. Remove the rear extension housing bolts and remove the extension housing with the rear mount attached.

6. Remove the control valve assembly as previously outlined.

7. Inspect and repair the parking mechanism components as required.

### Installation

1. After the necessary repairs to the parking mechanism components have been done, install the control valve assembly as previously outlined.

2. Install the rear extension housing with the rear mount attached. Torque the retaining bolts 14-18 ft. lbs.

3. Install the rear mount bolts and torque 43-58 ft. lbs.

4. Install the speedometer pinion and cable.

5. Install the propeller shaft.

6. Using a new gasket, install the oil pan and torque the retaining bolts 3.6-5.1 ft. lbs.

7. Refill the transmission to its correct level with Dexron® II fluid.

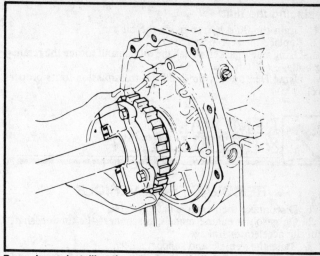

**Removing or installing the governor and oil distributor body (© Chrysler Corp.)**

## GOVERNOR VALVE ASSEMBLY

### Removal and Installation

1. Remove the propeller shaft and the rear extension housing as previously outlined.

2. Remove the governor assembly from the output shaft oil distributor.

3. Inspect and repair the governor assembly as required.

4. Install the governor assembly on the output shaft oil distributor body.

5. Torque the retaining bolts 3.6-5.1 ft. lbs.

6. Complete the assembly as outlined previously in the Parking Mechanism Component Removal and Installation section.

7. Correct the transmission fluid level as required.

## TRANSMISSION FLUID CHANGE

The L3N71B, L4N71B, 4N71B, JM600 and E4N71B transmissions do not have a specific or periodic fluid change interval for normal maintenance, only the checking of the fluid and correcting the level as required. However, at the time of any major repairs or if the vehicle is used in continuous service or driven under severe conditions, the transmission fluid should be changed every 30,000 miles or 24 months.

**NOTE: The time and mileage intervals are average. Each vehicle operated under severe conditions should be treated individually.**

**Inspection of debris in oil pan with the transmission out of the vehicle (© Nissan Motor Co. of USA)**

### Replacing the fluid

1. Drain the fluid by removing the oil pan.
2. Replace the screen as required.
3. Using a new gasket, install the oil pan and torque the retaining bolts, 3.6-5.1 ft. lbs.
4. Using Dexron® II fluid, fill the transmission to its proper level.

 **REMOVAL & INSTALLATION**

## REMOVAL FROM VEHICLE

1. Disconnect the negative battery cable.
2. On gasoline engine models, disconnect the torsion shaft from the accelerator linkage.
3. Raise the vehicle and support safely.
4. Remove the propeller shaft from the transmission and plug the opening in the rear extension to prevent fluid leakage.
5. Disconnect the front exhaust pipe.
6. Disconnect the wiring connections at the inhibitor switch, the downshift solenoid, O.D. solenoid, lock-up control solenoid and the O.D. indicator switch.
7. Disconnect the selector range lever from the manual control shaft.
8. Disconnect the speedometer from the rear extension and remove the vacuum hose from the vacuum diaphragm nipple.
9. Disconnect the fluid filler tube and remove the fluid cooler lines from the transmission case. Remove governor tube between converter housing and transmission case.

**NOTE: Plug all openings into the transmission to prevent foreign material to enter.**

10. Support the engine under the oil pan, using a wooden block and jack type tool. Support the transmission by means of a transmission jack or equivalent.
11. Remove the gussets between the engine and the transmission bell assemblies. Remove the converter housing dust cover.
12. Remove the bolts securing the drive plate to the converter assembly.

**NOTE: It is advisable to matchmark the converter and the drive plate to aid in the re-assembly.**

13. Remove the rear engine mount securing bolts and the crossmember mounting bolts.

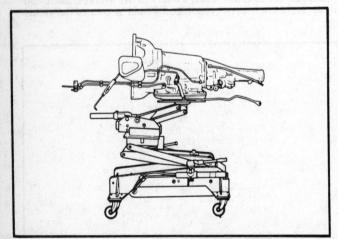

**Typical jack assembly for removal or installation of the transmission** (© Chrysler Corp.)

14. Remove the starter motor assembly.
15. Remove the bolts securing the transmission to the engine. Have the transmission secured on the jack assembly and slowly lower the assembly from the vehicle.
16. As the converter becomes accessible, retain it in the bell housing to avoid its dropping from the transmission.

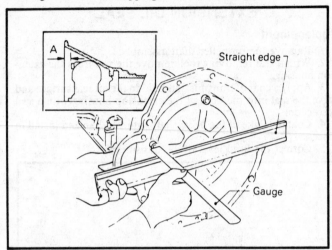

**Measuring converter-to-bell housing flange distance** (© Chrysler Corp.)

17. Remove the transmission assembly from under the vehicle for necessary service operations.

### Installation

1. Before installation of the transmission, the drive plate should be checked for run-out. The run-out, in one revolution of the crankshaft, should be no more than 0.020 inch.
2. The torque converter can be charged with approximately 2⅛ US quart of fluid and then installed on the transmission, lining up the notch in the torque converter with the notch in the oil pump.
3. The distance from the leading edge of the transmission bell housing and the leading edge of the bolt lugs of the converter should be no less than 1.38 inches, if the converter lugs and the oil pump lugs are correctly assembled.
4. With the converter properly installed, place the transmission on the jack and secure with a safety chain.
5. Raise the transmission into position and install the converter housing to engine attaching bolts. Torque the bolts to 29-36 ft. lbs.

**NOTE: The converter and the drive plate matchmarks should be aligned as the converter housing and the engine are joined.**

6. Install the starter assembly.
7. Install the rear engine mount securing bolts and the crossmember securing bolts.
8. Install the drive plate to converter bolts. Torque to 29-36 ft. lbs.
9. Install the converter dust cover and the engine to transmission gussets.
10. Remove the transmission jack from under the transmission and the support from under the engine.
11. Install the fluid cooler lines and the fluid filler tube. Install governor tube.
12. Install the speedometer cable to the rear extension housing and install the vacuum hose to the the vacuum diaphragm.
13. Connect the selector range lever to the manual control shaft.
14. Connect the wiring connectors and connections at the inhibitor switch, the downshift solenoid, O.D. solenoid, lock-up control solenoid and the O.D. indicator switch.

15. Connect the front exhaust pipe.

16. Install the propeller shaft and secure.

17. Recheck the assembly on the undercarriage and lower the vehicle.

18. On gasoline engines, connect the torsion shaft to the accelerator linkage.

19. Connect the negative battery cable.

20. Fill the transmission with Dexron® II fluid, start the engine, move the selector lever through all detents and re-check the fluid level. Correct as required.

21. Verify that no leakage is present and all components are operating properly. Re-check the fluid level and correct as necessary. Road test the vehicle.

# BENCH OVERHAUL

## Before Disassembly

Before removing the subassemblies from the transmission, thoroughly clean the outside of the case to prevent dirt from entering the mechanical parts during the overhaul and repair operation. If steam cleaning is used to remove the outside grime from the case, immediate disassembly of the transmission must be done to avoid internal rusting.

During the disassembly of the transmission and subassemblies, handle all the parts carefully to avoid nicking or burring the bearings or mating surfaces. Lubricate all internal parts of the transmission before assembly with either transmission fluid or petroleum jelly. Always use new gaskets and seals when assembling the transmission. Torque all bolts and nuts to their recommended torque.

## Converter Inspection

The welded construction of the torque converter prohibits the disassembly or service unless highly specialized converter equipment is available. If the transmission has been diagnosed as having a defective lock-up unit or defective stator overrunning clutch, through road test and/or stall test procedures, torque converter replacement is mandatory.

It is advisable to replace the torque converter, should the transmission be contaminated with clutch and band debris, unless a commercial torque converter cleaner and flushing unit is available.

## Transmission Disassembly

### L3N71B TRANSMISSION

1. Remove the torque converter and drain the transmission fluid through the end of the rear extension housing.

2. Place the transmission on a holding tool, if available, with the oil pan upright.

3. If not previously removed, remove the governor tube between the case and converter housing. Remove the converter housing from the front of the transmission.

4. Remove the downshift solenoid, the vacuum diaphragm and rod from the transmission case. Remove "O" rings.

5. Remove the lock plate retaining bolt and remove the speedometer pinion.

6. Remove the oil pan and inspect the residue on the inside of the pan.

**NOTE: An analysis of the residue can indicate the types of internal problems that will be encountered.**

7. Remove the control valve assembly, noting the position of the different length bolts. Remove the manual valve from the valve body to avoid dropping it during the control valve assembly removal.

8. Loosen the band servo stem locknut and tighten the piston stem to avoid the high-reverse (front) drum from dropping out when the front pump is removed.

9. Note the positioning of the input shaft in the front pump and remove it.

— CAUTION —
*During the assembly, do not install the shaft backwards.*

10. Remove the front pump retaining bolts. Install slide hammer type tools in the pump body and carefully pull the pump from the case.

— CAUTION —
*Do not allow the high-reverse (front) pump to drop.*

11. Remove the high-reverse (front) thrust washer and bearing race. Back off the band servo piston stem to release the band. Remove the brake band strut, then remove the brake band, high reverse (front) and forward (rear) clutch assemblies as a unit.

**NOTE: To avoid stretching the brake band unnecessarily, a clip is available to hold the open ends of the band in one position.**

12. Remove the pump thrust bearings and the forward (rear) clutch thrust washers.

13. Remove the forward (rear) clutch hub, front planetary carrier and connecting shell, the rear clutch thrust bearing, front planetary carrier thrust washer and thrust bearing.

14. Loosen the band servo cover bolts approximately one-half their lengths. With the use of an air gun, carefully apply air pressure to loosen the band servo. Remove the band servo cover retaining bolts and remove the band servo piston assembly.

15. Remove the rear planetary carrier retaining snap ring and remove the rear planetary carrier from the case.

16. Remove the output shaft snap ring and remove the rear connecting drum with the internal (annulus) gear.

17. Remove the snap ring from inside the transmission case, holding the low and reverse brake assembly. Tilt the rear of the transmission upward and remove the low and reverse brake assembly.

18. Remove the rear extension from the transmission case.

**NOTE: Do not lose the parking pawl, spring and retainer washer.**

19. Remove the output shaft with the governor assembly attached. Remove the governor thrust washer and needle bearing.

20. Remove the one-way clutch inner race attaching bolts. Remove the one-way clutch inner race, return thrust washer, low and reverse return spring and the spring thrust ring.

21. With the use of an air gun, apply air pressure to the proper port and remove the low and reverse piston.

22. Should the manual control and parking mechanism need to be removed, the snap rings must be removed from both ends of the parking brake lever in order to remove the lever. Back off the manual shaft locknut and remove the manual plate and parking rod. The inhibitor switch and the manual shaft can be removed by loosening the two securing bolts.

### L4N71B, E4N71B AND JM600 TRANSMISSIONS

1. Remove the torque converter and drain the transmission fluid through the end of the rear extension housing.

2. Place the transmission on a holding tool, if available, with the oil pan upright.

3. (L4N71B and JM600) remove the governor tube between the case and the converter housing. (E4N71B) remove the lock-up solenoid. Remove the converter housing from either model.

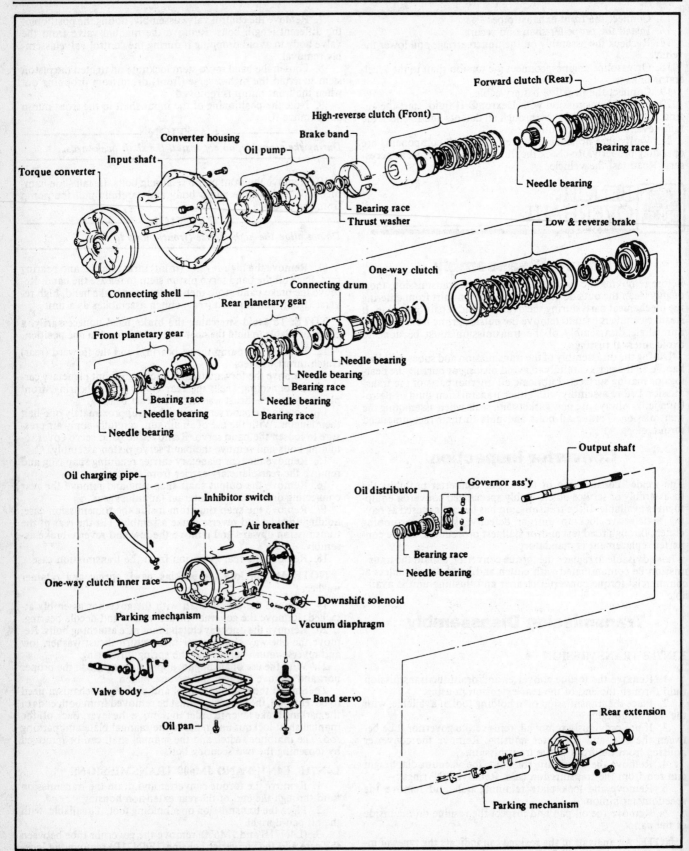

Exploded view of L3N71B models (© Nissan Motor Co. of USA)

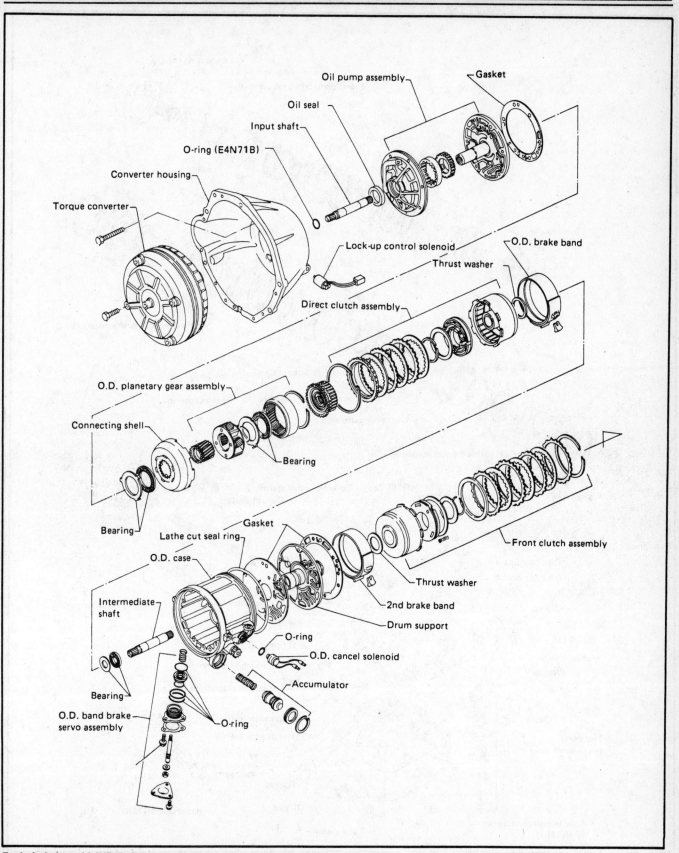

**Exploded view of L4N71B, E4N71B , JM600 models** (© Nissan Motor Co. of USA)

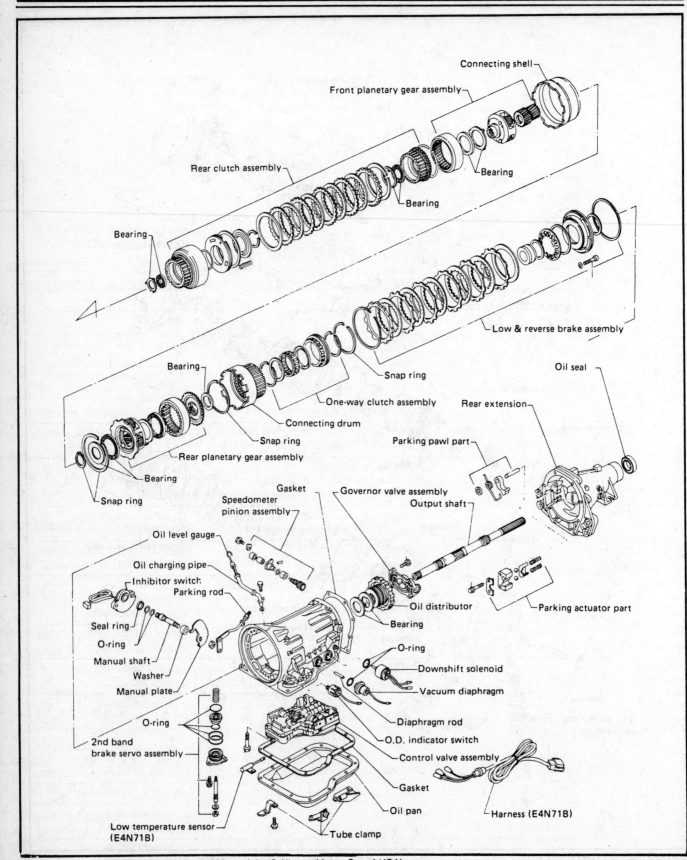

Connecting shell

Front planetary gear assembly

Rear clutch assembly

Bearing

Bearing

Bearing

Low & reverse brake assembly

Bearing

Oil seal

Snap ring

One-way clutch assembly

Rear extension

Connecting drum

Snap ring

Parking pawl part

Rear planetary gear assembly

Bearing

Governor valve assembly

Snap ring

Gasket

Output shaft

Speedometer
pinion assembly

Oil level gauge

Oil charging pipe

Inhibitor switch

Oil distributor

Parking rod

Bearing

Seal ring

O-ring

O-ring

Manual shaft

Downshift solenoid

Washer

Vacuum diaphragm

Manual plate

Diaphragm rod

O-ring

O.D. indicator switch

2nd band
brake servo assembly

Control valve assembly

Gasket

Oil pan

Low temperature sensor
(E4N71B)

Tube clamp

Harness (E4N71B)

Parking actuator part

**Exploded view of L4N71B, E4N71B, JM600 models** (© Nissan Motor Co. of USA)

4. Remove the overdrive component assembly. Remove the high-reverse (front) clutch thrust washer and needle bearing with race. Remove input and intermediate shafts. Put overdrive component assembly aside.

5. Remove the downshift solenoid, vacuum diaphragm with rod and the "O" rings.

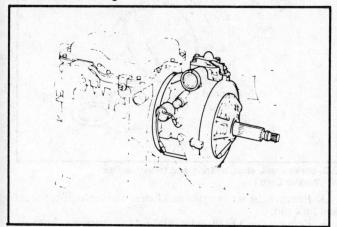

**Removing the O.D. case assembly (© Chrysler Corp.)**

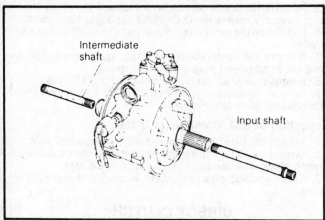

**Removing the intermediate and input shafts (© Chrysler Corp.)**

6. Remove the speedometer pinion.
7. Remove the oil pan and inspect the residue on the inside of the oil pan.

**NOTE: An analysis of the residue can indicate the types of internal problems that will be encountered.**

8. Remove the control valve assembly, noting the position of the three different length bolts. Remove the manual valve from the valve body to prevent its dropping during the control valve assembly removal.

9. Loosen the second band locknut and tighten the piston stem up to a maximum of two turns. If the stem can be turned more than two turns, the band is worn out. Back off the stem adjuster to release the band.

10. Remove the band strut. Remove the brake band, High-reverse (front) clutch, forward (rear) clutch and the front planetary gear assembly as a unit.

**NOTE: To avoid stretching the band unnecessarily, a clip is available to hold the open ends of the band in one position.**

11. Loosen the servo cover retaining bolts approximately one-half their length. Using an air gun, apply air into the servo apply port and raise the servo piston assembly. Remove the retaining bolts from the cover and remove the servo piston assembly from the case.

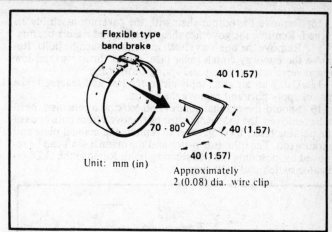

**Installation of the wire clip to the band**
(© Nissan Motor Co. of USA)

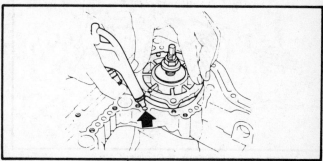

**Removing the servo assembly with air pressure**
(© Nissan Motor Co. of USA)

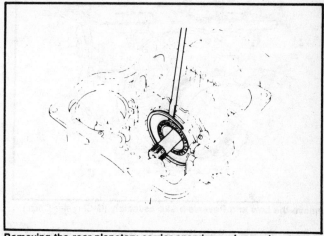

**Removing the rear planetary carrier snapring and rear planetary carrier (© Chrysler Corp.)**

12. Remove the rear planetary carrier snap ring and rear planetary carrier from the case.
13. Remove the output shaft snap ring and remove the connecting drum with the internal gear.
14. Remove the snap ring and tilt the transmission case upward in the rear and remove the low and reverse brake clutch assembly.
15. Remove the rear extension assembly.

— **CAUTION** —
*Do not lose the parking pawl spring and retainer washer from the rear extension.*

16. Remove the output shaft with the governor assembly attached. Remove the governor thrust washer and needle bearing.

17. Remove the one-way clutch inner race attaching bolts. Remove the one-way clutch inner race, return thrust washer, low and reverse return spring and spring thrust ring.

18. Using an air gun, apply air to the low and reverse brake piston apply port and remove the piston.

19. Should the manual control and parking mechanism need to be removed, the snap rings must be removed from both ends of the parking brake lever in order to remove the manual plate and parking rod. The inhibitor switch and the manual shaft can be removed by loosening the two securing bolts. Remove the O.D. indicator switch and "O" ring.

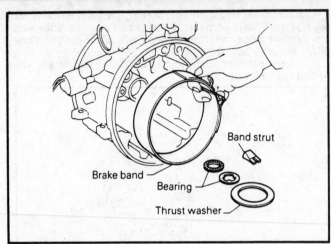

**O.D. brake band, strut, bearing and thrust washer** (© Chrysler Corp.)

3. Remove the servo cover and loosen the servo piston stem and lock nut.

4. Remove the O.D. planetary gear set and the direct clutch assembly.

5. Remove the needle bearing with race and the direct clutch thrust washer. Remove the O.D. brake band and band strut.

6. Lightly tap the servo retainer and remove the O.D. servo assembly.

7. Remove the accumulator snap ring, apply pressure to remove the accumulator plug, piston and spring.

8. Remove the O.D. cancel solenoid and its "O" ring.

9. Remove the drum support from the O.D. component body, after removal of its retaining bolts.

### Inspection of O.D. Component Units

1. Inspect the input and output shafts for abnormal wear.

2. Inspect the O.D. housing for wear points, cracks, damaged threads, blocked or damaged oil channels in the case.

3. Check one way plug in the O.D. housing and replace if required.

## DIRECT CLUTCH

### Disassembly

1. Remove the large clutch retaining plate snap ring.

2. Remove the clutch plate assembly from the drum.

3. Using a spring compressor tool, compress the clutch

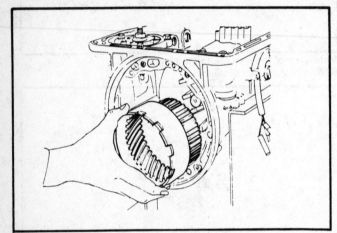

**Removing the connecting drum** (© Chrysler Corp.)

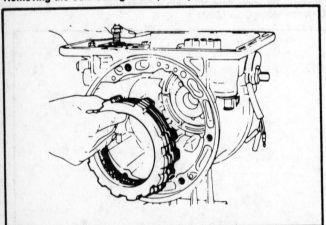

**Remove the Low and Reverse brake assembly** (© Chrysler Corp.)

## Unit Disassembly, Inspection and Assembly

**L4N71B, E4N71B, JM600 TRANSMISSIONS**

### OVERDRIVE COMPONENT UNIT

#### Disassembly

1. Remove the input and output shafts from the assembly, if not previously removed.

**NOTE: Mark and note the position of the shafts before removal for easier installation.**

2. Attach slide hammer type tool to the oil pump body and carefully remove the oil pump from the O.D. housing.

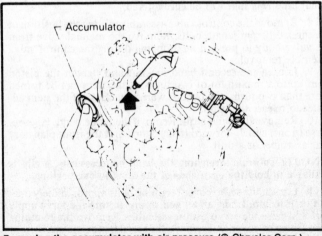

**Removing the accumulator with air pressure** (© Chrysler Corp.)

springs, remove the snap ring from the spring retainer.

4. Remove the compressing tool, the spring retainer and the springs (10).

5. Install the drum into the drum support and using an air gun, apply air into the apply port of the drum support to loosen the piston. Remove the piston from the drum.

6. Remove the clutch hub seal and the piston seal.

## Inspection

1. Inspect the clutch drive plates for wear. If the drive plates are to be used again, standard drive plate thickness must be 0.0591-0.065 inch (1.50-1.65 mm), with a service minimum thickness of 0.055 inch (1.4 mm).

2. Inspect the degree of wear of the snap rings and retaining grooves. Check all springs for being worn or having broken coils. Inspect the driven clutch plates for scores, burrs or being burned.

3. Check the operation of the check ball in the apply piston with air pressure. Air should pass freely in one direction and be blocked in the other.

## Assembly

1. With the clutch drum on a flat surface, lubricate the clutch hub and piston sealing surfaces. Install the seals on the clutch hub and on the piston. Use either transmission fluid or petroleum jelly as a lubricant.

### ─── CAUTION ───
*Do not stretch the seals during their installation.*

2. Install the piston into the clutch drum, being careful not to damage or kink the seal during the piston installation. After the piston installation, turn the piston by hand to ensure that no binding exists.

3. Install the springs (10) and the spring retainer into position. Install the spring compressing tool and carefully compress the springs and retainer. Install the snap ring and be sure it is secured. Remove the compressing tool.

4. Install the two dished plates next to the piston with the first dished plate facing away from the piston, the second dished plate facing the first dished plate with the outer circumferences touching each other.

5. Install a driven steel plate, a drive plate, a steel plate and finish with a driven plate. Install the retaining or pressure plate and retain it with the large snap ring.

**NOTE: Three driven and three drive plates are used when equipped with VG30E turbo engine.**

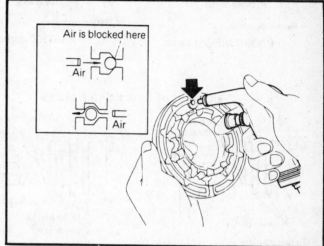

**Checking the apply piston check ball with air pressure**
(© Chrysler Corp.)

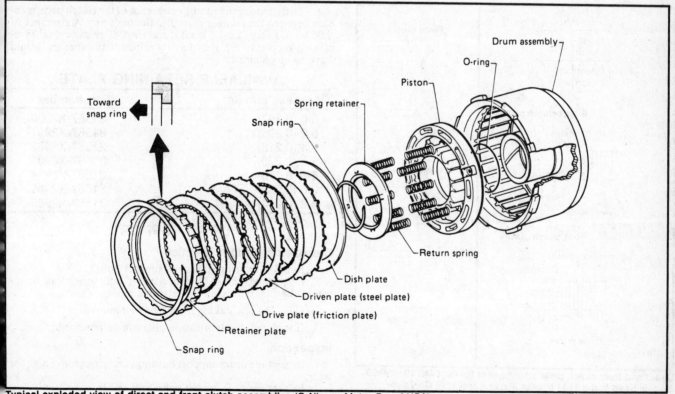

**Typical exploded view of direct and front clutch assemblies** (© Nissan Motor Co. of USA)

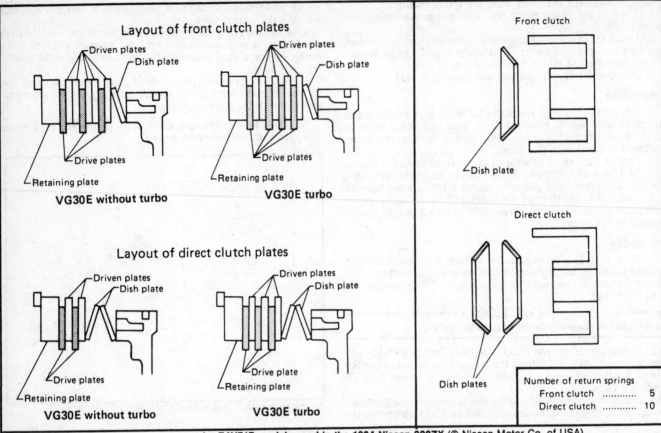

Layout of front clutch plates

**VG30E without turbo**

**VG30E turbo**

Layout of direct clutch plates

**VG30E without turbo**

**VG30E turbo**

Front clutch

Direct clutch

| Number of return springs | |
|---|---|
| Front clutch | 5 |
| Direct clutch | 10 |

**Direct and front clutch plate arrangement for E4N71B models used in the 1984 Nissan 300ZX** (© Nissan Motor Co. of USA)

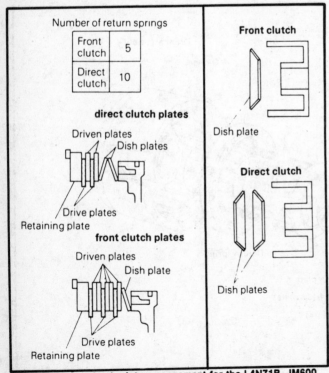

| Number of return springs | |
|---|---|
| Front clutch | 5 |
| Direct clutch | 10 |

**direct clutch plates**

Front clutch

**front clutch plates**

Direct clutch

**Direct and front clutch plate arrangement for the L4N71B, JM600 models used in the 1984 Nissan Maxima and 1984 Chrysler Conquest** (© Nissan Motor Co. of USA)

6. To determine the running clearance of the clutch pack, measure between the retainer plate and the snap ring. A clearance of 0.063-0.071 inch (1.6-1.8 mm) is specified. If necessary, other retaining or pressure plates, having different thicknesses, would have to be obtained.

## AVAILABLE RETAINING PLATE

| Thickness mm (in) | Part number |
|---|---|
| 5.0 (0.197) | 31567-X2900 |
| 5.2 (0.205) | 31567-X2901 |
| 5.4 (0.213) | 31567-X2902 |
| 5.6 (0.220) | 31567-X2903 |
| 5.8 (0.228) | 31567-X2904 |
| 6.0 (0.236) | 31567-X2905 |
| 6.2 (0.244) | 31567-X2906 |

## DRUM SUPPORT

### Disassembly and Inspection

1. Remove the rings from the support hub.
2. If required, the O.D. cancel valve and spring can be removed by first removing the retaining pin.

**NOTE: The pin staking must first be removed.**

3. If required, the lubrication plug can be removed.

### Inspection

1. Inspect the drum support bushings and ring groove area for wear.
2. Inspect the O.D. cancel valve and spring.
3. Inspect the internal surfaces for visible wear or damage.

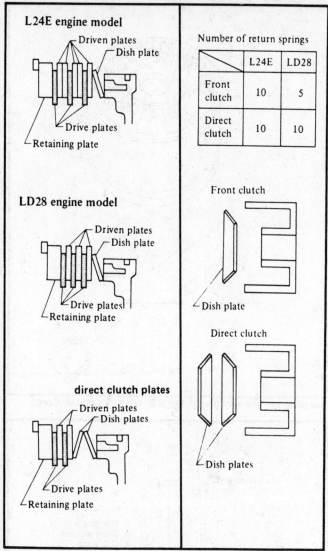

**L24E engine model**

**LD28 engine model**

**direct clutch plates**

| Number of return springs | | |
|---|---|---|
| | L24E | LD28 |
| Front clutch | 10 | 5 |
| Direct clutch | 10 | 10 |

Front clutch

Dish plate

Direct clutch

Dish plates

**Direct and front clutch plate arrangement for the L4N71B model used in 1983 Nissan Maxima (© Nissan Motor Co. of USA)**

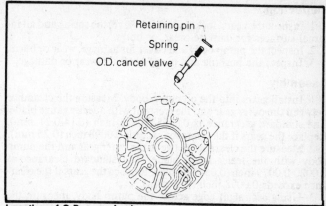

**Location of O.D. cancel valve assembly (© Chrysler Corp.)**

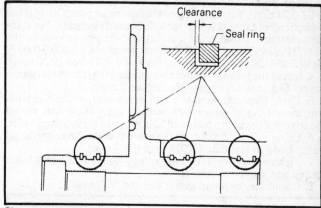

**Clearance check between the ring groove and the seal rings (© Chrysler Corp.)**

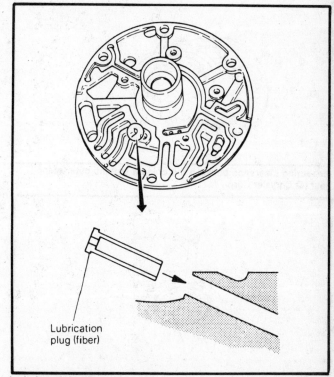

**Location of the fiber lubrication plug in the drum support (© Chrysler Corp.)**

4. Measure the clearance between the ring grooves and a new ring. The specified clearance should be 0.0020-0.0079 inch (0.05-0.20 mm). Replace the drum support if the clearance exceeds 0.0079 inch (0.20 mm).

## Assembly

1. If removed, install the O.D. cancel valve and spring. Tap in the retaining pin. Secure the pin.
2. If removed, install the fiber lubrication plug.
3. Install the sealing rings on the support hub.

## OIL PUMP

### Disassembly

**L4N71B, E4N71B, JM600 TRANSMISSIONS**

1. Remove the front pump gasket and the "O" ring.
2. Remove the pump cover from the pump body.
3. Remove the retaining pin, the lock-up control valve and spring.
4. Remove the drive and driven oil pump gears from the housing. Note the direction and location of the gears. Mark the gears as required.

## Inspection

1. Inspect the gears, lock-up control valve, the spring and all internal surfaces for damage, wear, or burrs.
2. Inspect the pump body and cover for damage, wear or burrs.
3. Inspect the bushing and pump shaft for wear or damage.

## Assembly

1. Install gears into the oil pump body. Measure the clearance between the outer gear and the crescent with a feeler gauge blade. The standard clearance is 0.0055-0.0083 inch (0.14-0.21 mm). Replace the gears if the clearance exceeds 0.0098 inch (0.25 mm).
2. Measure the clearance between the outer gear and the pump body with the feeler gauge blade. The standard clearance is 0.0020-0.0079 inch (0.05-0.20 mm). Replace the gears if the clearance exceeds 0.0098 inch (0.25 mm).
3. Using a straight edge across the pump body, measure the clearance between the gears and the pump body cover with a feeler gauge blade. The standard clearance is 0.0008-0.0016 inch (0.02-0.04 mm). Replace the gears, or cover, or pump body if the measurement exceeds 0.0031 inch (0.08 mm) clearance. The standard clearance between the seal ring and the ring groove for the L4N71B, JM600 and the E4N71B transmissions is 0.0020-0.0079 inch (0.05-0.20 mm) with a wear limit of 0.0079 inch (0.20 mm).
4. Install the lock-up control valve and spring into the oil pump cover. Tap in the retaining pin. Secure the pin.
5. Using a special mounting tool and spacer, or their equivalent, mount the oil pump body with the gears in the tool. Install the cover on the pump body and lightly install the retaining bolts.
6. Using a dial indicator, set the run-out of the cover on the oil pump body to less than 0.0028 inch (0.07 mm).
7. Tighten the cover retaining bolts to 4.3-5.8 ft. lbs. (6-8 N•m) torque and check the runout.
8. Install the oil pump gasket and the "O" ring.

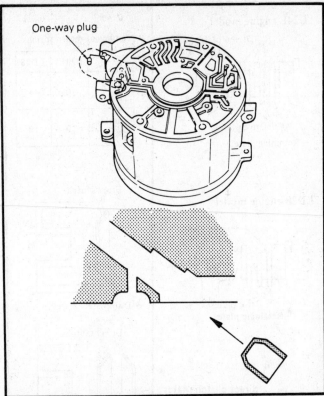

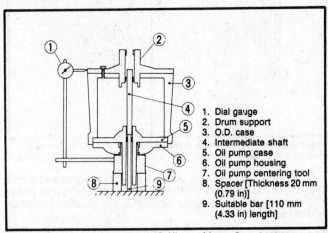

**Installing the one way plug in the O.D. case (© Chrysler Corp.)**

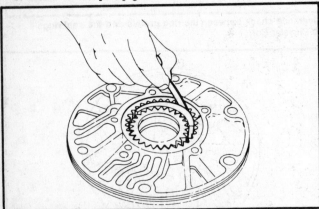

**Measuring clearance between the cresent and the outer pump gear (© Chrysler Corp.)**

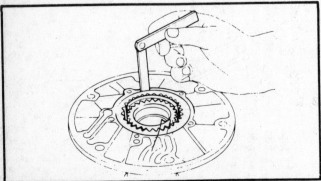

**Measuring the clearance between the outer gear and the pump body (© Chrysler Corp.)**

1. Dial gauge
2. Drum support
3. O.D. case
4. Intermediate shaft
5. Oil pump case
6. Oil pump housing
7. Oil pump centering tool
8. Spacer [Thickness 20 mm (0.79 in)]
9. Suitable bar [110 mm (4.33 in) length]

**Checking drum support runout (© Nissan Motor Co. of USA)**

## DRUM SUPPORT HUB TO O.D. CASE

### Assembly

1. Install the one way plug in the O.D. case, if it had been removed.
2. Mount the assembled oil pump into the special mounting tool and spacer, or their equivalent.
3. Mount the O.D. case, drum support and gasket in the oil pump assembly and temporarily assemble the drum support.

——————————— CAUTION ———————————
*Be sure the O.D. case is seated in the oil pump body properly.*

4. Install a 4.33 inch (110 mm) bar into the oil pump at the shaft location and install the intermediate shaft to set upon the top of the bar.

5. Using a dial indicator, set the run out of the drum support on the O.D. case to less than 0.0020 inch (0.05 mm).

6. Tighten the drum support bolts to 5.1-6.5 ft. lbs. (7-9 N•m).

7. Recheck the drum support run out. Correct as required.

8. Install the "O" ring and gasket.

9. Remove the assembly from the special tool and spacer.

10. Set the O.D. unit aside until the transmission is to be re-assembled.

## OIL PUMP

### Disassembly

#### L3N71B TRANSMISSIONS

1. Remove the "O" ring and the pump gasket.

2. Remove the pump body cover.

3. Remove the speed cut valve and the lock-up control valve from the pump body.

4. Remove the drive and driven gears from the pump body. Note the location and direction of the gears. Mark the gears as required.

### Inspection

1. Inspect the gears, speed cut control valve and the lock-up control valve, the springs and all internal surfaces for damage, wear or burrs.

2. Inspect the pump body and cover for damage, wear or burrs.

3. Inspect the bushing and pump shaft for wear or damage.

### Assembly

1. Install the drive and driven gears into the oil pump body. Measure the clearance between the outer gear and the crescent with a feeler gauge blade. The standard clearance is 0.0055-0.0083 inch (0.14-0.21 mm). Replace the gears if the clearance exceeds 0.0098 inch (0.25 mm).

2. Measure the clearance between the outer gear and the pump body with a feeler gauge blade. The standard clearance is 0.0020-0.0079 inch (0.05-0.20 mm). Replace the gears if the clearance exceeds 0.0098 inch (0.25 mm).

3. Using a straight edge across the pump body, measure the

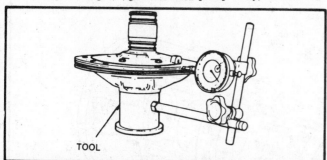

**Checking oil pump body runout—L3N71B models**

clearance between the gears and the pump body cover with a feeler gauge blade. The standard clearance is 0.0008-0.0016 inch (0.02-0.04 mm). Replace the gears, or cover or pump body if the measurements exceeds 0.0031 inch (0.08 mm) clearance.

4. Measure the clearance between the seal ring and the ring groove with a feeler gauge blade. The standard clearance for the L3N71B transmission is 0.0016-0.0063 inch (0.04-0.16 mm). Replace the oil pump body if the measurements exceed 0.0063 inch (0.16 mm) with the use of new rings as a measuring guide.

5. Install the speed cut control valve, the lock-up control valve and their springs. Install the retaining pins and secure.

6. Set the pump housing into a special holding tool, or its equivalent. With the use of a dial indicator, set the run out of the pump body cover to less than 0.0028 inch (0.07 mm).

7. Tighten the securing cover to body bolt to 4.3-5.8 ft. lbs. (6-8 N•m) torque. Recheck the cover run out. Re-set as required.

## Remaining Disassembly, Inspection and Assembly of Components

The remaining disassembly, inspection and assembly procedures of the L3N71B, E4N71B, JM600 and L4N71B transmission components are basically the same. Differences in assembly procedures will again be encountered during the re-assembly of the transmission components into the case. Each difference will be noted accordingly as the assembly procedure progresses.

### HIGH-REVERSE (FRONT) CLUTCH AND FORWARD (REAR) CLUTCH

#### Disassembly

1. Remove the large snap ring from the clutch housing, retaining the clutch pack.

2. Remove the clutch pack assembly from the clutch housing.

3. Using a compressing tool, compress the clutch springs and remove the snap ring from the spring retainer. Release the compressing tool and remove.

4. Remove the spring retainer and the springs.

5. Mount clutch housing on the front pump assembly and using an air gun, direct air to the piston apply port of the front pump and loosen the piston. Remove the piston from the clutch hub.

6. Remove the clutch housing hub seal and the piston seal.

#### Inspection

1. Inspect the clutch drive plates for wear. If the drive plates are to be used again, standard drive plate thickness must be 0.0591-0.0650 inch (1.50-1.65 mm), with a service thickness at a minimum of 0.055 inch (1.4 mm).

2. Inspect for the degree of wear of the snap rings and retaining grooves. Check all springs for being worn or having broken coils. Inspect the driven clutch plates for scores, burrs or being burned.

3. Check the operation of the check ball in the apply piston with air pressure. Air should pass freely in one direction and be blocked in the other.

## CLUTCH PISTON RETURN SPRINGS

| Transmission | Type | | Quantity |
|---|---|---|---|
| L3N71B | High-Reverse (Front) Clutch | | 10 coil springs |
| | Forward (Rear) Clutch | | 10 coil springs |
| | Low & Reverse Brake | | Bellville type spring |
| L4N71B, JM600① | Direct Clutch | | 10 coil springs |
| | High-Reverse (Front) Clutch | W/L24E Engine | 10 coil springs |
| | | W/LD28 Engine | 5 coil springs |
| | Forward (Rear) Clutch | | 8 coil springs |
| | Low & Reverse Brake | | Bellville type spring |
| E4N71B | Direct Clutch | | 10 coil springs |
| | High-Reverse (Front) Clutch | | 5 coil springs |
| | Forward (Rear) Clutch | | 8 coil springs |
| | Low & Reverse Brake | | Bellville type spring |

① JM600: No specifications

## Assembly

1. With the clutch drum on a flat surface, lubricate the clutch hub and piston sealing surfaces. Install the seals on the clutch hub and piston. Use either transmission fluid or petroleum jelly as a lubricant.

——— CAUTION ———

*Do not stretch the seals during their installation.*

2. Install the piston into the clutch housing, being careful not to damage or kink the seals during the piston installation. After the piston is installed, turn it by hand to ensure that no binding exists.

3. Install either the 10 or 5 return springs, depending upon engine model, and postion the spring retainer. Install the spring compressing tool and carefully compress the springs and retainer. Install the snap ring and be sure it is secured. Remove the compressing tool.

4. Install the dished plate with the dish facing outward.

5. Install a steel driven clutch plate, and then a drive friction plate. Repeat this order until the correct number of clutch plates have been installed.

NOTE: Refer to the Specifications for correct number of clutch plates.

——— CAUTION ———

*The L24E and VG30E engine models use two sets of driven steel clutch plates together in the high-reverse (front) clutch assembly in the following manner; the dished plate, a steel driven clutch plate, a drive friction clutch plate, two steel driven clutch plates, a drive friction clutch plate, two steel driven clutch plates and one drive friction clutch plate, followed by the retaining plate. The VG30E Turbo engine models only use one set of driven steel plates.*

6. Install the retainer or pressure plate and the snap ring.

7. Measure the clutch pack running clearance with a feeler gauge blade. The clearance between the retainer plate and snap ring should be 0.063-0.079 inch (1.6-2.0 mm) on the high-reverse (front) clutch and 0.031-0.059 inch (0.8-1.5 mm) on the high-reverse (front) clutch and 0.031-0.059 inch (0.8-1.5 mm) on the forward (rear) clutch. If necessary to correct the clearance, different thicknesses of retainer plates are available.

8. To test the high-reverse (front) or forward (rear) clutch, assemble the clutch onto the oil pump assembly. Direct a jet of air into the apply port of the oil pump and listen or feel the clutch action, under air pressure and when released.

## Control Valve Body Assembly

It is suggested that a valve and spring holding rack be available to the repairman during the disassembly, cleaning and re-assembly of the control valve body assembly, to maintain its sequence of assembly. Do not interchange valves, springs, sleeves or other internal parts, but return each component back to its original position to maintain the calibration of the control valve body assembly. There is no set sequence of control valve disassembly and assembly, but a general procedure is suggested.

### HIGH-REVERSE (FRONT) CLUTCH
### L4N71B, E4N71B, JM600 Transmissions

| Thickness mm (in) | Part number Nissan | Part number Chrysler |
| --- | --- | --- |
| 5.0 (0.197) | 31567-X2900 | MD610366 |
| 5.2 (0.205) | 31567-X2901 | MD610367 |
| 5.4 (0.213) | 31567-X2902 | MD610368 |
| 5.6 (0.220) | 31567-X2903 | MD610369 |
| 5.8 (0.228) | 31567-X2904 | MD610370 |
| 6.0 (0.236) | 31567-X2905 | MD610371 |
| 6.0 (0.244) | 31567-X2906 | MD610372 |

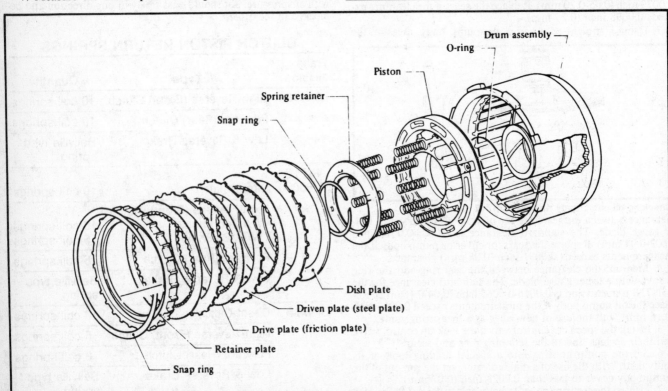

Exploded view of high-reverse (front) clutch assembly—typical (© Nissan Motor Co. of USA)

## DIRECT CLUTCH
### E4N71B Transmission

| Thickness mm (in) | Part number Nissan | |
|---|---|---|
| 5.8 (0.228) | 31567-X2904 | |
| 6.0 (0.236) | 31567-X2905 | |
| 6.2 (0.244) | 31567-X2906 | |
| 6.4 (0.252) | 31507-X8600 | |
| 6.6 (0.260) | 31507-X8601 | |
| 6.8 (0.268) | 31537-X2800 | |
| 7.0 (0.276) | 31537-X2801 | |
| 7.2 (0.283) | 31537-X0900 | VG30E turbo only |
| 7.4 (0.291) | 31537-X0901 | |

### L4N71B, JM600 Transmissions

| Thickness mm (in) | Part number Nissan | Part number Chrysler |
|---|---|---|
| 5.6 (0.220) | 31567-X2903 | MD610252 |
| 5.8 (0.228) | 31567-X2904 | MD610253 |
| 6.0 (0.236) | 31567-X2905 | MD610254 |
| 6.2 (0.244) | 31567-X2906 | MD610255 |
| 6.4 (0.252) | 31567-X8600 | MD610256 |
| 6.6 (0.260) | 31567-X8601 | MD610257 |
| 6.8 (0.268) | 31567-X2800 | MD610258 |
| 7.0 (0.276) | 31567-X2801 | MD610259 |

## LOCK-UP VALVE BODY

### Disassembly
**L3N71B**

1. Remove the oil strainer and its attaching screws, nuts and bolts.

2. Disassemble the valve body to separate the lower body, separation plate and the upper body.

3. During the separation of the components, do not lose the orifice check valve, servo orifice check valve, throttle relief check ball and the related springs.

4. Remove the side plate (A) retaining the pressure regulator valve, spring, spring seat, sleeve and plug, the second lock valve and spring. Maintain the correct sequence of the components.

5. Remove the side plate (B) retaining the vacuum throttle valve, throttle back-up valve and spring, the kickdown valve and its spring. Maintain the correct sequence of the components.

6. Remove the side plate (C) retaining the pressure modifier valve and spring, 2nd-3rd shift valve, spring and plug, 1st-2nd shift valve and spring. Maintain the correct sequence of the components.

### Inspection

1. Because of the close tolerances between the valves and the valve body bores, clearances greater than 0.0012 inch (0.03 mm) between the valves and the bores necessitates the replacement of the valve body assembly.

2. Always use crocus cloth to clean the valves and valve body bores, never use sandpaper or emery cloth.

3. Do not remove the sharp edges of the valves during the clean-up.

4. The valves can be cleaned with alcohol or lacquer thinner.

5. The valve body can be dip-cleaned with carburetor cleaner or lacquer thinner.

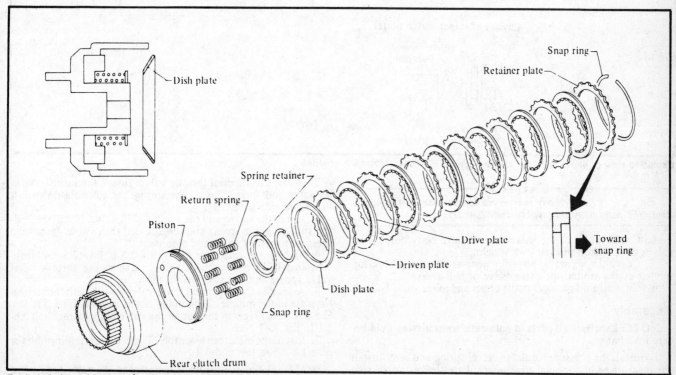

**Exploded view of forward (rear) clutch—typical (© Nissan Motor Co. of USA)**

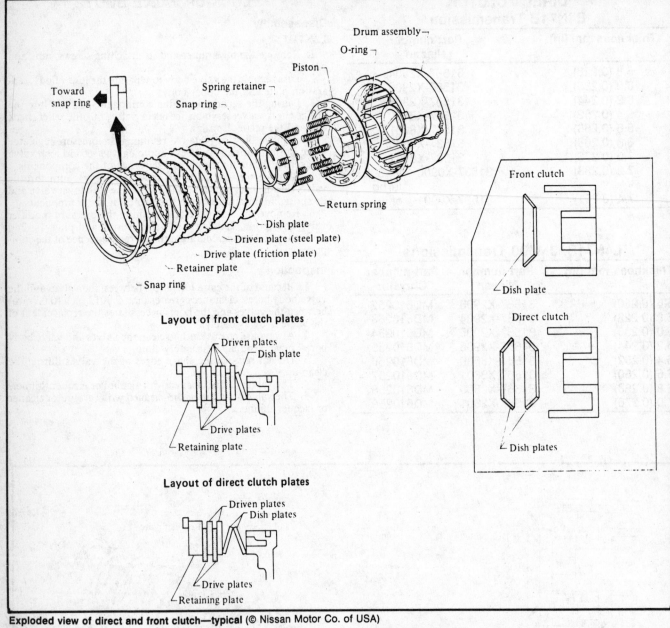

**Toward snap ring** ←

- Spring retainer
- Snap ring
- Drum assembly
- O-ring
- Piston
- Return spring
- Dish plate
- Driven plate (steel plate)
- Drive plate (friction plate)
- Retainer plate
- Snap ring

**Layout of front clutch plates**

- Driven plates
- Dish plate
- Drive plates
- Retaining plate

**Layout of direct clutch plates**

- Driven plates
- Dish plates
- Drive plates
- Retaining plate

**Front clutch**
- Dish plate

**Direct clutch**
- Dish plates

**Exploded view of direct and front clutch—typical** (© Nissan Motor Co. of USA)

---

**CAUTION**

*Do not leave the valve body submerged longer than five minutes. Rinse the valve body thoroughly and blow dry.*

---

6. Check the fit of the valves in the valve body bores. The valves should drop of their own weight.

7. Check the separator plate for wear or damage. Check for scratch marks around the check valve or ball areas.

8. Check the oil passages in the upper and lower valve bodies.

## Assembly

**NOTE: Lubricate all parts in automatic transmission fluid before installation.**

1. Install the pressure regulator valve, spring and seat. Install the pressure regulator plug, pressure regulator sleeve and the side plate "A".

2. Install the vacuum throttle valve. Install the throttle backup valve and spring. Install the spring, the solenoid downshift valve and side plate "B".

3. Install the spring and the 1st-2nd shift valve. Install the 2nd-3rd shift plug, the spring and the 2nd-3rd shift valve. Install the pressure modifier valve and side plate "C".

4. Tighten the side plate screws 1.8-2.5 ft. lbs. (2.5-3.4 Nm).

5. Install the orifice check valve, valve spring, throttle relief valve spring and the steel ball in the valve body.

6. Assemble the upper and lower valve bodies with the separator plate in the middle. Tighten the retaining bolts 1.8-2.5 ft. lbs. (2.5-3.4 Nm). Tighten the nut for the valve body reamer bolt 3.6-5.1 ft. lbs. (5-7 Nm).

7. Install the oil screen assembly. Tighten the retaining bolts or nuts 1.8-2.5 ft. lbs. (2.5-3.4 Nm).

**NOTE: The manual valve is installed in the valve body when the valve body is attached to the transmission case.**

## OVERDRIVE/LOCK-UP VALVE BODY

### Disassembly

**L4N71B, E4N71B, JM600**

1. Remove the oil strainer with its retaining bolts, nuts and screws.

2. Remove the retaining nuts and bolts to separate the upper and lower valve bodies. Remove the separator plate, noting the position of the orifice check valve, servo orifice check valve and the throttle relief check ball with spring.

3. Remove side plate "A" retaining screws and carefully remove the cover. Remove the pressure regulator valve, spring and spring seat. Remove the sleeve and plug, the second lock valve with spring. Place in a rack or tray to maintain the correct sequence.

4. Remove the side plate "B" carefully. Remove the 3rd-4th shift valve, the vacuum throttle valve, throttle back-up valve with spring and the kickdown valve with spring. Maintain the correct sequence.

5. Remove side plate "C" carefully. Remove the pressure modifier valve with spring, the 2nd-3rd shift valve, spring and plug, along with the 1st-2nd shift valve with spring. Maintain the sequence of assembly.

**NOTE: The manual valve was removed during the removal of the valve body from the transmission case.**

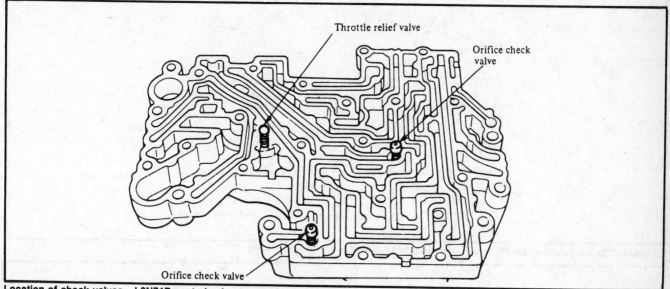

Location of check valves—L3N71B control valve assembly (© Nissan Motor Co. of USA)

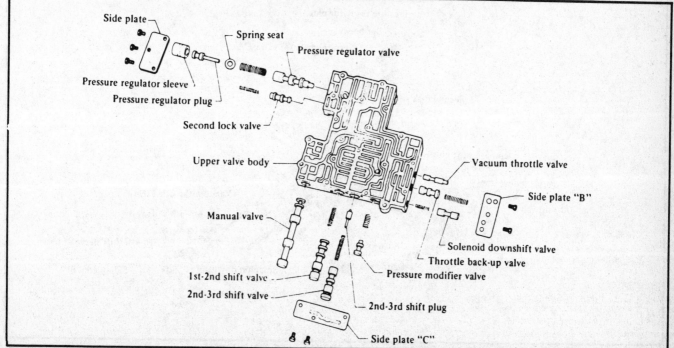

Exploded view of L3N71B control valve assembly (© Nissan Motor Co. of USA)

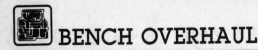

## Inspection

1. Because of the close tolerances between the valves and the valve body bores, clearances greater than 0.0012 inch (0.03 mm) between the valves and the bores necessitates the replacement of the valve body assembly.

2. Always use crocus cloth to clean the valves and valve body bores, never sandpaper or emery cloth.

3. Do not remove the sharp edges of the valves during the clean-up.

4. The valves can be cleaned with alcohol or lacquer thinner.

5. The valve body can be dip-cleaned with carburetor cleaner or lacquer thinner.

### — CAUTION —

*Do not leave the valve body submerged longer than five minutes. Rinse the valve body thoroughly and blow dry.*

6. Check the fit of the valves in the valve body bores. The

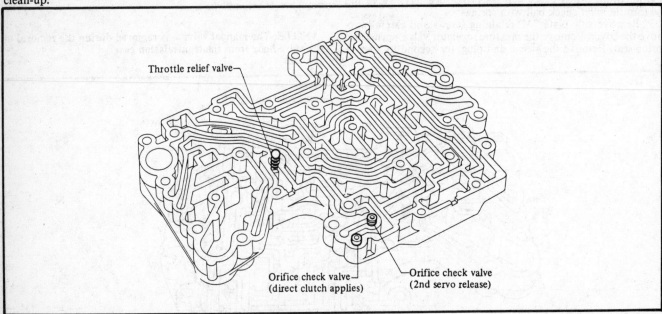

**Location of check valves—L4N71B control valve assembly** (© Nissan Motor Co. of USA)

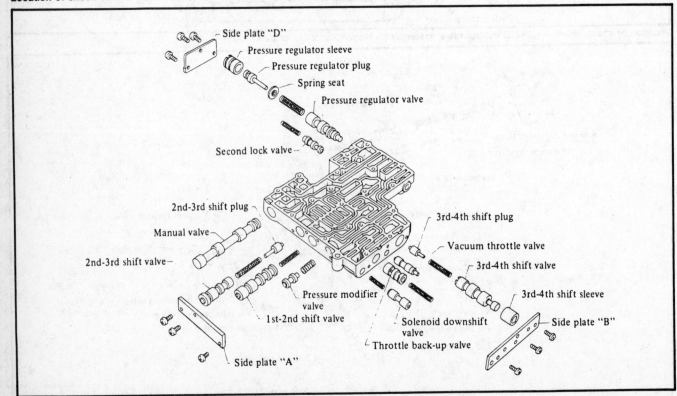

**Exploded view of L4N71B, E4N71B   JM600 control valve assembly** (© Nissan Motor Co. of USA)

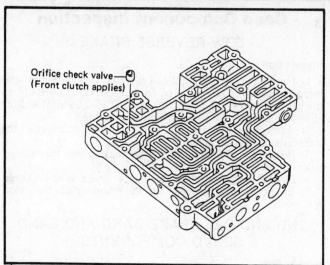

Location of check valves in the upper control valve assembly— E4N71B models (© Nissan Motor Co. of USA)

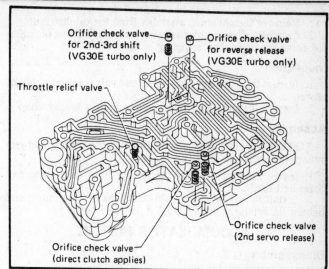

Location of check valves in the lower control valve body— E4N71B models (© Nissan Motor Co. of USA)

valves should drop of their own weight.

7. Check the separator plate for wear or damage. Check for scratch marks around the check valve or ball areas.

8. Check the oil passages in the upper and lower valve bodies.

9. Check the valve springs for weakened load conditions.

### Assembly

NOTE: Lubricate all parts in automatic transmission fluid before installation.

1. Install the 2nd-3rd shift plug, the spring and the 2nd-3rd shift valve, the spring and the 1st-2nd shift valve, the spring and the pressure modifier valve. Install the side plate "A" and its retaining screws.

2. Install the spring and the solenoid downshift valve, the throttle back-up valve with its spring. Install the 3rd-4th shift plug, the spring, the 3rd-4th shift valve, the 3rd-4th shift sleeve and install the side plate "B" and its retaining screws.

3. Install the second lock valve and spring. Install the pressure regulator valve with spring, the spring seat, the pressure regulator plug, the pressure regulator sleeve and install the side plate "C" with its retaining screws.

4. Tighten the side plate retaining screws on "A", "B", and "C" plates 1.8-2.5 ft. lbs. (2.5-3.4 N•m).

5. Install the orifice check valve, the 2nd servo check valve and the throttle relief ball with spring, into the valve body channels. Install the separator plate and assemble the valve bodies together. Tighten the retaining bolts, nuts or screws 1.8-2.5 ft. lbs. (2.5-3.4 N•m). Tighten the nut for the reamer-bolt 3.6-5.1 ft. lbs. (5-7 N•m).

6. Install the oil strainer and retain it with its bolts, nuts or screws. Tighten to 1.8-2.5 ft. lbs. (2.5-3.4 N•m).

NOTE: The manual valve is installed in the valve body when the valve body is installed on the transmission case.

## GOVERNOR

### Disassembly

NOTE: The governor assemblies from the L3N71B and the L4N71B/E4N71B/JM600 transmissions are basically the same in appearances, but differences do exist. Do not attempt to interchange any of the components.

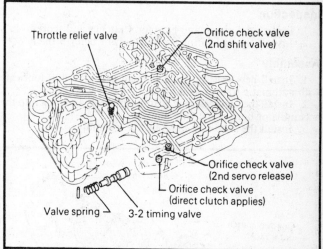

Location of the check valves—JM600 control valve assembly (© Chrysler Corp.)

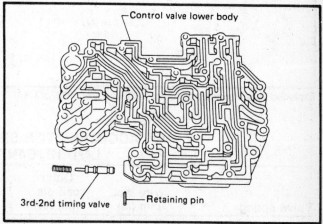

Lower control valve assembly—E4N71B models (© Nissan Motor Co. of USA)

1. Remove the governor assembly from the oil distributor.
2. Carefully, disassemble the governor body, keeping the internal components in their sequence of assembly.

### Inspection

1. Inspect the governor body bores and valves for scratches or scores.
2. Inspect the springs for weakness or having broken coils.

### Assembly

NOTE: Do not interchange components of the primary and secondary governor valves.

1. Install the proper springs and valves into their respective bores and retain.
2. Install the governor assembly onto the oil distributor and tighten the retaining bolts 3.6-5.1 ft. lbs. (5-7 N•m).

## ACCUMULATOR PISTON

### Disassembly

#### L4N71B, E4N71B, JM600

1. Remove the accumulator plug snap ring and apply air pressure to the apply port within the O.D. housing.
2. Remove the accumulator plug, piston with seals, spring and the spacer.

### Inspection

1. Inspect the piston and bore for scratches and scores.
2. Inspect the coil spring for weakness or being broken.

### Assembly

1. Install new seals on the accumulator piston and lubricate with automatic transmission fluid.
2. Install the spacer, spring, piston with seals and plug into the accumulator bore of the O.D. housing.
3. Install the snap ring to retain the assembly.

## Case Component Inspection
### LOW-REVERSE BRAKE

### Inspection

1. Inspect the steel and friction covered clutch plates for wear, being damaged or burned. The friction (drive) plate standard thickness is between 0.0748-0.0807 inch (1.90-2.05 mm) and the allowable thickness limit is 0.071 inch (1.8 mm).
2. Inspect the snap ring and groove in the clutch area of the transmission case for wear.
3. Inspect the piston and the clutch housing bore for damage, scores or scratches.
4. Inspect the piston return spring for weakness or breakage.
5. Inspect the thrust washer and the retainer plate for abnormal wear.

## 2ND AND O.D. BRAKE BAND AND BAND SERVO COMPONENTS

### Inspection

1. Inspect the brake band friction surface for wear, cracked areas, chipped or burned.
2. Inspect the pistons and the piston bores for wear, scores or scratches.
3. Inspect the servo piston return spring for weakness or breakage.

NOTE: There is no band servo return spring in the O.D. band servo on the LD28 diesel engine models.

## PLANETARY GEAR CARRIER ASSEMBLIES

### Inspection

1. Inspect the planetary gear set for damage or worn gears.
2. Inspect the clearance between the pinion washer and the

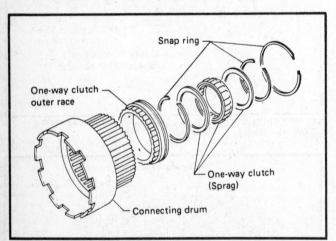

Exploded view of connecting drum (© Nissan Motor Co. of USA)

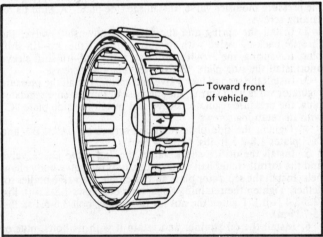

Correct direction of sprag assembly during installation
(© Nissan Motor Co. of USA)

## ACCUMULATOR SPRING SPECIFICATIONS
### L4N71B, E4N71B Transmissions

| Valve spring | Wire dia. mm (in) | Outer coil dia. mm (in) | No. of active coil | Free length mm (in) | Installed Length mm (in) | Installed Load N (kg, lb) |
|---|---|---|---|---|---|---|
| Accumulator spring | 1.8 (0.071) | 14.85 (0.5846) | 7.3 | 39.7 (1.563) | 30.5 (1.201) | 58.8 (6.0, 13.2) |

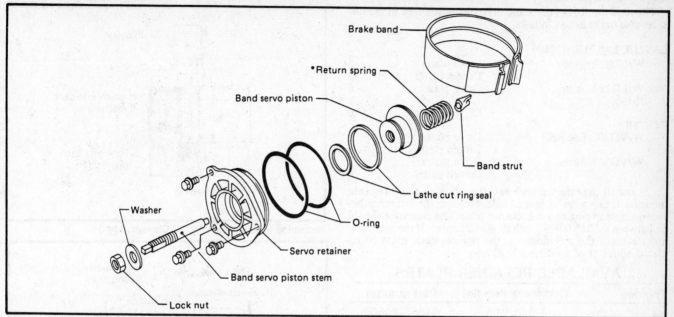

**Typical 2nd and O.D. brake band and band servo assembly** (© Nissan Motor Co. of USA)

planetary carrier, with a feeler gauge blade. The standard clearance is 0.0079-0.0276 inch (0.20-0.70 mm), with the maximum clearance of 0.0315 inch (0.80 mm).

**NOTE: Since the planetary gear carrier assemblies cannot be disassembled to replace worn parts, the entire assembly must be replaced, should damaged or worn parts require replacement.**

## CONNECTING DRUM ASSEMBLY

### Inspection

1. Remove the snap ring and remove the one-way clutch inner and outer races.

2. Inspect the one-way sprag and mating surfaces on the races for damage or wear. Replace the parts as required.

3. During the re-assembly of the one-way clutch, the arrow mark, located between two sprag segments, should be pointing towards the front of the vehicle and the one-way clutch should be free to rotate in a clockwise direction only.

## Transmission Assembly

### L3N71B, L4N71B, E4N71B, JM600

**NOTE: Before assembling the transmission components, verify that all internal parts and case are clean and ready for assembly. Use transmission fluid to lubricate seals and necessary parts before installation. Petroleum jelly (vaseline) should be used to secure thrust washers and bearings for assembly purposes.**

1. Lubricate the seals and components of the low & reverse brake piston and carefully install the piston into the case.

2. Install the thrust ring, piston return spring, thrust washer and one-way clutch inner race into the case.

3. Install the hex head bolts into the inner one-way clutch race from the rear of the case. Torque the bolts 9-13 ft. lbs. (13-18 N•m).

---
#### CAUTION
---

*Be sure the return spring is centered on the race before the bolts are tightened.*

---

4. Install the low & reverse brake clutches into position within the case, starting with the steel dished plate (no external lugs or internal splines), followed by a steel plate and a friction plate, alternating, until the total plates have been installed.

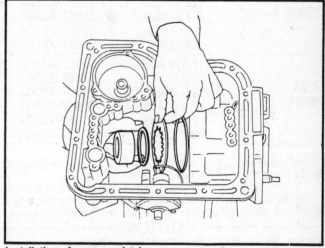

**Installation of one-way clutch race components** (© Nissan Motor Co. of USA)

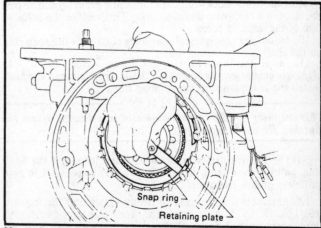

**Measuring low and reverse brake clearance** (© Nissan Motor Co. of USA)

The total number of drive and driven clutches used in the low & reverse brake are as follows:

**L3N71B, L4N71B, JM600**

| | | |
|---|---|---|
| W/L24E Engine | Drive plates | 5 |
| | Driven plates | 5 |
| W/LD28 Engine, JM600 | Drive plates | 6 |
| | Driven plates | 6 |

**E4N71B**

| | | |
|---|---|---|
| W/VG30E Engine | Drive plates | 6 |
| | Driven plates | 6 |
| W/VG30E Turbo | Drive plates | 7 |
| | Driven plates | 7 |

5. Install the retainer plate and the retaining snap ring into the case. Using a feeler gauge blade, measure the clearance between the snap ring and the retainer plate. The clearance should be between 0.0315-0.0492 inch (0.80-1.25 mm). If the measurement exceeds the specifications, the retainer plate must be replaced with one of a different thickness.

## AVAILABLE RETAINER PLATES

| Engines | Thickness mm (in) | Part number |
|---|---|---|
| | 7.8 (0.307) | 31667-X0500 |
| | 8.0 (0.315) | 31667-X0501 |
| L24E | 8.2 (0.323) | 31667-X0502 |
| VG30E Turbo | 8.4 (0.331) | 31667-X0503 |
| | 8.6 (0.339) | 31667-X0504 |
| | 8.8 (0.346) | 31667-X0505 |
| | 11.8 (0.465) | 31667-X0300 |
| | 12.0 (0.472) | 31667-X0301 |
| LD28 | 12.2 (0.480) | 31667-X0302 |
| VG30E | 12.4 (0.488) | 31667-X0303 |
| | 12.6 (0.496) | 31667-X0304 |
| | 12.8 (0.504) | 31667-X0305 |

6. Using an air gun, apply air pressure to the low & reverse brake assembly to check its operation.
7. Install the governor thrust washer and the needle bearing.
8. Slide the governor distributor assembly onto the output shaft and install the shaft assembly into the transmission case.

— CAUTION —

*Do not damage the governor distributor sealing rings.*

9. Install the connecting drum with the sprag into the case, by rotating the drum clockwise. The connecting drum should be free to rotate in a clockwise direction only. This verifies the installation of the sprag is correct.
10. Install the rear internal gear and retain with the snap ring on the shaft.
11. Install the thrust bearing and thrust washer on the rear planetary gear assembly and install the unit into place in the case. Install the rear planetary carrier snap ring.

— CAUTION —

*This snap ring is thinner than those used in a drum to retain the clutches. Do not interchange.*

**NOTE: If difficulty is experienced when installing the snap ring, pull the connecting drum forward as far as possible to gain sufficient groove clearance.**

12. Assemble the high-reverse (front) clutch and the forward (rear) clutch, the front internal gear, front planetary carrier and the connecting shell. Secure all thrust bearings with petroleum jelly.

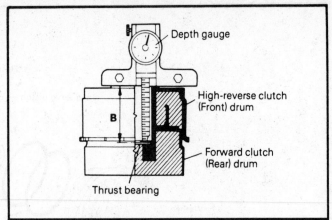

Measuring for dimension "B" (© Chrysler Corp.)

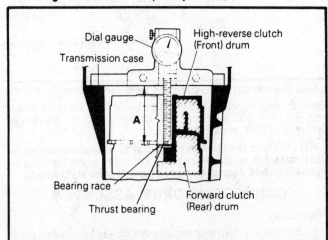

Measuring for dimension "A" (© Chrysler Corp.)

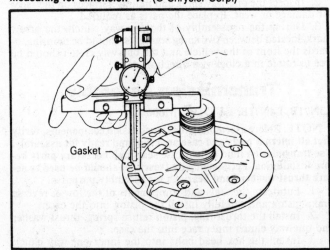

Measuring for dimension "C" (© Chrysler Corp.)

13. Lay the assembled high-reverse (front) clutch and the forward (rear) clutch flat on a level surface, with the high-reverse (front) clutch drum upward. With the rear hub thrust bearing properly seated, measure the distance from the face of the clutch drum to the top of the thrust bearing race, using a dial indicator gauge or a depth caliper with a seven inch post. This measurement is considered dimension "B".
14. Install the clutch drum assembly into the transmission

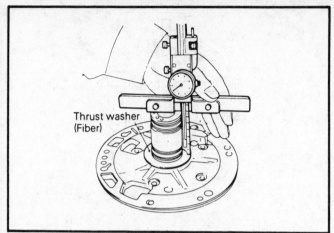

Measuring for dimension "D" (© Chrysler Corp.)

case, being sure all parts are properly seated.

15. Place the transmission in an upright position and measure from the rear hub thrust bearing race to the case oil pump flange. This measurement is considered dimension"A".

NOTE: The measuring procedure sequence to find the "A" and "B" dimensions can be reversed, depending upon the repairmans professional judgement.

16. Place the oil pump assembly flat on a level surface and install the gasket so as to include it in the measurement. Measure from the top of the drum support shaft (front clutch and rear clutch side) to the installed gasket. This measurement is considered dimension "C".

17. Install the fiber thrust washer over the drum support shaft and on to the oil pump body. Measure from the top of the drum support shaft to the top surface of the thrust washer. This dimension is considered dimension "D".

18. The difference between dimension "A" 0.004 inch or 0.1 mm) and dimension "C" minus dimension "D" is the front end play and must be within the specified of between 0.020-0.031 inch (0.5-0.8 mm). The front end-play can be adjusted with the high-reverse (front) clutch thrust washers of different sizes.

## AVAILABLE HIGH-REVERSE CLUTCH (FRONT) THRUST WASHER

| Thickness mm (in) | Part number |
|---|---|
| 1.3 (0.051) | 31528-X0107 |
| 1.5 (0.059) | 31528-X0106 |
| 1.7 (0.067) | 31528-X0105 |
| 1.9 (0.075) | 31528-X0100 |
| 2.1 (0.083) | 31528-X0101 |
| 2.3 (0.091) | 31528-X0102 |
| 2.5 (0.098) | 31528-X0103 |
| 2.7 (0.106) | 31528-X0104 |

NOTE: To properly handle the L3N71B transmission oil pump body for measurement of dimension "C" and "D", the stator support must be held stationary and level.

19. To adjust total end play, measure dimension "A" as previously outlined. Measure dimension "C" as previously outlined. The difference between dimension "A" (-0.004 inch or, 0.1 mm) and dimension "C" is considered total end play.

20. The specific value of total end play is 0.0098-0.0197 inch (0.25-0.50 mm).

21. If the difference between dimension "A" and dimension "C" is not within specifications, the proper sized oil pump cover bearing race can be selected from the following chart.

## AVAILABLE OIL PUMP COVER BEARING RACE

| Thickness mm (in) | Part number |
|---|---|
| 1.2 (0.047) | 31556-X0100 |
| 1.4 (0.055) | 31556-X0101 |
| 1.6 (0.063) | 31556-X0102 |
| 1.8 (0.071) | 31556-X0103 |
| 2.0 (0.079) | 31556-X0104 |
| 2.2 (0.087) | 31556-X0105 |

22. (L4N71B, E4N71B, JM600 Models)—Install the brake band, the band strut and the servo assembly. Pre-lubricate the servo seals before installation.

—————— CAUTION ——————
*Do not damage the servo "O" rings during their installation.*

23. Install the servo cover and torque the retaining bolts 3.6-5.1 ft. lbs. (5-7 N•m).

24. Finger tighten the servo piston stem enough to prevent the band and strut from dropping out of place.

NOTE: Do not adjust the band as yet.

25. Lubricate the bearing race and thrust washer, place them onto the drum support, if not previously done.

26. (L3N71B models)—Install the gasket on the oil pump and retain it with petroleum jelly. Align the pump to the transmission case and install two retaining bolts temporarily.

27. Adjust the brake band by torquing the piston stem to the specified torque of 9-11 ft. lbs. (12-15 N•m). Back the piston stem off two complete turns and secure the stem with the lock nut. Torque the nut to 11-29 ft. lbs. (15-39 N•m).

NOTE: Perform a final air check of the assembled components to verify tightness of bolts and to check against seal damage during the assembly.

28. (L4N71B, E4N71B, JM600 models)—Coat the drum support gasket with petroleum jelly and install on the drum support. Coat the drum support "O" ring with A/T fluid. Align the drum support with the O.D. case to the transmission case and install.

—————— CAUTION ——————
*Be sure the drum support and O.D. case has been centered properly before installation.*

29. Install two converter housing retaining bolts temporarily to hold O.D. case.

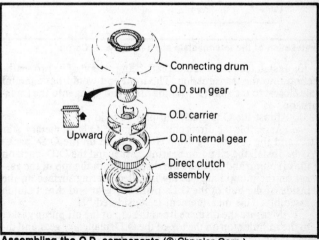

Assembling the O.D. components (© Chrysler Corp.)

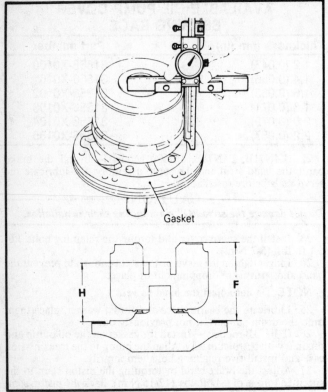

Measuring for dimension "H" and "F" (© Chrysler Corp.)

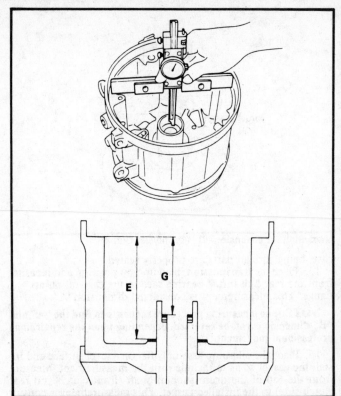

Measuring for dimension "E" and "G" (© Chrysler Corp.)

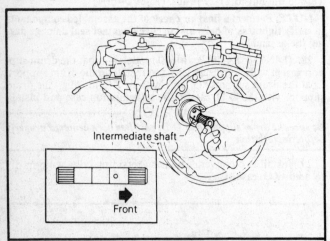

Installation of the intermediate shaft (© Chrysler Corp.)

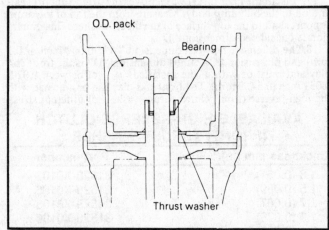

Location of the thrust bearing and washer on the O.D. pack
(© Chrysler Corp.)

30. Install the intermediate shaft, being careful of its proper direction into the transmission. The front end would have the oil hole closest to the splines, with the other end going into the transmission.

31. Adjust the O.D. pack end play as follows;

a. Assemble the direct clutch assembly, O.D. planetary gear set and the connecting drum. Install them on the O.D. pack.

b. Install the oil pump bearing, gasket and the O.D. pack on the oil pump and measure the distance from the top of the gasket on the pump flange to the installed bearing surface on the inside of the hub of the O.D. planetary gear and direct clutch assembly. This measurement is considered "H".

c. Measure the distance from the top of the oil pump gasket to the middle stop on the top of the O.D. planetary gear and direct clutch assembly. This measurement is considered "F".

d. Position the drum support so the front is upward and attach the thrust washer and needle bearing to the drum support and O.D. case.

e. Measure the distance from the outer flange surface of the O.D. case to the top of the O.D. case. This distance is considered "E".

f. Measure the distance from the outer flange surface of the O.D. case to the top of the needle bearing in the drum support. This measurement is considered "G".

g. The difference between the dimension "E" (0.004 inch or 0.1 mm) and "F" is the O.D. pack end play and must be between 0.020-0.031 inch (0.5-0.8 mm).

h. The O.D. pack end play can be adjusted with selective thrust washers, which are identified in the following chart.

## AVAILABLE O.D. THRUST WASHER

| Thickness mm (in) | Part number |
|---|---|
| 1.5 (0.059) | 31528-X0106 |
| 1.7 (0.067) | 31528-X0105 |
| 1.9 (0.075) | 31528-X0100 |
| 2.1 (0.083) | 31528-X0101 |
| 2.3 (0.091) | 31528-X0102 |
| 2.5 (0.098) | 31528-X0103 |
| 2.7 (0.106) | 31528-X0104 |

**NOTE: The O.D. pack selective washers are the same as used in the front clutch assembly.**

32. The O.D. total end play dimension is found by determining the difference between "G" (0.004 or 0.1 mm) and the "H" dimensions. The total end play must be between 0.0098-0.0197 inch (0.25-0.50 mm).

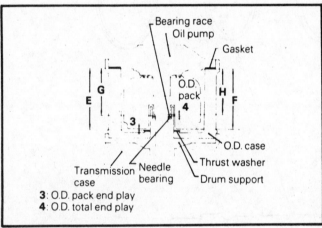

**O.D. pack end play** (© Chrysler Corp.)

33. Should the resulting measured tolerance not be within specifications, selected bearing races can be determined for use from the following chart.

## AVAILABLE O.D. BEARING RACES

| Thickness mm (in) | Part number |
|---|---|
| 1.2 (0.047) | 31556-X0100 |
| 1.4 (0.055) | 31556-X0101 |
| 1.6 (0.063) | 31556-X0102 |
| 1.8 (0.071) | 31556-X0103 |
| 2.0 (0.079) | 31556-X0104 |
| 2.2 (0.087) | 31556-X0105 |

34. Adjust the front band, making sure the band strut is positioned correctly. Torque the piston stem to 9-11 ft. lbs. (12-15 N•m). Back off the stem two full turns and tighten the stem lock nut to 11-29 ft. lbs. (15-39 N•m).

35. Lubricate the O.D. servo "O" rings with AT fluid and install the brake band, band strut and the O.D. band servo assembly.

36. Lubricate the seal ring of the direct clutch and install the O.D. bearing and race. Install the O.D. thrust washer and the O.D. pack on the drum support. Be sure the brake band strut is correctly installed.

37. Lubricate the "O" ring of the oil pump. Install the needle bearing and race. Position the oil pump and install.

---
**CAUTION**

*Before installing the oil pump housing and oil pump on the O.D. case, make certain the parts are properly centered.*
---

38. Adjust the O.D. brake band, making sure the band strut is properly positioned. Torque the piston stem to 5.1-7.2 ft. lbs. (7-10 N•m). Back off the piston stem two full turns and tighten the lock nut to 11-29 ft. lbs. (15-39 N•m).

39. Using an air gun, test the operation of the O.D. band servo.

40. Install the accumulator spring, piston, plug and the snap ring.

41. Remove the two bolts used to temporarily tighten the O.D. case. Apply sealant to the sealing surfaces of the converter housing at the bolt locations and install the converter housing on the O.D. case. Tighten the converter housing retaining bolts to specifications.

42. Install the input shaft into position.

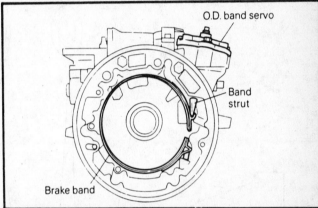

**O.D. band and servo assembly** (© Chrysler Corp.)

43. Perform an air check of the transmission assembled components before the installation of the valve body. Be sure the parking pawl, pin, spring and washer are correctly assembled.

44. Install the rear extension assembly and torque the retaining bolts to specifications.

45. Align the manual valve with the selector pin and install the valve body. Install the three sized retaining bolts in their proper locations. Torque the valve body retaining bolts to 4.0-5.4 ft. lbs. (5.4-7.4 N•m).

**NOTE: Be sure the manual control valve can be moved in all its positions.**

46. (L3N71B models) Check the pump to transmission case alignment and install the converter housing. Torque the retaining bolts 33-40 ft. lbs. (44-54 N•m).

47. (All Models) Before installing the vacuum diaphragm, measure the depth of the hole into which it is to be inserted. This measurement determines the correct rod length to be used with the diaphragm unit to ensure proper performance.

## VACUUM DIAPHRAGM ROD SELECTION

| Measured depth "L" mm (in) | Rod length mm (in) | Part number |
|---|---|---|
| Under 25.55 (1.0059) | 29.0 (1.142) | 31932 X0103 |
| 25.65-26.05 (1.0098-1.0256) | 29.5 (1.161) | 31932 X0104 |
| 26.15-26.55 (1.0295-1.0453) | 30.0 (1.181) | 31932 X0100 |
| 26.65-27.05 (1.0492-1.0650) | 30.5 (1.201) | 31932 X0102 |
| Over 27.15 (1.0689) | 31.0 (1.220) | 31932 X0101 |

48. Install the vacuum diaphragm with the correct length rod.

---
**CAUTION**

*Do not allow the vacuum diaphragm rod to interfere with the side plate of the valve body.*
---

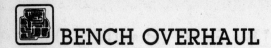
49. Install the downshift solenoid, being sure of its operation.

50. (L4N71B, E4N71B, JM600 models) Install the O.D. solenoid, the O.D. cancel solenoid, the lock-up solenoid, temperature sensing unit and the O.D. indicator switch.

51. (All models) Install the inhibitor switch and check for its proper operation in each gear position.

52. Install the oil pan using a new gasket. Tighten the retaining bolts to 3.6-5.1 ft. lbs. (5-7 N•m).

53. (L4N71B models) Install the governor tube and secure properly to the transmission case.

54. Install the converter, being sure the converter lugs are engaged with the oil pump drive gear.

**NOTE: The converter can be filled with fluid before installation.**

55. The transmission is ready for installation into the vehicle.

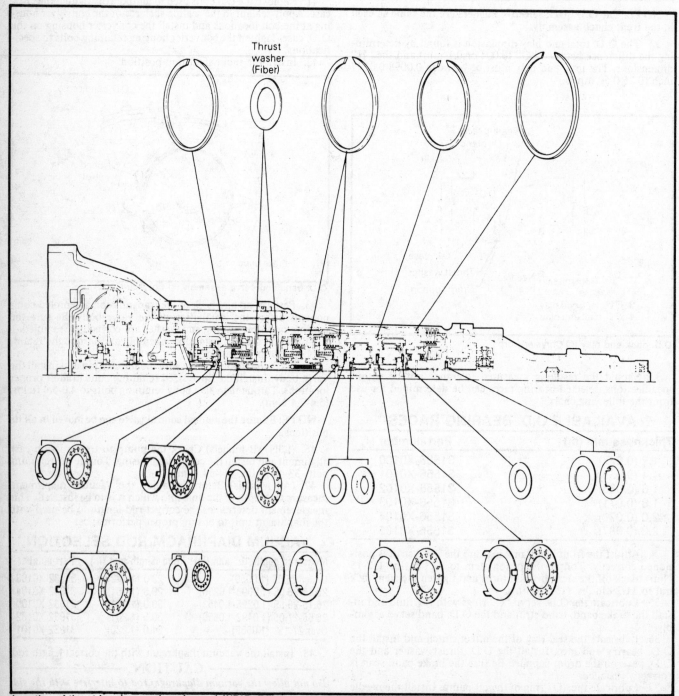

Location of thrust bearings and washers—L4N71B, E4N71B and JM600 models (© Chrysler Corp.)

# S SPECIFICATIONS

## TORQUE SPECIFICATIONS

| Component part | N•m | kg-m | ft-lb | Component part | N•m | kg-m | ft-lb |
|---|---|---|---|---|---|---|---|
| Transmission case to converter housing | 44-54 | 4.5-5.5 | 33-40 | Governor valve body to oil distributor | 5-7 | 0.5-0.7 | 3.6-5.1 |
| Transmission case to rear extension | 20-25 | 2.0-2.5 | 14-18 | Oil pump housing to oil pump cover | 6-8 | 0.6-0.8 | 4.3-5.8 |
| Oil pan to transmission case | 5-7 | 0.5-0.7 | 3.6-5.1 | Inhibitor switch to transmission case | 5-7 | 0.5-0.7 | 3.6-5.1 |
| 2nd servo piston retainer to transmission case | 7-9 | 0.7-0.9 | 5.1-6.5 | Drive plate to Crankshaft | 137-157 | 14.0-16.0 | 101-116 |
| 2nd piston stem (when adjusting band brake) ① | 12-15 | 1.2-1.5 | 9-11 | Drive plate to torque converter | 39-49 | 4.0-5.0 | 29-36 |
| 2nd piston stem lock nut | 15-39 | 1.5-4.0 | 11-29 | Converter housing to engine | 39-49 | 4.0-5.0 | 29-36 |
| Control valve body to transmission case | 5.4-7.4 | 0.55-0.75 | 4.0-5.4 | Rear mounting bracket to transmission | 31-42 | 3.2-4.3 | 23-31 |
| Lower valve body to upper valve body | 2.5-3.4 | 0.25-0.35 | 1.8-2.5 | Rear mounting bracket to rear insulator | 31-42 | 3.2-4.3 | 23-31 |
| O.D. servo piston retainer to O.D. case | 10-15 | 1.0-1.5 | 7-11 | Rear mounting member | 59-78 | 6.0-8.0 | 43-58 |
| O.D. stem (when adjusting band brake) | 7-10 | 0.7-1.0 | 5.1-7.2 | Gussets to transmission and engine | 25-35 | 2.6-3.6 | 19-26 |
| O.D. stem lock nut | 15-39 | 1.5-4.0 | 11-29 | Manual shaft lock nut | 29-39 | 3.0-4.0 | 22-29 |
| Side plate to control valve body | 2.5-3.4 | 0.25-0.35 | 1.8-2.5 | Oil cooler pipe to transmission case | 29-49 | 3.0-5.0 | 22-36 |
| Nut for control valve reamer bolt | 5-7 | 0.5-0.7 | 3.6-5.1 | Drum support to O.D. case | 7-9 | 0.7-0.9 | 5.1-6.5 |
| Oil strainer to lower valve body | 3-4 | 0.3-0.4 | 2.2-2.9 | | | | |

① Turn back two turns after tightening.

# SPECIAL TOOLS

| Tool number (Kent-Moore No.) | Tool name | |
|---|---|---|
| ST25420001 (J26063) (ST25420000) (J26063) | Clutch spring compressor |  |
| ST25580001 (J25719) | Oil pump assembling gauge | |
| ST2505S001 (J25695) | Oil pressure gauge set | |

# INDEX

# JATCO
# RN3F01A • RL3F01A
# Automatic Transaxle

## APPLICATIONS

**RN3F01A**
1982 Datsun 310

**RL3F01A**
1983-84 Nissan Stanza
1982-83 Nissan Sentra
1983-84 Nissan Pulsar, NX

## GENERAL DESCRIPTION

Both the RL3F01A and RN3F01A transaxle models are fully automatic units, consisting of two planetary gear sets, two multiple disc clutches, multiple disc brake, brake band and a one-way clutch. The RL3F01A transaxle model utilizes a lock-up clutch along with the usual three element torque converter used in both models. A hydraulic control system is used to operate the friction elements and automatic shift controls.

### Transaxle and Converter Identification

#### TRANSAXLE

The identification label is attached to the transaxle on the upper right face of the transaxle case. The first figure denotes the transaxle model with "O" representing "automatic". The second figure represents the month of production. 1 through 9 represents

January through September respectively, while X, Y, and Z represent the months of October, November and December respectively. The following five digits of the number designation representing the serial production number for the month of assembly.

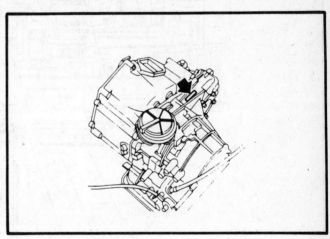

**Location of transaxle identification number label**
(© Nissan Motor Co. of USA)

### TORQUE CONVERTER

The torque converters are coded by the manufacturer and sold through varied parts networks. Specific part numbers are used to identify the converters and to allow proper match-up to the transaxle assembly. When replacing a converter, verify the replacement unit is the same as the one originally used with the engine/transaxle combination. Lock-up and non-lock-up torque converters cannot be interchanged.

### Transmission Metric Fasteners

Metric bolt sizes and thread pitches are used for all fasteners on the Jatco transaxles. The metric fastener dimensions are close to the dimensions of the familiar inch system fasteners, and for this reason, replacement fasteners must have the same measurement and strength as those removed.

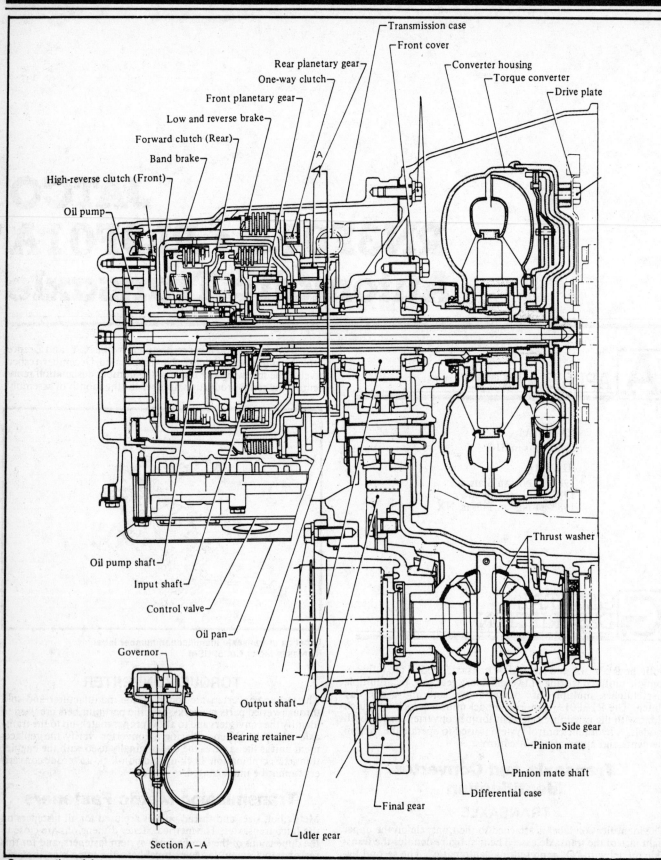

Rear planetary gear
One-way clutch
Front planetary gear
Low and reverse brake
Forward clutch (Rear)
Band brake
High-reverse clutch (Front)
Oil pump

Transmission case
Front cover
Converter housing
Torque converter
Drive plate

A

Oil pump shaft
Input shaft
Control valve
Oil pan
Governor

Output shaft
Bearing retainer

Section A–A

Idler gear
Final gear

Thrust washer

Side gear
Pinion mate
Pinion mate shaft
Differential case

**Cross section of Jatco automatic transaxle RL3F01A model with lock-up torque converter (© Nissan Motor Co. of USA)**

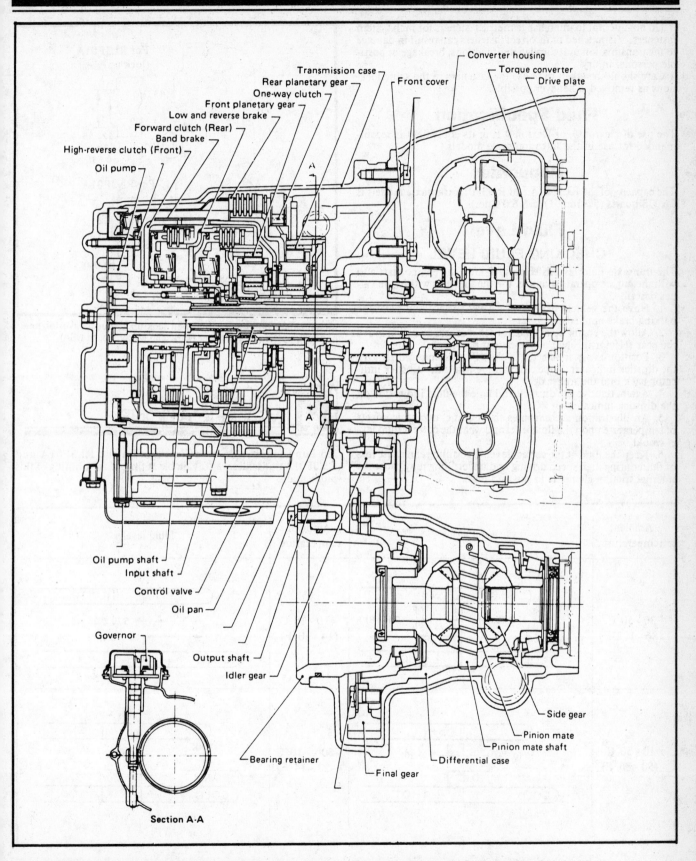

Cross section of Jatco automatic transaxle RN3F01A model without lock-up torque converter (© Nissan Motor Co. of USA)

Do not attempt to interchange metric fasteners for inch system fasteners. Mismatched or incorrect fasteners can result in damage to the transmission unit through malfunctions, breakage or possible personal injury.

Care should be taken to re-use the fasteners in the same locations as removed, whenever possible.

## Fluid Specification

The use of Dexron®, or Dexron® II or its equivalent is recommended for use in the Jatco transaxle models.

## Capacities

The capacity of the RL3F01A and RN3F01A transaxle models is 6⅜ US quarts (5¼ Imp. Quart, 6.0 Liter).

## Fluid Level

### CHECKING FLUID LEVEL

The transaxle fluid level is correct, if, after the engine start and with the engine operating at idle, the fluid level is within the values described.

1. Have the vehicle parked on a level surface and have the parking brake applied.

2. Allow the engine to operate for ten minutes and then move the gear selector through all the detent positions.

3. Position the gear selector in the "P" position and remove the dipstick indicator. Wipe clean and re-insert the dipstick indicator back into the transaxle.

4. Again, remove the dipstick and note the fluid indication on the dipstick indicator.

5. An illustration accompanies this outline, depicting effects of temperature upon the fluid level and what the correct fluid level would be.

6. Keep the fluid at the correct level. Overfilling can cause loss of fluid during high speed driving and underfilling may cause the internal friction elements to slip and burn.

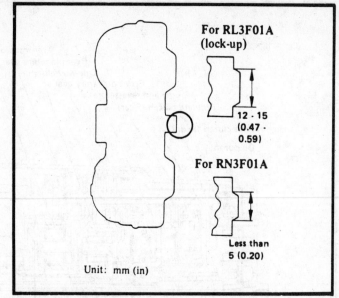

For RL3F01A (lock-up)

12 - 15 (0.47 - 0.59)

For RN3F01A

Less than 5 (0.20)

Unit: mm (in)

**Identification differences between lock-up torque converter and non-lock-up torque converter** (© Nissan Motor Co. of USA)

No known transaxle modifications for the RL3F01A and RN3F01A transaxles were available at time of the printing of this publication.

| Ambient temperature | Fluid level | | Ambient temperature | Fluid level |
|---|---|---|---|---|
| 30 - 50°C (86 - 122°F) | Type 1. \|L  H\|  2 (0.08) — 2 (0.08)  Type 2. O.K. COLD HOT | | −10 - 10°C (14 - 50°F) | \|L  H\|  O.K. — 5 (0.20)  20 (0.79)  COLD HOT |
| 10 - 30°C (50 - 86°F) | \|L  H\|  10 (0.39) — 5 (0.20)  O.K. COLD HOT | | −30 - −10°C (−22 - 14°F) | \|L  H\|  O.K. 15 (0.59)  O.K. COLD HOT |

**Temperature affect on fluid level readings** (© Nissan Motor Co. of USA)

**TROUBLE DIAGNOSIS**

## CLUTCH AND BAND APPLICATION CHART
### RL3F01A and RN4F01A Automatic Transaxles

| Range | | High-reverse clutch (Front) | Forward clutch (Rear) | Low & reverse brake | Lock-up | Band servo Operation | Band servo Release | One-way clutch | Parking pawl |
|---|---|---|---|---|---|---|---|---|---|
| Park | | | | | | | | | on |
| Reverse | | on | | on | | | | | |
| Neutral | | | | | | | | | |
| Drive | $D_1$ Low | | on | | | | | on | |
| | $D_2$ Second | | on | | | on | | | |
| | $D_3$ Top (3rd) | on | on | | on | (on) | on | | |
| 2 | $2_1$ Low | | on | | | | | on | |
| | $2_2$ Second | | on | | | on | | | |
| 1 | $1_1$ Low | | on | on | | | | on | |
| | $1_1$ Second | | on | | | on | | | |

The low & reverse brake is applied in "$1_1$" range to prevent free wheeling when coasting and allow engine braking.

## CHILTON'S THREE "C's" TRANSAXLE DIAGNOSIS CHART
### RL3F01A, RN3F01A Jatco Transaxles

| Condition | Cause | Correction |
|---|---|---|
| Engine does not start in "N", "P" ranges | a) Range select cable<br>b) Neutral safety switch<br>c) Ignition switch and starter motor | a) Adjust cable<br>b) Adjust or replace<br>c) Repair or replace |
| Engine starts in range other than "N" and "P" | a) Range select cable<br>b) Neutral safety switch | a) Adjust cable<br>b) Adjust or replace |
| Sharp shock shifting from "N" to "D" range | a) Misadjusted throttle cable<br>b) High engine idle<br>c) High line pressure control<br><br>d) Manual valve<br><br>e) Forward (rear) clutch | a) Adjust throttle linkage<br>b) Adjust the engine idle<br>c) Adjust or locate malfunction causing high line pressure<br>d) Adjust selector cable or renew manual control valve<br>e) Renew clutch as required |
| Vehicle will not move in "D" range (but moves in "2", "1" and "R" ranges) | a) Range select cable<br>b) Main line pressure<br><br>c) Manual control valve<br><br>d) One way clutch of transmission | a) Adjust cable<br>b) Correct main line pressure or passage per air test<br>c) Adjust range select renew valve<br>d) Renew clutch |

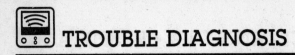

## CHILTON'S THREE "C's" TRANSAXLE DIAGNOSIS CHART
### RL3F01A, RN3F01A Jatco Transaxles

| Condition | Cause | Correction |
|---|---|---|
| Vehicle will not move in "D", "1" or "2" ranges but moves in "R" range Clutch slips, very poor acceleration | a) Oil level<br>b) Range select cable<br>c) Main line pressure<br><br>d) Manual control valve.<br><br>e) Leakage at fluid passage<br>f) Engine adjustment and brake defects<br>g) Forward (rear) Clutch<br>h) High-reverse (front) clutch | a) Add if needed<br>b) Adjust cable<br>c) Correct main line pressure or passage per air test<br>d) Adjust range select cable/renew valve<br>e) Correct as per air test<br>f) Repair as needed<br><br>g) Renew clutch as required<br>h) Renew clutch as required |
| Vehicle will not move in "R" range (but moves in "D", "2" and "1" ranges). Clutch slips, very poor acceleration | a) Oil level<br>b) Range select cable<br>c) Throttle valve pressure<br><br>d) Manual control valve<br><br>e) Leakage of passage<br>f) Forward (rear) clutch<br>g) High-reverse (front) clutch<br>h) Low and Reverse brake<br><br>i) High-reverse (front) clutch check ball | a) Add if needed<br>b) Adjust cable<br>c) Correct throttle valve or passage per air test<br>d) Adjust range select cable/renew valve<br>e) Correct as per air test<br>f) Renew clutch as required<br>g) Renew clutch as required<br>h) Renew low and reverse brake as required<br>i) Test and replace check ball as required |
| Vehicle will not move in any range | a) Oil level<br>b) Range select cable<br>c) Main line pressure or pressure loss<br>d) Manual control valve<br><br>e) Leakage of fluid passage<br>f) Oil pump<br>g) Parking linkage<br>h) Forward (rear) clutch | a) Add if needed<br>b) Adjust cable<br>c) Correct main line pressure or passage per air test<br>d) Adjust range select cable/renew valve<br>e) Correct as per air test<br>f) Repair or renew<br>g) Repair or renew<br>h) Renew clutch as required |
| Clutches or brakes slip somewhat in starting to move | a) Oil level<br>b) Range select cable<br>c) Throttle valve cable pressure<br>d) Manual control valve<br><br>e) Leakage of fluid passage<br>f) Oil pump<br>g) Main line pressure | a) Add if needed<br>b) Adjust cable<br>c) Correct throttle valve or passage per air test<br>d) Adjust range select cable/renew valve<br>e) Correct as per air test<br>f) Repair or renew<br>g) Correct main line pressure |
| Vehicle moves in "N" range | a) Range select cable<br>b) Manual control valve<br><br>c) Forward (rear) clutch | a) Adjust cable<br>b) Adjust range select cable/renew valve<br>c) Renew clutch as required |
| Excessive creep | a) High engine idle rpm | a) Adjust cable |
| Failure to change gear from "1st" to "2nd" | a) Range cable<br>b) Throttle cable misadjusted<br>c) Detent valve | a) Adjust cable<br>b) Adjust throttle cable<br>c) Repair or renew detent valve |

## CHILTON'S THREE "C's" TRANSAXLE DIAGNOSIS CHART
### RL3F01A, RN3F01A Jatco Transaxles

| Condition | Cause | Correction |
|---|---|---|
| Failure to change gear from "1st" to "2nd" | d) Manual control valve | d) Adjust range select cable/renew valve |
| | e) Band servo | e) Renew band servo |
| | f) Leakage of fluid passage | f) Correct as per air test |
| | g) High-reverse (front) clutch | g) Renew clutch as required |
| | h) Front clutch check (high-reverse) ball | h) Renew clutch check ball |
| | i) band brake | i) Replace band brake |
| | j) Governor valve | j) Governor overhaul or replace as required |
| Failure to change gear from "2nd" to "3rd" | a) Range select cable | a) Adjust cable |
| | b) Throttle cable misadjusted | b) Adjust throttle cable |
| | c) Detent valve | c) Repair or renew detent valve |
| | d) Manual control valve | d) Adjust range select cable/renew valve |
| | e) Governor valve | e) Overhaul governor/renew governor |
| | f) Band servo | f) Renew band servo |
| | g) Leakage of fluid passage | g) Correct as per air test |
| | h) Band brake | h) Renew band brake |
| | i) High-reverse (front) clutch | i) Renew clutch as required |
| | j) High-reverse (front) clutch check ball | j) Renew clutch check ball |
| Gear change directly from "1st" to "3rd" occurs | a) Manual control valve | a) Adjust range select cable/renew valve |
| | b) Governor valve | b) Overhaul governor/renew governor |
| | c) Leakage of fluid passage | c) Correct as per air test |
| | d) Band brake | d) Renew band brake |
| Too sharp shock in change from "1st" to "2nd" | a) Misadjusted throttle cable | a) Adjust throttle cable |
| | b) Manual control valve | b) Adjust range select cable/renew valve |
| | c) Band servo | c) Renew band servo |
| | d) Band brake | d) Renew band brake |
| | e) Engine stall rpm | e) Perform stall test |
| Too sharp shock in change from "2nd" to "3rd" | a) Misadjusted throttle cable | a) Adjust throttle cable |
| | b) Detent valve | b) Repair or renew detent valve |
| | c) Throttle valve pressure | c) Correct throttle valve or passage per air test |
| | d) Manual control valve | d) Adjust range select cable/renew valve |
| | e) Band servo | e) Renew band servo |
| | f) High-reverse (front) clutch | f) Renew clutch as required |
| Almost no shock or slipping in change from "1st" to "2nd" | a) Oil level | a) Add if needed |
| | b) Range select cable | b) Adjust cable |
| | c) Misadjusted throttle cable | c) Adjust throttle cable |
| | d) Low main line pressure | d) Correct main line pressure or passage per air test |
| | e) Manual control valve | e) Adjust range select cable/renew valve |
| | f) Band servo | f) Renew band servo |

## CHILTON'S THREE "C's" TRANSAXLE DIAGNOSIS CHART
### RL3F01A, RN3F01A Jatco Transaxles

| Condition | Cause | Correction |
|---|---|---|
| Almost no shock or engine runaway on "2nd" to "3rd" shift | g) Leakage of fluid passage<br>h) Band brake | g) Correct as per air test<br>h) Renew band brake |
| Almost no shock or engine runaway on "2nd" to "3rd" shift | a) Oil level<br>b) Range select cable<br>c) Misadjusted throttle cable<br>d) Low main line pressure<br><br>e) Manual control valve<br><br>f) Band servo<br>g) Leakage of fluid passage<br>h) High-reverse (front) clutch<br>i) Front clutch check (high-reverse) ball | a) Add if needed<br>b) Adjust cable<br>c) Adjust throttle cable<br>d) Correct main line pressure or passage per air test<br>e) Adjust range select cable/ renew valve<br>f) Renew band servo<br>g) Correct as per air test<br>h) Renew clutch as required<br>i) Renew front clutch check ball |
| Vehicle braked by gear change from "1st" to "2nd" | a) Manual control valve<br><br>b) Front clutch (high-reverse)<br>c) Low and reverse brake<br><br>d) One-way clutch of transaxle | a) Adjust range select cable/renew valve<br>b) Renew front clutch<br>c) Renew low and reverse brake<br>d) Renew one-way clutch of transaxle |
| Vehicle braked by gear change from "2nd" to "3rd" | a) Manual control valve<br><br>b) Band servo<br>c) Brake band | a) Adjust range select cable<br>b) Renew band servo<br>c) Renew brake band |
| Failure to change from "3rd" to "2nd" | a) Misadjusted throttle cable<br>b) Manual control valve<br><br>c) Governor valve<br><br>d) Band servo<br>e) Leakage of fluid pressure passage<br>f) Front clutch (high-reverse)<br>g) Band brake | a) Adjust throttle cable<br>b) Adjust range select cable/renew valve<br>c) Overhaul governor/ renew governor<br>d) Renew band servo<br>e) Correct as per air test<br><br>f) Renew front clutch<br>g) Renew band brake |
| Transaxle overheats | a) Oil level<br>b) Band servo<br>c) Main line pressure<br><br>d) Restricted or no rear lubrication<br>e) Manual control valve<br><br>f) Leakage of fluid pressure passage<br>g) Front clutch (high-reverse)<br>h) Band brake<br>i) Low and reverse brake<br><br>j) Engine stall rpm | a) Add if needed<br>b) Renew band servo<br>c) Correct main line pressure or passage per air test<br>d) Check passages<br><br>e) Adjust range select cable/renew valve<br>f) Correct as per air test<br><br>g) Renew front clutch<br>h) Renew band brake<br>i) Renew low and reverse brake<br>j) Locate malfunction and correct |

## CHILTON'S THREE "C's" TRANSAXLE DIAGNOSIS CHART
### RL3F01A, RN3F01A Jatco Transaxles

| Condition | Cause | Correction |
| --- | --- | --- |
| Transaxle overheats | k) Oil Pump<br>l) Torque converter<br>m) Planetary gears | k) Renew oil pump<br>l) Renew torque converter<br>m) Renew planetary gears |
| Transaxle noise in "P" and "N" ranges | a) Oil level<br>b) Main line pressure<br><br><br>c) Oil pump | a) Add if needed<br>b) Correct main line pressure or passage per air test test<br>c) Renew oil pump |
| Transaxle noise in "D", "2", "1" and "R" ranges | a) Oil level<br>b) Main line pressure<br><br><br>c) Rear clutch (forward)<br>d) Oil pump<br>e) One-way clutch of transaxle<br>f) Planetary gear | a) Add if needed<br>b) Correct main line pressure or passage per air test test<br>c) Renew rear clutch<br>d) Renew oil pump<br>e) Renew one-way clutch of transaxle<br>f) Renew planetary gear |
| Failure to change gear from "2nd" to "1st" or from "3rd" to "1st" | a) Misadjusted throttle cable<br>b) Manual control valve<br><br>c) Governor valve<br><br>d) Band servo<br>e) Band brake<br>f) Leakage of fluid pressure passage<br>g) One-way clutch of transaxle | a) Adjust throttle cable<br>b) Adjust range select cable/renew valve<br>c) Overhaul governor/ renew governor<br>d) Renew band servo<br>e) Renew band brake<br>f) Correct as per air test<br>g) Renew one-way clutch of transaxle |
| Races extremely or slips in changing from "3rd" to "2nd" | a) Misadjusted throttle cable<br>b) Main line pressure<br><br>c) Manual control valve<br><br>d) Band servo<br>e) Leakage of fluid pressure passage<br>f) Front clutch (high-reverse) | a) Adjust throttle cable<br>b) Correct main line pressure or passage as per air test<br>c) Adjust range select cable/renew valve<br>d) Renew band servo<br>e) Correct as per air test<br><br>f) Renew front clutch |
| Failure to change from "3rd" to "2nd" when changing lever into "2" range | a) Range select cable<br>b) Main line pressure<br><br>c) Manual control valve<br><br>d) Band servo<br>e) Band brake<br>f) Leakage of fluid pressure passage | a) Adjust cable<br>b) Correct main line pressure or passage per air test<br>c) Adjust range select cable/renew valve<br>d) Renew band servo<br>e) Renew band brake<br>f) Correct as per air test |
| No shock on change from "1" range to "2nd" range or engine races extremely | a) Oil level<br>b) Range select cable<br>c) Misadjusted throttle cable<br>d) Engine idle rpm<br>e) High stall speed | a) Add if needed<br>b) Adjust cable<br>c) Adjust throttle cable<br>d) Set idle rpm<br>e) Renew band brake |

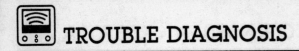

## CHILTON'S THREE "C's" TRANSAXLE DIAGNOSIS CHART
### RL3F01A, RN3F01A Jatco Transaxles

| Condition | Cause | Correction |
|---|---|---|
| No shock on change from "1" range to "2nd" range or engine races extremely | f) Manual control valve | f) Adjust range select cable/renew valve |
| | g) Transmission air check to determine if band servo is working | g) Repair or renew servo |
| | h) Oil pump | h) Repair or renew |
| Failure to shift from "3rd" to "2nd" when shifting lever into "1" range | a) Range select cable | a) Adjust cable |
| | b) Main line pressure | b) Correct main line pressure or passage per air test |
| | c) Manual control valve | c) Adjust range select cable/renew valve |
| | d) Governor valve | d) Overhaul governor/ renew governor |
| | e) Band servo | e) Renew band servo |
| | f) Leakage of fluid pressure passage | f) Correct as per air test |
| | g) High-reverse (front) clutch | g) Renew clutch as required |
| No engine braking in range "1" | a) Range select cable | a) Adjust cable |
| | b) Main line pressure | b) Correct main line pressure or passage per air test |
| | c) Manual control valve | c) Adjust range select cable/renew valve |
| | d) Leakage of fluid pressure passage | d) Correct as per air test |
| | e) Low and reverse brake | e) Renew low and reverse brake |
| Gear change from 2nd to 3rd in "2" range | a) Range select cable | a) Adjust cable |
| | b) Main line pressure | b) Correct main line pressure |
| | c) Manual valve | c) Adjust range select linkage/ renew valve |
| | d) Band servo | d) Renew band servo |
| | e) Fluid quality | e) Correct fluid quality and refill transaxle |
| | f) Band brake | f) Correct or renew band brake |
| | g) Leakage fluid pressure passage | g) Correct as per air test |
| Gear change from "1st" to "2nd" or from "2nd" to "3rd" in "1" range | a) Range select cable | a) Adjust cable |
| | b) Manual control valve | b) Adjust range select linkage/renew valve |
| | c) Leakage of fluid pressure passage | c) Correct as per air test |
| Does not change from "2nd" to "1st" in "1" range | a) Oil level | a) Add if needed |
| | b) Range select cable | b) Adjust cable |
| | c) Manual control valve | c) Adjust range select cable/renew valve |
| | d) Governor valve | d) Overhaul governor/ renew governor |
| | e) Band servo | e) Renew band servo |
| | f) Leakage of fluid pressure passage | f) Correct as per air test |
| | g) Low and reverse brake | g) Renew low and reverse brake |

## CHILTON'S THREE "C's" TRANSAXLE DIAGNOSIS CHART
### RL3F01A, RN3F01A Jatco Transaxles

| Condition | Cause | Correction |
|---|---|---|
| Large shock in changing from "2nd" to "1st" in "1" range | a) Misadjusted throttle cable<br>b) High engine stall rpm<br>c) Manual control valve<br><br>d) Low and reverse brake | a) Adjust throttle cable<br>b) Locate malfunction and correct<br>c) Adjust range select cable/renew valve<br>d) Renew low and reverse brake |
| Oil shoots out during operation. While smoke from exhaust during operation | a) Oil level<br>b) Misadjusted throttle cable<br>c) Main line pressure<br><br>d) Restricted or no rear lubrication<br>e) Manual control valve<br><br>f) Leakage of fluid pressure passage<br>g) Engine stall rpm<br>h) Band brake<br>i) Low and reverse brake<br><br>j) Oil pump<br>k) One-way clutch torque converter<br>l) Planetary gear | a) Add if needed<br>b) Adjust throttle cable<br>c) Correct main line pressure or passage per air test<br>d) Check passages<br><br>e) Adjust range select cable/renew valve<br>f) Correct as per air test<br><br>g) Locate malfunction and correct<br>h) Renew band brake<br>i) Renew low and reverse brake<br>j) Renew oil pump<br>k) Renew one-way clutch torque converter<br>l) Renew planetary gear |
| Vehicle moves changing into "P" range or parking gear does not disengage when shifted out of "P" range | a) Range select linkage<br>b) Parking linkage | a) Adjust linkage<br>b) Repair parking linkage |

## CHILTON'S THREE "C's" DIAGNOSIS CHART
### Jatco RL3F01A With Lock-up Torque Converter

| Condition | Cause | Correction |
|---|---|---|
| Torque converter not locked-up | a) Governor<br>b) Line pressure malfunctions<br><br>c) "O"-ring on input shaft<br>d) Torque converter<br>e) Speed cut valve<br>f) Lock-up control valve<br><br>g) Oil pump | a) Repair or renew governor<br>b) Locate malfunction and adjust line pressure<br>c) Renew "O" ring<br>d) Renew torque converter<br>e) Repair or renew speed cut valve<br>f) Repair or renew lock-up control valve<br>g) Repair or renew oil pump |
| Lock-up Piston slips | a) Line pressure malfunction<br><br>b) "O" ring on input shaft<br>c) Torque converter<br>d) Oil pump | a) Locate malfunction and adjust line pressure<br>b) Renew "O" ring<br>c) Renew torque converter<br>d) Repair of renew oil pump |

## CHILTON'S THREE "C's" DIAGNOSIS CHART
### Jatco RL3F01A With Lock-up Torque Converter

| Condition | Cause | Correction |
|---|---|---|
| Lock-up point is extremely high or low | a) Governor<br>b) Speed cut valve<br>c) Lock-up control valve | a) Repair or renew governor<br>b) Repair or renew speed cut valve<br>c) Repair or renew lock-up control valve |
| Engine is stopped in "R", "D", "2" and "L" range | a) Torque converter<br>b) Lock-up control valve | a) Renew torque converter<br>b) Repair or renew lock-up control valve |
| Transmission overheats | a) Line pressure malfunction<br>b) "O" ring on input shaft<br>c) Torque converter<br>d) Oil pump | a) Locate malfunction and adjust line pressure<br>b) Renew "O" ring<br>c) Renew torque converter<br>d) Repair or renew oil pump |

# Hydraulic Control System

Hydraulic pressure, clutch and band applications control the changing of gear ratios in the automatic transaxle. The clutches and the band are applied by the force of the fluid pressure, controlled by a system of valves, springs and other control mechanisms. Some of the controlling mechanisms and components are as follows:

1. Screen or filter to clean foreign material from the fluid supply before the fluid is drawn into the pump.
2. The oil pump supplies fluid pressure to the transaxle components.
3. Fluid pressure regulator valve is used to control main line pressure to the transaxle components.
4. A converter pressure relief valve is used to prevent fluid pressure build up in the torque converter.
5. The torque converter is used as a fluid coupling and torque multiplier between the engine and the transaxle gearing.
6. The forward (rear) clutch is applied in all forward gears.
7. The Low and reverse brake is applied in Reverse, and range "1" low gear.
8. The High-reverse (front) clutch is applied in reverse and the high gears.
9. The rear lubrication passages lubricate the rear transaxle components.
10. The front lubrication passages lubricate the front transaxle components.
11. The cooler system removes heat from the A/T fluid by having the fluid routed through a cooler unit within the vehicle's cooling system radiator and back into the transaxle.
12. Varied anti-drain back valves are used to prevent loss of fluid in the hydraulic circuits when the engine is stopped.
13. A throttle control valve regulates throttle pressure in relation to the position of the accelerator pedal through the use of a cable assembly.
14. The brake band is applied in the second speed, with the selector lever in the "D", "2" or "1" position. The brake band is pressure released when the transmission is in the third speed, "D" position.
15. Pressure modifier valve uses throttle pressure, controlled by governor pressure, to modify the main line pressure from the regulator valve. This modifies the harsh shifting caused by excessive pump pressure.
16. Timing valves are used to control shifting under heavy load conditions.

17. The governor circuit provides road speed signals to the transaxle hydraulic control system.
18. Throttle cable is connected to the valve body and along with controlling the T.V. pressure, upon wide open throttle position of the accelerator, the detent valve is moved to control forced downshifting of the transaxle.
19. The manual control valve is used to direct fluid pressure to the varied units to control the range selection of gearing. The control valve is connected mechanically to the shift lever, located within the drivers compartment.
20. The shift valves control the up and down shifting of the transaxle, from one ratio to another.
21. When the transaxle is equipped with the lock-up torque converter, Lock-up control valve, speed cut valve and fail safe valves are used to control the on and off of the converter clutch.

## MAJOR HYDRAULIC COMPONENTS

1. The main line control pressure system supplies fluid pressure to the transaxle and converter when the engine is operating.
2. Converter and lubrication systems regulates the converter fluid pressure, provides gear train lubrication and fluid cooling while the transaxle is operating.
3. Forward clutch pressure and governor pressure systems applies the forward clutch, which is applied in all forward speeds and applies pressure to the governor valve. The governor valve supplies regulated pressure to the rear side of the shift valves, dependent upon the road speed of the vehicle.
4. The low and reverse brake system applies the low and reverse brake in the "L" and "R" selector lever positions and locks out the second and third speed gears by directing pressure to the appropriate valves to prevent them from shifting.
5. The first gear lockout system allows the transaxle valve body to shift directly to the second speed and locks out the 1st and 3rd gears.
6. The brake band servo apply system applies the servo to hold the band to the surface of the reverse and high clutch cylinder.
7. Reverse pressure booster system increased the control or line pressure and applies the reverse and high clutch in the reverse range.
8. The shift valve train system applies and exhausts the fluid pressures to the servo and clutch assemblies for upshifts and downshifts automatically on demand.
9. The kickdown system forces downshift by overriding the governor/throttle valve control of the shift valves.

Oil Pressure Circuit Diagram - "N" range (Neutral)

Note: Marked X are drain.

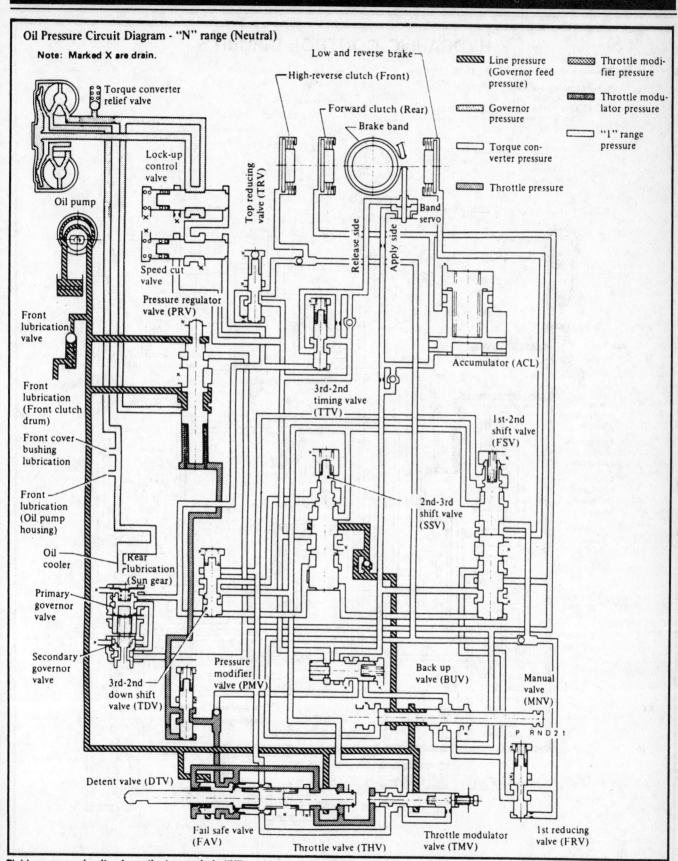

**Fluid pressure circuit schematic, transaxle in "N" position and equipped with lock-up torque converter (© Nissan Motor Co. of USA)**

# HYDRAULIC CONTROL CIRCUITS

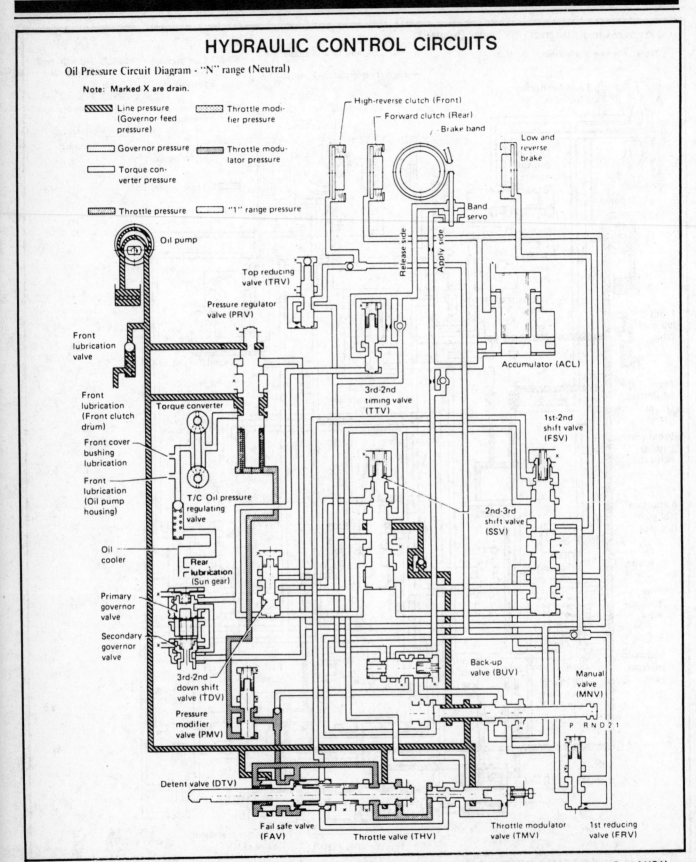

Oil Pressure Circuit Diagram - "N" range (Neutral)

Note: Marked X are drain.

Fluid pressure circuit schematic, transaxle in "N" position and not equipped with lock-up torque converter (© Nissan Motor Co. of USA)

10. The governor system provides a varying pressure proportional to the vehicle speed and throttle opening to help control the timing qualities of the transaxle shifts.

11. The throttle pressure (T.V.) system provides a varying pressure proportional to throttle opening and engine load to help control the timing qualities of the transaxle shifts.

12. The throttle modifier system and the pressure modifier systems compensates and adjust control pressure to insure smoother shifting under the various loads and throttle openings of the engine.

## Diagnosis Testing

### OIL PRESSURE CIRCUITS

Control (line) pressure is a regulated main line pressure, developed by the operation of the front pump. It is directed to the main regulator valve, where predetermined spring pressure automatically moves the regulator valve to control the pressure of the oil at a predetermined rate, by opening the valve and exhausting excessive pressured oil back into the sump and holding the valve closed to build up pressure when needed.

Therefore, it is most important during the diagnosis phase to test main line control pressure to determine if high or low pressure exists. Do not attempt to adjust a pressure regulator valve spring to obtain more or less control pressure. Internal transmission damage may result.

The main valve is the controlling agent of the transmission, which directs oil pressure to separate passages used to control the valve train.

### CONTROL PRESSURE SYSTEM TESTS

Control pressure tests should be performed whenever slippage, delay or harshness is felt in the shifting of the transmission. Throttle pressure changes can cause these problems also, but are generated from the control pressures and therefore reflect any problems arising from the control pressure system.

The control pressure is first checked in all ranges without any throttle pressure input, and then checked as the throttle pressure is increased.

The control pressure tests should define differences between mechanical or hydraulic failures of the transmission.

### PRESSURE PORTS

**RN3F01A**

The non-converter lock-up equipped transaxles are provided with three pressure ports on the transaxle case. The port identification is as follows:
1. Line pressure, high-reverse (front) clutch
2. Line pressure, forward (rear) clutch
3. Governor pressure

**RL3F01A**

The lock-up converter equipped transaxles are provided with four pressure ports on the transaxle case. The port identification is as follows:
1. Line pressure, high-reverse (front) clutch
2. Line pressure, forward (rear) clutch
3. Governor pressure
4. Torque converter lock-up pressure

**Testing Line Pressure**

1. Install a pressure gauge to the line pressure port as follows:
    a. When the selector lever is in the "D", "2" or "1" range, install the pressure gauge to the Forward (rear) clutch pressure port.
    b. When the selector lever is in the "R" range, install the pressure gauge to the high-reverse (front) clutch pressure port.
2. Locate the pressure gauge so it can be seen by the operator.

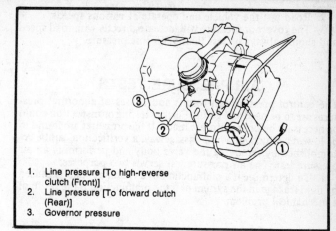

1. Line pressure [To high-reverse clutch (Front)]
2. Line pressure [To forward clutch (Rear)]
3. Governor pressure

**Pressure port locations—RN3F01A transaxle**
(© Nissan Motor Co. of USA)

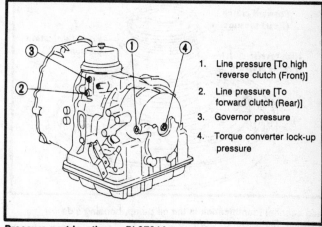

1. Line pressure [To high-reverse clutch (Front)]
2. Line pressure [To forward clutch (Rear)]
3. Governor pressure
4. Torque converter lock-up pressure

**Pressure port locations—RL3F01A transaxle**
(© Nissan Motor Co. of USA)

3. Measure line pressure at idle and at stall test speeds.
4. Road test the vehicle and note the pressure under different throttle and engine load conditions.
5. The key points of pressure testing are as follows:
    a. Look for a steady rise in line pressure as the car speed increases under light engine load.
    b. Pressure drop between shifts should not exceed 14 psi. Excessive leakage could be caused by an internal leak at a servo or clutch seal.
    c. Line pressure should be measured when the fluid temperature is 109-135°F. (43-57°C).

### Lock-up Pressure Test

1. Install the pressure gauge to the lock-up pressure port on the transaxle case.
2. Shift the selector lever to the "D" position and operate the vehicle to allow the lock-up converter to operate.
3. With the lock-up converter not applied, a pressure reading of 28 psi or more, should be registered.
4. With the lock-up converter applied, a pressure reading of 7 psi or less, should be registered.

### Governor Pressure Test

1. Install the pressure gauge to the governor pressure port on the transaxle case. Locate the gauge so it can be seen by the operator.

2. Road test the vehicle and operate at various speeds.

3. The governor pressure will increase directly with road speed and should always be less than main line pressure.

## AIR PRESSURE TESTS

The control pressure test results and causes of abnormal pressures are to be used as a guide. Further testing or inspection could be necessary before repairs are made. If the pressures are found to be low in a clutch, servo or passageway, a verification can be accomplished by removing the valve body and performing an air pressure test. The air pressure test serves two purposes:

1. To determine if a malfunction of a clutch or band is caused by fluid leakage in the system or if the malfunction is the result of a mechanical problem.

2. To test the transaxle for internal fluid leakage during the rebuilding process and to verify operation of the units before completing the assembly.

### Procedure

1. Obtain an air nozzle rated for 25-30 psi. Apply air pressure to the passages as illustrated.

## STALL TEST

The stall test is an application of the engine torque, through the transaxle and drive train to locked-up road wheels, held by the vehicle's service brakes. The engine speed is increased until the rpms are stabilized. Given ideal engine operating conditions and no abnormal slippage from the transaxle clutches, bands or torque converter, the engine speed will stabilize at a specific test rpm.

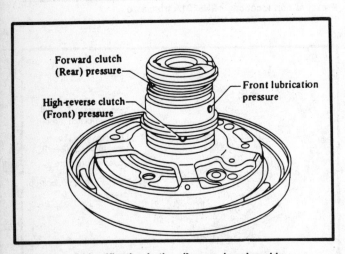

**Fluid channel identification in the oil pump, housing side** (© Nissan Motor Co. of USA)

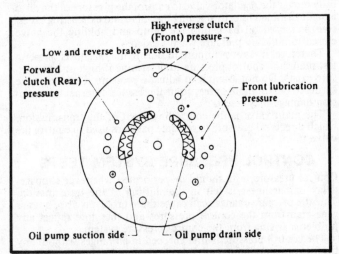

**Fluid channel identification in the oil pump, plate side** (© Nissan Motor Co. of USA)

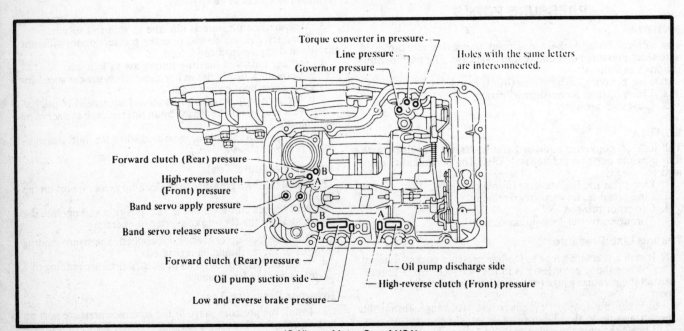

**Fluid passage identification in RN3F01A transaxle case** (© Nissan Motor Co. of USA)

## Performing the Stall Test

1. Check the engine oil level and start the engine, bringing it up to normal operating temperature.
2. Check the transaxle fluid level and correct as required.
3. Attach a calibrated tachometer to the engine and a pressure gauge to the transaxle main line pressure port.
4. Mark the specified maximum engine rpm on the tachometer cover plate with a grease pencil to easily check if the stall speed is over or under the specifications.
5. Apply the parking brake and block the front and rear wheels.

— CAUTION —

*Do not allow anyone to stand in front of the vehicle while performing the stall test.*

6. Apply the foot service brakes and accelerate to wide open throttle.

— CAUTION —

*Do not hold the throttle open for longer than five seconds.*

7. Quickly note the engine stall speed and the pressure reading. Release the accelerator.

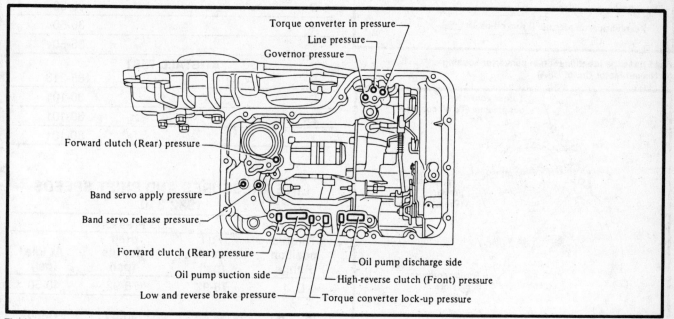

**Fluid passage identification in RL3F01A transaxle case** (© Nissan Motor Co. of USA)

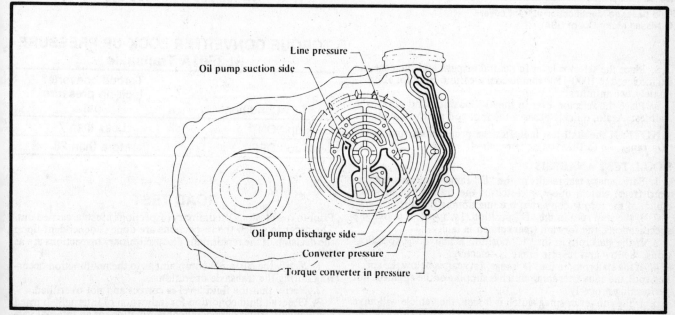

**Fluid passage identification in converter housing side of case** (© Nissan Motor Co. of USA)

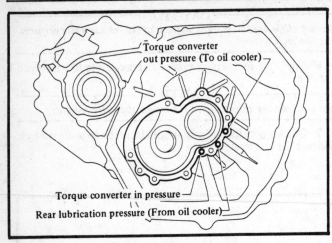

**Fluid passage identification in converter housing**
(© Nissan Motor Co. of USA)

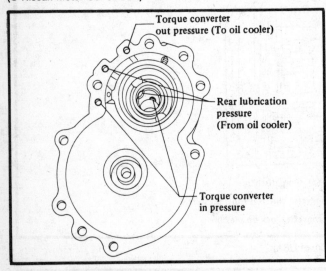

**Fluid passage identification in front cover**
(© Nissan Motor Co. of USA)

8. Place the selector lever in neutral or park and increase the engine speed to 1000-1500 rpm to cool the fluid. Hold for approximately two minutes.

9. Place the selector lever in the "R" position and repeat the stall test. Again, quickly observe the rpm and pressure readings.

**NOTE: If the stall test indicates the proper stall rpm in the "D" range, no further testing is required.**

## STALL TEST ANALYSIS

1. Satisfactory test results in the "D" range indicates the forward (rear) clutch, one-way clutch of the transaxle and sprag clutch of the torque converter, are functioning properly.

2. If the stall rpm in the "D" position, 1st speed, is above the specifications, the forward (rear) clutch is faulty.

3. If the stall rpm in the "R" position is above the specifications, the low and reverse brake is defective.

4. If the stall rpm, in the "D" range, 1st gear, is below the specified rpm, the converter sprag clutch is slipping or the engine is not performing properly.

5. If the converter sprag clutch is frozen, the vehicle will have poor high speed performance. If the sprag clutch is slipping, the vehicle will be sluggish up to 30-40 mph.

## STALL SPEED SPECIFICATIONS

| | |
|---|---|
| 1982 Datsun 310 | 1650-1950 RPM |
| 1983-84 Nissan Stanza | 2000-2300 RPM |
| 1982-84 Nissan Sentra | 1800-2100 RPM |
| 1983-84 Nissan Pulsar, NX | 1800-2100 RPM |

## LINE PRESSURE SPECIFICATIONS
### 1983-84 Pulsar and Stanza, 1982-84 Sentra

| Range | Line Pressure (psi) |
|---|---|
| **AT IDLING** | |
| R | 91-112 |
| D | 36-50 |
| 2 | 36-50 |
| 1 | 36-50 |
| **AT STALL TEST** | |
| R | 185-213 |
| D | 80-101 |
| 2 | 80-101 |
| 1 | 80-101 |

## LINE PRESSURES AND SHIFT SPEEDS
### 1982 310

| | Line Pressure | | |
|---|---|---|---|
| Throttle position Range | Full throttle (psi) | Half throttle (psi) | At idle (psi) |
| D, 1 | 78-92 | 78-92 | 40-50 |
| 2 (D1 → 22) | 80-92 | 80-92 | 78-92 |
| R | 192-206 | 192-206 | 85-107 |

## TORQUE CONVERTER LOCK-UP PRESSURE
### RL3F01A Transaxle

| Condition | Torque converter lock-up pressure psi |
|---|---|
| Lock-up "ON" | Less than 7 |
| Lock-up "OFF" | More than 28 |

## ROAD TEST

Prior to road testing, preliminary inspections must be carried out. The order in which the inspections are done is dependent upon the decision of the repairman. The preliminary inspections are as follows:

1. Verify the customer complaint as to the malfunction occurring during the transaxle operation.

2. Verify that the fluid level is correct and not overfilled.

3. Observe fluid condition for indication of internally burned components, water or coolant contamination, or an internal varnish condition.

4. Verify engine operation. Verify cooling and oiling systems are operating normally and that all levels are correct.

5. Verify selector lever positioning is correct and properly aligned.

6. Verify transaxle throttle valve control cable is free and properly adjusted.

7. Install a tachometer to the engine and a oil pressure gauge to the transaxle.

8. The road test should be performed on a pre-selected course that has been used in the diagnosis of other transmission/transaxle malfunctions.

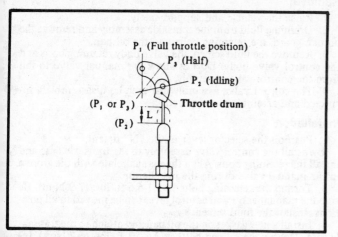

**Throttle cable positioning at varied throttle openings**
(© Nissan Motor Co. of USA)

## Road Testing Procedure

1. **Park**—Place the control lever in "P" range and start the engine. Stop the engine and repeat the procedure in all other ranges and neutral. In Park, the car should be locked in position, unable to roll or move. Note all results on the Symptom Chart.

2. **Reverse**—Manually shift the control lever from "P" to "R", and note shift quality. Drive the car in reverse long enough to detect slippage or other abnormalities. Note results.

3. **Neutral**—Manually shift the control lever from "P" to "N" and note quality. In neutral no clutches or bands are applied, and there should be no movement. Note results.

4. **Drive**—Manually shift the control lever to range "D", and note shift quality. Drive the car through all automatic shifts and in all gear ranges. Note shift quality and timing [km/h (MPH)], check for slippage, noise, or other abnormal conditions. If necessary, drive the test sequence under different throttle openings (e.g. light, medium or full throttle).

5. **Range "2"**—Manually shift the control lever to range "2". Check for slippage, hesitation or abnormal condition. When the lever is set at this position, the transaxle will be automatically shifted between 1st and 2nd gears in response to the depression of the accelerator pedal. However, the transaxle is not shifted to 3rd gear. When the car is slowing down, the transaxle will automatically down-shift.

6. **Range "1"**—Manually shift the control lever to range "1". Note shift quality. It should, however, downshift immediately to 2nd gear and downshift again to 1st gear as road speed decreases. Accelerate and decelerate in 1st gear to determine engine braking. Note results.

The transaxle should not shift into 1st gear from "D" range if the car road speed is above approximately 65 km/h (40 MPH).

7. Record line pressure and governor pressure at each range and at each throttle valve opening.

## LOCK-UP TORQUE CONVERTER

The lock-up of the clutch assembly to the torque converter occurs when the transaxle shifts into the third speed and the road speed is approximately 39-46 mph. During the transaxle downshifting, the lock-up will release at speeds of 44-37 mph.

Hydraulic fluid pressure is applied to both sides of the clutch plate assembly when in the released position and when applied, the pressure is exhausted from between the clutch and the converter front plate, allowing the clutch to lock-up mechanically.

## ON CAR SERVICES

## Adjustments

### THROTTLE CABLE

#### Adjustment

To adjust the throttle cable, double nuts are provided and are located on the carburetor side of the cable.

1. Loosen the throttle cable double nuts.

2. With the throttle positioned in the wide open mode, move the cable fitting towards the transaxle completely while adjusting the two locknuts.

3. Loosen the locknut on the transaxle side, between one and one-half turns. Tighten the locknut on the carburetor side securely to 5.8-7.2 ft. lbs.

4. Ensure the throttle cable stroke is within the specified range of 1.079-1.236 in. (27.4-31.4mm) during the idle and wide open throttle operations.

**NOTE: The throttle cable will be pulled outward when at wide open throttle position.**

### CONTROL CABLE

#### Adjustment

1. Place the selector lever in the "P" range.

2. Move the selector lever to the "1" range, feeling the detents in each position or range.

3. If the detents cannot be felt or the indicator is not properly aligned, the cable must be adjusted.

4. With the selector lever in the "P" position and the transaxle in the "P" position, adjust the control cable to the trunnion by loosening the locknuts on each side of the trunnion.

5. Center the trunnion in the transaxle lever and tighten the locknuts.

6. Move the selector lever from "P" position to the "1" position and check for detent feel and ease of cable operation.

7. Readjust as required. Lubricate the spring washer on the transaxle lever.

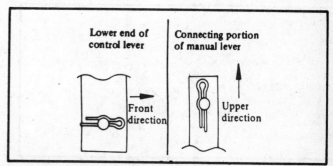

**Proper positioning of spring retaining clip**
(© Nissan Motor Co. of USA)

## NEUTRAL SAFETY (INHIBITOR) SWITCH

### Adjustment

1. Loosen the adjusting screws.
2. Position the selector lever in the "N" position.
3. Install a 0.098 in. (2.5mm) diameter pin into the adjusting holes in both the switch and the operating lever.
4. Tighten the adjusting screws to 1.4-1.9 ft. lbs. (2.0-2.5 N•m).
5. Check the operation of the switch in the "P" and "N" positions to allow the engine to start and the back-up lights to operate in the "R" position.

NOTE: An Ohmmeter can be used to check the continuity of the switch in the varied positions, if so desired.

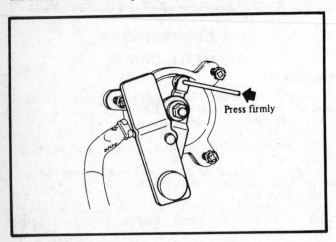

**Installation of pin in adjustment holes of switch**
(© Nissan Motor Co. of USA)

## BRAKE BAND

### Adjustment

1. Raise the vehicle and support safely. Drain the transaxle and remove the oil pan.
2. Remove the valve body and screen assembly from the transaxle.

NOTE: Refer to the valve body removal and installation procedure in the Service section of On Car Services.

3. Loosen the locknut.
4. Torque the anchor end pin to 2.9-4.3 ft. lbs. (4-6 N•m).
5. Back off the anchor end pin 2.5 complete turns.
6. While holding the anchor end pin, tighten the locknut to 12-16 ft. lbs. (16-22 N•m).

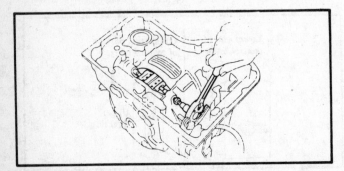

**Adjustment location of brake band** (© Nissan Motor Co. of USA)

7. Reinstall the valve body and screen assembly as per instructions in the Valve Body Removal and Installation section.
8. Install the oil pan, using a new gasket. Tighten the pan bolts to 3.6-5.1 ft. lbs. (5-7 N•m).
9. Fill the transaxle with fluid and verifty level after the units reach normal operating temperature.

## Services

### CONTROL VALVE ASSEMBLY

#### Removal

1. Raise the vehicle and support safely.
2. Drain the fluid from the transaxle assembly and remove the oil pan guard, the retaining bolts and the oil pan.
3. Remove the fluid screen, the valve body retaining bolts and the control valve body. Do not allow the manual valve to fall from the control valve assembly.
4. The control valve assembly can then be disassembled, inspected and assembled as required.

#### Installation

1. Position the selector lever in the "N" detent.
2. Install the control valve assembly to the transaxle case and install the retaining bolts. Align the manual plate with the groove in the manual valve during the installation.
3. Torque the retaining bolts to 5.1-6.5 ft. lbs. (7-9 N•m). Be sure the manual valve and control lever can be moved to all positions. Install the fluid screen.
4. Install a new gasket on the oil pan and attach to the transaxle case. Tighten the oil pan bolts to 3.6-5.1 ft. lbs. (5-7 N•m). Install the oil pan guard.
5. Install the drain plug if not previously installed. Tighten to 5.1-9.4 ft. lbs. (7-13 N•m).
6. Refill the transaxle, start the engine, move the selector lever through all detent positions and recheck the fluid level. Correct as required.

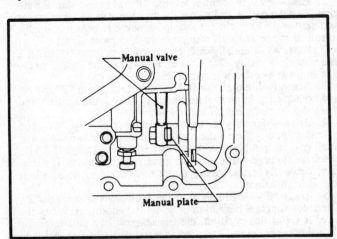

**Aligning manual valve and manual plate**
(© Nissan Motor Co. of USA)

## THROTTLE CONTROL CABLE

### Removal

1. Remove the control valve assembly as previously outlined.
2. Disconnect the throttle cable from the carburetor throttle lever and from the cable bracket.
3. Disconnect the transaxle end from the throttle lever in the case. Remove the cable assembly from the case.

## Installation

1. Install the cable in the reverse of its removal procedure.
2. Bend the locking plate within the case, after tightening the lock nut.
3. Adjust the cable as outlined in the adjustment section.

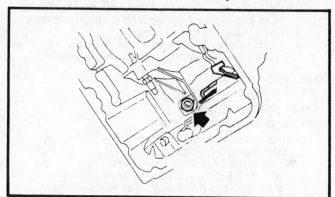

Location of bendable lockwasher on the throttle cable within the case (© Nissan Motor Co. of USA)

## GOVERNOR ASSEMBLY

### Removal

1. Disconnect the battery cables.
2. Remove the radiator reserve tank and remove the battery along with its support bracket.
3. Remove the snap retainer, governor cap with breather hose and the seal ring.
4. Remove the governor shaft retaining bolt.
5. Remove the governor shaft assembly from the transaxle.
6. The governor can now be replaced or repaired, as required.

### Installation

1. Install the governor shaft assembly into the transaxle case. Secure with the retaining bolts.
2. Install the O-ring, the governor cap with the breather hose and secure it with the snap.

**NOTE: Install the cap in the same direction as was removed.**

3. Install the battery support, the battery, the radiator reserve tank and connect the battery cables.

## NEUTRAL START (INHIBITOR) SWITCH

### Removal

1. Remove the lower panel.
2. Remove the control cable from the transaxle manual lever.
3. Disconnect the electrical harness from the switch and remove the retaining screws.
4. Remove the switch.

### Installation

1. Install the switch into position and install the retaining screws. Adjust the switch as described in the Adjustment section.
2. Tighten the screws to 1.4-1.8 ft. lbs. (2-2.5 N•m).
3. Install the wiring connector and the manual lever cable.
4. Test the switch for proper operation and movement.

## DRIVE AXLE OIL SEALS

The left and right transaxle drive shaft oil seals can be replaced with the drive shafts removed from the unit. Special seal pulling tools are used to remove the seals while special installation tools are used to install the seals into the case components.

**NOTE: Do not scratch the seal surface during the axle installation.**

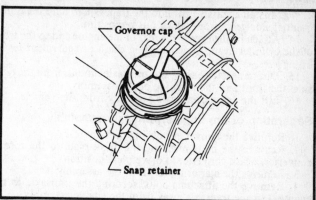

Governor snap retainer location. Note the position of the cap direction before removal (© Nissan Motor Co. of USA)

# REMOVAL & INSTALLATION

## TRANSAXLE ASSEMBLY

The transaxle assembly can be removed from the vehicle separately, except for the 1982 310 models, from which the engine and transaxle must be removed as a unit. When removing or installing the transaxle assembly, extreme care must be exercised to prevent damage to the unit or personal injury.

### Removal

**1982 310 MODELS**

1. Remove the hood, after marking its location on the hinges.
2. Remove the battery and support bracket.
3. Remove the air cleaner assembly and plug the carburetor air horn to prevent entrance of unwanted material.
4. Drain the cooling system, remove the radiator and cooling fan.
5. If equipped, remove the power steering oil pump. Do not disconnect the lines, but lay aside safely.
6. Without disconnecting the air conditioning lines, remove the compressor and support within the engine compartment to prevent its dropping.
7. Disconnect the exhaust front pipe from the exhaust manifold.
8. Disconnect the selector lever control cable at the transaxle.
9. Remove the speedometer cable with the driven gear attached. Plug the hole to prevent entrance of unwanted material.
10. Disconnect the throttle control cable from the carburetor.
11. Remove the vacuum and electrical wiring/hoses from the engine. Mark each wire and hose to prevent mix-up during assembly.
12. Disconnect the fuel hose from the fuel pump assembly.
13. Disconnect the right and left drive shafts from the transaxle in the following manner:
    a. Raise the vehicle and support safely.
    b. Remove the wheel assembly.
    c. Remove the retaining bolts holding the lower ball joint to the transverse link (lower control arm).
    d. Drain the fluid from the transaxle.
    e. Disconnect the tie rod end from each side of the steering linkage.
    f. Pulling outward on the wheel assembly while holding the drive shaft, remove the shaft from the transaxle.

g. Install a suitable bar into the transaxle to hold the differential side gears from falling out of position.

14. Attach lifting eyes to the rear of the engine and to the front of the cylinder head. Attach a lifting chain or equivalent to the lifting eyes.

15. Disconnect the engine and transaxle mounts from the right side, the front and the rear side of the assembly.

16. Lift the engine/transaxle assembly from the vehicle.

## Separation of the Engine/transaxle assembly

1. Remove the converter housing dust cover.

2. Remove the bolts retaining the drive plate to the torque converter. Mark converter to drive plate position.

3. Remove the starter motor from the assembly.

4. Remove the attaching bolts, securing the transaxle to the engine. Lift the transaxle away from the engine assembly.

## Assembly of Transaxle to the Engine

1. Measure the drive plate runout with a dial indicator. Runout should not exceed 0.020 in. (0.5mm).

2. Measure the distance from the edge of the converter housing to the attaching lug face on the converter. The distance should not be less than 0.831 in. (21.1mm).

3. When joining the converter to the drive plate, align the previously made marks if the same parts are used.

4. After the converter is installed and tightened, rotate the engine crankshaft several times to be sure the converter/transaxle is free to rotate without binding.

## Engine/Transaxle Installation

1. The installation of the engine/transaxle assembly is in the reverse order of its removal.

2. The following installation notes should be observed:

a. When installing the assembly, ensure that brake tubes, master cylinder, etc., do not interfere with the installation.

b. Align and tighten engine/transaxle mounts securely.

c. Verify rubber mount clearance.

d. Verify selector lever, neutral safety switch, starter and throttle cable operate properly before moving vehicle.

## Transaxle Removal

### 1983-84 NISSAN STANZA
### 1982-84 NISSAN SENTRA
### 1983-84 NISSAN PULSAR, NX

1. Disconnect the negative battery cable.

2. Raise the vehicle and support safely.

3. Remove the front wheel assemblies.

4. Drain the fluid from the transaxle.

5. Remove the left side fender inner panel protector.

6. Disconnect the drive axles in the following manner:

a. Remove the brake caliper assembly from each side and hang from the body with wire.

b. Remove the steering tie rod end stud from the steering arm on each side.

c. Remove the retaining bolts from the lower ball joints to lower control arms on each side.

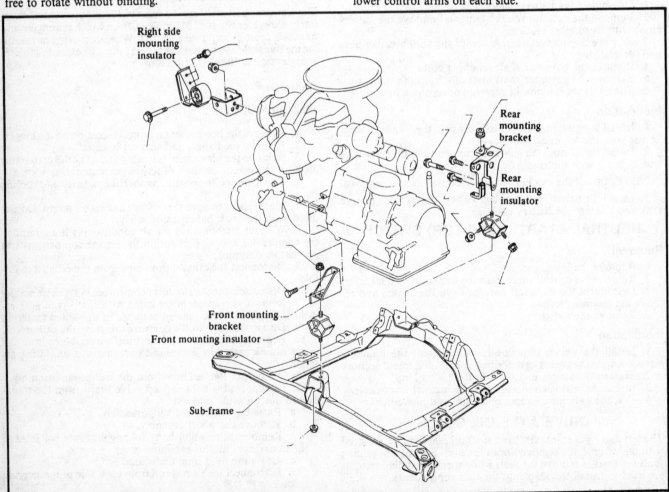

**Engine/transaxle mount locations—1982 310 models** (© Nissan Motor Co. of USA)

**NOTE: Use new nuts upon installation.**

d. Pulling outward on the wheel assemblies while holding the drive shafts, remove the shafts from the transaxle.

**NOTE: It may be necessary to pry the axle from the transaxle, along with the outward pressure applied to the wheel assemblies.**

e. With the drive shafts out of the transaxle, discard the circlips and install new ones before axle installation.

7. Remove the speedometer cable.
8. Disconnect the throttle control cable at the carburetor.
9. Remove the selector cable from the transaxle control lever.
10. Remove the dipstick tube assembly.
11. Support the transaxle with a transmission type jack unit.

### ——————— CAUTION ———————
*Do not place the support tool under the oil pan drain plug.*

12. Disconnect the oil cooler lines at the hose ends.
13. Matchmark the torque converter to the drive plate and remove the retaining bolts from the drive plate to converter.
14. Remove the engine mount securing bolts.
15. Remove the starter assembly.
16. Remove the engine to transaxle retaining bolts.
17. Gradually move the support tool to loosen the transaxle from the engine, lower sufficiently and remove the transaxle through the vehicle's wheel opening on the left side.

## Installation

1. The installation of the transaxle is in the reverse order of removal. The following installation notes must be adhered to:

a. Measure the drive plate runout with a dial indicator. The runout should not exceed 0.020 in. (0.5mm).

b. Measure the distance from the edge of the converter housing to the attaching lug face on the converter. The distance should not be less than 0.831 in. (21.1mm).

c. When joining the converter to the drive plate, align the previously made marks, if the same parts are used.

d. After the converter has been bolted to the drive plate, rotate the engine crankshaft several times to be sure the converter/transaxle is free to rotate without binding.

e. Upon assembly of the lower ball joints to the control arms, new nuts must be used to assure proper bolt torque retention.

f. Be sure of selector lever, neutral safety switch, starter and throttle cable operation before moving vehicle.

# BENCH OVERHAUL

## Before Disassembly

With the openings on the transaxle plugged to prevent contamination, clean the outside of the unit thoroughly. If a steam cleaning unit is used for cleaning, the transaxle must be disassembled as soon as possible to avoid internal rusting of components.

Disassembly must be done in a clean work area and the use of nylon cloth or paper towels to wipe parts, is recommended.

## Disassembly

1. Remove the converter assembly from the transaxle.
2. If the transaxle has not been drained, remove the oil pan plug and drain the unit. Re-install the plug into the oil pan when drained.
3. Remove the oil pump shaft and the input shaft.
4. Remove the snap retainer, governor cap with breather hose and the O-ring.

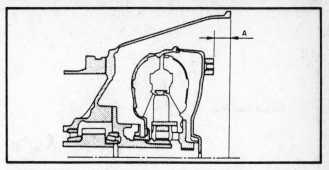

**Positioning of converter within the converter housing**
(© Nissan Motor Co. of USA)

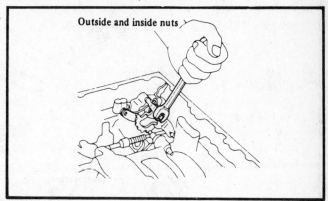

**Removing the manual shaft securing nuts**
(© Nissan Motor Co. of USA)

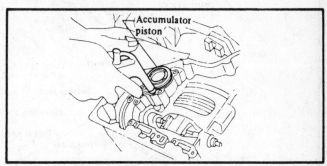

**Removing the accumulator piston with air pressure**
(© Nissan Motor Co. of USA)

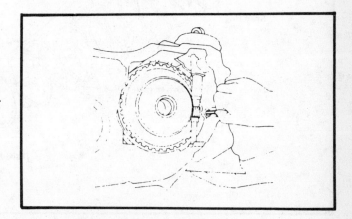

**Removing parking pawl shaft** (© Nissan Motor Co. of USA)

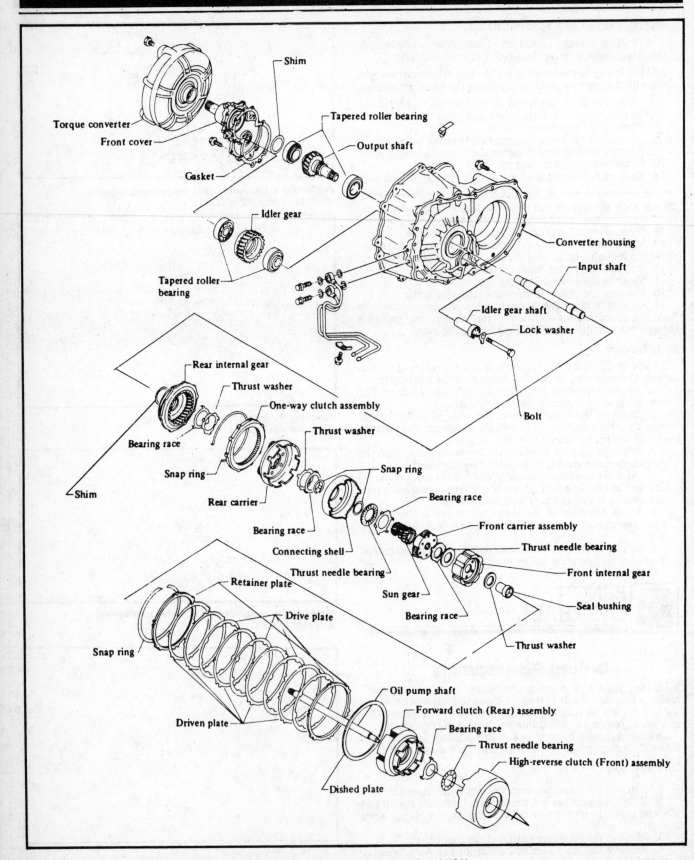

**Exploded view of the forward section of the transaxle assembly (© Nissan Motor Co. of USA)**

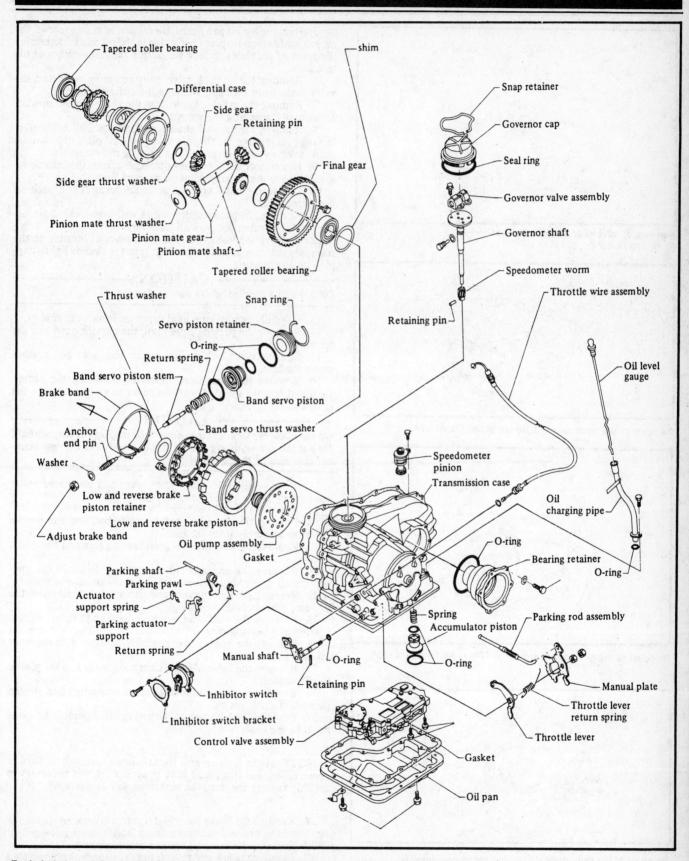

Tapered roller bearing
Differential case
Side gear
Retaining pin
Side gear thrust washer
Pinion mate thrust washer
Pinion mate gear
Pinion mate shaft
Final gear
Tapered roller bearing
shim

Snap retainer
Governor cap
Seal ring
Governor valve assembly
Governor shaft
Speedometer worm
Throttle wire assembly
Retaining pin
Oil level gauge

Thrust washer
Snap ring
Servo piston retainer
O-ring
Return spring
Band servo piston stem
Brake band
Band servo piston
Anchor end pin
Band servo thrust washer
Washer
Low and reverse brake piston retainer
Low and reverse brake piston
Adjust brake band
Oil pump assembly
Gasket

Speedometer pinion
Transmission case
Oil charging pipe
O-ring
Bearing retainer
O-ring

Parking shaft
Parking pawl
Actuator support spring
Parking actuator support
Return spring
Manual shaft
O-ring
Retaining pin
Inhibitor switch
Inhibitor switch bracket
Control valve assembly

Spring
Accumulator piston
O-ring
O-ring
Parking rod assembly
Manual plate
Throttle lever return spring
Throttle lever
Gasket
Oil pan

**Exploded view of the rear section of the transaxle assembly (© Nissan Motor Co. of USA)**

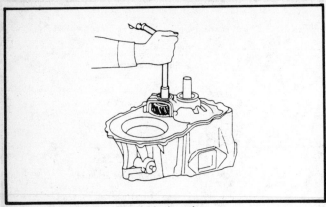

**Removal of idler gear bolt and lockwasher**
(© Nissan Motor Co. of USA)

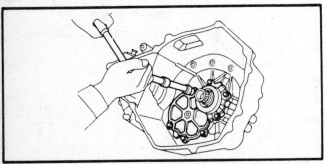

**Removal of the front cover** (© Nissan Motor Co. of USA)

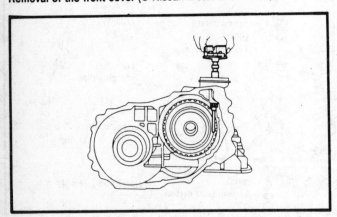

**Removal of the governor assembly** (© Nissan Motor Co. of USA)

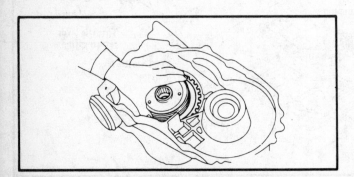

**Removal of the rear internal gear and thrust components**
(© Nissan Motor Co. of USA)

5. Remove the oil pan guard, the oil pan retaining screws, the oil pan and gasket. Inspect the residue in the oil pan to determine the types of problems to look for during the disassembly of the transaxle.

6. Remove the control valve body retaining bolts and the valve body from the case. Remove the sediment magnet.

7. Remove the manual valve from the valve body to prevent accidentally dropping the valve to the floor.

8. Remove the manual shaft securing nuts. Pull out the retaining pin, remove the throttle lever, manual plate, the manual shaft, selector range lever and the parking rod assembly.

9. Disconnect the throttle control cable from the throttle lever. Remove the parking actuator support from the case.

10. Loosen the band brake piston stem locknut and back off the piston stem.

11. Remove the accumulator piston with compressed air, being careful to catch piston with shop rag.

12. Remove the bolts retaining the converter housing to the transaxle case. Separate the housing from the case by lightly tapping on the housing.

— CAUTION —

*Do not allow the final drive unit to drop.*

13. Carefully remove the final drive unit from the case.

14. Remove the parking pawl shaft, the parking pawl and the return spring.

15. Straighten the lock washer on the idler gear bolt and remove the bolt.

16. Remove the front cover retaining bolts, tap the output shaft and remove the shaft and the cover as a unit. Remove the gasket.

— CAUTION —

*Do not allow the front cover to drop while tapping the output shaft. Do not lose the adjusting shim which is attached to the rear internal gear side of the output shaft.*

17. Remove the idler gear, idler gear shaft and taper roller bearings by tapping the idler gear shaft.

18. Remove the seal bushing.

19. Remove the governor shaft retaining bolt and remove the governor assembly from the case.

20. Remove the rear internal gear, bearing race and the thrust washer.

21. Remove the one-way clutch snapring. Remove the one-way clutch assembly together with the rear carrier assembly.

22. Remove the bearing race and thrust washer. Remove the low and reverse brake snapring.

23. Remove the shell and sun gear assembly, thrust needle bearing and bearing race.

24. Remove the front carrier assembly, together with the front internal gear.

25. Remove the forward (rear) clutch assembly and the plastic thrust washer.

26. Remove the low and reverse brake retaining plate, driven plates and drive plates.

27. Remove the high-reverse (front) clutch assembly by turning it in the case.

NOTE: If the high-reverse (front) clutch assembly is hard to remove, the seal rings may have expanded. If it is necessary to forcibly remove the unit, the seal rings will be damaged.

28. Remove the brake band and install a fabricated clip in the open ends to prevent the brake lining from cracking or peeling.

29. Remove the low and reverse brake retainer.

30. Remove the low and reverse brake piston with compressed air while holding a shop cloth to catch the piston.

31. Remove the oil pump assembly, the thrust washer and thrust needle bearing by lifting the assembly straight out of the case.

32. Remove the neutral safety switch and the band servo piston and return spring.

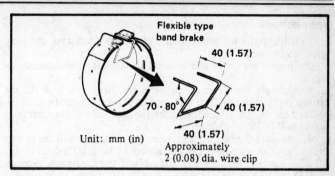

Unit: mm (in)
Approximately
2 (0.08) dia. wire clip

**Installation of the fabricated band holding clip**
(© Nissan Motor Co. of USA)

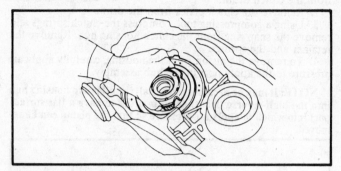

**Removal of the one-way clutch assembly**
(© Nissan Motor Co. of USA)

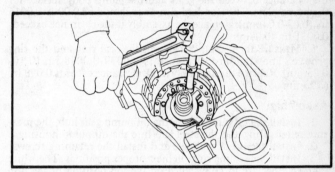

**Removal of the low and reverse brake retainer**
(© Nissan Motor Co. of USA)

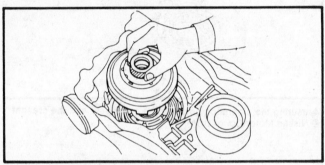

**Removal of the shell and sungear assembly**
(© Nissan Motor Co. of USA)

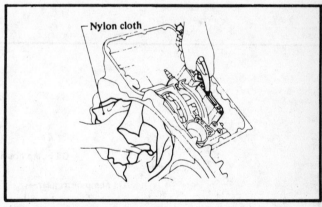

**Using air pressure to remove the low and reverse brake piston**
(© Nissan Motor Co. of USA)

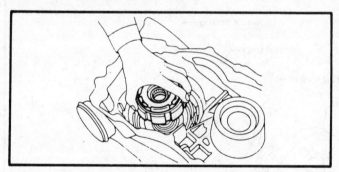

**Removal of the front carrier and front internal gear**
(© Nissan Motor Co. of USA)

# Disassembly, Inspection and Assembly of Internal Components
## OIL PUMP

### Disassembly

1. Remove the oil pump plate retaining screws and remove the plate.

2. Remove the oil pump gear hub, the pressure relief spring and the steel ball from the housing.

3. Remove the driven and drive gears from the oil pump housing.

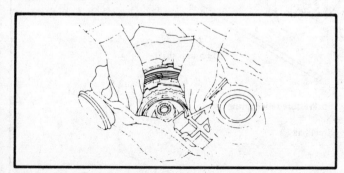

**Removal of the low and reverse brake assembly**
(© Nissan Motor Co. of USA)

## Inspection

1. Inspect the oil pump body, oil pump shaft and the ring grooves for wear.

2. Inspect the gears and internal surfaces for wear and damages.

3. Measure the clearance between the outer gear and the oil pump body crescent. The standard clearance should be 0.0079-0.0118 in. (0.20-0.30mm). Replace the assembly if the clearance exceeds 0.0138 in. (0.35mm).

4. Measure the clearance between the outer gear and the pump housing. The standard clearance should be 0.0079-0.0118 in. (0.20-0.30mm). Replace the assembly if the clearance exceeds 0.0138 in. (0.35mm).

5. Using a feeler gauge blade and a straightedge tool, measure the clearance between the gears and the pump body surface for the pump plate. The standard clearance should be 0.0008-0.0016 in. (0.02-0.04mm). Replace the assembly if the clearance exceeds 0.0031 in. (0.08mm).

6. Measure the clearance between the seal ring and the ring groove. The standard clearance is 0.0039-0.0098 in. (0.10-0.25mm). Replace the assembly if the clearance exceeds 0.098 in. (0.25mm).

## Assembly

1. Install the oil pump gears, the oil pump gear hub, the pressure relief spring and the steel ball into the oil pump housing.

2. Install the oil pump plate and install the retaining screws.

3. Install the sealing rings in their proper positions. The white marked rings are to be installed on the top position of the hub while the rings with no marks are to be installed on the lower part of the hub.

## HIGH-REVERSE (FRONT) CLUTCH

### Disassembly

1. Remove the large retaining snapring and the retainer plate from the clutch drum.

2. Remove the clutch plates from the drum.

3. Using a compressing tool, compress the clutch springs and remove the snap ring from the clutch housing hub. Remove the retainer and the springs.

4. To remove the piston from the housing, carefully apply air pressure to the apply port in the hub assembly.

**NOTE: It may be necessary to install the oil pump housing hub into the high-reverse (front) drum in order to have a flat surface port into which to apply air pressure so that the piston can be removed.**

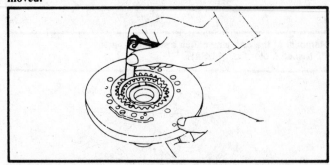

**Measuring the clearance between the outer gear and the cresent** (© Nissan Motor Co. of USA)

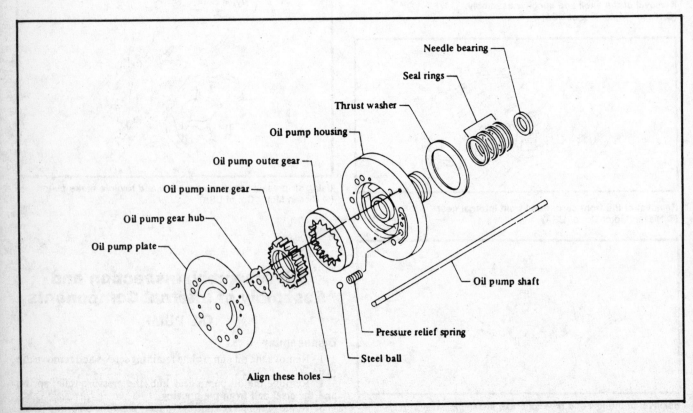

**Exploded view of the oil pump assembly** (© Nissan Motor Co. of USA)

### Inspection

1. Inspect the clutch plates for wear or damage. The standard plate thickness for the drive plate is 0.0591-0.0650 in. (1.50-1.65mm). The plate thickness must not be less than 0.055 in. (1.4mm).

**NOTE: It is good practice to install both the drive and driven clutch plates during the rebuilding process.**

2. Inspect the snap rings and springs for being broken, weak or twisted. Inspect the spring retainer for being warped.
3. Check the clutch housing for damage, wear or broken areas.
4. Check the piston for damage, wear or broken seal ring grooves. If equipped with a ball check, be sure ball seats properly and is free in its bore.

### Assembly

1. Install the piston lip seal and the clutch housing hub seal. Lubricate each seal with transmission fluid.

2. Install the piston into the clutch drum carefully, to avoid damaging the seals. Rotate the piston after it has been seated to be sure no binding exists.

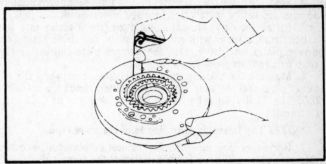

**Measuring the clearance between the outer gear and the pump housing** (© Nissan Motor Co. of USA)

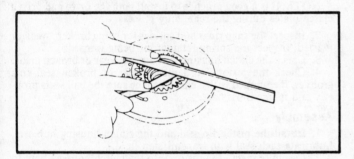

**Measuring the clearance between the gears and the pump body plate** (© Nissan Motor Co. of USA)

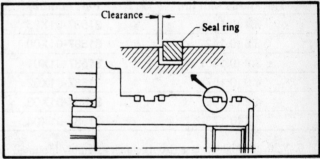

**Measuring the clearance between the seal ring and the pump body hub grooves** (© Nissan Motor Co. of USA)

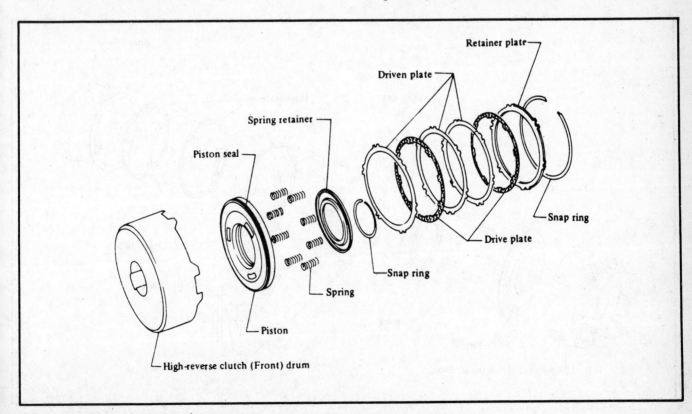

**Exploded view of the high-reverse (front) clutch assembly** (© Nissan Motor Co. of USA)

3. Install the springs, retainer and with the spring compressing tool installed, compress the springs and install the snap ring into its groove. Be sure the ring is properly seated.

4. Soak the drive (lined) plates in A/T fluid for approximately 15 minutes before installation into the clutch drum.

5. Install the drive (lined) and driven (steel) plates into the clutch drum, starting with one driven plate, one drive plate, two driven plates, one drive plate, the retainer plate and install the snap ring into its groove.

6. Measure the existing minimum clearance between the retainer plate and the snap ring. The standard clearance is 0.039-0.055 in. (1.0-1.4mm) with an allowable limit of 0.087 in. (2.2mm).

**NOTE: The retaining snap ring is of the wave type.**

7. If the specified measurement cannot be obtained, another retaining plate will have to be installed of the correct thickness. Retainer plates are available in the following thicknesses.

| Thickness mm (in) | Part number |
| --- | --- |
| 3.4 (0.134) | 31537-01X05 |
| 3.6 (0.142) | 31537-01X00 |
| 3.8 (0.150) | 31537-01X01 |
| 4.0 (0.157) | 31537-01X02 |
| 4.2 (0.165) | 31537-01X03 |
| 4.4 (0.173) | 31537-01X04 |

8. With the high-reverse (front) clutch assembly mounted on the oil pump housing, apply a jet of compressed air into the apply hole in the pump body to operate the clutch assembly.

## FORWARD (REAR) CLUTCH

### Disassembly

1. Remove the large retaining snap ring and the retainer plate from the clutch drum.

2. Remove the clutch pack assembly from the drum.

3. With the use of a compressing tool, remove the snap ring from the clutch drum hub, after compressing the springs.

4. Remove the retainer and springs.

5. The piston can be removed from the clutch drum with the use of air pressure, if required.

6. Discard the piston seals.

### Inspection

1. Inspect the clutch plates for wear or damage. The standard plate thickness for the drive plate is 0.0591-0.0650 in. (1.50-1.65mm). The plate thickness must not be less than 0.055 in. (1.4mm).

**NOTE: It is a good practice to install both the drive and driven clutch plates during the rebuilding process.**

2. Inspect the snap rings and springs for being broken, weak or twisted. Inspect the spring retainer for being warped.

3. Check the clutch housing for damage, wear or broken areas.

4. Check the piston for damage, wear or broken seal ring grooves. If equipped with a check ball, be sure the ball seats properly and is free in its bore.

### Assembly

1. Install the piston lip seal and the clutch housing hub seal. Lubricate each seal with transmission fluid.

2. Carefully install the piston into the clutch housing bore to avoid damaging the seals. Rotate the piston after it has been seated to be sure no binding exists.

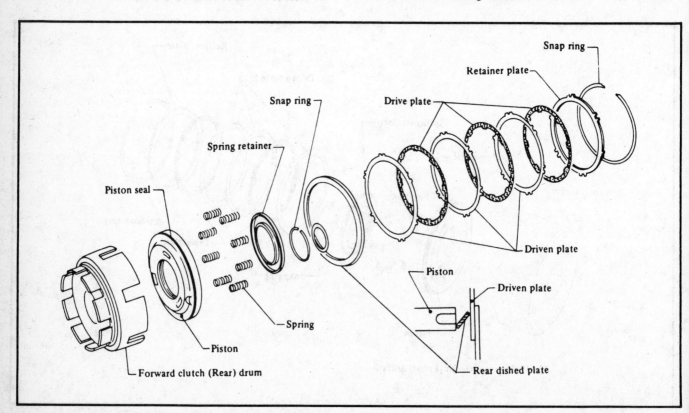

**Exploded view of the forward (rear) clutch assembly** (© Nissan Motor Co. of USA)

3. Install the springs and retainer. With the spring compressor tool installed, compress the springs and install the snap ring into its groove. Be sure the ring is properly seated.

4. Soak the lined drive plates in A/T fluid for approximately 15 minutes before installing into the clutch drum.

5. Install the drive (lined) plates and the driven (steel) plates into the clutch drum, starting with one driven plate, one drive plate, alternating with the remaining plates until a total of three driven (steel) and three drive (lined) plates have been installed. Position the retaining plate next to the last drive plate and install the snap ring. Be sure the ring is fully seated in its groove.

6. Measure the existing minimum clearance between the retainer plate and the snap ring. The standard clearance is 0.020-0.031 in. (0.5-0.8mm). The allowable limit is 0.094 in. (2.4mm).

**NOTE: The retaining snap ring is of the wave type.**

7. If the specified measurement cannot be obtained, another retaining plate will have to be used. Retainer plates are available in the following thicknesses:

| Thickness mm (in) | Part Number |
|---|---|
| 3.4 (0.134) | 31537-01X05 |
| 3.6 (0.142) | 31537-01X00 |
| 3.8 (0.150) | 31537-01X01 |
| 4.0 (0.157) | 31537-01X02 |
| 4.2 (0.165) | 31537-01X03 |
| 4.4 (0.173) | 31537-01X04 |

8. With the forward (rear) clutch mounted on the oil pump housing hub, apply a jet of compressed air into the apply hole for the forward (rear) clutch, testing its operation.

## LOW AND REVERSE BRAKE ASSEMBLY

### Disassembly

1. The low and reverse brake assembly is disassembled during the removal of the internal components of the transaxle.

### Inspection

1. Inspect the low and reverse brake for damaged clutch drive plate facings and worn snap ring. Replace the components as required.

2. Test the piston return spring for weakness or being broken.

3. The drive plate thickness should be between 0.0748-0.0807 in. (1.90-2.05mm). The allowable limit is 0.071 in. (1.8mm).

**NOTE: It is a good practice to replace the driving plates during the rebuilding process.**

### Assembly

1. The assembly of the low and reverse brake assembly will be outlined during the assembly of the transaxle.

## BRAKE BAND

### Disassembly and Assembly

1. The brake band is removed and replaced during the disassembly and assembly of the transaxle.

### Inspection

1. Inspect the band friction material for wear, cracks, chips or burned spots. Replace as required.

2. Inspect the band strut and the band apply pin for damage or wear. Replace as required.

## CONTROL VALVE ASSEMBLY

### Disassembly

1. Remove the oil filter and magnet.

2. Disassemble the valve body and its remaining attaching bolts and nuts. Carefully separate the lower body, separator plate and upper body.

3. During the separation, do not lose the six steel balls on the valve body upper section.

4. Using a stiff piece of wire, remove the parallel pins form the valve body bores. Remove the plugs, 3rd-2nd downshift valves, 2nd-3rd shift valve, 1st-2nd shift valve, 1st-2nd control valve and the respective springs.

**NOTE: Place each internal component on a rack to retain the correct sequence of assembly.**

5. Remove the parallel pins with wire, remove the plugs, fail-safe valve, throttle valve, detent valve, throttle valve modulator valve with the spring guide, pressure modifier valve, 1st reducing valve, top reducing valve, 3rd-2nd timing valve and the respective springs.

6. Remove the back-up valve retaining plate by pressing its spring with a small probe. Remove the parallel pin, the plug, pressure regulator valve and its spring.

**NOTE: Place each internal component on a rack to retain the correct sequence of assembly.**

### Inspection

1. If the inspection reveals excessive clearance between the valves and the bores in the valve body of over 0.0012 in. (0.03mm), replace the entire valve body rather than attempt a rework of the unit.

2. Clean the valves with alcohol or lacquer thinner. Clean the valve body with carburetor cleaner or lacquer thinner.

— CAUTION —

*Do not allow the parts to be submerged longer than five to ten minutes. Rinse thoroughly and dry.*

3. Check the valves for signs of burning. Clean with crocus cloth, but do not remove the sharp edges of the valve lands.

4. Check the separator plate for scratches or damage.

5. Check the bolt holes for damage or stripped threads.

6. Check the springs for distortion or being broken. Refer to the spring chart for specifications.

7. Check the worm tracks in the valve bodies for damage or sides broken, which would allow fluid pressure to cross into another channel.

### Assembly

1. Assemble all the internal components in the reverse order of their removal.

2. Install the six steel balls in the upper valve body as illustrated.

3. Assemble the separator plate and lower valve body on to the upper valve body. Install the bolts and tighten as follows.

   a. Lower valve body to upper valve body securing bolts. 5.1-6.5 ft. lbs. (7-9 N•m).

   b. Accumulator support plate securing bolt, 2.5-3.3 ft. lbs. (3.4-4.4 N•m).

4. Install the oil filter and magnet. Tighten the filter bolts to 1.8-2.5 ft. lbs. (2.5-3.4 N•m).

**NOTE: The manual valve is installed into the valve body during the valve body installation onto the transaxle case.**

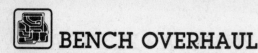

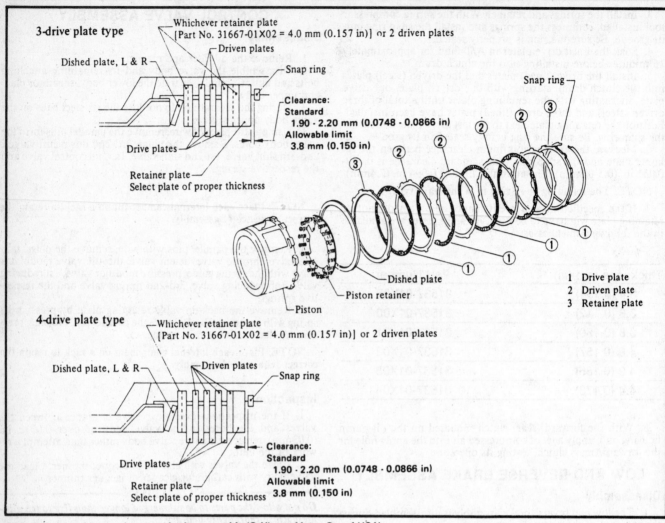

**3-drive plate type**

Whichever retainer plate
[Part No. 31667-01X02 = 4.0 mm (0.157 in)] or 2 driven plates

Driven plates

Dished plate, L & R

Snap ring

Drive plates

Clearance:
Standard
1.90 - 2.20 mm (0.0748 - 0.0866 in)
Allowable limit
3.8 mm (0.150 in)

Retainer plate
Select plate of proper thickness

Snap ring

Dished plate

Piston retainer

Piston

1 Drive plate
2 Driven plate
3 Retainer plate

**4-drive plate type**

Whichever retainer plate
[Part No. 31667-01X02 = 4.0 mm (0.157 in)] or 2 driven plates

Dished plate, L & R

Driven plates

Snap ring

Drive plates

Clearance:
Standard
1.90 - 2.20 mm (0.0748 - 0.0866 in)
Allowable limit
3.8 mm (0.150 in)

Retainer plate
Select plate of proper thickness

**Exploded view of low and reverse brake assembly** (© Nissan Motor Co. of USA)

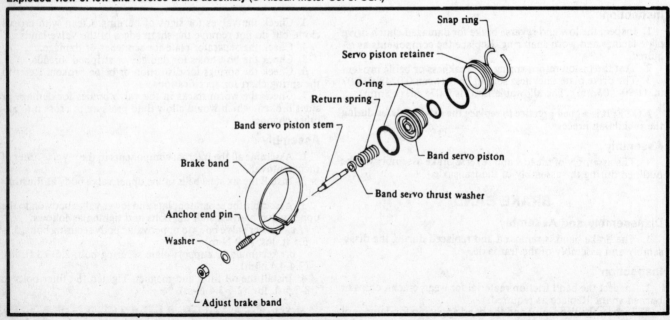

Snap ring

Servo piston retainer

O-ring

Return spring

Band servo piston stem

Brake band

Band servo piston

Band servo thrust washer

Anchor end pin

Washer

Adjust brake band

**Exploded view of band and servo assembly** (© Nissan Motor Co. of USA)

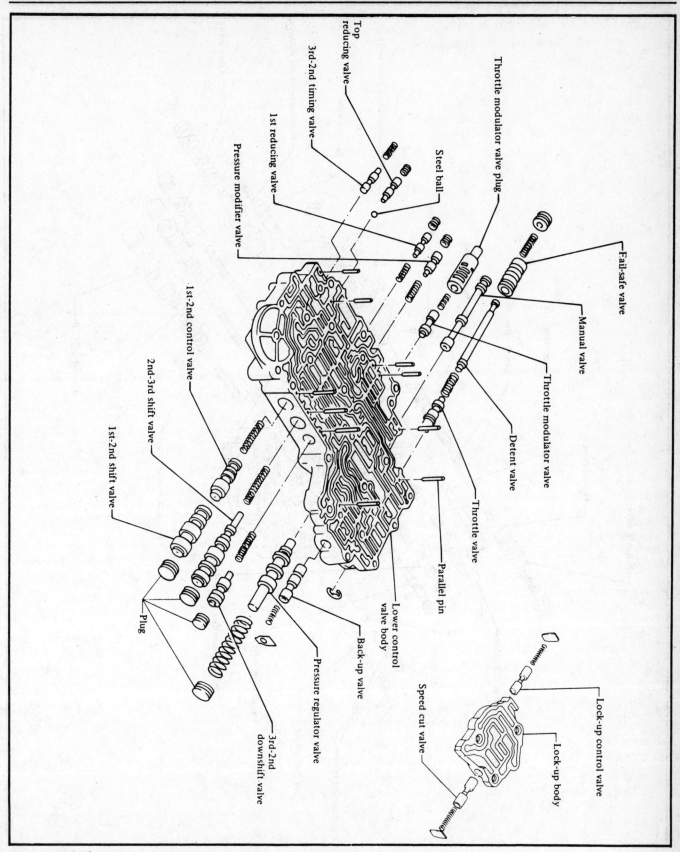

**Exploded view of control valve assembly with lock-up controls** (© Nissan Motor Co. of USA)

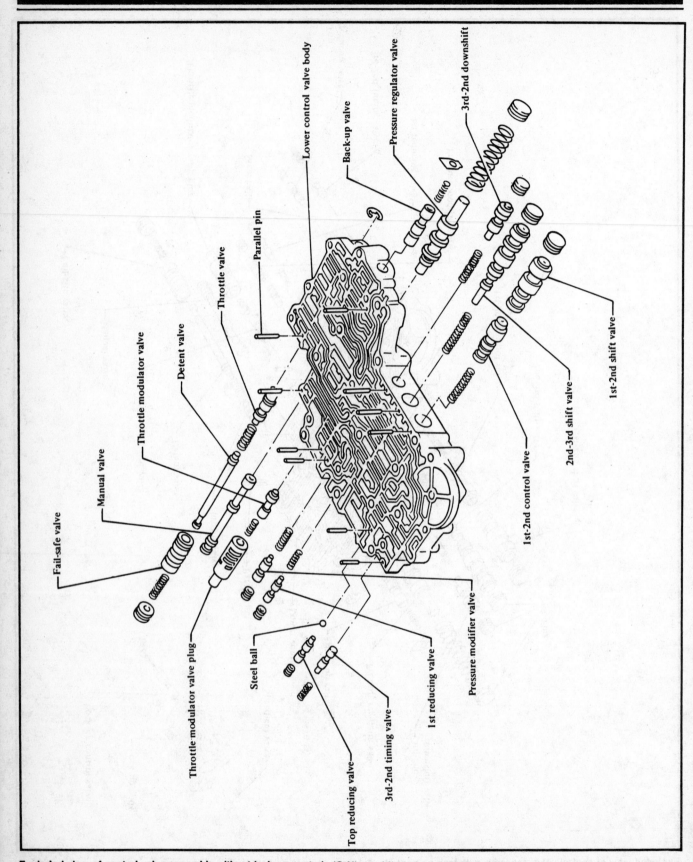

**Exploded view of control valve assembly without lock-up controls** (© Nissan Motor Co. of USA)

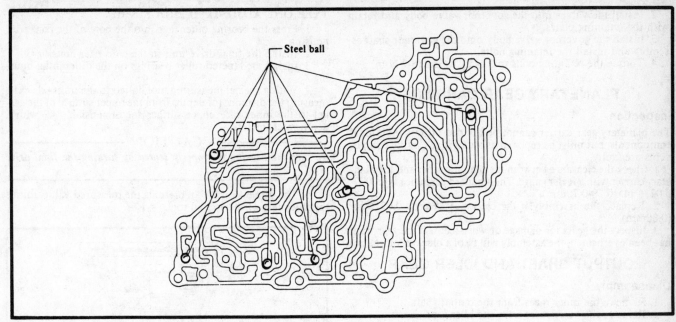

**Location of check balls in the valve body, with or without lock-up controls** (© Nissan Motor Co. of USA)

## FINE ADJUSTING SCREW

A fine adjusting screw is located on the end of the throttle modulator sleeve and provides a maximum fine adjustment of approximately 3 mph. Tightening of the screw causes the shift point to occur at a lower point (mph) and if loosened, would allow the shift point to occur at a higher point (mph), except when in the kickdown mode.

The standard position of the adjusting screw between the top of the screw and the top of the locknut is 0.492-0.512 in. (12.5-13.0mm). The locknut is secured with a torque of 2.5-3.3 ft. lbs. (3.4-4.4 N•m).

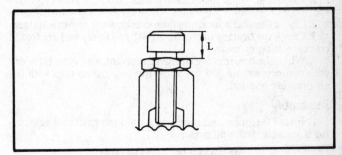

**Standard position (L) of fine adjusting screw on valve body** (© Nissan Motor Co. of USA)

## BAND SERVE PISTON

### Disassembly

1. The O-rings can be removed from the servo piston and the piston separated from the piston retainer.

### Inspection

1. Inspect the piston assembly and case bore for wear and/or scoring. If damages are present on the piston assembly, replace the unit. Inspect the return spring.
2. If the case bore is scored to the extent of being nonusable, the case would have to be replaced.

### Assembly

1. Assemble the piston to the piston retainer.
2. Lubricate and install the O-rings on the piston.

## GOVERNOR

### Disassemble

1. Remove the governor body from the governor shaft by removing the four retaining bolts.
2. Disassemble the governor valve body by removing the governor retaining plates. Matchmark valve positions.
3. If the governor gear is to be removed from the shaft, the roll pin must be driven from the gear/shaft assembly.

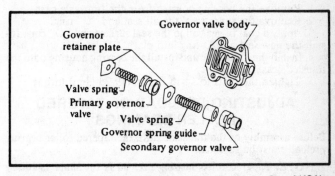

**Exploded view of governor assembly** (© Nissan Motor Co. of USA)

### Inspection

1. Check the valves for indications of burning or scratches. Inspect the springs for weakness or burning.
2. Replace the parts as required or if necessary, replace the complete governor assembly.

### Assembly

1. Install the governor gear on the shaft and align the roll pin holes. Install the roll pin.

2. Install the valves into the governor valve body and retain with the retaining plates.

3. Install the governor valve body onto the governor shaft assembly and install the retaining bolts.

4. Torque the retaining bolts to 3.6-5.1 ft. lbs. (5-7 N•m).

## PLANETARY GEAR CARRIERS

### Inspection

The planetary gear carrier cannot be divided into its individual components, but must be replaced as a unit if any of the components are faulty.

1. Check the clearance between the pinion washer and the planetary carrier with a feeler gauge. The standard clearance is 0.0079-0.0276 in. (0.20-0.70mm).

2. Replace the assembly if the clearance exceeds 0.0315 in. (0.80mm).

3. Inspect the gears for damage or worn teeth. If the gear train has been overheated, the assembly will be of a blue discoloration.

## OUTPUT SHAFT AND IDLER GEAR

### Disassembly

1. Remove the inner races from the output shaft.
2. Remove the outer races from the idler gear.

### Inspection

1. Inspect all gears for excessive wear, chips, cracks or breakage.

2. Check the shafts for distortion, cracks, wear or worn splines.

3. Check the bearing to be sure all will roll freely and are free of cracks, pitting or wear.

4. When the bearings are cleaned in solvent, air dry or blow dry with compressed air. Do not allow the bearings to spin with the air pressure applied.

### Assembly

1. Install the outer and inner races onto the shaft and gear, using a suitable drift and press.

## BEARING HOUSING

### Disassembly and Assembly

1. Remove the bearing housing from the transaxle case.
2. Remove the inner race, the oil seal and "O" ring.
3. Apply a coat of gear oil to the seal surface and "O" ring. Install the new seal and O-ring into place.
4. Install the inner race and install the bearing housing onto the transaxle case.
5. Tighten the bolts to 14-18 ft. lbs. (19-25 N•m) torque.

## ADJUSTING PRELOAD OF TAPERED ROLLER BEARINGS

Before assembly of the transaxle unit, the tapered roller bearing preload must be adjusted.

**NOTE: Tapered roller bearing preload is the same as rotary frictional force adjustment.**

If the transaxle case, bearing housing, tapered roller bearings, differential case or converter housing is replaced, the final drive unit must be adjusted. This adjustment is accomplished with the use of selected shims of varied thickness.

### Adjusting Procedure

Two types of adjusting procedures have been established by the manufacturer. It is the decision of the repair-person as to which procedure to follow.

### TYPE ONE ADJUSTING PROCEDURE

1. Press the bearing outer race into the bore of the converter housing.

2. Install the final drive unit in the converter housing.

3. Install the tapered roller bearings on the differential housing.

4. With a special measuring tool bolted to the transaxle case, measure the distance (or depth) from the upper surface of the gasket to the inner race upper surface for dimension "A" with a depth micrometer.

---- **CAUTION** ----

*Be sure the bearing is properly seated by turning the final drive gear.*

---

5. The dimension "A" represents the measured value, minus the thickness of the special tool.

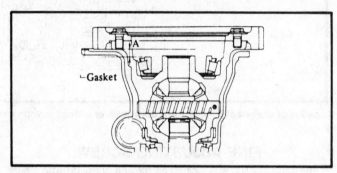

Dimension "A" measurement (© Nissan Motor Co. of USA)

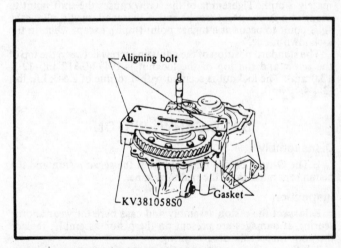

Use of the special tool mounted to the case
(© Nissan Motor Co. of USA)

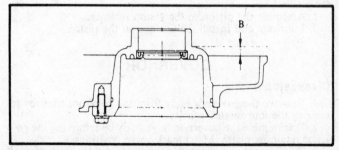

Measurement location to find dimension "B"
(© Nissan Motor Co. of USA)

6. Install the housing to the transaxle case.

7. Ensure the bearing is properly seated by turning the outer race while pushing on it.

8. The distance between the bearing seal on the bearing housing and the top surface of the transaxle case is considered dimension "B". The special tool is used to span the transaxle case surface and when used as a measuring tool, dimension "B" = thickness of the special tool, minus (-) the measured value.

9. Height "H" is the selective shim thickness needed to provide the proper preload. "H" is found by the following equation. H = A-B. The correct shim is selected from the charts in the specification section.

10. Remove the bearing retainer from the case and install the selected shim on the bearing housing. Seat the bearing assembly on the housing.

11. Lubricate the O-ring with vaseline and install it on the bearing housing.

12. Install the bearing housing to the transaxle case assembly.

13. Attach the converter housing gasket to the case. Install the retaining bolts and torque 10-13 ft. lbs. (14-18 N•m).

14. Turn the final drive assembly at least ten times and using a torque wrench, measure the preload (rotary frictional force) of the final drive tapered roller bearings. The torque should be 52-65 *inch* lbs. (5.9-7.4 N•m).

15. If the preload (rotary frictional force) is correct, disassemble the case, remove the final drive assembly and prepare for complete case reassembly.

**NOTE: Changes in the rotary frictional force of the final drive assembly should be within 8.7 inch lbs. (1.0 N•m) per revolution, without binding.**

## TYPE TWO ADJUSTING PROCEDURE

1. With the bearing housing removed from the transaxle case, remove the bearing and shim from the housing. Reinstall the bearing *without* the shim onto the housing.

2. Install the final drive assembly into the transaxle case.

3. Install the gasket, the converter housing and the retaining bolts. Torque the retaining bolts 10-13 ft. lbs. (14-18 N•m) in a criss-cross pattern.

4. Attach a dial indicator to the case assembly with the indicator stem through the bearing housing and touching the differential side gear.

5. Using a special preload adapter tool or its equivalent, position the tool into the side gear and move the tool and gear up and down, while observing the dial indicator deflection. This deflection indicates the size of the shim needed for the bearing housing to bearing distance.

6. Select the desired thickness shim from the chart in the specification section.

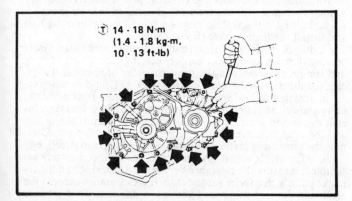

**Installation of converter housing for test**
(© Nissan Motor Co. of USA)

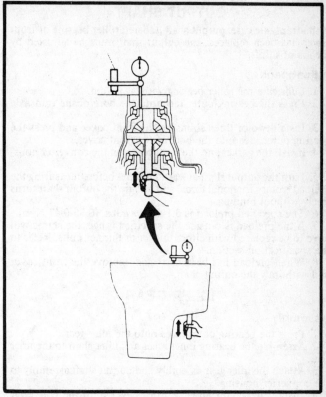

**Use of special tool and dial indicator to determine the proper sized shim to be used** (© Nissan Motor Co. of USA)

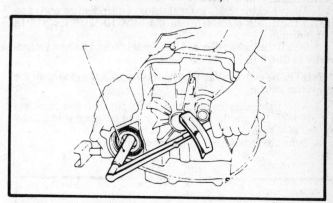

**Use of special tool and torque wrench to determine the preload (rotary frictional force) of the differential side bearing**
(© Nissan Motor Co. of USA)

7. Disassemble the bearing housing and remove the bearing from the housing. Install the shim and the bearing onto the bearing housing. Be sure both are properly seated.

8. With the use of the special turning tool and a torque wrench, turn the differential final drive unit and measure the preload (rotary frictional force) on the bearings.

9. The final drive unit must be turned at least ten times before measuring the preload. The changes in the reading of the preload per revolution should be within 8.7 *inch* lbs. (1.0 N•m) without binding.

10. The specified preload (rotary fricitional force) for the bearings is 52-65 *inch* lbs. (5.9-7.4 N•m). If the measurement is outside the specifications, the unit will have to be disassembled, re-checked and reassembled.

### OUTPUT SHAFT

If the transaxle case, output shaft, tapered roller bearing or front cover has been replaced, the output shaft must be adjusted by means of shims.

#### Adjustment

1. Lubricate the roller bearing with A/T fluid.
2. Press the bearing outer race into the bore of the transaxle case.
3. Install two or three shims on the front cover and press the bearing outer race into the bore of the front cover.
4. Install the gasket and the front cover on the converter housing.
5. Turn the output shaft at least ten times before measuring the preload (rotary frictional force) and be sure the output shaft turns freely without binding.
6. The specified preload is 3.1-4.2 *inch* lbs. (0.35-0.47 N•m).
7. If the preload is outside the specified range, the shims will have to be replaced with either thicker or thinner units. Refer to the specification section.
8. When preload has been corrected, remove the front cover and withdraw the output shaft.

### IDLER GEAR

#### Assembly

1. Press the bearing outer races onto the idler gear.
2. Assemble the bearing inner races and idler shaft to the idler gear.
3. Attach the idler gear assembly and output shaft assembly to the converter housing.
4. Install the gasket and the front cover onto the converter housing. Before installing the bolts, clean the threads and the converter housing with solvent.
5. Apply locking sealer to the threads of the retaining bolts and install them into place. Tighten the bolts 10-13 ft. lbs. (14-18 N•m) torque.
6. Install the lockwasher and idler gear bolt and tighten temporarily to 20-27 ft. lbs. (26-36 N•m).

**NOTE: Be sure to align the lockwasher with the groove on the converter housing.**

7. After tightening the bolt, turn the output shaft five complete revolutions. Loosen the idler gear bolt and retighten it to 2.2-2.9 ft. lbs. (3-4 N•m).
8. Bend the lockwasher to lock the bolt in place.

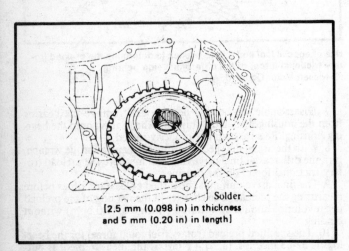

Solder
[2.5 mm (0.098 in) in thickness
and 5 mm (0.20 in) in length]

**Use of solder strip or solder plate to measure end play**
(© Nissan Motor Co. of USA)

### END PLAY OF OUTPUT SHAFT

#### Adjusting

After the adjustment of the preload on the output shaft tapered roller bearing, the end play of the output shaft must be checked. A strip of solder or a solder plate can be used to check the end play clearance.

1. Using a strip of solder or solder plate, at least 0.098 in. (2.5mm) in diameter or thickness and 0.200 in. (5.0mm) in length, as the maximum gear clearance is 0.091 in. (2.3mm). If the diameter or thickness of the test solder is smaller than 0.098 in. (2.5mm), also use shims.

**NOTE: Always use two strips or plates of solder, one on each side of the gear.**

2. With the solder strip or plate in place, install the converter housing and output shaft assembly as a unit on the transaxle case.
3. Torque the retaining bolts to 10-13 ft. lbs. (14-18 N•m).
4. Remove the retaining bolts and housing assembly.
5. Measure the thickness of the solder strips or plates and if necessary, select shims of appropriate thickness so that the end play of the output shaft is within the specified range of 0.0098-0.0217 in. (0.25-0.55mm).

### ASSEMBLY OF THE TRANSAXLE COMPONENTS

#### Before Assembly

1. Before proceeding with the final assembly of the transaxle, verify the case housing and all parts are free of dirt dust and other foreign material. Lubricate the parts in clean A/T fluid. Petroleum jelly (vaseline) can be used to secure thrust washers and bearings during the assembly.
2. All new seals and rings should have been installed on the individual components before the final assembly. If not, install them as the components are readied for assembly into the case.

#### Assembly

1. Lubricate the oil pump assembly and install it, along with the nylon washer and thrust bearing. Align the five bolt holes.
2. Lubricate the low and reverse brake piston seal. Install the piston into the case by lightly tapping upon it evenly.
3. Install the low and reverse piston retainer and springs. Align the holes and install the retaining bolts. Tighten to 5.1-6.5 ft. lbs. (7-9 N•m).
4. Apply air pressure to test the low and reverse brake piston. If the piston moves smoothly, the seal has not turned and is installed properly.
5. Install the brake band, the servo piston and "O" ring, the return spring and the snapring. Hold the piston into its bore with a small C-clamp until the snapring is installed into its groove.
6. Lubricate the sealing rings on the oil pump housing hub and install the high-reverse (front) clutch.
7. Install the forward (rear) clutch, front internal gear, thrust bearing, bearing race, front carrier, bearing race thrust bearing and sun gear assembly in their reverse order of removal. Lubricate the thrust washers and bearings with A/T fluid or vaseline.
8. Install the low and reverse brake dished retainer plate, drive and driven clutch plates, retainer plate and the snapring. Install the dished plate with the inner concave against the piston and the outer concave against the first driven (steel) plate. Alternate the remaining plates with a drive (lined), driven (steel), etc.
9. After the low and reverse brake has been completely assembled, measure the clearance between the snapring and the retainer plate with a feeler gauge blade. If the clearance exceeds the allowable limit of 0.150 in. (3.8mm), a different sized retainer plate must be installed. The preferred or standard clearance is 0.0748-0.0866 in. (1.90-2.20mm). The available plates are as follows:

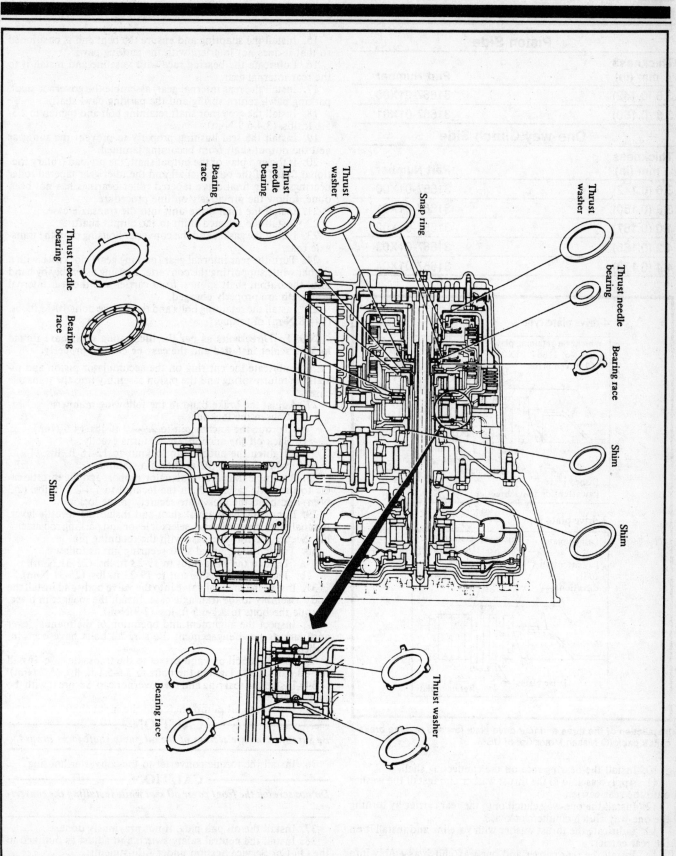

Thrust race bearing

Thrust needle bearing

Thrust washer

Snap ring

Thrust washer

Thrust needle bearing

Thrust needle bearing

Bearing race

Bearing race

Shim

Shim

Shim

Bearing race

Thrust washer

**Location of thrust bearings and washers within the drive train (© Nissan Motor Co. of USA)**

### Piston Side

| Thickness mm (in) | Part Number |
|---|---|
| 3.6 (0.142) | 31667-01X00 |
| 3.8 (0.150) | 31667-01X01 |

### One-way Clutch Side

| Thickness mm (in) | Part Number |
|---|---|
| 3.6 (0.142) | 31667-01X00 |
| 3.8 (0.150) | 31667-01X01 |
| 4.0 (0.157) | 31667-01X02 |
| 4.2 (0.165) | 31667-01X03 |
| 4.4 (0.173) | 31667-01X04 |

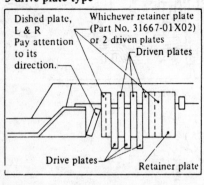

**4-drive plate type**

Whichever retaining plate (Part No. 31667 01X02) or 2 driven plates — Driven plate

Retainer plate

Drive plate

Dished plate
Pay attention to its direction

**3-drive plate type**

Dished plate, L & R
Pay attention to its direction.

Whichever retainer plate (Part No. 31667-01X02) or 2 driven plates — Driven plates

Drive plates

Retainer plate

**Installation of the three and four drive plate low and reverse brake clutch pack (© Nissan Motor Co. of USA)**

10. Install the bearing race on the connecting shell.
11. Apply vaseline to the thrust washer and install the washer onto the rear carrier.
12. Install the one-way clutch onto the rear carrier by turning the one-way clutch counterclockwise.
13. Lubricate the thrust washer with vaseline and install it on the rear carrier.
14. Install the rear carrier and one-way clutch assembly into the case by turning the one-way clutch/carrier assembly in a clockwise direction.

15. Install the snapring and ensure the bent end is positioned so that it does not interfere with the parking pawl.
16. Lubricate the bearing race with vaseline and install it to the rear internal gear.
17. Install the rear internal gear, assemble the governor shaft, parking pawl, return spring and the parking pawl shaft.
18. Install the governor shaft retaining bolt and tighten to 2.5-5.1 ft. lbs. (3.4-6.9 N•m).
19. Install the seal bushing properly to prevent the sun gear and the output shaft from becoming jammed.
20. If the end play of the output shaft, the preload (rotary frictional force) of the output shaft and the idler gear tapered roller bearings or the final drive tapered roller bearings has not been done, follow the previously outline procedure.
21. Install the final drive unit into the transaxle case.
22. Install the selected shim to the output shaft.
23. Install the gasket and the converter housing onto the transaxle case.
24. Turn the rear internal gear (parking gear) clockwise with a prybar while supporting the converter housing assembly by hand until the output shaft splines, front carrier and the rear internal gear teeth are properly engaged.
25. Install the retaining bolts and tighten the bolts 10-13 ft. lbs. (14-18 N•m) of torque.

**NOTE: Three bolts as per the illustration must have thread locking sealer installed and the case be cleaned properly.**

26. Lubricate the cut ring on the accumulator piston and install the return spring and the piston assembly into the transaxle case.
27. Adjust the brake band in the following manner:
    a. Loosen the locknut.
    b. Torque the anchor pin to 2.9-4.3 ft. lbs. (4-6 N•m).
    c. Back off the anchor pin 2.5 turns exactly.
    d. Tighten the anchor pin locknut to 12-16 ft. lbs. (16-22 N•m) while holding the anchor pin stationary.
28. Assemble the parking actuator support and the throttle cable to transaxle case. Tighten the locknut to 1.4-2.2 ft. lbs. (2-3 N•m) and bend the lock plate securely to the locknut.
29. Lubricate the manual shaft and install the throttle lever, manual plate, manual shaft, selector lever and parking rod assembly. Secure them to the case with the retaining pin.
30. Tighten the manual shift securing nut as follows:
    a. Tighten the inside nut to 19-23 ft. lbs. (25-31 N•m).
    b. Tighten the outside nut to 19-23 ft. lbs. (25-31 N•m).
31. Install the manual valve into the valve body and install the body assembly to the transaxle case. Install the magnet in place. Torque the bolts to 5.1-6.5 ft. lbs. (7-9 N•m).
32. Inspect the alignment and operation of the manual lever and parking pawl engagement. Be sure all bolts have been installed.
33. Install the oil pan and gasket to the transaxle case. Install the oil pan guard. Tighten the bolts to 3.6-5.1 ft. lbs. (5-7 N•m).
34. Install the seal ring and the governor cap. Secure it with the snap retainer.
35. Install the oil pump shaft and the input shaft.

— CAUTION —
*Be sure the concave section of the oil pump shaft faces inward.*

36. Install the torque converter to the converter housing.

— CAUTION —
*Do not scratch the front cover oil seal while installing the converter.*

37. Install the oil pan plug, if not previously done.
38. Install the neutral safety switch and adjust as outlined in the On-Car Service Section under Adjustments.
39. Verify the manual control lever is operating properly.
40. Prepare the transaxle for installation into the vehicle.

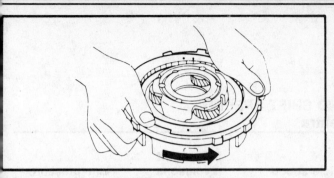

Installation of one-way clutch into the rear carrier
(© Nissan Motor Co. of USA)

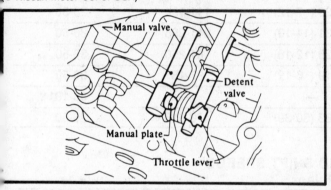

Alignment of manual valve and manual plate, along with the alignment of the throttle lever and the detent valve during the valve body installation (© Nissan Motor Co. of USA)

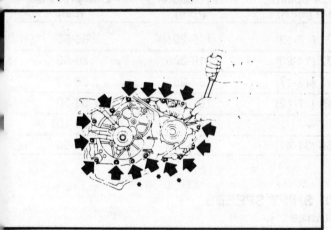

Use of a sealer is recommended on the star indicated bolts during the converter housing final assembly (© Nissan Motor Co. of USA)

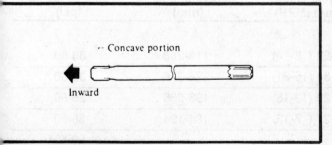

Direction of assembly for oil pump shaft
© Nissan Motor Co. of USA)

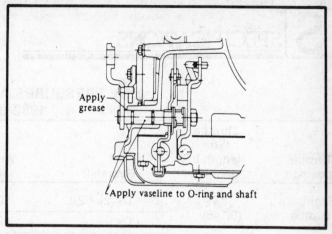

Apply grease

Apply vaseline to O-ring and shaft

Installation of manual shaft assembly (© Nissan Motor Co. of USA)

Projection should face upward

Installation of the one-way clutch/rear carrier assembly into the case (© Nissan Motor Co. of USA)

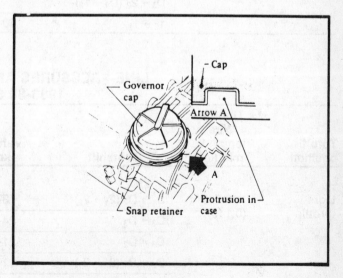

Cap

Governor cap

Arrow A

A

Protrusion in case

Snap retainer

Installation of the governor cap. Note the direction of cap during the installation (© Nissan Motor Co. of USA)

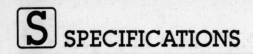

# S SPECIFICATIONS

### LINE PRESSURES AND SHIFT SPEEDS
### 1982 Sentra

| Throttle position | Throttle Wire length L mm (in) | Gearshift | Vehicle speed km/h (MPH) | Drive shaft revolutions (rpm) | Line pressure (psi) |
|---|---|---|---|---|---|
| Light throttle | 3.7 (0.146) | $D_1 \rightarrow D_2$ $(2_1 \rightarrow 2_2)$ | 12-20 ( 7-12) | 111-194 | 36-50 |
| | | $D_2 \rightarrow D_3$ | 22-31 (14-19) | 211-295 | 36-50 |
| | | $D_3 \rightarrow D_2$ | 19-26 (12-16) | 181-250 | 36-50 |
| | | $D_2 \rightarrow D_1$ $(2_2 \rightarrow 2_1)$ | 10-19 ( 6-12) | 97-181 | 36-50 |
| | | $D_3 \rightarrow 2_2$ $(D_3 \rightarrow 1_2)$ | — | — | 80-101 |
| | | $1_2 \rightarrow 1_1$ | 49-63 (30-39) | 470-610 | 36-50 |

### LINE PRESSURES AND SHIFT SPEEDS
### 1983-84 Pulsar

| Throttle position | Throttle Wire length L mm (in) | Gearshift | Vehicle speed km/h (MPH) | Drive shaft revolutions (rpm) | Line pressure (psi) |
|---|---|---|---|---|---|
| Light throttle (1/8 open) | 3.7 (0.146) | $D_1 \rightarrow D_2$ $(2_1 \rightarrow 2_2)$ | 12-21 ( 7-13) | 115-201 | 36-50 |
| | | $D_2 \rightarrow D_3$ | 23-32 (14-20) | 219-306 | 36-50 |
| | | $D_3 \rightarrow D_2$ | 19-27 (12-17) | 187-259 | 36-50 |
| | | $D_2 \rightarrow D_1$ $(2_2 \rightarrow 2_1)$ | 11-19 ( 7-12) | 101-188 | 36-50 |
| | | $D_3 \rightarrow 2_2$ $(D_3 \rightarrow 1_2)$ | — | — | 80-101 |
| | | $1_2 \rightarrow 1_1$ | 50-66 (31-41) | 487-632 | 36-50 |

### LINE PRESSURES AND SHIFT SPEEDS
### 1983-84 Stanza

| Throttle position | Throttle Wire length L mm (in) | Gearshift | Vehicle speed km/h (MPH) | Drive shaft revolutions (rpm) | Line pressure (psi) |
|---|---|---|---|---|---|
| Light throttle | 3.7 (0.146) | $D_1 \rightarrow D_2$ $(2_1 \rightarrow 2_2)$ | 13-22 ( 8-14) | 119-208 | 36-50 |
| | | $D_2 \rightarrow D_3$ | 24-34 (15-21) | 226-316 | 36-50 |
| | | $D_3 \rightarrow D_2$ | 21-29 (13-18) | 193-268 | 36-50 |
| | | $D_2 \rightarrow D_1$ $(2_2 \rightarrow 2_1)$ | 11-21 ( 7-13) | 104-194 | 36-50 |
| | | $D_3 \rightarrow 2_2$ $(D_3 \rightarrow 1_2)$ | — | — | 80-101 |
| | | $1_2 \rightarrow 1_1$ | 54-71 (34-44) | 503-653 | 36-50 |

### LINE PRESSURES AND SHIFT SPEEDS
### 1983-84 Sentra w/engine E16
### Transaxle Model 11X03

| Throttle position | Throttle Wire length L mm (in) | Gearshift | Vehicle speed km/h (MPH) | Drive shaft revolutions (rpm) | Line pressure (psi) |
|---|---|---|---|---|---|
| Light throttle | 3.7 (0.146) | $D_1 \rightarrow D_2$ ($2_1 \rightarrow 2_2$) | 12-21 ( 7-13) | 115-201 | 36-50 |
| | | $D_2 \rightarrow D_3$ | 23-32 (14-20) | 219-306 | 36-50 |
| | | $D_3 \rightarrow D_2$ | 19-27 (12-17) | 187-259 | 36-50 |
| | | $D_2 \rightarrow D_1$ ($2_2 \rightarrow 2_1$) | 11-19 ( 7-12) | 101-188 | 36-50 |
| | | $D_3 \rightarrow 2_2$ ($D_3 \rightarrow 1_2$) | — | — | 80-101 |
| | | $1_2 \rightarrow 1_1$ | 50-66 (31-41) | 487-632 | 36-50 |

### LINE PRESSURES AND SHIFT SPEEDS
### 1983-84 Sentra w/engine CD17
### Transaxle Model 03X17

| Throttle position | Throttle Wire length L mm (in) | Gearshift | Vehicle speed km/h (MPH) | Drive shaft revolutions (rpm) | Line pressure (psi) |
|---|---|---|---|---|---|
| Light throttle | 3.7 (0.146) | $D_1 \rightarrow D_2$ ($2_1 \rightarrow 2_2$) | 13-22 ( 8-14) | 119-208 | 36-50 |
| | | $D_2 \rightarrow D_3$ | 21-30 (13-19) | 198-288 | 36-50 |
| | | $D_3 \rightarrow D_2$ | 18-26 (11-16) | 170-245 | 36-50 |
| | | $D_2 \rightarrow D_1$ ($2_2 \rightarrow 2_1$) | 11-21 ( 7-13) | 104-194 | 36-50 |
| | | $D_3 \rightarrow 2_2$ ($D_3 \rightarrow 1_2$) | — | — | 80-101 |
| | | $1_2 \rightarrow 1_1$ | 46-62 (29-39) | 435-585 | 36-50 |

### SPECIFICATIONS FOR INTERNAL COMPONENTS
#### Codes

| Year/Model | Transaxle Code |
|---|---|
| 1982 310 | 01X05 |
| 1983-84 Stanza | 13X07 |
| 1983-84 Pulsar | 11X03 |
| 1982 Sentra | 11X00 |
| 1983-84 Sentra | |
| W/E16 engine | 11X03 |
| W/CD17 engine | 03X17 |

### STALL SPEED SPECIFICATIONS

| MODEL | RPM |
|---|---|
| 1982 Datsun 310 | 1650-1950 |
| 1983-84 Nissan Stanza | 2000-2300 |
| 1982-84 Nissan Sentra | 1800-2100 ① |
| 1983-84 Nissan Pulsar, NX | 1800-2100 |

① 1500-1800 RPM w/CD17 engine

## SPECIFICATIONS FOR INTERNAL COMPONENTS

### High-Reverse (Front) Clutch
**TRANSAXLE MODEL CODES—01X05, 11X00, 13X07, 11X03, 03X17**

| Number of drive plates | | 2 | |
|---|---|---|---|
| Number of driven plates | | 3 | |
| Clearance mm (in.) | Standard | 1.0-1.4 (0.039-0.055) | |
| | Allowable limit | 2.2 (0.087) | |
| Drive plate thickness mm (in.) | Standard | 1.80 (0.0709) | |
| | Allowable limit | 1.6 (0.063) | |
| Thickness for retaining plate | | Thickness mm (in) | Part number |
| | | 3.4 (0.134) | 31537-01X05 |
| | | 3.6 (0.142) | 31537-01X00 |
| | | 3.8 (0.150) | 31537-01X01 |
| | | 4.0 (0.157) | 31537-01X02 |
| | | 4.2 (0.165) | 31537-01X03 |
| | | 4.4 (0.173) | 31537-01X04 |

### Forward (Rear) Clutch
**TRANSAXLE MODEL CODES—01X05, 11X00, 13X07, 11X03, 03X17**

| Number of drive plates | | 3 ① | |
|---|---|---|---|
| Number of driven plates | | 3 ② | |
| Clearance mm (in.) | Standard | 0.8-1.2 (0.031-0.047) ③ | |
| | Allowable limit | 2.8 (0.110) ④ | |
| Drive plate thickness mm (in.) | Standard | 1.80 (0.0709) | |
| | Allowable limit | 1.6 (0.063) | |
| Thickness for retaining plate | | Thickness mm (in) | Part number |
| | | 3.4 (0.134) | 31537-01X05 |
| | | 3.6 (0.142) | 31537-01X00 |
| | | 3.8 (0.150) | 31537-01X01 |
| | | 4.0 (0.157) | 31537-01X02 |
| | | 4.2 (0.165) | 31537-01X03 |
| | | 4.4 (0.173) | 31537-01X04 |

① Code 11X00—Four drive plates
② Code 11X00—Four Driven plates
③ Code 13X07—0.5-0.8mm (0.020-0.031 inch)
④ Code 13X07—2.4mm (0.094 inch)

### Low and Reverse Brake
**TRANSAXLE MODEL CODES—01X05**

| Number of drive plates | 4 |
|---|---|
| Number of driven plates | 5 |
| Clearance mm (in) | 0.8-1.1 (0.031-0.043) |

### TRANSAXLE MODEL CODE—13X07

| Number of drive plates | | 5 |
|---|---|---|
| Number of driven plates | | 5 |
| Clearance mm (in.) | Standard | 1.90-2.20 (0.0748-0.0866) |
| | Allowable limit | 3.8 (0.150) |
| Drive plate thickness mm (in.) | Standard | 2.00 (0.0787) |
| | Allowable limit | 1.8 (0.071) |

### TRANSAXLE MODEL CODE—11X00, 11X03

| Number of drive plates | | 4 |
|---|---|---|
| Number of driven plates | | 4 (6) ① |
| Clearance mm (in.) | Standard | 1.90-2.20 (0.0748-0.0866) |
| | Allowable limit | 3.8 (0.150) |
| Drive plate thickness mm (in.) | Standard | 2.00 (0.0787) |
| | Allowable limit | 1.8 (0.071) |

### TRANSAXLE MODEL CODE—03X17

| Number of drive plates | | 3 |
|---|---|---|
| Number of driven plates | | 3 (7) ① |
| Clearance mm (in.) | Standard | 1.90-2.20 (0.0748-0.0866) |
| | Allowable limit | 3.8 (0.150) |
| Drive plate thickness mm (in.) | Standard | 2.00 (0.0787) |
| | Allowable limit | 1.8 (0.071) |

① In the case where two driven plates are used instead of the retaining plate.

## SPECIFICATIONS FOR INTERNAL COMPONENTS

### Oil Pump Clearance
**ALL TRANSAXLE MODEL CODES**
mm (in.)

| Outer gear-pump housing | Standard | 0.20-0.30 (0.0079-0.0118) |
|---|---|---|
| | Allowable limit | 0.35 (0.0138) |
| Outer gear-crescent | Standard | 0.20-0.30 (0.0079-0.0118) |
| | Allowable limit | 0.35 (0.0138) |
| Gears-pump plate | Standard | 0.02-0.04 (0.0008-0.0016) |
| | Allowable limit | 0.08 (0.0031) |
| Seal ring-ring groove | Standard | 0.10-0.25 (0.0039-0.0098) |
| | Allowable limit | 0.25 (0.0098) |

### Planetary Carrier Clearance
**ALL TRANSAXLE MODEL CODES**
mm (in.)

| Clearance between pinion washer and planetary carrier | Standard | 0.20-0.70 (0.0079-0.0276) |
|---|---|---|
| | Allowable limit | 0.80 (0.0315) |

### Identification marks on separator plate
Code 11X00 - U
Code 11X03 - W
Code 03X17 - R
Code 13X07 - AG

### PreLoad (Rotary Frictional Force)
**ALL MODEL CODES**

| | N•m | (in.-lb) |
|---|---|---|
| Output shaft | 0.35-0.47 | (3.1-4.2) |
| Final drive | 5.9-7.4 | (52-65) |

### Output Shaft End Play
**ALL MODEL CODES**

| 0.25-0.55 mm (0.0098-0.0217 in.) |
|---|

### Output Shaft End Play Adjusting Shims
**ALL MODEL CODES**

| Thickness of soldering plate −0.05mm (0.0020 in)① mm (in) | Thickness mm (in) | Part number |
|---|---|---|
| 0.55-0.85 (0.0217-0.0335) | 0.3 (0.012) | 31484-01x00 |
| 0.75-1.05 (0.0295-0.0413) | 0.5 (0.020) | 31484-01x01 |
| 0.95-1.25 (0.0374-0.0492) | 0.7 (0.028) | 31484-01x02 |
| 1.15-1.45 (0.0453-0.0571) | 0.9 (0.035) | 31484-01x03 |
| 1.35-1.65 (0.0531-0.0650) | 1.1 (0.043) | 31484-01x04 |
| 1.55-1.85 (0.0610-0.0728) | 1.3 (0.051) | 31484-01x05 |
| 1.75-2.05 (0.0689-0.0807) | 1.5 (0.059) | 31484-01x06 |
| 1.95-2.25 (0.0768-0.0886) | 1.7 (0.067) | 31484-01x07 |

① 0.05 mm (0.0020 in.) is the amount the soldering plate recovers due to its elasticity, and it must be subtracted from the thickness of soldering plate.

### Final Drive Adjusting Shims
**ALL MODEL CODES**

| H = A − B mm (in) | Thickness mm (in) | Part number |
|---|---|---|
| 0-0.07 (0-0.0028) | 0.38 (0.0150) | 38453-01X00 |
| 0.07-0.15 (0.0028-0.0059) | 0.46 (0.0181) | 38453-01X01 |
| 0.15-0.23 (0.0059-0.0091) | 0.54 (0.0213) | 38453-01X02 |
| 0.23-0.31 (0.0091-0.0122) | 0.62 (0.0244) | 38453-01X03 |
| 0.31-0.39 (0.0122-0.0154) | 0.70 (0.0276) | 38453-01X04 |
| 0.39-0.47 (0.0154-0.0185) | 0.78 (0.0307) | 38453-01X05 |
| 0.47-0.55 (0.0185-0.0217) | 0.86 (0.0339) | 38453-01X06 |
| 0.55-0.63 (0.0217-0.0248) | 0.94 (0.0370) | 38453-01X07 |

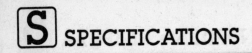

## SPECIFICATIONS FOR INTERNAL COMPONENTS

### Final Drive Adjusting Shims
#### ALL MODEL CODES

| H = A − B mm (in) | Thickness mm (in) | Part number |
|---|---|---|
| 0.63-0.71 (0.0248-0.0280) | 1.02 (0.0402) | 38453-01X08 |
| 0.71-0.79 (0.0280-0.0311) | 1.10 (0.0433) | 38453-01X09 |
| 0.79-0.87 (0.0311-0.0343) | 1.18 (0.0465) | 38453-01X10 |
| 0.87-0.95 (0.0343-0.0374) | 1.26 (0.0496) | 38453-01X11 |
| 0.95-1.03 (0.0374-0.0406) | 1.34 (0.0528) | 38453-01X12 |
| 1.03-1.11 (0.0406-0.0437) | 1.42 (0.0559) | 38453-01X13 |
| 1.11-1.19 (0.0437-0.0469) | 1.50 (0.0591) | 38453-01X14 |
| 1.19-1.27 (0.0469-0.0500) | 1.58 (0.0622) | 38453-01X15 |
| 1.27-1.35 (0.0500-0.0531) | 1.66 (0.0654) | 38453-01X16 |

### TORQUE SPECIFICATIONS

| Unit | | N•m | ft-lb |
|---|---|---|---|
| Drive plate to torque converter | | 49-69 | 36-51 |
| Converter housing to engine | M8 | 16-22 | 12-16 |
| | M10 | 39-49 | 29-36 |
| Engine gusset to cylinder block (CD17 engine model) | | 30-40 | 22-30 |
| Transaxle case to converter housing | | 14-18 | 10-13 |
| Transaxle case to front cover | | 14-18 | 10-13 |
| Oil pan to transaxle case | | 5-7 | 3.6-5.1 |
| Bearing retainer to transaxle case | | 19-25 | 14-18 |
| Piston stem (when adjusting band brake)① | | 4-5 | 2.9-3.6 |
| Piston stem lock nut | | 16-22 | 12-16 |

### TORQUE SPECIFICATIONS

| Unit | N•m | ft-lb |
|---|---|---|
| Low and reverse brake piston retainer | 7-9 | 5.1-6.5 |
| Control valve body to transaxle case | 7-9 | 5.1-6.5 |
| Lower valve body to upper valve body | 7-9 | 5.1-6.5 |
| Final gear bolt | 69-78 | 51-58 |
| Oil strainer to lower valve body | 5-7 | 3.6-5.1 |
| Governor valve body to governor shaft | 5-7 | 3.6-5.1 |
| Governor shaft securing nut | 3.4-6.9 | 2.5-5.1 |
| Idler gear when adjusting turning frictional force) | 26-36 | 20-27 |
| Idler gear lock nut② | — | — |
| Throttle wire securing nut | 5-7 | 3.6-5.1 |
| Control cable securing nut | 8-11 | 5.8-8.0 |
| Inhibitor switch to transaxle case | 2.0-2.5 | 1.4-1.9 |
| Manual shaft lock nut | 31-42 | 23-31 |
| Oil cooler pipe to transaxle case | 29-49 | 22-36 |
| Test plug (oil pressure inspection hole) | 5-10 | 3.6-7.2 |
| Support actuator (parking rod inserting position) to rear extension | 8-11 | 5.8-8.0 |
| Engine to gusset | 30-40 | 22-30 |
| Gusset to converter housing | 16-21 | 12-15 |

① Turn back 2.5 turns after tightening.
② Refer to Adjusting Turning Frictional Force of Tapered Roller Bearing.

# SPECIAL TOOLS

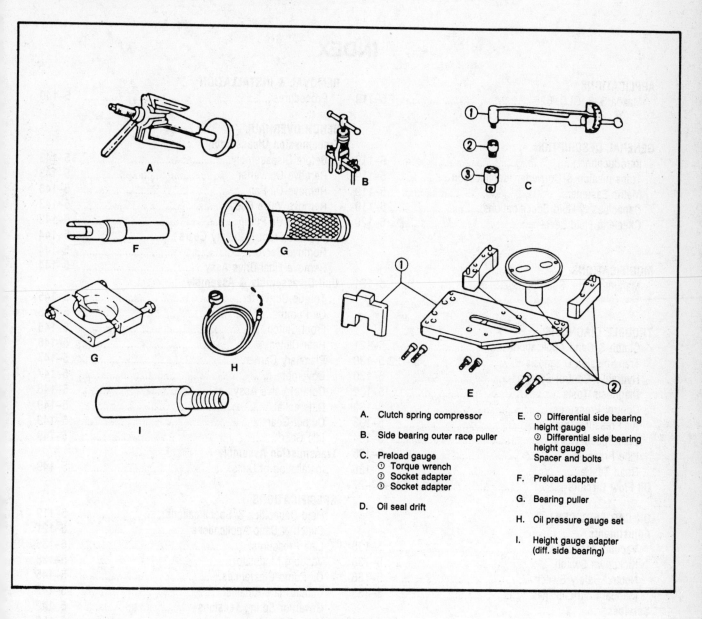

A. Clutch spring compressor

B. Side bearing outer race puller

C. Preload gauge
① Torque wrench
② Socket adapter
③ Socket adapter

D. Oil seal drift

E. ① Differential side bearing height gauge
② Differential side bearing height gauge
Spacer and bolts

F. Preload adapter

G. Bearing puller

H. Oil pressure gauge set

I. Height gauge adapter (diff. side bearing)

# INDEX

# JATCO
# F3A (MAZDA)
# Automatic Transaxle

## APPLICATIONS

Mazda 626
Mazda 323/GLC

## GENERAL DESCRIPTION

The Jatco F3A transaxle is a fully automatic unit, consisting of three forward speeds and one reverse speed. The internal components are similar to the 3N71B and R3A automatic transmissions. Some of the differences are as follows:

1. The torque converter is located on the engine side and the oil pump is located on the other end of the transaxle. The front clutch, the rear clutch, front planetary and rear planetary gears are arranged in the respective order from the front, or oil pump end of the transaxle. During the section outline, the oil pump end will be referred to as the front and the converter end, or engine end, will be referred to as the rear of the transaxle.

2. The control valve is located under the front clutch and the rear clutch assemblies.

3. The governor is located on the outside of the case and responds to the speed of the output shaft to control operating oil pressure.

4. The low and reverse brake band is located on the outside of the rear planetary gears to shorten the total length of the transaxle.

5. The three shafts that are contained within the case are the oil pump driveshaft which transmit engine speed directly to the oil pump via a quill shaft inside the input shaft, the input shaft which transmits power from the torque converter turbine and drives the front clutch cover. The third shaft is the output shaft which transmits power from the front planetary gear carrier and the rear planetary gear annulus, through the main drive idler gear to the differential drive gear.

6. Both the transaxle and the differential use a commond sump with ATF fluid as the lubricant.

## Transaxle and Converter Identification

### TRANSAXLE

Identification tags are located on the front of the transaxle, under the oil cooler lines and identify the transaxle type and model. It is most important to obtain the tag information when ordering parts for a rebuild operation, since different models are used with different engines.

### CONVERTER

The torque converter is a welded unit and cannot be disassembled unless special tools are available for that purpose. Identification codes are used by the manufacturer, but are not listed for general usage by the trade, other than type 12.

## Transaxle Metric Fasteners

Metric bolt sizes and thread pitches are used for all fasteners on the Jatco transaxles. The metric fastener dimensions are close to the dimensions of the familiar inch system fasteners, and for this reason, replacement fasteners must have the same measurement and strength as those removed. Do not attempt to interchange metric fasteners for inch system fasteners. Mismatched or incorrect fasteners can result in damage to the transmission unit through malfunctions, breakage or possible personal injury. Care should be taken to reuse the fasteners in the same locations as removed whenever possible.

## Fluid Specification

The use of type F automatic transmission fluid or its equivalent, is recommended for use in the F3A automatic transaxle models.

### CAPACITIES

The capacity of the F3A transaxle is 6.0 US quarts, 5.7 Liters, or 5.0 Imp. quarts.

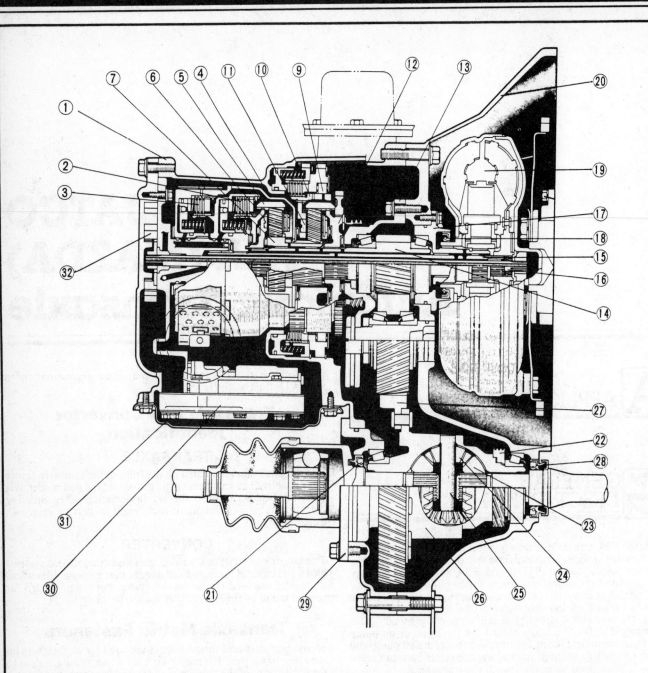

1. Transmission
2. Rear clutch
3. Front clutch
4. Connection shell
5. Rear clutch hub assembly
6. Planetary carrier
7. Sun gear
8. Low and reverse brake
9. One-way clutch
10. One-way clutch inner race
11. Planetary carrier
12. Drum hub assembly
13. Bearing housing
14. Output gear
15. Turbine shaft
16. Oil pump shaft
17. Bearing cover
18. Oil seal
19. Torque converter
20. Converter housing
21. Oil seal
22. Speedometer drive gear
23. Side gear
24. Pinion gear
25. Pinion shaft
26. Differential gear case
27. Ring gear
28. Oil seal
29. Side bearing housing
30. Control valve
31. Oil pan
32. Oil pump

**Cross section of the F3A transaxle** (©Toyo Kogyo Co. Ltd.)

**Location of identification tags** (©Toyo Kogyo Co. Ltd.)

## FLUID LEVEL

### Check the Fluid Level

With the engine/transaxle assemblies up to normal operating temperature, move the quadrant through all the selector positions and finish in the "P" position. The correct level is between the "F" and "L" marks on the dipstick. It is important to keep the level at, or slightly below, the "F" mark on the dipstick. Do not overfill the assembly.

Transaxle oil level should be checked, both visually and by smell, to determine that the fluid level is correct and to observe any foreign material in the fluid. Smelling the fluid will indicate if any of the bands or clutches have been burned through excessive slippage or overheating of the trans.

It is most important to locate the defect and its cause, and to properly repair them to avoid having the same problem recur.

In order to more fully understand the Jatco automatic transaxle and to diagnose possible defects more easily, the clutch and band applications chart and a general description of the hydraulic control system is given.

## MODIFICATIONS

### Transaxle Modifications

No known transaxle modifications for the F3A units were available at the time of printing of this publication.

## TROUBLE DIAGNOSIS

A logical and orderly diagnosis outline and charts are provided with clutch and band applications, shift speed and governor pressures, main control pressures and oil flow circuits to assist the repairman in diagnosing the problems, causes and extent of repairs needed to bring the automatic transaxle back to its acceptable level of operation.

Preliminary checks and adjustments should be made to the manual valve linkage, accelerator and downshift linkage.

## CLUTCH AND BAND APPLICATION CHART
### Jatco F3A Automatic Transaxle

| Range | | Front Clutch ① | Rear Clutch ② | Low & Reverse Brake Clutch | Brake Band Servo ③ Operation | Release | One-Way Clutch | Parking Pawl |
|---|---|---|---|---|---|---|---|---|
| Park | | — | — | On | — | — | — | On |
| Reverse | | On | — | On | — | On | — | — |
| Neutral | | — | — | — | — | — | — | — |
| Drive | Low D1 | — | On | — | — | — | On | — |
| | Second D2 | — | On | — | On | — | — | — |
| | Top D3 | On | On | — | (On) | On | — | — |
| 2 | Second | — | On | — | On | — | — | — |
| 1 | Second 1₂ | — | On | — | On | — | — | — |
| | Low 1₁ | — | On | On | — | — | — | — |

① Reverse and high clutch
② Forward clutch
③ Intermediate band

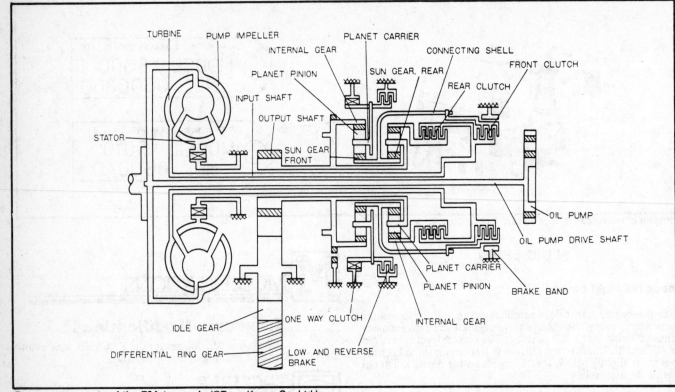

Power components of the F3A transaxle (©Toyo Kogyo Co. Ltd.)

## CHILTON'S THREE "C's" DIAGNOSIS CHART
### Jatco F3A Automatic Transaxle

| Condition | Cause | Correction |
|---|---|---|
| Engine does not start in "N", "P" ranges | a) Range select linkage<br>b) Neutral safety switch<br>c) Ignition switch and starter motor | a) Adjust linkage<br>b) Adjust or replace<br>c) Repair or replace |
| Engine starts in range other than "N" and "P" | a) Range select linkage<br>b) Neutral safety switch | a) Adjust linkage<br>b) Adjust or replace |
| Sharp shock shifting from "N" to "D" range | a) Vacuum diaphragm and hoses<br>b) Engine idle rpm<br>c) Throttle valve pressure<br>d) Manual control valve<br>e) Rear clutch | a) Renew diaphragm and hoses<br>b) Set engine idle rpm<br>c) Correct throttle valve or passage per air test<br>d) Repair or replace valve<br>e) Renew rear clutch |
| Vehicle will not move in "D" range (but moves in "2", "1" and "R" ranges) | a) Range select linkage<br>b) Throttle valve pressure<br>c) Manual control valve<br>d) One way clutch of transmission | a) Adjust linkage<br>b) Correct throttle valve or passage per air test<br>c) Adjust range select linkage/renew valve<br>d) Renew clutch |

## CHILTON'S THREE "C's" DIAGNOSIS CHART
### Jatco F3A Automatic Transaxle

| Condition | Cause | Correction |
|---|---|---|
| Vehicle will not move in "D", "1" or "2" ranges but moves in "R" range Clutch slips, very poor acceleration | a) Oil level<br>b) Range select linkage<br>c) Throttle valve pressure<br><br>d) Manual control valve<br><br>e) Leakage of fluid passage<br>f) Engine adjustment and brake defects<br>g) Rear clutch | a) Add if necessary<br>b) Adjust linkage<br>c) Correct throttle valve or passage per air test<br>d) Adjust range select linkage/renew valve<br>e) Correct as per air test<br>f) Repair as needed<br><br>g) Renew rear clutch |
| Vehicle will not move in "R" range (but moves in "D", "2" and "1" ranges). Clutch slips, very poor acceleration. | a) Oil level<br>b) Range select linkage<br>c) Throttle valve pressure<br><br>d) Manual control valve<br><br>e) Leakage of passage<br>f) Rear clutch<br>g) Front clutch<br>h) Low and reverse brake<br>i) Front clutch check ball | a) Add if needed<br>b) Adjust linkage<br>c) Correct throttle valve or passage per air test<br>d) Adjust range select linkage/renew valve<br>e) Correct as per air test<br>f) Renew rear clutch<br>g) Renew front clutch<br>h) Renew low and reverse brake<br>i) Repair or renew |
| Vehicle will not move in any range | a) Oil level<br>b) Range select linkage<br>c) Throttle valve pressure<br><br>d) Manual control valve<br><br>e) Leakage of fluid passage<br>f) Oil pump<br>g) Parking linkage | a) Add if needed<br>b) Adjust linkage<br>c) Correct throttle valve or passage per air test<br>d) Adjust range select linkage/renew valve<br>e) Correct as per air test<br>f) Repair or renew<br>g) Repair or renew |
| Clutches or brakes slip somewhat in starting to move | a) Oil level<br>b) Range select linkage<br>c) Throttle valve pressure<br>d) Vacuum diaphragm and hoses<br>e) Manual control valve<br><br>f) Leakage of fluid passage<br>g) Oil pump | a) Add if needed<br>b) Adjust linkage<br>c) Correct throttle valve or passage per air test<br>d) Renew as required<br>e) Adjust range select linkage/renew valve<br>f) Correct as per air test<br>g) Repair or renew |
| Vehicle moves in "N" range | a) Range select linkage<br>b) Manual control valve<br><br>c) Rear clutch | a) Adjust linkage<br>b) Adjust range select linkage/renew valve<br>c) Renew rear clutch |
| Maximum speed not attained, acceleration poor | a) Oil level<br>b) Range select linkage<br>c) Throttle valve pressure<br><br>d) High stall rpm<br>e) Manual control valve | a) Add if needed<br>b) Adjust linkage<br>c) Correct throttle valve or passage per air test<br>d) Renew torque converter<br>e) Adjust range select linkage/renew valve |

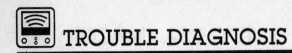
## CHILTON'S THREE "C's" DIAGNOSIS CHART
### Jatco F3A Automatic Transaxle

| Condition | Cause | Correction |
|---|---|---|
| Maximum speed not attained, acceleration poor | f) Band servo | f) Repair/renew band servo |
| | g) Rear clutch | g) Renew rear clutch |
| | h) Front clutch | h) Renew front clutch |
| | i) Band brake | i) Renew band brake |
| | j) Low and reverse brake | j) Renew low and reverse brake |
| | k) Oil pump | k) Repair or renew oil pump |
| Vehicle braked in "R" range | a) Band servo | a) Renew band servo |
| | b) Leakage of fluid passage | b) Correct as per air test |
| | c) Rear clutch | c) Renew rear clutch |
| | d) Band brake | d) Renew band brake |
| | e) Parking linkage | e) Repair/renew linkage |
| No creep at all | a) Oil level | a) Add if needed |
| | b) Range select linkage | b) Adjust linkage |
| | c) Low engine idle rpm | c) Adjust idle rpm |
| | d) Manual control valve | d) Adjust range select linkage/renew valve |
| | e) Rear clutch | e) Renew rear clutch |
| | f) Front clutch | f) Renew front clutch |
| | g) Oil pump | g) Repair or renew oil pump |
| | h) Leakage of fluid passage | h) Correct as per air test |
| Excessive creep | a) High engine idle rpm | a) Adjust idle rpm |
| Failure to change gear from "2nd" to "3rd" | a) Range select linkage | a) Adjust linkage |
| | b) Vacuum diaphragm and hoses | b) Renew diaphragm/hoses |
| | c) Downshift solenoid kickdown switch and wiring | c) Repair wiring and adjust or renew the downshift solenoid |
| | d) Manual control valve | d) Adjust range select linkage/renew valve |
| | e) Governor valve | e) Overhaul governor/renew governor |
| | f) Band servo | f) Renew band servo |
| | g) Leakage of fluid passage | g) Correct as per air test |
| | h) Band brake | h) Renew band brake |
| Failure to change gear from "1st" to "2nd" | a) Range linkage | a) Adjust linkage |
| | b) Vacuum diaphragm and hoses | b) Renew diaphragm/hoses |
| | c) Downshift solenoid kickdown switch and wiring | c) Repair wiring and adjust or renew the solenoid downshift kickdown switch |
| | d) Manual control valve | d) Adjust range select linkage/renew valve |
| | e) Band servo | e) Renew band servo |
| | f) Leakage of fluid passage | f) Correct as per air test |
| | g) Front clutch | g) Renew front clutch |
| | h) Front clutch check ball | h) Renew front clutch check ball |

## CHILTON'S THREE "C's" DIAGNOSIS CHART
### Jatco F3A Automatic Transaxle

| Condition | Cause | Correction |
|---|---|---|
| Too high gear change point from "1st" to "2nd" and from "2nd" to "3rd" | a) Vacuum diaphragm and hoses | a) Renew diaphragm/hoses |
| | b) Downshift solenoid kickdown switch and wiring | b) Repair wiring and adjust or renew the downshift solenoid kickdown switch |
| | c) Manual control valve | c) Adjust range select linkage/renew valve |
| | d) Governor valve | d) Overhaul governor/ renew governor |
| | e) Leakage of fluid passage | e) Correct as per air test |
| Gear change directly from "1st" to "3rd" occurs | a) Manual control valve | a) Adjust range select linkage/renew valve |
| | b) Governor valve | b) Overhaul governor/ renew governor |
| | c) Leakage of fluid passage | c) Correct as per air test |
| | d) Band brake | d) Renew band brake |
| Too sharp shock in change from "1st" to "2nd" | a) Vacuum diaphragm and hoses | a) Renew diaphragm/hoses |
| | b) Manual control valve | b) Adjust range select linkage/renew valve |
| | c) Band servo | c) Renew band servo |
| | d) Band brake | d) Renew band brake |
| Too sharp shock in change from "2nd" to "3rd" | a) Vacuum diaphragm and hoses | a) Renew diaphragm/hoses |
| | b) Downshift solenoid kickdown switch and wiring | b) Repair wiring and adjust or renew the downshift solenoid kickdown switch |
| | c) Throttle valve pressure | c) Correct throttle valve or passage per air test |
| | d) Manual control valve | d) Adjust range select linkage/renew valve |
| | e) Band servo | e) Renew band servo |
| | f) Front clutch | f) Renew front clutch |
| Almost no shock or slipping in change from "1st" to "2nd" | a) Oil level | a) Add if needed |
| | b) Range select linkage | b) Adjust linkage |
| | c) Vacuum diaphragm and hoses | c) Renew diaphragm/hoses |
| | d) Throttle valve pressure | d) Correct throttle valve or passage per air test |
| | e) Manual control valve | e) Adjust range select linkage/renew valve |
| | f) Band servo | f) Renew band servo |
| | g) Leakage of fluid passage | g) Correct as per air test |
| | h) Band brake | h) Renew band brake |
| Almost no shock or engine runaway on "2nd" to "3rd" shift | a) Oil level | a) Add if needed |
| | b) Range select linkage | b) Adjust linkage |
| | c) Vacuum diaphragm and hoses | c) Renew diaphragm/hoses |

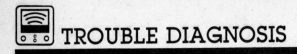
### CHILTON'S THREE "C's" DIAGNOSIS CHART
#### Jatco F3A Automatic Transaxle

| Condition | Cause | Correction |
|---|---|---|
| Almost no shock or engine runaway on "2nd" to "3rd" shift | d) Throttle valve pressure | d) Correct throttle valve or passage per air test |
| | e) Manual control valve | e) Adjust range select linkage/renew valve |
| | f) Band servo | f) Renew band servo |
| | g) Leakage of fluid passage | g) Correct as per air test |
| | h) Front clutch | h) Renew front clutch |
| | i) Front clutch check ball | i) Renew front clutch check ball |
| Vehicle braked by gear change from "1st" to "2nd" | a) Manual control valve | a) Adjust range select linkage/renew valve |
| | b) Front clutch | b) Renew front clutch |
| | c) Low and reverse brake | c) Renew low and reverse brake |
| | d) One-way clutch of transmission | d) Renew one-way clutch of transmission |
| Vehicle braked by gear change from "2nd" to "3rd" | a) Manual control valve | a) Adjust range select linkage |
| | b) Band servo | b) Renew band servo |
| | c) Brake band | c) Renew brake band |
| Failure to change from "3rd" to "2nd" | a) Vacuum diaphragm and hoses | a) Renew diaphragm/hoses |
| | b) Manual control valve | b) Adjust range select linkage/renew valve |
| | c) Governor valve | c) Overhaul governor/ renew governor |
| | d) Band servo | d) Renew band servo |
| | e) Leakage of fluid pressure passage | e) Correct as per air test |
| | f) Front clutch | f) Renew front clutch |
| | g) Band brake | g) Renew band brake |
| Failure to change gear from "2nd" to "1st" or from "3rd" to "1st" | a) Vacuum diaphragm and hoses | a) Renew diaphragm/hoses |
| | b) Manual control valve | b) Adjust range select linkage/renew valve |
| | c) Governor valve | c) Overhaul governor/ renew governor |
| | d) Band servo | d) Renew band servo |
| | e) Band brake | e) Renew band brake |
| | f) Leakage of fluid pressure passage | f) Correct as per air test |
| | g) One-way clutch of transmission | g) Renew one-way clutch of transmission |
| Gear change shock felt during deceleration by releasing accelerator pedal | a) Range select linkage | a) Adjust linkage |
| | b) Vacuum diaphragm and hoses | b) Renew diaphragm/hoses |
| | c) Downshift solenoid kickdown switch and wiring | c) Repair wiring and adjust or renew the downshift solenoid kickdown switch |
| | d) Throttle valve pressure | d) Correct throttle valve or passage per air test |

## CHILTON'S THREE "C's" DIAGNOSIS CHART
### Jatco F3A Automatic Transaxle

| Condition | Cause | Correction |
|---|---|---|
| Gear change shock felt during deceleration by releasing accelerator pedal | e) Manual control valve | e) Adjust range select linkage/renew valve |
| | f) Governor valve | f) Overhaul governor/renew governor |
| | g) Leakage of fluid pressure passage | g) Correct as per air test |
| Too high change point from "3rd" to "2nd" and from "2nd" to "1st" | a) Range select linkage | a) Adjust linkage |
| | b) Vacuum diaphragm and hoses | b) Renew diaphragm/hoses |
| | c) Downshift solenoid kickdown switch and wiring | c) Repair wiring and adjust or renew the downshift solenoid kickdown switch |
| | d) Throttle valve pressure | d) Correct throttle valve or passage per air test |
| | e) Manual control valve | e) Adjust range select linkage/renew valve |
| | f) Governor valve | f) Overhaul governor/renew governor |
| | g) Leakage at fluid passage | g) Correct per air test |
| No kickdown by depressing pedal in "3rd" within kickdown speed | a) Vacuum diaphragm and hoses | a) Renew diaphragm/hoses |
| | b) Downshift solenoid kickdown switch and wiring | b) Repair wiring and adjust or renew the solenoid downshift kickdown switch |
| | c) Manual control valve | c) Adjust range select linkage/renew valve |
| | d) Governor valve | d) Overhaul governor/renew governor |
| | e) Band brake | e) Renew band brake |
| | f) Leakage at fluid passage | f) Correct per air test |
| Kickdown operates or engine overruns when depressing pedal in "3rd" beyond kickdown speed limit | a) Range select linkage | a) Adjust linkage |
| | b) Vacuum diaphragm and hoses | b) Renew diaphragm/hoses |
| | c) Throttle valve pressure | c) Correct throttle valve or passage per air test |
| | d) Manual control valve | d) Adjust range select linkage/renew valve |
| | e) Governor valve | e) Overhaul governor/renew governor |
| | f) Leakage of fluid pressure passage | f) Correct as per air test |
| | g) Front clutch | g) Renew front clutch |
| Races extremely or slips in changing from "3rd" to "2nd" | a) Vacuum diaphragm and hoses | a) Renew diaphragm/hoses |
| | b) Throttle valve pressure | b) Correct throttle valve or passage as per air test |
| | c) Manual control valve | c) Adjust range select linkage/renew valve |
| | d) Band servo | d) Renew band servo |

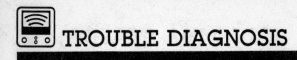

## CHILTON'S THREE "C's" DIAGNOSIS CHART
### Jatco F3A Automatic Transaxle

| Condition | Cause | | Correction | |
|---|---|---|---|---|
| Races extremely or slips in changing from "3rd" to "2nd" | e) | Leakage of fluid pressure passage | e) | Correct as per air test |
| | f) | Front clutch | f) | Renew front clutch |
| Failure to change from "3rd" to "2nd" when changing lever into "2" range | a) | Range select linkage | a) | Adjust linkage |
| | b) | Throttle valve pressure | b) | Correct throttle valve or passage per air test |
| | c) | Manual control valve | c) | Adjust range select linkage/renew valve |
| | d) | Band servo | d) | Renew band servo |
| | e) | Band brake | e) | Renew band brake |
| | f) | Leakage of fluid pressure passage | f) | Correct as per air test |
| Gear change from "2nd" to "1st" or from "3rd" to "2nd" | a) | Range select linkage | a) | Adjust linkage |
| | b) | Throttle valve pressure | b) | Correct throttle valve or passage per air test |
| | c) | Manual control valve | c) | Adjust range select linkage/renew valve |
| No shock on change from "1" range to "2" range or engine races extremely | a) | Oil level | a) | Add if needed |
| | b) | Range select linkage | b) | Adjust linkage |
| | c) | Vacuum diaphragm and hoses | c) | Renew diaphragm/hoses |
| | d) | Engine idle rpm | d) | Set idle rpm |
| | e) | High stall speed | e) | Renew band brake |
| | f) | Manual control valve | f) | Adjust range select linkage/renew valve |
| | g) | Transmission air check to determine if band servo is working | g) | Repair or renew servo |
| | h) | Oil pump | h) | Repair or renew |
| Failure to shift from "3rd" to "2nd" when shifting lever into "1" range | a) | Range select linkage | a) | Adjust linkage |
| | b) | Throttle valve pressure | b) | Correct throttle valve or passage per air test |
| | c) | Manual control valve | c) | Adjust range select linkage/renew valve |
| | d) | Governor valve | d) | Overhaul governor/renew governor |
| | e) | Band servo | e) | Renew band servo |
| | f) | Leakage of fluid pressure passage | f) | Correct as per air test |
| | g) | Low and reverse brake | g) | Renew low and reverse brake |
| No engine braking in range "1" | a) | Range select linkage | a) | Adjust linkage |
| | b) | Throttle valve pressure | b) | Correct throttle valve or passage per air test |
| | c) | Manual control valve | c) | Adjust range select linkage/renew valve |
| | d) | Leakage of fluid pressure passage | d) | Correct as per air test |
| | e) | Low and reverse brake | e) | Renew low and reverse brake |

## CHILTON'S THREE "C's" DIAGNOSIS CHART
### Jatco F3A Automatic Transaxle

| Condition | Cause | Correction |
|---|---|---|
| Gear change from "1st" to "2nd" or from "2nd" to "3rd" in "1" range | a) Range select linkage<br>b) Manual control valve<br><br>c) Leakage of fluid pressure passage | a) Adjust linkage<br>b) Adjust range select linkage/renew valve<br>c) Correct as per air test |
| Does not change from "2nd" to "1st" in "1" range | a) Oil level<br>b) Range select linkage<br>c) Manual control valve<br><br>d) Governor valve<br><br>e) Band servo<br>f) Leakage of fluid pressure passage<br>g) Low and reverse brake | a) Add if needed<br>b) Adjust linkage<br>c) Adjust range select linkage/renew valve<br>d) Overhaul governor/renew governor<br>e) Renew band servo<br>f) Correct as per air test<br><br>g) Renew low and reverse brake |
| Large shock in changing from "2nd" to "1st" in "1" range | a) Vacuum diaphragm and hoses<br>b) High engine stall rpm<br><br>c) Manual control valve | a) Renew diaphragm/hoses<br>b) Renew low and reverse brake<br>c) Adjust range select linkage/renew valve |
| Vehicle moves changing into "P" range or parking gear does not disengage when shifted out of "P" range | a) Range select linkage | a) Adjust linkage |
| Transmission overheats | a) Oil level<br>b) Band servo<br>c) Throttle valve pressure<br><br>d) Restricted or no rear lubrication<br>e) Manual control valve<br><br>f) Leakage of fluid pressure passage<br>g) Front clutch<br>h) Band brake<br>i) Low and reverse brake | a) Add if needed<br>b) Renew band servo<br>c) Correct throttle valve or passage per air test<br>d) Check passages<br><br>e) Adjust range select linkage/renew valve<br>f) Correct as per air test<br><br>g) Renew front clutch<br>h) Renew band brake<br>i) Renew low and reverse brake |
| Oil shoots out during operation. White smoke from exhaust during operation | a) Oil level<br>b) Vacuum diaphragm and hoses<br>c) Throttle valve pressure<br>d) Restricted or no rear lubrication<br>e) Manual control valve<br><br>f) Leakage of fluid pressure passage<br>g) Rear clutch | a) Add if needed<br>b) Renew vacuum diaphragm/hoses<br>c) Correct throttle valve or passage per air test<br>d) Check passages<br>e) Adjust range select linkage/renew valve<br>f) Correct as per air test<br><br>g) Renew rear clutch |

## CHILTON'S THREE "C's" DIAGNOSIS CHART
### Jatco F3A Automatic Transaxle

| Condition | Cause | Correction |
|---|---|---|
| Oil shoots out during operation. White smoke from exhaust during operation | h) Band brake<br>i) Low and reverse brake<br>j) Oil pump<br>k) One-way clutch torque converter<br>l) Planetary gear | h) Renew band brake<br>i) Renew low and reverse brake<br>j) Renew oil pump<br>k) Renew one-way clutch torque converter<br>l) Renew planetary gear |
| Offensive smell at fluid fill pipe | a) Oil level<br>b) Rear clutch<br>c) Front clutch<br>d) Band brake<br>e) Low and reverse brake<br>f) Oil pump<br>g) Leakage of fluid pressure passage<br>h) One-way clutch torque converter | a) Add if needed<br>b) Renew rear clutch<br>c) Renew front clutch<br>d) Renew band brake<br>e) Renew low and reverse brake<br>f) Renew oil pump<br>g) Correct as per air test<br>h) Renew one-way clutch torque converter |
| Transmission noise in "P" and "N" ranges | a) Oil level<br>b) Throttle valve pressure<br>c) Oil pump | a) Add if needed<br>b) Correct throttle valve or passage per air test<br>c) Renew oil pump |
| Transmission noise in "D", "2", "1" and "R" ranges | a) Oil level<br>b) Throttle valve pressure<br>c) Rear clutch<br>d) Oil pump<br>e) One-way clutch of transmission<br>f) Planetary gear | a) Add if needed<br>b) Correct throttle valve or passage per air test<br>c) Renew rear clutch<br>d) Renew oil pump<br>e) Renew one-way clutch of transmission<br>f) Renew planetary gear |

# HYDRAULIC CONTROL SYSTEM

Hydraulic pressure, clutch and band applications control the changing of gear ratios in the automatic transaxle. The clutches and bands are applied by the force of fluid pressure controlled by a system of values and control mechanisms.

1. Screen or filter cleans foreign material from the oil supply before entering the oil pump.
2. Oil pump supplies oil pressure to trans.
3. Converter pressure relief valve prevents converter pressure build up.
4. Torque converter is a fluid coupler and torque multiplier.
5. Rear clutch is applied in all forward gears.
6. Front clutch is applied in reverse and high gears.
7. Low and reverse brake (clutch) is applied in Park, Reverse and range "1" low gear.
8. Rear lubrication passages lubricate the rear transaxle components.
9. Front lubrication passages lubricate the front transaxle components.
10. Cooler system removes heat from converter by sending the transmission fluid through a cooler in the engine cooling system.
11. Drain back valve prevents loss of fluid in hydraulic circuits when engine is stopped.
12. Throttle control valve regulates throttle pressure in relation to the engine manifold vacuum through vacuum diaphragm (modulator).
13. Brake band servo is applied in 2nd gear and pressure released in high gear.
14. Pressure modifier valve uses throttle pressure, controlled by governor pressure, to modify the main line pressure from the regulator valve. Modifies harsh shifting caused by excessive pump pressure.
15. 2-3 timing valve slows down 2-3 shifts under heavy load condition.
16. Vacuum diaphragm (modulator) moves the throttle valve in relation to engine manifold vacuum changes.
17. Throttle backup valve increases throttle pressure output to delay the upshift at higher engine loads with engine vacuum low.
18. Governor provides road speed signal to the transaxle hydraulic control system.
19. Oil pressure regulator valve is used to control main line control pressure.
20. Throttle solenoid downshift valve overrides normal upshifts to provide forced downshifts on full acceleration.
21. Manual control valve moves with the shift selector and directs the line control pressure to the various oil passages.
22. 1-2 shift valve controls the upshift from first to second and the downshift from second to first.
23. 2-3 shift valve controls the upshift from second to third and downshift from third to second.

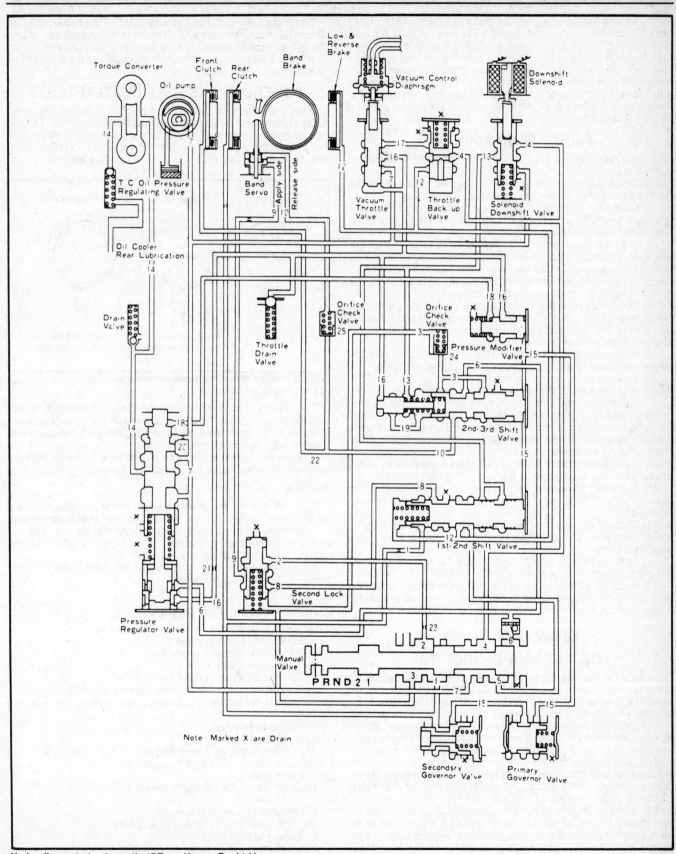

**Hydraulic control schematic** (©Toyo Kogyo Co. Ltd.)

24. Second lockup valve applies brake band servo in "D", "1" and "2" ranges. The second lockup valve locks out the 1-2 shift valve in the "2" range. In other words, the second lockup valve applies the brake band servo without regard to the position of the 1-2 shift valve when the manual lever is in the "2" range. In "D" range 3rd gear operation second lock up valve pressure remains applied at the brake band servo; however, the servo is inoperative because the release side of the brake servo is applied by pressure from 2-3 shift valve.

## Major Components

The hydraulic control system consists of the following major components.

1. Main control pressure system supplies pressure to the transaxle and converter when the engine is operating.
2. Converter and lubrication system regulates converter fluid pressure, provides gear train lubrication and fluid cooling while the transaxle is operating.
3. Forward clutch pressure and governor pressure system applies the forward clutch, which is applied in all forward speeds, and applies pressure to the governor valve. The governor valve supplies regulated pressure to the rear side of the shift valves, dependent upon the road speed of the vehicle.
4. Low and reverse brake apply system applies the low and reverse brake in "1" and "R" selector lever positions and locks out the second and third gears by directing pressure to the appropriate valves to prevent them from shifting.
5. First gear lock out system allows the transaxle to shift directly to second speed and locks out the 1st and 3rd gears.
6. Brake band servo apply system applies the servo to hold the band to the surface of the reverse and high clutch cylinder.
7. Reverse pressure booster system increases control (line) pressure and applies reverse and high clutch in the reverse range.
8. Shift valve train system applies and exhaust the fluid pressures to servos and clutch assemblies for upshifts and downshifts automatically on demand.
9. Kick-down system (downshift) forces downshift by overriding governor/throttle valve control of the shift valves.
10. Governor provides a varying pressure proportional to engine vacuum to help control the timing and quality of the transaxle shifts.
11. Throttle (TV) system provides a varying pressure proportional to engine vacuum to help control the timing quality of the transaxle shifts.
12. Throttle backup system compensates for lower rate of engine vacuum at ½ or more of throttle opening.
13. Pressure modifier system adjusts control (line) pressures and 2-3 shift timing valve operation to insure smoother shifting under various engine load and vacuum conditions.

## Diagnosis Tests

### OIL PRESSURE CIRCUITS

To utilize the oil flow charts for diagnosing transaxle problems, the repairman must have an understanding of the oil pressure circuits and how each circuit affects the operation of the transaxle by the use of controlled oil pressure.

Control (line) pressure is a regulated main line pressure, developed by the operation of the front pump. It is directed to the main regulator valve, where predetermined spring pressure automatically moves the regulator valve to control the pressure of the oil at a predetermined rate, by opening the valve and exhausting excessive pressured oil back into the sump and holding the valve closed to build up pressure when needed.

Therefore, it is most important during the diagnosis phase to test main line control pressure to determine if high or low pressure exits. Do not attempt to adjust a pressure regulator valve spring to obtain more or less control pressure. Internal transaxle damage may result.

The main valve is the controlling agent of the transaxle which directs oil pressure to one of six separate passages used to control the valve train. By assigning each passage a number a better understanding of the oil circuits can be gained from the diagnosis oil flow charts.

## CONTROL PRESSURE SYSTEM TESTS

Control pressure tests should be performed whenever slippage, delay or harshness is felt in the shifting of the transaxle. Throttle and modulator pressure changes can cause these problems also, but are generated from the control pressures and therefore reflect any problems arising from the control pressure system.

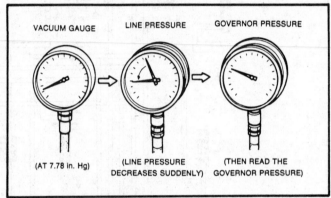

**Gauges needed to test the hydraulic circuits**
(©Toyo Kogyo Co. Ltd.)

The control pressure is first checked in all ranges without any throttle pressure input, and then checked as the throttle pressure is increased by lowering the vacuum supply to the vacuum diaphragm with the use of the stall test.

The control pressure tests should define differences between mechanical or hydraulic failures of the transaxle.

### Testing

1. Install a 0-400 psi pressure gauge to the main line control pressure tap, marked ML on the right side of the transaxle case.
2. Block wheels and apply both parking and service brakes.
3. Operate the engine/transaxle in the ranges on the following charts and at the manifold vacuum specified.
4. Record the actual pressure readings in each test and compare them to the given specifications.

### Control Pressure Test Results

Low pressure at idle in all ranges is caused by
1. EGR system, if equipped
2. Vacuum diaphragm modulator
3. Manifold vacuum line
4. Throttle valve or control rod
5. Sticking regulator boost valve (pressure modifier valve)
OK at idle in all ranges, but low at 10 in. of vacuum is caused by
1. Excessive leakage
2. Low pump capacity
3. Restricted oil pan screen or filter
Pressure low in "P" range is caused by
1. Valve body
Pressure low in "R" range is caused by
1. Front clutch
2. Low and reverse brake
Pressure Low in "N" range is caused by
1. Valve body
Pressure low in "D" range is caused by
1. Rear clutch

Pressure low in "2" range is caused by
1. Rear Clutch
2. Brake band servo

Pressure low in "1" range is caused by
1. Rear clutch
2. Low and reverse brake

High or low pressure in all test conditions is caused by
1. Modulator control rod broken or missing
2. Stuck throttle valve
3. Pressure modifier valve or regulator valve

### Precautions Before Idle Tests

1. Be sure manifold vacuum is above 15 in. Hg. If lower, check for engine conditions and/or vacuum leaks and repair.

2. Make sure the manifold vacuum changes with throttle plate opening. Check by accelerating quickly and observing the vacuum reading.

### Precautions If Stall Test Is Used
### On Pressure Rise Test

(Refer to stall test procedures.)

1. Do not operate engine/transaxle at stall for longer than 5 seconds per test.

2. Operate the engine between 1000 and 1200 rpm at the end of a test for approximately one to two minutes for cooling (in neutral).

3. Release the accelerator immediately in case of slippage or spin-up of the transaxle to avoid more damage to the unit.

## AIR PRESSURE TESTS

The control pressure test results and causes of abnormal pressures are to be used as a guide. Further testing or inspection could be necessary before repairs are made. If the pressures are found to be low in a clutch, servo or passageway, a verification can be accomplished by removing the valve body and performing an air pressure test. This test can serve two purposes:

1. To determine if a malfunction of a clutch or band is caused by fluid leakage in the system or is the result of a mechanical failure.

2. To test the transaxle for internal fluid leakage during the rebuilding and before completing the assembly.

### Procedure

1. Obtain an air nozzle and adjust for 25 psi.
2. Apply air pressure (25 psi) to the passages as listed.

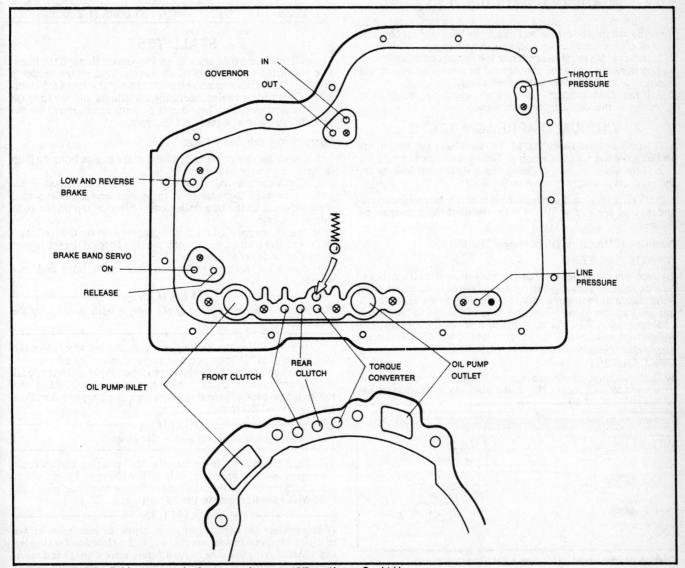

**Identification of the fluid passages in the transaxle case** (©Toyo Kogyo Co. Ltd.)

## Vacuum Diaphragm

The modulated throttle system, which adjusts throttle pressure for the control of the shift valves, is operated by engine manifold vacuum through a vacuum diaphragm and must be inspected whenever a transaxle defect is apparent.

### Preparation of Vacuum Test

Before the vacuum diaphragm test is performed, check the engine vacuum supply and the condition and routing of the supply lines.

With the engine idling, remove the vacuum line at the vacuum diaphragm and install a vacuum gauge. There must be a steady, acceptable vacuum reading for the altitude at which the test is being performed.

If the vacuum is low, check for a vacuum leak or poor engine performance. If the vacuum is steady and acceptable, accelerate the engine sharply and observe the vacuum gauge reading. The vacuum should drop off rapidly at acceleration and return to the original reading immediately upon release of the accelerator.

If the vacuum reading does not change or changes slowly, check the vacuum supply lines for being plugged, restricted or connected to a vacuum reservoir supply. Repair the system as required.

## MANIFOLD VACUUM TESTS

1. With the engine idling, remove the vacuum supply hose from the modulator nipple and check the hose end for the presence of engine vacuum with an appropriate gauge.

2. If vacuum is present, accelerate the engine and allow it to return to idle. A drop in vacuum should be noted during acceleration and a return to normal vacuum at idle.

3. If manifold vacuum is not present, check for breaks or restrictions in the vacuum lines and repair.

## VACUUM DIAPHRAGM TESTS

1. Apply at least 18 in. Hg. to the modulator vacuum nipple and observe the vacuum reading. The vacuum should hold.

2. If the vacuum does not hold, the diaphragm is leaking and the modulator assembly must be replaced.

**NOTE: A leaking diaphragm causes harsh gear engagements and delayed or no up-shifts due to maximum throttle pressure developed.**

### Additional Vacuum Diaphragm Testing

ON THE CAR TEST

The vacuum diaphragm is tested on the vehicle with the aid of an outside vacuum source, which can be adjusted to maintain a certain amount of vacuum. Apply 18 inches Hg. to the vacuum diaphragm vacuum nipple, through a hose connected to the outside vacuum source. The vacuum should hold at the applied level without any leakdown. If the vacuum level drops off, the vacuum diaphragm is leaking and must be replaced.

OFF CAR TEST

With the vacuum diaphragm removed from the automatic transmission, apply 18 inches Hg. to the diaphragm vacuum nipple.

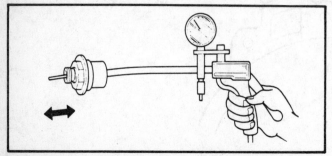

Testing vacuum modulator with a hand vacuum pump
(©Toyo Kogyo Co. Ltd.)

The vacuum level should remain and not drop off. If the vacuum level drops, the diaphragm is leaking and the unit should be replaced.

A second test can be made with the diaphragm removed from the transaxle. Insert the control rod into the valve end of the diaphragm and apply vacuum to the nipple. Hold a finger over the control rod and release the vacuum supply hose. The control rod should be moved outward by the pressure of the internal return spring. If the control rod does not move outward, a broken return spring is indicated.

## VACUUM MODULATOR DIAPHRAGM ROD SPECIFICATIONS

| Part No. | | | Diaphragm rod |
|---|---|---|---|
| 0338 | 19 | 828 | 29.0mm (1.140 in) |
| 0338 | 19 | 829 | 29.5mm (1.160 in) |
| 0338 | 19 | 830 | 30.0mm (1.180 in) |
| 0338 | 19 | 831 | 30.5mm (1.200 in) |
| 0338 | 19 | 832 | 31.0mm (1.220 in) |

## STALL TEST

The stall test is an application of engine torque, through the transaxle and drive train to locked-up wheels, held by the vehicle's brakes. The engine's speed is increased until the rpms are stabilized. Given ideal engine operating conditions and no slippage from transmission clutches, bands or torque converter, the engine will stabilize at a specified test rpm.

### Performing the Stall Test

1. Check the engine oil level and start the engine bringing it up to operating temperature.

2. Check the transaxle fluid level and correct as necessary. Attach a calibrated tachometer to the engine and a 0-400 psi oil pressure gauge to the transaxle control pressure tap on the right side of the case.

3. Mark the specified maximum engine rpm on the tachometer cover plate with a grease pencil to easily check if the stall speed is over or under specifications.

4. Apply the parking brake and block both front and rear wheels.

—————— CAUTION ——————
*Do not allow anyone in front of the vehicle while performing the stall test.*

5. While holding the brake pedal with the left foot, place the selector lever in "D" position and slowly depress the accelerator.

6. Read and record the engine rpm when the accelerator pedal is fully depressed and the engine rpm is stabilized. Read and record the oil pressure reading at the high engine rpm point. Stall speed—2200-2450 rpm.

—————— CAUTION ——————
*The stall test must be made within five seconds.*

7. Shift the selector lever into the "N" position and increase the engine speed to approximately 1000-1200 rpm. Hold this engine speed for one to two minutes to cool the transaxle and fluid.

8. Make similar tests in the "2", "1" and "R" positions.

—————— CAUTION ——————
*If at any time the engine rpm races above the maximum as per specifications, indications are that a clutch unit or band is slipping and the stall test should be stopped before more damage is done to the internal parts.*

### Results of Stall Test

#### HIGH ENGINE RPM

If a slipping condition occurs during the stall test, indicated by high engine rpm, the selector lever position at the time of slippage provides an indication as to what holding member of the transaxle is defective.

By determining the holding member involved, several possible causes of slippage can be diagnosed.

1. Slips in all ranges, control pressure low
2. Slips in "D", "1" or "2", rear clutch
3. Slips in "D1" only, one-way clutch
4. Slips in "R" only, front clutch or low and reverse brake

Perform a road test to confirm these conditions.

#### LOW ENGINE RPM

When low stall speed is indicated, the converter one-way clutch is not holding or the engine is in need of a major tune-up. To determine which is at fault, perform a road test and observe the operation of the transaxle and the engine. If the converter one-way clutch does not lock the stator, acceleration will be poor up to approximately 30 mph. Above 30 mph acceleration will be normal. With poor engine performance acceleration will be poor at all speeds. When the one-way clutch is seized and locks the stator from turning either way, the stall test rpm will be normal. However, on a road test the vehicle will not go any faster than 50-55 mph because of the 2:1 reduction ratio in the converter.

If slippage was indicated by high engine rpm, the road test will help identify the problem area observing the transaxle operation during upshifts, both automatic and manual.

### POSSIBLE LOCATIONS OF PROBLEMS DUE TO LINE PRESSURE

#### Malfunctions

1. Low pressure when in "D", "2", or "R" positions could be the result of a worn oil pump, fluid leaking from the oil pump, control valve or transaxle case, or the pressure regulator valve sticking.

### STALL TEST HOLDING MEMBER CHART

| Selector Lever Position | Holding Member Applied |
|---|---|
| "D" 1st Gear | Rear clutch<br>One-way clutch |
| "1" Manual | Rear clutch<br>Low and reverse brake clutch |
| "2" Manual | Rear clutch<br>Rear band |
| Reverse | Front clutch<br>Low and reverse brake clutch |

### Line Pressure At Stall Speed

| | |
|---|---|
| "D" Range | 128 to 156 psi |
| "2" Range | 114 to 171 psi |
| "R" Range | 228 to 270 psi |

### Line Pressure Before Stall Test—At Idle

| | |
|---|---|
| "D" Range | 43 to 57 psi |
| "2" Range | 114 to 171 psi |
| "R" Range | 57 to 110 psi |

2. Low pressure when in "D" and "2" only could result from fluid leakage from the hydraulic circuit of the two ranges selected. Refer to the hydraulic fluid schematics.

3. Low fluid pressure when in the "R" position could result from a fluid leakage in the reverse fluid circuit. Refer to the hydraulic fluid schematic.

4. High pressure when idling could be the result of a broken or disconnected vacuum hose to the modulator or a defective vacuum modulator assembly.

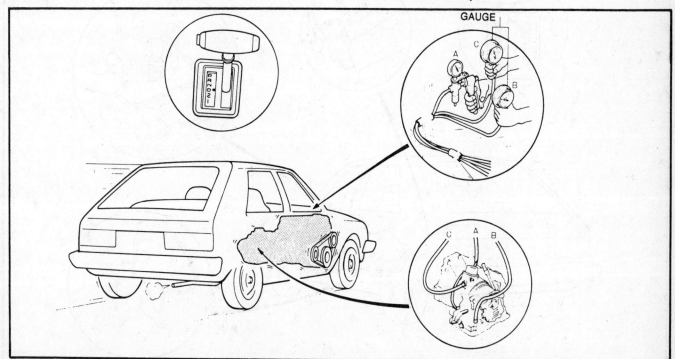

Line pressure cut back point (©Toyo Kogyo Co. Ltd.)

## Main Line Pressure Cut-Back Point Test

1. Connect the fluid pressure test gauge to the line pressure test port outlet of the transaxle case.

2. Connect a fluid pressure test gauge to the governor pressure test port on the transaxle case.

3. Position the gauges so that each can be seen from the driver's seat.

4. Disconnect the vacuum hose to the vacuum modulator and plug the hose.

5. Connect a vacuum pump to the vacuum modulator and position the pump so it can be operated from the driver's seat.

6. If the line pressure drops abruptly when the engine rpm is increased gradually while the selector lever is in the "D" position. Measure the governor pressure.

7. Measure the governor pressure when the vacuum is at 0 in. Hg and at 7.78 in. Hg. The specifications are as follows:

   0 in. Hg—14-23 psi
   7.78 in. Hg— 6-14 psi

8. If the specifications are not met, check to see that the diaphragm rod has been installed or that it is more than standard. Check for a sticking valve inside the control valve assemble if the rod is correct.

## Governor Pressure Test

1. Connect the fluid pressure gauge to the governor test port on the transaxle case. Position the gauge so that it is accessible to the operator.

2. Drive the vehicle with the selector lever in the "D" position.

3. Measure the governor pressure at the following speeds:

   20 mph—11.9-17.1 psi
   35 mph—19.9-28.4 psi
   55 mph—38.4-48.3 psi

4. If the test results do not meet the specifications, the following should be checked:

   a. Fluid leakage from the line pressure hydraulic circuit.
   b. Fluid leakage from the governor pressure hydraulic circuit.
   c. Governor malfunctions.

## ROAD TEST

The road test is used to confirm malfunctions do exist within the transaxle unit, or that repairs have been accomplished and the transaxle unit is either operating properly or will require additional adjustments or repairs. The road test must be performed over a pre-determined drive course that has been used before to evaluate transmission and/or transaxle operations.

Should malfunctions occur during the road test, the selector range and road speed should be noted, along with the particular gear or shift point. By applying the point of malfunction in the operation of the transaxle, to the Clutch and Band Application Chart and the Chilton's Three "C's" diagnosis chart, the probable causes can be pinpointed.

Some of the points to be evaluated during the road test are as follows:

1. The shift point should be smooth and have a positive engagement.

2. The shifts speed are within specifications.

3. All shifts occur during the upshifts and downshifts when in the selector lever detents, as required.

4. All downshifts occur when a forced downshift is demanded.

5. No upshift to third when the selector lever is in the "2" position and the transaxle is in the second speed.

6. Only one upshift from the first speed when the selector lever is in the "1" position.

7. The vehicle is firmly locked when the lever is in the "P" position.

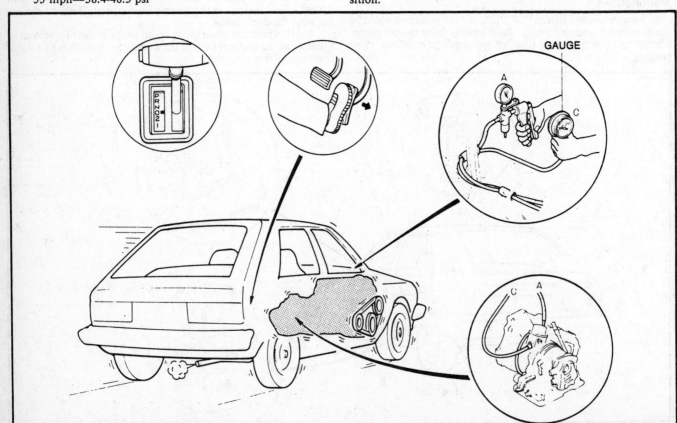

Governor pressure check (©Toyo Kogyo Co. Ltd.)

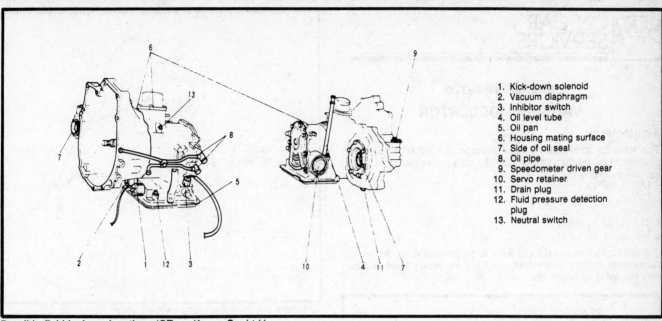

1. Kick-down solenoid
2. Vacuum diaphragm
3. Inhibitor switch
4. Oil level tube
5. Oil pan
6. Housing mating surface
7. Side of oil seal
8. Oil pipe
9. Speedometer driven gear
10. Servo retainer
11. Drain plug
12. Fluid pressure detection plug
13. Neutral switch

**Possible fluid leakage locations** (©Toyo Kogyo Co. Ltd.)

GAUGE

**Line pressure test** (©Toyo Kogyo Co. Ltd.)

## ON CAR SERVICES

## Adjustments

### VACUUM MODULATOR

**Adjustment**

The vacuum modulator has no adjustments other than the replacement of the diaphragm rod. The rods are available in varied lengths as follows:
1.160 in. or 29.5mm
1.180 in. or 30.0mm
1.200 in. or 30.5mm
1.220 in. or 31.0mm
1.240 in. or 31.5mm

NOTE: The transaxle will have to be drained down before the vacuum modulator is removed. Add the necessary fluid and correct the level as required.

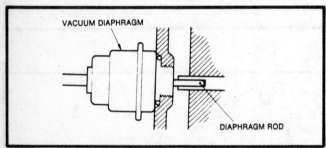

Installation of modulator assembly (©Toyo Kogyo Co. Ltd.)

### KICKDOWN SWITCH

**Adjustment**

1. Move the ignition switch to the ON position.
2. Loosen the kickdown switch to engage when the accelerator pedal is between 7/8 to 15/16 inch of full travel. The downshift solenoid will click when the switch engages.
3. Tighten the attaching nut and check for proper operation.

### NEUTRAL SAFETY SWITCH

**Adjustment**

No adjustment is possible on the neutral safety switch. If the engine will not start while the selector lever is in the "P" or "N" po-

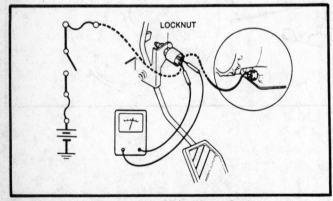

Checking the kickdown switch (©Toyo Kogyo Co. Ltd.)

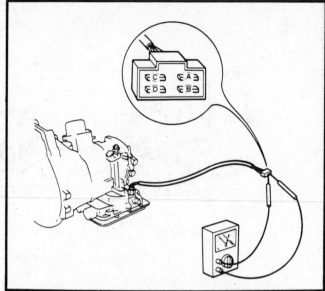

Checking the neutral starting switch (©Toyo Kogyo Co. Ltd.)

sitions and the back-up lamps do not operate, the switch is defective and must be replaced.

### MANUAL SHIFT LINKAGE

**Adjustment**

**GLC**

NOTE: The control linkage is of the rod type.

1. Shift the selector lever and the control rod to the "P" position.
2. Move the selector lever bracket forward and rearward until the indicator aligns properly.
3. Tighten the selector lever bracket retaining bolts.
4. Move the selector lever through all ranges and recheck the positioning.
5. Be sure the assembly moves freely and all detents are felt as the selector lever is moved.

**626**

NOTE: The control linkage is of the cable type.

1. Remove the console cover, exposing the cable end with the two adjusting locknuts.
2. Engage the parking brake and loosen the two locknuts.
3. Shift the selector lever to the "N" position and confirm the detent roller is in the "N" range.
4. Shift the selector lever on the transaxle to the "N" position.
5. Tighten the lower (A) locknut until it is in contact with the trunnion on the selector lever linkage.
6. Tighten the upper (B) locknut 5.8-8.0 ft. lbs. (8-11 N•m).
7. With the selector lever knob depressed, push the selector lever towards the "P" position until the selector lever on the transaxle begins to move. Measure the distance.
8. From the center position, move the selector lever towards the "D" position until the lever on the transaxle begins to move. Measure the distance.
9. If the forward and rearward movement is not equal, adjust the locknuts until both are equal.
10. Verify that the adjustment is correct.
11. If the button on the selector lever does not operate properly, set the selector lever to the "P" position, loosen the detent roller mounting nut and then adjust by moving the detent roller.

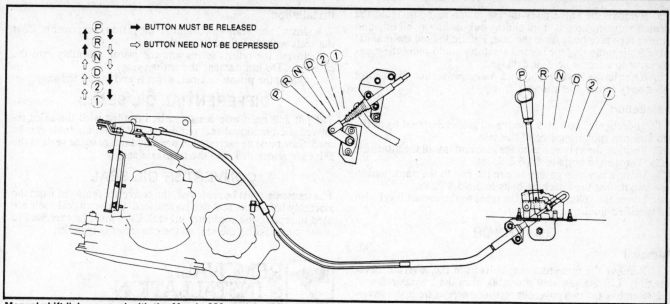

Manual shift linkage used with the Mazda 626 models (©Toyo Kogyo Co. Ltd.)

# Services

## TRANSAXLE FLUID CHANGE

The Jatco transaxle do not have a specific or periodic fluid change interval for the normal maintenance of the units. However, at the time of any major repairs or when the fluid has been contaminated, the converter, cooler and lines must be flushed to remove any debris and contaminated fluid. If the vehicle is used in continuous service or driven under severe conditions (police or taxi type operations), the transaxle should be drained, flushed and refilled at mileage intervals of 18,000-24,000 or at time intervals of 18-24 months.

**NOTE: The time or mileage intervals given are average. Each vehicle operated under severe conditions should be treated individually.**

### Procedure

1. Remove the speedometer cable and driven gear from the transaxle case.
2. Remove the drain plug at the bottom of the transaxle case.
3. Allow the fluid to drain completely and reinstall the drain plug.
4. Add type F fluid to the transaxle through the speedometer gear opening in the case until the desired level is reached.
5. Reinstall the speedometer cable and driven gear into the transaxle case.

## VACUUM DIAPHRAGM

**NOTE: Drain the transaxle before removing the vacuum modulator.**

### Removal

1. Raise the vehicle and support safely. Disconnect the vacuum hose from the diaphragm unit.
2. Turn the threaded diaphragm unit to remove it from the transmission case.
3. Pull the actuating pin and the throttle valve from the transmission case.
4. Remove the O-ring from the assembly.

### Installation

1. Install a new O-ring on the diaphragm unit.

2. Install the throttle valve, the actuating pin and the vacuum diaphragm tubes toward the transmission case and install the assembly into the case.
3. Tighten the vacuum diaphragm unit securely.

## OIL PAN

### Draining and Removal

1. Raise the vehicle and support safely.
2. Position a drain pan beneath the transaxle oil pan and starting at the rear, loosen, but do not remove the pan bolts.
3. Loosen the pan from the transaxle case and allow the fluid to drain gradually.
4. Remove all pan bolts except two at the front of the pan and allow the fluid to continue draining.
5. Remove the pan. Clean the remains of the old gasket from the pan and transaxle case.

### Installation

1. Install a new gasket on the pan and install it to the transaxle case.
2. Install all pan bolts and torque to 3.6-5.8 ft. lbs.
3. Install three quarts of transmission fluid, type F into the filler tube (converter not drained).
4. Start the engine and operate the engine at idle speed for approximately two minutes. Then raise the engine speed to approximately 1200 rpm until the engine and transaxle reach operating temperature.

————————— CAUTION —————————
*Do not overspeed the engine during warm-up.*
————————————————————————————

5. Check the fluid level after moving the gear selector through all ranges. Correct the fluid level as necessary.

## VALVE BODY

### Removal

1. Raise the vehicle so the transaxle oil pan is accessible.
2. Drain the transmission fluid by loosening the pan attaching bolts and allowing the fluid to drain.
3. Remove the pan attaching bolts, pan and gasket.
4. Remove the downshift solenoid, vacuum diaphragm, vacuum diaphragm rod and O-rings.

5. Remove the valve body-to-case attaching bolts. Hold the manual valve to keep it from sliding out of the valve body and remove the valve body from the case. Failure to hold the manual valve while removing the control assembly could cause the manual valve to become bent or damaged.

6. Refer to the Disassembly and Assembly section for control valve body repair operations.

### Installation

1. Thoroughly clean and remove all gasket material from the pan and pan mounting face of the case.

2. Position the valve body to the case and install the attaching bolts. Torque the bolts to 5.8-8.0 ft. lbs.

3. Using a new pan gasket, secure the pan to the transmission case and torque the attaching bolts to 3.6-5.8 ft. lbs.

4. Lower the vehicle and fill the trans to the correct level with the specified fluid.

## GOVERNOR

### Removal

1. Remove the three retaining bolts from the governor cover assembly. Lift the governor assembly from the transaxle case.

2. Remove the two governor retaining screws from the governor sleeve. Remove the governor valve body.

3. Disassemble the governor valve body as required.

### Installation

1. Reassemble the governor valve body.

2. Install the governor valve body to the governor sleeve.

3. Mount the governor to the transaxle case so that the sleeve projection is aligned with the mating mark on the transaxle case.

4. Install the three cover/governor retaining bolts and tighten to 3.6-5.8 ft. lbs. of torque.

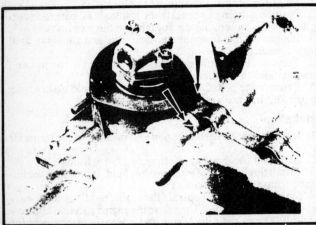

Governor to transaxle mating marks (©Toyo Kogyo Co. Ltd.)

## SERVO

### Removal

NOTE: Depending upon the configurations of the varied vehicle applications, the removal of the servo could require excessive movement of the engine/transaxle assembly. Perform this procedure as required.

1. With a pushing type tool, move the piston retainer inward and remove the snapring.

2. Remove the piston assembly from the case bore. Remove the return spring.

3. The seals can be removed and the piston assembly separated.

### Installation

1. Install new seals and assemble the piston components. Coat the seals with A/T fluid or vaseline.

2. Install the return spring and the piston assembly into the case bore. Do not damage the sealing rings.

3. Install the piston retainer, depress and install the snapring.

## DIFFERENTIAL OIL SEALS

The left and right axle seals can be installed with the axles removed. Conventional seal removing and installing tools can be used. Care must be exercised to prevent damage to the seals as the axles are reinstalled into the transaxle case.

## CONVERTER OIL SEAL

The transaxle must be removed, the converter removed from the assembly before the seal can be replaced. Conventional tools are used to replace the converter oil seal. Care must be exercised to prevent damage to the seal as the converter is installed.

## REMOVAL & INSTALLATION

### Removal of Transaxle
**MAZDA 626 MODELS**

1. Disconnect the negative battery cable and the speedometer cable.

2. Disconnect the selector control cable from the transaxle. Disconnect the ground wire from the transaxle.

3. Disconnect the neutral start (inhibitor) switch from the transaxle.

4. Remove the starter assembly.

5. Attach engine support assembly to the engine hanger eyelets and suspend the engine within the compartment.

6. Remove the vacuum line to the modulator.

7. Remove the upper bolts retaining the transaxle to the engine.

8. Loosen the pipe clip and disconnect the oil hose from the oil pipe.

9. Raise the vehicle and support safely at the desired working height. Drain the transaxle fluid from the unit.

10. Remove the front wheels and the left and right splash pans (shields).

11. Remove the control link of the stabilizer bar and remove the under cover pan.

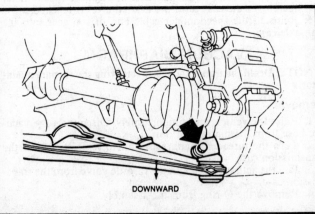

DOWNWARD

Removal of the lower ball joint retaining bolt (©Toyo Kogyo Co. Ltd.)

12. Remove the retaining bolts and nuts from the left and right lower arm ball joints to the steering knuckles. Pull the lower arms downward to separate them from the knuckles.

**NOTE: Do not damage the ball joint dust covers.**

13. Remove the left driveshaft from the transaxle in the following manner:

   a. Pull the front hub outward the move the drive shaft in the direction away from the transaxle, by tapping on it so that the coupling with the differential side gear is disconnected.

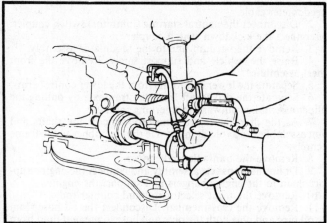

Removing the drive shaft from the transaxle (©Toyo Kogyo Co. Ltd.)

─────────── CAUTION ───────────
*Do not strike the drive shaft with a hard force to begin with, but tap on it with increasing force.*
───────────────────────────────

   b. Pull the front hub outward and pull the drive shaft out from the transaxle and set aside.

─────────── CAUTION ───────────
*To avoid damaging the oil seal, hold the joint with one hand while pulling the shaft straight out.*
───────────────────────────────

14. Remove the right drive shaft from the transaxle in the following manner:

   a. Insert a prybar between the driveshaft and the joint shaft. Pry the shaft assembly out of the joint shaft to start its movement.

   b. Pull the front hub outward and carefully remove the shaft from the joint shaft and set aside.

15. Remove the joint shaft bracket mounting bolts and pull the joint bracket from the transaxle as a complete assembly.

16. Remove the transaxle under cover pan.

17. Remove the retaining bolts between the torque converter and the drive plate.

18. Remove the crossmember and the left side lower arm to-

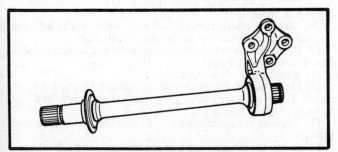

Joint shaft and bracket assembly (©Toyo Kogyo Co. Ltd.)

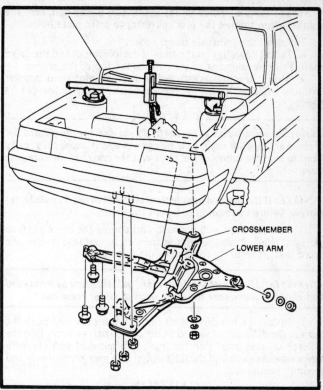

CROSSMEMBER

LOWER ARM

Removal or installation of crossmember and lower arm assembly (©Toyo Kogyo Co. Ltd.)

gether as an assembly after removing the nuts from the engine and transaxle.

19. It is suggested to attach a safety chain or rope to the transaxle during its removal from the vehicle, along with the use of a transmission type jack assembly.

─────────── CAUTION ───────────
*The added safety measure is suggested because of the unbalanced weight of the assembly.*
───────────────────────────────

20. Remove the two lower bolts retaining the transaxle to the engine.

21. Remove the transaxle from the vehicle, being careful not to disengage the converter as the unit is being removed.

22. After the transaxle has been removed, disconnect and remove the axle mount bracket from the transaxle.

### Installation

1. Install the transaxle mount bracket to the transaxle.

2. Position the transaxle on the jacking tool and secure with a safety chain or rope. Place the transaxle under the vehicle and carefully raise the assembly into place.

─────────── CAUTION ───────────
*Because the transaxle is not well balanced, be sure the assembly is properly secured to the lifting device and the converter assembly is held in place.*
───────────────────────────────

3. Install and tighten the two mounting bolts between the transaxle and the engine. Tighten to 66-86 ft. lbs. (91-119 N•m).

4. Remove the jacking device from under the transaxle while maintaining the rope or chain support.

5. Install the crossmember and transaxle mount nuts. Tighten the M10 nuts to 31.8-40 ft. lbs. (40-55 N•m) and the M12 nuts to 69-85 ft. lbs. (95-118 N•m).

6. Tighten the converter to drive plate bolts 25-36 ft. lbs. (35-50 N•m).

NOTE: With a wrench on the crankshaft pulley bolt, turn the crankshaft to tighten the four converter to drive plate bolts.

7. Install the transaxle under cover.

8. Install new clips on the ends of the joint shaft and the drive shaft. Position the gaps in the clips to the top of the groove.

9. Mount the joint shaft and install the joint shaft bracket onto the engine. Tighten the bracket bolts 31.1-46 ft. lbs. (43-63 N•m).

--- CAUTION ---

*During the installation of the shaft, do not damage the oil seal lip. If the shaft does not engage the side gear properly, move the gear by hand so that the center of the shaft and the center of the side gear meet.*

NOTE: If the preload adapter has been left in the transaxle, remove it before attempting to install the shaft.

10. Pull the front hub outward and couple the drive shaft to the joint shaft. Push the joint at the differential side so that the drive shaft is securely coupled to the joint shaft.

--- CAUTION ---

*After the installation of the drive shaft, pull the front hub outward and check to make sure the drive shaft does not come out.*

11. Install the left drive shaft into the transaxle and push the joint at the differential side to fit the drive shaft securely into the differential side gear. Pull the front hub outward and check to make sure the shaft and the differential side gear are properly and securely positioned.

--- CAUTION ---

*Be careful not to damage the oil seal.*

12. Attach the left and right lower ball joints to the knuckle and tighten the clinch bolts and nuts 32-40 ft. lbs. (44-55 N•m).

13. Attach the stabilizer bar control link. The bolt should protrude approximately 1 inch (25.5mm) from the top of the nut.

14. Install the left and right splash shields.

15. Install the left and right wheel assemblies.

16. Lower the vehicle and connect the oil hose to the pipe and tighten the hose clamp.

17. Install and tighten the five bolts retaining the transaxle to the engine to 66-86 ft. lbs. (91-119 N•m).

18. Install the vacuum line to the modulator and connect the wiring to the kickdown solenoid and the neutral safety (inhibitor) switch.

19. Connect the transaxle ground wire.

20. Connect the selector control cable to the transaxle.

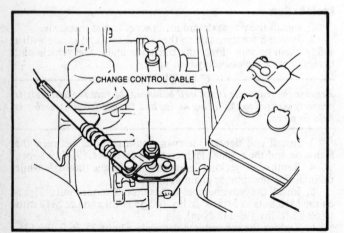

**Installing the change control cable (©Toyo Kogyo Co. Ltd.)**

21. Connect the speedometer cable to the transaxle.

22. Connect the battery cable and install the proper fluid into the transaxle.

23. Start the engine and correct the fluid level as required.

24. Adjust the manual linkage, the neutral starter switch and conduct a road test.

25. Verify correct operation and lack of fluid leakages.

## Removal
### GLC MODELS

1. Disconnect the negative battery cable. Disconnect the speedometer cable.

2. Disconnect the neutral starting (inhibitor) switch coupler. Disconnect the kickdown switch coupler.

3. Remove the vacuum line to the modulator assembly.

4. Raise the vehicle and support safely. Remove the front wheel assemblies.

5. Separate the lower ball joints from the lower control arms.

6. Separate the driveshaft from the transaxle by pulling the caliper assemblies outward in a jerking motion.

7. As the driveshafts are removed, support the shafts and joint assemblies to avoid damage. Tie the assemblies to the frame securely.

8. Remove the transaxle undercover.

9. Drain the transaxle assembly and connect the engine support chain to the engine hangers and support the engine.

10. Remove the front selector rod and counter rod.

11. Remove the crossmember. Disconnect the oil hose from the oil pipe and plug both the pipe and hose to prevent fluid from leaking.

12. Remove the upper front rubber mount from the left side of the transaxle.

13. Remove the starter motor from the engine assembly.

14. Remove the converter housing end cover and remove the bolts retaining the converter to the drive plates.

15. Support the transaxle with a jacking tool and secure the transaxle to the tool.

16. Remove the bell housing retaining bolts and remove the transaxle by slowly lowering the assembly from under the vehicle.

17. Do not allow the converter to drop from the assembly as it is being lowered from the vehicle.

## Installation

1. The installation of the transaxle is in the reverse procedure of its removal.

2. Raise the transaxle into position, being careful not to drop the converter as the transaxle is raised into position. Install the retaining bolts into the bell housing and tighten to 26.8-39.8 ft. lbs. (3.7-5.5 M-kg).

3. Install the bolts retaining the converter to the drive plate. Tighten to 25.3-36.2 ft. lbs. (3.5-5.0 M-kg). Install the end cover.

4. Install the starter assembly to the engine.

5. Install the front left upper rubber mount to the transaxle.

6. Install the cross member and connect the oil hose to the oil pipe.

7. Install the front selector rod and the counter rod.

8. Install the transaxle under cover and remove the supporting engine chain.

9. Carefully install the left and right drive shafts into the transaxle, being careful not to damage the oil seals.

10. Install the lower ball joint clinch bolts and tighten to 32.5-39.8 ft. lbs. (4.4-5.5 M-kg).

11. Install the front wheel assemblies.

12. Lower the vehicle and install the vacuum hose to the modulator. Install the neutral starting (inhibitor) switch and the kickdown switch couplers.

13. Connect the speedometer cable and the battery negative cable.

14. Install the proper fluid into the transaxle and start the engine. Verify that the fluid level is correct as the engine warms up.

15. Inspect the transaxle assembly for fluid leakage and correct, if necessary.

16. Road test the vehicle. Verify the manual linkage and the neutral starting switch operates properly.

## BENCH OVERHAUL

### Before Disassembly

Before removing any of the subassemblies, thoroughly clean the outside of the transaxle to prevent dirt from entering the mechanical parts during the repair operation.

During the repair of the subassemblies, certain general instructions which apply to all units of the transaxle must be followed. These instructions are given here to avoid unnecessary repetition.

Handle all transaxle parts carefully to avoid nicking or burring the bearing or mating surfaces.

Lubricate all internal parts of the transaxle before assembly with clean automatic transmission fluid. Do not use any other lubricants except on gaskets and thrust washers which may be coated with petroleum jelly to facilitate assembly. Always install new gaskets when assembling the transaxle.

Tighten all bolts and screws to the recommended torque.

## Transaxle Disassembly

### Disassembly

1. Remove the converter assembly. Do not spill the fluid within the unit.

2. Mount the transaxle on a stand assembly or on a clean work bench area.

3. Remove the neutral starter switch, the kickdown solenoid and the vacuum modulator.

4. Remove the oil level gauge (dipstick) and the tube.

5. Remove the speedometer driven gear and pull the oil pump shaft from the turbine shaft. Remove the turbine shaft.

6. Remove the oil pan and control valve assembly.

7. Remove the steel ball and spring from the transaxle case.

8. Remove the oil pump assembly from the end of the transaxle, after Steps 9 and 10.

9. Measure the front clutch drum end play before any further disassembly is made. Push the front drum towards the oil pump position with a pry bar. Measure the distance (clearance) between the front clutch drum and the connecting shell. This clearance is the front clutch drum end play. The standard clearance is 0.020-0.031 in. (0.5-0.8mm).

10. If the clearance is not within specifications, the proper sized shim must be selected for the assembly.

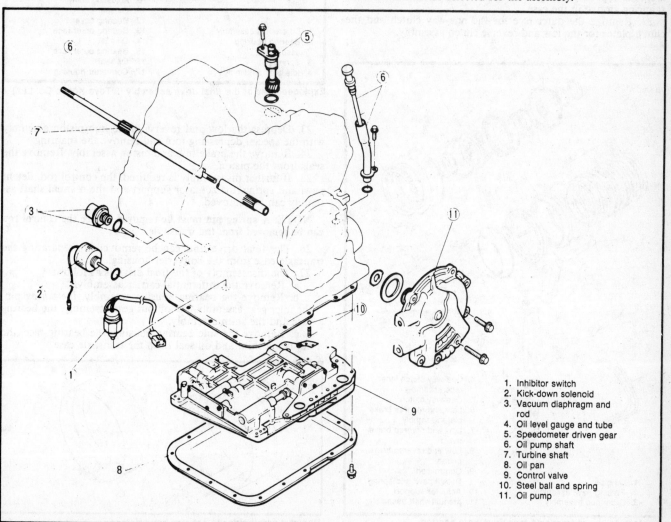

1. Inhibitor switch
2. Kick-down solenoid
3. Vacuum diaphragm and rod
4. Oil level gauge and tube
5. Speedometer driven gear
6. Oil pump shaft
7. Turbine shaft
8. Oil pan
9. Control valve
10. Steel ball and spring
11. Oil pump

Removal of exterior components of the transaxle (©Toyo Kogyo Co. Ltd.)

NOTE: A bearing race shim chart is included in the assembly procedure outline.

11. Should the oil pump be difficult to remove, tighten the brake band to anchor the front clutch. Slowly remove the oil pump.

12. The total end play will be checked during the assembly procedure.

13. Remove the brake band strut bolt and locknut.

14. Remove the brake band, the front clutch, the rear clutch and the hub assembly of the rear clutch, along with the thrust bearings and washers.

15. Remove the front planetary gear carrier assembly, the sun gear and spacer. Remove the connecting shell.

16. Remove the servo retaining snapring and remove the servo piston assembly.

17. Remove the governor retaining bolts and lift the governor from the transaxle case. Lift the cover from the governor assembly.

18. Remove the oil pipes from the case.

19. Remove the parking pawl assembly.

20. Remove the drum hub assembly from the case. Remove the one-way clutch assembly. Note the locations of the thrust bearings and washers.

21. Depress the low and reverse brake assembly with the use of a special type depressing tool. Remove the snapring from the snapring groove in the case.

22. Remove the outer race for the one-way clutch and the clutch plates for the low and reverse clutch assembly.

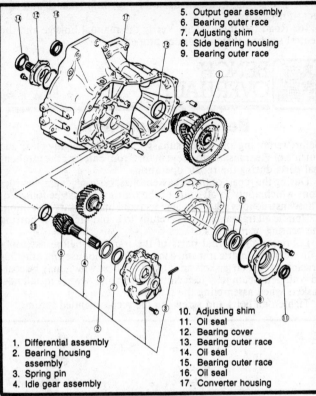

5. Output gear assembly
6. Bearing outer race
7. Adjusting shim
8. Side bearing housing
9. Bearing outer race

10. Adjusting shim
11. Oil seal
12. Bearing cover
13. Bearing outer race
14. Oil seal
15. Bearing outer race
16. Oil seal
17. Converter housing

1. Differential assembly
2. Bearing housing assembly
3. Spring pin
4. Idle gear assembly

**Exploded view of the final drive assembly** (©Toyo Kogyo Co. Ltd.)

23. Depress the low and reverse brake hub/piston assembly with the special depressing tool and remove the snapring.

24. Remove the brake hub and piston assembly. Remove the seals from the piston.

25. If further disassembly is required, the control rod, detent pawl and spring, the actuator support and the manual shaft assembly can be removed.

**NOTE: A spring pin must be removed before the control rod can be removed from the transaxle.**

26. The final drive unit can be removed by separating the transaxle case from the converter housing.

27. The disassembly of the final drive is as follows;

a. Remove the differential carrier assembly.

b. Remove the bearing housing assembly, the spring pin, the idler gear assembly, the output gear assembly, the bearing race and the shim assembly.

c. Remove the side bearing housing, the bearing race, the adjusting shim and oil seal from the transaxle case.

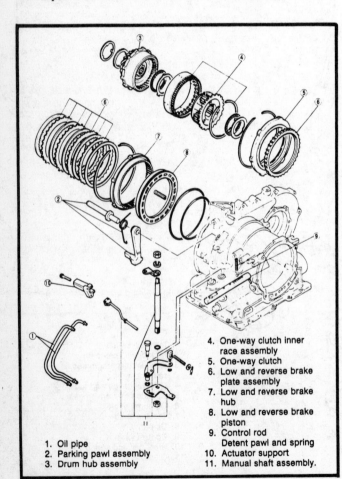

4. One-way clutch inner race assembly
5. One-way clutch
6. Low and reverse brake plate assembly
7. Low and reverse brake hub
8. Low and reverse brake piston
9. Control rod Detent pawl and spring
10. Actuator support
11. Manual shaft assembly.

1. Oil pipe
2. Parking pawl assembly
3. Drum hub assembly

**Exploded view of transaxle rear drive train section** (©Toyo Kogyo Co. Ltd.)

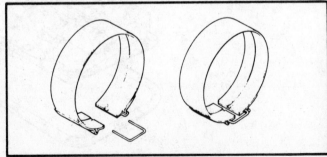

**Use of a wire holder to prevent band damage** (©Toyo Kogyo Co. Ltd.)

d. Remove the bearing cover, the bearing outer race, the oil seal, and the differential side bearing outer race from the converter housing.

**NOTE: The oil seals and bearing outer races are included in the bearing housings and must be pressed from the housings for removal.**

# Transaxle Component Disassembly, Inspection and Reassembly

## TORQUE CONVERTER

### Disassembly

1. The torque converter is welded together and cannot be disassembled.

**NOTE: Remanufacturing of torque converters is possible by specialty shops equipped to perform the necessary procedures.**

### Inspection

1. If the converter is to be reused, inspect the outer area of the converter for crack, inspect the bushing and seal surfaces for worn areas, scores, nicks or grooves.
2. The converter must be cleaned on the inside with cleaning solvent, dried, flushed with A/T fluid and drained until ready for installation.

## OIL PUMP

### Disassembly

1. Remove the pump cover and the drive flange. Mark the inner and outer gears.
2. Remove the inner and outer gears from the pump housing.
3. Remove the oil seals from the pump cover hub.

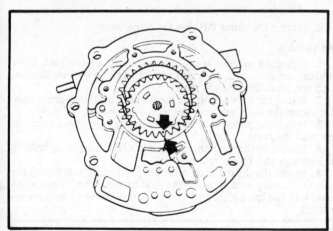

**Identifying marks on the inner and outer oil pump gears** (©Toyo Kogyo Co. Ltd.)

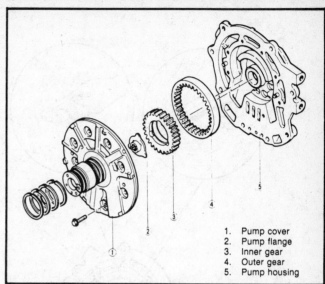

**Exploded view of the oil pump** (©Toyo Kogyo Co. Ltd.)

1. Pump cover
2. Pump flange
3. Inner gear
4. Outer gear
5. Pump housing

### Inspection

1. Check the housing and cover for cracks or worn areas.
2. Check the gears for wear, broken or damaged gear teeth.
3. Check the inner gear bushing of the pump housing sleeve for being worn or damaged.
4. Check the clearance of the inner gear to the pump cover and the outer gear to the pump cover. Refer to the specifications chart.
5. Check the clearance of the outer gear teeth head to the crescent dam. Refer to the specifications chart.
6. Check the clearance between the outer gear to the housing. Refer to the specifications chart.
7. Check the clearance between the new seal rings and the seal ring groove in the pump cover hub. Refer to the specifications chart.

### Assembly

1. The assembly of the oil pump is the reverse of the removal procedure.
2. Be sure the marks on the inner and outer gears are on the pump cover side.
3. Tighten the pump cover bolts 7.96-10.13 ft. lbs. (11-14 N•m).
4. After the assembly is complete, install the oil pump shaft and make sure the gears turn easily.

## FRONT CLUTCH

### Disassembly

1. Remove the retaining snapring from the drum.
2. Remove the retaining plate and the clutch plate assembly.

## CLEARANCE FOR OIL PUMP COMPONENTS

| Illus-tration | Measured location | Standard value | Limit |
|---|---|---|---|
| 1 | Inner gear to pump cover. Outer gear to pump cover | 0.02-0.04mm (0.001-0.002 in) | 0.08mm (0.003 in) |
| 2 | Head of outer gear teeth to Crescent dam | 0.14-0.21mm (0.006-0.008 in) | 0.25mm (0.010 in) |
| 3 | Outer gear to Housing | 0.05-0.20mm (0.002-0.008 in) | 0.25mm (0.010 in) |
| 4 | Seal ring to seal ring groove | 0.04-0.16mm (0.002-0.006 in) | 0.40mm (0.016 in) |

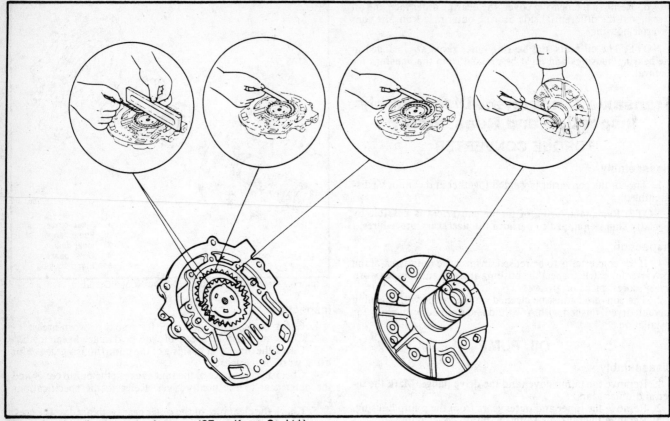

Measuring the oil pump gear clearance (©Toyo Kogyo Co. Ltd.)

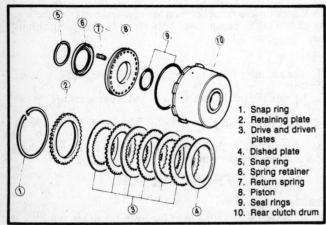

1. Snap ring
2. Retaining plate
3. Drive and driven plates
4. Dished plate
5. Snap ring
6. Spring retainer
7. Return spring
8. Piston
9. Seal rings
10. Rear clutch drum

Exploded view of the front clutch assembly (©Toyo Kogyo Co. Ltd.)

3. Remove the dished plate, noting the direction of the dish.
4. Remove the snapring from the drum hub with the use of a compressing tool.
5. Remove the piston from the drum by blowing compressed air into the apply hole in the drum. Remove the oil seals from the piston and drum hub.

## Inspection

1. Inspect for damaged or worn drive plates, broken or worn snaprings, deformed spring retainer, or weakened return springs.

**NOTE: The free length of the return springs is 0.992-1.071 in. (25.2-27.2mm).**

2. Inspect the drum bushing for being worn.

## Assembly

1. It is good practice to install new clutch plates, both drive and driven, during the overhaul of a transmission/transaxle unit, and not reuse the original plates.
2. Install the oil seals on the piston and the clutch drum hub. Lubricate the seals and grooves with vaseline or A/T fluid.
3. Install the piston into the drum, being careful not to cut or damage the seals.
4. Install the compressing tool and install the snapring holding the springs and spring retainer.
5. Install the dished plate with the protruding side facing the piston. Starting with a steel plate next to the dished plate, alternate with the lined plate and steel plate until three of each are installed.

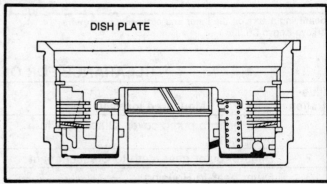

DISH PLATE

Direction of the dished plate in the front clutch
(©Toyo Kogyo Co. Ltd.)

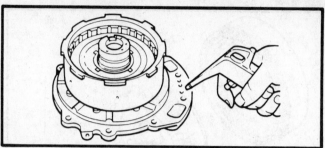

**Checking the front clutch piston with air pressure**
(©Toyo Kogyo Co. Ltd.)

6. Install the retaining plate and the retaining snapring.

7. Measure the front clutch clearance between the retaining plate and the snap ring. The standard clearance is 0.063-0.071 in. (1.6-1.8mm). If the clearance is not correct, adjust it with the proper sized retaining plate.

## FRONT CLUTCH RETAINER PLATE SPECIFICATIONS

| Part Number | Thickness of Retaining Plate |
|---|---|
| 3959 19 504 | 5.2mm (0.2047 in) |
| 3959 19 505 | 5.4mm (0.2126 in) |
| 3959 19 506 | 5.6mm (0.2205 in) |
| 3959 19 507 | 5.8mm (0.2284 in) |
| 3959 19 508 | 6.0mm (0.2362 in) |
| 3959 19 509 | 6.2mm (0.2441 in) |

## REAR CLUTCH

### Disassembly

1. The disassembly of the rear clutch is in the same manner and procedure as the disassembly of the front clutch.

### Inspection

1. Inspect the rear clutch components as was done for the front clutch components.

### Assembly

1. Install the oil seals on the piston and the clutch drum hub. Lubricate the seals and grooves with vaseline or A/T fluid.

2. Install the piston into the drum, being careful not to cut or damage the oil seals.

3. Continue the assembly of the rear clutch in the same manner and procedure as was done for the front clutch.

4. A total of four steel and four lined clutch plates are used in the rear clutch assembly. (3 plates each for 1,300 cc engine equipped vehicles).

5. Measure the clutch clearance in the same manner as was done for the front clutch. The standard clearance is 0.031-0.059 in. (0.8-1.5mm).

6. If the clearance is not correct select the correct sized retaining plate for installation into the drum.

## DRUM HUB

### Disassembly

1. Remove the parking gear spring.

2. Remove the parking gear by pushing the two pins which project from the drive hub.

3. Remove the snapring, the internal gear and the drive hub.

### Inspection

1. Inspect the components for broken or worn snaprings, damaged or worn gears, or broken teeth.

### Assembly

1. Assembly of the drum hub is in the reverse of its disassembly procedure.

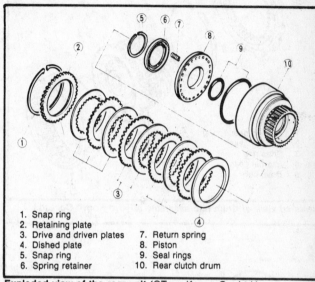

1. Snap ring
2. Retaining plate
3. Drive and driven plates
4. Dished plate
5. Snap ring
6. Spring retainer
7. Return spring
8. Piston
9. Seal rings
10. Rear clutch drum

**Exploded view of the rear unit** (©Toyo Kogyo Co. Ltd.)

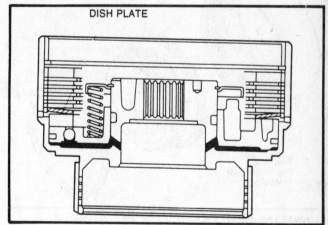

DISH PLATE

**Direction of dished plate in rear unit** (©Toyo Kogyo Co. Ltd.)

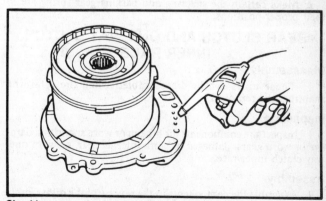

**Checking rear unit with air pressure** (©Toyo Kogyo Co. Ltd.)

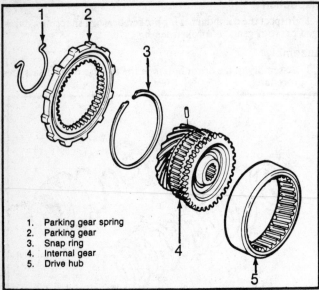

1. Parking gear spring
2. Parking gear
3. Snap ring
4. Internal gear
5. Drive hub

**Exploded view of drum hub assembly** (©Toyo Kogyo Co. Ltd.)

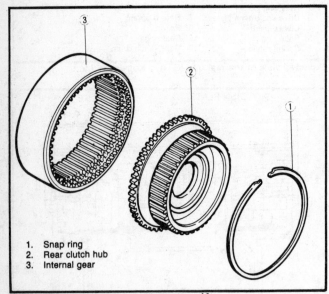

1. Snap ring
2. Rear clutch hub
3. Internal gear

**Exploded view of rear clutch hub assembly** (©Toyo Kogyo Co. Ltd.)

2. Make certain the snapring and parking gear spring are in their proper positions.

## REAR CLUTCH AND ONE-WAY CLUTCH INNER RACE

### Disassembly

1. These units can be disassembled when the retaining snaprings are removed.

### Inspection

1. Inspect the components for broken or worn snaprings, damage or worn gears, damaged or worn internal gear, or worn one-way clutch inner race.

### Assembly

1. Assemble the components in the reverse of the disassembly procedure.

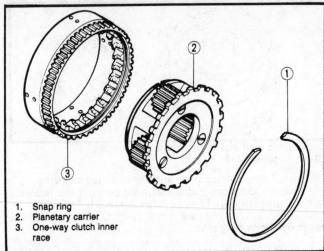

1. Snap ring
2. Planetary carrier
3. One-way clutch inner race

**Exploded view of clutch inner race and planetary gear carrier** (©Toyo Kogyo Co. Ltd.)

## PLANETARY CARRIER

### Inspection

1. Inspect the rotation of the gears and the clearance between the pinion washer and the planetary carrier.
2. The standard clearance is 0.031 in. (0.8mm).

## GOVERNOR

### Disassembly

1. The governor can be completely disassembled, with the removal of the shaft and gear, if required.
2. Remove the valve assembly from the governor shaft platform. Disassemble the valves from the body.
3. Should the shaft and gear need to be removed, drive the retaining pin from the gear-to-shaft and pull the gear from the shaft. Do not lose the shims, bearing and sleeve.

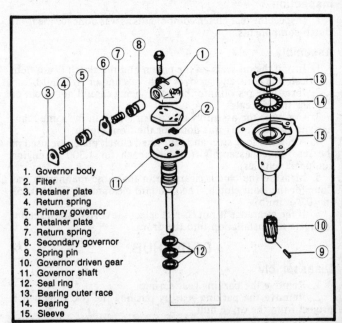

1. Governor body
2. Filter
3. Retainer plate
4. Return spring
5. Primary governor
6. Retainer plate
7. Return spring
8. Secondary governor
9. Spring pin
10. Governor driven gear
11. Governor shaft
12. Seal ring
13. Bearing outer race
14. Bearing
15. Sleeve

**Exploded view of governor assembly** (©Toyo Kogyo Co. Ltd.)

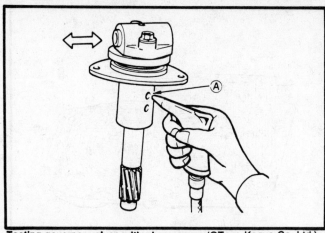

Testing governor valves with air pressure (©Toyo Kogyo Co. Ltd.)

## Inspection

1. Inspect the governor assembly for damaged or worn valves, clogged filter, weakened return spring and the sliding condition of the valve.

## Assembly.

1. The assembly of the governor assembly is in the reverse of the removal procedure.

2. Tighten the governor valve body-to-governor shaft platform to 5.79-7.96 ft. lbs. (8-11 N•m).

## GOVERNOR SPRING TENSION SPECIFICATIONS

| Spring | Outer diameter | Free length |
|---|---|---|
| Primary spring | 8.7-9.3mm (0.350-0.366 in) | 12.5-14.5mm (0.492-0.728 in) |
| Secondary spring | 9.2-9.8mm (0.362-0.386 in) | 12-14mm (0.472-0.551 in) |

## CONTROL VALVE ASSEMBLY

### Disassembly

1. The valve body is a precision unit within the transaxle and must be handled with extreme care. It must not be disassembled unless a reason exists to perform the procedure.

2. No specific order of disassembly is outline, but the repairman must rely upon his the professional expertise and judgement that dictates such repairs.

3. The valves and springs should be arranged in a channeled block or tray, in their disassembled order, to provide an assembly sequence.

4. Note the position of the check balls and the worm tracks that each were removed.

### Inspection

1. Inspect the valve body assembly for damaged or worn valves, damaged oil passages, cracked or damaged valve body, weakened springs and the operation of each valve in its bore of the valve body.

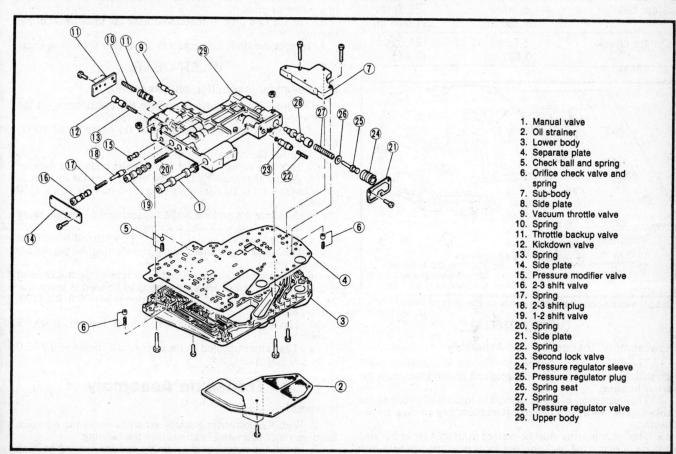

1. Manual valve
2. Oil strainer
3. Lower body
4. Separate plate
5. Check ball and spring
6. Orifice check valve and spring
7. Sub-body
8. Side plate
9. Vacuum throttle valve
10. Spring
11. Throttle backup valve
12. Kickdown valve
13. Spring
14. Side plate
15. Pressure modifier valve
16. 2-3 shift valve
17. Spring
18. 2-3 shift plug
19. 1-2 shift valve
20. Spring
21. Side plate
22. Spring
23. Second lock valve
24. Pressure regulator sleeve
25. Pressure regulator plug
26. Spring seat
27. Spring
28. Pressure regulator valve
29. Upper body

Exploded view of control valve assembly (©Toyo Kogyo Co. Ltd.)

## Assembly

1. Assemble the valves and springs into the valve body bores as were removed.
2. Install the two steel balls and springs into their positions in the valve body, along with the orifice check valve. Install the separator plate and the upper valve body.

### VALVE BODY SPRING TENSION SPECIFICATIONS

| Name of spring | Outer diameter | Free length |
|---|---|---|
| Throttle backup | 7.3mm (0.287 in) | 36.0mm (1.417 in) |
| Downshift | 5.55mm (0.218 in) | 22.0mm (0.866 in) |
| Pressure modifier | 8.4mm (0.331 in) | 18.5mm (0.728 in) |
| 2-3 shift | 6.9mm (0.272 in) | 41.0mm (1.614 in) |
| 1-2 shift | 6.55mm (0.258 in) | 32.0mm (1.260 in) |
| Second lock | 5.55mm (0.218 in) | 33.5mm (1.319 in) |
| Pressure regulator | 11.7mm (0.461 in) | 43.0mm (1.693 in) |
| Steel ball | 6.5mm (0.256 in) | 26.8mm (1.516 in) |
| Orifice check | 5.0mm (0.197 in) | 21.5mm (0.846 in) |

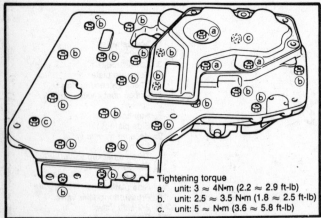

Tightening torque
a. unit: 3 ≈ 4N•m (2.2 ≈ 2.9 ft-lb)
b. unit: 2.5 ≈ 3.5 N•m (1.8 ≈ 2.5 ft-lb)
c. unit: 5 ≈ N•m (3.6 ≈ 5.8 ft-lb)

Control valve bodies attaching screw torque (©Toyo Kogyo Co. Ltd.)

## DIFFERENTIAL

### Disassembly, Inspection and Assembly

1. The differential is disassembled in the conventional manner, with the removal of the ring gear and pinion gears from the carrier housing.
2. The inspection of the components consists of checking for broken teeth, worn gears and thrust washers, or a cracked carrier housing.
3. The roller bearing must be pressed from the carrier housing and new ones pressed back on. New races must be used with new bearings.

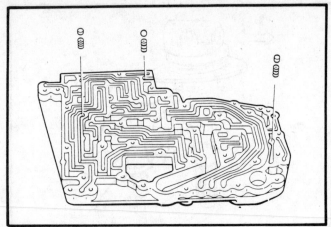

Location of steelballs and orifice check valve
(©Toyo Kogyo Co. Ltd.)

4. The backlash of the pinion gears is 0.0-0.039 in. (0.0-0.1mm).
5. If the backlash of the pinions are not correct, replace all the thrust washers with new ones and recheck. If excessive clearance still exists, check the carrier for wear.

## OUTPUT GEAR

### Disassembly, Inspection and Assembly

1. The bearings must be removed from the shaft with the use of a puller or press.
2. The use of a press is required during the installation of the bearings.
3. Inspect the shaft for broken or worn gear teeth or splines.

## IDLER GEAR

### Disassembly, Inspection and Assembly

1. Remove the locknut and remove the components on the shaft with the use of a puller or press as required.
2. Do not lose the adjusting shims as the components are removed.
3. Replace the components as required.
4. Check and adjust the idler gear bearing preload as follows:
   a. Secure the assembly in a vise and tighten the locknut to the lower limit of its tightening torque which is 94 ft. lbs. (130 N•m).
   b. Measure the preload while tightening the locknut, using special measuring tools and a spring scale.
   c. If the specified preload cannot be obtained within the specified tightening torque, adjust by selecting the proper adjusting shims.
   d. The preload can be reduced by increasing the thickness of the shims. A total of allowable shims to be used is seven.
   e. The tightening torque specification is 94-130 ft. lbs. (130-180 N•m).
   f. The preload specification is 0.3-7.8 inch lb. (0.03-0.9 N•cm).
   g. The value indicated on the spring scale should be 0.07-2.0 lbs. (30-900 grams).

## Transaxle Assembly

### Assembly

1. With the converter housing secured, install the oil seals, bearings outer races and bearings into the housing.
2. Install the output gear assembly and the bearing housing assembly. Install the idler gear assembly.

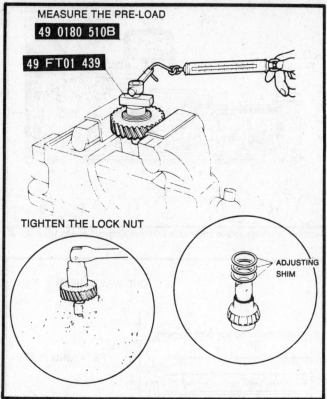

**MEASURE THE PRE-LOAD**

`49 0180 510B`

`49 FT01 439`

**TIGHTEN THE LOCK NUT**

ADJUSTING SHIM

Adjusting idler gear preload (©Toyo Kogyo Co. Ltd.)

3. Install the differential assembly.

4. Install the seal into the side bearing housing and install the bearing outer race, and adjusting shims onto the transaxle case.

**NOTE: The transaxle manufacturer has designed special tools for use during the assembly of the final drive unit. This repair procedure should not be attempted unless these tools or their equivalents, along with their use instructions are present. It is suggested the special tools be obtained before the transaxle is overhauled.**

5. The tolerances for the final drive are as follows:

a. Side bearing tightening torque—13.7-18.8 ft. lbs. (19-26 N•m).

b. Output gear bearing preload—0.3-7.8 in. lbs. (0.03-0.9 N•m).

c. Reading on spring scale for preload—0.07-2.0 lbs. (30-900 grams).

d. The differential side gear bearing preload—1.8-2.5 inch lbs. (2.1-2.9 N•m).

e. The reading on the spring scale—4.6-6.4 lbs. (2.1-2.9 Kg.).

## OUTPUT GEAR BEARING SHIM SPECIFICATIONS

| Part Number | | | Thickness of Shim |
|---|---|---|---|
| FT01 | 19 | 224 | 0.10mm (0.004 in) |
| FT01 | 19 | 225 | 0.12mm (0.005 in) |
| FT01 | 19 | 226 | 0.14mm (0.006 in) |
| FT01 | 19 | 227 | 0.16mm (0.007 in) |
| FT01 | 19 | 228 | 0.20mm (0.008 in) |
| FT01 | 19 | 229 | 0.50mm (0.020 in) |

6. If the manual shaft, actuator support, control rod, detent ball and spring have been removed previously, install the components in their proper order.

## DIFFERENTIAL SIDE BEARING SHIM SPECIFICATIONS

| Part Number | | | Thickness of Shim |
|---|---|---|---|
| G001 | 27 | 401 | 0.10mm (0.004 in) |
| G001 | 27 | 411 | 0.12mm (0.005 in) |
| G001 | 27 | 412 | 0.14mm (0.006 in) |
| G001 | 27 | 413 | 0.16mm (0.007 in) |
| G001 | 27 | 402 | 0.20mm (0.008 in) |
| G991 | 27 | 405 | 0.50mm (0.020 in) |

7. With the seals on the low and reverse brake piston, install the piston into the transaxle case, being careful not to damage or cut the lubricated oil seals.

8. Install the low and reverse brake hub and secure with the snapring.

9. Install the dished plate so that the protruding side faces the driven plates.

10. Starting with a steel plate, install the clutch plate pack into the transaxle case, alternating steel to lined and lined to steel, until a total of four steel and four lined plates have been installed.

11. Install the retaining plate and the one-way clutch. Push the one-way clutch down with the use of a compressing tool and install the snapring into its groove.

12. Measure the clearance of the low and reverse brake clutch pack between the retaining plate and the one-way clutch with a feeler gauge blade. The clearance should be 0.032-0.041 in. (0.8-1.05mm).

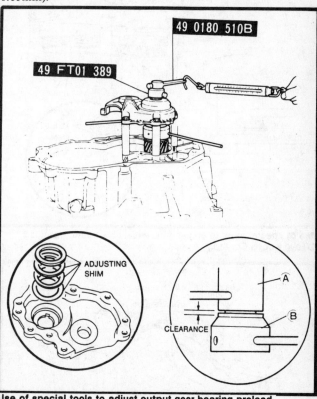

`49 0180 510B`

`49 FT01 389`

ADJUSTING SHIM

CLEARANCE

A
B

Use of special tools to adjust output gear bearing preload (©Toyo Kogyo Co. Ltd.)

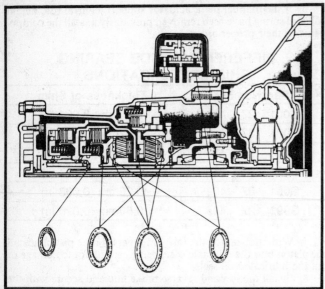

Needle bearing location within transaxle (©Toyo Kogyo Co. Ltd.)

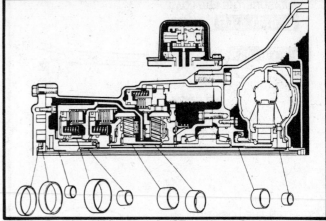

Bushing location within transaxle (©Toyo Kogyo Co. Ltd.)

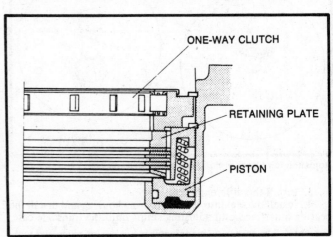

ONE-WAY CLUTCH

RETAINING PLATE

PISTON

Assembly of low and reverse brake set (©Toyo Kogyo Co. Ltd.)

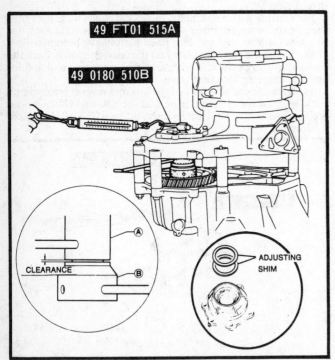

49 FT01 515A

49 0180 510B

CLEARANCE

A

B

ADJUSTING SHIM

Use of special tools to adjust differential side bearing preload (©Toyo Kogyo Co. Ltd.)

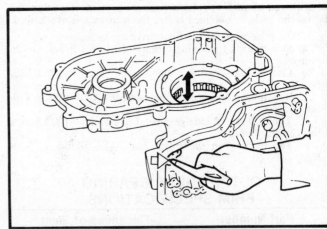

Checking low and reverse brake operation with air pressure (©Toyo Kogyo Co. Ltd.)

13. If the clearance is not within the specified tolerance, adjust it by selecting a different sized retaining plate.

14. Check the operation of the low and reverse brake by blowing compressed air into the apply port of the case.

15. Install the one-way clutch inner race assembly and the drum hub assembly. Slight movement may have to be accomplished to fit the units properly.

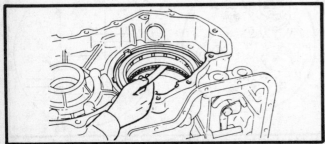

Measuring low and reverse brake clearance (©Toyo Kogyo Co. Ltd.)

16. Install the parking pawl assembly and the oil pipes.

17. Install the governor assembly into the case. Tighten the governor retaining bolts to 3.6-5.8 ft. lbs. (5-8 N•m).

**NOTE: Mount the governor so that the sleeve projection on the governor is aligned with the mating mark on the transaxle case.**

18. Apply a thin coat of sealant to the surface of the clutch housing which faces the transaxle case. Mount the case to the converter housing and install the retaining bolts. Tighten the bolts to a torque of 26.8-40 ft. lbs. (37-40 N•m).

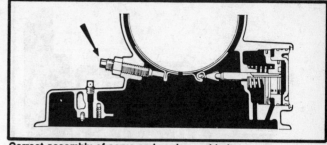
**Correct assembly of servo and anchor end bolt** (©Toyo Kogyo Co. Ltd.)

---
### CAUTION
---

*The preload adaptor tool or its equivalent, must be installed into the driveshaft coupling hole and secured by using wire, to prevent the side differential gear from turning the top of the pinion gear inside the differential gear case. Should this occur, the drive shaft coupling of the side gear will move and the transaxle may have to be disassembled again to correct the problem.*

19. Install new seals on the servo components and install into the case. Install the snap ring and cover with the help of a compressing tool.

20. Install the connecting shell, the sun gear and spacer, the planetary carrier and the rear clutch hub.

21. Install the thrust washer and bearing. Install the rear clutch assembly and its thrust bearing.

22. Install the front clutch and the brake band.

23. Install the anchor end bolt and the locknut for the brake band.

24. The total end play must be checked in the following manner:

   a. Remove the pump cover from the oil pump.

   b. Install the bearing into the rear clutch drum.

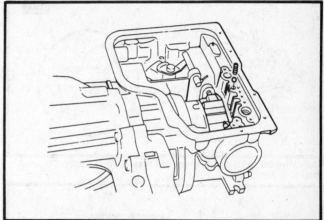
**Installing steel ball and spring in case** (©Toyo Kogyo Co. Ltd.)

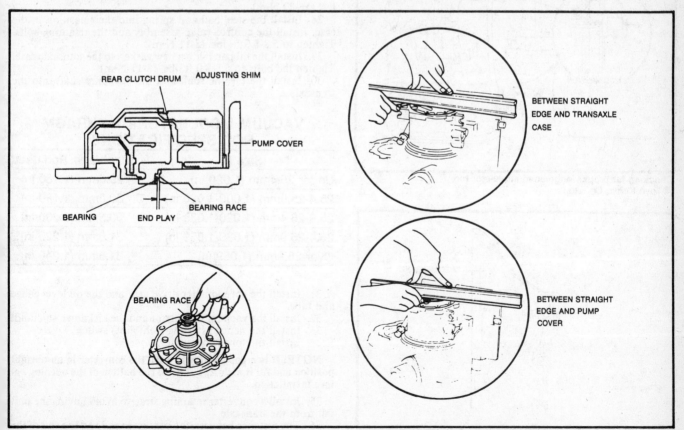
**Measuring for total end play** (©Toyo Kogyo Co. Ltd.)

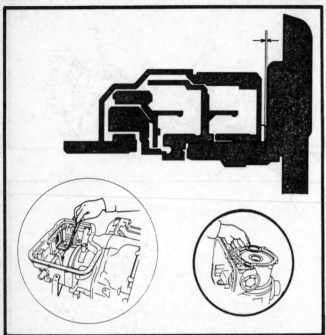

Measuring for front clutch drum end play (©Toyo Kogyo Co. Ltd.)

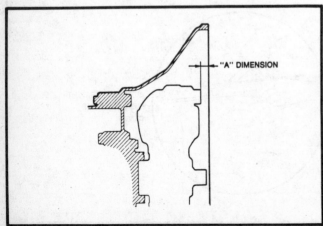

Checking for proper lengthened modulator rod
(©Toyo Kogyo Co. Ltd.)

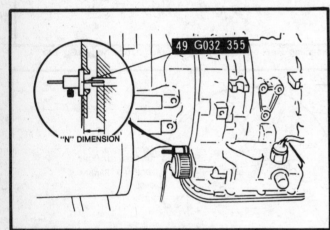

Dimension A = 0.79 in. (20mm) (©Toyo Kogyo Co. Ltd.)

c. Mount the bearing race to the pump cover and then install this inside the rear clutch drum.

d. Note that adjusting shims are not to be used between the pump cover and the brake drum.

e. Position a straight edge on the transaxle case and measure the clearance between the straight edge and either the pump cover or the transaxle case.

Between the straight edge and the pump cover—less than 0.004 in. (0.1mm).

Between the straight edge and the transaxle case—less than 0.006 in. (0.15mm).

## CAUTION

*Do not position the straight edge on the screws for mounting the oil pump to the case.*

f. The total end play must be 0.010-0.020 in. (0.25-0.5mm). If the end play does not agree with the standard value, adjust it by selecting a suitable bearing thrust race.

25. Assemble the oil pump assembly and install it onto the transaxle case with the correct bearing thrust race. Tighten the bolts to 10.8-15.9 ft. lbs. (15-22 N•m).

26. With oil pump installed, check the front clutch drum end play. This is accomplished in the following manner.

a. Push the front clutch drum towards the oil pump with a prybar.

b. Measure the clearance between the front clutch drum and the connecting shell. This is considered front clutch drum end play. The standard end play is 0.020-0.031 in. (0.5-0.8mm).

c. If the end play is not specified, adjust it by selecting a proper adjusting shim.

27. Tighten the anchor end bolt to a torque of 8.7-10.8 ft. lbs. (12-15 N•m) and loosen it two complete turns. While holding the end bolt securely, tighten the locknut to a torque of 40.5-59.3 ft. lbs. (56-82 N•m).

28. Install the steel ball and spring into their position in the case. Install the control valve assembly and the retaining bolts. Tighten to 5.8-8.0 ft. lbs. (8-11 N•m).

29. Install the oil pan (with a new gasket) to the transaxle case. Tighten the bolts to 5.8-8.0 ft. lbs. (8-11 N•m).

30. Install the turbine shaft and the oil pump shaft into the transaxle.

## VACUUM MODULATOR DIAPHRAGM ROD SPECIFICATIONS

| Size N | Diaphragm Rod Used |
| --- | --- |
| Under 25.4mm (1.000 in) | 29.5mm (1.160 in) |
| 25.4-25.9mm (1.000-1.020 in) | 30.0mm (1.180 in) |
| 25.9-26.4mm (1.020-1.039 in) | 30.5mm (1.200 in) |
| 26.4-26.9mm (1.039-1.059 in) | 31.0mm (1.220 in) |
| Over 26.9mm (1.059 in) | 31.5mm (1.240 in) |

31. Install the speedometer drive gear and the oil level gauge and tube.

32. Install the vacuum modulator and the kickdown solenoid.

33. Install the neutral starting (inhibitor) switch.

34. Install the torque converter.

**NOTE: It is a good policy to have the converter in an upright position and fill it with A/T fluid to the bottom of the opening before installation.**

35. Install a converter retaining strap to avoid having the unit fall from the transaxle.

36. The distance between the converter end and the end of the converter housing should be approximately 0.79 in. (20.0mm).

# S SPECIFICATIONS

## SPECIFICATIONS
## Jatco F3A Transaxle

| Item | Transaxle | | Specification |
|---|---|---|---|
| Model | | | F3A |
| Gear Ratio | 1st | | 2.842 |
| | 2nd | | 1.541 |
| | 3rd | | 1.000 |
| | Reverse | | 2.400 |
| Oil capacity liters (U.S. qts.) | | | 5.7 (6.0) |
| Fluid type | | | A.T.F. type F (M2C33F) |
| Fluid level<br>*Engine idling condition at "P" position | | | Between "F" and "L" marks on gauge |
| **STALL REVOLUTION** | | | |
| Before brake in | | rpm | 2,150-2,400 |
| After brake in | | rpm | 2,200-2,450 |
| **LINE PRESSURE** | | | |
| "R" | Idling condition | kPa (psi) | 400-700 (57-100) |
| | Stall condition | kPa (psi) | 1,600-1,900 (228-270) |
| "D" | Idling condition | kPa (psi) | 300-400 (43-57) |
| | Stall condition | kPa (psi) | 900-1,100 (128-156) |
| "2" | Idling condition | kPa (psi) | 800-1,200 (114-171) |
| | Stall condition | kPa (psi) | 800-1,200 (114-171) |
| "1" | Idling condition | kPa (psi) | 300-400 (43-57) |
| | Stall condition | kPa (psi) | 900-1,100 (128-156) |
| **CUT BACK POINT** | | | |
| Vacuum of vacuum pump | | | Governor pressure kPa (psi) |
| 0 mm-Hg (0 in-Hg) | | | 100-160 (14-23) |
| 200 mm-Hg (7.87 in-Hg) | | | 40-100 (6-14) |
| **GOVERNOR PRESSURE** | | | |
| Driving speed mph | | | Governor pressure kPa (psi) |
| 20 | | | 80-120 (11-17) |
| 35 | | | 140-200 (20-28) |
| 55 | | | 270-340 (38-48) |
| **SHIFT POINT SPEED** | | | |
| Throttle condition | | | Shift point km/h (mph) |
| Wide open throttle | D¹ → D² | | 54-76 (33-47) |
| | D² → D³ | | 100-131 (62-81) |
| | D³ → D² | | 87-115 (55-71) |
| | D² → D¹ | | 25-50 (15-31) |
| Half throttle<br>200 mm-Hg (7.87 in-Hg) | D¹ → D² | | 17-36 (10-32) |
| | D² → D³ | | 28-67 (17-41) |

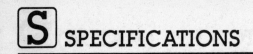 

## SPECIFICATIONS
### Jatco F3A Transaxle

| Item | Transaxle | Specification |
|---|---|---|
| **SHIFT POINT SPEED** | | |
| Fully closed throttle | $D^3 \to D^1$ | 9-20 (5-12) |
| | $1_2 \to 1_1$ | 41-56 (25-34) |
| **TORQUE CONVERTER** | | |
| Stall torque ratio | | 2,100 |
| Bushing diameter | Standard | 33.00-33.025 (1.299-1.300) |
| mm (in) | Wear limit | 33.075 |
| **OIL PUMP** | | |
| Clearance | | |
| Gear end float | Standard | 0.02-0.04 (0.0008-0.0016) |
| mm (in) | Limit | 0.08 (0.0031) |
| Outer gear and crest | Standard | 0.14-0.21 (0.0055-0.0083) |
| mm (in) | Limit | 0.25 (0.0098) |
| Outer gear and housing | Standard | 0.05-0.20 (0.002-0.0079) |
| mm (in) | Limit | 0.25 (0.0098) |
| Oil seal ring and ring groove | Standard | 0.04-0.16 (0.0016-0.0063) |
| mm (in) | Limit | 0.40 (0.0157) |
| Pump housing sleeve diameter | Standard | 37.950-37.975 (1.4941-1.4951) |
| mm (in) | Limit | 37.900 (1.4922) |
| Inner gear bushing inner diameter | Standard | 38.0-38.025 (1.4961-1.4971) |
| mm (in) | Limit | 38.075 (1.499) |
| **FRONT CLUTCH** | | |
| Number of driven and drive plates | | 3 |
| Front clutch clearance | mm (in) | 1.6-1.8 (0.063-0.071) |
| Clearance adjusting retaining plate mm (in) | | 5.2(0.205) 5.4(0.213) 5.6(0.220) 5.8(0.228) 6.0(0.236) 6.2(0.244) |
| Return spring free length | mm (in) | 25.2-27.2 (0.996-1.075) |
| Drum bushing inner diameter | Standard | 44.0-44.025 (1.7322-1.7331) |
| mm (in) | Limit | 44.075 (1.7354) |
| Front clutch drum end prary mm (in) Clearance between drum and connecting shell. | | 0.5-0.8 (0.020-0.032) |
| End play adjusting shim mm (in) | | 1.3(0.051) 1.5(0.059) 1.7(0.067) 1.9(0.075) 2.1(0.083) 2.3(0.091) 2.5(0.098) 2.7(0.106) |
| **REAR CLUTCH** | | |
| Number of driven and drive plates | | 4 |
| Rear clutch clearance | mm (in) | 0.8-1.5 (0.031-0.059) |
| Return spring free length | mm (in) | 25.2-27.2 (0.992-1.071) |
| **LOW AND REVERSE BRAKE** | | |
| Number of friction and steel plates | | 4 |
| Clearance mm (in) Total clearance measured between retaining plate and stopper. | | 0.8-1.05 (0.031-0.041) |

## SPECIFICATIONS
### Jatco F3A Transaxle

| Item | Transaxle | Specification |
|---|---|---|
| | **LOW AND REVERSE BRAKE** | |
| Clearance adjusting retaining plates | mm (in) | 4.6(0.181) 4.8(0.189) 5.0(0.197) 5.2(0.205) 5.4(0.213) 5.6(0.221) |
| Free length of return spring | mm (in) | 26.7-28.7 (1.051-1.130) |
| | **SERVO** | |
| Free length of return spring | mm (in) | 47.0-49.0 (1.85-1.929) |
| | **GOVERNOR** | |
| Primary spring | Outer diameter | 8.7-9.3 (0.343-0.366) |
| mm (in) | Free length | 16.5-18.5 (0.65-0.728) |
| Secondary spring | Outer diameter | 8.95-9.55 (0.352-0.376) |
| mm (in) | Free length | 12.4-14.4 (0.488-0.567) |
| | **ONE-WAY CLUTCH** | |
| Bushing diameter | Standard | 12.987-130.013 (5.1177-5.1187) |
| mm (in) | Limit | 130.063 (5.1207) |
| | **GEAR ASSEMBLY** | |
| Total end play | mm (in) | 0.25-0.50 (0.010-0.020) |
| End play adjusting race | mm (in) | 1.2(0.047) 1.4(0.055) 1.6(0.063) 1.8(0.071) 2.0(0.079) 2.2(0.087) |
| Idle gear bearing preload | kg (in-lb) | 0.03-0.09 (0.3-7.8) |
| Preload adjusting shims | mm (in) | 0.10(0.004) 0.12(0.005) 0.14(0.006) 0.16(0.007) 0.50(0.020) 0.20(0.008) |
| Output gear bearing preload | kg (in-lb) | 0.03-0.9 (0.3-7.8) |
| | **CONTROL VALVE** | |
| Throttle backup valve spring | Diameter | 7.3 (0.287) |
| mm (in) | Free length | 36.0 (1.417) |
| Down shift valve spring | Diameter | 5.55 (0.219) |
| mm (in) | Free length | 22.0 (0.866) |
| Pressure modifier valve spring | Diameter | 8.4 (0.331) |
| mm (in) | Free length | 18.5 (0.728) |
| 2 → 3 shift valve spring | Diameter | 6.9 (0.272) |
| mm (in) | Free length | 41.0 (1.614) |
| 1 → 2 shift valve spring | Diameter | 6.55 (6.258) |
| mm (in) | Free length | 32.0 (1.260) |
| Second lock valve spring | Diameter | 5.55 (0.219) |
| mm (in) | Free length | 33.5 (1.319) |
| Pressure regulator valve spring | Diameter | 11.7 (0.461) |
| mm (in) | Free length | 43.0 (1.693) |
| Steel ball spring | Diameter | 6.5 (0.256) |
| mm (in) | Free length | 26.8 (1.055) |
| Orifice check valve spring | Diameter | 5.0 (0.197) |
| mm (in) | Free length | 21.5 (0.846) |
| | **VACUUM DIAPHRAGM** | |
| Available diaphragm rods | mm (in) | 29.0(1.142) 29.5(1.161) 30.0(1.181) 30.5(1.200) 31.0(1.220) |

## SPECIFICATIONS
### Jatco F3A Transaxle

| Item | Transaxle | Specification |
|---|---|---|
| **DRIVE AND DIFFERENTIAL** | | |
| Final gear | Type | Helical gear |
| | Reduction ratio | 3.450 |
| Side bearing preload | kg (in-lb) | 2.1-2.9 (4.62-6.39) |
| Preload adjusting shims | mm (in) | 0.1(0.004) 0.2(0.008) 0.3(0.012) 0.4(0.016) 0.5(0.020) 0.6(0.024) 0.7(0.028) 0.8(0.031) 0.9(0.035) 0.12(0.0047) 0.14(0.0055) 0.16(0.0063) |
| Backlash of side gear and pinion | mm (in) | 0-0.1 (0-0.004) |
| Backlash adjusting thrust washers | mm (in) | 2.0(0.079) 2.1(0.083) 2.2(0.087) |

## TIGHTENING TORQUE SPECIFICATIONS
### Jatco F3A Transaxle

| Item | Nm (ft. lb.) |
|---|---|
| Drive plate to crankshaft | 98-105 (70-75) |
| Drive plate to torque converter | 35-50 (25.3-36.2) |
| Converter housing to engine | 91-119 (65-86) |
| Converter housing to transaxle case | 37-55 (26.8-39.8) |
| Bearing housing to converter housing | 19-26 (13.7-18.8) |
| Side bearing housing to transaxle case | 19-26 (13.7-18.8) |
| Bearing cover to transaxle case | 11-14 (8.0-10.1) |
| Oil pump to transaxle case | 19-26 (13.7-18.8) |
| Governor coker to transaxle case | 5-8 (3.6-5.8) |
| Oil pan | 5-8 (3.6-5.8) |
| Anchor end bolt (when adjusting band brake) | 12-15 (8.7-10.8) |
| Anchor end bolt lock nut | 56-82 (41-59) |
| Control valve body to transaxle case | 8-11 (5.8-8.0) |
| Lower valve body to upper valve body | 2.5-3.5 (1.8-2.5) |
| Side plate to control valve body | 2.5-3.5 (1.8-2.5) |
| Reamer bolt of control valve body | 5-7 (3.6-5.1) |
| Oil strainer of control valve | 3-4 (2.2-2.9) |
| Governor valve body to governor shaft | 8-11 (5.8-8.0) |
| Oil pump cover | 11-14 (8.0-10.1) |
| Inhibitor switch | 19-26 (13.7-18.8) |
| Neutral switch | 10-15 (7.2-8.0) |
| Manual shaft lock nut | 30-40 (21.7-29.0) |
| Oil cooler pipe set bolt | 16-24 (11.6-17.4) |
| Actuator for parking rod to transaxle case | 12-16 (8.7-11.6) |
| Idle bear bearing lock nut | 130-180 (94-130) |

## SPECIAL TOOLS

## SPECIAL TOOL APPLICATION

| Tool Number | Identification |
|---|---|
| 49 FT01 377 | Replacer Lo. & Rev. Piston |
| 49 FT01 439 | Holder Idle Gear Shaft |
| 49 FT01 361 | Remover Bearing |
| 38MM or 1½" | Socket Wrench |
| 4MM 3.2MM | Pin Punch |
| 49 B001 795 | Installer Oil Seal |
| 49 FT01 376 | Lifter Servopiston |
| 49 FT01 377 | Replacer Lo. Rev. Piston |
| 49 0839 425 | Bearing Puller Set |
| 49 F401 330 | Bearing Installer Set |
| 49 F401 365 | Bearing Remover |
| 49 FT01 380 | Shim Selector Set |
| 49 F401 380 | Shim Selector Set |

## SPECIAL TOOL APPLICATION

| Tool Number | Identification |
|---|---|
| 49 FT01 515 | Preload Adaptor |
| 49 0180 510A | Preload Adaptor |
| Welding Rod | Drive Shaft Hanger |

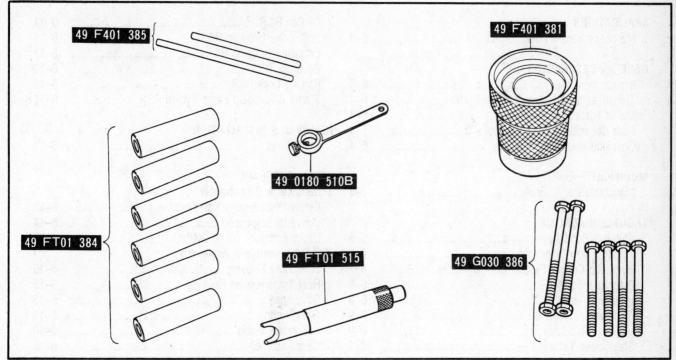

**Differential side bearing preload tool set** (©Toyo Kogyo Co. Ltd.)

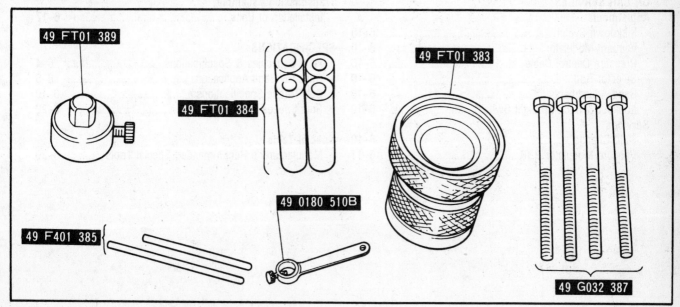

**Output gear bearing preload tool set** (©Toyo Kogyo Co. Ltd.)

# INDEX

# MERCEDES-BENZ W4A040

## APPLICATIONS

### TRANSMISSION APPLICATION CHART
### W4A-040, W4A-020

| Year | Model | Transmission |
|---|---|---|
| '81 and later | 300D Turbodiesel | W4A-040 |
| '81 and later | 300CD Turbodiesel | W4A-040 |
| '81 and later | 300TD Turbodiesel | W4A-040 |
| '81 and later | 300SD Turbodiesel | W4A-040 |
| '81-'82 | 380SLC | W4A-040 |
| '81-later | 380SL | W4A-040 |
| '81-'83 | 380SEL | W4A-040 |
| '81-'83 | 380SEC | W4A-040 |
| '84 and later | 380SE | W4A-040 |
| '84 and later | 500SEC | W4A-040 |
| '84 and later | 500SEL | W4A-040 |
| '84 and later | 190E | W4A-020 |
| '84 and later | 190D | W4A-020 |

## GENERAL DESCRIPTION

The W4A-040 transmission is a fully automatic four-speed unit consisting primarily of a three element welded torque converter and a compound planetary gear set. Two multiple disc clutches, one overrunning clutch, and three bands provide friction ele-

ments required to obtain desired function of the planetary gear set. A hydraulic system, pressurized by a primary gear type pump and secondary piston type pump provides working pressure required to operate friction elements and automatic controls.

The W4A-020 is very similar to the W4A-040. The similarities apply to the layout of the planetary gear sets, brake bands and clutches and the shift valves. It is a 5-speed converter type transmission with an input torque of 147.5 ft. lbs. (200 N•m).

On vehicles equipped with the gas engine, with the shift lever in positions "D" and "3", the transmission starts in second gear

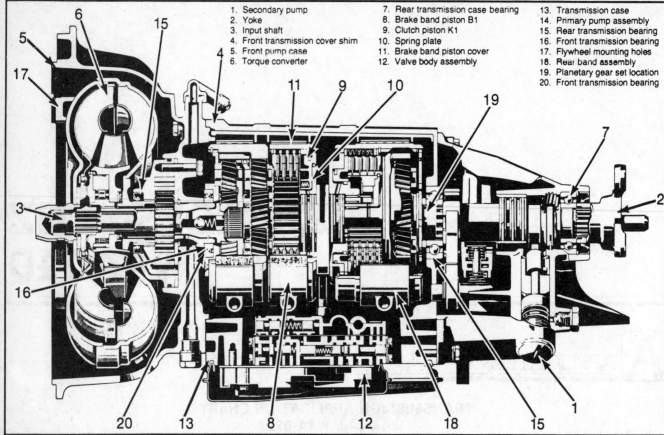

1. Secondary pump
2. Yoke
3. Input shaft
4. Front transmission cover shim
5. Front pump case
6. Torque converter
7. Rear transmission case bearing
8. Brake band piston B1
9. Clutch piston K1
10. Spring plate
11. Brake band piston cover
12. Valve body assembly
13. Transmission case
14. Primary pump assembly
15. Rear transmission bearing
16. Front transmission bearing
17. Flywheel mounting holes
18. Rear band assembly
19. Planetary gear set location
20. Front transmission bearing

Typical automatic transmission (© Mercedes-Benz of America)

when driving in the lower load range and in first gear when in the higher load range.

On vehicles equipped with the diesel engine, the transmission starts in first gear in all forward driving positions. When the vehicle is stopped the transmission will remain in second gear to prevent creeping. The ratio in first gear has been changed to 4.25:1 to accommodate the lower rear axle ratio.

## Transmission and Converter Identification

### TRANSMISSION

The W4A-040 and W4A-020 transmissions can be identified by a tag that is attached to the transmission case, near the center servo cover. The lower line of the tag shows the transmission build number and the top line of the tag shows the transmission assembly part number.

### CONVERTER

The torque converter used with the Mercedes-Benz automatic transmission is a sealed unit and cannot be disassembled for service. If the hub of the converter is scored, or if metal particles are found in the transmission fluid, replace the torque converter.

A smaller torque converter is used on the W4A-020 with the pump gear diameter being 9.6 in. (245mm.).

## Transmission Fasteners

Metric bolts and fasteners are used in attaching the transmission to the engine and also in attaching the transmission to the chassis crossmember mount.

The metric fastener dimensions are very close to the dimensions of the familiar inch system fasteners, and for this reason, replacement fasteners must have the same measurement and strength as those removed.

Do not attempt to interchange metric fasteners for inch system fasteners. Mismatched or incorrect fasteners can result in damage to the transmission unit through malfunctions, breakage or possible personal injury.

Care should be taken to reuse the fasteners in the same locations as removed, whenever possible.

**NOTE: At an oil temperature of 20-30 degrees C the maximum fluid level is 30mm below the lower dipstick mark. This information is provided as an aid during an oil change, which is generally made at this temperature.**

Wipe the dipstick with a clean lint free cloth, immerse it fully for measuring, pull the dipstick out again and read the oil level.

## Fluid Type Specifications

Only type A, Dexron® or Dexron® II automatic transmission fluid should be used in the Mercedes-Benz automatic transmission. Failure to use the proper grade and type automatic transmission fluid could result in serious internal transmission damage.

## Checking Transmission Fluid Level

Check the automatic transmission fluid level at least every 6,000 miles. This fluid check is made with the engine running, the parking brake on, and the selector lever in the "P" position. The vehicle must also be on level ground and in an unloaded condition. The automatic transmission must also be at operating temperature which is about 80 degrees centigrade. Prior to inspection run the engine for about 1-2 minutes at idling speed so that the torque converter can fill up.

Fill the transmission as required. Actuate the service brake, when the upper dipstick mark is attained after adding transmission fluid. Move the selector lever in all range positions. Then move it back to position "P", so that the working pistons of the servo members are charged with transmission fluid. Check the transmission fluid once again and make corrections if necessary.

NOTE: A fully cooled down transmission will show an oil level below the bottom dipstick mark even when correctly filled with oil.

If the oil level is too low the oil pump will suck up air which can be clearly heard. The oil will foam and provide wrong results during an oil level checkup. Wait unitl the oil foam is down (for approx. 2 minutes), add oil and check oil level.

Excessive transmission fluid must be drained otherwise the transmission gears would be splashing in oil. The temperature will increase unnecessarily until the foaming oil will be ejected through breather. Continuous operation under such circumstances will lead to transmission damage.

## Fluid Capacity

All W4A-020 and W4A-040 automatic transmissions have a fluid capacity of 12.9 pts.

## MODIFICATIONS

### Brake Band B3 Adjusting Bolt

The adjusting bolt for brake band B3 has been modified. On the modified version, the bolt head is "sheared off" after the brake band adjustment has been made. This prevents a subsequent alteration of the brake band setting (no readjustment is possible). The previous version adjusting bolt should be replaced by the modified version only during the course of any transmission repairs that might be performed requiring the removal of the automatic transmission from the vehicle.

## TROUBLE DIAGNOSIS

NOTE: On all automatic transmissions, this brake band may now only be adjusted on transmissions removed from the vehicle.

Adjust brake band B3 using the procedure below.
1. Remove the transmission.
2. Remove the valve body.
3. Remove solenoid from transmission if solenoid is installed in an inclined position.
4. Remove the previous version adjusting bolt and replace with the modified version.
5. Tighten the adjusting bolt to 3.6 ft. lbs.
6. Measure the brake band gap and record the measurement.
7. Back off the adjusting bolt by 1¾ turns and tighten the lock nut, making sure in doing so that the adjusting bolt is not turned.
8. Measure the gap again. It must be 0.118 in. (3mm) wider than the gap measured previously.
9. Twist off (shear off) the head of the adjusting bolt.
10. Install the solenoid and the valve body and install the transmission.

## Brake Band Piston B2

The seal ring for the brake band piston B2 is made out of teflon. It has a very wide sealing surface and because of this the piston is not in direct contact with the housing and cannot seize.

## Fluid Line Connection Bore Relocation

The connection bore of the right transmission fluid line to the transmission fluid cooler has been relocated by 0.43 in. On transmissions with a wide fluid pan the connection to the transmission has been changed to an inlet union fitting (banjo fitting) and is fastened directly to the transmission with the inlet union screw. The previously used elbow fitting is now being omitted from production. Replacement transmissions are being supplied with the previous as well as with the relocated fitting bores. Should the transmission require replacement the following should be noted.

On transmissions with narrow oil pans, the oil line must be slightly rebent if installing a replacement transmission with relocated connection bore. On transmissions with wide oil pans and when a previous version is replaced by a modified version transmission, a new oil line with an inlet union fitting must be installed. Also, when a modified version is replaced by the previous version transmission, an oil line with an elbow fitting and a nut must be installed.

## CLUTCH AND BAND APPLICATION CHART
### W4A-040, W4A-020

| Gear Range | Front Brake | Center Brake | Rear Brake | Front Clutch | Rear Clutch | Overdrive Clutch |
|---|---|---|---|---|---|---|
| First gear | | X | | | X | X |
| Second gear | X | X | | | | |
| Third gear | | X | | X | | |
| Fourth gear | | | | X | X | |
| Reverse | | | X | | X | X |
| Neutral/Park | | | | | | |

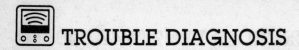
## CHILTON'S THREE "C's" TRANSMISSION DIAGNOSIS CHART
### Mercedes-Benz Model W4A-040

| Condition | Cause | Correction |
| --- | --- | --- |
| Slips in all selector positions | a) Incorrect modulating pressure<br>b) Modulating pressure control valve or pressure relief | a) Adjust modulator or replace<br>b) Clean or replace problem valve |
| Rough jerking when changing gear | a) Check modulating and line pressure<br><br>b) Vacuum lines or connections leaking or broken<br>c) Control pressure linkage out of adjustment<br>d) Control valve converter adjustment incorrect | a) Adjust pressure as necessary; if line pressure is to high replace valve body assembly<br>b) Replace as necessary<br><br>c) Adjust control pressure linkage as required<br>d) Correct problem as required |
| Rough jerk on 3-2 downshift | a) Rear servo piston sealing ring worn or damaged<br>b) Defective rear servo piston | a) Replace defective component as required<br>b) Replace as required |
| No upshifts | a) Incorrect governor pressure<br>b) Defective governor assembly<br>c) Valve body dirty or valves sticking | a) Correct pressure as necessary<br>b) Repair or replace governor<br>c) Repair or replace components as necessary |
| Upshifts only in upper speed range of gears | a) Control pressure linkage out of adjustment<br>b) Defective governor assembly | a) Adjust linkage as required<br><br>b) Repair or replace governor |
| Upshifts only in lower speed range of gears | a) Control speed linkage damaged or out of adjustment<br>b) Accelerator linkage out of adjustment<br>c) Defective governor assembly | a) Repair or adjust linkage as necessary<br>b) Adjust linkage as required<br><br>c) Repair or replace governor |
| No kickdown shifts | a) Fuse for power supply to the solenoid valve blown<br>b) Defective solenoid valve<br>c) Control pressure linkage damaged or out of adjustment<br>d) Kickdown control valve in the valve body sticking | a) Replace fuse<br><br>b) Replace solenoid valve<br>c) Repair or adjust control pressure linkage<br>d) Repair or replace control valve as required |
| No engine braking on downshifts | a) Control pressure linkage out of adjustment<br>b) Defective servo piston(s)<br><br>c) Defective valve body assembly | a) Adjust control pressure linkage as required<br>b) Repair or replace piston(s) as necessary<br>c) Repair or replace valve body as required |
| Slips in all selector positions | valve for modulating pressure dirty or sticking<br>c) Line to transmission vacuum unit clogged or leaking<br>d) Line pressure control valve dirty or sticking<br>e) Defective primary pump | <br><br>c) Clean or replace vacuum line<br>d) Clean or replace line pressure control valve<br>e) Repair or replace pump |
| Transmission grabs or vehicle shakes when starting off from a complete stop | a) Incorrective modulating pressure<br>b) Check transmission vacuum unit | a) Correct pressure as required<br>b) If fluid is found replace the unit; if fuel is found check and adjust the injection system |

## CHILTON'S THREE "C's" TRANSMISSION DIAGNOSIS CHART
### Mercedes-Benz Model W4A-040

| Condition | Cause | Correction |
|---|---|---|
| Transmission slips in 1st gear | a) Dirty or sticking valves in valve body<br>b) Defective center servo piston or piston sealing ring damage<br>c) Defective center band or thrust body<br>d) Bleed valves for the front clutch supporting flange sticking | a) Correct as required<br>b) Repair servo piston and sealing ring as required<br>c) Repair center band or thrust body as required<br>d) Correct or replace components as necessary |
| Transmission slips on upshifts | a) Incorrect modulator or line pressure<br>b) Faulty valve body assembly<br>c) Defective front or rear clutch<br>d) Oil distribution sleeve damage | a) Correct modulator and/or line pressure as required<br>b) Replace sealing bushings on plug pipes<br>c) Repair or replace front or rear clutch, as required<br>d) Repair as necessary |
| Transmission slips in 3rd gear | a) Valve body sealing bushings worn or damaged<br>b) Defective rear clutch assembly<br>c) Oil distributing sleeve damaged | a) Replace valve body or sealing bushings as required<br>b) Repair or replace as required<br>c) Repair as necessary |
| Transmission slips in 1st and 2nd gears | a) Rear band worn or damaged<br>b) Adjust brake band | a) Replace rear band as required<br>b) Install a longer thrust pin |
| Transmission slips in all gears | a) Incorrect modulating pressure<br>b) Defective modulator pressure relief valve or control valve | a) Correct pressure as required<br>b) Replace problem valve |
| No positive engagement in Reverse | a) Front band out of adjustment<br>b) Front servo piston sealing ring worn or damaged<br>c) Defective one-way clutch in gear unit assembly | a) Correct front band adjustment<br>b) Replace front servo piston sealing ring as required<br>c) Repair or replace one-way clutch as required |
| Rough jerk when engaging selector lever in "D" position | a) Engine idle speed too high<br>b) Incorrect modulating and/or line pressure<br>c) Defective pressure receiving piston located in the extension housing | a) Correct as required<br>b) Correct modulating and/or line pressure as required<br>c) Correct the pressure receiving piston as necessary |

# Hydraulic Control System
## TORQUE CONVERTER

The torque converter operates as an automatic clutch, a variable torque converter, and as a vibration damper between the engine and the transmission at the same time.

## CLUTCHES AND BANDS

Two multiple-disc clutches, one overrunning clutch, and three brake bands provide the friction elements required to obtain the desired function of the planetary gear set.

## OIL PUMP

This particular automatic transmission uses a conventional gear-type oil pump, which is mounted just behind the torque converter. The oil pump draws filtered oil from the fluid pan and sends it under pressure to the main pressure valve and the manual valve in the control valve body.

The hydraulic system is also composed of a secondary piston-type pump, which provides, along with the primary pump, the line pressure to operate the friction elements and the automatic controls of the automatic transmission. The secondary pump is located in the rear transmission extension housing.

## GOVERNOR ASSEMBLY

The governor is a conventional design in that it has weights and springs, and is mounted on the output shaft. In this way, the governor only turns when the vehicle is moving. It produces an oil pressure in relation to the road speed of the vehicle. This pressure is then directed into the valve body and used to control gearshift timing and operation. The main pressure coming from the oil pump acts against the centrifugal force until the proper governor pressure is set between the different valve surfaces. During moderate speeds, the increasing centrifugal force from the governor valve alone accounts for more increase in pressure. In this way, the governor can provide an exact amount of pressure at low road speeds, and prevent high pressure at high road speeds.

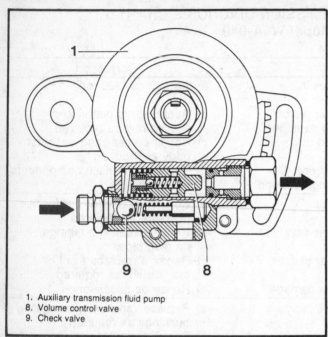

1. Auxiliary transmission fluid pump
8. Volume control valve
9. Check valve

**Cross section of auxiliary pump and check valves**
(© Mercedes-Benz of America)

## AUXILIARY OIL PUMP

An auxiliary oil pump is used to insure proper cooling and adequate lubrication of the internal components of the transmission. It is installed in the transmission fluid circuit between the transmission and the oil cooler which is located within the radiator. The auxiliary pump is driven by the air conditioning pulley and also serves as an idler pulley for the compressor.

Should the auxiliary pump fail, check valves are used to route the fluid through the normal cooling and lubrication circuits to prevent fluid and transmission overheating.

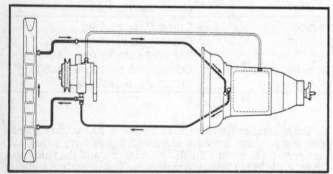

**Fluid route with auxiliary pump inoperative**
(© Mercedes-Benz of America)

## VALVE BODY

The main valve body is located in the lower part of the transmission. The valve body is a two piece design, using two separator plates as well as an oil distributing plate. The separator plates serve as a seal between the upper and lower valve bodies, as well as a connection for the different oil passages and openings. There are a number of different valves in the valve body, each with a specific function.

## Diagnosis Tests

To troubleshoot automatic transmissions, it is important that several basic points be understood to save the technician's time.

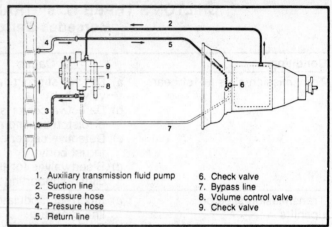

1. Auxiliary transmission fluid pump
2. Suction line
3. Pressure hose
4. Pressure hose
5. Return line
6. Check valve
7. Bypass line
8. Volume control valve
9. Check valve

**Fluid route with auxiliary pump operating**
(© Mercedes-Benz of America)

A road test should be performed if the vehicle's condition allows it. Use care so that more damage is not done on the road test than has already occurred. Inspect carefully for leaks and other signs of obvious damage. Make sure that all the cable and linkages are attached. Pull out the dipstick and check the color and smell of the fluid. Be sure that the engine is in at least a reasonable state of tune. When road testing, pick a route that will show all the transmission operations, and try the unit in each range, including kickdown and reverse. If the trouble cannot be pinpointed after using the Clutch and Band Application Chart in conjunction with the road test, then further testing will be required. This means that the shift points, stall speed and oil pressure will have to be checked.

## CONTROL LINE (WORKING) PRESSURE

**NOTE: Before making any hydraulic pressure tests, be sure that the transmission fluid level and fluid condition are up to specification. Also, make sure that manual and throttle linkages, EGR system, and neutral safety/back-up light switch are checked and adjusted as required.**

The working pressure of the automatic transmission is not adjustable. Line pressure is automatically established when the vacuum modulator is correctly adjusted. To check the line pressure, drive the vehicle in the indicated range and speed that is shown in the chart. Record the pressure readings on the gauge.

## GOVERNOR PRESSURE TEST

**NOTE: Before making and hydraulic pressure tests, be sure that the transmission fluid level and fluid condition are up to specification. Also, make sure that manual and throttle linkages, EGR system, and neutral safety/back-up light switch are checked and adjusted as required.**

The governor pressure is a partial pressure of the line pressure and is set to the required value by the centrifugal governor, which is attached to the output shaft of the transmission. The governor pressure can never exceed the line pressure and for this reason the upper pressure valves can be measured only while driving at full throttle. In measuring the governor pressure, an accurate oil pressure gauge is required.

## THROTTLE VALVE CONTROL PRESSURE TEST

**NOTE: Before making any hydraulic pressure tests, be sure that the transmission fluid level and fluid condition are up to specification. Also, make sure that manual and throttle linkages, EGR system, and neutral safety/back-up light switch are checked and adjusted as required.**

The throttle valve control pressure is a partial pressure of the modulating pressure. It is mechanically controlled by the position of the accelerator pedal. If the control pressure rod linkage is adjusted correctly the control pressure will be correct.

For correct control rod linkage adjustment follow the following procedure.

### Four Cylinder Models

1. Remove the vacuum control unit from the carburetor.
2. Disconnect the automatic choke connecting rod so the throttle valve rests against the idle stop.
3. Loosen the screw and turn the levers against each other so the control rod rests against the idle stop.
4. Tighten the screw and depress the accelerator to the kickdown position. The throttle valve must rest against the full throttle stop.
5. Install the vacuum control unit on the distributor and connect the automatic choke rod.

### Five Cylinder Models

1. Disconnect the control pressure rod.
2. Push the angle lever toward the front of the vehicle.
3. Push the control pressure rod rearward against the stop and adjust its length so there is no binding.
4. Tighten the counter nut after adjustment.

### Eight Cylinder Models

1. Remove the air filter and disconnect the control pressure linkage.
2. The throttle valve should rest against the idle speed stop.
3. Push the regulating lever and angle lever to the idle position.
4. Push the control pressure rod completely rearward against the stop and adjust the length of the rod so there is no tension.
5. When checking the rod for length, hold it to the left of the socket, not above to compensate for rotary motion of the linkage.

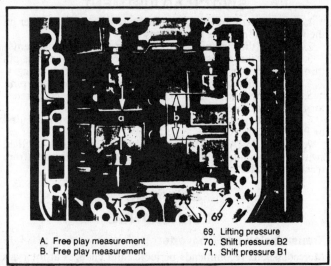

| | |
|---|---|
| A. Free play measurement | 69. Lifting pressure |
| B. Free play measurement | 70. Shift pressure B2 |
| | 71. Shift pressure B1 |

**Measurement of band free-play (© Mercedes-Benz of America)**

## AIR PRESSURE TEST

Air pressure is used to determine free play of the center and rear bands. To check the rear band free play, introduce air pressure into the rear band release pressure passage located inside the transmission case. Mark the position of the band end on the drum. Apply air pressure to the rear band apply pressure passage in the transmission case. Mark the position of the band end on the drum. Measure the distance between the two marks; measurement is the rear band free play. To find the center band free play, measure the position of the band end on the drum in its released position. Apply air pressure to the center servo apply passage in the transmission case. Mark the position of the band end on the drum. The distance between the two marks is the center band free play.

**NOTE: This free play should be 3 or 4mm. If not, install a pressure pin of the correct length to bring the free play within its required specification.**

## STALL SPEED TEST

**NOTE: Before making any hydraulic pressure tests, be sure that the transmission fluid level and fluid condition are up to specification. Also, make sure that manual and throttle linkages, EGR system, and neutral safety back-up light switch are checked and adjusted as required.**

A stall speed test is a quick test of the torque converter but since it is a demanding test on the transmission, it should only be done if the vehicle accelerates poorly or it fails to reach high speed. A tachometer will be required that is compatible with the ignition system that is used on the vehicle. Never perform this test any longer than the time it takes to look at the gauges and record the reading. When making the test, do not hold the throttle open longer than five seconds or severe transmission damage may result from the heat that is generated. If engine speed exceeds maximum limits, release the accelerator immediately as this is an indication of clutch or band slippage. With the engine at normal operating temperature, vacuum line disconnected, tachometer installed, and parking brake applied firmly, stall test the transmission by pushing the accelerator pedal to the floor and noting the engine speed on the tachometer. If the stall speed is higher than specified, general transmission problems are indicated and hydraulic pressure tests should be made to locate the faulty internal parts of the transmission. If the stall speed is lower than specified, the torque converter roller clutch is at fault.

**NOTE: Make sure that the engine performance is adequate before concluding that the torque converter is the problem. The torque converter is a sealed unit and cannot be taken apart for repair.**

## MODULATOR PRESSURE TEST

**NOTE: Before making any hydraulic pressure tests, be sure that the transmission fluid level and fluid condition are up to specification. Also make sure that manual and throttle linkages, EGR system, and neutral safety/back-up light switch are checked and adjusted as required.**

Modulator pressure must be measured and corrected before making line pressure and governor pressure tests. To check the modulator pressure, accelerate the vehicle on the road or on a dynamometer to 40 mph. Read the regulating pressure on the gauge, which is attached to the modulating pressure take-off point on the transmission. The pressure reading should be 40 psi in "D" for the W4A-040 transmission. As transmission oil temperature increases, a bimetallic spring attached to the modulating sleeve housing (on rear face of case, inside extension housing) applies pressure to the modulator valve stem. This will move it toward the full load position. This increases modulator pressure and stabilizes the line pressure at high fluid temperatures. To insure that the spring does not influence the modulator pressure, the test must be performed with the fluid temperature between 140°F and 195°F. Pressure may be adjusted by removing the vacuum line from the vacuum unit and turning the adjusting screw in or out using a 4mm Allen wrench. One complete turn of the adjusting screw changes the modulating pressure about 3 psi. It may be necessary to remove the vacuum modulator cover and the locking plate before performing the adjustment procedure.

 ON CAR SERVICES

# Adjustments

## KICKDOWN SWITCH ADJUSTMENT

The kickdown position of the solenoid valve is controlled by the accelerator pedal. Push the accelerator pedal against the kickdown limit stop. In this position the throttle lever should rest against the full load stop of the venturi control unit. Adjustments are made by loosening the clamping screw on the return lever which is on the accelerator pedal shaft and turning the shaft. Tighten the clamping screw again.

## VACUUM MODULATOR ADJUSTMENT

Original equipment modulators are not adjustable on this unit. Often, aftermarket replacements have a set screw in the vacuum pipe so that the shifting quality can be "fine-tuned." Modulator service is generally confined to replacement.

On transmission models having an adjustable modulator, remove the vacuum line from the modulator and insert a 4mm Allen wrench into the modulator nipple and engage the adjusting screw. One complete turn of the adjusting screw changes the modulating pressure approximately 3 psi.

Whenever the modulator is inspected, always check the rubber hose connector for cracks or other deterioration.

## PRESSURE CONTROL CABLE

The pressure control cable can be replaced without removing the valve body. It is secured to the transmission housing by a locking lever. To remove, push the locking lever toward the sleeve and turn counterclockwise. Pull out in an upward direction.

## CONTROL PRESSURE ROD ADJUSTMENT

### Four Cylinder Models

1. Remove the vacuum control unit from the carburetor.
2. Disconnect the automatic choke connecting rod so the throttle valve rests against the idle stop.
3. Loosen the screw and turn the levers against each other so the control rod rests against the idle stop.
4. Tighten the screw and depress the accelerator to the kickdown position. The throttle valve must rest against the full throttle stop.
5. Install the vacuum control unit on the distributor and connect the automatic choke rod.

### Five Cylinder Models

1. Disconnect the control pressure rod.
2. Push the angle lever toward the front of the vehicle.
3. Push the control pressure rod rearward against the stop and adjust its length so there is not binding.
4. Tighten the counter nut after adjustment.

### Eight Cylinder Models

1. Remove the air filter and disconnect the control pressure linkage.
2. The throttle valve should rest against the idle speed stop.
3. Push the regulating lever and angle lever to the idle position.
4. Push the control pressure rod completely rearward against the stop and adjust the length of the rod so there is no tension.
5. When checking the rod for length, hold it to the left of the socket, not above to compensate for rotary motion of the linkage.

## SELECTOR ROD LINKAGE ADJUSTMENT

NOTE: The vehicle must be standing with the weight normally distributed on all four wheels. No jacks may be used.

1. Disconnect the selector rod from the selector lever.
2. Set the selector lever in Neutral and make sure that there is approximately 1mm clearance between the selector lever and the N stop of the selector gate.
3. Adjust the length of the selector rod so that it can be attached free of tension.
4. Retighten the counternut.

## BAND ADJUSTMENT AND INTERVAL

The adjusting bolt for brake band B3 has been modified. The bolt head is "sheared off" after the brake band adjustment is made. Brake band B3 can only be adjusted when the transmission has been removed from the vehicle.

1. Remove the transmission.
2. Remove the valve body.
3. Remove solenoid from transmission if solenoid is installed in an inclined position.
4. Remove the previous version adjusting bolt and replace with the modified version.
5. Tighten the adjusting bolt to 3.6 ft. lbs.
6. Measure the brake band gap and record the measurement.
7. Back off the adjusting bolt by 1¾ turns and tighten the lock nut, making sure in doing so that the adjusting bolt is not turned.
8. Measure the gap again. It must be 0.118 in. (3mm) wider than the gap measured previously.
9. Twist off (shear off) the head of the adjusting bolt.
10. Install the solenoid and the valve body and install the transmission.

## STARTER LOCKOUT & BACK-UP LIGHT SWITCH ADJUSTMENT

1. Disconnect the selector rod and move the selector lever on the transmission to the Neutral position.
2. Tighten the clamping screw prior to making adjustments.
3. Loosen the adjusting screw and insert the locating pin through the driver into the locating hole in the shift housing.
4. Tighten the adjusting screw and remove the locating pin.
5. Move the selector lever to position N and connect the selector rod so that there is no tension.
6. Check to be sure that the engine cannot be started in Neutral or Park.
7. On the W4A-020, the starter lockout and back-up light switch can be adjusted from below. A gasket prevents water from reaching the electrical connections.

# Services

## FLUID CHANGE

### Transmission and Converter

Mercedes-Benz recommends periodic fluid changes at intervals of 27,000 miles. Type A, Dexron® or Dexron® II automatic transmission fluid meeting Mercedes-Benz quality standard must be used in the automatic transmission. Failure to use the proper grade and type fluid could cause serious internal automatic transmission damage.

For vehicles that are subjected to aggravated conditions (such as taxis, trailer pulling vehicles, or vehicles used on mountain roads) additional fluid change is necessary.

NOTE: The miles given for fluid change are average. Each vehicle operated under severe driving conditions should be treated individually.

When the automatic transmission has been removed for repairs, the unit should be drained completely. The converter, cooler and cooler lines should be flushed to remove any particles or dirt that might have entered the components as a result of transmission malfunction or failure.

## VACUUM DIAPHRAGM

### Removal

1. Raise the vehicle on a hoist and support it safely.
2. Disconnect the vacuum line from the vacuum modulator.

**NOTE: As the vacuum line is being disconnected from the modulator, the modulator unit must be held steady.**

3. Remove the vacuum modulator and thrust pin from the transmission case.

### Installation

1. Install the vacuum modulator unit in the transmission case.
2. Screw the vacuum line to the modulator, using care so as not to turn the modulator.
3. Lower the vehicle from the hoist. Road test the vehicle as required.

## OIL PAN DRAINING

### Removal

1. Raise the vehicle on a hoist and support it safely.
2. Drain the automatic transmission fluid by loosening the dipstick tube.
3. Remove the transmission fluid pan.
4. If you are going to replace the transmission fluid filter, remove the bolts that retain the fluid filter to the transmission and remove the fluid filter.

### Installation

1. Install the new transmission fluid filter in its place.
2. Clean the old gasket material from the transmission case and the transmission fluid pan.
3. Install the transmission fluid pan to the transmission case using a new pan gasket. Install the dipstick tube.
4. Lower the vehicle from the hoist. Fill the transmission with the proper grade transmission fluid.
5. Start the engine and check for leaks. Correct as required.

## SHIFT VALVE HOUSING

### Removal

1. Raise the vehicle on a hoist and support it safely. Drain the transmission fluid.
2. Remove the transmission fluid pan and the old pan gasket. Remove the fluid filter.
3. Move the selector lever to position "P". Remove the shift valve housing bolts. Remove the shift valve housing from the case.
4. Remove the plug pipes with the sealing bushings and pull the sealing bushings from the plug pipes.

### Installation

1. Install new sealing bushings on the plug pipes and insert them into the transmission case.
2. Insert a locating pin for the control pressure valve into the shift valve housing.
3. Carefully install the shift valve housing into the transmission.

**NOTE: Make sure that the range selector valve enters correctly into the detent plate.**

4. Install the shift valve housing bolts with the spring washers and torque the bolts to 9.4 foot pounds.

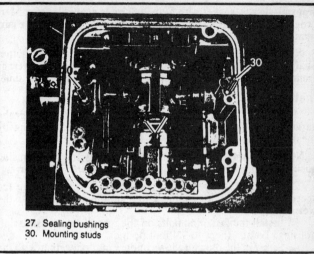

27. Sealing bushings
30. Mounting studs

**Location of sealing bushing** (© Mercedes-Benz of America)

5. Remove the locating pin.
6. Install a new fluid filter. Install the transmission fluid pan using a new pan gasket. Torque the pan bolts 5.1 foot pounds. Install the fluid filler pipe to the transmission pan.
7. Lower the vehicle from the hoist. Fill the transmission with the proper grade transmission fluid.
8. Start the engine and check for leaks. Road test the vehicle and check the shifting pattern. Correct as required.
9. Check the transmission fluid level at normal operating temperature. Correct as needed.

## EXTENSION HOUSING

### Removal

1. Raise the vehicle on a hoist and support it safely. Drain the transmission fluid.
2. Slightly raise the engine/transmission unit. Remove both the bolts for the rear engine mount. Remove the 12 tunnel closing plate bolts and remove the tunnel closing plate. On models with the W4A-040 automatic transmission, remove the rear engine mount along with the engine carrier and also remove the mounting bracket for the front exhaust pipe.
3. Loosen the speedometer shaft on the rear of the transmission case and pull it off.
4. Disconnect the selector rod on the range selector lever and move the range selector lever to position "P".
5. Loosen both fastening bolts of the universal shaft intermediate bearing, but do not screw them out. Loosen the universal shaft clamping nut. Unscrew the universal shaft on the transmission, but leave the universal plate on the universal shaft.
6. Slide the universal shaft to the rear, as far as the center bearing and the clamping piece permit.
7. Place a piece of wood under the front of the universal shaft in such a way that the shaft is completely pushed up.
8. Unlock and remove the slotted nut on the three-legged flange. Remove the three-legged flange.
9. Disconnect the vacuum line on the vacuum modulator. If equipped, remove the vacuum modulator mounting bracket. Remove the vacuum modulator.
10. Unscrew the plug for the secondary pump and remove the compression spring.
11. Lower the transmission enough to remove the bolts from the rear transmission housing.
12. Pull off the rear transmission housing using Mercedes-Benz tool No. 115-589-03-33-00, or equivalent.

**NOTE: On the W4A-020, the three legged flange is attached with a double hex nut instead of the slot nut used on the W4A-040**

transmission. A socket with ¾ inch drive is available from Mercedes-Benz as a special tool for this double hex. It carries the part number 126 589 02 09 00.

NOTE: The centrifugal governor should remain on the output shaft, that is, when pulling off the housing, also pull the governor from the guide of the rear transmission housing at the same time.

### Installation

1. Install a new rear transmission housing gasket. Center the gasket on the sealing surface of the transmission housing by means of two screws.

NOTE: In order to install the new transmission rear housing gasket, you must remove the modulating pressure valve housing.

2. Mount the rear transmission housing while moving the speedometer drive with a suitable tool until it is in mesh with the worm gear.

3. Install the fastening bolts on the rear of the transmission housing. Torque them to 9.4 foot pounds.

4. Screw in the plug for the secondary pump together with the compression spring.

5. Coat the vacuum modulator with sealing compound and screw it into the rear of the transmission housing. Connect the vacuum line to the modulator. Install the mounting bracket, if equipped.

6. Place the range selector lever in the "P" position.

7. Place the three-legged flange on the output shaft and torque the slotted nut to 86.2 foot pounds.

8. Attach the selector rod to the range selector lever. Connect the speedometer shaft to the transmission housing.

9. Lift the engine/transmission unit as required. Remove the wooden support from under the propeller shaft and install the propeller shaft to the transmission.

10. Check the rubber mount and screw to the transmission. Install the rear end of the tunnel closing plate. Install the fastening bolts for the rubber mount on the end plate.

11. Lower the vehicle and move it back and forth and tighten the propeller shaft clamping nut. Torque the fastening bolts on the propeller shaft intermediate bearing to 14.5 foot-pounds.

12. Fill the transmission with the proper grade and type automatic transmission fluid. Shift through all gears and correct the fluid level.

13. Check the modulating pressure and adjust, if necessary. Screw on the front end of the tunnel closing plate.

## Governor

### Removal

1. Raise the vehicle on a hoist and support it safely.
2. Remove the transmission extension housing.
3. Remove the plate spring, worm gear of the speedometer drive, eccentric ring for the secondary pump and the governor from the output shaft.

### Installation

1. Attach the governor, eccentric ring, worm gear of the speedometer drive and the plate spring to the output shaft.

NOTE: The flange of the worm gear should face the governor and the curvature of the plate spring should face the worm gear.

2. Reinstall the rear transmission housing.
3. Lower the vehicle from the hoist and fill with the proper grade transmission fluid.
4. Start the engine and check for any leaks. Correct as required.

NOTE: The drive gears on the W4A-020 transmission are made of plastic. A lock ring holds the drive gears in the axial direction. The drive gear of the output shaft is driven by two lugs.

## PARKING LOCK

### Removal

1. Raise the vehicle on a hoist and support it safely.
2. Remove the transmission extension housing along with the governor.
3. Unscrew the fastening bolt from the holder and remove the holder together with the leaf spring. Remove the resilient linkage.
4. Remove the parking pawl together with the clamping spring.
5. Pull the parking lock gear from the output shaft.

### Installation

1. Attach the parking lock gear to the output shaft and slide the parking lock with the clamping spring on the bearing pin.
2. Install the resilient linkage.
3. Install the leaf spring. Install the needle bearing supported roller and holder. Torque the bolts to 7.2 ft. lbs.
4. Place the range selector lever in the "P" position to check if the parking lock engages correctly.
5. Install the governor and the rear transmission housing.
6. Lower the vehicle from the hoist. Fill the transmission with the proper grade fluid.
7. Start the engine and check for leaks. Correct as required.

### STARTER LOCK AND BACK-UP LIGHT SWITCH

### Removal

1. Raise the vehicle on a hoist and support it safely.
2. Disconnect the selector rod at the range selector lever. Remove the range selector lever from the shaft by loosening the clamping screw.
3. Remove the screws from the starter locking switch. Remove the switch from the shaft.

### Installation

1. Install the starter locking switch to the transmission housing.

15. Worm gear of speedometer drive
16. Eccentric ring for the secondary pump
17. Governor assembly
85. Plate spring
19. Parking lock pawl
18. Parking lock gear
20. Modulator pressure housing

**Governor and attaching parts** (© Mercedes-Benz of America)

2. Place the range selector lever on the switch and tighten it with the clamping screw. Adjust the switch as indicated in the adjustment section of this chapter.

3. Attach the selector rod to the range selector lever and secure it.

4. Lower the vehicle from the hoist and road test as required.

# REMOVAL & INSTALLATION

## REMOVAL

1. Disconnect the negative battery cable. Raise the vehicle and support it safely.

2. Drain the automatic transmission fluid.

**NOTE: To do this, unscrew the fluid filler pipe on the sump of the transmission fluid pan. Also remove the fluid drain plug which is located on the torque converter.**

3. Remove the mounting bracket for the front exhaust pipes.

4. Remove the oil cooler pipes and cap them with plastic plugs to prevent leakage.

5. Loosen the fastening bolts on the propeller shaft intermediate bearing, but do not remove them.

6. Loosen the propeller shaft clamping nut. Unscrew the fastening bolts from the engine mounting and remove the engine carrier.

7. Unscrew the propeller shaft on the transmission. Leave the universal plate on the propeller shaft. Slide the propeller shaft toward the rear, as far as the center bearing and clamping piece will permit. Place a suitable piece of wood underneath the propeller shaft at the front of the tunnel, in such a way that the propeller shaft is completely pushed upwards.

8. Pull out the plug for the starter lock and the back-up light switch. Unscrew the clamping screw from the lever-for-control pressure and pull the lever from the shaft.

9. Remove the cable from the kickdown solenoid valve. Disconnect the shift rod on the range selector lever and set the range selector lever to the "P" position. Disconnect the speedometer shaft on the transmission.

**NOTE: During removal and installation of the W4A-020, when the vehicle is equipped with a diesel engine, the torque converter must be retained to the transmission. Insert the holding device into the cutout of the vent grille in the converter housing. Remove the holding device before starting the engine.**

10. Unscrew the vacuum line from the vacuum diaphragm, while holding a suitable tool on the vacuum diaphragm unit. Unscrew the fastening clips from the mounting bracket.

11. Pull the covering plug from the intermediate flange. Separate the hydraulic clutch from the driven plate by removing the plate bolts.

12. Slightly raise the engine-transmission unit. Remove all the bolts attaching the transmission to the intermediate flange. The two lateral bolts should be removed last.

13. Push the transmission with the torque converter in the direction of the rear axle until the bearing journal of the hydraulic clutch can no longer touch the intermediate flange.

14. Carefully lower the automatic transmission unit with the torque converter. Pull the unit out of the vehicle in the forward direction.

15. Place the transmission in a vertical position. Screw on the holding plate (Mercedes-Benz tool No. 116-589-02-62-00) on the torque converter and pull the torque converter out in an upward direction.

## INSTALLATION

1. Install the torque converter to the transmission using the holding tool (Mercedes-Benz tool No. 116-589-02-62-00). Grease the centering pin and the drive flange of the torque converter with molly lube or equivalent.

**NOTE: If the torque converter is properly installed, dimension "K" should be approximately 0.157 in. (4mm). Also make sure that when installing the torque converter, the sealing lip of the radial sealing ring in the primary pump housing is not damaged. Check dimension "K" again prior to flanging-on transmission.**

2. Place the automatic transmission on the transmission jack. Turn the torque converter in such a manner that the two fastening bores are at the bottom.

3. Rotate the engine until the two bores in the driven plate for fastening the engine to the torque converter are at the bottom.

4. Move the transmission until the bolts of the clutch housing are in alignment with the bores in the intermediate flange. Push the transmission forward until the clutch housing is well seated. Do not use force.

5. After installing the engine and the transmission to the round centering of the clutch bowl, force the torque converter, using a suitable tool, through the cooling slots on the clutch bowl in a forward direction so that distance "A" is eliminated. Install the six bolts into the torque converter.

6. Connect the vacuum modulator to the vacuum line. Connect the fastening clips to the mounting bracket. Connect the speedometer hook-up to the transmission.

7. Attach the selector rod to the range selector lever. Connect the cable to the kickdown solenoid valve. Slide the control pressure lever on the shaft and attach it with the clamping screw. Attach the plug for the starter lock and the back-up light switch.

8. Remove the wooden support from under the universal shaft and screw the universal shaft to the transmission.

9. Bolt the rear engine mount to the transmission. Install the rear engine mounting bolts. Install the rear engine carrier, then install the mounting bracket for the front exhaust pipes.

10. Tighten the universal shaft clamping nut. Tighten the fastening bolts of the universal shaft intermediate bearing.

11. Remove the plastic plugs from the oil cooler pipes and install them. Use the fastening clips to secure the pipes to their proper location.

12. Install the fluid filler pipe to the sump of the transmission. Install the fluid drain plug into the torque converter.

13. Lower the vehicle and connect the negative battery cable.

14. Fill the transmission with the proper type automatic transmission fluid.

15. Start the engine and check for leaks. Correct as required. Road test the vehicle.

# BENCH OVERHAUL

## Before Disassembly

1. Clean the exterior of the automatic transmission unit before any attempt is made to disassemble it. This procedure is done to prevent dirt and other foreign material from entering the automatic transmission and damaging any internal parts.

2. Handle all automatic transmission parts carefully to avoid nicking or burring the bearing or mating surfaces.

3. Lubricate all internal parts of the automatic transmission with fresh automatic transmission fluid before assembling the automatic transmission unit.

4. Use new gaskets and seals when assembling the automatic transmission.

5. Tighten all bolts and screws to their recommended torque specification.

**NOTE: If steam cleaning is done to the exterior of the automatic transmission unit, immediate disassembly should be done to avoid rusting from condensation which has formed on the internal parts of the unit.**

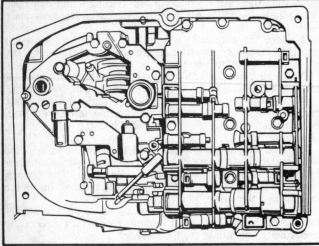

Valve body assembly (© Mercedes-Benz of America)

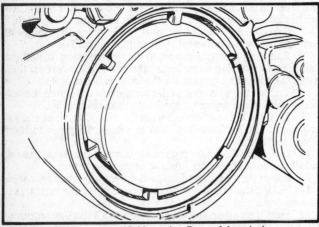

Brake band piston cover (© Mercedes-Benz of America)

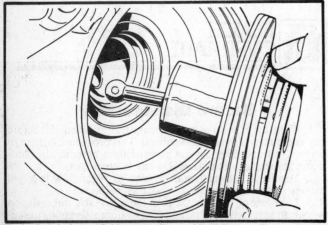

Brake band piston (© Mercedes-Benz of America)

## Converter Inspection

1. If the fluid in the torque converter is discolored but does not contain metal bits or particles, the torque converter is not damaged and need not be replaced, as long as trouble-shooting does not point to an internal failure.

2. Color is no longer a good indicator of the transmission fluid condition. In the past, dark color was associated with overheated transmission fluid. It is not considered a positive sign of transmission failure today because of the newer fluids that are available in today's market.

3. If fluid from the torque converter contains metal particles, the torque converter is damaged internally and must be replaced.

4. If the cause of fluid contamination was burned clutch plates or overheated fluid, the torque converter is contaminated and should, in most cases, be replaced.

## Transmission Disassembly

1. Mount the automatic transmission unit in a suitable automatic transmission holding fixture.

2. Remove the transmission fluid pan and gasket. Remove the fluid filter.

3. Unscrew the valve body bolts and remove the valve body. Unbolt, the shift lever mechanism and remove with the retaining spring.

4. Remove the lower cover with the intermediate plate and oil pipe. Remove the one-way valve with the brake band guide (B2).

5. Push in the brake band piston cover (B2) and remove the locking ring. Pull out the brake band piston (B2).

6. Using a suitable tool unclamp the B1 brake band locking ring, and remove the B1 brake piston with the cover and the back pressure springs.

7. Pull out the B1 brake band guide.

8. Unscrew the thrust bolt closing plug and remove the range selector lever. Remove the starter lockout switch.

9. Remove the vacuum control unit and the modulating pressure control valve. Detach the kickdown solenoid valve.

10. Unscrew the slotted nut and pull off the three legged flange from the output shaft. Remove the rear transmission extension housing.

11. Remove the plate spring with the worm gear of the speedometer drive. Remove the eccentric ring for the secondary pump and the governor assembly from the output shaft. Remove the secondary pump.

12. Remove the parking lock gear with the parking lock pawl and the expanding spring.

13. Remove the resilient linkage lock ring and remove the resilient linkage.

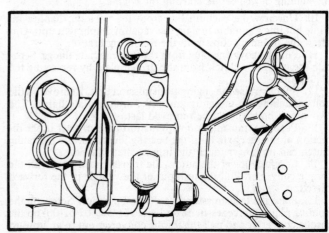

Range selector lever (© Mercedes-Benz of America)

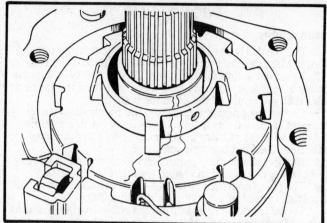

Parking lock pawl with parking lock gear
(© Mercedes-Benz of America)

Secondary pump intermediate plate (© Mercedes-Benz of America)

14. Remove the needle bearing. Remove the starter lock and back-up light assembly.

15. Unlock brake band piston cover B3. Remove the locking ring and pull off the cover. Remove brake band piston B3 and the truncated or blunt cone spring.

16. Pull out the clip for the bearing pin from brake band lever B3 and knock the bearing pin out in the forward direction. Remove brake band lever B3 from the transmission housing.

17. Remove the locking clip for thrust body B1 and B2. Remove both of these thrust bodies.

Resilient linkage (© Mercedes-Benz of America)

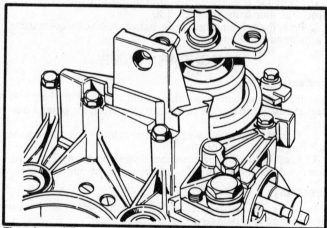

Three legged flange (© Mercedes-Benz of America)

## Unit Disassembly

NOTE: After disassembly of each unit, wash all parts in cleaning solvent. Blow dry with compressed air. Inspect all parts for excessive wear or damage and replace parts as needed.

### SHIFT VALVE HOUSING

#### Disassembly

NOTE: The shift valve housing has 18 valve balls. During disassembly make sure that the balls do not roll around. Wash all parts in unused cleaning solvent. Blow dry with compressed air.

1. Remove the bolts from the bottom of the shift valve housing assembly, except for two bolts opposite each other. Position the shift valve housing on an assembly fixture or another suitable disassembly device.

2. Remove the two remaining bolts from the bottom of the shift valve housing and lift off the top together with the intermediate plate.

3. Remove the intermediate plate from the top of the unit. Remove the filter along with its spring from inside the top of the shift valve housing.

4. Lift the bottom of the shift valve housing from the assembly fixture and remove the filter modulating pressure screen. Remove all the valve balls.

#### Assembly

1. Insert the valve balls into their proper location. Install the filter modulating pressure screen and shift pin.

2. Install the filter with its spring in the top of the shift valve housing. Install the intermediate plate on the shift valve housing.

3. Place the top of the shift valve housing on the intermediate plate and insert two opposite bolts and tighten slightly.

4. Insert the remaining bolts. Torque the bolts to 5.8 ft. lbs. (8 N•m).

### REAR TRANSMISSION HOUSING

#### Disassembly

1. Remove the bolt from the cover plate of the locking piston and remove the locking piston together with the spring. Remove the spring plate along with its two springs. Remove the pressure receiving piston from the rear of the transmission case cover.

2. Remove the bolt for the speedometer drive. Pull the speed-

ometer drive out of the rear transmission case. Remove the speedometer pinion from the bearing body.

3. Remove the bolt for the secondary pump. This bolt is located inside the rear transmission housing. Remove the secondary pump from the transmission case.

**NOTE: If the thrust pin (plastic pin) binds or drops out, be sure to replace it. New transmission covers are already provided with the thrust pin (plastic pin), compression spring, ball, and the closing plug.**

4. Remove the rear transmission housing seal with a suitable seal removal tool. Remove the locking ring and press out the ball bearing.

5. Unscrew all measuring screw connections and closing plugs with their ball valves.

6. Unscrew the closing plug and remove the steel ball. Check the thrust pin (plastic pin) for smooth operation.

## Assembly

1. Press a new ball bearing into the rear transmission case housing, using Mercedes-Benz tool No. 108-589-02-43-00 or equivalent. Install the locking ring. Install a new sealing ring.

2. Insert the locking piston with the spring and screw down the holding plate.

3. Install the secondary pump into the rear transmission case until the fastening bore is in alignment with the bore in the transmission case. Torque the fastening bolt to 5.8 ft. lbs.

4. Insert the speedometer pinion into the bearing body. Install the speedometer drive into the rear transmission case until the fastening bore is in alignment with the bore in the transmission case. Torque the fastening bolt to 5.8 ft. lbs.

5. Install all measuring screw connections and closing plugs with their ball valves.

6. Insert the pressure receiving piston by first inserting the compression spring into the piston and then installing both components into the transmission case.

## GOVERNOR

### Disassembly

1. Replace the sealing rings as required by disconnecting them and removing them from the governor body.

2. Remove the bolts that hold the unit together. Remove the shift valve housing and the governor housing from the flange.

3. Remove the lock washer, compression spring and the shift valve from the shift valve housing.

4. Remove the spring plate, centrifugal weight and the compression spring in the upward direction from the governor housing.

5. Remove the compression spring with the compensating washers and the control valve in the downward direction from the governor housing.

### Assembly

1. Insert the control valve into the governor housing. Install the centrifugal weight with the compression spring in the control valve. Insert the compression washers with compression spring into the control valve.

**NOTE: Do not change the number of compensating washers.**

2. Attach the spring plate making sure it seats properly. Insert the shift valve with the compression spring and push on the lock washer.

3. Position the shift housing on the flange making sure that the outer oil slots are facing the oil seal rings and the oil ducts are in alignment.

4. Insert the strainer into the seat provided in the oil duct and mount the governor housing. Replace the oil sealing rings if they were dislodged during removal. Torque the bolts to 5.8 ft. lbs. (7.5 N•m).

## FRONT PUMP

### Disassembly

1. Pull the ball bearing from the front of the transmission cover using Mercedes-Benz tool No. 116-589-07-33-00 or equivalent.

2. Remove the four fastening bolts. Install two bolts approximately 50mm long, opposite each other, in two of the four bolt holes that you removed the fastening bolts from.

3. Loosen the primary pump from the transmission cover by means of tapping the two 50mm bolts lightly with a hammer.

4. Remove the primary pump housing with the intermediate plate from the front transmission cover.

5. Remove the primary pump gears from the pump housing. Remove the O-ring and the radial sealing ring if necessary.

6. The pump housing on the W4A-020 transmission has a roller bearing instead of a bushing for the drive flange.

7. To reduce possible leaks from the roller bearing, a sealing plate is to be installed behind the bearing and is held in place with a steel disc.

### Assembly

1. Install a new O-ring and radial sealing ring into the primary pump housing. Lubricate the primary pump gears and insert them into the pump housing.

**NOTE: The bevelled outer edge of the pump gear should face the bronze bushing.**

2. Insert the intermediate plate in such a manner that the fastening bores for the primary pump are in alignment.

3. Place the installation sleeve, Mercedes-Benz tool No. 116-589-19-61-00 or equivalent, onto the stator shaft and screw in the two studs for guiding the primary pump into place.

4. Insert the primary pump into the transmission cover and torque the four bolts to 14.5 ft. lbs.

5. Press the ball bearing into the transmission case cover using a suitable installation tool.

## SECONDARY PUMP

### Disassembly

1. Place the secondary pump on a flat surface with the pump gears exposed. Lift out the two pump gears from the pump housing.

2. Turn the pump housing over and remove the cover plate lock ring and the cover plate.

3. Remove the shut-off piston, compression spring, spring retainer and the check ball from the inside of the pump housing.

### Assembly

1. Check the O-rings in the shut-off piston and the pump housing and replace if damaged.

2. Insert the shut-off piston into the pump housing.

3. Install the compression spring with the spring retainer and the check ball into the shut-off piston.

4. Install the cover plate and insert the lock ring.

5. Turn the pump unit over and insert the pump gears making sure of gear engagement.

## GEAR ASSEMBLY

### Disassembly

1. Remove the output shaft together with the rear planetary gear carrier. Place the gear assembly with the input shaft in an upward direction on the assembly stand.

2. Remove the circlip and lift off the planetary gear set. Remove the axial bearing and input shaft.

3. Remove the output shaft radial bearing and the axial bearing and lift out the output shaft.

4. Remove the sun gear bearing and the sun gear. Remove the

plate carrier snap ring and lift the plate carrier and one-way clutch out of the connecting carrier.

5. Detach the supporting disc and remove the compensating ring and O-ring.

6. Turn the one-way clutch in an anticlockwise direction and pull out. Remove the cylindrical rollers.

## Assembly

1. Insert the cylindrical rollers into the compensating ring and install the locking plates.

2. Install the inner race of the one-way clutch while rotating in anticlockwise direction. Pull out the locking plates and insert the compensating ring and O-ring.

3. Mount the supporting plate making sure that the pin on the back side of the plate enters into bore of the one-way clutch outer race.

4. Insert the compensating washer into the connecting carrier and place the one-way clutch into connecting carrier.

5. Install the circlip into the outside groove and check for end play of the one-way clutch.

6. Install the sun gear in the roller clutch and insert the axial bearing on the sun gear. Install the output shaft into the roller clutch.

7. Install the axial bearing and the radial bearing on the output shaft. Mount the input shaft and the input shaft axial bearing.

8. Install the front gear set and lock with a circlip. Install the axial bearing on the input shaft.

## CLUTCH K1

### Disassembly

1. Push the circlip out of the groove with a suitable tool and remove it from the assembly. Remove the plate assembly by tilting the supporting flange.

2. Place a press on the spring retainer in such a manner that the pressure ring is uniformly seated. Push the spring retainer down with the press until the circlip is exposed and can be removed. Carefully release the press and remove the spring retainer and its springs.

3. Hold the piston with a pair of pliers and pull it out of the supporting flange, until it can be held manually.

4. Lift the piston with the lip sealing ring out of the supporting flange. Check the condition of the seal.

### Assembly

1. Install a new lip sealing ring, if necessary. Do not use a sharp edged tool when installing, as damage could result.

**NOTE: The lip sealing ring should be correctly resting in the groove with the lip pointing in the downward direction.**

2. Insert the introducing ring into the supporting flange. Install a new lip sealing ring, if necessary. The lip sealing ring should point in the downward direction. Lubricate the piston and the lip sealing rings. Install and push on the housing bottom without canting.

**NOTE: Do not use force since this might damage the lip sealing ring.**

3. Insert the piston return spring into the piston. Position the spring retainer in such a manner that each spring is centered in one prominence of the spring retainer.

**NOTE: Do not confuse the springs with those of clutch K2.**

4. Push the spring retainer carefully without canting, down under the press until the circlip can be installed. Carefully release the press and check for the correct seating of the circlip.

5. Assemble the plate assembly for clutch K1. Soak the new lining plates in clean automatic transmission fluid for a short time before installing them.

6. Insert the plate assembly into the outer plate carrier. Insert

the undulated circlip into the groove and push down into the groove with a suitable tool to secure the clip.

**NOTE: The resilient circlips of clutches K1 and K2 are different in spring force and should not be interchanged. The circlip of K1 has six undulations (waves).**

## CLUTCH K2

### Disassembly

1. Push down on the supporting flange, until the circlip can be removed.

2. Remove the plate package by tilting the outside plate carrier.

3. Remove the spring retainer circlip using a suitable tool. Remove the spring retainer along with the compression springs.

4. Remove the piston from the outside of the plate carrier.

### Assembly

1. Insert the sealing ring into the piston making sure it is not twisted. Install the lip sealing ring to the inside of the piston.

2. Insert the installation sleeve on the outside of the plate carrier and lubricate the sleeve and the sealing rings with automatic transmission fluid.

3. Place the piston into the outside of the plate carrier. Remove the installation sleeve.

4. Install the compression springs and compress them using a suitable tool until the spring retainer can be inserted. Secure with a circlip and remove the compression tool.

5. Insert the plate package into the outside of the plate carrier. Install the circlip and push into the circlip groove.

## Transmission Assembly

1. Mount the transmission unit in a suitable automatic transmission holding fixture.

2. Screw in the closing plug with a new aluminum sealing ring and torque to 2-3 ft. lbs. (10 N•m).

3. Place the O-ring and the sealing ring into the transmission casing.

**NOTE: Lubricate all rings and clutch discs with automatic transmission fluid prior to assembling.**

4. Install the Teflon rings in the rear clutch supporting flange. Install the supporting flange in accordance with the hole pattern of the fastening bore.

5. Insert the thrust body with the thrust body plate in an upward direction. Insert and tighten the end casing bolts to 8 ft. lbs. (11 N•m).

Placement of sealing rings and O-rings
(© Mercedes-Benz of America)

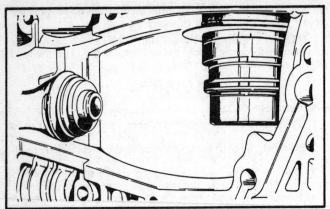

Supporting flange location (© Mercedes-Benz of America)

6. Install the thrust washer into the casing and position it so that the plate for the torsion lock is secured within the transmission casing.

7. Compress the rear brake assembly and install in the transmission casing.

8. Place the rear brake assembly and install in the transmission casing.

**NOTE: Check the installation of the gear set by making sure the upper edge of the connecting carrier is lower than the supportive surface of the outside plate.**

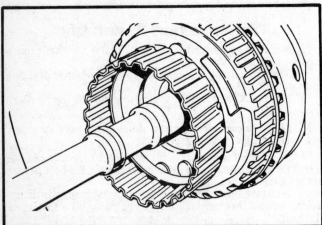

Gearset with input shaft (© Mercedes-Benz of America)

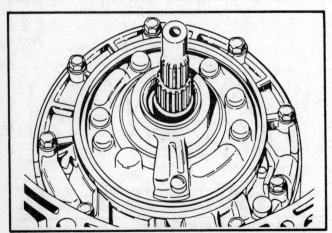

Location of front cover on input shaft (© Mercedes-Benz of America)

9. Place the axial bearing into the planetary gear carrier and insert the pressure ring in the groove located on the input shaft.

10. Install the front brake (B1) band in a manner that the assembly lock pin is facing the thrust body.

11. Install the Teflon rings on the front cover and install the front cover with gasket. Tighten to 10 ft. lbs. (13 N•m).

12. Turn the transmission in its holder so that the output shaft is facing up and slip the circlip up to the output shaft groove.

**NOTE: To reduce noise on the W4A-020 automatic transmission, the output shaft has an additional bearing. It is a one piece needle bearing with a plastic cage. It is open which will help ease installation.**

13. Install the helical gear on the output shaft. Install the axial holder on the shaft directly next to the output shaft.

14. Install a new O-ring in the governor housing and insert the governor. Insert the axial holder in the governor shaft groove.

15. Install the governor cover and secure with the locking ring.

16. Install the secondary pump and torque to 5.9 ft. lbs. (8 N•m). Check the axial holder for proper position.

17. Install the oil pipe and the detent plate with the shaft and torque to 6 ft. lbs. (8.5 N•m).

18. Mount the resilient linkage roller on the resilient linkage and install the linkage on the detent plate. Install lock ring.

19. Install the compensating washers on the helical gear and mount the parking lock pawl with the expanding spring.

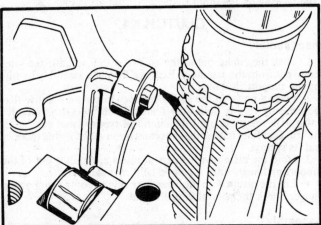

Resilient linkage roller (© Mercedes-Benz of America)

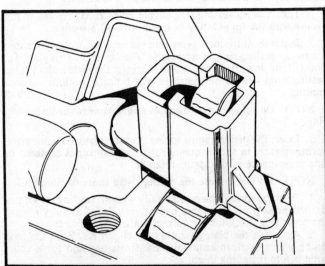

Resilient linkage guide (© Mercedes-Benz of America)

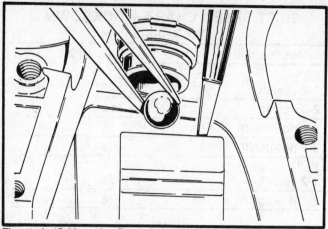

**Thrust pin** (© Mercedes-Benz of America)

20. Install the parking lock wheel on the output shaft and slip on the shaft sleeve. Torque the slotted nut to 73.8 ft. lbs. (100 N•m).

21. Install rear cover with the washer and torque to 14.8 ft. lbs. (20 N•m).

22. Insert the O-ring into the three legged flange and mount the three legged flange to the output shaft. Torque the slot nut to 88.5 ft. lbs. (120 N•m).

23. Screw in the kick down solenoid and torque to 14.8 ft. lbs. (20 N•m).

24. Insert the thrust pin into the thrust body and install a new O-ring. Install the thrust body assembly along with the modulating pressure control valve in the transmission casing.

25. Mount the vacuum control unit with the holding plate and torque to 5.9 ft. lbs. (8 N•m). Install the starter lockout switch.

26. Mount the range selector lever and place in position "N". Tighten to 5.9 ft. lbs. (8 N•m).

27. Install the front brake band guide and install the front brake (B1). A compression tool to compress the springs can be used.

**NOTE: During assembling make sure that the thrust pin of the brake band piston (B1) enters the brake band and that the sealing ring is not damaged.**

28. Using the compression tool, squeeze the piston in and insert the locking ring. Insert the thrust pin with the larger diameter towards the brake band B2.

29. Install the brake band B2 making sure that the thrust pin is engaged with the thrust pin.

30. Install the brake band piston cover and secure with a locking ring.

31. Install the one-way valve and the brake band guide B2.

32. Install a new O-ring on the control pressure cable and attach to the connecting rod. Push the plastic sleeve of the control cable into the transmission casing until it engages.

33. Assemble the lower cover, making sure it engages. Center the valve body and torque to 6 ft. lbs. (8 N•m).

34. Install the oil filter and torque to 3 ft. lbs. (4 N•m).

35. Install the oil pan and torque to 5.9 ft. lbs. (8 N•m).

# S SPECIFICATIONS

## TORQUE SPECIFICATIONS
### W4A-040

| Item | | Foot Pounds | N•m |
|---|---|---|---|
| Valve body to case | | 5.9 | 8 |
| Oil pan to case | | 5.9 | 8 |
| Oil pan drain plug | | 10.5 | 14 |
| Lower cover bolts | | 5.9 | 8 |
| Oil filter | | 3.0 | 4 |
| Universal shaft clamping nut | | 22.1 | 30 |
| Three legged flange nut | | 88.5 | 120 |
| Rear cover bolts | | 14.8 | 20 |
| Governor bolts | | 5.9 | 8 |
| Secondary pump bolts | | 5.9 | 8 |
| Axial holder nut | | 5.9 | 8 |
| Converter housing to case | | 30.5 | 42 |
| Torque converter drain plug | | 12.0 | 14 |
| Transmission to engine fastening bolts | M10 | 33.0 | 55 |
| | M12 | 48.0 | 65 |
| Primary pump, front cover bolts | | 15.0 | 21 |
| Detent plate | | 5.9 | 8 |
| Kickdown solenoid | | 14.8 | 20 |

## SHIFT SPEED CHART—MINIMUM THROTTLE W4A-040

| Selector Position | Approx. MPH |
|---|---|
| In "D" | |
| 2-3 upshift | 14 |
| 3-4 upshift | 20 |
| 3-2 downshift | 10 |
| 4-3 downshift | 14 |
| In "S" | |
| 1-2 upshift | 8 |
| 2-3 upshift | 14 |
| 2-1 downshift | — |
| 3-2 downshift | 10 |
| In "L" | |
| 1-2 upshift | 28 |
| 2-1 downshift | 8 |

## SHIFT SPEED CHART—FULL THROTTLE W4A-040

| Selector Position | Approx. MPH |
|---|---|
| In "D" | |
| 2-3 upshift | 40 |
| 3-4 upshift | 80 |
| 3-2 downshift | 14 |
| 4-3 downshift | 45 |
| In "S" | |
| 1-2 upshift | 26 |
| 2-3 upshift | 50 |
| 2-1 downshift | 7 |
| 3-2 downshift | 14 |
| In "L" | |
| 1-2 upshift | 28 |
| 2-1 downshift | 12 |

## SHIFT SPEED CHART—KICKDOWN W4A-040

| Selector Position | Approx. MPH |
|---|---|
| In "D" | |
| 1-2 upshift | 28 |
| 2-3 upshift | 50 |
| 3-4 upshift | 80 |
| 2-1 downshift | 12 |
| 3-2 downshift | 38 |
| 4-3 downshift | 75 |

## SHIFT SPEED CHART—KICKDOWN W4A-040

| Selector Position | Approx. MPH |
|---|---|
| In "S" | |
| 1-2 upshift | 28 |
| 2-3 upshift | 50 |
| 2-1 downshift | 12 |
| 3-2 downshift | 38 |
| In "L" | |
| 1-2 upshift | 28 |
| 2-1 downshift | 18 |

## SPECIAL TOOLS

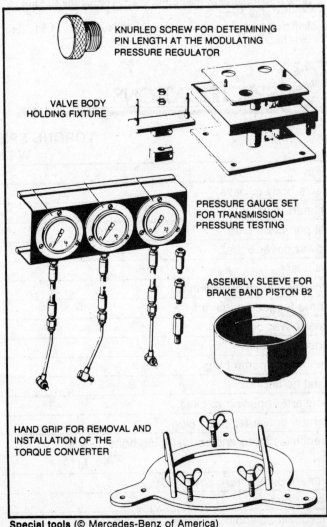

KNURLED SCREW FOR DETERMINING PIN LENGTH AT THE MODULATING PRESSURE REGULATOR

VALVE BODY HOLDING FIXTURE

PRESSURE GAUGE SET FOR TRANSMISSION PRESSURE TESTING

ASSEMBLY SLEEVE FOR BRAKE BAND PISTON B2

HAND GRIP FOR REMOVAL AND INSTALLATION OF THE TORQUE CONVERTER

**Special tools** (© Mercedes-Benz of America)

1. Input shaft
2. Front gear set
3. Circlip
4. Axial bearing
5. Radial bearing
6. Axial bearing
7. Connecting carrier
8. Output shaft
9. Axial bearing
10. Sun gear rear gear set
11. Supporting plate
12. O-ring

13. One-way clutch inner race
15. Compression springs
16. Cylindrical rollers
17. Compensating ring
19. Inside plate carrier K2 with one-way clutch outer race
21. Circlip
22. Compensating washer
23. Axial bearing
95. Lubricating pressure ring

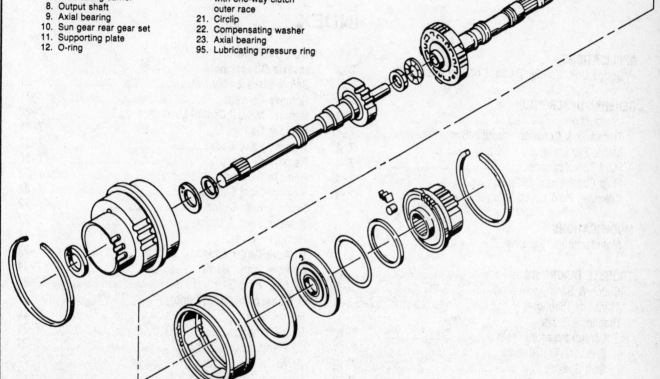

**Gear assembly—exploded view** (© Mercedes-Benz of America)

# INDEX

# MITSUBISHI KM-171 • 172 Automatic Transaxle

## APPLICATIONS

### APPLICATION CHART

| Year/Model | Engine Size | Transaxle Model |
|---|---|---|
| 1982-83 Dodge Colt | 1.4 Litre | KM-171 |
| 1983-84 Mitsubishi Cordia (L) | 1.8 Litre | KM-171 |
| 1983-84 Mitsubishi Cordia (LS) | 1.8 Litre | KM-171 |
| 1983-84 Mitsubishi Tredia | 1.8 Litre | KM-171 |
| 1983-84 Dodge Colt Vista | 1.4 Litre | KM-172 |

## GENERAL DESCRIPTION

The KM-171, 172 is also referred to as the KM-170-1 and the KM-170-2 transaxles. The KM-171, 172 models use an electronically controlled torque converter coupled to a fully automatic 3 speed transmission, including transfer gearing and differential into a compact front wheel transaxle unit.

There are four centers of rotation in the KM-171, 172:
1. Main center line plus valve body
2. Idler gear center line
3. Transfer shaft center line
4. Differential center line

The center distances between these main rotating parts are held precisely to maintain a low noise level through smooth accurate mesh of connecting the center lines.

The transaxle consists of two multiple disc clutches, an overrunning clutch, a hydraulic accumulator, multiple disc brakes, band brake, and planetary gearset. The unit provides three forward ratios and one reverse ratio. The reverse sun gear of the planetary gearsets is connected to the front clutch by a kickdown drum which is splined to the sun gear and to the front clutch retainer. The forward sun gear is connected to the rear clutch by the clutch hub which is splined to the sun gear. The planetary gearset carries a parking sprag on the outside surface of the annulus (ring) gear.

The hydraulic system consists of an oil pump and a valve body which contains all of the valves except the governor valve assembly.

Venting of the transmission sump is done through a vent hole located in the top of the oil pump.

Output torque from the main center line is delivered through helical gears to the transfer shaft. This transfer shaft carries the governor.

An integral helical gear on the transfer shaft drives the differential drive gear; these gears are factors of the final drive ratio. The gear ratio's for the KM-171-172 transaxle are the same except for the final drive gear ratio.

| Lever Position | KM-171 Gear Ratio | KM-172 Gear Ratio |
|---|---|---|
| 1st | 2.846 | 2.846 |
| 2nd | 1.581 | 1.581 |
| 3rd | 1.000 | 1.000 |
| Reverse | 2.176 | 2.176 |
| Final drive gear | 2.800 | 3.187 |

**NOTE:** On the 1982 Colt 1st and 2nd gear ratio's on the KM-170-2 have been changed. 1st speed is 2.551 and 2nd speed is 1.488.

The torque converter, transmission area, and differential are housed in an aluminum die-cast housing and transmission case.

**NOTE:** The transmission oil sump is common with the differential sump.

The torque converter is attached to the crankshaft through a flexible driving plate. The assembly is of metric design and special tools will be required to service and overhaul the unit. The converter cooling is through an oil to coolant cooler located in the radiator lower tank. The torque converter is a sealed unit and can not be disassembled by the average repair shop.

## Transmission and Converter Identification

### TRANSMISSION

The transmission can be identified by the 12th digit in the vehicle identification number located on the left top side of the instrument panel and visible through the windshield. The transaxle model can be found on the vehicle information plate riveted onto the headlight support panel. The plate shows model code, engine model, transaxle model, and body color code. The KM-171, 172 3 speed automatic transmission 12th digit code is as follows:

1. 49 states—code 7
2. California—code 8
3. Canada—code 9

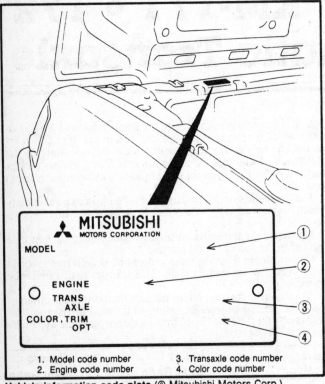

1. Model code number
2. Engine code number
3. Transaxle code number
4. Color code number

Vehicle information code plate (© Mitsubishi Motors Corp.)

### CONVERTER

The torque converter is the integeral damper clutch type.

## Transmission Fasteners

Metric bolt sizes and thread pitches are used for all fasteners on the KM-171, 172 transmissions. The metric fasteners dimensions are very close to the dimensions of the familiar inch system fasteners, and for this reason, replacement fasteners must have the same measurement and strength as those removed.

Do not attempt to interchange metric fasteners for inch system fasteners. Care should be taken to reuse the fasteners in the same locations as removed, whenever possible. Mismatched or incorrect fasteners can result in damage to the transmission unit through malfunctions, breakage or possible personal injury.

## Fluid Specifications

Use only automatic transmission fluids of the type marked

Dexron® or Dexron® II or their equivalent. Chrysler corporation does not recommend the use of any additives other than the use of a dye to aid in the determination of fluid leaks.

## Capacity
### CAPACITIES CHART

| Transaxle | U.S. (qts) | Imp. (qts) | Liter |
|---|---|---|---|
| Automatic | 5.8 | 6.1 | 5.1 |
| Differential | 1.0 | 1.2 | 1.1 |

## Checking Fluid Levels

### 1980-84

Place the selector in "PARK" and allow engine to idle. Run the engine at idle speed (minimum operating time of six minutes) to bring the vehicle to normal operating temperature. Then place the vehicle on a level surface with the parking brakes applied. Move selector sequentially to every position to fill the torque converter and hydraulic circuit with fluid, then place lever in "N" Neutral position. This operation is necessary to be sure that the fluid level check is accurate.

Remove the dipstick, wipe it clean and reinsert it into the dipstick hole. Then pull the dipstick out and check to see if the level is on the "HOT" range on the dipstick.

**NOTE: Make sure the fluid is at normal operating temperature 50-80°C (120-180°F). If the fluid is low, add ATF until level reaches "HOT" range.**

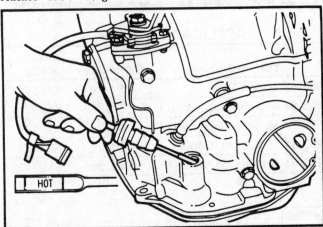

Checking the fluid level (© Chrysler Corp.)

Low fluid level can cause a variety of conditions because it allows pump to take in air along with fluid. Air trapped in hydraulic circuit forms bubbles which make fluid spongy. Therefore, pressures will be erratic. Improper filling can also raise fluid level too high. When transaxle has too much fluid, gears churn up foam and cause same conditions which occur with low fluid level, resulting in accelerated deterioration of ATF. In either case, air bubbles can cause overheating, fluid oxidation, and varnishing, which can interfere with normal valve, clutch, and servo operation. Foaming can also result in fluid escaping from transaxle vent where it may be mistaken for a leak.

Along with fluid level, it is important to check the condition of the fluid. When fluid smells burned, and is contaminated with metal bushing or friction material particles, a complete transaxle overhaul is needed. Be sure to examine fluid on dipstick closely. If there is any doubt about its condition, drain out sample for double check. After fluid has been checked, seat dipstick fully to seal out water and dirt.

# MODIFICATIONS

The 1982 Colt with the KM-170-1 automatic transaxle has been revised into the KM-170-2 transaxle. The main changes are in the 1st and 2nd gear ratios.

| Reduction ratio | KM-170-2 | KM-170-1 |
|---|---|---|
| 1st speed | 2.551 | 2.846 |
| 2nd speed | 1.488 | 1.581 |

# TROUBLE DIAGNOSIS

### CLUTCH AND BAND APPLICATION CHART
### KM-171 and 172 Transaxle

| Lever Position | Front Clutch | Rear Clutch | One-Way Clutch | Kickdown Band | Low-Reverse Band |
|---|---|---|---|---|---|
| P—Parking | — | — | — | — | — |
| R—Reverse | Applied | — | — | — | Applied |
| N—Neutral | — | — | — | — | — |
| **D—Drive** | | | | | |
| First | — | Applied | Holding | — | — |
| Second | — | Applied | — | Applied | — |
| Third (Direct) | Applied | Applied | — | — | — |
| **2—Second** | | | | | |
| First | — | Applied | Holding | — | — |
| Second | — | Applied | — | Applied | — |
| L—Lockup (First) | — | Applied | — | — | Applied |

### CHILTON'S THREE "C's" TRANSMISSION DIAGNOSIS CHART
### KM-171 and 172 Transaxle

| Condition | Cause | Correction |
|---|---|---|
| No starter action in Park or Neutral | a) Faulty or maladjusted safety switch<br>b) Manual linkage out of adjustment | a) Adjust or replace safety switch<br>b) Adjust manual linkage |
| Abnormal shock in selection of Drive, Second, Low or Reverse | a) Engine idle speed too high<br>b) Throttle control cable out of adjustment<br>c) Line pressure too high | a) Adjust engine idle speed to specification<br>b) Adjust throttle control cable<br>c) Adjust regulator valve and/or repair or replace line pressure relief valve |
| Noise originating within transaxle case | a) Worn or broken gears or other rotating parts | a) Replace parts as needed |
| Clutch slips in Drive (high stall rpm) | a) Throttle control cable out of adjustment<br>b) Low fluid level<br>c) Manual linkage out of adjustment | a) Adjust throttle control cable<br>b) Correct fluid level<br>c) Adjust manual linkage |

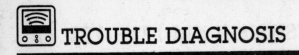

### CHILTON'S THREE "C's" TRANSMISSION DIAGNOSIS CHART
#### KM-171 and 172 Transaxle

| Condition | Cause | Correction |
|---|---|---|
| Clutch slips in Drive (high stall rpm) | d) Line pressure too low | d) Adjust regulator valve and/or repair or replace oil pump |
| | e) Faulty rear clutch and piston | e) Repair or replace rear clutch and piston |
| | f) Faulty planetary overrunning clutch | f) Replace planetary overrunning clutch |
| | g) Valve body malfunction | g) Repair or replace valve body |
| Clutch slips in Reverse | a) Throttle control cable out of adjustment | a) Adjust throttle control cable |
| | b) Low fluid level | b) Correct fluid level |
| | c) Manual linkage out of adjustment | c) Adjust manual linkage |
| | d) Line pressure too low | d) Adjust regulator valve. Repair or replace oil pump |
| | e) Valve body malfunction | e) Repair or replace valve body |
| | f) Faulty front clutch and piston | f) Replace front clutch and/or piston |
| | g) Faulty low-reverse brake and piston | g) Replace low-reverse brake and/or piston |
| | h) Absence of O-ring in front clutch circuit, between valve body and case | h) Replace O-ring |
| Low stall rpm | a) Throttle control cable out of adjustment | a) Adjust throttle control cable |
| | b) Lack of engine output | b) Repair engine as needed |
| | c) Faulty torque converter | c) Replace torque converter |
| No drive in Drive | a) Throttle control cable out of adjustment | a) Adjust throttle control cable |
| | b) Low fluid level | b) Correct fluid level |
| | c) Manual linkage out of adjustment | c) Adjust manual linkage |
| | d) Line pressure too low | d) Adjust pressure regulator Repair or replace oil pump |
| | e) Faulty rear clutch and piston | e) Replace rear clutch and/or piston |
| | f) Faulty planetary overrunning clutch | f) Replace planetary overrunning clutch |
| | g) Valve body malfunction | g) Repair or replace valve body |
| No drive in Reverse | a) Throttle control cable out of adjustment | a) Adjust throttle control cable |
| | b) Low fluid level | b) Correct fluid level |
| | c) Manual linkage out of adjustment | c) Adjust manual linkage |
| | d) Line pressure too low | d) Adjust pressure regulator Repair or replace oil pump |
| | e) Valve body malfunction | e) Repair or replace valve body |
| | f) Faulty front clutch and piston | f) Replace front clutch and/or piston |
| | g) Faulty low-reverse brake and piston | g) Replace low-reverse brake and/or piston |
| | h) Absence of O-ring in front clutch circuit between valve body and case | h) Replace O-ring |

## CHILTON'S THREE "C's" TRANSMISSION DIAGNOSIS CHART
### KM-171 and 172 Transaxle

| Condition | Cause | Correction |
|---|---|---|
| 1-2 upshift at wrong speed or no upshift to 2nd gear | a) Throttle control cable out of adjustment<br>b) Low fluid level<br>c) Line pressure too low<br><br>d) Valve body malfunction<br>e) Governor valve malfunction<br>f) Faulty kickdown band or servo<br>g) Kickdown band out of adjustment | a) Adjust throttle control cable<br>b) Correct fluid level<br>c) Adjust pressure regulator Repair or replace oil pump<br>d) Repair or replace valve body<br>e) Repair or replace governor valve<br>f) Replace kickdown band and/or repair or replace kickdown servo<br>g) Adjust kickdown band servo |
| Slips in 1-2 upshift (delayed upshift) | a) Throttle control cable out of adjustment<br>b) Low fluid level<br>c) Line pressure too low<br><br>d) Valve body malfunction<br>e) Faulty kickdown band or servo<br>f) Kickdown band out of adjustment | a) Adjust throttle control cable<br>b) Correct fluid level<br>c) Adjust pressure regulator Repair or replace oil pump<br>d) Repair or replace valve body<br>e) Replace kickdown band and/or replace kickdown servo<br>f) Adjust kickdown band |
| 2-3 shift at wrong vehicle speeds or no upshift to 3rd gear | a) Throttle control cable out of adjustment<br>b) Low fluid level<br>c) Line pressure too low<br><br>d) Valve body malfunction<br>e) Faulty front clutch and piston<br>f) Governor valve malfunction | a) Adjust throttle control cable<br>b) Correct fluid level<br>c) Adjust pressure regulator Repair or replace oil pump<br>d) Repair or replace valve body<br>e) Replace front clutch and repair or replace piston<br>f) Repair or replace governor valve |
| Slips in 2-3 upshift (delayed upshift) | a) Throttle control cable out of adjustment<br>b) Low fluid level<br>c) Line pressure too low<br><br>d) Valve body malfunction<br>e) Faulty front clutch and piston | a) Adjust throttle control cable<br>b) Correct fluid level<br>c) Adjust pressure regulator Repair or replace oil pump<br>d) Repair or replace valve body<br>e) Replace front clutch and/or piston |
| Poor performance or overheat in Drive 3rd gear | a) Faulty torque converter | a) Replace torque converter |
| No downshift in Drive 3rd to Low | a) Manual linkage out of adjustment<br>b) Valve body malfunction<br>c) Faulty kickdown band or servo<br>d) Kickdown band out of adjustment | a) Adjust manual linkage<br>b) Repair or replace valve body<br>c) Replace kickdown band and repair or replace kickdown servo<br>d) Adjust kickdown band |
| Slip or shudder on start up in low | a) Throttle control cable out of adjustment<br>b) Low fluid level<br>c) Manual linkage out of adjustment<br>d) Valve body malfunction | a) Adjust throttle control cable<br>b) Correct fluid level<br>c) Adjust manual linkage<br>d) Repair or replace valve body |

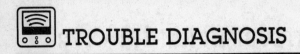

## CHILTON'S THREE "C's" TRANSMISSION DIAGNOSIS CHART
### KM-171 and 172 Transaxle

| Condition | Cause | Correction |
|---|---|---|
| Upshift in Low | a) Manual linkage out of adjustment | a) Adjust manual linkage |
| Severe shock in Drive 3-2 kickdown | a) Throttle control cable out of adjustment | a) Adjust throttle control cable |
| | b) Low fluid level | b) Correct fluid level |
| | c) Line pressure too low | c) Adjust pressure regulator Repair or replace oil pump |
| | d) Valve body malfunction | d) Repair or replace valve body |
| | e) Kickdown band out of adjustment | e) Adjust kickdown band |
| No lock-up in Park | a) Manual linkage out of adjustment | a) Adjust manual linkage |
| | b) Faulty parts in parking mechanism | b) Replace parts as needed |
| Converter housing groan with increases in engine rpm | a) Defective operation of oil pump | a) Repair or replace oil pump |
| | b) Interference of oil pump gear teeth and wear of bushing | b) Replace oil pump parts as needed |
| Metallic noises (chatter) from converter housing | a) Cracked or warped drive plate | a) Replace drive plate |
| | b) Loose drive plate bolt | b) Retorque all drive plate bolts |
| Hard to put control lever in P position | a) Worn dog of parking sprag | a) Replace |
| KM-171 Transaxle slips due to excessive wear of sprag (KM-172) | a) Broken ribbon spring of sprag clutch | a) Replace |
| **LOCK-UP TORQUE CONVERTER PROBLEMS** | | |
| No drive at any position due to lock-up torque converter engaged | a) Abnormal signal slippage in lock-up torque converter system | a) Replace |
| | b) Malfunctioning sealing in solenoid valve torque converter | b) Repair or replace as required |
| Excessive vibration | a) Decreased signal slippage from C.P.U. (Computer Processing Unit) | a) Replace |
| Inoperative lock-up torque converter system | a) No signal lock-up from C.P.U. | a) Replace |
| | b) Lock-up line pressure low | b) Restore to proper pressure |
| | c) Opened or shorted circuit of solenoid valve | c) Replace |
| Increased fuel consumption | a) Lock-up torque converter does not engage because of a stuck valve | a) Clean up |
| Lock-up torque converter does not release | a) Decreased driving effort in facing of clutch plate | a) Replace |
| | b) Burn out clutch disc | b) Release |
| | c) Lock-up torque converter system solenoid valve stuck open | c) Repair or replace as required |
| Increased vibration due to no control of slipping ratio | a) Sticking shaft in throttle opening sensor | a) Repair or replace as required |

## CHILTON'S THREE "C's" TRANSMISSION DIAGNOSIS CHART
### KM-171 and 172 Transaxle

| Condition | Cause | Correction |
|---|---|---|
| No drive at any position | a) Seized or stuck thrust bearing in torque converter | a) Replace |
| | b) Deformed crankshaft bushing in torque converter | b) Replace |
| | c) Broken or cracked drive plate | c) Replace |
| | d) Low oil level | d) Refill with fluid |
| Increased noise due to in-operative lock-up torque converter | a) Deformed or worn locking-ring in torque converter | a) Replace |
| Excessive slips when starting | a) Low oil level | a) Refill with fluid |
| | b) Worn over-running clutch in torque converter | b) Replace |
| Hunting | a) Oil leakage from valve body | a) Repair or replace as required |

# TROUBLE DIAGNOSIS

In order to properly diagnose transmission problems and avoid making second repairs for the same problem, all of the available information and knowledge must be used. Included is a list of the components of the transmission and their functions. Also, test procedures and their accompanying specification charts aid in finding solutions to problems. Further answers are found by road testing vehicles and comparing results of the above KM-171-172 Transaxle Diagnosis Chart. This chart gives conditions, cause and correction to most possible trouble conditions in the KM-171, 172 transaxle.

In order to diagnose transmission trouble, the hydraulic control circuits (passages) must be traced. The main components of the hydraulic system are the oil pump, the governor and the valve body assembly.

The oil pump delivers the hydraulic fluid to the torque converter, lubricates the planetary gearsets, overrunning clutch, and friction elements, and produces a pressure for hydraulic control.

This oil pump uses a gear within a ring gear. The pump drive gear is driven by two pawls of the pump drive hub welded to the center of the torque converter shell. Therefore hydraulic pressure is produced throughout engine operation.

The governor is a centrifugal hydraulic unit designed to turn with the rotation of the transfer shaft. The governor valve receives main line pressure and produces governor pressure. Governor pressure increases when transfer shaft (vehicle) speed increases. Governor pressure acts on the 1-2 shift valve, 2-3 shift valve, range control valve, and shuttle valve. The governor body incorporates a filter in order to prevent "valve sticking" caused by foreign material in the fluid.

The valve body assembly consists of a valve body, separating plate, transfer plate, and various valves.

The functions of the valves are

1. The regulator valve controls oil pump pressure to produce regulated main line pressure. The valve operates by varying throttle pressures opposing set spring pressure in the valve. Thus throttle opening changes cause changes in main line pressure. There is an adjusting screw on the end of the regulator valve. The procedure for adjusting the valve is covered in the On Car Services section.

2. The torque converter control valve maintains constant fluid pressure to the torque converter. Fluid coming out of the torque converter flows through the oil cooler and is used to lubri-

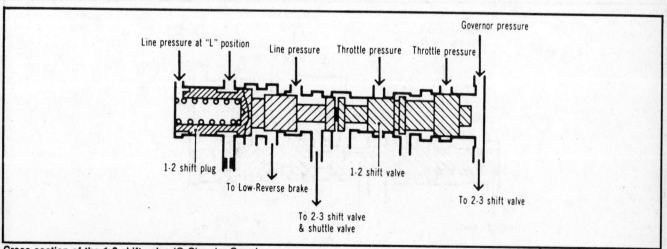

Cross section of the 1-2 shift valve (© Chrysler Corp.)

cate the planetary gearsets, overrunning clutch, and friction elements.

3. The throttle valve controls throttle pressure depending on carburetor throttle opening. Throttle pressure is directed to the regulator valve, 1-2 shift valve, 2-3 shift valve and shuttle valve. Depending on which valve is affected this causes increases in main line pressure, thereby changing shift points and shift timing.

4. The kickdown valve operates in sequence with the throttle valve. This valve is moved by the throttle control cable connected to accelerator linkage. At W.O.T. (wide open throttle) line pressure is directed to each shift valve, delaying the shift points.

5. Manual valve operation is connected to the selector lever in the vehicle. The valve receives main line pressure and delivers it to various valves and elements according to selector lever position.

6. 1-2 shift valve movement is controlled by spring pressure, governor pressure and throttle pressure. This valve controls 1-2 upshift and 2-1 downshifts.

7. The range control valve determines the vehicle speed for downshifting to first gear when "L" range is selected.

8. The 2-3 shift valve shifts the transmission from second to third or from third to second depending on governor pressure and throttle pressure.

9. Shuttle valve operation controls the feed and discharge pressure to the kickdown servo and front clutch to ensure smooth shifting.

## Diagnosis Tests

Automatic transmission failures may be caused by four basic conditions; hydraulic malfunctions, poor engine performance, improper adjustments, and mechanical failures. Diagnosis of these problems should always begin by checking easily accessible variables; fluid level and condition, throttle control cable adjustment, and manual control cable adjustment. After all these conditions are checked, perform a road test to see if the problems have been corrected. If the problem still exists after the road test and checks are completed, then hydraulic pressure tests should be performed.

### CONTROL PRESSURE TEST

Before performing the control pressure test do the following procedures, bring the engine and transaxle up to normal operating temperature, and install an engine tachometer. Raise the vehicle so that the front wheels can turn and position the tachometer so it can be read. Disconnect the linkage from the manual control lever on the transmission and also the throttle control cable from the carburetor so they can be controlled from outside the vehicle.

### Low Reverse Brake Pressure Test With Selector In "L"

1. Attach oil pressure gauge and oil pressure gauge adapter to low-reverse brake and line pressure takeoff ports.

2. Operate engine at 2,500 rpm for test, with the manual control lever all the way rearward to the "L" position.

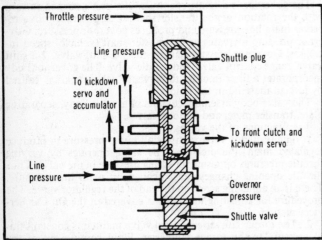

**Cross section of the shuttle valve** (© Chrysler Corp.)

**Transaxle right side pressure ports** (© Chrysler Corp.)

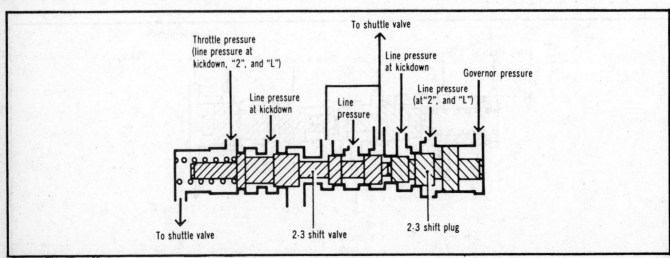

**Cross section of the 2-3 shift valve** (© Chrysler Corp.)

3. Read the pressures on the gauge as the throttle control cable is pulled from idle to wide open throttle position.

4. When throttle cable is in idle position the line pressure should read between 58-67 psi. and when the throttle cable is pulled to wide open position the line pressure should increase between 98-100 psi.

5. Low-reverse brake pressure should read between 24-33 psi.

6. This test pump output, pressure regulation, condition of the rear clutch and low-reverse hydraulic brake circuit.

### Low-Reverse Brake Pressure Test With Selector In "R"

1. Attach oil pressure gauge to low reverse brake pressure take-off port.

2. With engine operating at 2,500 rpm move manual control lever forward to the "R" position.

3. Low-reverse brake pressure should read between 199-284 psi. regardless of throttle opening.

4. This tests pump output, pressure regulation, condition of front clutch and low reverse brake hydraulic circuit.

### Line Pressure Test With Selector In "D"

1. Attach oil pressure gauge to line pressure posts.

2. With engine operating at 2,500 rpm, move manual control lever to the "D" position.

3. Read pressure on gauge as throttle control cable is pulled from idle position to the wide-open position.

4. Line pressure should read between 58-67 psi. with cable in idle position and gradually increased, as the throttle cable is pulled toward the wide-open position.

5. This tests pump output, pressure regulation, condition of front and rear clutches and hydraulic circuit.

### Lubrication Pressure Test With Selector In "2"

1. Attach oil pressure gauge to line pressure takeoff port and tee (3-way joint) into cooler line (transaxle cooler) fitting to read lubrication pressure.

2. With engine operating at 2,500 rpm move the manual control lever to the 2 position.

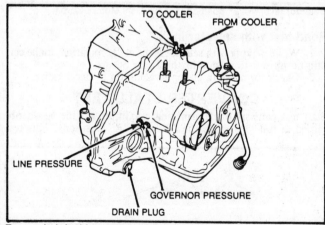

Transaxle left side pressure ports (© Chrysler Corp.)

3. Read pressure on gauge as throttle control cable is pulled from idle to wide-open position.

4. Line pressure should read between 58-67 psi. with throttle cable in idle position and 98-100 psi. in the wide-open position.

5. Lubrication pressure should read 7-21 psi. regardless of the throttle position.

6. This tests pump output, pressure regulation, condition of rear clutch and lubrication hydraulic circuit.

### Governor Pressure Test

Governor pressure test should be taken if the transaxle shifts at the wrong vehicle speeds when the control cable is adjusted properly. After the other pressure test are completed, be sure to reconnect the manual linkage and the control cable and properly adjust both.

1. Connect the oil pressure gauge to the governor pressure port.

2. Operate the vehicle in third gear to read the pressures and compare the vehicle speeds shown in the chart.

3. If governor pressures are incorrect at given speeds the governor valve is sticking or the filter in the governor body is clogged.

### GOVERNOR PRESSURE ①

| Pressure | Vehicle Speed |
| --- | --- |
| 14 psi | 16-18 MPH |
| 43 psi | 32-40 MPH |
| 71 psi | 53-62 MPH |

① Governor pressure should be from 0 to 3 psi when the vehicle stands still. Changes in tire size will cause shift points to occur at corresponding higher or lower vehicle speeds.

4. Governor pressure should respond smoothly to changes in vehicle speeds and should return to 0-2.8 psi when the vehicle is stopped.

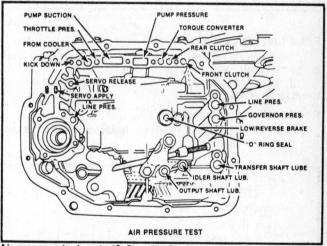

Air pressure test ports (© Chrysler Corp.)

### OVERALL PRESSURE TEST RESULT INDICATIONS

1. Low pressure in "D", "L" and "2", but correct pressure in "R" indicates rear clutch circuit leakage.

2. Low pressure in "D" and "R" but correct pressure in "L" indicates front clutch circuit leakage.

3. Low pressure in "R" and "L" but correct pressure in "2" indicates low-reverse brake circuit leakage.

4. Low line pressure in all selector positions indicates a defective pump, a clogged filter, or a stuck pressure regulator valve.

5. If proper line pressure, minimum to maximum, is found in any test, the pump and pressure regulator are working properly.

### ROAD TEST

Before starting a road test, check to see that the fluid level condition and the control cable adjustments are correct. During a road test the transaxle should be operated in each position to check for slipping and hard shifting. Approximate shift speeds for various modes of operation are shown in the Automatic shift speed chart below.

## AUTOMATIC SHIFT SPEEDS CHART
### KM-171, 172

| Engine | 1.8 liter |
|---|---|
| Axle ratio | 3.166 |
| Standard tire | 155SR13 |
| | km/h (mph) |
| Closed throttle 1-2 | 12-19 (7-12) |
| Closed throttle 2-3 | 17-23 (11-14) |
| Part throttle 1-2 | 26-33 (16-21) |
| Part throttle 2-3 | 38-51 (23-32) |
| Wide open throttle 1-2 | 44-54 (27-34) |
| Wide open throttle 2-3 | 88-89 (54-60) |
| Kickdown limit 3-2 | 80-90 (49-56) |
| Kickdown limit 2-1 | 33-44 (20-27) |
| Closed throttle 3-1 | 9-15 (6-9) |

### Road test with selector in "P"

1. With vehicle parked on a small grade, put the selector lever in the "P" position and release the parking brake.
2. If the vehicle does not roll backwards, the parking system is working properly.

### Road test with selector in "R"

1. Start the engine and stall test the transaxle to see if the friction element is slipping or not.

Selector lever in "P" position (© Mitsubishi Motors Corp.)

### Road test with selector In "D"

1. Increase speed of vehicle and while holding the accelerator pedal steady check to see if transaxle makes 1-2 and 2-3 upshift at correct vehicle speeds. Also check for hard shifting or slipping at this time.
2. While driving in third gear, check for noise and vibration.
3. With selector lever in second or third gear, check to see if 2-1, 3-1 and 3-2 kickdown shifts occur properly at specified kickdown limit vehicle speeds.
4. Drive in third gear, and select "2" range, than "L" range to check if engine brake is effective.
5. Drive in third gear at 31 mph. or higher speeds, and select

Selector lever in "D" position (© Mitsubishi Motors Corp.)

"L" range to check if 2-1 downshift occurs at proper vehicle speed.

### Road test with selector in "2"

1. While driving with selector lever in "2" position increase vehicle speed. Make sure that the transaxle makes 1-2 upshift at the proper vehicle speed. Also check for noise and shock at the time of shifting.
2. Check to see if 2-1 kickdown occurs at correct limit vehicle speed.

Selector lever in "2" position (© Mitsubishi Motors Corp.)

### Road test with selector in "L"

1. While driving with selector lever in "L" position, make certain no upshift to second or third gear occurs.
2. Check for noise in either acceleration or deceleration.

## CONVERTER STALL TEST

Stall test consists of determining maximum engine speed obtained at full throttle in the "D" and "R" positions. This test

Selector lever in "L" position (© Mitsubishi Motors Corp.)

checks torque converter stator overrunning clutch operation, and holding ability of transaxle clutches and low-reverse brake.

---
#### CAUTION
---

*During this test let no one stand in front of or behind the vehicle.*

---

1. Check the transmission fluid level at normal transmission and engine operating temperatures.
2. Apply chocks to both front and rear wheels.
3. Attach engine tachometer.
4. Apply parking and service brakes fully.
5. Start the engine.
6. With the selector in Drive position, depress the accelerator pedal fully and read the maximum engine rpm.

---
#### CAUTION
---

*Do not hold the throttle wide open any longer than is necessary to obtain a maximum engine rpm reading, and never longer than 10 seconds at a time. If more than one stall test is required, operate the engine at approximately 1,000 rpms in neutral to cool the transmission fluid between tests.*

---

7. Follow the same procedure in Reverse position.

**NOTE:** The stall speed for the KM-171 is 2,100 ± 200 rpm. and the stall speed for the KM-172 is 2,200 ± 200 rpm.

## INTERPRETATION OF STALL TEST RESULTS

### Stall speed above specification in "D"

1. Rear clutch or overrunning clutch is slipping.

### Stall speed above specification in "R"

1. Front clutch or low-reverse brake is slipping.

**NOTE:** If the stall speed is higher than specification in "D" and "R" position, perform a hydraulic test to locate the cause of slippage.

### Stall speed below specification in "D" and "R"

1. If stall speed is lower than specification, poor engine performance or a defective torque converter is the suspected problem.
2. Check for engine misfiring, ignition timing and other engine related problems. If these are good then the torque converter is defective.

## LOCK-UP TORQUE CONVERTER

The new 3-speed automatic transaxle incorporates a new Mitsubishi development known as ELC (Electronic Control). The system has a built-in damper clutch that operates in 2nd and 3rd gears to keep the torque converter's slip ratio very low, thus helping to improve fuel economy.

The lock-up feature on the automatic transmissions produced by other manufactures operates only at speeds over 25-35 mph, because of vibration problems. One of the design features of the ELC system is that it works at a very low speed. The damper clutch in the ELC system is so effective that it functions without perceptible vibration at speeds as low as 12 mph.

**NOTE:** The lock-up torque converter will not operate when the coolant temperature is below 50°C (122°F) or when the vehicle is travelling in 1st gear. It also will not operate when in the "R" position.

The ELC computer continuously processes all important information such as engine speed, kickdown drum speed, output shaft speed, throttle position and the coolant temperature. With this information, the ELC computer then provides instructions to the oil pressure valve that controls the damper clutch.

**NOTE:** Tests done by the manufacturer indicates that a vehicle with the ELC lock-up torque converter uses about 10% less fuel than one without ELC.

A comparison of slip ratios between automatic transaxles without ELC, and transaxles with ELC is shown below:

## COMPARISON OF SLIP RATIOS
### At a constant speed of—

|  | 25 mph | 35 mph | 55 mph |
| --- | --- | --- | --- |
| Automatic with ELC | 2.5:1 | 1.1:1 | 1.0:1 |
| Automatic without ELC | 9.0:1 | 5.0:1 | 3.0:1 |
| **ACCELERATION AT 50% THROTTLE:** | | | |
| Automatic with ELC | 4.0:1 | 1.1:1 | 1.0:1 |
| Automatic without ELC | 30.0:1 | 13.0:1 | 5.0:1 |

## DIAGNOSIS OF THE LOCK-UP TORQUE CONVERTER

### Lock-Up Torque Converter Operations Test

1. Engage the parking brake and position the selector lever in the "P" or "N" position and start the engine.
2. With the vehicle at normal operating temperature of 122°F (50°C), firmly depress the brake pedal and shift the selector lever to "D" or "R" position. Check to see if the engine stays running or stalls.
3. If the engine stays running then the torque converter is operating correctly.

### Engine Stalls

1. Replace the solenoid valve if the valve is not completely closed.
2. Overhaul the valve body when the lock-up torque converter control valve is stuck.
3. Replace the torque converter assembly when the lock-up torque converter is seized (heat seized).
4. Adjust the idle if the idle is incorrectly adjusted.

### Lock-Up Solenoid Valve Test

1. With the engine running at normal operating temperature and the selector lever in "N" position, disconnect the connector of the lock-up solenoid valve.
2. Connect a 12 volt battery between the valve connector and the transaxle case.

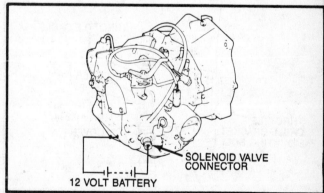

**Battery connection for lock-up solenoid test**
(© Mitsubishi Motors Corp.)

---
#### CAUTION
---

*Do not apply voltage to the solenoid over 5 seconds because the solenoid will burn out.*

3. Firmly depress the brake pedal and shift the selector lever into the "D" or "R" position. If the engine stalls, the lock-up clutch operates correctly.

### Engine Running

1. Check and repair any broken wires on solenoid valve. If the wires are not broken and incorrect solenoid valve operation still occurs replace the solenoid valve.
2. Overhaul the valve body when the lock-up torque converter control valve is stuck.
3. Replace the torque converter assembly due to abnormal abrasion of lock-up converter.

### Lock-Up Torque Converter Circuit Tester

1. Find the inspection connector located in the engine compartment and connect the circuit tester to it.
2. Operate the vehicle in the "2" position at 14 mph and shift to the "D" position at 28 mph.
3. If the circuit tester shows the same voltage as the battery, the lock-up torque converter control system is operating correctly.
4. If the circuit tester shows no value, there is a malfunction in the lock-up torque converter control system.

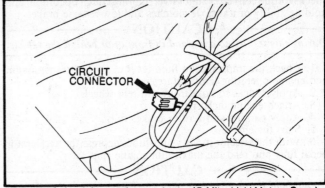
Location of circuit inspection connector (© Mitsubishi Motors Corp.)

3. Turn switch body until the wide end (A) of the manual control lever ovelaps the switch body flange.
4. While keeping the switch body flange and manual lever aligned, torque the two attaching bolts to 10-11.5 N•m (7.5-8.5 ft. lbs.).

## Adjustments

Proper adjustment of the manual linkage, neutral (inhibitor) safety switch, throttle control cable, kickdown band and line pressure will ensure proper operation and normal service life of the KM-171, 172 transaxle.

### NEUTRAL SAFETY (INHIBITOR) SWITCH

1. Place the manual control lever in neutral position.
2. Loosen the two switch attaching bolts.

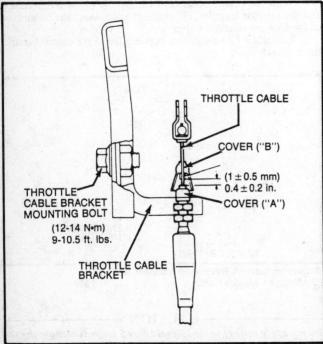
Throttle control cable adjustment (© Mitsubishi Motors Corp.)

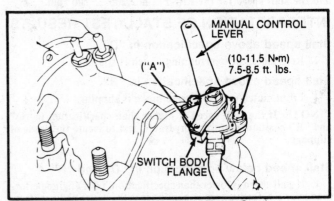
Inhibitor switch adjustment (© Mitsubishi Motors Corp.)

### THROTTLE CONTROL CABLE

1. With engine at normal operating temperature, place carburetor throttle lever in the curb idle position.
2. Raise cover (B) of the throttle cable upward to expose the nipple.
3. Loosen lower cable bracket mounting bolt.
4. Move lower cable bracket until distance between nipple and top of cover (A) on throttle cable is adjusted to 0.04 ±0.02 in.
5. Torque lower cable bracket mounting bolt to 9-10.5 ft. lbs.
6. Check the cable for freedom of movement. With the carburetor at wide open throttle, pull the control cable upward away from the transaxle.
7. If the cable is binding or sticking, it may need repair or replacement.

### KICKDOWN BAND

1. Wipe all dirt and other contamination from the kickdown servo cover and surrounding area.
2. Remove the snap ring and then the cover.
3. Loosen the lock nut.
4. Holding the kickdown servo piston from turning tighten the adjusting screw to 7 ft. lbs. and then back it off. Repeat the tightening and backing off two times in order to ensure seating of the band on the drum.
5. Tighten the adjusting screw to 3.5 ft. lbs. and back it off 3.5 turns (counterclockwise).

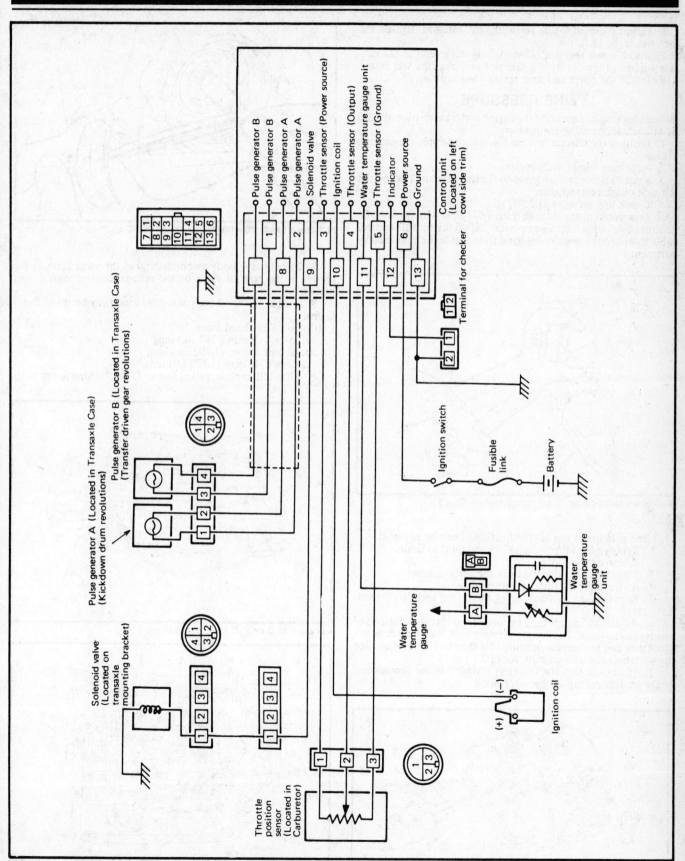

**Electronic control lock-up torque converter wiring diagram** (© Mitsubishi Motors Corp.)

6. Holding the adjusting screw against rotation, tighten the lock nut to 11-15 ft. lbs.

7. Install a new seal ring (D-shaped) in the groove in the outside surface of the cover. Use care not to distort the seal ring.

8. Install the cover and then install the snap ring.

## LINE PRESSURE

Before checking line pressure the engine and transmission should be at normal operating temperature.

1. Position the selector lever in Neutral and apply the parking brake.

2. Attach an engine tachometer.

3. Attach an oil pressure gauge to the line pressure port on the left side of the transmission.

4. Check line pressure at 2,500 rpm.

5. Line pressure should read from 98-100 psi with the throttle control cable in the wide open position. (Pull the throttle control cable to wide open position by hand from inside the engine compartment.)

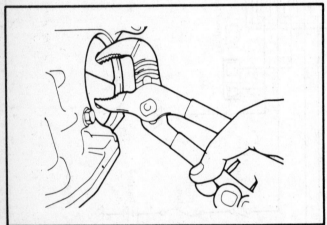

**Kickdown servo cover** (© Mitsubishi Motors Corp.)

If line pressure is out of specification, it can be adjusted.

1. Remove the oil pan and allow the fluid to drain.

2. Remove the oil pan.

3. Disconnect the throttle from the throttle cam.

4. Remove the oil filter and filter plate.

5. Remove the valve body being careful not to drop the manual valve.

6. Adjust the line pressure by turning the screw on the end of the regulator valve. To increase pressure turn the screw counterclockwise and to decrease pressure turn the screw clockwise. One turn changes the line pressure about 3.7 psi.

7. Make sure that the O-ring is installed in the low-reverse brake passage on top of the valve body.

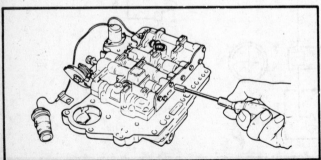

**Line pressure adjustment** (© Mitsubishi Motors Corp.)

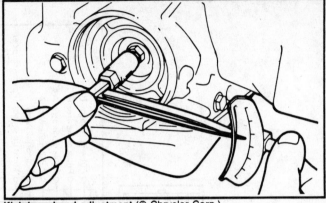

**Kickdown band adjustment** (© Chrysler Corp.)

8. Install valve body assembly, and at the same time fit the groove of the manual valve on the manual control shaft detent plate pin.

9. Torque the valve body assembly mounting bolts to 7.5-8.5 ft. lbs.

10. Bolt Size (head mark 7):
    a. A bolt 20mm (.787 in.) long
    b. B bolt 28mm (1.102 in.) long
    c. C bolt 45 mm (1.772 in.) long.

11. Install filter plate, gasket and oil filter. Tighten flange bolts to 4-5 ft. lbs.

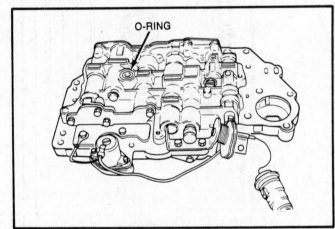

**Location of O-ring** (© Mitsubishi Motors Corp.)

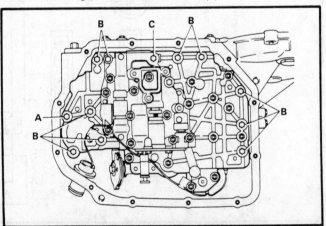

**Valve body mounting bolts** (© Mitsubishi Motors Corp.)

12. Reconnect throttle control cable to throttle cam.

13. Install a new oil pan gasket and reinstall the oil pan. Then tighten the bolt washer assemblies to 7.5-8.5 ft. lbs. of torque.

14. Refill the transaxle to the proper level with Dexron® or Dexron® II ATF.

## MANUAL LINKAGE

The transaxle manual control linkage removal, inspection, installation and adjustment are covered in this section.

### Removal

1. Remove the selector handle from the selector lever.
2. Remove the console box.
3. Remove the indicator panel and disconnect the connector for the position indicator light.
4. Disconnect the control cable from the lever.
5. Remove the control cable from the transaxle and the transaxle mount bracket.
2. Check for detent plate wear.
3. Check for worn contact surface of the pushbutton and the sleeve.
4. Check the pin at the end of the selector lever for wear or damage.

### Installation

1. Apply grease to all sliding parts.
2. With the selector lever in the "N" position turn the selector handle while pressing downward, so that clearance (0.008-0.035

in.) between the detent plate and the selector lever end pin is within the standard value range.

**NOTE: Make sure the selector handle is attached to selector lever so that the pushbutton is at the driver side.**

3. After making the adjustment, check to see that the pushbutton free play is within standard value range.

**NOTE: The free play range is 0.008-0.063 in.**

4. Move the selector lever and the inhibitor switch to the "N" position, and install the control cable.

6. Raise the vehicle, and then remove the bolt mounting the control cable to the floor and the plate assembly mounting nuts.

7. Remove the plate assembly from inside the vehicle, and remove the control cable from underneath the vehicle.

### Inspection

1. Check the control cable for excessive bend or damage.

**NOTE: Make sure that the tooth washer is in the correct position when connecting the control cable to the transaxle mounting bracket.**

5. Turn the adjusting nut to remove the slack from the manual control cable.

6. Place the selector lever in the "N" position, and then mount the indicator panel so that the "N" indication is properly aligned.

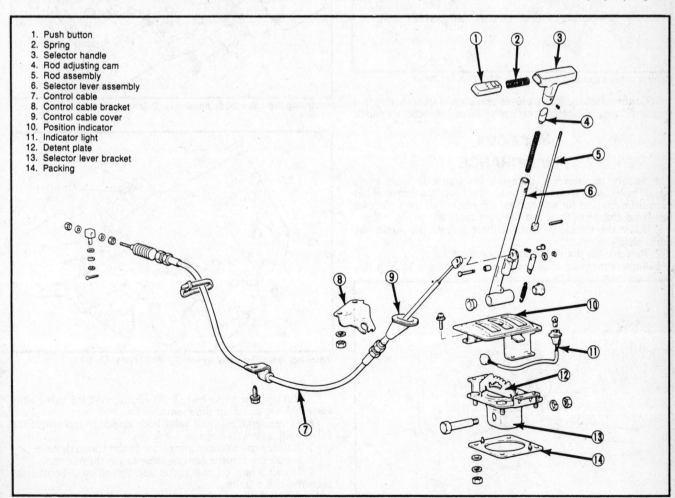

1. Push button
2. Spring
3. Selector handle
4. Rod adjusting cam
5. Rod assembly
6. Selector lever assembly
7. Control cable
8. Control cable bracket
9. Control cable cover
10. Position indicator
11. Indicator light
12. Detent plate
13. Selector lever bracket
14. Packing

**Manual shift control parts** (© Chrysler Corp.)

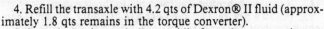

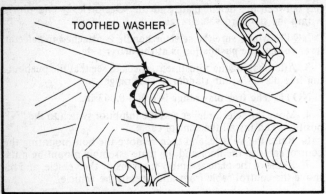

Control cable lock washer (© Mitsubishi Motors Corp.)

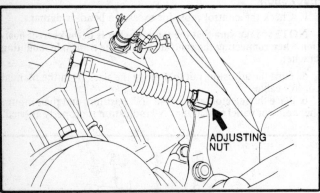

Control cable adjusting nut (© Mitsubishi Motors Corp.)

7. Confirm that the selector lever operation is smooth, and that the correct gear is selected at each position on the indicator panel.

## Services

### FLUID CHANGE

The factory recommends changing the transaxle fluid every 30,000 miles using Dexron® II fluid. Whenever the transaxle has been disassembled for any reason, adjustment of the kickdown band and change of fluid and filter are required.

1. Raise the vehicle on a hoist. Place a drain pan under the drain plug.
2. Remove the drain plug and drain the fluid.
3. Replace the drain plug. Torque the drain plug to 22-25 ft. lbs.

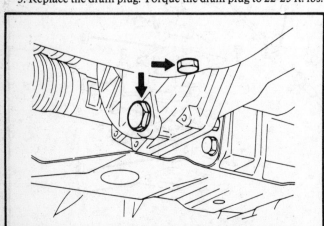

Transaxle fluid drain plugs (© Mitsubishi Motors Corp.)

4. Refill the transaxle with 4.2 qts of Dexron® II fluid (approximately 1.8 qts remains in the torque converter).
5. Start the engine and allow to idle for at least two minutes. With the parking brake applied, move the selector lever to each position, ending in Neutral.
6. Add sufficient fluid to bring the lever to the lower mark. Recheck the fluid level after the transaxle is up to normal operating temperature.

## VALVE BODY

### Removal and Installation

1. Drain ATF fluid and remove the oil pan.
2. Disconnect the throttle control cable from the throttle cam.
3. Remove the solenoid connector from transaxle case.
4. Remove oil filter and filter plate.

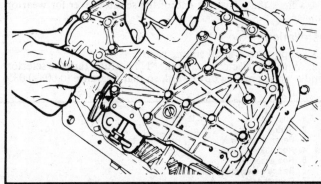

Removing the valve body assembly (© Chrysler Corp.)

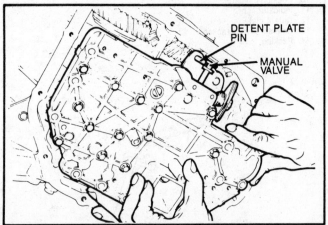

Installing the valve body assembly (© Chrysler Corp.)

5. Remove the valve body bolts and remove the valve body assembly. Do not drop the manual valve.
6. To reassemble, install valve body assembly and torque the valve body assembly bolts to 3-4 ft. lbs.
7. Replace the solenoid connector to the transaxle case.
8. Install the throttle control cable to the throttle cam.
9. Install a new oil pan gasket and the oil pan. Torque the bolts to 7.5-8.5 ft. lbs.
10. Add 4.2 quarts of recommended ATF into the transaxle case through the dipstick hole.

## ACCUMULATOR

### Removal and Installation

To remove the accumulator, first drain the ATF fluid and remove the oil pan and valve body assembly as previously outlined. With the valve body assembly removed, proceed as follows:

1. Remove the snap ring and accumulator plug.
2. Remove the accumulator springs and piston from the transaxle case.
3. Assembly is reverse, being sure to lube the seals with ATF or petroleum jelly.

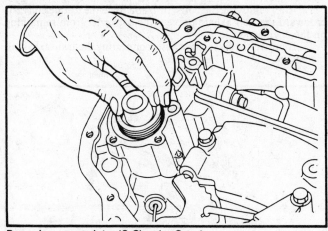

**Removing accumulator** (© Chrysler Corp.)

## KICKDOWN SERVO

### Removal and Installation

1. Drain ATF fluid and remove kickdown servo cover snap ring.
2. Remove kickdown servo cover.
3. Using special tool (MD 998303 or its equivalent), push in kickdown servo and remove snap ring.
4. Remove kickdown servo piston, sleeve and spring.
5. Assembly is reverse, being sure to lube the seals with ATF or petroleum jelly.

## SPEEDOMETER GEAR

### Removal and Installation

1. Drain ATF fluid.
2. Disconnect the speedometer cable and remove the speedometer gear assembly.
3. Drive spring pin out to disassemble the gear and the sleeve (do not reuse O-rings and spring pin).
4. Install new O-rings to the speedometer driven gear sleeve, inner and outer diameters and insert sleeve onto drive gear.

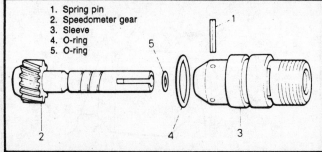

1. Spring pin
2. Speedometer gear
3. Sleeve
4. O-ring
5. O-ring

**Speedometer assembly** (© Chrysler Corp.)

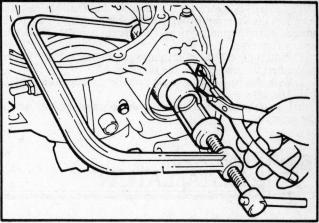

**Removing the kickdown servo snap ring** (© Chrysler Corp.)

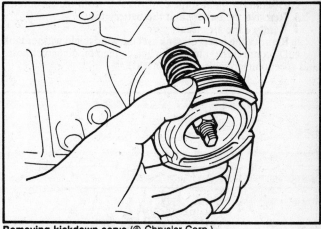

**Removing kickdown servo** (© Chrysler Corp.)

5. Align pin hole in sleeve with pin slot in gear shaft, and drive in spring pin.
6. Replace the speedometer gear assembly into the transaxle case, and connect speedometer cable.
7. Add recommended ATF fluid.

## PULSE GENERATORS "A" AND "B"

### Removal and Installation

The pulse "A" generator is located in the transaxle case and monitors the kickdown drum revolutions in the transaxle, for the ELC system.

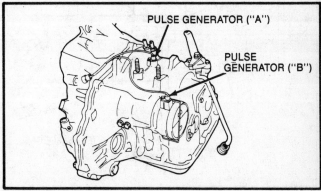

PULSE GENERATOR ("A")

PULSE GENERATOR ("B")

**Locations of pulse generators "A" and "B"** (© Chrysler Corp.)

The pulse "B" generator is located in the transaxle case and monitors the Transfer driven gear revolutions for the ELC (Electronic Control System) system. This system controls the lock-up torque converter.

1. Find the locations of the pulse generators "A" or "B" and disconnect the lead wire to the generator.

2. With lead wire disconnected, remove the generator from the transaxle case.

3. Install the new pulse generator and connect the lead wire to the generator.

 **REMOVAL & INSTALLATION**

### Removal from Vehicle

1. Disconnect the control cable from the transaxle.

2. Disconnect the throttle control cable from the carburetor.

3. Remove the battery and the battery tray.

4. Remove the air cleaner case.

5. Remove the reservoir tank and the windshield washer tank.

6. Disconnect the inhibitor switch connector, oil cooler hoses, and speedometer cable from transaxle.

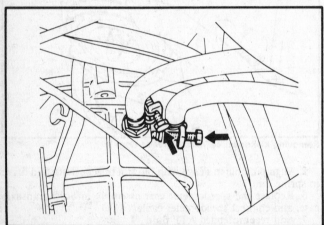

Oil cooler hoses (© Mitsubishi Motors Corp.)

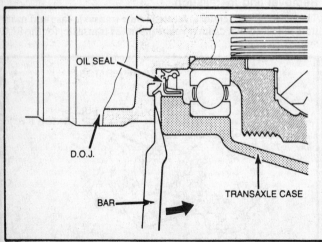

Removal of drive shaft from transaxle (© Chrysler Corp.)

**NOTE: Be sure to plug the oil cooler lines, so that no foreign matter enters the lines. It will also keep the oil from draining out of the oil cooler.**

7. Remove the starter motor.

8. Raise the vehicle and remove the front wheels and drain the transmission fluid.

9. Remove the strut bars and the stabilizer bar from the lower arms.

10. Remove the right and left driveshafts from the transaxle and place them in a safe place.

11. Remove the bell housing cover and then remove the three bolts connecting the torque converter to the drive plate.

12. After removing the bolts, turn and force the torque converter toward the transaxle to prevent the converter from remaining on the engine side.

13. Remove the five upper bolts connecting the transaxle with the engine.

Upper five connecting bolts (© Mitsubishi Motors Corp.)

14. Using a transmission jack or equivalent, support the lower part of the transaxle and remove the remaining bolts that connect the engine to the transaxle.

**NOTE: Support a wide area of the transaxle so that the oil pan is not distorted when supported.**

15. Remove the transaxle mount insulator bolts and the mount bracket.

16. Remove the blank cap from inside the right fender shield and remove installation bolts.

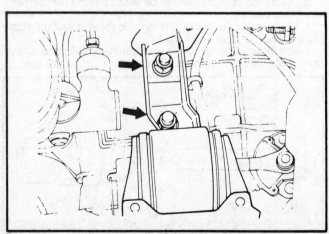

Transaxle mount insulator bolts (© Mitsubishi Motors Corp.)

# MITSUBISHI KM-171 • 172 SECTION 7

17. Slide the transaxle assembly to the right and lower it to remove it. Do not allow the converter to fall from the unit.

## Installation

The transaxle and converter should be installed as a unit. Connecting the torque converter to engine first could cause damage to the oil seal on the transaxle and the drive plate.

1. Place the transaxle on the removing jack or equivalent and raise it into position in the vehicle.

2. Replace the transaxle mounting bolts and torque them to 32-39 ft. lbs., if the bolts are marked 7 on the head. Torque to 22-25 ft. lbs., if the bolts are marked 10 on the head.

3. Install the 3 bolts that connect the torque converter to the drive plate and torque to 25-30 ft. lbs.

4. Reinstall the bell housing cover and torque bolts to 7.5-8.5 ft. lbs.

5. Install starter motor and torque bolts to 16-23 ft. lbs.

6. Install the speedometer cable at the transaxle, and reinstall the oil cooler lines.

7. Reinstall the strut bars and the stabilizer bar.

8. Fill the transaxle with Dexron® II ATF fluid.

9. Reinstall the inhibitor switch connector.

10. Reinstall the throttle control cable to the carburetor. Adjust the cable per adjustment section.

11. Install the control cable to the transaxle, and adjust the slack out of the cable.

12. Install the battery, the battery tray and the air cleaner case.

13. Reinstall the reservoir tank and the windshield washer tank.

14. Confirm ignition switch starter action in the "P" and "N" positions. Make sure that the starter does not engage in any other positions.

15. Check to see that the selector lever operates smoothly and is properly shifting into every selector position.

16. Check the transmission fluid level again.

## BENCH OVERHAUL

## Before Disassembly

1. Prior to disassembling the transaxle, thoroughly remove all dirt from the exterior to prevent the dirt from entering the transmission.

2. The automatic transaxle consists of many precision parts. Care should be taken not to scratch, nick or impair the parts during overhaul of the transmission.

3. Make sure bench work areas are clean.

4. Do not use cloth gloves or shop towels during overhaul operations. Use nylon cloth or paper waste if necessary.

5. Clean all metal parts in suitable solvent and dry with compressed air.

6. Clean all clutch discs, plastic thrust plates and rubber parts in automatic transmission fluid.

7. All rubber gaskets and oil seals should be replaced with new at every re-installation.

**NOTE: The rubber seal at the oil level dipstick need not be replaced.**

8. Do not use grease other than pertroleum jelly.

9. Apply Dexron® II fluid to the friction elements, rotating parts and sliding parts before installation.

10. Do not apply a sealer on adhesive to gaskets.

11. A new clutch disc should be immersed in fluid for more than two hours before installation.

12. When replacing a bushing replace the complete bushing assembly.

## Disassembly

### Disassembly of Unit

1. Remove the torque converter.

2. Measure and record the input shaft end play. Attach the dial indicator to the converter housing and adjust it to measure input shaft end play.

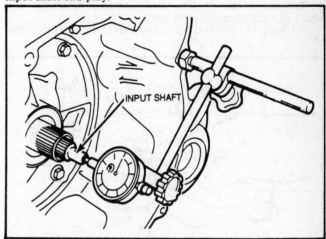

**Measure input shaft end play** (© Chrysler Corp.)

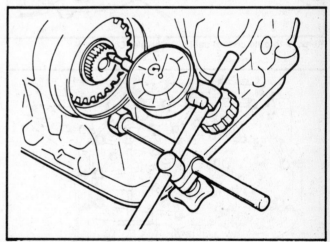

**Measure transfer shaft end play** (© Chrysler Corp.)

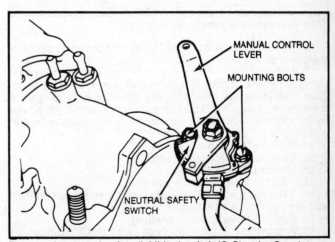

**Remove the neutral safety (inhibitor) switch** (© Chrysler Corp.)

7-21

3. Remove the transfer shaft cover holder and cover.

4. Measure and record the transfer shaft end play.

5. Remove the manual control lever and then the neutral safety switch.

6. Take out 13 bolts to remove the converter housing.

7. Remove the oil pan and gasket.

8. Remove the oil filter.

9. Disconnect the throttle control cable from the throttle cam which is attached to the valve body.

10. Unbolt 11 valve body assembly bolts and remove the valve body.

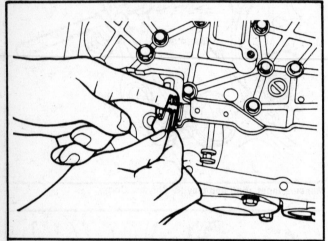

**Remove throttle control cable** (© Chrysler Corp.)

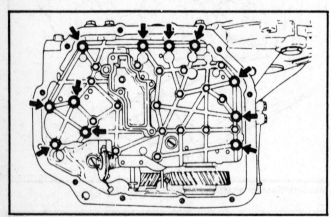

**Valve body mounting bolts** (© Chrysler Corp.)

11. Set the transmission on the bench, with the input shaft facing upwards.

12. Remove the six oil pump mounting bolts. Screw the special pump remover tool bolts into the two oil pump removing holes. Turn both removers simultaneously and uniformly to remove the oil pump assembly. If the pump moves to the side of the two tools, tap the case lightly on that side or tilt the remover tools to compensate for their off center position.

13. Remove the oil pump gasket.

14. Take out the differential assembly.

15. Detach the fiber thrust washers.

16. Remove the front clutch assembly.

17. Take out the one fiber washer, two metal thrust washers and the caged needle bearing.

18. Remove the rear clutch assembly.

19. Remove the thrust washer and caged needle bearing.

20. Lift out the clutch hub.

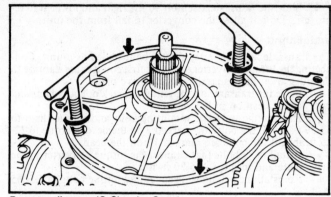

**Remove oil pump** (© Chrysler Corp.)

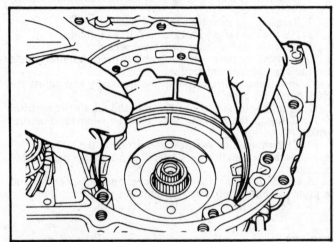

**Remove kickdown band** (© Chrysler Corp.)

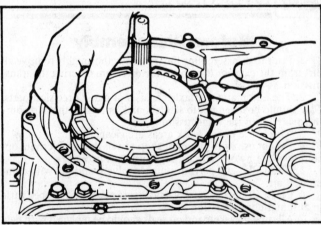

**Remove front clutch** (© Chrysler Corp.)

21. Take out the next two thrust washers and the needle bearing.

22. Remove the kickdown drum.

23. Take out the kickdown band.

24. Remove the kickdown servo cover snap ring.

25. Pull out the kickdown servo cover.

26. Using special tool, servo spring compressor (MD998303 or equivalent), push in the kickdown servo and remove the snap ring.

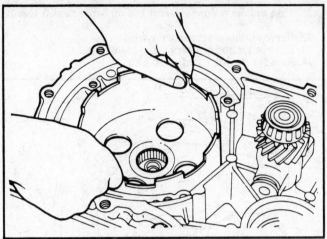

**Remove kickdown drum** (© Chrysler Corp.)

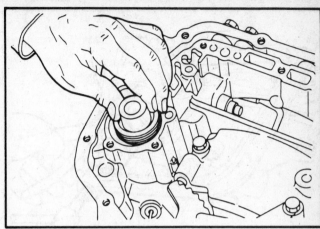

**Remove accumulator** (© Chrysler Corp.)

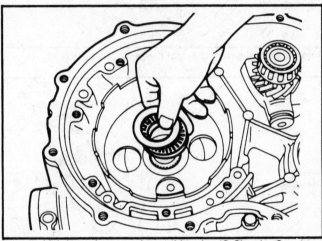

**Remove kickdown drum  washer and bearing** (© Chrysler Corp.)

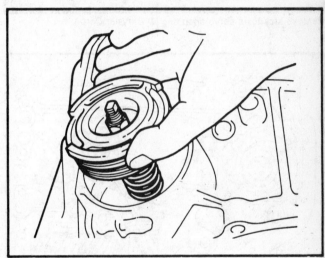

**Remove kickdown servo** (© Chrysler Corp.)

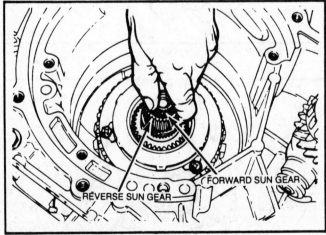

FORWARD SUN GEAR

REVERSE SUN GEAR

**Remove sun gears** (© Chrysler Corp.)

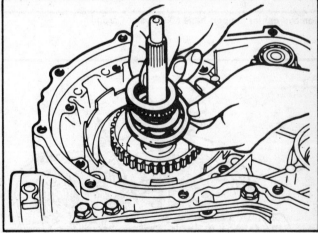

**Remove rear clutch thrust washers** (© Chrysler Corp.)

27. Remove the kickdown servo piston, sleeve, and spring.

── **CAUTION** ──

*Do not turn transaxle upside down as planetary thrust washers could fall out of place.*

28. Remove accumulator piston and spring from transmission case.

29. Remove two center support bolts.

30. Attach special tool, center support remover and installer, to the center support. Holding the handle of the tool, pull out the center support straight upward.

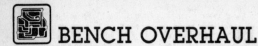

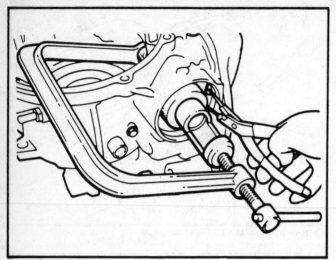

**Remove kickdown servo snap ring** (© Chrysler Corp.)

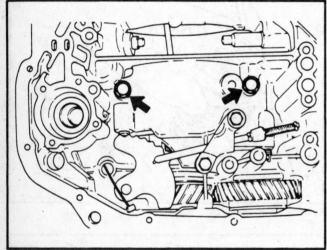

**Remove center support bolts** (© Chrysler Corp.)

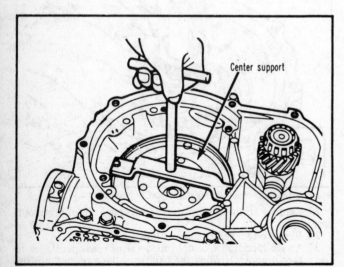

Center support

**Remove center support** (© Chrysler Corp.)

31. Take out the reverse sun gear and forward sun gear together.
32. Remove the planet carrier assembly.
33. Lift out the thrust bearing and thrust race.
34. Remove the idler shaft lock plate.

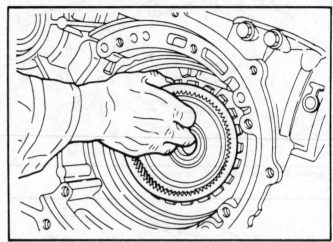

**Remove internal gear and output flange** (© Chrysler Corp.)

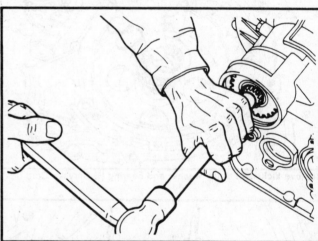

**Remove transfer shaft** (© Chrysler Corp.)

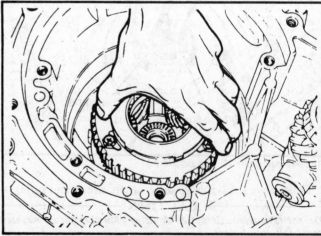

**Remove planet carrier** (© Chrysler Corp.)

35. Using special tool, wrench adapter (MD998344 or equivalent) loosen the transfer idler shaft.

36. Draw out the transfer idler shaft. Remove the transfer idler gear, bearing inner races (2 pieces), and spacer from inside the case. Use special tool L-4518 or equivalent to remove each bearing outer race. Use special tool C-4628 with handle C-4171 (or equivalent) to install each bearing outer race.

37. Remove the bearing retainer.

38. Remove the snap ring from the bearing.

39. Draw out the internal (ring) gear, output flange, transfer drive gear, and bearing as an assembly, from the case.

40. Remove the transfer shaft rear end snap ring.

41. Using a brass drift on the rear end of the transfer shaft, drive out the transfer shaft toward the engine mounting surface. The transfer driven gear comes off.

42. Remove the snap ring from the transmission case, then remove the taper roller bearing inner and outer races.

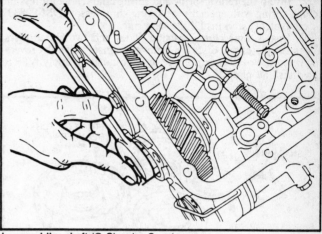

Loosen idler shaft (© Chrysler Corp.)

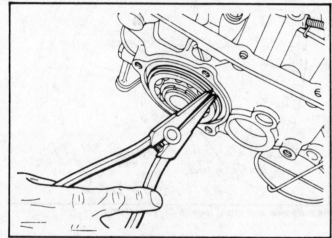

Remove bearing snap ring (© Chrysler Corp.)

# Unit Disassembly and Assembly
## FRONT CLUTCH

### Disassembly and Assembly

1. Remove the snap ring, then remove three clutch reaction plates and two clutch discs. When the clutch reaction plates and clutch discs are to be reused, keep the order and direction of their installation straight.

2. With the return spring compressed with special tool, spring compressor (MD-998337 or equivalent), remove the snap ring, then the spring retainer and return spring.

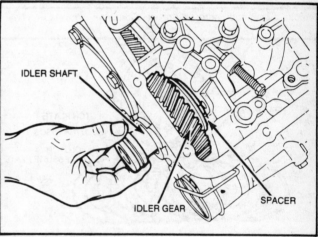

Remove transfer idler gear (© Chrysler Corp.)

3. Remove the piston.

4. Remove the D-section rings from the outside of the piston and the front clutch retainer.

5. Install the D-section ring in the groove in the outside surface of the piston with its round side out. Install another D-section ring to the front clutch retainer.

6. With ATF applied to the surface of the D-section rings, push the piston into the front clutch retainer by hand.

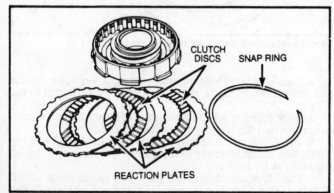

Remove reaction clutches (© Chrysler Corp.)

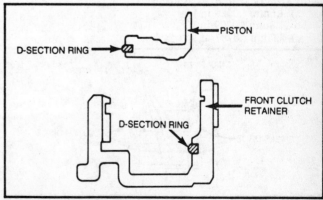

Install D-section rings (© Chrysler Corp.)

7. Install the return spring and spring retainer. Compress the return spring with special tool, spring compressor (DM-998337 or equivalent), and install the snap ring.

8. Install three clutch reaction plates and two clutch discs. When the plates and discs are removed, reinstall them by reversing the order of disassembly. Prior to installation apply ATF to the discs and plates.

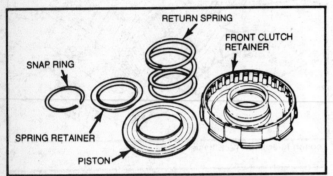

**Remove piston and spring** (© Chrysler Corp.)

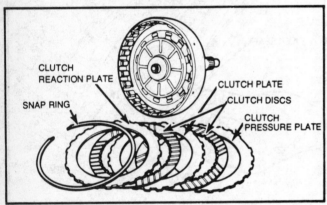

**Remove clutch discs** (© Chrysler Corp.)

— CAUTION —

*When new clutch discs are used, they should be soaked in ATF for more than two hours before installation.*

9. After installing the snap ring, check to see if there is a 0.4-0.6mm (.0156-.0234 in.) clearance between the snap ring and the clutch reaction plate. To check clearance, hold the entire clutch reaction plate down with 11 lbs. of force. If the clearance is out of specification, select a snap ring for correct clearance.

10. Sizes of snap rings available:
    a) 1.6mm (.0629 in.)
    b) 1.8mm (.0709 in.)
    c) 2.0mm (.0787 in.)

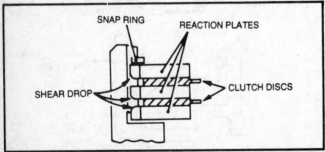

**Install front clutches** (© Chrysler Corp.)

d) 2.2mm (.0866 in.)
e) 2.4mm (.0945 in.)
f) 2.6mm (.1024 in.)
g) 2.8mm (.1102 in.)
h) 3.0mm (.1181 in.)

## REAR CLUTCH

### Disassembly and Assembly

1. Remove the snap ring. Remove the clutch reaction plate, two clutch discs, clutch plate, and clutch pressure plate.

2. After removing the seal ring, remove the snap ring and then remove the thrust race.

3. Using an appropriate pry bar, remove the waved spring.

4. Remove the return spring and piston.

5. Remove two D-section rings from the piston.

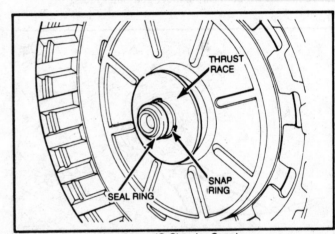

**Remove seal and thrust race** (© Chrysler Corp.)

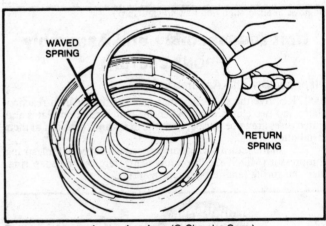

**Remove return and waved springs** (© Chrysler Corp.)

6. Install the new D-section rings in the grooves in the outside and inside surfaces of the piston (rounded edge of D-ring to the outside).

7. After applying ATF to the outside of piston and seals, push the piston into the rear clutch retainer by hand.

8. Install the return spring, then compress the return spring with the waved snap ring by pushing down and seating the waved snap ring in its groove.

9. Install the clutch pressure plate, two clutch discs, clutch plate, and clutch reaction plate to the rear clutch retainer. When reaction plate, clutch plate, and clutch discs are removed, rein-

stall them by reversing the order of disassembly. Prior to installing, apply ATF to plates and discs.

### CAUTION

*When new clutch discs are used, soak them in ATF for more than two hours before installation.*

10. Install the snap ring. Check to see that the clearance between the snap ring and the clutch reaction plate is 0.3-0.5mm (.0118-.020 in.). To check the clearance, hold the entire clutch reaction plate down with 11 lbs. of force. If the clearance is out of specifications, adjust it by selecting the proper size snap ring. The snap rings are common to those used for the front clutch.

11. Install the thrust race, then the snap ring. Always use a new seal ring.

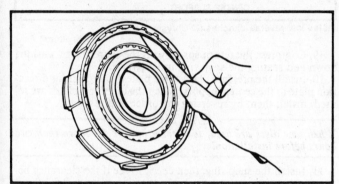

**Measure snap ring to reaction plate clearance** (© Chrysler Corp.)

## OIL PUMP

### Disassembly and Assembly

1. Remove the five bolts to separate the pump housing from the reaction shaft support.

2. Take the oil pump drive and driven gears from the pump housing. When the gears are to be reused, draw mating marks (with a felt pen) on the side surfaces of the gears so that they can be reinstalled in their original positions.

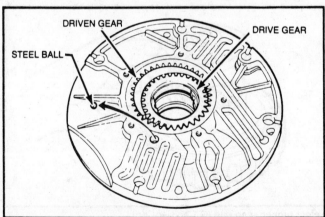

**Remove oil pump drive gear** (© Chrysler Corp.)

3. Remove the steel ball from the pump housing.
4. Take the two seal rings out of the reaction shaft support.
5. Using an appropriate tool pry out the pump housing oil seal.
6. Using special tool (MD-998334 or equivalent) install the oil seal to the pump housing. Apply a thin coat of transmission fluid to the oil seal lip before installation.

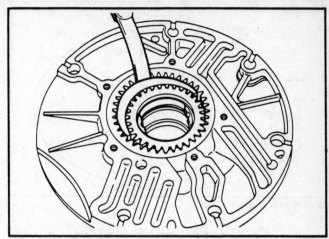

**Measure oil pump clearance** (© Chrysler Corp.)

7. After coating the drive and driven gears with transmission fluid, install them in the pump housing. When reusing the gears, install them with the mating marks properly aligned.

8. Measure the following clearances:

| | |
|---|---|
| a. Driven gear O.D.-to-housing clearance | 0.08-0.15mm .0031-.0059 in. |
| b. Driven gear tooth top-to-crescent clearance | 0.11-0.24mm .0043-.0094 in. |
| c. Driven gear side clearance | 0.025-0.05mm .001-.002 in. |
| d. Drive gear tooth top-to-crescent clearance | 0.22-0.34mm .0087-.0118 in. |
| e. Drive gear side clearance | 0.025-0.05mm .001-.002 in. |

9. Put the steel ball in the 9mm (.354 in.) diameter hole in the pump housing.

10. Install two seal rings coated with ATF to the reaction support shaft.

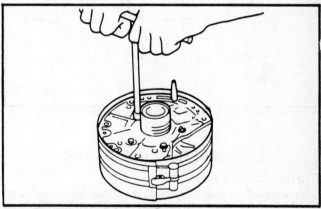

**Assemble oil pump** (© Chrysler Corp.)

11. Temporarily install the reaction shaft support on the pump housing. Tighten the five bolts fingertight.

12. With the reaction shaft support properly positioned on the pump housing using special tools, oil pump band (C-3759 or equivalent) and guide pin (MD-998336 or equivalent), torque the five bolts to 7.5-8.5 ft. lbs.

13. Make sure that the oil pump gear turns freely.

14. Install a new O-ring in the groove provided in the outer edge of the pump housing. Before installing apply petroleum jelly on the O-ring.

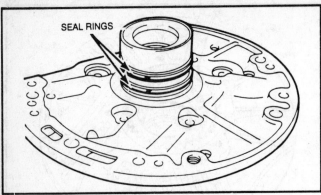

Remove seal rings (© Chrysler Corp.)

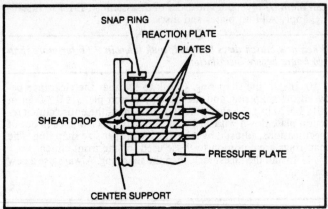

Install low-reverse clutches (© Chrysler Corp.)

## KICKDOWN SERVO PISTON

### Disassembly and Assembly

1. Remove the jam nut and the adjusting screw.
2. Remove the sleeve and the piston, removing the O-ring from the sleeve and the D-rings from the piston.
3. Apply ATF to the new D-rings and the O-ring.
4. Install new D-rings to the piston and a new O-ring to the sleeve.
5. Install the piston into the sleeve, then insert the adjusting screw into the piston and screw the jam nut on to secure the unit.

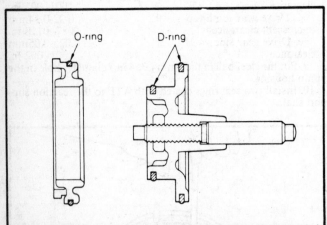

Kickdown servo piston assembly (© Mitsubishi Motors Corp.)

## LOW AND REVERSE BRAKE

### Disassembly and Assembly

1. Remove the snap ring. Remove the brake reaction plate, four discs, three plates, and pressure plate. Keep the discs and plates in order for purposes of reassembly.
2. Using an appropriate pry bar, remove the snap ring.
3. Remove the return spring and waved spring.
4. Remove the piston. If the piston is hard to remove, place the center support on the bench with the piston side down, and blow air into the oil passage to force the piston out.
5. Remove the D-section rings from the piston.
6. Install new D-section rings on the piston with rounded side of each seal directed to the outside.
7. Apply ATF to the piston and rings, and install the piston into the center support by hand.
8. Install the waved spring and the return spring.

9. Compress the return spring with the snap ring by pushing down and seating the snap ring in its groove.
10. Install the pressure plate, three plates, four discs, and reaction plate to the center support. When the discs and plates are reused, install them by reversing the order of diassembly.

---
### CAUTION

*When new discs are used, soak them in AFT for more than two hours before installation.*

---

11. Install the snap ring, then check to see if the clearance between the snap ring and the brake reaction plate is 0.8-1.0mm (.0315-.0394 in.). To check the clearance, hold the entire clutch reaction plate down with 11 lbs. force. If the clearance is out of specification, adjust by selecting a proper size snap ring.
12. Sizes of snap rings available:
   a) 1.6mm (.0629 in.).
   b) 1.8mm (.0709 in.).
   c) 2.0mm (.0787 in.).
   d) 2.2mm (.0866 in.).
   e) 2.4mm (.0945 in.).
   f) 2.6mm (.1024 in.).
   g) 2.8mm (.1102 in.).
   h) 3.0mm (.1181 in.).

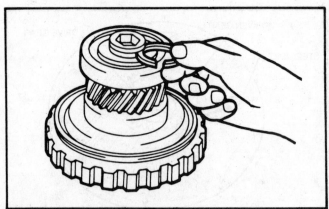

Select proper snap ring (© Chrysler Corp.)

## PLANET CARRIER ASSEMBLY

### Disassembly and Assembly

1. Pry the tabs of the stopper plate straight to remove the stopper plate.
2. Remove two bearing end plates and the overrunning clutch.

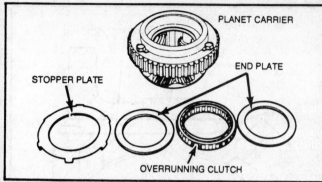

**Disassemble overrunning clutch** (© Chrysler Corp.)

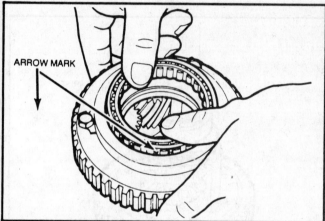

**Install overrunning clutch** (© Chrysler Corp.)

3. Prior to installing the overrunning clutch, check the sprag, ribbon spring, and the outer race, for damage.
4. Insert the end plate into the carrier assembly.
5. Press the overrunning clutch into the carrier assembly, in the direction of the arrow stamped on the outside surface of the cage.
6. Install the end plate.
7. Install the stopper plate, then bend the tabs to secure the stopper plate to the planet carrier.

## INTERNAL GEAR AND TRANSFER DRIVE GEAR

### Disassembly and Assembly

1. Remove the snap ring from the rear end of the output flange.
2. Using special tool, bearing and gear puller (MD-998348 or its equivalent) pull off the ball bearings and remove the transfer drive gear from the output flange.

**Removal of snap ring from internal gear** (© Mitsubishi Motors Corp.)

3. Remove the snap ring and separate the internal gear from the output flange.
4. Using special tool (MD-998349 or its equivalent) press fit the two ball bearings and the transfer drive gear onto the output flange.

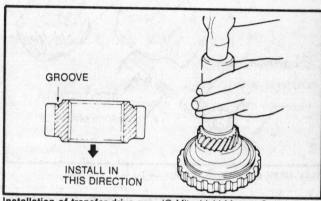

**Installation of transfer drive gear** (© Mitsubishi Motors Corp.)

— CAUTION —
*Replace the output flange and the transfer drive gear as a set.*

5. Install transfer drive gear in the proper direction with attention paid to groove on the side of the gear surface.
6. Select a snap ring, that will be the thickest one that can be installed in the groove.

## TRANSFER SHAFT AND GOVERNOR

### Disassembly and Assembly

1. Remove three seal rings.
2. Loosen the governor set screws to remove the governor assembly.
3. Remove the snap ring, and disassemble the governor into governor weight, spring retainer, governor valve and governor spring.

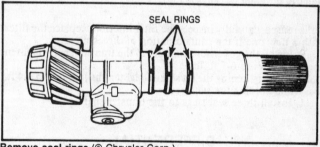

**Remove seal rings** (© Chrysler Corp.)

4. Pull off the governor filter. Replace the filter if clogged with dirt.
5. Use special tools, bearing puller (MD-998354 or its equivalent) and bearing installer (MD-998322 or its equivalent) to replace the taper roller bearing inner race assembly.

— CAUTION —
*Replace the taper roller bearing inner and outer races as a set.*

6. Install the taper roller bearing inner race assembly using special tool (MD-998322 or its equivalent).
7. Install the governor valve, spring, spring retainer, and governor weight to the governor body, then install the snap ring.
8. Install the governor filter. When the removed governor fil-

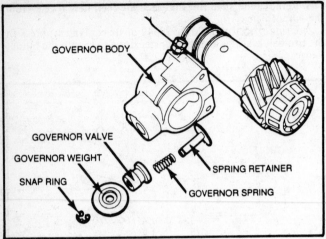

Disassemble governor (© Chrysler Corp.)

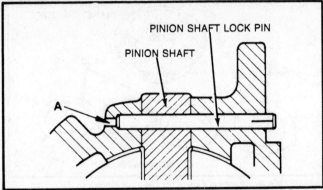

Removal location of pinion shaft lock pin (© Mitsubishi Motors Corp.)

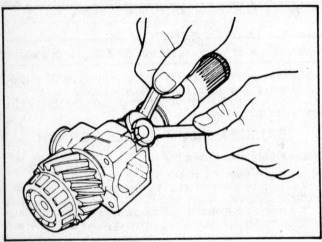

Remove governor (© Chrysler Corp.)

ter is reused, carefully inspect the filter interior. Replace the filter with a new one if the contamination of dirt is present.

9. Install the governor assembly to the transfer shaft. Tighten the set screws to 6-7 ft. lbs.

10. After tightening the set screws, tighten the jam nut to 3-4 ft. lbs. while holding the set screw.

11. Install three seal rings to the transfer shaft.

## DIFFERENTIAL

### Disassembly and Assembly

1. Using special tool (MD-998329 or its equivalent) remove the ball bearings from the differential.

2. Using a punch, drive out the pinion shaft lock pin.

3. Remove the pinion shaft, then remove the pinion gear and the washer.

4. Remove the eight bolts and lock washers from the differential drive gear and remove the drive gear.

5. Press ball bearings in both ends of the differential housing.

NOTE: When pressing the bearings, apply the load to the inner race. Do not apply load to outer race.

6. Install spacer to the back of each side gear and install the side gears in the differential housing. When reusing the side gears and the spacers, be sure that they are in their original position.

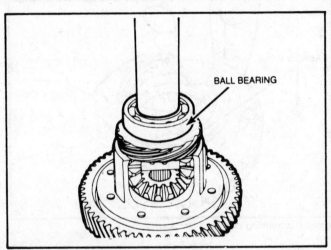

Install ball bearing (© Chrysler Corp.)

NOTE: If using new differential side gears, install spacers of medium thickness 1.0-0.07mm (0.039-0.003 in.).

7. Put a washer on the back of the pinion gear and install the pinion gear. Turn the pinion gear to bring it into mesh with the side gears.

8. Insert the pinion shaft.

9. Measure the backlash between the side gear and the pinion gear. The backlash should be 0-0.076mm (0-.0030 in.), and the right and left-hand gear pairs should have an equal backlash. If

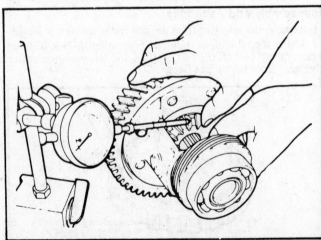

Measure backlash (pinion-to-side gear) (© Chrysler Corp.)

the backlash is out of specification disassemble the gears and re-assemble them using the spacers selected for correct backlash.

10. Install the pinion shaft lock pin, and after installation check to see that projection of the lock pin is less than 3mm (0.118 in.).

**NOTE: Do not reuse the lock pin, install a new lock pin at reassembly.**

11. Install differential drive gear.
12. After applying ATF to their threads, temporarily tighten down the drive gear bolts.
13. Torque the drive gear bolts to 47-54 ft. lbs. in the sequence shown below.

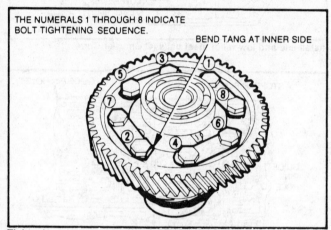

THE NUMERALS 1 THROUGH 8 INDICATE BOLT TIGHTENING SEQUENCE.

BEND TANG AT INNER SIDE

**Tightening sequence (drive gear bolts)** (© Chrysler Corp.)

## VALVE BODY

### Disassembly and Assembly

**NOTE: Do not place any parts of the valve body or the transfer plate in a vise or any other form of clamp. The slightest distortion of the valve body or the transfer plate will cause sticking valves, excessive leakage or both.**

1. Remove the throttle cam assembly.
2. Remove the 13 bolts (one is shorter) to separate the transfer plate and separating plate from the valve body.
3. Take off the stiffener plate, then the separating plate. Remove the two steel balls and two springs.
4. Remove the manual valve.
5. Remove the kickdown valve, throttle valve and two springs.
6. Remove two regulator plugs.

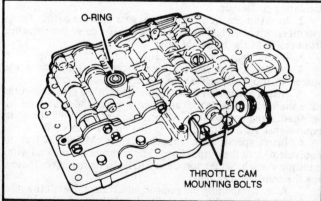

O-RING

THROTTLE CAM MOUNTING BOLTS

**Remove throttle cam** (© Chrysler Corp.)

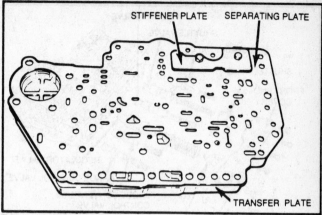

STIFFENER PLATE     SEPARATING PLATE

TRANSFER PLATE

**Remove stiffener plate** (© Chrysler Corp.)

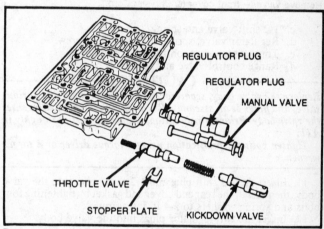

REGULATOR PLUG

REGULATOR PLUG

MANUAL VALVE

THROTTLE VALVE

STOPPER PLATE

KICKDOWN VALVE

**Remove valves** (© Chrysler Corp.)

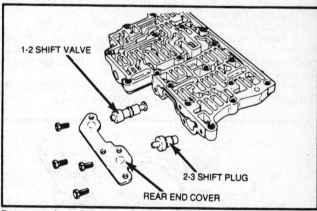

1-2 SHIFT VALVE

2-3 SHIFT PLUG

REAR END COVER

**Remove valves—rear cover** (© Chrysler Corp.)

7. Take off the rear end cover and gasket.
8. Pull out the 1-2 shift valve and the 2-3 shift plug.
9. Remove the front end cover. Remove each valve, spring and plug. Remove the shuttle valve after removal of the snap ring.
10. Install the valves, springs, and plugs shown below to the valve body. Then install the front end plate by tightening seven bolts to 3-4 ft. lbs.
   a. 2-3 shift valve and spring.
   b. Shuttle valve, spring, shuttle plug, and snap ring.

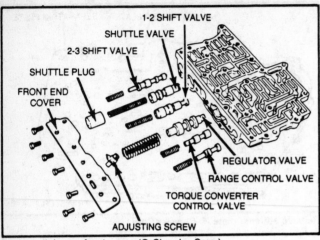

**Remove valves—front cover** (© Chrysler Corp.)

c. 1-2 shift valve and spring.
d. Regulator valve, spring, and adjusting screw.
e. Torque converter control valve and spring.
f. Range control valve and spring.

— CAUTION —

*Replace the valve body, separator plate, transfer plate and various valves and plugs as an assembly. Be careful that no impurities enter the valve body. Prior to installation, wash each part thoroughly in ATF.*

*Tighten bolts to specification using a torque driver or a torque wrench.*

11. Insert the 2-3 shift plug and 1-2 shift valve into the valve body, then install the rear end cover and gasket by tightening four bolts and spring washers to 2-4 ft. lbs. torque.
12. Insert the two regulator plugs into the valve body.
13. Insert the manual valve into the valve body.
14. Place the kickdown spring, throttle valve, throttle spring, and kickdown valve into the valve body. Install the stopper plate to the position next to the guide pin hole.
15. Install four steel balls in the valve body.
16. Install the line relief and low relief steel balls and springs to the transfer plate. For spring identification see the spring identification table. The four steel balls are identical to those installed in the valve body.
17. Insert two guide pins special tools (MD-998266 or equivalent) into the transfer plate guide pin holes.

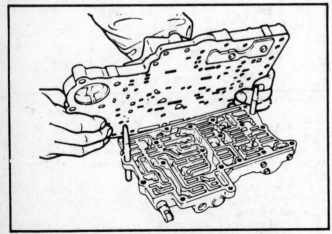

**Assemble transfer plate and valve body** (© Chrysler Corp.)

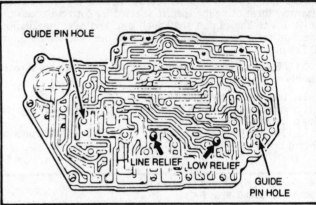

**Install line and low-relief steel balls** (© Chrysler Corp.)

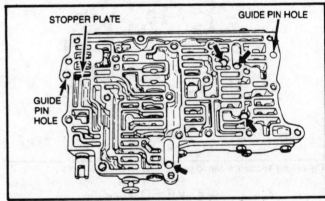

**Stopper plate and steel ball location** (© Chrysler Corp.)

18. Using the guide pins to align the plates, install the separator plate.
19. Install the stiffener plate, and then temporarily tighten two bolts. Pull off pin.
20. Insert two guide pins (MD-998266 or equivalent) into guide pin holes in the valve body. Using the guide pins as a guide, install the transfer plate and separating plate as a unit to the valve body.
21. Torque the 19 bolts (one shorter) to 3-4 ft. lbs.

## Reassembly

### Assembly of Unit

1. Place the transaxle case on the bench with the oil pan mounting surface up.
2. Insert in position the internal gear and the output flange assembly, with two ball bearings and transfer drive gear attached from inside of the transaxle case.
3. Install snap ring on the output flange rear bearing.
4. Install the two bearing outer races, two inner races and spacer, in proper directions, to the transfer idler gear.
5. Install assembled transfer idler gear in the case. Insert the idler shaft from outside the case, then screw in and tighten the idler shaft using special tool, wrench adapter (MD-998344 or its equivalent). Also install a new O-ring on the idler shaft.
6. Insert special tool, wrench adapter (MD-998343 or its equivalent) into the output flange and measure the preload using a torque wrench. Set the torque at 1 ft. lb. by tightening or loosening the transfer idler shaft.
7. After completing the preload adjustment, install the idler shaft lock plate. Tighten the lock plate bolt to 15-19 ft. lbs. of torque.

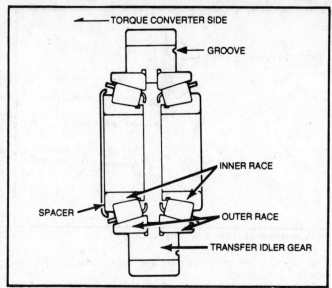

**Direction to install transfer idler gear** (© Chrysler Corp.)

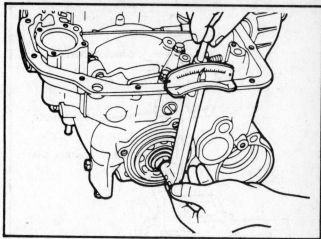

**Preload adjustment** (© Chrysler Corp.)

8. Install a new O-ring in the groove in the rear end of the transaxle case (output flange area).

9. Install the transfer shaft bearing retainer and tighten the three bolts to 11-15 ft. lbs.

10. Insert transfer shaft (with governor and taper bearing inner race) into the case.

11. Install special tool, transfer shaft retainer (MD-998351 or its equivalent) to the converter mating surface of the transaxle case.

12. Using special tool, bearing installer (MD998350 or equivalent), fit the bearing inner race on the transfer shaft.

13. Install the taper roller bearing outer race, then install the snap ring.

14. Using special tool, bearing installer (MD998350 or equivalent), install the transfer driven gear on the transfer shaft.

15. Install the snap ring to the end of the transfer shaft. Turn the transaxle so that the engine side is up.

16. Apply petroleum jelly to the thrust race and affix it to the output flange.

17. After attaching the thrust races and needle roller bearings to the front and rear of the planet carrier assembly, install the assembly, being careful not to drop the bearings out of place.

18. After attaching the thrust bearing to the forward sun gear

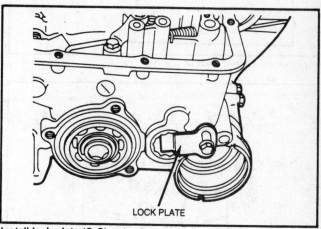

**Install lock plate** (© Chrysler Corp.)

with petroleum jelly, assemble the forward sun gear with the reverse sun gear, and then install both sun gears in the planet carrier assembly.

19. Check the position of the tooth area of the reverse sun gear to see that it is nearly level with the planet gear long pinion.

20. Attach special tool, center support remover and installer (MD998340 or equivalent) to the center support.

21. Apply ATF to the overrunning clutch inner race fitting area of the center support. Insert the center support (low and reverse brake) assembly into the case by holding the handle of the tool.

22. Install the two center support locking bolts. Tighten the bolts to 15-19 ft. lbs. while pressing the center support firmly with about 22 lbs. of pressure.

— CAUTION —

*Do not turn transaxle upside down as planetary gearset thrust washers could fall out of place.*

23. Install special tool (MD-998345 or its equivalent) to retain reverse sun gear firmly.

24. Insert the manual control shaft into the transaxle case and push it fully toward the manual control lever. At this time, do not install the O-ring (larger of two) on the manual control shaft. If the O-ring is installed before inserting the shaft, it can be damaged by the set screw hole.

25. Install the new O-ring on the manual shaft from the outside of the case. Draw the shaft back into the case and install the

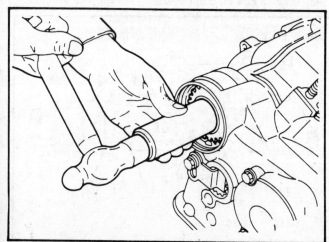

**Install transfer driven gear** (© Chrysler Corp.)

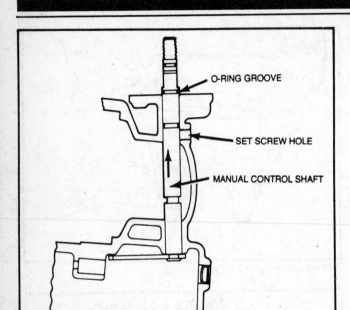

Install manual control shaft (© Chrysler Corp.)

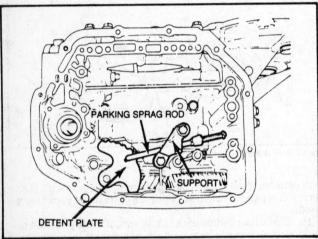

Install parking sprag rod (© Chrysler Corp.)

set screw and gasket. Also install the detent steel ball and spring at this time.

26. Place the case with oil pan mounting surface up.

27. Install the parking sprag rod to the detent plate (manual control shaft).

28. Install the sprag rod support and torque the two bolts to 15-19 ft. lbs.

29. Install the accumulator piston and spring.

30. Install the O-ring at the center of the top of the valve body assembly (low-reverse brake passage).

31. Install the valve body assembly to the case, fitting the detent plate (manual control shaft) pin in the slot of the manual valve.

32. Torque the valve body bolts (11 pieces) to 7.5-8.5 ft. lbs. (one bolt is shorter).

33. Firmly install the throttle control assembly into the transaxle case.

34. Connect the throttle control cable inner cable to the throttle cam.

35. Install the oil filter. Torque bolts to 4-5 ft. lbs.

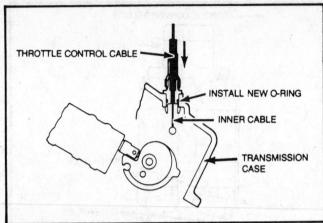

Install throttle control cable (© Chrysler Corp.)

36. Install a new oil pan gasket and the oil pan. Torque the bolts to 7.5-8.5 ft. lbs.

37. Place the case with converter housing mounting surface up.

38. Install the kickdown servo spring, piston and sleeve into the transaxle case. Install one large and one small new D-section ring on the piston and a new O-ring in the groove of the sleeve before installation into the case.

39. Using a special tool, servo spring compressor (MD-998303 or its equivalent), push in the kickdown servo piston and sleeve, then install the snap ring.

40. Install the kickdown band; attach the ends of the band to the ends of the anchor rod and servo piston adjusting screw.

41. Install the kickdown drum with its splines in mesh with the reverse sun gear. Place the kickdown band on the kickdown drum and tighten the kickdown servo adjusting screw to keep the band in position.

42. Apply petroleum jelly to the thrust races and thrust bearings and attach them to the kickdown drum.

43. Attach the thrust races with petroleum jelly to both ends of the clutch hub. Attach the thrust bearing to the engine side thrust race. Install the clutch hub to the forward sun gear splines.

44. Install the rear clutch assembly.

45. Attach the plastic thrust washer with petroleum jelly to the rear clutch retainer. Next, attach the thrust race and thrust bearing with petroleum jelly, to the rear clutch retainer.

46. Install the front clutch assembly.

47. Install the differential assembly.

48. Install a new oil pump gasket.

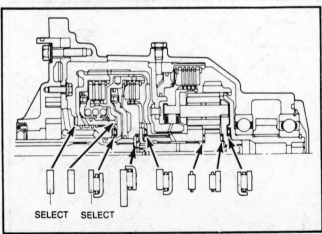

Location of thrust bearings, races and washers (© Chrysler Corp.)

49. Attach the fiber thrust washer with petroleum jelly to the rear end of the oil pump assembly. If the end play which was measured and recorded at the time of disassembly is out of specifications, bring the end play into specification by using the proper size thrust washer and race. Install the correct size thrust race and washer in pairs.

50. When the thrust race is replaced with a race of a different thickness, also replace the thrust washer located between the oil pump and the front clutch. Be sure to use a thrust washer of the proper thickness corresponding to the thrust race.

51. Attach the thrust washer to the front clutch.

52. Install a new O-ring in the groove of the oil pump housing, and apply ATF lightly on the outside surface of the O-ring.

53. Install the oil pump assembly by tightening the six bolts evenly to 11-15 ft. lbs. When installing this oil pump assembly, be careful that the thrust washer will not drop.

54. Prior to installation of the converter housing, make certain that transfer shaft end play measured and recorded at the time of disassembly is the same. If the measurement is out of specification, pull off the taper roller bearing outer race from the converter housing, and replace the spacer with a spacer that will correct the end play. Transfer shaft end play should fall between 0.025mm (0.0010 in.) tight and loose.

55. Place spacer on the differential bearing outer race.

56. Install a new transaxle case gasket on the case.

57. Install the converter housing and torque the 13 bolts to 14-16 ft. lbs.

58. Check the input shaft for correct end play and also the transfer shaft end play and the differential case end play. Readjust if it is necessary.
   a. Input shaft end play—0.5-1.4mm (0.020-0.055 in.)
   b. Transfer shaft end play—0.025mm (0.0010 in.) tight or loose.
   c. Differential end play—0-0.15mm (0-0.006 in.)

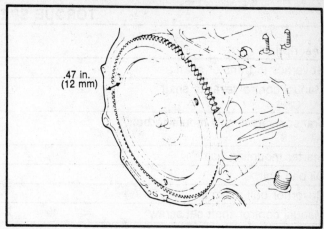

.47 in. (12 mm)

**Install torque converter** (© Mitsubishi Motors Corp.)

59. Install transfer shaft cover, then the cover holder.

60. Using special tool, oil seal installer (MD-998325 or its equivalent), drive two drive shaft oil seals into the transaxle case and converter housing.

61. Install the neutral (inhibitor) safety switch and the manual lever. Adjust the neutral safety switch (see Adjustments).

62. After applying ATF to the outside surface of the oil pump-side cylindrical portion of the torque converter, install the torque converter carefully so as not to damage the oil seal lip. Make certain the torque converter is in mesh with the oil pump drive gear. Measure the distance betwen the ring gear end to the converter housing end. The torque converter has been properly installed when the measurement is about 12mm (0.47 in.).

# S SPECIFICATIONS

## TORQUE SPECIFICATIONS

| Description | Head Mark | Torque N•m (ft-lbs.) |
|---|---|---|
| Drive plate to ring gear | — | 35-41 (26-30) |
| Transaxle to engine | 7 | 43-53 (32-39) |
| | 10 | 30-34 (22-25) |
| Bell housing cover | 7 | 10-11.5 (7.5-8.5) |
| Drain plug on transaxle case | — | 30-34 (22-25) |
| Drain plug on oil pan | — | 25-29 (18-21) |
| Pressure check plug | — | 8-9.5 (6-7) |
| Bearing retainer to transaxle case | 7 | 15-21 (11-15) |
| Oil cooler connector | — | 15-21 (11-15) |
| Converter housing to transaxle case | 7 | 19-22 (14-16) |
| Oil pan to transaxle case | 7 | 10-11.5 (7.5-8.5) |
| Kickdown servo | — | 15-21 (11-15) |
| Center support to transaxle case | 8 | 20-26 (15-19) |
| Lock plate to transaxle case | 7 | 20-26 (15-19) |
| Differential drive gear to differential case | 10 | 64-73 (47-54) |

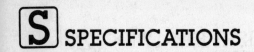 

## TORQUE SPECIFICATIONS

| Description | Head Mark | Torque N•m (ft-lbs.) |
|---|---|---|
| Governor to transfer shaft | 7 | 8-9.5 (6-7) |
| Manual control lever to shaft | — | 4-5.5 (3-4) |
| | — | 17-20 (13-15) |
| Transaxle assembly mounting bolt | 7 | 43-53 (32-39) |
| | 10 | 30-34 (22-25) |
| Starter mounting bolt | — | 22-32 (16-23) |
| Oil pan bolt | — | 10-11 (7.5-8.5) |
| Governor bolt locknut | — | 4.0-5.5 (3-4) |
| Manual control shaft set screw | — | 8-9.5 (6-7) |
| Inhibitor switch to transaxle case | 7 | 10-11.5 (7.5-8.5) |
| Sprag rod support to transmission case | 7 | 20-26 (15-19) |
| Oil pump housing to reaction shaft support | 7 | 10-11.5 (7.5-8.5) |
| Oil pump assembly to transmission case | 7 | 15-21 (11-15) |
| End plate to valve body | 7 | 4-5.5 (3-4) |
| Valve body to transfer plate | 7 | 4-5.5 (3-4) |
| Stiffener plate to transfer plate | — | 4-5.5 (3-4) |
| Throttle cam bracket to transfer plate | — | 4-5.5 (3-4) |
| Throttle cam to bracket | — | 8-9.5 (6-7) |
| Valve body assembly to transfer case | 7 | 10-11.5 (7.5-8.5) |
| Oil filter to transfer plate | 7 | 5-6.5 (4-5) |
| Speedometer gear sleeve locking plate to converter housing | 4 | 3-4.5 (2.5-3.5) |

## AUTOMATIC SHIFT SPEEDS CHART
### KM-171, 172 Automatic Transaxles

| Throttle Position | Gear Shift | Vehicle Speed |
|---|---|---|
| Minimum | 1-2 upshift | 7-12 MPH |
| | 2-3 upshift | 11-14 MPH |
| | 3-1 downshift | 6-9  MPH |
| Wide Open | 1-2 upshift | 27-24 MPH |
| | 2-3 upshift | 54-60 MPH |
| Wide Open Throttle Kickdown | 3-2 downshift | 49-56 MPH |
| Part Throttle Kickdown | 3-2 downshift | 32-40 MPH |
| Wide Open Throttle Kickdown | 3-1 downshift | 24-29 MPH |

## SELECT RACE AND WASHER CHART
### Input Shaft End Play ①

| Symbol | Thickness mm (in.) | Part number |
|--------|--------------------|-----------|
| **THRUST WASHER (FIBER)** | | |
| K | 1.8 (.071) | MD707290 |
| L | 2.2 (.087) | MD707291 |
| M | 2.6 (.102) | MD707292 |
| N | 3.0 (.118) | MD707293 |
| **THRUST RACE (METAL)** | | |
| E | 0.8 (.031) | MD707265 |
| F | 1.2 (.047) | MD707266 |
| G | 1.6 (.063) | MD707267 |
| H | 2.0 (.079) | MD707268 |

① Select in pairs (race and washer on the same line).

## SPRING IDENTIFICATION TABLE

| Location of Spring | O.D. mm (in.) | Free Length mm (in.) |
|--------------------|---------------|----------------------|
| Throttle | 9.5 (.374) | 32.4 (1.276) |
| Kickdown | 6.4 (.252) | 26.1 (1.028) |
| Torque converter control | 8.4 (.331) | 24.1 (0.949) |
| Range control | 8.4 (.331) | 24.1 (0.949) |
| Regulator | 15.4 (.606) | 51.4 (2.024) |
| 1-2 shift | 7.6 (.299) | 39.0 (1.535) |
| Shuttle | 6.6 (.260) | 59.5 (2.343) |
| 2-3 shift | 6.8 (.268) | 30.2 (1.189) |
| Low relief | 6.6 (.260) | 16.8 (0.661) |
| Line relief | 7.0 (.276) | 24.4 (0.961) |

## SPECIAL TOOLS

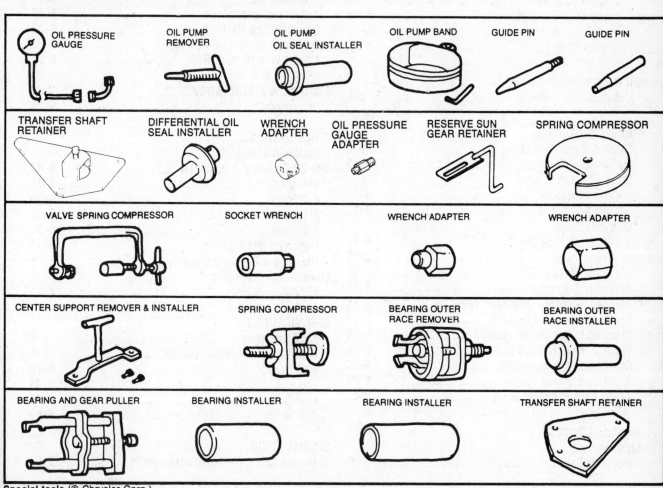

Special tools (© Chrysler Corp.)

# INDEX

# RENAULT MB1 • MJ Automatic Transaxle

##  APPLICATIONS

Model MB-1

Model MJ-1, 3

Renault Alliance

Renault 18 and 18i

Renault Fuego

##  GENERAL DESCRIPTION

The model MB-1 automatic transaxle and engine are mounted in a transverse position while the models MJ-1 and MJ-3 automatic transaxles are mounted in a longitudinal position in their respective vehicles. Each transaxle has three forward speeds and one reverse. The forward speeds are controlled in their upshifting and downshifting by mechanical, hydraulic and electrical controls.

### Transaxle and Converter Identification

#### TRANSAXLE

The identification plates, located under external bolt heads on both the MB and MJ transaxles, are stamped with information for the model and type, the type suffix and the fabrication (serial) number. The plates can be oval or rectangular in appearance.

#### CONVERTER

No known markings are present on the converters.

### Metric Fasteners

The transaxles are designed and assembled using metric fasteners. Metric measurements are used to determine clearances with-

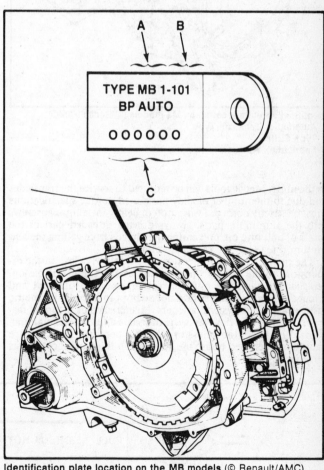

Identification plate location on the MB models (© Renault/AMC)
A-Automatic Transaxle Type
B-Type Suffix
C-Fabrication Number

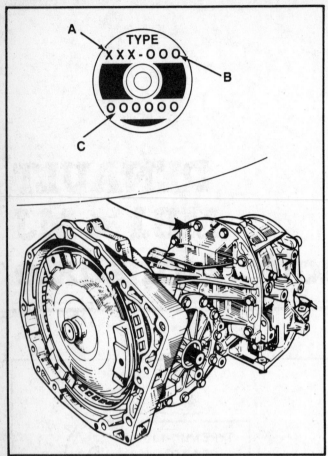

Identification plate location on MJ models (© Renault/AMC)
A-Automatic Transaxle Type
B-Type Suffix
C-Fabrication Number

## Fluid Capacities

| Transaxle Model | Car line | Dry Fill Qts. (Liter) | Refill Qts. (Liter) |
|---|---|---|---|
| MB-1 | Alliance | 4.5 (4.3) | 3.7 (3.5) |
| MJ-1, MJ-3 | 18, 18i, Fuego | 5.6 (5.3) | 3.7 (3.5) |

## RECOMMENDED CHANGE INTERVAL AND RECOMMENDED FLUID TYPE

The recommended change interval is 30,000 mile (48,000 KM) or every 24 month. The only fluid types recommended for the MB and MJ models are Dexron® II, Mobil 220 ATF or AMC/Jeep/Renault ATF. It is recommended by the manufacturer that AMC/Jeep/Renault ATF or Mobil 220 ATF be used as the initial fill for new replacement automatic transaxles of the MB and MJ models.

## Checking Fluid Levels

The automatic transaxle dipstick is located on the left side of the vehicle, in the engine compartment. Check the fluid level with the engine/transaxle at normal operating temperature and the engine idling. Have the vehicle on a level surface.

1. Remove the dipstick and determine the temperature of the fluid. Wipe the dipstick clean and reinsert it into the fill tube.
2. Remove the dipstick and read the indicated level of the fluid. Again, determine the temperature of the fluid.
3. If the dipstick is too hot to hold, the transaxle is at its normal operating temperature of 160°-170°F. (71°-77°C.) and the level should be between the ADD to FULL marks on the dipstick.
4. If the dipstick is warm, room temperature to 100°F. (38°C.). The fluid level should be in the ADD range of the dipstick.
5. Add enough transmission fluid to fill the transaxle to its proper level. With the transaxle at normal operating temperature, one-half pint of fluid is needed to raise the level from the ADD (B) mark to the FULL (A) mark. Do not overfill.

### Precautions

**Overfilling of the transaxle can cause any of the following:**
    a. Foaming of the fluid.
    b. Loss of fluid.
    c. Damage to the transaxle.

**Low fluid level can cause the following:**
    a. Slipping of the transaxle internal components.
    b. Loss of drive.
    c. Damage to the transaxle.

**The correct fluid level cannot be obtained if:**
    a. The vehicle has been driven for a long period of time at high speed.
    b. The vehicle has been driven in city traffic in hot weather for a long period of time.
    c. The vehicle has stopped after towing a trailer and the fluid is immediately checked.

in the units. Metric tools will be required to service the transaxles and due to the number of alloy parts used, torque specifications must be strictly observed when noted. Before installing capscrews into the aluminum parts, always dip the threaded part of the screw or bolt into oil, preventing the threads from galling the aluminum threads in the case and components.

The metric fastener dimensions are extremely close to the dimensions of the familiar inch system fasteners. For this reason, replacement fasteners must have the same measurement and strength as those removed. Do not attempt to interchange metric fasteners for inch system fasteners. Mismatched or incorrect fasteners can result in damage to the transaxle unit through malfunctions, breakage, looseness or possible personal injury. Care should be exercised to use the fasteners in the same locations as removed.

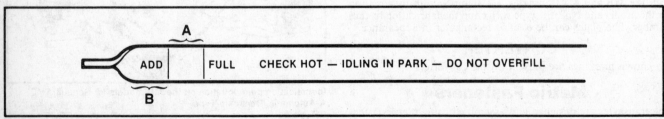

Dipstick indicator (© Renault/AMC)

d. If any of the above has occurred, wait 30 minutes until the fluid has cooled and stabilized at an even temperature before checking.

**To check the fluid level:**

a. Apply the parking brake.

b. Place the transaxle in the P position and start the engine.

c. With the vehicle stationary, move the selector lever through all the gear ranges and return it to the P position.

d. Check the fluid level as outlined in the Checking Fluid Level section.

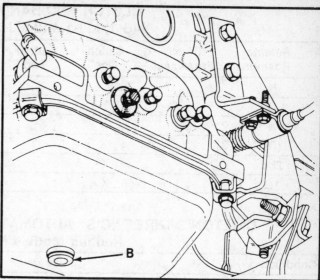

Drain plug (B) location on oil pan (© Renault/AMC)

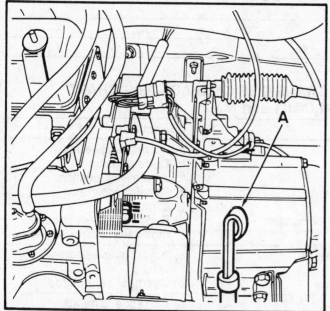

Dipstick location (A) on Alliance (© Renault/AMC)

# MODIFICATIONS

## Electrical System Inspection

When inspecting and checking for electrical problems in the transaxle electrical components, the battery must be fully charged, since a low-charged battery may not produce enough voltage to ensure proper Electronic Control Unit operation, resulting in loss of 1st and 2nd gears.

## Torque Converter Removal and Installation

Before removing the transaxle from the engine, mark the converter and drive plate for assembly alignment. These components must be properly aligned to ensure the correct operation and function of the ignition system. The ignition control module input is dependent upon the correct signal from the converter circumference and TDC sensor.

## Rear Case Locator Bolt "O" Ring

When overhauling the transaxle, the rear case locator bolt "O" ring must be replaced with a new one during the assembly.

## Differential Case Snapring Slot

Two different width snapring slots are used on the differential cases to retain the small bearings. The early production cases have a slot which measures 0.069 inch (1.75mm) in width. The later production cases have a slot which measures 0.099 inch (2.5mm) in width. It is most important to install the correct sized snapring.

# TROUBLE DIAGNOSIS

## CLUTCH AND BAND APPLICATION CHART
### MB-1, MJ-1 and MJ-3 Automatic Transaxles

| Selector Position | Clutch Freewheel | Clutch One | Clutch Two | Brake One | Brake Two | Solenoid EL-1 | Solenoid EL-2 |
|---|---|---|---|---|---|---|---|
| P | | | | | | | X |
| R | | | X | X | | | X |

## CLUTCH AND BAND APPLICATION CHART
### MB-1, MJ-1 and MJ-3 Automatic Transaxles

| Selector Position | | Clutch Freewheel | Clutch One | Clutch Two | Brake One | Brake Two | Solenoid EL-1 | Solenoid EL-2 |
|---|---|---|---|---|---|---|---|---|
| N | | | | | | | | X |
| A | 1 | X | X | | | | | X |
| | 2 | | X | | | X | X | X |
| (D) | 3 | | X | X | | | | |
| 2nd | | | X | | | X | X | X |
| 1st | | | X | | X | | | X |

## CHILTON'S THREE "C'S" AUTOMATIC TRANSMISSION DIAGNOSIS CHART
### Renault Models MB-1, MJ-1 and MJ-3

| Condition | Cause | Correction |
|---|---|---|
| Engine Stalls and has uneven idle | a) Engine idle<br>b) Ignition System<br>c) Accelerator control<br>d) Vacuum modulator and/or hoses | a) Correct engine Idle<br>b) Correct ignition system malfunction<br>c) Repair accelerator control<br>d) Repair or renew vacuum modulator and/or hoses |
| Creeps in "N" position | a) Gear selector lever<br>b) E-1/E-2 Clutches | a) Adjust gear selector lever<br>b) Overhaul as required |
| Excessive creep in "D" | a) Engine Idle<br>b) Accelerator control<br>c) Converter | a) Correct engine idle<br>b) Correct accelerator control<br>c) Renew converter assembly |
| Slippage when starting in "D" or "R" | a) Fluid level<br>b) Fluid pressure<br>c) Valve body<br>d) Converter | a) Correct fluid level<br>b) Adjust fluid pressure<br>c) Clean, repair or renew valve body assembly<br>d) Renew converter assembly |
| Slippage when starting off in "D" only | a) Fluid level<br>b) E-1/E-2 clutches<br>c) Overrunning clutch | a) Correct fluid level<br>b) Correct or renew clutches<br>c) Renew overrunning clutch |
| Slippage during shift | a) Fluid pressure<br>b) Modulator<br>c) Valve body<br>d) Oil pump screen<br>e) E-1/E-2 or overrunning clutches | a) Correct fluid pressure<br>b) Adjust or renew modulator assembly<br>c) Clean, repair or renew valve body<br>d) Clean or renew oil pump screen<br>e) Overhaul and renew as required |
| No 1st gear hold | a) Selector lever<br>b) Harness, plugs, grounds<br>c) Computer control unit<br>d) Multifunction switch | a) Adjust selector lever<br>b) Clean, repair, or renew components as required<br>c) Test and/or renew computer control unit<br>d) Clean, repair or renew components as required |

## CHILTON'S THREE "C'S" AUTOMATIC TRANSMISSION DIAGNOSIS CHART
### Renault Models MB-1, MJ-1 and MJ-3

| Condition | Cause | Correction |
|---|---|---|
| No 1st gear hold | e) Valve body | e) Clean, repair or renew valve body assembly |
| No 2nd gear hold | a) Selector lever | a) Adjust selector lever |
| | b) Harness, plugs, grounds | b) Clean, repair, or renew components as required |
| | c) Computer control unit | c) Test and/or renew computer control unit |
| | d) Multifunction switch | d) Clean, repair or renew components as required |
| | e) Valve body | e) Clean, repair or renew valve body assembly |
| Remains in 1st gear when in "D" position | a) Harness, plugs grounds | a) Clean, repair or renew components as required |
| | b) Computer control unit | b) Test and/or renew computer control unit |
| | c) Solenoid valves | c) Clean, repair or renew solenoid valves |
| | d) Road speed indicator | d) Test, repair or renew indicator assembly |
| | e) Valve body | e) Clean, repair or renew valve body assembly |
| Remains in 3rd gear | a) Fuses | a) Test circuits and renew fuses |
| | b) Harness, plugs, grounds | b) Clean, repair, or renew components as required |
| | c) Computer control assembly | c) Test and/or renew computer control unit |
| | d) Oil pump | d) Repair or renew oil pump |
| | e) Valve body | e) Clean, repair or renew valve body assembly |
| Some gear ratios unobtainable and selector lever out of position | a) Selector lever | a) Adjust selector lever |
| | b) Selector control | b) Adjust or repair selector control |
| | c) Manual valve mechanical control | c) Repair or renew components as required |
| Park position not operating | a) Selector lever | a) Adjust selector lever |
| | b) Broken or damaged components | b) Repair or renew components as required |
| Starter not operating and/or back-up lights not operating | a) Selector lever | a) Adjust selector lever |
| | b) Selector control | b) Adjust or repair selector control |
| | c) Harness, plugs, grounds | c) Clean, repair, or renew components as required |
| | d) Computer control unit | d) Test and/or renew computer control unit |
| | e) Multifunction switch | e) Clean, repair or renew components as required |
| No 1st in "D" position, operates—2nd to 3rd to 2nd | a) EI-1 solenoid ball valve stays open | a) Test and/or renew EI-1 solenoid ball valve |

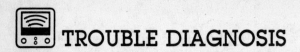

### CHILTON'S THREE "C'S" AUTOMATIC TRANSMISSION DIAGNOSIS CHART
#### Renault Models MB-1, MJ-1 and MJ-3

| Condition | Cause | Correction |
|---|---|---|
| No 2nd in "D" position, operates—1st to 3rd to 1st | a) El-1 solenoid ball valve stays closed<br><br>b) Solenoid ball valves reversed | a) Test and/or renew El-1 solenoid ball valve<br><br>b) Reverse solenoid ball valves |
| Operates in 3rd only | a) El-2 solenoid ball valve stays open | a) Test and/or renew El-2 solenoid ball valve |
| No 3rd, operates 1st to 2nd to 1st | a) El-2 solenoid ball valve stays closed | a) Test and/or renew El-2 solenoid ball valve |
| Surge when starting off | a) Idle speed<br>b) Accelerator controls<br><br>c) Fluid level | a) Correct idle speed<br>b) Correct the accelerator controls<br>c) Correct fluid level |
| Surge during shifting | a) Modulator valve and/or hoses<br><br>b) Valve body assembly | a) Adjust or renew modulator assembly and/or hoses<br>b) Clean, repair or renew valve body assembly |
| Incorrect shifting speeds | a) Accelerator controls<br><br>b) Load Potentiometer setting<br><br>c) Harness, plugs or grounds<br><br>d) Kickdown switch<br><br>e) Computer control units<br><br>f) Road speed | a) Correct accelerator controls<br>b) Adjust setting of load potentiometer<br>c) Clean, repair or renew components as required<br>d) Adjust or renew kickdown switch<br>e) Test and/or renew computer control<br>f) Bring vehicle to correct road speed. |
| No drive | a) Selector lever ad<br>b) Fluid level<br>c) Valve body<br><br>d) Oil pump<br>e) Oil pump screen<br><br>f) Oil pump shaft broken<br>g) Turbine shaft broken<br>h) Final Drive<br><br>i) Converter drive plate broken<br><br>j) Converter<br>k) E-1/E-2 clutches | a) Adjust selector lever<br>b) Correct fluid level<br>c) Clean, repair or renew valve body assembly<br>d) Repair or renew oil pump<br>d) Clean or renew oil pump screen<br>f) Renew oil pump shaft<br>g) Replace turbine shaft<br>h) Correct final drive malfunction<br>i) Replace converter drive plate<br>j) Renew converter<br>k) Correct or renew clutches |
| No drive in 1st gear hold or in "D" position | a) Valve body<br><br>b) E-1/E-2 Clutches<br>c) Overrunning clutch | a) Clean, repair or renew valve body assembly<br>b) Correct or renew clutches<br>c) Renew overrunning clutch |

### CHILTON'S THREE "C'S" AUTOMATIC TRANSMISSION DIAGNOSIS CHART
#### Renault Models MB-1, MJ-1 and MJ-3

| Condition | Cause | Correction |
|---|---|---|
| No drive in "R" or 3rd gear | a) Valve body | a) Clean, repair or renew valve body assembly |
| | b) E-1/E-2 clutches | b) Correct or renew clutches |
| No reverse or engine braking in 1st gear hold | a) Multifunction switch | a) Test, repair or renew multifunction switch |
| | b) Valve Body | b) Clean, repair or renew valve body assembly |
| | c) F-1 Brake | c) Correct or renew brake |
| No 1st gear in "D" position | a) Harness, plugs or grounds | a) Clean, repair or renew components as required |
| | b) Solenoid valves | b) Clean, repair or renew solenoid valves |
| | c) Overrunning clutch | c) Renew overrunning clutch |
| No 2nd gear in "D" position | a) Harness, plugs or grounds | a) Clean, repair or renew components as required |
| | b) Valve body assembly | b) Clean, repair or renew valve body assembly |
| | c) F-2 brake | c) Correct or renew brake |
| No 3rd gear in "D" position | a) Harness, plugs or grounds | a) Clean, repair or renew components as required |
| | b) Computer control unit | b) Test and/or renew computer control |
| | c) Solenoid valves | c) Clean, repair or renew solenoid valves |
| | d) Multifunction switch | d) Test, repair or renew multifunction switch |
| | e) Valve body | e) Clean, repair or renew valve body assembly |

# HYDRAULIC AND ELECTRICAL CONTROLS

## Hydraulic Controls

### OIL PUMP

The oil pump is driven directly from the engine and supplies fluid to the transaxle hydraulic system. Pressure is directed to the converter assembly, to the brakes and clutches and for lubricating the internal components of the transaxle. The oil pump has internally toothed gears and is located at the rear of the transaxle.

### VALVE BODY

The hydraulic valve body regulates the fluid pressure according to the engine load, through the pressure regulator and the vacuum modulator. The valve body components routes the fluid to operate the clutches and the brake clutches, through varied passages. Gear ratio changes are determined by the operation of the two solenoid valves, E-1 and E-2, called the solenoid ball valves. The electrical signal to operate the solenoid ball valves are routed from the governor and computer assemblies.

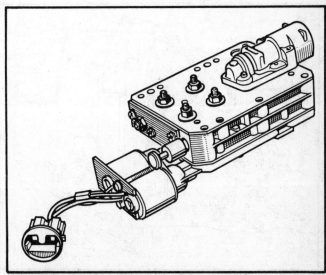

Valve body assembly—MJ models (© Renault/AMC)

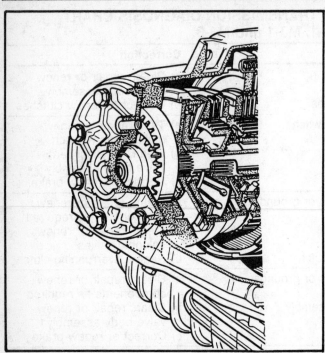

Oil pump location—MJ models (© Renault/AMC)

## VACUUM MODULATOR AND PRESSURE REGULATOR

To produce the circuit pressure, the vacuum modulator and the pressure regulator are used to determine the pressure to the varied components and control valves, depending upon engine load and the vehicle speed. Both units control the quality of the transaxle shift, both up and down.

## Electrical Controls

### GOVERNOR

The governor is a small low-wattage alternator which supplies to the computer an alternating current (AC) which varies accordingly to the engine load, dependent upon the accelerator pedal position, and the vehicle speed.

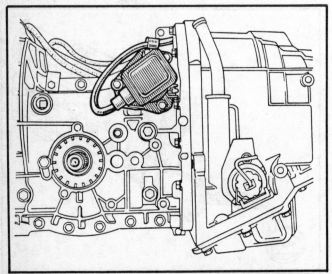

Location of governor assembly on MJ models (© Renault/AMC)

### COMPUTER

The computer transmits electrical impulses to the solenoid ball valves according to the strength of the alternating current (AC) supplied by the governor through vehicle speed and engine load. The position of the gear selector lever allows current to flow to pre-designated areas of the transaxle. The computer is made up of electronic and mechanical components.

### KICKDOWN SWITCH

The kickdown switch is activated by the accelerator pedal at the end of its travel. It grounds a circuit in the computer to allow a lower gear ratio to be selected in certain conditions.

### SOLENOID BALL VALVES

Upon an electrical signal, the ball valves open or close hydraulic circuits to allow the gear shifting.

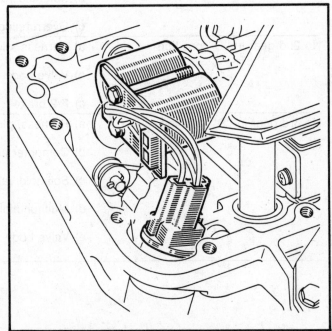

Solenoid ball valves mounted on valve body (© Renault/AMC)

### MULTIFUNCTION SWITCH

This switch is driven by the gear shift linkage and allows the opening and closing of different electrical circuits, depending upon the linkage position. It controls the engine start-up circuit when the selector lever is in the "P" or "N" position, the back-up light circuit when the selector lever is in the "R" position and also controls the initial operation of the EL-1 and EL-2 solenoid ball valves.

### IGNITION SWITCH

The transaxle electrical components are energized when the ignition switch is turned on.

### KICKDOWN CONTROL

A kickdown position is provided for command downshifting.

### ENGINE LOAD POTENTIOMETER

This is a unit that provides variable voltage based on the throttle position to the computer control unit.

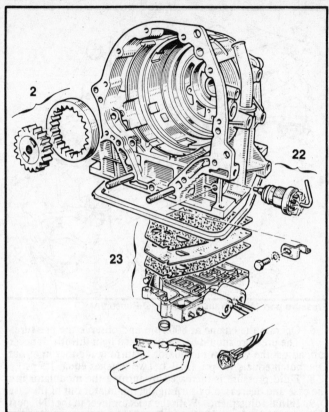

**Oil pump (2), Vacuum Diaphragm Capsule (22), Valve body (23) on MB models** (© Renault/AMC)

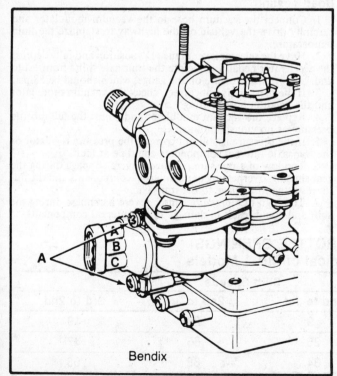

**Bendix type potentiometer. (A) screws are used for adjustment** (© Renault/AMC)

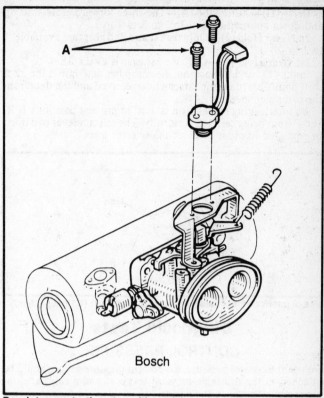

**Bosch type potentiometer, with retaining screws (A)** (© Renault/AMC)

## ROAD SPEED SENSOR

The road speed sensor is a magnetic unit, fitted opposite the "park" ring with signals sent to the computer control unit.

## SELECTOR LEVER

The selector lever has six positions for controlling the transaxle operation.

**Park (P)**—The transaxle is mechanically locked. The starter can be operated to start the engine.

**Reverse (R)**—The vehicle may be driven backward and the back-up lights are illuminated.

**Neutral (N)**—No power flow through the transaxle. The starter can be operated to start the engine.

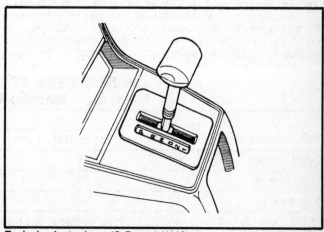

**Typical selector lever** (© Renault/AMC)

**Drive (D)—Automatic (A)**—The three forward gears shift up and down automatically. 1 to 2 to 3 to 2 to 1.

**2nd Gear Hold (2)**—Only the 1st and 2nd gears are available. 1 to 2 to 1.

**1st Gear Hold (1)**—Only the 1st gear is available.

In the "D" or "A" position, the computer determines the ideal shift points based on the information received and the data from the computer memory.

An interlocking mechanism is used to prevent positions 1, R, and P from being selected accidently. The selector lever pad must be squeezed in order to move the selector lever.

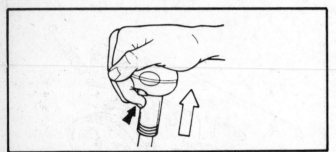

Use of interlock mechanism on the gear shift lever (© Renault/AMC)

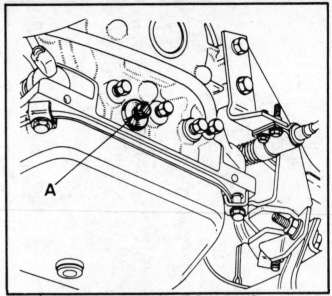

Pressure port (A) on transaxle case (© Renault/AMC)

## Diagnosis Tests

### CONTROL PRESSURE

To test the control pressure, a 0-300 psi pressure gauge should be attached to the transaxle pressure test port and a calibrated tachometer attached to the engine.

The transaxle fluid must be at 176°F (80°C.) or above. The vacuum modulator and the vacuum circuits must be in good condition. Regulated fluid pressure varies with the fluid temperature. It is therefore normal to fluid pressures higher than the indicated value if the fluid temperature has not reached its normal checking temperature.

### CHECKING OF THE FLUID PRESSURE

The fluid pressure is checked in two steps:
1. Initial adjustment in the shop.
2. Road testing at full throttle.

### Initial Adjustment

1. Connect the pressure gauge to the transaxle and correct the fluid level as required. Install a tachometer to the engine.
2. Lock the parking and service brakes, start the engine.
3. High pressure test—Move the selector lever to the "P" position. The fluid pressure must be 58 psi minimum at 800 rpm.
4. Accelerate the engine and the fluid pressure should rise rapidly until it reaches the maximum pressure of 189-203 psi.
5. Light throttle pressure—Disconnect the vacuum modulator vacuum hose and move the selector lever to the "N" position.

6. Operate the engine at 800 rpm and observe the pressure.
7. The pressure should be 36-39 psi at a light throttle. If necessary adjust the vacuum modulator by turning it either in or out. One notch equals 1.5 psi. (MB-1, Two notches equal 1.5 psi).
8. Fluid pressure is increased by turning the modulator into the case and decreased by turning the modulator out of the case.
9. Initial adjustment—With the selector lever in the "N" position, run the engine at 3800 rpm. The fluid pressure must be close to the full throttle pressure. The final tests and adjustments must be made during the road test.

### Road Testing

1. Connect the vacuum hose to the vacuum modulator and carefully drive the vehicle on the highway to stabilize the fluid temperature.
2. Have the selector lever in the "D" position and fully depress the accelerator pedal. Just before the transaxle shifts from 1st to 2nd, observe the pressure on the gauge, which should be 58 psi.
3. If the pressure is not correct, check the vacuum modulator and the vacuum hose routing.
4. Replace the vacuum modulator and adjust the full throttle pressure as previously outlined.
5. If the pressure is still not correct, the pressure regulator or the transaxle internal components could be at fault.
6. Too low of a pressure produces severe slippage during the gear shifting, overheating of the internal components and the fluid, resulting in damage to the transaxle.
7. Too high of a pressure causes severe harshness during the shift and could result in damage to the internal components.

### SHIFT SPEEDS AT THROTTLE OPENINGS
#### MJ-1, MJ-3 Models, Typical of MB-1 Models

| | Shift Speeds | | | |
|---|---|---|---|---|
| Throttle Position | 1st to 2nd | 2nd to 1st | 2nd to 3rd | 3rd to 2nd |
| Light throttle | 15 | 9 | 28 | 19 |
| Full throttle | 37 | 25 | 65 | 47 |
| Kickdown | 40 | 34 | 68 | 65 |

**NOTE:** These speeds may vary depending upon tolerances allowed in the various units, such as the governor, computer, speedometer and size of tires.

# DIAGNOSIS TOOLS

Should the transaxle operation suggest a malfunction of the internal components, three test boxes are available through the manufacturer, to test the electrical components and their affect upon the hydraulic components, while the vehicle is operating.

## Type One

Type one test box (B.VI. 454-06, B.VI. 797) contains an electrical circuit assembly connected to indicator lights, a dial, switches and a storage compartment for the required test wiring.

### INDICATOR LIGHTS

The indicator lights operate as follows:

1. The red indicator light represents current from the battery and is on when the test box is operating.
2. The blue light represents current being applied to the solenoid ball valve EL-1.
3. The white light represents current being applied to the solenoid ball valve EL-2.
4. The green light represents the activation of the emission control system, if equipped (not used in U.S.).
5. The orange light represents current being applied to the kickdown switch.

### C-1 SWITCH

This switch has two positions for test purposes.

**Position A**—Allows the transaxle to be operated in the normal manner with the use of the selector lever.

**Position 1-2-3**—Move the selector lever to the "A" ("D" or Drive) position. By turning the switch knob to the number 1, 2 or 3 position, the transaxle gear ratio can be controlled.

### C-2 SWITCH

This switch allows the checking of the battery current at position one, current through the solenoid ball valves (EL-1 and EL-2) at position two, the fluid temperature at position six, while positions four and five are not used.

### GALVANOMETER

The dial has scales that allows successive readings of the following:

1. Transmission fluid temperature.
2. Battery voltage with the engine stopped or operating.
3. Current passing through the solenoid ball valves in amperes.

### TEST CABLE

A special test cable is used to plug into the diagnostic socket of the automatic transaxle and to the test cable of the test box.

### THERMOMETER

A special thermometer replaces the transaxle dipstick in its tube. A connector wire is used between the thermometer and the test box.

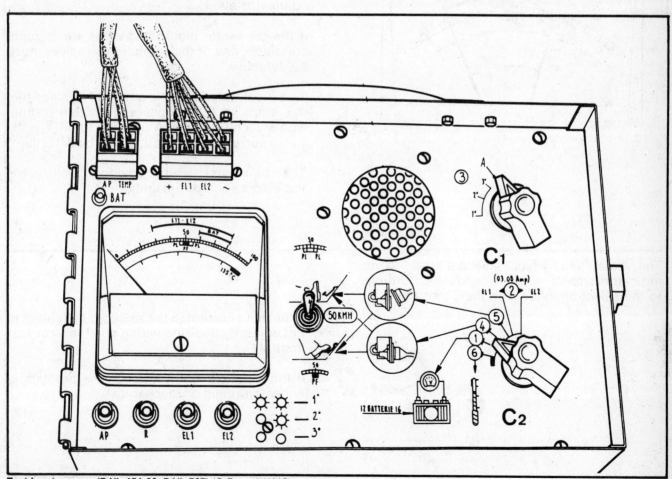

Test box type one (B.VI. 454-06, B.VI. 797) (© Renault/AMC)

| READING | REMARKS |
|---|---|

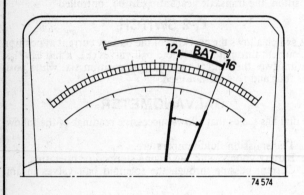

74 574

Incorrect battery voltage (outside the 12 volt to 16 volt range) may cause the automatic transmission to malfunction.

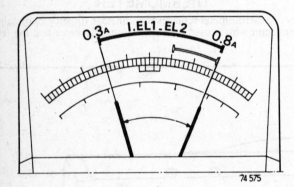

74 575

If the current is normal (between 0.3 amps and 0.8 amps ), the solenoid ball valves are in good electrical condition.

If the current is abnormal, check the wires and connector blocks.

If the connector blocks and wires are in good condition, one of the solenoid ball valves must be defective.

If an incorrect reading is obtained (outside the 0.3 amps to 0.8 amps range) when testing with switch C1 in the A position (the C1 tests being correct) the computer may be defective.

The blue and white solenoid ball valve indicators should remain lit.

The blue and white solenoid ball valve indicators should remain lit or go out according to the selection made with the C1 switch.

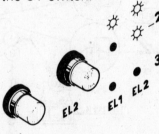

If the input current to the solenoid ball valves is not correct, check the wiring and the electrical controls.

If the input current is correct, the problem is either hydraulic or mechanical.

## Type Two

The type two test box (B.VI. 797-01, B.VI. 797-02) contains function indicator lights, a potentiometer, a galvanometer dial, a digital display, switches, two leads for connection to the vehicle and three safety fuses.

### INDICATOR LIGHTS

1. The EL-1 yellow indicator light represents current being applied to the solenoid ball valve EL-1.
2. The EL-2 yellow light indicator represents current being applied to the solenoid ball valve EL-2.
3. The red AP indicator light indicates current to the emission control system, if used (Not in U.S.).
4. The RC green indicator light indicates current to the kickdown switch and that it is operating.

### DIGITAL DISPLAY

The digital display indicates multifunction switch operation and the computer condition.

### POTENTIOMETER

The potentiometer is not used while testing the transaxle units.

### CIRCUIT BREAKER

The circuit breaker is not used while testing the transaxle units.

### GALVANOMETER

The galvanometer has four scales to allow successive readings of the following:
1. Battery voltage with the engine stopped or operating.
2. Measurement of current passing through the solenoid ball valves.
3. The third is not used during the tests.
4. Measures the transaxle fluid temperature. A red zone is indicated and the transaxle fluid temperature must not exceed it.

### SWITCH

The switch is used to select the test modes that can be performed with the test instrument.
1. Position 0—indicates battery voltage with the engine stopped or operating.
2. Position 1—Measures the current in EL-1 and its input.
3. Position 2—Measures the current in EL-2 and its input.
4. Position 3—Places the vehicle in the third gear ratio when the selector lever is in the "D" position (EL-1 and EL-2 are not activated).
5. Position 4—Not used.
6. Position 5—Not used.
7. Position 6—Not used.
8. Position 7—Allows transaxle fluid temperature to be measured.

### FUSES

1. Fuse a—Protects test box input (1A).
2. Fuse b—Protects EL-1 current (1A).
3. Fuse c—Protects EL-2 current (1A).

### THERMOMETER

A special thermometer replaces the transaxle dipstick in its tube. A connector wire is used between the thermometer and the test box.

### TEST CABLE

A special test cable is used between the diagnostic socket of the transaxle and the test box.

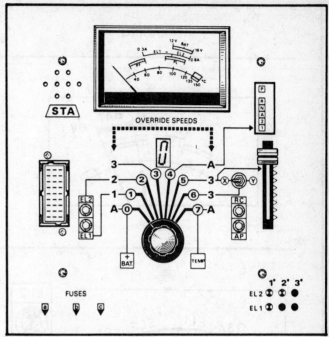

**Test box type two (B.VI. 797-01 or B.VI. 797-2)** (© Renault/AMC)

## Type Three

The type three test box (B.VI. 958) has a self checking feature. By connecting terminal 14 to the battery and switching the I1 switch to the TEST position, test lights 1, 2, 3, 4, 5, 6, 7, 8 and the positive (+) red zone should illuminate. If they do not illuminate, the test box is defective.

### DESCRIPTION

**Zone A** is used to test MB and MJ transaxles.
1. Solenoid valves
2. Road speed sensor
3. Potentiometer
4. 2nd gear hold switch    gear selector
4&5. 1st gear hold switch    lever position
6. Multifunction switch
15. Diagnostic socket
14. Control box feed
RAZ. Return to zero for check lights 1 to 6
TEST. B.VI. 958 check
DIAG. Instrument panel check light

**Zone B** is used to measure the solenoid valve windings and voltage and to test the multifunction switch on all RENAULT automatic transaxles.
7-8. Reading control lights
  P. Control harnesses
 P1. Control input sockets

**Zone C** is used to check types 4139 and 4141 transaxles. Additional wiring is required.

**Zone D** is used to check and adjust the load potentiometer on MB and MJ transaxles.
12. Inverter
 9. Adjustment check light
+. Feed light (MB-MJ)
F. Fuse (3.15A)
16. Test harness connectors

| READING | REMARKS |
|---|---|
| | Incorrect battery voltage (outside the 12 volt to 16 volt range) can cause the automatic transmission to malfunction.<br><br>**Note:**<br>This test may also be performed with the vehicle moving.<br><br>If there is no voltage, check test box fuses a, b, and c. |
| | If the current is normal (between 0.3 amps. and 0.8 amps.), the solenoid ball valves are in good electrical condition.<br><br>If the current is abnormal:<br>• check the wires and the connector blocks<br>• if the wires and blocks are in good condition, one of the solenoid ball valves must be defective.<br><br>If there is no current, check test box fuses a, b, and c. |
| | If the current is normal (between 0.3 amps. and 0.8 amps.), the solenoid ball valves are in good electrical condition.<br><br>If the current is abnormal:<br>• check the wires and the connector blocks<br>• if the wires and blocks are in good condition, one of the solenoid ball valves must be defective.<br><br>If there is no current, check test box fuses a, b, and c. |
| | If the input current to the solenoid ball valves is not correct, check the leads and the electrical controls.<br><br>If the input current is correct, the problem is either hydraulic or mechanical. |

| READING | REMARKS |
|---|---|

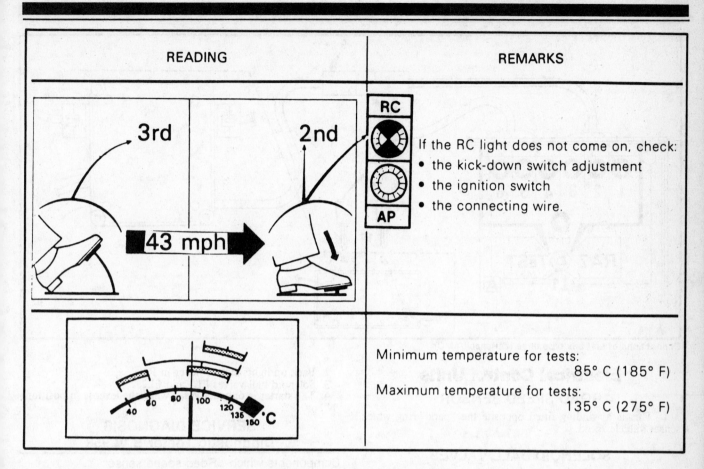

If the RC light does not come on, check:
- the kick-down switch adjustment
- the ignition switch
- the connecting wire.

Minimum temperature for tests:
85° C (185° F)
Maximum temperature for tests:
135° C (275° F)

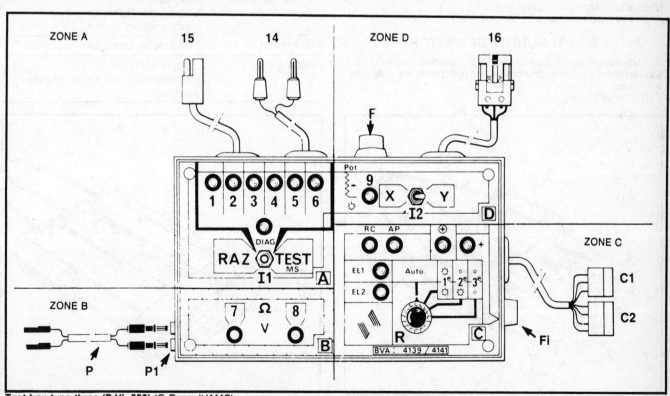

Test box type three (B.VI. 958) (© Renault/AMC)

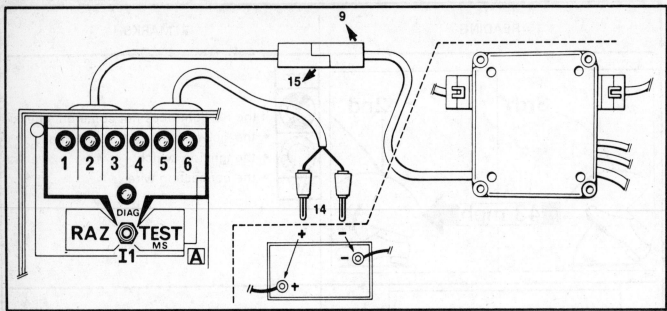

Connections of test box type three (© Renault/AMC)

## Electrical Control Units

### ROAD SPEED SENSOR

1. This is a winding fitted opposite the "park" ring which senses vehicle speed.

### SOLENOID BALL VALVES

1. These are solenoid-operated ball valves which open or close hydraulic channels to change gears.
2. They are controlled by the computer.

### MULTI-FUNCTION SWITCH

Its cam, moved by the gear selector lever, opens or closes the various electrical circuits depending on the position of the gear selector lever:
1. Starter circuit.

2. Back up lights circuit (lever in R).
3. Solenoid ball valves EL1 and EL2.
4. The starter is only activated when the lever is in positions "N" or "P".

## SERVICE DIAGNOSIS
### Diagnostic Tester B.VI.958

| Components which may be tested | Road speed sensor<br>Solenoid valves<br>Load potentiometer<br>Multifunction switch |
|---|---|
| Adjustment | Load potentiometer |
| Readings | Supply voltage<br>Continuity in the solenoid valve winding |

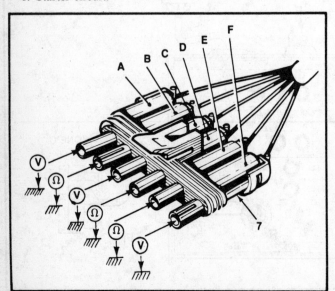

Checking the 6-way connector (© Renault/AMC)

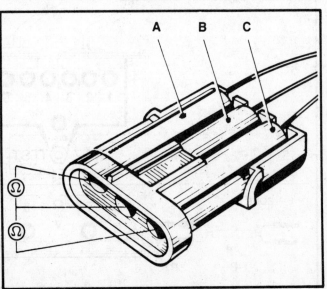

Checking the load potentiometer (© Renault/AMC)

## COMPUTER

This is an electronic calculator which interprets information from the following sources:
1. The road speed sensor.
2. The engine load potentiometer.
3. The multifunction switch.

The computer then changes the information into electrical instructions to the solenoid ball valves to change the gear ratios.

## ENGINE LOAD POTENTIOMETER

1. It is a simple potentiometer which provides variable voltage based on throttle position.

## CHECKING THE 6-WAY CONNECTOR

Unplug connector from the computer and make the following checks.

| Action on vehicle | Check | Diagnosis |
|---|---|---|
| Ignition switched off | B-Ground = 4 ohm ± 3 | Backup lamps |
| Ignition switched off | A-Ground = 12V ± 2 | Backup lamps |
| Ignition switched on | E-Ground = 0 ohm | Ground |
| Ignition switched on | F-Ground = 12V ± 2 | Current feed to module |
| Operate starter | C-Ground = 12V ± 2 | Starter |

## CHECKING ENGINE LOAD POTENTIOMETER
(Unplug connector)

| Check | Diagnosis |
|---|---|
| C to B = 4k ohm ± 1<br>A to B = 2,5k ohm ± 1<br><br>A to B: open throttle slowly; the ohmmeter should never show infinite resistance ($\infty$) | If the readings are different the potentiometer is faulty or incorrectly adjusted. |

## RESULTS OF THE READINGS
### Diagnostic Tester B.VI.958

(Road test the vehicle, but do not shut the engine off after the test.)

**Vehicle Stopped (Engine Running)**

| Checks | Check light(s) | Good | Bad | Faulty components | Oper-ation |
|---|---|---|---|---|---|
| Solenoid Valves | 1 | O | ★ | Solenoid valves<br>Harness | IX-X-XI |
| Road Speed Sensor | 2 | O | ★ | Faulty road speed sensor | |
| Potentio-meter | 3 | O | ★ | Load potentiometer harness | XII-XV |

**Engine Not Running—Ignition Switch On**

| Position of the control lever | Check light(s) | Good | | Faulty components | Oper-ation |
|---|---|---|---|---|---|
| 2nd hold | 4 | 4 ★ | 5 O | If bad, multifunction switch and harness | V-XIV |
| 1st hold | 4 and 5 | 4 ★ | 5 ★ | If bad, check multifunction switch and harness | V-XIV |
| P L N D | 4 and 5 | 4 O | 5 O | If bad, check multifunction switch and harness | III-IV<br>XIII-XIV |
| P—N | 6 | ★ | | If bad, check selector lever adjustment and multifunction switch operation | II |

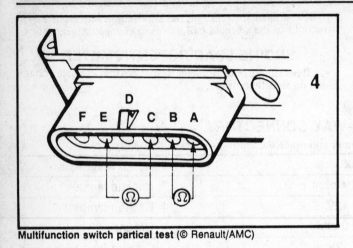

Multifunction switch partical test (© Renault/AMC)

## CONTROL OF THE POTENTIOMETER

| Test | |
| --- | --- |
| | Check light |
| Press accelerator to floor | 9 |
| Good | ★ |
| Bad or badly adjusted | O |

## PARTIAL CHECK OF MULTI-FUNCTION SWITCH
(Unplug the 6-way connector and check computer socket.)

| Check | Diagnosis |
| --- | --- |
| A to B = 0 ohm (selector in R) <br> E to C = 0 ohm (selector in P or N) | Replace multifunction switch |

## CHECKING THE 3-WAY CONNECTOR

| Action on vehicle | Check | Diagnosis |
| --- | --- | --- |
| Ignition switched on | B-Ground = 4.3 V ± 0.5 | If this check proves a problem exists, check 6 way connector. Replace the computer if connector is satisfactory. <br> Replace computer. |

## CHECKING THE SOLENOID VALVES AND HARNESS
(Unplug connector from the computer.)

| Check | Diagnosis | |
| --- | --- | --- |
| A to C = 30 ohm ± 10 | If 0 ohm | :Replace wiring or solenoid valves |
| | 60 ohm ± 20 | :Poor connection |
| B to C = 30 ohm ± 10 | | :Replace wiring or solenoid valves |
| C to Ground = ∞ | If not ∞: | |
| | There is a short circut between the solenoid valve windings and ground: | |
| | Replace the wiring or solenoid valves | |

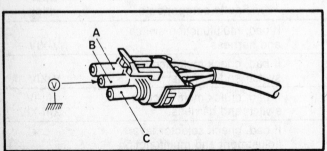

Checking the three way connector (© Renault/AMC)

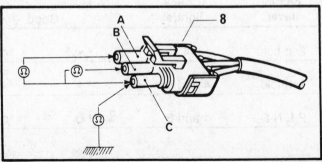

Checking the solenoid ball valves and harness (© Renault/AMC)

## CHECKING THE SOLENOID VALVES

| Test points | | Diagnosis |
|---|---|---|
| A - C = 30 ohm ± 10 | Si 0 ohm | :Replace the Solenoid Valves |
| | 60 ohm ± 20 | :Bad connection |
| B - C = 30 ohm ± 10 | ∞ | :Replace the Solenoid Valves |
| C - Ground = ∞ | | :If different from ∞ |
| | | —Solenoid valves short between ground and windings. |
| | | Replace the solenoid valves. |

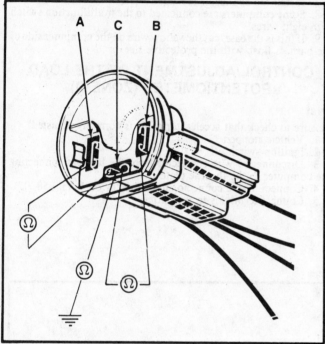

Checking the solenoid valves (© Renault/AMC)

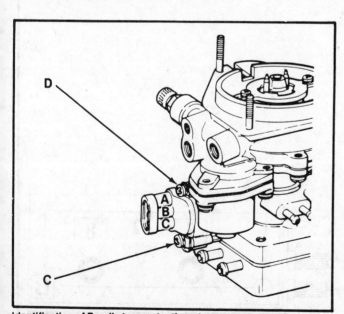

Identification of Bendix type potentiometer connector terminals and adjusting screws (C & D) (© Renault/AMC)

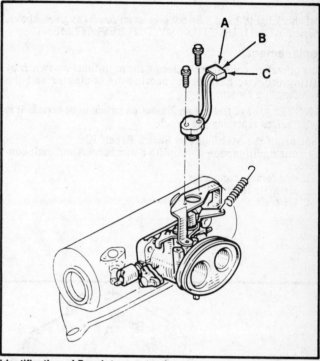

Identification of Bosch type potentiometer connector terminal (© Renault/AMC)

### Adjustment of The Potentiometer

1. Partially unscrew the 2 screws attaching the potentiometer (on the throttle plate housing).
2. Keep the throttle plate fully open and slowly rotate the potentiometer until check light 9 comes on. Tighten the 2 screws V in the position when 9 is on.
3. If check light 9 does not come on, check the potentiometer wiring or replace the potentiometer.
4. Each time the potentiometer is removed or replaced, it has to be adjusted.

## CONTROL OF THE MULTIFUNCTION SWITCH (ZONE B)

### Backup lights not working test

NOTE: Be sure to check that the governor cable is correctly adjusted.

1. Vehicle stopped.
2. Ignition switch off.
3. B.Vi. 958 connected to battery.
4. Disconnect 6 wire connector from the auto trans computer.
5. Connect control harness to B.Vi 958 (male red connector to red terminal).

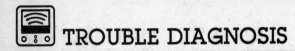
6. If backup light not working, readings to be taken between A and B.

| Gear Selector | Check Lights | |
|---|---|---|
| | 7 | 8 |
| D/1/2/N/P | O | O |
| R | O | ★ |

If check lights 7 and 8 do not give exact results as given above, refer to MULTIFUNCTION SWITCH REPLACEMENT.

## Replacement

This operation consists of replacing the multifunction switch by cutting the wire harness connecting the computer and the multifunction switch.

NOTE: Always test the multifunction switch to be certain it is faulty before replacing the switch.

Contents of the Multifunction Switch Repair Kit:
1. one multifunction switch with a wire harness and male connector.
2. one female connector.
3. six male terminals.
4. six seals.

### Removal and Installation

1. Remove the multifunction switch from the transaxle.
2. Cut the harness the same length as the replacement harness.
3. On the computer side, remove 65mm (2.6 in.) of outer insulation from the cable end.
4. Remove 5mm (0.20 in.) of insulation from each wire.
5. Install a seal on each wire.
6. Install and crimp the six male terminals on the wire ends.

NOTE: When installing the wires in the connector, be sure the wire color codes are not mismatched.

7. Install the connector locking device.
8. Some computers are connected to the multifunction switch with eight wires.
9. If this is the case, cut the yellow wire on the computer side of the harness flush with the protective sleeve.

## CONTROL/ADJUSTMENT OF THE LOAD POTENTIOMETER (ZONE D)

### Test

Be sure to check that accelerator cable is correctly adjusted.
1. Vehicle stopped
2. Ignition switch off
3. Disconnect 3 wire connector from the harness connecting the computer to the throttle plate
4. Connect 3 wire connector to connector on B.Vi. 958
5. Connect terminals to the battery

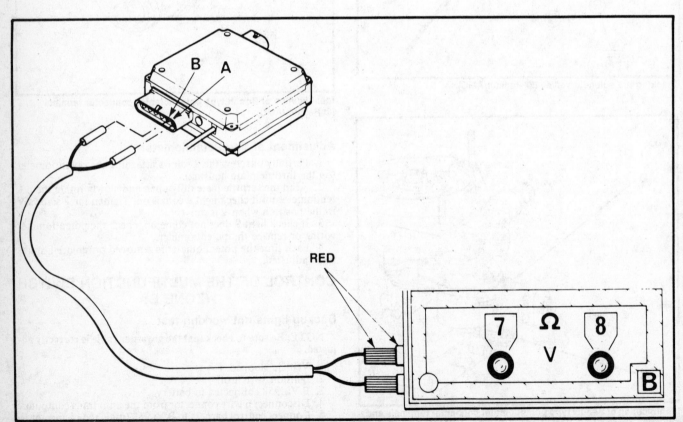

**Control of the multifunction switch with the type three test box in zone "B"** (© Renault/AMC)

| Press accelerator to floor | Check light 9 |
|---|---|
| Good | ✪ |
| Bad or badly adjusted | ○ |

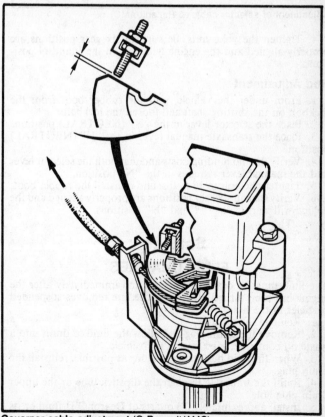

Control adjustment of the load potentiometer with the type three test box in zone "D" (© Renault/AMC)

## Adjustments

### GOVERNOR CABLE

1. Before adjusting the governor cable, inspect the accelerator cable to be sure it is adjusted properly.
   a. Depress the accelerator to the fully wide open position.
   b. Measure the compression on the cable spring which should be 0.080 in. (2 mm) from the released position.
   c. Check for proper kickdown switch operation.
2. When adjusting the governor, cable, complete the following:
   a. Adjust the cable locknuts on both the governor and throttle sides to the midway position.
   b. Adjust the cable stop to obtain a clearance of 0.008-0.028 in. (0.2-0.7mm) between the screw and the lever with the throttle fully open.
   c. Tighten the locknuts.

   d. Verify that the length of the governor cable is approximately 0.788 in. (20mm) between the wide open throttle position and the closed position.

### CAUTION

*The screw has been preset at the time of manufacture and must not be adjusted under any circumstances.*

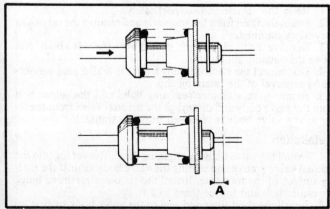

Accelerator cable adjustment (© Renault/AMC)

Governor cable adjustment (© Renault/AMC)

## KICKDOWN SWITCH

NOTE: Adjustment is made with the accelerator cable.

1. Be sure the accelerator cable has sufficient play to allow about 1/16 inch (3-4mm) movement in the stop sleeve when the accelerator pedal is completely depressed.
2. Properly install the sealing cover in position to prevent corrosion of the contacts.

—————————— CAUTION ——————————

*Accelerator cable/pedal travel, kickdown switch adjustment and the governor control cable adjustments are all closely related. Be sure each is properly adjusted whenever any of the adjustments are changed.*

## MANUAL LINKAGE

### Cable Adjustment

1. Place the transaxle manual lever in the P (PARK) position.
2. Place the selector lever in the P (PARK) position.
3. Adjust the cable assembly by loosening the adjusting yoke nuts and sliding the cable and the yoke forward to remove the slack in the cable.

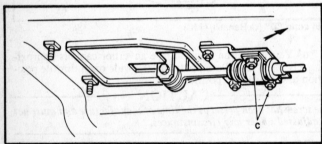

**Adjustment of selector cable** (© Renault/AMC)

4. Tighten the yoke nuts. Be sure all six gear positions are properly aligned and the engine will start in the P and N positions.

### Rod Adjustment

1. From under the vehicle, pull the rubber boot from the lockbolt on the shifting shaft and loosen the lockbolt.
2. Place the selector lever in the "N" (NEUTRAL) position.
3. Place the transaxle manual lever in the "N" (NEUTRAL) position.
4. Verify that no binding exists and that both the selector lever and the manual lever remains in the "N" position.
5. Tighten the bolt to 13 ft. lbs. and reinstall the rubber boot.
6. Verify that all six gear positions are properly aligned and the engine will start in the "P" and "N" positions.

## Services

### FLUID CHANGES

The fluid must be drained when hot and immediately after the engine has been turned off. This procedure removes suspended particles in the fluid.

1. Remove the dipstick.
2. Remove the drain plug and allow the fluid to drain into a waste oil container, after raising the vehicle.
3. When the fluid has drained as long as possible, reinstall the drain plug.
4. Refill the transaxle through the dipstick tube or the upper drain plug hole.
5. Install approximately 2⅔ quarts of Dexron® II fluid or its equivalent.

6. Start the engine and allow it to idle. Check the fluid level after running the selector lever through all the gear positions.
7. Correct the fluid level as necessary.

## OIL PAN

### Removal and Installation

1. Raise the vehicle and support safely.
2. Drain the transmission as previously outlined. Reinstall the drain plug. Remove transaxle mount bolt and raise the assembly to gain clearance for pan removal, as required (Alliance).
3. Remove the retaining bolts from the oil pan and bump the oil pan to loosen.
4. Remove the oil pan and the gasket.
5. Clean the gasket from the oil pan and the mating surface of the transaxle.

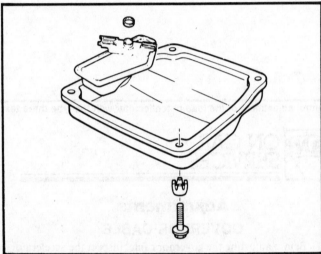

**Typical oil pan and filter assembly** (© Renault/AMC)

6. Install a new gasket on the oil pan and fit into position on the mating surface of the transaxle.
7. Install the retaining bolts and tighten to 54 *inch* lbs. Install mount bolt, if removed.
8. Install fluid as outlined previously.

NOTE: With the oil pan off the transaxle, the filter unit can be changed.

## VALVE BODY

### Removal

1. Raise the vehicle and support safely.
2. Drain the fluid from the transaxle and remove the oil pan as previously outlined.
3. Remove the fluid filter and its seal from the valve body. Remove the vacuum modulator.
4. Disconnect the electrical plug from the sealed plug connector by removal of the retaining clip.
5. Remove the six outer retaining bolts and the center bolt from the valve body and disengage the manual valve from the lever as the valve body is removed from the transaxle.

### Installation

1. Install the valve body by engaging the shift lever lug into the manual valve groove and seating the valve body against the mating surface of the transaxle. Install the six outer retaining bolts, the center bolt and torque them to 5 ft. lbs.
2. Install the fluid filter and seal to the valve body by first lubricating the "O" ring for the filter suction pipe and installing it

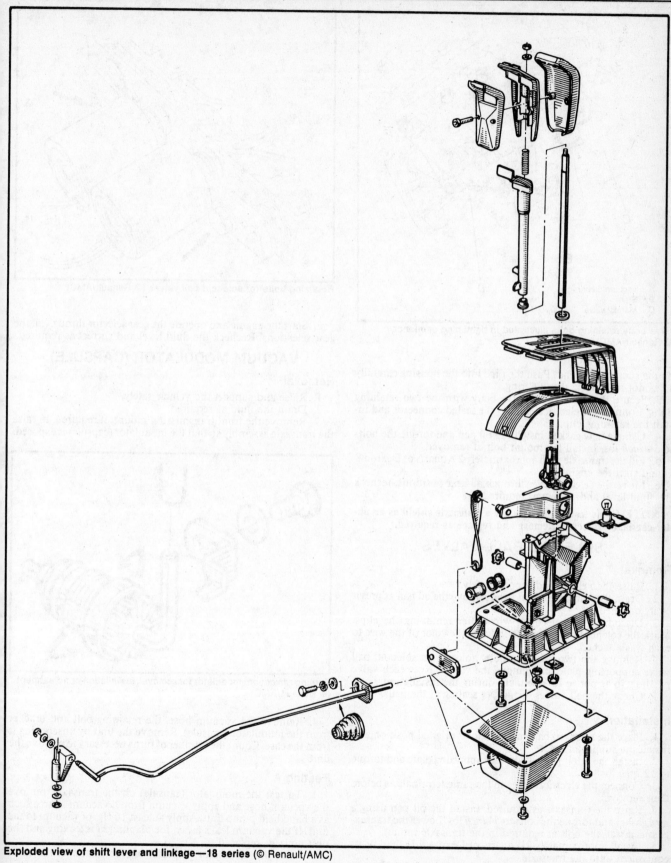

**Exploded view of shift lever and linkage—18 series** (© Renault/AMC)

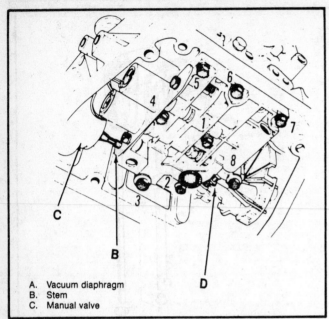

A. Vacuum diaphragm
B. Stem
C. Manual valve

**Valve body retaining bolts illustrated in tightening sequence**
(© Renault/AMC)

on the suction pipe end. Push the pipe into the housing carefully so as not to damage the "O" ring.

3. Secure the filter to the valve body with the two retaining bolts. Connect the electrical plug to the sealed connector and install the retaining clip.

4. Using a new gasket, install the oil pan and torque the bolts to 54 *inch* lbs. Install the mount bolt, if removed.

5. Fill the transaxle with approximately 2⅔ quarts of Dexron® II and start the engine.

6. Move the selector lever through all gear positions, recheck the fluid level and correct as required.

NOTE: Some transaxles may use a transaxle shield as an under-carriage protector. Remove and replace as required.

## SOLENOID BALL VALVES

### Removal

1. Raise the vehicle and support safely.

2. Drain the transaxle of fluid and remove the oil pan as previously outlined.

3. Disconnect the electrical wires after removing the clips. Mark the solenoid ball valves to indicate the color of the wire to each was attached.

4. Remove the two retaining bolts holding the solenoid ball valve supporting plate and remove the valves. Note each valve position so as not to reverse them during the installation.

5. Check the ball valves for proper sealing of the balls.

### Installation

1. Place the solenoid ball valves in their original position and install the supporting plate.

2. Install the retaining bolts in the supporting plate and torque to 12 *inch* lbs.

3. Connect the electrical wires to the same terminals as before their removal.

4. Raise the transaxle as required, install the oil pan using a new gasket and torque the bolts to 54 *inch* lbs. Lower the transaxle and install the bolt as required in the transaxle mount.

5. Install approximately 2⅔ quarts of Dexron® II fluid or its equivalent, into the transaxle.

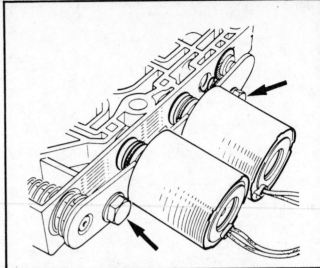

**Retaining bolts for solenoid ball valves** (© Renault/AMC)

6. Start the engine and operate the gear selector through all the gear selections. Recheck the fluid level and correct as required.

## VACUUM MODULATOR (CAPSULE)

### Removal

1. Raise and support the vehicle safely.

2. Drain the fluid as required.

3. Remove the front transmission mount, if required, to raise the transaxle assembly so that the modulator (capsule) is exposed.

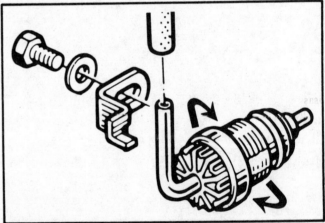

**Turning of vacuum modulator for removal, installation or adjustment**
(© Renault/AMC)

4. Remove the vacuum hose, the retaining bolt and bracket from the modulator (capsule). Remove the unit by unscrewing it from the case. Count the number of turns necessary to remove the unit.

### Testing

1. To test the modulator (capsule) on the transaxle, remove the vacuum hose and apply vacuum from a vacuum source such as a hand held pump unit. Apply at least 16 Hg. of vacuum to the unit. If the vacuum leaks away, the diaphragm is leaking and the unit must be replaced.

2. With the modulator (capsule) off the transaxle, the same

test can be performed. If the vacuum cannot be held or the operating pin does not move, the unit is defective and must be replaced.

### Installation

1. Install the modulator (capsule) into the transaxle by screwing the unit in the same number of turns as was counted when the unit was removed.
2. Install the retaining bracket and bolt. Attach the vacuum hose to the unit.
3. Lower the transaxle, if raised, and install the front mount bolt.
4. Lower the vehicle and install 2⅔ quarts of Dexron® II or its equivalent, into the transaxle. Start the engine, operate the gear selector lever through all of the gear positions and recheck the level of the fluid. Correct as required.

## SPEEDOMETER DRIVE SHAFT SEAL

### Removal

1. Disconnect the speedometer cable at the transaxle and remove.
2. Insert a special tool, part number B.VI. 905 or its equivalent into the case opening.
3. Insert the end of the tool into the seal and by turning part of the tool and holding the second part, the seal can be removed from the case bore.

### Installation

1. Lubricate the seal and push it downward into the case bore, until it seats squarely at the bottom.
2. Install the speedometer cable and tighten the assembly.

## SELECTOR LEVER

### Removal

#### FUEGO AND 18i

1. Position the selector lever at the "N" position.
2. Working under the vehicle, remove the circlip from the transaxle lever, remove the protective cover at the bracket, remove the bracket retaining bolt and remove the bracket arm.
3. From inside the vehicle, remove the selector lever grille by sliding it out.
4. Remove the selector lever housing. The lever can then be disassembled by removing a drift pin from its bottom.

### Installation

1. Install the selector lever to its base and install the drift pin.
2. Check to be sure the transaxle lever and the selector lever is set at the "N" position.
3. Mount the boot and selector lever housing onto the rod and insert the control rod in the bearing at the control end.
4. Attach the control rod at the transaxle side and install the circlip.
5. Reconnect the arm and tighten the bolt to 13 ft. lbs.
6. Install the protective cover and secure it to the rod.
7. Complete the assembly inside the vehicle for the gear selector housing.

#### ALLIANCE

### Removal

1. Disconnect the negative battery cable, raise the vehicle and support safely.
2. Disconnect the selector lever cable from the selector lever and lower the vehicle.
3. Remove the selector lever grille, the console bezel, the radio and the console itself.
4. Remove the two selector lever bracket retaining bolts and spacers. Remove the selector lever assembly.

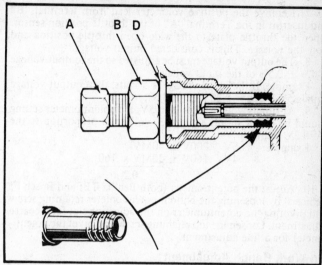

Use of special tool (A-extractor, B-nut and D-spacer) to remove speedometer drive shaft oil seal (© Renault/AMC)

### Installation

1. Install the following in this order, the selector lever assembly, the spacers and retaining bolts, the console, the radio, the control bezel and the selector lever grille.
2. Raise the vehicle and support safely. Connect the selector lever cable.
3. Lower the vehicle and connect the battery cable.
4. Check the gear selector lever operation and make adjustments as required.

## THROTTLE POSITION POTENTIOMETER

### Removal

#### VEHICLES WITH BENDIX TBI AND BOSCH FI

1. Remove the air filter assembly (vehicles equipped with Bendix TBI only).
2. Separate the wire connector from the potentiometer.
3. Remove the two retaining screws and the potentiometer.

### Installation

1. Install the potentiometer and the two retaining screws.
2. Install the wire connector.
3. If the vehicle is equipped with the Bendix TBI, install the air filter assembly.

### Adjustment.

1. On vehicles equipped with Bendix TBI, remove the air filter assembly.
2. Turn the ignition to the "ON" position.
3. Using a digital volt-ohm meter, insert the negative (−) voltmeter lead into the terminal "C" of the potentiometer.

**NOTE: Do not disconnect the connector. Insert the voltmeter lead (−) into the back of the connector and push it in to contact the terminal.**

4. Insert the positive (+) voltmeter lead into terminal "B" of the throttle position sensor.
5. Move the throttle plate to the wide open throttle position by hand. Be sure the throttle contacts the stop.

─────── **CAUTION** ───────

*Do not have the engine operating.*

6. Note the exact voltmeter reading. This is input voltage and should be approximately 4.3 volts.

7. Remove the positive voltmeter lead from terminal "B" and insert it in the Terminal "A" of the throttle position sensor. Open the throttle plate to the wide open throttle position and note the voltage. This is considered output voltage.

8. The output voltage must be adjusted so that output voltage is 4% ± 0.5% of the input voltage.

Example: If the input voltage is 5 volts, then output voltage equals 5V x 4% = 0.20V ± 0.03 V.

9. At supply voltages less than 5V, the potentiometer setting should be 4% of supply voltage ± voltage in proportion to the 5V/0.2V setting.

**Example:** 5V .200V ± 30MV

$$4V \quad .160V \pm \frac{30MV \times .160}{0.2}$$

10. Adjust the potentiometer (both Bendix TBI and Bosch FI vehicles) by loosening the bottom potentiometer retaining screw and pivoting the potentiometer on the adjusting slot for a coarse adjustment. Loosen the top retaining screw and pivot the potentiometer for a fine adjustment.

### On Work Bench Adjustment

1. Using a regulated power source, such as the vehicle battery, connect a lead between the positive (+) terminal of the power source and the terminal "B" of the potentiometer.

2. Connect a lead from the negative (−) terminal of the power source and terminal "C" of the potentiometer.

3. Open the throttle to the wide open position.

4. Using a digital volt/ohm meter, read the input voltage between terminals "B" and "C." Close the throttle.

5. Remove the positive (+) lead from terminal "B" and insert it in terminal "A."

6. Open the throttle plate to its wide open position.

7. Read the voltage on the voltmeter. This is output voltage and should be 4% ± 0.5% of the input voltage. Close the throttle.

**Example:** 12.5V x 4% = 0.5V ± .062V

## KICKDOWN SWITCH

### Adjustment

1. The kickdown switch must operate with the accelerator pedal fully depressed.

2. Be sure the accelerator cable has approximately 1/16 inch (3–4mm) movement in the stop sleeve when the accelerator pedal is completely depressed. The switch is adjusted by the cable setting.

3. Be certain the electrical connector cover is properly positioned to prevent corrosion.

### Removal

1. Remove the accelerator cable and electrical wire.

2. Disconnect the wire from the kickdown switch.

3. Remove the switch retaining bolts and remove the switch.

### Installation

1. Install the switch and the retaining bolts.

2. Install the electrical wire.

3. Install the accelerator cable and adjust the cable and switch.

## CONVERTER OIL SEAL

### Removal

The converter oil seal can be removed after the transaxle has been removed from the vehicle and the converter removed from the transaxle. The seal is pryed from the housing bore and with the use of a special seal installer tool, the seal can be reinstalled to its proper depth.

## DIFFERENTIAL BEARING NUT AND OIL SEAL

**NOTE: The differential bearing nut may be removed with the transaxle in the vehicle.**

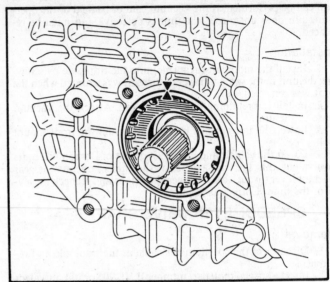

**Matchmarking position of differential bearing nut (© Renault/AMC)**

### Removal

1. Raise the vehicle and support safely.

2. Drain the transaxle of fluid.

3. Insert a special spacer tool or its equivalent, between the lower shock absorber attaching base and the lower suspension arm pivot shaft.

4. Remove the brake caliper and punch out the drive shaft roll pins.

5. With appropriate tools, loosen the steering tie rod ends, the upper suspension ball joints and tilt the stub axle carriers to disengage the drive shafts from the side gears.

6. Match mark the position of the differential bearing nut with respect to the housing. Remove the "O" ring from the side gear.

7. Remove the lockstop and unscrew the nut, counting the number of turns required to remove it.

8. Remove the oil seal and "O" ring from the differential nut.

### Installation

1. Lubricate the seal and "O" ring. Install both on the differential nut.

**NOTE: The seal is positioned in the differential nut with the seal lip pointing inward.**

2. Carefully install the differential nut and tighten it the same number of turns as required to remove it.

**NOTE: A seal protector cannot be used on vehicles equipped with automatic transaxles.**

3. Install the lockstop and install the "O" ring onto the side gear.

4. Position the drive shaft to line up the roll pin holes. Insert the roll pins and seal the holes.

5. Install the steering and upper suspension ball joints. Tighten the nuts securely to a torque of 48 ft. lbs. on the upper suspension ball joint nuts; 26 ft. lbs. on the steering tie rod ball joint nuts; 59 ft. lbs. on the wheel lugs and 45 ft. lbs. on the brake caliper bolts.

6. Install the brake caliper and road wheels. Tighten the bolts to the above torque.

7. Remove the special tool spacer from the suspension and lower the vehicle.

8. Fill the transaxle with Dexron® II fluid or its equivalent to its correct level.

9. Apply the brakes several times before driving off to road test.

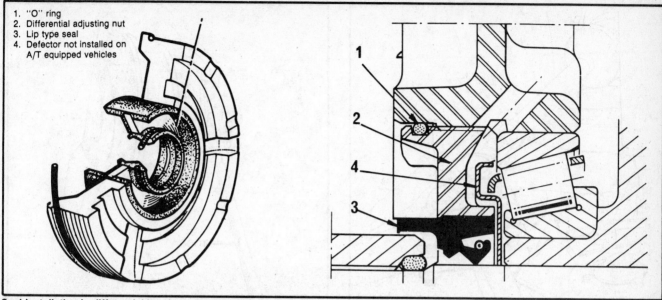

1. "O" ring
2. Differential adjusting nut
3. Lip type seal
4. Deflector not installed on A/T equipped vehicles

**Seal installation in differential bearing nut** (© Renault/AMC)

## MOLDED WIRE HARNESS

The wiring used to control the varied electrical components has molded sockets and most require the complete replacement of the wire assembly, should a malfunction occur within the wire assembly.

The governor/computer/multifunction switches and wiring can be removed separately, therefore, not requiring the removal of the lower unit housing of the transaxle when the solenoid valve wiring or the sealed plugs are not the cause of the malfunction.

# REMOVAL & INSTALLATION

## Transaxle Removal

### FUEGO, 18i MODELS

NOTE: The transaxle can either be removed with the engine from above or can be removed separately from under the vehicle. The procedures outlines are directed to the removal of the transaxle separately.

1. Disconnect the battery cables.
2. Raise the vehicle and support safely. Drain the fluid from the transaxle unit.
3. Disconnect the vacuum hose to the vacuum modulator.
4. Disconnect the transaxle electrical wiring connectors and remove the support.
5. Insert the suspension spacers between the lower shock absorber fixing base and the lower control arm pivot shaft.
6. Have the vehicle in a position or on a lift to raise the vehicle as required.
7. Drive the roll pins out of the drive shafts.
8. Remove the suspension upper ball joints and the steering tie rod ends.
9. Tilt the stub axles to free the drive shafts from the side gears.

10. Remove the selector linkage from the transaxle selector lever.
11. Remove the fluid dipstick tube.
12. Remove the converter protective plate and remove the three retaining bolts.
13. Remove the exhaust pipe bracket nut which is attached to the transaxle.
14. If not already positioned, place the transmission jack assembly under the rear of the transaxle. Remove the two supports and gently lower the transaxle from the installed position, enough to remove the speedometer and governor cables.
15. Remove the engine to transaxle bolts and slowly lower the transaxle from under the vehicle.
16. As soon as the converter is exposed, install a converter retaining strap to hold the converter in place.

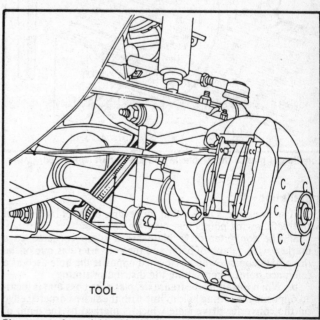

**Placement of special tool in the front suspension** (© Renault/AMC)

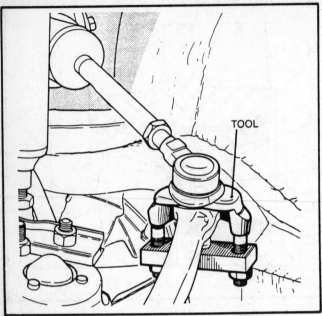

Separating the tie rod end—typical (© Renault/AMC)

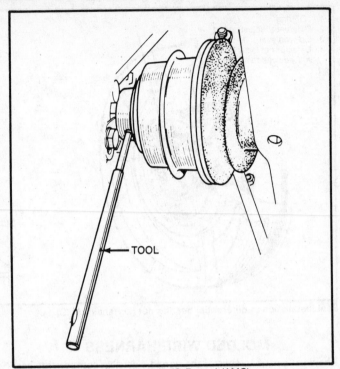

Removing the pins from the axle (© Renault/AMC)

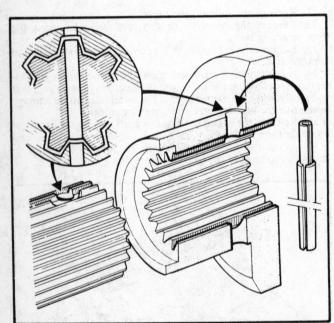

Location of pins in the stub axle and drive shaft (© Renault/AMC)

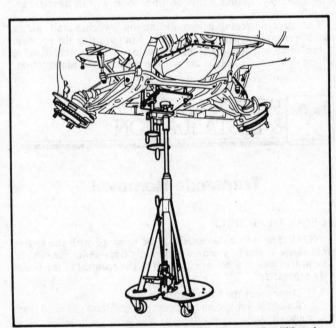

Removing or installing the transaxle with the use of a lifting device—typical (© Renault/AMC)

## Installation

1. The transaxle is replaced in the reverse order of its removal with the following points that must be noted:

a. The converter drive plate has a sharp cornered edge marked with a daub of paint and the converter has one of the three fixing bosses which is located opposite the hole used as a reference point when setting the distributor timing.

b. When installing the transaxle, place the boss that is located opposite the timing hole in line with the sharp cornered edge on the converter drive plate which is marked by the daub of paint.

c. Install new lock washers during the installation.

d. Tighten the converter bolts gradually and to a torque of 30 ft. lbs.

e. If the vehicle is equipped with a TDC sensor, position the sensor approximately 0.039 in. (1mm) from the engine flywheel. If a new sensor is used, three pegs are on the sensor which allows the position of the sensor to be set correctly.

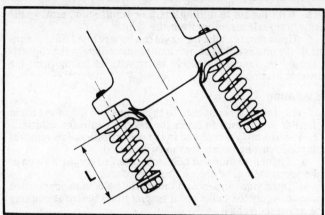

**Exhaust pipe to manifold retaining bolts and springs**
(© Renault/AMC)

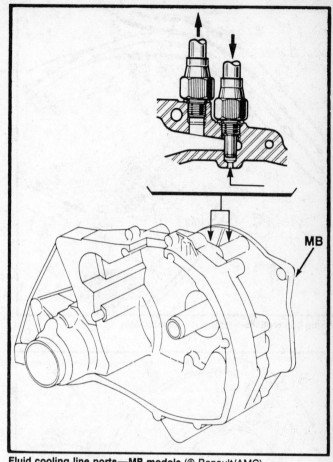

**Fluid cooling line ports—MB models** (© Renault/AMC)

f. Adjust the selector lever and the governor cable as previously outlined.

g. Be sure the computer and governor connections are correctly made and the grounding wires are in place.

h. Fill the unit with Dexron® II fluid and start the engine.

i. After the engine has operated a short time, move the selector lever through all the gear positions and recheck the fluid level. Correct as required.

j. Road test the vehicle and correct any malfunctions as required.

## Removal

### ALLIANCE, ENCORE

1. Disconnect the battery cables.
2. Raise the vehicle and support safely.
3. Drain the transaxle fluid, the engine oil, the cooling system, both the radiator and the block.
4. Remove the air intake assembly and the radiator.
5. Disconnect the wire harness connectors, the vacuum hoses, the accelerator cable and the heater house.

**NOTE: Mark the wiring, vacuum hoses and heater hoses to aid in the assembly.**

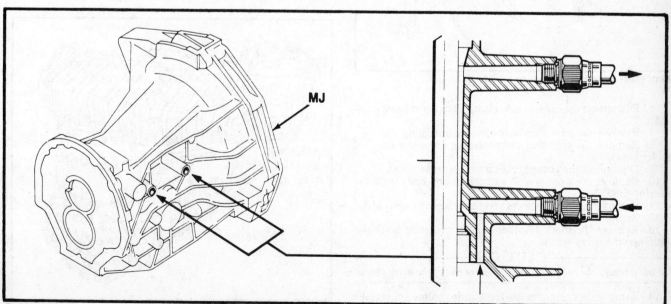

**Fluid cooling line ports—MJ models** (© Renault/AMC)

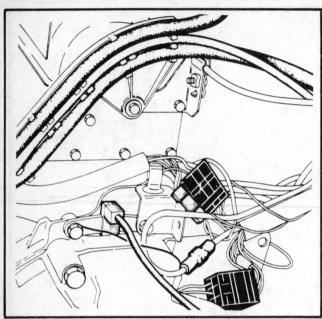

**Wiring connections—typical** (© Renault/AMC)

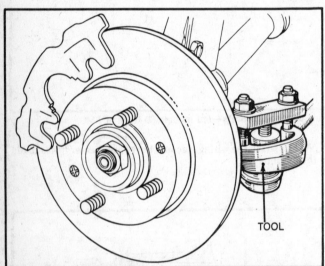

**Removal of tie rod end—Alliance models** (© Renault/AMC)

6. Disconnect the exhaust pipe clamp from the exhaust manifold.

7. Remove the power brake booster vacuum hose.

8. Remove the gear shift mechanism and the transaxle oil cooler hoses.

9. Disconnect the ground cable from the transaxle.

10. Remove the front wheels and the tie rod ends from the steering links.

11. Remove the brake calipers and hang them from the body.

12. Remove the drive shaft retaining roll pins.

13. Remove the shock absorber bottom mounting bolts and withdraw the drive shafts.

------- CAUTION -------

*Do not damage the rubber boot at the outer end of the drive shafts.*

14. Remove the engine/transaxle mounting bolts or nuts at the front mounting and at the rear mounting.

15. With the aid of a lifing chain or similar tool, remove the engine/transaxle assembly from the vehicle.

16. Upon removal, the transaxle can be separated from the engine. If the unit is not to be overhauled immediately, the converter should be strapped securely to prevent its falling from the transaxle assembly.

### Installation

1. The transaxle is attached to the engine and the lifting chain or similar tool is used to lower the assembly into the vehicle.

2. The assembly is replaced in the reverse order of its removal with the following points that must be noted:

   a. Tighten all nuts and bolts to a specified torque if given in the specifications or the outline procedures.

   b. Install the calipers and torque the bolts to their specified torque. Apply the brake pedal several times before attempting to move the vehicle.

   c. Fill the engine and the transaxle with oil and fluid.

   d. Fill the cooling system with proper coolant.

   e. New bolts must be used when installing the exhaust pipe clamp.

**NOTE: With the springs installed on the exhaust pipe clamp, the distance between the clamp and the lower part of the hex bolt head should be 1.71 in. (43.5mm).**

   f. After the roll pins have been installed in the drive shafts, the holes must be plugged with a sealer.

   g. Be certain the rubber boots on the drive shafts are in good condition and not torn or damaged.

# BENCH OVERHAUL

## MJ-1, MJ-3 TRANSAXLE MODELS

### Before Disassembly

1. Remove the converter from the transaxle.
2. Remove the dipstick tube and the wiring.

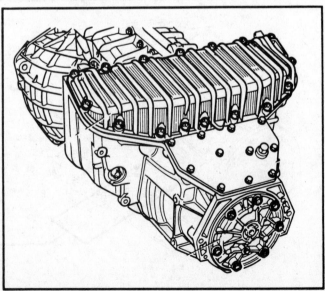

**Inverted MJ transaxle models** (© Renault/AMC)

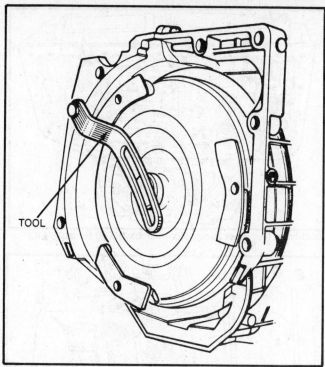

Use of bracket tool to hold torque converter (© Renault/AMC)

3. Remove the governor-computer from the assembly by the removal of the three upper bolts.
4. Remove the multifunction switch, leaving only the sealed plug on the housing.
5. Remove the vacuum modulator (capsule).

## Disassembly.

1. Invert the transaxle and remove the oil pan retaining bolts, the oil pan, the bottom cover and the gasket.
2. Remove the filter and seal. Do not discard the suction tube seal.
3. Disconnect the sealed plug socket and remove the moulded wiring.
4. Remove the outer valve body bolts from each side and remove the valve body assembly. Disengage the manual valve from the inner selector lever.

**NOTE: A center retaining bolt may be encountered on some transaxle models.**

5. From the outer end, remove the pump cover and remove the pump drive shaft. Inspect for wear on the slots for the lugs of the drive pump gear.
6. Remove the driven pump gear, marking its direction, if to be used again by the direction of the chamfer.
7. Remove the four inner differential assembly bolts from inside the transmission case.
8. Remove the two roll pins, the bolt and the parking gear latch from the gear control linkage.
9. Remove the connecting arm without separating the ball joints. Remove the gear control linkage.
10. Pull the shaft, but do not remove the toothed quadrant.

## ——— CAUTION ———
*The socket containing the locking ball must not be removed unless it is to be replaced.*

11. Set the transaxle on the transmission at the pump housing end. Remove the transaxle/transmission case assembly bolts.

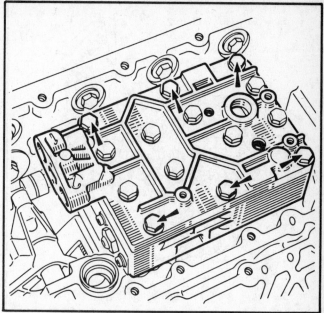

Valve body attaching bolts—MJ models (© Renault/AMC)

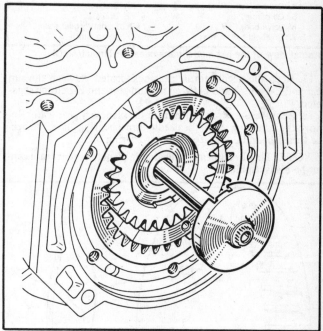

Removal of the oil pump drive shaft (© Renault/AMC)

12. Separate the differential and transmission cases.
13. Remove the parking latch by taking out the centering pin. A slide hammer type tool is used for this operation.
14. Remove the parking latch shaft, the parking latch and the return spring.
15. Remove the brake mechanism retaining bolts (10) and remove the drive train while holding the turbine shaft. Leave the needle thrust bearing inside the case.
16. Position the drive train on a support. Remove the planetary gear train, the sun gear (P-1), the F-1 and F-2 brake assemblies, clutch E-2, clutch E-1 and the turbine shaft.

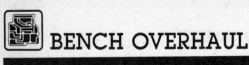

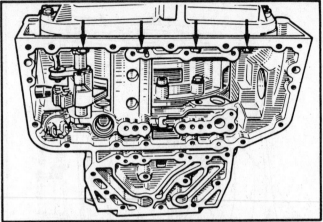

Location of four inner case bolts—MJ models (© Renault/AMC)

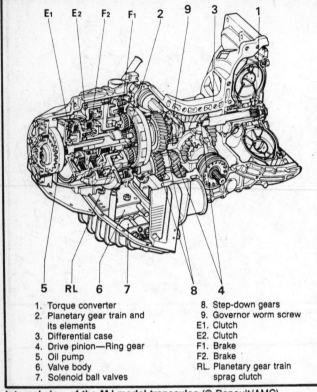

1. Torque converter
2. Planetary gear train and its elements
3. Differential case
4. Drive pinion—Ring gear
5. Oil pump
6. Valve body
7. Solenoid ball valves
8. Step-down gears
9. Governor worm screw
E1. Clutch
E2. Clutch
F1. Brake
F2. Brake
RL. Planetary gear train sprag clutch

Internal view of the MJ model transaxles (© Renault/AMC)

17. Keep the needle thrust bearings located between the sun gear and E-1 clutch and between the sun gear and E-2 clutch separated.

18. Remove the sprag clutch from the planetary gear train. Remove the adjusting shim, the needle thrust bearing plate, the needle thrust bearing, the needle thrust bearing plate.

NOTE: The thrust bearing inside the planetary gear train cannot be disassembled.

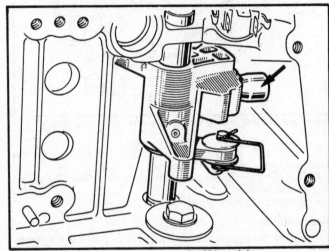

Do not remove the locking ball (arrow)—MJ models (© Renault/AMC)

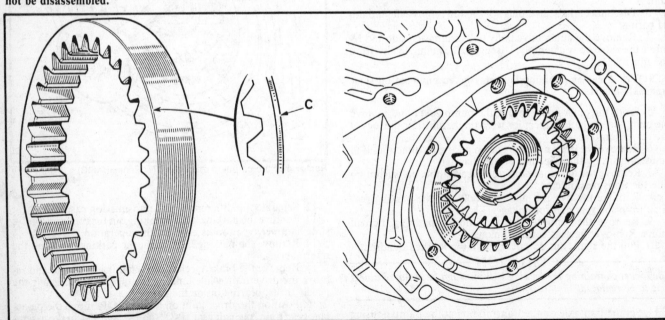

Removal or installation of the oil pump gears. Note beveled edge (C)  (© Renault/AMC)

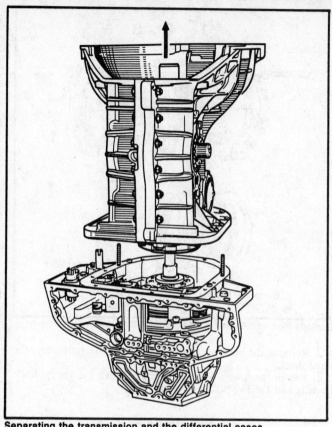

**Separating the transmission and the differential cases**
(© Renault/AMC)

## Component Disassembly

### E-1 CLUTCH

#### Disassembly

1. Remove the compression ring from the needle thrust bearing before removing the needle thrust bearing plate.

2. The turbine shaft and the hub are one piece and cannot be disassembled.

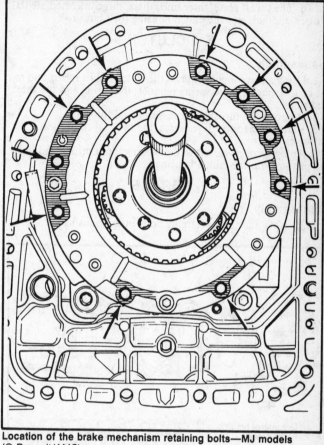

**Location of the brake mechanism retaining bolts—MJ models**
(© Renault/AMC)

3. Push downward on the E-1 piston housing and remove the retaining ring.

4. Disassemble the following after the retaining ring removal:

a. The housing, and shaft.

b. Apply compressed air to the piston housing input orifice and remove the piston.

c. The diaphragm spring.

3. Compression ring
4. Thrust bearing plate
6. Turbine shaft
7. Retaining ring
8. Hub
9. Piston
10. Spring
11. Thrust plate
12. Three lined discs
13. Three intermediate flat discs
14. Hub
15. Bell (clutch) housing

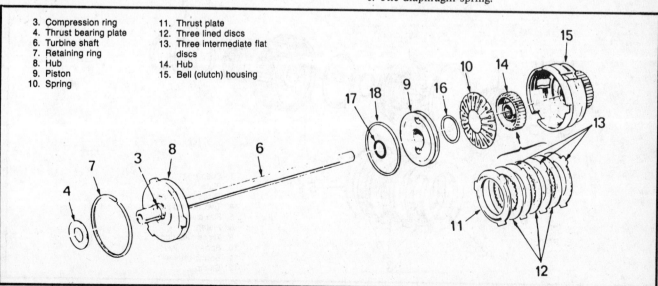

**Exploded view of E-1 clutches—MJ models** (© Renault/AMC)

d. The thrust plate, three lined discs, three intermediate flat discs, the hub and the clutch housing (bell housing).

## E-2 CLUTCH

### Disassembly

1. Using a press tool, compress the clutch return spring and remove the snapring, the spring retainer, the spring and the three seal rings.
2. Remove the thrust plate snapring and the plate.
3. Remove the three lined discs, the two waved discs and the flat disc.
4. Apply compressed air to the bearing input orifice and push the piston from the clutch housing.

## F-1 BRAKE

### Disassembly

1. Remove the three retaining bolts in the housing.

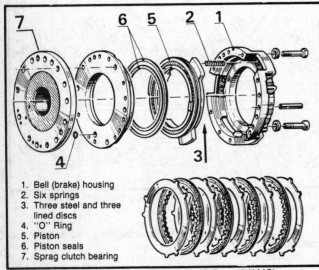

1. Bell (brake) housing
2. Six springs
3. Three steel and three lined discs
4. "O" Ring
5. Piston
6. Piston seals
7. Sprag clutch bearing

**Explode view of F-1 brake—MJ models** (© Renault/AMC)

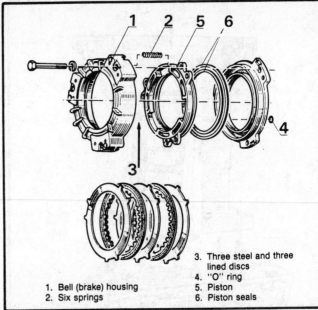

1. Bell (brake) housing
2. Six springs
3. Three steel and three lined discs
4. "O" ring
5. Piston
6. Piston seals

**Explode view of F-2 brake—MJ models** (© Renault/AMC)

2. Remove the housing, the six springs, the steel discs and the lined discs.
3. Retain the small "O" ring from between the sprag clutch bearing and the F-2 piston housing.

## F-2 BRAKE

### Disassembly

1. Remove the three retaining bolts in the housing.
2. Remove the housing, the six springs the steel and lined discs.
3. Retain the "O" ring located between the sprag clutch bearing and the F-1 piston housing.
4. Push the pistons out of the housings with compressed air. Remove the piston seals.

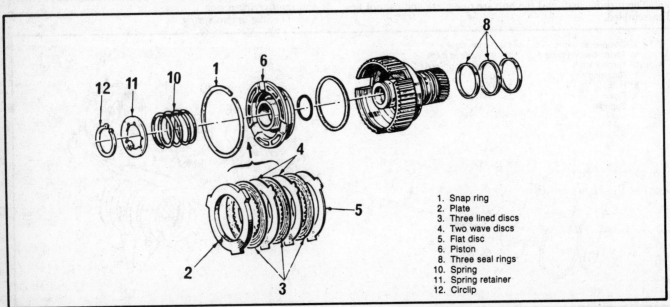

1. Snap ring
2. Plate
3. Three lined discs
4. Two wave discs
5. Flat disc
6. Piston
8. Three seal rings
10. Spring
11. Spring retainer
12. Circlip

**Exploded view of E-2 clutches—MJ models** (© Renault/AMC)

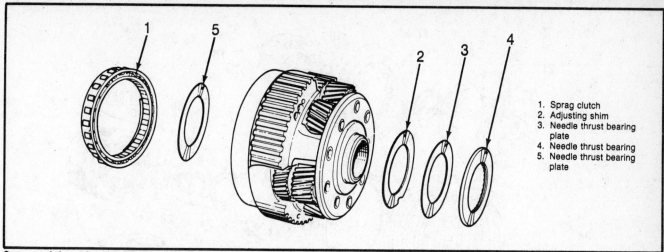

**Sprag and thrust bearings and washers—MJ models** (© Renault/AMC)

1. Sprag clutch
2. Adjusting shim
3. Needle thrust bearing plate
4. Needle thrust bearing
5. Needle thrust bearing plate

## MB-1 MODELS

### Disassembly

1. Place the transaxle on a clean work bench area and remove the converter.

2. Remove the four bolts on the step-down drive case and the remaining bolts on the converter and differential case. Separate the cases.

3. Remove the oil pan assembly.

4. Remove the sealed connection and its retaining clip from the valve body area.

5. Remove the valve body assembly from the case. Remove the two seals and plate.

**NOTE: The center valve body bolts on the pressure outlet side and the bolt next to the inlet screen tube are locator bolts and must be replaced in the same location during the reassembly.**

6. Remove the "Park" latch shaft and spring.

7. Remove the needle roller thrust bearing, snapring, reverse drive train, overrunning clutch and the F-1 clutch disc pack as a unit.

8. Remove the F-1 piston with air pressure applied through the apply port in the valve body case channels.

9. Remove the friction washer, the E-2 bell (clutch) housing the 1.5 mm thrust friction washer, the forward drive train and the E-1, E-2 clutch packs.

**NOTE: The E-1 and E-2 clutch assemblies cannot be disassembled and must be replaced as a unit. Only the needle roller bearing can be replaced.**

10. Remove the snapring, the F-1 piston holder sleeve, the F-2 clutch disc pack, the needle roller thrust bearing, the feed hub support and the F-2 cup assembly.

11. Remove the F-2 piston assembly and the oil pump gears.

12. The shift linkage and remaining parking linkage can be removed as required.

## INSPECTION AND CLEANING

### ALL TRANSAXLE MODELS
#### ——— CAUTION ———

*Do not use Trichlorethylene to clean the transaxle case and components. Harmful deposits can be left on the oil seals. Do not use rags with lint, only lint free shop rags.*

1. Use alcohol, mineral spirits or a professional cleaning agent to clean the case and components.

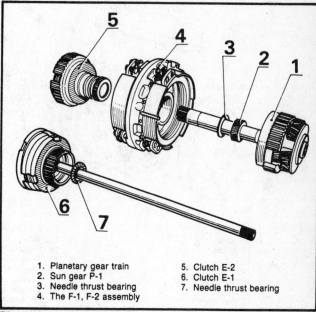

**Disassembly of the drive train—MJ models** (© Renault/AMC)

1. Planetary gear train
2. Sun gear P-1
3. Needle thrust bearing
4. The F-1, F-2 assembly
5. Clutch E-2
6. Clutch E-1
7. Needle thrust bearing

2. Use compressed air to dry the case and components after the cleaning process has been completed.

3. Use compressed air to blow out all the holes and channels in the following components;
   a. The transaxle case.
   b. The sprag clutch bearing.
   c. The forward sun gear.
   d. The reverse sun gear.
   e. The E-2 bell housing (ball valves).
   f. The E-1 piston (ball valves).
   g. The E-1 hub.
   h. The pump cover.
   i. The pump shaft.
   j. The turbine shaft.
   k. The stator support.
   l. The Converter oil return calibrating jet.
   m. The planetary gear carrier.

4. It is a normal overhaul procedure to replace the lined and unlined clutch discs during the disassembly and assembly of the transaxle.

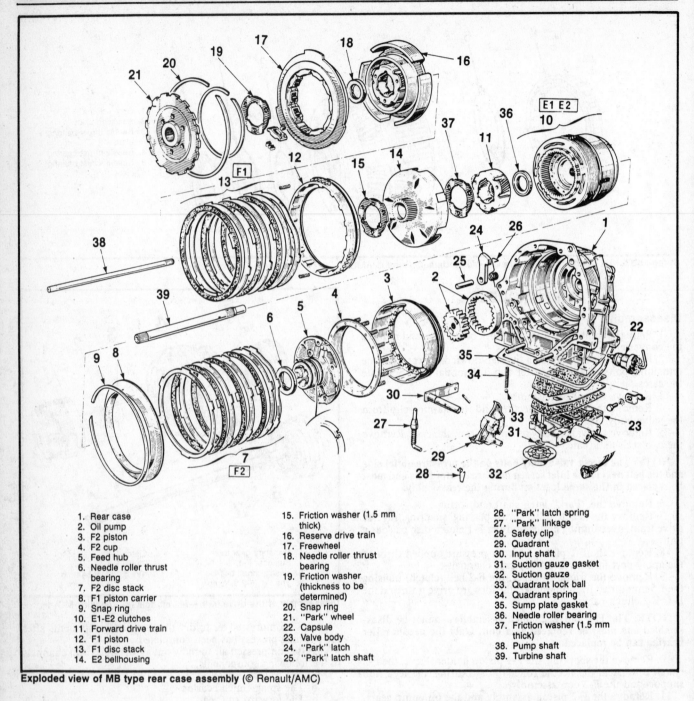

**Exploded view of MB type rear case assembly (© Renault/AMC)**

1. Rear case
2. Oil pump
3. F2 piston
4. F2 cup
5. Feed hub
6. Needle roller thrust bearing
7. F2 disc stack
8. F1 piston carrier
9. Snap ring
10. E1-E2 clutches
11. Forward drive train
12. F1 piston
13. F1 disc stack
14. E2 bellhousing
15. Friction washer (1.5 mm thick)
16. Reserve drive train
17. Freewheel
18. Needle roller thrust bearing
19. Friction washer (thickness to be determined)
20. Snap ring
21. "Park" wheel
22. Capsule
23. Valve body
24. "Park" latch
25. "Park" latch shaft
26. "Park" latch spring
27. "Park" linkage
28. Safety clip
29. Quadrant
30. Input shaft
31. Suction gauze gasket
32. Suction gauze
33. Quadrant lock ball
34. Quadrant spring
35. Sump plate gasket
36. Needle roller bearing
37. Friction washer (1.5 mm thick)
38. Pump shaft
39. Turbine shaft

5. After the cleaning of the components, lubricate the parts immediately with fluid to prevent rusting of metal components.

6. Inspect all sealing ring and "O" ring grooves for the condition of the seating areas. Replace any component showing worn or damaged grooves.

7. Check the condition of the gear teeth on the planetary gear unit and the gear cluster on their shafts.

8. To clean the converter without a professional cleaner, fill the converter with the proper grade of fluid. Invert the converter and allow it to drain for a period of time. Again, place the converter upright and remove the remaining fluid with a syringe from the center of the turbine hub.

9. Check the sealing surfaces on the converter, the stator support housing and the housing breather.

10. Inspect the condition of the oil pump gears and their housing. Be sure the drive shaft is re-useable, along with the cover.

11. The transmission case, the oil pump and ring gear wheel assembly are matched and the changing of one part always entails the replacement of the whole assembly.

12. Inspect the white metal sleeve on the E-1 clutch, the ring groove, the contact surfaces on the sealed junction box, the engagement shaft and all the sealing surfaces.

13. Check the condition of the intermediate clutch discs and that they slide easily on the hub splines and in the clutch housings (bell housings).

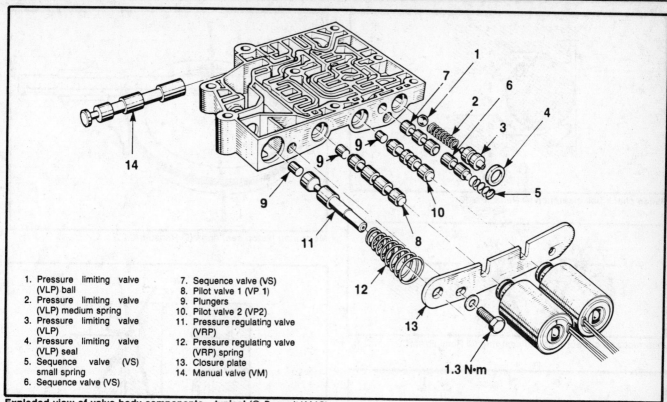

1. Pressure limiting valve (VLP) ball
2. Pressure limiting valve (VLP) medium spring
3. Pressure limiting valve (VLP)
4. Pressure limiting valve (VLP) seal
5. Sequence valve (VS) small spring
6. Sequence valve (VS)
7. Sequence valve (VS)
8. Pilot valve 1 (VP 1)
9. Plungers
10. Pilot valve 2 (VP2)
11. Pressure regulating valve (VRP)
12. Pressure regulating valve (VRP) spring
13. Closure plate
14. Manual valve (VM)

1.3 N•m

**Exploded view of valve body components—typical** (© Renault/AMC)

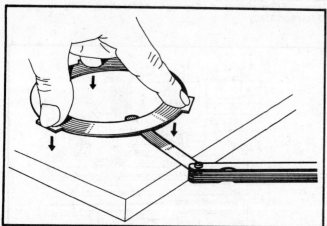

**Checking the wave clearance of disc** (© Renault/AMC)

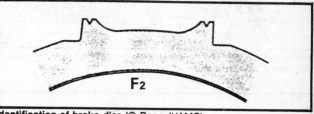

F₂

**Identification of brake disc** (© Renault/AMC)

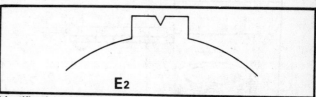

E₂

**Identification of clutch disc** (© Renault/AMC)

14. When installing the new steel wave plates, check the wave with a feeler gauge. Lay the disc flat on a flat surface and without exerting pressure on the disc, slip a feeler gauge blade between the disc and the flat surface. The clearance must be between 0.010-0.018 in. (0.25-0.45mm).

15. Change any bearing plates and thrust plates showing signs of overheating, poor surface conditions, run-out or taper.

— CAUTION —

*If one of the assemblies has overheated, all needle bearings or thrust bearings must be replaced.*

16. Be sure the oil seals fit tightly in their grooves. Measure the seal diameter at two points at right angles to each other, but do not squeeze the seal. Take an average of the two readings and compare it with the seal groove dimension.

17. The seal groove dimension should be 0.008-0.028 in. (0.2-0.7mm).

18. Change the seals without hesitation during the reassemble to avoid internal leak problems.

19. Check the clutch pistons for free movement of their relief check balls. Each ball should move freely in its socket and should not stick to its seat or to the crimped side. The ball travel should be approximately 0.0039 in. (1mm). Should the check balls not operate properly, the entire piston must be replaced.

20. The E-1 clutch bearing and the E-2 clutch bell housing have seal rings. Check the amount of wear on the ring sides, the condition of the bottoms of the ring grooves and the fit of the ring gaps, which must fit together in a flat manner. The gap play should be between 0.002-0.014 in. (0.05-0.35mm).

21. In addition to the checks as outlined in Step 20, inspect the

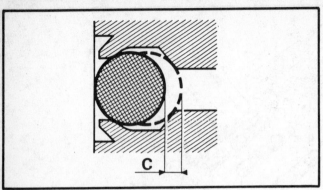

Piston check ball clearance (© Renault/AMC)

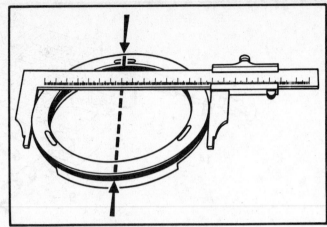

Measuring piston seal rings (© Renault/AMC)

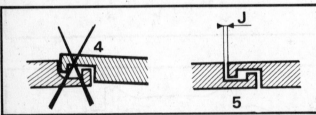

Incorrect and correct fitting of seal ring (© Renault/AMC)

Incorrect (4) and correct (5) fittings of rings. J represents allowable tolerance (© Renault/AMC)

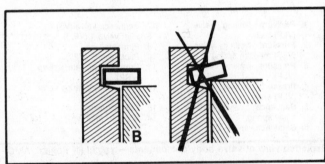

Correct (B) installation of snaprings and incorrect fitting (© Renault/AMC)

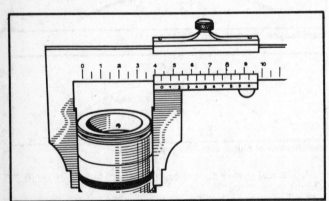

Measuring of white metal sleeve (© Renault/AMC)

surface condition of the piston bore, the diaphragm spring for breakage, the hub, the fit of the two sleeves in the piston housing and the fit of the turbine shaft on the E-1 clutch assembly.

22. On the E-2 clutch assembly, check the piston bore, the return spring, spring retainer and the snapring.

23. In addition to checking the gears on the planetary gear assembly, check the condition of the white metal sleeves, the sprag clutch, its race surface, the needle bearing and its bearing plate.

**NOTE: The sprag clutch can be replaced if necessary, but the planetary gear assembly must be replaced as a unit.**

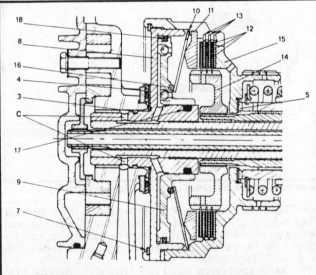

| | |
|---|---|
| 3. Seal ring | 12. Lined discs (3) |
| 4. Needle thrust bearing plate | 13. Flat intermediate discs (3) |
| 5. Needle thrust bearing | 14. Hub |
| 7. Circlip | 15. Connecting bell housing |
| 8. Piston housing | 16. Diaphragm thrust ring |
| 9. Piston | 17. O ring |
| 10. Diaphragm spring | 18. Rectangular seal |
| 11. Thrust plate | C. E1 piston oil feed hole |

Assembly of E-1 clutch unit—typical (© Renault/AMC)

24. The valve body and regulator assembly must not be disassembled, according to the manufacturer. Only the solenoid balls can be changed. Should poor quality of shifting or damage to the clutches and brakes occur, the valve body and its regulator assembly must be changed.

## Assembly of Components

**MJ-1, MJ-3, MB-1 MODELS**

### E-1 CLUTCH

#### Assembly

1. Place the thrust ring on the piston.
2. Lubricate and install the two piston seals. Install the rectangular seal on the piston and the "O" ring on the E-1 piston sleeve.

**NOTE: Lightly lubricate the bore and the part of the hub in which the piston will slide.**

3. Place the piston into its housing with the flange upward, by pushing it in with the thumbs while tilting it back and forth.
4. Assemble the following into the housing, in their proper order;
    a. The hub with the recessed part facing upward.
    b. A lubricated steel disc followed by a lubricated lined disc, continuing until a total of three each have been installed.
    c. The thrust plate with the smooth side towards the lined disc.
    d. The diaphragm spring.
5. Install the piston into the connecting bell housing.
6. Install the snapring, positioning the ends between the two lugs on the piston housing. Be sure the snapring is properly seated in its groove.
7. Install the bearing plate for the needle thrust bearing. Install the seal ring after checking the ring gap play.
8. Check the operation of the E-1 components by applying air pressure to the piston through the apply hole in the hub.

### E-2 CLUTCH

#### Assembly

1. After checking the ring gap play and the condition of the three grooves in the bell housing, install the three seal rings on the E-2 bell housing.
2. Lubricate the two piston seals and install the rectangular seal on the piston and the "O" ring on the piston hub in the E-2 bell housing.

**NOTE: Be sure the seals fit properly in their grooves.**

3. Install the piston into the bell housing and using a press, compress the spring to install the snapring. Guide the spring retainer during the compression.
4. Align the slots in the piston with the slots in the bell housing. Install in the following order, the following components:
    a. The thrust plate.
    b. A lubricated steel disc, followed by a lubricated lined disc, until a total of three steel discs and three lined discs are installed.
    c. Install the thrust plate with the punched mark surface towards the outside of the housing.
5. Install the snapring with the ends fully engaged with its groove.
6. Check the operation of the E-2 components by applying compressed air to the piston through the apply hole in the hub.

### CHECKING AND ADJUSTING THE OPERATING ENDPLAY OF THE E-2 CLUTCH

#### Assembly

1. Place the assembly on a flat surface. The end play is checked

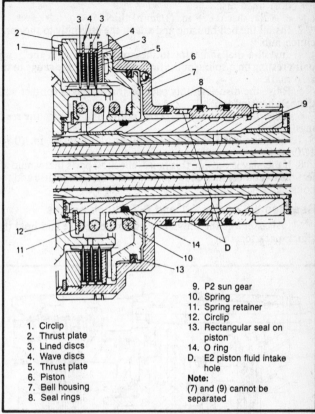

| | |
|---|---|
| 1. Circlip | 9. P2 sun gear |
| 2. Thrust plate | 10. Spring |
| 3. Lined discs | 11. Spring retainer |
| 4. Wave discs | 12. Circlip |
| 5. Thrust plate | 13. Rectangular seal on piston |
| 6. Piston | 14. O ring |
| 7. Bell housing | D. E2 piston fluid intake hole |
| 8. Seal rings | **Note:** (7) and (9) cannot be separated |

**Assembly of E-2 clutch unit—typical** (© Renault/AMC)

with either a dial indicator and a special plate or with the use of a feeler gauge blade.

2. The clearance to be checked is between the piston and the steel disc, with the clutch pack against the snapring, without compressing the wave discs.
3. The play should be between 0.043-0.083 in. (1.1-2.1mm)
4. If the play is greater than specifications, a thicker thrust plate must be used.

#### Checking and Adjusting F-2 Operating Endplay

1. Install the piston without its seal into the F-2 piston housing.
2. Install in order:
    a. A flat disc 0.059 in. (1.5mm) thick.
    b. A lined disc.
    c. A waved disc, marked with two notches, 0.079 in. (2.0mm) thick.

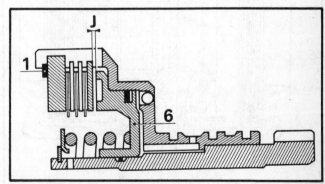

**Checking operating clearance (J) between clutch disc and piston (G)—typical** (© Renault/AMC)

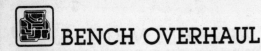
d. A lined disc.

e. A flat disc 0.059 in. (1.5mm) thick.

3. Install the bell housing and attach the assembly to the sprag clutch hub.

4. Install a dial indicator to the housing and with the gauge point resting on a spline of the first lined disc, set the gauge to the zero mark.

5. Raise the disc assembly pack so that it makes contact with the bell housing top.

6. Take measurements at several points and average the readings.

7. The end play should be between 0.028-0.067 in. (0.70-1.70mm).

8. If the play is outside this range, check all parts that would affect the tolerance, such as the piston, wave disc, lined disc and the housing.

## Reassembly of the F-1 and F-2 Clutch brakes

1. Disassemble the previously assembled brake and hold the clutch pack together.

2. Lubricate the four seals for the F-1 and F-2 pistons and install them on the pistons and housings. Be sure the seals fit tightly into their grooves.

3. Place the "O" ring between the sprag clutch hub and the F-1 housing.

4. Install the F-1 piston into its housing carefully so as not to damage the seals.

5. Install the steel discs 0.059 in. (1.5mm) thick and the lined discs.

6. Place the six springs in the housing and cap the assembly with the F-1 bell housing.

7. Install the three F-1 assembly bolts into the sprag clutch hub.

**NOTE: F-1 operating clearance is between 0.043-0.122 in. (1.1-3.1mm).**

8. Invert the assembly and rest it on the F-1 bell housing.

9. Place the "O" ring between the sprag clutch hub and the F-2 housing.

10. Install the F-2 piston into its housing being careful not to damage the seals.

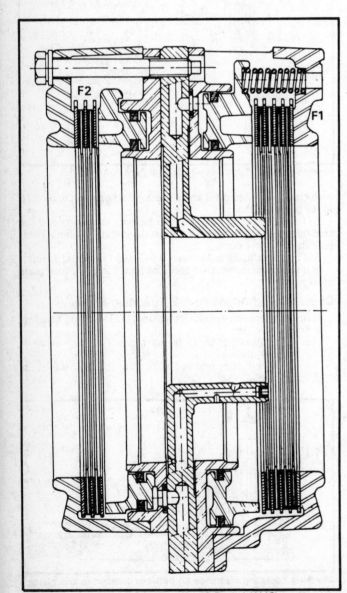

Assembly of F-1 and F-2 brake units (© Renault/AMC)

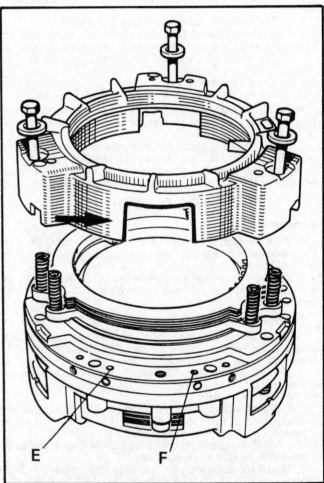

Air applied to E port to check F-1 piston operation and air applied to F port to check F-2 piston operation (© Renault/AMC)

11. Install the clutch pack previously selected, into the F-2 housing.

12. Place the six springs in their housings and cap the assembly with the F-2 bell housing. Install the three bolts into the F-1 sprag clutch assembly.

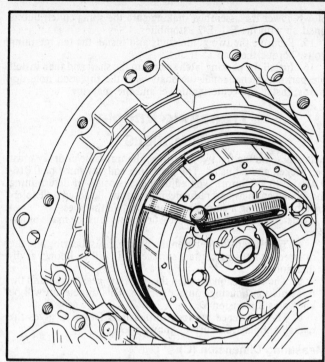

Checking the F-2 brake operating clearance—typical
(© Renault/AMC)

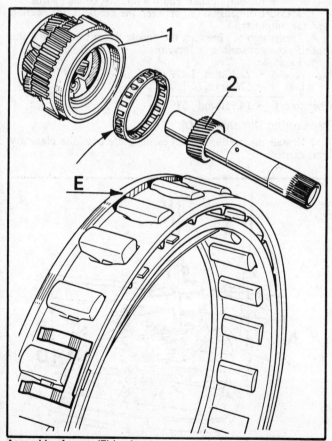

Assembly of sprag (E) in planetary gear train (1) along with P1 sun gear (2) (© Renault/AMC)

13. Check the F-1 and F-2 components with air pressure.

14. The air pressure is applied to the apply ports on the clutch housing.

### PLANETARY GEAR

**Assembly**

1. Install the sprag clutch on the planetary gear train. The shoulder of the cage should face towards inside or bottom of the carrier.

2. Correctly install the thrust bearing plate.

3. Install the sun gear so that it centers and holds the inner thrust bearing.

## Assembly of the Units into the Transaxle

**MJ-1, MJ-3, MODELS**

1. Place the E-1 assembly and the turbine shaft on a tube or pipe approximately 4 inches (100mm) in diameter.

2. Place the needle thrust bearing between the E-1 and P-2, with the pins facing towards P-2.

3. Roughly center the E-2 discs and slide the assembly onto the splines in the E-1 connecting bell housing.

4. Gently turn the assembly, without forcing, to avoid damaging the discs.

5. When all the discs have been properly placed, a play of approximately ⅛ in. (4mm) should exist between E-1 and E-2.

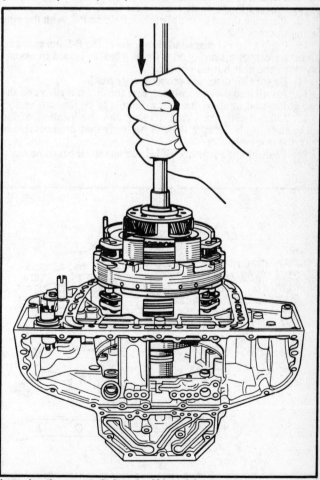

Lowering the gear train into the MJ model rear case
(© Renault/AMC)

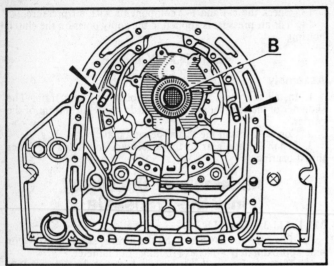

Location of needle thrust bearing (B) and use of the two guide bolts
(© Renault/AMC)

6. Lubricate the E-2 rings and their bearing surfaces on the sprag clutch hub.

7. Roughly center the F-2 discs and slowly lower the brake assembly onto E-2.

8. Proceed in the same manner for the E-2 unit.

9. Place the thrust bearing between P-2 and P-1, with the pins facing towards P-2.

10. Center the F-1 discs and slowly lower the P-1 sun gear and planetary carrier assembly onto the F-1 brake. To aid in assembly, turn the unit but do not force it.

11. Be sure all discs are properly aligned.

12. Install into the transmission case the thrust washer and the two guide stud to allow the unit assembly to be lowered easily.

13. Lubricate the seal ring housing and the location of the sprag clutch hub. Be sure there is no burrs that might interfere with the assembly.

14. Position the assembly while holding it by the turbine shaft.

Slowly lower the assembly, making sure the sprag clutch hub is lined up with the E-1, E-2 assemblies.

15. Remove the two guide studs and install the ten retaining bolts. Torque them to 15 ft. lbs.

16. Install the parking latch spring on the shaft and then install the parking latch. Install the shaft with the threaded hole upwards. Install the centering dowel and the snapring.

## Transaxle Endplay
### MJ MODELS

Before assembling the two-housings, the transaxle endplay must be checked and adjusted. The operating endplay must be 0.016-0.031 in. (0.4-0.8mm). The adjustment consists of determining the overall endplay and reducing it to within the acceptable tolerance by installing a shim of the appropriate thickness.

To determine the endplay, measurements must be made as follows:

a. The dimension between the needle thrust bearing and the differential housing contact surface. This will be known as dimension C.

b. The dimension between the planetary gear carrier and the transmission housing contact surface. This dimension will be known as dimension D.

c. The difference between dimensions D and C gives the overall endplay dimension, known as JT.

**Measuring Dimension (C):**

1. Install main shaft needle thrust bearing.

2. Using a straight edge and a depth gauge, measure dimension (A) between the output shaft and the housing contact surface.

3. Measure dimension (B) between the needle thrust bearing and the output shaft.

4. Dimension (C) between the needle thrust bearing and the housing contact surface is, therefore: $C = A - B$.

5. Example:

$$
\begin{array}{ll}
A = 72.10\text{mm} & (2.839 \text{ in.}) \\
\text{minus } B = 57.15\text{mm} & (2.250 \text{ in.}) \\
\hline
\text{therefore } C = 14.95\text{mm} & (0.589 \text{ in.})
\end{array}
$$

**Measuring Dimension (D):**

1. Install the needle thrust bearing plate onto the planetary gear carrier.

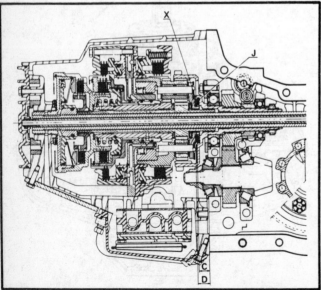

Location of selective shim (X) to control end play tolerance (J)—MJ models (© Renault/AMC)

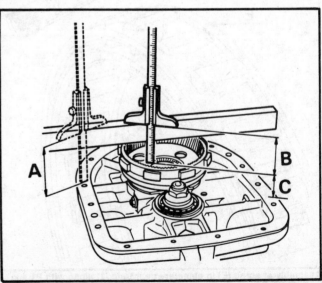

Measuring dimension A, B and C—MJ models (© Renault/AMC)

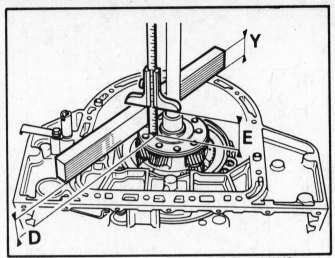

**Measuring dimension D and Y—MJ models** (© Renault/AMC)

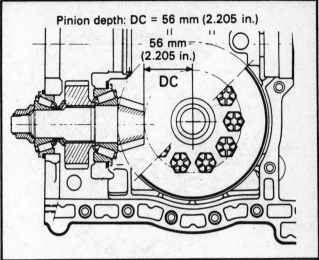

**Pinion depth—MJ models** (© Renault/AMC)

2. Measure dimension (E) on the transmission case between the straight edge and the plate on the planetary gear carrier: $D = E - Y$
3. Y is the thickness of the straight edge.
4. Example:
$$E = 41.85mm \ (1.648 \ in.)$$
$$\text{minus } Y = 25.00mm \ (0.984 \ in.)$$
$$\text{therefore } D = 16.85mm \ (0.664 \ in.)$$

## Overall End Play:

1. Overall end play (JT) between the planetary gear carrier and the needle thrust bearing is: $JT = D - C$.
2. Example:
$$D = 16.85mm \ (0.664 \ in.)$$
$$\text{minus } C = 14.95mm \ (0.589 \ in.)$$
$$\text{therefore } JT = 1.90mm \ (0.075 \ in.)$$

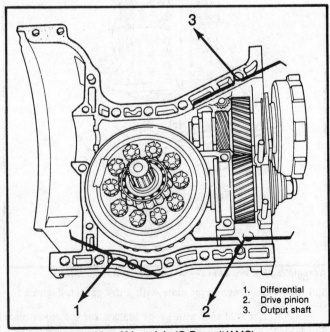

1. Differential
2. Drive pinion
3. Output shaft

**Differential assembly—MJ models** (© Renault/AMC)

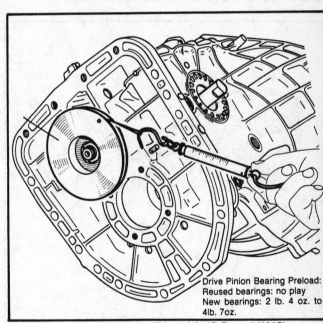

Drive Pinion Bearing Preload:
Reused bearings: no play
New bearings: 2 lb. 4 oz. to 4lb. 7oz.

**Drive pinion bearing preload—MJ models** (© Renault/AMC)

## Determining Shim Thickness:

1. The desired operating end play, lets say 0.6mm (0.024 in.), will be obtained by inserting a shim (X) which will be equal to: $X = JT - 0.6mm \ (0.024 \ in.)$.
2. Example: $X = 1.90mm - 0.6mm = 1.30mm$
$$(X = 0.075 \ in. - 0.024 \ in. = 0.051 \ in.)$$
3. Shims are available in the following thicknesses: 0.25, 0.50, 0.80, 1.00, 1.30, 1.50, 1.75, 2.00, 2.25, 2.50mm
4. So as not to be confused with the needle thrust bearing plate, the adjustment shims are brown and have a notch.
5. If the shim calculation comes out to zero or greater than 2.5mm (0.098 in.), check that:
   a. all needle thrust bearings are in position
   b. the sun gears are properly meshed
   c. the discs are properly seated on the splines.

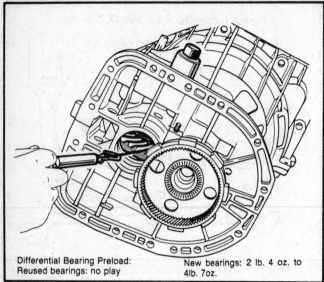

Differential Bearing Preload:
Reused bearings: no play

New bearings: 2 lb. 4 oz. to
4lb. 7oz.

**Differential bearing preload—MJ models** (© Renault/AMC)

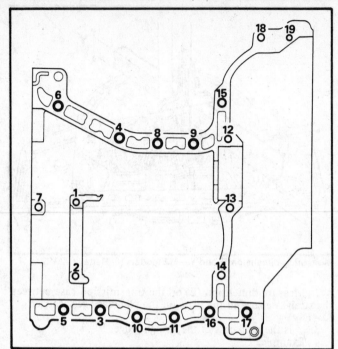

**Sequence of bolt tightening to 14 ft. lbs. torque —MJ models**
(© Renault/AMC)

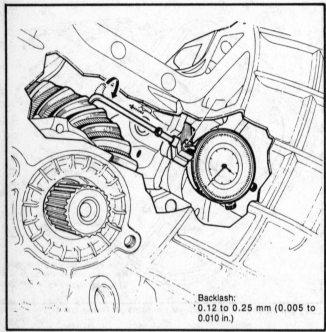

Backlash:
0.12 to 0.25 mm (0.005 to
0.010 in.)

**Ring and pinion back lash—MJ models** (© Renault/AMC)

## Assembling the Two Cases

1. Install the needle thrust bearing on the output shaft in the differential case.

2. Install the endplay adjusting shim that was previously selected. Shim should have a notch.

3. Install the needle thrust plate.

4. Be sure the oil seal is correctly installed on the transmission case.

5. Install the 0.276 in. (7.0mm) diameter guide studs on the transmission case.

6. Install the centering dowels and coat the sealing surface with gasket sealer. Install the gasket.

7. Lubricate the turbine shaft and slowly lower the differential case onto the transmission case. Tighten the attaching bolts

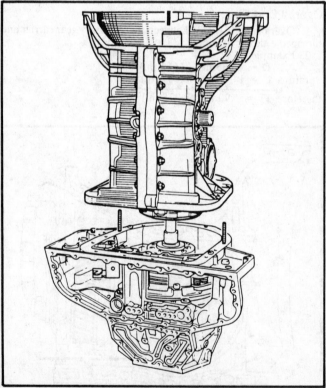

**Assembling the two cases—MJ models** (© Renault/AMC)

and install the lower cover plate with a dry gasket. Tighten the cover plate bolts.

8. Place the dial indicator gauge bracket on the cover plate and set the point of the gauge on the E-1 shaft.

9. Pull on the turbine shaft and set the gauge to zero.

10. Push the turbine shaft back into the unit and read the endplay on the dial indicator gauge. The endplay should be 0.016-0.032 in. (0.4-0.8mm).

11. When the endplay is correct, finish assembling the two housings and arrange the wiring clips correctly.

12. Install the sealed junction plug equipped with a new "O" ring.

13. Install the assembled sector and control shaft, being sure the "O" ring is in place. Install the assembled parking rod with its end in its housing and the control sector. Install the roll pin.

14. Install the valve body, being sure that both centering dowels are positioned on the valve body and that the two toothed quadrants are properly meshed when the selector lever is in *park* position.

15. Install the valve body on the housing and engage the manual valve on its ball joint. Tighten the bolts to their proper torque.

16. Connect the sealed junction plug and check that the marks on the valve body, the solenoid ball valves and on the plugs all match. Position the magnet on the solenoid ball valve retaining clamp.

17. Lubricate and install the inner and outer gears, aligning the marks made during the disassembly. Chamfer face downward into housing.

18. Install the pump drive shaft and engage the drive shaft lugs to the inner gear lugs.

19. Lubricate the "O" ring for the filter suction pipe and a slip it over the end of the pipe. Push the pipe into the housing carefully to avoid damage to the "O" ring.

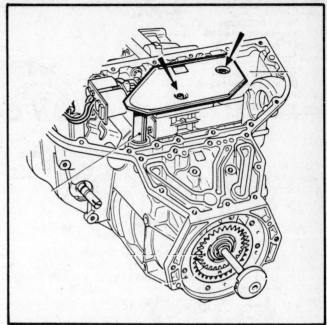

**Installation of the oil pump drive shaft and filter assembly—MJ models** (© Renault/AMC)

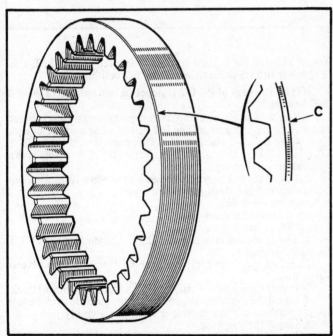

**Chamfer on pump gear edge is to be placed downward into the housing—MJ models** (© Renault/AMC)

20. Install the oil filter and secure it with its two bolts.

21. Install the oil pan and retain it with the retaining bolts.

22. Install the stator support with the aid of a guide bolt in one of the bolt holes. Lubricate the turbine shaft and install the stator support.

23. Lubricate the converter oil seal and install the seal with a seal installer tool.

24. Lubricate the converter white metal sleeve, the turbine shaft and the pump shaft splines. Install the converter assembly and install a converter holding tool.

25. Install the governor/computer with its seal, the vacuum diaphragm (capsule), the wiring and the dipstick.

## Assembly

**MB-1 MODELS**

1. Install the oil pump gears and make sure they rotate freely in the case.

2. Install the clutches and brakes into their housings in the same manner as outlined in the Assembly of Component Section.

3. Install the F-2 piston and the piston cup into the case. Be sure the springs enter their seats properly.

4. Using guide bolts, install the feed support hub with its rings installed, into the case. Install the bolts and tighten alternately and evenly.

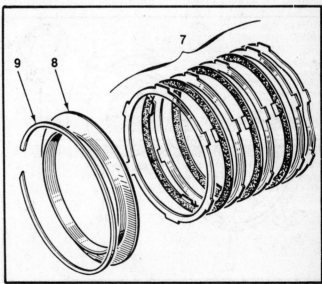

**Assembly of the F-2 discs (7), piston carrier (8) and snapring (9)— MB models** (© Renault/AMC)

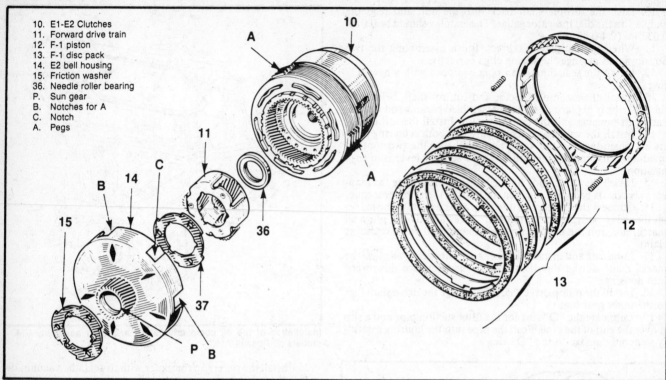

10. E1-E2 Clutches
11. Forward drive train
12. F-1 piston
13. F-1 disc pack
14. E2 bell housing
15. Friction washer
36. Needle roller bearing
P. Sun gear
B. Notches for A
C. Notch
A. Pegs

Assembly of the planetary gear drive train—MB models (© Renault/AMC)

5. Install the needle roller bearing and the F-2 brake steel clips. Install one wave form disc, one plain disc and one lined disc alternately as follows:
  a. One wave form disc.
  b. Four plain discs.
  c. Three lined discs.
6. Install the F-1 piston sleeve and the snapring.
7. Check the F-2 operating clearance which should be 0.050-0.130 in. (1.3-3.2mm). Check and replace the disc assembly if the clearance is incorrect.
8. Assemble the E-1, E-2 clutches, install the needle roller bearing, the forward drive train, the friction thrust washer (1.5

mm thick), and the E-2 bell housing. The three pegs of the E-1, E-2 clutches fit into the notches of the E-2 bell housing.
  **NOTE: The pegs of the F-2 clutches fit into notches of the E-2 bell housing.**
9. Check that the assembly is correct by measuring between the face of the hub gear on the E-2 bell housing and the outside face of the E-1, E-2 clutches. The clearance should be 1.598 ± 0.028 in. (40.6 ± 0.07mm). Check the order of assembly if this dimension is incorrect.
10. Install the F-1 piston followed by the wave form disc, one plain disc and one lined disc as follows:
  a. One wave disc.
  b. Three plain discs.
  c. Three lined discs.
11. The operating clearance for the F-1 assembly is 0.03-0.10 in. (0.8-2.7mm).
12. Install the freewheel overrunning clutch on the reverse drive train.
13. Install the friction washer which is 0.05 in. (1.5mm) thick.
14. Install the freewheel assembly into the case. Be sure the lugs on the washer inter the reverse drive train assembly.
15. Install the snapring.
16. Install the sealed junction box and its clip.
17. Install the manual valve of the valve body into the toothed quadrant. Position the valve body in position with the two seals and the plate.
18. Hand tighten the remaining valve body bolts in sequence to their proper torque.
19. The oil pan and gasket can be installed along with the other outside components.

## Adjustment of the Rear Case

Before Attachment To the Differential Assembly

  **NOTE: If any of the internal components of the transmission assembly have been replaced, the following two adjustments outlined must be performed with the use of a special measured tool.**

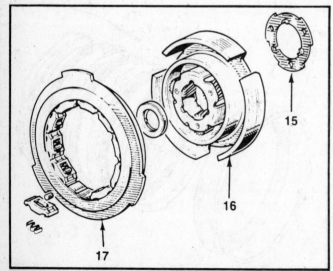

Assembly of freewheel (17) into the reverse drive train (16) with thrust washer (15) (© Renault/AMC)

## MB-1 Transaxle

### REVERSE GEAR TRAIN ADJUSTMENT

1. Shim 19 is used for adjustment.
2. 18 is the needle roller thrust bearing.
3. 16 is the reverse drive train.
4. Measure dimensions A and B. Subtract B from A. $X = A - B$
5. Overall clearance: $JT = X + C$

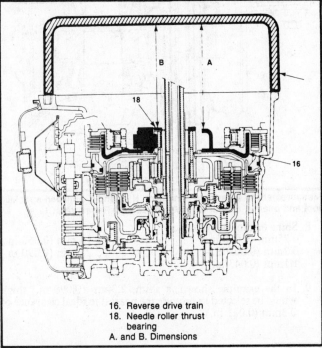

16. Reverse drive train
18. Needle roller thrust bearing
A. and B. Dimensions

**Reverse gear train adjustment with special tool to find A and B dimensions—MB models** (© Renault/AMC)

6. The average reverse gear train operating clearance is 0.4mm (.016 in.).
7. The shim (19) thickness is: JT—0.4mm (.016 in.)
8. Example:
   A = 158.2mm (6.228 in.)
   B = 156.9mm (6.177 in.)
   C = 1.3mm (0.051 in.)
   X = A-B = 158.2mm (6.228 in.)-156.9mm (6.177 in.) = 1.3mm (0.015 in.)
   JT = X + C = 1.3mm (0.015 in.) + 1.3mm (0.015 in.) = 2.6mm (0.102 in.)
9. Shim thickness required: 2.6mm (0.102 in.)-0.4mm (0.016 in.) = 2.2mm (0.086 in.)
10. Shim thicknesses available: 1.5 (0.059 in.)-2 (0.079 in.)-2.6 (0.102 in.) and 3.2mm (0.126 in.).
11. In the above example, a shim is selected which gives an operating clearance as close to the ideal as possible, in this case one of 2mm (0.079 in.)
12. Measure dimension (C) on "park" wheel (21).

### END PLAY ADJUSTMENT

1. Shim (K) is used for end play adjustment.
2. Measure dimension G. It equals F-H.
3. Measure dimension E. It equals H-D.
4. Over end play equals G-E.
5. Average operating clearance equals 0.8 mm (0.031 in.)
6. Based on the information above, the thickness of shim (K). = overall end play—0.8 mm (0.031 in.)

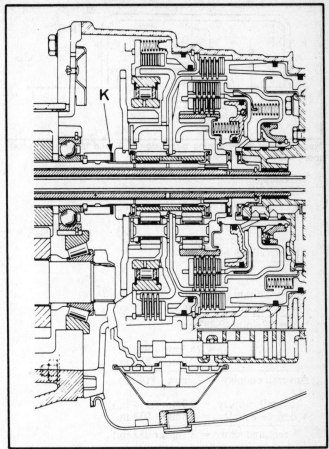

**Location of shim "K"—MB models** (© Renault/AMC)

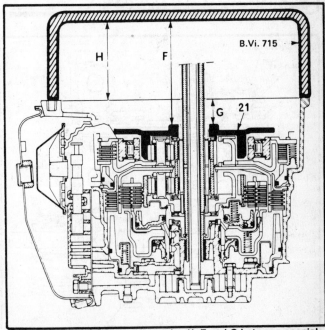

**Measurement to determine dimension H, F and G between special tool and the park gear—MB models** (© Renault/AMC)

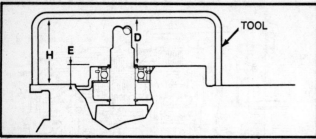

Measurement to determine dimension H, E and D, using special tool—MB models (© Renault/AMC)

7. **Example:**
H = 120mm (4.724 in.)
F = 145.3mm (5.720 in.)
D = 97.6mm (3.843 in.)

$$\frac{\begin{array}{l}F = 145.3mm\ (5.720\ in.)\\H = 120mm\ (4.724\ in.)\end{array}}{G = 25.3mm\ (0.996\ in.)}$$

$$\frac{\begin{array}{l}H = 120mm\ (4.725\ in.)\\D = 97.6mm\ (3.843\ in.)\end{array}}{E = 22.4mm\ (0.882\ in.)}$$

$$\frac{\begin{array}{l}G = 25.3mm\ (.996\ in.)\\E = 22.4mm\ (.882\ in.)\end{array}}{overall\ endplay = 2.9mm\ (.114\ in.)}$$

$$\frac{\begin{array}{l}overall\ endplay = 2.9mm\ (.114\ in.)\\desired\ endplay = 0.8mm\ (.032\ in.)\end{array}}{required\ shim = 2.1mm\ (.082\ in.)}$$

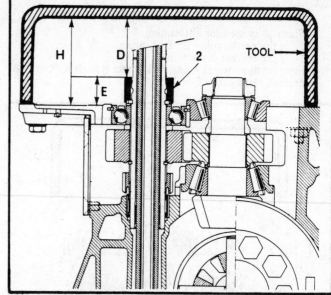

Measurement to determine dimension H, D and E between special tool and bearing spacer (2)—MB models (© Renault/AMC)

8. Shim thickness available:
0.25mm (0.010 in.)          1.7mm (0.066 in.)
0.7mm (0.003 in.)          2.3mm (0.090 in.)
1.1mm (0.043 in.)

9. In the example shown, a shim, 2.3mm (0.090 in.) thick would be selected to provide the nearest to ideal clearance of 0.3mm (0.031 in.).

# SPECIAL TOOLS

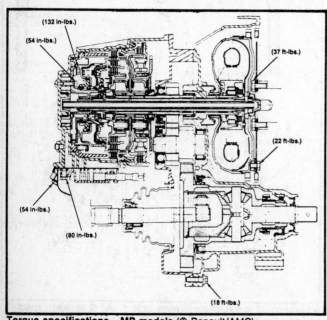

Torque specifications—MB models (© Renault/AMC)

Mot. 50—Torque wrench or equivalent beam type torque wrench

Mot. 593—Drain plug wrench (8 mm square drive)

B.Vi. 466-04—Oil pressure gauge

B.Vi. 31-01—Set of 3 roll pin drifts

B.Vi. 465—Converter oil seal replacement tool and converter holding lug

B.Vi. 883—Differential outside band installer

B.Vi. 905—Speedometer shaft seal replacement tool

B.Vi. 945—Planetary oil seal installing mandrel

B.Vi. 946—Planetary snap ring installer

B.Vi. 947—Intermediary case bearing installer

B.Vi. 955—Differential pinion bearing preload measuring tool

B.Vi. 951—Differential oil seal installer

B.Vi. 958—Diagnostic Tester

B.Vi. 959—Output shaft circlip installing tool

B.Vi. 952—Feed hub aligning dowels and front piston removing tool

B.Vi. 953—Step down driven gear holding tool

B.Vi. 961—Differential pinion bearing race installing tool

B.Vi. 715—Tool from B.Vi. 710 kit

B.Vi. 962—Converter oil seal installing tool

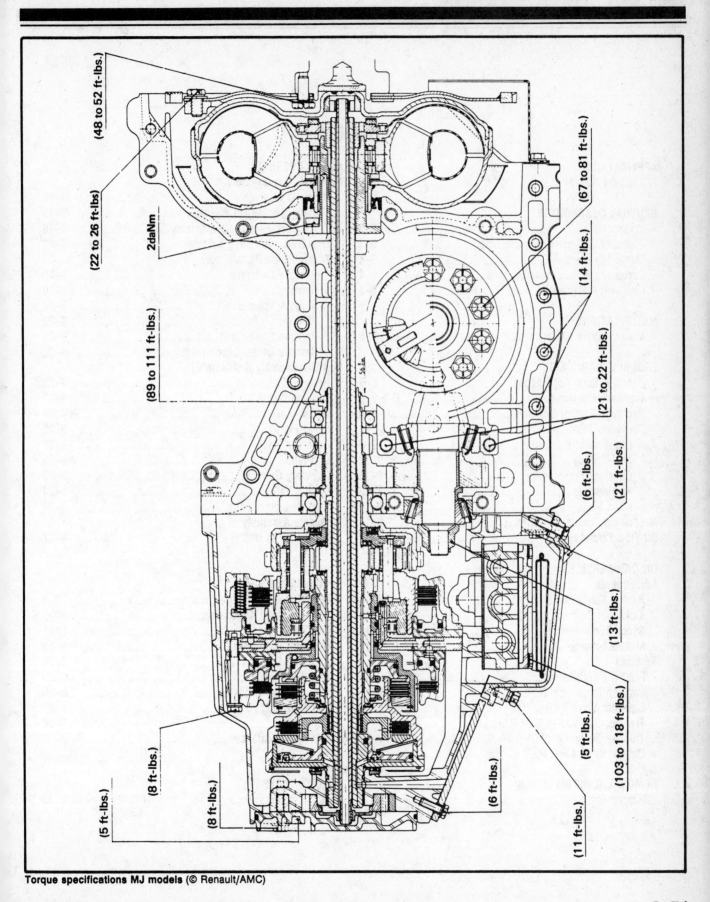

(48 to 52 ft-lbs.)

(22 to 26 ft-lbs.)

2daNm

(89 to 111 ft-lbs.)

(67 to 81 ft-lbs.)

(14 ft-lbs.)

(21 to 22 ft-lbs.)

(6 ft-lbs.)

(21 ft-lbs.)

(13 ft-lbs.)

(103 to 118 ft-lbs.)

(5 ft-lbs.)

(6 ft-lbs.)

(5 ft-lbs.)

(8 ft-lbs.)

(8 ft-lbs.)

(11 ft-lbs.)

**Torque specifications MJ models (© Renault/AMC)**

# INDEX

# SUBARU
# 3 SPEED • 4 SPEED
# Automatic Transaxle

## APPLICATIONS

1981-84 SUBARU

## GENERAL DESCRIPTION

The 4WD automatic transmission is basically composed of the conventional Subaru front wheel drive automatic transmission. The basic construction is unchanged from the current automatic transmission. Along with the adoption of the 4WD system, the final reduction case and transmission case have been changed thoroughly, and an oil seal holder has been newly introduced in the reduction drive gear portion. The hydraulic clutch, planetary gear, control valve and other elementary components of the automatic transmission section are unchanged from those of the current automatic transmission.

The centrifugal lockup torque converter and the transfer clutch are the main differences on the 4WD automatic transmission. The transfer clutch is operated by a transfer valve and a solenoid. When the solenoid is not energized, the transfer valve is closed and there is no line pressure to the transfer clutch circuit. When the transfer clutch is not engaged the vehicle will be in front wheel drive (FWD). When the solenoid is energized by depressing the 4WD selector switch, the transfer valve is opened allowing the line pressure to flow to the transfer clutch circuit. This will engage the transfer clutch and put the vehicle in 4WD.

The automatic transmission can be separated into two assemblies, the transmission assembly, and the differential and reduction assemblies. Each assembly can be replaced as an assembly and each may be disassembled or assembled independently of the other.

Some of the easy servicing features that are mentioned are as follows.

1. The governor valve which may cause trouble is installed on

the outside of the transmission. It can easily be removed and installed.

2. The brake band can be adjusted from the outside of the transmission.

3. The number of adjusting points has been decreased through the use of multi-disc clutches instead of brake bands.

4. Use of only one oil pump and a greater number of efficient needle bearings reduces transmission internal loss to a minimum.

5. The throttle pressure in the control valve assembly, which varies with the accelerator opening, is controlled by intake-manifold vacuum. This eliminates the need of linkage or control cables and makes accelerator operation easy.

6. As automatic transmission fluid cannot be used as a lubricating oil for the hypoid gear, this circuit has been simplified by making the transmission fluid pass through the hollow oil pump drive shaft.

The differential mechanism with a final reduction system is installed between the torque converter and the automatic transmission. The differential case contains the first reduction gear and the governor and speedometer drive gear, which can be removed as an assembly.

Since hypoid gears are used for the final reduction system, hypoid gear oil must be used for proper lubrication. For this reason the final reduction system is separated by oil seals from the other parts of the transmission where an automatic transmission fluid is used.

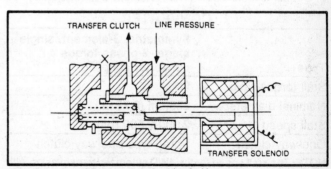

**Transfer valve** (©Fuji Heavy Industries Ltd.)

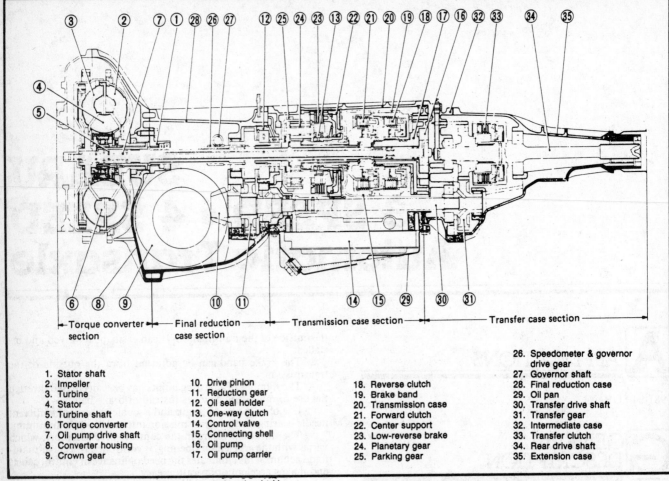

**4WD Automatic Transmission (©Fuji Heavy Industries Ltd.)**

1. Stator shaft
2. Impeller
3. Turbine
4. Stator
5. Turbine shaft
6. Torque converter
7. Oil pump drive shaft
8. Converter housing
9. Crown gear
10. Drive pinion
11. Reduction gear
12. Oil seal holder
13. One-way clutch
14. Control valve
15. Connecting shell
16. Oil pump
17. Oil pump carrier
18. Reverse clutch
19. Brake band
20. Transmission case
21. Forward clutch
22. Center support
23. Low-reverse brake
24. Planetary gear
25. Parking gear
26. Speedometer & governor drive gear
27. Governor shaft
28. Final reduction case
29. Oil pan
30. Transfer drive shaft
31. Transfer gear
32. Intermediate case
33. Transfer clutch
34. Rear drive shaft
35. Extension case

## Transmission and Converter Identification

### TRANSMISSION

The transmission can be identified by the 11th letter in the vehicle identification number located on the bulkhead panel of the engine compartment. The automatic transmission 11th letter code is as follows.

C. Gunma manufacture—Automatic transmission
F. Gunma manufacture—4WD Automatic transmission

### CONVERTER

| Type | Symmetric, 3-element, single stage, 2-phase torque converter coupling |
| --- | --- |
| Stall torque ratio | 2:1 |
| Nominal diameter | 236mm (9.29 in.) |
| Stall speed | 2,300-2,500 rpm |
| One-way clutch | Sprag type one-way clutch |

**NOTE:** The stall speed for the 4WD automatic transmission with a turbo charged engine is 2,700-2,900 rpm.

## Metric Fasteners

The metric fastener dimensions are very close to the dimensions of the familiar inch system fasteners. For this reason, replacement fasteners must have the same measurement and strength as those removed.

Do not attempt to interchange metric fasteners for inch system fasteners. Mismatched or incorrect fasteners can result in damage to the transmission unit through malfunctions, breakage or possible personal injury.

Care should be taken to reuse the fasteners in the same location as removed.

## Capacities

The conventional Subaru automatic transmission has a fluid capacity of 5.9-6.3 US qts. (5.6-6.0 liters). The 4WD automatic transmission has a fluid capacity of 6.3-6.8 US qts. (6.0-6.4 liters).

### FLUID SPECIFICATIONS

Texaco: Texamatic Fluid 6673—Dexron®
Caltex: Texamatic Fluid 6673—Dexron®
Castrol: Castrol TQ—Dexron®
BP: BP Autran—Dexron®
Mobil: Mobil ATF—220

## Checking Fluid Level

Checking ATF level and quality is essential to prevent various kinds of transmission trouble resulting from lack or deterioration of fluid.

1. If fluid level in the transmission is too low, clutches and band will slip and ultimatley be damaged. This is because the air sucked by the oil pump and mixed into the fluid will deteriorate the quality of fluid by producing sludge.

2. Too much fluid causes the same problem as to little fluid, because excessive fluid is stirred up by gears to generate air bubbles.

## PROCEDURE FOR CHECKING FLUID LEVEL

1. Warm the transmission up until the fluid temperature comes into the range of from 60-80°C (140-176°F). Generally, this will be attained after 5-10 km (3-6 miles) running.

2. Stop the car on level ground.

3. Shift the selector lever to the "P" position and check the fluid level while the engine is kept idling.

4. If necessary, refill the recommended fluid up to the upper level mark on the level gauge with the engine idling and selector lever in "P" position. Be careful not to add fluid beyond the upper level mark. The capacity difference between the lower and upper marks on the level gauge corresponds to a fluid capacity of 0.4 liter.

5. Change fluid at the specified intervals.

NOTE: Use a nylon rag to wipe the dipstick so that the level gauge is kept free from waste threads. Push the level gauge all the way into the filler tube and quickly pull it out before it is splashed with fluid beyond the true indication of fluid level. If it becomes necessary to frequently refill the fluid it is an indication of a leak in the transmission. Immediate repair is required to prevent damage to the transmission. The amount of fluid that can be changed is usually 2.5-3.0 liters (2.6-3.2 US qt, 2.2-2.6 Imp qt).

## DIFFERENTIAL

The kind of oil is API classification GL-5 and the SAE viscosity number is 75W-80. The capacity is 0.8-1.2 liter (1.3 US qt, 1.1 Imp qt). Inspect oil level at the specified intervals and, if necessary, refill with the recommended oil, up to the upper level mark on the level gauge. The capacity difference between the lower and upper marks on the level gauge corresponds to an oil capacity of 0.4 liter. Replace the differential gear oil at the specified intervals.

## TROUBLE DIAGNOSIS

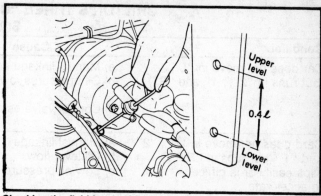

Checking the fluid levels (©Fuji Heavy Industries Ltd.)

NOTE: When replenishing the gear oil, always fill it up to the upper level mark (1.2 liter) on the level gauge. When replenishing or checking the gear oil, always keep the car in level.

## MODIFICATIONS

## The Governor Driven Gear

The 1979 governor driven gear is being incorrectly installed in the 1980 and later vehicles. The problem with this procedure is that this gear will last approximately 700-1,000 miles due to improper contact with the drive gears. The major difference between these two gears is the diameter. The 1979 governor driven gear (part no.# 440-847-000) is easily recognized by a groove cut in the metal portion of the governor shaft. The difference between these two gears are as follow: The 1977-79 governor driven gear (part no.# 440-847-000) diameter is 0.690 in. and the diameter for the 1980 and later governor driven gear (part no.# 440-847-100) is 0.765 in. The length for both of these gears is 1.683 in.

### CLUTCH AND BAND APPLICATION CHART
#### Subaru 2WD and 4WD

| Selector Position | Reverse Clutch | Forward Clutch | Brake Band | Low/Reverse Brake | One-Way Clutch |
|---|---|---|---|---|---|
| Neutral | Off | Off | Off | Off | Off |
| Park | Off | Off | Off | On | Off |
| Reverse | On | Off | Off | On | Off |
| D (1st gear) | Off | On | Off | Off | On |
| D (2nd gear) | Off | On | On | Off | Off |
| D (3rd gear) | On | On | Off | Off | Off |
| D (kickdown) | Off | On | On | Off | Off |
| 2 range | Off | On | On | Off | Off |
| 1 range | Off | On | Off | On | Off |

## CHILTON'S THREE "C's" DIAGNOSIS CHART
### Subaru

| Condition | Cause | Correction |
|---|---|---|
| Car does not move in "D" (but runs in "2", "1" and "R") | a) Manual linkage adjustment<br>b) Oil pressures low<br><br>c) Control valve assembly | a) Adjust as required<br>b) Check pressure readings to make determination<br>c) Clean or overhaul control valve assembly |
| Card does not move in "D", "2" and "1" (but runs in "R"), slips easily or is difficult to accelerate | a) Manual linkage<br>b) Oil level flow<br>c) Low oil pressure<br><br>d) Control valve assembly malfunction<br>e) Engine performance poor | a) Adjust manual linkage<br>b) Check and add fluid<br>c) Check pressure readings to make determination<br>d) Clean or overhaul valve body<br>e) Tune up engine |
| Car does not move in "R" (but runs in "D", "2" and "1"), slips easily or is difficult to accelerate | a) Manual linkage adjustment<br>b) Low oil pressure<br><br>c) Control valve assembly malfunction | a) Adjust manual linkage<br>b) Check pressure readings to make determination<br>c) Clean or overhaul valve body |
| Car does not move in all speed ranges or car moves sluggishly | a) Transmission fluid level<br><br>b) Manual linkage<br>c) Low oil pressure<br><br>d) Control valve assembly malfunction | a) Check fluid level and add as required<br>b) Adjust manual linkage<br>c) Check pressures to make determination<br>d) Clean or overhaul valve body |
| Maximum speed too low or insufficient acceleration | a) Transmission fluid level<br><br>b) Manual linkage<br>c) Low oil pressure<br><br>d) Stall speed<br>e) Brake band adjustment<br>f) Control valve assembly malfunction<br>g) Engine performance poor | a) Check fluid level and add as required<br>b) Adjust manual linkage<br>c) Check pressures to make determination<br>d) Check and adjust stall speed<br>e) Adjust brake band<br>f) Clean or overhaul valve body<br>g) Tune up engine |
| Car is braked when shifted to "R" | a) Oil condition<br><br><br>b) Brake band adjustment | a) Check oil, add if necessary; change and clean oil screen if necessary<br>b) Adjust brake band |
| Failure to shift automatically from 1st to 2nd speed | a) Manual linkage<br>b) Vacuum diaphragm<br><br>c) Downshift solenoid, kickdown switch | a) Adjust manual linkage<br>b) Check and replace vacuum diaphragm<br>c) Check and adjust, or replace downshift solenoid or kickdown switch |
| Failure to shift automatically from 2nd to 3rd speed | a) Manual linkage<br>b) Vacuum diaphragm<br><br>c) Downshift solenoid, kickdown switch<br><br>d) Control valve assembly malfunction<br>e) Governor valve<br>f) Brake band adjustment<br>g) Low oil pressure | a) Adjust manual linkage<br>b) Check and replace vacuum diaphragm<br>c) Check and adjust or replace downshift solenoid or kickdown switch<br>d) Clean or overhaul valve body<br>e) Replace governor valve<br>f) Adjust brake band<br>g) Check oil pressure to make determination |

## CHILTON'S THREE "C's" DIAGNOSIS CHART
### Subaru

| Condition | Cause | Correction |
|---|---|---|
| Running speed at which shifting occurs from 1st to 2nd or 2nd to 3rd is too high | a) Vacuum diaphragm | a) Check and replace vacuum diaphragm |
| | b) Downshift solenoid, kickdown switch | b) Check and adjust or replace downshift solenoid or kickdown switch |
| | c) Low oil pressure | c) Check pressures to make determination |
| | d) Control valve assembly malfunction | d) Clean or overhaul valve body |
| | e) Governor valve | e) Check and replace governor valve |
| Shifting straight from 1st to 3rd | a) Ignition switch and starter motor | a) Check ignition switch and starter motor operation |
| | b) Control valve assembly malfunction | b) Clean or overhaul valve body |
| | c) Governor valve | c) Check and replace governor valve |
| | d) Brake band | d) Adjust brake band |
| | e) Servo feed pipes | e) Check and replace servo feed pipes |
| Excessive shock is felt when shifting from 1st to 2nd or from 2nd to 3rd | a) Vacuum diaphragm | a) Check and replace vacuum diaphragm |
| | b) Low oil pressure | b) Check pressure to make determination |
| | c) Stall speed | c) Check and adjust stall speed |
| | d) Control valve assembly | d) Clean or overhaul valve body |
| | e) Brake band | e) Adjust brake band |
| Failure to shift from 3rd to 2nd | a) Vacuum diaphragm | a) Check and replace vacuum diaphragm |
| | b) Control valve assembly | b) Clean or overhaul valve body |
| | c) Governor valve | c) Check and replace governor valve |
| | d) Low oil pressure | d) Check pressures to make determination |
| Failure to shift from 2nd to 1st or from 3rd to 1st | a) Vacuum diaphragm | a) Check and replace vacuum diaphragm |
| | b) Control valve assembly | b) Clean or overhaul valve body |
| | c) Governor valve | c) Check and replace governor valve |
| | d) Brake band | d) Adjust brake band |
| Occurrence of downshifting from 2nd to 1st or upshifting from 2nd to 3rd when selector lever is placed in "2" position | a) Manual linkage | a) Check and adjust manual linkage |
| | b) Low oil pressure | b) Check pressures to make determination |
| | c) Control valve assembly | c) Clean or overhaul valve body |
| Failure to shift down from 3rd to 2nd when selector lever is shifted to "1" | a) Fluid level | a) Check and add fluid as necessary |
| | b) Manual linkage | b) Check and adjust manual linkage |
| | c) Control valve assembly | c) Clean or overhaul valve body |
| | d) Governor valve | d) Check and replace governor valve |
| | e) Brake band | e) Adjust brake band |

## CHILTON'S THREE "C's" DIAGNOSIS CHART
### Subaru

| Condition | Cause | Correction |
|---|---|---|
| Downshifting from 2nd to 1st is accomplished by excessive shock when selector lever is placed in "1" position | a) Vacuum diaphragm<br>b) Stall speed<br>c) Control valve assembly<br>d) Governor valve | a) Check and replace vacuum diaphragm<br>b) Check and adjust stall speed<br>c) Clean or overhaul valve body<br>d) Check and replace governor valve |
| Excessive chatter in "P" or "N" position of selector lever, excessive chatter in "D", "2", "1" or "R" positions | a) Fluid level low<br>b) Low oil pressure<br>c) Control valve assembly | a) Check and add fluid as necessary<br>b) Check pressures and make determination<br>c) Clean or overhaul valve body |
| Oil spurts or exhaust contains whitish smoke while car is running | a) Fluid level too high or too low<br>b) Vacuum diaphragm<br>c) Low or high oil pressure<br>d) Stall speed<br>e) Control valve assembly | a) Check and add fluid or drain fluid as necessary<br>b) Check and replace vacuum diaphragm<br>c) Check oil pressures and make determination<br>d) Check and adjust stall speed<br>e) Clean or overhaul valve body |

## Hydraulic Control System

Signals of the selector lever position, driving speed, and accelerator pedal operation are all conveyed to the control valve assembly, which distributed hydraulic pressure to the forward clutch, reverse clutch, transfer clutch, low & reverse brake, or brake band according to the current driving conditions, thereby achieving automatic transmission control.

### LINE PRESSURE

The pressure of oil discharge from the oil pump is regulated by the pressure regulating valve. This is the line pressure and works as the basic oil pressure for the hydraulic controls which govern the operation of the transmission clutches, brake band, etc.

### THROTTLE PRESSURE

The throttle pressure is produced and regulated by the vacuum throttle valve, which is actuated by the vacuum diaphragm to which the intake manifold vacuum is applied. Thus, the throttle pressure varies according to the intake manifold vacuum that varies with the carburetor throttle opening and engine speed. The oil is directed to the 2-3 shift valve, in which it performs gear shift in conjunction with the governor pressure. It is also delivered to the pressure regulating valve to control the line pressure.

### GOVERNOR PRESSURE

The governor pressure is generated by the governor valve and varies according to car speed. It is directed to the 1-2 shift valve and the 2-3 shift valve, which control gear shifting, and also the pressure regulating valve, which controls the line pressure.

### TRANSFER VALVE

The transfer valve is a valve which opens and closes the line pressure circuit to the transfer clutch, and is operated by a solenoid. When the transfer valve is closed, the transfer clutch is not engaged. When the transfer valve is opened, the transfer clutch is engaged and the vehicle will be in 4WD.

### TRANSFER CLUTCH

When the line pressure is applied to the transfer clutch, the clutch capacity varies, like the other hydraulic clutches, with the throttle opening and the vehicle speed.

## TRANSFER CLUTCH CONTROL CIRCUIT

The transfer clutch circuit and transfer valve have been added to the line pressure circuit between the oil pump discharge side and the control valve.

## Major Components

### OIL PUMP

The oil pump is installed at the rear end of the transmission. It pressurizes the oil to be delivered to the torque converter and the transmission through the control valve.

The oil pump is an internal gear drive involute gear pump. It is driven at the same speed as the engine by the hollow oil pump drive shaft splined to the converter cover of the torque converter assembly.

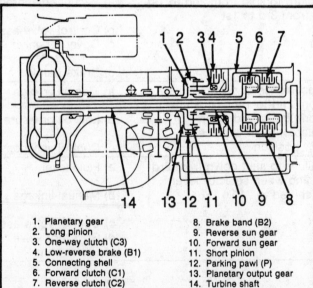

1. Planetary gear
2. Long pinion
3. One-way clutch (C3)
4. Low-reverse brake (B1)
5. Connecting shell
6. Forward clutch (C1)
7. Reverse clutch (C2)
8. Brake band (B2)
9. Reverse sun gear
10. Forward sun gear
11. Short pinion
12. Parking pawl (P)
13. Planetary output gear
14. Turbine shaft

**Hydraulic and mechanical power transmitting mechanism**
(©Fuji Heavy Industries Ltd.)

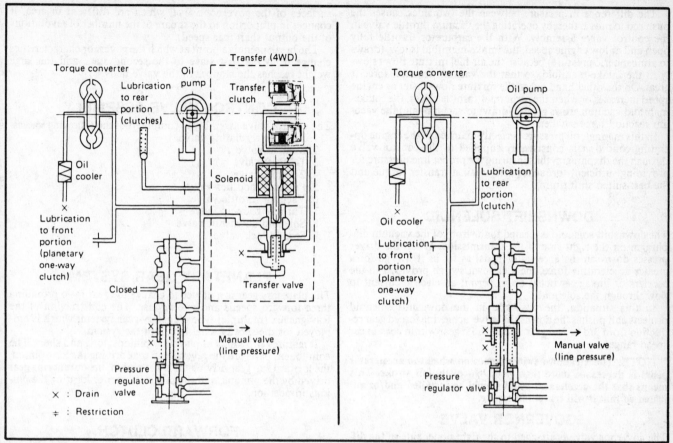

**Comparison of hydraulic circuits (A) 4WD automatic transmission for 1983-84 (B) FWD automatic transmission for 1982 & earlier** (©Fuji Heavy Industries Ltd.)

Oil admitted from the inlet port flows into part A is directed to part B through the rotation of the inner and outer gears and is then discharged from the outlet port.

Discharged oil from the oil pump is used for functioning the torque converter, for lubricating the parts, and for actuating the friction elements (the clutches and brake band) and the control system.

## MANUAL LINKAGE

The movement of the selector lever, mechanically transmitted through the manual linkage, turns the selector arm on the left center of the transmission case, by which the manual plate inside the case is turned through the manual shaft. When the selector lever is in the "P" and "N" range, the inhibitor switch closes the starter circuit and enables the engine to start. With the lever in the "R" range, the switch closes the back-up light circuit, turning the back-up light on.

## VACUUM DIAPHRAGM

The vacuum diaphragm is installed in the right center of the transmission. It is actuated by intake-manifold vacuum to operate the vacuum throttle valve. The vacuum diaphragm has a rubber diaphragm, on one side of which the engine intake-manifold vacuum and the force of the diaphragm spring act, while on the other side atmospheric pressure acts.

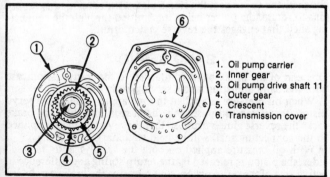

1. Oil pump carrier
2. Inner gear
3. Oil pump drive shaft 11
4. Outer gear
5. Crescent
6. Transmission cover

**Oil pump** (©Fuji Heavy Industries Ltd.)

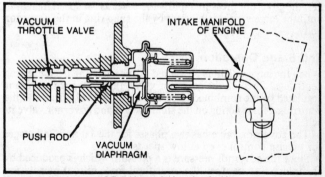

**Vacuum diaphragm** (©Fuji Heavy Industries Ltd.)

The difference in pressure between the two sides causes the push rod to move, thereby operating the vacuum throttle valve in the control valve assembly. With the carburetor throttle fully open and at low engine speed, the intake-manifold is low, (draws to atmospheric pressure) because the air-fuel mixture flows slowly in the intake-manifold, so that the vacuum reaction force is great. On the other hand, when the mixture flows faster as engine speed increases or when the carburetor throttle closes, the intake-manifold vacuum grows greater (draws to vacuum) and the vacuum reaction force smaller.

In this manner, oil pressure perfectly matched to the engine operating condition is consistently supplied to the control valve through the diaphragm, thus insuring the proper line pressure for providing sufficient torque capacity against transfer torque and the best-suited shift timing.

## DOWNSHIFT SOLENOID

The downshift solenoid is located to the front of the vacuum diaphragm on the right side of the transmission. When the driver presses down on the accelerator pedal as far as it will go for a greater accelerating force, the kickdown switch provided in the accelerator linkage switches on to permit an electric current to flow through the solenoid.

In this situation, the push rod in the downshift solenoid projects and pushes the downshift valve, achieving forced gear reduction from 3rd to 2nd gear or 2nd to 1st gear within certain car speed range.

**NOTE: The kickdown switch comes on when the accelerator pedal is depressed more than 7/8 or 15/16 of its full stroke. This means that the accelerator pedal should be installed and/or adjusted so that it will travel full stroke.**

## GOVERNOR VALVE

The governor valve is attached to the right upper side of the differential housing. It is driven by the speedometer and governor drive gear on the reduction drive gear shaft.

The governor valve regulates the line pressure in response to car speed. It also produces the governor pressure that exerts effect on the 1-2 and 2-3 shift valves for automatic gear shifting.

When the car is at a stop and the centrifugal force acting on the valve is zero, the large weight is pushed toward the center of the governor housing by the spring. In this case, the force of the spring is zero.

### 1st Stage Operation

As car and governor speeds increase, the centrifugal force acting on the large weight is transmitted to the governor valve through the spring, and centrifugal force also acts on the small weight and the governor valve itself.

In this condition, the governor pressure acting on the two annular surfaces of the governor valve, which are different in area, is regulated by the above combined centrifugal force. In this manner, the governor pressure rapidly increases as car speed increases until the large weight is blocked by the snap ring in the governor body.

### 2nd Stage Operation

When the large weight is prevented by the snap ring from exerting centrifugal force on the governor valve, the governor pressure is regulated by the combined force of the compressed spring and the centrifugal force acting on the small weight and governor valve itself.

The governor valve has two phases for the 1st and 2nd stages for precise control even at low speeds.

Since the governor pressure is a pressure which is produced by the interaction between the centrifugal force caused by rotation and the thrust caused by oil pressure acting on the two annular surfaces of the governor valve, which are different in area, it changes in proportion to the square of the number of revolutions of the output shaft (car speed).

The break point is a point at which the governor characteristics change from the first stage to the second stage and the large weight reaches the stopper in the valve body.

## CONTROL VALVE ASSEMBLY

The control valve assembly is composed of the following valves.
1. Pressure regulating valve
2. Manual valve
3. 1-2 shift valve
4. 2-3 shift valve
5. Pressure modifier valve
6. Vacuum throttle valve
7. Throttle back-up valve
8. Solenoid downshift valve
9. Second lock valve

## PLANETARY GEAR SYSTEM

The planetary gear is a device to change the gear ratio providing three forward speeds and one reverse. The construction of the Ravigneaux (multiple) type planetary-gear system, which is employed for the shorter axial length of the system.

It features two kinds of planetary pinions, long and short. The component parts are the reverse sun gear driving the long pinion, the forward sun gear driving the short pinion, the output ring gear driven by the pinions, and the planetary carrier locating the pinions in position.

## FORWARD CLUTCH

The forward clutch is always engaged during forward driving.

When the forward clutch has the piston released and the clutch plates are slipping due to clearance between them, no power is transmitted.

When the forward clutch applies hydraulic pressure to the piston so that the clutch plates are held tightly against each other, the drum rotation is transmitted to the clutch hub. When the hydraulic pressure applied to the piston is released, the return spring acts to return the clutch assembly to the original position. When the forward clutch piston is moved by hydraulic pressure to connect the clutch plates, the forward sun gear connected to the clutch hub begins to rotate, providing input to the planetary gears.

## REVERSE CLUTCH

The reverse clutch engages in the 3rd forward gear position and reverse gear position, its function being the same as that of the forward clutch. When hydraulic pressure is applied to the reverse clutch piston to connect the clutch plates, the reverse sun gear begins to rotate, the power being transmitted through the connecting shell that engages the reverse clutch drum.

## BAND SERVO

One end of the brake band is attached to the transmission case with the band adjusting screw serving as an anchor.

When oil pressure is applied to the "apply" side of the servo piston, the piston rod pushes the band strut and the band brake locks the reverse clutch drum so that the reverse sun gear splined to the connecting shell will be held stationary. (2nd gear)

With oil pressure applied on both the "apply" and "release" sides, the piston is released by the return spring and difference in active area of the servo piston, thus releasing the brake band. (3rd gear)

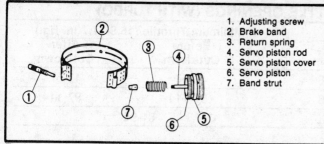

1. Adjusting screw
2. Brake band
3. Return spring
4. Servo piston rod
5. Servo piston cover
6. Servo piston
7. Band strut

**Exploded view of band servo** (©Fuji Heavy Industries Ltd.)

## LOW AND REVERSE BRAKE

When oil pressure acts on the piston of the low & reverse brake, the multi-disc brake is engaged, and the planetary carrier united with the one-way clutch outer race is locked by the transmission case ($D_1$ and reverse gears). The return spring in the low & reverse brake is a slit diaphragm spring instead of coil springs as used in the forward and reverse clutches.

## ONE-WAY CLUTCH

A sprag type one-way clutch is installed between the planetary carrier and the center support. The clutch prevents the planetary carrier from turning counterclockwise as viewed from the engine side.

It rotates or freewheels in the clockwise direction and does not rotate, locks up, in the counterclockwise direction.

# Diagnosis Tests

## MAIN LINE PRESSURE

Checking the main line pressure with an appropriate gauge while the transmission is being operated, will give indications of normal and abnormal operation.

A main line pressure plug is located on the rear of the transmission cover, nearly centered on the early models and located at the bottom of the cover on later models.

### Line Pressure Test

1. Temporarily attach a oil pressure gauge to a suitable place in the driver's compartment, remove the blind plug located in the front floorboard and pass the hose of the oil pressure gauge to the engine compartment.
2. Remove the pressure check plug from the transmission cover.
3. Attach the oil pressure gauge adapter to the pressure check plug hole in the transmission cover.
4. Connect the oil pressure gauge to the gauge adapter.
5. Run the engine and check the line pressures with the engine at a full-throttle and a minimum throttle. Refer to the accompanying chart for the proper oil pressure reading.

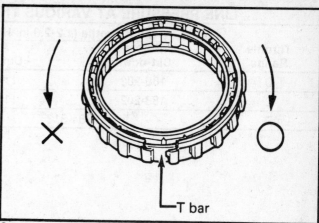

**One-way clutch operation** (©Fuji Heavy Industries Ltd.)

### OVERALL LINE PRESSURE TEST RESULT INDICATIONS IN FWD

1. Low pressure with the engine at idle speed indicates, a worn oil pump or clearance not adjusted to specs, a leak in the oil pressure circuit or a inoperative pressure regulator valve.
2. High line pressure with the engine at idle speed indicates, a leak in a vacuum hose or in the vacuum diaphragm or the diaphragm rod is too long, and the pressure regulator valve could be jamming.
3. When the line pressure will not rise with the engine at full throttle, check to see if the vacuum diaphragm rod has been installed or not.
4. If the line pressure does rise but will not come up to specified range, the vacuum throttle valve is jamming or the pressure regulator valve or the pressure regulator is plugged up.

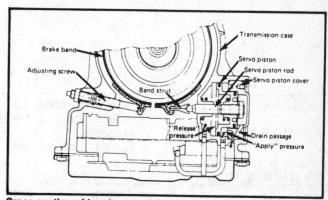

**Cross section of band servo** (©Fuji Heavy Industries Ltd.)

## LINE PRESSURE AT VARIOUS THROTTLE OPENINGS (NON-TURBO)

| Throttle Range | Full Throttle (1.2-2.0 in. Hg.) | | Minimum Throttle (16.9-17.7 in. Hg.) | |
| | Before Cut-down | After Cut-down | Before Cut-down | After Cut-down |
|---|---|---|---|---|
| D | 121-142 | 78-92.5 | 43-57 | 43-57 |
| 2 | 145-168 | 84-98 | 145-168 | 84-98 |
| R | 200-227 | | 67-81 | |

**NOTE:** Line pressure in drive ranges of D, 2 and Reverse will change in steps when the pressure modifier valve operates. These points are called "cut-down points." Before cut-down points denotes slow driving and after cut-down denotes vehicle speed of more than 22 MPH.

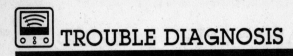 

## LINE PRESSURE AT VARIOUS THROTTLE OPENINGS (WITH TURBO)

| Throttle Range | Full Throttle (1.2-2.0 in. Hg.) | | Minimum Throttle (16.9-17.7 in. Hg.) | |
| --- | --- | --- | --- | --- |
| | Before Cut-down | After Cut-down | Before Cut-down | After Cut-down |
| D | 188-202 | 114-128 | 43-57 | 43-57 |
| 2 | 188-202 | 114-128 | 97-114 | 97-114 |
| R | 284-313 | | 81-95 | |

## STALL TEST RESULTS

| Stall Speed | Results | Possible Cause |
| --- | --- | --- |
| Higher than 2,500 rpm (Non-TURBO) or 2,900 rpm (TURBO) | a. Splippage of automatic transmission clutch, brake band, etc. (Further stall tests are not necessary.) | a. Low line pressure (If stall speed is higher than specified range at any shift position). <br> b. One-way clutch spliggage. (If stall speed is higher than specified range only in the D range). <br> c. Brake band slippage (If stall speed is higher than specified range only in the 2 range.) <br> d. Slippage of low & reverse brake or reverse brake (If stall speed is higher than specified range only in the R range.) |
| 2,300-2,500 rpm (Non-TURBO) or 2,700-2,900 rpm (TURBO) | a. Control members are in good order in the D, 2, 1 and R ranges. <br> b. Engine in good order. | |
| Lower than 2,300 rpm (Non-TURBO) or 2,700 rpm (TURBO) | a. Throttle not fully opened. <br> b. Erroneous engine operation or one-way clutch slippage. | |
| Road test | a. Acceleration is not properly made up to 50 km/h (31 MPH). <br> b. Car speed does not attain more than 80 km/h (50 MPH). <br> c. Operation is not proper at all car speeds. | a. One-way clutch slippage. <br> b. One-way clutch jamming. <br> c. Erroneous engine operation. |

## OVERALL LINE PRESSURE TEST RESULT INDICATIONS IN 4WD

1. With the engine at idle speed if the line pressure difference between 4WD and FWD is more than 4 psi. Then the transfer pipe is disconnected or the rear shaft seal ring has not been installed.

2. If the line pressure difference between the 4WD and FWD at engine idle speed is less than 4 psi., the solenoid or transfer valve is not working.

## GOVERNOR PRESSURE

The governor pressure reading should be taken if a malfunction of the governor pressure system is indicated.

### Governor Pressure Test

1. Remove the test plug from the right side of the final reduction case and install the oil pressure gauge adapter and the oil pressure gauge.

2. Warm up the engine by letting the engine idle for several minutes until the oil reaches operating temperature.

3. With the vehicle moving shift to the "2" range and check the governor pressure. Refer to the accompanying chart for the proper governor pressure readings.

## GOVERNOR PRESSURE AT VEHICLE SPEED

| Speed (mph) | PSI |
| --- | --- |
| 6 mph | 0 psi |
| 25 mph | 18-27 psi |
| 50 mph | 53-67 psi |

## AIR PRESSURE TESTS

Air pressure tests can be made to the various fluid passages, located within the transmission unit, separately or with the unit assembled, depending upon the exposed passage.

## CHANGE OF LINE PRESSURE WITH INTAKE MANIFOLD VACUUM CHANGES (N AND D RANGES)

| Intake Manifold Vacuum (in. HG) | Line Pressure (PSI) |
| --- | --- |
| 11 | 74-85 |
| 12 | 70-81 |
| 13 | 64-75 |
| 14 | 60-71 |
| 15 | 53-64 |
| 16 | 48-60 |
| 17 | 46-53 |
| 18 | 46-47 |

## STALL TEST

The purpose of the stall test is to check the clutch and band slippage, the engine performance and to determine if the torque converter is functioning properly.

### Procedure

1. Have the engine and the transaxle running at normal operating temperature.

2. Block all four wheels and apply hand brake.

3. Attach a tachometer to the engine and place it in a position to been seen.

NOTE: It is advisable to temporarily mark the specified stall speed (2,300-2,500 rpm) on the meter face.

4. Apply the foot brake and shift the selector lever to the "D" position.

5. With the foot brake applied gradually depress the accelerator pedal until the engine reaches full throttle.

6. When the engine speed is stabilized, read that speed quickly and release the accelerator pedal.

7. Shift the selector valve to the "N" neutral position, and cool down the engine by letting the engine idle for 2-5 minutes.

8. Record the stall speed and perform the stall tests with the selector lever in "2", "1" and "R" positions.

— CAUTION —

*Do not hold the stall test longer than 5 seconds as damage to the band and clutches can occur. Allow at least two to five minutes before attempting further stall tests.*

NOTE: If a relatively high stall speed is noted and internal transmission damages are suspected, that would necessitate tranmission removal and repair, do not continue the stall tests.

## ROAD TEST

The following descriptions concerning the road test should be observed correctly to make an accurate diagnosis of the automatic transmission.

### Gear Shift Feeling

The feeling of gear shifting as well as running speeds should be carefully checked, whether either of the following abnormalities is remarkable or not.

1. Shifting is not smooth but accompanied with a considerable shock.

2. Shifting is not sharp but accompanied with dragging.

These abnormalities indicate the presence of inaccurate throttle pressure or other related defects.

### Checking for Normal Shifting Conditions

1. Running speeds should be stepped up in the sequence of D1 to D2 to D3 when the selector lever is kept in the D position. No up-shifting should arise in the R position of the lever.

2. Kickdown operation should be achieved normally.

3. Running speeds should be stepped down in the sequence of D3 to 2 ($1_2$) to $1_1$ when the selector lever is shifted from the D to 1 position through 2 position.

The engine brake should be in effect throughout the $1_2$ and $1_1$ gears.

4. No up-shifting should arise in the 1 position of the selector lever.

5. Running speeds should be fixed to the second gear speed when the selector lever is shifted to the 2 position.

6. The car should be locked sufficiently from movement when the selector lever is shifted to the P position.

If any abnormal condition is felt on the second gear speed during the road test, the brake band should be adjusted.

If the defect still remains even through the brake band is in normally adjusted condition, oil leakage from the servo piston sealing parts should be checked.

### Checking The 4WD Operation

With the vehicle operating in 4WD, turn the vehicle in a circle while lightly depressing the accelerator pedal, and then shift the vehicle into the FWD position. When the vehicle is shifted into FWD a light shock should be felt. This shock is normal and will be felt everytime this operation takes place. Whenever the transfer clutch facing is replaced with a new one, the above test should be conducted, for the run-in purpose, two or three times with the vehicle set in the 4WD mode and the steering wheel fully turned.

# LOCK-UP TORQUE CONVERTER

This lock-up torque converter has a centrifugal lock up clutch built into the torque converter assembly. The lock up clutch has a very simple construction, consisting of five components: shoes and weights with paper facing pasted on their outer surfaces, two leaf springs (main and retractor springs) and pins. A total of eight shoes are used. The lock up clutch transmits torque by the centrifugal force acting on the shoes that slide along the inner circumference of the turbine cover. The shoes rotate at the same speed as the torque converter turbine. The shoes sometimes become completely engaged with the turbine cover, however they usually slide in a half clutch condition. The engine torque is transmitted from the turbine cover through the shoes to the reaction plate and then to the output shaft. The weight's primary job is to increase the transfer torque capacity in the medium and low-speed ranges. The centrifugal force acting on the weight is transmitted to the shoes through the main spring. The retractor spring always function to pull the shoe inward, which, in the low-speed range where the centrifugal force is small, prevents the shoes from touching the turbine drum. The pin holds the shoes in place so that the shoes will not come off the reaction plate, and also serves as a weight stopper.

NOTE: The lock-up torque converter is a sealed unit and can not be disassembled by the average repair shop.

### Diagnosis of the Lock-Up Torque Converter

If the following problems frequently occur with the transmission, the problem could be contributed to the torque converter. If the problem is found with the torque converter it should be removed and replaced.
1. Low maximum speed or poor acceleration.
2. Transmission overheating.
3. ATF fluid spills out while the vehicle is running.
4. Vehicle exhaust emits white smoke while running.

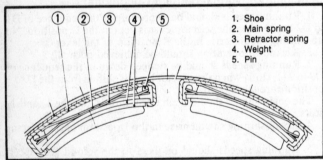

1. Shoe
2. Main spring
3. Retractor spring
4. Weight
5. Pin

**Exploded view of the lock-up clutch (©Fuji Heavy Industries Ltd.)**

ON CAR SERVICES

## Adjustments

### NEUTRAL SAFETY (INHIBITOR) SWITCH

**Adjustment**

If the manual valve detent position is not aligned with the guide plate groove position, perform the adjustment as follows.
1. Set the selector lever to the "N" position.
2. Loosen the adjusting nut of the linkage rod.

3. Set the detent position so the selector arm is aligned with the "N" location mark of the transmission case (within the range of a 0.24 in. (6mm diameter).
4. Adjust the rod so that the "N" mark of the guide plate is aligned correctly with this detent position.
5. If the indicator needle does not line up with the guide plate marking, remove the console box, loosen the four indicator mounting screws and adjust the position of the indicator assembly.

## KICKDOWN SWITCH AND DOWNSHIFT SOLENOID

### Testing

An audible click should be heard from the solenoid on the right side of the transmission, when the accelerator pedal is pushed down all the way with the engine off and the ignition switch on. The switch is operated by the upper part of the accelerator lever inside the car. The position of the switch can be varied to give quicker or slower kickdown response.

## SECOND GEAR BAND

### Adjustment

1. Hold the adjusting screw above the pan on the left side of the transmission.
2. Loosen the locknut.
3. Tighten the adjusting screw to a torque of 6.5 ft. lbs. and back off two complete turns.
4. Tighten the locknut, while holding the screw.

## MANUAL LINKAGE

The transmission manual control linkage removal, inspection, installation and adjustments are covered in this section.

### Removal

1. Remove the selector handle from the selector lever.
2. Remove the parking brake cover and the console box.
3. Disconnect the electrical connectors for the inhibitor switch and the position indicator light.
4. Remove the adjusting rod from transmission selector arm.
5. Remove the mounting screws and take out the selector lever assembly.

NOTE: Be sure that the selector lever is in the "N" position before removing the selector lever assembly.

### Disassembly

1. Remove the selector rod, position indicator and the inhibitor switch from the selector lever assembly.
2. Drive out the spring pin to the position where it is detached from the guide plate.
3. Remove the selector lever installing bolt and detach the boot by pushing it from underneath, then disconnect the selector lever from the plate.
4. Install the selector lever handle and release button to the selector lever temporarily, and drive the spring pin out from the selector rod, making sure not to damage the connected parts.

### Inspection

1. Check the selector lever rod for excessive bends or damage.
2. Check the detent plate for wear.
3. Check for worn contact surface of the pushbutton and the sleeve.
4. Check the pin at the end of the selector lever rod for wear or damage.

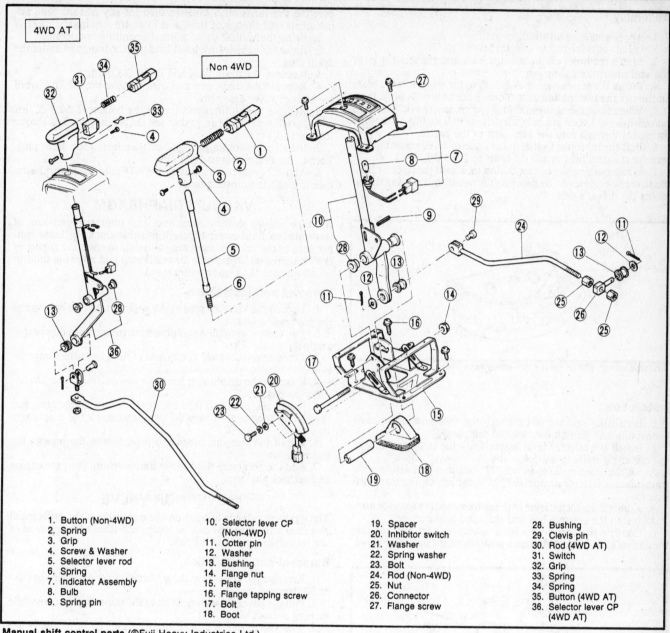

1. Button (Non-4WD)
2. Spring
3. Grip
4. Screw & Washer
5. Selector lever rod
6. Spring
7. Indicator Assembly
8. Bulb
9. Spring pin
10. Selector lever CP (Non-4WD)
11. Cotter pin
12. Washer
13. Bushing
14. Flange nut
15. Plate
16. Flange tapping screw
17. Bolt
18. Boot
19. Spacer
20. Inhibitor switch
21. Washer
22. Spring washer
23. Bolt
24. Rod (Non-4WD)
25. Nut
26. Connector
27. Flange screw
28. Bushing
29. Clevis pin
30. Rod (4WD AT)
31. Switch
32. Grip
33. Spring
34. Spring
35. Button (4WD AT)
36. Selector lever CP (4WD AT)

**Manual shift control parts** (©Fuji Heavy Industries Ltd.)

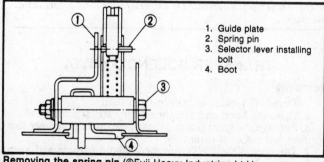

1. Guide plate
2. Spring pin
3. Selector lever installing bolt
4. Boot

**Removing the spring pin** (©Fuji Heavy Industries Ltd.)

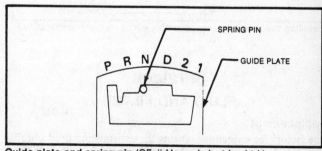

**Guide plate and spring pin** (©Fuji Heavy Industries Ltd.)

## Assembly

1. Apply grease to all sliding parts.
2. Install selector rod to selector lever.
3. Match the holes on the selector lever and the selector lever rod and insert the spring pin.
4. Install the selector lever assembly to the selector lever plate and insert the installation bolt. Torque the bolt to 9-14 ft. lbs.
5. When assembling the inhibitor switch, insert a 0.08 in. drill bit through the knock pin hole, turn the switch slightly so that the bit passes through into the back part of the switch.
6. Bolt the inhibitor switch to the selector lever assembly and remove the drill bit (torque the bolts to 2.9-5.8 ft. lbs.)
7. While pushing the release button in, install the selector handle to the selector lever. Be sure that the release button is installed facing the driver's side.

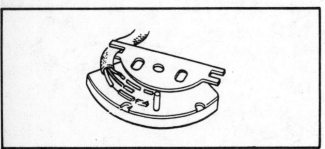

Inhibitor switch (©Fuji Heavy Industries Ltd.)

## Installation

1. Install the selector rod through the transmission selector connection and tighten the lock nut temporarily.
2. Install the selector lever assembly to the body and torque the mounting bolts to 3.3-5.4 ft. lbs.
3. Set the selector lever in the "N" position and also set the transmission selector arm in the "N" position on the transmission case.
4. Adjust the selector lever with the transmission selector arm.
5. Install the console box and the hand brake cover.
6. Confirm that the selector lever operation is smooth and that the correct gear is selected at each position on the indicator panel.

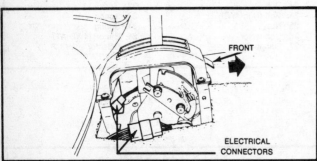

Installing the selector lever assembly (©Fuji Heavy Industries Ltd.)

## Services

### FLUID AND FILTER

#### Replacement

The factory recommends changing the transmission fluid and filter every 30,000 miles using the recommended ATF fluid. When-

ever the transmission is disassembled for any reason, band adjustments and change of fluid and filter are required.
1. Bring the vehicle up to normal operating temperature.
2. Raise the vehicle on a hoist, and place a drain pan under the drain plug.
3. Remove the drain plug and drain the fluid.
4. Remove the drain pan and then remove the oil filter from the control valve assembly.
5. Replace the oil filter and torque the bolts to 2.2-2.9 ft. lbs.
6. Install a new oil pan gasket and install oil pan, and torque the bolts to 8 ft. lbs.
7. Install a new drain plug gasket, then install the drain plug. Torque the drain plug to 18 ft. lbs.
8. Add 4.2 quarts of recommended ATF into the transmission case through the dipstick hole.

## VACUUM DIAPHRAGM

If rough idling, shifting harshness and undetermined loss of transmission fluid is experienced, possible cracks or loose connections of the vacuum lines may allow air to enter the engine or the vacuum diaphragm may be punctured and allowing fluid to be drawn into the engine and burned.

### Removal and Installation

1. Loosen the vacuum pipe at the engine/transaxle bolt and at the governor cover.
2. Pull the vacuum tube and pipe from the vacuum diaphragm assembly.
3. Drain approximately two quarts of fluid from the transmission.
4. Unscrew the diaphragm from the transmission case. Do not drop the push-rod.
5. Install the push-rod into the new vacuum diaphragm, seat the rod on the vacuum throttle valve and screw the diaphragm into place.
6. Install the vacuum tubes and pipe. Secure the pipe to the transmission.
7. Add the necessary fluid to the transmission. Start the engine and recheck the level.

## GOVERNOR VALVE

The governor valve is located on the right side of the differential and reduction case and can be removed without the removal of the transmission or the oil pan.

### Removal and Installation

1. Remove the bolts from the governor cover and turn the cover 90 degrees.
2. Pull the governor assembly from the transmission case while turning it clockwise.
3. The valve, sleeve and sealing ring can be inspected or replaced.
4. The installation is in the reverse of the removal procedure.

### ——— CAUTION ———

*Do not damage the seal ring, gear or the O-ring when installing the governor assembly. Lubricate the assembly with fluid before installation.*

## TRANSFER SOLENOID (4WD)

### Removal

1. Drain off 1 quart of transmission fluid.
2. Open the hood and disconnect the battery ground cable.
3. Remove the spare tire and loosen the pitching stopper to a position just before it comes off.
4. Disconnect the 4WD selector solenoid harness and keep the harness suspended.

5. Remove the upper cover, the cover must be removed in order to remove the exhaust pipe.

6. Remove the exhaust pipe.

7. Remove the intermediate side cable clamp.

8. Remove the rear crossmember, to ensure safety support the oil pan with a transmission jack or its equivalent.

9. Remove the side cable from the body clip.

10. Push the transmission to the left and insert a piece of wood between the clearance just achieved.

11. Remove the solenoid valve.

12. Installation of the transfer solenoid is just the reverse sequence of the removal procedures.

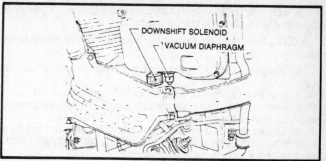

Removing the vacuum diaphragm (©Fuji Heavy Industries Ltd.)

2. Disconnect the vacuum hose and remove the downshift solenoid and the vacuum diaphragm together with the diaphragm rod.

3. Remove the oil pan and disconnect the servo pipes.

4. Remove the 6 mounting bolts and remove the control valve assembly.

**NOTE: Be careful not to drop the manual valve or damage the oil strainer.**

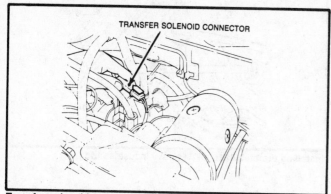

Transfer solenoid connector (©Fuji Heavy Industries Ltd.)

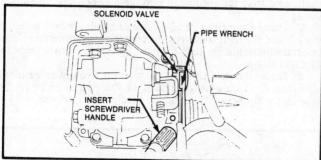

Removing the solenoid valve (©Fuji Heavy Industries Ltd.)

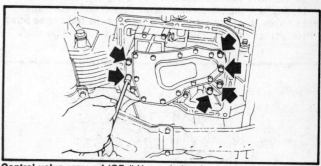

Control valve removal (©Fuji Heavy Industries Ltd.)

## Installation

1. Install the control valve assembly and torque the 6 mounting bolts equally at 4.3-5.8 ft. lbs.

2. Install the servo pipes (always use new servo pipes).

3. Install a new oil pan gasket and then install the oil pan.

4. Install the vacuum diaphragm.

5. Install the downshift solenoid and connect the vacuum hose.

**NOTE: Make sure to install a new O-ring on the downshift solenoid and the vacuum diaphragm.**

6. Refill with the recommended ATF and check the fluid level (approximately 4.2 quarts).

## TRANSFER SECTION (4WD)

### Removal and Installation

1. Completely drain the ATF from the transmission.

2. Remove the transfer solenoid (see transfer solenoid removal and installation for details).

3. Remove the temperature switch harness from the harness clamp.

4. Remove the 8 mounting bolts and remove the transfer section and the extension assembly as a unit from the intermediate case.

5. Installation of the transfer section is the reverse sequence of the removal procedures.

6. Refill the transmission with the recommended ATF and check the fluid level.

## CONTROL VALVE ASSEMBLY

### Removal

1. Raise the vehicle with a jack or a hoist and drain the ATF from the transmission.

## REMOVAL & INSTALLATION

### Transmission Removal

1. Open the hood as far as possible and secure it. Remove the spare wheel and disconnect the battery.

2. Remove all fluid lines, vacuum lines and tubes. Mark the lines and tubes for later installation.

3. Disconnect all wiring connections.

4. Disconnect the speedometer cable and unfasten the clip on the speedometer cable.

5. Remove the four bolts connecting the torque converter to the drive plate through the timing hole.

**NOTE: Be careful not to drop the bolts into the converter housing.**

6. Disconnect and plug the oil cooler hose from the transmission.

7. Remove the starter with the battery cable attached.

8. Remove the upper bolts which secure engine to transmission and loosen the lower nuts.

9. Loosen nut (10mm-0.39 in.) which retains the pitching stopper to the transmission side and slightly tilt the engine backward in order to remove transmission.

10. Disconnect the $O_2$ sensor harness and unclamp it.

11. Raise the front end of the vehicle and remove the exhaust assembly.

**NOTE: Do not strike the $O_2$ sensor against any parts during removal and a helper is needed to assist in removing the exhaust, due to the weight of the system.**

12. Drain the transmission fluid and then disconnect the oil supply pipe.

13. Move the selector to the "P" position and mark the location of the connector nut and separate the manual lever from the linkage rod.

14. Remove the stabilizer.

15. Remove the bolts which secure the left and right transverse links to the front crossmember, and lower the transverse links.

16. Drive both left and right spring pins out of axle shaft.

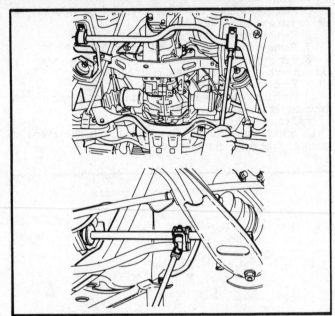

**Installing the stabilizer** (©Fuji Heavy Industries Ltd.)

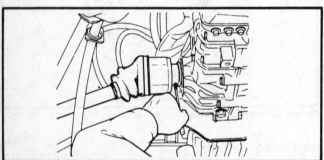

**Installing the axle shaft** (©Fuji Heavy Industries Ltd.)

**NOTE: Use new spring pins, do not reuse the old spring pins.**

17. While pushing the wheels toward the outer side, separate the axle shaft from the drive shaft.

18. Remove the mount retaining nut from the rear crossmember.

19. Support the transmission by placing a transmission jack or its equivalent, under the transmission.

20. Remove the crossmember.

21. Remove the two lower nuts that secure the engine to the transmission, and move the transmission away from the engine far enough so that the mainshaft of the transmission does not interfere with the engine.

22. Lower the transmission jack or its equivalent, and remove the transmission from the vehicle.

**Transmission Installation**

1. Place the transmission on the removing jack and raise into position in the vehicle.

2. When the transmission is aligned with the engine, secure the transmission to the engine.

3. Install the rear crossmember on the vehicle body.

4. Remove the jack from under the transmission.

5. Clamp the parking brake cable to the body.

6. Align the spring pin holes on the axle shaft and the drive shaft, and drive the spring pin into the holes (always use a new spring pin).

7. Using a punch or its equivalent, line up the bolt holes on the left and the right transverse links with the crossmember, and insert the bolts into the holes from the front side. Torque the bolts to 43-51 ft. lbs.

8. Install the stabilizer and position the two center bushings with their slits facing the rear side of the vehicle and the two outer bushings with their slits facing the inside of the vehicle.

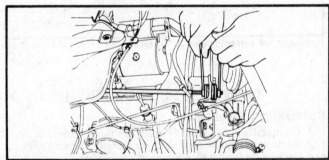

**Adjusting the pitching stopper** (©Fuji Heavy Industries Ltd.)

9. With the selector in the "P" position, insert the linkage rod into the manual lever, then set the selector at the "N" position, and torque the nut to 7-13 ft. lbs.

10. Connect the oil supply pipe (wipe ATF around the O-ring first).

11. Install the exhaust pipe assembly.

12. Connect the $O_2$ sensor harness to the $O_2$ sensor and clamp it.

13. Connect the hot air intake hose and lower the vehicle.

14. Tighten the bolts and nuts which retain the engine to the transmission (torque is 34-40 ft. lbs.). Also install the starter at this time.

15. With the bolt holes on the torque converter and the drive plate properly aligned, install the converter to the drive plate and torque the bolts to 17-20 ft. lbs.

16. Adjust the pitching stopper to 0.071-0.087 in. (1.8-2.2 mm) and torque the adjusting nuts to 7-13 ft. lbs.

17. Connect the speedometer cable and route the cable under the pitching stopper and then clamp it to the pitching stopper.

18. Make all necessary wire connections.

19. Connect the vacuum diaphragm hose and the oil cooler hose.

20. Connect the battery ground cable.

21. Refill the transmission with the recommended ATF.

22. Start the engine and check the exhaust system for any leaks.

23. Check to see that the selector lever operates smoothly and is properly shifting into every selector position.

24. Check the transmission fluid again and if it is low, add ATF until the fluid is at the proper level.

25. Install the spare tire and complete installation.

# BENCH OVERHAUL

## Before Disassembly

### All Models

When disassembling or assembling the automatic transmission, select a place that is clean and free from dust. Clean the exterior of the unit with steam or solvent.

During disassembly or assembly check the condition of each part. Apply a coat of automatic transmission fluid to parts before assembling. Torque all bolts and screw to their specified torque valves. Use petroleum jelly if necessary to hold parts in position when assembling. Be certain to use all new seals and gaskets.

The automatic transmission is divided into two sections, the transmission section and the differential and reduction sections. When replacing or overhauling the transmission separate the transmission from the differential.

## Transfer Section

### Disassembly
#### 4WD MODELS

1. Remove the rear engine mount and put the transfer unit on a work bench with the oil pan facing down.

2. Remove the solenoid from the transfer unit by turning the solenoid counter-clockwise by hand.

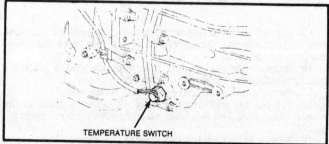

Removing the temperature switch (©Fuji Heavy Industries Ltd.)

3. Remove the temperature switch.

4. Remove the 8 mounting bolts and remove the transfer section together with extension assembly.

**NOTE: Make sure to remove the washer from the bearing bore on the upper side of the intermediate case. Do not place the opening of the extension assembly face down, because this may cause the rear shaft assembly to drop.**

5. Remove the extension assembly from the transmission section.

6. Remove the rear shaft assembly from the extension housing.

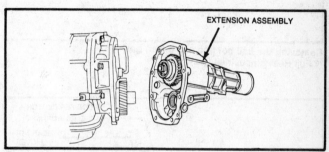

Removing the extension assembly (©Fuji Heavy Industries Ltd.)

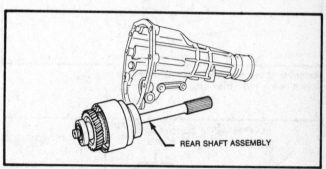

Removing the rear shaft assembly (©Fuji Heavy Industries Ltd.)

**NOTE: Be sure not to damage the oil seal in the rear of the extension housing.**

7. Remove the seal ring.

8. Using a bearing remover or its equivalent, drive out the ball bearing, washer and transfer driven gear.

9. Using the same bearing remover or its equivalent, remove the transfer clutch assembly drum and ball bearing.

10. Disassemble the transfer clutch assembly by, prying off the inner snap ring, removing the front pressure plate, the three clutch drive plates, the two clutch driven plates and the rear pressure plate.

## Transmission Case Section

### Disassembly
#### 4WD MODELS

1. With all the ATF drained remove the rear extension assembly.

2. Remove the turbine output shaft and the oil pump drive shaft (pull them straight out).

**NOTE: If the shafts cannot be pulled out by hand, wrap a nylon cloth around their splines and use a pair of pliers to remove the shafts. Do not damage the splines in any way.**

3. Remove the oil cooler pipe from the transmission case.

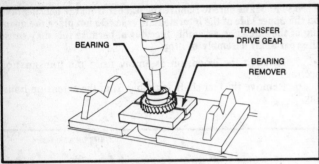

**Removing the ball bearing and driven gear**
(©Fuji Heavy Industries Ltd.)

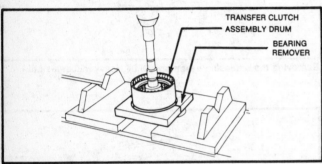

**Removal of the transfer clutch assembly drum**
(©Fuji Heavy Industries Ltd.)

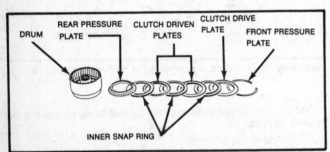

**Parts of the transfer clutch assembly** (©Fuji Heavy Industries Ltd.)

4. Remove the nuts which secure the transmission case to the final reduction case, and remove the downshift solenoid, transfer solenoid and temperature switch lead wire clips.
5. Remove the vacuum pipe and the ground lead wire.
6. Remove the oil supply pipe.
7. Drain the differential gear oil completely.
8. Place the transmission on a work bench with the housing face down.

## Final Reduction Case Section

### Disassembly
#### 4WD MODEL
1. With the extension assembly removed, remove the oil pan and the control valve assembly.
2. Wrap a nylon cloth around the spline portion of the drive pinion rear end in order not to damage the oil seal.
3. Remove the transmission case section from the final reduction case section.

## Transmission Disassembly

### FWD Models
NOTE: Before separating the cases, be sure to drain the differential gear oil.

1. Remove the torque converter assembly from the converter housing.
2. Remove the turbine shaft and oil pump drive shaft. Be careful not to damage the splines when removing the shaft.
3. Remove the nuts securing the transmission case to the differential and reduction case, and detach the downshift solenoid wire.
4. Remove the oil cooler pipes.
5. Remove the vacuum pipe and governor cover.
6. Separate the transmission from the differential and reduction section. Remove the washer located on the planetary output gear.
7. Place the transmission on a stand, drain the transmission fluid and remove the oil pan.
8. Remove the downshift solenoid valve and vacuum diaphragm by turning them with hand. Also remove the diaphragm rod and two O-rings.
9. Carefully pry out the servo apply and release pipes. Note that these pipes are aluminum and must be handled carefully.
10. Remove the six control valve body retaining bolts and lift off the valve body. Be certain not to drop out the manual valve.
11. Remove the transfer valve and loosen the brake band adjusting screw.
12. Remove the rear mounting rubber from the bracket.
13. Take out the bolts securing the transmission cover, turn the cover slightly while tapping rear mounting bucket. Remove the cover and the oil pump carrier as an assembly.
14. Move the transfer drive shaft upward and remove transfer coupling from the rear spline of the drive pinion. Remove the transfer drive shaft and remove the strut band.

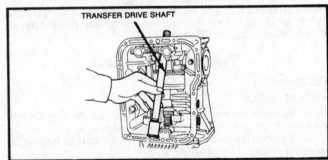

**Removing the transfer drive shaft** (©Fuji Heavy Industries Ltd.)

15. Pry out the snap ring securing the servo piston cover. Use two bolts to remove the cover and detach the servo piston by pushing its rod from the inside of the transmission case.
16. Remove the brake band, reverse clutch, clutch assembly and forward clutch assembly in that order.
17. Remove the connective shell and clutch hub.
18. Pry out the snap ring securing the center support to the transmission case. Use two bolts to remove the center support assembly.
19. Remove the forward and reverse sun gears.
20. Remove the planetary gear assembly and low and reverse brake plates as an assembly.
21. Remove the low and reverse brake retaining plate.
22. Take out the planetary gear output shaft.
23. Remove the nut and bolts securing the selector arm and neutral safety switch and remove them.

24. Remove the clip and lock nut from the manual shaft and remove the manual shaft and manual plate.

25. Remove the parking rod and lever.

26. Remove the clip from the parking pawl shaft, remove the pawl, the pawl return spring and parking rod support plate.

## TRANSFER SECTION

### Assembly 4WD Model

1. Apply a coat of recommended ATF to all parts and assemble the transfer clutch.

2. To assemble the transfer clutch, first install the transfer clutch assembly drum and bearing to the rear shaft. Install the rear pressure plate, the two clutch driven plates, the three clutch drive plates and the front pressure plate.

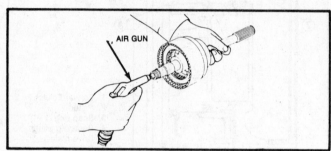

**Checking the piston for proper movement**
(©Fuji Heavy Industries Ltd.)

**NOTE: Apply compressed air into the oil hole to check proper piston movement. Pay attention to the directions of the front and rear pressure plates.**

3. After the transfer clutch has been assembled, measure the clearance between the outer snap ring and the front pressure plate. Install a suitable pressure plate to bring the clearance within specifications (transfer clutch clearance 0.4-0.8mm, 0.016-0.031 in.).

### PRESSURE PLATES

| Plate Thickness mm (in.) | Part Number |
|---|---|
| 4.7 (0.185) | 447677000 |
| 5.0 (0.197) | 447677001 |
| 5.3 (0.209) | 447677002 |
| 5.6 (0.220) | 447677003 |
| 5.9 (0.232) | 447677004 |

4. Using a bearing installer or its equivalent, install the transfer drive gear, the washer and the ball bearing.

5. Install the seal ring onto the rear drive shaft.

6. Install the rear shaft assembly into the extension housing.

7. Install a suitable washer so that the clearance between the rear shaft assembly and the intermediate case is 0-0.012 in. (0-0.3mm)—standard clearance.

8. Measure dimension "M" using a depth gauge and low-reverse brake gauge made by the manufacture (or use a flat piece of metal).

    a. Place the low-reverse brake gauge or its equivalent, from the rear shaft assembly to the extension mounting surface.

b. Using the depth gauge measure the distance (depth) between the low-reverse brake gauge or its equivalent, to the extension housing moutning surface.

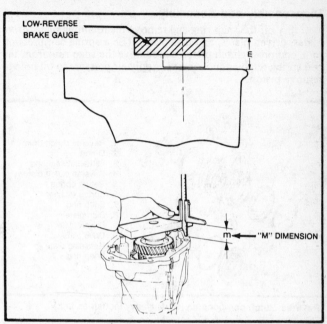

**Measuring the "M" dimension** (©Fuji Heavy Industries Ltd.)

c. The distance (depth) between the gauge and the extension mounting surface ("M" dimension) will determine what washer thickness to choose, so that the clearance between the rear shaft assembly and the intermediate case will be within specifications.

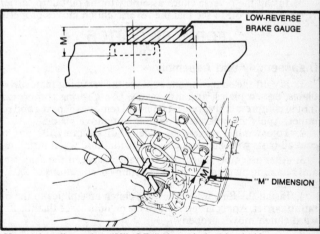

**Measuring dimension "M"** (©Fuji Heavy Industries Ltd.)

### WASHER THICKNESS

| Thickness—mm (in.) | Part Number |
|---|---|
| 0.2 (0.008) | 803242010 |
| 0.5 (0.020) | 803242011 |

9. Install the rear drive gear thrust plate and transfer gear onto the intermediate case.

## Unit Disassembly and Assembly
### REVERSE CLUTCH

#### Disassembly and Assembly

1. Pry off the snap ring and remove the retaining plate, drive plates, driven plates, and dish plates. Use a spring compression tool, compress clutch piston and remove the snap ring from the coil spring retainer and remove. Apply air pressure to oil hole to remove piston.

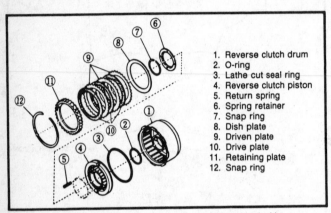

1. Reverse clutch drum
2. O-ring
3. Lathe cut seal ring
4. Reverse clutch piston
5. Return spring
6. Spring retainer
7. Snap ring
8. Dish plate
9. Driven plate
10. Drive plate
11. Retaining plate
12. Snap ring

Reverse clutch components (©Fuji Heavy Industries Ltd.)

2. To assemble, reverse the order of disassembly. Be sure to coat all parts with automatic transmission fluid when installing.
3. Install the driven plates to the clutch drum and align the driven plate missing tooth portion with the oil hole in the clutch drum.
4. Check the clearance between the snap ring and retaining plate to ensure it is within specifications 0.063-0.071 in. If not, change the retaining plate with a proper one.
5. Install the reverse clutch assembly to the oil pump carrier. Apply air into oil to see that the reverse clutch moves properly.

### FORWARD CLUTCH

#### Disassembly and Assembly

1. Pry off the snap ring and remove the retaining plate, drive plates, driven plates, and dish plates. Use a spring compressor tool to compress coil spring retainer and remove snap ring and retainer. Apply air pressure to oil hole to remove piston.
2. To assemble, reverse the order of disassembly. Be sure to coat all parts with automatic transmission fluid when installing.
3. After assembly, check the clearance between the snap ring and retaining plate to see that it is within specifications of 0.039-0.059 in.
4. Install the forward and reverse clutch assemblies to the oil pump carrier. Apply air pressure to the oil hole to see that the forward clutch moves properly.

### RETAINING PLATES

| Thickness—mm (in.) | Part Number |
| --- | --- |
| 10.6 (0.417) | 453710100 |
| 10.8 (0.425) | 453710101 |
| 11.0 (0.433) | 453710102 |
| 11.2 (0.441) | 453710103 |
| 11.4 (0.449) | 453710104 |

### PRESSURE PLATES

| Plate Thickness mm (in.) | Part Number |
| --- | --- |
| 11.6 (0.457) | 453710105 |

NOTE: Retaining plates are available in six different sizes.

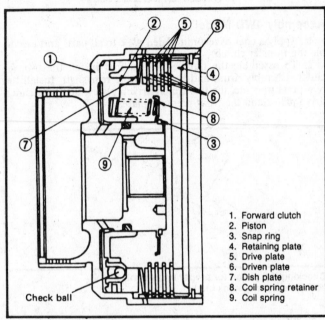

1. Forward clutch
2. Piston
3. Snap ring
4. Retaining plate
5. Drive plate
6. Driven plate
7. Dish plate
8. Coil spring retainer
9. Coil spring

Check ball

Sectional view of forward clutch (©Fuji Heavy Industries Ltd.)

# LOW AND REVERSE BRAKE

#### Disassembly and Assembly

1. Use the necessary tools to remove the snap ring from the center support. Remove the low and reverse brake piston by applying air pressure into the oil hole in the center support.
2. Replace any damaged parts.
3. To assemble, reverse the order of disassembly. Be sure to coat all parts with automatic transmission fluid when installing.

### SERVO PISTON

#### Disassembly and Assembly

1. Pry out the snap ring securing the servo piston cover and use two bolts to remove the cover. Detach the servo piston by pushing its rod from inside the transmission case.
2. To assembly, reverse the order of disassembly. Be sure to coat all parts with automatic transmission fluid when installing.
3. Before assembling the servo piston parts install the two O-rings coated with ATF.

### GOVERNOR VALVE

#### Disassembly and Assembly

1. Remove the screws securing the governor shaft to the governor body.
2. Remove the two snap rings and clip, and disassemble the governor valve assembly. Remove the governor valve, small weight, spring and large weight from the governor body.
3. To assemble reverse the order of disassembly and tighten the governor shaft screw to 3.3-4.0 ft. lbs.

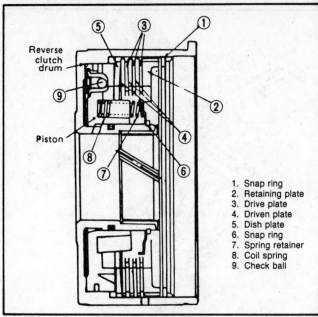

Sectional view of reverse clutch (©Fuji Heavy Industries Ltd.)

1. Snap ring
2. Retaining plate
3. Drive plate
4. Driven plate
5. Dish plate
6. Snap ring
7. Spring retainer
8. Coil spring
9. Check ball

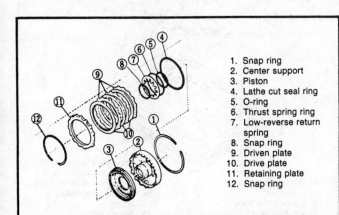

1. Snap ring
2. Center support
3. Piston
4. Lathe cut seal ring
5. O-ring
6. Thrust spring ring
7. Low-reverse return spring
8. Snap ring
9. Driven plate
10. Drive plate
11. Retaining plate
12. Snap ring

Low and reverse brake components (©Fuji Heavy Industries Ltd.)

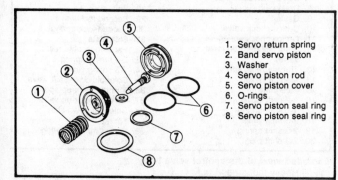

1. Servo return spring
2. Band servo piston
3. Washer
4. Servo piston rod
5. Servo piston cover
6. O-rings
7. Servo piston seal ring
8. Servo piston seal ring

Band servo components (©Fuji Heavy Industries Ltd.)

## OIL PUMP

### Disassembly and Assembly

NOTE: When disassembling the oil pump note the positions of the side faces of inner gear and outer gear so that they may be installed with their faces facing the same way.

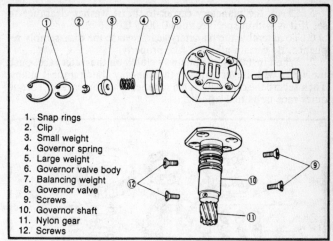

1. Snap rings
2. Clip
3. Small weight
4. Governor spring
5. Large weight
6. Governor valve body
7. Balancing weight
8. Governor valve
9. Screws
10. Governor shaft
11. Nylon gear
12. Screws

Governor valve assembly components (©Fuji Heavy Industries Ltd.)

1. Remove the bolts and disassemble the oil pump carrier and transmission cover.
2. Remove the inner and outer gears from the pump carrier.
3. Check gears and pump carrier bushings. If they are damaged, replace them. Also inspect needle bearings and replace if necessary.
4. When replacing inner or outer gear adjust clearance by selecting its thickness.
5. Check clearances of the gears. Clearance should be 0.08-0.0016 in. between inner/outer gear and transmission cover. Clearance between crescent and tooth tip of outer gear should be 0.0055-0.0083 in. Radial clearance between outer gear and oil pump carrier should be 0.0020-0.0079 in. Clearance between seal ring and groove should be 0.0016-0.0063 in.
6. After installing the gears place the oil pump drive shaft into the pump carrier.
7. When installing the transmission cover, tighten the cover bolts to 4.3-5.8 ft. lbs.

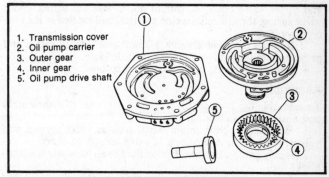

1. Transmission cover
2. Oil pump carrier
3. Outer gear
4. Inner gear
5. Oil pump drive shaft

Oil pump components (©Fuji Heavy Industries Ltd.)

## PLANETARY GEAR

### Disassembly and Assembly

1. Remove the bolts securing the one-way clutch outer race to the planetary carrier.
2. Push the pinion pin out toward the one-way clutch side, and detach the short pinions, long pinions, thrust washers, needle roller bearings and spacers.
3. Remove the one-way clutch from the outer race.
4. Check all parts and bushings for damage and wear; replace if necessary.

5. Check the planetary carrier-to-thrust washer clearance to see if it is within specifications 0.0059-0.0236 in.

6. To assemble the planetary gear, reverse the disassembly sequence. Be certain all parts face properly.

7. When installing the one-way clutch on the outer race, push the T-bar with finger to insert the one-way clutch until it snaps. Then secure the one-way clutch retainer in the outer race. Torque outer race bolts to 11 ft. lb.

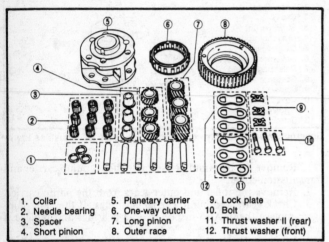

| | | |
|---|---|---|
| 1. Collar | 5. Planetary carrier | 9. Lock plate |
| 2. Needle bearing | 6. One-way clutch | 10. Bolt |
| 3. Spacer | 7. Long pinion | 11. Thrust washer II (rear) |
| 4. Short pinion | 8. Outer race | 12. Thrust washer (front) |

**Planetary gear components** (©Fuji Heavy Industries Ltd.)

## CONTROL VALVE BODY

### Disassembly

The control valve is composed of parts which are accurately machined to a high degree and should be handled carefully. Make sure that the valves are clean and free from any foreign material before assembly.

1. Remove the bolts and nut securing the oil strainer and lift off.

2. Remove the bolts and separate the lower valve body, plate, and upper valve body. Be careful not to lose the orifice check valve spring, throttle relief spring and steel ball located in the lower valve body.

3. Remove the manual valve, 1-2 shift and 2-3 shift valves and pressure modifier valve. Remove the side plate.

4. Remove the side plate valves and springs.

### Assembly

To assemble the control valve, reverse the order of disassembly and observe the following.

1. When assembling minor parts, such as valve springs and valves, refer to the description of valve springs in chart.

2. Apply automatic transmission fluid to all parts when assembling.

3. When tightening all parts do not force them into place, but lightly push into place with hand.

4. Install the side plates and torque to 1.8-2.5 ft. lbs.

5. Install the orifice check valve and spring, throttle relief spring and steel ball to lower valve body.

6. Assemble the upper and lower valve bodies and torque bolts to 1.8-2.5 ft. lbs.

7. Install the oil strainer and torque bolt to 1.8-2.5 ft. lbs.

## FINAL REDUCTION CASE SECTION

### Disassembly

1. Place the final reduction assembly on a differential stand or its equivalent, and remove the ten bolts that secure the final reduction housing to the converter housing.

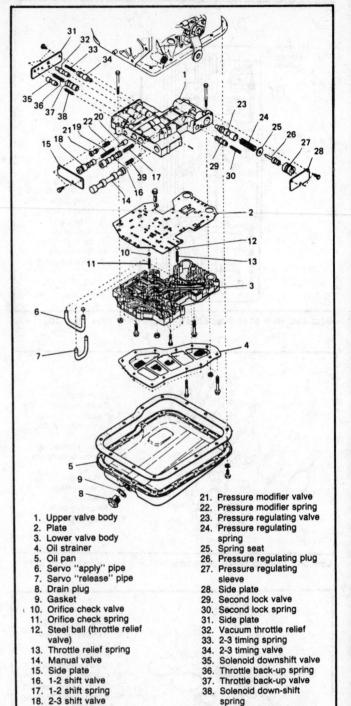

| | |
|---|---|
| 1. Upper valve body | 21. Pressure modifier valve |
| 2. Plate | 22. Pressure modifier spring |
| 3. Lower valve body | 23. Pressure regulating valve |
| 4. Oil strainer | 24. Pressure regulating |
| 5. Oil pan | spring |
| 6. Servo "apply" pipe | 25. Spring seat |
| 7. Servo "release" pipe | 26. Pressure regulating plug |
| 8. Drain plug | 27. Pressure regulating |
| 9. Gasket | sleeve |
| 10. Orifice check valve | 28. Side plate |
| 11. Orifice check spring | 29. Second lock valve |
| 12. Steel ball (throttle relief | 30. Second lock spring |
| valve) | 31. Side plate |
| 13. Throttle relief spring | 32. Vacuum throttle relief |
| 14. Manual valve | 33. 2-3 timing spring |
| 15. Side plate | 34. 2-3 timing valve |
| 16. 1-2 shift valve | 35. Solenoid downshift valve |
| 17. 1-2 shift spring | 36. Throttle back-up spring |
| 18. 2-3 shift valve | 37. Throttle back-up valve |
| 19. 2-3 shift spring | 38. Solenoid down-shift |
| 20. 2-3 shift plug | spring |
| | 39. Detent manual spring |
| | 40. Gasket |

**Exploded view of the control valve body**
(©Fuji Heavy Industries Ltd.)

2. Remove the bolts that secure the governor cover, and remove the governor body assembly.

**NOTE: While removing the governor assembly, slowly turn it to the right.**

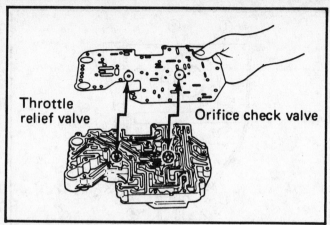

Installation of orifice, check and throttle relief valves
(©Fuji Heavy Industries Ltd.)

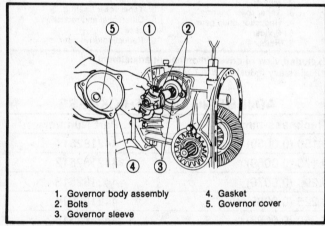

1. Governor body assembly     4. Gasket
2. Bolts                      5. Governor cover
3. Governor sleeve

**Removal of governor valve assembly** (©Fuji Heavy Industries Ltd.)

3. Remove the parking actuator.
4. Remove the three bolts securing the reduction gear oil seal holder.
5. Remove the snap rings from the axle drive shafts in the differential housing.
6. Remove the lock plates, then remove the axle shaft oil seal holders and the axle drive shafts as an assembly.
7. After moving the differential assembly to one side, remove the final reduction housing.
8. Remove the drive pinion lock nut and press out the drive pinion.
9. Remove the snap ring from the end of the speedometer shaft, and remove the speedometer driven gear and the steel ball.
10. Remove the reduction gear.
11. Remove the stator shaft.
12. Check the gears, bearings, seals, O-rings, and gaskets. If they are damaged, replace them.

## Installation

1. Press the thrust bearing retainer assembly and the reduction driven gear into the final reduction housing.

**NOTE: Be sure that the projection of the retainer flange is aligned with the groove of the final reduction housing.**

2. Install the transmission case front gasket and reduction drive gear on the final reduction housing, and snugly tighten the 8 mounting bolts.

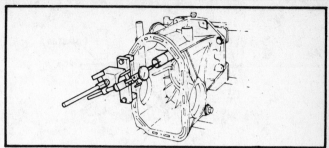

Measuring of run-out (©Fuji Heavy Industries Ltd.)

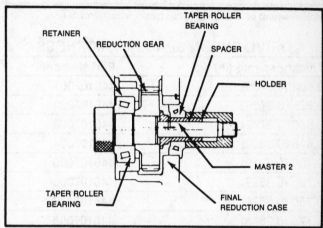

TAPER ROLLER BEARING

RETAINER

REDUCTION GEAR

SPACER

HOLDER

MASTER 2

TAPER ROLLER BEARING

FINAL REDUCTION CASE

**Preload adjustment of the drive pinion** (©Fuji Heavy Industries Ltd.)

3. With the final reduction housing secured to the differential stand or its equivalent, install the speedometer drive gear.
4. Be sure that the run-out at the tip of the reduction drive gear shaft is 0-0.0031 in. (0-0.08mm). With a dial indicator connected to the drive gear shaft, turn the shaft and watch the dial indicator to get the run-out reading.
5. Install the drive pinion assembly into the final reduction housing.
6. After the drive pinion assembly is installed, a pre-load adjustment of the drive pinion bearings must be performed.
7. Attach the preload check pulley or its equivalent, to the head of the final reduction case holder. Then tighten the holder so that the tension of the spring balance reads 7-9 ft. lbs. to give the specified preload.

**NOTE: The torque on the holder to give the specified preload is 7-9 ft. lbs. (10-12 N•m).**

8. Measure the clearance between the spacer and the rear bearing (which is preloaded). Slide the spacer rearward and install a dial indicator.
9. Once the clearance has been measured, select a combination of a shim and spacer to ensure a proper preload adjustment.

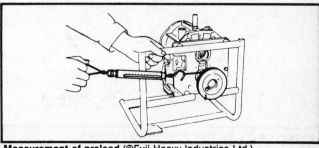

Measurement of preload (©Fuji Heavy Industries Ltd.)

**9-25**

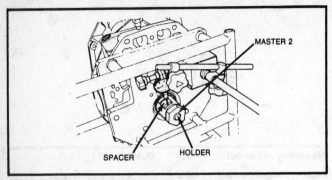

**Measurement of clearance (©Fuji Heavy Industries Ltd.)**

## DRIVE PINION SPACER THICKNESS

| Thickness-mm (in) | Part Number |
|---|---|
| 9.600 (0.3780) | 446107001 |
| 9.625 (0.3789) | 446107002 |
| 9.650 (0.3799) | 446107003 |
| 9.675 (0.3809) | 446107004 |
| 9.700 (0.3819) | 446107005 |
| 9.725 (0.3829) | 446107006 |
| 9.750 (0.3839) | 446107007 |
| 9.775 (0.3848) | 446107008 |

## DRIVE PINION SHIM THICKNESS

| Thickness-mm (in) | Part Number |
|---|---|
| 0.6 (0.024) | 441967001 |
| 0.8 (0.031) | 441967002 |
| 1.0 (0.039) | 441967003 |

10. After the preload adjustments have been made, the drive pinion height adjustment must be made.

11. The drive pinion height adjustment is made by inserting shims between the front bearing cone and the back face of the pinion gear.

12. Set the master drive pinion tool or its equivalent, and the low-reverse brake tool or its equivalent, to measure the clearance (N) between the master and the gauge using a thickness gauge (feeler gauge).

13. To ensure the correct pinion height adjustment select the proper size adjusting shim.

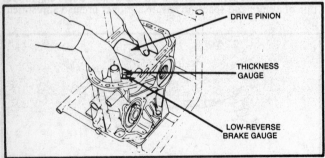

**Measurement of the drive pinion height clearance**
(©Fuji Heavy Industries Ltd.)

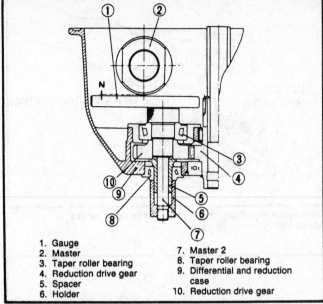

1. Gauge
2. Master
3. Taper roller bearing
4. Reduction drive gear
5. Spacer
6. Holder
7. Master 2
8. Taper roller bearing
9. Differential and reduction case
10. Reduction drive gear

**Exploded view of drive pinion height adjustment**
(©Fuji Heavy Industries Ltd.)

## ADJUSTING SHIM THICKNESS

| Thickness-mm (in) | Part Number |
|---|---|
| 0.150 (0.0059) | 442182511 |
| 0.175 (0.0069) | 442182512 |
| 0.200 (0.0079) | 442182513 |
| 0.225 (0.0089) | 442182514 |
| 0.250 (0.0098) | 442182515 |
| 0.275 (0.0108) | 442182516 |
| 0.300 (0.0118) | 442182517 |
| 0.500 (0.0197) | 442182518 |

14. With the drive pinion installed and the reduction gear in place, install the shim and spacer determined during the preload adjustment, and install the rear bearing cone onto the drive pinion.

15. Install the drive pinion lock nut and lock washer and torque the nut to 87 ft. lbs.

16. Recheck the preload.

17. Install the differential assembly.

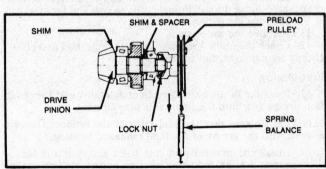

**Rechecking the preload adjustment (©Fuji Heavy Industries Ltd.)**

18. Install the right and left axle shafts and secure them with the snap rings.

**NOTE: Check to see if the clearance between the differential pinion shaft and the axle shaft is within specifications. (Specified clearance 0-0.2mm 0-0.008 in).**

19. There are two snap rings available for the adjustment of the clearance between the differential pinion shaft and the axle shaft.

## SNAP RING THICKNESS

| Thickness—mm (in) | Part Number |
|---|---|
| 1.00-1.10 (0.0394-0.0433) | 805026010 |
| 1.15-1.25 (0.0453-0.0492) | 031526000 |

20. Install the axle shaft oil seal holder.
21. Install the governor assembly and the governor cover, torque the governor cover bolts to 10-12 ft. lbs.

**NOTE: Before installing the governor cover, attach the washer to the cover with vaseline and replace the old gasket with a new one.**

22. Install the stator shaft to the converter housing with the new gasket in place and with the flange of the shaft facing upward (torque the flange bolts to 17-20 ft. lbs.).
23. Apply a coat of differential gear oil to the reduction drive gear shaft assembly and install a new mating surface gasket. Install the final reduction case to the converter housing and torque the mounting bolts to 17-20 ft. lbs.
24. Install the parking actuator with the spacer on the final reduction case and torque the parking actuator support bolt to 5.8-8.0 ft. lbs.

## Transmission Assembly

Clean and thoroughly check all parts and replace all seals and gaskets during assembly.

To assemble transmission, reverse the disassembly procedures and observe the following points.

1. Install the parking rod support plate and return spring to the case, set the clip to the parking pawl shaft and install the parking rod.
2. Check the one-way clutch for proper operation. It should turn clockwise only, as viewed from the front with the planetary carrier assembly assembled to the center support.
3. When installing the low and reverse brake parts into the case, install the snap ring, retaining plate, drive plates, driven plates, center support assembly and snap ring. There are three drive plates and three driven plates.

**NOTE: Before installing low and reverse brake, use a special gauge and select a proper retaining plate so that distance "H" shown in illustration is within specifications (2.778-2.801 in.).**

**NOTE: When installing the center support, screw two bolts into the center support, then install it into the transmission case while turning the center support gradually.**

4. After assembly, measure the clearance between the snap ring and retaining plate. The clearance should be within specifications, 0.0020-0.047 in.

5. The center support is engaged with the transmission case by splines at one position. When installing the center support, be careful not to damage the one-way clutch and bushing.
6. Apply air into the oil hole in the low and reverse brake to see that the piston moves properly.
7. Install the connecting shell and clutch hub as an assembly to the transmission case.
8. Install the forward clutch assembly to the clutch hub.
9. Install the reverse clutch assembly to the forward clutch assembly.
10. Match the projected portions of the brake band with the notches in the transmission case to install the brake band.
11. Select a proper washer to be used at the end of the oil pump carrier until the total end play is within specifications, 0.01-0.02 in.

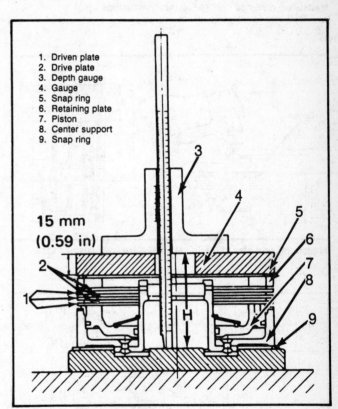

1. Driven plate
2. Drive plate
3. Depth gauge
4. Gauge
5. Snap ring
6. Retaining plate
7. Piston
8. Center support
9. Snap ring

15 mm (0.59 in)

**Selection of retaining plate** (©Fuji Heavy Industries Ltd.)

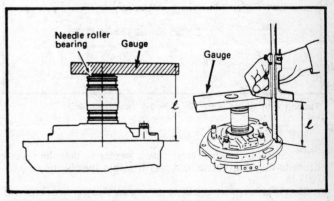

Needle roller bearing    Gauge    Gauge

**Measuring distance "L"** (©Fuji Heavy Industries Ltd.)

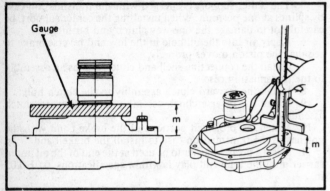

**Measuring distance "M"** (©Fuji Heavy Industries Ltd.)

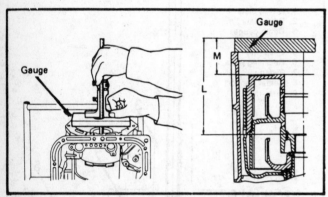

**Measuring end play "L" and "M"** (©Fuji Heavy Industries Ltd.)

**Testing with air pressure** (©Fuji Heavy Industries Ltd.)

12. Select a proper reverse clutch washer so that the reverse drum-to-oil pump carrier end play is within specifications, 0.02-0.03 in.

13. Apply petroleum jelly to the washer and pump carrier end, and put the washer on the pump carrier side before installing.

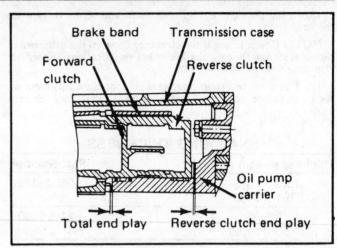

**Measuring position of end plays** (©Fuji Heavy Industries Ltd.)

**NOTE: Do not forget to install the needle bearing.**

14. Insert the servo piston cover assembly into the case, using the piston rod as a guide.

**NOTE: Two O-rings of the same size are used on the servo piston cover. An O-ring which is used for inner end of servo piston cover must be inserted into the transmission case side in advance.**

15. Install the band strut properly. Tighten the adjusting screw to 6.5 ft. lbs. torque, then turn it back 2 turns. Tighten the locknut to 18-1 ft. lbs. torque.

16. Adjust the clearance between the manual plate and the spacer by shims until it is within 0.012 in. Install the safety switch.

17. Install the manual valve groove to the manual plate pin and install to the transmission case. Torque valve body attaching bolts to 4.3-5.8 ft. lbs.

18. Push the vacuum throttle valve in and measure the distance from the rod end to the outer face of the case. Then select a diaphragm rod of the proper length and install it with the vacuum diaphragm. Install the solenoid.

19. Make sure that the servo apply and release pipes are properly installed. Check the height of the pipes above the mating surface of the oil pan to insure that it is 0.83 in. or less.

20. Install oil pan and torque pan retaining bolts to 2.53-3.25 ft. lbs.

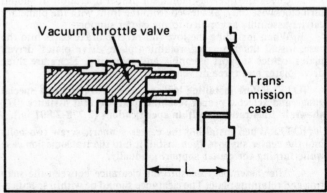

**Measurement of throttle valve depth** (©Fuji Heavy Industries Ltd.)

# S SPECIFICATIONS

## GEAR SPECIFICATIONS

| | | Backlash ① |
|---|---|---|
| Planetary gear | Forward sun gear to short pinion | 0.15-0.22mm (0.0059-0.0087 in) |
| | Reverse sun gear to long pinion | 0.15-0.22mm (0.0059-0.0087 in) |
| | Short pinion to long pinion | 0.15-0.22mm (0.0059-0.0087 in) |
| | Long pinion to planetary output gear | 0.18-0.25mm (0.0071-0.0098 in) |
| 1st reduction gears | | 0.05-0.12mm (0.0020-0.0047 in) |
| 2nd reduction gears | | 0.13-0.18mm (0.0051-0.0071 in) |
| Governor gears and Speedometer gears | | 0.30-0.81mm (0.0118-0.0319 in) |
| Transfer gears | | 0.051-0.125mm (0.0020-0.0049 in) |

①Units: mm (in)

## VACUUM DIAPHRAGM ROD

| Measurement "L"① | Part No. | Length① |
|---|---|---|
| 25.55 (1.0059) or less | 493210103 | 29 (1.14) |
| 25.65 to 26.05 (1.0098 to 1.0256) | 493210104 | 29.5 (1.16) |
| 26.15 to 26.55 (1.0295 to 1.0453) | 493210100 | 30 (1.18) |
| 26.65 to 27.05 (1.0492 to 1.0650) | 493210102 | 30.5 (1.20) |
| 27.15 (1.0689) or more | 493210101 | 21 (1.22) |

① Units: mm (in.)

## REVERSE CLUTCH THRUST WASHER

| Part No. | Thickness ① |
|---|---|
| 452810100 | 1.9 (0.075) |
| 452810101 | 2.1 (0.083) |
| 452810102 | 2.3 (0.091) |
| 452810103 | 2.5 (0.098) |
| 452810104 | 2.7 (0.106) |
| 452810105 | 1.5 (0.059) |
| 452810106 | 1.7 (0.067) |

① Units: mm (in)

## SPRING SPECIFICATIONS
(Low-Reverse Return Spring)

| Part No. | 465110101 |
|---|---|
| Plate thickness | 1.27 (0.050)① |
| Free height | 5.54 (0.218)① |
| Outer diameter | 93.98 (3.70)① |
| Inner diameter | 55.88 (2.20)① |

① Units: mm (in)

## RETAINING PLATE

| Part No. | Thickness ① |
|---|---|
| 344268701 | 7.2 (0.2834) |
| 344268702 | 7.4 (0.2913) |
| 344268703 | 7.6 (0.2992) |
| 344268704 | 7.8 (0.3070) |
| 344268705 | 8.0 (0.3149) |
| 344268706 | 8.2 (0.3228) |

① Units: mm (in)

## WASHER

| Part No. | Thickness ① |
|---|---|
| 803021048 | 1.0 (0.039) |
| 803021049 | 1.2 (0.047) |
| 803021040 | 1.4 (0.055) |
| 803021044 | 1.6 (0.061) |
| 803021045 | 1.8 (0.171) |
| 803021046 | 2.0 (0.079) |
| 803021047 | 2.2 (0.087) |

① Units: mm (in)

## OIL PUMP CLEARANCES

| Inner gear, Part Number | 434610100 | 434610101 | 434610102 |
|---|---|---|---|
| Outer gear, Part Number | 434710100 | 434710101 | 434710102 |
| Thickness mm, | 16-15.99 | 15.99-15.98 | 15.98-15.97 |
| in | 0.6299-0.6295 | 0.6295-0.6291 | 0.6291-0.6287 |

## SPECIAL TOOLS

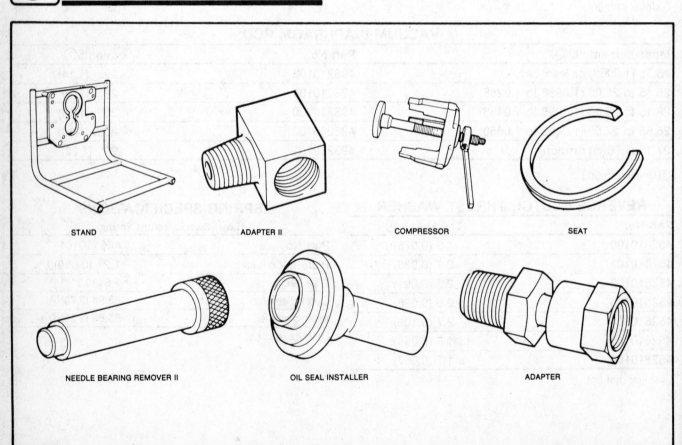

STAND

ADAPTER II

COMPRESSOR

SEAT

NEEDLE BEARING REMOVER II

OIL SEAL INSTALLER

ADAPTER

Special tools (©Fuji Heavy Industries Ltd.)

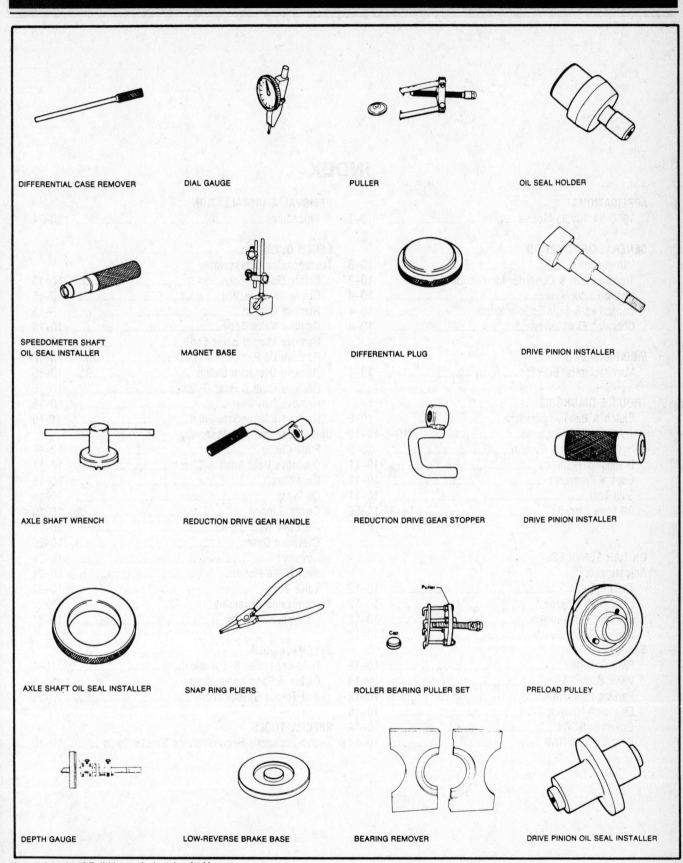

DIFFERENTIAL CASE REMOVER

DIAL GAUGE

PULLER

OIL SEAL HOLDER

SPEEDOMETER SHAFT
OIL SEAL INSTALLER

MAGNET BASE

DIFFERENTIAL PLUG

DRIVE PINION INSTALLER

AXLE SHAFT WRENCH

REDUCTION DRIVE GEAR HANDLE

REDUCTION DRIVE GEAR STOPPER

DRIVE PINION INSTALLER

AXLE SHAFT OIL SEAL INSTALLER

SNAP RING PLIERS

ROLLER BEARING PULLER SET

PRELOAD PULLEY

DEPTH GAUGE

LOW-REVERSE BRAKE BASE

BEARING REMOVER

DRIVE PINION OIL SEAL INSTALLER

**Special tools** (©Fuji Heavy Industries Ltd.)

# INDEX

# TOYOTA A40, A43D, A43DL, A43DE

##  APPLICATIONS

Toyoglide 4-Speed Automatic Transmissions
A-40D   A-43D   A-43DL   A-43DE

### TRANSMISSION APPLICATION
### A-40D, A-43D, A-43DL, A-43DE

| Model | Year | Engine Number | Transmission Number |
|-------|------|---------------|---------------------|
| Corolla | '82 | 3T-C | A-40D |
| Corolla | '83 | 4A-C | A-40D |
| Corona | '80-'82 | 22R | A-40D |
| Celica | '80-'81 | 22R | A-40D |
| Celica | '82-'84 | 22R & 22R-E | A-40D |
| Supra | '80-'81 | 5M-E | A-40D |
| Supra | '83-'84 | 5M-GE | A-43DE & A-43DL |
| Cressida | '83-'84 | 5M-GE | A-43DE |
| Trucks | '83-'84 | 22R & 22R-E | A-40D, A-43D & A-43DL |

##  GENERAL DESCRIPTION

The A-40D, A-43D, A-43DL and the A-43DE transmissions all consist of the following major units: the torque converter, the clutches, bands, and the planetary gear set and the hydraulic control system.

The torque converter is filled with transmission fluid pressure.

It transforms engine torque automatically and continuously to conform with vehicle torque resistance.

The planetary gear unit serves as an auxiliary transmission. It is located behind the torque converter. The planetary gear unit is controlled by the hydraulic pressure with the help of the operation of the front and rear multiple disc clutches, front and rear bands and the one-way clutch.

The hydraulic control system consists of the front oil pump, the torque converter, the governor and the cooler and lubrication circuits. Further main components are the valve body and the applying clutches and bands.

The selector lever has six ranges, which include "P", "R", "N", "D", "2", and "L". All shifting is automatic and regulated by engine load and vehicle speed.

In the A-43DE there is a solenoid that is electronically controlled which permits more precise control of shift points and torque converter lock-up operation. It will also allow improved response to road changes, engine conditions, driver demands and will improve fuel economy.

The electronically controlled transmission system measures the vehicle speed and the angle of the fuel injection throttle valve. These measurements are then fed to the electronically controlled transmission computer where they are analyzed. The computer then selects the best gear and shift speed to match the driving condition. The computer also monitors engine temperature, brake pedal position, shift lever position and the shift pattern select switches which are located on the dash. This monitoring allows for slight modifications in the "shifting programs."

The A-43DL has a lock up torque converter which automatically engages in third gear to provide a 1 to 1 gear ratio. The lock up torque converter also eliminates any slippage between the engine and the transmission. This action improves fuel economy whenever the lock up converter is engaged.

### Transmission and Converter Identification

#### TRANSMISSION

An identification plate is located on the left side of the transmission, with the model and serial number stamped on the plate. Should a transmission be encountered without an identification plate, examine the case for identifying code letters or digits. Also, obtain the vehicle model and serial number before obtaining replacement parts.

## CONVERTER

The converter is a welded unit and cannot be disassembled. The torque converter is a fluid drive coupling between the engine and transmission. It is designed to slip at low speeds, such as when the engine is idling. As engine speed increases, the torque converter will engage the engine to the transmission. There is also a hydraulically controlled mechanical clutch inside the torque converter. This clutch locks the transmission to the engine with almost no slippage. The clutch is controlled by the electronically controlled transmission computer. This clutch is applied in second, third and fourth gears.

## Metric Fasteners

Metric bolt sizes and thread pitches are used for all fasteners on the A-40D, A-43D, A-43DL and A-43DE automatic transmissions. Do not attempt to interchange metric fasteners for inch system fasteners. Mismatched or incorrect fasteners can result in damage to the transmission unit through malfunctions, breakage or personal injury.

The metric fasteners dimensions are very close to the inch system fasteners, and for this reason replacement fasteners must have the same measurement and strength as those removed.

Care should be taken to reuse the fasteners in the same locations as removed, whenever possible.

## Fluid Specifications

The fluid used in the A-40, A-43D, A-43DL and the A-43DE transmissions is Dexron® II. This applies to all units starting with July 1983 production. Transmissions used prior to July 1983, use Type F automatic transmission fluid.

**NOTE:** The drain plugs on certain models using Dexron® II have been marked with "DII." All others use Type F automatic transmission fluid. The drain plug change is for the A-40 series transmissions only.

### FLUID CAPACITY CHART

| Model | Liter | US Qts. | Imp. Qts. |
|---|---|---|---|
| A-43D, A-43DE, A-43DL | 6.5 | 6.9 | 5.7 |
| A-40D | 4.0 | 4.2 | 3.5 |

## Checking Fluid Level

The A-40D, A-43D, A-43DL and A-43DE transmissions are designed to operate with the fluid level between the "Add" and "Full" marks on the dipstick indicator. The fluid level should be checked with the transmission at normal operating temperature.

1. With the vehicle on a level surface, engine idling, foot brake applied, wheels blocked move the transmission gear selector through the gear positions to engage each gear and to fill the oil passages with fluid.

2. Place the selector lever in the Park position and apply the parking brake. Do not turn off the engine.

3. Clean the dipstick area of dirt and remove the dipstick from the filler tube. Wipe the dipstick clean and replace in the filler tube making sure to seat it firmly.

4. Again remove the dipstick from the filler tube and check the fluid level as indicated on the dipstick. The level should be between the "Add" and "Full" marks. If needed, add fluid through the filler tube to bring the fluid level to its proper height.

5. When the fluid level is correct, fully seat the dipstick in the filler tube.

# M MODIFICATIONS

## Adjustable Line Pressure Sleeve

The A-40D, A-43D, A-43DL and the A-43DE have had an adjustable line pressure sleeve added beginning in February 1983. This sleeve permits fine tuning of the line pressure, during assembly, by the factory. When disassembling and assembling the unit, make sure that the pre-set position is maintained. When adjusting the sleeve, a quarter of a turn in the counterclockwise direction will lower line pressure approximately four pounds per square inch.

## 1-2 Shift Valve A-40 Series

The 1-2 shift valve has been replaced with a new two piece type. This will eliminate sticking when cold. The two piece valve became effective in the A-40D, A-43D and A-43DL in October of 1981.

## Valve Body Design Change (A-40D only)

Beginning February 1983, the valve body of the A-40D automatic transmission has been modified. These modifications will allow the 3-4 upshift at wide open throttle to occur. It will also eliminate the delayed engagement of the neutral/reverse shift when the engine is hot.

## Governor Line Pressure Strainer (A-40 series)

A strainer has been added to the line pressure circuit of the automatic transmission. This will prevent the governor valve from sticking.

## Governor Valve (A-40 series)

A lock plate and bolt have been added to the governor valve. This will reduce fluid leakage.

### PART NUMBER INFORMATION:

| Transmission | Previous P/N | New P/N | Part Name |
|---|---|---|---|
| A40 | 35480-30051 | 35480-26010 | Governor assy |
| A40D | 35480-22010 | 35480-30060 | Governor assy |
| A40/A40D | 35770-22012 | 35770-14010 | Output Shaft |
| A40/A40D | — | 90101-05417 | Bolt |
| A40/A40D | — | 90215-11001 | Washer, screw location |

## Detent Spring Retaining Bolt (A-40 series)

Beginning in July of 1981, the detent spring retaining bolt has been lengthened from 1.377 in. (35mm) to 1.574 in (40mm).

## Extension Housing Modification (A-40 series)

Effective July 1981, the inside extension housing ribs have been extended. The extension housing bushing oil grooves have been repositioned. This will improve lubrication of the bushing.

## Coasting Downshift Shock (A-40D)

When coasting to a stop in drive range, the transmission may exhibit a clunking type noise. The transmission is designed to shift from third to first gear when coasting, but may shift into second gear and then first gear. This is caused by the B-1 brake engaging at the third to second gear downshift. In some transmissions this is caused by an improperly adjusted transmission throttle cable or high throttle pressure. Adjust as required.

## Clutch Piston Outer "O" Ring (A-40, A-40D, A-43D, A-43DL)

As of August 1981 the "O" ring for the front clutch (C1), overdrive clutch (C0), and rear clutch has had the cross-sectional diameter increased.

## Clutch Piston Return Spring (A-40)

Beginning August of 1981, the return spring for the front clutch (C1) and the rear clutch (C2) has been modified from a single spring type to a multiple spring type. This improves the return action of the clutch piston.

## Clutch Cylinder Oil Seal Ring (A-40, A-40D, A-43D, A-43DL)

The cylinder bore, ring groove diameters and oil seal ring grooves have been increased in diameter. This improves performance of the overdrive clutch (C0), front clutch (C1) and the rear clutch.

## Clutch Discs and Clutch Plates (A-40)

Due to the change in automatic transmission fluid, clutch discs and clutch plates have been modified. Automatic transmission overhaul gasket kits have also been changed. The new gasket kits can be used in old and new automatic transmissions while rebuilding.

### GASKET KIT PART NUMBERS
### A-40 series

| Previous Part Number | New Part Number | Transmission Type |
|---|---|---|
| 04351-22022 ① | 04351-22023 | A-40 |
| 04351-22031 ② | 04351-22032 | A-40D |
| 04351-30070 ① | 04351-30071 | A-43D |
| 04351-14011 ① | 04351-14012 | A-43DL |

① Parts may be used on previous vehicles
② Parts not interchangeable to previous vehicles

## Clutch Hub (multiple disc clutch only)

As of April 1984, the spline length of the clutch hub has been changed from 0.843 in. (21.4mm) to 0.901 in. (22.9mm). The new part number is 35631-30050 and it is interchangeable with previous parts.

## Lock-Up Relay Valve Sleeve (A-43D and A-43DE)

Effective June 1983, in order to reduce torque converter lock-up shock, the drain hole diameter in the lock-up valve sleeve has been changed from 0.007 in. (2mm) to 0.059 in. (1.5mm) the new part number is 35215-30012 and it is changeable with the old part.

**NOTE: When rebuilding any of the A-40 or A-43 series automatic transmissions, be sure to order the correct gasket rebuilding kit. When ordering replacement parts, be sure of the part number.**

 TROUBLE DIAGNOSIS

In order to properly diagnose transmission problems and avoid making second repairs for the same problem, all of the available information and knowledge must be used. Included is a working order of the components of the transmission. Test procedures and the accompanying specification charts aid in finding solutions to problems. Further answers are found by road testing the vehicle and comparing all of the results to the Chilton's Three "C's" Transmission Diagnostic Chart. The diagnostic chart gives condition, cause and correction to most possible trouble conditions in the Toyota A-40D, A-43D, A-43DL and A-43DE transmissions.

## Hydraulic Control System

The main parts of the hydraulic control system are the oil pump, valve body, governor and the various servo systems, together with the fluid passages connecting these units. The end result of the fluid pressure is to move the clutches and bands of the transmission. The clutches and bands control the planetary gear units which determine the gear ratio of the transmission.

### MAJOR COMPONENTS

The major components of the A-40D, A-43D, A-43DL and the A-43DE hydraulic system are the oil pump, the torque converter, governor, cooler and lubrication circuits, valve body and the applying clutches and bands.

The oil pump has the high output necessary to operate the low and reverse gears. The converter pump impeller which is driven by engine rotation is attached to the oil pump. The oil pump provides pressure to shift control valves and apply clutches and bands.

The torque converter consists of three main units; the pump impeller, turbine runner and the stator. The torque converter is a sealed unit and cannot be repaired. It must be replaced as a complete unit when found to be defective.

The pump impeller is driven by the engine crankshaft through the flywheel. The flywheel is bolted to the engine crankshaft.

The turbine, which is mounted to the input shaft, is driven by the pump impeller. The stator is mounted on a one-way clutch. All of these parts are enclosed and operate in a fluid filled housing which is part of the impeller.

The governor valve is installed on the output shaft and operates to produce fluid pressure in relation to vehicle speed. At low vehicle speed, the outer and inner weights act together as a single unit. The centrifugal force on these weights equals the fluid pressure.

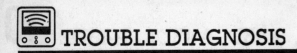

## CLUTCH APPLICATION CHART
### A-43D, A-43DE and A-43DL

| Selector Position | Overdrive Clutch (CO) | Clutch 1 | Clutch 2 I.P. | Clutch 2 O.P. | Overdrive Brake (BO) | Brake 1 | Brake 2 | Brake 3 I.P. | Brake 3 O.P. | One-way Clutch (F0) | One-way Clutch (F1) | One-way Clutch (F2) |
|---|---|---|---|---|---|---|---|---|---|---|---|---|
| Park | Applied | | | | | | | | | | | |
| Reverse | Applied | | Applied | Applied | | | | Applied | Applied | | | |
| Neutral | Applied | | | | | | | | | | | |
| Drive-1st | Applied | Applied | | | | | | | | Applied | | Applied |
| Drive-2nd | Applied | Applied | | | | | Applied | | | Applied | Applied | |
| Drive-3rd | Applied | Applied | Applied | | | | Applied | | | Applied | | |
| Overdrive | | Applied | Applied | | Applied | | Applied | | | | | |
| Manual 2 | Applied | Applied | Applied | | | Applied | Applied | | | | Applied | |
| Low | Applied | Applied | | | | | | Applied | | Applied | | Applied |

## CLUTCH APPLICATION CHART

| Selector Position | Overdrive Clutch (CO) | Clutch 1 | Clutch 2 I.P. | Clutch 2 O.P. | Overdrive Brake (BO) | Brake 1 | Brake 2 | Brake 3 I.P. | Brake 3 O.P. | One-way Clutch (F0) | One-way Clutch (F1) |
|---|---|---|---|---|---|---|---|---|---|---|---|
| Park | Applied | | | | | | | Applied | Applied | | |
| Reverse | Applied | | Applied | Applied | | | | Applied | Applied | | |
| Neutral | Applied | | | | | | | | | | |
| Drive-1st | Applied | Applied | | | | | | | | Applied | |
| Drive-2nd | | Applied | | | | | Applied | | | Applied | Applied |
| Drive-3rd | Applied | Applied | Applied | | | | | | | | |
| Overdrive | | Applied | Applied | | Applied | | Applied | | | | |
| Manual 2 | Applied | Applied | | | | Applied | | | | | Applied |
| Low | Applied | Applied | | | | | | Applied | Applied | | |

## CHILTON'S THREE "C's" TRANSMISSION DIAGNOSIS CHART
### Toyota A-40 Series

| Condition | Cause | Correction |
|---|---|---|
| Vehicle fails to move in any forward range | a) Extremely low oil discharge pressure from front oil pump<br>b) Pressure regulator valve frozen<br>c) Improper operation of manual shift linkage<br>d) Locked by parking lock pawl<br>e) Fluid insufficient<br>f) Front clutch does not operate | a) Repair or replace front oil pump<br>b) Repair valve or replace valve body assembly<br>c) Adjust or repair manual shift linkage<br>d) Repair or replace parking linkage as needed<br>e) Add fluid<br>f) Replace front clutch discs |
| Vehicle fails to move in "R" range | a) Rear clutch does not operate<br>b) Rear band does not operate | a) Replace rear clutch discs<br>b) Replace rear band or repair rear band servo |
| Fails to downshift from 2nd to 1st gear | a) Extremely high governor pressure<br>b) 1-2 shift valve does not operate<br>c) Governor valve does not operate<br>d) Throttle valve does not operate | a) Overhaul governor valve assembly<br>b) Repair 1-2 valve or replace valve body assembly<br>c) Overhaul governor valve assembly<br>d) Repair throttle valve or replace valve body assembly |

## CHILTON'S THREE "C's" TRANSMISSION DIAGNOSIS CHART
### Toyota A-40 Series

| Condition | Cause | Correction |
|---|---|---|
| Improper shifting point | a) Fluid insufficient<br>b) 1-2 shift valve does not operate<br>c) 2-3 shift valve does not operate<br>d) Throttle modulator valve does not operate<br><br>e) Throttle connecting rod out of adjustment<br>f) Governor pressure is abnormal<br>g) Throttle modulator pressure is abnormal | a) Add fluid<br>b) Repair 1-2 shift valve or replace valve body assembly<br>c) Repair 2-3 valve or replace valve body assembly<br>d) Repair throttle modulator valve or replace valve body assembly<br>e) Adjust throttle connecting rod<br>f) Overhaul governor valve assembly<br>g) Repair throttle modulator valve or replace valve body assembly |
| Fails to upshift from 1st to 2nd gear | a) 1-2 shift valve does not operate<br>b) Governor valve does not operate<br>c) Throttle valve does not operate<br><br>d) Front band does not operate | a) Repair 1-2 shift valve or replace valve body assembly<br>b) Overhaul governor valve assembly<br>c) Repair throttle valve or replace valve body assembly<br>d) Replace front band or repair front band servo |
| Fails to upshift from 2nd to 3rd gear | a) 2-3 shift valve does not operate<br>b) Governor valve does not operate<br>c) Throttle valve does not operate<br>d) Extremely high throttle modulator pressure<br><br>e) Rear clutch does not operate | a) Repair 2-3 valve or replace valve body assembly<br>b) Overhaul governor valve assembly<br>c) Repair throttle valve or replace valve assembly<br>d) Repair throttle modulator valve or replace valve body assembly<br>e) Replace rear clutch discs |
| Fails to downshift from 3rd to 2nd gear | a) Extremely high governor pressure<br>b) 2-3 shift valve does not operate<br>c) Governor valve does not operate<br>d) Throttle valve does not operate<br>e) Front band does not operate<br>f) Extremely low throttle modulator pressure | a) Overhaul governor valve assembly<br>b) Repair 2-3 shift valve or replace valve body assembly<br>c) Overhaul governor valve assembly<br>d) Repair throttle valve or replace valve body assembly<br>e) Replace front band or repair front band servo<br>f) Repair throttle modulator valve or replace valve body assembly |

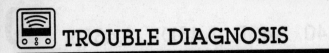 

## CHILTON'S THREE "C's" TRANSMISSION DIAGNOSIS CHART
### Toyota A-40 Series

| Condition | Cause | Correction |
|---|---|---|
| Oil pressure system noise | a) Air in oil pump suction side is mixing with oil | a) Overhaul oil pump |
| | b) Pressure regulator valve vibrates and causes resonance | b) Replace pressure regulator valve or replace valve body assembly |
| | c) Oil leakage in line pressure passage | c) Correct failed part as diagnosed by inspection and air pressure tests |
| Poor acceleration | a) Engine misses | a) Repair engine as needed |
| | b) Throttle connecting out of adjustment | b) Adjust throttle connecting rod |
| | c) Improper operation of one-way clutch | c) Replace one-way clutch |
| | d) Wrong type of transmission fluid | d) Drain and replace transmission fluid |
| Oil leakage from front transmission housing | a) Front oil pump body O-ring damaged | a) Replace front oil pump body O-ring |
| | b) Front oil pump body Type "T" oil seal damaged | b) Replace front oil pump body Type "T" oil seal |
| | c) Improper installation of front oil pump body | c) Remove front oil pump body and reinstall per procedure |
| | d) Engine rear oil seal damaged | d) Replace rear engine oil seal |
| | e) Torque converter damaged | e) Replace torque converter |
| Slips during engine braking | a) Improper operation of rear band | a) Replace rear band or repair rear band servo |
| | b) Improper operation of front band | b) Replace front band or repair front band servo |
| Slips during rapid acceleration | a) Fluid insufficient | a) Add fluid |
| | b) Low throttle pressure | b) Repair throttle valve or replace valve body assembly |
| | c) Improper operation of throttle relay valve | c) Repair throttle relay valve or replace valve body assembly |
| | d) Shift control rod out of adjustment | d) Adjust shift control rod |
| Mechanical noise | a) Excessive play due to worn planetary gears | a) Replace planetary gears |
| | b) Excessive wear of oil pump gears and other related parts | b) Replace oil pump gears and other related parts |
| | c) Turbine tube converter clearance | c) Replace torque converter |
| | d) Parking rod out of adjustment | d) Adjust parking linkage |
| Oil leakage from transmission housing | a) Loose bolts and nuts | a) Torque bolts and nuts to specifications |
| | b) Damaged gasket | b) Replaced gasket |
| | c) Improper installation of union bolts and test plugs | c) Remove, reseal, and reinstall bolts and plugs |
| | d) Damaged oil seal | d) Replace oil seal |
| | e) Excessive fluid | e) Remove excess fluid |

## CHILTON'S THREE "C's" TRANSMISSION DIAGNOSIS CHART
### Toyota A-40 Series

| Condition | Cause | Correction |
|---|---|---|
| Grinding shifts from 2nd to 3rd gear | a) Rear clutch slips<br>b) Throttle cable disengaged or maladjusted<br>c) Oil level too low<br>d) Oil pressure too low<br>e) Throttle pressure valve stuck<br>f) No. 1 one-way clutch defective | a) Replace rear clutch<br>b) Connect or adjust throttle cable<br>c) Correct oil level<br>d) Disassemble transmission<br>e) Replace valve body<br>f) Disassemble transmission |
| 3rd gear slips | a) Rear clutch slips<br>b) Throttle cable disengaged or maladjusted<br>c) Oil level too low<br>d) Oil pressure too low<br>e) Throttle pressure valve stuck | a) Disassemble transmission<br>b) Connect or adjust throttle cable<br>c) Correct oil level<br>d) Disassemble transmission<br>e) Replace valve body |
| Stall speed too high | a) Oil level too low<br>b) Engaged clutch slips<br>c) No. 1 or no. 2 one-way clutch slips | a) Correct oil level<br>b) Disassemble transmission<br>c) Disassemble transmission |
| Stall speed too low | a) Torque converted defective<br>b) Engine output insufficient | a) Replace torque converter<br>b) Test engine |
| Drive in 2nd gear only | a) 1-2 and 2-3 shift valves stuck | a) Replace valve body |
| Drive in 3rd gear only | a) 1-2 and 2-3 shift valves stuck<br>b) Governor bushing seized | a) Replace valve body<br>b) Clean or replace governor |
| Grinding shifts | a) Throttle cable disengaged or maladjusted<br>b) Oil level too low<br>c) Throttle pressure valve stuck<br>d) Front clutch defective | a) Connector or adjust throttle cable<br>b) Correct oil level<br>c) Replace valve body<br>d) Disassemble transmission |
| Grinding shifts from 1st to 2nd gear | a) Brake 1 and brake 2 slip<br>b) Clutch valve and damper malfunction<br>c) Throttle cable disengaged or maladjusted<br>d) Oil level too low<br>e) Throttle pressure valve stuck<br>f) One-way clutch F defective | a) Disassemble transmission<br>b) Disassemble transmission<br>c) Connect or adjust throttle cable<br>d) Correct oil level<br>e) Replace valve body<br>f) Disassemble transmission |
| Hard engagement jolt or definite double knock when engaging Reverse gear | a) Damper defective or wrong cover parts | a) Replace valve body |
| Car cannot be started in "N" | a) Transmission switch defective | a) Replace transmission switch |
| Car creeps or runs in "N" | a) Selector rod setting wrong<br>b) Front clutch defective (bonded) | a) Adjust selector rod<br>b) Disassemble transmission |
| Drive in 1st gear only when in "D" | a) 1-2 shift valve stuck<br>b) Governor bushing seized | a) Replace valve body<br>b) Clean or replace governor |
| Drive in 1st and 2nd gear only when in "D" | a) 2-3 shift valve stuck | a) Replace valve body |
| No kickdown shifts | a) Throttle cable setting wrong<br>b) Control unit setting wrong<br>c) Throttle pressure valve sticks<br>d) Plastic balls in transfer plate leak | a) Adjust throttle cable<br>b) Adjust valve body<br>c) Replace valve body<br>d) Replace valve body |

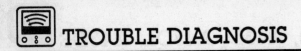 

## CHILTON'S THREE "C's" TRANSMISSION DIAGNOSIS CHART
### Toyota A-40 Series

| Condition | Cause | Correction |
|---|---|---|
| Selector lever cannot be moved to "P" | a) Selector linkage setting wrong<br>b) Locking device defective | a) Adjust selector linkage<br>b) Repair locking device |
| Parking position will not disengage | a) Parking lock pawl caught in teeth of output shell<br>b) Excessive friction in parking lock device | a) Replace parking lock pawl<br><br>b) Repair parking lock device |
| Parking position does not hold (slips) | a) Selector rod setting wrong | a) Adjust selector rod |
| Shift points too high | a) Throttle cable setting wrong<br>b) Governor bushing seized<br>c) Governor piston rings defective or worn<br>d) Throttle pressure valve malfunctions<br>e) Shift valves jammed | a) Adjust throttle cable<br>b) Clean or replace governor<br>c) Replace piston rings<br><br>d) Replace valve body<br>e) Replace valve body |
| Shift points too low | a) Throttle cable setting wrong<br>b) Governor bushing seized<br>c) Throttle pressure valve malfunctions<br>d) Plastic balls in transfer plate leak | a) Adjust throttle cable<br>b) Clean or replace governor<br>c) Replace valve body<br>d) Replace valve body |
| Shift points too high or too low and shift movements too long and too soft | a) Brake 1 and brake 2 are damaged by 1-2 gear shifts<br>b) Rear clutch damaged by 2-3 gear shifts | a) Replace brakes<br><br>b) Replace clutch |
| No drive in Reverse and 2nd gear | a) Shift valve stuck in 3rd gear position | a) Replace valve body Disassemble transmission if metal particles or abrasion are found in oil sump |
| No braking effect from 1st gear when in "2" and "1" | a) Clutch valve and damper defective<br>b) Brake 3 defective | a) Replace valve body<br>b) Replace brake 3 |
| No braking effect from 2nd gear when in "2" and "1" | a) Brake 2 defective | a) Replace brake 2 |
| Rattling noise in Neutral | a) Drive plate broken<br>b) Welded drive tabs on converter damaged | a) Replace drive plate<br>b) Replace converter |
| Growling noise in Neutral, eliminated when accelerating in "N" | a) Valve chatter in control unit<br>b) Oil pump draws in air | a) Correct oil level<br>b) Tighten valve body mounting screws, check gaskets |
| Harsh downshift to 1st gear | a) Improper operation of the one-way clutch | a) Repair or replace the one-way clutch |
| Slips when starting to move in "D", "2" and "L" range | a) Fluid insufficient<br>b) Improper operation of front oil pump<br>c) Improper operation of pressure regulator valve<br>d) Improper operation of front clutch<br>e) Improper operation of one-way clutch in "D" or "2" range | a) Add fluid<br>b) Overhaul or replace front oil pump<br>c) Repair or replace pressure regulator valve<br>d) Replace front clutch<br><br>e) Replace one-way clutch |

The oil pump supplies pressure to the regulator valves which will direct fluid to the torque converter. Fluid from the torque converter flows through the oil cooler to lubricate the planetary gear components.

The valve body assembly consists of the manual valve, pressure regulator valve, check valves and the automatic shift control valves. The automatic shift control valves are provided to actuate the upshift or downshift automatically.

## Diagnosis Tests

### OIL PRESSURE TEST

Certain general precautions should be taken when doing oil pressure testing.

1. The transmission should be filled with the specified transmission fluid to the proper level.
2. Be sure to have all four wheels blocked.
3. Perform the tests with the transmission warmed up to operating temperature.

### LINE PRESSURE TESTS

1. Block the front and rear wheels.
2. Apply the parking brake.
3. Make sure the throttle lever will move to the point marked on the transmission case when the carburetor is fully opened.
4. Connect a pressure gauge to the line pressure port.
5. Start the engine.
6. Shift to "D" range and move the throttle valve to the wide open position. Record the pressure.
7. Shift into "2" range and move the throttle valve to wide open position. Record the pressure.
8. Shift to "L" range and move the throttle valve to wide open position. Record the pressure.

--- CAUTION ---

*Do not run the tests longer than 5 seconds at a time. Never make range shifts when the throttle valve is wide open.*

With the pressure gauge still connected to the line pressure port, run the tests in the "R", "N" and "P" ranges.

Run the engine at 1,000 rpm and stall rpm in "D" and "R" ranges. Read the oil pressures in each range and record them when done.

### Evaluation

When all ranges show higher than specified pressures:
1. Pressure regulator valve defective.
2. Throttle valve defective.
3. Throttle cable out of adjustment. When all ranges show lower than specified pressures:
1. Defective oil pump.
2. Throttle valve defective.
3. Pressure regulator valve defective.

When the pressure at either range is too low, it is usually due to fluid leakage in the said range hydraulic circuit.
1. When the pressure is low in the "D" range, it is an indication of a defective front clutch or overdrive clutch.
2. When the pressure is low in the "R" range, it indicates a defective rear clutch, overdrive clutch or brake number three.

### GOVERNOR PRESSURE TESTS

Connect a pressure gauge to the governor pressure port and attach a tachometer to the engine. Shift into "D" range and measure the governor pressure.

--- CAUTION ---

*Decision can be reached with 1000 rpm test. But, if tests are to be made at 1800 and 3500 rpm, it would be safer to test on road or chassis dynamometer, as on-stand test could be hazardous.*

When the governor pressure is low or high:
1. Line pressure is defective.
2. Fluid leakage in the governor circuit.
3. The governor valve is defective.

### TIME LAG TEST

1. Check the transmission fluid level and adjust if necessary.
2. Block the front and rear wheels.
3. Apply the parking brake. Start the engine.
4. Check the idling speed. Adjust if needed.
5. Move the shift lever from "N" to "D" range. Measure the time it takes from shifting the lever until the shock is felt using a stopwatch. The lag time should be less than 1.2 seconds.
6. In the same fashion, check the lag time for the "N" to "D" range. The lag time should be less than 1.5 seconds.

### Evaluation

1. If the "N" to "D" lag time is longer than specified, then the front clutch or the overdrive clutch is defective. Line pressure could also be low.
2. If the "N" to "R" lag time is longer than specified, then the rear clutch, overdrive clutch, or number three brake is defective. Line pressure could also be excessively low.

### STALL TEST

The purpose of the stall test is to check transmission and engine performance. This is done by measuring maximum engine rpm against the transmission in "D", "2", "L", and "R" ranges.
1. Check the transmission fluid at normal operating temperature and adjust if necessary.
2. Check the accelerator and throttle linkage and adjust if necessary.
3. Apply the parking brake and block all four wheels.
4. Attach a tachometer to engine.
5. Apply foot brake and accelerator to floor until highest rpm reading is obtained.
6. Compare reading to specifications.

### Evaluation

If the stall speed is the same at all ranges but lower than specified:
1. The engine lacks sufficient power.
2. Stator one-way clutch is not operating.

**NOTE: If test results show a drop of more than 600 rpm below the specified value, the torque converter could be defective.**

When the stall speed at the "D" range is higher than specified:
1. The overdrive one-way clutch is not operating properly.
2. The line pressure is too low.
3. The front clutch is not operating properly.
4. The one-way clutch number 2 is not operating properly.

If the stall speed in the "R" range is higher than specified:
1. The rear clutch or brake number 3 is slipping.
2. Low line pressure.
3. Overdrive one-way clutch defective.

## ON CAR SERVICES

## Adjustments

A number of adjustments can be made without removing the transmission from the vehicle. These include adjustments to the throttle cable, shift linkage and the neutral safety switch.

### THROTTLE CABLE

#### Adjustment

1. Set the carburetor throttle lever and cable bracket to make sure they are not bent.
2. Check to see that the rubber boot is installed correctly.
3. Depress the accelerator fully and check for the throttle valve opening fully.

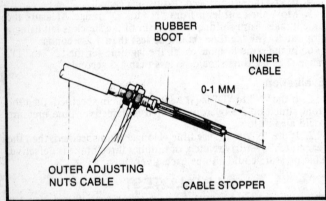

Throttle cable (© Toyota Motor Sales Co. Ltd.)

4. Open the throttle valve fully.
5. Adjust the distance between the boot end face and inner cable stopper or painted mark to 0.04 in.
6. Lock the adjusting nuts.

### FLOOR SHIFT LINKAGE

#### Adjustment

1. Raise the vehicle and support safely.
2. Loosen the connecting rod nut located on the right side of the transmission.
3. Push the manual lever to the front of the vehicle and return it three notches to the neutral position.
4. Set the shift selector to "N".
5. Tighten the connecting rod nut.
If the shift lever fails to move properly, check the following:

Connecting rod location (© Toyota Motor Sales Co. Ltd.)

1. Disconnect the control rod from the shift lever.
2. Operate the shift lever to see that it moves smoothly.
3. Operate the control rod to see that it moves properly.
4. Lubricate, repair or replace parts as needed.

### COLUMN SHIFT LINKAGE

#### Adjustment

When the transmission is in Neutral, the indicator should be accurately indicating the "N" position. It should not be possible to bring the shift lever to the "L", "R" or "P" range unless it is pulled back toward the driver. When shifted to the Park range, the parking pawl should mesh into the parking gear and lock the vehicle. The shift lever should operate smoothly and move properly into the various ranges, with the position indicator showing the ranges correctly.

If the indicator fails to show the transmission range correctly make the following adjustments.

1. Check the bushings, shafts, and linkage for wear and deformation.
2. Loosen the lock nut at the connecting rod swivel and move the shift lever to verify that the position indicator shows the ranges corresponding to the shift lever movement. Also verify that the position indicator is pointing accurately to the "N" range when the control shaft lever is at the Neutral position.
3. Set the transmission manual valve lever to "N" range and adjust the length of the first control rod so that the control position indicator in front of the driver will be pointing accurately to "N" range. Then tighten the lock nut at the connecting rod swivel.

### NEUTRAL SAFETY SWITCH

#### Adjustment

When the shift lever is at the "N" or "P" position, it should be possible to start the engine. But, when at any other position, it should not be possible to start the engine. If the switch is out of adjustment, use the following procedures.

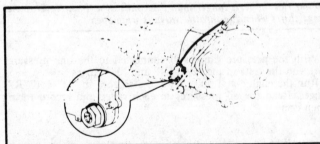

Neutral start switch location (© Toyota Motor Sales Co. Ltd.)

1. Loosen the attaching bolt.
2. Set the shift lever in the neutral position.
3. Align the switch shaft groove to the neutral basic line.
4. Torque the attaching bolt to 35-61 inch pounds.
5. Check for continuity between the terminals with an ohmmeter. Replace the switch if a problem is detected.

## Services

### FLUID CHANGE

#### Procedure

The normal service interval for changing transmission fluid and replacing or cleaning oil screens is 24,000 miles. Under more severe operating conditions, the services should be done more often. With heavy city mileage, hill climbing or trailer pulling, the fluid should be checked frequently for blackness or burned smelled. When these conditions occur, change fluid and service the transmission immediately.

1. Raise the vehicle and support safely.
2. Position a suitable drain pan under the transmission.
3. Remove the drain plug and allow the fluid to drain.

— **CAUTION** —

*If the vehicle has been driven recently, the transmission fluid will be hot.*

4. Remove the oil pan bolts and remove the pan and gasket. Discard the gasket.
5. Take out the oil tubes by prying gently on them using a suitable tool. Inspect and clean the tubes.
6. Unbolt the five oil strainer retainer bolts and remove the oil strainer. Inspect the strainer and clean or replace it.
7. Install the oil strainer. Torque the five bolts to 43-52 inch pounds.
8. Install the oil tubes by gently tapping them into place with a suitable tool.
9. Install a new pan gasket on the pan and install the pan. Torque them to 34-44 inch pounds.

**NOTE: When tightening the bolts, torque them by skipping every other one. Repeat procedure to complete tightening sequence.**

10. Replace the drain plug. Torque to 14-16 ft. lbs.
11. Add two quarts of the specified fluid and start the engine. Check the fluid level and correct as required.

## SERVICING THE VALVE BODY AND SOLENOID

### ALL MODELS

The valve body can be cleaned and serviced without removing the transmission from the vehicle on the transmission models. The Disassembly of the valve body can be accomplished by referring to the "Transmission Disassembly and Assembly" section.

### Removal

1. Raise the vehicle and support safely. Drain the fluid and remove the oil pan.
2. Gently remove the oil tubes from the valve body and transmission case area.
3. Loosen the oil strainer bolts; remove the bolts and the oil strainer.

**NOTE: At this point the solenoids can be replaced on A-43DE automatic transmission. Disconnect the solenoid connections. Remove the solenoid retaining bolts. Remove the solenoid with the gasket.**

4. Loosen the valve body retaining bolts and lower the valve body. Disconnect the throttle wire nipple from the throttle pan and take out the valve body.
5. Remove the second clutch accumulator piston spring.

### Installation

1. Install the second clutch accumulator piston spring into the valve body.
2. Connect the throttle cable nipple to the pan.
3. Align the manual valve lever with the manual valve and install the valve body. Torque the bolts to 70-104 inch pounds.
4. Make sure that the oil strainer is clean. Install the oil strainer and torque the bolts to 44-52 inch pounds.

**NOTE: Install the solenoids into their proper locations. Make sure that the gaskets are seated, and the valve springs are installed correctly. Torque the bolts to 4-7 ft. lbs. Make all wire connections.**

5. Install the oil tubes into their proper bores.

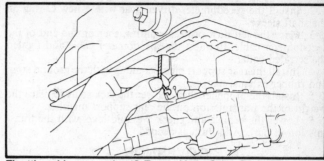

**Throttle cable connection (© Toyota Motor Sales Co. Ltd.)**

— **CAUTION** —

*Make sure that the oil tubes are inserted in the bores far enough so as not to interfere with the oil pan.*

6. Inspect the oil pan to make sure of the location of the two magnets. Install the oil pan with a new pan gasket. Torque the bolts evenly to 35-45 inch pounds.
7. Install the drain plug. Torque to 14-16 ft. lbs.
8. Fill the transmission with the specified fluid. Start the engine and shift through all the gears. Correct the fluid level as necessary.

## PARKING PAWL

### Removal

1. Raise the vehicle and support safely.
2. Remove the valve body.
3. Loosen the two bolts on the parking lock pawl bracket and remove the bracket.
4. Remove the spring from the pivot pin.
5. Remove the pivot pin and the parking pawl.

### Installation

1. Install the parking pawl and the pivot pin.
2. Insert the pivot spring on the pivot pin.
3. Push the lock rod into the forward position and loosely install the two bolts into the parking lock pawl bracket.
4. Check the pawl for smooth operation and torque the bolts 53-78 inch pounds.
5. Install the valve body. Fill the transmission with the specified fluid and correct as necessary.

## Extension Housing

### Removal

1. Raise the vehicle and support safely. Position a suitable drain pan under the transmission to catch any fluid that may drip.
2. Remove the propeller shaft. Place a block of wood under the transmission oil pan and jack up the transmission enough to remove the weight from the rear support member.
3. Loosen the serrated collar and disconnect the speedometer cable. Be sure not to lose the felt dust protector and washer.
4. Take out the speedometer driven gear.
5. Remove the rear support member along with the rubber exhaust hanger and ground strap.
6. Remove the extension housing and gasket. Discard the gasket.

### Installation

1. Install a new gasket on the extension housing. Install the extension housing on the transmission. Install the extension housing bolts and torque to 20-30 ft. lbs.

**NOTE: The two lower bolts are shorter than the upper bolts.**

2. Install the speedometer driven gear with a new O-ring on the shaft sleeve.

3. Place the felt dust protector and washer on the end of the speedometer cable. Connect the speedometer cable and tighten the serrated collar.

4. Install the rear support member along with the ground strap and rubber exhaust hanger.

5. Install the propeller shaft. Lower the jack so as to place the weight of the transmission on the rear support member.

6. Lower the vehicle and check the fluid level with the transmission in park. Add fluid as needed.

## GOVERNOR

### Removal

1. Raise the vehicle and support safely.
2. Remove the extension housing.
3. Using snap ring pliers, remove the speedometer drive gear snap ring. Slide the speedometer gear off.
4. Remove the other snap ring and lock ball.
5. Remove the governor lock bolt. Using a suitable tool, loosen the governor retaining clip. Slide the governor off of the shaft.

### Installation

1. Using a suitable tool, lift the governor retaining clip and slide the governor onto the shaft.

NOTE: When installing the governor, make sure that the retaining ring faces the end of the shaft. Position the governor in a fashion so that the retaining clip seats properly in the hole in the output shaft.

2. Install the governor lock bolt. Torque to 27-43 inch pounds.
3. Install the lock ball and snap ring on the output shaft. Slip the speedometer drive gear on the shaft.
4. Install the outer snapring.
5. Install the extension housing.

## REAR OIL SEAL

### Removal

1. Raise the vehicle and support safely.
2. Remove the drive shaft.
3. Take out the oil seal using tool SST 09308-10010 or its equivalent. Remove the dust seal.

### Installation

1. Lubricate the new seal with multi-purpose grease and install it.
2. Lubricate the new dust seal with transmission fluid. Install it flush with the housing.
3. Install the drive shaft.
4. Lower the vehicle. Check the transmission fluid. Adjust it to the proper level if necessary.

### Removal

1. Disconnect the negative battery cable.
2. Disconnect the upper radiator hose.
3. Drain out some of the coolant.
4. Loosen the transmission throttle cable adjusting nuts. Disconnect the cable housing from the bracket.
5. Disconnect the throttle cable from the throttle linkage.
6. Raise the vehicle and support safely.
7. Drain out the transmission fluid.

8. Disconnect the wiring connections for the back-up lights and the neutral safety switch.

9. Disconnect the starter motor wires. Remove the starter mounting bolts. Pull the starter to the front of the vehicle.

10. Remove the drive shaft. Remove the center bearing if applicable.

11. Disconnect the front exhaust pipe clamp and remove the front exhaust pipe.

12. Remove the oil cooler lines from the radiator.

13. Remove the manual linkage from the transmission.

14. Disconnect the speedometer cable.

15. Remove the right and left stiffener plates from the front of the transmission.

16. Jack up the transmission and remove the rear engine support crossmember.

NOTE: If a transmission jack is not available, place a block of wood between the oil pan and the jack to act as a buffer.

17. Remove the engine under cover plate if so equipped.

18. Disconnect the six torque converter mounting bolts through the service hole at the front side of the drive plate and ring gear.

NOTE: A rubber plug is installed in the service hole and will have to be removed before disconnecting the torque converter mounting bolts.

19. Using one of the bolt holes as access, install a guide pin in the torque converter.

20. Remove the transmission mounting bolts and remove the transmission and torque converter together.

21. Place a suitable container under the converter housing and pull the torque converter straight off its hub.

22. Remove the transmission oil filler tube.

### Installation

1. If the torque converter was removed, check to see that it has been properly inserted in the transmission case. Measure the distance between the installed surface of the torque converter to the front surface of the transmission case. The correct distance should be 1.02 in. (26mm).

2. Install a guide pin in one of the lower torque converter mounting holes.

3. Install the transmission oil filler tube.

4. Mount the transmission to the engine so that the guide bolt will pass through a drive plate hole.

--- CAUTION ---

*Do not allow the transmission to tilt forward during installation as the torque converter can slip out.*

5. Install the transmission housing mounting bolts. Torque to 37-57 ft. lbs. (500-800 kg. cm.).

6. Install the starter. Remove the guide pin.

7. Install the six torque converter bolts. Torque to 11-15 ft. lbs. (150-220 kg. cm.).

8. Install the engine under cover plate.

9. Install the rear transmission support member on the body. Connect the ground strap.

10. Lower the transmission onto the crossmember and install the remaining mounting bolts.

11. Install the converter cover and any exhaust pipe clamps that were removed earlier.

12. Attach the right and left stiffener plates to the front of the transmission.

13. Connect the manual shift linkage and the speedometer cable.

14. Attach the oil cooler lines and torque to 21-28 ft. lbs. (300-400 kg. cm.).

15. Connect the oil cooling line brackets.

16. Install the front exhaust pipe clamp and the front exhaust pipe.

17. Install the drive shaft and the center bearing if equipped.

18. Make the wiring connections for the neutral safety switch and the back-up lights.

19. Connect the transmission throttle cable to the throttle linkage. Install the throttle cable to the throttle cable bracket.

20. Lower the vehicle and connect the upper radiator hose. Fill the radiator with coolant.

21. Connect the negative battery cable.

22. Fill the transmission with approximately 4 quarts of the specified automatic transmission fluid.

23. Start the engine and shift into each gear. Check the fluid level and correct if necessary.

24. Road test the vehicle and check for slippage or other abnormal noises.

 **BENCH OVERHAUL**

## Before Disassembly

Before removing any subassemblies, thoroughly clean the outside of the transmission to prevent dirt from contaminating parts during repair. Handle all transmission parts carefully to avoid nicking or burring the bearing or mating surfaces. Lubricate all internal parts before assembly with clean automatic transmission fluid. Do not use any other fluid or lubricants except on gaskets or thrust washers which may be coated with petroleum jelly. Always install new gaskets when assembling the transmission. Torque all bolts to specification.

## Converter

### Inspection and Removal

1. Make certain that the transmission is held securely.

2. Pull the converter straight out of the transmission. Be careful since the converter contains a large amount of oil. There is no drain plug on the converter so the converter should be drained through the hub.

The fluid drained from the torque converter can help diagnose transmission problems.

1. If the oil in the converter is discolored but does not contain metal bits or particles, the converter is not damaged and need not be replaced. Remember that color is no longer a good indicator of transmission fluid condition. In the past, dark color was associated with overheated transmission fluid. It is not a positive sign of transmission failure with the newer fluids.

2. If the oil in the converter contains metal particles, the converter is damaged internally and must be replaced. The oil may have an "aluminum paint" appearance.

3. If the cause of oil contamination was due to burned clutch plates or overheated oil, the converter is contaminated and should be replaced.

## Transmission Disassembly

### OIL PAN

#### Removal

1. With the transmission resting on a flat surface, remove the oil pan bolts.

2. In order to remove the oil pan, lift the transmission from the pan.

**NOTE: The transmission is lifted from the oil pan so as not to contaminate the valve body with any foreign materials located in the oil pan.**

3. Remove the discard the gasket. Using a suitable tool remove any remaining gasket material left on the transmission case.

4. Remove the oil pan magnet. Examine any particles found in the oil pan. Magnetic particles (brass) will indicate bushing wear, while nonmagnetic particles (steel) will show evidence of gear, bearing and clutch plate wear.

### Solenoid

#### Removal (A-43DE only)

1. Place the transmission in a suitable holding fixture. Turn the transmission so that the oil tubes are facing up.

2. Using a suitable tool remove the oil tubes from the valve body. The solenoid wiring will now be visible.

3. Remove the solenoid grommet from the transmission case.

4. Disconnect the wiring from the number one, two and three solenoid. Remove the solenoids from the transmission case.

5. Remove the solenoid valve from the left side of the transmission.

Solenoid location circled (© Toyota Motor Sales Co. Ltd.)

### VALVE BODY

#### Removal

1. Turn the transmission so that the oil tubes are facing up. Using a suitable tool remove the oil tubes.

2. Loosen the oil strainer bolts; remove the bolts and the oil strainer.

3. Remove the valve body retaining bolts and remove the valve body.

4. Remove the second clutch accumulator piston. Remove the accumulator springs.

**NOTE: By using compressed air, the pistons can be dislodged more easily. Force the air into the air holes located in the transmission case.**

5. Detach the throttle cable from the throttle cable cam. Remove the plastic throttle cable cam.

6. Remove the parking lock rod bolt and remove the parking lock rod. Detach the parking lock pawl, spring and pivot pin.

### MANUAL LEVER SHAFT (OPTIONAL)

#### Removal

1. Using an appropriate tool, remove the manual lever shaft pin.

2. Slide the shaft out of the transmission case.

3. Remove the detent plate.

### GOVERNOR

#### REMOVAL

1. Remove the extension housing.

2. Remove the speedometer drive gear snap ring.

3. Detach the lock ball and the next snap ring.

4. Remove the governor lock bolt.

5. Using a suitable tool, loosen the governor retaining clip. Remove the governor from the output shaft.

## OIL PUMP

### Removal

1. Remove the oil pump housing bolts.

2. Using Toyota tool number SST 09610-20012 or its equivalent, remove the oil pump from the transmission case.

### CAUTION

*Care must be exercised during the oil pump removal so as not to crack the oil pump housing.*

3. Remove the oil pump bearing which is located behind the oil pump.

4. Remove the six converter housing bolts. Lift off the converter housing.

## OVERDRIVE CLUTCH

### Removal

1. Place a straight edge across the overdrive case and measure the distance between the straight edge and the front clutch. Record the measurement for use during reassembly.

2. Grip the input shaft and remove the overdrive clutch assembly.

3. Remove the bearing races located on both sides of the assembly.

4. Remove the overdrive case by pulling it out of the transmission case. Check for bearing races on both sides of the overdrive assembly.

## FRONT CLUTCH

### Removal

1. Place a straight edge across the transmission case and the front clutch and measure the distance between the straight edge and the front clutch. Record the figure for use during reassembly.

2. Grasp the input shaft and pull out the front clutch assembly.

3. Check for bearings and races on both sides of the assembly.

Front clutch (© Toyota Motor Sales Co. Ltd.)

## REAR CLUTCH

### Removal

1. Carefully grasp the rear clutch hub.

2. Pull the rear clutch assembly from the transmission case.

3. The rear clutch hub and the rear clutch assembly are removed from the transmission case as one unit.

Rear clutch (© Toyota Motor Sales Co. Ltd.)

## CENTER SUPPORT AND SUN GEAR

### Removal

1. Turn the transmission over in the stand and remove the two center support bolts.

2. Grasp the center support assembly and pull the assembly towards the front of the case.

3. Using a suitable tool remove the reaction plate retaining ring.

4. Check the end of the sun gear for the bearing races and any needle bearings.

Center support bolt removal (© Toyota Motor Sales Co. Ltd.)

Center support and sun gear removal
(© Toyota Motor Sales Co. Ltd.)

## INTERMEDIATE SHAFT

### Removal

1. Carefully grasp the rear intermediate shaft.

2. Pull the rear intermediate shaft out of the transmission case.

3. The intermediate shaft and the rear parts group will be removed from the transmission as one unit.

4. Remove the brake apply tube. Remove the rear thrust bearings from the transmission case.

**NOTE: The transmission case should be inspected for internal case damage. Check for wear, scoring or any other internal damage that might affect the operation of the transmission after assembly is complete.**

# Unit Disassembly and Assembly
## FRONT CLUTCH

### Disassembly

1. From both sides of the clutch, remove the thrust bearings and races.

2. Remove the snap ring from the front clutch hub and remove the front and rear clutch hub.

3. Remove the thrust bearings and races along with the clutch plate.

4. Remove the snap ring and lift out the remaining clutch plates and discs.

5. Using a suitable tool, compress the piston return springs and remove the snap ring.

6. Remove the spring retainer and the return springs.

7. Place the front clutch on the overdrive case and using compressed air, blow out the piston. Remove the O-rings from the piston.

### Inspection

1. Make sure that the check ball is free in the front clutch piston. Shake the piston and listen for the check ball moving.

2. Wash all parts in cleaning solvent and blow dry using compressed air.

3. Inspect the piston for nicks, burrs, scores and wear. Inspect the piston springs for distortion.

4. Repair or replace any damaged parts as required.

### Assembly

1. Install new O-rings on the front clutch piston. Install the piston in the front clutch drum with the cup side up.

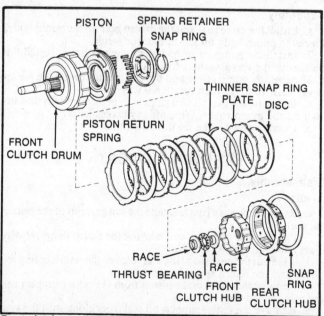

**Front clutch—exploded view (© Toyota Motor Sales Co. Ltd.)**

2. Install the piston return springs and the spring retainer.

3. Compress the return springs and retainer using a suitable tool and install the snap ring.

4. Install the clutch discs and plates and install the snap ring. Be sure that the clutch discs and the plates are assembled in the same manner as they were disassembled.

5. Place the front clutch drum onto the overdrive case and with a dial indicator or its equivalent measure the piston stroke. Maxmum piston stroke should be 0.0917 in. (2.33mm).

6. Install the inner snap ring in the clutch drum.

7. Install the clutch plate (A-40D) or the clutch disc (A-43D and A-43DE) into the clutch drums.

8. Install the inner thrust bearings and races.

9. Install the front clutch hub and the rear clutch hub. Make sure that the hub teeth align with the disc lugs.

10. Install the outer snap ring. Install the thrust bearings and races.

## OVERDRIVE INPUT SHAFT AND CLUTCH

### Disassembly

1. Remove the thrust bearings and races from the overdrive input shaft.

2. Remove the snap ring and hub from the overdrive clutch assembly. Remove the overdrive clutch assembly from the input shaft.

3. Remove the thin snapring, disc, flange and plate from the hub assembly.

4. Using a piston spring compressor or its equivalent, compress the piston return springs and remove the snapring.

5. Remove the spring retainer and the return springs.

6. Remove the overdrive clutch piston from the overdrive clutch assembly. Remove the clutch piston O-rings.

7. Remove the snapring from the overdrive planetary gear assembly and remove the thrust washers and one-way clutch.

8. Remove the four plugs located in the overdrive planetary gear assembly.

### Inspection

1. Wash all parts in cleaning solvent and blow dry using compressed air.

2. Inspect all parts for nicks, scores, burrs and wear. Inspect the piston springs for distortion.

3. Make sure that the check ball can be heard when shaking the piston.

4. Repair or replace any damaged parts as required.

### Assembly

1. Install the four plugs in the overdrive planetary gear assembly.

2. Install the thrust washer and bearing on the input shaft.

3. Install the one-way clutch and the thrust washer on the input shaft. Secure with the snapring.

4. Lubricate the new O-ring with automatic transmission fluid and install the O-ring on the overdrive clutch piston.

5. Install the overdrive clutch piston in the overdrive clutch drum. Make sure that the cup side is facing up.

6. Install the piston return springs and secure them with the spring retainer and snap ring.

7. Install the plate, disc and flange without inserting the thinner snapring.

8. With a dial indicator or its equivalent, measure the piston stroke of the overdrive clutch. Maximum piston stroke should be 0.0898 in. (2.28mm).

9. Install the thinner snapring. Install the hub and outer snapring.

10. Install the overdrive clutch assembly onto the input shaft along wiith the thrust bearings and races.

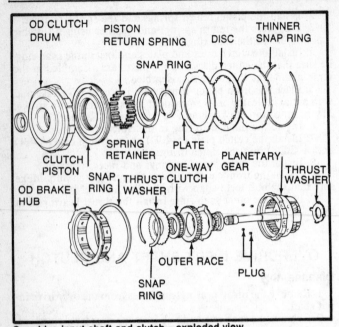

Overdrive input shaft and clutch—exploded view
(© Toyota Motor Sales Co. Ltd.)

NOTE: At this point, check the operation of the one-way clutch by holding the clutch drum with the right hand and turning the input shaft with the left hand. The input shaft should turn clockwise but not turn counterclockwise.

## REAR CLUTCH

### Disassembly

1. Remove the outer snapring which holds the outer clutch pack to the drum.
2. Remove the clutch discs, plates and flange.
3. Using a suitable tool, compress the piston spring retainer and remove the snapring. Remove the return springs.
4. Remove the rear clutch piston from the rear clutch drum.

NOTE: All A-40D automatic transmissions will have two rear clutch pistons, while the A-43D, A-43DL and A-43DE automatic transmissions will have only one piston.

5. Remove the O-rings from the rear clutch piston. Discard the O-rings.

### Inspection

1. Wash all parts in cleaning solvent and blow dry using compressed air.
2. Inspect the piston return springs for distortion. Inspect all parts for burrs, scoring or other wear.
3. Make sure that the check ball can be heard when shaking the piston.
4. Repair or replace any damaged parts as required.

### Assembly

1. Install new O-rings on the rear clutch piston.
2. Install the clutch pistons into the rear clutch drum.
3. Install the piston return springs with the piston return spring retainer and set in place with the snap ring.
4. Install the plate, discs and flange in the following order: plate-disc-plate-disc-plate-disc-flange.
5. Install the snapring making sure that the snapring ends are not aligned with a cutout in the rear clutch piston.

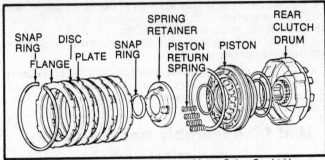

Rear clutch—exploded view (© Toyota Motor Sales Co. Ltd.)

6. Install a dial indicator or its equivalent, measure the piston stroke of the rear clutch. Maximum piston for the A-40D should be 0.059 in. (1.5mm). Maximum piston stroke for the A-43D, A-43DL and A-43DE should be 0.0835 in. (2.12mm).

## OIL PUMP

### Disassembly

1. Using the torque converter as a work stand, remove the two oil seal rings from the pump cover.
2. Remove the pump cover. Remove the O-ring from the pump.
3. Remove the oil pump drive gear and the oil pump driven gear.

### Inspection

1. Wash all parts in cleaning solvent and blow dry using compressed air.
2. Inspect the front oil seal for damage or other signs of wear. Replace if necessary.
3. Measure the body side clearance to a limit of 0.012 in. (0.3mm).
4. Measure the tip of the driven gear to the crescent for a clearance to a limit of 0.012 in. (0.3mm).
5. Measure the pump to side clearance to a limit of 0.004 in. (0.1mm).

### Assembly

1. Install the drive gear and the driven gear on the pump body. Place the pump body on the torque converter.
2. Install the pump cover and align the bolt holes. Install the bolts with the wave washers finger tight.
3. Align the pump cover and the pump and torque the pump cover bolts to 53-78 inch lbs. (0.6-0.9 kg-m).
4. Lubricate the two oil seal rings with petroleum jelly and install on the pump cover. Wipe off any excess jelly.
5. Install a new O-ring on the oil pump.

## CENTER SUPPORT

### Disassembly

A-40D

1. Remove the snap ring and take the sun gear out of the center support.
2. Remove the snap ring and take out the clutch flange, clutch discs and clutch plates.
3. Take out the next snap ring and remove the return spring retainer and the return springs.
4. Remove the No. 1 brake piston from the center support using compressed air.
5. Remove the center support oil seal rings along with the sun gear oil seal rings.

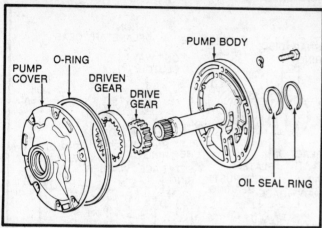

**Oil pump—exploded view** (© Toyota Motor Sales Co. Ltd.)

## Inspection

1. Wash all parts in cleaning solvent and blow dry using compressed air.
2. Inspect the return springs for distortion or other signs of wear.
3. Inspect the sun gear and the center support for any scores, nicks or burrs.
4. Repair or replace any defective parts as needed.
5. Lubricate any new clutch discs with automatic transmission fluid.

## Assembly

1. Install new oil seal rings on the center support and the sun gear. Install new O-rings on the brake piston and the center support.

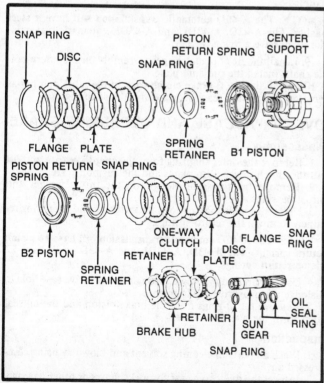

**Center support assembly—exploded view**
(© Toyota Motor Sales Co. Ltd.)

2. Install the No. 1 brake piston in the center support being careful not do damage the O-rings and with the cup side facing up.
3. Install the piston return springs and hold in place with the return spring retainer and snapring.
4. Install the No. 1 brake plates, clutch discs and clutch flange.
5. Install the snapring on the center support.
6. Check the piston stroke of the No. 1 brake piston by applying 57-114 psi of compressed air into the side oil hole of the center support. Piston stroke should be between 0.0394-0.0472 in. (1.00-1.20mm).
7. Install the center support on the sun gear shaft and install the snapring on the end of the sun gear shaft.

## CENTER SUPPORT

### Disassembly

**A-43D, A-43DL AND A-43DE**

1. Remove the snapring from the sun gear shaft and remove the center support from the shaft.
2. Remove the snapring from the front of the center support assembly.
3. Remove the clutch flange, clutch disc and clutch plates from the center support.
4. Using a suitable tool, compress the piston return spring retainer and remove the piston return spring, snapring and the piston return springs.
5. Using compressed air blown through the center support oil hole, remove the No. 1 brake piston. Remove the brake piston O-rings.
6. Turn the center support assembly over and remove the No. 2 brake snapring. Remove the clutch flange clutch discs and clutch plates from the No. 2 brake.
7. Using a suitable tool, compress the piston return spring retainer and remove the piston return spring snapring and the piston return springs.
8. Using compressed air blown through the center support oil hole, remove the No. 2 brake piston. Remove the brake piston O-rings.
9. Remove the one-way clutch assembly.
10. Remove the oil seal rings from the sun gear and the center support.

### Inspection

1. Wash all parts in cleaning solvent and blow dry using compressed air.
2. Inspect the return springs for distortion or other signs of wear.
3. Inspect the sun gear and the center support for any scores, nicks or burrs.
4. Check the function of the one-way clutch by holding it and turning the sun gear. The sun gear should turn freely counterclockwise, and should lock in the clockwise direction.
5. Repair or replace any defective parts as needed.
6. Lubricate any new clutch discs with automatic transmission fluid.

### Assembly

1. Install the new oil seal rings on the center support and the sun gear. Install new O-rings on the brake piston.
2. Install the one-way clutch on the sun gear. Install the No. 1 brake piston in the center support.
3. Install the piston return springs and using the snapring, secure the retainer in place.
4. Install the new O-rings on the center support and the piston.
5. Turn the center support over and install the No. 2 brake piston. Install the piston return springs and the return spring retainer with the snapring.

6. Turn the center support over again and install the No. 1 brake piston plate, disc and flange. Install the snapring in the center support.

7. Check the piston stroke of the No. 1 brake piston by applying 57-114 psi of compressed air into the side oil hole of the center support. Piston stroke should be between 0.0256-0.0512 in. (0.65-1.30mm).

8. Turn the center support over and install the No. 2 brake plates, discs and flange. Install the snapring in the center support.

9. Check the piston stroke of the No. 2 brake. Using a dial indicator or its equivalent, measure the piston stroke while applying compressed air (57-114 psi) to the center support oil hole. Piston strokes should measure between 0.0488-0.0835 in. (1.24-2.12mm).

10. Install the center support on the sun gear shaft and install the snapring on the end of the sun gear shaft.

## PLANETARY GEAR OUTPUT SHAFT

### Disassembly

1. Remove the reaction plate snapring and remove the No. 3 brake disc/plate pack and the front planetary pinion gears.

2. Remove the thrust washer from the planetary gears and lift out the brake discs and plates. Remove the reaction plate.

3. Remove the snapring from the front planetary pinion case and lift out the one-way clutch. Remove the nylon thrust washer from the front planetary pinion gears.

4. Remove the clutch pressure plate and the clutch apply tube.

5. Remove the snapring from the front planetary ring gear and remove the ring gear. Remove the washer inside of the ring gear.

**NOTE: THE A-40D automatic transmission will have a steel washer. The A-43D, A-43DL and A-43DE automatic transmission will have a nylon washer.**

6. Remove the output shaft from the intermediate shaft assembly. Remove the thrust bearings and races from the output shaft.

7. Remove the oil seal rings from the output shaft.

8. Remove the thrust bearings and races from the intermediate shaft.

9. Remove the rear planetary ring gear and bearing race from the intermedaite shaft along with the rear set ring.

10. Remove and discard all oil seal rings from the output shaft.

### Inspection

1. Wash all parts in cleaning solvent and blow dry using compressed air.

2. Inspect all discs and plates and replace any that are excessively worn.

3. Check all gears and shafts for any scoring, wears or burrs.

4. Repair or replace any defective parts as needed.

5. Lubricate new clutch discs with automatic transmission fluid.

### Assembly

1. Install the thrust bearing race and rear planetary ring gear on the intermediate shaft. Install the rear set ring.

2. Turn the intermediate shaft over and install the thrust bearing and race on the inside of the ring gear. Install the pinion gear assembly thrust washer on the rear planetary gear carrier.

3. Install the oil seal rings on the output shaft. Install the thrust bearing and race on the output shaft.

4. Install the intermediate shaft in the output shaft. Install the rear planetary gear carrier in the output shaft. Install the snapring.

5. Install the front planetary ring gear. Make sure that the notches align with the lugs. Install the snapring.

6. Install the washer in front of the planetary ring gear and install the front planetary pinion gear. Install the nylon washer, one-way clutch and the snapring.

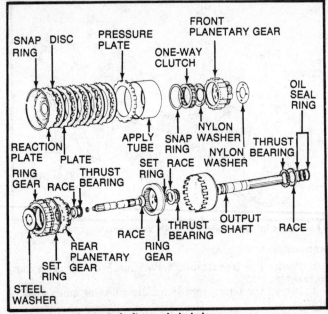

**Planetary gear output shaft—exploded view**
(© Toyota Motor Sales Co. Ltd.)

7. Install the reaction plate without the disc/plate pack to check the operation of the one-way clutch. The planetary gear must lock in the counterclockwise direction, but must rotate freely in the clockwise direction. If the clutch does not work properly, it must be replaced. Remove the reaction plate.

8. Install the thrust washer on the front planetary gear carrier. Petroleum jelly can be used to hold the washer in place during assembly.

**NOTE: The A-40D automatic transmission will have a steel washer. The A-43D, A-43DL and A-43DE automatic transmissions will have a nylon washer.**

9. Install the front planetary gear assembly on the intermediate shaft. Install the pressure plate.

10. Install the No. 3 brake clutch pack in the same manner as removed. Install the reaction plate and the snapring.

## OVERDRIVE CASE AND OVERDRIVE BRAKE

### Disassembly

1. Remove the outer snapring from the overdrive case and lift out the clutch flange, disc plates and the cushion plate.

2. Remove the ring gear along with the thrust washer and thrust bearings.

3. Using a suitable tool, remove the snapring and the spring retainer. Remove the return springs.

**NOTE: The A-40D automatic transmission will have 16 piston return springs. The A-43D, A-43DL and A-43DE will have 12 piston return springs.**

4. Use compressed air blown through an overdrive case hole to dislodge the overdrive brake piston.

5. Remove the O-rings from the brake piston and the oil seal rings form the overdrive case.

### Inspection

1. Wash all parts in cleaning solvent and blow dry using compressed air.

2. Inspect the overdrive case for nicks, burrs or other damage.

3. Check the piston return springs for any distortion.

4. Replace or repair defective parts as needed.

## Assembly

1. Install new oil seal rings on the overdrive case and new O-rings on the brake piston.

2. Install the return springs with the spring retainer and insert the snapring.

3. Install the thrust bearing and races on the ring gear and install the ring gear in the overdrive case.

4. Install the cushion plate, discs, plates and flange. Install the snapring.

**NOTE: Lubricate new clutch discs and plates with automatic transmission fluid before installing. Install the cushion plate with the rounded end down.**

5. Using a feeler gauge or its equivalent, measure the distance between the snapring and the flange. Maximum clearance should be 0.083 in. (2.1mm).

**NOTE: The thrust washer not used during reassembly of the overdrive case and overdrive brake will be used during the transmission assembly.**

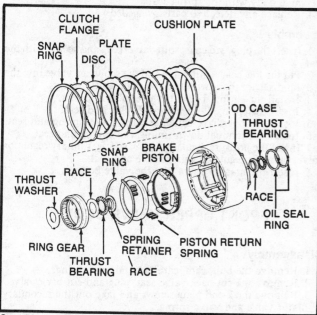

**Overdrive case and overdrive brake—exploded view**
(© Toyota Motor Sales Co. Ltd.)

## GOVERNOR

### Disassembly

1. Remove the E-ring and the governor weight from the governor body.

2. Slide the governor valve, spring and the governor valve shaft through the governor bore. Remove from the bottom.

3. Remove the retaining clip from the governor body being careful not to scrap the governor body.

4. Remove the lock plate and bolt from the side of the governor body.

### Inspection

1. Wash all parts in a cleaning solvent and blow dry using compressed air.

2. Check all parts for burrs, wear or other signs of excessive damage.

3. Check the oil passages for clogging.

4. Replace any parts that are found to be defective.

## Assembly

1. Install the lock plate and bolt to the side of the governor body.

2. Install the retaining clip being careful not to scrape the governor body.

3. Assemble the governor valve shaft, spring and the governor valve and install into the governor body.

4. Install the governor weight and the E-ring in the governor body.

## REAR BRAKE PISTONS

### Disassembly

1. Using a suitable tool, compress the return spring retainer and remove the snapring. Remove the return spring retainer and the piston return springs.

2. Apply compressed air to the outer and inner piston oil holes. This will dislodge the reaction sleeve and the outer piston. If the piston and sleeve do not come out using the compressed air, lift these units out using needle-nose pliers.

3. Remove the O-rings from the inner and outer pistons and the reaction sleeve.

### Inspection

1. Wash all parts in cleaning solvent and blow dry using compressed air.

2. Check return springs for any distortion.

3. Inspect all parts for any burrs, scoring and other signs of damage.

4. Remove the manual shaft oil seals with a suitable tool and install new right and left oil seals with a drift, making sure that they are flush with the transmission case.

5. Repair or replace any defective parts as needed.

### Assembly

1. Install new O-rings on the reaction sleeve and the inner and outer pistons. Install the inner and outer pistons in the reaction sleeve.

2. Install the reaction sleeve in the transmission with the spring seats facing up. Be careful not to damage the O-rings.

3. Install the piston return springs and the piston spring retainer. Using a suitable tool, compress the piston return springs and install the snapring.

4. Check the snapring to make sure it is seated on the piston spring retainer.

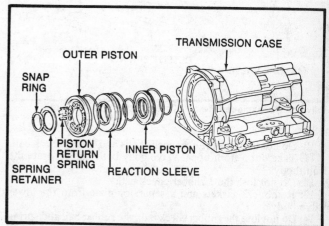

**Rear brake piston—exploded view** (© Toyota Motor Sales Co. Ltd.)

## VALVE BODY

### Disassembly

**A-40D**

1. Invert the transmission case so the valve body is in a horizontal position. Remove the necessary oil delivery tubes.
2. Remove the oil strainer by taking out five mounting bolts.
3. Remove the 17 valve body mounting bolts.

---
**CAUTION**
---

*Since there are five different lengths of mounting bolts, be sure to keep them in the same order as they came out.*

---

4. Carefully remove the valve body. After disconnecting the throttle wire nipple from the throttle pan, take out the valve body.

---
**CAUTION**
---

*When removing the valve body, prevent the number one accumulator piston from falling out.*

---

5. Remove the 9 bolts from the valve body cover and separate cover from valve body.
6. Do not lose the 4 rubber check balls.
7. Remove the 5 rear upper valve body bolts and take off the rear upper body.
8. Turn the valve body over and remove the remaining lower bolts.
9. Separate the lower valve body from the rear upper valve body.

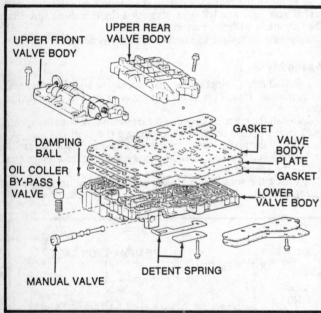

UPPER REAR VALVE BODY

UPPER FRONT VALVE BODY

GASKET

VALVE BODY PLATE

DAMPING BALL

GASKET

OIL COLLER BY-PASS VALVE

LOWER VALVE BODY

MANUAL VALVE

DETENT SPRING

**Valve body—exploded view (© Toyota Motor Sales Co. Ltd.)**

10. Do not lose the 4 rubber check balls and 1 steel check ball.
11. Take out 5 front upper valve body bolts and separate the front body.
12. Do not lose the 1 rubber check ball.
13. Remove 2 gaskets and a separator plate from the lower valve body.
14. Do not lose the rubber check ball, the rubber ball and spring set, and the check valve and spring set.

## LOWER VALVE BODY

### Disassembly

1. Remove the manual valve.
2. Remove the valve seat, valve sleeve, primary regulator valve, spring and pressure regulator valve.
3. Remove the seat, plug and manual down timing valve.
4. Remove the seat, spring and overdrive clutch exhaust valve.
5. Remove the seat, plug, 3-4 shift valve and spring.
6. Remove the seat, plug, 1-2 shift valve and spring.
7. Remove the 2 screws from the end plate and pull out the sequence valve and low coast shift valve.
8. Remove the seat, plug, 3rd coast shift valve and plug.
9. Remove the spring seat, spring and pressure relief ball.

### Inspection

1. Wash all parts in cleaning solvent and blow dry using compressed air.
2. Inspect all parts for damage and excessive wear.
3. Inspect the pressure relief spring and ball and secure them in the valve body with the spring seat.
4. Replace any defective parts as needed.

### Assembly

1. Insert the plug, 3rd coast shift valve, plug and secure with the seat.
2. Put the low coast shift valve and the sequence valve into the body and secure them with the end plate and 2 screws.
3. Install the spring, 1-2 shift valve, plug and seat.
4. Insert the spring, 3-4 shift valve, plug and seat.
5. Install the overdrive clutch exhaust valve, spring and seat.
6. Install the manual down timing valve, plug and seat.
7. Insert the pressure regulator valve, spring, primary regulator valve, pressure regulator valve sleeve and seat.
8. Insert the manual valve into the valve body.

## FRONT UPPER VALVE BODY

### Disassembly

1. Remove the bolt, cam, cam pin and cam spring.
2. Remove the cut-back valve seat, plug and cut-back valve.
3. Remove the 2 end plate screws and take out the secondary regulator valve and valve spring.
4. Remove the downshift plug, spring, clip, throttle valve, E-ring and spring.

**NOTE:** Count the number of E-rings because they are used as spacers.

### Inspection

1. Wash all parts in cleaning solvent and blow dry using compressed air.
2. Inspect all parts for any signs of excessive wear or damage.
3. Inspect the valve spring for any rust or compressed coils.
4. Replace any defective parts as required.

### Assembly

5. Hook the end of the cam spring over the valve body and install cam pin, cam and bolt.
6. Hook the other end of the cam spring into the hole in the cam.
7. Install the cut-back valve with the larger diameter land toward the outside of the valve body.
8. Install the secondary regulator valve and valve spring and secure it with the end plate and 2 screws.
9. Replace the E-rings, throttle valve, spring, clip and downshift plug.

## REAR UPPER VALVE BODY

### Disassembly

1. Remove the rear upper valve body end plate and pull out the detent valve seat, valve and spring.
2. Remove the 2-3 timing valve, plug and spring.
3. Remove the sequence valve spring and sequence valve.
4. Remove the governor modulator valve and spring and valve.
5. Remove the low modulator valve spring and valve.
6. Remove the 2-3 shift valve retaining spring, plugs, spring and the 2-3 shift valve.
7. Remove the lower 2-3 shift valve plug, seat and valve.
8. Remove the 3-2 kickdown orifice control valve seat, plug, valve and spring.

### Inspection

1. Wash all parts in cleaning solvent and blow dry using compressed air.
2. Inspect the valve springs for any signs of rust or excessive wear. Inspect for any collapsed coils.
3. Inspect the valve body housing for any warping or other damage.
4. Replace any defective parts as required.

### Assembly

1. Reinstall the 3-2 kickdown orifice control valve spring, valve, plug and seat.
2. Put in the 2-3 shift valve, plug and seat.
3. Install the 2-3 shift valve, spring, plugs and retaining seat.
4. Put the low modulator and governor modulator valves and springs in the upper valve body.
5. Install the 2-3 timing valve and sequence valve with their springs.
6. Install the upper valve body end plate with 2 screws.
7. Install the detent valve, spring and valve seat.

### Assembly of the Valve Body

1. Install the check balls in the area under the valve body cover, place the cover on the body and fasten with the 7 bolts.
2. Install the rubber ball, rubber ball and spring and valve and spring into the upper side of the lower valve body.
3. Install the 2 gaskets and separator plate on the lower valve body. Temporarily bolt it down with several bolts.
4. Install 1 rubber check ball and 1 steel check ball into the rear upper valve body. Bolt the lower valve body onto the rear upper valve body.
5. Turn the valve body over and install 5 bolts into the rear upper valve body.
6. Remove the temporary bolts and install 1 rubber check ball in the front upper valve body.
7. Install the lower valve body onto the front upper valve body and fasten it with 3 bolts.
8. Turn the valve body over and install 5 bolts into the front upper valve body.
9. Turn the valve body over and install the final 2 bolts into the valve cover.

**NOTE: Torque all valve body bolts to 3.6-4.3 ft. lbs.**

## VALVE BODY

### Disassembly

**A-43D, A-43DL AND A-43DE**

1. Invert the transmission case so that the valve body is in a horizontal position. Remove the necessary oil delivery tubes.
2. Remove the detent spring along with the manual valve. Remove the oil strainer.
3. Remove the lower valve body bolts.

4. Turn the assembly over and remove the bolts from the upper rear valve body and the upper front valve body.
5. Carefully remove the valve body components. Separate the lower valve body from the upper valve body.
6. Do not lose any of the rubber check balls during disassembly. Remove and discard all of the gasket material.

## LOWER VALVE BODY

### Disassembly

1. Disconnect and remove the lower valve body plate and gaskets. Remove the cooler by-pass check valve and spring.
2. Turn the assembly over and remove the 7 set bolts and remove the lower body cover, plate and gaskets. Remove the check balls being careful not to scratch the grooves.
3. Remove the pressure relief spring retainer and take out the pressure relief spring and ball.
4. Remove the plate and gasket along with the primary regulator valve. Remove the plunger, spring and sleeve from the primary regulator valve bore.
5. Remove the D-2 down timing valve.
6. Remove the locating pin for the 3-4 shift valve and take out the 3-4 shift valve and spring.
7. Remove the 1-2 shift valve retainer and take out the 1-2 shift valve and spring.
8. Remove the reverse brake plug along with the cover plate and the low coast shift valve.
9. Remove the third coast shift valve and the 3-4 shift control valve.

### Inspection

1. Wash all parts in cleaning solvent and blow dry using compressed air.
2. Inspect the valve springs for compressed coils and any distortion.
3. Inspect the valve body housing for any warping or other damage.
4. Replace any defective parts as required.

### Assembly

1. Install the low coast shift valve with the small end in first. Install the 3-4 shift control valve in the housing bore with the cup side first.
2. Install the third coast shift valve with the small end first. Install the cover plate.
3. Assemble the 1-2 shift valve and install with the 1-2 shift valve retainer plug.
4. Install the D-2 down timing valve and plug. Install the down timing valve retainer.
5. Install the primary regulator valve and spring. Install the gasket and plate.
6. Install the pressure relief ball, spring and retainer. Make sure that the retainers and pins are installed correctly.
7. Turn the valve body over and install the check balls. Install the gasket, plate and lower body cover.

## FRONT UPPER VALVE BODY

### Disassembly

1. Remove the check ball and the cut back valve retainer. Remove the cut back valve.
2. Remove the secondary regulator valve and spring. Be careful not to lose the valve since it is spring loaded.
3. Depress the down shift plug into the valve body and while holding in the throttle valve, remove the throttle cam. Remove the down shift plug and spring.
4. Pull out the throttle valve retainer and remove the throttle valve. Remove the throttle valve spring and adjusting rings.

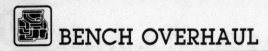
## Inspection

1. Wash all parts in cleaning solvent and blow dry using compressed air.
2. Inspect the valve springs for compressed coils and any other noticeable distortion.
3. Inspect the valve body housing for any warping or cracks.
4. Replace any defective parts as required.

## Assembly

1. Install the throttle valve and the retainer. Place the adjusting rings on the throttle valve shaft. Install the small spring on the throttle valve shaft.
2. Install the spring on the down shift plug and insert the down shift plug into the valve body.
3. Assemble the throttle cam and insert it into the front upper valve body. Torque the throttle cam bolt to 53-78 inch lbs.
4. Install the secondary regulator valve into its bore on the valve body. Depress the valve and place the cover plate over it. Install the cover plate bolt and torque to 44-52 inch lbs.
5. Install the cut back valve, plug and retainer.

**NOTE: Retainers can be coated with petroleum jelly during assembly to hold them in place.**

## REAR UPPER VALVE BODY

### Disassembly

1. Remove the check balls from the valve body along with intermediate shift valve retainer.
2. Remove the plug, intermediate shift valve and spring.
3. Remove the 2-3 shift valve retainer and the 2-3 shift valve assembly.
4. From the side of the valve body, remove one bolt and slide the valve cover to one side. Remove the low coast modulator valve and the governor modulator valve.
5. Slide the valve cover further and remove the rear clutch valve assembly.
6. Remove the cover plate and take out the intermediate modulator valve assembly.
7. Remove the detent regulator valve retainer and the detent regulator valve assembly.

### Inspection

1. Wash all parts in cleaning solvent and blow dry using compressed air.
2. Inspect the valve springs for collapsed coils or other damage.
3. Inspect the valve body housing for any warping or cracks.
4. Inspect the remaining parts for any rust, burrs or nicks.
5. Replace any defective parts as required.

### Assembly

1. Install the detent regulator valve assembly. Make sure that the retainer fully covers the spring.
2. Install the intermediate modulator valve and spring. Insert the valve with the round end in first.
3. Install the valve body side cover using one bolt. Install the rear sequence valve and spring.
4. Install the governor modulator valve, round end first, then insert the spring.
5. Install the low modulator valve and spring. Place the cover over the valve and install the second bolt through the cover. Torque to 44-52 inch lbs.
6. Install the 2-3 shift valve and insert the 2-3 shift valve plug. Depress the plug and install the intermediate shift valve retainer in the valve body.
7. Install the check balls in the valve body.

## Assembly of the Valve Body

1. Place a new gasket on the upper rear valve body.
2. Place the lower valve body with the plate on top of the upper rear valve body.
3. Install the lower valve body bolts to hold the upper rear valve body. Finger tighten only.
4. Turn the valve body over and install the 5 upper rear valve body bolts. Finger tighten only.
5. Position the lower and upper rear valve body assembly on top of the upper front valve body.
6. Install the 4 valve body bolts and finger tighten only.
7. Turn the assembly over and finger tighten the 5 bolts in the upper front valve body.
8. Check the alignment of the gasket and torque the upper front and upper rear valve body bolts to 44-52 inch lbs.
9. Turn the valve body assembly over and check the alignment of the gasket. Torque the lower valve body bolts to 44-52 inch lbs.
10. Install the manual valve and the detent spring.

# Transmission Assembly

Soak all new clutches and discs in transmission fluid, use new gaskets and O-rings. Apply transmission fluid on all sliding and rotating surfaces before assembly. Petroleum jelly should be used to hold the thrust washers and needle bearings in their proper location.

1. Place the transmission on a suitable fixture and make sure it is properly secured.
2. Install the thrust washer and bearing in the transmission case. Make sure the thrust washer is installed with the cup facing down.
3. Install the apply tube in the transmission case making sure that the locking tabs align with the transmission case.
4. Install the output shaft assembly into the transmission case aligning the clutch plate notches with the slot in the transmission case.

**NOTE: The A-40D automatic transmission does not have the clutch plate notches.**

5. Check the clutch pack clearance against the transmission case ledge. Maximum clearance for the A-40D, A-43D, A-43DL and the A-43DE should be 0.0866 in. (2.20mm).
6. Install the reaction plate with the notched tooth facing the valve body. Install the snap ring.
7. Install the center support assembly into the transmission case and install the center support bolts. Torque the bolts to 18-20 ft. lbs. (2.4-2.8 kg-m.).
8. Install the rear clutch in the transmission case. Rotate the clutch to engage the hub with the center support.

**NOTE: The rear clutch is installed correctly if the splined center of the clutch is flush with the end of the sun gear shaft.**

9. Install the needle bearing race using petroleum jelly to hold it in place.
10. Using petroleum jelly, install the thrust bearing and race on the front clutch. Install the front clutch in the transmission case.
11. Place a straight edge across the transmission case and the front clutch. Measure the distance between the straight edge and the front clutch. Maximum distance for the A-40D should be 1.34 in. (34mm). Distance for the A-43D, A-43DL and A-43DE should be 0.08 in. (2mm).
12. Install the thrust bearing on the front clutch. Use petroleum jelly to hold the thrust washer in place.
13. Install the guide bolts on the transmission case and finger tighten.
14. Install the thrust washer on the end of the overdrive case and install the overdrive case.

15. Install one thrust washer on the overdrive clutch and one washer on the overdrive case. The washer lugs are to be inserted in the clutch holes.

16. Install the overdrive clutch in the transmission case. Place a straight edge across the top of the transmission case and measure the distance between the overdrive clutch and the straight edge. Approximate distance for the A-40D automatic transmission should be 0.08 in. (2mm). Distance for the A-43D and the A-43DE automatic transmissions should be 0.138 in. (3.5mm).

17. Install the O-ring on the outside of the overdrive case.

18. Set the converter housing on the transmission case and secure it with 6 bolts. Torque the short bolts to 20-30 ft. lbs. (2.7-4.2 kg-m.) and the long bolts to 35-49 ft. lbs. (4.8-6.8 kg-m.).

19. Install the thrust washer and bearing on the overdrive clutch.

20. Install the thrust washer on the front of the oil pump and install the oil pump. Remove the guide bolts from the transmission case. Torque the oil pump bolts to 14-18 ft. lbs. (1.8-2.5 kg-m.).

21. Drive in a new pin to hold the manual shaft on the manual lever.

22. Install the parking lock pawl, pin and spring into the case. Install the parking pawl bracket on the case. Torque the 2 bolts to 53-78 in. lbs. (0.6-0.9 kg-m.).

23. Install a new O-ring on the throttle cable and install the throttle cable in the transmission case.

24. Insert the accumulator pistons and springs into the transmission case. Insert the valve body to case O-rings with the rounded edge towards the case.

25. Install the valve body and torque the bolts in 2 or 3 stages to 70-104 in. lbs. (0.8-1.2 kg-m.). Install the oil screen and oil tubes.

26. Install the magnet in the oil pan and install the oil pan with a new gasket. Install the oil pan drain plug.

27. Slide the governor onto the output shaft while prying up on the retaining ring.

28. Install the speedometer drive gear and snap ring on the output shaft.

29. Using a new gasket, install the extension housing. Torque the bolts to 20-30 ft. lbs.

30. Install the neutral safety switch and the shift handle.

31. Install the kick down switch. Install the solenoid switch with new O-rings.

# S SPECIFICATIONS

## TORQUE SPECIFICATIONS

| Bolt Class | Basic Diameter | Thread Pitch | Torque Limit m-kg | (ft-lb) |
|---|---|---|---|---|
| 4T | 6 | 1 | 0.4– 0.7 ( | 2.9– 5.0) |
| | 8 | 1.25 | 1.0– 1.6 ( | 7.3– 11.6) |
| | 10 | 1.25 | 1.9– 3.1 ( | 13.7– 22.4) |
| | 10 | 1.5 | 1.8– 3.0 ( | 13.0– 21.7) |
| | 10 | 1.25 | 3.5– 5.5 ( | 25.3– 39.8) |
| | 12 | 1.5 | 3.5– 5.0 ( | 25.3– 36.2) |
| | 12 | 1.75 | 3.0– 5.0 ( | 21.7– 36.2) |
| | 13 | 1.5 | 4.5– 7.0 ( | 32.5– 50.6) |
| | 14 | 1.5 | 5.0– 8.0 ( | 36.2– 57.8) |
| | 14 | 2 | 4.7– 7.7 ( | 34.0– 55.7) |
| | 16 | 1.5 | 7.5–11.0 ( | 54.2– 79.6) |
| | 16 | 2 | 7.1–10.6 ( | 51.3– 76.7) |

## TORQUE SPECIFICATIONS

| Bolt Class | Basic Diameter | Thread Pitch | Torque Limit m-kg | (ft-lb) |
|---|---|---|---|---|
| 5T | 6 | 1 | 0.6– 0.9 ( | 4.4– 6.5) |
| | 8 | 1.25 | 1.5– 2.2 ( | 10.9– 15.9) |
| | 10 | 1.25 | 3.0– 4.5 ( | 21.7– 32.5) |
| | 10 | 1.5 | 2.7– 4.2 ( | 19.5– 30.4) |
| | 12 | 1.25 | 5.0– 8.0 ( | 36.2– 57.8) |
| | 12 | 1.5 | 5.0– 7.0 ( | 36.2– 50.6) |
| | 12 | 1.75 | 4.8– 6.8 ( | 34.7– 49.2) |
| | 13 | 1.5 | 6.5– 9.0 ( | 47.0– 65.1) |
| | 14 | 1.5 | 7.5–11.0 ( | 54.2– 79.6) |
| | 14 | 2 | 7.0–10.5 ( | 50.6– 75.9) |
| | 16 | 1.5 | 12.0–17.0 ( | 86.8–123.0) |
| | 16 | 2 | 11.5–16.5 ( | 83.2–119.2) |
| 6T | 6 | 1 | 0.6– 0.9 ( | 4.4– 6.5) |
| | 8 | 1.25 | 1.5– 2.2 ( | 10.9– 15.9) |
| | 10 | 1.25 | 3.0– 4.5 ( | 21.7– 32.5) |
| | 10 | 1.5 | 2.7– 4.2 ( | 19.5– 30.4) |
| | 12 | 1.25 | 5.0– 8.0 ( | 36.2– 57.8) |
| | 12 | 1.5 | 5.0– 7.0 ( | 36.2– 50.6) |
| | 12 | 1.75 | 4.8– 6.8 ( | 34.7– 49.2) |
| 7T | 6 | 1 | 0.8– 1.2 ( | 5.8– 8.6) |
| | 8 | 1.25 | 2.0– 3.0 ( | 14.5– 21.7) |
| | 10 | 1.25 | 4.0– 5.5 ( | 28.9– 39.8) |
| | 10 | 1.5 | 3.7– 5.2 ( | 26.8– 37.6) |
| | 12 | 1.25 | 7.5–10.5 ( | 54.2– 75.9) |
| | 12 | 1.5 | 7.0– 9.0 ( | 50.6– 65.1) |
| | 12 | 1.75 | 6.0– 8.5 ( | 43.3– 61.4) |
| | 13 | 1.5 | 8.0–12.0 ( | 57.8– 86.8) |
| | 14 | 1.5 | 10.0–15.0 ( | 72.3–108.5) |
| | 14 | 2 | 9.5–14.0 ( | 68.7–101.2) |
| | 16 | 1.5 | 15.0–23.0 ( | 108.5–166.2) |
| | 16 | 2 | 14.0–22.0 ( | 101.2–159.0) |

# INDEX

# TOYOTA AW55
# AUTOMATIC TRANSAXLE

## APPLICATIONS

| Model | Year | Engine Number | Transmission Number |
|-------|------|---------------|---------------------|
| Tercel | 1980 | 1AC | A-55 |
| Tercel | 1981-84 | 3AC | A-55 |

## GENERAL DESCRIPTION

The Toyota A-55 transaxle is a fully automatic 3 speed transmission consisting of a torque converter, two sets of clutches, three sets of disc brakes, two sets of one-way clutches, valve body, oil pump and planetary gears. The A-55 transaxle is a six detent position type having the following shift positions, "P", "R", "N", "D", "2", "L". The torque converter consists of a pump and a turbine with a stator located in between, and all encased in a common housing. The planetary gear unit is provided with a wet type multiple disc clutch and disc brake for the purpose of controlling the speed ratio. Control of the power flow to attain first, second, and third speeds is effected by hydraulic pressure. In order to determine the required hydraulic pressure circuits, the passages for the ATF fluid have been collected in the valve body and the flow controlled by numerous valves. This part of the transaxle is called the hydraulic control system. These valves are controlled in accordance with the engine output condition and the vehicle speed. When the engine output condition changes, the throttle valve opening at that time is converted into hydraulic pressure signal.

When the vehicle speed changes, the speed of the governor turning together with the output shaft is converted into a hydraulic pressure signal. The transaxle has been made to automatically change speed to conform with these hydraulic pressure signals.

Factors causing the speed change are governor pressure produced in accordance with the vehicle speed and throttle pressure produced by changes in the carburetor throttle valve opening or accelerator pedal travel. This throttle pressure is controlled by the throttle valve cam connected to the carburetor by a cable.

## Transmission and Converter Identification

### TRANSMISSION

An identification plate is normally located on the left side of the transaxle case, with the model and serial number stamped on the plate. Should a transaxle be encountered without an identification plate, check the identification information plate on the firewall in the engine compartment and also the plate on the top of the instrument panel and driver's door post. If there is still no transaxle model number found, examine the transaxle case for identifying code letters or digits. Also, obtain the vehicle model and serial number before ordering replacment parts.

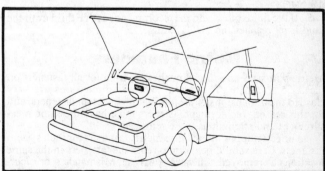

**Identification information plate** (© Toyota Motor Corporation)

### CONVERTER

The torque converter is a 3 element, single stage, 2 phase type. The converter is a welded unit and cannot be disassembled by the average repair shop.

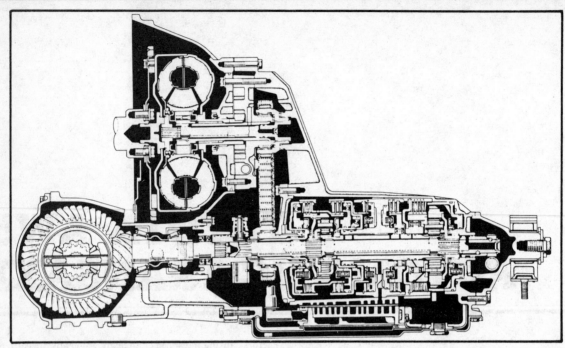

A-55 transaxle (© Toyota Motor Corporation)

## FLUID CAPACITY CHART

|                | Liters | US Qts. | Imp. Qts. |
|----------------|--------|---------|-----------|
| Drain and refill | 2.2    | 2.3     | 1.9       |
| Dry refill     | 4.5    | 4.8     | 4.0       |

## Checking Fluid Level

The fluid level should be checked when the transaxle is at normal operating temperature.

1. With the engine idling and the parking brake engaged, depress the brake pedal and shift the selector into each position from park to low and then return to park.
2. Now pull out the transaxle dipstick and wipe it clean.
3. With the dipstick clean push it back fully into the dipstick tube.
4. Pull the dipstick out again and check to see if the fluid is in the "HOT" range.
5. If the fluid is low, add the recommended ATF fluid until the fluid level reaches the "HOT" range.

## Metric Fasteners

Metric bolt sizes and thread pitches are used for all fasteners on the A-55 transaxle. The metric fasteners dimensions are very close to the dimensions of the familiar inch system fasteners, and for this reason, replacement fasteners must have the same measurement and strength as those removed.

Do not attempt to interchange metric fasteners for inch system fasteners. Care should be taken to reuse the fasteners in the same locations as removed, whenever possible. Mismatched or incorrect fasteners can result in damage to the transmission unit through malfunctions, breakage or possible personal injury.

## Fluid Specifications

The fluid used in the 1980-82 A-55 transaxle is ATF type F. The fluid used in the 1983-84 A-55 transaxle is Dexron® II. No other fluid should be used in this transaxle, unless specified by the manufacturer.

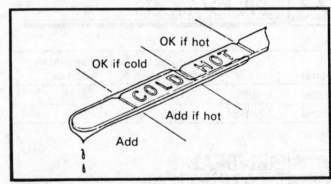

Checking the fluid level (© Toyota Motor Corporation)

## M MODIFICATIONS

There have been no major modifications to the A-55 transaxle at the time of this printing.

## TROUBLE DIAGNOSIS

In order to properly diagnose transmission problems and avoid making second repairs for the same problem, all of the available information and knowledge must be used. Included is a list of the components of the transaxle and their functions. Also, test procedures and their accompanying specification charts aid in finding solutions to problems. Further answers are found by road testing vehicles and comparing results of the above A-55 transaxle diagnosis chart. This chart gives conditions, cause and correction to most possible trouble conditions in the A-55 transaxle.

## CLUTCH APPLICATION CHART
### Toyota A-55

| Gear | Clutch 1 | Clutch 2 | Brake 1 | Brake 2 | Brake 3 | One-way Clutch 1 | One-way Clutch 2 |
|------|----------|----------|---------|---------|---------|------------------|------------------|
| P | — | — | — | — | — | — | — |
| R | — | Applied | — | — | Applied | — | — |
| N | — | — | — | — | — | — | — |
| D 1st | Applied | — | — | — | — | — | Holding |
| D 2nd | Applied | — | — | Applied | — | Holding | — |
| D 3rd | Applied | Applied | — | Applied | — | — | — |
| D 3-2 Kickdown | Applied | — | — | Applied | — | — | — |
| (2) 1st | Applied | — | — | — | — | — | Holding |
| (2) 2nd | Applied | — | Applied | Applied | — | — | Holding |
| L (low) | Applied | — | — | — | Applied | — | Holding |

## CHILTON'S THREE "C's" DIAGNOSIS CHART
### Toyota A-55 Transaxle

| Condition | Cause | Correction |
|-----------|-------|------------|
| Harsh down-shift | a) Throttle linkage out of adjustment<br>b) Accumulator pistons faulty<br>c) Valve body faulty<br>d) Transmission faulty | a) Adjust throttle linkage<br>b) Inspect accumulator pistons<br>c) Inspect valve body<br>d) Disassemble and inspect transmission |
| No down-shift when coasting | a) Governor faulty<br>b) Valve body faulty | a) Inspect governor<br>b) Inspect valve body |
| Down-shift occurs too quick or too late while coasting | a) Throttle linkage out of adjustment<br>b) Governor faulty<br>c) Valve body faulty<br>d) Transmission faulty | a) Adjust throttle linkage<br>b) Inspect governor<br>c) Inspect valve body<br>d) Disassemble and inspect transmission |
| No 3-2 or 2-1 kickdown | a) Throttle linkage out of adjustment<br>b) Governor faulty<br>c) Valve body faulty | a) Adjust throttle linkage<br>b) Inspect governor<br>c) Inspect valve body |
| No engine braking in "2" range | a) Valve body faulty<br>b) Transmission faulty | a) Inspect valve body<br>b) Disassemble and inspect transmission |
| Harsh engagement into any drive range | a) Throttle linkage out of adjustment<br>b) Valve body or primary regulator faulty<br>c) Accumulator pistons faulty<br>d) Transmission faulty | a) Adjust throttle linkage<br>b) Inspect valve body<br>c) Inspect accumulator pistons<br>d) Disassemble and inspect transmission |
| Delayed 1-2 or 2-3 up-shift, or down-shifts from 3-2 then shifts back to 3 | a) Throttle linkage out of adjustment<br>b) Governor faulty<br>c) Valve body faulty | a) Adjust throttle linkage<br>b) Inspect governor<br>c) Inspect valve body |
| Slips on 1-2 or 2-3 up-shift, or slips or shudders on take-off | a) Manual linkage out of adjustment<br>b) Throttle linkage out of adjustment<br>c) Transmission faulty | a) Adjust linkage<br>b) Adjust throttle linkage<br>c) Disassemble and inspect transmission |

## CHILTON'S THREE "C's" DIAGNOSIS CHART
### Toyota A-55 Transaxle

| Condition | Cause | Correction |
|---|---|---|
| Drag, binding or tie-up on 1-2 or 2-3 up-shift | a) Manual linkage out of adjustment<br>b) Valve body faulty<br>c) Transmission faulty | a) Adjust linkage<br>b) Inspect valve body<br>c) Disassemble and inspect transmission |
| Fluid discolored or smells burnt | a) Fluid contamination<br>b) Torque converter faulty<br>c) Transmission is faulty | a) Replace the fluid<br>b) Replace the torque converter<br>c) Disassemble and inspect the transmission |
| Vehicle does not move in any forward range or reverse | a) Manual linkage out of adjustment<br>b) Valve body or primary regulator faulty<br>c) Transmission faulty | a) Adjust the linkage<br>b) Inspect valve body<br>c) Disassemble and inspect transmission |
| Vehicle does not move in any range | a) Park lock pawl faulty<br>b) Valve body or primary regulator faulty<br>c) Torque converter faulty<br>d) Broken converter drive plate<br>e) Oil pump intake screen blocked<br>f) Transmission faulty | a) Inspect park pawl<br>b) Inspect valve body<br>c) Replace the torque converter<br>d) Replace the torque converter<br>e) Clean the screen<br>f) Disassemble and inspect transmission |
| Shift lever position is incorrect | a) Manual linkage out of adjustment<br>b) Manual valve and lever faulty<br>c) Transmission faulty | a) Adjust linkage<br>b) Inspect valve body<br>c) Disassemble and inspect transmission |
| Vehicle does not hold in "P" | a) Manual linkage out of adjustment<br>b) Parking lock pawl cam and spring faulty | a) Adjust linkage<br>b) Inspect cam and spring |

# HYDRAULIC CONTROL SYSTEM

The main parts of the hydraulic control system for the A-55 transaxle are the torque converter, oil pump, governor, cooler and lubrication circuits, valve body and applying clutches and brakes.

## Major Components

### OIL PUMP

The oil pump is used to send the ATF fluid to the torque converter, to lubricate the planetary gear units, and to supply the operating (line) pressure for hydraulic control. The oil pump drive gear, together with the torque converter impeller, is constantly driven by the engine. The pump has the capacity to supply the necessary hydraulic pressure for operating from low speed to high speed and when reversing.

### VALVE BODY

The valve body distributes the hydraulic pressure delivered by the oil pump to the various parts, and to perform automatic gear changes by regulating the hydraulic pressure in accordance with the throttle valve opening and vehicle speed.

1. The manual valve is linked to the shift lever in the driver's compartment and is used to charge the fluid passages, according to the movement of the shift lever.
2. The control valve check ball prevents loss of fluid from the torque converter when the engine is not running.
3. The primary regulator valve automatically controls the hydraulic pressure to the other valves and units of the transaxle as required by changing speed and torque conditions in the transaxle.
4. The oil pump safety relief check ball limits the maximum pressure output of the oil pump.
5. The detent regulator valve controls pressure passing through the downshift plug and acting on the 1-2 and 2-3 shift valves at kickdown.
6. The accumulators lessen the shock when the rear clutch and the number 2 brake are applied.
7. The cut-back valve regulates the cut-back pressure acting on the throttle valve by applying cut-back pressure to the throttle valve. The throttle pressure is lowered to prevent any unnecessary power loss from the oil pump.
8. The throttle valve operates in relation to engine load and creates the throttle pressure corresponding to the load. This valve is connected to the accelerator linkage. The throttle valve inner lever pushes the downshift plug in relation to accelerator pedal travel. Two springs on the inner valve oppose the inner lever pressure. When the throttle valve is partially closed a passage on the discharge side is closed and a passage for line pressure is opened to produce throttle pressure. Throttle pressure passing through the throttle modulator valve is routed to the shift valves. This pressure opposes governor pressure at the shift valves.
9. When the accelerator pedal is depressed fully, the downshift plug pushes strongly against the throttle valve to open the line pressure passage, causing throttle pressure to equal line pressure.
10. The 1-2 shift valve provides automatic shifting from 1st to 2nd and from 2nd to 1st. This valve is controlled by governor pressure, throttle modulator pressure and line pressure. When

governor pressure is high and throttle modulator pressure is low, the 1-2 shift valve is moved, which causes the brake number 2 passage to open. This results in the transmission shifting to 2nd gear. When governor pressure is low and throttle pressure is high, the 1-2 shift valve moves to close the brake number 2 passage, resulting in the transmission downshifting to 1st gear.

11. The 2-3 shift valve provides automatic shifting from 2nd to 3rd gear and from 3rd to 2nd gear. The valve is controlled by governor pressure, line pressure, throttle pressure and spring tension. When governor pressure is high and overcomes spring tension and throttle pressure the valve opens the line pressure passage to the rear clutch shifting to 3rd gear. When governor pressure is low, the 2-3 shift valve moves to close the line pressure passage to the rear clutch downshifting to 2nd gear.

## Diagnosis Tests

### TIME LAG TEST

When the shift lever is shifted while the engine is idling, there will be a certain time delay (lag) before the shock on the transaxle can be felt. This time delay (lag) is used for checking the condition of the front clutch, rear clutch and brake number 3.

#### Measuring Lag Time

1. Start the vehicle and bring the engine and transaxle up to normal operating temperature.
2. With the parking brake fully engaged, shift the shift lever from "N" to "D" range.
3. Using a stop watch or a wrist watch, measure the time it takes from shifting the lever until the shock is felt (average lag time is less than 1.2 seconds).
4. Now shift the shift lever from "N" to "R" range and measure the time lag (average lag time is less than 1.5 seconds).

**NOTE: Allow at least one minute intervals between tests. Make three measurements and then calculate the average lag time.**

#### Time Lag Test Result Indications

If the shift from "N" to "D" time lag is longer than specified, the problems could be:
1. The line pressure is too low.
2. The front clutch could be badly worn.

If the shift from "N" to "R" time lag is longer than specified, the problems could be:
1. The rear clutch is worn.
2. Brake number could be worn.
3. The line pressure is too low.

## Hydraulic Tests

#### Governor Pressure Test

1. Engage the parking brake and chock all four wheels.
2. Connect a oil pressure gauge to the governor pressure port on the transaxle.
3. Start the engine and bring it up to normal operating temperature.
4. Shift the shift lever into the "D" range and measure the governor pressure at the speeds specified in the chart below:

### GOVERNOR PRESSURE AT VEHICLE SPEED

| Speed (mph) | PSI |
|---|---|
| 19 mph | 17-26 psi |
| 31 mph | 26-34 psi |
| 63 mph | 54-71 psi |

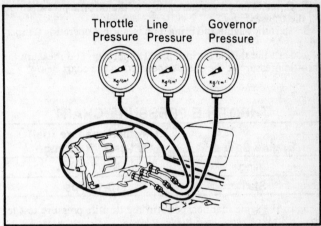

**Pressure test plug location** (© Toyota Motor Corporation)

#### Governor Pressure Test Result Indications

If the governor pressure is not within specifications:
1. The line pressure could be too low.
2. A possible fluid leakage in the governor pressure circuit.
3. The governor valve is not operating correctly.

#### Line Pressure Test

1. Engage the parking brake and chock all four wheels.
2. Connect an oil pressure gauge to the line pressure port on the transaxle.
3. Start the engine and bring it up to normal operating temperature.
4. Shift the shift lever into the "D" position and measure the line pressure at the speeds specified in the chart below:

### LINE PRESSURE CHART

| Engine Speed | Line Pressure (psi) | |
|---|---|---|
| | "D" Range | "R" Range |
| Idling | 57-65 | 95-107 |
| Stall | 132-161 | 223-259 |

5. In the same manner, perform the line pressure test for the "R" range.

**NOTE: If the measured line pressures are not within specifications, recheck the throttle link adjustment and retest.**

#### Line Pressure Test Result Indications

1. If the line pressure is higher than specified:
   a. Regulator valve is not operating correctly.
   b. Throttle link is out of adjustment.
   c. The throttle valve is not operating correctly.
2. If the line pressure is lower than specified:
   a. The oil pump may be defective.
   b. The throttle link is out of adjustment.
   c. The throttle valve is not operating correctly.
   d. The regulator valve is not operating correctly.
3. If the line pressure is low in the "D" range only:
   a. The front clutch is not operating correctly.
   b. There is a possible fluid leakage in the "D" range circuit.
4. If the line pressure is low in the "R" range only:
   a. The rear clutch is not operating correctly.
   b. Brake number 3 is not operating correctly.
   c. There is a possible fluid leakage in the "R" range circuit.

#### Throttle Pressure Test

1. Engage the parking brake and chock all four wheels.

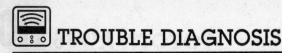 

2. Connect an oil pressure gauge to the throttle pressure port on the transaxle.

3. Start the engine and bring it up to normal operating temperature.

4. Shift the shift lever into the "D" position and measure the throttle pressure at the speeds specified in the chart below:

### THROTTLE PRESSURE CHART

| Engine Speed | Throttle Pressure (psi) "D" and "R" Range |
|---|---|
| Idling | 0-4.3 psi |
| Stall | 110-118 psi |

5. In the same manner, perform the throttle pressure test for the "R" range.

**NOTE: If the measured throttle pressures are not within specifications, recheck the throttle link adjustment and retest.**

### Throttle Pressure Test Result Indications

1. If the throttle pressure is higher than specified:
   a. The throttle valve is not operating correctly.
   b. The throttle circuit orifice could be clogged.
2. If the throttle pressure is lower than specified:
   a. Oil pump may be defective.
   b. The regulator valve is not operating correctly.
   c. The throttle valve is not operating correctly.

## ROAD TEST

### Road Test With Selector in "P"

1. With the vehicle parked on a small grade, put the selector lever in the "P" position and release the parking brake.
2. If the vehicle does not roll backwards, the parking system is working properly.

### Road Test With Selector in "R"

1. Start the engine and while running at full throttle, check the transaxle for slipping.

### Road Test With Selector in "D"

1. Increase speed of vehicle and while holding the accelerator pedal steady, check to see if transaxle makes 1-2 and 2-3 upshifts at correct vehicle speeds. Also check for hard shifting or slipping at this time.
2. While driving in third gear, check for noise and vibration.
3. With selector lever in second or third gear, check to see if 2-1, 3-1 and 3-2 kickdown shifts occur properly at specified kickdown limit vehicle speeds.
4. Drive in third gear, and select 2 range, than L range to check if engine brake is effective.
5. While driving in the "D" range, shift the selector to the "L" range to check if the 3-2 and the 2-1 downshift occurs at the proper vehicle speed.

### Road Test with Selector in "2"

1. While driving with the selector lever in the "2" position, increase the vehicle speed and check to see that the transaxle makes the 1-2 upshift at the proper vehicle speed. Also check for noise and shock at the time of shifting.
2. Check to see if the 2-1 kickdown occurs at correct vehicle speed limit.

### Road Test With Selector in "L"

1. While running in the "L" range, check to see that there is no up-shift to 2nd gear.
2. Check for noise in either acceleration or deceleration.

### AUTOMATIC VEHICLE SPEED SHIFT CHART (MPH) km/h

| "D" Range (throttle valve full open) | | | | "L" Range |
|---|---|---|---|---|
| 1-2 | 2-3 | 3-2 | 2-1 | 2-1 |
| (26-36) | (59-68) | (54-64) | (20-30) | (22-31) |
| 42-58 | 96-110 | 88-103 | 33-49 | 35-51 |

## STALL TEST

The object of this test is to check the overall performance of the transaxle and the engine by measuring the maximum engine speeds at the "D" and "R" ranges.

### Measuring Stall Speed

1. Engage the parking brake and chock all four wheels.
2. Attach a tachometer to the engine and place it in a position to be seen by the operator.
3. Start the engine and bring the vehicle up to normal operating temperature.
4. Apply the foot brake and shift the selector lever to the "D" position.
5. With foot brake applied, gradually depress the accelerator pedal until the engine reaches full throttle.
6. When the engine speed is stabilized, read the engine speed quickly and release the accelerator pedal. Hold no longer than 5 seconds. Stall speed should be 2,200 ± 150 rpm.
7. Shift the selector lever to the "N" position, and cool down the transaxle fluid by letting the engine run for 2-5 minutes at fast idle speed.
8. Record the stall speed and perform the stall test with the selector lever in the "R" position.

**NOTE: Do not perform the stall test longer than 5 seconds as damage to the transaxle can occur.**

### Interpretation of Stall Test Results

1. If the stall speed is lower than specified:
   a. Engine output could be insufficient.
   b. Stator one-way is not operating correctly.

**NOTE: If the stall speed is more than 600 rpm below the specified stall speed, the torque converter could be defective.**

2. If the stall speed in the "D" position is higher than specified:
   a. The front clutch could be slipping.
   b. One-way clutch number 2 is not operating correctly.
   c. The line pressure could be too low.
3. If the stall speed in the "R" position is higher than specified:
   a. The rear clutch could be slipping.
   b. Brake number 3 could be slipping.
   c. The line pressure could be too low.

## STATOR ONE-WAY CLUTCH TEST

### (CONVERTER REMOVED)

1. Fill the torque converter with the recommended ATF up to the top of the stator splines.
2. Insert the one-way clutch test tool or its equivalent into the stator spline.
3. Turn the one-way clutch tool rapidly to the left, the one-way clutch is not functioning and the stator is turning, creating resistance against the ATF fluid.
4. Now turn the one-way clutch tool rapidly to the right. At this time there should be no resistance felt when turning the one-way clutch to the right.
5. If there is resistance when turning the one-way clutch to the right, the one-way clutch is not sliding freely and therefore not operating correctly.

 **ON CAR SERVICES**

# Adjustments

## THROTTLE LINK

### Adjustment

1. Remove the air cleaner and check to see if the throttle lever and the throttle link are bent or damaged.
2. Push on the throttle lever and see if the throttle valve opens fully.
3. Using a pedal jack or its equivalent, fully depress and hold the accelerator pedal to the floor.
4. Loosen the turnbuckle lock nut and adjust the throttle linkage length by turning the turnbuckle.
5. The adjustment will be correct when the throttle valve lever indicator lines up with the mark on the transaxle case.
6. Now tighten the turnbuckle lock nut and recheck the adjustment.
7. Install the air cleaner and remove the pedal jack from the accelerator pedal.

## FLOOR SHIFT LINKAGE

### Adjustment

1. From underneath the vehicle check the shift linkage connecting rod bushing for wear or deformation.
2. Loosen the lock nut on the connecting rod.
3. Move the manual shift lever all the way forward and return the shift lever to the "N" neutral position (3 notches).
4. Set the shift selector to the "N" position.

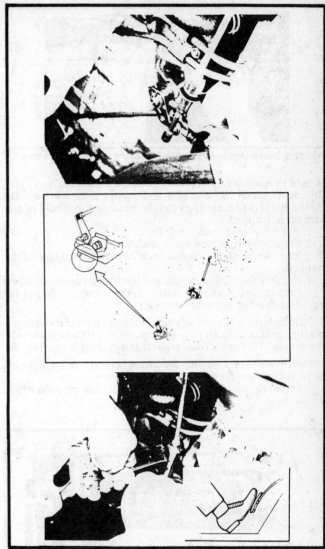

Adjusting the throttle linkage (© Toyota Motor Corporation)

5. While holding the selector slightly toward the "R" position, tighten the connecting rod lock nut.

## NEUTRAL SAFETY SWITCH

### Adjustment

Whenever it is possible to start the engine with the shift selector in any position other than the "P" or "N" positions, adjustment of the neutral safety switch is required.

1. Loosen the neutral safety switch hold down bolt.
2. Set the shift selector lever to the "N" position.
3. Align the switch shaft groove with the neutral base line on the transaxle.
4. Hold the switch in the align position and torque the hold down bolt to 9 ft. lbs.

# Services

## OIL PAN, FLUID AND FILTER

### Removal and Change

The normal service interval for changing transmission fluid and replacing or cleaning oil filters is 24,000 miles. When the vehicle

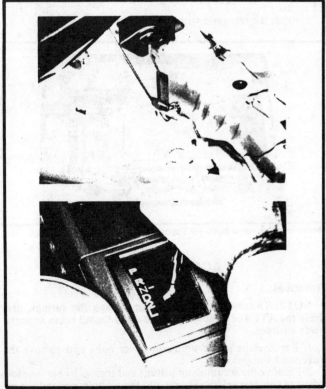

Floor shift linkage adjustment (© Toyota Motor Corporation)

Installing the neutral safety switch (© Toyota Motor Corporation)

is used in more severe operating conditions such as, heavy city driving, constant hill climbing and pulling a trailer the fluid should be checked more often and the transmission should be serviced more frequently.

1. Raise the vehicle on a safe lift.
2. Place a oil drain pan under the transaxle.
3. Remove the drain plug and drain all the ATF fluid out of the transaxle.
4. Remove the 17 oil pan bolts and remove the pan and gasket.
5. Inspect the pan and the magnet in the bottom of the pan for any steel chips or any other particles.

**NOTE: If there is any steel chips in the pan it could mean that a bearing, gear or a clutch plate are wearing out. If there is brass in the bottom of the pan it could mean that a bushing is wearing out.**

6. Remove the six oil filter mounting bolts and remove the oil filter. Inspect the filter and clean or replace it.
7. Install the oil filter and torque the six mounting bolts to 53-78 in. lbs.

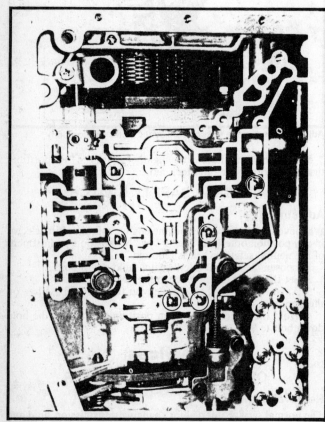

Location of the steel balls (© Toyota Motor Corporation)

### Installation

1. Install the oil pan with a new gasket to the transaxle case. Torque the 17 oil pan bolts to 65 in. lbs.
2. Install the drain plug with a new gasket and torque the drain plug to 22 ft. lbs.
3. Refill the transaxle with 2.3 U.S. quarts of the recommended ATF fluid. Start the engine and run it at idle. Check the fluid level and if the level is low add the necessary fluid to bring the level up to the "HOT" range on the dipstick.

## VALVE BODY

### Removal

The valve body can be removed from the transaxle while the transaxle is still attached to the vehicle. This procedure is not advisable because during removal, some of the valves and the steel check balls may fall out of the valve body, becoming lost or maybe installed in the wrong position in the valve body during installation.

1. Raise the vehicle and support safely. Drain the ATF from the transaxle.
2. Pry up both ends of the oil pressure tubes with a screwdriver and remove the six oil tubes.

**NOTE: When removing the valve body, be careful not to lose the pin and shift valve plug seat. Also try to keep the valve body gasket and separator plate attached to the transaxle, because this will hold the six steel balls in place in the upper valve body.**

### Installation

1. Install the valve body assembly and torque the 14 valve body bolts to 48 in. lbs.
2. Install the oil tubes by pressing the tubes into position by hand (do not bend or damage the tubes).
3. Install a new oil pan gasket and the oil pan, torque the oil pan bolts to 65 in. lbs.
4. Install the drain plug and gasket and torque the drain plug to 22 ft. lbs.
5. Refill the transaxle with the recommended ATF.

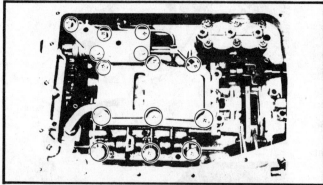

Removing the valve body (© Toyota Motor Corporation)

## ACCUMULATOR

### Removal

**NOTE: To remove the accumulator pistons and springs, first drain the ATF and remove the oil pan and the oil tubes as previously outlined.**

1. Remove the six accumulator cover bolts and remove the cover and the gasket.
2. Remove the accumulator pistons and springs by blowing low pressure compressed air (14 psi) into the air holes around the accumulator cylinders.

Accumulator piston removal (© Toyota Motor Corporation)

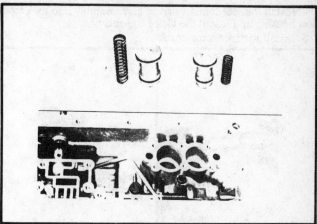

Inspecting the accumulator pistons (© Toyota Motor Corporation)

Installing the accumulator pistons (© Toyota Motor Corporation)

Installing the accumulator cover (© Toyota Motor Corporation)

3. Position a rag under the accumulator pistons to catch the pistons as they come out of the cylinders.

**NOTE: Do not use high pressure air to remove the accumulator pistons and keep face away from pistons to avoid injury.**

### Installation

Before installing the accumulator pistons and springs, check the pistons, springs, cover and cylinder for wear or damage.

1. Install new O-rings around the accumulator pistons and coat the O-rings with ATF.

2. Press the accumulator pistons and springs into the accumulator cylinder by hand.

**NOTE: Be sure to install the accumulator pistons and springs in the same cylinder that they came out of.**

3. Install a new accumulator cover gasket and then the cover and the six bolts. Torque the bolts to 30-60 in. lbs.

4. Install the oil tubes and oil pan. Add the recommended ATF to the transaxle and recheck level.

## SPEEDOMETER GEARS

### Removal

1. Place a drain pan under the extension housing to catch any ATF that might drain out.

2. Remove the speedometer cable.

3. Remove the bolt and lock plate that hold the speedometer driven gear to the extension housing and remove the driven gear.

4. Remove the extension housing and gasket.

Installing the extension housing (© Toyota Motor Corporation)

5. Remove the snap ring from the output shaft sleeve and remove the speedometer drive gear.

### Installation

1. Install the speedometer drive gear and snap ring.

2. Install the extension housing with a new gasket and torque the housing bolts to 14 ft. lbs.

3. Install new O-rings and bushings to the speedometer driven gear shaft sleeve.

4. Install the speedometer driven gear assembly into the extension housing and install the lock plate and bolt.

5. Install the speedometer cable.

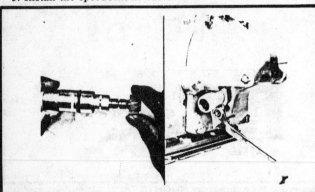

**Installing the speedometer driven gear with housing**
(© Toyota Motor Corporation)

# REMOVAL & INSTALLATION

## TRANSAXLE REMOVAL AND INSTALLATION

### Removal

1. Disconnect the positive battery cable.
2. Drain out some of the coolant from the radiator.
3. Remove the upper radiator hose from the engine.
4. Disconnect the electrical connectors to the neutral safety switch and the back-up light switch.
5. Remove the air cleaner assembly.
6. Remove the throttle link.
7. Remove the oil cooler pipe clamp.
8. Using two wrenches disconnect the oil cooler inlet pipe.
9. Remove the upper transaxle set bolts.
10. Raise the vehicle and support it safely. Drain the ATF.
11. Remove both drive shafts.
12. Remove the exhaust flange nuts and the clamp on the side of the transaxle. Remove the front exhaust pipe.
13. Remove the stiffener plate.
14. Disconnect the control link at the rear connection.
15. Disconnect the speedometer cable.
16. Remove the engine under cover.
17. Remove the three torque converter cover bolts and remove the converter cover.
18. Remove the six torque converter set bolts by turning the crankshaft to gain access to each bolt.
19. Disconnect the oil cooler outlet pipe.

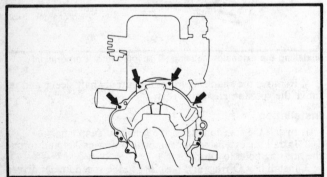

**Location of the upper transaxle bolts** (© Toyota Motor Corporation)

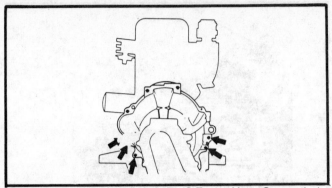

**Location of the lower transaxle bolts** (© Toyota Motor Corporation)

20. Remove the 5 transaxle mounting bolts.
21. Disconnect the rear bond cable.
22. Place a wooden block between the engine and the firewall panel.
23. Position a transmission jack or its equivalent under the transaxle and remove the rear engine support.
24. While turning the crankshaft, pry on the torque converter to separate it from the drive plate.
25. With the transaxle free of any obstructions, lower the jack and remove the transaxle from the vehicle.

## INSTALLATION

NOTE: Before installing the transaxle, apply grease to the center hub of the torque converter and the pilot hole in the crankshaft.

1. Insert a guide pin in the most outward converter mounting hole.
2. With the transaxle on the removing jack, raise the transaxle into position in the vehicle.

NOTE: The transaxle and the torque converter should be installed as a unit.

3. Align the guide pin with one of the holes in the drive plate and install the transaxle to the engine.

NOTE: The transaxle should be installed to the engine so that the tip of the converter goes into the hole in the end of the crankshaft.

4. Remove the guide pin and install two torque converter set bolts about half way in and tighten them evenly.
5. Install the 5 transaxle mounting bolts and torque the bolts to 47 ft. lbs.
6. Install the rear support member and torque the bolts to 70 ft. lbs.
7. Loosen the temporarily installed torque converter set bolts and install the other four bolts by turning the crankshaft to gain access to the bolt holes. After tightening the bolts evenly, torque the bolts to 13 ft. lbs.
8. Install the torque converter cover.
9. Using two wrenches, connect the oil cooler outlet pipe. The torque for the nuts is 16 ft. lbs.
10. Install the engine under cover and install the stiffener plate.
11. Install the exhaust clamp on the side of the transaxle and the exhaust flange nuts and install the front exhaust pipe.
12. Connect the speedometer cable and the rear bond cable.
13. Align the shift lever and control lever at the "N" position and connect the control link.
14. Install both drive shafts.
15. Lower the vehicle and install the upper transaxle set bolts. Torque the set bolts to 47 ft. lbs.
16. Using two wrenches, connect the oil cooler inlet pipe.
17. Install the oil cooler pipe clamp.
18. Connect the throttle link.

19. Connect the electrical connectors to the neutral safety switch and the back-up light switch.
20. Install the upper radiator hose and refill the cooling system with coolant.
21. Adjust the throttle link (see adjustment section).
22. Install the air cleaner assembly and connect the positive battery cable.
23. Refill the transaxle with 2.3 U.S. quarts of the recommended ATF.

**NOTE: If the torque converter has been drained, then the transaxle should be refilled with 4.8 U.S. quarts of the recommended ATF.**

24. Perform a road test to check the operation of the transaxle.
25. Check for fluid leaks and for differential gear oil leaks.

# BENCH OVERHAUL

## Before Disassembly

1. Before disassembling the transaxle, thoroughly remove all dirt from the exterior to prevent the dirt from entering the transaxle.
2. The transaxle consists of many precision parts. Care should be taken not to scratch, nick or damage the parts during the overhaul of the transaxle.
3. Make sure that the bench work area is clean.
4. Clean all metal parts in a suitable solvent and dry with compressed air.
5. Clean all clutch discs, thrust plates and rubber parts in automatic transmission fluid.
6. All rubber gaskets and oil seals should be replaced with new at every reinstallation.
7. Apply automatic transmission fluid to the friction elements, rotating parts and sliding parts prior to installation.
8. During disassembly, always keep the parts in order.
9. A new clutch disc should be immersed in fluid for more than two hours before installation.
10. When replacing a bushing, replace the complete bushing assembly.

## Disassembly

1. Remove the torque converter.
2. Remove the transmission case from the transaxle.
3. Remove the neutral safety switch.
4. Remove the speedometer driven gear and remove the extension housing.

**Manual lever shaft removal** (© Toyota Motor Corporation)

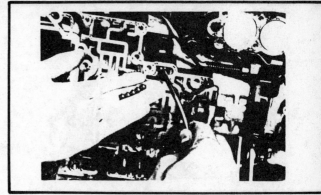

**Removing the steel balls** (© Toyota Motor Corporation)

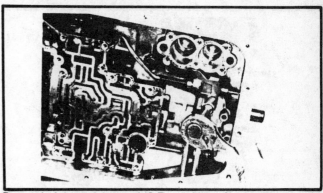

**Removal of the park lock rod** (© Toyota Motor Corporation)

5. Remove the speedometer drive gear and the output shaft sleeve (do not lose the locking ball on the shaft sleeve).
6. With the transaxle oil pan face down on the bench, remove the oil pan bolts and lift the transaxle up to separate the transaxle from the oil pan.
7. Turn the transaxle over and remove the oil tubes.
8. Remove the oil filter and the valve body assembly.
9. Remove the six steel balls and the valve vibrating stopper from the valve body and set them aside.
10. Remove the accumulator pistons and springs.
11. Remove the parking lock rod, spring, pivot pin and parking lock pawl.
12. Remove the spacer and turn the ring 90 degrees.
13. With a hammer and punch, drive out the slotted spring pin and remove the manual valve shaft lever.

**Oil pump delivery & pressure tube removal**
(© Toyota Motor Corporation)

Removal of the oil pump (© Toyota Motor Corporation)

Removing the center support bolts (© Toyota Motor Corporation)

Input shaft and sprocket removal (© Toyota Motor Corporation)

Center support and sun gear removal (© Toyota Motor Corporation)

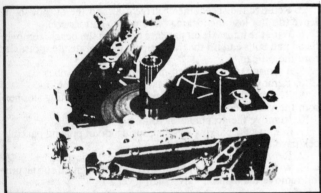

Front clutch removal (© Toyota Motor Corporation)

No. 2 one-way clutch removal (© Toyota Motor Corporation)

Rear clutch removal (© Toyota Motor Corporation)

14. Remove the oil pump suction tube.
15. Remove the oil pump delivery tube and the pressure tube.
16. Remove the oil pump.
17. Remove the snap ring and pull out the input shaft, driven sprockets and chain.
18. Remove the front transaxle support and place the transaxle standing up on a wooden block.
19. Measure the distance between the top of the transaxle case and the front clutch (make a note of the distance for reassembly).
20. Remove the front clutch and bearings.
21. Remove the output shaft and the front planetary gear.
22. Remove the rear clutch.
23. Remove the two center support bolts.
24. Remove the center support and the sun gear assembly.
25. Remove the snap ring and remove the reaction plate retaining ring.

Brake No. 3 disc removal (© Toyota Motor Corporation)

Measuring the body clearance (© Toyota Motor Corporation)

Planetary ring gear removal (© Toyota Motor Corporation)

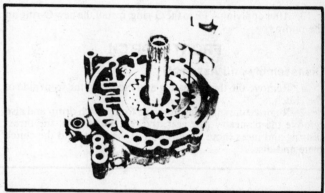

Measuring the tip clearance (© Toyota Motor Corporation)

26. Remove the rear number 2 one-way clutch and the rear planetary gear.
27. Remove the brake number 3 disc, plate and cushion plate.
28. Remove the rear planetary ring gear.
29. The basic disassembly is complete.

# Unit Disassembly and Assembly
## OIL PUMP

### Disassembly and Assembly

1. Remove the three oil pump cover bolts and remove the pump cover.
2. Remove the check ball, priming valve and spring.
3. Remove the pressure regulator valve assembly.
4. Remove the two oil seal rings from the front support.

5. Pull the driven gear to one side of the pump body and using a feeler gauge, measure the body clearance of the driven gear. Standard clearance is 0.0028-0.0059 in. (0.07-0.15mm).
6. Measure between the gear teeth and crescent shaped part of the pump, to check the tip clearance of both gears. Standard tip clearance is 0.0043-0.0055 in. (0.11-0.14mm.)
7. Using a steel straightedge and a feeler gauge, measure the side clearance of both gears. Standard side clearance is 0.0008-0.0020 in. (0.02-0.05mm).
8. Remove and replace the front oil seal on the pump.
9. After checking to see that the measurments of the oil pump gears are within specifications, install the priming valve and the check ball valve.
10. Install the oil pump cover and torque the pump cover bolts to 13 ft. lbs. (19 N•m).
11. Install the pressure regulator valve assembly.
12. Apply petroleum jelly to the oil seal rings and install the oil seal rings on the front support on the pump.

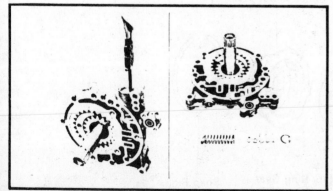

Removing the pressure regulator assembly
(© Toyota Motor Corporation)

Measuring the side clearance (© Toyota Motor Corporation)

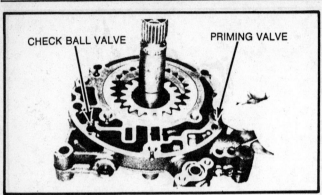

**Installing the check ball valve and priming valve**
(© Toyota Motor Corporation)

**Measuring front clutch clearance** (© Toyota Motor Corporation)

13. After applying ATF to the O-ring, install the new O-ring on the pump.

## FRONT CLUTCH

### Disassembly and Assembly

1. Remove the thrust bearing and race from the front side of the clutch.

2. Remove the snap ring from the front clutch drum and also remove the planetary ring gear, the rear clutch hub, the thrust bearing and races (note the position of the races) and the clutch plate and disc.

3. Remove the thinner snap ring and remove the remaining clutch plates and discs.

4. Compress the piston return spring using special Toyota tool SST 09350-20013 or its equivalent, in a press. Then remove the snap ring with an appropriate snap ring removing tool.

5. Remove the piston by inserting air pressure into the piston apply hole of the clutch drum.

6. Inspect the front clutch piston, disc, plate, return spring and clutch drum.

7. Install new O-rings on the piston and install the piston in the front clutch drum (apply ATF to the O-rings).

8. Place the clutch drum in an arbor press.

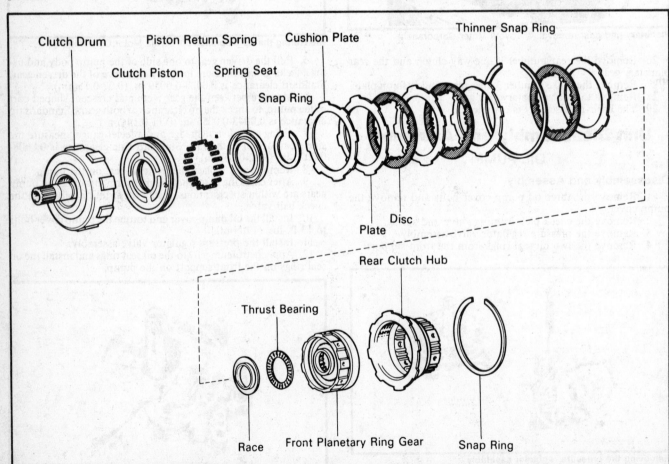

**Front clutch components** (© Toyota Motor Corporation)

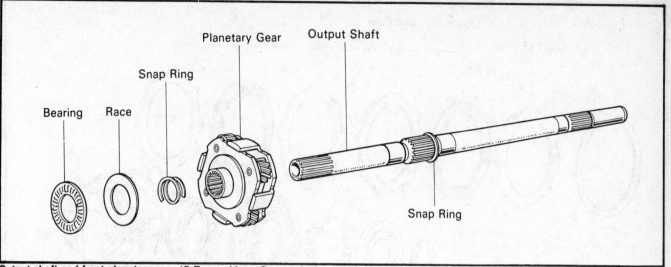

**Output shaft and front planetary gear** (© Toyota Motor Corporation)

9. Install the piston return springs, spring seat and snap ring in place.

10. Using the special Toyota tool SST 09350-20013 or its equivalent, compress the return springs and install the snap ring in the groove.

11. Install the clutch discs and plates and measure the clearance of the front clutch. Standard clearance is 0.0118-0.0587 in. (0.30-1.49mm).

12. Install the thinner snap ring and the inner bearing and race. Coat the parts with petroleum jelly to keep them in place. Face the lip of the race towards the front clutch body.

13. Install the planetary gear and make sure the hub meshes with all the discs and is fully inserted.

14. Install the rear clutch hub and the outer snap ring.

## OUTPUT SHAFT AND FRONT PLANETARY GEAR

### Disassembly and Assembly

1. Remove the thrust bearing and race from the front side of the planetary gear.

2. Remove the planetary gear snap ring and pull the planetary gear off the output shaft.

3. Measure the planetary gear thrust clearance. The standard clearance is 0.0079-0.0197 in. (0.20-0.50mm).

4. Position the planetary gear assembly on the output shaft and install the planetary gear snap ring.

5. Install the thrust bearing and race.

## REAR CLUTCH

### Disassembly and Assembly

1. Remove the outer clutch pack retaining snap ring from the clutch drum and remove the clutch flange, discs and plates from the drum. If the clutch plates and discs are to be reused, they must be kept in the original order for assembly.

2. Compress the piston return spring using special Toyota tool SST 09350-20013 or its equivalent, in a press. Then remove the snap ring with an appropriate snap ring removal tool.

3. Remove the piston by inserting compressed air into the center support. If the piston does not come out completely, use a pair of pliers to remove it.

4. Remove the rear clutch from the center support and remove the O-rings from the rear clutch piston.

5. Inspect the rear clutch piston, discs, plates, return springs and clutch drum.

6. Install new O-rings and install the inner and outer piston in the clutch drum.

7. Install the piston return springs, spring seat and snap ring in place.

8. Using special Toyota tool SST 09350-20013 or its equivalent, compress the return spring and install the snap ring.

9. Install the clutch discs, plates and flange and install the snap ring.

10. Install the rear clutch onto the center support and using a dial indicator, measure the piston stroke of the rear clutch while applying and releasing compressed air. The standard piston stroke is 0.0386-0.0748 in. (0.98-1.90mm).

**NOTE:** If the piston stroke is higher than the limit, the clutch pack is probably worn. If the stroke is less than the limit, the parts may be assembled wrong or there may be excess ATF on the clutch discs.

## CENTER SUPPORT ASSEMBLY

### Disassembly and Assembly

1. Remove the center support assembly from the sun gear.

2. Remove the snap ring from the front of the center support assembly and remove the clutch flange, disc and plate (No. 1 brake).

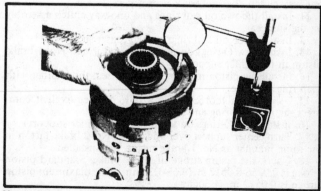

**Measuring the piston stroke** (© Toyota Motor Corporation)

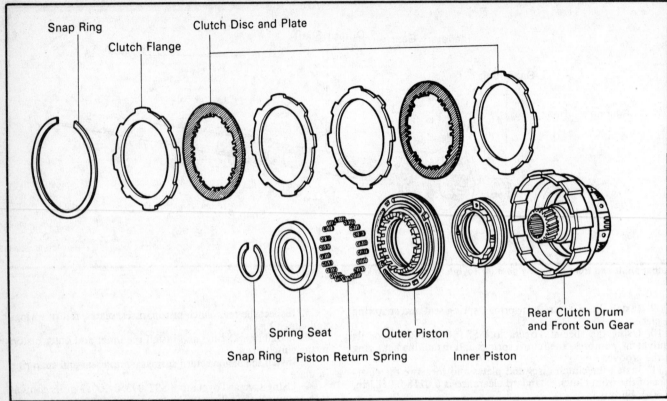

**Rear clutch components** (© Toyota Motor Corporation)

3. Compress the piston return springs using special Toyota tool SST 09350-20013 or its equivalent, in a press. Remove the snap ring with an appropriate snap ring removal tool.

4. Remove the No. 1 brake piston by inserting compressed air into the center support. If the piston does not pop out, use a pair of pliers to remove the piston.

5. Remove the No. 1 brake piston O-rings.

6. Turn the center support assembly over and remove the rear snap ring on No. 2 brake.

7. Disassemble the No. 2 brake assembly in the same manner as the procedure for the No. 1 brake assembly.

8. Remove the three oil seal rings from the center support.

9. Remove the one-way clutch assembly and oil seal rings from the sun gear.

10. Check the operation of the one-way clutch by holding the No. 2 brake hub and turning the sun gear. The sun gear should turn freely counter clockwise and should lock clockwise. If the one-way clutch does not work properly, replace it.

11. Install the two oil seal rings and one-way clutch assembly on the sun gear.

12. Install three oil seal rings on the center support.

13. Install new O-rings on the piston and install No. 1 brake piston in the center support.

14. Install the piston return springs and seat the retainer with snap ring, in place.

15. Using special tool SST 09350-20013 or its equivalent, compress the return spring and install the snap ring.

16. Install new O-rings on the piston and center support.

17. Turn center support over and install No. 2 brake piston in the same manner as No. 1 brake piston was installed.

18. Check the piston stroke of No. 1 brake. Standard piston stroke is 0.0256-0.0512 in. (0.65-1.30mm). The maximum piston stroke is 0.0512 in. (1.30mm).

19. Check the piston stroke of No. 2 brake. Standard piston

stroke is 0.0366-0.0677 in. (0.93-1.72mm). The maximum piston stroke is 0.0677 in. (1.72mm).

20. Assemble the center support and sun gear shaft.

## REAR NO. 2 ONE-WAY CLUTCH AND PLANETARY GEAR

### Disassembly and Assembly

1. Remove the snap ring and remove the one-way clutch.

2. Remove No. 2 thrust washer from rear planetary gear.

3. Install No. 2 thrust washer in front of the planetary pinion gear. Be sure to face the lugs downward and match them with the slots in the back of the planetary gear.

4. Install the one-way clutch into the outer race facing the spring cage toward the front.

5. Make sure that the one-way clutch operates properly and then install the reaction plate on the planetary.

## TRANSAXLE CASE AND REAR BRAKE PISTON

### Disassembly and Assembly

1. Using special tool 09350-20013 or its equivalent, compress the return springs and remove the spring retainer snap ring, spring retainer and the eighteen springs.

2. Insert compressed air into the oil hole in the transaxle case to remove the outer piston and reaction sleeve.

3. Inspect the transaxle case and remove and replace the manual shaft oil seals.

4. Install new O-rings on the piston and install the piston into the transaxle case.

5. Align the portion of the piston marked "A" with the groove on the transaxle case marked "B".

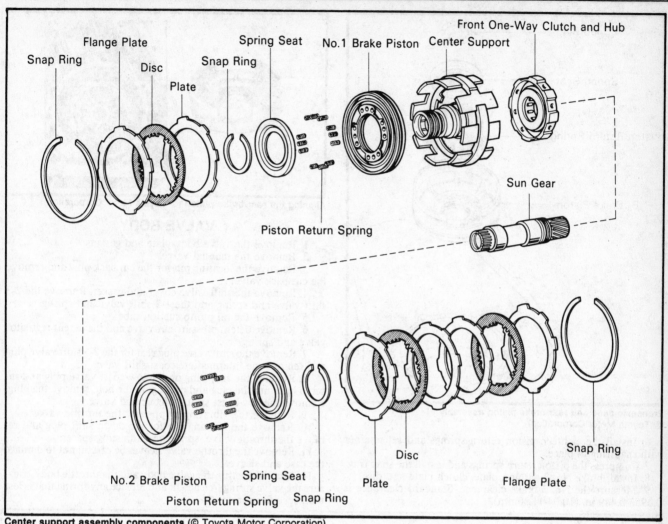

**Center support assembly components** (© Toyota Motor Corporation)

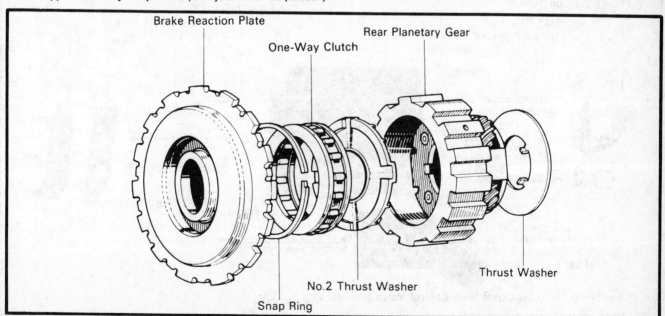

**Rear No. 2 one-way clutch and planetary gear assembly** (© Toyota Motor Corporation)

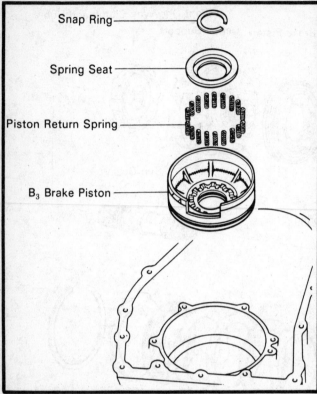

Snap Ring

Spring Seat

Piston Return Spring

B₃ Brake Piston

**Transaxle case and rear brake piston assembly**
(© Toyota Motor Corporation)

6. Install the eighteen piston return springs and set retainer with snap ring in place.

7. Compress the piston return springs and install the snap ring.

8. Install brake No. 3 cushion plate, clutch plate and disc.

9. Measure the No. 3 brake clearance. Standard clearance is 0.3953-0.449 in. (10.04-11.30mm).

**Aligning the rear brake piston** (© Toyota Motor Corporation)

## VALVE BODY

1. Remove the valve body plate and gaskets.

2. Remove the manual valve.

3. Remove the locating pin for the cut back plug and remove the cut back valve.

4. Remove the shift valve cover and gasket. Remove the 2-3 shift valve and spring and the 1-2 shift valve and spring.

5. Remove the oil pump suction tube.

6. Remove detent pressure cut valve and the detent regulator valve and spring.

7. Remove the shift valve plug seat for the 2-3 shift valve plug and remove the intermediate-coast shift valve.

8. Remove the snap ring on the low-coast valve plug and insert a bolt into the plug and pulling on the bolt, remove the plug. Remove the low-coast spring, sleeve and valve.

9. Remove the vibrating stopper for the throttle valve.

10. Remove the locating pin for the down shift plug and remove the throttle valve, spring and adjusting spacer.

11. Remove the throttle valve sleeve. Be careful not to damage the case and sleeve.

12. After inspecting the valve body and the throttle body, measure the valve spring free height and replace any spring that is less than specifications:

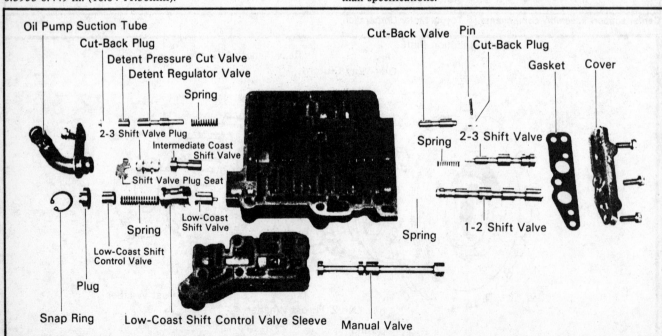

**Valve body assembly** (© Toyota Motor Corporation)

Oil Pump Suction Tube
Cut-Back Plug
Detent Pressure Cut Valve
Detent Regulator Valve
Spring
2-3 Shift Valve Plug
Intermediate Coast Shift Valve
Shift Valve Plug Seat
Spring
Low-Coast Shift Control Valve
Plug
Snap Ring
Low-Coast Shift Valve
Low-Coast Shift Control Valve Sleeve
Manual Valve
Spring
Cut-Back Valve    Pin
Cut-Back Plug
Gasket    Cover
Spring    2-3 Shift Valve
1-2 Shift Valve

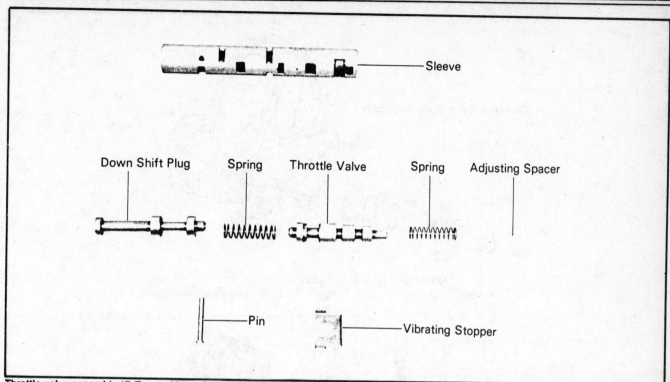

**Down Shift Plug** | **Spring** | **Throttle Valve** | **Spring** | **Adjusting Spacer**

Sleeve

Pin

Vibrating Stopper

**Throttle valve assembly** (© Toyota Motor Corporation)

## VALVE SPRING FREE LENGTH

| Valve Spring | Free Length in. (mm) |
|---|---|
| Throttle valve spring (Rear) | 1.0827 (27.50) |
| Throttle valve spring (Front) | 1.1823 (30.03) |
| Detent regulator valve spring | 1.0787 (27.40) |
| 2-3 shift valve spring | 0.8701 (22.10) |
| 1-2 shift valve spring | 1.0236 (26.00) |
| Low-coast shift valve | 1.4370 (36.50) |

13. Install the low-coast shift valve and the low-coast shift control valve.

14. Install the 1-2 shift valve plug and snap ring.

15. Install the intermediate-coast shift valve.

16. Install the 2-3 shift valve plug and the 2-3 shift valve plug seat.

17. Install detent regulator valve with spring and the detent pressure cut valve.

18. Install the oil pump suction tube.

19. Install the 1-2 shift valve and spring and the 2-3 shift valve and spring.

20. Install the shift valve cover and gasket. Torque the bolts to 48 in. lbs. (5.4 N•m).

21. Install the cut-back valve with plug and the cutback retainer. Coat the pin with petroleum jelly to keep it in place.

22. When assembling the throttle valve, be sure to use the same amount of adjusting spacers that were removed at disassembly.

23. Install the throttle valve and spring into the throttle sleeve and assemble the sleeve to the transaxle case.

24. Push down shift plug forward and install the location pin.

25. Install the valve vibrating stopper. Apply petroleum jelly to keep it in place and check to see that the throttle valve slides smoothly.

## GOVERNOR

### Disassembly and Assembly

1. Remove the snap ring and remove the governor body support.

2. Remove the retaining ring and pull the governor body from the governor support.

3. Remove the E-ring and the governor weight.

4. Slide it down through the bore and remove the governor valve.

5. Measure the governor spring free-height and replace it if it is less than specifications. Standard free-height 0.7717 in. (19.60mm).

6. Check the governor body and support and oil seal ring for wear or damage.

7. Check the governor pressure adapter and oil seal for wear or damage. Remove and replace the oil seal.

**Installing the vibrating stopper** (© Toyota Motor Corporation)

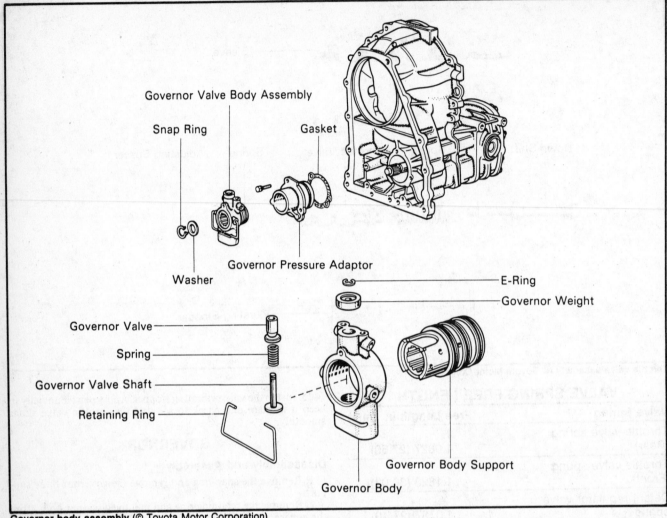

Governor Valve Body Assembly

Snap Ring

Gasket

Governor Pressure Adaptor

Washer

E-Ring

Governor Weight

Governor Valve

Spring

Governor Valve Shaft

Retaining Ring

Governor Body Support

Governor Body

**Governor body assembly** (© Toyota Motor Corporation)

8. Install the governor valve, spring and shaft to the governor body.

9. Compress the governor valve spring and install the governor weight and E-ring on the governor shaft.

10. Install the governor body to the governor support.

11. Install a new O-ring on the governor pressure adapter and coat the O-ring and the drive pinion with grease. Install the governor pressure adapter.

12. Insert the oil strainer into the adapter and torque the adapter mounting bolts to 48 in. lbs. (5.4 N•m).

13. Install the governor valve assembly and check to see that the governor assembly is operating smoothly.

## Transaxle Assembly

1. Install the thrust washer, facing the cup side downward, and the bearing. Use petroleum jelly to keep the small parts in place.

2. Install the rear planetary ring gear and No. 3 brake cushion plate, disc and plate.

3. Install the thrust bearing and coat the race with petroleum jelly and attach it to the ring gear.

4. After aligning the notch and the tab, install the rear planetary gear and thrust washer.

5. With the disc flukes aligned, install the rear planetary gear.

6. Measure the clearance of No. 3 brake. Standard clearance is 0.3953-0.4449 in. (10.04-11.30mm).

7. Align the portion of the reaction plate marked "A" with the portion of the transaxle case marked "B" and install the reaction plate and snap ring.

8. Align the oil hole and the bolt hole of the center support with those of the body side and insert the center support assembly into the transaxle case.

9. Install the two center support bolts and washers. Torque the bolts to 19 ft. lbs. (25 N•m).

10. Install the rear clutch assembly into the transaxle case and install the thrust bearing race.

11. Install the output shaft and the front planetary gear. Install the thrust bearing and race.

12. Install the front clutch assembly into the transaxle case.

13. Using a clutch drum height gauge or its equivalent, measure the distance between the top surface of the transaxle case and the front clutch assembly. If the distance is within specifications, the front clutch is installed correctly.

**NOTE: Also use the measurement found at disassembly. Height: 0.024-0.063 in. (0.6-1.6mm).**

14. Install the thrust bearing and race. Install an O-ring on the transaxle case.

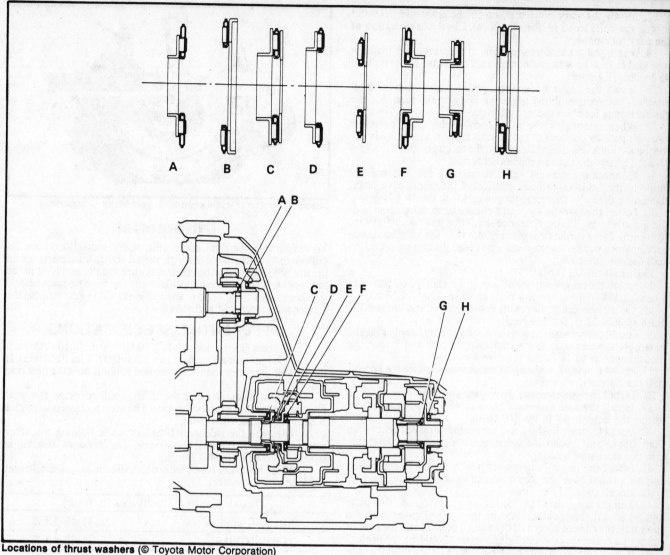

Locations of thrust washers (© Toyota Motor Corporation)

15. Install the thrust washer on the front support and install the front support on the transaxle case.

**NOTE: If there is a clearance between the surfaces of the front support and the transaxle case when installing the front support, the front clutch is not completely installed.**

16. Tighten the front support bolts in a diagonal order a little at a time, with the final torque being 14 ft. lbs. (19 N•m).

17. Check the front clutch input shaft thrust play. Thrust play: 0.0094-0.0378 in. (0.24-0.96mm).

18. Check the front clutch output shaft thrust play. Thrust play: 0.0122-0.0602 in. (0.31-1.53mm).

19. Install the bearing on the drive sprocket and install the thrust race on the transaxle case.

20. Install input shaft, drive sprocket chain and driven sprocket and install the snap ring.

21. Check the thrust clearance between the snap ring and the driven sprocket. Thrust clearance is 0.0043-0.0272 in. (0.11-0.69mm).

22. Install the thrust race on the oil pump and install the oil pump. Torque the oil pump bolts gradually to 13 ft. lbs. (18 N•m).

23. Check to see that the oil pump drive gear rotates smoothly and then check the input shaft thrust play. Thrust play is 0.0039-0.0276 in. (0.10-0.70mm).

24. Install the oil pump delivery tube and the oil pump pressure tubes.

25. Install the manual lever shaft into the transaxle case and drive in the slotted spring pin. After assembly, turn the spacer 90° degrees and stake it.

**NOTE: Always replace the spacer and the slotted spring pin with a new one. Never reuse a slotted spring pin.**

26. Install the park pawl, pivot pin and spring into the transaxle case.

Measuring the thrust clearance (© Toyota Motor Corporation)

27. Install the park pawl bracket on the transaxle case and torque the bolts to 65 in. lbs. (7.4 N•m). Check the operation of the park lock pawl.

28. Install the accumulator pistons and springs and install a new gasket and the accumulator cover. Torque the cover bolts to 48 in. lbs. (5.4 N•m).

29. Install the valve body plate, gasket, valve body and oil strainer (before assembling the valve body, make sure that the cut-back plug lock pin did not fall out).

30. When assembling the valve body to the upper transaxle case, be sure to connect the oil pump suction pipe. Gradually torque the bolts in a diagonal order to the torque of 48 in. lbs. (5.4 N•m). Tighten the suction pipe bracket bolt.

31. Connect the manual valve connecting rod and manual valve to the front valve body and install the front valve body, tightening the bolts to a final torque of 48 in. lbs. (5.4 N•m).

32. Install the throttle lever and check the thrust clearance of the throttle lever. Thrust clearance should be less than 0.0197 in. (0.50mm). If the thrust clearance is more than the specified clearance, insert a washer on the outer side of the throttle lever and install the throttle cover.

33. Install the oil tubes.

34. Install the magnets in the oil pan and install the oil pan with a new gasket. Torque the pan bolts to 65 in. lbs. (7.4 N•m).

35. Install the drain plug with a new gasket and torque the drain plug to 22 ft. lbs. (29 N•m).

36. Install the transaxle gasket and the governor apply gaskets. Assemble the transaxle to the transmission case and torque the mounting bolts to 14 ft. lbs. (19 N•m).

37. Install a new oil seal ring to the output shaft sleeve and install the output shaft sleeve.

38. Install the speedometer drive gear and snap ring.

39. Install the rear extension housing with a new gasket and torque the bolts to 14 ft. lbs. (19 N•m).

40. Install O-rings, bushing and speedometer driven gear to the shaft sleeve and install the speedometer driven gear assembly into the extension housing.

41. Install the neutral safety switch with the slit in the switch and the neutral base line match up and tighten the bolt and nut.

42. Install the oil filler tube.

43. Temporarily install the torque converter to the drive plate and set up a dial indicator. Measure the torque converter sleeve runout. If the runout exceeds 0.0118 in. (0.30mm) and the runout cannot be corrected, the torque converter should be replaced.

44. If the torque converter has been drained, then refill the converter with 1.1 U.S. quarts of the recommended ATF and install the converter in the transaxle.

45. Check the torque converter installation by using calipers and a straight edge. Measure from the installed converter center piece surface to the front surface of the transaxle housing. Correct distance is more than 0.31 in. (8mm).

**Checking converter installation** (© Toyota Motor Corporation)

## Differential

To reassemble the final drive unit, many special tools are required and are available through varied sources. Instructions on the use of the tools during reassembly are usually included in the tool packs. The required specifications for bearing preload and gear backlash are included in the outline to aid in determining the proper tolerances and preloads.

### DIFFERENTIAL SPECIFICATIONS

1. The ring gear backlash is 0.0039-0.0059 in. (0.10-0.15mm).

2. The maximum ring gear run out is 0.0028 in. (0.07mm). If the runout is greater than the specified runout, install a new ring gear.

3. Before disassembling the differential, measure the total preload on the drive pinion bearing. The total preload (starting) is 5.2-8.7 in. lbs. (0.6-1.0 N•m).

4. Measure the side gear backlash while holding the other side gear towards the differential case. The standard backlash is 0.0016-0.0094 in. (0.04-0.24mm).

5. If the backlash is not within specifications, use a different thickness thrust washer.

| Thrust Washer Thickness in. (mm) | |
| --- | --- |
| 0.0583-0.0598 | (1.48-1.52) |
| 0.0602-0.0618 | (1.53-1.57) |
| 0.0622-0.0638 | (1.58-1.62) |
| 0.0642-0.0657 | (1.63-1.67) |
| 0.0661-0.0667 | (1.68-1.72) |
| 0.0681-0.0697 | (1.73-1.77) |

**Measuring the sleeve run-out** (© Toyota Motor Corporation)

**Measuring the preload** (© Toyota Motor Corporation)

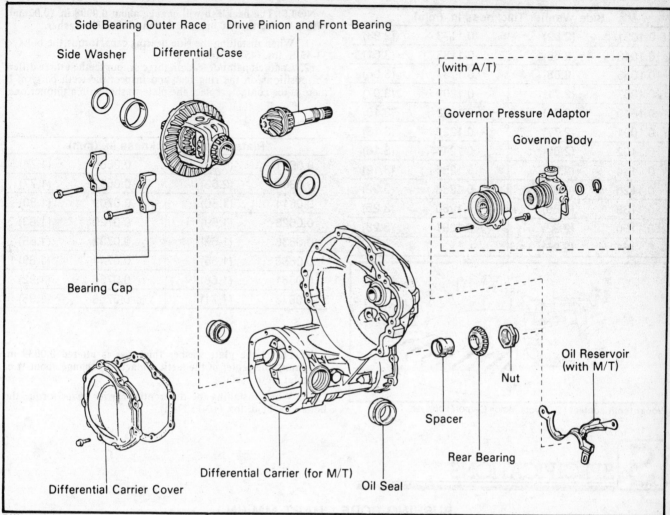

**Differential components** (© Toyota Motor Corporation)

6. The torque for the ring gear set bolts is 67-75 ft. lbs. (91-102 N•m).

7. The torque for the drive pinion lock nut is 108 ft. lbs. (147 N•m).

8. Drive pinion bearing preload:
New bearing: 4.3-8.7 in. lbs. (0.5-1.0 N•m).
Reused bearing: 2.6-4.3 in. lbs. (0.3-0.5 N•m).

9. Push the side bearing boss on the teeth surface of the ring gear and measure the backlash: 0.0039 in. (0.10mm).

10. Select a ring gear back side washer using the backlash as reference.

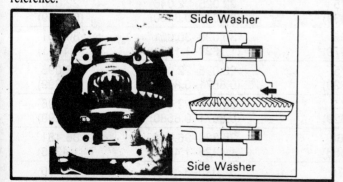

**Location of the side washers** (© Toyota Motor Corporation)

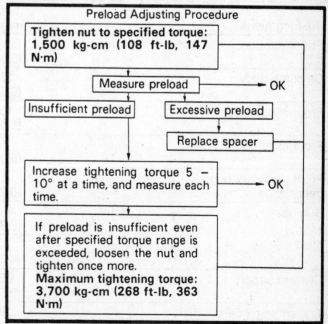

**Preload adjusting procedures** (© Toyota Motor Corporation)

### Side Washer Thickness in. (mm)

| | | | |
|---|---|---|---|
| 0.1031 | (2.62) | 0.1173 | (2.98) |
| 0.1043 | (2.65) | 0.1185 | (3.01) |
| 0.1055 | (2.68) | 0.1197 | (3.04) |
| 0.1067 | (2.71) | 0.1209 | (3.07) |
| 0.1079 | (2.74) | 0.1220 | (3.10) |
| 0.1091 | (2.77) | 0.1232 | (3.13) |
| 0.1102 | (2.80) | 0.1244 | (3.16) |
| 0.1114 | (2.83) | 0.1256 | (3.19) |
| 0.1126 | (2.86) | 0.1268 | (3.22) |
| 0.1138 | (2.89) | 0.1280 | (3.25) |
| 0.1150 | (2.92) | 0.1291 | (3.28) |
| 0.1161 | (2.95) | | |

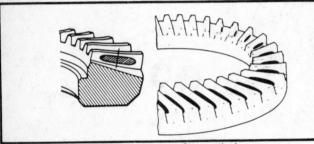

Proper teeth contact (© Toyota Motor Corporation)

**NOTE:** The backlash will change about 0.0008 in. (0.02mm) with a 0.0012 in. (0.03mm) variation of the side washer.

11. When installing the side bearing caps, torque the bolts to 33-39 ft. lbs. (45-53 N•m).

12. Coat red paint or lead on three or four teeth at three different positions on the ring gear and inspect the teeth pattern. If there is toe contact, replace the plate washer with a thinner one.

### Plate Washer Thickness in. (mm)

| | | | |
|---|---|---|---|
| 0.0591 | (1.50) | 0.0685 | (1.74) |
| 0.0602 | (2.53) | 0.0697 | (1.77) |
| 0.0614 | (1.56) | 0.0709 | (1.80) |
| 0.0626 | (1.59) | 0.0720 | (1.83) |
| 0.0638 | (1.62) | 0.0732 | (1.86) |
| 0.0650 | (1.65) | 0.0744 | (1.89) |
| 0.0661 | (1.68) | 0.0756 | (1.92) |
| 0.0673 | (1.71) | 0.0768 | (1.95) |

**NOTE:** If the plate washer thickness is altered 0.0039 in. (0.10mm), the center of the teeth contact will change about ⅛ of the total teeth surface.

12. When installing the differential carrier cover torque the bolts to 8-11 ft. lbs. (10-15 N•m).

# S SPECIFICATIONS

## BUSHING BORE CHART MM (IN.)

| Bushing name | | Length mm (in.) | Finished bore mm (in.) | Bore limit mm (in.) |
|---|---|---|---|---|
| Stator support | Front | 9.75 (0.3839) | 16.000–16.018 (0.6299–0.6306) | 16.068 (0.6326) |
| Oil pump body | | 13.46 (0.5299) | 38.125–38.150 (1.5010–1.5020) | 38.200 (1.5039) |
| Front support | | 10.75 (0.4232) | 31.038–31.063 (1.2220–1.2230) | 31.113 (1.2249) |
| Front clutch drum | | 9.75 (0.3839) | 22.025–22.046 (0.8671–0.8680) | 22.096 (0.8699) |
| Front planetary ring gear flange | | 6.55 (0.2579) | 30.025–30.051 (1.1821–1.1831) | 30.101 (1.1851) |
| Sun gear | Front | 9.75 (0.3839) | 22.025–22.046 (0.8671–0.8680) | 22.096 (0.8699) |
| | Rear | 9.75 (0.3839) | 22.025–22.046 (0.8671–0.8680) | 22.096 (0.8699) |
| Center support | | 65.68 (2.5858) | 36.386–36.411 (1.4325–1.4335) | 36.461 (1.4355) |
| Transmission case | | 10.75 (0.4232) | 32.025–32.050 (1.2608–1.2618) | 32.100 (1.2638) |

## SPRING SPECIFICATIONS
### Coil Spring

| Item | Piston Return Spring (Forward-Reverse Clutch) in. (mm) | Brake Piston Return Spring (B1,B2) in. (mm) | (B3) |
|---|---|---|---|
| Free Length | 1.1378 (28.90) | 0.6346 (16.12) | 1.0303 (26.17) |
| Coil Outside Diameter | 0.315 (8.00) | 0.0315 (8.00) | 0.3110 (7.90) |
| Number of Coils | 12 | 6 | 9 |

## SPECIFICATION OF SPRINGS IN THE VALVE BODY ASSEMBLY

| Item | Free length mm (in.) | Coil outside diameter mm (in.) | No. coils | Wire Diameter mm (in.) |
|---|---|---|---|---|
| Regulator valve | 55.80 (2.1968) | 18.10 (0.7126) | 8.5 | 1.6 (0.063) |
| Valve body | | | | |
| 1-2 shift valve | 26.00 (1.0236) | 5.15 (0.2028) | 14.5 | 0.5 (0.020) |
| Low-coast valve | 36.50 (1.4370) | 8.60 (0.3386) | 16 | 1.2 (0.047) |
| 2-3 shift valve | 22.10 (0.8701) | 6.40 (0.2520) | 9.5 | 0.6 (0.024) |
| Detent regulator | 27.40 (1.0787) | 8.00 (0.3150) | 10 | 1.0 (0.039) |
| Throttle valve | | | | |
| Front | 30.03 (1.1823) | 8.55 (0.3366) | 8.9 | 0.9 (0.035) |
| Rear | 27.50 (1.0827) | 7.40 (0.2913) | 10.25 | 0.6 (0.024) |
| Accumulator | | | | |
| Front | 67.00 (2.6378) | 17.80 (0.7008) | 12.5 | 2.3 (0.091) |
| Rear | 38.42 (1.5126) | 14.03 (0.5524) | 10 | 2.03 (0.0799) |
| Governor valve | 19.60 (0.7717) | 9.40 (0.3701) | 6 | 0.80 (0.0315) |
| T/C check ball valve | 26.20 (1.0315) | 6.60 (0.2598) | 14 | 0.60 (0.0236) |
| Priming valve | 19.20 (0.7559) | 6.30 (0.2480) | 9 | 0.65 (0.0256) |

## TORQUE SPECIFICATIONS

| Description | Torque |
|---|---|
| Transaxle mount bolts | 14 ft. lbs. (19 N•m) |
| Extension housing bolts | 14 ft. lbs. (19 N•m) |
| Neutral safety swtich | 9 ft. lbs. (13 N•m) |
| Drive plate bolts | 47 ft. lbs. (64 N•m) |
| Torque converter bolts | 13 ft. lbs. (18 N•m) |
| Oil pump bolts | 13 ft. lbs. (18 N•m) |
| Center support | 19 ft. lbs. (25 N•m) |
| Valve body bolts | 48 in. lbs. (5.4 N•m) |
| Oil pan bolts | 65 in. lbs. (7.4 N•m) |

## TORQUE SPECIFICATIONS

| Description | Torque |
|---|---|
| Oil pump cover bolts | 13 ft. lbs. (18 N•m) |
| Front support bolts | 14 ft. lbs. (19 N•m) |
| No. 3 valve body cover bolt | 48 in. lbs. (5.4 N•m) |
| Accumulator piston cover | 48 in. lbs. (5.4 N•m) |
| Governor pressure adapter | 48 in. lbs. (5.4 N•m) |
| Oil cooler pipe nut | 25 ft. lbs. (34 N•m) |
| Pressure testing plug | 65 in. lbs. (7.4 N•m) |
| Parking lock pawl bracket | 65 in. lbs. (7.4 N•m) |
| Oil pan drain plug | 22 ft. lbs. (29 N•m) |

# INDEX

# TOYOTA A140E AUTOMATIC TRANSAXLE

##  APPLICATIONS

| Model | Year | Engine Number | Transmission Number |
|-------|------|---------------|---------------------|
| Camry | 1983-84 | 2S-E | A-140-E |

##  GENERAL DESCRIPTION

The Toyota A-140-E transaxle is housed in a one piece aluminum die-cast case. The oil sump is divided by two oil seals on the transfer shaft to maintain a proper oil level in the transfer area and for efficient lubrication of the differential gear area. The transaxle is composed of a simple planetary gear set, an overdrive direct clutch disengaging in 4th gear, a one-way clutch and an overdrive brake engaging in 4th gear. The 4th gear unit and the transfer drive gear are arranged on the output shaft of the 3-speed unit in a compact package. It is supported by a long span of the ball bearing and the needle bearing. This transaxle also incorporates a electro-hydraulic control system and a electronically controlled torque converter. The electro-hydraulic control system is intended to improve fuel economy, performance and shift quality by precise control of the shift points and timing according to the signals from nine sensors through a preprogrammed microprocessor, located on the fire wall on the passenger side of the vehicle. The lock-up torque converter is also controlled by the electro-hydraulic control system and is applied in second, third and fourth gears.

### Transmission and Converter Identification

#### TRANSMISSION

An identification plate is normally located on the left side of the transaxle case, with the model and serial number stamped on the plate. Should a transaxle be encountered without an identification plate, check the identification information plate on the firewall in the engine compartment and also this plate is on the top of the instrument panel and driver's door post. If there is still no transaxle model number found, examine the transaxle case for identifying code letters or digits. Also, obtain the vehicle model and serial number before ordering replacement parts.

#### CONVERTER

The converter is a welded unit and cannot be disassembled by the average repair shop. This converter incorporates a lock up clutch which is controlled by the electro-hydraulic control system. If internal malfunctions occur, the converter must be replaced. No specific identification is given for quick identification by the repairman. Should converter replacement be necessary, order from the information given on the model and the serial number plate.

### Metric Fasteners

Metric bolt sizes and thread pitches are used for all fasteners on the A-55 transaxle. The metric fasteners dimensions are very close to the dimensions of the familiar inch system fasteners, and for this reason, replacement fasteners must have the same measurement and strength as those removed.

Do not attempt to interchange metric fasteners for inch system fasteners. Care should be taken to reuse the fasteners in the same locations as removed, whenever possible. Mismatched or incorrect fasteners can result in damage to the transmission unit through malfunctions, breakage or possible personal injury.

### Fluid Specifications

The fluid used in the 1983-84 A-140-E transaxle is Dexron® II. No other fluids should be used in this transaxle, unless specified by the manufacturer.

#### FLUID CAPACITY CHART

|  | Liters | U.S. Qts. | Imp. Qts. |
|---|--------|-----------|-----------|
| Drain and refill | 2.4 | 2.5 | 2.1 |
| Dry refill | 6.0 | 6.3 | 5.3 |

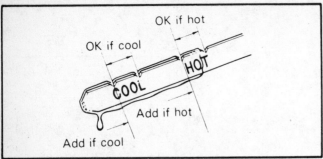

**Checking the fluid level** (© Toyota Motor Sales Co. Ltd.)

## Checking Fluid Level

The fluid level should be checked when the transaxle is at normal operating temperature.

1. With the engine idling and the parking brake engaged, de- press the brake pedal and shift the selector into each position from park to low and then return to park.

2. Pull out the transaxle dipstick and wipe it clean.

3. With the dipstick clean, push it back fully into the dipstick tube.

4. Pull the dipstick out again and check to see if the fluid is in the "HOT" range.

5. If the fluid is low, add the recommended ATF fluid until the fluid level reaches the "HOT" range.

# M MODIFICATIONS

There have been no major modifications to the A-140-E transaxle at the time of this printing

# TROUBLE DIAGNOSIS

## CLUTCH APPLICATION CHART
### Toyota A-140-E

| Gear | Clutch 0 | Clutch 1 | Clutch 2 | Brake 0 | Brake 1 | Brake 2 | Brake 3 | One-way Clutch 1 | One-way Clutch 2 |
|---|---|---|---|---|---|---|---|---|---|
| P | Off | Off | Off | Off | Off | Off | Off | Off | Off |
| R | On | Off | On | Off | Off | Off | On | Off | Off |
| N | Off | Off | Off | Off | Off | Off | Off | Off | Off |
| D-1st | On | On | Off | Off | Off | Off | Off | Off | Holding |
| D-2nd | On | On | Off | Off | On | Off | Off | Holding | Off |
| D-3rd | On | On | On | Off | Off | On | Off | Off | Off |
| O-D Lock-up | Off | On | On | On | Off | On | Off | Off | Off |
| 2-1st | On | On | Off | Off | Off | Off | Off | Off | Holding |
| 2-2nd | On | On | Off | Off | On | On | Off | Holding | Off |
| 2-3rd | On | On | On | Off | Off | On | Off | Off | Off |
| L-1st | On | On | Off | Off | Off | Off | On | Off | Holding |

## CHILTON'S THREE "CS" DIAGNOSIS CHART
### Toyota A-140-E

| Condition | Cause | Correction |
|---|---|---|
| Fluid discolored or smells burnt | a) Fluid contamination<br>b) Torque converter faulty<br>c) Transmission is faulty | a) Replace the fluid<br>b) Replace the torque converter<br>c) Disassemble and inspect the transmission |
| Vehicle does not move in any forward range or reverse | a) Manual linkage out of adjustment<br>b) Valve body or primary regulator faulty<br>c) Transmission faulty | a) Adjust the linkage<br>b) Inspect valve body<br>c) Disassemble and inspect transmission |

## CHILTON'S THREE "CS" DIAGNOSIS CHART
### Toyota A-140-E

| Condition | Cause | Correction |
|---|---|---|
| Vehicle does not move in any range | a) Park lock pawl faulty<br>b) Valve body or primary regulator faulty<br>c) Torque converter faulty<br>d) Broken converter drive plate<br>e) Oil pump intake screen blocked<br>f) Transmission faulty | a) Inspect park pawl<br>b) Inspect valve body<br><br>c) Replace the torque converter<br>d) Replace the torque converter<br>e) Clean the screen<br>f) Disassemble and inspect transmission |
| Shift lever position is incorrect | a) Manual linkage out of adjustment<br>b) Manual valve and lever faulty<br>c) Transmission faulty | a) Adjust linkage<br>b) Inspect valve body<br>c) Disassemble and inspect transmission |
| Slips on 1-2, 2-3 or 3-OD up-shift, or slips or shudders on take-off | a) Control cable out of adjustment<br>b) Throttle cable out of adjustment<br>c) Valve body faulty<br>d) Solenoid valve faulty<br>e) Transmission faulty | a) Adjust control cable<br>b) Adjust throttle cable<br>c) Inspect valve body<br>d) Inspect valve body<br>e) Disassemble and inspect transmission |
| Drag, binding or tie-up on 1-2, 2-3 or 3-OD up-shift | a) Control cable out of adjustment<br>b) Valve body faulty<br>c) Transmission faulty | a) Adjust control cable<br>b) Inspect valve body<br>c) Disassemble and inspect transmission |
| No lock-up in 2nd, 3rd or OD | a) Electric control faulty<br>b) Valve body faulty<br>c) Solenoid valve faulty<br>d) Transmission faulty | a) Inspect electric control<br>b) Inspect valve body<br>c) Inspect valve body<br>d) Disassemble and inspect transmission |
| Harsh down-shift | a) Throttle cable out of adjustment<br>b) Throttle cable and cam faulty<br>c) Accumulator pistons faulty<br>d) Valve body faulty<br>e) Transmission faulty | a) Adjust throttle cable<br>b) Inspect throttle cable and cam<br>c) Inspect accumulator pistons<br>d) Inspect valve body<br>e) Disassemble and inspect transmission |
| No down-shift when coasting | a) Valve body faulty<br>b) Solenoid valve faulty<br>c) Electric control faulty | a) Inspect valve body<br>b) Inspect solenoid valve<br>c) Inspect electric control |
| Down-shift occurs too quick or too late while coasting | a) Throttle cable faulty<br>b) Valve body faulty<br>c) Transmission faulty<br><br>d) Solenoid valve faulty<br>e) Electric control faulty | a) Inspect throttle cable<br>b) Inspect valve body<br>c) Disassemble and inspect transmission<br>d) Inspect solenoid valve<br>e) Inspect electric control |
| No OD-3, 3-2 or 2-1 kickdown | a) Solenoid valve faulty<br>b) Electric control faulty<br>c) Valve body faulty | a) Inspect solenoid valve<br>b) Inspect electric control<br>c) Inspect valve body |
| Harsh engagement into any drive range | a) Throttle linkage out of adjustment<br>b) Valve body or primary regulator faulty<br>c) Accumulator pistons faulty<br>d) Transmission faulty | a) Adjust throttle linkage<br>b) Inspect valve body<br><br>c) Inspect accumulator pistons<br>d) Disassemble and inspect transmission |

## CHILTON'S THREE "CS" DIAGNOSIS CHART
### Toyota A-140-E

| Condition | Cause | Correction |
|---|---|---|
| No engine braking in "2" or "L" range | a) Solenoid valve faulty<br>b) Electric control faulty<br>c) Valve body faulty<br>d) Transmission faulty | a) Inspect the solenoid valve<br>b) Inspect the electric control<br>c) Inspect the valve body<br>d) Disassemble and inspect the transmission |
| Vehicle does not hold in "P" | a) Control cable is out of adjustment<br>b) Parking lock pawl cam and spring faulty | a) Adjust the control cable<br>b) Inspect the cam and spring |

In order to properly diagnose transmission problems and avoid making second repairs for the same problem, all of the available information and knowledge must be used. Included is a list of the components of the transaxle and their functions. Also, test procedures and their accompanying specification charts aid in finding solutions to problems. Further answers are found by road testing vehicles and comparing results of the above A-140-E transaxle diagnosis chart. This chart gives conditions, cause and correction to most possible trouble conditions in the A-140-E transaxle.

### ELECTRONICALLY CONTROLLED TRANSMISSION

When trouble occurs with the ECT system, the trouble can be caused by either the engine, ECT electronic control or the auto-

matic transmission itself. These areas should be distinctly isolated before proceeding with troubleshooting the ECT system. Troubleshoot the ECT system as follows:

1. Remove the instrument panel box and the right side speaker box.
2. Turn the ignition switch to the on position.
3. Using the proper circuit tester measure the voltage at each electrical terminal.

### Hydraulic Control System

The main parts of the hydraulic control system for the A-140-E transaxle are the, torque converter, oil pump, cooler and lubrication circuits, valve body and applying clutches and brakes. The system is controlled by the Electro-hydraulic control system. This

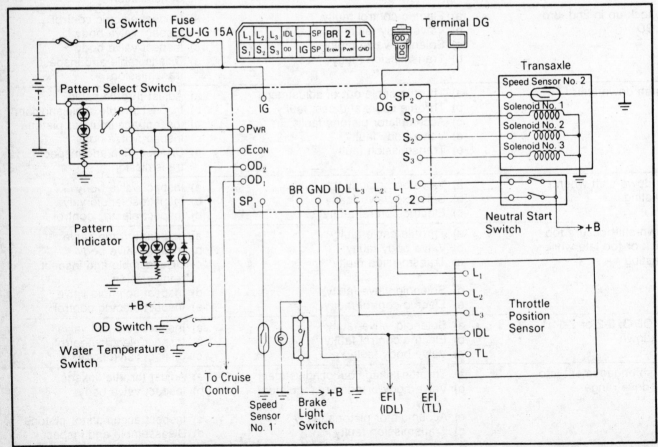

Electronic control circuit (© Toyota Motor Sales Co. Ltd.)

## ELECTRONIC CONTROL CIRCUIT TROUBLESHOOTING CHART
### Toyota A-140-E

| Terminal | Measuring condition | Voltage (V) | |
|---|---|---|---|
| | | DENSO type computer | AISIN type computer |
| L₁-GND | Throttle valve fully closed | 5 | 12 |
| | Throttle valve fully closed full open | 5 to 0 | 12 to 0 |
| | Throttle valve fully open | 0 | 0 |
| L₂-GND | Throttle valve fully closed | 5 | 12 |
| | Throttle valve fully closed to full open | 5 to 0 to 5 | 12 to 0 to 12 |
| | Throttle valve fully open | 5 | 12 |
| L₃-GND | Throttle valve fully closed | 5 | 12 |
| | Throttle valve fully closed to full open | 5 to 0 to 5 to 0 to 5 | 12 to 0 to 12 to 0 to 12 |
| | Throttle valve fully open | 5 | 12 |
| IDL-GND | Standing still | 0 | 12 |
| | Throttle valve opening above 1.5° | 4 | 4 |
| SP₁-GND | Standing still | 12 or 0 | 12 or 0 |
| | Engine running, vehicle moving | 6 | 6 |
| BR-GND | Brake pedal depressed | 12 | 12 |
| | Brake pedal not depressed | 0 | 0 |
| 2-GND | 2 range | 9 to 16 | 9 to 16 |
| | Except 2 range | 0 to 2 | 0 to 2 |
| L-GND | L range | 9 to 16 | 9 to 16 |
| | Except L range | 0 to 2 | 0 to 2 |
| S₁-GND | — | 12 | 12 |
| S₂, S₃-GND | — | 0 | 0 |
| OD₁-GND | Coolant temp. below 70°C | 0 | 0 |
| | Coolant temp. above 70°C | 5 | 12 |
| OD₂-GND | OD switch turn ON | 12 | 12 |
| | OD switch turn OFF | 0 | 0 |
| IG-GND | Standing still | 12 | 12 |
| SP₂-GND | Standing still | 5 or 0 | 12 or 0 |
| | Engine running | 4 | 10 |
| PWR-GND | PWR pattern | 12 | 12 |
| | Except PWR pattern | 1 | 1 |
| ECON-GND | ECON pattern | 12 | 12 |
| | Except ECON pattern | 1 | 1 |

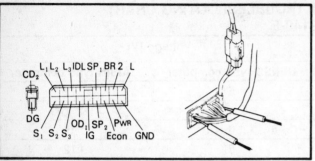

**Measuring the voltage** (© Toyota Motor Sales Co. Ltd.)

conventional involute gear pump. The pump has the capacity to supply the necessary hydraulic pressure for operating from low speed to high speed and when reversing.

## Diagnosis Tests
### TIME LAG TEST

When the shift lever is shifted while the engine is idling, there will be a certain time delay (lag) before the shock on the transaxle can be felt. This time delay (lag) is used for checking the condition of the overdrive clutch, forward clutch, direct clutch and first and reverse brake.

**Measuring Lag Time**

1. Start the vehicle and bring the engine and transaxle up to normal operating temperature.
2. With the parking brake fully engaged, shift the shift lever from "N" to "D" range.
3. Using a stop watch or a wrist watch, measure the time it takes from shifting the lever until the shock is felt, (average lag time is less than 1.2 seconds).
4. Now shift the shift lever from "N" to "R" range and measure the time lag, (average lag time is less than 1.5 seconds).

**NOTE: Allow at least one minute intervals between tests. Make three measurements and then calculate the average lag time.**

**TIME LAG TEST RESULT INDICATIONS**

If the shift from "N" to "D" time lag is longer than specified, the problems could be,
1. The line pressure is too low.
2. The front clutch could be badly worn.
3. The OD one-way clutch is not operating properly.

system incorporates nine sensors and electronic signals, from these nine sensors are inputted into an ECU (Electronic Control Unit), which outputs its computation results into three solenoid valves. Two of these three valves control the transmission clutch and one controls the lock-up clutch inside the torque converter. These three shift valves are a simple straight type. They operate by solenoid and clutch pressures, both of which acts as a signal pressure in the normal drive "D" range. The lock-up clutch engages in 2nd, 3rd and 4th gears. These engagements are controlled by the solenoid switching clutch pressure which is generated as a signal pressure of the lock-up relay valve in 2nd, 3rd and 4th gears.

The oil pump is used to send the ATF fluid to the torque converter, to lubricate the inner working parts of the transaxle and to supply the operating pressure for the hydraulic control. The oil pump drive gear has a special tooth profile, this tooth profile is originated from the hypocychloid curve instead of the involute curve. Since the gear features an enlarged displacement per tooth, its width is narrowed to approximately two-thirds of that of a

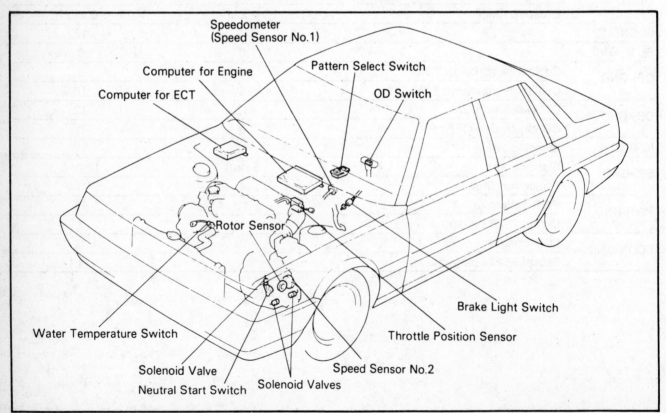

**Electronic control circuit components** (© Toyota Motor Sales Co. Ltd.)

If the shift from "N" to "R" time lag is longer than specified, the problems could be,
1. The line pressure is too low.
2. The direct clutch is badly worn.
3. The OD one-way clutch is not operating properly.

## HYDRAULIC TESTS

### Line Pressure Test

1. Engage the parking brake and chock all four wheels.
2. Connect an oil pressure gauge to the line pressure port on the transaxle.
3. Start the engine and bring it up to normal operating temperature.
4. Shift the shift lever into the "D" position and measure the line pressure at the speeds specified in the chart below:

### LINE PRESSURE CHART

| Engine Speed | Line Pressure "D" Range | PSI "R" Range |
|---|---|---|
| Idling | 53-61 | 77-102 |
| Stall | 131-152 | 205-239 |

5. In the same manner, perform the line pressure test for the "R" range.

**NOTE: If the measured line pressures are not within specifications, recheck the throttle cable adjustment and retest.**

### LINE PRESSURE TEST RESULT INDICATIONS

If the line pressure is higher than specified,
1. The throttle cable is out of adjustment.
2. The throttle valve is defective.
3. The regulator valve is not operating properly.
If the line pressure is lower than specified,
1. The throttle valve is defective.
2. The throttle cable is out of adjustment.
3. The regulator valve is not operating properly.
4. The oil pump could be defective.
5. The over-drive clutch is not operating properly.
If the line pressure is low in the "D" range only.
1. There is a possible fluid leakage in the "D" range circuit.
2. The forward clutch is defective.
If the line pressure is low in the "R" range only.
1. There is a possible fluid leakage in the "R" range circuit.
2. The first and reverse brake is not operating properly.
3. The direct clutch is defective.

## ROAD TEST

### Road Test With Selector in "P"

1. With the vehicle parked on a small grade, put the selector lever in the "P" position and release the parking brake.
2. If the vehicle does not roll backwards then the parking system is working properly.

### Road Test With Selector in "R"

1. Start the engine and while running at full throttle check the transaxle for slipping.

### Road Test With Selector in "D"

1. Increase speed of the vehicle and while holding the accelerator pedal steady check to see if the transaxle makes the 1-2, 2-3, 3-OD and lock-up upshifts at the correct vehicle speed.
2. If there is no 1-2 upshift:
   a. The No. 2 solenoid is stuck.
   b. The 1-2 shift valve is not operating properly.

3. If there is no 2-3 upshift:
   a. The No. 1 solenoid is stuck.
   b. The 2-3 shift valve is not operating properly.
4. If there is no 3-OD upshift:
   a. The 3-OD shift valve is not operating properly.
5. If the lock-up is defective:
   a. The No. 3 solenoid is stuck.
   b. The lock-up relay valve is stuck.
6. While running in the "D" range, 2nd and 3rd gears and over-drive check to see if the 2-1, 3-1, 3-2, OD-3 and OD-2 kickdown shifts occur properly at the specified kickdown limit vehicle speeds.
7. Drive in third gear, and select "2" range than the "L" range to check if the engine brake is effective. Also check for hard shifting and slipping at this time.
8. While driving in the "D" range shift the selector to the "L" range to check if the OD-3, 3-2 and 2-1 downshifts occur at the proper vehicle speed.

### Road Test With Selector in "2"

1. While driving with the selector lever in the "2" position increase the vehicle speed, and check to see that the transaxle makes the 1-2 upshift at the proper vehicle speed. Also check for noise and shock at the time of shifting.
2. Check to see if the 2-1 kickdown occurs at correct vehicle speed limit.

### Road Test With Selector in "L"

1. While running in the "L" range, check to see that there is no up-shift to 2nd gear.
2. Check for noise in either acceleration or deceleration.

## Converter Stall Test

The object of this test is to check to the overall performance of the transaxle and the engine by measuring the maximum engine speeds at the "D" and "R" ranges.

### Measuring Stall Speed

1. Engage the parking brake and chock all four wheels.
2. Attach a tachometer to the engine and place it in a position to be seen.
3. Start the engine and bring the vehicle up to normal operating temperature.
4. Apply the foot brake and shift the selector lever to the "D" position.
5. With foot brake applied gradually depress the accelerator pedal until the engine reaches full throttle.
6. When the engine speed is stabilized, read that speed quickly and release the accelerator pedal.
7. Shift the selector lever to the "N" position, and cool down the engine by letting the engine idle for 2 to 5 minutes (specified stall speed 2,200 ± 150 rpm).
8. Record the stall speed and perform the stall test with the selector lever in the "R" position.

**NOTE: Do not perform the stall test longer than 5 seconds as damage to the transaxle can occur.**

### Interpretation of Stall Test Results

If the stall speed is lower than specified.
1. Engine output could be insufficient.
2. Stator one-way is not operating correctly.

**NOTE: If the stall speed is more than 600 rpm below the specified stall speed, the torque converter could defective.**

If the stall speed in the "D" position is higher than specified.
1. The front clutch could be slipping.
2. One-way clutch number 2 is not operating correctly.
3. The line pressure could be too low.

4. The over-drive one-way clutch is not operating properly.

If the stall speed in the "R" position is higher than specified.

1. The line pressure could be too low.
2. Improper fluid level.
3. The over-drive one-way clutch is not operating properly.

## THE LOCK-UP TORQUE CONVERTER

To eliminate power loss and fuel waste, Toyota has added a mechanical clutch inside the torque converter. It firmly locks the engine to the transaxle with virtually no slippage, and that means less fuel waste. The lock-up clutch is controlled by the ECT system, which applies the clutch in 2nd, 3rd, and 4th gears. Along with the lock-up torque converter there's the ECT shift pattern select switches. Located on the dash or console in the Camry, the switches allows the driver to select normal, power and economy shift patterns to suit the drivers immediate driving needs. In the normal pattern the ECT shifts according to a computer program developed by the manufacture. In the economy pattern the computer is instructed to introduce a modified lock-up torque converter schedule, causing the torque converter to lock-up at a lower speed. In this way less slippage occurs during city driving, result-

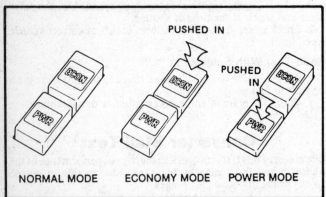

Shift pattern select switches (© Toyota Motor Sales Co. Ltd.)

ing in better fuel economy. In the power pattern the ECT computer adopts an entirely different shift pattern, instead of concentrating on vehicle speed the computer concentrates on the driver's demand on the throttle pedal. Lock-up operation occurs just as in the normal pattern and the result is later upshifts and more responsive downshifts to better respond to the driver's commands.

**NOTE:** The ETC provides identical fuel economy in all three patterns when driving on the open highway. Its effect is only noticeable during around-town and city driving.

## Adjustments

### NEUTRAL SAFETY SWITCH

**Adjustment**

1. Connect an Ohmmeter between the two electrical terminals on the neutral safety switch.
2. Shift the selector lever into the "N" position.
3. Adjust the switch to the point where there is continuity between the terminals.
4. Lock down the switch with the two mounting bolts.

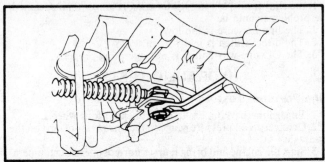

Adjusting the shift linkage (© Toyota Motor Sales Co. Ltd.)

## TRANSAXLE SHIFT LINKAGE

**Adjustment**

1. Loosen the swivel nut on the shift linkage lever.
2. Push the manual lever fully forward toward the right side of the vehicle and return the lever two notches to the neutral position.
3. Set the shift lever to the "N" position and while holding the lever lightly toward the "R" position, tighten the swivel nut.

## THROTTLE LINK

**Adjustment**

1. Remove the air cleaner and check to see if the throttle lever and the throttle link are not bent or damaged.
2. Push on the throttle lever and see if the throttle valve opens fully.
3. Using a pedal jack or its equivalent, fully depress and hold the accelerator pedal to the floor.
4. Loosen the turnbuckle lock nut and adjust the throttle linkage length by turning the turnbuckle.
5. The adjustment will be correct when the throttle valve lever indicator lines up with the mark on the transaxle case.
6. Now tighten the turnbuckle lock nut and recheck the adjustment.
7. Install the air cleaner and remove the pedal jack from the accelerator pedal.

## THROTTLE CABLE

**Adjustment**

1. Remove the air cleaner hose, then depress the accelerator pedal all the way to see if the throttle valve opens fully.
2. Fully depress the accelerator pedal and loosen the adjustment nuts on the throttle cable.
3. Adjust the throttle cable so that the distance between the end of the cable boot and the stopper on the cable is 0.04 in. (0-1mm).
4. Tighten the adjusting nuts, recheck the adjustments and install the air cleaner hose.

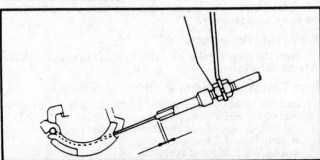

Adjusting the throttle cable (© Toyota Motor Sales Co. Ltd.)

## Services

### FLUID AND FILTER CHANGE

The normal service interval for changing transmission fluid and replacing or cleaning oil filters is 24,000 miles. When the vehicle is used in more severe operating conditions such as, heavy city driving, constant hill climbing and pulling a trailer the fluid should be check more often and the transmission should be service more frequently.

#### Procedure

1. Raise the vehicle on a safe lift.
2. Place a oil drain pan under the transaxle.
3. Remove the drain plug and drain all the ATF fluid out of the transaxle.
4. Remove the 15 oil pan bolts and remove the pan and gasket.
5. Inspect the pan and the magnet in the bottom of the pan for any steel chips or any other particles.

**NOTE: If there is any steel chips in the pan it could mean that a bearing, gear or a clutch plate are wearing out. If there is brass in the bottom of the pan it could mean that a bushing is wearing out.**

6. Remove the three oil filter mounting bolts and remove the oil filter. Inspect the filter and clean or replace it.
7. Install the oil filter and torque the three mounting bolts to 7 ft. lbs. (10 N•m).
8. Install the oil pan with a new gasket to the transaxle case. Torque the 15 oil pan bolts to 43 inch lbs. (4.9 N•m).
9. Install the drain plug with a new gasket and torque the drain plug to 22 ft. lbs.
10. Refill the transaxle with 2.5 U.S. quarts of the recommended ATF fluid. Start the engine and run it at idle. Check the fluid level and if the level is low add the necessary fluid to bring the level up to the "HOT" range on the dipstick.

### VALVE BODY

#### Removal & Installation

1. Raise the vehicle on a safe hoist, drain the ATF and remove the oil pan.
2. Remove the oil filter and disconnect the solenoid connectors.
3. Pry up both ends of the oil pressure tubes with a screwdriver and remove the oil tubes.
4. Remove the manual detent valve, manual valve and valve body.
5. Disconnect the throttle cable from the cam, remove the 12 valve body bolts and remove the valve body.
6. Remove the second brake apply gasket.
7. Install the second brake apply gasket and place the valve body on the transaxle.
8. Connect the throttle cable to the cam and with the valve body in position install the 12 valve body bolts. Torque the bolts to 7 ft. lbs.

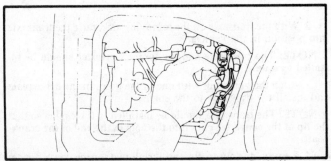

**Disconnecting the solenoid** (© Toyota Motor Sales Co. Ltd.)

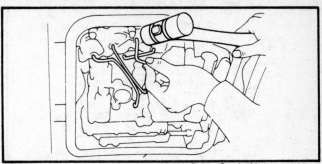

**Installing the oil tubes** (© Toyota Motor Sales Co. Ltd.)

9. Connect the two solenoid connectors to each solenoid.
10. Align the manual valve with the pin on the manual shift lever and torque the manual valve body bolts to 7 ft. lbs. (10 N•m).
11. Instal lthe detent spring and torque the hold down bolts to 7 ft. lbs. (10 N•m).
12. Using a plastic hammer install the oil tubes in their proper positions.
13. Install the oil filter and the oil pan with a new gasket to the transaxle case, torque the oil pan bolts to 43 inch lbs. (4.9 N•m).
14. Refill the transaxle with 2.5 U.S. quarts of the recommended ATF fluid. Start the engine and run it at idle, check the fluid level and if the level is low add the necessary fluid to bring the level up to the "HOT" range on the dipstick.

### ACCUMULATOR

#### Removal and Installation

To remove the accumulator pistons and springs, first drain the ATF and remove the oil pan and the oil tubes as previously outlined.

1. Remove the five accumulator cover bolts one turn at a time until the spring tension is released, then remove the cover and the gasket.
2. Remove the accumulator pistons and springs by blowing low pressure compressed air (14 psi) into the air holes around the accumulator cylinders.
3. Position a rag under the accumulator pistons to catch the pistons as they come out of the cylinders.

**NOTE: Do not use high pressure to remove the accumulator pistons and keep face away from pistons to avoid injury.**

Before installing the accumulator pistons and springs, check the pistons, springs, cover and cylinder for wear or damage.

4. Install new O-rings around the accumulator pistons and coat the O-rings with ATF.
5. Install the springs and pistons into their bores, and install the cover with a new gasket. Torque the bolts gradually to 7 ft. lbs. (10 N•m).
6. Install the oil tubes and oil pan and refill the transaxle with the recommended ATF.

### SPEED SENSOR

#### Removal and Installation

1. Remove the left front drive shaft and remove the transaxle dust cover.
2. Remove the two bolts and the support bracket and remove the speed sensor and O-ring.
3. Inspect the speed sensor by connecting an ohmmeter to the speed sensor and check that the meter deflects when the sensor is brought close to a magnet and removed from it.
4. Install the speed sensor with a new O-ring and coat the O-ring with ATF.

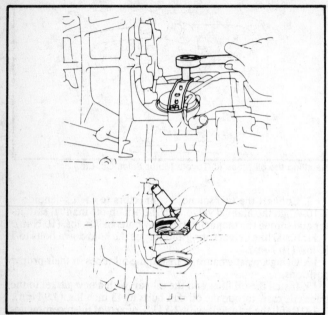

Speed sensor removal or installation (© Toyota Motor Sales Co. Ltd.)

5. Install the support bracket and the bracket bolts and torque the bolts to 9 ft. lbs. (13 N•m).
6. Install the transaxle dust cover and the left front drive shaft.

## THROTTLE CABLE

### Removal and Installation

1. Disconnect the throttle cable from the bracket and the throttle linkage.
2. Remove the clip and disconnect the transaxle control cable from the manual shift lever and remove the shift lever.
3. Remove the neutral safety switch.
4. Drain the ATF and remove the valve body as previously outlined.
5. Remove the one bolt retaining plate and pull the cable out of the transaxle case.
6. Push the new throttle cable all the way in the transaxle and install the one bolt retaining plate.
7. Install the valve body (as previously outlined).
8. Connect the throttle bracket to the throttle linkage and to the housing bracket. Adjust the throttle cable (see adjustment section.)
9. Install the neutral safety switch and the manual shift lever. Adjust the neutral safety switch (see adjustment section).
10. Connect the transaxle control cable and adjust the cable (see adjustment section), then test drive the vehicle.

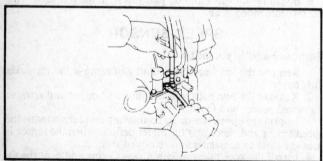

Installing the retainer plate (© Toyota Motor Sales Co. Ltd.)

# REMOVAL & INSTALLATION

## REMOVAL

1. Disconnect the positive battery cable.
2. Disconnect the electrical connectors to the neutral safety switch and the back-up light switch.
3. Remove the air cleaner assembly.
4. Remove the throttle link.
5. Remove the oil cooler pipe clamp.
6. Using two wrenches disconnect the oil cooler inlet pipe.
7. Remove the upper transaxle set bolts.
8. Raise the vehicle and support it safely, and drain the ATF.
9. Position a transmission jack or its equivalent under the transaxle and remove the front and rear transaxle mounts.
10. Remove the left side dust cover and mounting bracket.
11. Remove the side gear shaft, intermediate shaft and universal joint from the transaxle.
12. Remove the transaxle control cable bracket and stiffener plate.
13. Remove the torque converter dust cover and locking plate, then remove the six torque converter mounting bolts (turn the crankshaft to gain access to each bolt).
14. Remove the starter motor and the lower transaxle mounting bolts.
15. While turning the crankshaft, pry on the torque converter to separate it from the drive plate.
16. With the transaxle free of any obstructions, lower the jack and remove the transaxle from the vehicle.

### Installation

Before installing the transaxle, apply grease to the center hub of the torque converter and the pilot hole in the crankshaft.
1. Insert a guide pin in the most outward converter mounting hole.

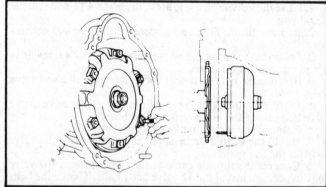

Installing the guide pin (© Toyota Motor Sales Co. Ltd.)

2. With the transaxle on the removing jack, raise the transaxle into position in the vehicle.
**NOTE: The transaxle and the torque converter should be installed as a unit.**
3. Align the guide pin with one of the holes in the drive plate and install the transaxle to the engine.
**NOTE: The transaxle should be installed to the engine so that the tip of the converter goes into the hole in the end of the crankshaft.**
4. Remove the guide pin and install two torque converter set bolts about half way in and tighten them evenly.

5. Install the 5 transaxle mounting bolts and torque the bolts to 47 ft. lbs.

6. Install the starter motor and the other four torque converter mounting bolts (do not forget to remove the guide pin) torque the bolts to 13 ft. lbs. (18 N•m).

7. Install the torque converter cover.

8. Using two wrenches connect the oil cooler outlet pipe, the torque for the nuts is 16 ft. lbs., and install the stiffener plate.

9. Install the control cable bracket.

10. Install the side gear shaft, intermediate shaft and universal joint.

11. Install the left side dust cover and mounting bracket.

12. Install the front and rear transaxle mounting and remove the removing jack.

13. Lower the vehicle and install the upper transaxle mounting bolts, torque the bolts to 47 ft. lbs.

14. Using two wrenches connect the oil cooler inlet pipe and install oil cooler pipe clamp.

15. Connect the throttle link and the electrical connectors to the neutral safety switch and the back-up light switch.

16. Adjust the throttle link (see adjustment section).

17. Install the air cleaner assembly and connect the positive battery cable.

18. Refill the transaxle with 2.5 U.S. quarts of the recommended ATF.

**NOTE: If the torque converter has been drained, then the transaxle should be filled with 6.3 U.S. quarts of the recommended ATF.**

19. Perform a road test to check the operation of the transaxle and to check the front end alignment.

20. Check for fluid leaks and for differential gear oil leaks.

# Unit Disassembly and Assembly

## OIL PUMP

When disassembling and assembling the oil pump be sure to replace all O-rings and seals. Inspect all oil pump gears and check the gear clearances. Driven gear body clearance: 0.0028-0.0059 (0.07-0.15mm). Gear tip clearance: 0.0043-0.0055 in. (0.11-0.14mm). Gear side clearance: 0.0008-0.0020 in. (0.02-0.05mm).

## DIRECT CLUTCH

Replace all O-rings with new ones and apply ATF to the O-rings when installing them. Using a feeler gauge measure the clearance of the direct clutch. Direct Clutch Clearance: 0.0173-0.0437 in. (0.44-1.11mm).

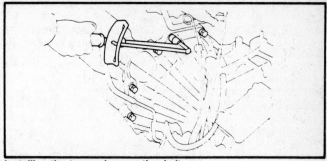

Installing the transaxle mounting bolts (© Toyota Motor Sales Co. Ltd.)

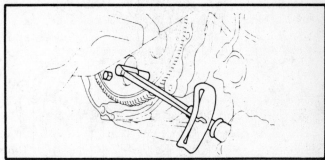

**Installing the torque converter** (© Toyota Motor Sales Co. Ltd.)

## FORWARD CLUTCH

When reassembling the forward clutch make sure that the check ball in the clutch piston is free by shaking the piston and check to see if the valve leaks, by applying low pressure compressed air. Also measure the clearance of the forward clutch. Forward Clutch Clearance: 0.0163-0.0429 in. (0.414-1.090mm).

## NO. 1 ONE-WAY CLUTCH AND SUN GEAR

When disassembling and assembling the one-way clutch and sun gear, check the operation of the one-way clutch by holding the sun

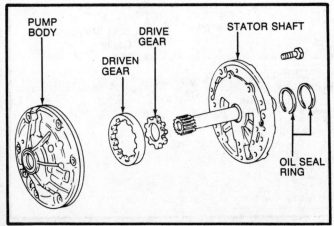

**Exploded view of the oil pump** (© Toyota Motor Sales Co. Ltd.)

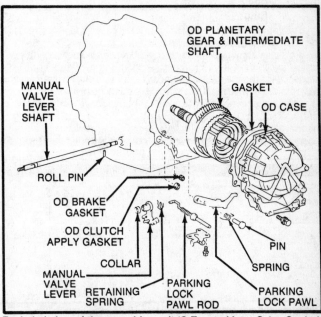

**Exploded view of the over drive unit** (© Toyota Motor Sales Co. Ltd.)

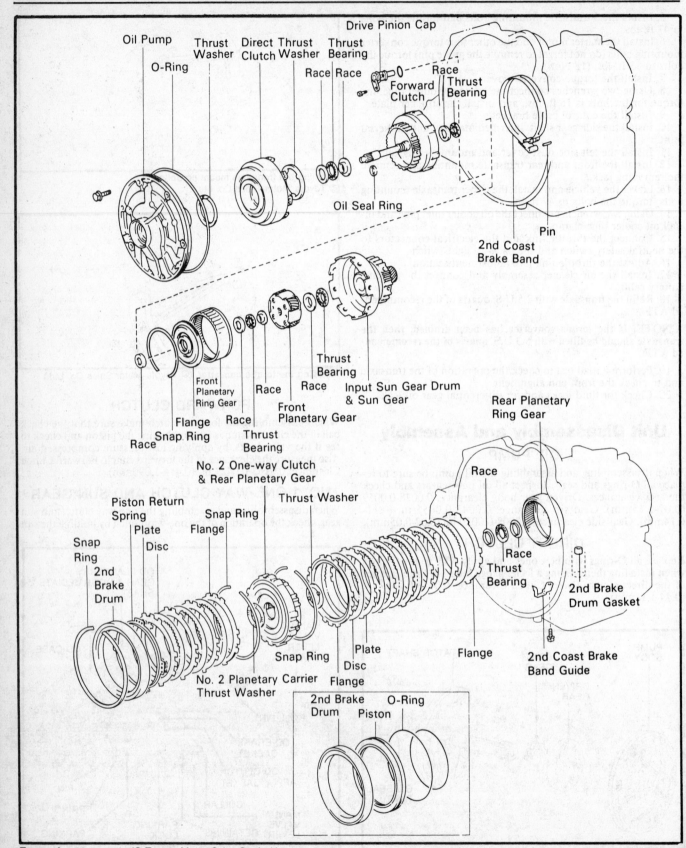

Transaxle components (© Toyota Motor Sales Co. Ltd.)

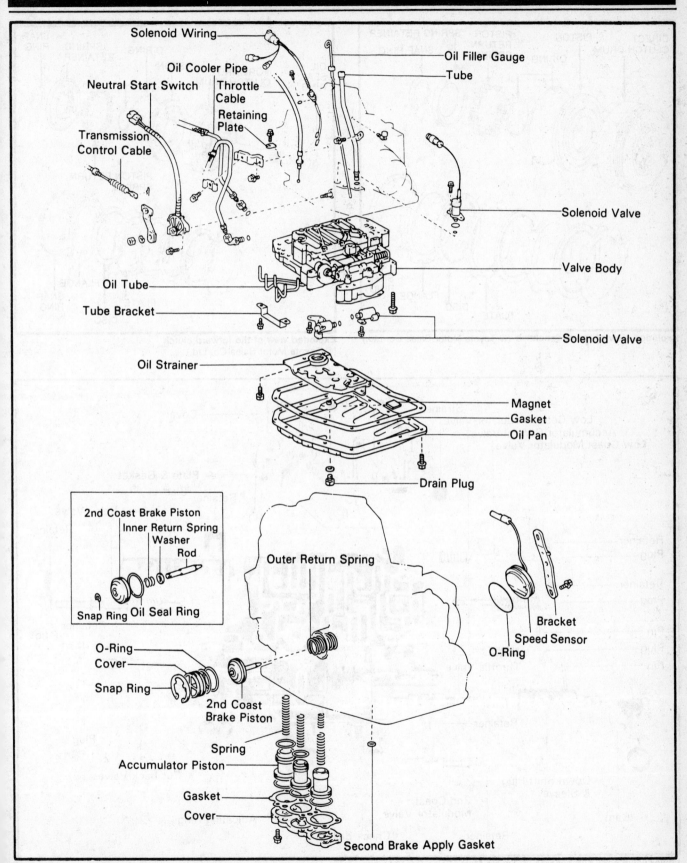

Transaxle components (© Toyota Motor Sales Co. Ltd.)

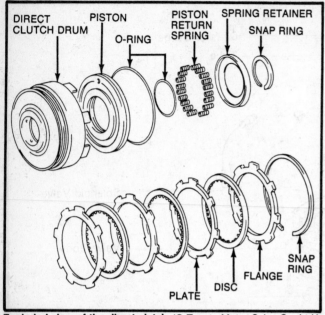

**Exploded view of the direct clutch** (© Toyota Motor Sales Co. Ltd.)

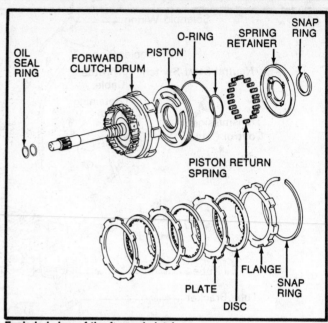

**Exploded view of the forward clutch**
(© Toyota Motor Sales Co. Ltd.)

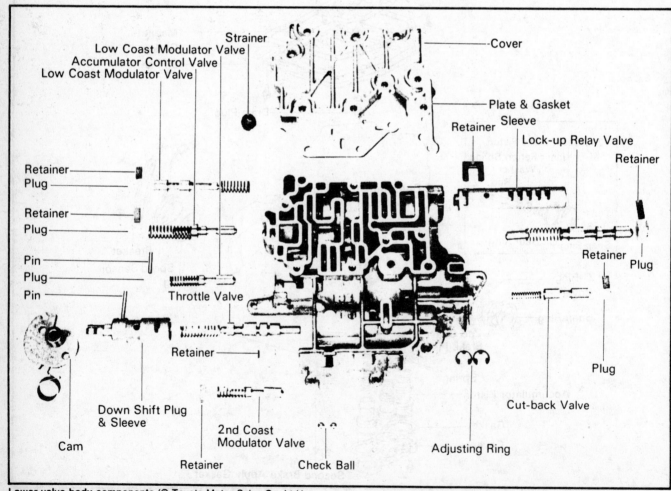

**Lower valve body components** (© Toyota Motor Sales Co. Ltd.)

gear input drum and turning the hub. The hub should turn freely clockwise and should lock-up when turned counterclockwise. If the one-way clutch does not operate properly, it should be replaced.

## NO. 2 ONE-WAY CLUTCH AND REAR PLANETARY GEAR

Check the operation of the No. 2 one-way clutch in the same manner as the No. 1 one-way clutch was checked. When assembling the one-way clutch, be sure to install the one-way clutch into the outer race, facing the flange cage toward the oil pump side.

## FIRST AND REVERSE BRAKE PISTON

When removing the piston from the transaxle case compressed air must be applied to the oil passage of the transaxle case in order to remove the piston. If the piston does not pop out with the compressed air, use needle nose pliers to remove it. Install new O-rings and apply ATF when installing them.

## OVERDRIVE UNIT

When disassembling and assembling the overdrive unit be sure to measure the clearance of the overdrive brake. To measure the clearance, use a feeler gauge and check the clearance between the cushion plate and the piston. Clearance: 0.0201-0.0661 in. (0.51-1.68mm). Again using a feeler gauge measure the clearance of the overdrive clutch, measure the clearance between the piston and the end of the plate. Clearance: 0.0283-0.0661 in. (0.72-1.68mm). Install all new O-rings and coat the O-rings with ATF. The pre-load for the counter drive bearing is, 2.0-3.4 ft. lbs. (9-15 N•m). If the overdrive gear assembly is properly installed to the overdrive case, the clearance between them will be about 0.138 in. (3.5mm).

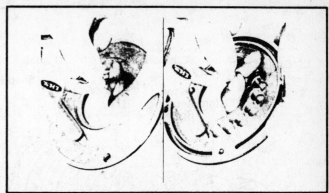

Checking the clutch piston check ball (© Toyota Motor Sales Co. Ltd.)

Checking one-way clutch operation (© Toyota Motor Sales Co. Ltd.)

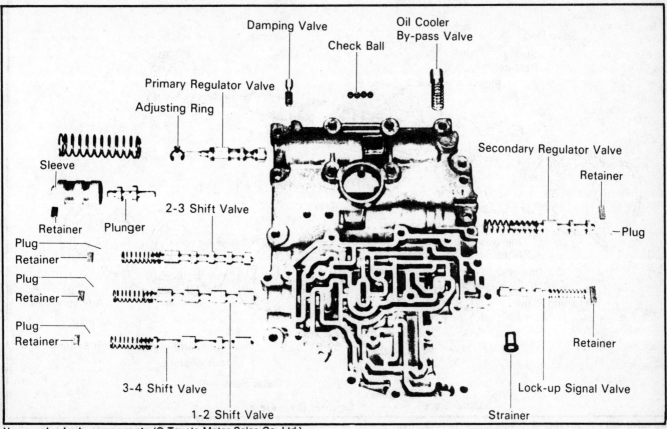

Upper valve body components (© Toyota Motor Sales Co. Ltd.)

- Damping Valve
- Check Ball
- Oil Cooler By-pass Valve
- Primary Regulator Valve
- Adjusting Ring
- Secondary Regulator Valve
- Retainer
- Sleeve
- Retainer
- Plunger
- 2-3 Shift Valve
- Plug
- Retainer
- Plug
- Retainer
- Plug
- Retainer
- Plug
- Retainer
- 3-4 Shift Valve
- 1-2 Shift Valve
- Lock-up Signal Valve
- Strainer

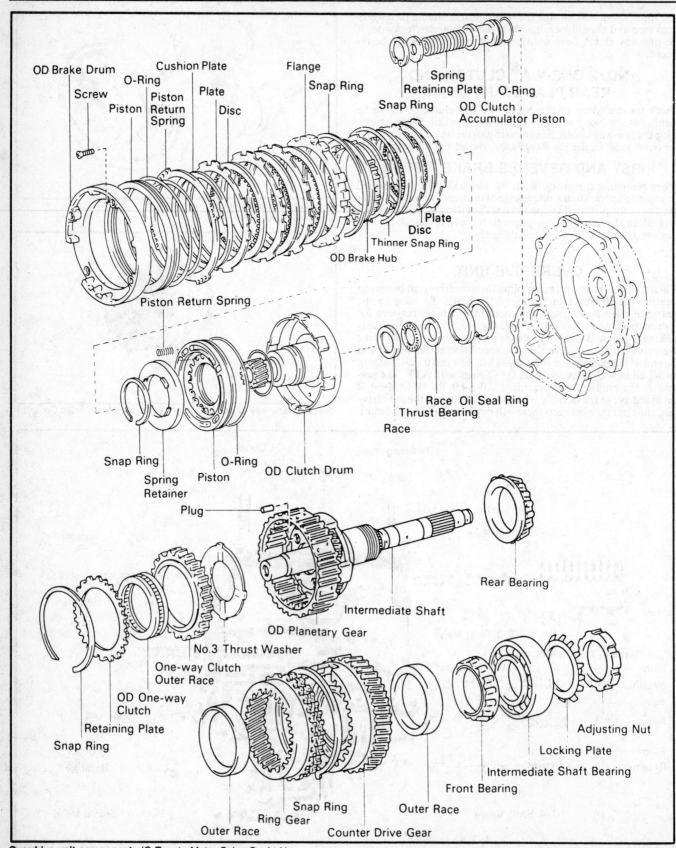

**Overdrive unit components** (© Toyota Motor Sales Co. Ltd.)

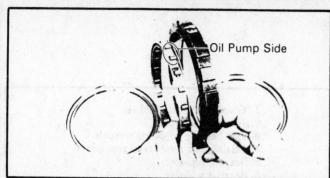

Installing the one-way clutch (© Toyota Motor Sales Co. Ltd.)

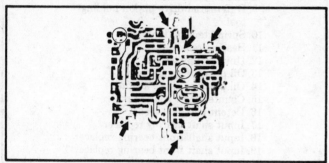

Location of the steel check balls (© Toyota Motor Sales Co. Ltd.)

# S SPECIFICATIONS

## DIFFERENTIAL SPECIFICATIONS
### Toyota A-140-E

|  | In. lbs. | N•m |
|---|---|---|
| **SIDE BEARING PRELOAD** | | |
| New bearing | 8.7-13.9 | 1.0-1.6 |
| Reused bearing | 4.3-6.9 | 0.5-0.8 |
| **DRIVE PINION PRELOAD** | | |
| New bearing | 8.7-13.9 | 1.0-1.6 |
| Reused bearing | 4.3-6.9 | 0.5-0.8 |
| **TOTAL PRELOAD** | | |
| New bearing | 2.5-3.6 | 0.3-0.4 |
| Reused bearing | 1.2-1.7 | 0.1-0.2 |
| **BACKLASH** | | |
| Pinion to side gear | 0.0020-0.0079 | 0.05-0.20mm |

## TORQUE SPECIFICATIONS CHART
### Toyota A-140E

| Description | ft-lb | N•m |
|---|---|---|
| Transmission case x Transaxle case | 22 | 29 |
| Transmission case x Case cover | 13 | 18 |
| Transmission case protector | 13 | 18 |
| Rear bearing retainer | 13 | 18 |
| Output shaft bearing lock plate | 13 | 18 |
| Input shaft oil receiver | 65 in.-lb | 7.4 |
| 5th driven gear lock nut | 90 | 123 |
| Reverse idler shaft lock bolt | 18 | 25 |
| Control shaft cover | 27 | 37 |
| Reverse shift arm bracket | 13 | 18 |
| Reverse shift arm pivot | 13 | 18 |
| Shift fork No. 3 | 9 | 13 |
| Ring gear x Differential case | 71 | 97 |
| Lock ball assembly | 27 | 37 |
| Control shift lever | 56 in.-lb | 6.4 |
| Filler plug | 36 | 49 |
| Drain plug | 36 | 49 |
| Back-up light switch | 33 | 39 |
| Side bearing retainer | 13 | 18 |
| Clutch release bearing retainer | 65 in.-lb | 7.4 |
| Speedometer driven gear lock plate | 48 in.-lb | 5.4 |
| Transaxle case x Lock plate | 18 | 25 |
| Straight screw plug (Shift fork shaft No. 2) | 9 | 13 |
| (Reverse restrict pin holder) | 9 | 13 |
| Transaxle case x Engine          12 mm | 47 | 64 |
| 10 mm | 25 | 34 |
| Bolt locking plate x transaxle | 18 | 25 |
| Stiffener plate x Engine | 27 | 37 |
| Stiffener plate x Transaxle case | 27 | 37 |
| Drive plate | 61 | 37 |
| Torque converter | 13 | 18 |
| Oil pump x Transaxle case | 16 | 22 |
| Oil pump body x Stator shaft | 7 | 10 |
| Second coast brake band guide | 48 in.-lb | 5.4 |
| Upper valve body x Lower valve body | 48 in.-lb | 5.4 |
| Valve body | 7 | 10 |
| Accumulator cover | 7 | 10 |
| Oil strainer | 7 | 10 |
| Oil pan | 43 in.-lb | 4.9 |
| Oil pan drain plug | 22 | 29 |
| Cooler pipe union nut | 25 | 34 |
| Testing plug | 65 in.-lb | 7.4 |
| Parking lock pawl bracket | 65 in.-lb | 7.4 |
| Overdrive case x Transaxle case | 18 | 25 |
| Overdrive brake drum x Overdrive case | 48 in.-lb | 5.4 |

## SPECIAL TOOLS

| | |
|---|---|
| 1 | |
| 2 | |
| 3 | |
| 4 | |
| 5 | |
| 6 | |
| 7 | |
| 8 | |

1. Toyota transaxle tool set
2. Side bearing puller
3. Side bearing adjusting wrench
4. Side washer remover & replacer
5. Bearing replacer
6. Bearing replacer
7. Rear wheel bearing replacer
8. Drive pinion holding tool
9. Differential drive pinion holding tool
10. Spring tension tool
11. Bearing remover
12. Universal puller kit
13. Oil pressure gauge set
14. Oil pressure gauge adapter
15. Counter shaft bearing puller
16. Detent ball plug socket
17. Input shaft bearing replacer
18. Input shaft front bearing replacer
19. Input shaft front bearing replacer
20. Bushing replacer
21. Oil seal puller
22. Oil seal puller
23. Pinion bearing tool set
24. Bearing replacer tool set
25. Tilt handle bearing replacer
26. Transmission oil seal plug
27. Suspension bushing tool set
28. Drive pinion lock nut wrench

| | |
|---|---|
| 9 | |
| 10 | |
| 11 | |
| 12 | |

Special tools (© Toyota Motor Corporation)

| 13 | | 21 | |
|----|----|----|----|
| 14 | | 22 | |
| 15 | | 23 | |
| 16 | | 24 | |
| 17 | | 25 | |
| 18 | | 26 | |
| 19 | | 27 | |
| 20 | | 28 | |

# INDEX

# VOLVO
# AW70 • AW71

GENERAL DESCRIPTION

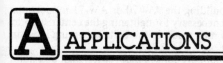

## A APPLICATIONS

| Year | Model Usage | Transmission |
|------|-------------|--------------|
| 82 and later | Volvo GLT Turbo | AW71 |
| 82 and later | Volvo GLT, GL, DL | AW70 |

## G GENERAL DESCRIPTION

The AW70 and AW71 are both three speed automatics with overdrive as the fourth speed. The AW71 is used for somewhat heavier duty applications than the AW70, such as with the higher torque B21F Turbo engine.

The following major components are used:
1. Hydrodynamic torque converter.
2. Hydraulically controlled planetary gear transmission, which includes the overdrive and is located ahead of the three speed planetary gear transmission. The overdrive gear is automatically engaged when a controlling switch is energized.
3. Gear Selector—The sequence being P-R-N-D-2-1.

The entire transmission is contained in a single housing which is bolted to the rear of the engine, and operated using a single mechanical hookup. A starter inhibitor switch and reverse light switch is also provided. Valve bodies on both units are located on the bottom. The overdrive gear ratio of 0.69:1 is obtained in fourth gear.

## Transmission and Converter Identification

### TRANSMISSION

The AW70 automatic transmission model is used in the Volvo

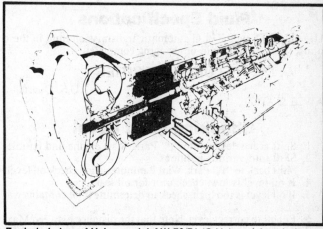

**Exploded view of Volvo model AW-70/71** (© Volvo of America)

models DL, GL, and GLT when equipped with the B21F engine. The AW71 transmission model is used in the Volvo model GLT when equipped with the B21F Turbo engine.

A plate carrying the letter reference and serial number is fixed to the left-hand side of the transmission case.

### CONVERTER

The effective diameter is 9.764 in. (248mm). The converter acts as an automatic clutch. It also multiplies engine torque to an extent determined by throttle position, engine speed and driving conditions. Additional torque multiplication is provided by the planetary gearsets, located within the transmission, when first, second, or reverse gears are in use.

Torque multiplication by the converter reaches a maximum of approximately 2 to 1 when the engine is running at full throttle and the turbine is "stalled", i.e. is prevented from turning by holding the car on the brakes with one of the gears engaged. Under running conditions the multiplication of torque varies with the speed ratio between the impeller and turbine and responds automatically to the input from the engine and the output needed to propel the car. When the rotational speed of the turbine approaches 90 per cent of the impeller speed, the input and output torque become equalized, the stator starts to revolve in unison (as permitted by the one-way clutch) and the converter acts as a fluid coupling.

Energy is transmitted from a vaned impeller, driven by the engine, to a vaned turbine (which drives the gearset) by the rapid circulation of fluid which then returns to the impeller through the vanes of a central stator carried on a fixed hub. A sprag—or one-way clutch—prevents the stator from rotating backwards under fluid pressure. All three elements (impeller, turbine and stator) are completely enclosed in a circular impeller cover which carries the mounting bosses (or ring) and contains the fluid. Fluid from the converter is circulated through a cooling element installed in the main radiator and releases heat to the engine cooling system, the capacity of which may need up-rating to carry the extra duty.

## Metric Fasteners

The metric fastener dimensions are very close to the dimensions of the familiar inch sytem fasteners, and for this reason, replacement fasteners must have the same measurement and strength as those removed.

Do not attempt to interchange metric fasteners for inch system fasteners. Mismatched or incorrect fasteners can result in damage to the transmission unit through malfunctions, breakage or possible person injury.

Care should be taken to reuse the fasteners in the same locations as removed.

## Fluid Specifications

Use only ATF type F or G automatic transmission fluid in these units, when adding fluid or changing completely.

### FLUID CAPACITIES

| | Litres | U.S. Quarts |
|---|---|---|
| AW70 & AW71 | 7.5 | 7.9 |

## Checking Fluid Level

1. Shift gear selector into "P" Park. Start engine and let idle.
2. Shift into various positions.
3. Shift back to "P" Park. Wait 2 minutes, then check oil level.
4. If oil level is low, check unit for oil leak.
5. If oil level is too high, check to determine if oil contains water.
6. Fill oil to correct level. Note that the distance between Max. and Min. marks corresponds to only 0.2 qt. of oil. Use only ATF type F or G automatic transmission fluid.

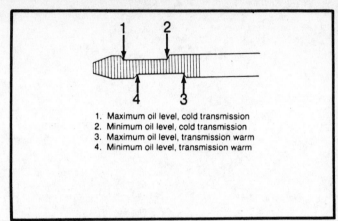

1. Maximum oil level, cold transmission
2. Minimum oil level, cold transmission
3. Maximum oil level, transmission warm
4. Minimum oil level, transmission warm

**Oil level indicator** (© Volvo of America)

# M MODIFICATIONS

## Tightening Center Support Bolts

When servicing or rebuilding the AW-70 or AW-71 models, the following procedure is necessary for tightening the center support bolts. Failure to do so may result in the bolts becoming loose in service.

1. Assemble center support bolts in main case. Align bolt holes and finger tighten the bolts. Do not torque the bolts at this stage.
2. Assemble clutches and pump to the main case and torque the pump bolts.
3. Torque the center support location bolt to a torque of 17-20 ft. lbs. Then tighten the opposite bolt to the same torque.

## Selector Lever/Cross Shaft Nut

When assembling the cross shaft lever to the transmission, the cross shaft nut must not be overtightened or internal damage to the transmission may result. The correct procedure is to place the transmission in the Neutral position and, with the opposite end of the cross shaft held, assemble the lever, washer, and nut and tighten.

## CLUTCH APPLICATION CHART
### AW-70 and AW71 Automatic Transmission

| Selector Position | Clutch OD | Forward C-1 | Direct C-2 | Brake OD | Brake B-1 | Brake B-2 | Brake B-3 | One-way Clutch (OD) | One-way Clutch (1) | One-way Clutch (2) |
|---|---|---|---|---|---|---|---|---|---|---|
| Park | X | | | | | | X | | | |
| Reverse | X | | X | | | | X | X | | |
| Neutral | X | | | | | | | | | |
| **Drive** | | | | | | | | | | |
| 1st | X | X | | | | | | X | | X |
| 2nd | X | X | | | | X | | X | X | |
| 3rd | X | X | X | | | X | | X | | |
| 4th | | X | X | X | | X | | | | |
| **Manual 2** | | | | | | | | | | |
| 1st | X | X | | | | | | X | | X |
| 2nd | X | X | | X | X | | | X | X | |
| **Manual 1** | | | | | | | | | | |
| 1st | X | X | | | | | X | X | | X |

## CHILTON'S THREE C's TRANSMISSION DIAGNOSIS CHART
### AW-70 and AW-71

| Condition | Cause | Correction |
|---|---|---|
| Shift points too high | a) Accelerator cable setting wrong<br>b) Governor bushing seized<br>c) Governor piston rings defective or worn<br>d) Throttle pressure valve malfunctions<br>e) Shift valves jammed | a) Adjust accelerator cable<br>b) Clean or replace governor<br>c) Replace piston rings<br><br>d) Replace valve body control unit<br>e) Replace valve body control unit |
| Shift points too low | a) Accelerator cable setting wrong<br>b) Governor bushing seized<br>c) Throttle pressure valve malfunctions<br>d) Plastic balls in transfer plate leak | a) Adjust accelerator cable<br>b) Clean or replace governor<br>c) Replace valve body control unit<br>d) Replace valve body control unit |
| Shift points too high or too low and shift movements too long and too soft | a) Clutch C + C damaged by 1-2 gear shifts<br>b) Clutch B damaged by 2-3 gear shifts | a) Replace clutches<br><br>b) Replace clutch B |
| No kickdown shifts | a) Accelerator cable setting wrong<br>b) Control unit setting wrong<br>c) Throttle pressure valve sticks<br>d) Plastic balls in transfer plate leak | a) Adjust accelerator cable<br>b) Adjust valve body control unit<br>c) Replace valve body control unit<br>d) Replace valve body control unit |
| Selector lever cannot be moved to "P" | a) Selector linkage setting wrong<br>b) Locking device defective | a) Adjust selector linkage<br>b) Repair locking device |
| Parking position will not disengage | a) Parking lock pawl caught in teeth of output shell<br>b) Excessive friction in parking lock device | a) Replace parking lock pawl<br><br>b) Repair parking lock device |

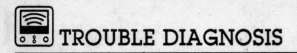 

## CHILTON'S THREE C's TRANSMISSION DIAGNOSIS CHART
### AW-70 and AW-71

| Condition | Cause | Correction |
|---|---|---|
| Parking position does not hold (slips) | a) Selector rod setting wrong<br>b) Lock pin defective | a) Adjust selector rod<br>b) Replace lock pin |
| Car cannot be started in 0 or N | a) Transmission switch defective | a) Replace transmission switch |
| Car creeps or runs in 0 or N | a) Selector rod setting wrong<br>b) Clutch A released too slowly<br>c) Clutch A defective (bonded) | a) Adjust selector rod<br>b) Disassemble transmission<br>c) Disassemble transmission |
| Drive in 1st and 2nd gear only when in A or D | a) 2nd-3rd shift valves stuck | a) Replace valve body control unit |
| Drive in 2nd gear only | a) 1st-2nd and 2nd-3rd shift valves stuck | a) Replace valve body control unit |
| Drive in 3rd gear only | a) 1st-2nd and 2nd-3rd shift valves stuck<br>b) Governor bushing seized | a) Replace valve body control unit<br>b) Clean or replace governor |
| No forward or reverse drive | a) Oil level insufficient<br>b) Pump drive defective<br>c) Drive plate broken<br>d) Parking lock pawl stuck<br>e) Clutches A and B defective | a) Correct oil level<br>b) Replace converter and pump<br>c) Replace drive plate<br>d) Replace pawl<br>e) Disassemble transmission |
| No forward drive | a) Selector linkage setting wrong<br>b) Clutch OD defective or oil lost through leak in supply line | a) Adjust selector linkage<br>b) Replace clutch OD |
| No reverse drive | a) Selector linkage setting wrong<br>b) Clutch B or D defective<br>c) Brake B3 defective<br>d) Oil level too low, pump cannot draw in oil | a) Adjust selector linkage<br>b) Disassemble transmission<br>c) Disassemble transmission<br>d) Correct oil level |
| Hard engagement jolt or definite double knock when engaging reverse gear | a) Damper B defective or wrong cover parts | a) Replace valve body control unit |
| Slipping or shaking in Reverse gear | a) Clutch B or D damaged<br>b) Serious loss of oil in supply line to B or D | a) Disassemble transmission<br>b) Disassemble transmission |
| No drive in Reverse and 2nd gear | a) Shift valve stuck in 3rd gear position | a) Replace valve body control unit Disassemble transmission if metal particles or abrasion are found in oil sump |
| Grinding shifts | a) Accelerator cable disengaged or maladjusted<br>b) Oil level too low<br>c) Throttle pressure valve stuck<br>d) Clutch A defective | a) Connect or adjust accelerator cable<br>b) Correct oil level<br>c) Replace valve body control unit<br>d) Disassemble transmission |
| Grinding shifts from 1st to 2nd gear | a) Clutches C and C' slip<br>b) Clutch valve and damper C malfunction<br>c) Accelerator cable disengaged or maladjusted<br>d) Oil level too low<br>e) Throttle pressure valve stuck<br>f) One-way clutch F defective | a) Disassemble transmission<br>b) Disassemble transmission<br>c) Connect or adjust accelerator cable<br>d) Correct oil level<br>e) Replace valve body control unit<br>f) Disassemble transmission |

## CHILTON'S THREE C's TRANSMISSION DIAGNOSIS CHART
### AW-70 and AW-71

| Condition | Cause | Correction |
|---|---|---|
| Grinding shifts from 2nd to 3rd gear | a) Clutch B slips<br>b) Accelerator cable disengaged or maladjusted | a) Replace clutch B<br>b) Connect or adjust accelerator cable |
| Rattling noise in Neutral | a) Drive plate broken<br>b) Welded drive dogs on converter damaged | a) Replace drive plate<br>b) Replace converter |
| Growling noise in Neutral, eliminated when accelerating in 0 or N | a) Valve chatter in control unit<br>b) Oil pump draws in air | a) Correct oil level<br>b) Tighten valve body mounting screws, check gasket |
| Oil on torque converter bell housing | a) Shaft seal shot<br>b) Primary pump body O-ring shot<br>c) Converter leaks at welded seams<br>d) Plug leaks | a) Replace shaft seal<br>b) Replace O-ring<br>c) Replace converter<br>d) Replace seal |
| Oil on output flange | a) Shaft seal shot | a) Replace shaft seal |
| Oil on speedometer drive | a) O-ring shot<br>b) Shaft seal in speedometer bushing shot | a) Replace O-ring<br>b) Replace speedometer bushing |
| Grinding shifts from 2nd to 3rd gear | c) Oil level too low<br>d) Oil pressure too low<br>e) Throttle pressure valve stuck<br>f) One-way clutch E defective | c) Correct oil level<br>d) Disassemble transmission<br>e) Replace valve body control unit<br>f) Disassemble transmission |
| 3rd gear slips | a) Clutch B slips<br>b) Accelerator cable disengaged or maladjusted<br>c) Oil level too low<br>d) Oil pressure too low<br>e) Throttle pressure valve stuck | a) Disassemble transmission<br>b) Connect or adjust accelerator cable<br>c) Correct oil level<br>d) Disassemble transmission<br>e) Replace valve body control unit |
| Stall speed too high | a) Oil level too low<br>b) Engaged clutch slips<br>c) One-way clutch (F or G) slips | a) Correct oil level<br>b) Disassemble transmission<br>c) Disassemble transmission |
| Stall speed too low | a) Torque converter defective<br>b) Engine output insufficient | a) Replace torque converter<br>b) Test engine |
| No braking effect from 2nd gear when in 2 and 1 | a) Clutch C'' defective | a) Replace clutch C' |
| Transmission shifts too early when downshifting from 2nd to 1st gear manually | a) Locking valve pressure too high<br>b) Loss of pressure in governor supply line between governor and shift valves | a) Replace valve body control unit<br>b) Disassemble transmission |
| Transmission shifts too late when downshifting from 2nd to 1st gear manually | a) Locking valve pressure too low<br>b) Governor pressure too high | a) Replace valve body control unit<br>b) Disassemble transmission |
| Transmission vibrates at fast move-offs | a) Clutch A defective<br>b) Propeller shaft center bearing defective<br>c) One-way clutch F or G defective | a) Replace clutch A<br>b) Replace center bearing<br>c) Disassemble transmission |
| Transmission shifts hard or down | a) Accelerator cable setting wrong<br>b) Clutch A defective | a) Adjust accelerator cable |
| Drive in 0 or N | a) Selector linkage setting wrong<br>b) Clutch A (forward) bonded<br>c) Clutch B (reverse) bonded | a) Adjust selector linkage<br>b) Disassemble transmission<br>c) Disassemble transmission |

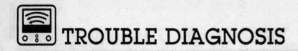

### CHILTON'S THREE C's TRANSMISSION DIAGNOSIS CHART
### AW-70 and AW-71

| Condition | Cause | Correction |
|---|---|---|
| No braking effect from 1st gear when in 2 and 1 | a) Clutch valve and damper D defective<br>b) Clutch D defective | a) Replace valve body body control unit<br>b) Replace clutch D |
| Stall speed in forward too high | a) Clutch A or 1st gear one-way clutch slips | a) Disassemble transmission |
| Stall speed in forward too low | a) Engine output not sufficient<br>b) Converter one-way clutch defective | a) Check engine tuning<br>b) Replace converter |
| Whining depending on speed | a) Center bearing of propeller shaft defective | a) Replace center bearing |
| Vehicle does not hold in park position | a) Linkage play excessive<br>b) Rod length needs adjustment<br>c) Damaged lock pin<br>d) Damaged valve body<br>e) Locking device defective<br>f) Parking pawl, spring defective | a) Replace bushings<br>b) Adjust sleeve<br>c) Replace lock pin<br>d) Replace valve body<br>e) Repair locking device<br>f) Replace defective parts |
| Oil on torque converter bell housing | a) Shaft seal shot<br>b) Primary pump body O-ring shot<br>c) Converter leaks at welded seams<br>d) Plug leaks | a) Replace shaft seal<br>b) Replace O-ring<br>a) Replace converter<br>d) Replace seal |
| Oil on output flange | a) Shaft seal shot | a) Replace shaft seal |
| Oil on speedometer drive | a) O-ring shot<br>b) Shaft seal in speedometer bushing shot | a) Replace O-ring<br>b) Replace speedometer bushing |

# POWER FLOW

## Neutral/Park

### UNITS APPLIED—OVERDRIVE CLUTCH, REAR BRAKE

When the selector lever is in the park position, a lock pawl engages with the front ring gear, which prevents the output shaft from rotating and thus immobilizes the vehicle.

## Reverse

### UNITS APPLIED—OVERDRIVE CLUTCH, REAR CLUTCH, ONE-WAY CLUTCH, REAR BRAKE

Planet pinions drive their ring gear in a counterclockwise direction, which transmits power to the output shaft at a speed ratio of 2.21:1, in reverse.

## Drive, First Gear

### UNITS APPLIED—OVERDRIVE CLUTCH, FRONT CLUTCH, ONE-WAY OD CLUTCH, ONE-WAY CLUTCH 2

Planet pinions of the rear train drive their carrier in a clockwise direction, and also drives the sun gear counterclockwise, at a speed controlled by the front planetary train.

## Drive, Second Gear

### UNITS APPLIED—OVERDRIVE CLUTCH, FRONT CLUTCH, BRAKE B2, ONE-WAY OD CLUTCH, ONE-WAY CLUTCH 2

The front clutch is applied and transmits power from the input shaft to the rear ring gear. The sun gear is held against counterclockwise rotation by brake B2 and the front brake. Planet pinions then transmit power to the output shaft at a speed ratio of 1.45:1.

## Drive, Third Gear

### UNITS APPLIED—OVERDRIVE CLUTCH, FRONT CLUTCH, REAR CLUTCH, REAR BRAKE, ONE-WAY OD CLUTCH

Front and rear clutches are both applied. The entire planetary gear assembly rotates as a unit. The rear brake is applied to assist in gear changing. Ratio will be 1:1.

## Drive, Fourth Gear (Overdrive)

### UNITS APPLIED—FRONT CLUTCH, REAR CLUTCH, OVERDRIVE BRAKE, BRAKE B2

The overdrive engages automatically to provide a fourth gear. The overdrive brake is applied which will cause the sun gear to stop rotating. Power is then transmitted to the front clutch and then transferred to the output shaft. Drive ratio is reduced from 1:1 to 0.69:1.

## Second Gear, Position 2

### UNITS APPLIED—OVERDRIVE CLUTCH, FRONT BRAKE, BRAKE B2, ONE-WAY OVERDRIVE CLUTCH, ONE-WAY CLUTCHES 1 AND 2

The difference in comparison to gear selector position "D", is the fact that the front brake is also applied. Brake B2 prevents the sun gear from rotating counterclockwise. First gear is not locked out.

## First Gear, Position 1

### UNITS APPLIED—OVERDRIVE CLUTCH, FRONT CLUTCH, REAR BRAKE, ONE-WAY OVERDRIVE CLUTCH

The difference in this position as opposed to "D" is that the rear brake is also applied and the planetary gear is prevented from rotating. Power is then transferred from the output shaft to the input shaft.

## Hydraulic Control System

The power required to apply and hold the clutches and brakes which control the action of the planetary gears is provided by an engine-driven pump which draws fluid from the oil pan through a strainer and delivers it, under regulated pressure, to a system of valves, ports and passages. The pump also supplies fluid to the torque converter, a cooler, and the lubrication system of the gearset. Most of the hydraulic circuits and all valves (except the governor) are contained in the valve bodies assembly which is attached to the base of the transmission case and can be removed as a complete unit.

In addition to the primary function of automatic gearshifting, the hydraulic system is designed to make the shifts smoothly and to vary the hydraulic loading applied to the clutches and brakes in a manner appropriate to the torque which is imposed on them under a wide range of operating conditions. These requirements are met by using a variety of automatic valves which respond to variations in hydraulic pressure. The refinement in control obtained in this way is an important operational advantage.

The hydraulic system is controlled by the following basic controls:

1. Primary and secondary regulator valves automatically determine the pressure of the fluid in various parts of the system in relation to a number of operational requirements.
2. Governor valve, carried by the output shaft, provides a variable pressure signal (governor pressure) which is regulated in relation to car speed.
3. Throttle valve provides a variable pressure signal (throttle pressure) primarily dependent on the extent to which the carburetor throttle is opened.
4. Manual valve, operated by a selector lever, enables the driver to choose various modes of operation, including neutral and park.

### GOVERNOR

The governor is mounted on the output shaft which is, at all times connected to the road wheels which drive the vehicle and therefore revolves at a speed proportional to the speed of the vehicle. In all forward gears, fluid at line pressure is routed to the governor by the manual valve. From the governor, fluid is directed to the shift valves, the governor modulator valve and the cut-back valve at a regulated governor pressure which rises as the speed of the vehicle increases.

A two-stage governor mechanism is used which controls governor pressure through the speed range.

When the vehicle is at rest, the output shaft is stationary and an inlet port is closed by the valve. At low vehicle speeds the valve moves to an intermediate position in which it is cracked open to admit fluid at line pressure against the opposition of the centrifugal force produced by the governor weight, valve and spring acting in unison. Fluid is directed to the outlet port at a regulated governor pressure which increases as the speed of the shaft rises in response to the rapid build-up of centrifugal force.

When a pre-determined speed is reached, a disc, which is part of the stem to which the governor weight is attached, makes contact with the governor body. From this stage onwards, regulation is maintained by a balance between governor pressure acting on the differential areas of the valve and the spring load (plus the small centrifugal force of the valve itself), with the net result that governor pressure continues to rise with vehicle speed and can approach (but never reach) the level of line pressure. Excess pressure will force the valve towards the shaft, so opening an exhaust port and closing the supply port.

### PRIMARY REGULATOR VALVE

1. Valve closed by spring load, cutting off line 1 from line 1A.
2. Valve in regulating position, allowing fluid to reach circuits

supplying secondary regulator valve, lubrication system and torque converter-coupling.
3. At high speeds, valve permits any surplus fluid to return to pump inlet circuit.

### SECONDARY REGULATOR VALVE

1. Valve closed by spring load, cutting off return circuit from torque converter-coupling.
2. Valve in intermediate position, allowing hot fluid from torque converter-coupling to flow to cooler.
3. Valve fully opened, allowing surplus fluid to reach cooler circuit.

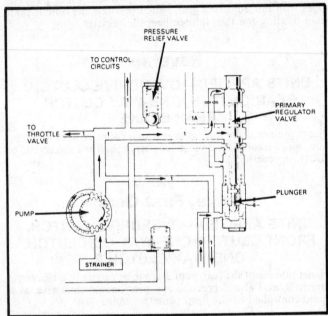

**Primary regulator valve** (© Volvo of America)

### MANUAL VALVE

The manual valve is linked mechanically to the gear selector lever (operated by the driver) and is precisely located, relative to a series of ports, by a local detent device which must not be over-ridden by the operating linkage. One port receives fluid at line pressure from the primary regulator valve. The other ports are connected to various parts of the hydraulic system.

### PRIMARY REGULATOR VALVE

The primary regulator valve receives fluid from the engine-driven pump and directs it, at a regulated line pressure, to the manual valve, throttle valve, second speed brake (B.2) accumulator and direct clutch (C.2) accumulator. Also directs fluid to the lubrication system of the planetary gearset, the torque converter, the secondary regulator valve and to the cooler. Fluid surplus to requirements is re-circulated through the primary regulator valve to the suction port of the pump when the demand is low.

The primary regulating function provides for an increase in line pressure when the engine torque is high and a reduction at normal driving speeds. Line pressure is also increased to a suitably high value when reverse gear is engaged manually.

### THROTTLE VALVE AND KICKDOWN VALVE

Fluid is fed at line pressure to the throttle valve from the primary regulator valve and is directed at regulated throttle pressure to the primary and secondary regulator valves, the shift valves, the cutback valve, and the kickdown valve. A damping valve is included in the line which serves the primary regulator valve.

The primary function of the throttle valve is to send a pressure signal to the shift valves which acts in opposition to governor pressure. An upshift or a downshift takes place when hydraulic unbalance allows governor pressure to overcome throttle pressure, or vice versa.

A cable connects the carburetor throttle lever to a cam which is in contact with a roller mounted at one end of a kickdown valve, located in tandem with the throttle valve in the valve bodies assembly.

## General Arrangement of the Gear Set

Various rotating parts of the transmission are arranged in groups that always turn in unison. Some are permanently connected by welding and others by the interlocking of splines (or castellations) which enable the parts to be separated during dismantling and reengaged on assembly. The rotating parts which are grouped in these various ways are listed below:

1. Torque converter turbine, input shaft, forward clutch cylinder and direct clutch (inner member).
2. Forward clutch (inner member), intermediate shaft and rear ring gear.
3. Direct clutch cylinder, brake hub (B.1) and sun gear.
4. Front planet carrier and brake hub (B.3.)
5. Front planet ring gear, rear planet carrier, cover and output shaft.

Power enters the transmission through the input shaft and forward clutch cylinder assembly. This cylinder is the outer (driving) member of the forward clutch and is coupled to the inner member of the neighbouring direct clutch assembly by shallow, interlocking projections or keys.

The gear set consists of two planetary trains which are located end to end at the rear of the transmission case. Each train consists of four planet pinions, located in a carrier, which are in mesh with the internal teeth of a ring gear. Both sets of planet pinions are in mesh with a single, lengthy sun gear, the teeth of which are integral with the rear end of a hollow shaft within which the intermediate shaft is located. Helical involute tooth forms are used throughout.

When the forward clutch is engaged, power is transmitted through its inner member to the intermediate shaft and thence to the ring gear of the rear planetary train. Engagement of the direct clutch transmits power to the sun gear through the hollow shaft of which it is an intergral part. These are the two routes through which power can flow into the transmission. No matter which gear is in use, power leaves the transmission through the output shaft which passes through the extension housing and is connected to the front universal joint of the propeller shaft.

Three forward speed ratios, one reverse speed ratio and a neutral condition are obtained by the selective engagement of two clutches and three brakes, all of which are of the multi-disc type, running in oil. One-way sprag clutches act in association with two of the brakes to permit rotation in one direction only.

Fluid supplied under pressure from a pump, through a control system, operates the multi-disc clutches and brakes by means of pistons which are retracted by springs when the pressure is released. As the pump is driven from the impellor member of the torque converter, hydraulic pressure is generated whenever the engine is running. A manual valve, and a large number of automatic valves, direct the hydraulic pressure selectively to the clutches and brakes and so determine the action of the gearing.

The overdrive unit is located ahead of the 3-speed transmission, between the oil pump and the front clutch (C.1), within the transmission casing. This is essentially a fourth gear and will automatically engage when driving in third gear with a throttle opening less than 85 percent. Overdrive can be disengaged, by a push button on the gear selector, to obtain a three speed unit. This

is indicated to the driver by a light on the instrument panel which reads "OD-OFF". The overdrive will remain disengaged until the button on the gear selector is pushed again or the ignition switch is turned off. The transmission will always return to the fourth speed range when the ignition is switched off.

### BY-PASS VALVE

The by-pass valve protects the oil cooler from excessive pressure.

### PRESSURE RELIEF VALVE

The pressure relief valve is located immediately after the oil pump. It will open automatically at a preset pressure.

### CUTBACK VALVE

The cutback valve on the AW-70 and AW-71 is acted on by pressure from the governor modulator valve. The cutback valve on both transmissions have the same function: to lower the throttle pressure and the line pressure at normal and high speeds. This causes a reduction in line pressure which is needed to drive the oil pump. It also improves the gear changing qualities.

## Shift Valves—Operating Principles

The function of a shift valve is to signal changes of gear (upshifts and downshifts) in response to variations in governor pressure and throttle pressure. Each valve has only two operative positions so that two valves are required in a three-speed transmission (1-2 and 2-3). A "snap" action is essential in order that the valve does not hesitate, or "hunt" between the two gears that it controls.

### 1-2 SHIFT VALVE

This valve controls the oil flow to engage gears 1 and 2. The throttle pressure, which varies with the throttle opening, acts on one end of this valve. On the other end, the governor pressure acts. At the middle of the valve there are passages leading to the clutches and brakes which controls the planetary gear operation when in first and second gears. Which gear is used depends on line, throttle and governor pressure.

### 2-3 SHIFT VALVE

The 2-3 shift valve occupies the downshift position when the vehicle is driven in 1st, 2nd and reverse gear. There is no governor pressure in reverse.

In 2nd gear, throttle pressure, spring tension, and governor pressure are applied to the 2-3 shift valve. Fluid received from the 1-2 shift valve is able to pass to the intermediate coast modulator valve through adjacent ports. Other intermediate ports provide a fluid route for the direct clutch. In the middle of the valve there are passages that lead to the clutch and brakes. These clutch and brakes control the planetary gear operation in second and third speeds. The position of the 2-3 shift valve is determined by line, throttle and governor pressure.

### 3-4 SHIFT VALVE (AW-71)

Throttle pressure, which varies with the throttle opening acts on one end of this valve. On the other end acts the governor pressure, which varies with the vehicle speed. In the middle of the valve are two oil passages. These passages direct oil to the overdrive clutch (CO) and overdrive brake (BO). Which passage is used depends on the strength of the line pressure.

### LOW COAST SHIFT VALVE

The low cost shift valve is acted on by modulated line pressure.

The low coast shift valve is located above, and in alignment with, the 1-2 shift valve, a compressed coil spring is placed between them and normally holds the low-coast shift valve in its upper position where it acts as a stop to limit the upshift travel of the 1-2 shift valve.

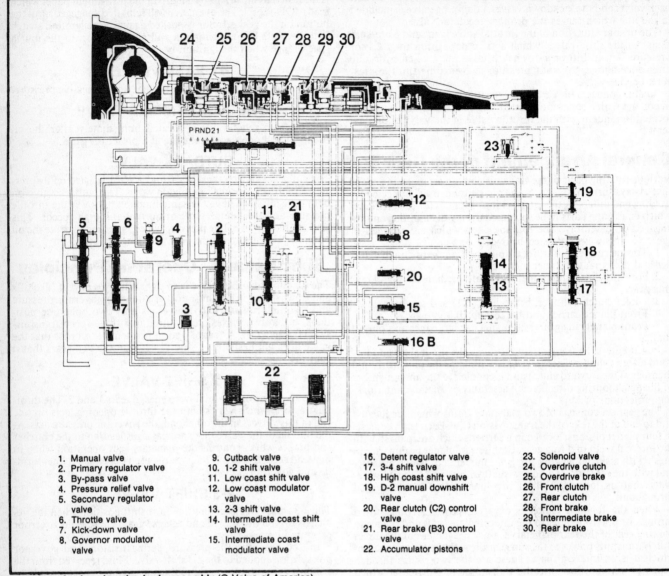

PRND21

1. Manual valve
2. Primary regulator valve
3. By-pass valve
4. Pressure relief valve
5. Secondary regulator valve
6. Throttle valve
7. Kick-down valve
8. Governor modulator valve
9. Cutback valve
10. 1-2 shift valve
11. Low coast shift valve
12. Low coast modulator valve
13. 2-3 shift valve
14. Intermediate coast shift valve
15. Intermediate coast modulator valve
16. Detent regulator valve
17. 3-4 shift valve
18. High coast shift valve
19. D-2 manual downshift valve
20. Rear clutch (C2) control valve
21. Rear brake (B3) control valve
22. Accumulator pistons
23. Solenoid valve
24. Overdrive clutch
25. Overdrive brake
26. Front clutch
27. Rear clutch
28. Front brake
29. Intermediate brake
30. Rear brake

**Location of valves in valve body assembly** (© Volvo of America)

When the manual valve is placed in first gear, fluid at directed line pressure passes through the low coast modulator valve and acts upon unequal areas of the low coast shift valve. If the vehicle is stationary, or being operated in 1st gear, the low coast shift valve will move downwards into contact with the 1-2 shift valve, which is then in the downshift position. Ports are opened which allow this pressurized fluid to apply both pistons of brake B3, the former feed being controlled by the orifice shown on the schematic drawings.

If the manual valve is placed in 1st gear while the vehicle is being operated in 2nd gear (1-2 shift valve in upper position) the hydraulic pressure acting on the top of the low coast shift valve is opposed by governor pressure acting on the bottom of the 1-2 shift valve. The large and small pistons of brake B3 are both open to exhaust. As the vehicle speed falls, modulated line pressure overcomes governor pressure, at a pre-determined value, and forces both the low coast and 1-2 shift valves down to their low positions. Ports are opened to allow fluid at modulated line pressure to apply both pistons of brake B3.

When the manual valve is placed in reverse gear, fluid passes directly to the low coast shift valve. If this valve is in its upper position the pressurized fluid has direct access, through ports, to brake B3. If the manual valve is shifted directly from 1st to reverse, the pressurized fluid overcomes the modulated line pressure and forces the low coast shift valve into its upper position. This shift does not involve "stroking" the pistons of brake B3, but increases the pressure already acting on them.

## INTERMEDIATE COAST SHIFT VALVE

The intermediate coast shift valve is located above, and in alignment with, the 2-3 shift valve. A compressed coil spring is placed between them and normally holds the intermediate coast shift valve in its upper position where it acts as a stop to limit the upshift travel of the 2-3 shift valve.

When the manual valve is placed either in 1st gear or 2nd gear, (vehicle stationary), fluid at directed line pressure acts directly on the large upper surface of the intermediate coast shift valve and imposes an hydraulic load which forces the valve downwards to its lower position and thus prevents the 2-3 shift valve from moving upwards to engage top gear, regardless of vehicle speed.

If the vehicle is being operated in 3rd gear when the manual valve is placed either in 1st gear or 2nd gear, a similar action takes place, almost regardless of vehicle speed or throttle opening. The intermediate coast shift valve forcing the 2-3 shift valve downwards to the 2nd gear position. For all practical purposes there is no inhibition on obtaining this manually activated 3-2 shift. This is because the line pressure which acts downwards on a large area of the intermediate cost shift valve, is higher than the governor pressure which acts upwards on the smaller area of the 2-3 shift valve.

## HIGH COAST SHIFT VALVE

The high coast shift valve is manually controlled by a push button on the gear selector, or automatically when the electric kickdown switch is engaged. When switching the overdrive unit off manually, the high coast shift valve will depress the 3-4 shift valve to its lower position. This will disengage the fourth gear. The high coast shift valve will remain in the lower position until the solenoid valve is disengaged. In both cases, the high coast shift valve is acted on by line pressure.

## DETENT REGULATOR VALVE

The detent regulator valve is located ahead of the kick down valve and is under constant line pressure. It reduces line pressure to a point where it can act on the kick down valve. The detent regulator valve receives fluid at throttle pressure from the kick down valve and regulates the detent pressure at which fluid is applied to the 2-3 shift valve. Detent pressure increases the vehicle speed at which a 3-2 shift can occur.

## INTERMEDIATE COAST MODULATOR VALVE

The intermediate coast modulator valve modulates line pressure to a lower value before it is applied to brake B1 when second gear is engaged (either automatically or manually) in order to ensure a smooth shift. Brake B1 is used at all times, in second gear, and supplements the thermal capacity of brake B2 on an automatic 1-2 shift. Total torque capacity would be higher than necessary if full line pressure were applied to brake B1.

If the vehicle is being driven in third gear when the gear selector is moved to position 2, the downshift to second gear will occur, regardless of the throttle opening or vehicle speed.

## D-2 MANUAL DOWNSHIFT VALVE

This valve controls manual downshifting from fourth gear to second gear. Third gear is used only for a short time. This eliminates the risk of the engine over-revving during the braking period. Downshift valve D-2 is influenced by pressures at both ends; control pressure from the high coast shift valve at one end, and pressure for overdrive clutch (CO) at the other end.

## REAR CLUTCH (C2) CONTROL VALVE

Rear clutch (C2) is composed of two piston surfaces. When engaging third gear, the smaller of the two surfaces is used. In position "R," both surfaces must be used to prevent the clutch from slipping. This valve provides a smooth engagement of reverse gear by applying the rear clutches.

## REAR BRAKE B-3) CONTROL VALVE

This valve provides smooth engagement of the reverse gear, by using two hydraulic pistons. These pistons are applied in stages and are fed by separate oil passages. This valve serves as a restrictor in the piston oil passages. This valve also divides the oil flow to the pistons. The front piston is applied before the rear piston which results in B3 being applied for an additional period of time. The reverse gear engagement is therefore smooth.

## ACCUMULATOR PISTONS

Accumulator pistons are found in all oil circuits for the front clutch, rear clutch, and brake B2.

## SOLENOID VALVE

The solenoid valve controls the engagement and disengagement of the fourth gear (overdrive). It is engaged by a switch on the gear selector. When engaged, the solenoid relieves line pressure from one end of the 3-4 shift valve. When disengaged, the solenoid then supplies, the end of the 3-4 shift valve with line pressure. The solenoid valve does not return to the engaged position until it receives a new impulse from the gear selector switch or the ignition is switched off/on.

# Diagnostic Tests

## LINE PRESSURE

### Excessive Pressure

Usually caused by a seizing valve (provided the throttle cable is correctly adjusted).
It might be one of the following two valves.
    a. Throttle Valve
    b. Primary Regulator Valve

**THROTTLE VALVE**

As the throttle valve influences line pressure, it is possible to check the throttle valve operation as follows.
1. Let engine idle, gear selector position "N."
2. Pull the transmission cable by hand, not influencing throttle opening (and engine speed).
3. Pressure should increase. If not, the throttle valve seizes.

**PRIMARY REGULATOR VALVE**

Increase engine speed. If the primary regulator valve seizes, the normal control of the pressure will fail. Pressure will vary directly in proportion to the oil pump speed (engine speed).

### Test Procedure

1. Remove front plug and connect nipple. Attach the pressure gauge to the door window. Route the hose behind the splash guard, over the steering control rod and between oil pipes to transmission. Connect to the pressure nipple.
2. Start engine and let idle. Gear selector in position "N" and idle speed approx. 900 rpm.
3. Depress the brake pedal and shift gear selector into "D". Note reading.
4. Shift gear selector into "R." Note reading.

**TOO LOW PRESSURE**

Too low pressures may be caused by seizing primary regulator valve or throttle valve. Test as described under "Excessive Pressure".

If these two tests verify that the too low pressure is not caused by any of these valves, the fault may be:
1. Defective pressure relief valve (only early versions).
2. Defective oil pump.
**NOTE: A defective oil pump usually makes noise.**

## GOVERNOR PRESSURE

The governor pressure is a modified line pressure. So governor pressure will be incorrect if line pressure is incorrect. Therefore, an incorrect line pressure must be corrected before governor pressure is checked.

### Procedures

1. Attach pressure gauge to the door window. Route the hose behind splash shield, over control arm and into transmission. Remove rear plug on transmission and connect nipple.

2. Test drive the vehicle in "D" and note readings. Pressure should be 0 when vehicle is standing still, also in position "R."

## LOW GOVERNOR PRESSURE

1. Governor leaks or jams.
2. Oil leak at cover for governor oil ducts.
3. Governor seals on output shaft are defective.

## EXCESSIVE GOVERNOR PRESSURE

Govenor jams. Remove and check governor.

## LINE PRESSURE CHART

| Selector Position | Model AW-70 | Model AW-71 |
|---|---|---|
| D | 50-63 psi | 65-77 psi |
| R | 71-91 psi | 106-117 psi |

## STALL SPEED TEST

### Prepare Vehicle for Stall Test

Install an engine tachometer and connect a 0 to 300 psi test pressure gauge to line pressure fitting on transmission. Install chocks in front of and behind both front wheels and set hand brake.

### —— CAUTION ——

*Do not maintain stall rpm longer than five seconds*

### Perform Stall Test in "D" Range

Start engine and set selector lever to "D". Firmly apply the foot brake, and press the accelerator pedal to full throttle position. Quickly read the highest line pressure and engine rpm obtained. AW-70 stall speed should fall between 1,800-2,300 rpm with the line pressure between 137-160 psi. AW-71 stall speed should fall between 2,000-2,500 rpm with the line pressure between 140-205 psi.

### Perform Stall Test In "R" Range

Set selector lever to "R". Firmly apply foot brake and press accelerator pedal to full throttle position. Quickly read the highest line pressure and engine rpm obtained. Stall rpm for the AW-70 should fall between 1,800-2,300 and line pressure 195-242 psi. AW-71 stall rpm should fall between 2,000-2,500 and line pressure should be between 213-270 psi.

### Perform Time Lag Test

Obtain a stop watch. With engine idling and selector lever in "N", simultaneously shift to "D" and start stop watch. Stop the watch when transmission engagement shock is felt. Time should be less than 1.2 seconds.

Set selector back to "N" and repeat test for shift from "N" to "R". Time should be less than 1.5 seconds.

### Perform Hydraulic Pressure Tests

Using an engine tachometer, and a 0-100 psi test gauge for governor pressure port for governor pressure test, and a 0-300 psi test gauge to line pressure port for line pressure test. Ensure chocks are in front of and behind both front wheels.

### LINE PRESSURE CHECK IN "D" RANGE

Set the parking brake. Set the selector lever to "D". Apply the foot brake and allow the engine to idle (900 rpm). Line pressure for the AW-70 should be 50-63 psi. Line pressure for the AW-71 should be 65-77 psi.

### LINE PRESSURE CHECK IN "R" RANGE

Set the parking brake. Set the selector lever in "R". Apply the foot brake and allow the engine to idle (900 rpm). Line pressure for the

## STALL TEST EVALUATION

| Malfunction | Action |
|---|---|
| Grinding or grating noise from transmission | Troubleshoot noise problems |
| Stall speed higher than specified maximum with clutch or brake squawk in "D" range | Troubleshoot front clutch |
| Stall speed higher than specified maximum with no apparent clutch or brake slippage | Check torque converter |
| Stall speed higher than specified maximum with clutch or brake in squawk in "R" range | Troubleshoot reverse range elements |
| Time lag in shift from "N" to "D" is longer than specified | Troubleshoot valve body |
| Time lag in shift from "N" to "R" is longer than specified | Troubleshoot valve body |
| Incorrect governor pressure | Troubleshoot governor |
| Line pressure higher than specified in all ranges | Troubleshoot valve body |
| Line pressure lower than specified in all ranges | Troubleshoot valve body |
| Line pressure lower than specified in "D" range | Troubleshoot front clutch |
| Line pressure lower than specified in "R" range | Troubleshoot "R" range elements |

AW-70 should be 106-117 psi. be 71-91 psi. Line pressure for the AW-71 should.

### Perform Governor Pressure Test

Jack up rear of vehicle and install stands so rear wheels are free to rotate. Release hand brake. Start engine and set selector to "D". Operate vehicle to obtain speedometer readings equal to 1,400 and 2,400 output shaft rpm, when governor pressure test readings should be 13-21 and 58-75 psi.

## ROAD TEST

### Check Upshift Points at Full Throttle in "D" Range

Set selector lever to "D" Drive vehicle at full throttle from standing start and observe road speeds at shift points. Speeds at shift points should be specified.

### Check Upshift Points at Half Throttle in "D" Range

With selector in "D" range, drive vehicle at approximately half throttle and observe road speeds at shift points. Speeds at shift points should be near nominal speeds specified.

### Check Coast Downshift Speed

With vehicle running in 3rd gear, release accelerator and allow speed to decrease. Engine rpm should decrease in direct relation to vehicle speed, and a downshift from 3rd to 2nd, 2nd to 1st should occur as specified.

## ROAD TEST EVALUATION

| Malfunction | Action |
|---|---|
| Shift lever position indicator incorrect | Troubleshoot manual linkage |
| Vehicle moves forward with shift lever in "N" | Troubleshoot manual linkage |
| Vehicle moves backward with shift lever in "N" | Troubleshoot manual linkage |
| Harsh engagement into any drive ranges | Troubleshoot for pressure surges |
| Noise in transmission when engine is running | Troubleshoot for noise problems |
| Delayed 1-2 upshift | Troubleshoot "D" range |
| Delayed 2-3 upshift | Troubleshoot "D" range |
| Delayed 3-4 upshift | Troubleshoot "D" range |
| Downshifts from 3rd speed to 2nd speed, then shifts back to 3rd speed | Troubleshoot "D" range |
| Slip on 1-2 upshift | Troubleshoot 2nd speed |
| Slip on 2-3 upshift | Troubleshoot 3rd speed |
| Drag, binding, or tie-up on 1-2 shift | Troubleshoot 1st speed |
| Drag, binding, or tie-up on 2-3 shift | Troubleshoot 2nd speed |
| Slip, squawk, or shudder on full throttle take-off in forward ranges | Troubleshoot 1st speed |
| Transmission noisy during operation | Troubleshoot noise problems |
| Slip, squawk, or shudder on take-off in "R" range | Troubleshoot "R" range |
| Harsh downshifts | Troubleshoot valve body |
| No coast downshift | Troubleshoot governor |
| Noisy during coastdown | Troubleshoot noise problems |
| No 4-3 kickdown | Troubleshoot throttle valve |
| No 3-2 kickdown | Troubleshoot throttle valve |
| No 2-1 kickdown | Troubleshoot throttle valve |
| No downshift | Inspect governor |

## ROAD TEST EVALUATION

| Malfunction | Action |
|---|---|
| Downshift to first speed occurs above specified maximum speed when "1" range is manually selected | Inspect governor |
| No engine braking in "2" range | Troubleshoot coast brake |
| Automatic 2-3 upshift in "2" range | Inspect valve body |
| Coast downshift occurs above specified maximum speed | Troubleshoot valve body |
| Coast downshift occurs below specified minimum speed | Troubleshoot valve body |

### Check Kickdown Speeds in "D" Range

With vehicle decelerating from high speed in 3rd gear, attempt kickdown (press accelerator to full throttle) at 5 mph (8 kph) intervals. Record highest speed at which kickdown from third to second occurs, then repeat for kickdown from second to first. Kickdown speeds should be as specified.

### Check Manual Downshift Points

--------- CAUTION ---------

*Manual 3-2 downshift is possible at any speed. Shifting into "2" range at speeds in excess of 90 mph may cause damage to transmission.*

While in 3rd gear in "D" range, manually shift into "2" range. A 3-2 downshift should occur immediately, and engine braking should decelerate vehicle. Manually shift into "1" range. A 2-1 downshift should occur after vehicle has decelerated to speed specified and engine braking should continue.

### Check Automatic Upshift Point at Half Throttle in "2" Range

With range selector lever in "2", drive vehicle at approximately half throttle. Observe road speed at 1-2 upshift. Upshift should occur near nominal speed specified.

### Check "1" Range Operation

With selector lever in "1", drive vehicle and accelerate to approximately 40 mph. Transmission should remain in first gear. Release accelerator and check for engine braking effect.

### Check "R" Range Operation

Set selector lever to "R". Drive vehicle in reverse and check for slipping.

### Check Parking Lock

Stop vehicle on a hill with a grade of at least 5°. Set selector lever to "P" and release brake. Vehicle should not move when brake is released. Check parking lock with vehicle heading uphill and downhill.

### Check Converter Function

Inability to start on steep grades combined with poor acceleration from rest indicates that the converter stator one-way clutch is slipping or that the stator support is fractured. This condition permits the stator to rotate in an opposite direction to the turbine and torque multiplication cannot occur. Check the stall speed, and if it is more than 50% below normal, the converter assembly must be renewed.

Below standard acceleration in top gear above 30 mph combined with a substantially reduced maximum speed indicates that the stator one-way clutch has locked in the engaged condition.

The stator will then not rotate with the turbine and impeller, therefore the fluid flywheel phase of the converter performance cannot occur. This condition will also be indicated by severe overheating of the transmission, although the stall speed will remain normal. The converter assembly must be replaced.

 ON CAR SERVICES

## Adjustments

### SHIFT LEVER LINKAGE

**Adjustment**

Start engine and release hand brake. Hold foot on foot brake. Set selector lever to "N". Vehicle should not attempt to move. Set selector lever to "R". Vehicle should attempt to move backward.

Set selector lever to "D", "2", and to "1". Vehicle should attempt to move forward in each range.

### THROTTLE CABLE AND KICKDOWN CABLE

**Adjustment**

1. Disconnect link and cable at throttle control pulley.
2. Loosen locknut screw out throttle shaft adjusting screw, then turn in the screw until it just touches the boss and make one additional turn. Lock with the locknut. Check that throttle valve does not seize or bind.
3. Adjust the throttle control link until it fits on pulley ball and does not influence pulley position.
4. Attach cable to pulley. Adjust cable sheath. The cable should be stretched but not influence pulley position.
5. Depress throttle pedal to full throttle position. The pulley should touch the full throttle abutment.
6. Adjust the cable to the transmission. At idle there should be 0.40" clearance between clip and adjusting sheath. The clip must not touch the sheath.

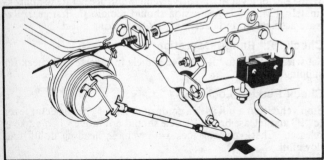

Throttle control link adjustment (© Volvo of America)

### NEUTRAL SAFETY SWITCH

The neutral safety switch is located at and directly controlled by the gear shift control lever.

1. Select gear shift position "P". Adjust switch to set P-mark at the center of the switch lever.

2. Select gearshift position "N". Check that the N mark is at the center of the switch lever.
3. Move gearshift selector from "P" to "1" and back again. Check that the control pin does not slide out of the switch lever.
4. Check that engine starts in gearshift positions "P" and "N" only; and that back-up lights operate in position "R".

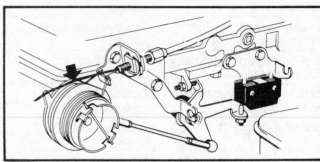

Throttle cable adjustment (© Volvo of America)

## Services

### FLUID CHANGE

1. If transmission has been overhauled or completely drained, fill with 9.8 qts. of type F or G automatic transmission fluid.
2. Shift gear selector to position "P", start engine and let idle. If converter has been emptied or a new converter has been installed add 2.6 qts. of ATF.
3. Shift gear selector to various positions.
4. Place gear selector in "P", wait 2 minutes and then check transmission oil level. Use measuring range "COLD" and dipstick.
5. Add oil as necessary. Note that distance between "Max." and "Min." marks on dipstick corresponds to only 0.2 qt. of oil.
6. Recheck oil level.

### OIL PAN

**Removal**

1. Raise the vehicle and support safely, disconnect oil filler pipe from oil pan and drain fluid.
2. Remove the oil pan retaining bolts and carefully remove the pan from the case. Remove and clean the oil strainer.

**Installation**

1. Clean the oil pan.
2. Install the oil strainer.
3. Place a new gasket and the oil pan in place and install the oil pan retaining bolts.
4. Connect the oil filler pipe to the oil pan, and fill the transmission with the recommended automatic transmission fluid.

### OVERDRIVE SOLENOID VALVE

**Removal**

1. Raise the vehicle and support safely.
2. It may be necessary to drain a certain amount of transmission fluid from the unit.
3. Remove the shift lever linkage as required.
4. Disconnect the electrical connector at the gear selector.
5. Clean the area around the solenoid. Remove the solenoid retaining bolts and O-rings.
6. Check the solenoid with an ohmmeter. The resistance should be 13 ohms. When electrical current is disconnected, the air passage on the face of the valve should be blocked. If this does not occur, replace the valve.

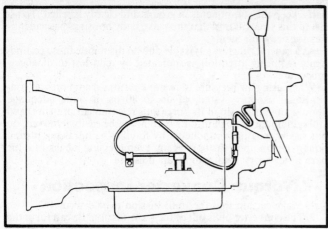

**Location of solenoid valve on transmission** (© Volvo of America)

## Installation

1. Lubricate the O-rings with clean automatic transmission fluid before installation. This will hold the O-rings in place.

2. Install the solenoid assembly. Torque the retaining bolts to 9 ft. lbs. (13 N•m).

3. Connect the electrical connector at the gear selector.

4. Install the shift lever linkage as required.

5. Lower the vehicle and check the fluid level. Replace lost fluid as required.

6. Start the engine and check for leaks.

7. Road test the vehicle, and check for positive engagement of the overdrive gear.

## VALVE BODY

### Removal

1. Raise the vehicle and support safely, disconnect the oil filler pipe from the oil pan and drain the fluid.

2. Remove the oil pan and oil strainer.

3. Remove all the valve body retaining bolts except the one behind the detent spring for the manual valve.

4. Loosen the final bolt and install the plate retaining tool which holds the accumulator pistons in place. Otherwise the accumulator pistons will drop out.

5. Remove remaining bolt, disconnect the throttle cable from the cam and remove the valve body assembly.

### Installation

1. Hold the valve body assembly in place and connect the throttle cable to the cam.

2. Position the selector cam pin within the recess on the manual valve.

3. Position the valve body and install retaining bolts finger tight. Remove the plate retaining tool and tighten bolts to the specified torque: 3.5-6 ft. lbs. Install particle magnet.

4. Install oil strainer bolts.

5. Place oil pan with new gasket in position and install pan retaining bolts.

6. Connect oil filler pipe and fill transmission with the recommended automatic transmission fluid.

## EXTENSION HOUSING/GOVERNOR

### Removal

1. Raise vehicle and support safely.

2. Disconnect propeller shaft a'   ir drive flange and remove shaft.

3. Remove exhaust pipe clamps as necessary.

4. Support engine and remove the bolts securing transmission support member. Pull back, twist and lift out.

5. Remove rear engine mount and bracket for exhaust pipes.

6. Use a puller and pull off drive flange, after removing retaining nut.

7. Disconnect speedometer cable at drive gear.

8. Remove the extension housing to case bolts and lift off extension housing. Replace extension housing oil seal.

9. Remove speedometer drive gear and spacer ring.

10. Unhook drive spring and slide governor off output shaft.

11. Remove cover for governor oil ducts.

### Installation

1. Place governor on output shaft and hold out lock spring in order to position governor on shaft.

2. Slide speedometer drive gear spacer and drive gear on shaft.

3. With new oil seal installed in extension housing, place housing with new gasket against rear of case and install retaining bolts.

4. Connect speedometer cable at drive gear.

5. Push drive flange onto output shaft and install and tighten retaining nut.

6. Install rear engine mount and hook up exhaust pipe bracket.

7. Place transmission support member into position and install retaining bolts.

8. Install exhaust pipe clamps as necessary.

9. Slide propeller shaft into place and connect at rear flange with retaining bolts.

10. Lower vehicle, check transmission fluid level and road test.

**Removing governor spring clip** (© Volvo of America)

## REMOVAL & INSTALLATION

### Removal

1. Remove carburetor air cleaner.

2. Disconnect throttle cable at pulley and cable sheath at bracket.

3. Remove the two upper converter housing to engine bolts.

4. Disconnect transmission oil filler pipe from the engine.

5. Raise the vehicle and support safely. Disconnect oil filler pipe from oil pan and drain transmission oil.

6. Remove the retaining bolts and take off the splash guard.

7. Pry off the rubber suspension rings from the front muffler.

8. Mark the flanges and disconnect the drive shaft at the rear flange. Remove drive shaft.

9. Remove the exhaust pipe clamps.

10. Remove the bolts securing the transmission support member. Pull support member back, twist and lift out.

11. Remove the rear engine mount securing bolts. Remove attachment and bracket.

12. Disconnect speedometer cable at transmission extension.

13. Remove transmission oil cooler pipes.

14. Remove transmission neutral safety switch. On later models the switch is located at, and directly controlled by the gearshift control lever.

15. Disconnect gearshift control rod.

16. Remove cover plate between engine and transmission, remove starter motor blind cover and remove starter motor.

17. Remove bolts attaching converter to drive plate.

18. Position a transmission fixture under transmission and remove the lower retaining bolts and separate the converter from the drive plate.

19. Lower the transmission assembly and slide it out from under vehicle.

### Installation

1. Position the transmission and converter assembly on a transmission fixture. Raise and position the transmission behind the engine.

2. Line up and install the lower transmission retaining bolts, adjust the plate between the starter motor and casing and install the starter motor.

3. Connect the oil filler pipe at the lower end.

4. Install the upper transmission to the engine bolts.

5. Install the converter to the drive plate bolts and torque to 30-36 ft. lbs.

6. Install the starter motor blind plate and lower cover plate.

7. Move gear selector lever into position "2".

8. Attach the control rod at the front end, and adjustable clevis to the gear selector lever.

9. Check control adjustment. The clearance from "D" stop should be approximately the same as from "2" to stop. Move lever to position "1" and then to "P". Recheck clearance in position "D" and "2". Readjust if necessary.

10. Install starter neutral safety switch. Torque to 4-7 ft. lbs.

11. Install oil cooler pipes. Torque to 14-22 ft. lbs.

12. Install drive shaft and attach at rear flange.

13. Install exhaust pipe brackets, rear engine mount and the speedometer cable.

14. Install transmission support member and torque bolts to 30-37 ft. lbs.

15. Install exhaust pipe clamps and muffler hanger.

16. Install engine splash guard.

17. Attach throttle cable to bracket and adjust cable.

18. Fill the transmission with the recommended transmission fluid.

19. Install carburetor air cleaner.

20. Road test vehicle and recheck the fluid level.

## Before Disassembly

Prior to the removal of any components, the outside of the transmission must be thoroughly cleaned. High standards of cleanliness are required when handling or storing components and care is necessary to avoid damage to light-alloy parts. Bench surfaces and tools must be scrupulously clean.

Unless requiring replacement, clutch and brake plate packs should be kept in their correct relationships.

When dismantling sub-assemblies, particularly the valve body

parts, keep the components in groups and clearly labelled. To assist in this you will find that the valve body housings have identifications cast on them.

As a general rule it is advisable only to dismantle those components requiring attention as indicated by road test or diagnosis procedure.

When using air pressure to remove pistons from bores a "conventional" supply system of up to 80 psi is quite adequate. Should any piston tip in its bore (thus releasing air pressure) and still remain far enough into its bore not to be easily removed, do not risk damaging components by forcibly withdrawing piston. Square piston up in the bore again, even pressing it back into the bore if necessary, and reapply air pressure.

## Torque Converter Inspection

1. Make certain that the transmission is held securely.

2. The converter pulls out of the transmission. Be careful of the weight since the converter contains a large amount of oil. There is no drain plug on the converter so the converter should be drained through the hub.

The transmission fluid drained from the converter can help diagnose transmission problems.

1. If the oil in the converter is discolored but does not contain metal bits or particles, the converter is not damaged and need not be replaced. Remember that color is no longer a good indicator of transmission fluid condition. In the past, dark color was associated with overheated transmission fluid. It is not a positive sign of transmission failure with the newer fluids that are being used today.

2. If the oil in the converter contains metal particles, the converter is damaged internally and must be replaced. The oil may have an "aluminum paint" appearance.

3. If the cause of oil contamination was burned clutch plates or overheated oil, the converter is contaminated and should be replaced.

## EXTENSION HOUSING AND GOVERNOR

### Removal

1. With the transmission mounted in a secure fixture, remove the propeller shaft and coupling flange.

2. Remove the speedometer cable and rear extension housing. Discard the housing gasket.

3. Loosen the large speedometer driven gear and the spacer. Remove these and place aside.

4. Unsnap the drive ring and remove the screw and lock plate.

5. Withdraw the governor from the shaft. It may be necessary to use a puller to remove it.

## OIL PAN AND OIL TUBES

### Removal

1. Position the transmission in order to gain access to the oil pan retaining bolts.

2. Remove the pan bolts and discard the pan gasket.

3. Carefully remove the oil pipes and check for blockage with compressed air. Discard the oil filter.

## VALVE BODY

### Removal

1. Remove all valve body retaining bolts except one behind cam spring.

2. Loosen the final bolt and install special tool retainer plate to hold accumulator pistons in place. Otherwise the accumulator pistons will drop out.

3. Remove the valve body assembly and remove the final bolt.

4. Remove the kick down cable from the throttle cam and lift away the valve body assembly.

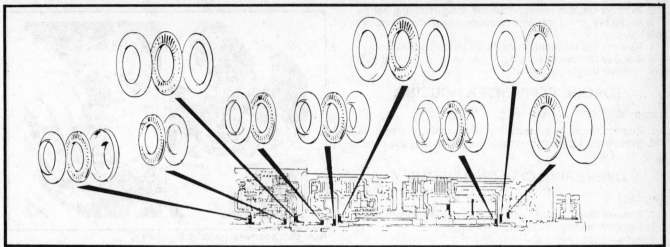

**Thrust bearing locations** (© Volvo of America)

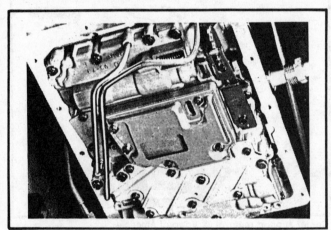

**Oil pipe locations** (© Volvo of America)

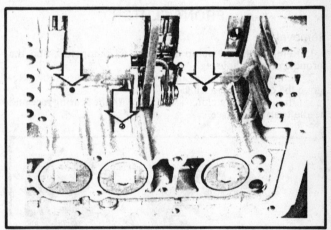

**Feed hole locations** (© Volvo of America)

## ACCUMULATOR PISTONS

### Removal

1. Remove the retainer plate and lift out the accumulator pistons.

2. If removal is difficult, compressed air can be used to dislodge the accumulator pistons.

3. Clean and check the pistons for scoring or other damage. Replace if damaged.

## GEAR SELECTOR MECHANISM (OPTIONAL)

### Removal

1. Loosen the lock plate bolts (2) and remove with the thrust rod. Remove the parking pawl.

2. Remove the lock ring that holds the cam and tap out the pin with a punch.

3. Remove the oil seals that surround the gear selector shaft and remove the shaft.

## OIL PUMP

### Removal

1. Turn transmission on the fixture so that the oil pump faces up.

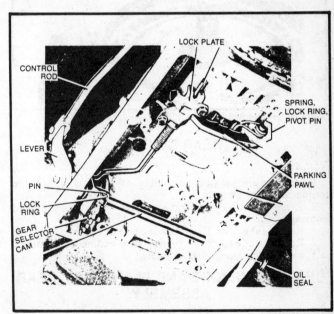

**Gear selector mechanism and related components**
(© Volvo of America)

2. Remove the hub seals and the oil pump retaining bolts.

3. Install two dowel pins into two opposing oil pump retaining bolt holes.

4. Remove the oil pump using an oil pump removal tool.

5. Remove the two dowel pins. Using an oil pump seal puller tool, remove the oil pump seal.

## TORQUE CONVERTER HOUSING

### Removal

1. Remove the oil pump assembly. Remove the oil pump seal.

2. Remove the torque converter housing by pulling and turning at the same time.

## OVERDRIVE CLUTCH ASSEMBLY

### Removal

1. Remove the oil pump assembly. Remove the oil pump seal.

2. Remove the torque converter housing.

3. Remove the O-ring and overdrive clutch assembly.

4. Remove the overdrive housing by lifting out with both hands.

## FRONT CLUTCH

### Removal

1. Remove the oil pump assembly, oil pump seal, and the torque converter housing.

2. Remove the "O"-ring and overdrive clutch assembly. Remove the overdrive housing.

3. Lift out the front clutch assembly, with the bearing race and needle bearing in place.

**Rear clutch removal** (© Volvo of America)

**Center support removal** (© Volvo of America)

**Front clutch removal** (© Volvo of America)

## REAR CLUTCH

### Removal

1. Remove the oil pump assembly, oil pump seal, and the torque converter housing.

2. Remove the "O"-ring and overdrive clutch assembly and housing.

3. Remove the front clutch bearing race and needle bearings.

4. Remove the rear clutch bearing races and needle bearing.

5. Lift out the rear clutch assembly.

## CENTER SUPPORT AND PLANETARY GEAR ASSEMBLY

### Removal

1. Remove the 2 bolts securing the center support to the case.

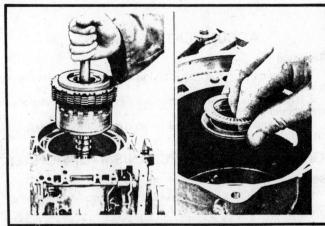

**Planetary gearset removal** (© Volvo of America)

2. Remove center support assembly by gripping and pulling on the "nose" on which the sealing rings are fitted.

**NOTE:** The planetary sun gear will come out with the center support.

3. Retrieve the thrust race and plates between rear of planetary sun gear and rear carrier assembly ring gear.

## REAR BRAKE AND COUNTERSHAFT

### Removal

1. Remove the countershaft retaining ring and lift out the rear brake countershaft. Remove the needle bearing and bearing race.
2. Remove lock ring which holds the rear brake return springs. A press tool is used to release the tension of the return springs.
3. Remove the return spring thrust plate and the 16 return springs.
4. Remove the pistons with a suitable tool. It may be necessary to use compressed air (maximum 14 psi) to loosen the pistons.
5. Remove the nipples for the tubes which lead to the oil cooler.

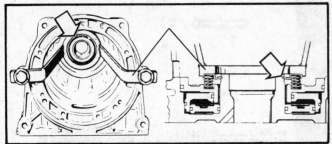

**Press tool location for removal of return springs** (© Volvo of America)

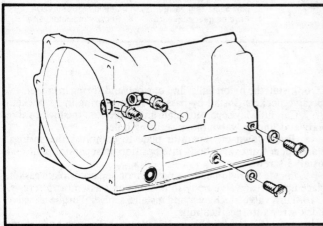

**Location of oil cooler tubes** (© Volvo of America)

# Unit Disassembly and Assembly
## GOVERNOR

### Disassembly

1. Remove the drive ring, governor weight, shaft, spring and governor.
2. Inspect all parts for signs of wear, abrasions, and cracks.
3. Clean all parts with unused solvent.

### Assembly

1. Lubricate all parts with automatic transmission fluid.
2. Install the shaft, spring and governor in the body.
3. Check that the governor does not bind.

## EXTENSION HOUSING

### Disassembly

1. Remove the oil seal with a suitable tool.

2. Clean the extension housing with the proper solvent and inspect for scoring. If the unit is damaged it must be replaced.
3. Remove the bushing with a drift or punch.

### Assembly

1. Install the new bushing with a drift or punch.
2. Install the oil seal in the extension housing.

**Governor parts** (© Volvo of America)

## VALVE BODY

### Disassembly—Lower Valve Body

1. Place valve body on a clean bench, lower valve body uppermost. Remove detent spring and lower valve body cover.
2. Remove 5 screws partly securing upper valve bodies to lower.
3. Turn assembly over and remove 5 screws securing rear upper valve body to lower valve body and put body aside; retrieve the nylon balls.
4. Loosen 5 screws securing front upper valve body, then holding against spring pressure, remove screws.
5. Allow spring pressure to release, and lift off valve body.
6. Remove separator plate and gasket, the nylon balls, one spring and by pass valve and spring.
7. Compress pressure relief valve and spring. Remove retainer, spring and ball. Take out the manual valve.
8. Compress primary regulator valve sleeve and remove retainer. Remove sleeve, plunger, spring and primary regulator valve.
9. Take out 2 screws securing low coast shift valve cover and remove cover. Remove low coast shift valve and 1-2 shift valve spring. Remove 1-2 shift valve retainer plug and 1-2 shift valve.

### Disassembly—Upper Rear Valve Body

1. Remove 2 screws securing rear valve cover and remove cover.
2. Remove 4 valves and their springs, intermediate coast modulator, reverse sequence, governor modulator and low coast modulator valves.

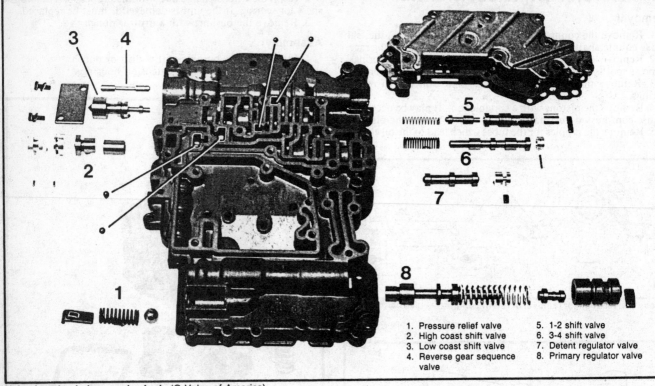

1. Pressure relief valve
2. High coast shift valve
3. Low coast shift valve
4. Reverse gear sequence valve
5. 1-2 shift valve
6. 3-4 shift valve
7. Detent regulator valve
8. Primary regulator valve

**Valve location in lower valve body** (© Volvo of America)

3. Remove detent regulator valve retainer, valve spring and valve.

4. Take out the 2-3 shift valve retainer plug, the 2-3 shift valve and spring.

5. Remove the intermediate coast shift valve retainer, plug and valve.

NOTE: On some installations the intermedaite coast valve will be working within a sleeve.

### Disassembly—Upper Front Valve Body

1. Remove screw securing downshift cam to valve body; remove cam, spacer and spring.

2. Withdraw kickdown valve and spring, and throttle valve.

NOTE: A small quantity of clips will be found on the spring stem of the throttle valve. These clips are fitted when the valve body is built. If they are removed, the same quantity must be replaced or the transmission will malfunction.

3. Remove cut-back valve retainer plug, valve and spring.

4. Remove 2 screws securing secondary regulator valve cover, and remove cover, valve and spring.

### Assembly—Lower Valve Body

1. Assemble pressure relief ball and spring and secure with retainer.

2. Install primary regulator valve and spring. Assemble plunger to sleeve and locate sleeve behind primary regulator valve spring. Press sleeve into bore to compress spring, and install retainer.

3. Install low coast shift valve, cover and plate. Secure with 2 screws and washers.

4. Assemble 1-2 shift valve spring, valve and plug. Press plug into bore to compress spring and secure with retainer.

5. Install manual valve.

6. Install the nylon balls, and one ball and spring into their respective pockets. Install by-pass valve and spring in its pocket.

7. Carefully lay separator plate and gaskets on the lower valve body and line up valve block securing holes.

8. Press down on separator plate to compress the springs. Place upper front valve body into position on separator plate and install 5 screws.

9. Locate the nylon balls in position on separator plate gasket. Place upper rear valve body in position and assemble 5 screws.

10. Turn valve block over and install 5 screws. Torque all valve block screws to specifications.

11. Assemble lower valve body cover with 2 screws and assemble detent spring with 1 screw. Be sure spring fits into machined step in lower valve body.

NOTE: Do not use petroleum jelly or any form of grease to assist in the assembly of the balls. Grease will cause balls to stick and the transmission will not function properly.

### Assembly—Upper Rear Valve Body

1. Assemble detent regulator valve and retainer.

2. Assemble intermediate coast modulator, reverse sequence, governor modulator, and low coast modulator valves and springs. Fit cover plate and secure with 2 screws and washers.

3. Assemble 2-3 shift valve, plug and retainer. Install 2-3 shift valve spring from opposite end of bore, and assemble intermediate coast shift valve sleeve (if equipped). Install intermediate coast shift valve and plug. Push plug into bore to compress spring and install retainer.

NOTE: Spring specifications can be used only to identify new springs. Do not use the free length of a spring as a measurement on condition. Only a special measuring device can decide whether a spring is faulty or not.

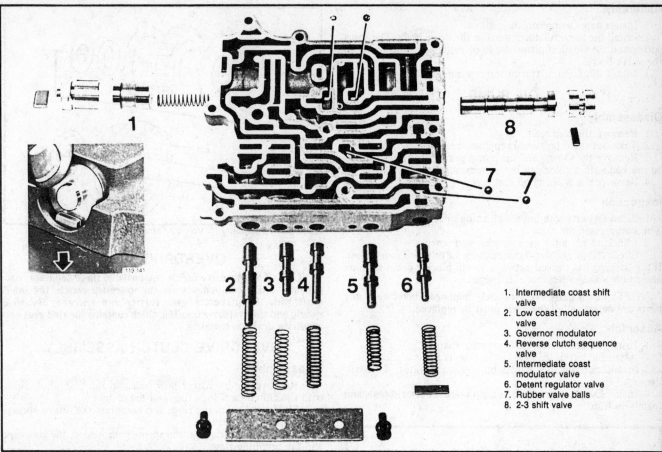

1. Intermediate coast shift valve
2. Low coast modulator valve
3. Governor modulator
4. Reverse clutch sequence valve
5. Intermediate coast modulator valve
6. Detent regulator valve
7. Rubber valve balls
8. 2-3 shift valve

**Layout of upper rear valve body** (© Volvo of America)

NOTE: Valve retainers can easily be removed with a magnet. Force must not be used at any time.

## Assembly—Upper Front Valve Body

1. Locate spring in cup end of cut-back valve and assemble the valve upward into its bore. Place the plug into position and hold it against spring tension to install its retaining ring.
2. Place secondary regulator valve spring into bore. Assemble valve and install cover.
3. Remove the clips from the spring end of the throttle valve and place valve in its bore.
4. Locate the valve spring in position and install the same number of clips removed. Assemble kickdown valve and spring.
5. Assemble washers, cam spring and spacer to hex-headed screw.

NOTE: Hooked leg of spring to engage in cam, compress kickdown valve and assemble cam to valve block. Position cam so that straight leg of spring will lie on unmachined surface of valve block, with slight tension on the spring, the step of the cam will lie against the kickdown valve roller when it is released. Roller of kickdown valve must run squarely on profile of cam.

6. Fit keep plate to throttle valve.

## ACCUMULATOR PISTONS

### Disassembly

1. Remove the valve body assembly using the accumulator piston retaining tool.

2. Lift out the accumulator pistons and remove the retaining tool. If the pistons are difficult to remove, compressed air (maximum 14 psi), applied to the feed hole can be used to dislodge them.
3. Remove the accumulator piston springs.

### Inspection

1. The pistons are constructed of either white metal or aluminum, and can be cleaned with the springs in unused solvent.
2. Check the pistons for scoring, burrs and any other damage or wearing. Replace any parts that are found to be defective.
3. Blow dry all parts with compressed air.

## Assembly

1. Install new O-rings on the pistons.
2. Install the accumulator pistons in the valve body. The short spring and the smallest piston are to be installed in the center of the valve body.
3. Install the accumulator piston retaining tool.

### OIL PUMP

### Disassembly

1. Remove the hub seals.
2. Take out the 6 bolts and separate the pump.
3. Remove the O-ring and the pump gears. Note gears should be marked with a color pen before removing.
4. Remove the housing oil seal.

### Inspection

1. Clean all parts with unused cleaning solvent. Blow dry parts with compressed air.
2. Check all parts for wear, cracks, and scoring.
3. Check the torque converter bushing for outward movement. If the bushing has moved outward, it will block a drain channel and cause leakage. Replace if damaged.

NOTE: Pump parts are accurately matched, therefore if any parts are defective, all the parts must be replaced.

### Assembly

1. Install oil seal on torque converter shaft.
2. Assemble pump loosely; install 6 bolts finger tight.
3. Install centering tool, tighten bolts. Torque bolts to 4.4-6.6 ft. lbs.
4. Install O-ring in groove on pump body. Lubricate seals and install on hub.

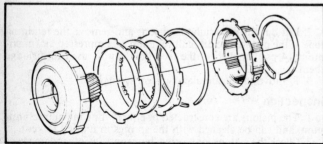

Oil pump disassembled (© Volvo of America)

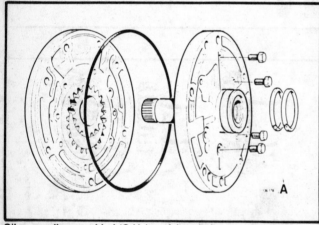

Layout of overdrive clutch (© Volvo of America)

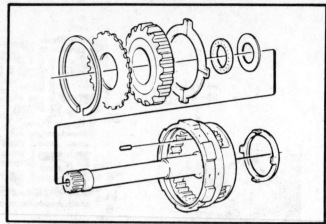

Input shaft assembly (© Volvo of America)

### OVERDRIVE UNIT

NOTE: The overdrive unit is composed of three separate components. These components are the overdrive clutch, the input shaft with the planetary gear carrier and one-way overdrive clutch, and the overdrive housing which contains the ring gear and overdrive brake assemblies.

### OVERDRIVE CLUTCH ASSEMBLY

#### Disassembly

1. Remove the overdrive lock ring and the brake hub along with the clutch pack lock ring and the clutches.
2. Unclip the retaining rings and compress the return springs with a spring compressor.
3. Remove the lock ring, the spring compressor, the ring cage and the retaining rings.
4. Remove the clutch piston from its housing. Blow compressed air through the feed hole on the inside of the housing to dislodge the piston.
5. Remove the O-rings from the piston.

#### Inspection

1. Clean all parts, except the clutches, with cleaning solvent. Blow dry all parts with compressed air.
2. Check all parts for wear, cracks or other damage. Replace as necessary.
3. Check the clutch piston by shaking. The piston ball should move freely.
4. Check that the friction discs are flat and not damaged. Replace any that are damaged.

#### Assembly

1. Lubricate all parts with automatic transmission fluid prior to assembly.
2. Install the new O-rings on the clutch piston. The O-rings should not be turned in the grooves during assembly.
3. Insert the clutch piston into its housing being careful not to damage or dislodge the O-rings.
4. Install the return springs and their retainer, making sure the rings are vertical.
5. Using the spring compressor, load the springs and install the lock ring.
6. Install the unlined clutch disc at the bottom, the friction lining and the steel bevelled disc outermost.

NOTE: Minimum disc thickness is 0.82 in. (2.1mm) for used discs. New disc thickness is 0.91 in. (2.3mm).

7. Install the clutch pack lock ring, the brake hub and the brake hub lock ring.

8. Check the piston function by blowing compressed air (maximum 14 psi) through the feed hole located on the inside of the clutch drum. Block the opposite hole. A click should be heard when air passes through. This indicates that the piston is functioning.

## INPUT SHAFT ASSEMBLY

### Disassembly

1. Remove the pressure plate lock ring, the pressure plate, and the one-way clutch.
2. Remove the thrust washer with the needle bearing and bearing race.
3. Remove the oil passage plugs located in the planetary gear shaft.
4. Remove the other thrust washer from the planetary gear carrier. Keep all parts in their correct order.

### Inspection

1. Clean all parts with cleaning solvent and dry using compressed air.
2. Inspect all parts for cracks, scoring or other signs of wear.
3. Check the gear teeth and splines for burrs and wear.
4. Replace any damaged parts as needed.

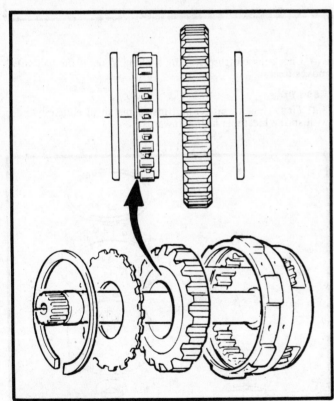

**Exploded view of one-way clutch and bearing race**
(© Volvo of America)

### Assembly

1. Lubricate all parts with automatic transmission fluid prior to assembly.
2. Install the oil passage plugs in the planetary gear shaft.
3. Install the bearing race, needle bearing and thrust washer. The grooves on the thrust washer are to be facing up.
4. Place the bearing race in the one-way clutch and assemble with the outer race.
5. Install the one-way clutch and outer race in the planetary gear carrier.

**NOTE: The collar part on the one-way clutch must face outward and away from the planetary gear carrier.**

6. Install the pressure plate and lock ring.
7. Assemble the overdrive clutch to the input shaft of the planetary gear carrier, making sure that the carrier fits properly into the clutch pack.

**NOTE: At this point check the function of the one-way clutch by holding the carrier and turning the input shaft. The shaft should be able to turn clockwise but not counterclockwise.**

8. Install the thrust washer in the rear of the planetary gear carrier.
9. Install the bearing race and the needle bearing on the input shaft, with any washer plugs facing out.

**NOTE: Two types of bearing washers are being used for the AW-70 and AW-71.**

## OVERDRIVE ASSEMBLY

### Disassembly

1. Remove the brake pack lock ring and thrust plate.
2. Disassemble the brake pack with the thrust ring and remove the bearing race from the ring gear.
3. Remove the ring gear along with the bearing races and needle bearing.
4. Remove the brake piston lock ring.
5. Remove the spring retainer and the return springs.
6. Dislodge the brake piston by blowing compressed air (maximum 14 psi) through the feed hole located in the overdrive housing.
7. Remove the O-rings from the piston and unclip the sealing rings from the overdrive housing.

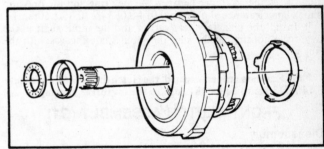

**Thrust washer, bearing race and needle bearing location**
(© Volvo of America)

### Inspection

1. Clean all parts with cleaning solvent and blow dry with compressed air.
2. Inspect all parts for scoring, or other damage and replace if necessary.
3. Check the return springs and piston ring groove.
4. Check all discs for warping and replace if found to be distorted. Minimum thickness is 0.83 in. (2.1mm)
5. Check that the overdrive housing plugs are mounted properly.

### Assembly

1. Install new sealing rings in the overdrive housing. These rings should slide smoothly once they are in the groove.
2. If needed install new needle bearings in the overdrive housing. Do this with the housing in a vise and tap the bearings in with a 29mm socket.
3. Install new O-rings on the piston.
4. Lubricate the remaining parts with automatic transmission fluid.

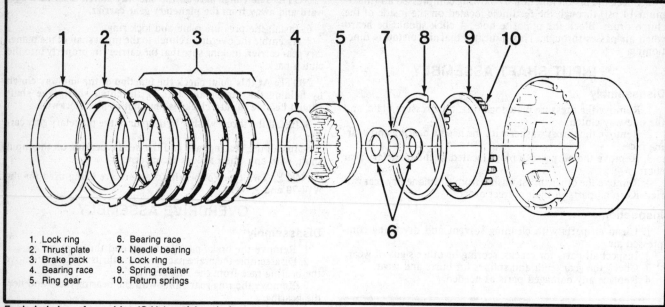

1. Lock ring
2. Thrust plate
3. Brake pack
4. Bearing race
5. Ring gear
6. Bearing race
7. Needle bearing
8. Lock ring
9. Spring retainer
10. Return springs

**Exploded view of overdrive** (© Volvo of America)

5. Install the piston in the overdrive housing, being careful not to damage the O-rings.

6. Install the return springs, retainer and the lock ring.

7. Press the lock ring into position making sure that the gap is not in one of the recesses of the body.

8. Check the clearance between the lock ring and the pressure plate. The clearance should be 0.014-0.063 in. (0.35-1.60mm).

9. Install the planetary gear carrier and the input shaft in the overdrive housing. Make sure the input shaft engages with the ring gear.

**NOTE: When properly seated, the clutch drum should measure 0.14 in. (3.5mm) below the edge of the overdrive housing.**

## FRONT CLUTCH ASSEMBLY (C1)

### Disassembly

1. Remove the snap ring from C-1 clutch cylinder and remove C-2 clutch input hub.

2. Remove C-1 clutch hub from inside clutch pack by pulling on splined center flange.

3. Take out the thrust bearing and race plate between input shaft end and C-1 clutch hub.

4. Remove the clutch plates.

5. Using a spring compressor tool, compress clutch spring sufficiently to remove snap ring; carefully release spring compressor tool and remove 18 springs.

6. Using air pressure blow through drilling in inside wall of piston, while holding fingers over other holes, piston will be blown out.

7. Remove O-rings from piston. Do not disturb ball valve inserted in piston.

### Inspection

1. Wash all parts, except the clutch discs, with cleaning solvent. Blow all parts dry with compressed air.

2. Check that the clutch discs are not distorted or damaged. Minimum thickness is 0.83 in. (2.1mm). Replace if necessary.

3. Inspect the return springs, input shaft, hub and clutch drum for any signs of damage or unusual wearing, such as scoring or burrs. Replace any damaged components.

4. Check the clutch piston by shaking to see if the ball valve moves freely.

### Assembly

1. Fit O-rings to piston and install piston in clutch cylinder with spring locations facing upwards.

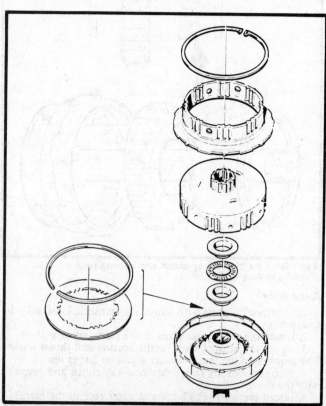

**Exploded view front clutch** (© Volvo of America)

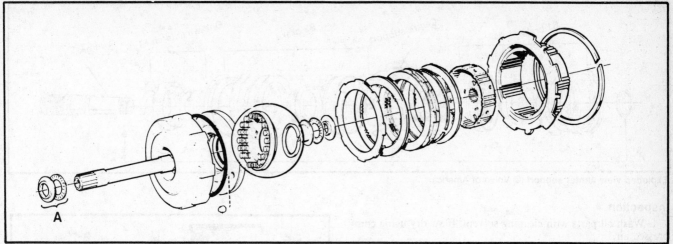

**Exploded view clutch pack** (© Volvo of America)

2. Place 8 springs in locations in piston and stand retainer plate and snap ring in top of piston.

3. Use spring compressor tool to compress spring, then install snap ring.

4. Place the bearing, then the race plate with flange protruding through bearing to locate input shaft counter bore, to end face of input shaft.

5. Assemble clutch pack into cylinder: start with unlined plate, then alternate with lined and unlined plates.

6. Locate clutch hub into center of clutch pack onto thrust bearing.

7. Finish assembling clutch with direct clutch hub then install retaining ring.

## REAR CLUTCH ASSEMBLY (C2)

### Disassembly

1. Remove snap ring from clutch cylinder.
2. Invert cylinder and shake or tap out clutch plates.
3. Use a spring compressor tool to compress clutch spring and remove snap ring.
4. Remove 18 springs.
5. Apply air pressure to the drilling and cylinder inside wall while holding fingers over other drillings; the piston will blow out.
6. Remove O-rings from piston. Do not disturb the ball valve assemblies inserted in pistons.

### Inspection

1. Wash all parts, except the clutches, with cleaning solvent. Blow dry with compressed air.
2. Check that the clutch discs are flat and not distorted. Minimum thickness is 0.82 in. (2.1mm).
3. Inspect the return springs and the clutch drum for any scoring, burrs or other damage. Replace as needed.
4. Check the clutch piston by shaking; make sure the ball valve moves freely.

### Assembly

1. Fit O-rings to front and rear of piston and assemble piston in clutch cylinder. Rear (smaller) piston diameter is entered first.
2. Place 18 springs in place and stand retainer and snap ring on top of springs.
3. Use a spring compressor tool to compress springs and retainer, then install snap ring.

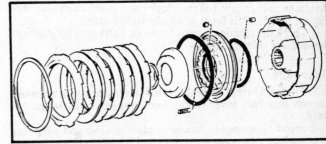

**Exploded view rear clutch** (© Volvo of America)

4. Assemble clutch pack starting with unlined plate against piston, then alternate with lined and unlined plates, finishing with thicker backing plate.

## CENTER SUPPORT

### Disassembly

1. Remove 3 sealing rings from forward nose of center support.
2. Remove retaining ring from forward rim of center support and remove B-1 brake pack.
3. Use a spring compressor tool to compress brake springs, then remove the snap ring.
4. Apply air pressure to brake apply hole in outside wall of center support to blow out piston.
5. Remove O-rings from piston and remove brake hub complete with one-way clutch assembly.
6. Remove retaining ring from rear rim of center support and remove B-2 brake pack.
7. Use a spring compressor tool to compress brake spring, then remove snap ring.
8. Unload spring compressor tool to release 12 coil springs.
9. Apply air pressure to brake feed hole in outside wall of center support and blow out B-2 brake piston.

--- **CAUTION** ---
*When removing pistons with air pressure, do not remove both retainer rings and then blow out pistons. Holding the center support with a heavy clutch is a wise precaution.*

10. Remove O-rings from pistons.

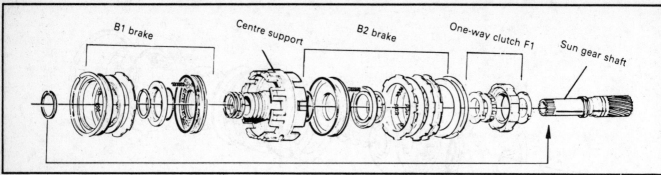

Exploded view center support (© Volvo of America)

## Inspection

1. Wash all parts with cleaning solvent. Blow dry using compressed air.

2. Check the clutch discs for warping, distortion, or other damage. Minimum thickness is 0.83 in. (2.1mm). Replace as needed.

3. Check the one-way clutch while its on the sun gear. The shaft should be able to turn counter-clockwise but not clockwise. Replace if the clutch is loose or grinds while rotating.

4. Check the remaining parts for nicks, burrs or other damage. Replace any damaged parts.

## Assembly

1. Fit new O-rings on brake piston; assemble piston to center support rear bore (over shorter hub) with spring locations upward.

2. Stand 12 springs in locations; place retainer and snap ring over springs, compress the springs and install the snap ring.

3. Assemble B-2 brake pack, unlined plate to piston first, then alternating with lined and unlined plates. Finish with thicker backing plate, then install snap ring.

4. Fit O-rings to B-1 brake piston, assemble piston to center support front bore (over hub with sealing ring grooves, with spring locations uppermost).

5. Stand 12 springs in locations, place retainer and snap ring over springs, compress springs and install snap ring.

6. Assemble B-1 brake pack, unlined plate to piston first then alternating with a lined and unlined plate. Finish with a thicker (backing) plate, then install snap ring.

## PLANETARY GEAR ASSEMBLY

### Disassembly

1. Remove the rear brake discs (B3), one-way clutch (F2) and the front planetary gear. Place the planetary gear assembly on the intermediate shaft and remove the front brake pack with the front planetary gear assembly.

2. Compress the front ring gear lock ring and remove the front ring gear.

3. Remove the rear planetary gear thrust washer. Leave the front planetary gear washer in place.

4. Separate the input shaft from the output shaft and remove the needle bearing and the bearing race from the output shaft.

5. Remove the rear planetary gear assembly from the rear ring gear. Remove the bearing washer and needle bearing.

6. Unclip the rear ring gear lock and remove the rear ring gear.

7. Remove the bearing race from the output shaft.

8. Remove three oil sealing rings from the output shaft. Unclip the retaining rings and lift of the hub.

9. Remove the thrust washer from the front planetary gear carrier, along with the brake pack.

10. Divide the front planetary gear carrier from the brake pack thrust/reaction plate.

Brake disc and one-way clutch (© Volvo of America)

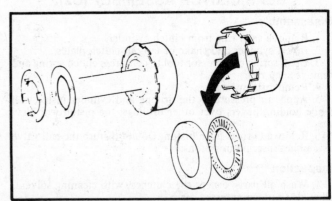

Bearing washer and needle bearing locations (© Volvo of America)

11. Remove the lock that holds the bearing cages and one-way clutch and remove these. The thrust washer should now be free to come out.

### Inspection

1. Wash all parts, except the brake discs, with cleaning solvent. Blow dry with compressed air.

2. Check that the clutch discs are not damaged or warped. Minimum thickness should be 0.83 in. (2.1mm).

3. Inspect all remaining parts for burrs, cracks or other damage. Replace any damaged parts.

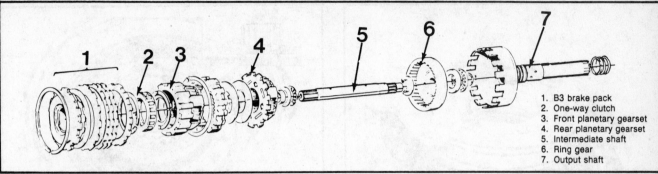

**Planetary gear assembly** (© Volvo of America)

1. B3 brake pack
2. One-way clutch
3. Front planetary gearset
4. Rear planetary gearset
5. Intermediate shaft
6. Ring gear
7. Output shaft

## Assembly

1. Lubricate all parts with automatic transmission fluid prior to assembly.

2. Install the thrust washer with the lugs facing down. Washer can only be installed one way.

3. Install the lower bearing cage.

4. Install the one-way clutch, using hand pressure to seat it.

**NOTE: The arrow on the outside of the clutch must point down. This indicates that the flange is facing up.**

5. Install the upper bearing cage and lock ring.

6. Assemble the brake pack reaction plate to the front of the planetary gear carrier.

7. Place the rear brake (B3) on the front planetary gear carrier. Thrust disc should be outermost.

8. Install new oil seal rings on the output shaft.

9. Install the rear bearing race and ring gear on the intermediate shaft. Secure with the lock ring.

10. Place the needle bearing and bearing race on the intermediate shaft.

11. Install the rear planetary gear carrier in the rear ring gear.

12. Position the needle bearing and bearing race on the output shaft. Assemble the intermediate shaft to the output shaft.

13. Place the front ring gear above the rear ring gear and install the thrust washer on the rear planetary gear.

14. Place the thrust washer on the front planetary gear and assemble the front and rear planetary gears.

### REAR BRAKE

#### Disassembly

1. Separate the three pistons from each other by hand and lay aside.

2. Remove the O-rings and discard them.

#### Inspection

1. Wash all parts with cleaning solvent. Blow dry using compressed air.

2. Check the pistons for scoring or any other signs of damage.

3. Replace any damaged parts with new parts.

#### Assembly

1. Lubricate all parts with automatic transmission fluid.

2. Install new O-rings in the piston grooves.

3. Assemble the piston by hand in the reverse order as disassembly.

## Transmission Assembly

Check all parts before assembling, making sure that all needle bearings and thrust washers are secure and located properly. Soak any new discs in automatic transmission fluid before installing.

**Three brake pistons** (© Volvo of America)

**Assembly of piston** (© Volvo of America)

Petroleum jelly may be used only to keep needle bearings and thrust washers in place during assembly.

Whenever possible use new O-rings, gaskets and sealing rings during assembly. Do not use gasket sealer in place of a regular gasket.

Dry all parts using compressed air. Do not use rags or any other material which can leave lint behind. This could cause a malfunction later.

1. Turn the transmission casing to a vertical position for assembling. Clean the casing prior to assembling.

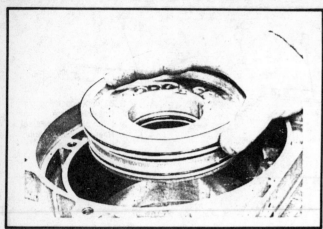

Rear brake piston (© Volvo of America)

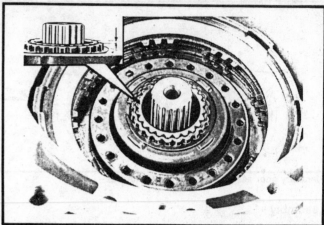

Rear clutch lying flush with sun gear (© Volvo of America)

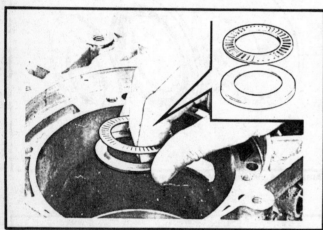

Rear bearing and bearing race (© Volvo of America)

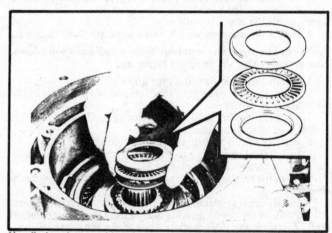

Needle bearings and bearing races on the front clutch (© Volvo of America)

Location of compressed air feed hole (© Volvo of America)

Overdrive housing with bearing races (© Volvo of America)

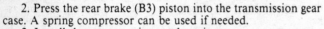

2. Press the rear brake (B3) piston into the transmission gear case. A spring compressor can be used if needed.

3. Install the return springs and retainer.

4. Off load the return springs with a spring compressor and install the retaining ring.

5. Tighten the screws crosswise using the proper wrench, while making sure the retaining plate is installed square.

6. Fit the rear bearing and bearing race onto the intermediate shaft and place the shaft in the rear brake piston.

7. Lower the planetary gear carrier with the rear brake pack (B3) into the gear case, making sure the recess in the brake pack faces the oil pan.

8. Install the lock, making sure that the gap in the lock ring is between two recesses in the casing.

**NOTE: Apply compressed air (maximum 14 psi) to the feed hole located in the casing. If a clear click is heard then the piston is installed properly. If not, then remove and check the rear brake assembly.**

9. Install the center support assembly by lowering into the casing above the rear brake pack. Move the center support around to engage the sun gear in the planetary gears and to line up the front one-way clutch.

10. Install the center support retaining bolts. These bolts should be installed loosely while moving the center support around. This will ensure correct alignment of the center support. Do not torque bolts at this time.

11. Carefully assemble the rear clutch assembly (C2) to the nose of the center support. Rotate to be sure all the brake plates are engaged by their hub.

**NOTE: When fully engaged, face of clutch hub (outer spline) will lie flush with, or just rearward of, front and middle sun gear assembly splines (externally splined tube).**

12. Assemble the needle bearing and the bearing races to the hub of the front clutch assembly (C1). Petroleum jelly can be used to help hold them in place.

13. Assemble the front clutch (C1) and input shaft to the transmission. Turn slowly to ensure engagement of the splines in the front clutch (C1) and the rear clutch (C2) which both connect to the direct clutch plates.

14. Install the bearing race in the rear of the overdrive housing. A small amount of petroleum jelly can be used to hold the bearing race in place.

15. Install the guide pins in the overdrive. The guide pins will centralize the overdrive during installation.

16. Place the overdrive in the transmission casing and check that the overdrive clutch (CO) is approximately 0.14 in. (3.5mm) beneath the edge of the overdrive housing. Install the O-ring making sure it seats properly.

17. Lubricate the overdrive surfaces with petroleum jelly and install the torque converter casing. Torque the 4 upper bolts to 25 ft. lbs. (35 N•m). Torque the 2 lower bolts to 43 ft. lbs. (60 N•m).

18. Fit thrust bearing to input shaft and its race plate to pump with flange lip locating in bore of stator support.

19. Install 2 sealing rings to nose of pump cover; be certain rings are free.

20. Install O-ring to O.D. of pump assembly and smear with petroleum jelly.

21. Fit pump to transmission; orientate pump by aligning suction and delivery ports between pump and maincase.

22. Assemble pump part way over input shaft. Carefully ease pump inwards up to rubber O-ring while turning input shaft by hand.

23. Install 7 pump to case bolts and hand tighten.

24. Using hand pressure, work pump into case bore. Use a blunt "pusher" to work O-ring into its groove.

25. Once fully seated the pump flange will project approximately 6mm behind case. Torque pump retaining bolts to specifications.

26. Torque center support bolts to 5 ft. lbs. at a time until proper torque reading is obtained.

27. Check that both input and output shafts are free to rotate and have end float.

**NOTE: The input and output shafts will not necessarily each have the same amount of end float. Both shafts will offer a little resistance to turning, particularly the output shaft in the overrun direction.**

28. Install the gear selector shaft and cam. A new pivot is required to hold it in place.

29. Install the gear selector lock ring, making sure it seats properly.

30. Install the gear selector shaft oil seals with a suitable tool.

31. Locate the pivot end of the parking brake pawl in the case and fit the pivot pin through the spring and pawl and secure with a snap ring.

32. Install the thrust rod to the gear selector cam and install the lock plate. Torque the bolts to 5 ft. lbs. (7 N•m).

33. Connect the kick down cable to the gear case. The type of kick down cable may vary with the type of engine.

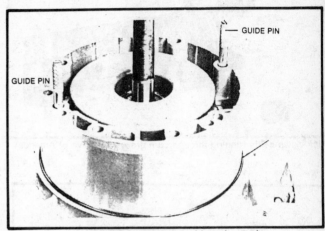

**Center support assembly being lowered into the casing** (© Volvo of America)

**Fitting race to pump** (© Volvo of America)

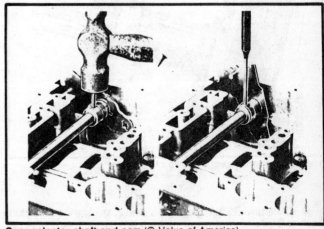

**Gear selector shaft and cam** (© Volvo of America)

Kick-down cable running through cam groove (© Volvo of America)

Checking converter for fit. Distance should be 0.64-0.77 in. (© Volvo of America)

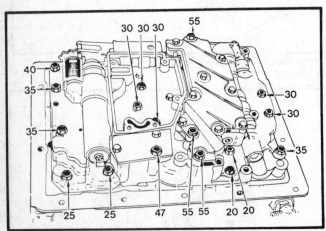

Location of valve body bolts. Numbers refer to length in millimeters (© Volvo of America)

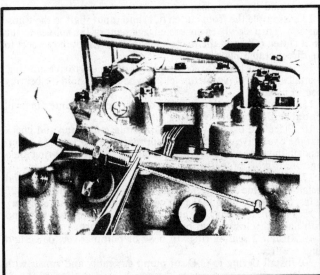

Free play on kick-down cable (© Volvo of America)

Speedometer drive gear (© Volvo of America)

34. Once through the gear case, connect the cable to the cam. The cable must run through the cam groove.

35. Lower the valve body down into position on the case. Be certain that the accumulators and springs close properly.

36. Install the valve body bolts in their proper locations as to length. Check that the valve body is sitting flush on all its mating surfaces, then tighten the bolts to 7 ft. lbs. (10 N•m).

37. Install the gasket, spacer and oil filter and tighten the bolts to 3.6 ft. lbs. (5 N•m).

38. Install the oil pipes into their proper position in the valve body.

39. Carefully pull the kick down cable until the cam barely moves and install the cable clip 0.04 in. (1.0mm) from the end of the bolt thread.

40. Install the oil pan magnet in the oil pan directly under the oil filter.

41. Install a new gasket on the oil pan and install the oil pan. Torque the bolts to 3.6 ft. lbs. (5 N•m).

42. Fit gasket, cover plate and screws to rear face of case to close off governor feed and return ports in case and torque retaining bolts to specifications.

43. Install governor retaining and drive ring to governor body by first inserting lower leg of clip into tapered "through" hole in governor body. Then insert short leg into blind hole on opposite side of governor body.

44. Carefully slide governor over output shaft while holding

clip leg out to allow governor to seat. Clip leg has to be located in small drilling in shaft opposite the governor feed and return drilling. It may be necessary to ease governor to and fro on shaft to engage clip leg in its hole in the shaft.

45. Install speedometer drive gear with drive ball, retaining clip and spacers. If drive gear is press fit, use a special driving tool to install it on shaft.

46. Install new gasket to rear face of case and a new seal in transmission extension housing.

47. Assemble extension housing to case and install the retaining bolts. Torque bolts to specifications.

48. Fit coupling flange and install retaining bolt/nut.

49. Using new O-rings, install the nipples for the oil cooler tubes.

50. Place new O-rings on the plugs for the pressure gauge connections. Install these in the transmission casing and tighten to 5.8 ft. lbs. (8 N•m).

51. Place the torque converter on the input shaft and turn it slowly until it engages with the output shaft splines.

52. Install the gear shift selector lever and torque to 10 ft. lbs. (14 N•m).

**NOTE: When placing torque converter on the transmission take care so as not to damage the oil pump seal or bushing.**

53. Lubricate the solenoid O-rings with petroleum jelly and install the solenoid. Torque to 9.4 ft. lbs. (13 N•m).

54. Reconnect the solenoid wire, and secure the wire to the transmission case with the proper fasteners.

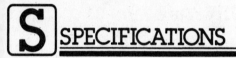

# SPECIFICATIONS

## REDUCTION RATIOS

| | |
|---|---|
| 1st speed | 2.45:1 |
| 2nd speed | 1.45:1 |
| 3rd speed | 1:1 |
| Overdrive | 0.69:1 |
| Reverse | 2.21:1 |
| Converter ratio | 1-2:1 |
| Converter size | 9.764 in (248 mm) |
| Lubricant | ATF Type F or G |

## TORQUE CHART

| Description | | ft. lbs. | N•m |
|---|---|---|---|
| Converter casing-engine | | 25-36 | 35-50 |
| Drive plate to torque converter | | 30-36 | 41-50 |
| Center support to gear case | | 17-20 | 24-28 |
| Pump cover to pump body | | 4-6 | 6-9 |
| Pump assembly to gear case | | 13-18 | 18-25 |
| Parking pawl plate | | 4-6 | 6-9 |
| Converter casing to gear case | M 10 | 19-34 | 26-47 |
| | M 12 | 35-49 | 48-68 |
| Rear extension housing to gear case | | 20-30 | 27-42 |
| Valve bodies for cam | M 6 | 4-6 | 6-9 |
| | M 5 | 3.5-4 | 5-6 |
| Oil strainer to lower valve body | | 3.5-4 | 5-6 |
| Cover plate to gear case | | 4-6 | 6-9 |
| Valve body to gear case | | 6-9 | 8-12 |
| Oil pan to gear case | | 3-3.5 | 4-5 |

# S SPECIFICATIONS

## TORQUE CHART

| Description | ft. lbs. | N•m |
|---|---|---|
| Coupling flange to output shaft | 30-36 | 40-50 |
| Blind plug for pressure test | 3.5-6 | 5-9 |
| Oil cooler nut to gear case | 14-22 | 20-30 |
| Speedometer drive | 3-4 | 4-6 |
| Oil dipstick nut | 58-72 | 80-100 |
| Solenoid valve | 7-12 | 10-16 |
| Oil pan drain plug | 13-17 | 18-23 |

## SHIFT SPEEDS
### km/h (mph)

| Limits for shift points | AW 70 (3.73) | AW 70 (3.91) | AW 71 (3.73) | AW 71 (3.91) | Throttle opening % |
|---|---|---|---|---|---|
| 1-2 | 65 (41) | 62 (39) | 63 (40) | 60 (38) | 100 ① (63) |
| 2-3 | 108 (68) | 103 (65) | 105 (66) | 100 (63) | 100 ① (63) |
| 3-4 | 114 (72) | 109 (69) | 111 (70) | 105 (66) | 75 (47) |
| 4-3 | 40 (25) | 38 (24) | 39 (25) | 37 (23) | 0 (0) |
| 3-2 | 102 (64) | 97 (61) | 99 (62) | 94 (59) | 100 ① (63) |
| 2-1 | 51 (32) | 49 (31) | 50 (32) | 48 (30) | 100 ① (63) |

① Kick-down position

## CLEARANCES

| Component | Clearance in. (mm) |
|---|---|
| Oil pump: pump body-outer gear wheel | 0.083 (2.1) |
| arc segment-large gear wheel | 0.0043-0.0055 (0.11-0.14) |
| axial clearance | 0.0008-0.0019 (0.02-0.05) |
| Brake BO: between clutch pressure plate and lock ring | 0.0138-0.063 (0.35-1.60) |
| Clutch C2, brakes B1 & B2: between clutch pressure plate and lock ring | 0.0118-0.0472 (0.3-1.2) |
| Input shaft, clutch CO: axial clearance | 0.0118-0.0354 (0.3-0.9) |
| Output shaft: axial clearance | 0.0118-0.0354 (0.3-0.9) |

## SPRING IDENTIFICATION CHART
### AW70, AW71

| Spring | Free length mm (in.) | Active coils | Wire dia mm (in.) | Spring OD mm (in.) | Remarks |
|---|---|---|---|---|---|
| Accumulator B2 | 66.68 (2.625) | 14.00 | 2.80 (0.110) | 17.34 (0.682) | AW70: 020, 033 |
| | 68.35 (2.691) | 13.00 | 2.60 (0.102) | 17.91 (0.705) | AW70: 055 |
| | 66.68 (2.625) | 12.00 | 3.20 (0.126) | 20.4 (0.803) | AW71 |
| Accumulator C2 | 61.21 (2.410) | 11.5 | 2.50 (0.098) | 16.54 (0.651) | AW70 |
| | 55.18 (2.172) | 8.5 | 2.00 (0.079) | 15.87 (0.625) | AW71 |
| Accumulator C1 | 68.56 (2.700) | 15.5 | 2.03 (0.080) | 17.53 (0.690) | AW70, AW71 |
| | 64.80 (2.551) | 13.0 | 2.00 (0.079) | 17.20 (0.677) | AW70: 053 |
| Governor | 20.63 (0.812) | 1.5 | 0.90 (0.035) | 9.05 (0.356) | |
| Throttle valve, secondary | 21.94 (0.864) | 8 | 0.71 (0.028) | 8.58 (0.338) | |
| Throttle valve, primary | 43.0 (1.693) | 15.5 | 1.19 (0.047) | 10.80 (0.429) | |
| Detent regulator valve | 31.39 (1.236) | 13.5 | 0.90 (0.035) | 8.85 (0.348) | |
| Intermediate coast modulator valve type 1 | 25.6 (1.008) | 11.5 | 1.14 (0.045) | 9.00 (0.354) | AW70 |
| type 2 | 27.26 (1.073) | 9.5 | 1.10 (0.043) | 9.04 (0.356) | AW71 |
| Reverse clutch sequence valve | 37.55 (1.478) | 14.5 | 1.17 (0.046) | 9.17 (0.361) | |
| Governor modulator valve | 36.07 (1.420) | 12.0 | 0.71 (0.028) | 9.09 (0.358) | Yellow |
| Intermediate coast modulator valve | 42.35 (1.667) | 15.0 | 0.84 (0.033) | 9.24 (0.364) | |
| Intermediate coast shift valve | 35.10 (1.382) | 12.5 | 0.76 (0.030) | 8.96 (0.353) | |
| Low coast shift valve | 34.62 (1.363) | 13.0 | 0.56 (0.022) | 7.56 (0.298) | |
| Line pressure relief valve | 32.14 (1.265) | 9.0 | 2.03 (0.080) | 13.14 (0.517) | |
| Pressure relief valve | 33.32 (1.312) | 7.0 | 1.32 (0.052) | 13.82 (0.544) | |
| Shift valve 3-4, type 1 | 37.88 (1.491) | 14.5 | 1.10 (0.043) | 10.60 (0.417) | AW70 |
| type 2 | 33.65 (1.325) | 14.5 | 1.10 (0.043) | 10.60 (0.417) | AW71 |
| Primary regulator valve, type 1 | 73.30 (2.886) | 15 | 1.588 (0.063) | 16.72 (0.658) | AW70 |
| type 2 | 61.20 (2.409) | 13 | 1.80 (0.071) | 17.2 (0.677) | AW71 (AW70 transmission: 055) |
| Secondary regulator valve | 71.27 (2.806) | 15 | 1.93 (0.076) | 17.43 (0.686) | |

 SPECIAL TOOLS

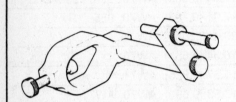

END-FLOAT CHECKING GAUGE

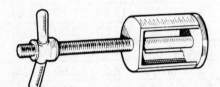

CLUTCH SPRING COMPRESSOR

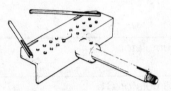

TRANSMISSION MOUNTING BRACKET

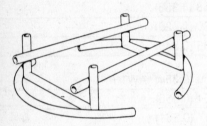

BENCH CRADLE

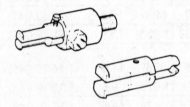

BUSH AND NEEDLE
BEARING REMOVER

PRESSURE TEST EQUIPMENT

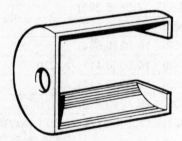

CLUTCH SPRING COMPRESSOR

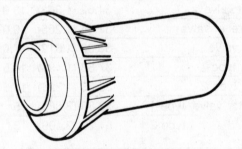

FRONT PUMP SEAL INSTALLER

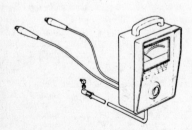

TACHOMETER AND PRESSURE
TEST EQUIPMENT

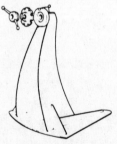

ENGINE STAND

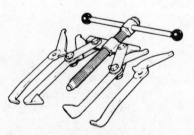

TWO LEGGED PULLER

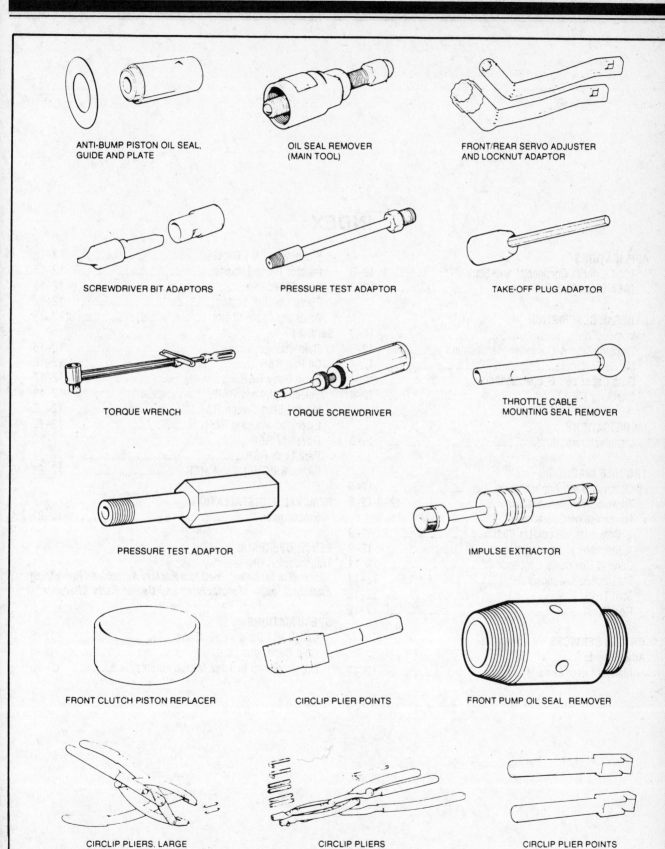

ANTI-BUMP PISTON OIL SEAL,
GUIDE AND PLATE

OIL SEAL REMOVER
(MAIN TOOL)

FRONT/REAR SERVO ADJUSTER
AND LOCKNUT ADAPTOR

SCREWDRIVER BIT ADAPTORS

PRESSURE TEST ADAPTOR

TAKE-OFF PLUG ADAPTOR

TORQUE WRENCH

TORQUE SCREWDRIVER

THROTTLE CABLE
MOUNTING SEAL REMOVER

PRESSURE TEST ADAPTOR

IMPULSE EXTRACTOR

FRONT CLUTCH PISTON REPLACER

CIRCLIP PLIER POINTS

FRONT PUMP OIL SEAL REMOVER

CIRCLIP PLIERS, LARGE

CIRCLIP PLIERS

CIRCLIP PLIER POINTS

# INDEX

# ZF
# 4HP-22

##  APPLICATIONS

1984 Lincoln Continental, Mark VII W/2.4L Turbocharged Diesel Engine
1984 Volvo 760 GLE W/D24T Diesel Engine

##  GENERAL DESCRIPTION

The ZF 4HP22 automatic transmission is a four speed transmission incorporating a lock-up clutch, located in the torque converter and is engaged only when the transmission is operating in the fourth gear range. The fourth gear is an overdrive ratio. This transmission is only available coupled to a diesel engine at the present time.

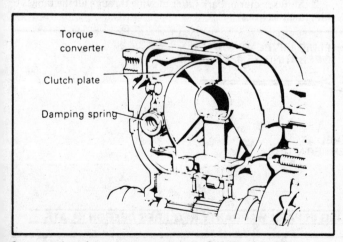

**Cross section of converter components** (© Volvo of America)

ZF 4HP 22 AUTOMATIC
TRANSMISSION IDENTIFICATION TAG
(ADJACENT TO MANUAL LEVER)

22-XXX     SERIAL NO.   ZF
1043 010 008   MODEL NO.
4HP-22

FORD ASSY.   ZF Getriebe GmbH
NO. E4LP-CA    Saarbrucken

PART NO. PREFIX AND SUFFIX
ALSO USED AS MODEL NUMBER

**ZF transmission identification tag** (© Ford Motor Co.)

## Transmission and Converter Identification

### TRANSMISSION

The transmission identification tag is located adjacent to the manual lever on the left side of the unit. Both Volvo and Ford Motor Company have part numbers and model identifications stamped on the tag. The prefix and suffix of the part number is used as the model number for the Ford Motor Company's parts identifications program.

### CONVERTER

The torque converter is a 10¼ inch diameter unit with a 2.55:1 ratio at full stall speed. Identification numbers or symbols are either stamped into the cover or inkstamped on the cover surface.

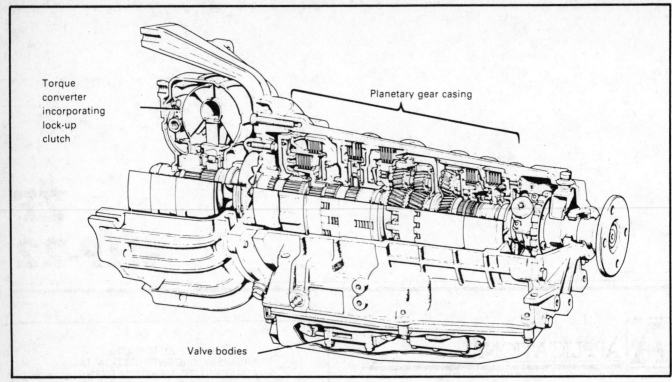

Cutaway view of ZF 4HP22 automatic transmission (© Volvo of America)

## Metric Fasteners

The ZF 4HP22 transmission models are designed and assembled using metric fasteners. Metric measurements are used to determine clearances within the unit during the initial assembly. Metric tools are required to service the unit and torque specifications must be strictly adhered to. Before installing capscrews into aluminum parts, always dip the threaded part of the screw or bolt into oil or anti-seize compound to prevent the threads from galling the aluminum threads in the case or component.

The metric thread is extremely close to the dimensions of the familiar inch system threads and for this reason, extreme care must be exercised to prevent the interchanging of inch system bolts or screws to that of the metric type. Mismatched or incorrect fasteners can result in damage to the transmission unit through malfunctions, breakage, looseness or possible personal injury. The fasteners should be used in the same location as re-

moved from, or with fasteners of the same measurement and strength as the ones removed.

## Fluid Capacities and Fluid Specifications

The fluid fill capacity with the transmission dry, is 8 quarts (US) or 7.7 Liters. The fluid type to be used is Dexron® II or its equivalent.

### FLUID LEVEL INSPECTION

#### Pre-Road Test Check

The fluid level should ideally be checked with the transmission at operating temperatures. Test conditions are:
1. Engine at hot curb idle.
2. Shift selector in Park (after moving through all the ranges to fill clutch cavities).

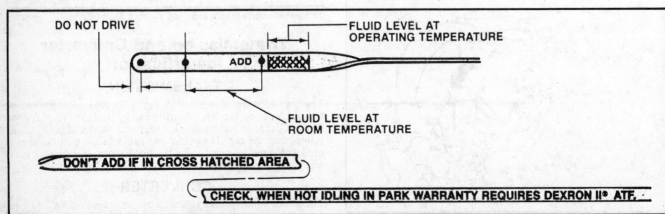

Fluid level dipstick indicator rod markings (© Ford Motor Co.)

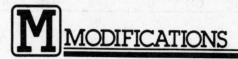

For road testing, a cold check can be made. The fluid level should be between the inner holes. If the level is at or below the lowest hole, the vehicle should **not** be driven without adding fluid.

### Hot Fill

After the vehicle is driven some 20 minutes, the fluid temperature should be close to 150 degrees Fahrenheit (65°C). The final fill should be in the cross-hatched area at operating temperature. DO NOT OVERFILL. DO NOT ADD FLUID IF IT IS IN THE CROSS-HATCHING.

### Leak Check

If the fluid is low, check for and repair any repairable leak.

### Fluid Condition

If the fluid is burnt or discolored, or if it has clutch residue, the transmission should be replaced. Be sure to note the fluid condition on the warranty return Diagnostic Form.

# MODIFICATIONS

No transmission modifications have been published by the manufacturer at time of this publication.

# TROUBLE DIAGNOSIS

The ZF 4HP22 Automatic transmission torque converter and gear train are not to be serviced by the manufacturers' new car dealerships at this time. If diagnosis determines damages or malfunctions are present in the converter or drive train, the entire transmission assembly must be removed from the vehicle and re- placed through the dealership parts department exchange program. As the supply of transmissions become more plentiful, the overhaul by the independent repair shops will be required to fulfill the requirements of the motoring public.

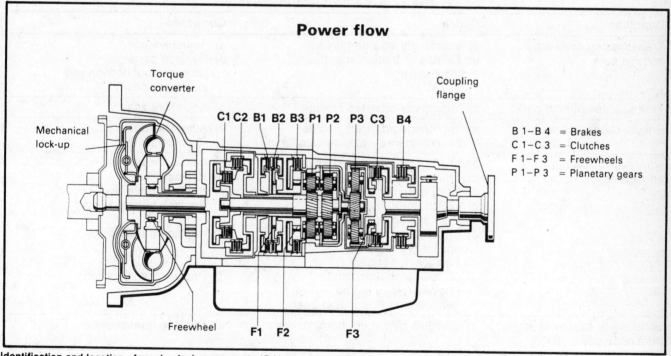

**Identification and location of mechanical components** (© Volvo of America)

## CLUTCH AND BRAKE APPLICATION CHART
### ZF 4HP22 Automatic Transmission

| Gear Selector Position and Gear | Clutch | | | Brake | | | | Overrunning Clutch | | | Parking Pawl |
|---|---|---|---|---|---|---|---|---|---|---|---|
| | C-1 | C-2 | C-3 | B-1 | B-2 | B-3 | B-4 | F-1 | F-2 | F-3 | |
| P | | | ON | | | | | | | | ON |
| R | | ON | ON | | | ON | | | | | |
| N | | | ON | | | | | | | | |

## CLUTCH AND BRAKE APPLICATION CHART
### ZF 4HP22 Automatic Transmission

| Gear Selector Position and Gear | | Clutch C-1 | C-2 | C-3 | Brake B-1 | B-2 | B-3 | B-4 | Overrunning Clutch F-1 | F-2 | F-3 | Parking Pawl |
|---|---|---|---|---|---|---|---|---|---|---|---|---|
| D | 1st | ON | | ON | | | | | | ON | ON | |
|   | 2nd | ON | | ON | ON | ON | | | ON | | ON | |
|   | 3rd | ON | ON | ON | | ON | | | | | ON | |
|   | 4th | ON | ON | | | ON | | ON | | | | |
| 3 | 1st | ON | | ON | | | | | | ON | ON | |
|   | 2nd | ON | | ON | ON | ON | | | ON | | ON | |
|   | 3rd | ON | ON | ON | | ON | | | | | ON | |
| 2 | 1st | ON | | ON | | | | | | ON | ON | |
|   | 2nd | ON | | ON | ON | ON | | | ON | | ON | |
| 1 | 1st | ON | | ON | | | ON | | | | ON ① | |

① Only transfers power when engine is pulling

## CHILTONS THREE "C's" TRANSMISSION DIAGNOSIS CHART
### ZF 4HP22 Automatic Transmission

| Condition | Cause | Correction |
|---|---|---|
| Transmission does not engage park | a) Improperly adjusted linkage<br>b) Excessive friction in park mechanism | a) Adjust linkage<br>b) Replace parts (cam and connection rod, eventually pawl) |
| Trans. does not hold park | a) Improperly adjusted linkage | a) Adjust linkage |
| Engine cannot be started | a) Improperly adjusted linkage<br>b) Neutral start switch malfunctioning | a) Adjust linkage<br>b) Replace switch |
| No/delayed reverse engagement | a) Improperly adjusted linkage<br>b) Transmission filter plugged<br>c) Body dirty/sticking valves<br>d) Clutch burnt/worn, in this case no 3rd gear<br>e) Clutch burnt/worn, no engine braking in Position 1, 1st gear<br>f) Clutch burnt/worn, no engine braking in 2nd + 3rd gear, also in Pos. 1, 1st gear | a) Adjust linkage<br>b) Replace filter<br>c) Replace valve body<br>d) Replace transmission<br>e) Replace transmission<br>f) Replace transmission |
| Slippage or chatter at start in reverse gear | a) Clutches damaged, burnt or worn | a) Replace transmission |
| Harsh engagement P-R or N-R, or distinct double jerk at P-R or N-R (below 1500 RPM engine speed) | a) Valve body malfunction (will give the same symptoms when changing from 2nd to 3rd gear) | a) Replace valve body |
| Back-up lights do not operate, Bulbs, wiring and fuses O.K. | a) Improperly adjusted linkage<br>b) Neutral start switch malfunctioning | a) Adjust the linkage<br>b) Replace switch |
| Engine cannot be started in the "N" position | a) Improperly adjusted linkage<br>b) Neutral start switch malfunctioning | a) Adjust linkage<br>b) Replace switch |

# CHILTONS THREE "C's" TRANSMISSION DIAGNOSIS CHART
## ZF 4HP22 Automatic Transmission

| Condition | Cause | Correction |
|---|---|---|
| Vehicle moves in Position N | a) Improperly adjusted linkage<br>b) Clutch seized | a) Adjust linkage<br>b) Replace transmission |
| No drive in "D" position | a) Improperly adjusted linkage<br>b) Transmission filter plugged<br>c) Clutch burnt/worn<br>d) One way clutch 1st gear slips | a) Adjust linkage<br>b) Replace filter<br>c) Replace transmission<br>d) Replace transmission |
| Slipping or chatter at driveway | a) Clutch burnt/worn | a) Replace transmission |
| Strong jerk N-D (below 1500 RPM engine speed) | a) Clutch damper malfunction<br>b) Clutch burnt/worn | a) Replace valve body<br>b) Replace transmission |
| No or erratic shifts | | |
|   No 1-2/2-1 | a) Governor valve sticking<br>b) Shift valve 1-2 sticking | a) Replace governor<br>b) Replace valve body |
|   No 1-2 | a) Clutches burnt/worn | a) Replace transmission |
|   No 2-3/3-2 | a) Governor valve sticking<br>b) Shift valve 2-3 sticking | a) Replace governor<br>b) Replace valve body |
|   No 2-3 | a) Clutch burnt/worn | a) Replace transmission |
|   No 3-4/4-3 | a) Governor valve sticking<br>b) Shift valve 3-4 sticking | a) Replace governor<br>b) Replace valve body |
|   No 3-4 | a) Clutch burnt/worn | a) Replace transmission |
| Vehicle starts in 2nd gear | a) Sticking governor<br>b) 1-2 Shift valve sticking | a) Replace governor<br>b) Replace valve body |
| Vehicle starts in 3rd gear | a) Sticking governor<br>b) 1-2, 2-3 Shift valves sticking | a) Replace governor<br>b) Replace valve body |
| Shifts 1-3 in ⒟ , D ranges | a) 2-3 Shift valve sticking | a) Replace valve body |
| Shift Speeds | | |
|   No upshifts | a) Stuck governor<br>b) Shift valves sticking | a) Replace governor<br>b) Replace valve body |
|   Shift points incorrect at full throttle | a) Throttle cable setting incorrect | a) Re-adjust throttle cable |
|   No 1-2/2-1 shift at kickdown | a) Throttle cable setting incorrect | a) Re-adjust throttle cable |
|   No 2-3/3-2 shift at kickdown | a) Throttle cable setting incorrect | a) Re-adjust throttle cable |
|   No 4-3 shift at kickdown | a) 4-3 Kickdown valve sticking | a) Replace valve body |
| Shift quality | | |
|   Harsh shifts at light throttle | a) Valve body malfunction | a) Replace valve body |
|   Harsh shifts at full throttle and kickdown | a) Valve body malfunction<br>b) Clutch plates burnt/worn | a) Replace valve body<br>b) Replace transmission |
|   Soft shifts at full throttle and kickdown | a) Valve body malfunction<br>b) Clutch plates burnt/worn | a) Replace valve body<br>b) Replace transmission |
| Position D<br>3rd Gear<br>No engine braking | a) Clutch burnt/worn | a) Replace transmission |
| Position L<br>No manual 2-1 downshift | a) Dirty/sticking valve body<br>b) Governor sticking | a) Replace valve body<br>b) Replace governor |
| No engine braking | a) Clutch burnt/worn | a) Replace transmission |
| Torque Converter<br>Lockup points incorrect for lockup clutch | a) Valve body malfunction<br>b) Governor pressure incorrect | a) Replace valve body<br>b) Replace governor |

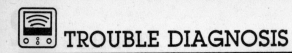

## CHILTONS THREE "C's" TRANSMISSION DIAGNOSIS CHART
### ZF 4HP22 Automatic Transmission

| Condition | Cause | Correction |
|---|---|---|
| Shift too harsh | a) Damper malfunction<br>b) Torque converter malfunction | a) Replace valve body<br>b) Replace transmission |
| No lockup | a) Valve body malfunction<br>b) Torque converter malfunction | a) Replace valve body<br>b) Replace transmission |
| Throttle cable sticking | a) Too much friction in sleeve of throttle cable<br>b) Throttle pressure valve sticking | a) Replace cable<br><br>b) Replace valve body |
| Noisy and no drive after long journey | a) Oil filter on valve body dirty | a) If there is no burnt clutch plate lining in oil sump, then replace filter, otherwise replace transmission |
| Very noisy and no drive | a) Flex plate is damaged<br>b) Pump drive worn | a) Replace flex plate or transmission<br>b) Replace transmission |
| Oil dripping from converter housing | a) Seal ring in pump housing damaged<br>b) Pump housing porous<br>c) Converter leaking from welded seam | a) Replace seal<br><br>b) Replace transmission<br>c) Replace transmission |
| Leakage between transmission and oil pan | a) Incorrect torque of bolts<br>b) Pan gasket damaged | a) Tighten bolts<br>b) Replace gasket |
| Leakage between intermediate plate and main housing (esp. at pump pressure point) | a) Converter housing bolts have worked loose | a) Tighten bolts |
| Oil loss at speedo | a) Damaged O-ring on speedo | a) Replace O-ring |
| Oil leak at throttle connection cable | a) O-ring connection damaged | a) Replace O-ring or complete cable |
| Oil leak at extension housing | a) Output oil seal damaged | a) Replace seal |
| Loss of oil through breather | a) Oil level too high<br>b) No breather cap<br>c) O-ring breather damaged<br><br>d) Securing clip broken/damaged | a) Check and correct oil level<br>b) Replace cap or change breather<br>c) Remove extension housing and replace O-ring<br>d) Replace clip |
| Leakage in cooler lines | a) Loose connections | a) Re-tighten |
| Oil leak at intermediate | a) Plugs loose | a) Tighten plugs, replace washers |
| Leakage between main case and extension housing | a) Loose bolts<br>b) Gasket damaged | a) Re-tighten<br>b) Replace gasket |
| High pitched noise in all positions, esp. if oil is cold | a) Low oil level<br>b) Leaking valve body | a) Top off as required<br>b) Replace valve body |
| High-pitched squeaking noise (dependent on engine RPM) in all gears when oil is warm, accompanied by intermittent no drive after long journey | a) Dirty filter | a) If no debris in sump, just replace filter, otherwise replace transmission |
| Loud noise when in lockup | a) Torsional damper malfunction | a) Replace transmission |
| Torsional vibrations from engine when in lockup | a) Engine RPM is too low, lockup shift point incorrect | a) Replace valve body |

# TRANSMISSION OPERATION

## Torque Converter With Lock-up Clutch

The torque converter serves as both a clutch and a hydraulic gear, linking the engine to the gearbox. Due to the slip between the impeller and turbine there is always some power loss in the torque converter when it is operating hydraulically. The lock-up unit, which is very similar to a manual gearbox clutch, makes it possible to mechanically transfer power and thereby eliminate this power loss. This has the added benefit of lowering engine rpm, fuel consumption and oil temperature.

The lock-up function can only be engaged when cruising at high speed in 4th gear. Moreover the transmission oil temperature must exceed 20°C (68°F).

The mechanical lock-up unit consists of a lined clutch plate and damping spring. The plate is pressed against the torque converter casing when the clutch is engaged.

A special valve in the valve body system beneath the transmission, controls the engagement and disengagement of the clutch. To the driver, lock-up engagement feels like a gear change.

### DISENGAGED LOCK-UP CLUTCH

Power is transferred from the impeller by the turbine to the transmission input shaft. Hydraulic oil under pressure, directed by a valve in the valve body, passes through the hollow input shaft and grooves in the front thrust washer, to the front side of the clutch plate. This prevents the plate from contacting the torque converter front face. The oil returns through grooves at the bottom of the stator.

### ENGAGED LOCK-UP CLUTCH

The oil flow is reversed when lock-up is engaged. Oil flows through the stator grooves and pushes the lock-up clutch plate forwards so that its friction face is pressed against the torque converter body.

Springs on the clutch plate take up the shock of engagement, and the engine torque is now transferred mechanically to the input shaft. Surplus oil returns through the hollow input shaft.

## Transmission Mechanical Power Flow

### 1ST SPEED, GEAR SELECTOR IN D

1. C1 front clutch is applied.
2. C3 clutch for 4th gear is applied.
3. P1 planetary gear carrier is locked against gear case through F2 freewheel when engine is pulling. But is overrun when engine is coasting.
4. P3 planetary gear rotates with planetary gear carrier.
5. F3 freewheel is engaged.

### GEAR SELECTOR IN POSITION 1

1. B3 brake is applied and engine braking is obtained.

### 2ND SPEED, GEAR SELECTOR IN D

1. C1 front clutch is applied.
2. C3 clutch for 4th gear is applied.
3. B1 and B2 brakes are applied.
4. F2 freewheel is not locked.
5. Intermediate shaft, which is splined to sun gear shaft for P1 and P2 planetary gears is locked. P3 planetary gear rotates as a solid block.

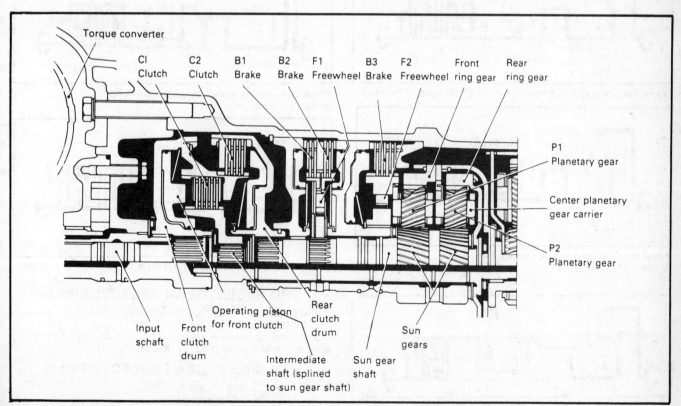

**First to third gear components** (© Volvo of America)

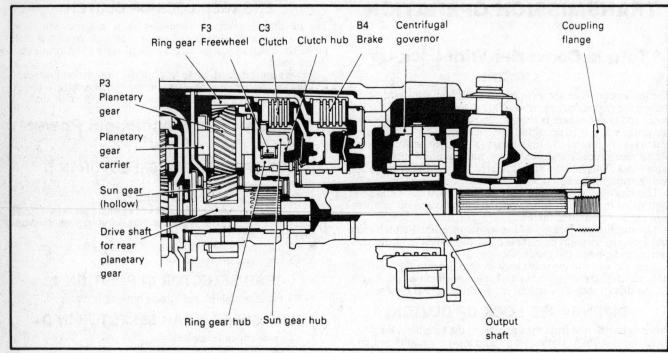

Overdrive components (© Volvo of America)

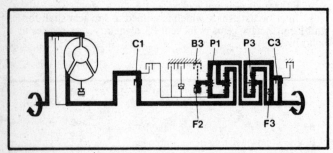

Power flow—first speed, selector lever in "D" (© Volvo of America)

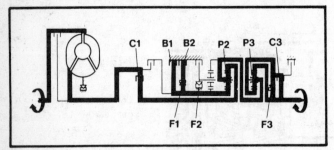

Power flow—second speed, selector lever in "D"
(© Volvo of America)

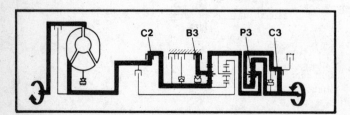

Power flow— selector lever in reverse (© Volvo of America)

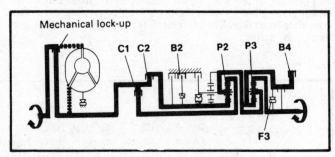

Power flow—fourth speed, selector lever in "D"
(© Volvo of America)

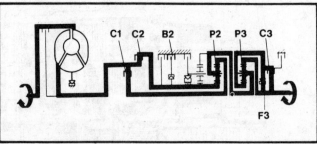

Power flow—third speed, selector lever in "D" (© Volvo of America)

## 3RD SPEED, GEAR SELECTOR IN D

1. C1, C2 and C3 clutches are applied.
2. B2 brake is applied.
3. F1 and F2 freewheels are overrun. P1, P2 and P3 planetary gears rotate as a solid block so that ratio is 1:1.

## 4TH SPEED, GEAR SELECTOR IN D

1. C1 and C2 clutches are applied.
2. B2 and B4 brakes are applied.
3. No freewheels are locked.

4. B4 brake prevents P3 planetary gear sun wheel from rotating. Planetary gear, driven by planetary gear carrier, transfers power via ring gear to output shaft, achieving a reduction ratio 0.73:1.

5. At speeds above a preset value the torque converter is locked to prevent slipping.

## REVERSE

1. C2 and C3 clutches are applied.
2. B3 brake is applied.
3. Front planetary gear carrier is locked and the output shaft rotates counter clockwise. P3 planetary gear rotates as a solid block.

## SHIFT SELECTOR POSITIONS AND OPERATION

### FORD MOTOR CO.

The ZF transmission is fully automatic in either the Ⓓ (overdrive) or D (overdrive lockout) positions. Manual upshifting and downshifting is available through the forward drive positions Ⓓ, D, L.

Ⓓ **(Overdrive)**—This is the normal driving position for an automatic overdrive transmission. In this position the transmission starts in first gear and as the vehicle accelerates, automatically upshifts to second, third and fourth gears. The transmission will automatically downshift as vehicle speed decreases.

NOTE: The transmission will not shift into or remain in overdrive (fourth) gear when the accelerator is pushed to the floor.

**D (Overdrive Lockout)**—In this position the transmission operates as in Ⓓ(OVERDRIVE) except there will be no shift into the overdrive gear and no converter clutch lockup. This position may be used when driving up or down mountainous roads to provide better performance and greater engine braking than the overdrive position. The transmission may be shifted from Ⓓ to D or D to Ⓓ at any vehicle speed.

**L (Low)**—This position can be used when maximum engine braking is desired. To help brake the vehicle on hilly roads where D (Overdrive Lockout) does not provide enough braking, shift the selector lever to L (Low). At vehicle speeds above approximately 20 mph the transmission will shift to second gear, and remain in second gear. When vehicle speed drops below approximately 20 mph the transmission will downshift to first gear, and remain in first gear. Upshifts from L (Low) can be made by manually shifting to Ⓓ (Overdrive) or D (Overdrive Lockout). When the L (Low) position is selected for initial driveaway, the transmission will remain in the selected gear range until the selector is moved into another gear position.

**P, R AND N**—These positions operate the same as other Ford automatics.

**Reverse Inhibitor**—If the selector is moved to R with the vehicle moving forward at 19 mph or more, the transmission will not shift to reverse gear.

## FORCED DOWNSHIFTS

1. At vehicle speeds from approximately 50 mph to 20 mph in Ⓓ(Overdrive) or D (Overdrive Lockout) the transmission will downshift to second gear when the accelerator is pushed to the floor.

2. At vehicle speeds above approximately 50 mph the transmission will not downshift to second gear.

3. At vehicle speeds below approximately 20 mph the transmission will downshift to first gear when the accelerator is pushed to the floor.

4. At most vehicle speeds in Ⓓ(Overdrive) the transmission will downshift from fourth gear to third gear when the accelerator is pushed for moderate to heavy acceleration.

## GEAR SELECTOR

### VOLVO

1. The gear selector has 7 positions. The overdrive fourth gear and the lock-up clutch are only available when the lever is placed in "D".

2. The start inhibitor switch is located in the housing. It is an electrical switch which prevents the engine from starting unless "N" or "P" is selected.

3. There is no electrical selection of overdrive (4th) gear, all gear selections are made through a linkage rod.

4. Adjustment of the linkage rod is done in same way as on the AW71 gearbox.

## GENERAL DIAGNOSIS SEQUENCE

The general diagnosis sequence is the same as for Ford automatics, except that there is *no line pressure test*:

1. Fluid level and condition
2. Injection pump linkage adjustment
3. Free movement of T.V. cable/cable adjustment
4. Manual linkage check
5. Road test
6. Stall test
7. Visual inspection (as appropriate)
8. Do not drive the vehicle unless:
   a. Fluid level is correct.
   b. Manual selector lever is in synchronization with detents in the transmission.
   c. Kickdown (T.V.) cable moves free of all obstructions.

NOTE: Experienced technicians can use the operation of a C3 or C5 automatic transmission with an added gear set for fourth

## STALL SPEED DIAGNOSIS
## ZF 4HP22 Automatic Transmission

| Selector Positions | Stall Speed(s) High (Slip) | Stall Speeds Low |
|---|---|---|
| Forward Ranges Ⓓ, D, L | Clutch Slippage: Replace Transmission | 1. Check engine for proper tune-up. |
| All Driving Ranges | Check T.V. Adjustment; if okay Replace Transmission | 2. Check injector pump linkage for proper adjustment. |
| R Only | Clutch Slippage: Replace Transmission | 3. If okay, replace transmission assembly due to torque converter one-way clutch slip. |

gear in the diagnosis. A major difference is the hydraulic application of the converter clutch, which can be definitely felt coming on. Most conditions that would lead to overhaul of a C5 or C3 would lead to replacement of the ZF transmission.

## STALL TEST

The stall test checks for clutch slippage, for engine performance and for torque converter operation. It should be done only with the engine coolant and transmission fluid at proper levels and at operating temperature, and with the T.V. cable set properly. Apply the service and parking brakes firmly for each stall test.

1. Look up the specified stall RPM for the vehicle (minimum 2600 RPM, maximum 2900 RPM). Use a grease pencil to mark the RPM on the dial of a diesel tachometer.

2. Connect the tachometer to the engine and position it for easy reading from the driver's seat.

3. In each of the driving ranges, press the accelerator to the floor and hold it just long enough to let the engine get to full RPM.

### ———————— CAUTION ————————

*If the needle goes past the mark, something is slipping. Release the accelerator immediately.*

4. Record the results in each range on the Diagnosis Check Sheet.

5. Run the engine at fast idle, in neutral, between each test to cool the fluid.

6. Refer to the diagnosis chart for further checks or corrective action to take.

## ROAD TEST

### Before Road Test
#### KICKDOWN (T.V.) CABLE

1. Bead must be tightly crimped to cable.
2. Cable must move freely both ways when accelerator is depressed and released.
3. Clearance must be as specified between bead and barrel end.

### ———————— CAUTION ————————

*If the shifts are mushy, do not drive the vehicle until the adjustment is correct.*

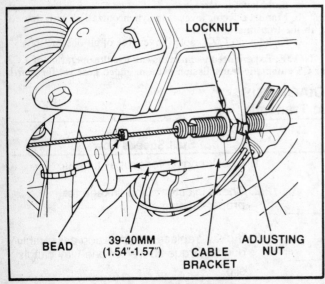

LOCKNUT

BEAD  39-40MM (1.54"-1.57")  CABLE BRACKET  ADJUSTING NUT

Kickdown (T.V.) cable adjustment (© Ford Motor Co.)

## MANUAL LINKAGE

Check before road test. Engine can be off.

1. Pull the column shift lever toward you to "ungate" it. On vehicles with a floor shift, depress the button the "T" handle. Move it through all the ranges.

2. Feel the detents in the transmission. Are they synchronized with the markings on the shift selector?

3. Shift to the ⑩ (overdrive) position detent and let the lever drop into position.

4. Check if the shift gate pawl is against the ⑩ stop by trying to move the lever toward position ⑩ without ungating it.

If there is free movement to the ⑩ stop; or if the pawl is up on the D land; an adjustment is required.

### ———————— CAUTION ————————

*Do not drive the car if the adjustment is not correct.*

### ROAD TEST

Drive the vehicle in all ranges and through all gears. Use the Diagnosis Check Sheet and check for:

1. Proper Engagement
2. Correct Upshift and Downshift Speeds
3. Any Signs of Slip, Harshness, Mushiness or other Shift Feel Condition
4. Engagement and Disengagement of Converter Clutch

# ON CAR SERVICES

## Adjustments

FORD MOTOR COMPANY VEHICLES

### MANUAL LEVER LINKAGE

#### Adjustment

1. Put the selector lever in the ⑩ position, tight against the stop and retain it with a weight. With floor shift, block the lever rearward.

2. Disconnect the linkage at the manual lever on the transmission or the bellcrank.

3. Shift the lever fully counterclockwise; then back three detents to Overdrive ⑩.

**NOTE: The ZF transmission has an extra detent position, marked "X" on the illustration. This detent position is not used on Ford vehicle applications. It is equivalent to Manual low.**

4. Connect the linkage; check the selector is still in ⑩; tighten the nut securely.

### KICKDOWN (T.V.) CABLE

#### Installation and Adjustment

**NOTE: If a new cable is used, the reference bead will be loose on the cable. Proceed as follows:**

#### NEW CABLE

1-A. With cable reconnected at transmission and transmission bolted up to engine, follow steps B4-B5 and set adjusting nuts approximately in the center of the threaded barrel.

2-A. Pull the "T" head until you feel the wide-open throttle "full" stop, (about 6.4mm or .25 inch before maximum cable travel). Do not pull any farther.

3-A. Slide the bead along the cable until there is a gap of 39-40mm (1.54 to 1.57 inch) between the end of the threaded barrel and the end of the bead closest to the barrel.

4-A. Crimp the bead to the braided cable core with a wire ter-

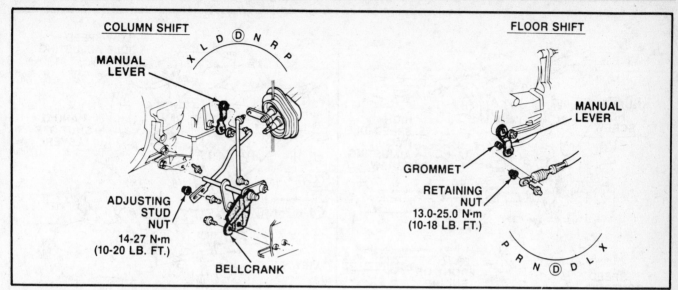

**Adjustment of manual shift linkage** (© Ford Motor Co.)

minal crimper. Be careful to distort the bead as little as possible.

5-A. Remove the cable from the bracket and proceed to B.

### WITH A USED CABLE, REFERENCE BEAD CRIMPED TIGHT TO CABLE

1-B. Rest the braided cable core wire on the split in the white plastic lever insert (7L109) with the "T" head on the trunnion side and pull it through.

2-B. Snap the "T" head into the insert trunnions.

3-B. Snap the insert into the lower rectangular hole in the injector pump side lever after threading the braided cable core through the slot.

4-B. Spin the rearward adjusting nut back to end of the threaded barrel and place the threaded barrel through the slot in the cable bracket.

5-B. Pull the threaded barrel into the 10.2mm diameter hole in the bracket.

### Cable Adjustment

6-C. Set the injector pump top lever at the full throttle position.

7-C. Tighten the rear adjusting nut on the threaded barrel until

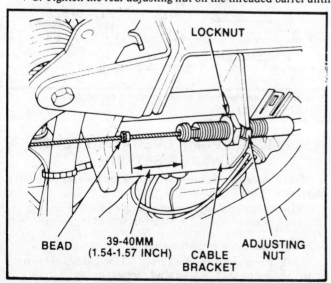

**Bead clearance on kickdown (T.V.) cable** (© Ford Motor Co.)

a gap of 39-40mm (1.54-1.57 inch) exists between the edge of the crimped bead on the cable closest to the barrel and the end of the threaded barrel.

8-C. Tighten the forward adjusting nut to lock the cable assembly to the bracket. Torque to 9-12 N•m (80-106 lb-in).

9-C. Recheck 39-40mm (1.54-1.57 inch) dimension and reset if necessary.

## INJECTOR PUMP LINKAGE

### Adjustment

Three adjustments affect the transmission performance and the transmission shift speeds: Low-Speed Idle Adjustment, High Engine "W.O.T." (Wide Open Throttle) Speed Adjustment and Injector Pump Operating Lever Linkage Setting. All these adjustments are performed on the injector pump. The Low-Speed Idle Adjustment and the High Engine "W.O.T." Speed Adjustment must be performed before the Injector Pump Operating Lever Linkage Setting. All three adjustments must be performed prior to adjusting the Kickdown (T.V.) Cable.

Before proceeding with any of these adjustments the following must be verified:

1. The engine must be at the normal operating temperature.
2. The valve clearance must be at the specified dimensions.
3. All electrical equipment must be in the OFF position.
4. A tachometer, such as the Diesel Tach/Timing Meter, Rotunda 78-0116 or equivalent, must be attached to the diagnostic plug connector of the diesel engine.

## LOW-SPEED IDLE

### Adjustment

1. Start the engine.
2. Loosen the locknut on the low-speed idle adjusting screw (located on the top inboard side of the injector pump). Adjust the idle speed by turning the low-speed adjusting screw until 750-800 rpm is obtained.
3. Turn the knurled head screw until the clearance between the knurled head and the speed control lever is 0.5-1.0mm (0.020-0.040 inch).
4. Check, and if required, adjust the High Engine "W.O.T." Speed and the Injector Pump Operating Lever Setting.

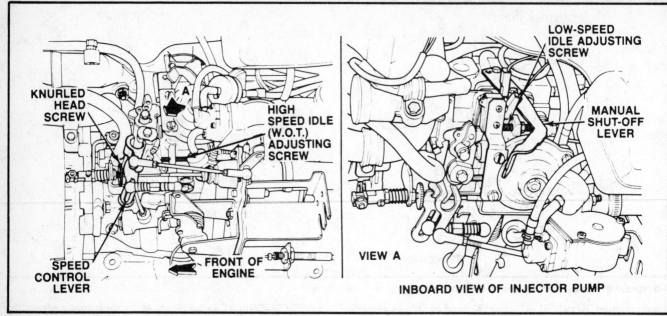

Speed controls on diesel engine injector pump (© Ford Motor Co.)

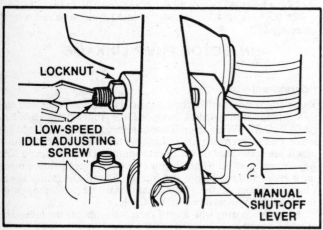

Low speed adjusting screw location (© Ford Motor Co.)

## HIGH ENGINE "W.O.T." (WIDE OPEN THROTTLE) SPEED

### Adjustment

**NOTE: Before adjusting the High Engine "W.O.T." speed, make sure the engine is at normal operating temperature.**

1. Start the engine.
2. Move the speed control lever to the full load or "W.O.T." (Wide Open Throttle) position.
3. Loosen the locknut and turn the engine high idle speed ("W.O.T.") adjusting screw (located on the outboard side of the injector pump) until 5350 ± 100 rpm is obtained.
4. Check the throttle cable so that the stop on the speed control lever rests on the engine high idle speed ("W.O.T.") adjusting screw when the lever is in the full load or "W.O.T." position
5. Check to verify that the speed control lever is at the full load or "W.O.T." position when the accelerator is depressed fully to the floor.

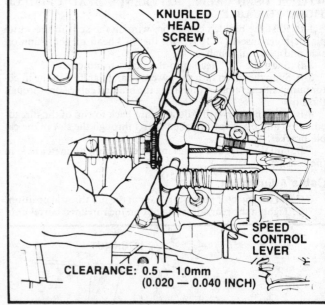

Clearance for knurled head screw to speed control lever (© Ford Motor Co.)

## INJECTOR PUMP OPERATING LEVER LINKAGE SETTING

**NOTE: Prior to adjusting the injector pump operating lever, make sure of the following:**

1. Low-Speed Idle Adjustment is at the specified setting.
2. High Engine "W.O.T." Speed Adjustment is at the specified setting.
3. The engine is at normal operating temperature.

**NOTE: For the purpose of accuracy, it is recommended that the metric setting be used in taking all measurements.**

1. Measure distance "A" from the front face of the pump brack-

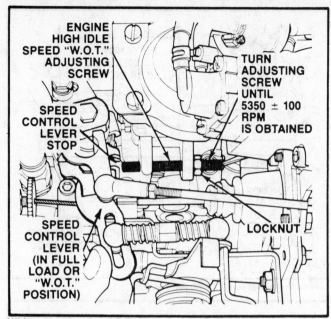

Wide open throttle (W.O.T.) speed adjustment (© Ford Motor Co.)

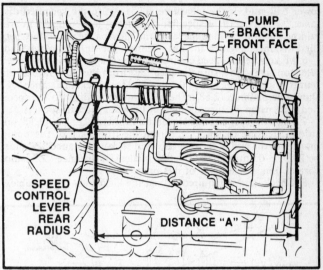

Measuring dimension "A" (© Ford Motor Co.)

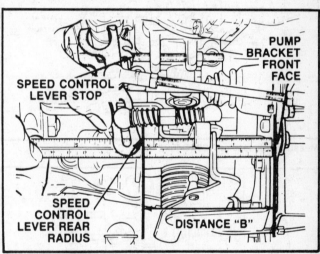

Measuring dimension "B" (© Ford Motor Co.)

et to the rear radius of the speed control lever Record distance "A".

2. Push the speed control lever against the full load or the "W.O.T." stop and measure distance "B" from the front face of the pump bracket to the rear radius of the speed control lever, Record distance "B".

3. Subtract distance "B" from distance "A" to find distance "Y" ("A" − "B" = "Y"). For example: if distance "A" is 128mm (5.03 inches) and distance "B" is 81.0mm (3.18 inches), then by subtracting distance "B" from distance "A", distance "Y" is 47.0mm (1.85 inches) (128mm − 81mm = 47.0mm or 5.03 inches − 3.18 inches = 1.85 inches).

4. Find distance "C" by finding distance "Y" in the appropriate chart. For example: if distance "Y" is 47.0mm (1.85 inches) then distance "C" is 67.0mm (2.64 inches).

5. Disconnect the linkage from the lower stud on the speed control lever and measure distance "C" from the centerline of the lever shaft (on top of the injector pump) to the centerline of the

## DISTANCE "C" ADJUSTING TABLE CHARTS
### Ford Motor Company

| Measurements in Inches | | | | | | | | | | | |
|---|---|---|---|---|---|---|---|---|---|---|---|
| Y (in.) | 1.61 | 1.63 | 1.65 | 1.67 | 1.69 | 1.71 | 1.73 | 1.75 | 1.77 | 1.79 | 1.81 | 1.83 |
| C (in.) | 3.07 | 3.03 | 3.00 | 2.94 | 2.90 | 2.87 | 2.83 | 2.79 | 2.76 | 2.73 | 2.70 | 2.66 |
| Y (in.) | 1.85 | 1.87 | 1.89 | 1.91 | 1.93 | 1.95 | 1.97 | 1.99 | 2.01 | 2.03 | 2.05 | 2.07 |
| C (in.) | 2.64 | 2.61 | 2.58 | 2.55 | 2.53 | 2.50 | 2.47 | 2.45 | 2.42 | 2.40 | 2.38 | 2.35 |
| Y (in.) | 2.09 | 2.11 | 2.13 | 2.15 | 2.17 | 2.19 | 2.20 | | | | | |
| C (in.) | 2.33 | 2.31 | 2.29 | 2.27 | 2.26 | 2.24 | 2.22 | | | | | |

| Measurements in MM | | | | | | | | | | | |
|---|---|---|---|---|---|---|---|---|---|---|---|
| Y (mm) | 41 | 41.5 | 42 | 42.5 | 43 | 43.5 | 44 | 44.5 | 45 | 45.5 | 46 | 46.5 |
| C (mm) | 78.1 | 77.0 | 76.0 | 74.9 | 73.9 | 73.0 | 72.0 | 71.1 | 70.3 | 69.4 | 68.6 | 67.8 |
| Y (mm) | 47 | 47.5 | 48 | 48.5 | 49 | 49.5 | 50 | 50.5 | 51 | 51.5 | 52 | 52.5 |
| C (mm) | 67.0 | 66.3 | 65.6 | 64.9 | 64.2 | 63.5 | 62.9 | 62.3 | 61.6 | 61.0 | 60.5 | 59.9 |
| Y (mm) | 53 | 53.5 | 54 | 54.5 | 55 | 55.5 | 56 | | | | | |
| C (mm) | 59.4 | 58.8 | 58.3 | 57.8 | 57.3 | 56.8 | 56.4 | | | | | |

lower ball stud. If the measurement is not to the specified distance "C", adjust to the specified distance by loosening the nut retaining the lower stud to the lever and moving the nut to the specified distance. Tighten the nut. Connect the linkage to the stud.

6. Make sure the speed control lever rests against the low-speed idle stop screw. Measure distance "X" from the front face of the pump bracket to the end of the rear ball stud socket Distance "X" should be 68.0mm (2.68 inches). If required, adjust to the specified dimension by turning the nut between the ball sockets.

7. Place the speed control lever in the full load or "W.O.T." position. Measure distance "Z" from the front face of the pump bracket to the end of the rear ball stud socket. Distance "Z" must be $29.0 \pm 0.5$mm ($1.14 \pm 0.020$ inches). If distance "Z" is not correct, repeat Steps 1-4 of this procedure.

8. Check, and if required, adjust the kickdown (T.V.) cable.

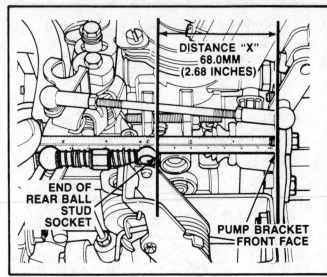

Measuring dimension "X" (© Ford Motor Co.)

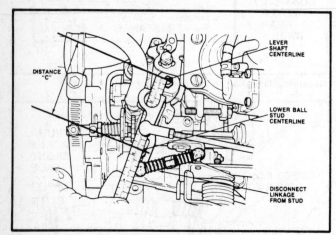

Measuring dimension "C" (© Ford Motor Co.)

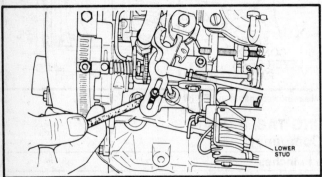

Adjusting dimension "C" (© Ford Motor Co.)

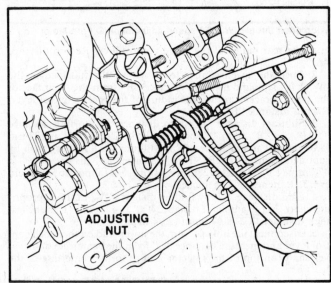

Adjusting dimension "X" (© Ford Motor Co.)

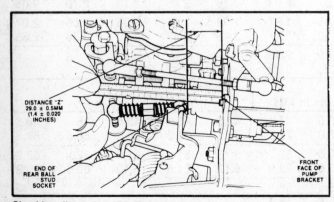

Checking dimension "Z" (© Ford Motor Co.)

## Services

### FLUID CHANGE

1. Change fluid at 30,000 miles. Remove and clean oil pan.
2. Remove and inspect screen; replace if damaged or clogged.
3. Use only DEXRON® II fluid. Fill with approximately 3 or 4 quarts (does not include converter) and check fluid level (see Diagnosis section) with transmission hot.

### OIL PAN AND SCREEN

#### Removal

1. Remove drain plug to drain out most of the fluid.
2. Remove the bolt attaching the filler stub tube to the converter housing.
3. Disconnect the stub tube from the oil pan.
4. Remove (6) bolts and clamps with 10mm socket.
5. Use Torx bit 27 to remove three bolts attaching oil screen to valve body.

## Installation

1. Install new screen O-ring.
2. Pan gasket is reusable if it is not damaged. Gasket should be installed onto oil pan.
3. Tighten bolts at assembly:
4. Screen: 8 N•m (71 inch pounds).
5. Pan: 8 N•m (71 inch pounds).

B7390BP11-Transmission-Copy 11-15-Galley 3

**NOTE: Two identical clamps without inner radius mount on sides of oil pan. Four long clamps with radius mount on corners. Corner clamps and bolts are to be installed first.**

6. Connect the filler stub tube to the oil pan and the converter housing. Tighten the tube bracket bolt to 23 N•m (17 ft. lbs.) and the pan nut to 100-110 N•m (74-85 ft. lbs.)

## VALVE BODY (MAIN CONTROL ASSEMBLY)

### Removal

1. Drain and remove oil pan.
2. Remove oil pan screen bolts (3) with Torx bit 27.
3. Remove 13 more attaching bolts to remove valve body.

**NOTE: Remove only the large head bolts with Torx bit 27**

4. Clean case and valve body mating surfaces. Inspect for burrs and distortion.

### Installation

1. Position valve body under case to engage detent plate pin in manual valve Ⓐ
2. Pull on kickdown cable to position accelerator cam so that roller on throttle piston clears the cam Ⓑ
3. Then install valve body against the case.
4. Install 13 valve body bolts finger tight to hold the valve body to the case for alignment length identification.

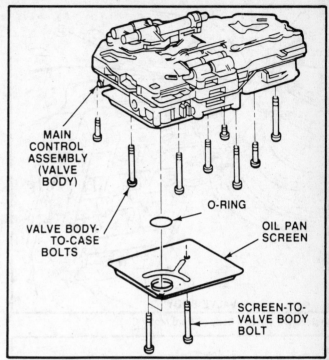

Valve body and screen assembly (© Ford Motor Co.)

### Alignment of Valve Body

1. Align the valve body by inserting the valve body gauge (special service tool #T84P-77003-A) between the throttle piston pin and the valve body housing. If the piston pin interferes with the gauge and does not allow it to pass through, use the notch in the gauge handle to grip the pin and draw the throttle piston farther out of its bore.

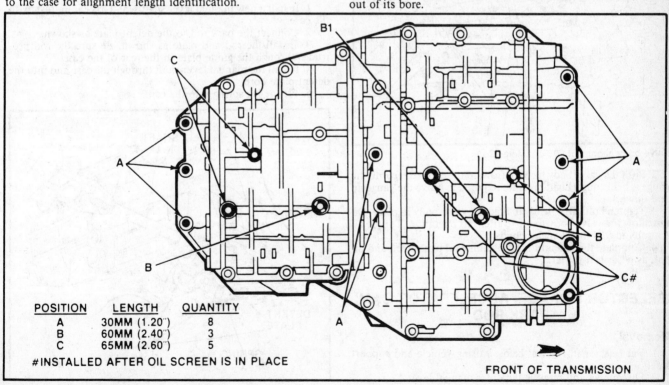

| POSITION | LENGTH | QUANTITY |
|----------|--------|----------|
| A | 30MM (1.20") | 8 |
| B | 60MM (2.40") | 3 |
| C | 65MM (2.60") | 5 |

#INSTALLED AFTER OIL SCREEN IS IN PLACE

FRONT OF TRANSMISSION

Valve body retaining bolt location (© Ford Motor Co.)

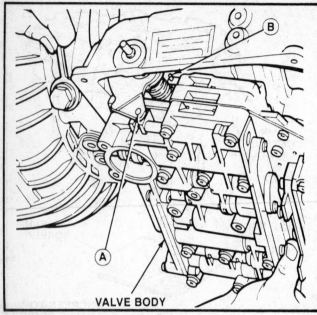

**Installation of valve body** (© Ford Motor Co.)

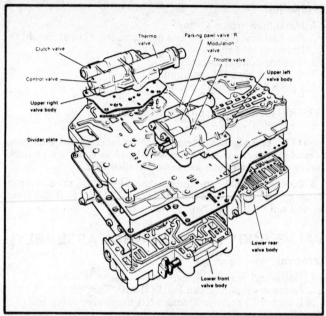

**Valve body assembly** (© Volvo of America)

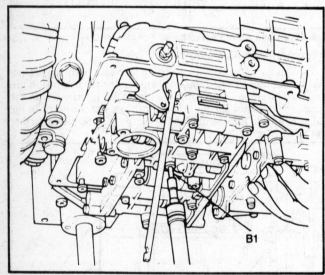

**Valve body alignment** (© Ford Motor Co.)

2. Push the valve body forward (toward the converter) until the gauge is held snug. (Light pressure required to move the gauge up and down.)

3. Tighten bolt "B1" firmly to hold the valve body in place. Do not allow the valve body to move after this operation. Torque all 13 bolts to 8 N•m (71 inch pounds.)

4. Complete this operation by installing oil pan screen and oil pan as described earlier.

## SELECTOR LINKAGE, ACCELERATOR CAM, PARK ROD

### Removal

1. Put selector in Neutral before raising vehicle and support safely.

2. Disconnect and remove the outer manual lever.

3. Remove the oil pan, sump screen and valve body.

4. Disconnect the T-bar end of the kickdown cable from its seat in the accelerator cam.

5. Punch out the roll pin from the detent plate and manual lever shaft.

6. Pull out the shaft to remove the leg spring, cam and detent plate.

7. Unhook the parking pawl rod and pull it out of the case.

8. Remove and discard the shaft seal.

### Installation

1. Install a new manual lever shaft seal. Drive it in flush with the case.

2. Connect the park rod to the detent plate as shown.

3. Install the rod and plate as shown. Be sure the rod protrudes through the guide plate in the rear of the case.

4. Install the manual lever shaft through the case and into the detent plate bore.

5. Fit the leg spring into the cam.

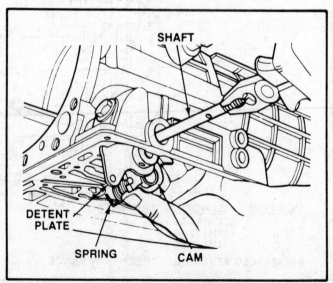

**Removing manual lever shaft** (© Ford Motor Co.)

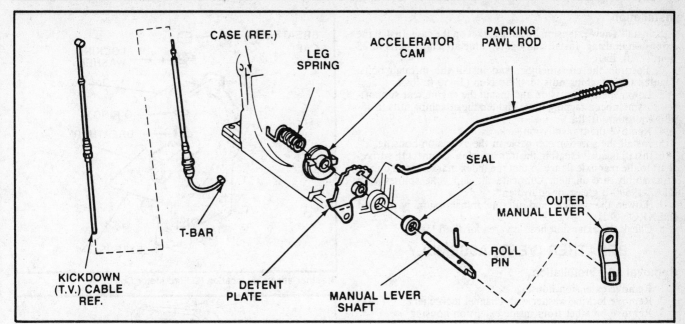

**Exploded view of selector internal linkage** (© Ford Motor Co.)

6. Install the cam and spring in the case, with the leg of the spring on the cast support.

7. Push the shaft in until it stops.

8. Align the holes in the shaft and detent plate.

9. Install a new roll pin with the slot to the rear of the transmission.

10. Revolve the cam once to tension the leg spring; then seat the T-bar end of the cable in the cam.

11. Install the valve body, screen and oil pan.

## NEUTRAL START SWITCH

1. The switch is located just forward of the manual lever, near the cooler return line fitting.

2. There is no switch adjustment.

### Replacement

1. Disconnect the electrical connector and remove the bolt, washer and retainer plate to remove the switch. Reverse the procedure to install it. Tighten the bolt to 10 N•m (88 inch pounds) torque.

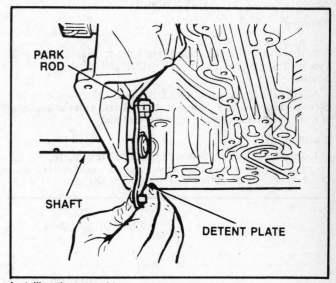

**Installing the manual lever shaft** (© Ford Motor Co.)

## EXTENSION HOUSING

### Removal

1. Raise the vehicle and support safely.

2. Remove the driveshaft. To maintain initial driveshaft balance, mark the rear driveshaft yoke and axle companion flange so they can be installed in their original position.

3. Position a transmission jack to support the transmission.

4. Remove the speedometer cable from the extension housing.

5. Remove the engine rear support to crossmember attaching nuts.

6. Raise the transmission and remove the rear support to body bracket through bolts. Remove the crossmember.

7. Loosen the extension housing attaching bolts and allow the transmission to drain.

8. Remove the nine extension housing-to-case attaching bolts and remove housing.

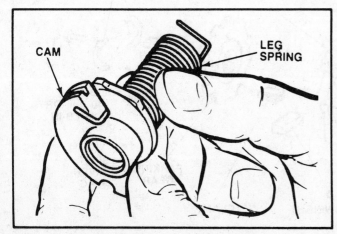

**Fitting the spring leg to the cam** (© Ford Motor Co.)

## Installation

1. Install a new extension housing gasket on the case. Install the extension housing. Install and tighten nine attaching bolts to 23 N•m (17 ft. lbs.).

2. Position the crossmember and install the through bolts. Tighten the attaching nuts to 48-88 N•m (36-50 ft. lbs.).

3. Lower the transmission and install the engine rear support-to-crossmember attaching nuts. Tighten the attaching nuts to 48-68 N•m (30-50 ft. lbs.).

4. Remove the transmission jack.

5. Install the speedometer cable in the extension housing.

6. Install the driveshaft in the transmission. Connect the driveshaft to the rear axle flange so that the index marks, made during disassembly, are aligned. Lubricate the slip yoke splines with C1AZ-19590-B grease or equivalent.

7. Lower the vehicle and fill the transmission with fluid (DEXRON® II).

8. Check the extension housing area for fluid leakage.

## BREATHER (VENT) ASSEMBLY

### Removal and Installation

1. Remove extension housing.
2. Remove locking washer with channel lock pliers.
3. Remove breather from inside extension housing.
4. Use new O-ring and new locking washer for assembly.

## GOVERNOR

### Removal

1. Remove driveshaft and extension housing.
2. Remove interlocking snap ring behind parking gear; and slide parking gear and governor off of shaft and hub of rear clutch housing.

**NOTE: If necessary, pry split driver spline rings out from between parking gear and shaft: one at a time. Use a plastic hammer at installation, if needed, to tap rings into place.**

### Installation

1. Replace any of the following that are damaged.
   a. O-ring on output shaft forward of park gear splines.
   b. Steel ring on output shaft forward of O-ring.

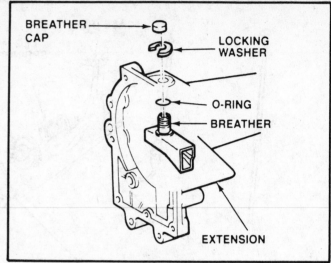

**Breather assembly location** (© Ford Motor Co.)

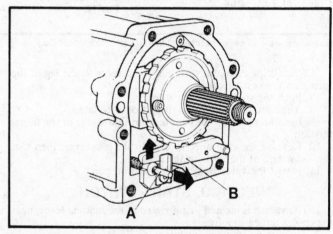

**Parking pawl mechanism** (© Volvo of America)

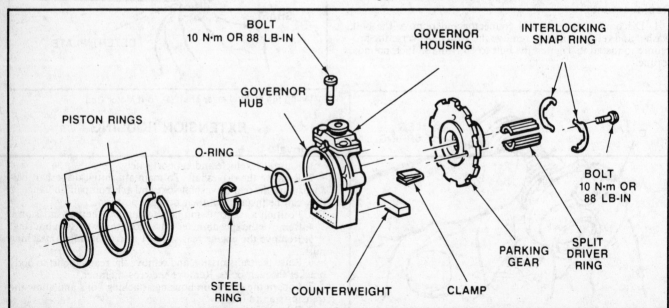

**Exploded view of governor assembly** (© Ford Motor Co.)

c. Piston rings on hub of rear clutch housing.

2. Unbolt parking gear if necessary for access to clamp and counterweight. Governor housing may be unbolted from hub for inspection. Torque governor housing and parking gear bolts to 10 N•m (88 inch lbs.).

## PARK LOCK

### Removal and Installation

1. Remove extension housing and parking gear/governor assembly.

2. Unbolt guide plates from case and remove.

3. Pull pawl and spring off shaft; remove shaft from case.

4. Reverse procedure to install. Set the spring tension by placing the 90° leg of the spring into the hole in the pawl (twist clockwise).

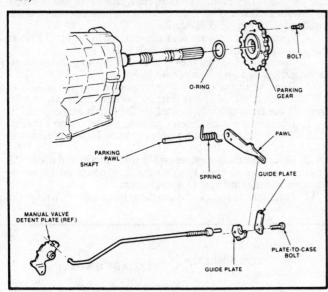

Exploded view of park lock components (© Ford Motor Co.)

## KICKDOWN (T.V.) CABLE

### Removal and Installation

1. In the engine compartment, remove the cable and insert from the injector pump side lever and cable bracket.

2. Raise the vehicle and support safely.

3. Remove the oil pan, sump screen and valve body as described earlier.

4. Carefully pry the cable out of the case with two screwdrivers as shown. (Push in by hand when reinstalling the cable.)

5. Unhook the T-bar end of the cable from the accelerator cam and remove the cable.

6. Reverse the above procedure to connect the cable.

NOTE: Before installing and adjusting the kickdown (T.V.) cable, perform the Injector Pump Linkage Adjustment.

## REMOVAL & INSTALLATION

### Removal

#### FORD MOTOR COMPANY VEHICLES

1. Remove the Kickdown (T.V.) Cable and insert from the injector pump side lever and cable bracket to the engine compartment.

2. Place the transmission selector lever in N (Neutral). Raise the vehicle and support safely.

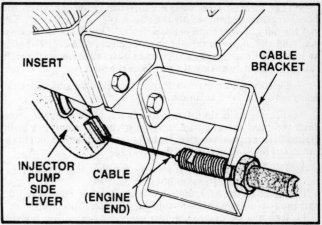

Engine compartment end of kickdown (T.V.) cable (© Ford Motor Co.)

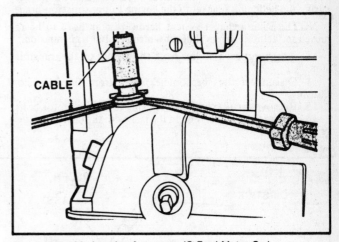

Removing cable housing from case (© Ford Motor Co.)

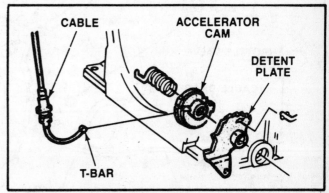

Removal of "T" bar from the accelerator cam (© Ford Motor Co.)

3. Remove the outer manual lever and nut from the transmission selector shaft.

4. Remove the engine brace from the lower end of the converter housing and engine block.

5. Place a transmission jack under the transmission.

6. Remove the converter-to-flywheel attaching nuts. Place a wrench on the crankshaft pulley attaching bolt to turn the converter to gain access to the nuts.

NOTE: The converter studs are installed in the converter with Loc-Tite. During disassembly the nuts may override the Loc-Tite and the nut and stud come out as a "bolt." This poses no concern. The stud and converter threads are to be cleaned, Loc-Tite applied and the "bolt" can be reinstalled and tightened to normal specifications without removing the nut from the stud.

7. Disconnect the driveshaft from the rear axle and slide shaft rearward from the transmission.

NOTE: To maintain driveshaft balance, mark the rear driveshaft yoke and axle companion flange so the driveshaft can be installed in its original position. Install a seal installation tool in the extension housing to prevent fluid leakage.

8. Disconnect the neutral start switch electrical connector.
9. Remove the extension housing damper.
10. Remove the rear mount-to-crossmember attaching nuts and the two crossmember-to-side support attaching bolts.
11. Remove the two engine rear support-to-extension housing attaching bolts and remove the rear mount from the exhaust system.
12. On Continental with column shift, remove the two bolts securing the bellcrank bracket to the engine to transmission brace.

NOTE: Some exhaust system hardware may have to be removed to facilitate removal of crossmember and transmission.

13. Disconnect each oil line from the fittings on the transmission.
14. Disconnect the speedometer cable from the extension housing.
15. Remove the (2) converter housing to starter motor bolts.
16. Secure the transmission to the jack with the chain and lower it slightly.

17. Remove the (4) converter housing-to-cylinder block attaching bolts.
18. Remove the filler tube and dipstick.
19. Carefully move the transmission and converter assembly away from the engine and, at the same time, lower the jack to clear the underside of the vehicle.

### Installation

1. Place the transmission on the jack. Secure the transmission to the jack with a chain.
2. Rotate the converter until the studs are in alignment with the holes in the flywheel and flexplate.
3. Move the converter and transmission assembly forward into position, using care not to damage the flywheel, flexplate, and the converter pilot. The converter face must rest squarely against the flexplate. This indicates that the converter pilot is not binding in the engine crankshaft.
4. Install the filler tube and dipstick, position bracket over the upper right housing to engine bolt hole.
5. Install and tighten the (4) converter housing-to-engine attaching bolts to 52-65 N•m (38-48 ft. lbs.).
6. Remove the safety chain from around the transmission.
7. Connect the oil cooler lines by pushing them into the fittings on the transmission (located on the intermediate plate).
8. Connect the speedometer cable to the extension housing.
9. Install the extension housing damper. Torque the bolts to 24-34 N•m (18-25 ft. lbs.).
10. Secure the crossmember on the side support and install the attaching bolts and nuts. Position the rear mount on the crossmember and tighten nuts to specification.
11. Install the rear mount on to the exhaust system. Secure the

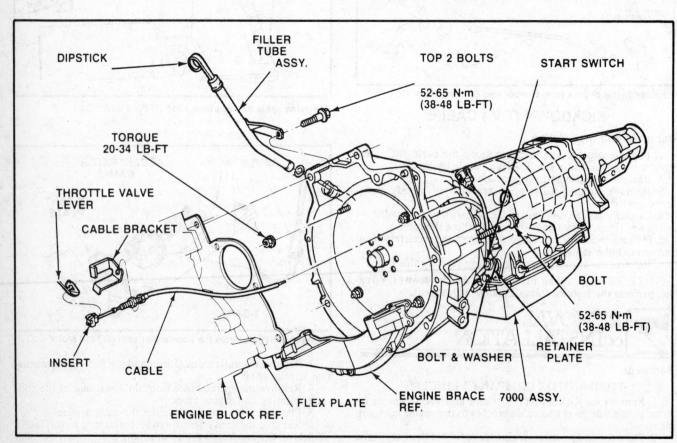

DIPSTICK
FILLER TUBE ASSY.
TOP 2 BOLTS
52-65 N•m (38-48 LB-FT)
START SWITCH
TORQUE 20-34 LB-FT
THROTTLE VALVE LEVER
CABLE BRACKET
INSERT
CABLE
FLEX PLATE
ENGINE BLOCK REF.
ENGINE BRACE REF.
7000 ASSY.
BOLT & WASHER
RETAINER PLATE
BOLT
52-65 N•m (38-48 LB-FT)

Removal or installation of transmission and converter assembly (© Ford Motor Co.)

engine rear support to the extension housing and tighten the bolts to specification.

12. If removed, install exhaust system hardware.

13. Lower the transmission and remove the jack.

14. On Continental column shift, position the bellcrank to the engine to transmission brace and install the two attaching bolts. Torque the bolts to 14-27 N•m (10-20 ft. lbs.).

15. Guide the Kickdown (T.V.) Cable up into the engine compartment.

16. Install the outer manual lever on the transmission selector shaft. Torque the nut to 14-27 N•m (10-20 ft. lbs.).

17. Install the converter to flywheel attaching nuts (or "bolts") and torque them to 27-46 N•m (20-34 ft. lbs.)

18. Install the engine brace on the lower end of the converter housing and engine block. Torque the bolts to 20-24 N•m (15-18 ft. lbs.).

19. Connect the neutral start switch harness at the transmission.

20. Connect the driveshaft to the rear axle. Install the driveshaft so the index marks, made during removal, are correctly aligned.

**NOTE: Lubricate the yoke splines.**

21. Adjust the manual shift linkage.

22. Lower the vehicle and adjust the Kickdown (T.V.) Cable.

23. Fill the transmission to the correct level with the specified fluid (Dexron® II). Start the engine and shift the transmission to all ranges, then recheck the fluid level.

# CONVERTER HOUSING AND INTERMEDIATE PLATE GASKET

## Removal

Remove transmission and converter assembly from car as just described. (If the studs come out of the converter cover, screw them back in.)

Use tool handles to remove converter assembly from the transmission.

**NOTE: Oil will be running out of converter. Handle carefully to avoid damage to pump bushing and oil seal lip.**

Place transmission on work bench.

## To Service Gasket Only

Remove 12 long 17mm bolts closest to pump shaft. Pull converter housing and intermediate plate assembly away as a unit. Be careful not to disturb input shaft and clutch cylinder.

To install, be sure thrust washers and thrust bearing are properly positioned as in inset view. Use petroleum jelly to hold in place while plate is assembled to transmission.

## To Replace Converter Housing

Remove 6 short 17mm bolts farthest from pump shaft.

Tighten all bolts to 46 N•m (34 ft. lbs.).

With the transmission in a horizontal position, use handles to install converter. Guide it carefully onto pump shaft until it seats.

## Removal

### VOLVO MODELS

1. Remove air cleaner.

2. Disconnect throttle cable at pulley and cable sheath at bracket.

3. Remove the two upper converter housing to engine bolts.

4. Disconnect tranmission oil filler pipe from the engine.

5. Raise the vehicle and support safely. Disconnect oil filler pipe from oil pan and drain transmission oil.

6. Remove the retaining bolts and take off the splash guard.

7. Pry off the rubber suspension rings from the front muffler.

8. Mark the flanges and disconnect the drive shaft at the rear flange. Remove drive shaft.

9. Remove the exhaust pipe clamps.

10. Remove the bolts securing the transmission support member. Pull support member back, twist and lift out.

11. Remove the rear engine mount securing bolts. Remove attachment and bracket.

12. Disconnect speedometer cable at transmission extension.

13. Remove transmission oil cooler pipes.

14. Remove transmission neutral safety switch. On later models the switch is located at, and directly controlled by the gearshift control lever.

15. Disconnect gearshift control rod.

16. Remove cover plate between engine and transmission, remove starter motor blind cover and remove starter motor.

17. Remove bolts attaching converter to drive plate.

18. Position a transmission fixture under transmission and remove the lower retaining bolts and separate the converter from the drive plate.

19. Lower the transmission assembly and slide it out from under vehicle.

## Installation

1. Position the transmission and converter assembly on a transmission fixture. Raise and position the transmission behind the engine.

2. Line up and install the lower transmission retaining bolts, adjust the plate between the starter motor and casing and install the starter motor.

3. Connect the oil filler pipe at the lower end.

4. Install the upper transmission to the engine bolts.

5. Install the converter to the drive plate bolts and torque to 30-36 ft. lbs.

6. Install the starter motor blind plate and lower cover plate.

7. Move gear selector lever into position 2.

8. Attach the control rod at the front end, and adjustable clevis to the gear selector lever.

9. Check control adjustment. The clearance from "D" stop should be approximately the same as from "2" to stop. Move lever to position "1" and then to "P". Recheck clearance in position "D" and "2". Readjust if necessary.

10. Install starter neutral safety switch. Torque to 4-7 ft. lbs.

11. Install oil cooler pipes. Torque to 14-22 ft. lbs.

12. Install drive shaft and attach at rear flange.

13. Install exhaust pipe brackets, rear engine mount and the speedometer cable.

14. Install transmission support member and torque bolts to 30-37 ft. lbs.

15. Install exhaust pipe clamps and muffler suspender.

16. Install engine splash guard.

17. Attach throttle cable to bracket and adjust cable.

18. Fill the transmission with the recommended transmission fluid.

19. Install air cleaner.

20. Road test vehicle and recheck the fluid level.

# AUTOMATIC TRANSMISSION THROTTLE CABLE

## Adjust

1. Check for wear.

2. Depress accelerator pedal to floor. Do not move throttle control by hand as incorrect adjustment may result.

3. With accelerator pedal fully depressed measurement between cable sheath and clip should be 50.4-52.6mm (1.98-2.07 in.).

# Metric Tables

## SI METRIC TABLES

The following tables are given in SI (International System) metric units. SI units replace both customary (English) and the older gavimetric units. The use of SI units as a new worldwide standard was set by the International Committee of Weights and Measures in 1960. SI has since been adopted by most countries as their national standard.

These tables are general conversion tables which will allow you to convert customary units, which appear in the text, into SI units.

The following are a list of SI units and the customary units, used in this book, which they replace:

| To measure: | Use SI units: | Which replace (customary units): |
| --- | --- | --- |
| mass | kilograms (kg) | pounds (lbs) |
| temperature | Celsius (°C) | Fahrenheit (°F) |
| length | millimeters (mm) | inches (in.) |
| force | newtons (N) | pounds force (lbs) |
| capacities | liters (l) | pints/quarts/gallons (pts/qts/gals) |
| torque | newton-meters (N·m) | foot pounds (ft lbs) |
| pressure | kilopascals (kPa) | pounds per square inch (psi) |
| volume | cubic centimeters (cm³) | cubic inches (cu in.) |
| power | kilowatts (kW) | horsepower (hp) |

If you have had any prior experience with the metric system, you may have noticed units in this chart which are not familiar to you. This is because, in some cases, SI units differ from the older gravimetric units which they replace. For example, newtons (N) replace kilograms (kg) as a force unit, kilopascals (kPa) replace atmospheres or bars as a unit of pressure, and, although the units are the same, the name Celsius replaces centigrade for temperature measurement.

If you are not using the SI tables, have a look at them anyway; you will be seeing a lot more of them in the future.

## ENGLISH TO METRIC CONVERSION: FORCE

Force is presently measured in pounds (lbs.). This type of measurement is used to measure spring pressure, specifically how many pounds it takes to compress a spring. Our present force unit (the pound) will be replaced in SI metric measurements by the Newton (N). This term will eventually see use in specifications for electric motor brush spring pressures, valve spring pressures, etc.

To convert pounds (lbs.) to Newton (N): multiply the number of lbs. by 4.45

| lbs | N | lbs | N | lbs | N | oz | N |
|---|---|---|---|---|---|---|---|
| 0.01 | 0.04 | 21 | 93.4 | 59 | 262.4 | 1 | 0.3 |
| 0.02 | 0.09 | 22 | 97.9 | 60 | 266.9 | 2 | 0.6 |
| 0.03 | 0.13 | 23 | 102.3 | 61 | 271.3 | 3 | 0.8 |
| 0.04 | 0.18 | 24 | 106.8 | 62 | 275.8 | 4 | 1.1 |
| 0.05 | 0.22 | 25 | 111.2 | 63 | 280.2 | 5 | 1.4 |
| 0.06 | 0.27 | 26 | 115.6 | 64 | 284.6 | 6 | 1.7 |
| 0.07 | 0.31 | 27 | 120.1 | 65 | 289.1 | 7 | 2.0 |
| 0.08 | 0.36 | 28 | 124.6 | 66 | 293.6 | 8 | 2.2 |
| 0.09 | 0.40 | 29 | 129.0 | 67 | 298.0 | 9 | 2.5 |
| 0.1 | 0.4 | 30 | 133.4 | 68 | 302.5 | 10 | 2.8 |
| 0.2 | 0.9 | 31 | 137.9 | 69 | 306.9 | 11 | 3.1 |
| 0.3 | 1.3 | 32 | 142.3 | 70 | 311.4 | 12 | 3.3 |
| 0.4 | 1.8 | 33 | 146.8 | 71 | 315.8 | 13 | 3.6 |
| 0.5 | 2.2 | 34 | 151.2 | 72 | 320.3 | 14 | 3.9 |
| 0.6 | 2.7 | 35 | 155.7 | 73 | 324.7 | 15 | 4.2 |
| 0.7 | 3.1 | 36 | 160.1 | 74 | 329.2 | 16 | 4.4 |
| 0.8 | 3.6 | 37 | 164.6 | 75 | 333.6 | 17 | 4.7 |
| 0.9 | 4.0 | 38 | 169.0 | 76 | 338.1 | 18 | 5.0 |
| 1 | 4.4 | 39 | 173.5 | 77 | 342.5 | 19 | 5.3 |
| 2 | 8.9 | 40 | 177.9 | 78 | 347.0 | 20 | 5.6 |
| 3 | 13.4 | 41 | 182.4 | 79 | 351.4 | 21 | 5.8 |
| 4 | 17.8 | 42 | 186.8 | 80 | 355.9 | 22 | 6.1 |
| 5 | 22.2 | 43 | 191.3 | 81 | 360.3 | 23 | 6.4 |
| 6 | 26.7 | 44 | 195.7 | 82 | 364.8 | 24 | 6.7 |
| 7 | 31.1 | 45 | 200.2 | 83 | 369.2 | 25 | 7.0 |
| 8 | 35.6 | 46 | 204.6 | 84 | 373.6 | 26 | 7.2 |
| 9 | 40.0 | 47 | 209.1 | 85 | 378.1 | 27 | 7.5 |
| 10 | 44.5 | 48 | 213.5 | 86 | 382.6 | 28 | 7.8 |
| 11 | 48.9 | 49 | 218.0 | 87 | 387.0 | 29 | 8.1 |
| 12 | 53.4 | 50 | 224.4 | 88 | 391.4 | 30 | 8.3 |
| 13 | 57.8 | 51 | 226.9 | 89 | 395.9 | 31 | 8.6 |
| 14 | 62.3 | 52 | 231.3 | 90 | 400.3 | 32 | 8.9 |
| 15 | 66.7 | 53 | 235.8 | 91 | 404.8 | 33 | 9.2 |
| 16 | 71.2 | 54 | 240.2 | 92 | 409.2 | 34 | 9.4 |
| 17 | 75.6 | 55 | 244.6 | 93 | 413.7 | 35 | 9.7 |
| 18 | 80.1 | 56 | 249.1 | 94 | 418.1 | 36 | 10.0 |
| 19 | 84.5 | 57 | 253.6 | 95 | 422.6 | 37 | 10.3 |
| 20 | 89.0 | 58 | 258.0 | 96 | 427.0 | 38 | 10.6 |

# METRIC INFORMATION

## ENGLISH TO METRIC CONVERSION: LENGTH

To convert inches (ins.) to millimeters (mm): multiply number of inches by 25.4

To convert millimeters (mm) to inches (ins.): multiply number of millimeters by .04

| Inches | Decimals | Milli-meters | inches | mm | Inches | Decimals | Milli-meters | inches | mm |
|---|---|---|---|---|---|---|---|---|---|
| | 1/64 0.051625 | 0.3969 | 0.0001 | 0.00254 | | 33/64 0.515625 | 13.0969 | 0.6 | 15.24 |
| 1/32 | 0.03125 | 0.7937 | 0.0002 | 0.00508 | 17/32 | 0.53125 | 13.4937 | 0.7 | 17.78 |
| | 3/64 0.046875 | 1.1906 | 0.0003 | 0.00762 | | 35/64 0.546875 | 13.8906 | 0.8 | 20.32 |
| 1/16 | 0.0625 | 1.5875 | 0.0004 | 0.01016 | 9/16 | 0.5625 | 14.2875 | 0.9 | 22.86 |
| | 5/64 0.078125 | 1.9844 | 0.0005 | 0.01270 | | 37/64 0.578125 | 14.6844 | 1 | 25.4 |
| 3/32 | 0.09375 | 2.3812 | 0.0006 | 0.01524 | 19/32 | 0.59375 | 15.0812 | 2 | 50.8 |
| | 7/64 0.109375 | 2.7781 | 0.0007 | 0.01778 | | 39/64 0.609375 | 15.4781 | 3 | 76.2 |
| 1/8 | 0.125 | 3.1750 | 0.0008 | 0.02032 | 5/8 | 0.625 | 15.8750 | 4 | 101.6 |
| | 9/64 0.140625 | 3.5719 | 0.0009 | 0.02286 | | 41/64 0.640625 | 16.2719 | 5 | 127.0 |
| 5/32 | 0.15625 | 3.9687 | 0.001 | 0.0254 | 21/32 | 0.65625 | 16.6687 | 6 | 152.4 |
| | 11/64 0.171875 | 4.3656 | 0.002 | 0.0508 | | 43/64 0.671875 | 17.0656 | 7 | 177.8 |
| 3/16 | 0.1875 | 4.7625 | 0.003 | 0.0762 | 11/16 | 0.6875 | 17.4625 | 8 | 203.2 |
| | 13/64 0.203125 | 5.1594 | 0.004 | 0.1016 | | 45/64 0.703125 | 17.8594 | 9 | 228.6 |
| 7/32 | 0.21875 | 5.5562 | 0.005 | 0.1270 | 23/32 | 0.71875 | 18.2562 | 10 | 254.0 |
| | 15/64 0.234375 | 5.9531 | 0.006 | 0.1524 | | 47/64 0.734375 | 18.6531 | 11 | 279.4 |
| 1/4 | 0.25 | 6.3500 | 0.007 | 0.1778 | 3/4 | 0.75 | 19.0500 | 12 | 304.8 |
| | 17/64 0.265625 | 6.7469 | 0.008 | 0.2032 | | 49/64 0.765625 | 19.4469 | 13 | 330.2 |
| 9/32 | 0.28125 | 7.1437 | 0.009 | 0.2286 | 25/32 | 0.78125 | 19.8437 | 14 | 355.6 |
| | 19/64 0.296875 | 7.5406 | 0.01 | 0.254 | | 51/64 0.796875 | 20.2406 | 15 | 381.0 |
| 5/16 | 0.3125 | 7.9375 | 0.02 | 0.508 | 13/16 | 0.8125 | 20.6375 | 16 | 406.4 |
| | 21/64 0.328125 | 8.3344 | 0.03 | 0.762 | | 53/64 0.828125 | 21.0344 | 17 | 431.8 |
| 11/32 | 0.34375 | 8.7312 | 0.04 | 1.016 | 27/32 | 0.84375 | 21.4312 | 18 | 457.2 |
| | 23/64 0.359375 | 9.1281 | 0.05 | 1.270 | | 55/64 0.859375 | 21.8281 | 19 | 482.6 |
| 3/8 | 0.375 | 9.5250 | 0.06 | 1.524 | 7/8 | 0.875 | 22.2250 | 20 | 508.0 |
| | 25/64 0.390625 | 9.9219 | 0.07 | 1.778 | | 57/64 0.890625 | 22.6219 | 21 | 533.4 |
| 13/32 | 0.40625 | 10.3187 | 0.08 | 2.032 | 29/32 | 0.90625 | 23.0187 | 22 | 558.8 |
| | 27/64 0.421875 | 10.7156 | 0.09 | 2.286 | | 59/64 0.921875 | 23.4156 | 23 | 584.2 |
| 7/16 | 0.4375 | 11.1125 | 0.1 | 2.54 | 15/16 | 0.9375 | 23.8125 | 24 | 609.6 |
| | 29/64 0.453125 | 11.5094 | 0.2 | 5.08 | | 61/64 0.953125 | 24.2094 | 25 | 635.0 |
| 15/32 | 0.46875 | 11.9062 | 0.3 | 7.62 | 31/32 | 0.96875 | 24.6062 | 26 | 660.4 |
| | 31/64 0.484375 | 12.3031 | 0.4 | 10.16 | | 63/64 0.984375 | 25.0031 | 27 | 690.6 |
| 1/2 | 0.5 | 12.7000 | 0.5 | 12.70 | | | | | |

## ENGLISH TO METRIC CONVERSION: TORQUE

To convert foot-pounds (ft. lbs.) to Newton-meters: multiply the number of ft. lbs. by 1.3

To convert inch-pounds (in. lbs.) to Newton-meters: multiply the number of in. lbs. by .11

| in lbs | N·m | in lbs | N·m | in lbs | N·m | in lbs | N·m | in lbs | N·m |
|---|---|---|---|---|---|---|---|---|---|
| 0.1 | 0.01 | 1 | 0.11 | 10 | 1.13 | 19 | 2.15 | 28 | 3.16 |
| 0.2 | 0.02 | 2 | 0.23 | 11 | 1.24 | 20 | 2.26 | 29 | 3.28 |
| 0.3 | 0.03 | 3 | 0.34 | 12 | 1.36 | 21 | 2.37 | 30 | 3.39 |
| 0.4 | 0.04 | 4 | 0.45 | 13 | 1.47 | 22 | 2.49 | 31 | 3.50 |
| 0.5 | 0.06 | 5 | 0.56 | 14 | 1.58 | 23 | 2.60 | 32 | 3.62 |
| 0.6 | 0.07 | 6 | 0.68 | 15 | 1.70 | 24 | 2.71 | 33 | 3.73 |
| 0.7 | 0.08 | 7 | 0.78 | 16 | 1.81 | 25 | 2.82 | 34 | 3.84 |
| 0.8 | 0.09 | 8 | 0.90 | 17 | 1.92 | 26 | 2.94 | 35 | 3.95 |
| 0.9 | 0.10 | 9 | 1.02 | 18 | 2.03 | 27 | 3.05 | 36 | 4.0/ |

## ENGLISH TO METRIC CONVERSION: TORQUE

Torque is now expressed as either foot-pounds (ft./lbs.) or inch-pounds (in./lbs.). The metric measurement unit for torque is the Newton-meter (Nm). This unit—the Nm—will be used for all SI metric torque references, both the present ft./lbs. and in./lbs.

| ft lbs | N-m | ft lbs | N-m | ft lbs | N-m | ft lbs | N-m |
|--------|-----|--------|-----|--------|-----|--------|-----|
| 0.1 | 0.1 | 33 | 44.7 | 74 | 100.3 | 115 | 155.9 |
| 0.2 | 0.3 | 34 | 46.1 | 75 | 101.7 | 116 | 157.3 |
| 0.3 | 0.4 | 35 | 47.4 | 76 | 103.0 | 117 | 158.6 |
| 0.4 | 0.5 | 36 | 48.8 | 77 | 104.4 | 118 | 160.0 |
| 0.5 | 0.7 | 37 | 50.7 | 78 | 105.8 | 119 | 161.3 |
| 0.6 | 0.8 | 38 | 51.5 | 79 | 107.1 | 120 | 162.7 |
| 0.7 | 1.0 | 39 | 52.9 | 80 | 108.5 | 121 | 164.0 |
| 0.8 | 1.1 | 40 | 54.2 | 81 | 109.8 | 122 | 165.4 |
| 0.9 | 1.2 | 41 | 55.6 | 82 | 111.2 | 123 | 166.8 |
| 1 | 1.3 | 42 | 56.9 | 83 | 112.5 | 124 | 168.1 |
| 2 | 2.7 | 43 | 58.3 | 84 | 113.9 | 125 | 169.5 |
| 3 | 4.1 | 44 | 59.7 | 85 | 115.2 | 126 | 170.8 |
| 4 | 5.4 | 45 | 61.0 | 86 | 116.6 | 127 | 172.2 |
| 5 | 6.8 | 46 | 62.4 | 87 | 118.0 | 128 | 173.5 |
| 6 | 8.1 | 47 | 63.7 | 88 | 119.3 | 129 | 174.9 |
| 7 | 9.5 | 48 | 65.1 | 89 | 120.7 | 130 | 176.2 |
| 8 | 10.8 | 49 | 66.4 | 90 | 122.0 | 131 | 177.6 |
| 9 | 12.2 | 50 | 67.8 | 91 | 123.4 | 132 | 179.0 |
| 10 | 13.6 | 51 | 69.2 | 92 | 124.7 | 133 | 180.3 |
| 11 | 14.9 | 52 | 70.5 | 93 | 126.1 | 134 | 181.7 |
| 12 | 16.3 | 53 | 71.9 | 94 | 127.4 | 135 | 183.0 |
| 13 | 17.6 | 54 | 73.2 | 95 | 128.8 | 136 | 184.4 |
| 14 | 18.9 | 55 | 74.6 | 96 | 130.2 | 137 | 185.7 |
| 15 | 20.3 | 56 | 75.9 | 97 | 131.5 | 138 | 187.1 |
| 16 | 21.7 | 57 | 77.3 | 98 | 132.9 | 139 | 188.5 |
| 17 | 23.0 | 58 | 78.6 | 99 | 134.2 | 140 | 189.8 |
| 18 | 24.4 | 59 | 80.0 | 100 | 135.6 | 141 | 191.2 |
| 19 | 25.8 | 60 | 81.4 | 101 | 136.9 | 142 | 192.5 |
| 20 | 27.1 | 61 | 82.7 | 102 | 138.3 | 143 | 193.9 |
| 21 | 28.5 | 62 | 84.1 | 103 | 139.6 | 144 | 195.2 |
| 22 | 29.8 | 63 | 85.4 | 104 | 141.0 | 145 | 196.6 |
| 23 | 31.2 | 64 | 86.8 | 105 | 142.4 | 146 | 198.0 |
| 24 | 32.5 | 65 | 88.1 | 106 | 143.7 | 147 | 199.3 |
| 25 | 33.9 | 66 | 89.5 | 107 | 145.1 | 148 | 200.7 |
| 26 | 35.2 | 67 | 90.8 | 108 | 146.4 | 149 | 202.0 |
| 27 | 36.6 | 68 | 92.2 | 109 | 147.8 | 150 | 203.4 |
| 28 | 38.0 | 69 | 93.6 | 110 | 149.1 | 151 | 204.7 |
| 29 | 39.3 | 70 | 94.9 | 111 | 150.5 | 152 | 206.1 |
| 30 | 40.7 | 71 | 96.3 | 112 | 151.8 | 153 | 207.4 |
| 31 | 42.0 | 72 | 97.6 | 113 | 153.2 | 154 | 208.8 |
| 32 | 43.4 | 73 | 99.0 | 114 | 154.6 | 155 | 210.2 |

# METRIC INFORMATION

## STANDARD TORQUE SPECIFICATIONS AND CAPSCREW MARKINGS

Newton-Meter has been designated as the world standard for measuring torque and will gradually replace the foot-pound and kilogram-meter torque measuring standard. Torquing tools are still being manufactured with foot-pounds and kilogram-meter scales, along with the new Newton-Meter standard. To assist the repairman, foot-pounds, kilogram-meter and Newton-Meter are listed in the following charts, and should be followed as applicable.

### U.S. BOLTS

| SAE Grade Number | 1 or 2 | | | 5 | | | 6 or 7 | | | 8 | | |
|---|---|---|---|---|---|---|---|---|---|---|---|---|
| **Capscrew Head Markings** Manufacturer's marks may vary. Three-line markings on heads below indicate SAE Grade 5.  |  | | |  | | |  | | | | | |
| **Usage** | Used Frequently | | | Used Frequently | | | Used at Times | | | Used at Times | | |
| **Quality of Material** | Indeterminate | | | Minimum Commercial | | | Medium Commercial | | | Best Commercial | | |
| **Capacity Body Size** | Torque | | | Torque | | | Torque | | | Torque | | |
| (inches)–(thread) | Ft-Lb | kgm | Nm | Ft-Lb | kgm | Nm | Ft-Lb | kgm | Nm | Ft-Lb | kgm | Nm |
| 1/4–20 | 5 | 0.6915 | 6.7791 | 8 | 1.1064 | 10.8465 | 10 | 1.3630 | 13.5582 | 12 | 1.6596 | 16.2698 |
| –28 | 6 | 0.8298 | 8.1349 | 10 | 1.3830 | 13.5582 | | | | 14 | 1.9362 | 18.9815 |
| 5/16–18 | 11 | 1.5213 | 14.9140 | 17 | 2.3511 | 23.0489 | 19 | 2.6277 | 25.7605 | 24 | 3.3192 | 32.5396 |
| –24 | 13 | 1.7979 | 17.6256 | 19 | 2.6277 | 25.7605 | | | | 27 | 3.7341 | 36.6071 |
| 3/8–16 | 18 | 2.4894 | 24.4047 | 31 | 4.2873 | 42.0304 | 34 | 4.7022 | 46.0978 | 44 | 6.0852 | 59.6560 |
| –24 | 20 | 2.7660 | 27.1164 | 35 | 4.8405 | 47.4536 | | | | 49 | 6.7767 | 66.4351 |
| 7/16–14 | 28 | 3.8132 | 37.9629 | 49 | 6.7767 | 66.4351 | 55 | 7.6065 | 74.5700 | 70 | 9.6810 | 94.9073 |
| –20 | 30 | 4.1490 | 40.6745 | 55 | 7.6065 | 74.5700 | | | | 78 | 10.7874 | 105.7538 |
| 1/2–13 | 39 | 5.3937 | 52.8769 | 75 | 10.3725 | 101.6863 | 85 | 11.7555 | 115.2445 | 105 | 14.5215 | 142.3609 |
| –20 | 41 | 5.6703 | 55.5885 | 85 | 11.7555 | 115.2445 | | | | 120 | 16.5860 | 162.6960 |
| 9/16–12 | 51 | 7.0533 | 69.1467 | 110 | 15.2130 | 149.1380 | 120 | 16.5960 | 162.6960 | 155 | 21.4365 | 210.1490 |
| –18 | 55 | 7.6065 | 74.5700 | 120 | 16.5960 | 162.6960 | | | | 170 | 23.5110 | 230.4860 |
| 5/8–11 | 83 | 11.4789 | 112.5329 | 150 | 20.7450 | 203.3700 | 167 | 23.0961 | 226.4186 | 210 | 29.0430 | 284.7180 |
| –18 | 95 | 13.1385 | 128.8027 | 170 | 23.5110 | 230.4860 | | | | 240 | 33.1920 | 325.3920 |
| 3/4–10 | 105 | 14.5215 | 142.3609 | 270 | 37.3410 | 366.0660 | 280 | 38.7240 | 379.6240 | 375 | 51.8625 | 508.4250 |
| –16 | 115 | 15.9045 | 155.9170 | 295 | 40.7985 | 399.9610 | | | | 420 | 58.0860 | 568.4360 |
| 7/8–9 | 160 | 22.1280 | 216.9280 | 395 | 54.6285 | 535.5410 | 440 | 60.8520 | 596.5520 | 605 | 83.6715 | 820.2590 |
| –14 | 175 | 24.2025 | 237.2650 | 435 | 60.1605 | 589.7730 | | | | 675 | 93.3525 | 915.1650 |
| 1–8 | 236 | 32.5005 | 318.6130 | 590 | 81.5970 | 799.9220 | 660 | 91.2780 | 894.8280 | 910 | 125.8530 | 1233.7780 |
| –14 | 250 | 34.5750 | 338.9500 | 660 | 91.2780 | 849.8280 | | | | 990 | 136.9170 | 1342.2420 |

### METRIC BOLTS

**Description** — Torque ft-lbs. (Nm)

| Thread for general purposes (size x pitch (mm)) | Head Mark 4 | | Head Mark 7 | |
|---|---|---|---|---|
| 6 x 1.0 | 2.2 to 2.9 | (3.0 to 3.9) | 3.6 to 5.8 | (4.9 to 7.8) |
| 8 x 1.25 | 5.8 to 8.7 | (7.9 to 12) | 9.4 to 14 | (13 to 19) |
| 10 x 1.25 | 12 to 17 | (16 to 23) | 20 to 29 | (27 to 39) |
| 12 x 1.25 | 21 to 32 | (29 to 43) | 35 to 53 | (47 to 72) |
| 14 x 1.5 | 35 to 52 | (48 to 70) | 57 to 85 | (77 to 110) |
| 16 x 1.5 | 51 to 77 | (67 to 100) | 90 to 120 | (130 to 160) |
| 18 x 1.5 | 74 to 110 | (100 to 150) | 130 to 170 | (180 to 230) |
| 20 x 1.5 | 110 to 140 | (150 to 190) | 190 to 240 | (160 to 320) |
| 22 x 1.5 | 150 to 190 | (200 to 260) | 250 to 320 | (340 to 430) |
| 24 x 1.5 | 190 to 240 | (260 to 320) | 310 to 410 | (420 to 550) |

CAUTION: Bolts threaded into aluminum require much less torque

## ENGLISH TO METRIC CONVERSION: MASS (WEIGHT)

Current mass measurement is expressed in pounds and ounces (lbs. & ozs.). The metric unit of mass (or weight) is the kilogram (kg). Even although this table does not show conversion of masses (weights) larger than 15 lbs, it is easy to calculate larger units by following the data immediately below.

To convert ounces (oz.) to grams (g): multiply th number of ozs. by 28
To convert grams (g) to ounces (oz.): multiply the number of grams by .035

To convert pounds (lbs.) to kilograms (kg): multiply the number of lbs. by .45
To convert kilograms (kg) to pounds (lbs.): multiply the number of kilograms by 2.2

| lbs | kg | lbs | kg | oz | kg | oz | kg |
|---|---|---|---|---|---|---|---|
| 0.1 | 0.04 | 0.9 | 0.41 | 0.1 | 0.003 | 0.9 | 0.024 |
| 0.2 | 0.09 | 1 | 0.4 | 0.2 | 0.005 | 1 | 0.03 |
| 0.3 | 0.14 | 2 | 0.9 | 0.3 | 0.008 | 2 | 0.06 |
| 0.4 | 0.18 | 3 | 1.4 | 0.4 | 0.011 | 3 | 0.08 |
| 0.5 | 0.23 | 4 | 1.8 | 0.5 | 0.014 | 4 | 0.11 |
| 0.6 | 0.27 | 5 | 2.3 | 0.6 | 0.017 | 5 | 0.14 |
| 0.7 | 0.32 | 10 | 4.5 | 0.7 | 0.020 | 10 | 0.28 |
| 0.8 | 0.36 | 15 | 6.8 | 0.8 | 0.023 | 15 | 0.42 |

## ENGLISH TO METRIC CONVERSION: TEMPERATURE

To convert Fahrenheit ( F) to Celsius (°C): take number of °F and subtract 32; multiply result by 5; divide result by 9

To convert Celsius (°C) to Fahrenheit (°F): take number of °C and multiply by 9; divide result by 5; add 32 to total

| Fahrenheit (F) | Celsius (C) | | | Fahrenheit (F) | Celsius (C) | | | Fahrenheit (F) | Celsius (C) | | |
|---|---|---|---|---|---|---|---|---|---|---|---|
| °F | °C | °C | °F | °F | °C | °C | °F | °F | °C | °C | °F |
| −40 | −40 | −38 | −36.4 | 80 | 26.7 | 18 | 64.4 | 215 | 101.7 | 80 | 176 |
| −35 | −37.2 | −36 | −32.8 | 85 | 29.4 | 20 | 68 | 220 | 104.4 | 85 | 185 |
| −30 | −34.4 | −34 | −29.2 | 90 | 32.2 | 22 | 71.6 | 225 | 107.2 | 90 | 194 |
| −25 | −31.7 | −32 | −25.6 | 95 | 35.0 | 24 | 75.2 | 230 | 110.0 | 95 | 202 |
| −20 | −28.9 | −30 | −22 | 100 | 37.8 | 26 | 78.8 | 235 | 112.8 | 100 | 212 |
| −15 | −26.1 | −28 | −18.4 | 105 | 40.6 | 28 | 82.4 | 240 | 115.6 | 105 | 221 |
| −10 | −23.3 | −26 | −14.8 | 110 | 43.3 | 30 | 86 | 245 | 118.3 | 110 | 230 |
| −5 | −20.6 | −24 | −11.2 | 115 | 46.1 | 32 | 89.6 | 250 | 121.1 | 115 | 239 |
| 0 | −17.8 | −22 | −7.6 | 120 | 48.9 | 34 | 93.2 | 255 | 123.9 | 120 | 248 |
| 1 | −17.2 | −20 | −4 | 125 | 51.7 | 36 | 96.8 | 260 | 126.6 | 125 | 257 |
| 2 | −16.7 | −18 | −0.4 | 130 | 54.4 | 38 | 100.4 | 265 | 129.4 | 130 | 266 |
| 3 | −16.1 | −16 | 3.2 | 135 | 57.2 | 40 | 104 | 270 | 132.2 | 135 | 275 |
| 4 | −15.6 | −14 | 6.8 | 140 | 60.0 | 42 | 107.6 | 275 | 135.0 | 140 | 284 |
| 5 | −15.0 | −12 | 10.4 | 145 | 62.8 | 44 | 112.2 | 280 | 137.8 | 145 | 293 |
| 10 | −12.2 | −10 | 14 | 150 | 65.6 | 46 | 114.8 | 285 | 140.6 | 150 | 302 |
| 15 | −9.4 | −8 | 17.6 | 155 | 68.3 | 48 | 118.4 | 290 | 143.3 | 155 | 311 |
| 20 | −6.7 | −6 | 21.2 | 160 | 71.1 | 50 | 122 | 295 | 146.1 | 160 | 320 |
| 25 | −3.9 | −4 | 24.8 | 165 | 73.9 | 52 | 125.6 | 300 | 148.9 | 165 | 329 |
| 30 | −1.1 | −2 | 28.4 | 170 | 76.7 | 54 | 129.2 | 305 | 151.7 | 170 | 338 |
| 35 | 1.7 | 0 | 32 | 175 | 79.4 | 56 | 132.8 | 310 | 154.4 | 175 | 347 |
| 40 | 4.4 | 2 | 35.6 | 180 | 82.2 | 58 | 136.4 | 315 | 157.2 | 180 | 356 |
| 45 | 7.2 | 4 | 39.2 | 185 | 85.0 | 60 | 140 | 320 | 160.0 | 185 | 365 |
| 50 | 10.0 | 6 | 42.8 | 190 | 87.8 | 62 | 143.6 | 325 | 162.8 | 190 | 374 |
| 55 | 12.8 | 8 | 46.4 | 195 | 90.6 | 64 | 147.2 | 330 | 165.6 | 195 | 383 |
| 60 | 15.6 | 10 | 50 | 200 | 93.3 | 66 | 150.8 | 335 | 168.3 | 200 | 392 |
| 65 | 18.3 | 12 | 53.6 | 205 | 96.1 | 68 | 154.4 | 340 | 171.1 | 205 | 401 |
| 70 | 21.1 | 14 | 57.2 | 210 | 98.9 | 70 | 158 | 345 | 173.9 | 210 | 410 |
| 75 | 23.9 | 16 | 60.8 | 212 | 100.0 | 75 | 167 | 350 | 176.7 | 215 | 414 |

# METRIC INFORMATION

## ENGLISH TO METRIC CONVERSION: PRESSURE

The basic unit of pressure measurement used today is expressed as pounds per square inch (psi). The metric unit for psi will be the kilopascal (kPa). This will apply to either fluid pressure or air pressure, and will be frequently seen in tire pressure readings, oil pressure specifications, fuel pump pressure, etc.

To convert pounds per square inch (psi) to kilopascals (kPa): multiply the number of psi by 6.89

| Psi | kPa | Psi | kPa | Psi | kPa | Psi | kPa |
|-----|-----|-----|-----|-----|-----|-----|-----|
| 0.1 | 0.7 | 37 | 255.1 | 82 | 565.4 | 127 | 875.6 |
| 0.2 | 1.4 | 38 | 262.0 | 83 | 572.3 | 128 | 882.5 |
| 0.3 | 2.1 | 39 | 268.9 | 84 | 579.2 | 129 | 889.4 |
| 0.4 | 2.8 | 40 | 275.8 | 85 | 586.0 | 130 | 896.3 |
| 0.5 | 3.4 | 41 | 282.7 | 86 | 592.9 | 131 | 903.2 |
| 0.6 | 4.1 | 42 | 289.6 | 87 | 599.8 | 132 | 910.1 |
| 0.7 | 4.8 | 43 | 296.5 | 88 | 606.7 | 133 | 917.0 |
| 0.8 | 5.5 | 44 | 303.4 | 89 | 613.6 | 134 | 923.9 |
| 0.9 | 6.2 | 45 | 310.3 | 90 | 620.5 | 135 | 930.8 |
| 1 | 6.9 | 46 | 317.2 | 91 | 627.4 | 136 | 937.7 |
| 2 | 13.8 | 47 | 324.0 | 92 | 634.3 | 137 | 944.6 |
| 3 | 20.7 | 48 | 331.0 | 93 | 641.2 | 138 | 951.5 |
| 4 | 27.6 | 49 | 337.8 | 94 | 648.1 | 139 | 958.4 |
| 5 | 34.5 | 50 | 344.7 | 95 | 655.0 | 140 | 965.2 |
| 6 | 41.4 | 51 | 351.6 | 96 | 661.9 | 141 | 972.2 |
| 7 | 48.3 | 52 | 358.5 | 97 | 668.8 | 142 | 979.0 |
| 8 | 55.2 | 53 | 365.4 | 98 | 675.7 | 143 | 985.9 |
| 9 | 62.1 | 54 | 372.3 | 99 | 682.6 | 144 | 992.8 |
| 10 | 69.0 | 55 | 379.2 | 100 | 689.5 | 145 | 999.7 |
| 11 | 75.8 | 56 | 386.1 | 101 | 696.4 | 146 | 1006.6 |
| 12 | 82.7 | 57 | 393.0 | 102 | 703.3 | 147 | 1013.5 |
| 13 | 89.6 | 58 | 399.9 | 103 | 710.2 | 148 | 1020.4 |
| 14 | 96.5 | 59 | 406.8 | 104 | 717.0 | 149 | 1027.3 |
| 15 | 103.4 | 60 | 413.7 | 105 | 723.9 | 150 | 1034.2 |
| 16 | 110.3 | 61 | 420.6 | 106 | 730.8 | 151 | 1041.1 |
| 17 | 117.2 | 62 | 427.5 | 107 | 737.7 | 152 | 1048.0 |
| 18 | 124.1 | 63 | 434.4 | 108 | 744.6 | 153 | 1054.9 |
| 19 | 131.0 | 64 | 441.3 | 109 | 751.5 | 154 | 1061.8 |
| 20 | 137.9 | 65 | 448.2 | 110 | 758.4 | 155 | 1068.7 |
| 21 | 144.8 | 66 | 455.0 | 111 | 765.3 | 156 | 1075.6 |
| 22 | 151.7 | 67 | 461.9 | 112 | 772.2 | 157 | 1082.5 |
| 23 | 158.6 | 68 | 468.8 | 113 | 779.1 | 158 | 1089.4 |
| 24 | 165.5 | 69 | 475.7 | 114 | 786.0 | 159 | 1096.3 |
| 25 | 172.4 | 70 | 482.6 | 115 | 792.9 | 160 | 1103.2 |
| 26 | 179.3 | 71 | 489.5 | 116 | 799.8 | 161 | 1110.0 |
| 27 | 186.2 | 72 | 496.4 | 117 | 806.7 | 162 | 1116.9 |
| 28 | 193.0 | 73 | 503.3 | 118 | 813.6 | 163 | 1123.8 |
| 29 | 200.0 | 74 | 510.2 | 119 | 820.5 | 164 | 1130.7 |
| 30 | 206.8 | 75 | 517.1 | 120 | 827.4 | 165 | 1137.6 |
| 31 | 213.7 | 76 | 524.0 | 121 | 834.3 | 166 | 1144.5 |
| 32 | 220.6 | 77 | 530.9 | 122 | 841.2 | 167 | 1151.4 |
| 33 | 227.5 | 78 | 537.8 | 123 | 848.0 | 168 | 1158.3 |
| 34 | 234.4 | 79 | 544.7 | 124 | 854.9 | 169 | 1165.2 |
| 35 | 241.3 | 80 | 551.6 | 125 | 861.8 | 170 | 1172.1 |
| 36 | 248.2 | 81 | 558.5 | 126 | 868.7 | 171 | 1179.0 |

## ENGLISH TO METRIC CONVERSION: LIQUID CAPACITY

Liquid or fluid capacity is presently expressed as pints, quarts or gallons, or a combination of all of these. In the metric system the liter (l) will become the basic unit. Fractions of a liter would be expressed as deciliters, centiliters, or most frequently (and commonly) as milliliters.

To convert pints (pts.) to liters (l): multiply the number of pints by .47
To convert liters (l) to pints (pts.): multiply the number of liters by 2.1
To convert quarts (qts.) to liters (l): multiply the number of quarts by .95

To convert liters (l) to quarts (qts.): multiply the number of liters by 1.06
To convert gallons (gals.) to liters (l): multiply the number of gallons by 3.8
To convert liters (l) to gallons (gals.): multiply the number of liters by .26

| gals | liters | qts | liters | pts | liters |
|------|--------|-----|--------|-----|--------|
| 0.1 | 0.38 | 0.1 | 0.10 | 0.1 | 0.05 |
| 0.2 | 0.76 | 0.2 | 0.19 | 0.2 | 0.10 |
| 0.3 | 1.1 | 0.3 | 0.28 | 0.3 | 0.14 |
| 0.4 | 1.5 | 0.4 | 0.38 | 0.4 | 0.19 |
| 0.5 | 1.9 | 0.5 | 0.47 | 0.5 | 0.24 |
| 0.6 | 2.3 | 0.6 | 0.57 | 0.6 | 0.28 |
| 0.7 | 2.6 | 0.7 | 0.66 | 0.7 | 0.33 |
| 0.8 | 3.0 | 0.8 | 0.76 | 0.8 | 0.38 |
| 0.9 | 3.4 | 0.9 | 0.85 | 0.9 | 0.43 |
| 1 | 3.8 | 1 | 1.0 | 1 | 0.5 |
| 2 | 7.6 | 2 | 1.9 | 2 | 1.0 |
| 3 | 11.4 | 3 | 2.8 | 3 | 1.4 |
| 4 | 15.1 | 4 | 3.8 | 4 | 1.9 |
| 5 | 18.9 | 5 | 4.7 | 5 | 2.4 |
| 6 | 22.7 | 6 | 5.7 | 6 | 2.8 |
| 7 | 26.5 | 7 | 6.6 | 7 | 3.3 |
| 8 | 30.3 | 8 | 7.6 | 8 | 3.8 |
| 9 | 34.1 | 9 | 8.5 | 9 | 4.3 |
| 10 | 37.8 | 10 | 9.5 | 10 | 4.7 |
| 11 | 41.6 | 11 | 10.4 | 11 | 5.2 |
| 12 | 45.4 | 12 | 11.4 | 12 | 5.7 |
| 13 | 49.2 | 13 | 12.3 | 13 | 6.2 |
| 14 | 53.0 | 14 | 13.2 | 14 | 6.6 |
| 15 | 56.8 | 15 | 14.2 | 15 | 7.1 |
| 16 | 60.6 | 16 | 15.1 | 16 | 7.6 |
| 17 | 64.3 | 17 | 16.1 | 17 | 8.0 |
| 18 | 68.1 | 18 | 17.0 | 18 | 8.5 |
| 19 | 71.9 | 19 | 18.0 | 19 | 9.0 |
| 20 | 75.7 | 20 | 18.9 | 20 | 9.5 |
| 21 | 79.5 | 21 | 19.9 | 21 | 9.9 |
| 22 | 83.2 | 22 | 20.8 | 22 | 10.4 |
| 23 | 87.0 | 23 | 21.8 | 23 | 10.9 |
| 24 | 90.8 | 24 | 22.7 | 24 | 11.4 |
| 25 | 94.6 | 25 | 23.6 | 25 | 11.8 |
| 26 | 98.4 | 26 | 24.6 | 26 | 12.3 |
| 27 | 102.2 | 27 | 25.5 | 27 | 12.8 |
| 28 | 106.0 | 28 | 26.5 | 28 | 13.2 |
| 29 | 110.0 | 29 | 27.4 | 29 | 13.7 |
| 30 | 113.5 | 30 | 28.4 | 30 | 14.2 |

## ENGLISH TO METRIC CONVERSION: PRESSURE

The basic unit of pressure measurement used today is expressed as pounds per square inch (psi). The metric unit for psi will be the kilopascal (kPa). This will apply to either fluid pressure or air pressure, and will be frequently seen in tire pressure readings, oil pressure specifications, fuel pump pressure, etc.

To convert pounds per square inch (psi) to kilopascals (kPa): multiply the number of psi by 6.89

| Psi | kPa | Psi | kPa | Psi | kPa | Psi | kPa |
|-----|------|-----|------|-----|------|-----|------|
| 172 | 1185.9 | 216 | 1489.3 | 260 | 1792.6 | 304 | 2096.0 |
| 173 | 1192.8 | 217 | 1496.2 | 261 | 1799.5 | 305 | 2102.9 |
| 174 | 1199.7 | 218 | 1503.1 | 262 | 1806.4 | 306 | 2109.8 |
| 175 | 1206.6 | 219 | 1510.0 | 263 | 1813.3 | 307 | 2116.7 |
| 176 | 1213.5 | 220 | 1516.8 | 264 | 1820.2 | 308 | 2123.6 |
| 177 | 1220.4 | 221 | 1523.7 | 265 | 1827.1 | 309 | 2130.5 |
| 178 | 1227.3 | 222 | 1530.6 | 266 | 1834.0 | 310 | 2137.4 |
| 179 | 1234.2 | 223 | 1537.5 | 267 | 1840.9 | 311 | 2144.3 |
| 180 | 1241.0 | 224 | 1544.4 | 268 | 1847.8 | 312 | 2151.2 |
| 181 | 1247.9 | 225 | 1551.3 | 269 | 1854.7 | 313 | 2158.1 |
| 182 | 1254.8 | 226 | 1558.2 | 270 | 1861.6 | 314 | 2164.9 |
| 183 | 1261.7 | 227 | 1565.1 | 271 | 1868.5 | 315 | 2171.8 |
| 184 | 1268.6 | 228 | 1572.0 | 272 | 1875.4 | 316 | 2178.7 |
| 185 | 1275.5 | 229 | 1578.9 | 273 | 1882.3 | 317 | 2185.6 |
| 186 | 1282.4 | 230 | 1585.8 | 274 | 1889.2 | 318 | 2192.5 |
| 187 | 1289.3 | 231 | 1592.7 | 275 | 1896.1 | 319 | 2199.4 |
| 188 | 1296.2 | 232 | 1599.6 | 276 | 1903.0 | 320 | 2206.3 |
| 189 | 1303.1 | 233 | 1606.5 | 277 | 1909.8 | 321 | 2213.2 |
| 190 | 1310.0 | 234 | 1613.4 | 278 | 1916.7 | 322 | 2220.1 |
| 191 | 1316.9 | 235 | 1620.3 | 279 | 1923.6 | 323 | 2227.0 |
| 192 | 1323.8 | 236 | 1627.2 | 280 | 1930.5 | 324 | 2233.9 |
| 193 | 1330.7 | 237 | 1634.1 | 281 | 1937.4 | 325 | 2240.8 |
| 194 | 1337.6 | 238 | 1641.0 | 282 | 1944.3 | 326 | 2247.7 |
| 195 | 1344.5 | 239 | 1647.8 | 283 | 1951.2 | 327 | 2254.6 |
| 196 | 1351.4 | 240 | 1654.7 | 284 | 1958.1 | 328 | 2261.5 |
| 197 | 1358.3 | 241 | 1661.6 | 285 | 1965.0 | 329 | 2268.4 |
| 198 | 1365.2 | 242 | 1668.5 | 286 | 1971.9 | 330 | 2275.3 |
| 199 | 1372.0 | 243 | 1675.4 | 287 | 1978.8 | 331 | 2282.2 |
| 200 | 1378.9 | 244 | 1682.3 | 288 | 1985.7 | 332 | 2289.1 |
| 201 | 1385.8 | 245 | 1689.2 | 289 | 1992.6 | 333 | 2295.9 |
| 202 | 1392.7 | 246 | 1696.1 | 290 | 1999.5 | 334 | 2302.8 |
| 203 | 1399.6 | 247 | 1703.0 | 291 | 2006.4 | 335 | 2309.7 |
| 204 | 1406.5 | 248 | 1709.9 | 292 | 2013.3 | 336 | 2316.6 |
| 205 | 1413.4 | 249 | 1716.8 | 293 | 2020.2 | 337 | 2323.5 |
| 206 | 1420.3 | 250 | 1723.7 | 294 | 2027.1 | 338 | 2330.4 |
| 207 | 1427.2 | 251 | 1730.6 | 295 | 2034.0 | 339 | 2337.3 |
| 208 | 1434.1 | 252 | 1737.5 | 296 | 2040.8 | 240 | 2344.2 |
| 209 | 1441.0 | 253 | 1744.4 | 297 | 2047.7 | 341 | 2351.1 |
| 210 | 1447.9 | 254 | 1751.3 | 298 | 2054.6 | 342 | 2358.0 |
| 211 | 1454.8 | 255 | 1758.2 | 299 | 2061.5 | 343 | 2364.9 |
| 212 | 1461.7 | 256 | 1765.1 | 300 | 2068.4 | 344 | 2371.8 |
| 213 | 1468.7 | 257 | 1772.0 | 301 | 2075.3 | 345 | 2378.7 |
| 214 | 1475.5 | 258 | 1778.8 | 302 | 2082.2 | 346 | 2385.6 |
| 215 | 1482.4 | 259 | 1785.7 | 303 | 2089.1 | 347 | 2392.5 |

## GENERAL CONVERSION TABLE

| Multiply By | To Convert | To | |
|---|---|---|---|
| | | **Length** | — |
| 2.54 | Inches | Centimeters | .3937 |
| 25.4 | Inches | Millimeters | .03937 |
| 30.48 | Feet | Centimeters | .0328 |
| .304 | Feet | Meters | 3.28 |
| .914 | Yards | Meters | 1.094 |
| 1.609 | Miles | Kilometers | .621 |
| | | **Volume** | |
| .473 | Pints | Liters | 2.11 |
| .946 | Quarts | Liters | 1.06 |
| 3.785 | Gallons | Liters | .264 |
| .016 | Cubic inches | Liters | 61.02 |
| 16.39 | Cubic inches | Cubic cms. | .061 |
| 28.3 | Cubic feet | Liters | .0353 |
| | | **Mass (Weight)** | |
| 28.35 | Ounces | Grams | .035 |
| .4536 | Pounds | Kilograms | 2.20 |
| | | **Area** | |
| .645 | Square inches | Square cms. | .155 |
| .836 | Square yds. | Square meters | 1.196 |
| | | **Force** | |
| 4.448 | Pounds | Newtons | .225 |
| .138 | Ft./lbs. | Kilogram/meters | 7.23 |
| 1.36 | Ft./lbs. | Newton-meters | .737 |
| .112 | In./lbs. | Newton-meters | 8.844 |
| | | **Pressure** | |
| .068 | Psi | Atmospheres | 14.7 |
| 6.89 | Psi | Kilopascals | .145 |
| | | **Other** | |
| 1.104 | Horsepower (DIN) | Horsepower (SAE) | .9861 |
| .746 | Horsepower (SAE) | Kilowatts (KW) | 1.34 |
| 1.60 | Mph | Km/h | .625 |
| .425 | Mpg | Km/1 | 2.35 |
| — | To obtain | From | Multiply by |

## TAP DRILL SIZES

| NATIONAL COARSE OR U.S.S. | | | | | | NATIONAL FINE OR S.A.E. | | | | | |
|---|---|---|---|---|---|---|---|---|---|---|---|
| Screw & Tap Size | Threads Per Inch | Use Drill Number | Screw & Tap Size | Threads Per Inch | Use Drill Number | Screw & Tap Size | Threads Per Inch | Use Drill Number | Screw & Tap Size | Threads Per Inch | Use Drill Number |
| No. 5 | 40 | 39 | 1/2 | 13 | 27/64 | No. 5 | 44 | 37 | 1/2 | 20 | 29/64 |
| No. 6 | 32 | 36 | 9/16 | 12 | 31/64 | No. 6 | 40 | 33 | 9/16 | 18 | 33/64 |
| No. 8 | 32 | 29 | 5/8 | 11 | 17/32 | No. 8 | 36 | 29 | 5/8 | 18 | 37/64 |
| No. 10 | 24 | 25 | 3/4 | 10 | 21/32 | No. 10 | 32 | 21 | 3/4 | 16 | 11/16 |
| No. 12 | 24 | 17 | 7/8 | 9 | 49/64 | No. 12 | 28 | 15 | 7/8 | 14 | 13/16 |
| 1/4 | 20 | 8 | 1 | 8 | 7/8 | 1/4 | 28 | 3 | 1 1/8 | 12 | 1 3/64 |
| 5/16 | 18 | F | 1 1/8 | 7 | 63/64 | 5/16 | 24 | 1 | 1 1/4 | 12 | 1 11/64 |
| 3/8 | 16 | 5/16 | 1 1/4 | 7 | 1 7/64 | 3/8 | 24 | Q | 1 1/2 | 12 | 1 27/64 |
| 7/16 | 14 | U | 1 1/2 | 6 | 1 11/32 | 7/16 | 20 | W | | | |

# MECHANICS DATA

## TAP DRILL SIZES

### NATIONAL COARSE OR U.S.S.

| Screw & Tap Size | Threads Per Inch | Use Drill Number |
|---|---|---|
| No. 5 | 40 | 39 |
| No. 6 | 32 | 36 |
| No. 8 | 32 | 29 |
| No. 10 | 24 | 25 |
| No. 12 | 24 | 17 |
| 1/4 | 20 | 8 |
| 5/16 | 18 | F |
| 3/8 | 16 | 5/16 |
| 7/16 | 14 | U |
| 1/2 | 13 | 27/64 |
| 9/16 | 12 | 31/64 |
| 5/8 | 11 | 17/32 |
| 3/4 | 10 | 21/32 |
| 7/8 | 9 | 49/64 |
| 1 | 8 | 7/8 |
| 1 1/8 | 7 | 63/64 |
| 1 1/4 | 7 | 1 7/64 |
| 1 1/2 | 6 | 1 11/32 |

### NATIONAL FINE OR S.A.E.

| Screw & Tap Size | Threads Per Inch | Use Drill Number |
|---|---|---|
| No. 5 | 44 | 37 |
| No. 6 | 40 | 33 |
| No. 8 | 36 | 29 |
| No. 10 | 32 | 21 |
| No. 12 | 28 | 15 |
| 1/4 | 28 | 3 |
| 5/16 | 24 | 1 |
| 3/8 | 24 | Q |
| 7/16 | 20 | W |
| 1/2 | 20 | 29/64 |
| 9/16 | 18 | 33/64 |
| 5/8 | 18 | 37/64 |
| 3/4 | 16 | 11/16 |
| 7/8 | 14 | 13/16 |
| 1 1/8 | 12 | 1 3/64 |
| 1 1/4 | 12 | 1 11/64 |
| 1 1/2 | 12 | 1 27/64 |

## DECIMAL EQUIVALENT SIZE OF THE NUMBER DRILLS

| Drill No. | Decimal Equivalent | Drill No. | Decimal Equivalent | Drill No. | Decimal Equivalent |
|---|---|---|---|---|---|
| 80 | .0135 | 53 | .0595 | 26 | .1470 |
| 79 | .0145 | 52 | .0635 | 25 | .1495 |
| 78 | .0160 | 51 | .0670 | 24 | .1520 |
| 77 | .0180 | 50 | .0700 | 23 | .1540 |
| 76 | .0200 | 49 | .0730 | 22 | .1570 |
| 75 | .0210 | 48 | .0760 | 21 | .1590 |
| 74 | .0225 | 47 | .0785 | 20 | .1610 |
| 73 | .0240 | 46 | .0810 | 19 | .1660 |
| 72 | .0250 | 45 | .0820 | 18 | .1695 |
| 71 | .0260 | 44 | .0860 | 17 | .1730 |
| 70 | .0280 | 43 | .0890 | 16 | .1770 |
| 69 | .0292 | 42 | .0935 | 15 | .1800 |
| 68 | .0310 | 41 | .0960 | 14 | .1820 |
| 67 | .0320 | 40 | .0980 | 13 | .1850 |
| 66 | .0330 | 39 | .0995 | 12 | .1890 |
| 65 | .0350 | 38 | .1015 | 11 | .1910 |
| 64 | .0360 | 37 | .1040 | 10 | .1935 |
| 63 | .0370 | 36 | .1065 | 9 | .1960 |
| 62 | .0380 | 35 | .1100 | 8 | .1990 |
| 61 | .0390 | 34 | .1110 | 7 | .2010 |
| 60 | .0400 | 33 | .1130 | 6 | .2040 |
| 59 | .0410 | 32 | .1160 | 5 | .2055 |
| 58 | .0420 | 31 | .1200 | 4 | .2090 |
| 57 | .0430 | 30 | .1285 | 3 | .2130 |
| 56 | .0465 | 29 | .1360 | 2 | .2210 |
| 55 | .0520 | 28 | .1405 | 1 | .2280 |
| 54 | .0550 | 27 | .1440 | | |

## DECIMAL EQUIVALENT SIZE OF THE LETTER DRILLS

| Letter Drill | Decimal Equivalent | Letter Drill | Decimal Equivalent | Letter Drill | Decimal Equivalent |
|---|---|---|---|---|---|
| A | .234 | J | .277 | S | .348 |
| B | .238 | K | .281 | T | .358 |
| C | .242 | L | .290 | U | .368 |
| D | .246 | M | .295 | V | .377 |
| E | .250 | N | .302 | W | .386 |
| F | .257 | O | .316 | X | .397 |
| G | .261 | P | .323 | Y | .404 |
| H | .266 | Q | .332 | Z | .413 |
| I | .272 | R | .339 | | |

## DECIMAL EQUIVALENTS OF THE COMMON FRACTIONS

| | | | | | |
|---|---|---|---|---|---|
| 1/64 = .0156 | | 21/64 = .3281 | | 43/64 = .6719 | |
| | 1/32 = .0313 | | 11/32 = .3438 | | 11/16 = .6875 |
| 3/64 = .0469 | | 23/64 = .3594 | | 45/64 = .7031 | |
| | 1/16 = .0625 | | 3/8 = .3750 | | 23/32 = .7188 |
| 5/64 = .0781 | | 25/64 = .3906 | | 47/64 = .7344 | |
| | 3/32 = .0938 | | 13/32 = .4063 | | 3/4 = .7500 |
| 7/64 = .1094 | | 27/64 = .4219 | | 49/64 = .7656 | |
| | 1/8 = .1250 | | 7/16 = .4375 | | 25/32 = .7813 |
| 9/64 = .1406 | | 29/64 = .4531 | | 51/64 = .7969 | |
| | 5/32 = .1563 | | 15/32 = .4688 | | 13/16 = .8125 |
| 11/64 = .1719 | | 31/64 = .4844 | | 53/64 = .8281 | |
| | 3/16 = .1875 | | 1/2 = .5000 | | 27/32 = .8438 |
| 13/64 = .2031 | | 33/64 = .5156 | | 55/64 = .8594 | |
| | 7/32 = .2188 | | 17/32 = .5313 | | 7/8 = .8750 |
| 15/64 = .2344 | | 35/64 = .5469 | | 57/64 = .8906 | |
| | 1/4 = .2500 | | 9/16 = .5625 | | 29/32 = .9063 |
| 17/64 = .2656 | | 37/64 = .5781 | | 59/64 = .9219 | |
| | 9/32 = .2813 | | 19/32 = .5938 | | 15/16 = .9375 |
| 19/64 = .2969 | | 39/64 = .6094 | | 61/64 = .9531 | |
| | 5/16 = .3125 | | 5/8 = .6250 | | 31/32 = .9688 |
| | | 41/64 = .6406 | | 63/64 = .9844 | |
| | | | 21/32 = .6563 | | |

# Transmission/Transaxle
# Oil Flow Circuits

## INDEX

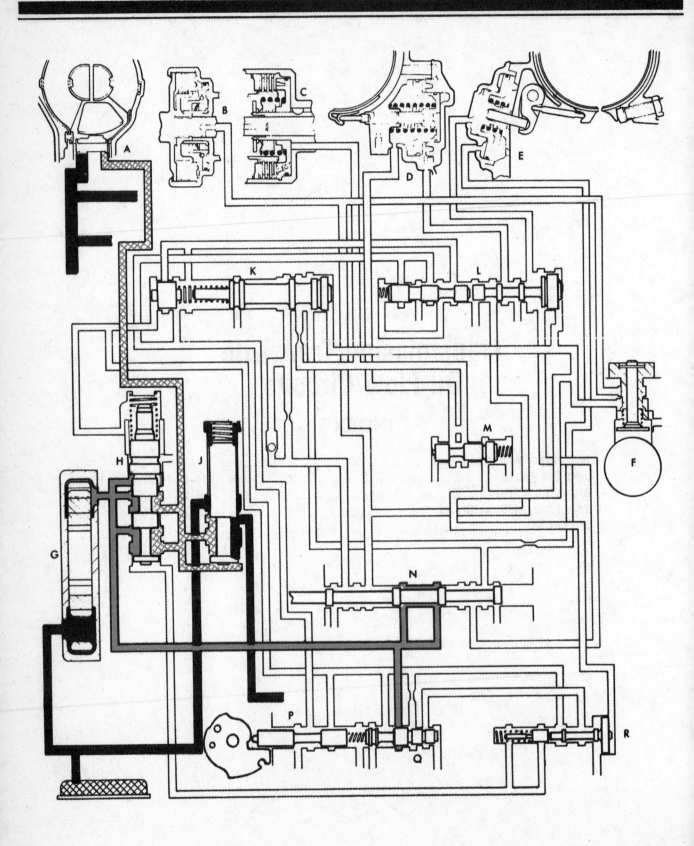

**Neutral**

# Neutral

## UNITS APPLIED—NONE

The selector lever is in Neutral and the engine speed is at idle. The foot brake is applied and the vehicle is at rest.

## PRESSURE SUPPLY SYSTEM

The oil pump (G) is supplying fluid pressure to the primary regulator valve (H), the manual valve (N) and the throttle valve (Q).

## PRESSURE REGULATING SYSTEM

The primary regulator valve (H) is controlling the pressure valve of line pressure and supplying the secondary regulator valve (J). The secondary regulator valve (J) is directing pressure to the converter (A) and the lubrication circuits. The secondary regulator valve (J) also acts as a high pressure relief valve for the system.

## FLOW CONTROL SYSTEM

None of the flow control valves are operating in Neutral.

## CLUTCH AND BAND SERVO SYSTEM

No clutches or bands are applied in Neutral.

---

A. Torque converter
B. Front clutch
C. Rear clutch
D. Front servo
E. Rear servo
F. Governor
G. Pump
H. Primary regulator valve

J. Secondary regulator valve
K. 2-3 shift valve
L. 1-2 shift valve
M. Servo orifice control valve
N. Manual valve
P. Downshift valve
Q. Throttle valve
R. Modulator valve

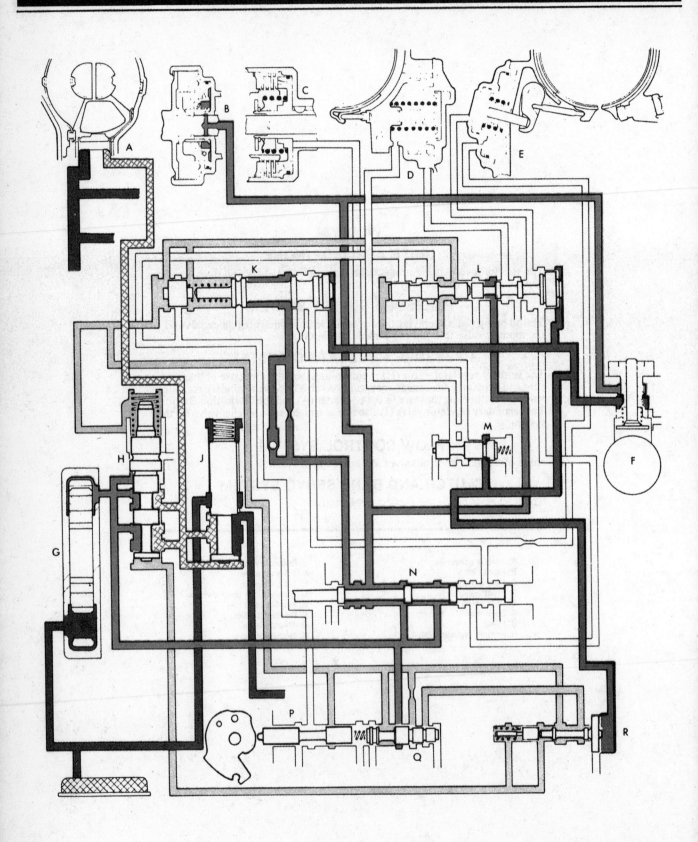

**Drive—First Gear**

# Drive—1st Gear

## Units Applied—Front Clutch, One-Way Clutch

The selector lever is in "D", the vehicle speed is less than 8 mph and engine speed is at half throttle.

### PRESSURE SUPPLY SYSTEM

The oil pump (G) is supplying fluid pressure to the primary regulator valve (H) and the manual valve (N). The oil pump (G) also supplies fluid directly the throttle valve (Q).

### PRESSURE REGULATING SYSTEM

The primary regulator valve (H) is controlling line pressure and supplying pressure to the secondary regulator valve (J). The secondary regulator valve (J) acts as a pressure relief valve and supplies pressure to the converter (A) and lubrication circuits.

### FLOW CONTROL SYSTEM

The manual valve (N) is supplying pressure to the 1-2 shift valve (L), the 2-3 shift valve, the front clutch (B) and the governor (F).

The governor (F) is supplying pressure to the 1-2 shift valve (L), the 2-3 shift valve (K), the servo orifice control valve (M) and the modulator valve (R).

The throttle valve (Q) is directing pressure to the modulator valve (R), the primary regulator valve (H), the 1-2 shift valve (L) and the 2-3 shift valve (K).

The throttle and governor pressures are acting on the shift valves to control subsequent upshifts and downshifts.

### CLUTCH AND BAND SERVO SYSTEM

In Drive 1st gear, the front clutch (D) is applied by the manual valve and the one-way clutch is holding.

A. Torque converter
B. Front clutch
C. Rear clutch
D. Front servo
E. Rear servo
F. Governor
G. Pump
H. Primary regulator valve

J. Secondary regulator valve
K. 2-3 shift valve
L. 1-2 shift valve
M. Servo orifice control valve
N. Manual valve
P. Downshift valve
Q. Throttle valve
R. Modulator valve

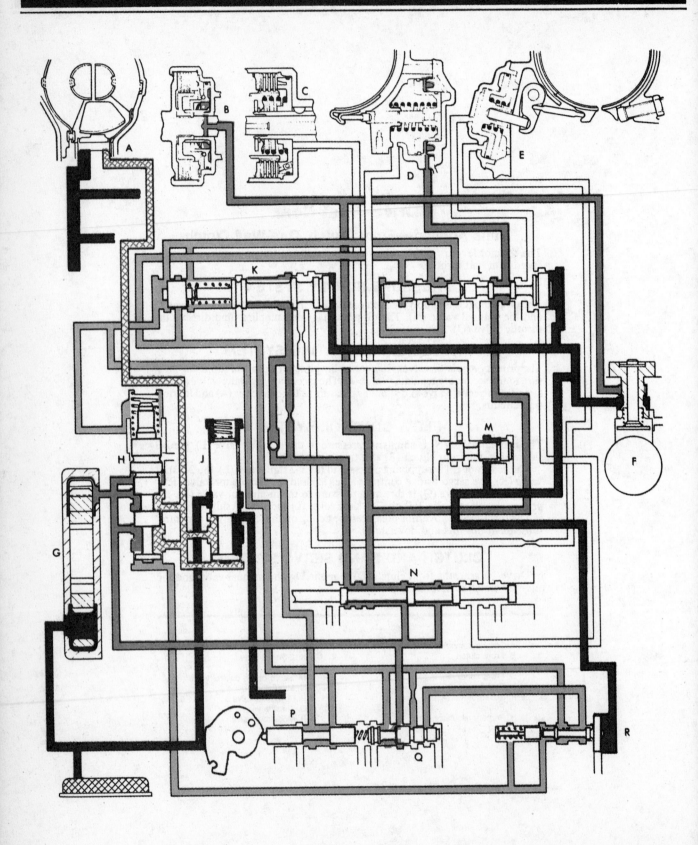

**Drive—Second Gear**

## Drive—2nd Gear

### UNITS APPLIED—FRONT CLUTCH, FRONT BAND

The selector lever is in Drive and the vehicle is traveling between 25-34 MPH with engine speed at half throttle.

### PRESSURE SUPPLY SYSTEM

The oil pump (G) is supplying fluid pressure to the primary regulator valve (H) and the manual valve (N). The oil pump (G) is also supplying fluid directly to the throttle valve (Q).

### PRESSURE REGULATING SYSTEM

The primary regulator valve (H) is controlling line pressure and supplying pressure to the secondary regulator valve (J). The secondary regulator valve also acts as a pressure relief valve and supplies fluid to the torque converter (A) and the lubrication circuits.

### FLOW CONTROL SYSTEM

The manual valve (N) is directing pressure to the 2-3 shift valve (K). Also, the manual valve (N) is directing pressure to the 1-2 shift valve (L), the front clutch (B) and the governor (F). Governor pressure is present at the modulator valve (R), the servo orifice control valve (M), 1-2 shift valve (L), and the 2-3 shift valve (K). Throttle pressure is present at the modulator valve (R), both ends of the primary regulator valve (H), the downshift valve (P), the 1-2 shift valve (L) and the 2-3 shift valve (K). The governor pressure has overcome throttle pressure at the 1-2 shift valve (L) and moved it to open a passage to the apply side of the front servo (E).

### CLUTCH AND BAND SERVO SYSTEM

The transmission is in Drive 2nd gear with the front clutch (B) and the front band (D) applied.

A. Torque converter
B. Front clutch
C. Rear clutch
D. Front servo
E. Rear servo
F. Governor
G. Pump
H. Primary regulator valve

J. Secondary regulator valve
K. 2-3 shift valve
L. 1-2 shift valve
M. Servo orifice control valve
N. Manual valve
P. Downshift valve
Q. Throttle valve
R. Modulator valve

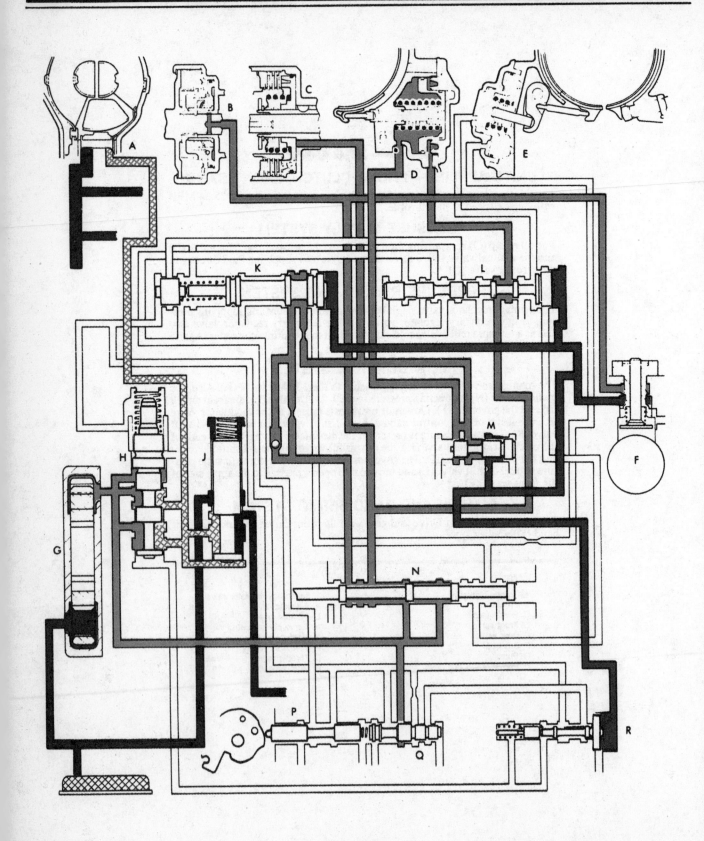

Drive—Third Gear

## Drive-3rd Gear

### UNITS APPLIED—FRONT CLUTCH, REAR CLUTCH

The selector lever is in "D" position and the vehicle speed is between 33-49 MPH. Also, the engine speed is at half throttle.

### PRESSURE SUPPLY SYSTEM

The oil pump (G) is supplying fluid pressure to the primary regulator valve (H) and the manual valve (N). The oil pump (G) also supplies fluid to the throttle valve (Q).

### PRESSURE REGULATING SYSTEM

The primary regulator valve (H) is controlling line pressure and supplying pressure to the secondary regulator valve (J). The secondary regulator valve (J) acts as a pressure relief valve and supplies pressure to the converter (A) and the lubrication circuits.

### FLOW CONTROL SYSTEM

The manual valve (N) is directing pressure to the 1-2 shift valve (L), the 2-3 shift valve (K), the front clutch (B) and the governor (F).

Governor pressure is present at the modulator valve (R), the servo orifice control valve (M), the 1-2 shift valve (L) and the 2-3 shift valve (K).

Although throttle pressure is not shown in this drawing, it is present at both ends of the primary regulator valve (H), the modulator valve (R), the downshift valve (P), the 1-2 shift valve (L) and the 2-3 shift valve (K). Throttle pressure is at a minimum and has been overcome by governor pressure at the 2-3 shift valve (K). This opens a passage from the 2-3 shift valve (K) to the orifice control valve (M) and the rear clutch (C). The filling of the large release cavity on the front servo (D) occurs before and times the application of the rear clutch (C) after the release of the front band (D) to avoid tie-up of both 2nd and 3rd gears. The orifice restricts the pressure build-up for a few seconds to soften the release and application of the front band (D) and rear clutch (C).

### CLUTCH AND BAND SERVO SYSTEM

The front clutch (B) and the rear clutch (C) are applied in drive 3rd gear. There are no accumulator pistons in the Model 66; however, the release cavity on the front servo (D) is used in connection with the servo orifice control valve for the same purpose as an accumulator.

A. Torque converter
B. Front clutch
C. Rear clutch
D. Front servo
E. Rear servo
F. Governor
G. Pump
H. Primary regulator valve

J. Secondary regulator valve
K. 2-3 shift valve
L. 1-2 shift valve
M. Servo orifice control valve
N. Manual valve
P. Downshift valve
Q. Throttle valve
R. Modulator valve

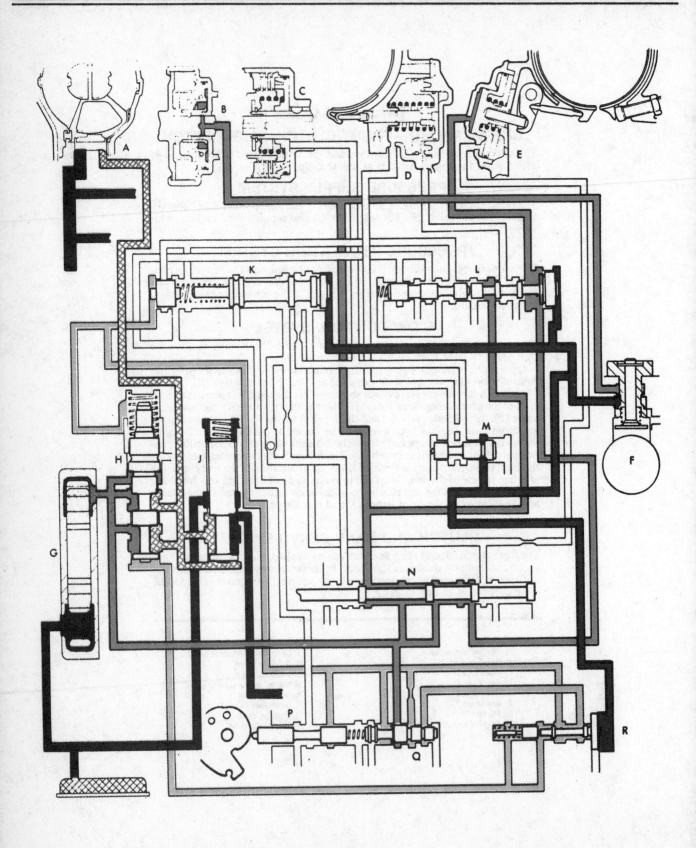

Manual 1—First Gear

## Manual 1—1st Gear

### UNITS APPLIED—FRONT CLUTCH, REAR BAND

The selector lever is in "1" position and the vehicle is starting to move.

### PRESSURE SUPPLY SYSTEM

The oil pump (G) is supplying fluid pressure to the primary regulator valve (H), the manual valve (N) and the throttle valve (Q).

### PRESSURE REGULATING SYSTEM

The primary regulator valve (H) is supplying pressure to the secondary regulator valve (J) and the secondary regulator valve (J) is directing pressure to the torque converter (A) and lubrication circuits. The secondary regulator valve (J) also acts as a high pressure relief valve for the system.

### FLOW CONTROL SYSTEM

The manual valve (N) is directing pressure to the 1-2 shift valve (L). The manual valve (N) is also supplying pressure to the front clutch (B), the governor (F) and another land on the 1-2 shift valve (L). The two pressures on the 1-2 shift valve (L) including pressure on the wider land opposing governor pressure, lock out upshifts. The 1-2 shift valve (L) has an apply passage open to the rear servo (E).

### CLUTCH AND BAND SERVO SYSTEM

With the front clutch (B) and rear servo (E) applied the transmission is in "1"— low gear.

---

A. Torque converter
B. Front clutch
C. Rear clutch
D. Front servo
E. Rear servo
F. Governor
G. Pump
H. Primary regulator valve

J. Secondary regulator valve
K. 2-3 shift valve
L. 1-2 shift valve
M. Servo orifice control valve
N. Manual valve
P. Downshift valve
Q. Throttle valve
R. Modulator valve

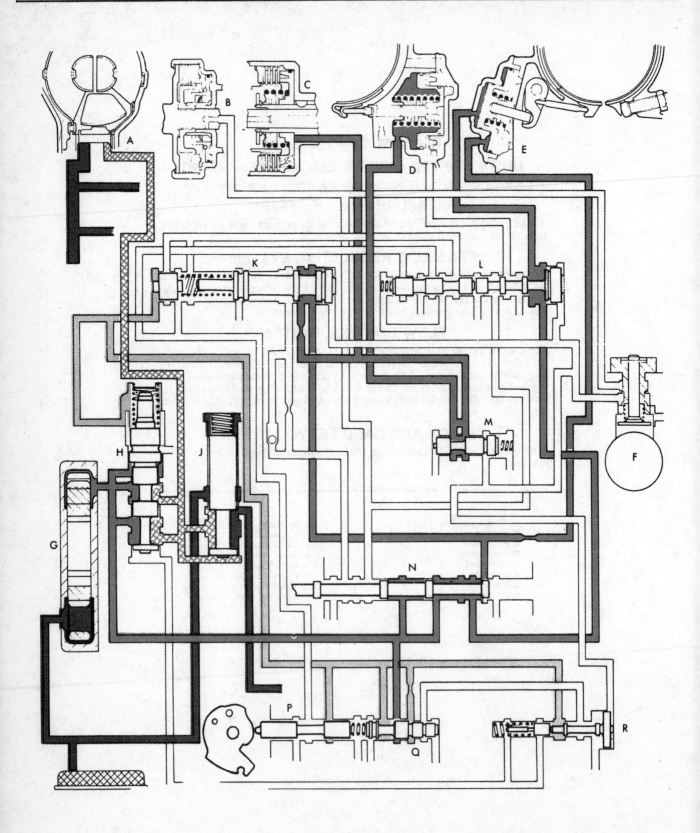

Reverse

# Reverse

### UNITS APPLIED—REAR CLUTCH, FRONT BAND

The selector lever is in Reverse and the engine speed is at idle. It is assumed that the foot brake is applied.

### PRESSURE SUPPLY SYSTEM

The oil pump (G) is supplying fluid pressure to the primary regulator valve (H), the manual valve (N) and the throttle valve (Q).

### PRESSURE REGULATING SYSTEM

The primary regulator valve (H) is controlling line pressure and supplying the secondary regulator valve (J). The secondary regulator valve (J) is directing pressure to the torque converter (A) and the lubrication circuits. The secondary regulator valve also acts as a high pressure relief valve for the system.

### FLOW CONTROL SYSTEM

The manual valve (N) is directing pressure ot the 2-3 shift valve (K), the release side of the rear servo (E) and the 1-2 shift valve (L). The 2-3 shift valve (K) is supplying pressure to the orifice control valve (M) and the rear clutch (C). The servo orifice control valve (M) is supplying pressure to the front servo apply (D). There is no governor pressure in Reverse. Throttle pressure is directed to the modulator valve (R), the 2-3 shift valve (K) and the increase end of the primary regulator valve (H). This means that the primary regulator valve (H) is controlling line pressure to a higher level to compensate for the greater torque in Reverse.

### CLUTCH AND BAND SERVO SYSTEM

The rear servo is not applied since both the apply and release side of the servo are pressurized. The front servo is applying the band and the rear clutch is applied. This means that the transmission is in Reverse gear.

| | |
|---|---|
| A. Torque converter | J. Secondary regulator valve |
| B. Front clutch | K. 2-3 shift valve |
| C. Rear clutch | L. 1-2 shift valve |
| D. Front servo | M. Servo orifice control valve |
| E. Rear servo | N. Manual valve |
| F. Governor | P. Downshift valve |
| G. Pump | Q. Throttle valve |
| H. Primary regulator valve | R. Modulator valve |

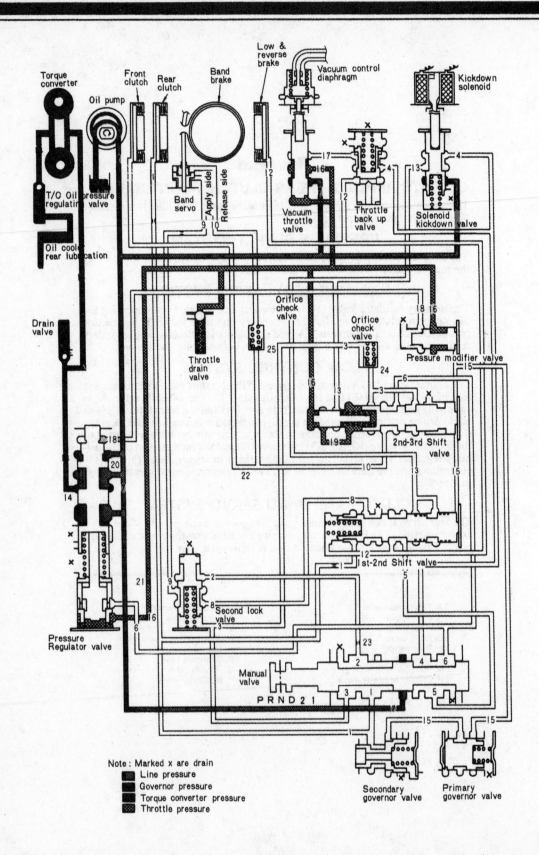

Note : Marked x are drain
▪ Line pressure
▪ Governor pressure
▪ Torque converter pressure
▪ Throttle pressure

**Neutral**

# Neutral

## Units Applied

### NONE

The transaxle is not transmitting torque to output shaft in Neutral range.

The oil pump is operating and has charged the main line control pressure system. Pressure is regulated.

The converter and cooler systems are charged. Control pressure is also routed to the vacuum throttle valve and the solenoid downshift valve.

The manual control valve is in the Neutral position and control pressure ⑦ is stopped at the manual valve.

Vacuum throttle valve pressure ⑯ is directed to the pressure modifier valve, 2-3 shift valve, 2-3 timing valve and the bottom of the pressure regulator valve. The pressure pushing up on the pressure regulator valve increases regulated line pressure. Since no clutches or bands are engaged, the transaxle is in Neutral.

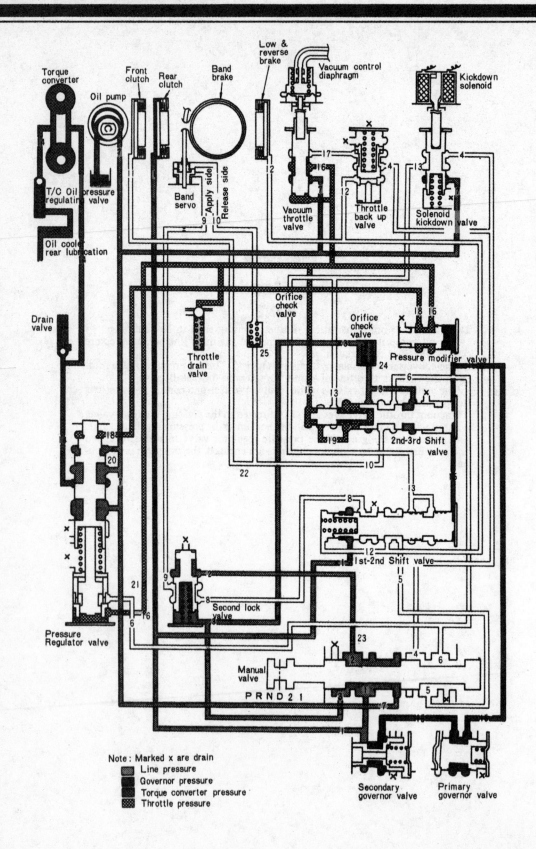

Torque converter

Oil pump

Front clutch

Rear clutch

Band brake

Low & reverse brake

Vacuum control diaphragm

Kickdown solenoid

T/C Oil pressure regulating valve

Band servo

Apply side

Release side

Vacuum throttle valve

Throttle back up valve

Solenoid kickdown valve

Oil cooler rear lubrication

Drain valve

Throttle drain valve

Orifice check valve

Orifice check valve

Pressure modifier valve

2nd-3rd Shift valve

1st-2nd Shift valve

Second lock valve

Pressure Regulator valve

Manual valve

P R N D 2 1

Secondary governor valve

Primary governor valve

Note: Marked x are drain
- Line pressure
- Governor pressure
- Torque converter pressure
- Throttle pressure

**D₁ range, first gear**

# DRIVE—1ST GEAR

## Units Applied

### REAR CLUTCH, ONE-WAY CLUTCH

It is assumed the vehicle is moving at low speed (10-15 mph) and at a light throttle opening.

The oil pump is operating and has charged the main control pressure circuit. The fluid is being regulated.

The converter and cooler systems are charged with control pressure, which is also routed to the vacuum throttle valve and solenoid downshift valve.

The manual valve has been positioned to open passage ① leading to the governor secondary valve, the rear of the 1-2 shift valve and to apply the rear clutch.

The manual valve is positioned so that fluid pressure ② is directed to the second lock valve.

Passage ③ is charged. Fluid pressure is directed to the opposite end of the second lock valve, opposing and equalizing pressure ②.

Passage ③ fluid pressure is directed through the orifice check valve and to the 2-3 shift valve, where it is stopped by the valve lands and grooves.

Throttle valve pressure ⑯ is directed to the pressure modifier valve, 2-3 shift valve, 2-3 timing valve and the pressure regulator valve.

Governor pressure, generated in proportion to vehicle speed, is transmitted to the end of the 1-2 shift valve, 2-3 shift valve, 2-3 timing valve and the pressure modifier valve.

After initial start up and under hard acceleration, the oil pump output ⑦ may be high. The higher pump pressure causes higher line pressure ⑦ and harsh application of bands and clutches. The pressure modifier valve is designed to reduce line pressure ⑦ under these conditions. When governor pressure ⑮ overcomes throttle pressure ⑯ and spring force in the pressure modifier valve, then throttle pressure ⑱ is allowed to flow to the top of the pressure regulator valve. This new pressure pushing down on the pressure regulator valve reduces line pressure.

The 1-2 shift valve is not modulated by vacuum throttle valve pressure in the Jatco transaxle. Therefore, the 1-2 shift depends on governor pressure opposing spring and line pressure to regulate the 1-2 shift.

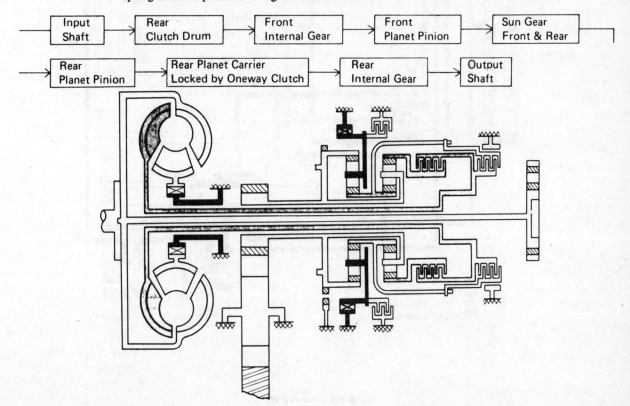

| Input Shaft | → | Rear Clutch Drum | → | Front Internal Gear | → | Front Planet Pinion | → | Sun Gear Front & Rear | → |
| Rear Planet Pinion | → | Rear Planet Carrier Locked by Oneway Clutch | → | Rear Internal Gear | → | Output Shaft | |

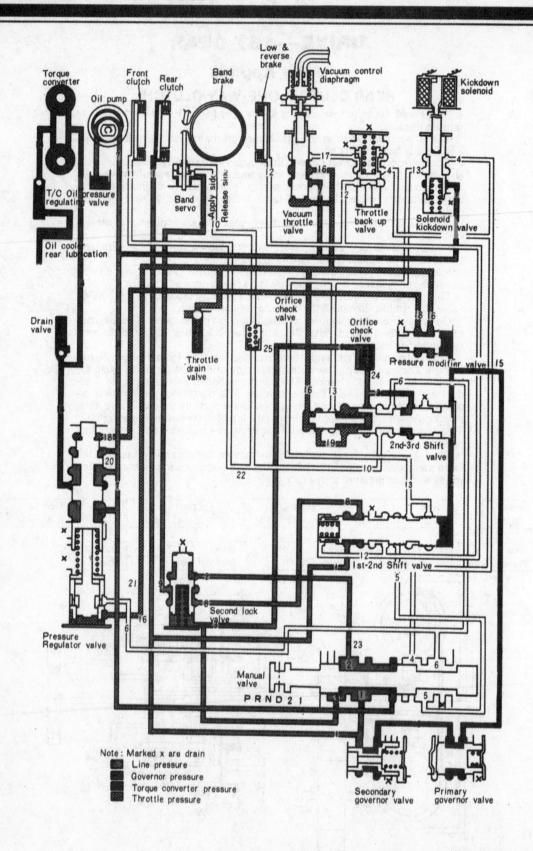

D₂ range, second gear

# DRIVE—2ND GEAR
## Units Applied
### REAR CLUTCH, BAND SERVO

The transaxle is now in 2nd speed and the vehicle is moving approximately 35 mph at light throttle.

The oil pump is charging the main control system and pressure is regulated.

The converter and cooler systems are charged. Control pressure is routed to the vacuum throttle valve and the downshift solenoid valve.

The manual valve has been positioned to open passage ① to the secondary governor valve, the rear of the 1-2 shift valve and the apply side of the rear clutch.

Passage ② is charged and fluid pressure is directed to the end of the second lock valve.

Passage ③ is directed to the other end of the second lock valve. Fluid pressure ③ opposes and equalizes fluid pressure ② at the second lock valve.

Fluid pressure ③ is also directed through orifice check valve to the 2-3 shift valve where it is stopped by the valves lands and grooves.

Vacuum throttle valve pressure ⑯ is directed to the pressure modifier valve, 2-3 shift valve, 2-3 timing valve and pressure regulator valve.

Governor pressure ⑮, generated in proportion to vehicle speed, is transmitted to the end of the 1-2 shift valve, 2-3 shift valve and the pressure modifier valve.

After initial start up and under hard acceleration, the oil pump output ⑦ may be higher. The higher pump pressure causes harsh application of clutches and bands. The pressure modifier valve is designed to reduce regulated pressure ⑦ under these conditions. When governor pressure ⑮ overcomes throttle pressure ⑯ and spring pressure in the pressure modifier valve, then throttle pressure ⑱ is allowed to flow to the top of the pressure regulator valve. This new pressure pushing down on the pressure regulator valve reduces line pressure, thereby modulating the harsh shift.

As the governor pressure increases on the 1-2 shift valve, passage ⑧ opens and is directed through the center of the second lock valve ⑨ and to the apply side of the brake band servo. The brake band is applied and the transaxle is in 2nd speed.

| Input Shaft | → | Rear Clutch Drum | → | Front Internal Gear | → | Front Sun Gear Locked by Brake Band | → | Front Planet Pinion |

| Front Planet Carrier | → | Output Shaft |

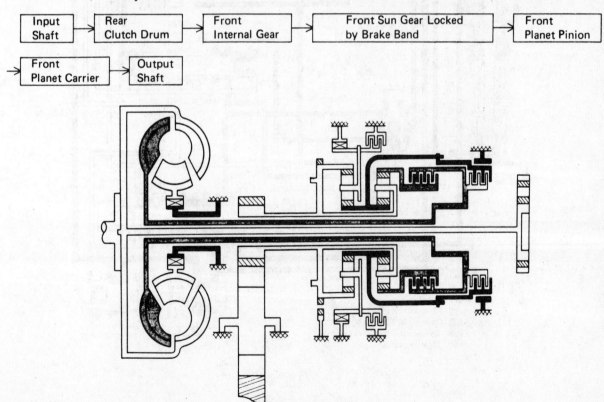

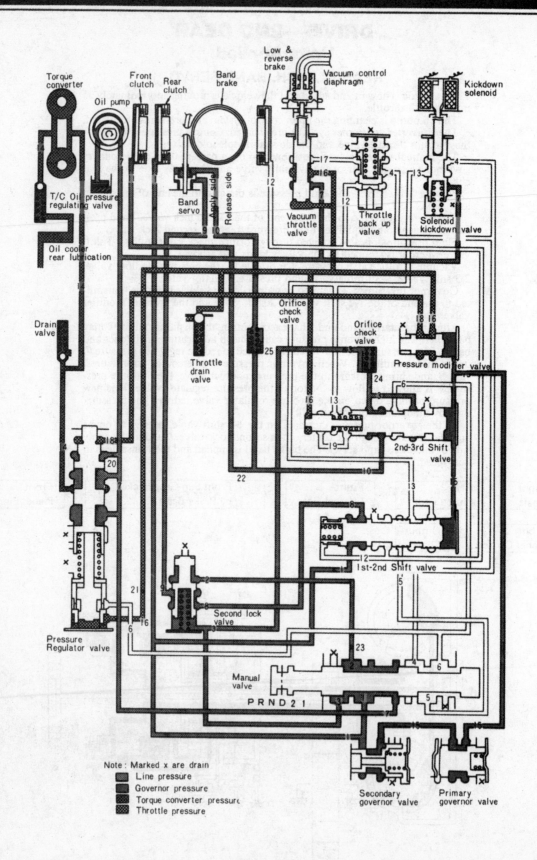

**D₃ range, third gear**

# DRIVE—3RD GEAR
## Units Applied
### FRONT CLUTCH, REAR CLUTCH

The transaxle has shifted to 3rd speed and the vehicle is moving approximately 50 mph at ½ throttle.

The oil pump is charging the main control system and pressure is regulated.

The converter and cooler systems are charged. Control pressure is also routed to the vacuum throttle valve and the downshift solenoid valve.

The manual valve has been positioned to open passage ① to the secondary governor valve, the rear of the 1-2 shift valve and the apply side of the rear clutch.

Passage ② is charged and fluid pressure is directed to the end of second lock valve.

Passage ③ is directed to the other end of the second lock valve. Fluid pressure ③ opposes and equalizes fluid pressure ② at the second lock valve.

Fluid pressure ③ is also directed through the orifice check valve to the 2-3 shift valve where it is stopped by the valve lands and grooves.

Vacuum throttle valve pressure ⑯ is directed to the pressure modifier valve, 2-3 shift valve, 2-3 timing valve and pressure regulator valve.

Governor pressure ⑮, generated in proportion to vehicle speed, is transmitted to the end of the 1-2 shift valve, 2-3 shift valve and the pressure modifier valve.

After initial start up and under hard acceleration, the oil pump output ⑦ may be higher. The pressure modifier valve is designed to reduce regulated pressure ⑦ under these conditions. When governor pressure ⑮ overcomes throttle pressure ⑯ and spring pressure, the pressure modifier valve allows throttle pressure ⑱ to flow to the top of the pressure regulator valve. This new pressure pushing down on the pressure regulator valve reduces line pressure and modulates the harsh shift.

As vehicle speed increases, so does governor pressure on the 2-3 shift valve. When the valve is pushed to the left, passage ⑩ opens, directing fluid pressure to the release side of the brake band servo. At the same time that the second speed brake band is being released, the third speed ⑪ front clutch is being applied. Thus, the transaxle is shifted into 3rd speed.

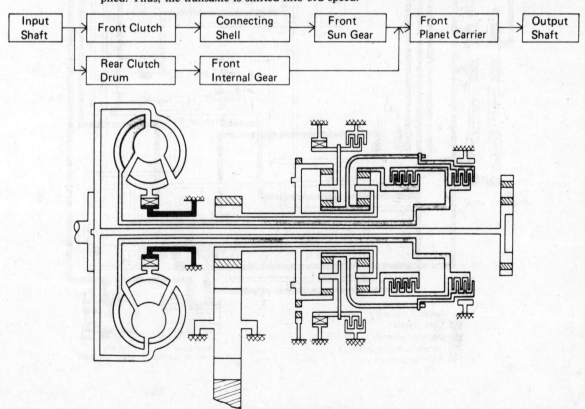

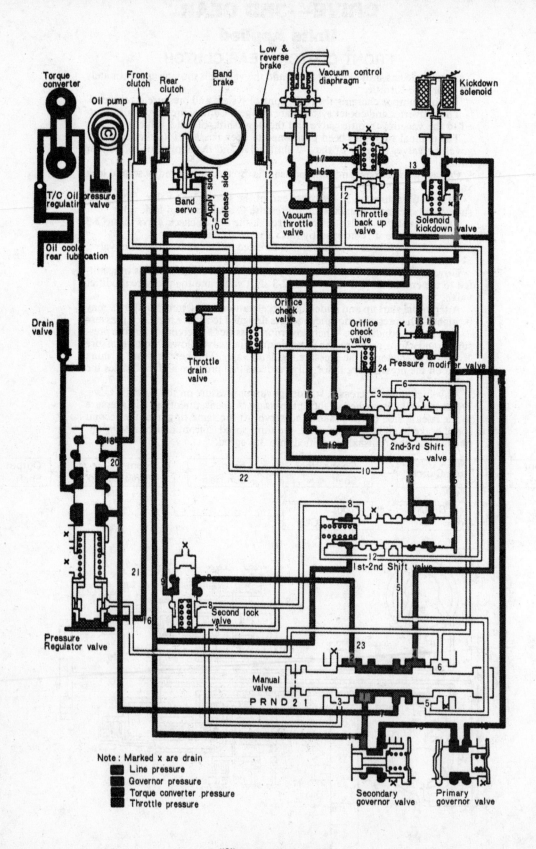

"2" range, second gear

# MANUAL "2"—2ND GEAR

## Units Applied

### REAR CLUTCH, BAND SERVO

The "2" range means that the transaxle is locked in 2nd gear, regardless of the engine and vehicle speed conditions. This is accomplished totally by fluid pressure from manual valve passages opened in the "2" range position of the manual valve.

The oil pump is supplying pressure and pressure is regulated.

The converter and cooling systems are charged. Main line control pressure is also directed to the vacuum throttle valve and the solenoid downshift valve.

Manual valve passage① supplies the secondary governor valve.

Passage① directs fluid pressure to the rear clutch.

Passage① also supplies fluid pressure to the 1-2 shift valve.

The manual valve passage② directs fluid pressure to the upper end of the second lock valve. The downward fluid pressure locks the transmission in 2nd speed since it also allows passage② pressure to flow through to passage⑨, which is the apply side of the brake band servo. With the rear clutch and brake band applied, without regard to the position of the 1-2 shift valve, the transaxle is locked-up out of 1st and into 2nd gear. However, there is also provision for preventing upshifts into 3rd gear. The "2" range provides 2-3 upshift lock-out.

In the "2" range, two pressures combine to provide 2-3 upshift lockout. Passage④ supplies fluid pressure to the solenoid downshift valve and the throttle backup valve.

Through passage⑰, the throttle backup valve boosts the pressure in the throttle vacuum valve passage⑯.

Vacuum throttle valve pressure⑯, and solenoid downshift valve pressure⑬ both oppose the governor upshift pressure⑮ at the 2-3 shift valve. The two fluid pressures combine with spring pressure to lock out the 2-3 upshift. The transaxle is locked in 2nd speed.

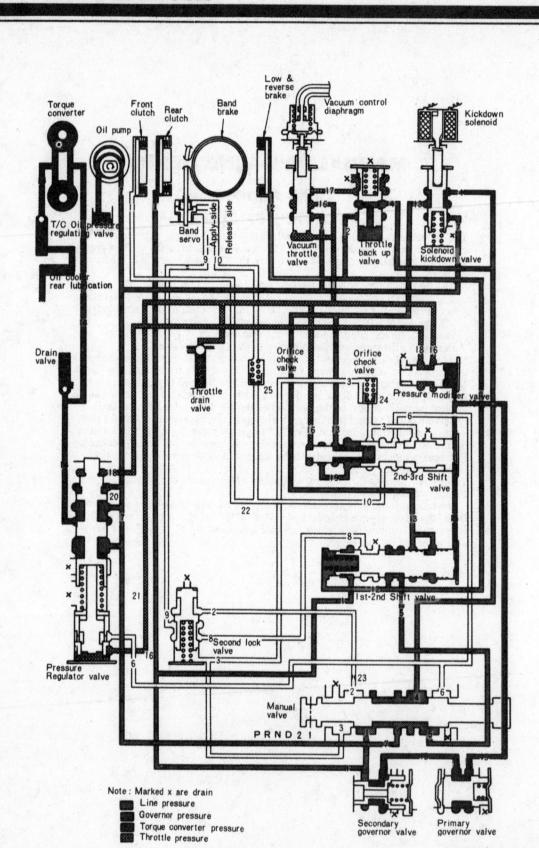

Note : Marked x are drain
- Line pressure
- Governor pressure
- Torque converter pressure
- Throttle pressure

**1₁ range, first gear**

# MANUAL "1"—1ST GEAR

## Units Applied

### REAR CLUTCH, LOW-REVERSE BRAKE

It is assumed the vehicle speed is less than 16 mph at light throttle. The shift lever is moved to the "1" range position and the transaxle is locked in Low gear.

The oil pump pressure is present and pressure is regulated.

Converter and cooler systems are charged. Main line control pressure is supplied to the throttle back up valve and the solenoid downshift valve.

The manual valve supplies passage①. Passage directs fluid pressure to the secondary governor valve, the rear clutch and the 1-2 shift valve.

Passage④ routes fluid pressure to the solenoid downshift valve and the throttle back up valve.

In "1" range, the manual valve applies fluid pressure to passage⑤. Passage⑤ directs fluid pressure to the 1-2 shift valve.

Passage⑫ routes fluid pressure from the 1-2 shift valve to the other end of the 1-2 shift valve. This pressure, plus solenoid downshift pressure⑬, is overcome to provide the upshift to 2nd speed.

Passage⑫ also directs fluid pressure to the throttle backup valve and the low and reverse brake.

Two pressures combined with spring pressure to lock out 2-3 upshifts in the "1" range. Solenoid downshift valve pressure⑬ is applied to the 2-3 and 1-2 shift valves.

Vacuum throttle valve pressure⑯ combined with throttle back-up valve pressure⑰ are applied to the 2-3 shift valve.

The rear clutch and the low and reverse brake are applied. The transaxle is locked in Low (1st) gear.

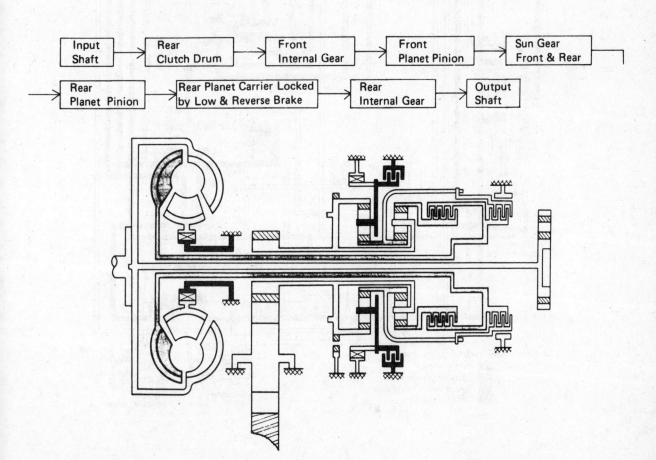

```
┌────────────┐   ┌────────────┐   ┌────────────┐   ┌────────────┐   ┌────────────┐
│ Input      │ → │ Rear       │ → │ Front      │ → │ Front      │ → │ Sun Gear   │
│ Shaft      │   │ Clutch Drum│   │ Internal Gear│ │ Planet Pinion│ │ Front & Rear│
└────────────┘   └────────────┘   └────────────┘   └────────────┘   └────────────┘

   ┌────────────┐   ┌────────────────────────────┐   ┌────────────┐   ┌────────────┐
→  │ Rear       │ → │ Rear Planet Carrier Locked │ → │ Rear       │ → │ Output     │
   │ Planet Pinion│ │ by Low & Reverse Brake     │   │ Internal Gear│ │ Shaft      │
   └────────────┘   └────────────────────────────┘   └────────────┘   └────────────┘
```

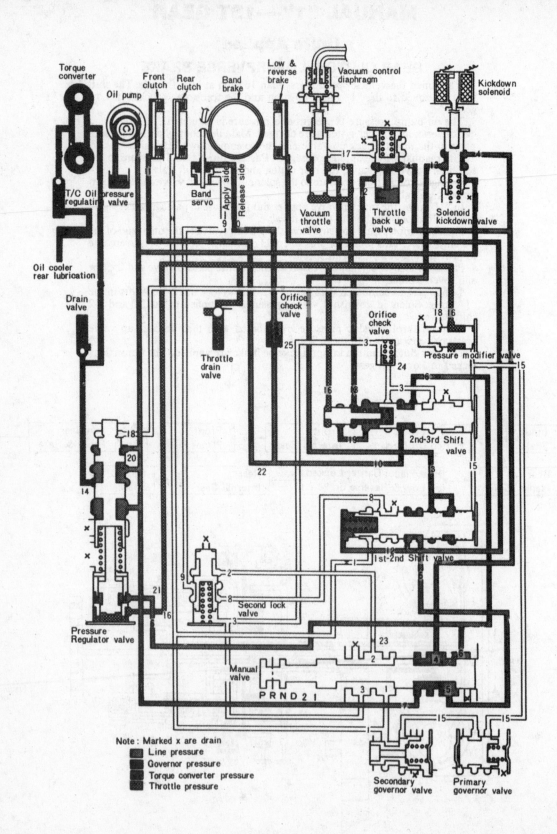

Torque converter
Oil pump
Front clutch
Rear clutch
Band brake
Low & reverse brake
Vacuum control diaphragm
Kickdown solenoid

T/C Oil pressure regulating valve
Band servo
Apply side
Release side
Vacuum throttle valve
Throttle back up valve
Solenoid kickdown valve

Oil cooler rear lubrication

Drain valve

Throttle drain valve

Orifice check valve

Orifice check valve

Pressure modifier valve

2nd-3rd Shift valve

1st-2nd Shift valve

Second lock valve

Manual valve

P R N D 2 1

Pressure Regulator valve

Note : Marked x are drain
■ Line pressure
■ Governor pressure
■ Torque converter pressure
■ Throttle pressure

Secondary governor valve
Primary governor valve

**Reverse**

14-26

# REVERSE

## Units Applied

### FRONT CLUTCH, LOW-REVERSE BRAKE

The pump is supplying mainline control pressure and the pressure is being regulated.

The converter and cooler systems are charged.

The manual valve is in the Reverse position, and passages④, ⑤ and ⑥ are charged.

Passage④ supplies control line pressure to the throttle backup valve and the solenoid downshift valve.

Passage⑤ supplies control pressure to the 1-2 shift valve. The 1-2 shift valve routes the fluid pressure to passage⑫, which supplies pressure to the throttle backup valve and the low and reverse brake.

Passage⑥ supplies pressure to the 2-3 shift valve, the front clutch⑪ and the release side of the brake band servo⑩.

Passage⑥ also supplies pressure to one end of the regulator valve, thus increasing control pressure. More control pressure is needed in Reverse because of increased torque on the output shaft.

The application of pressure to the release side of the brake band servo serves only to ensure the release of the brake band. The front clutch and the low and reverse brake are the operating members of the power train in this gear.

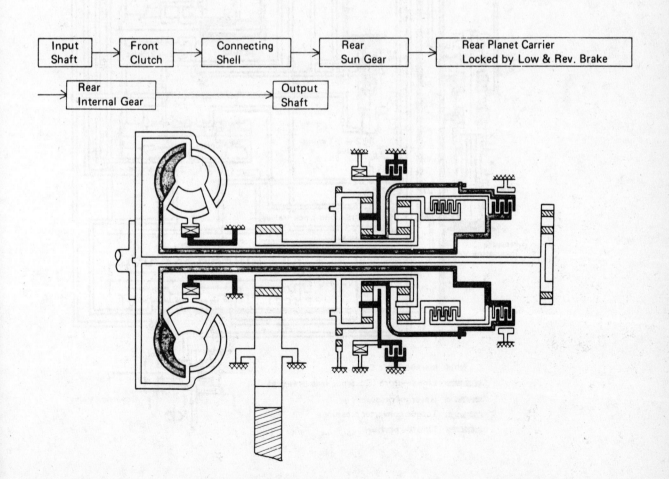

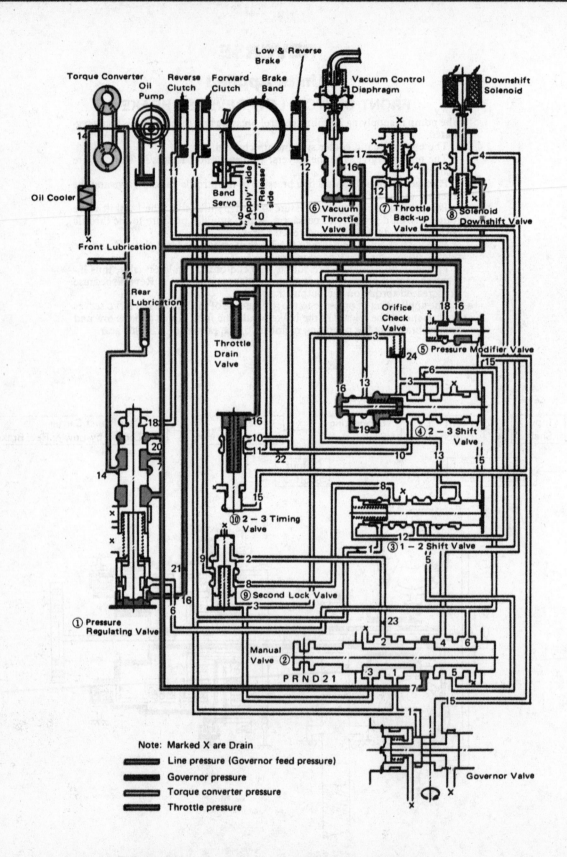

Note: Marked X are Drain

- Line pressure (Governor feed pressure)
- Governor pressure
- Torque converter pressure
- Throttle pressure

**FWD automatic transmission in neutral** (©Fuji Heavy Industries Ltd.)

# NEUTRAL

When the transmission is in the N range, the clutches are released, as pressure oil is not delivered from the oil controlling mechanism to the speed controlling elements (clutches and brake band). Therefore, the power from the input shaft (turbine shaft) is not transmitted to the output shaft.

The pressure of the oil discharged from the oil pump is regulated by the pressure regulating valve ① and the pressurized oil, called line pressure 7, is delivered to the manual valve ②, vacuum throttle valve ⑥, and solenoid downshift valve ⑧. The oil then travels to the torque converter as torque converter oil 14, and, on the way to the converter, part of the oil is supplied to the forward and reverse clutches as rear lubricating oil. Other part of the oil is directed as front lubricating oil to the planetary gears, one-way clutch and low & reverse brake through the oil pump shaft. Since the oil pump is rotating at the same speed as the engine, the volume of oil from the oil pump increases with engine speed, excess oil being returned through the pressure regulating valve ① directly to the oil pan.

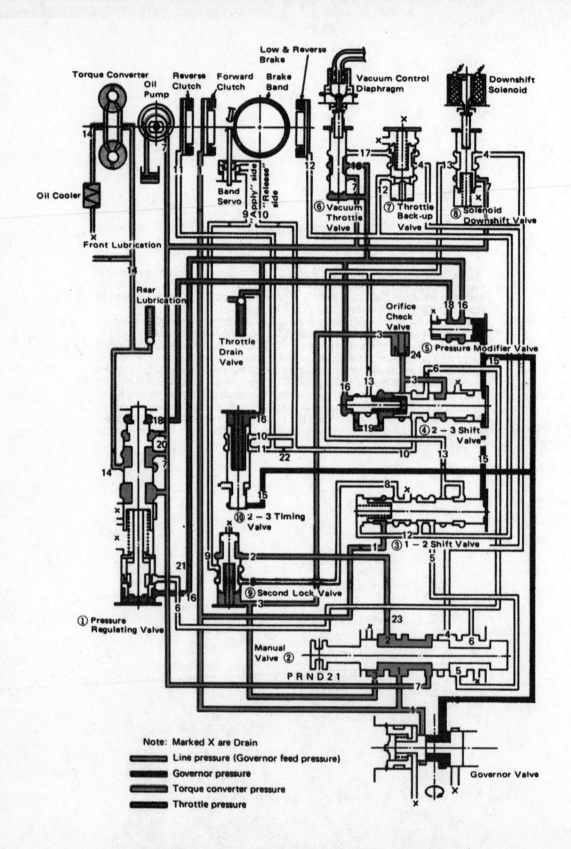

**FWD automatic transmission in drive—1st gear** (©Fuji Heavy Industries Ltd.)

# DRIVE—1ST GEAR

When the transmission is the D (1st gear) range, the forward clutch is engaged and power from the turbine shaft is transmitted to the forward sun gear. The planetary carrier is locked to the transmission case through the one-way clutch outer race, one-way clutch and center support.

The planetary gear system in this range provides a ratio of 2.6:1. Since the planetary carrier tends to turn clockwise when the car is coasting, the one-way clutch is released and runs idle. In this condition, no reverse drive is transmitted to the engine so that the engine brake will not be applied.

With the manual valve ② in the D position, the line pressure 7 admitted into the manual valve ② flows through the line pressure passages 1, 2 and 3. The line pressure passing through the passage 1 acts on the forward clutch, the governor, and the 1-2 shift valve ③ to achieve gear shifting.

The line pressure through the passage 2, enters the second lock valve ⑨. The line pressure through the passage 3, acts on the 2-3 shift valve ④ to perform 2-3 gear shifting and locks the second lock valve ⑨ as well.

The throttle pressure 16, which varies with accelerator pedal depression, acts on the pressure regulating valve ①, pushing the regulating valve ① to cause a rise in the pressure 7.

With an increase in car speed, the governor pressure 15 derived from the line pressure passage 1 actuates the 1-2 shift valve ③, 2-3 shift valve ④, and pressure modifier valve ⑤.

With high governor pressure, the pressure modifier valve ⑤ operates to compress its spring, and the throttle pressure 16 is carried to the passage 18 to act against the spring of the pressure regulating valve ① and the throttle pressure 16, so that the line pressure 7 will drop.

As car speed increases, the governor pressure 15 increases and pushes one side of the 1-2 shift valve ③ counteracting the throttle pressure 19, line pressure 1 and spring. When the governor pressure overcomes these forces, the gear changes from 1st to 2nd.

When the throttle pressure 19 is higher, or the accelerator pedal is depressed farther, the governor pressure rises higher, moving the shifting point to the higher speed side.

**NOTE: When the selector lever is placed in the "1" range, the forward clutch is engaged and the planetary gear is locked by the low and reverse clutch brake, instead of being locked by the one-way clutch.**

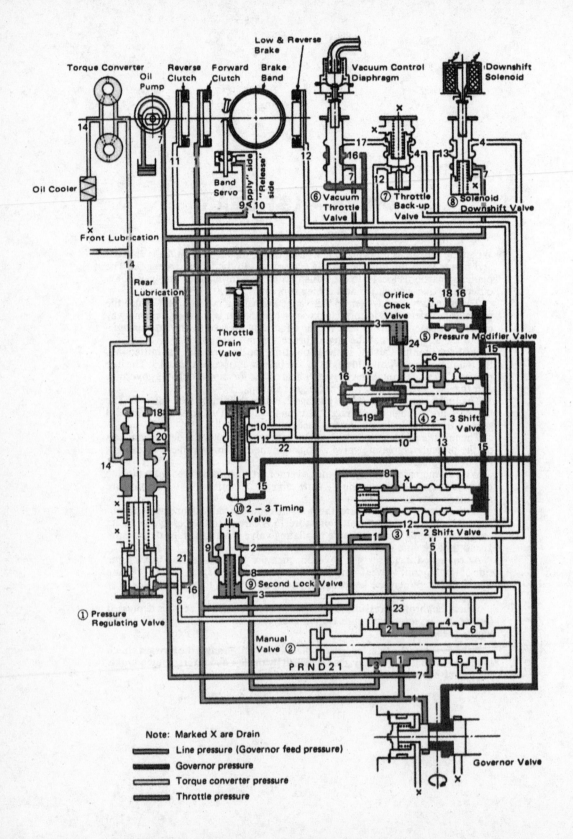

Note: Marked X are Drain

| | |
|---|---|
| | Line pressure (Governor feed pressure) |
| | Governor pressure |
| | Torque converter pressure |
| | Throttle pressure |

**FWD automatic transmission in drive 2nd gear and manual 2—2nd gear (©Fuji Heavy Industries Ltd.)**

# DRIVE—2ND GEAR AND MANUAL 2—2ND GEAR

When the transmission is in the D (2nd gear) range, the forward clutch is engaged and power from the turbine shaft is transmitted to the forward sun gear. Also, the brake band is applied to hold stationary the reverse clutch drum interlocked with the reverse sun gear and connecting shell.

The power also flows in the same manner with the transmission in the 2 and 1 (2nd gear) range. With the reverse sun gear held stationary, the planetary carrier rotates clockwise as the pinions circle around the reverse sun gear. Thus, the one-way clutch outer race runs idle and a gear ratio of 1.505 to 1 is obtained in this gear position.

When the governor pressure 15 increases with an increase in car speed while traveling in the D (1st gear) range, the 1-2 shift valve ③ moves to permit the line pressure 1 to run through the valve to the line pressure passage 8. The line pressure 8 is delivered to the line pressure passage 9 through the second lock valve ⑨, applying the band servo to shift up to the 2nd gear.

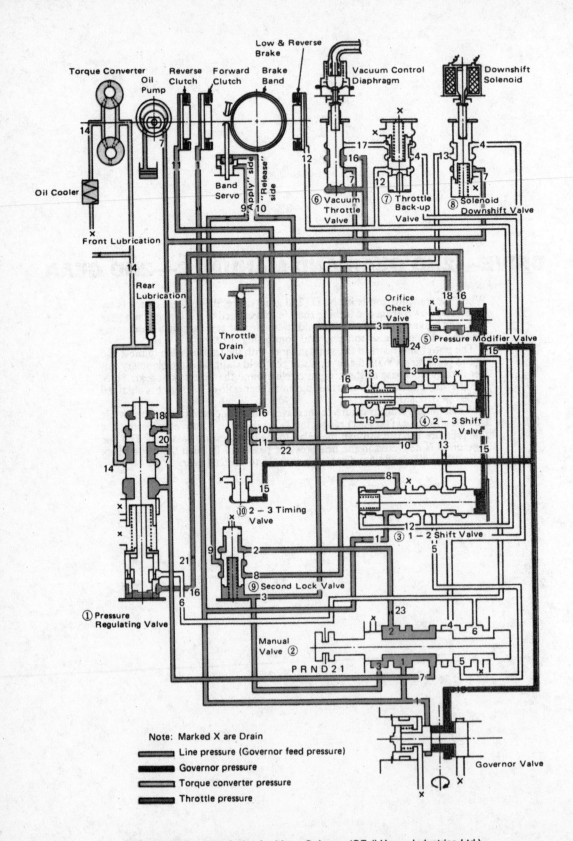

**FWD automatic transmission in drive—3rd gear (©Fuji Heavy Industries Ltd.)**

# DRIVE—3RD GEAR

With the transmission in the D (3rd gear) range, the forward clutch and the reverse clutch are engaged. Although oil pressure is applied to the servo piston on both the "apply" and "release" sides, the brake band is released as the servo piston is released by the combined releasing force which consists of the return spring force and the thrust caused by oil pressure acting on the annular surfaces of the governor valve which are different in area.

The power transmitted from the turbine shaft to the forward clutch drum is divided into two streams; one is transmitted from the forward clutch to the forward sun gear and the other from the reverse clutch to the reverse sun gear through the connecting shell.

Since the forward sun gear and the reverse sun gear make the rotation, the planetary-gear system turns as a unit and the output ring gear also turns in the same direction at the same speed. Hence, there is no gear reduction in the transmission and a gear ratio of 1 to 1 is achieved.

As car speed increases while traveling in the D (2nd gear) range, the governor pressure 15 grows greater than the spring force of the 2-3 shift valve ④ and the throttle pressure 19. When this takes place, the 2-3 shift valve ④ moves to apply the line pressure 3 to the reverse clutch and the "release" side of the band servo through the line pressure passage 10.

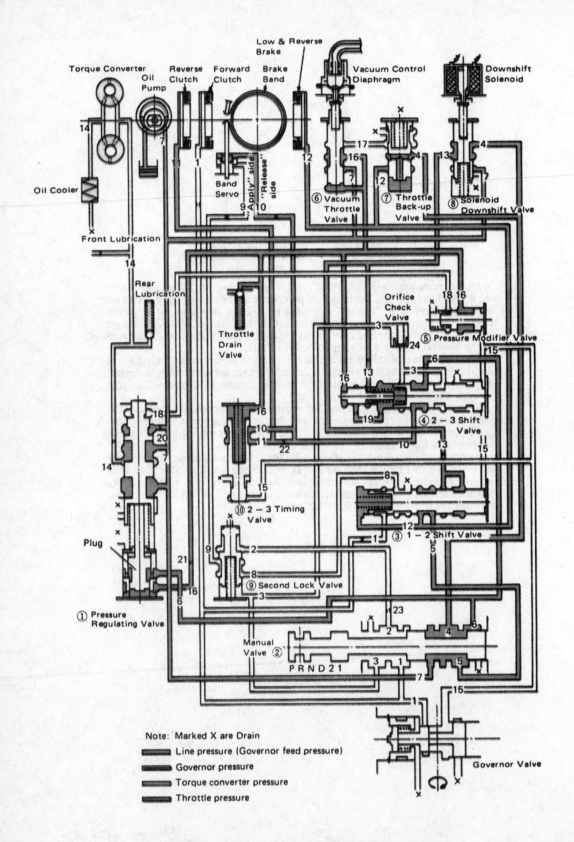

**FWD automatic transmission in reverse (©Fuji Heavy Industries Ltd.)**

# REVERSE

The reverse clutch and the low & reverse brake are engaged when the transmission is in the R range. The power flow is from the turbine shaft, through the reverse clutch, and from the connecting shell to the reverse sun gear. As the planetary carrier is held stationary by the low & reverse brake, the reverse sun gear turns clockwise. This causes the output ring gear to turn counterclockwise at a reduced speed, providing a gear ratio of 2.167 to 1.

With the manual valve ② in the R position, the line pressure 7 entering the manual valve ② flows in the line pressure passages 5, 6. The line pressure flowing through the passage 5 is diverted to the line pressure passage 12 through the 1-2 shift valve ③ to act on the low & reverse brake.

The oil running in the passage 6 passes through the 2-3 shift valve ④ to the line pressure passage 10 and acts on the "release" side of the band servo and the reverse clutch. The throttle pressure 16 and line pressure 6, which vary according to pedal depression, are applied to the plug in the pressure regulating valve ① to push the valve ① to cause a rise in the line pressure 7.

Since there is no governor pressure in the R range, the 1-2 shift valve ③, 2-3 shift valve ④, and the pressure modifier valve ⑤ are not functioning as a valve.

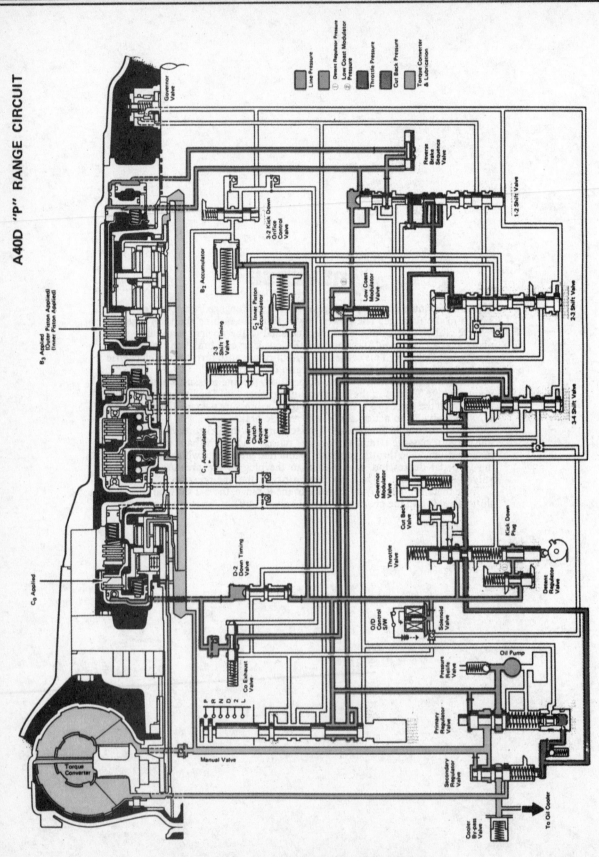

Oil flow circuit park range A-40D automatic transmission

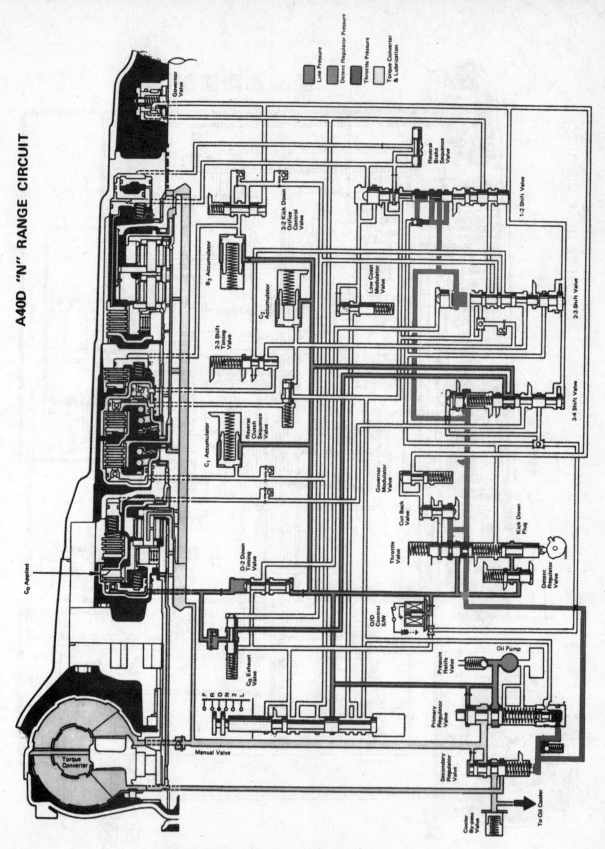

**A40D "N" RANGE CIRCUIT**

Governor Valve

Reverse Brake Sequence Valve

3-2 Kick Down Orifice Control Valve

1-2 Shift Valve

B₂ Accumulator

C₂ Accumulator

Low Coast Modulator Valve

2-3 Shift Valve

2-3 Shift Timing Valve

Reverse Clutch Sequence Valve

C₁ Accumulator

3-4 Shift Valve

Governor Modulator Valve

Cut Back Valve

Kick Down Plug

C₀ Applied

Throttle Valve

Detent Regulator Valve

D-2 Down Timing Valve

O/D Control S/W

C₀ Exhaust Valve

Pressure Relief Valve

Oil Pump

P R D 2 L

Primary Regulator Valve

Manual Valve

Secondary Regulator Valve

Torque Converter

Cooler By-pass Valve

To Oil Cooler

Line Pressure | Detent Regulator Pressure | Throttle Pressure | Torque Converter & Lubrication

**Oil flow circuit neutral range A-40D automatic transmission**

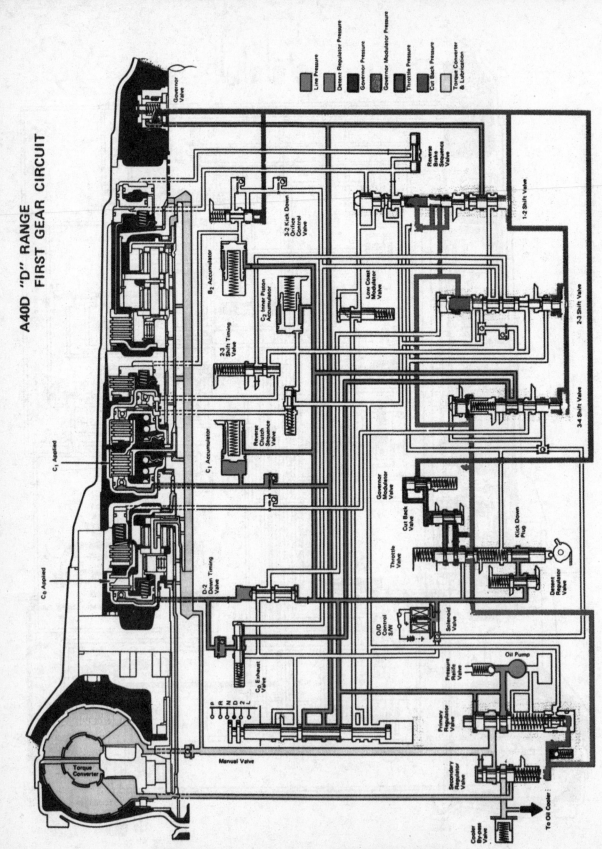

**A40D "D" RANGE FIRST GEAR CIRCUIT**

Oil flow circuit drive range 1st gear A-40D automatic transmission

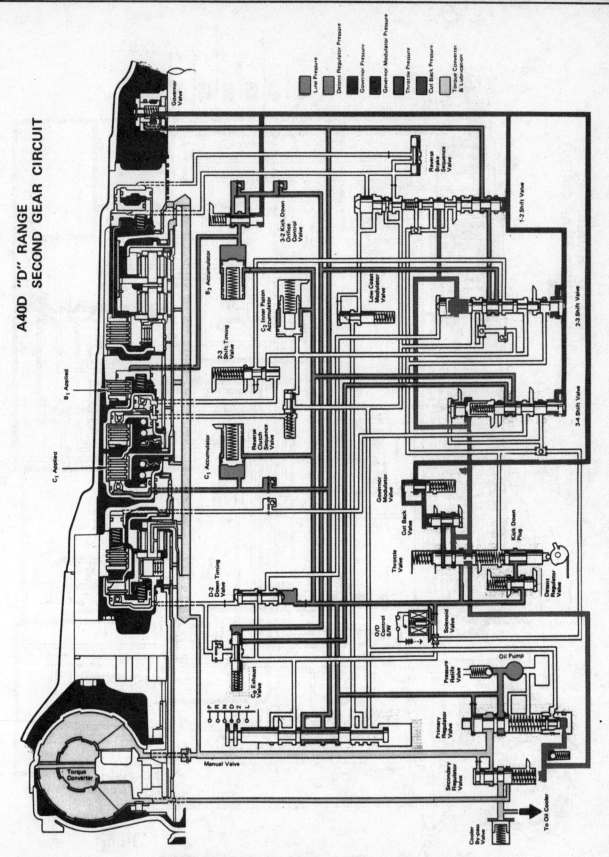

**Oil flow circuit drive range 2nd gear A-40D automatic transmission**

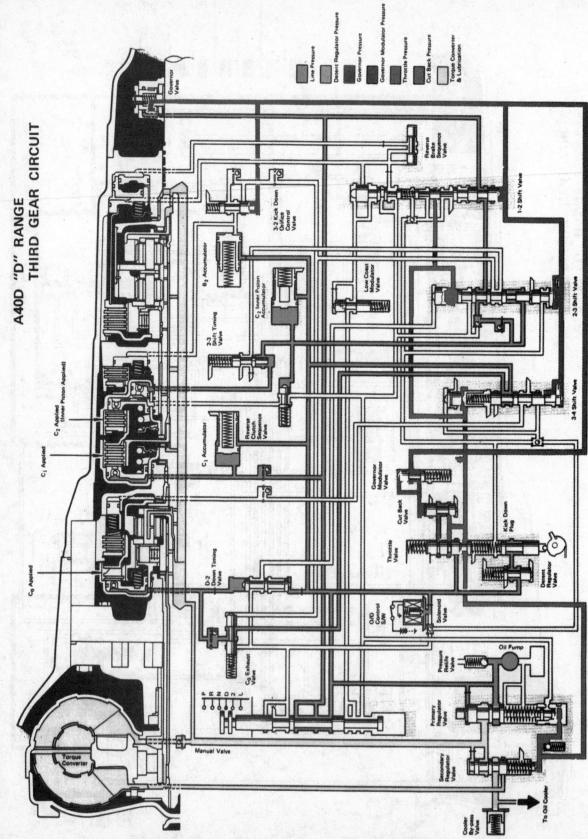

Oil flow circuit drive range 3rd gear A-40D automatic transmission

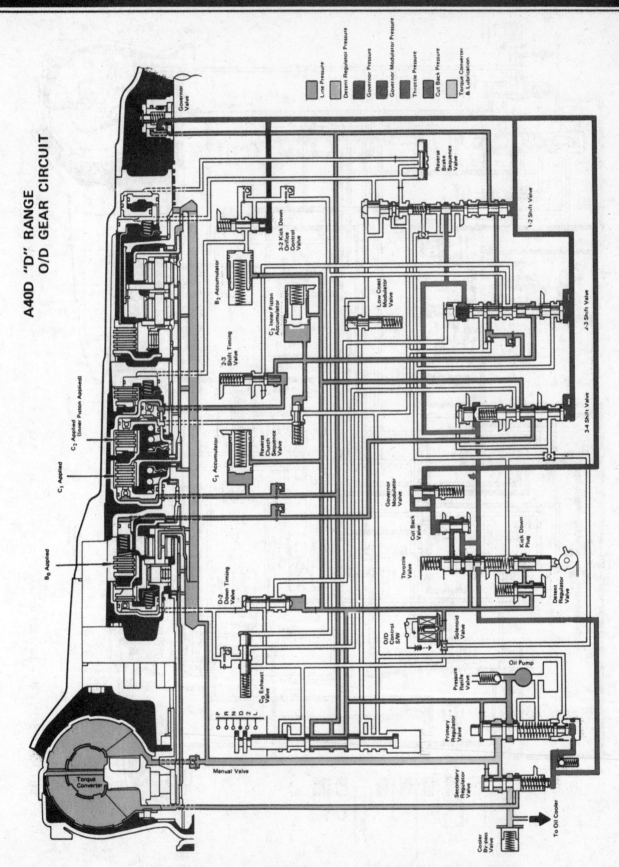

Oil flow circuit drive range overdrive gear A-40D automatic transmission

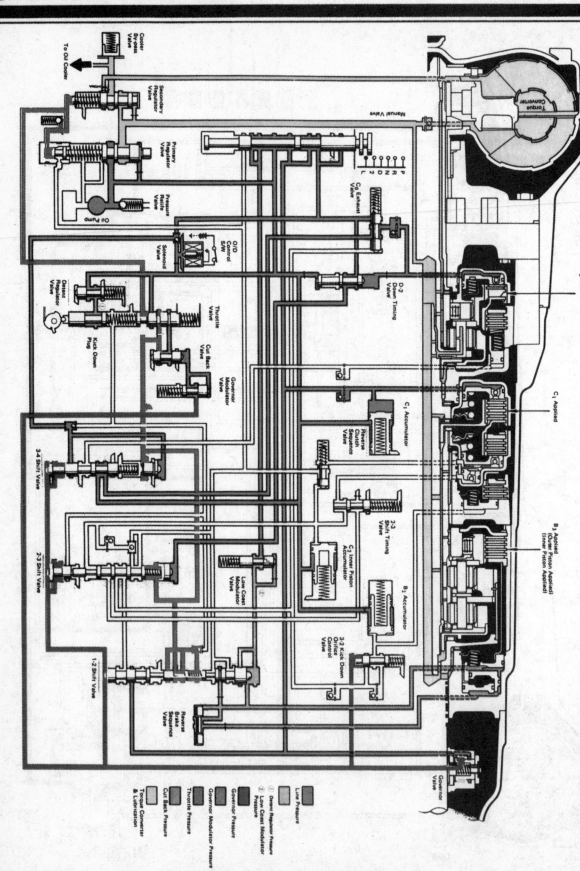

Oil flow circuit low range A-40D automatic transmission

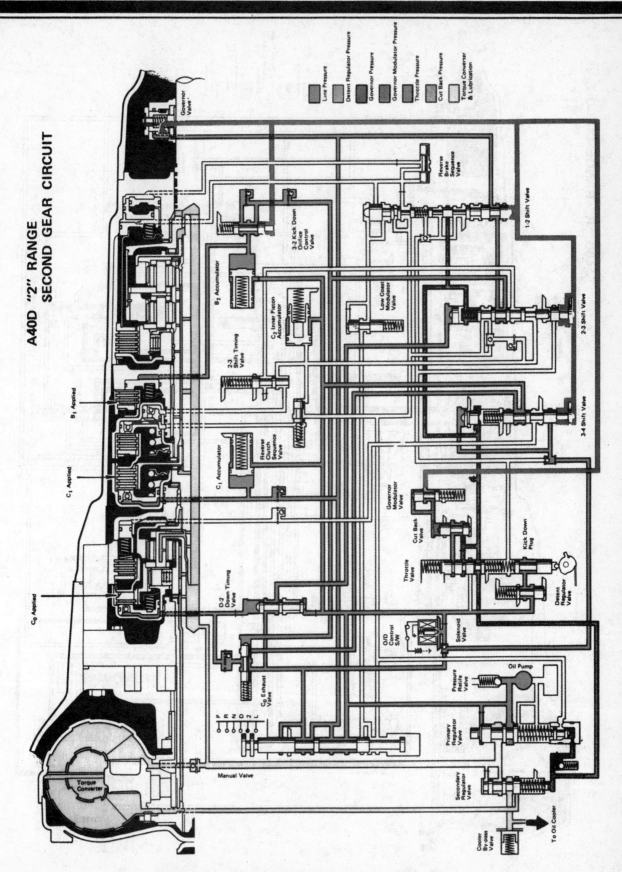

Oil flow circuit manual 2 range A-40D automatic transmission

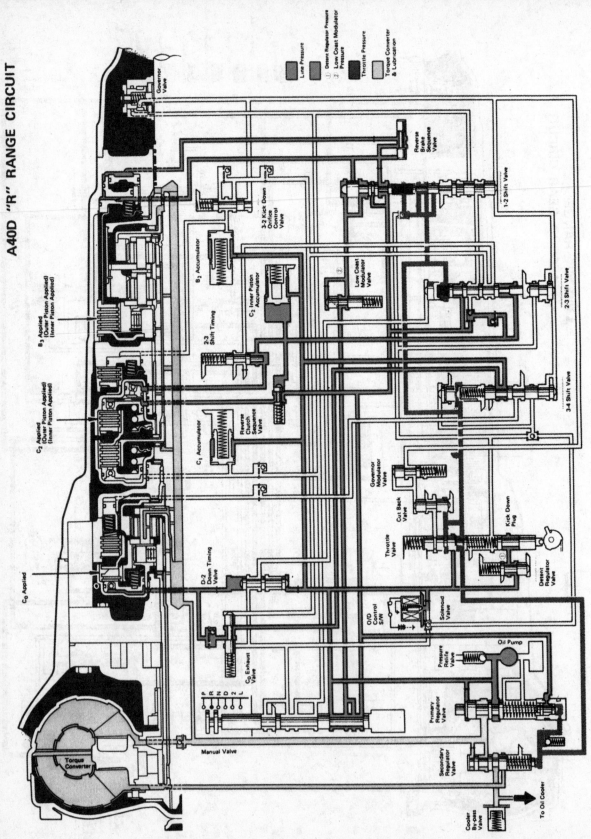

**A40D "R" RANGE CIRCUIT**

Line Pressure
① Desent Regulator Pressure
② Low Coast Modulator Pressure
Throttle Pressure
Torque Converter & Lubrication

Oil flow circuit reverse range A-40D automatic transmission

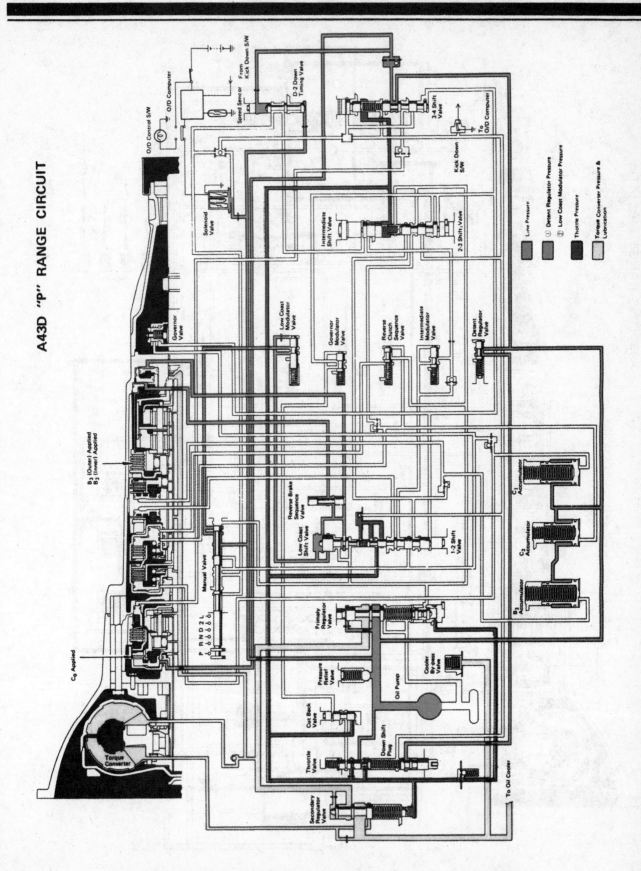

A43D "P" RANGE CIRCUIT

Oil flow circuit park range A-43D, A-43DL and A-43DE automatic transmission

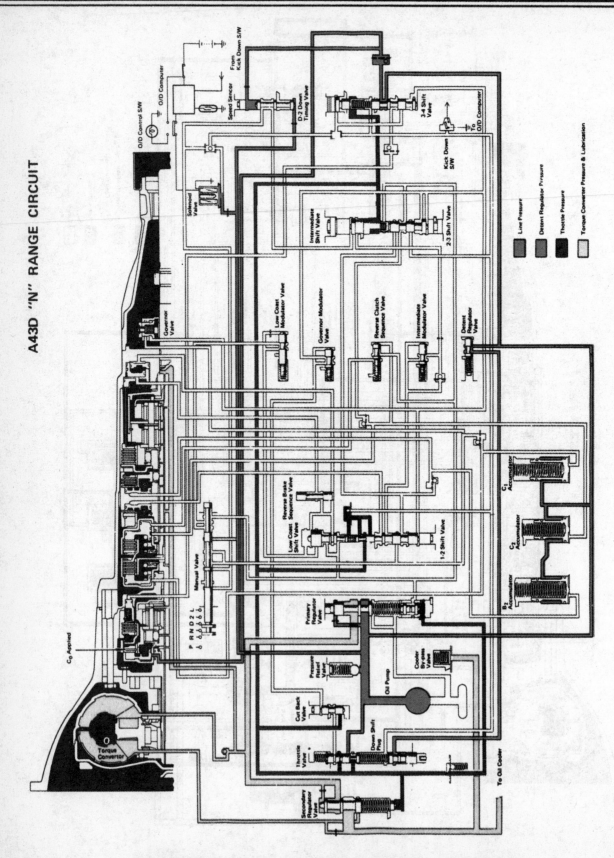

Oil flow circuit neutral range A-43D, A-43DL and A-43DE automatic transmission

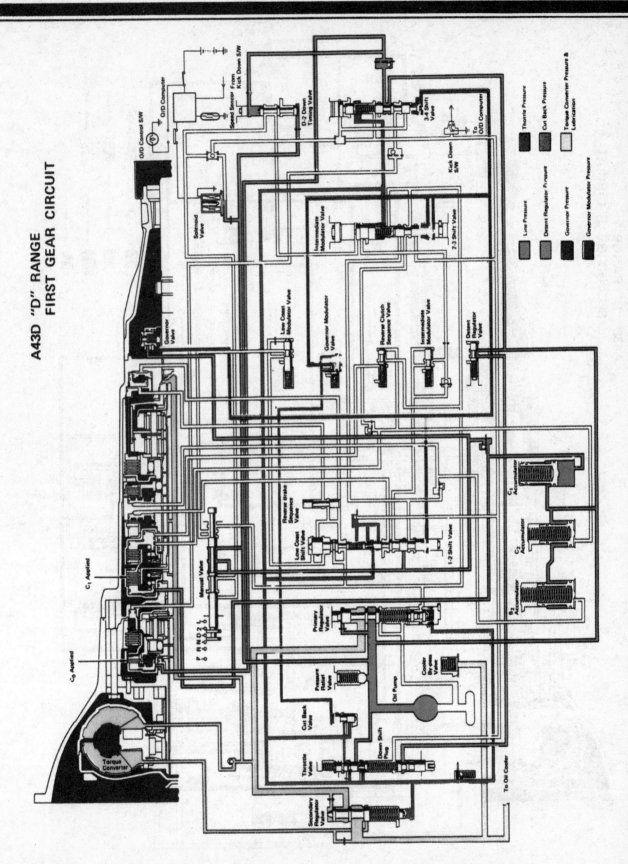

A43D "D" RANGE
FIRST GEAR CIRCUIT

Thortle Pressure
Cut Back Pressure
Torque Converter Pressure & Lubrication

Line Pressure
Detent Regulator Pressure
Governor Pressure
Governor Modulator Pressure

**Oil flow circuit drive range 1st gear A-43D, A-43DL and A-43DE automatic transmission**

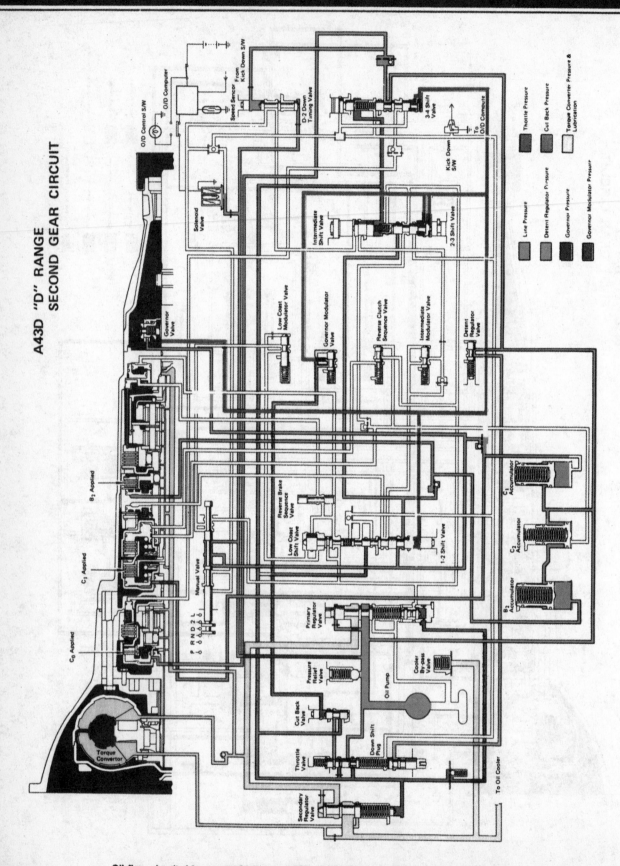

Oil flow circuit drive range 2nd gear A-43D, A-43DL and A-43DE automatic transmission

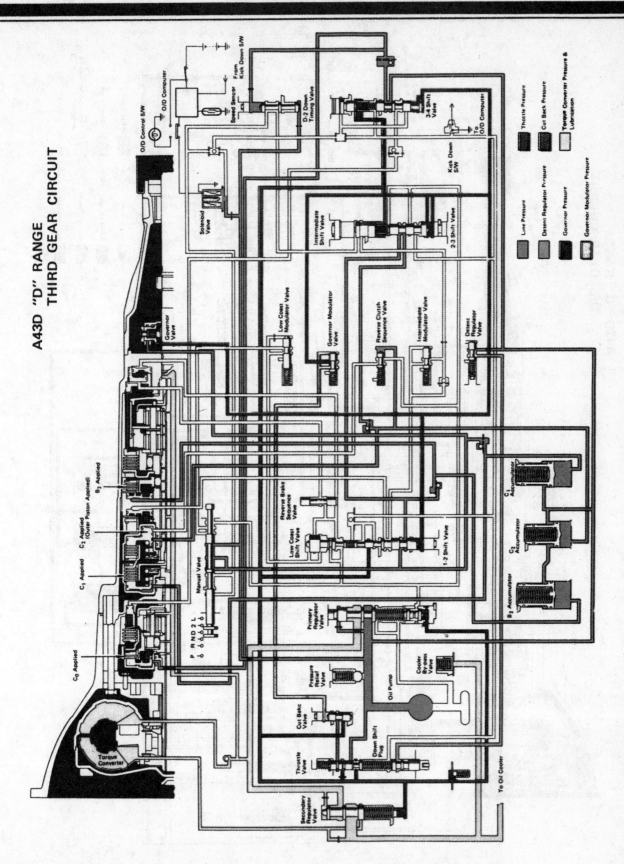

A43D "D" RANGE
THIRD GEAR CIRCUIT

**Oil flow circuit drive range 3rd gear A-43D, A-43DL and A-43DE automatic transmission**

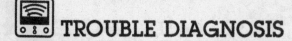

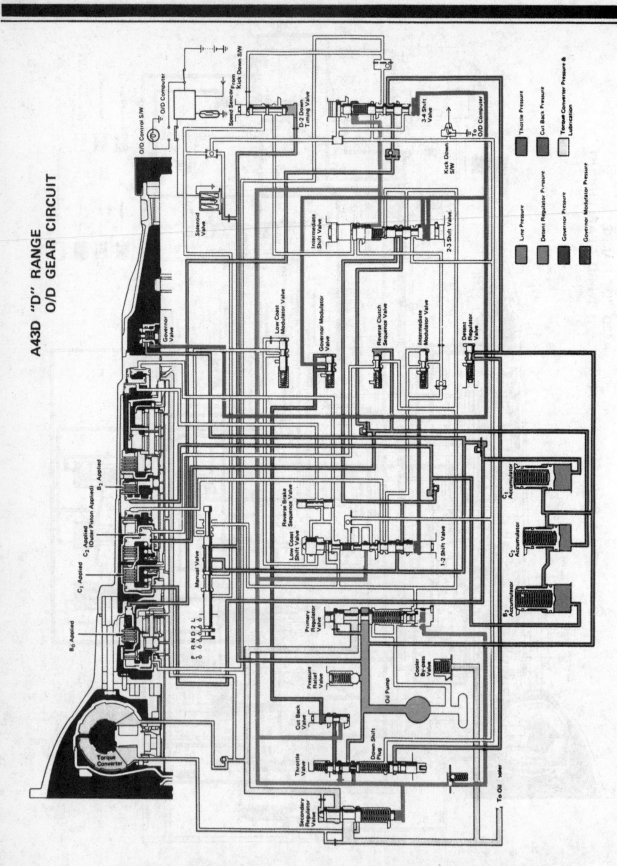

**Oil flow circuit drive range overdrive gear A-43D, A-43DL and A-43DE automatic transmission**

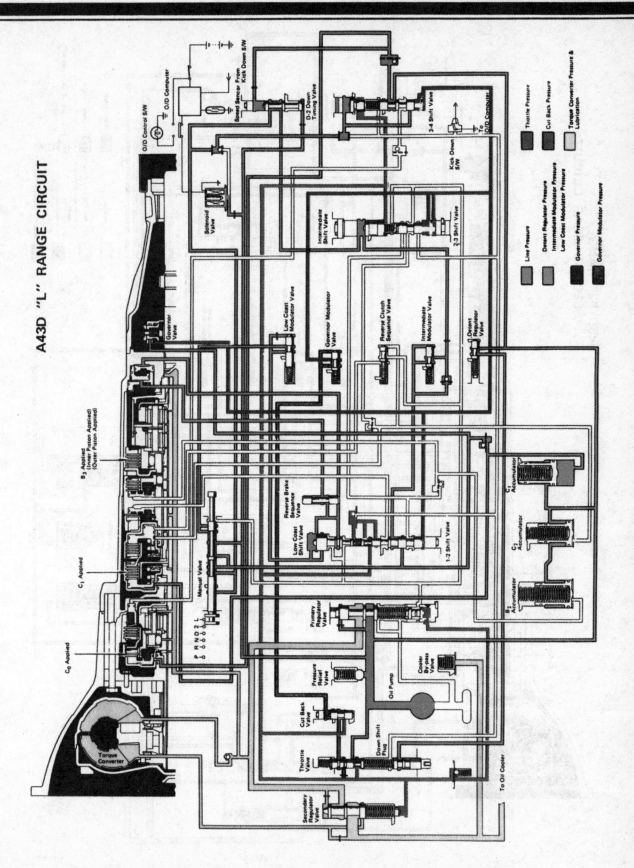

Oil flow circuit low range A-43D, A-43DL and A-43DE automatic transmission

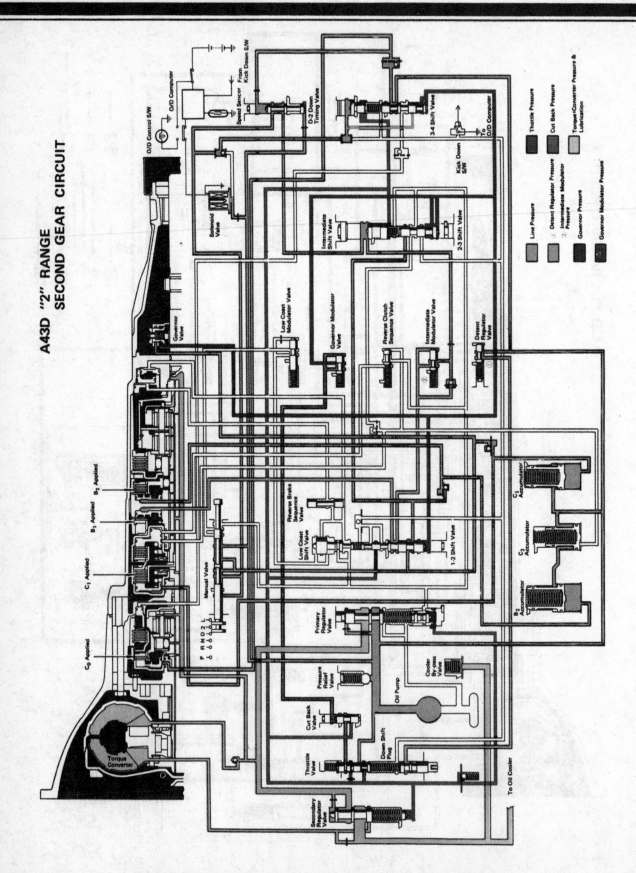

**A43D "2" RANGE SECOND GEAR CIRCUIT**

Oil flow circuit manual 2 range A-43D, A-43DL and A-43DE automatic transmission

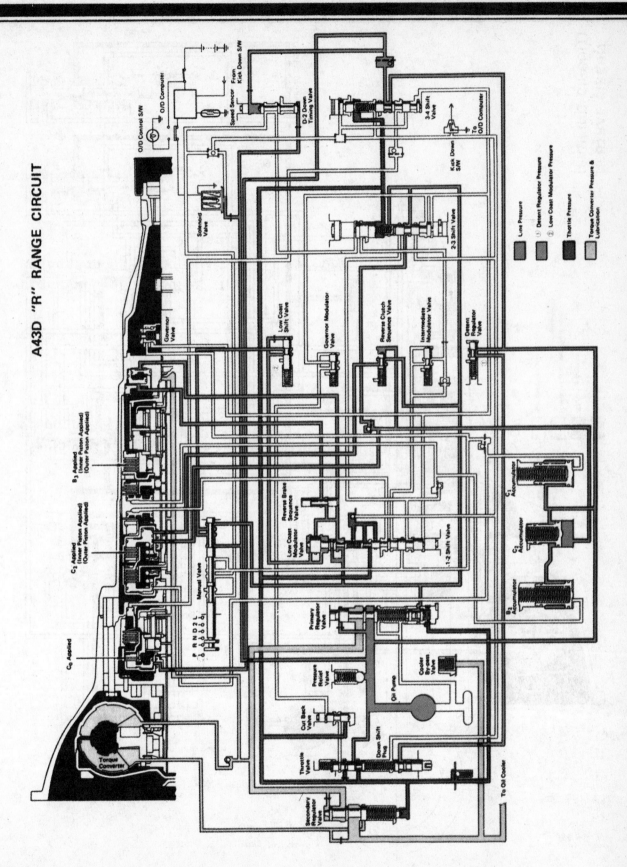

Oil flow circuit reverse range A-43D, A-43DL and A-43DE automatic transmission

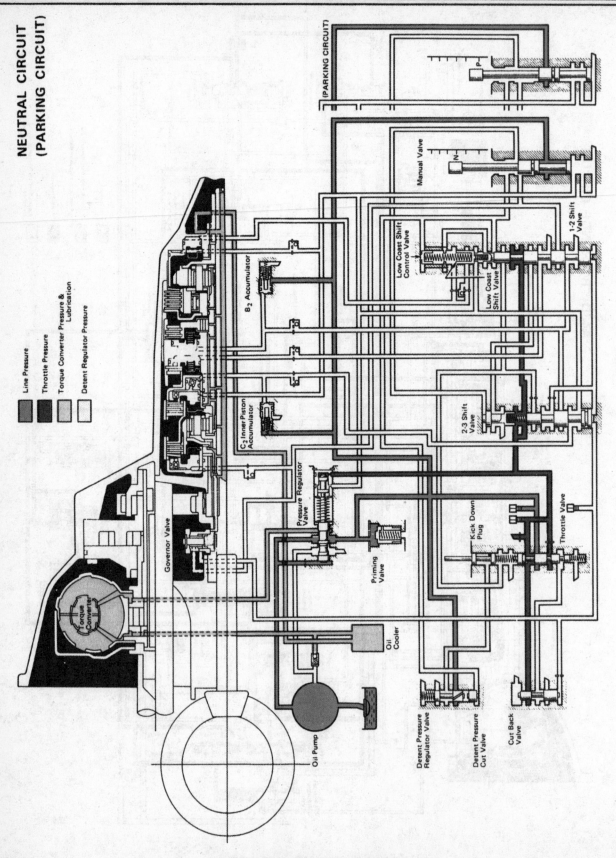

NEUTRAL CIRCUIT
(PARKING CIRCUIT)

(PARKING CIRCUIT)

Manual Valve

Low Coast Shift Control Valve

Low Coast Shift Valve

1-2 Shift Valve

2-3 Shift Valve

B₂ Accumulator

C₂ Inner Piston Accumulator

Governor Valve

Torque Converter

Pressure Regulator Valve

Priming Valve

Kick Down Plug

Throttle Valve

Oil Cooler

Oil Pump

Detent Pressure Regulator Valve

Detent Pressure Cut Valve

Cut Back Valve

Line Pressure

Throttle Pressure

Torque Converter Pressure & Lubrication

Detent Regulator Pressure

**Automatic transaxle in "N" neutral range**

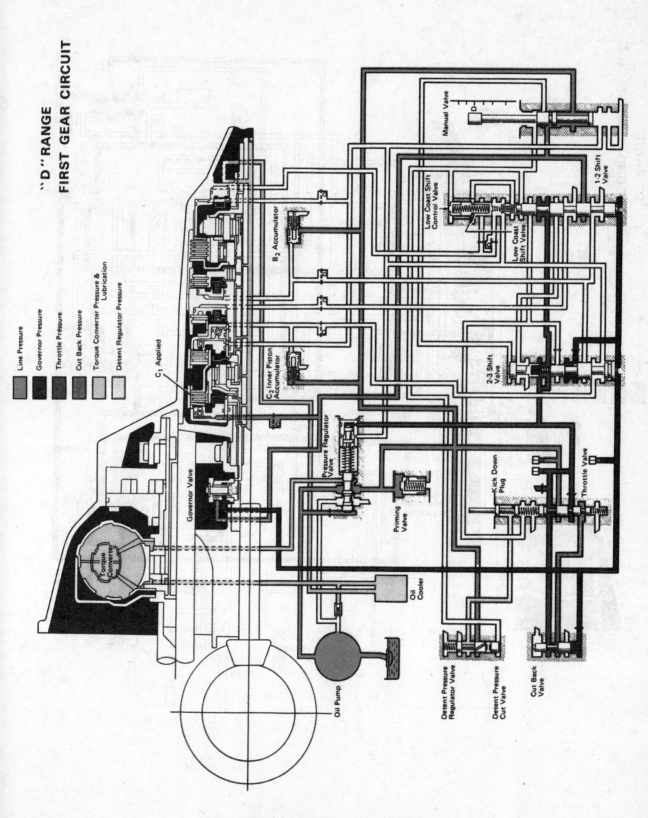

"D" RANGE
FIRST GEAR CIRCUIT

Line Pressure
Governor Pressure
Throttle Pressure
Cut Back Pressure
Torque Converter Pressure & Lubrication
Detent Regulator Pressure

Manual Valve
Low Coast Shift Control Valve
Low Coast Shift Valve
1-2 Shift Valve
2-3 Shift Valve
B₂ Accumulator
C₂ Inner Piston Accumulator
C₁ Applied
Governor Valve
Pressure Regulator Valve
Priming Valve
Kick Down Plug
Throttle Valve
Torque Converter
Oil Cooler
Oil Pump
Detent Pressure Regulator Valve
Detent Pressure Cut Valve
Cut Back Valve

**Automatic transaxle in "D" range 1st gear**

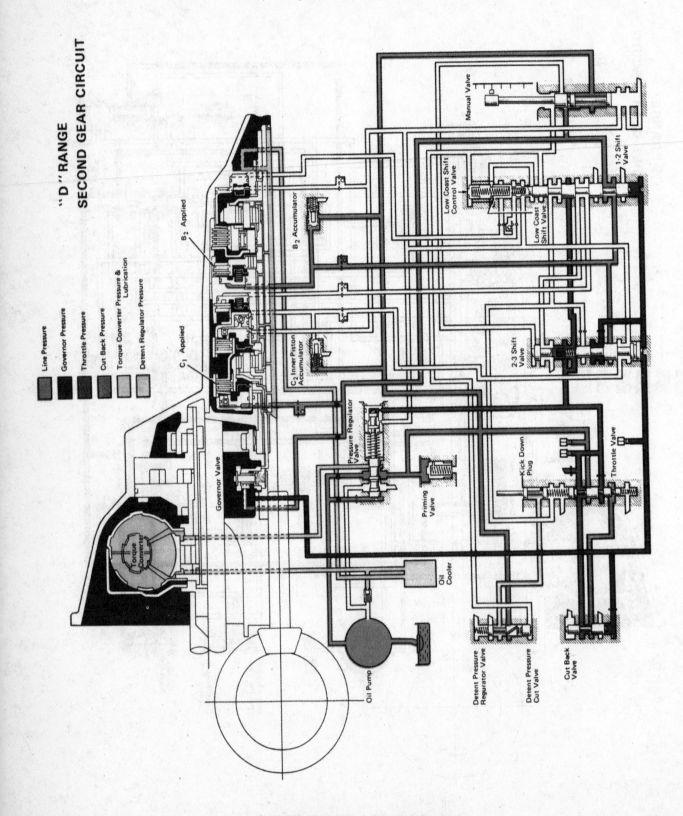

**"D" RANGE SECOND GEAR CIRCUIT**

Line Pressure
Governor Pressure
Throttle Pressure
Cut Back Pressure
Torque Converter Pressure & Lubrication
Detent Regulator Pressure

**Automatic transaxle in "D" range 2nd gear**

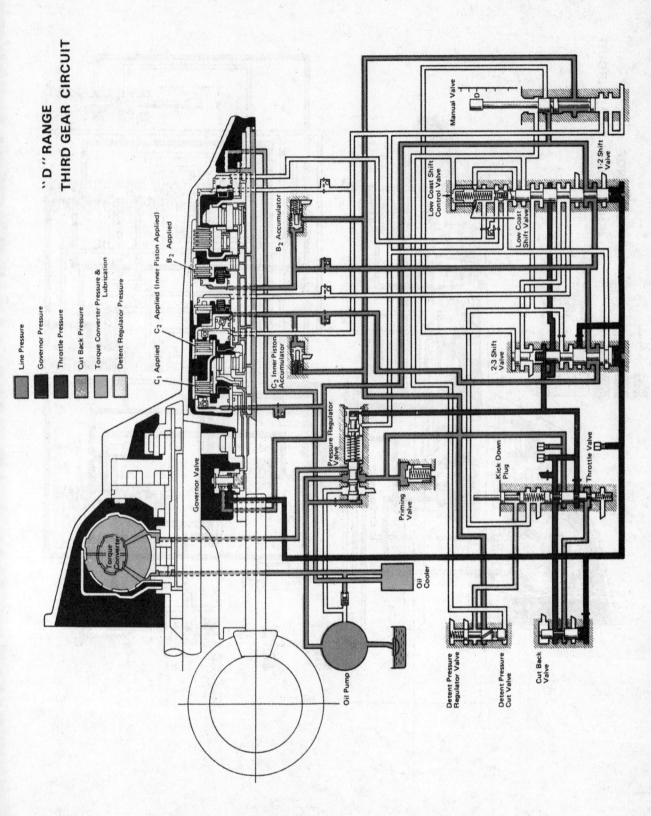

"D" RANGE
THIRD GEAR CIRCUIT

Line Pressure
Governor Pressure
Throttle Pressure
Cut Back Pressure
Torque Converter Pressure & Lubrication
Detent Regulator Pressure

Automatic transaxle in "D" range 3rd gear

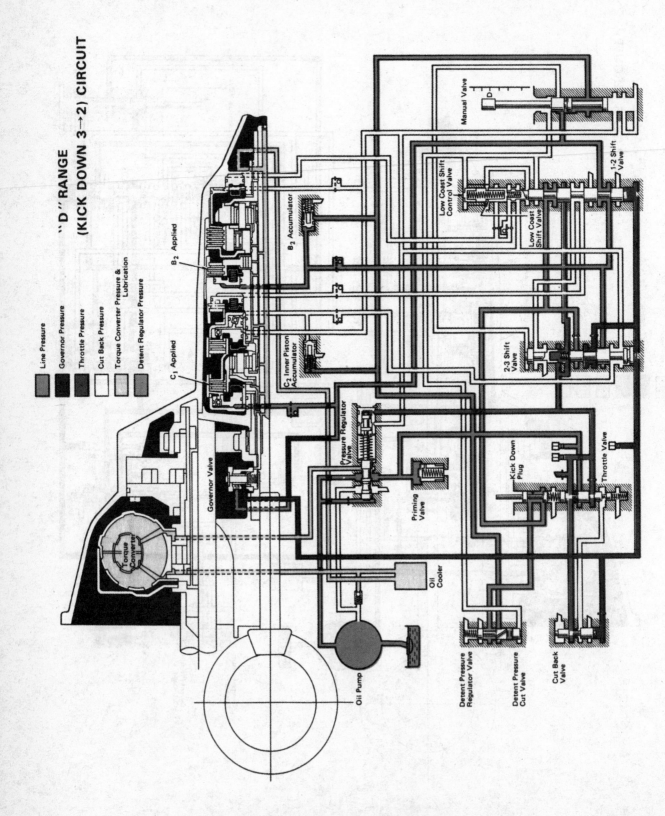

"D" RANGE
(KICK DOWN 3→2) CIRCUIT

Line Pressure
Governor Pressure
Throttle Pressure
Cut Back Pressure
Torque Converter Pressure & Lubrication
Detent Regulator Pressure

**Automatic transaxle in "D" range kickdown**

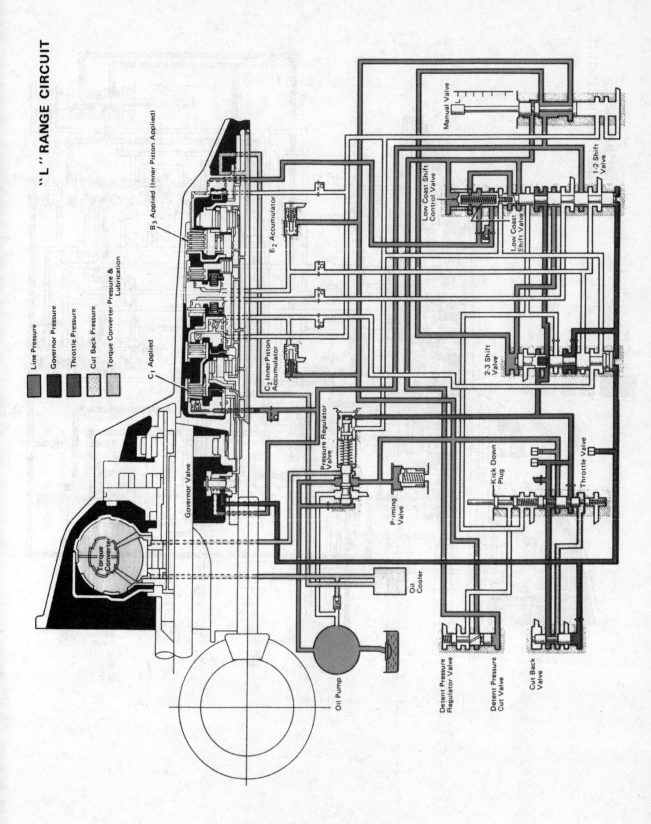

## "L" RANGE CIRCUIT

**Line Pressure**
**Governor Pressure**
**Throttle Pressure**
**Cut Back Pressure**
**Torque Converter Pressure & Lubrication**

B₃ Applied (Inner Piston Applied)

C₁ Applied

E₂ Accumulator

C₂ Inner Piston Accumulator

Governor Valve

Torque Converter

Pressure Regulator Valve

Priming Valve

Oil Cooler

Oil Pump

Manual Valve

Low Coast Shift Control Valve

Low Coast Shift Valve

1-2 Shift Valve

2-3 Shift Valve

Kick Down Plug

Throttle Valve

Detent Pressure Regulator Valve

Detent Pressure Cut Valve

Cut Back Valve

**Automatic transaxle in "L" low range**

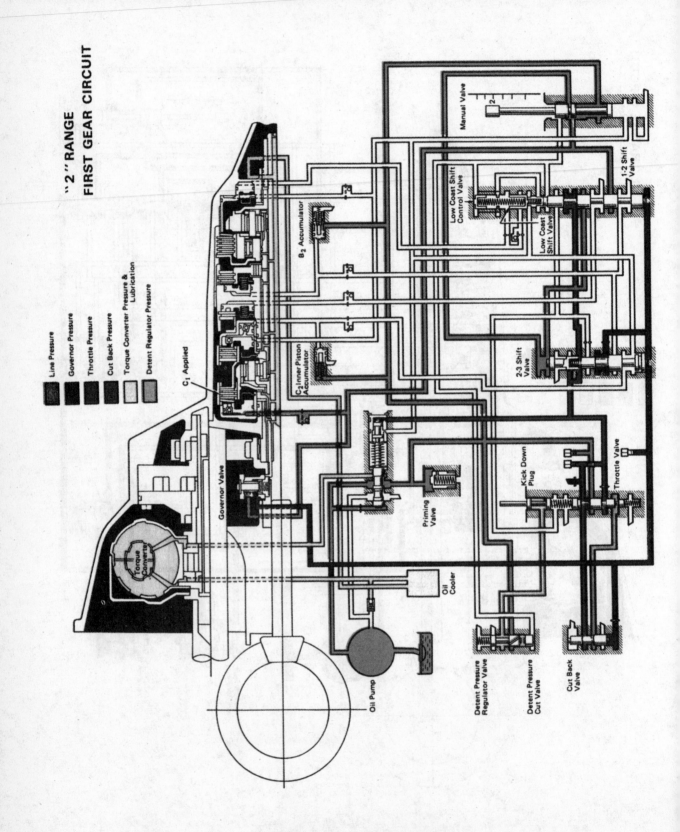

"2" RANGE
FIRST GEAR CIRCUIT

Line Pressure
Governor Pressure
Throttle Pressure
Cut Back Pressure
Torque Converter Pressure & Lubrication
Detent Regulator Pressure

Manual Valve

Low Coast Shift Control Valve

Low Coast Shift Valve

1-2 Shift Valve

2-3 Shift Valve

B₂ Accumulator

C₂ Inner Piston Accumulator

C₁ Applied

Governor Valve

Torque Converter

Priming Valve

Kick Down Plug

Throttle Valve

Oil Cooler

Oil Pump

Detent Pressure Regulator Valve

Detent Pressure Cut Valve

Cut Back Valve

**Automatic transaxle in "2" range 1st gear**

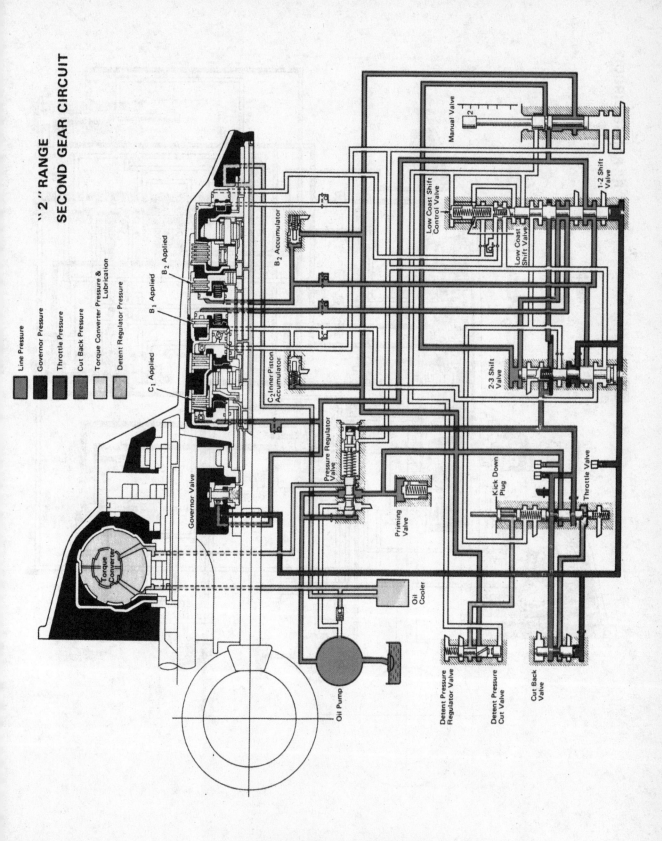

## "2" RANGE SECOND GEAR CIRCUIT

**Legend:**
- Line Pressure
- Governor Pressure
- Throttle Pressure
- Cut Back Pressure
- Torque Converter Pressure & Lubrication
- Detent Regulator Pressure

**Labels:**
- Torque Converter
- Governor Valve
- C₁ Applied
- B₁ Applied
- B₂ Applied
- B₂ Accumulator
- C₁ Inner Piston Accumulator
- Pressure Regulator Valve
- Priming Valve
- Oil Pump
- Oil Cooler
- Manual Valve
- Low Coast Shift Control Valve
- Low Coast Shift Valve
- 1-2 Shift Valve
- 2-3 Shift Valve
- Kick Down Plug
- Throttle Valve
- Detent Pressure Regulator Valve
- Detent Pressure Cut Valve
- Cut Back Valve

**Automatic transaxle in "2" range 2nd gear**

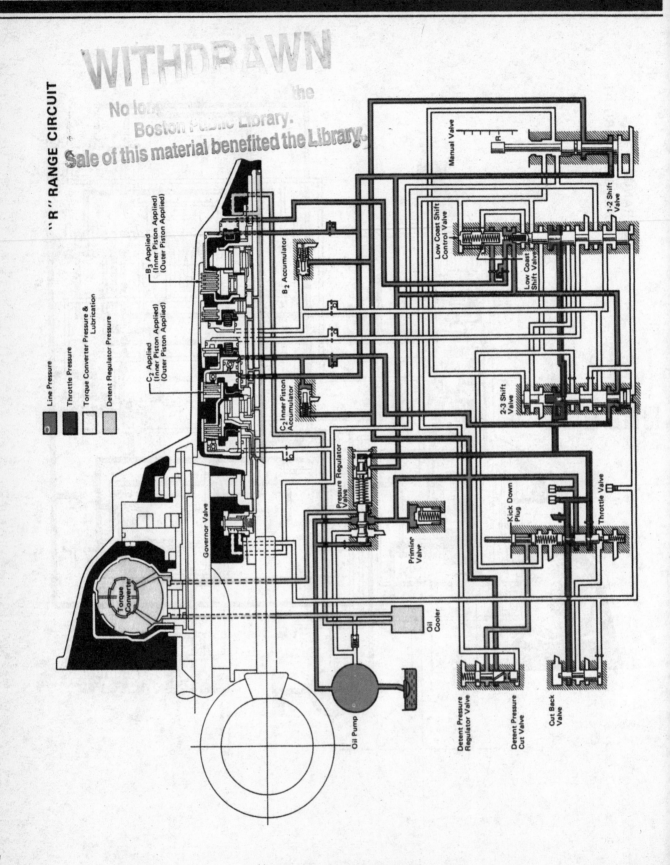

**Automatic transaxle in "R" reverse**